THE
TRIBES OF YAHWEH

THE
TRIBES OF YAHWEH

A Sociology of the Religion
of Liberated Israel
1250-1050 B.C.E.

Norman K. Gottwald

ORBIS BOOKS
Maryknoll, New York 10545

Second Printing, August 1981

Library of Congress Cataloging in Publication Data

Gottwald, Norman Karol, 1926-
  The Tribes of Yahweh

  Includes bibliographical references and indexes.
  1. Sociology, Biblical. 2. Bible. O.T.—
Theology. 3. Twelve tribes of Israel. 4. Jews—
History—1200-953 B.C. I. Title.
BS1199.S6G67   301.5'8   78-24333
ISBN 0-88344-498-4
ISBN 0-88344-499-2 pbk.

THIS STUDY IS DEDICATED TO THE MEMORY AND TO
THE HONOR
OF THE FIRST ISRAELITES

Think of them laughing, singing
    loving their people
        and
    all people who put love
        before power
    then
put love with power
    which is necessary
        to destroy power without love.

—from an anonymous tribute to the people of Vietnam.

The chronological limits of the inter-tribal period are conventionally set at 1250 to 1000 B.C.E. and are so referred to in the body of this work. The title sets the date at 1250 to 1050 B.C.E. because, according to the author's understanding, the major development in cult, religious ideology, and social organization took place by the mid-eleventh century.

Contents

LITERARY-HISTORICAL FOUNDATIONS
SYNCHRONIC SOCIAL STRUCTURE (PARTS I—VII)

PART I

BIBLICAL HISTORY AND BIBLICAL SOCIOLOGY

PART II

THE HISTORICAL STARTING POINT AND A SOURCE COMPENDIUM

PART III

THE CULTIC-IDEOLOGICAL FRAMEWORK OF THE SOURCES

PART VII

MODELS OF THE SOCIAL STRUCTURE (II): ALL ISRAEL, AMPHICTYONY OR CONFEDERACY?

DIACHRONIC-COMPARATIVE SOCIAL STRUCTURE SOCIOLOGY OF RELIGION VS. BIBLICAL THEOLOGY (PARTS VIII—XI)

PART VIII

COMPARATIVE SOCIAL SYSTEMS AND ECONOMIC MODES: THE SOCIOHISTORIC MATRICES OF LIBERATED ISRAEL

        in the Israelite Highlands   580

46. *The Israelite Countryside: Heartland of the Yahwistic Socioeconomic
    Revolution*   584

PART X

THE RELIGION OF THE NEW EGALITARIAN SOCIETY: IDEALIST,
STRUCTURAL-FUNCTIONAL, AND HISTORICAL CULTURAL-MATERIALIST MODELS

47. *A Preliminary View*   591

48. *Religious Idealism: Yahwism as an Autonomous Self-Generative
    "Faith"*   592

    48.1 Israelite Religion Severed from Israelite Society   592

    48.2 Israelite Society Derived from Israelite Religion   599

    48.3 Social Influences on "Nonessential" Features of Israelite Religion   602

49. *Structural Functionalism: Mutual Reinforcement of Yahwism
    and Social Egalitarianism*   608

    49.1 Structural-Functional Societal Models   608

    49.2 Mono-Yahwism as the Function of Sociopolitical Equality   611

    49.3 Sociopolitical Equality as the Function of Mono-Yahwism   618

50. *Historical Cultural Materialism: Yahwism as the Symbolization
    of Egalitarian Social Struggle*   622

    50.1 Durkheim: Collective Representations   624

    50.2 Weber: Elective Affinity and Co-Determination   627

    50.3 Marx: Lawfully Interacting and Evolving Inter-Human Totalities   631

    50.4 Priority of Cultural-Material Conditions and Social Struggle: Yahwism
          as a Societal "Feedback" Servomechanism   642

51. *A Program of Historical Cultural-Material Research into Early Israel*   650

    51.1 An Economic and Cultural-Material Inventory   650

    51.2 Historico-Territorial and Topological Studies   652

    51.3 Biblical Archaeology and "the New Archaeology"   653

    51.4 Population Size and Distribution   654

    51.5 Technological Factors: Iron and Waterproof Plaster—Terracing
          and Irrigation Systems   655

    51.6 The Socioeconomic Shift from Amarna to Israelite Canaan: A Provisional
          Historical Cultural-Material Hypothesis   660

PART XI

BIBLICAL THEOLOGY OR BIBLICAL SOCIOLOGY?

List of Charts

Abbreviations

AA	*American Anthropologist*
AAb	*Aegyptologische Abhandlungen*
AASOR	*Annual of the American Schools of Oriental Research*
AB	*Analecta Biblica*
ABR	*Australian Biblical Review*
AES	*Archives Européennes de Sociologie*
AFO	*Archiv für Orientforschung*
AION	*Annali del' Instituto Orientale di Napoli*
AJA	*American Journal of Archaeology*
AJBA	*Australian Journal of Biblical Archaeology*
ALUOS	*Annual of the Leeds University Oriental Society*
ANET	*Ancient Near Eastern Texts Relating to the Old Testament*, 3rd ed., 1969 (ed. J. B. Pritchard)
ANVAOT	*Avhandlinger utgitt av Det Norske Videnskaps Akademi i Oslo*
AO	*Analecta Orientalia*
AOS	*American Oriental Series*
ARM	*Archives Royales de Mari*, 1946– (ed. A. Parrot and G. Dossin)
ArO	*Archiv Orientální*
ARSI	*Annual Report of the Smithsonian Institution*
AS	*Antiquity and Survival*
ASR	*American Sociological Review*
ASTI	*Annual of the Swedish Theological Institute in Jerusalem*
ASV	American Standard Version of the Bible
AT	*The Alalakh Tablets*, 1953 (ed. D. J. Wiseman)
ATANT	*Abhandlungen zur Theologie des Alten und Neuen Testaments*
AVTR	*Aufsätze und Vorträge zur Theologie und Religionswissenschaft*
AZT	*Arbeiten zur Theologie*
BA	*The Biblical Archaeologist*
BAR	*The Biblical Archaeologist Reader*
BASOR	*Bulletin of the American Schools of Oriental Research*
BBB	*Bonner Biblische Beiträge*
BDB	F. Brown, S. R. Driver, and C. A. Briggs, *A Hebrew and English Lexicon of the Old Testament*, 1906
BJPES	*Bulletin of the Jewish Palestine Exploration Society* = *Yedioth*
BSOAS	*Bulletin of the School of Oriental and African Studies*
BWANT	*Beiträge zur Wissenschaft vom Alten und Neuen Testament*
BZAW	*Beihefte zur Zeitschrift für die Alttestamentliche Wissenschaft*
CAH	*The Cambridge Ancient History*
CB	*Coniectanea Biblica*

CBQ	*Catholic Biblical Quarterly*
CnB	*The Century Bible*
CnBN	*The Century Bible, New Edition*
CTM	*Concordia Theological Monthly*
CV	*Communio Viatorum*
DMOA	*Documenta et Monumenta Orientis Antiqui*
DOTWSA	Proceedings of *Die Ou-Testamentiese Werkgemeenskap in Suid-Afrika*
EA	El Amarna letters cited according to the numbering system in J. A. Knudtzon, *Die El-Amarna-Tafeln* 1907 / 1915 and in A. F. Rainey, *El Amarna Tablets 359–379*, 1970.
EB	*Estudios Biblicos*
EG	*Economic Geography*
EI	*Eretz Israel*
EJ	Encyclopaedia Judaica
EM	*'Entsiqlopedyah Miqra'ith* (Encyclopaedia Biblica)
EOTHR	A. Alt, *Essays in Old Testament History and Religion*, 1966
ETL	*Ephemerides Theologicae Lovanienses*
EvT	*Evangelische Theologie*
Ex	*The Expositor*
FRLANT	*Forschungen zur Religion und Literatur des Alten und Neuen Testaments*
GR	*Geography Review*
HAT	*Handbuch zum Alten Testament*, Tübingen
HTR	*Harvard Theological Review*
HUCA	*Hebrew Union College Annual*
HZAT	*Handkommentar zum Alten Testament*, Göttingen
IB	*The Interpreter's Bible*
ICC	*The International Critical Commentary*
IDB	The Interpreter's Dictionary of the Bible
IDBSV	The Interpreter's Dictionary of the Bible, Supplementary Volume
IEJ	*Israel Exploration Journal*
IESS	The International Encyclopedia of the Social Sciences
IOCB	*The Interpreter's One-Volume Commentary on the Bible*
JAAR	*Journal of the American Academy of Religion*
JAGS	*Journal of the American Geographic Society*
JANES	*Journal of the Ancient Near Eastern Society of Columbia University*
JAOS	*Journal of the American Oriental Society*
JB	The Jerusalem Bible
JBL	*Journal of Biblical Literature*
JCS	*Journal of Cuneiform Studies*
JES	*Journal of Ecumenical Studies*
JESHO	*Journal of the Economic and Social History of the Orient*

JJS	*Journal of Jewish Studies*
JNES	*Journal of Near Eastern Studies*
JPOS	*Journal of the Palestine Oriental Society*
JPS	*A New Translation of the Holy Scriptures: The Torah.* The Jewish Publication Society of America, 1962
JR	*Journal of Religion*
JRAI	*Journal of the Royal Anthropological Institute*
JSS	*Journal of Semitic Studies*
JTS	*Journal of Theological Studies*
K	*K^{e}thiv*, Heb. for "what is written," referring to consonantal MT at points where Massoretes note a corrected reading by *Q^{e}re* (Q), "what is to be read."
KD	*Kerygma und Dogma*
KF	*Kleinasiatische Forschungen*
KS	A. Alt, *Kleine Schriften zur Geschichte des Volkes Israel*, 1953–1959; O. Eissfeldt, *Kleine Schriften*, 1962–1968
KZSS	*Kölner Zeitschrift für Sociologie und Sozialpsychologie*
LTQ	*Lexington Theological Quarterly*
LXX	Septuagint
MANE	*Monographs on the Ancient Near East*
MGWJ	*Monatsschrift für Geschichte und Wissenschaft des Judentums*
MIO	*Mitteilungen des Instituts für Orientforschung*
MS(S)	Manuscript(s)
MT	Massoretic Text of the Hebrew Bible
MUSJ	*Mélanges de l'Université Saint Joseph*
NAB	*The New American Bible*
NEB	The New English Bible
NYSMB	*New York State Museum Bulletin*
OA	*Oriens Antiquus*
OBL	*Orientalia et Biblica Lovaniensia*
Or	*Orientalia*
OTL	*The Old Testament Library*
OTS	*Oudtestamentische Studien*
PEQ	*Palestine Exploration Quarterly*
PH	*Pennsylvania History*
PJ	*Palästinajahrbuch*
PTMS	The Pittsburgh Theological Monograph Series
PWRE	*Paulys Real-Encyclopädie der klassischen Altertumswissenschaft.* Neue Bearbeitung begonnen von G. Wissowa
Q	*Q^{e}re*, Heb. for "what is to be read," a notation by Massoretes to correct the consonantal MT or *K^{e}tive* (K), "what is written."

RA	*Revue Archéologique*
RAAO	*Revue d'Assyriologie et d'Archéologie Orientale*
RB	*Revue Biblique*
RE	*Review and Expositor*
RHPR	*Revue d'Histoire et de Philosophie Religieuses*
RR	*Radical Religion*
RSCPT	Royal Society of Canada. Proceedings and Transactions
RSO	*Rivista degli Studi Orientali*
RSV	Revised Standard Version of the Bible
RT	*Revue Thomiste*
RV	English Revised Version of the Bible
SAWW	*Sitzungsberichte der Akademie der Wissenschaften in Wien*
SBLDS	Society of Biblical Literature Dissertation Series
SBT	*Studies in Biblical Theology*
SGI	*Studies in the Geography of Israel*
SH	*Scripta Hierosolymitana*
SJA	*Southwestern Journal of Anthropology*
SNTSMS	Society for New Testament Studies Monograph Series
SS	*Studi Semitici*
ST	*Studia Theologica*, Lund
STKM	*Die Studierstube: Theologische und Kirchliche Monatsschrift*
SVT	Supplements to *Vetus Testamentum.*
TB	*Tyndale Bulletin*
TDNT	*Theological Dictionary to the New Testament*, 1932– (ed. G. Kittel and G. Friedrich)
TLZ	*Theologische Literaturzeitung*
TPQ	*Theologisch Praktische Quartalschrift*
VT	*Vetus Testamentum*
TvT	*Tijdschrift voor Theologie*
WHJP	*The World History of the Jewish People*, 1970– (ed. B. Mazar)
WMANT	*Wissenschaftliche Monographien zum Alten und Neuen Testament*
WO	*Die Welt des Orients*
WZMLU	*Wissenschaftliche Zeitschrift der Martin-Luther-Universität* (Halle)
ZA	*Zeitschrift für Assyriologie und verwandte Gebiete*
ZAW	*Zeitschrift für die Alttestamentliche Wissenschaft*
ZDMG	*Zeitschrift der Deutschen Morgenländischen Gesellschaft*
ZDPV	*Zeitschrift des Deutschen Palästinavereins*
ZS	*Zeitschrift für Semitistik*
ZThK	*Zeitschrift für Theologie und Kirche*

NOTE: special abbreviations used in the précis of the Books of Joshua and Judges in Part IV are explained in notes 88 and 90.

Preface

Does it require deep intuition to comprehend that man's ideas, views, and conceptions, in one word, man's consciousness, changes with every change in the conditions of his material existence, in his social relations and in his social life?

What else does the history of ideas prove, than that intellectual production changes its character in proportion as material production is changed? The ruling ideas of each age have ever been the ideas of its ruling class.

When people speak of ideas that revolutionize society, they do but express the fact that within the old society the elements of a new one have been created, and that the dissolution of the old ideas keeps even pace with the dissolution of the old conditions of existence. (Karl Marx and Friedrich Engels, *The Manifesto of the Communist Party*, 1848.)

In Exodus 1—24, a religious revolt and a social revolt clearly go hand in hand. A people decides no longer to accept passively their difficult social situation because they hear that a God, previously unknown to them (at least by his true name) wants to change their social position in a short time. Likewise, they welcome this new god who is proclaimed to them by one who has received a revelation because it is from him that the change in their social situation is expected. A new religion makes a people revolutionary. And on the other side, the difficult social situation of this people makes them ready for a new religion.

. . .even though there are no classical parallels for the religious-social revolution illustrated in Exodus, there are Middle Age and modern parallels. We can see no better clarification of this remarkable circumstance than the fact that we have before us in Exodus 1—24 a report (although greatly impaired) of the *first* ideologically based socio-political revolution in the history of the world. (Jan Dus, "Moses or Joshua? On the Problem of the Founder of the Israelite Religion," *Radical Religion* 2.2/3 [1975] 28 = *Radical Religion Reader*, 1976, p. 28.)

A formative period is by definition one which is concerned to *break* with the contemporary and recent past, partly because it is intolerable or unsatisfactory, but more importantly because there comes about a vision and conviction that something much more excellent is not only possible but necessary. Discontent movements are a constant, as the history of revolt, war, and rebellion indicates. But rare indeed are those movements in history that result in such creative breaks with the past that they survive for centuries and expand over large population areas to create some sort of social unity or unified tradition that did not exist before. The first such movement to survive was the biblical one, and this religious revolution urgently needs more adequate *historical* study. (George E. Mendenhall, *The Tenth Generation: The Origins of the Biblical Tradition*, 1973, p. 12.)

Judging by the impact on the daily lives and thoughts of millions of people, there has been more rapid and significant social change in the last two hundred years than in the entirety of preceding human history. Not surprisingly, one of the marks of this accelerating and deepening change is inquiry and reflection concerning the conditions of social change. What sector of human life, or what combination of sectors, spearheads and shapes social change, and with what consequences? Of particular fascination has been the question of the role of ideas in social change—among which religious ideas have held a special prominence. Increasing attention is focused on contemporary and historic religion in its total setting under the pressure of social change.

The present study takes up precisely the challenge of clarifying the place of religious ideas and practices within the changeful social totality at one of the critical origin points in Western history and culture. By combining traditional literary, historical, and theological methods of inquiry with more unaccustomed sociological methods, I shall attempt to reconstruct the origins and early development of that remarkable ancient socioreligiously mutant people who called themselves Israel. Such a study is necessarily not only a study of *social totality* but a study of *radical social change* that was also *liberating social change*.

METHODS AND AREAS OF INQUIRY. The following procedural steps decisively determine the shape of my inquiry:

1. Because Israel's origins are obscure and controversial, my initial goal is to assemble the most reliable information about *the rise of Israel* as determined by recognized methods of biblical science, including literary criticism, form criticism, tradition history, history, and history of religion.

2. To this body of data and theory developed within biblical science, I shall apply the methods of the social sciences in order to delineate and to conceptualize *early Israel as a total social system.* Correspondingly, the religion of Israel will be viewed, not as the isolated datum and arbitrary oddity it is usually taken to be, but rather as an integral dimension of the Israelite social system, lawfully and intelligibly correlated with other elements of that system.

3. In particular, I shall examine the major proposals that have been offered about the character of early Israelite society, such as the hypothesis that Israelites were *pastoral nomads* in transition to agriculture and to village and city life, the hypothesis that Israelites were *confederated tribes bonded together in a sacral league* dedicated to the cult of the god Yahweh, and the hypothesis that Israelites were *Canaanite peasants in revolt* against the political economy in which they were exploited participants. In the course of examining these hypotheses, I employ not only data from the Hebrew Bible and from the Canaanite and ancient Near Eastern environment, but also anthropological and sociological analyses of kinship, pastoral nomadism, tribalism, peasant society, statism, social evolution, and intra-systemic social conflict.

4. Finally, explanatory social theory is introduced for making sense out of the Israelite mutation. Initially, *a structural-functional model* is proposed by which Israel's religion can be viewed in working congruence with the other elements of the social structure. Eventually, however, it becomes crucial to introduce *an historical cultural-material model* to account for the mutant appearance of Israel in its

time and place as the successful convergence of several antistatist sectors of the populace in the imperial-feudal Canaanite society of the fourteenth to thirteenth centuries B.C. Techno-environmental and techno-economic elements in this historical cultural-material hypothesis include the topography of the Israelite highlands, the introduction of improved iron tools, the intensive use of waterproof cisterns and of small-scale irrigation systems, and the extended use of rock terracing in agriculture.

PRESUPPOSITIONS. My approach is influenced throughout by the following fundamental assumptions: (1) that humanistic and sociological methods are equally valuable and complementary methods for reconstructing the ancient Israelite mutation; (2) that religion is best approached as an aspect of a wider network of social relations in which it has intelligible functions to perform; (3) that changes in religious behavior and thought are best viewed as aspects of change in the wider network of social and economic relations; and (4) that religion is intelligible to the degree that it exhibits lawful behavior and symbolic forms which can be predicted and retrodicted within parameters set by changing total mixes of social and economic relations.

MAJOR CONCLUSIONS. Among the findings of this study, too numerous and nuanced to be summarized here in their totality, the following deserve particular emphasis: (1) that early Israel was an eclectic formation of marginal and depressed Canaanite people, including "feudalized" peasants (*ḫupshu*), *'apiru* mercenaries and adventurers, transhumant pastoralists, tribally organized farmers and pastoral nomads (*shosu*), and probably also itinerant craftsmen and disaffected priests; (2) that Israel was emergent from and a fundamental breach within Canaanite society and not an invasion or an immigration from without; (3) that Israel's social structure was a deliberate and highly conscious "retribalization" process rather than an unreflective unilinear carry-over from pastoral nomadic tribalism; (4) that the religion of Yahweh was a crucial societal instrument for cementing and motivating the peculiar constellation of unifying and decentralizing sociocultural patterns necessary to the optimal functioning of the social system and, *in extremis,* to the sheer survival of the system; and (5) that a sociology of Israel's religion, rooted in an historical cultural-material understanding of religious symbols and praxis, accounts for all those "distinctives" of Israelite religion that the biblical theology movement tried to accentuate and characterize, but with imprecise and muddled results.

ORGANIZATION. The study is structured serially in the following manner: 1. The aims and methods of the project, together with a prospectus, are set forth in the context of a brief history of scholarly study of Israelite origins (Part I). 2. The possibilities for conceptualizing Israelite society are formulated on the basis of the results of two centuries of intensive inquiry in the several humanities-based branches of Old Testament science, and a prospectus of the sociological tasks and methods for the remainder of the study is presented (Parts II–V). 3. A largely synchronic structural design of early Israelite society is set forth, together with a pinpointing of developmental problems to be treated (Parts VI–VII). 4. The emergence of early Israelite society is traced in continuity and discontinuity with its immediate antecedents and contemporaries, with particular attention to the major socioeconomic component groups of Israel (Parts VIII–IX). 5. The religion of earliest Israel is elucidated in its social context vis-à-vis ancient Near Eastern religion, and the substantial contributions of sociology of religion toward evaluating the pertinence of ancient Israelite religion for contemporary purposes are indicated (Parts X–XI).

ACKNOWLEDGMENTS. Although this immediate study has been eight years in the making, I consider my entire past engagement in Old Testament scholarship to be contributory to the results. I shall not repeat here what is stated in the prefaces to two previous books: *A Light to the Nations: An Introduction to the Old Testament,* 1959, and *All the Kingdoms of the Earth: Israelite Prophecy and International Relations in the Ancient Near East,* 1964. The acknowledgments there noted continue to be integral aspects of my analysis and outlook, most especially the foundational influence of James Muilenburg, my teacher at Union Theological Seminary, New York City (1949–1953) and my colleague in the Graduate Theological Union, Berkeley, California (1966–1972), who taught me methodological rigor and the utmost respect for the human subjectivity of the ancient Israelites, as well as giving me some initial glimpses into the possibilities of sociological study of the Old Testament (cf., e.g., Muilenburg's Prolegomenon to the KATV reprint of W. Robertson Smith's *Lectures on the Religion of the Semites: The Fundamental Institutions,* 3rd ed. with introduction and notes by S. A. Cook, reprinted 1969).

My immense debt to previous and contemporary generations of biblical specialists, archaeologists, sociologists, and anthropologists will be abundantly clear from the text, especially in Parts I and X. I owe a special word of credit to Marvin Chaney, my colleague in the Graduate Theological Union, Berkeley, California, who is acknowledged on specific points throughout the notes. For the past six years he and I have shared a common interest in the sociology of premonarchic Israel and have had ample occasion to share ideas and to try out hypotheses in jointly taught courses and in private conversations. Similarly, I have profited from three years of participation in an informal biblical sociology faculty study group composed of John H. Elliott (University of San Francisco), Donald Stoike (Concordia College, Oakland), John P. Brown (Ecumenical Peace Institute, and formerly of the Graduate Theological Union and the Berkeley Free Church), and Marvin Chaney, Herman C. Waetjen, Anne C. Wire and myself (Graduate Theological Union). The final stages of the argument in Parts X and XI, with some subsequent amplification, were worked out in connection with a seminar conducted at the Ecumenical Institute for Advanced Theological Studies, Jerusalem, and a lecture course given in the Overseas Students Program of the Hebrew University of Jerusalem in 1973–74. I am also grateful to have had the opportunity to share major results of this study in a lecture at the Eighth Congress of the International Organization for the Study of the Old Testament in Edinburgh (August 18–23, 1974), subsequently published in the *Supplements to Vetus Testamentum,* Eighth Congress volume (1975), pp. 89–100, under the title "Domain Assumptions and Societal Models in the Study of Pre-Monarchic Israel." Likewise, I acknowledge the privilege of co-authoring (with Frank S. Frick of Albion College) an orientation paper for the 1975 Society of Biblical Literature Consultation on the Social World of Ancient Israel, published in *SBL 1975 Seminar Papers,* vol. 1, pp. 165–178, in which some aspects of the history of sociological study of ancient Israel treated in Part I of this study are elaborated.

Finally, I want to identify three persisting sources of influence on my sociological interest in ancient Israel: 1. Three year-long stays in the land of ancient Israel (1960–61; 1968–69; 1973–74) have been of incalculable value in informing my work with a sense of time and place and with a feel for the unique blend of material and spiritual conditions that constitute the warp and woof of human meaning. 2. Two decades of involvement in civil rights struggles, in opposition to the war in Vietnam, in anti-imperialist efforts, in analysis of North American capitalism, and in the rough-and-tumble of ecclesial and educational politics have constituted an ever-informative "living laboratory" for discerning related social struggles in ancient Israel. 3. Immersion in the macro-sociological theories of Emile Durkheim, Max Weber, and Karl Marx has provided me a rich body of analytic tools and substantive conclusions with which to reflect on my own social experience and on the social experience of ancient Israel. In the absence of any of these three decisive inputs, I do not believe that this study would have been either conceived or accomplished.

NEXT STEPS. Although it is ambitious and comprehensive, I view this work as no more than the first tentative step toward an understanding of the grossly neglected sociology of ancient Israel, including the sociology of its mutant religion. That after two hundred years of herculean efforts in the scientific study of ancient Israel our knowledge should remain so rudimentary in important regards is indeed a delicious irony on how social norms dictate what we deem worthy of study. Particularly in Part X, Chapter 51, under the title, "A Program of Historical Cultural-Material Research into Early Israel," I indicate whole classes of data which have yet to be assembled and systematically studied if we are to grasp the society and the religion of ancient Israel in the depth and detail which their impact on our lives categorically merits. In short, the basic tenet for future research and theory is clear and commanding: only as the full *materiality* of ancient Israel is more securely grasped will we be able to make proper sense of its *spirituality.*

Norman K. Gottwald
Berkeley, California
December 29, 1975

Part I

Biblical History and Biblical Sociology

Obstacles to a Comprehensive Understanding of Early Israel

A comprehensive and coherent historical and socioreligious understanding of the people Israel prior to the united monarchy has yet to be developed. In spite of a wealth of detailed information about Israel in its formative period, the actual course of events and, beyond that, the structural and functional reality of Israelite society, as well as its defining rationale as a radical socioreligious mutation, still elude our grasp.

Of course there has been no lack of literary, historical, and religious inquiries into the period of Israel's history marked off by the rather nebulous figure of Moses on the one side and by the more sharply etched figure of David on the other, a period to be delimited as approximately 1250–1000 b.c. The literary sources in the so-called historical books of the Old Testament—particularly in Joshua, Judges, and I Samuel—have been examined in the minutest detail, and seemingly endless dissections and reconstructions of the component strands have been attempted. Scholars have reached behind the written sources to dissolve the continuous strands of narration into separate units of oral composition and cultic formulation and have further striven to connect these units with festivals celebrated at one or another of the many shrines in ancient Israel. Hypothetical reconstructions of the stages in the occupation of the land of Canaan and the sequences in the joining together of the tribes to form Israel have been plentifully proposed. Theories about the relation of the religion of Yahweh to the gods of the surrounding peoples and to the gods of the peoples who became Israelites have been propounded almost beyond reckoning. Our difficulties in comprehending early Israel do not stem from a lack of industry in inquiry or of ingenuity in theorizing. With all that said, we still do not know the straightforward history of the time and, even more strikingly, premonarchic Israel continues to escape our efforts to visualize it as a totality, to locate its deepest roots, and to account for its cohesion and vitality.

How is it that such intensive study has yielded such overall disappointing results? Basically, there are two reasons for our bafflement over the origins of Israel. One has to do with the nature of the sources of our knowledge about early Israel. The other concerns scholarly and religious aversion to, and hesitancy in, conceiving ancient Israel as a social totality.

3

1.1 The Problem of Sources

The problem of the sources of our knowledge about early Israel is at first glance scarcely conceivable. Are we not, after all, provided with innumerable stories, laws, and poems which crowd the pages of the Hebrew Bible from Genesis to Samuel? Hardly any other people has produced so much material about its beginnings. The central difficulty is that these materials come to us in the form of a corpus of religious documents deriving from the monarchy and still later periods of Israel's history. The finished form of the writings Genesis through Samuel comes from no earlier than the sixth century B.C. This late compilation of the traditions is incredibly complex, and the earliest continuous sources we can identify are not earlier than about 950 B.C. at best, a time already falling outside the period of premonarchic origins and one strongly imprinted by the historical circumstances and mental horizons of the monarchy which so greatly altered the earlier life conditions of Israel.

It is now well known that the earliest sources in Genesis-Samuel contain rich materials from the premonarchic era. But it is equally evident that none of these materials is in unaltered form, although the alteration may be so subtle as to escape instant detection. The traditional sequences tend to break into units without certain chronological connection; and the more they are examined, the more certain it is that an idealized conception of Israel's unity has been cast back into the earlier traditions, thereby lending them all the impression that their subject is a single people, stemming from a single line of ancestors and united in a tribal system from the days of their Egyptian bondage. A harmonization of traditions from the perspective of Israel united in Canaan bars the way to immediate access to the historic growth of unity in premonarchic Israel.

This fundamental condition on all our study of the early history of Israel is not changed by the fact that some scholars have posited a premonarchic narrative source lying behind the continuous sources composed under the monarchy (generally designated "G" after Noth's *Grundlage* or "foundation," assumed to be common to J and E). While the hypothesis has plausibility, the exact contours of the premonarchic source have yet to be delineated, so thoroughly and freely has it been worked into the major monarchic J and E sources in a manner peculiar to each. And even such a premonarchic foundation source, were it reconstructable in detail, would have to be seen as the latest stage in a long premonarchic development of tradition. It would be helpful primarily for the immediate half-century before Saul; it could probably tell us much less about the period prior to 1075–1050 B.C.

Fortunately we are able to detect distinctions between the later fiction of united Israel and the discrepant traditions of the segmented groups which only gropingly and often belatedly came together in the one people Israel. But the task of unraveling the diverse histories from the unified traditional history is no easy one. Lacking the controls of external data, these efforts must remain conjectural and problematic. Our attempts at a history of premonarchic Israel have not gotten much farther than a history of the traditions of premonarchic Israel. The struggle to find our way in the morass of traditional materials, amenable as they are to varied interpretations, leads often to an exhaustion of energy and insight in efforts at oversubtleness of analysis and cleverness of theorizing. In the absence of anything that can be firmly known, scholars have grasped at straws and built ingenious theories on the crumbling foundations of possibilities which, while they cannot always be disproved, have certainly yet to be demonstrated. The parameters of conjecture and fantasy have been considerably narrowed by an increasing understanding of the natural and human environment of early Israel. Nevertheless, there is as yet no single commanding version of the origins of Israel. We may speak at most of a number of widely shared assumptions on the basis of which scholars organize the source materials into a range of partly congruous and partly competing histories of premonarchic Israel.

1.2 The Scandal of Sociological Method

Greatly complicating the ambiguous and fragmentary sources of knowledge about early Israel is ingrained hesitancy at trying to envision the people of Israel as a living social totality, as human beings in a network of lived relationships and shared meanings. One root of this inhibition is the canonical sanctity that still surrounds ancient Israel as the forerunner of Judaism and Christianity. The very patterns of our thinking about Israel have been imbued with religiosity, or with its defensive counterpart, anti-religiosity. It is most difficult not to think of Israel as a people wholly apart from the rest of humanity. While our scholarly or secular minds may know better, our psychosocial milieu impels us to look for abstract religious phenomena and for all-encompassing theological explanations as indices to the meaning of Israel. As a result, the radical historic mutation of Israel in human history is accounted for by the supernatural, or by retrojected theological meanings from later Israel, or simply not accounted for at all.

Yet another root of our lack of total vision of early Israel is the myopia of academic overspecialization. Biblical studies, largely freed from the immediate grip of religious dogma, have fallen into yet another dogma: the enslaving hold of hyperspecialization disconnected from a larger framework which could relate means and ends, parts and wholes. Each scholar pursues particular skills and interests, as linguist, exegete, literary critic, form critic, historian, or historian of religion. The specialist circles around a narrowly circumscribed field of study while focusing on it with a single, highly refined methodology. There are few who take responsibility for synthesizing the discoveries of the specialists. So limited and arcane have the specializations become in biblical studies that it borders on anathema to try to encompass enough of what the specialists have found to dare a large-scale interpretative model.

Fragmented lines of inquiry are reinforced by scholarly vanity and the encrusted traditions of learning. Students of the Bible are socialized to believe that it is "scholarly" to limit sharply the scope of what is researched. The self-restricting mentality and practices developed during graduate study tend to become hardened into lifelong career habits. Such self-limitation for tactical purposes, with a view to contributing specialized results to a total effort at synthesis, is eminently defensible. Regrettably, tactical self-limitation has become strategic self-limitation, and the larger possible designs of Israel as an historic phenomenon of the first magnitude are increasingly lost to the workaday mentality and method of biblical scholarship. The widest and deepest understandings, the significances and uses of what is studied microscopically, are now largely matters for hours of avocation and offhand speculation.

In the face of questions about the total structure and import of early Israel, biblical specialists are virtually as mute as those who have never taken up specialized biblical studies. It is not surprising, and not altogether unjust, that religious laity, humanists, historians, and theologians have taunted us with having labored inordinately long in the biblical mines while having produced so little precious ore. It is only partly a defense when we object that much immediately unproductive digging is necessary in order to turn up any precious metal at all. The really stinging question in the criticism is this: Have we biblical specialists forgotten what it was we set out to find? Maybe there is a fair amount of refinable metal lying about on our slag heaps. Maybe we persist in digging in familiar but exhausted veins. And perhaps we have been operating largely as solo prospectors, each intent on striking it rich, jealous and fearful lest we invade one another's claims.

We must beware of treating scholarly overspecialization as a moral issue of guilt and blame. The problem has solid intellectual, cultural, and sociological dimensions. When an individual specialist resolves to look at the larger meaning of ancient Israel, at base one is limited by the remarkable degree to which the language and habits of biblical study have been shaped by the humanities. There is an almost irresistible instinct to split all approaches and conclusions with respect to the biblical materials into literary, historical, or religious (theological/philosophical) channels. Everything in one's training as a biblical scholar impels toward one or the other, or some combination, of those well-worn approaches. Simultaneously, everything in one's training militates against formulation of the object of study in holistic terms.

Having identified and decried our myopia toward early Israel, what alternative approach is available? Have we not canvassed the phenomena when we examine the literature of Israel, the history of Israel, and the religion or theology of Israel?

Is not everything encompassed in these categories? In terms of one way of formulating the data, namely, the schema provided by the venerable tradition of the humanities, it is true that such a tripartite division of the subject matter presents a reasonably ample "coverage." Anyone who carefully studies the literature, history, and religion of Israel over their total range will normally have amassed an immense amount of information in the process and, if at all perceptive, will have acquired a richly textured conception of the data. Unquestionably such a humanities-oriented inquirer will know a great deal about Israel, but at the price of a certain compartmentalization of knowledge in which the impulse to account for ancient Israelites as actual psychosocial beings will have been severely attenuated.

A humanities perspective on ancient Israel gets at important dimensions of the phenomenon. The Israelites wrote engrossing literature. The Israelites experienced an eventful history. The Israelites developed a novel and consequential religion. Beyond that, the humanities approach roots the literature and the religion in the unfolding history of Israel and sees these three dimensions of ancient Israel as vitally interrelated.

Yet what is this "history of Israel"? History is a welter of events in endless succession and in problematic interconnection. Why are some events remembered by a people and not others? And how are the newly discovered events and factors of Israel's world, uncovered by modern research, to be related to those events and factors which Israel identified and proclaimed in an overarching cultural schema? Are the significant events and forces at work in the history of a people always those of which they are themselves aware? Or, if they are aware of them, do they always choose to give direct expression to them? And what are the transactions by which the events through which a people pass, especially in their beginnings, are transmuted into symbolic structures of collective identity and meaning? What are the forms of living together and thinking about the communal life which take ever-changing shapes and orientations in the course of historical experience? And how are the social interaction patterns and the thought patterns of a people related? How can a student of ancient Israel take its total existence as a social system of interacting doers and thinkers into account and still give the inquiry a boundable controlled form? The humanities as such give very little help in answering such questions.

2

Complementarity of Humanistic and Sociological Studies of Early Israel

There are many facets of human experience which cannot be gotten at directly within the compass of the humanities. The social sciences enable us to approach human life and to reflect upon it in yet another way. Biblical scholars have been slow to approach their subject matter in terms of social science. This is partly due to the fear that a social-scientific approach will undercut the primacy of theology. In direct proportion to the degree that the scholar holds the religious views of the Old Testament in high regard, he or she is likely to shy away from subjecting them to the immanent categories of sociological analysis.

Furthermore, social sciences came rather late to the company of the sciences. Humanities derived from the ancient Greeks and burst upon Western Europe with renewed fervor in the Renaissance of the fourteenth to sixteenth centuries. By contrast, sociology and anthropology are not much older than the middle of the nineteenth century. Ecclesiastical theology made its peace with the humanities and somewhat more grudgingly with the natural sciences, whereas ecclesiastical theology continues to suspect that a pact with the social sciences will mean its own subservience or subversion. Moreover, by comparision with the refinements of method in the humanities and in the natural sciences, the social sciences have seemed too crude and imprecise for specialists versed in apparently more exact methods. Where should a humanities-oriented biblical specialist begin in order to penetrate the protean world of the social sciences? Which of the many competing forms of sociology should be applied to Old Testament studies?

A closer look at the legacy of the humanities approach to biblical studies seems necessary if we are to understand the current hesitancy and lag in viewing the Bible sociologically. The rise of the humanities in a vast renewal during the Renaissance must be understood over against the domination of biblical studies by myth and dogma—a domination which the new forms of study shattered by introducing rational empirical inquiry into human subject matters, including the Bible itself. To study literature, history, and religion or philosophy as human products was an intellectually and culturally liberating experience. And so it has been ever since.

Nonetheless, there has always been a curious ambivalence built into the

humanities. On the one side, they proceed with exact modes of inquiry: grammar and syntax, rhetoric and logic, and the rules of historical evidence. One can only be a humanistic scholar by doing something precise with exacting methods. At the same time, from their inception in the classical world and their renewal in the Renaissance, the humanities have been moved by large human ideals, often of heroic proportions. Man as a rational, aesthetic, and spiritual being has been, however vaguely expressed, the lodestone which promised the transformation of humanistic pedantry and archaism into sources of inspiration and models for wise and humane persons and for a just and fulfilling society. The general editor of an ambitious survey of American humanistic scholarship put it this way:

> The job of the humanist scholar is to organize our huge inheritance of culture, to make the past available to the present, to make the whole of civilization available to men who necessarily live in one small corner for one little stretch of time, and finally to judge, as a critic, the actions of the present by the experience of the past.[1]

Such an articulation of the task of the humanities sounds remote and unreal for very good reasons. Academic overspecialization has gotten the upper hand, and it is a minority of humanistic scholars, principally historians and philosophers, who think of their work in these large terms. In this respect academicians have participated in that wider current in Western experience which Marx called "alienation" and Weber called "rationalization" and whose specially virulent forms we know as professional specialization and bureaucratization. This process has both fractured the wholeness of the scholar and the wholeness of the subject matter and cut the dialectical interchange between scholar and subject matter. Each of us does a narrow bit of work, either not greatly caring or, more often, simply trusting that it will relate to the bits of work done by others, and generally without much understanding of how it might all fit together or toward what ends. Thus a vision and a promise implicit in the humanities of creating whole persons in a whole society have suffered attrition and neglect. Biblical scholars, who are in effect humanist scholars, have participated in the general decline of comprehensive vision. Insofar as they have such a vision at all, it tends to be cast in theological terms which are not squared either with contemporary human experience or with humanistic learning.

Generally unacknowledged in the assessment of why biblical scholars approach their subject matter as they do is the factor of the social-class position of biblical scholars. A recent presidential address to the Society of Biblical Literature and Exegesis touched upon this factor but failed to develop it. The relevant insight was briefly put:

> It is not always realized, or kept in mind, that biblical research, no less than any other branch of group activity, is subject to the social forces—the term "social," of course, represents the longer phrase and concept: social, economic, political, cultural, religious, and the like—at work within the community at large. . . . This principle of

social forces, rather than the personal whim of a scholar here and there, being the decisive factor in the shaping of a discipline such as ours, applies of course to every epoch in history, be it the Middle Ages, the Renaissance, the Reformation, the demise of feudalism, or the birth of capitalism in Western Europe.[2]

A perusal of major modern studies on the history of biblical research and interpretation corroborates Orlinsky's judgment that the social factors in biblical study have been either unrealized or untreated—which amounts to the same thing in practice. To be sure, the broad intellectual, cultural, and religious currents receive a fair amount of attention, but the specifically social, economic, and political factors are virtually unmentioned or unfocused. Even Orlinsky's rebuke does not specify the crucial factor of the social-class identity of the biblical scholar.

What can be hazarded about the social-class position of biblical scholars since the Renaissance? In spite of the absence of detailed inquiry on the matter, some estimations are possible. Biblical scholars from the Renaissance to the bourgeois revolutions of the seventeenth through the nineteenth centuries were generally the intellectual adjuncts of monarchic, aristocratic, or clerical class interests. Increasingly in the nineteenth century, they became one functional group among many academicians and intellectuals who shared in the bourgeois revolutions against monarchic and aristocratic domination. A broadly bourgeois democratic political and cultural perspective shaped their outlook, although the specifically democratic component was very late in developing in Germany. By and large the position of biblical scholars, as a professional and intellectual elite, was oppositional both toward the declining monarchies and aristocracies and toward the rising underclasses of the industrial proletariat and, later, the peasantry. In contrast to the formerly dominant classes they were liberative and progressive, but toward the classes below them they were conservative and reactionary. An informed guess is that the greater proportion of biblical scholars was drawn from clerical or artisan circles, or from the families of government officials and bureaucrats, i.e., from groups shaped by a petty-bourgeois outlook.

Given such a social-class position, biblical scholars found that the humanities vision of the whole person in a just society blended tolerably well with the emerging bourgeois cultures, which tended toward the politics of parliamentary democracy. Without taking serious account of the sociopolitical tensions in industrialized capitalist Europe, they naively clung to the goal of the disinterested humanities without facing the reality that large segments of the European population were effectively omitted from their vision. Where biblical scholars have taken the underclass perspective into account, it has generally been in terms of ameliorative reformism in the bourgeois system, combined often with a biblically inspired concept of public charity. By contrast, socialist societies, breaking with the explicit or implicit ecclesiastical framework of bourgeois societies, have shown little interest in biblical scholarship. Of course, the picture varied considerably from country to country in Western Europe and in North America—where most biblical research originated—and it should be one of the unfinished tasks of a history of biblical research to plot these variations in detail. But the massive datum is that biblical scholars of the last two centuries have been firmly located in the middle class and have synthesized their scholarly humanistic ideals with bourgeois capitalism and, furthermore, have done so with surprisingly little sense of the inherent tensions and contradictions in such a synthesis.

I have cited the original humane and holistic vision of the humanities to suggest that there is nothing about the humanistic methods or the humanistic subject matters that requires a narrow pedantic vision. The narrowness has been a function of academic habit, general cultural pressure, and specific class location. Indeed, because the things which the humanist scholar studies are human products, there is every reason for the total human situation to engage even the specialist's attention. The logic of integrated human experience is so much stronger than the logic of discrete academic inquiry.

> No matter how technically a scholar may operate in his own limited area, that area, by virtue of its coextension with human experience in general, is never a self-contained entity except for procedural purposes. The dimensions of scholarship are not first of all divisions of human experience. They are the products of man's need to examine wide ranges of experience in a disciplined, piecemeal fashion in order to grasp and to penetrate to the significance of the whole.[3]

There remains an additional obstacle within the tradition of the humanities to broadening scientific inquiry concerning human historical and cultural products. I refer to the distinctly individualizing perspective of the humanities, a perspective reinforced and complicated by the attachment of biblical scholars first to monarchic and aristocratic class interests and then to bourgeois class interests. After all, the humanities treat of the most distinctive human creations. They deal with brilliant literary achievements. They reconstruct histories which are so often reported to us in terms of energetic leaders, larger-than-life, who "made history." They expound the thoughts of imaginative philosophers and religious leaders. The humanities have a bias toward idiosyncratic and even egocentric individuality. Thus, the humanities do not find it easy to relate to social science, whose bias is the typically rather than the individually human, and whose perspective is on people in groups rather than on persons as single creative integers. Consequently, biblical scholars trained as humanist scholars react against sociology not only on theological grounds but on humanist methodological grounds as well. They fear that the force and flavor of biblical writings, the vigor and distinctiveness of biblical persons, and the uniqueness and concreteness of biblical beliefs will be inundated in an indiscriminate sea of generality and abstraction. Literary, historical, and religious/theological jargons thus seem a little more colorful and true to the subject in its concreteness than does sociological jargon.

Indeed, it would be a lusterless and finally valueless sociology which levelled all human individuality by proceeding as though its typical understanding of humankind in groups was the only truth to be known. Clearly, to reverse Holbrook's terms in the above quote, all our "divisions of scholarship" are arbitrary ways of getting at "dimensions of human experience." Sociology also includes some things and excludes others. Its virtue is that it can bring a higher order of inclusiveness, which permits a grasp of otherwise unrelated data. Its weakness is that it may generalize at so high a level that the concrete data are violated or untreated. So the question is: Are there dimensions of human experience in ancient Israel which only the typically generalizing approach to human relations can treat? And can we build into our understanding of general systems of human relations a recognition that they are the social relations of individual human beings which take on various conformations in the course of human history? Can the individual be subsumed justly and meaningfully in the typical and can the typical be adequately nuanced by the individual? I think I have shown that while there are sentiments and habits of mind, as well as powerful class interests, which make it difficult for humanistic biblical scholars to respond to a sociological perspective on biblical studies, there is absolutely nothing in the nature of what is studied that requires this suspicion. On the contrary, there is every reason to believe that an interpenetration, a symbiotic partnership, of the two approaches will achieve a fuller understanding of early Israel than either could attain alone.

While my analysis is directed primarily toward the limitations of humanistic scholarship, I should not want to be understood as implying that "sociology" is a single monolithic discipline or that sociologists are immune to the splintering and rootless effects of overspecialization. As a matter of fact there have always been intense internal struggles among social theorists over the nature of social systems and the interrelationships and priorities among the several segments or dimensions of social systems. Some forms of "statistical" or "empirical" sociology, particularly strong on the American scene, have tried to avoid theoretical entanglements by focusing on circumscribed descriptive studies. Indeed, many educated people who have had no more than a college introduction to sociology still think of it as a study of statistical information about sex and family, work and leisure, and rural and city living.

Nevertheless, the old theoretical questions about social community (its structure and distribution of power, the relation of its specialized segments to the whole, its equilibrium and its tendency to change, etc.) have re-emerged more insistently than ever in a milieu of social chaos, engaging the energies of many schools and tendencies of thought, while other sociologists continue to treat narrow ranges of phenomena in disregard of the theoretical and value context of their workaday choices and methods in just as limiting and hyperspecialized a manner as any comparably oriented humanistic or biblical scholar. On the American scene the re-emergence of critical theoretical sociology is associated with the work of C. Wright Mills in the late 1940s and 1950s[4] and is perhaps best known in theological circles through the work of Peter Berger.[5] Today the revival of comprehensive critical social theory is in full tide and includes many forms of radical and neo-Marxist thought.

Since this is not primarily a work on sociology, or even on social theory, I shall not systematically review these sociological tendencies and disputes, nor the closely related developments in anthropological theory and political science.[6] I shall not, however, conceal my commitment to the larger need for large-scale social theory of the sort associated with Marx, Durkheim, and Weber and their successors, while emphasizing that all the theory in the world is only as good as the empirical observations on which it is based. It will become evident, especially in Parts X and XI, which forms of sociological and anthropological theory I believe to be most pertinent to an understanding of early Israel as a social system.

If a partnership of humanist and sociological approaches to the Bible be granted as desirable, or at least possible, we may now consider what the social-scientific approach to the Bible has produced to date. What we discover is a number of social-scientific thrusts into the biblical field which broke new ground but which were handicapped either by the undeveloped state of social science at the time or by the failure of biblical scholars to pursue the issues in an adequate framework. There simply has not been a cumulative biblical-sociological tradition of scholarship in any way comparable to the tradition of higher-critical biblical study rooted in the humanities. We must speak rather of sporadic and isolated upthrusts, abortive and undeveloped explorations, and a glaring absence of disciplined continuity in tackling issues and methods.

Anthropology and sociology have been applied to the Old Testament erratically since the end of the nineteenth century. W. Robertson Smith and J. Wellhausen opened the way to comparing the customs and rites of the Israelites with the ethnography of the pre-Islamic bedouin Arabs.[7] Their gross comparative methods and crude evolutionary models led to simplistic results which discouraged others from attempting to refine their approach. Max Weber, in the course of his monumental inquiry into the connections between religion and economics, sought to delineate the social groups and forces that interacted with the religious ideas and practices of the ancient Israelites.[8] His sophisticated approach conceded very little to clarity of expression, and in spite of significant anticipations of the role of the cult in Israel's social system, his general systematic approach was allowed to lapse with his death. The Social Gospel movement in American Christianity drew heavily upon biblical sources, and Walter Rauschenbusch's incisive treatment of the Hebrew prophets suggested new lines for biblical scholarship to explore.[9] American individualism was too strong and the pre-prophetic roots of Israel's social faith too poorly understood, however, for the stimulus of the Social Gospel to greatly affect biblical studies.

Biblical scholars at the University of Chicago, where sociology made its first significant penetration into the American academic scene, tried for a time in the 1920s and 1930s to combine a broadly social approach with comparative religion in order to discern Israel or the early church as total communities.[10] The achievements were more extensive in New Testament studies than in Old Testament studies. Overall, however, this effort lacked a sharp sociological focus, moved more in the direction of comparative cultural studies, and seems finally to have been cut short by the rise of biblical theology under the impetus of neo-orthodox theology as it reached America in force in the late 1930s and the 1940s. Form criticism, with its concern for the life-setting of traditional materials in both Testaments, flirted with social perspectives. Remaining mired, however, in a formal literary orientation, it has regrettably made little progress in getting at the systemic communal milieu of the traditions and the symbolic constructs which the traditions enshrined. Cult, as one aspect of the social system, has tended to be treated by form critics as a self-contained entity without much regard for social organization, economics, politics, and communal symbolizing.[11]

Yet the total sociologically relevant yield of biblical scholarship is far from as negative as a survey of the explicitly biblical-sociological approach implies. As a wealth of ancient Near Eastern written and material remains has become available in this century, scholars have moved cautiously toward a consideration of the implications of these materials for reconstructing early Israel as a total society. Fifty years ago, Albrecht Alt,[12] with his form-critical and historico-territorial approach, and William F. Albright,[13] with his archaeological and linguistic approach, independently set in motion significant streams of scholarship which, in spite of their major differences on several points, have cultivated a continuing interest in a comprehensive grasp of early Israel. From the Alt stream of scholarship has come Martin Noth's attempt to reconstruct the social system of early Israel as a twelve-tribe religious league or "amphictyony."[14] From the Albright stream of scholarship have come George Mendenhall's proposals that the Israelite covenant was a religious analogue of a suzerain-vassal political treaty[15] and that the Israelite conquest was a peasant's revolt.[16] Furthermore, numerous detailed studies have treated a great range of Israelite sociopolitical texts, offices, practices, and institutions in relation to cognate phenomena in other ancient Near Eastern societies.[17] In particular, great progress has been made in clarifying pastoral nomadism as an economic mode in the ancient Near East.

All in all, however, there has been surprisingly little practical application and overall synthesis of the significant detailed studies. Most biblical scholars still write about pastoral nomadism as if nothing on the subject had been learned in the last fifty years. Even Noth's generally accepted amphictyonic theory and Mendenhall's generally rejected peasant revolt model have drawn surprisingly little evaluation informed by social observation and theory. Moreover, many of the most important contributions to an adequate sociology of early Israel remain unassimilated to the mainstream of biblical scholarship for the simple reason that they are buried in unpublished academic dissertations.[18] Thus, the recovery and advancement of sociological study of the Bible comes as a logical extension of the preceding rich discoveries from early Israel's environment. The enterprise of biblical sociology is able to draw upon considerable materials, already partly digested and at points loosely integrated in the body of biblical studies, but its challenge is to do interpretative justice to these materials through a new social model of early Israel.

The failure of biblical sociology to become a persisting substantive and methodological force in biblical studies is well illustrated by what now generally passes for a sociology of Israel's religion. I refer, of course, to materials about the daily life, customs, institutions, and general culture of Israel collected in introductory handbooks and consistently lacking in critical theoretical depth which would necessarily include how these data relate to the main lines of Old Testament inquiry.[19] These "social" materials are thought of as prolegomena or adjuncts to the serious literary, historical, and religious study of the Bible; they do not shape or modify the basic structure of research and theory. Economics and politics are rather assiduously avoided as systematic perspectives on ancient Israel. If Israel was "social," these handbooks seem to be saying, in the trite sense that it had social institutions such as the family, clan, and tribe, room can be made in the existing scholarly framework to comment on those institutions. But if "social" encompasses a whole network of relations and activities in the production of goods, services, and ideas and in group decision-making and norm-building, the framework of scholarly "business as usual" may have to be stretched beyond recognition or shattered altogether.

As an encompassing systemic understanding of "social" emerges, it becomes increasingly impossible to restrict sociology to prolegomenon. Sociology demands recognition as a constitutive aspect of all biblical study, and moreover it offers one important way of organizing the contributions of the humanities to illuminate the big underlying questions about the rationale of the historic mutation of Israel. Although the subject matters and methods of the social sciences have hovered around the periphery of biblical studies, to date they have not been admitted to the core of the sustained inquiry. Those who have done most with biblical sociology have generally been thought of within the discipline of biblical studies as ill-equipped interlopers. Frequently there was justice to that criticism; what we who criticized them from within the discipline failed to notice was our own ill-equipped professionalism securely protected within the established discipline, as though the social-scientific demand could be dismissed along with some of its bungling practitioners. That Israel's religion was deeply involved with and systematically correlated to its economic, social, and political situation as a people has not often been seriously proposed from within the biblical discipline proper, and the systematic empirical testing and elaboration of that insight engages the full attention of very few biblical scholars even yet, in spite of the current renewed social interest in the Old Testament.

It is the goal of this study to incorporate the substantive conclusions of the humanities in biblical studies with the methodological and theoretical contributions of the social sciences in order to give specificity to the claim that Israel was a total socioreligious system of active symbolizers or, if one prefers, of symbolizing actors. It is argued that when we take the significant results of literary, historical, and religious study of the Bible and present them within the framework of a social-scientific approach, new and illuminating patterns of interpretation emerge. While social science cannot resolve the impasse into which particular lines of literary, historical, and religious inquiry have fallen by producing new data out of whole cloth, it can set the tentative and fragmentary results of what the humanities have to say about the origins of biblical religion in an entirely new contextual light. Furthermore, it can sometimes call attention to data which do not appear pertinent to a humanistic formulation of biblical problems but which become pertinent to a social formulation of biblical problems. Ancient Israel begins to stand out as a distinctive social system that is illuminative of many vexed questions in biblical studies.

Max Weber commented appropriately when he remarked of his intrusion as a sociologist of religion into biblical territory:

> From the outset, in our attempt to present developmental aspects of Judaic religious history relevant to our problem [i.e., how did Jews develop into a "pariah" people with highly specific peculiarities?], we entertain but modest hopes of contributing anything essentially new to the discussion, apart from the fact that, here and there, some source data may be grouped in a manner to emphasize some things differently than usual. Our questions may, of course, vary in some points from those which Old Testament scholars legitimately raise.[20]

The English translators of Weber's volume add, by way of qualifying the rather too modest tone of the original:

> This emphasis, a genuine theoretical contribution, is sociological. New relations are perceived between old facts when Weber brings the varied talents of jurist, economist, historian, linguist and philosopher to the task of integration.[21]

As long as we understand that sociology can contribute to grasping new relations between old facts, it is of small moment whether these new relations are described as a matter of emphasis or as an essentially new element. Probably no single generalization holds good for all such sets of new relations in the biblical data;

some may strike us as merely lending reinforcement or nuance to what is already known, while others may appear as truly novel patterns with far-reaching interconnections and implications. The extent and import of the new relations perceived by sociology must be determined from case to case.

Consequently, while reiterating that sociology cannot supply literary and historical solutions when literary and historical data are absent, it is possible to say that what must remain uncertain in specifically literary or historical terms can take on another kind of certitude in social terms. We need not wait for the future resolution of historical questions for the social significance of the religion of ancient Israel to be demonstrated. At the same time, it is not to be overlooked that a rebirth of social study of biblical religion, which would be its actual birth as a focused discipline and method, could conceivably have beneficial effects in stimulating historical studies to look at old questions in new ways. It is well recognized that the topics and sources considered valid for historical investigation, and even its methods, are modified substantially according to the larger intellectual and cultural context in which the historian works. Wherever divergent disciplines have focused intently on a common subject matter, the tendency has been for the disciplines to modify one another by the incorporation of one another's angles of approach and methods of working.

Historical and sociological approaches to the Old Testament are methodologically differentiated but compatible disciplines. Moreover, where the intent is to study the total experience of a people, they are essential complementary disciplines. Historical study of the Old Testament will aim at the sequential discreteness of Israel's experience and the rich variety of its cultural products; sociological study of the Old Testament will aim at the total structure and function of Israel as a social system in twofold form: the structure and function of the human relations in Israelite society and the structure and function of the societal values and ideas. Indeed, it is the contention of this study that the longstanding interest of humanistically trained biblical scholars in the religion or theology of Israel requires a sociological approach if it is to be satisfactorily pursued. Scientific sociology brings the means for reflecting on the structure and function of Israel's thought in tandem with the structure and function of its interaction patterns as those patterns underwent change in the course of Israel's historic experience. Only by such a method can the thought system of Israel be intelligibly related to its action system. By whatever route we approach the core of ancient Israel, history and sociology present themselves as the indispensable twin methodologies for getting at the subject. It is inviting to paraphrase Kant's dictum concerning percepts and concepts: sociology without history is empty; history without sociology is blind. By wedding history and sociology we strive for an understanding of ancient Israel that is both full of content and perceptive of form and meaning.

3

Aims and Methods: Overview of Contents

All in all, we know enough about the historical circumstances of the emergence of Israel and its faith to offer a reasonably full account of the structure and function of Israel's religion in its total social system and, thereby, to see Israel's religion, so often treated in isolation, in relation to those dimensions of collective life which we arbitrarily characterize as economic, social, and political. I contend that we are able to connect up the forms and functions of Yahwism with the other life factors and forces in a way and to a degree which have been heretofore unattained. In part I say "unattained" because only in the last few decades have we gained enough historical knowledge from biblical studies and enough sociological sophistication from the social sciences to make such a sociological analysis of biblical Israel credible. But I also say "unattained" because, given the scholarly and ecclesiastical tendencies of the last two centuries, not many persons have thought it important to strive for an understanding of religion in ancient Israel as a basically social reality. The current mounting interest in a social understanding of Israel's religion can at last be joined to our historical knowledge of Israel's religion to open the way for sociological reflection on a subject matter long reserved for linguists, historians, and theologians.

As implied above, when I say "social system," I refer to the whole complex of communal interaction involving functions, roles, institutions, customs, norms, and symbols. A social system may be understood as active in the communal production of goods, services, and ideas and in the communal control of the distribution and uses of goods, services, and ideas. A social system so viewed encompasses the spheres of economics, social order, political order, and religion, and includes such specialized communal activities as law and warfare. The social system of ancient Israel thus includes social order, in the sense of the basic functional and conceptual units (whether organized by kinship or by residence), but it is much broader than kinship and residence groups.

"Sociology of religion" here means viewing religion in the context of the social system as a totality and specifically aims at uncovering the concrete and theoretical connections between religion and all the other aspects of the social system, insofar as these can be known. The theoretical connections between religion and the rest of the social system may refer either to the connections identified and generalized by the Israelites themselves or to connections identified and generalized by the

18

observing social inquirer. Such a sociology of religion seeks to establish patterns of correlation among the various social phenomena, and especially to note the specific ways in which the historically mutant religion of Israel served the socially expressed needs of the historically mutant community of Israel. Seeing Israel's religion as one form of communal production and control will enable us to make some contributions to answering the vexed question: Why did Israel's religion bulk so large as its most enduring and distinctive mode of social production and control? And, more precisely, did Israel's religion hold so prominent a position in the social system at the beginning as it did at later stages in its history? I maintain that the question about the form and function of Israel's religion as a social complex is the sociological equivalent of the theological question: Wherein lay the uniqueness of Israel's faith? Whereas the theological question can only be "answered" in the last analysis by divine mystery, the sociological question is capable of a straightfoward empirical answer—although I would be the first to acknowledge that even this "answer" immediately becomes in itself the basis of a new set of questions.

Having set for myself a task of overwhelming magnitude, I must explain the form in which this study unfolds. The aim being to grasp the religion of premonarchic Israel within its total social system, it was my original hope to construct this study deductively from a number of complex and nuanced interlocking propositions about the social system of ancient Israel and the place of religion within it. In the chapters on synthetic egalitarianism (Part IX) and on the religion of Yahwism in the social system (Part X), I come close to the form which I once envisioned for the entire work. Instead of working *out of* such a deductive system, however, I finally decided to work *toward* it. For one thing, I was unsure that I could say all I wanted to say within the complex symmetry of such a deductive system. But beyond that, I felt it necessary to recapitulate in part the course of my own intellectual adventures in the sociology of Israel's earliest religion.

For me it has been a process of involvement and discovery by stages in which I have had to keep working through the methods and results of prevailing Old Testament scholarship in order to give proper formulation to my sociological concern. I am, after all, trained as a humanistic biblical scholar and, as I have sought to show, I am convinced that the results of humanistic study of the Bible are of profound and indispensable importance to a proper understanding of ancient Israel. Thus, the form of this work is in part an unfolding of the humanistic-historical method of study in dialectical relation to the sociological method of study. I concluded that I could only expect my readers to follow me if they were led along the same course of inquiry I have followed through the years in which this approach to ancient Israel has been maturing in my mind. So I have chosen to discuss method at relevent points in the course of developing the historical and sociological arguments which are the substance of the study.

The given fact of contemporary Old Testament studies is that clearly marked divisions of inquiry exist in the form of literary criticism, form criticism, tradition history, history, history of religion, and theology. It is not my intent, nor would one study suffice, to survey all that these divisions of inquiry entail and all that they have concluded. Nor am I insensitive to the various conceptions of aim, scope, and method with which practitioners work in these variously demarcated channels of inquiry. My beginning point rather is to summarize and assess what these divisions or channels of Old Testament study tell us about premonarchic Israel, what distinctive shape they give to a scientific formulation of Israel's emergence as an historical and social entity.

In making this assessment of previous biblical studies, I have two chief interests. The first is to specify our knowledge of ancient Israel supplied by the respective divisions of Old Testament study—its nature and extent, the degrees of certainty according to categories of evidence, the levels of specificity and generality, and the sizable gaps. For example, what is the kind and range of information supplied by form criticism, how certain are its judgments, and how detailed are its applications in reconstructing Israelite life before the monarchy? The second is to present the results of each division of study in such a way that they can be reflected on sociologically; or, if that proves difficult or impossible, to indicate why there is little or no point of contact between the historical result and sociological analysis. This second interest is somewhat muted in the early chapters, although it can be detected as a formative element from the very start; but it will be observed that these chapters form a sequence which gathers momentum and increases in sociological explicitness as it builds toward the model of Israelite society as synthetic egalitarianism.

Parts II through IV are concerned with the literary and form-critical study of the sources for a social history of premonarchic Israel; they focus on the cultic-ideological production and refraction of the sources. Part V sets forth and critiques the chief models for understanding the settlement of Israel in Canaan and concludes with questions about the relation of the settlement to the social system, which in turn set the stage for an extended examination of the internal structure of Israel's society in Parts VI and VII. After an examination of the sub-units of tribe, protective association of families (*not* "clan"), and extended family, the comprehensive totality is explored by means of a critique of Noth's hypothesis of a twelve-tribe amphictyony.

The results of the preceding study of sources, settlement models, and social structure are then marshalled in Part VIII for a comparative analysis of early Israelite and non-Israelite social systems and socioeconomic types. Particular attention is given to the interlock between Egyptian imperialism and Canaanite feudalism, to the *'apiru* (social "outlaw") adaptation to this interlock, to the Philistines as heirs of the Egyptian-Canaanite symbiosis, and to the hypothesis of an original Israelite "pastoral nomadism." A model of social morphemes for Canaan is proposed involving the coexisting forms of agriculture and of pastoral nomadism (dimorphemes) and the antagonistic morphemes of urban statism and rural tribalism (antimorphemes). In Part IX a synthetic egalitarian model is advanced which interprets liberated Israel as the conjunction and coalition of previously fragmented and chiefly rural tribal populations culminating a long history of underclass social struggle in Canaan. The transition from Amarna Age Canaan through Elohistic Israel to Yahwistic Israel is hypothesized. The synthetic egalitarian model is supported by textual data on the enemies, component members, and allies of early Israel, and a new category of Canaanite "neutrals" is proposed. The implications of this historically based social model for the construction of a proper model of the settlement and for grasping the genetics of social organization in early Israel are spelled out.

Although the religion of liberated Israel will necessarily be treated throughout the study, a systematic examination of Yahwism as social organization and ideology is undertaken in Part X. The sociopolitical function and significance of mono-Yahwism and covenant are delineated. It is shown that a provisional "structural-functional" sociology of Israel's religion must be absorbed into a "historical-dialectical" sociology of Israel's religion if the socioreligious mutation involved is to be adequately interpreted and explained. In Part XI the issues between biblical sociology and biblical theology are joined. It is argued that early Israel's "historical faith," its passionate belief in the liberating God, its self-understanding as "a chosen people," and its insistent hope for the future are best understood as cultic-ideological dimensions of its novel synthetic egalitarian society. A theory of religious symbolization is proposed for interpreting Yahwism. Biblical theology becomes "historical-dialectical" biblical sociology.

One major difficulty in this form of presentation is that there is more repetition than would have occurred in a strictly deductive study. I sympathize as never before with all those who have attempted to incorporate the historical dimensions of Israel in a systematic theoretical framework. In the main, however, I find the repetitions necessary reiterations in the building of a sociological understanding of early Israel. The resulting structure will seem as strange to many readers as it did to me and will demand much reflection and reconsideration before it is fully understood, its implications grasped, and its argument accepted or rejected in part or in whole. For the same reason, I have often detailed aspects of the biblical text or of biblical scholarship, even when it is probable that many readers will already know the facts of which I speak. My point is to be as completely clear about every step in the argument as I possibly can be. It is hoped that the novel turns in argument to be met with along the way, the perceptions of "new relations . . . between old facts," will compensate for the occasional recital of familiar data.

Lastly, I must mention that many facets of the subject have only been lightly touched upon, and some of those most fascinating to me have been deliberately omitted or sharply curtailed. For example, I had originally hoped to include an extended treatment of Israelite law. When it became clear that its inclusion would inflate the book to impossible proportions, I confined myself to a few points where my social model of early Israel touches most directly on the law, e.g., in the discussion on covenant. Moreover, early on in the study I encountered an intriguing assortment of sociopolitical models suggested by various scholars as analogues for understanding early Israel: the Greek amphictyonies, the Arab bedouin tribes, the Near Eastern 'apiru, the Philistine amphictyony, the Iroquois Confederation, the Swiss federal union, the Gypsies, African tribal leagues, African secret societies, etc. Given that these analogues are drawn from such widely divergent cultures and historical periods, I soon decided that it was totally beyond the scope of this initial study in a sociology of early Israel's religion to examine them all with the care they deserve. Consequently, a decision was made to treat only those analogues closest in time and space to premonarchic Israel, namely the 'apiru, the Philistine amphictyony, and the prototypes or ancestors of the pre-Islamic Arab bedouins thought to have been contemporary with early Israel. Although they are geographically, and in large part temporally, more remote than the other analogues, I could not disregard the Greek amphictyonies, since they have been made the basis of the most comprehensive previous attempt by a biblical scholar to understand the structure of early Israel's society. I refer, of course, to Noth's scheme of Israel as a twelve-tribe sacral league formally analogous to the Greek amphictyonies or sacral leagues.

As it developed, the vast range of proposed social analogues for early Israel lured me into ever widening circles of anthropological, sociological, and historical literature. It will be evident that I have drawn heavily and unabashedly on anthropological and sociological research and theory, especially for an understanding of key socioeconomic categories integral to the study of early Israel: clan, lineage system, tribe, pastoral nomadism, urbanism, social stratification, and state. It has become abundantly clear to me that previous social studies of early Israel have repeatedly foundered on a lack of empirically informed anthropological and sociological theory. Many scholars have been able to cite all kinds of "parallels" between Israel and other peoples; far fewer have been able to assimilate and assess the comparative phenomena within an adequate theoretical framework. Because of the great scope of this undertaking, I am well aware that my own grasp of the appropriate theories is far from complete. Consequently, I have sought to nuance my proposals according to varying degrees of probability and have tried wherever possible to suggest what additional study is necessary to test them. I fully recognize that what I offer is no more than the initial anatomy of a subject whose ramifications appear to spread out endlessly. It is up to my readers to confirm, rebut, refine, or elaborate the model, or to develop alternative models.

Part II

The Historical Starting Point
and a Source Compendium

4

Evaluating the Historical Sources:
Temporal Distance and Cultic-Ideological Roots

Our task has been formulated as the examination of the place of the religion of Yahweh in the dynamics of the Israelite social system in the premonarchic period. The only way we can hope to realize our aim is to seek valid models based on the historical data available for the period. For our purposes, historical reconstruction of early Israel is prolegomenon to sociology of religion, but it is not "introductory" in the popularly entertained sense that, once sketched, the history can be forgotten about. The history of the formation of early Israel is the vital and foundational substructure for sociological characterization. The two concerns intersect in the area where history involves social history and where sociology involves social genetics and social evolution.

Cumbersome though the task is, we must survey the state of our historical knowledge about early Israel. We are asking: How precise can we be in delineating the stages and processes by which the people Israel, espousing the religion of Yahweh, came into being in the highlands of Canaan from the Negeb in the south to Upper Galilee in the north, and in Transjordan between the Wadi Arnon and the Wadi Yarmuk, within the approximate period 1250–1000 B.C.? Our reasons for fixing on this period as the proper historical starting point for our study will become evident as we consider the extent and solidity of our historical information about early Israel. Our attention in this and the following two parts will be focused on the character of our sources and the state of current thinking about their reliability for reconstructing the period. In Part II we shall attempt a general assessment of the historical problem in the course of staking out the field of study and offering a compendium of sources. In Part III we shall concentrate on the cultic character of the sources and their decided ideological shape. In Part IV we shall examine the sources in Joshua and Judges which ostensibly concern the formation of Israel in Canaan. In these sections we focus the concern with literary and form-critical studies in terms of their essential contributions to a proper assessment and use of the traditions of early Israel as historical sources.

There are valuable secondary sources of knowledge about the Israelite settlement and formation in Canaan. Archaeology has reconstructed phases of the material culture and thereby effectively illuminated intellectual and social culture to a certain extent, especially when its results are supplemented by nonbiblical texts from the period.[22] These political, economic, and religious texts are a productive source of information, although they must be used with the proviso that most of them derive from a time somewhat earlier than the upper limit of our period, i.e., prior to 1250 B.C., and many of them come from the northerly reaches of Syria-Palestine and thus fall outside the immediate region of Israelite development. Historians assess the pertinence of these documents variously according to the degree that they think the conditions of Israelite Canaan held good in earlier centuries and in the regions of Syria north of Canaan.

Scholars have sometimes tried to use archaeology and nonbiblical texts as direct historical witnesses to the Israelite settlement, but their efforts have proved facile and simplistic and at times simply mistaken. The fact is that, apart from one statement in the victory stele of Pharaoh Merneptah, the nonbiblical texts contain no reference to Israel nor even any certain reference to a single one of the component groups in Israel. Egyptian records may allude to Asher by name[23] and may describe Issachar's origins, without naming the group.[24] The identifications in both instances are problematic, however. The chief value of such texts as the Tell el-Amarna diplomatic correspondence[25] is to enrich our knowledge of the country and its peoples—their social, political, and religious forms, their modes of thought and experience—and to tell us enough about historical forces and movements to suggest analogies for understanding Israel's beginnings in at least some respects.

Such background knowledge is of inestimable value for analyzing Israel's social structure. It enables us to see Israel in a broad family of successive social and political movements in Canaan, which included the Amorites, the Hyksos, the 'apiru, and the Philistines. Those family relationships will be examined more closely in Parts V, VIII, and IX. Nonetheless, the background information so acquired is *not* translatable into direct historical judgments about Israel. The problems involved in employing this archaeological and comparative textual material for historical purposes will be explored when we review the chief models for reconstructing the Israelite settlement in Part V. The possibilities and challenges for archaeology in helping to contribute to a much needed, more fully rounded, cultural-material understanding of Israelite society will be adumbrated in Part X.

Accordingly, while we wish it were otherwise, the primary source of our knowledge about Israel's beginnings remains the Hebrew Bible. Without it we should not even have guessed from all the other sources combined that so energetic and unique a people as Israel appeared in Canaan at the dawn of the Iron Age. With it we possess an embarrassing richness of literary traditions. As we have already adumbrated, when we inquire about the historical information which the Bible contains for the period 1250–1000 B.C., we come up abruptly against the reality that this literature is not directly historical in its form and content. The literature is to a large extent narrative in that it offers a series of incidents linked at times by a chronological framework of a sort, but, for all their air of factuality, even the narratives are not directly or primarily historical. They are at most quasi-historical, materials for history. Most of the incidents are viewed from a temporal distance, and all of them are shaped in one way or another by cultic and ideological considerations. These crucial factors of temporal distance and of cultic-ideological production will be returned to again and again in the course of our study, and pointedly so in Part III. For the moment, we make some brief, initially clarifying observations.

By *temporal distance* we mean that these traditions of early Israel appear in a written form which was given them, with perhaps a very few exceptions, anywhere from decades to centuries after their initial formulation as separate items of tradition. By itself, a large time gap would not be an insuperable obstacle to the historicity of the traditions. Where written sources are available and where there is the instinct for historical research, it is possible for a historian, removed from the primary sources by generations or centuries, to do an estimable job of writing the history of an earlier age. In point of fact, early Israel did not have written sources on anything like the scale or of the sort characteristic of more politically developed societies. Furthermore, Israel's later so-called historians were not moved by the same notions of "objective" historiography that characterize the humanistic discipline of historical writing. When the monarchic "historians" gathered the available data about earlier Israel they were content to record the meaning-bearing accounts of Israel's beginnings, which must originally be approached as legendary or saga-like, however much they contain the reflections and refractions of actual events.[26] Those units of the tradition which have a documentary archival cast turn out, on examination, to be generally among the latest materials. They are often presented out of proper context and are influenced by the urge for recording typical of the more developed political life of Israel under the monarchy. We shall illustrate this process in considerable detail with respect to the tribal allotment lists of Joshua 13—19 and the fragmentary settlement annals of Judges 1, which are to be analyzed in Part IV.

By *cultic-ideological production* we mean that these early traditions of Israel stem from the peculiar structure and the peculiar needs of premonarchic Israel as a cult community. Without trying to anticipate all that our subsequent analysis will show, we simply state that the peculiar structure of Israel consisted in its being a social movement with a well-articulated religious cult. The peculiar need of that cult community was the development of traditions which would cement its component members together by nourishing their common identity at points of critical shared interests, while simultaneously protecting the local autonomy of the component members. We stress the immediate and primary origins of tradition in the

group-cementing cult community. We do not deny that primary historical material can secondarily serve cultic-ideological needs. We are claiming simply that no
such primary historical instinct existed in early Israel apart from the cult community.

The materials typical of cultic-ideological production are liturgies, poems,
myths, sagas, legends, and genealogies, although myth in the technical sense has
been so suppressed in early Israel that form critics generally speak at most of
"broken myths" or of "mythical" elements or motifs lodged in other forms. That
these traditions tend to describe a past is much less significant than that they
employ the past to reinforce tendencies in the present. When past events are
recounted, as is often the case with early Israel, the controlling factor is how that
past posits and contributes to particular present developments; indeed, how that
past lives in and through the present recollection and recital of it. In Part III we
shall formulate our working definitions of cult and of ideology as they specifically
apply to early Israel.

When these twofold factors of temporal distance and cultic-ideological production join in the formation and articulation of tradition, *substantive and editorial
alterations* inevitably and intentionally occur. These alterations were not the result
of careless craftmanship with respect to either the casual or the willful disregard of
criteria of historical accuracy otherwise accepted as normative; but rather the
imaginative folk refraction of communal experience, entirely consonant with and
appropriate to the structure and needs of a nascent social system which, although
it knew of writing and made use of it, was basically preliterary in its impulses.[27] By
distinguishing for analytic purposes between substantive and editorial alterations,
we are pointing to alterations in the perception of lived-through events in the
initial traditional forms, *and* we are pointing to alterations in the structure and
meaning of the initial traditional forms in the course of their incorporation in
successively larger complexes of tradition.

Substantively, the events related are altered as a matter of course by selective
emphases which delete, introject, condense, transpose, join what was once separate, and separate what was once joined, in order to serve immediate cultic-
ideological needs. Editorially, the initially separate units are strung together one
after the other or spliced together in frequent rearrangements of material and
shifts of context so complex that any given unit will tend to contain two or more
meanings, depending upon the stage of its transmission or the scope of the
context in which it is read and interpreted. Admittedly, documentary historians
must practice a formally similar selectivity in the sources they use and the form in
which they communicate their versions of history. The point is that cultic-
ideological selectivity is of a different sort than documentary historical selectivity.
When later more literary attention is given to the cultic-ideologically produced

traditions, that literary attention (as in the case of the J or E writers) is not in the form of original research into yet older written sources which can be used to correct the received accounts by a more accurate historical picture.

Instead of a fundamental historical reshaping of tradition, the later literary traditionist builds upon the early cultic-ideological foundation, introducing perhaps a fresh perspectival understanding, but without basically questioning that received traditional foundation. The literary enlargement and qualification of the traditions occurs by way of linking and grouping materials, by editorial frameworks and notations, all of which may add new perspectives but none of which can be understood as the result of fundamentally new historical research. From the work of the literary traditionist J, E, or D we get an enlarged interpretative perspective with a distinctive slant and color. We also get the agglomeration of previously separate traditions which, now joined in a single frame, introduces new contradictions and tensions that demand our independent historical assessment. Yet in no case do these editorial alterations lead us back behind the traditional process to a point where the traditionist critically corrects the substantive alterations of remembered events in terms of freshly arrived at principles of historical analysis.

Of course, we are at liberty to qualify this seeming harshness of judgment by saying that early Israelite traditionists were as historically critical as they could be under the circumstances. In no case, however, does that allow us to hedge on the basic recognition that what they wrote was not a documentary history of early Israel, even though some documentation appears incorrectly retrojected into earlier contexts and even though, from our perspective as humanistic historians, we can make historical use of their work. This confusing and somewhat disheartening situation has led some biblical scholars to retreat into the illusion of the outright historical value of the early accounts. Since the early biblical accounts are based on presumably good memory and are often highly circumstantial, the reality of the cultic-ideological production of the materials is swept aside and the traditions are posited as "historical." Such grasping for historical security by fiat, in spite of its sincerity of intention, leads only to historical conclusions by fiat.

Form criticism and tradition history, about which we shall have more to say in the next part, have fully validated their fundamental insight into the immense multilevel cultural and historical complexity of the traditions. There can be no denying that the strict historical implications of their discoveries are catastrophic for all attempts to write a history of early Israel which merely sum up and underline the surface biblical account treated as straightforward documentary evidence. Our basic biblical sources for early Israel are legendary, cultic-ideological products, wholly comprehensible in their formal communal framework, magnificently architectonic in conception and execution, and without ques-

tion rich in sources of information about the earliest times. It remains the necessary task of the historian to sift this information and to supply a spatio-temporal
framework for understanding the stages by which Israel came into existence.

All efforts to supply a spatio-temporal framework for the refracted historical
data discerned within the cultic-ideological formulations of the early Israelite
traditions are necessarily rough approximations. Occasionally it is possible to
detect single striking historical items which stand out pronouncedly against the
surrounding historically indistinct material, such as the comment in Exodus 1:11
that Israelites (we should prefer to say proto-Israelites) helped build the Egyptian
store cities of Pithom and Raamses.[28] Characteristically, however, it is difficult
to draw a firm line between what is historical and what is not historical within
accounts which almost everyone senses to possess some foundation in actual
events. We have to do with a spectrum or continuum along which the accounts
appear as now more or less historical in one respect or another. It is understandable that competent humanist historians differ in the weight they give to the
various factors involved in judging the historicity of the tradition. The synthetic
historical judgments entailed are complex calculations or estimates involving
different kinds of evidence and different processes of reasoning.[29] Historical
judgment strives for objectivity, but it is always a judgment as to probability. The
more the historical elements are mixed into the work of communal imagination,
the more difficult it is to control the probabilities. The virtual absence of nonbiblical texts synchronized with the premonarchic origins of Israel, in contrast to
their comparative frequency in the monarchic period, contributes to the relatively
low-probability confidence that historians must acknowledge for their reconstructions of premonarchic Israelite history.

The sociologist of Israel's religion is dependent upon the work of the historian,
being unable to escape altogether the difficulties which arise from the lack or
obscurity of historical data. Yet the sociologist's interest in historical data is
different from the historian's interest.[30] The sociological interest is determined by
the goal of discerning the religion of premonarchic Israel in its social system.
Insofar as that goal requires analysis of the social system of Israel as a developmental phenomenon in ancient Near Eastern history and culture, the sociologist
cannot avoid taking positions on many crucial historical questions. The version of
Israel's early history regarded by the sociologist as most probable will indeed make
a great difference to the resulting sociological constructions.

The differing interests of historians and sociologists in historical detail can best
be expressed in the difference between the degree of spatio-temporal detail which
the historian seeks in order to achieve an optimal historical reconstruction and the
degree of spatio-temporal detail which the sociologist seeks as the *sine qua non* for
analyzing a social system at some stated level of complexity or with reference to a

particular clustering of social relations. On the average, as a matter of disciplinary procedure, I think it can be said that the historian strives for fuller detail than does the sociologist. The sociologist, while seriously concerned with the range and distribution of available historical detail, can survive on less historical detail than the historian, provided it is of the sort that facilitates understanding of the social system from some clearly articulated analytic perspective, whether in developmental profile or in functional cross-section. A period of history which looks rather sparsely documented from the viewpoint of the professional historian may, if certain data are known, appear rather more amply known to the sociologist. In history and in sociology, as in all disciplined human efforts to know, the aim of the inquiry determines whether we feel informed and how fully we feel informed. Only when we know the question are we able to say if a given datum or theory is an "answer." As Noth has succinctly remarked, "The right way of posing the question . . . is above all the most important matter and the fundamental presupposition for correct solutions."[31]

A basic methodological question for our study is now evident: Do we possess sufficient historical knowledge about premonarchic Israel of the right kinds to allow us to construct an account of the Israelite social system and the place of Yahwism within it? And what are "the right kinds" of historical information pertinent to sociological analysis? Instead of discussing this question in the abstract, I prefer to let it stand as a question for the reader who follows my own working answer to the questions in the historical and sociological analysis to follow. I merely note for the present that the mode in which our sociological interest requires us to cast our historical analysis will necessitate our conceiving the historical task in the study of Israelite origins rather differently than is usually done and will allow us to treat as relatively inconsequential for our purposes some of the finer points of historical inquiry which are still unresolved and which are still worth pursuing in their own right. This, I take it, is one of the things Weber had in mind when he remarked, "Our questions may, of course, vary in some points from those which Old Testament scholars legitimately raise."[32] The decision, or more properly the series of synthetic decisions composed of many factors, as to which historical data and problems in the early history of Israel are pertinent for the sociology of its religion is a critical one for our study. It is my intention to be as open and self-critical as possible about those historical data and problems I include and those I omit.

5

The Historical Subject:
Israel in Canaan 1250–1000 B.C.

The fundamental historical anchor point for reconstructing the object of our study is the formation of the social system of Israel in Canaan during the period 1250–1000 B.C. Endeavors to push back behind that era of the self-conscious independent emergence of the Yahwistic "tribes" of Israel on Canaanite soil are shadowed by so much uncertainty that they cannot constitute a firm alternative starting point. Neither the traditions about the fathers or patriarchs of Israel (Genesis 12—50) nor the traditions about Moses (Exodus-Deuteronomy) are sufficiently secure historically to permit us to begin with them as dependable historical foundations.[33] We begin necessarily with a body of people in a social movement which includes diverse traditions focused on the unifying cult of Yahweh and making various claims about how Yahwism was introduced to Israel by Moses and/or by Israel's ancestors in the cults of the patriarchs. The traditional claims in that regard must remain prehistory in a methodologically necessary suspension of historical judgment. Once we have explicated the community of Israel in the land of Canaan it may be possible to examine the traditions of Israel's prehistory, the accounts of the fathers and of Moses, with a view to determining retrospectively what historical solidity they contain concerning the fortunes of some of the peoples who entered into the social system of Israel.

Not only is a starting point with Israel in Canaan the only proper one in terms of historical sources but equally it is the only proper one in terms of sociological method. We are concerned with the social system called Israel, and whatever historical worth there may be in the traditions of the fathers and of Moses, they do not present us with a distinct integral social system such as appears in the banding together of the "tribes" of Israel in Canaan beginning in the period 1250–1200 B.C. The traditions of the fathers and of Moses tend either to give us traits of a social system which look suspiciously like naive retrojections of later Israelite features, or they suggest fragmentary aspects of a social system conspicuously different from that of later Israel. Given the reality that the patriarchal and Mosaic eras are represented in the present form of the traditions by confused retrojections of a later period or by sketches of fundamentally different proto-Israelite social forms—or by a bewildering admixture of both—we must conclude that they are not a clearly determinable part of the social history of Israel per se.

Obviously that does not end the problem. From a sociological viewpoint, the earlier traditions may be sifted in an effort to locate elements which contributed to the social system of Israel or elements which were rejected by that system. Our contention is that such a critical analysis of the earlier traditions can only be carried out adequately after the emergent social system of Israel in Canaan is characterized organizationally and structurally in its own terms. So far as I can judge, the prehistoric patriarchal and Mosaic eras will not yield much historical or sociological data as the consequence of a direct approach to them which ignores the locus of the traditions about those eras precisely in the social system and cult of Yahwistic Israel in Canaan.

Indeed by approaching our subject through the social system of Yahwistic Israel, I believe it is possible to hypothesize a pre-Yahwistic stage of confederated peoples which also bore the name of Israel. This hypothesis, adumbrated if not fully stated by Noth, will be advanced and elaborated in IX.43. The delineation of this pre-Yahwistic Israel is not, however, the result of merely compiling data from the patriarchal legends. It stems rather from a rigorous analysis of Yahwistic Israel in Canaan, secondarily employing data from the episodes concerning the patriarchs, viewed in the light of general sociopolitical and religio-cultic data on pre-Yahwistic Canaan.

My hypothesized dividing line between fully formed Israel and the Mosaic and patriarchal prehistories is an admittedly arbitrary one. It is arbitrary, in the first place, because Israel emerged as a social system in Canaan *by stages*. It is impossible to point to a single date when Israel came fully into being, and it is necessary to conceive its course as a social system in terms of decades of development which continued up to the verge of the monarchy under Saul. Israel's premonarchic social system was never altogether the same from one decade to the next, and it never attained a finished form, since it was aborted by the introduction of the political form of monarchy. It is arbitrary, in the second place, because the prehistory of peoples who joined Israel in its later stages undoubtedly *overlapped chronologically* with the history of the emerging social system Israel. Thus, aspects of proto-Israelite life reflected in the patriarchal stories, for example, may well have been contemporary with the early stages of the social system of Israel. It is arbitrary, in the third place, because when a new group entered Israel, it brought its cultural heritage and fund of experience with it and thereby contributed to the total social system of Israel while it was reciprocally altered in those fundamental respects which defined membership in Israel. So we must be at pains not to give either the impression of a hermetically sealed wall between Israelite and pre- or proto-Israelite phases or the impression that the Israelite phase, although methodologically separable from the proto-Israelite phases, was monolithic and unchanging.

Having made all the above qualifications, there is nevertheless compelling necessity and value in the analytic distinction between Israel's history and social maturation as a Yahwistic community in Canaan, on the one hand, and the prehistory of its component peoples as proto-Israelite Yahwists or non-Yahwists within or without Canaan, on the other hand. Simply stated, the distinction permits us a proper stress upon Israel's emergence as a recognizably novel and coherent social system in Canaan. It further provides a base for estimating whether the traditions pointing to the prehistorical situations of proto-Israelites, either before they were in Canaan or before they accepted Yahwism, contain actual memories or are retrojections into prehistory of traditions drawn from a later Israelite experience. Within the analytic parameters of the Israelite social system in Canaan we can respect both the changes and tensions within the system and the contributions of the proto-Israelites to the larger system.

It is apparent, then, that we have a delicate task in assessing the relationship between Israel as a total coherent system and the prehistories of its component peoples. Evidently we must come to terms with two seemingly contrary tendencies: a tendency to retain certain proto-Israelite memories and a tendency to retroject later Israelite conditions into the proto-Israelite accounts. The enormous difficulty of judging whether the preservative or the anachronizing tendency is at work in a given case, or how they are associated in other instances, does not vitiate the historical and sociological import of these interacting tendencies of the tradition. These tendencies are clearly rooted in objective conditions in ancient Israel; they reflect the formation of a social system involving composite populations, cultural elements, religious features, and psychosocial needs which sought a novel equilibrium.

The traditional view of the Hebrew Bible is that Israel's history began with the patriarchs and Moses. Some biblical scholars still begin the history with the patriarchs. Others, probably a majority, begin it with Moses. Accordingly, it is advisable for me to explain more exactly why this study posits the historical beginning, as qualified above, only with Israel's development in Canaan. The following paragraphs apply the preceding formal distinctions to the concrete situation of the traditions about the patriarchs and Moses.

5.1 Patriarchal Episodes

First, I would not deny that there are historical data in the traditions about the patriarchs.[34] It is evident that in the Abraham, Isaac, and Jacob traditions there are traces of the life circumstances of some groups that eventually found their way into the larger formation of Israel. Some of those traces evidently refer to the actual experiences and social forms of groups while they were still proto-Israelite, or pre-Yahwistic, i.e., before they joined in an association of Yahweh-worshipping peoples. To acknowledge this historical dimension is not, of course, to say anything precise about the temporal period to which these traces refer, since we only know that they stem from a time prior to the group's incorporation in Israel and thus in principle could derive from times as late as the last increment to the membership of Israel, i.e., in my opinion about 1050 B.C. The geographical factor is far more explicit, since the patriarchal traditions are often tied to specific locales within and adjacent to Canaan, but it is a matter of dispute whether the events and social forms recounted were originally attached to the places named or were secondarily connected. Many of these purportedly "historical" traces in the patriarchal accounts are evidently the naive retrojection of later Israelite experiences and social forms, a process facilitated by the later Israelite canonical division of the "history" of all Israel into patriarchal, Mosaic, and settlement phases.

In other words, the first type of historical traces are strictly proto-Israelite in that they do not tell us about the distinctively constructed people Israel, but only about the life of some people who became Israelites. The second type of historical traces are Israelite, to be sure, but their actual chronological reference point is not to a period predating the formation of Israel proper. The actuality of the full Israelite origins of these historical traces is obscured by their tradition-historical separation from context and their canonical phasing in the cultic-ideological frame of the traditions. These understandings of historical traces in the patriarchal narratives need not exclude the possibility that some elements recollected from proto-Israelite contexts became important in fully Israelite contexts. The point is that such elements bridging the proto-Israelite and Israelite phases can only be known by dealing explicitly with the cultic-ideological shape of all the traditions.

5.2 Moses and the Moses Group of Yahwists

Secondly, I would not deny that there are historical data in the traditions about Moses.[35] In my view some of these historical traces stand out rather clearly. Moses is recalled as an actual person who was of Levitical kinship, who intermarried with Midianite "semi-nomads," who led a slave revolt, who was reportedly buried in Transjordan, and whose grandson Jonathan was a priest to the tribe of Dan after it settled in northern Canaan (reading "Moses" in Judges 18:30 with some LXX MSS, Vulgate, and Old Latin[L] instead of "Manasseh" as in MT). Many scholars go on to regard as solidly historical the identification of this Moses with a great religious movement of salvation from bondage, covenant-making, and law-giving, as testified in the traditions of the exodus and Sinai. Now the Israelite tradition certainly makes this identification in innumerable ways; it is an historical datum in the broad sense that later Israelites traced the immediate origins of Yahwism to Moses. Clearly, however, to follow this Israelite traditional attribution is to adopt a far-reaching synthetic historical judgment without much specific underpinning. It is unsupported by precise historical data, inasmuch as the points we acknowledged above about Moses' kinship, marriage, burial, and priestly line over three generations do not directly support the great superstructure of the later tradition. Only Moses' leadership in the slave revolt seems directly related to the massive tradition, and neither the revolt nor Moses' part in it is dealt with adequately in the traditions.

As I see it, the historical situation which can be calculated on the basis of the Mosaic traditions is such that we can have more confidence about the experience and religious belief and practice of a proto-Israelite "Moses group" than we can have about the specific person Moses. There remains an unclosed disjunction between the few details known about Moses and the way in which he serves as a cipher for a whole order of experience, belief, and practice which Levites, and perhaps other proto-Israelites, brought with them when they entered Canaan and which served both as a catalyst and as an instrument for the formation of Israel proper. For my part, I am prepared to say it is highly probable that the notion of Yahweh as a god who delivers from oppression was introduced first among a group of proto-Israelites for whom Moses was one, although not necessarily the only, leader. I say that, however, while simultaneously insisting that the present accounts about Moses and his group tell of the introduction of Yahweh and his deliverance from oppression in a form overwhelmingly determined by what those beliefs meant to the peoples who formed the community of Israel in Canaan. In short, I think we have only the faintest glimpses of how those later stock beliefs of Yahwism were really held and what they really meant to the Moses group who first introduced them to Israel.

I am also prepared to say that it is at least possible, conceivably probable, that notions of covenanting between god and people and of divine law-giving were introduced in some form among that same group of proto-Israelites in which Moses was a leader. The probabilities of the presence of some version of covenant and law in the Moses group might be put in this way: (1) Since the Moses group contributed the cult of Yahweh to Israel in Canaan, it is reasonable to believe that it concurrently contributed covenant and law; (2) since the Moses group was self-ruling once it escaped Egypt, it would have required some instruments for self-rule similar to those provided by covenant and law; and (3) the Exodus traditions explicitly claim that Moses introduced covenant and law. By rebuttal, however, it must be asserted: (1) It is not logically or historically necessary to posit covenant and law as features of Yahwism from its inception; (2) there are other forms of self-rule for small groups besides the fully articulated covenant and law attributed to Moses; and (3) the covenant and law texts in Exodus exhibit such literary-critical and form-critical difficulties that they do not yield any demonstrable evidence of going back to pre-Canaanite tradition.

My sense as historian is that for the proto-Israelite Moses group, covenanting and law-giving were relatively undeveloped as compared with what the instrumentalities of covenant and law came to mean during the great confederation of Israelite peoples in Canaan. How they were conceived of and practiced in the wilderness of Sinai, if they did function at that time and under those circumstances, is so far irrecoverable except by picking out this or that feature of later covenant and law and asserting it to be Mosaic. In saying this I do not mean that efforts to ascertain what forms covenant and law may have taken in the Moses group should be abandoned. I am simply stating that in my opinion the efforts to date have been unconvincing.

And of course there remains in the traditions more than a hint that covenant and law-giving may after all have been associated with another southern group of proto-Israelites connected with Kadesh who may not have been involved in the Egyptian exodus at all.[36] So I make this problematic historical concession to the Moses group while simultaneously insisting that the present accounts about what happened at Sinai-Kadesh are in a form overwhelmingly determined by what those beliefs meant to the peoples who formed the community of Israel in Canaan. As with the beliefs about Yahweh the deliverer from Egypt, so with the beliefs about Yahweh who covenants and gives law, I think we have only the faintest glimpses of how such later stock beliefs and forms of Yahwism may have been held and practiced and what they may actually have meant to the Moses group (or alternatively, to a separate Kadesh group) if in fact that group first introduced them to Israel.

Bluntly put, we are not in a position to calculate the part that the historical Moses actually played in introducing Yahweh, in explicating him as a deliverer from oppression, as one with whom to covenant, and as a law-giver. This is another way of saying that we do not know precisely how those notions, and their operational corollaries, actually arose and functioned in the proto-Israelite Moses group. Possibly the later tradition is correct in believing that Moses had the decisive part to play in all these respects. But only possibly. The historical difficulty in discerning the role of Moses is enormous. Very soon, apparently within two or three generations, he underwent the fate of a legendary figure of archetypal proportions. He became a sacred figure for legitimating virtually everything regarded as normative by later Yahwists. That fate as a sacred cipher has decisively shaped the legendary accounts of his work. They abound in edifying and aetiological tales with the intent of locating the fraternal unity and religious totality of later Israel in its normative beginnings. In particular, they focus in the person of Moses many of the later offices of Israelite religion and sociopolitical organization, and they attribute to him practices and institutions known only certainly to have been operative in much later times.

As we have noted, historical judgments must be drawn from among contending, more or less probable, alternatives. In this instance, a possible judgment is that Moses bulks so large in later tradition because historically he did play the central role. Even when such a formal possibility is accepted as probable, we merely move the problem of Yahwistic origins one stage back and into an obscure period where it is extremely tenuous to give the work of Moses any exact content that is clearly distinguishable from his traditional archetypal function. Thus it seems fully as logical an inference, and in the end more convincing, to attribute the primacy of the role of Moses to the impact of the Yahweh cult in Canaan in which there existed a central office (or offices) occupied by one (or more) who articulated the traditions and instructions of the faith and who was (were) conceived in the august role of Moses, "the covenant mediator" or "law proclaimer."[37] Under the circumstances, we can readily understand the practical cult-functional impetus for vastly enlarging the "historical" figure of Moses and in the process irretrievably obscuring it in the contemporary needs of the religious community.

In our analysis of the patriarchal and Mosaic eras as obscure and insubstantial starting points for the history of Israel, an important difference between the two eras has been uncovered. With respect to the patriarchal period we are unable to identify the operational presence of any criterion of fully formed premonarchic Israel which is not, in one way or another, simply a pseudohistorical retrojection of tradition. The patriarchal "history" is either material for proto-Israelite history or it is veiled, temporally misplaced reflections of later Israelite history and experience. The Mosaic locus, however, is of a substantially different order. Setting aside any necessity of resting the significance of that age on the single figure of Moses, we nonetheless have clearly identified it as the locus which introduced some of the decisive features that were to be taken over in later Israel. Among these we would specify Yahweh as the deliverer of oppressed peoples from imperial-feudal thraldom into autonomous egalitarian "tribal" existence.

According to our best calculations, the Moses group was the bearer of the experience of the god Yahweh as a deliverer from political oppression. Very possibly the Moses group, or a somewhat similarly situated Kadesh group, was also the bearer of some forms of covenanting between god and people and some forms of divine law-giving. These were features of central importance to the all-Israelite cult, which gave structural and functional cohesion to the many peoples who joined with the Moses group in Canaan. These Yahwistic features were differentiating criteria of Israel over against other peoples in Israel's environment. We can say therefore, that the pre-Canaanitic Yahwistic experience of the Moses group was a proper part of the history of later Israel only in the restricted sense that it was the experience of this Moses group, interpreted through its cult of Yahweh, which provided the basic, immediate historical catalyst, the communal focus, and probably a significant part of the repertory of cult symbols and practices for emerging Israel.

If we must concede so much historical importance to the pre-Israelite Moses group, why should that group's experience be denied as the proper starting point for the history of Israel? The answer is simply this: although it was Yahwistic, the

Moses group was not Israelite and, therefore, even its Yahwism was not simply coterminous with the more fully elaborated Israelite Yahwism. We must not be misled by the anachronizing periodization of the canonical traditions into assuming that the religion of Yahweh among the Mosaic Levites outside of Canaan was the same phenomenon as the religion of Yahweh among the greatly expanded congeries of mixed pastoralists and agriculturalists who came to practice it in succeeding generations in Canaan. Important continuity there was, but the critically important discontinuity can be grasped best by comparing the two confessing Yahwistic communities: on the one hand, a small, relatively homogeneous, group forged out of a common experience of Egyptian oppression; and, on the other hand, ethnically, culturally, economically, and historically variegated groups in Canaan with highly tenuous grounds for unity. The small, historically focused Moses group was *not* the large variegated people of Israel, even though its members became a part of greater Israel. Correspondingly, while bearing the same name and some of the same traits, and even being confessed by some of the same peoples in the two settings, the Yahweh of the Moses group and the Yahweh of variegated larger Israel were in important respects two different Yahwehs. We are dealing here with a subtle, easily overlooked combination of continuity and discontinuity not unlike the dialectical relationship between the pre-resurrection Jesus and the post-resurrection Christ of Christian beginnings.

When it is said that the Moses group was not yet Israel we mean it in at least three respects. For one thing, the Moses group in my view did not bear the name Israel. Although it has seldom occurred to biblical scholars, it is a matter of fairly conclusive demonstration that the name Israel was given to the Yahweh-worshipping association of peoples for the first time on the soil of Canaan. Secondly, the Moses group was not a people mainly engaged in intensive farming on its own home ground and defending itself with success against sociopolitical oppression from adjacent city-states, as was the case with Israel in Canaan. From the limited evidence available, the Moses group appears to have been composed of a mixture of stock-breeders (sheep, goats, and cattle), small gardeners, and fishermen, including war captives or migrants from Canaan, who were forced by the harsh imposition of state slavery in Egypt into migratory habits for survival. They lived for some years in the sparsely populated Sinai peninsula where they were not immediately threatened with extermination or with inundation by other, more politically organized, peoples, cultures, or religious cults. Once free of Egypt, the military struggles they had were with similar small groups of people and, in truth, their main dangers were from a hostile natural environment and from the shock of adapting their social forms to a precarious freedom. Thirdly, they were not a large conglomerate of people coming from widely disparate historical and cultural experiences, such as was the situation of Israel in Canaan.

This is not to deny that the Moses group included people from various back-

grounds prior to their common oppression by the Egyptians. The point is that the Levitical worshippers of Yahweh were relatively few in number, perhaps no more than a few hundreds or thousands at most. They had a common historical experience as a guest people on the border of Egypt who were eventually depressed into the status of state slaves. They constituted in the desert a small sovereign group in a compact region in which leadership could be directly and strongly asserted in face-to-face relationships. Once the Moses group entered Canaan and joined with other peoples to form the larger community of Israel, the distinguishing earlier traits, if they were not lost altogether, were either sharply attenuated as only one set of cultural norms and historical experiences within the larger body of Israel or re-formed in the design of a vastly expanded social system.

These differentia between the proto-Israelite Yahweh community of the Moses group and the Israelite Yahweh community in Canaan must be kept clearly in mind when reading the biblical accounts and when constructing historical and sociological models for early Israel. When biblical tradition presents "Israel" under Moses, it eliminates the sharp differences in scope and structure and experience between the two essentially different historical and sociocultural communities, naively picturing "Israel" in the desert as identical with Israel in the settled land—except for the fact that Israel in the desert had been a wandering people. Even the wandering is pictured as movement toward that goal which the writers themselves had long since experienced as the remarkable domination of Israel in Transjordan and in the Canaanite highlands. Thus we must resolutely struggle against the thoroughly understandable tendency of the biblical traditions, and the less excusable tendency of biblical scholars who too uncritically follow those traditions, to flatten out and to unify the historical discreteness and the sociocultural developmental differentia into an account of a monolithic people under a changeless deity.

The above analysis, which exposes the inadequacy of the patriarchal and Mosaic periods as historical starting points for a history of early Israel, may be summarized in this way: The patriarchal period is not a separate autonomous phase in the history of Israel. It is a synthetic creation of canonical Israelite tradition in which scattered memories of the proto-Israelite experiences of some Israelite groups are inter-mixed with later Israelite experiences and beliefs and cast in the form of "a history of genealogically related eponymous ancestors." The Mosaic age is not a separate autonomous phase in the history of Israel, although it is a separate autonomous phase in the history of Yahwism which contributed basic beliefs and practices to the later Yahwism of united Israel. Insofar as the Mosaic age's autonomy as a phase of Yahwism is cast as a phase in the history of all Israel, the Mosaic age is also a synthetic creation of canonical Israelite tradition in which the authentic continuity between the two phases of Yahwism is transformed into monolithic unity in the form of "a history of all the tribes of Israel under the single prototypical leader Moses."

The methodological consequences of this understanding are as follows: From the patriarchal traditions we can derive information as to the prehistory of some peoples in Israel, as well as hints as to how some peoples in later Israel thought of their earlier fortunes. It also means that from the Mosaic traditions we can derive information as to the pre-Israelite phase of Yahwism as the source of key all-Israelite beliefs, as well as abundant evidence concerning the cultic-ideological forces at work in later Israel. The available information in these various categories is uneven in quantity and quality. From neither set of traditions, however, can we derive a straightforward history of Israel. The information in the partriarchal and Mosaic traditions will be helpful historically only when we have established the early history of Israel in Canaan from other sources.

5.3 The United Monarchy

To round out this explanation of why premonarchic Israel in Canaan is the proper starting point for reconstructing Israel's early history, it is necessary to rebut the less commonly advanced, but formally possible, contention that the history of Israel begins with the monarchy. Documented history, which is at the base of the humanistic discipline of history, arises only where there is sufficient political development to replace or to supplement the rather schematic traditions of the cult with more secular accounts of what men and women said and did in a discernible spatio-temporal framework. For Israel this stage of political secularity arrived with the monarchy, approximately two hundred years after the formation of Israel. The monarchy's central institutions provided archives preserving administrative, diplomatic, and military information.[38] Beyond this technical sphere of political documentation, the monarchy introduced a cultured, urbane interest in unifying traditions and tracing origins which went far beyond the initial stirrings of such interests in old Israel.[39] It is in this climate that the first extensive "histories" of Israel's origins were prepared by the so-called J and E traditionists. We can observe the persisting concerns of the centralized monarchy in the way their work is organized and in their editorial contributions in the form of frames and notations. Why, then, should we not simply conclude that the history of Israel begins with the archives of David's and Solomon's reigns and with the traditionist J who worked in the Jerusalem court, and to a lesser extent with the traditionist E who worked in the cultural sphere of the northern monarchy, if not directly under monarchic aegis, after it split away from David's dynasty?

In a sense we do begin with the monarchy. We begin with the monarchy in that we have to take up our task of assessing and analyzing the sources which come to us in the great sequences that the traditionists of monarchic times prepared, including those of the D traditionist from late monarchic times. Accordingly, we have to be constantly alert to the politically centralizing monarchic filter through which the earlier traditions passed. We must test those traditions to see what alteration they have undergone because of the context in which the great traditionists of the monarchy worked. This assessment will be in part our task in Part IV. But these admissions and cautions are by no means tantamount to claiming that Israel had no discernible history prior to the monarchy. On the contrary, the main outlines of a premonarchic, and in critical respects an anti-monarchic, form of Israelite life conflict so fundamentally with the pre-suppositions and impulses of the monarchic traditionists that we cannot possibly understand them as a late fabrication. Such a body of traditions about old Israel makes sense only as the direct product of a premonarchic form of life and thought which carries on in the monarchy in part as an archaic cultural survival, in part as a religio-national norm, and in part as a continuing social struggle within Israel.

I shall now try to summarize all that has been said on the proper historical starting point in early Israel by drawing together the several strands of argument. The legitimacy of beginning Israel's history with the period 1250–1000 B.C. can be established by comparing the premonarchic and monarchic periods in correlation with the patriarchal and Mosaic ages, which have been naively included within an all-Israelite frame. The two earliest periods, the patriarchal and Mosaic, we have seen to be fictitious pre-extensions of the valid history of Israel, useful as material for Israelite prehistory. In addition, the Mosaic age belonged to the history of Yahwism, which became the religion of later Israel, and in that regard may contribute something to our understanding of the central religious features of old Israel. The later period of the monarchy is that separate phase of the history of Israel in which the people attained a developed centralized political form, aspects of which are documented in enough fullness to hearten the strictest historian.

Unlike the patriarchal and Mosaic ages, but in common with the monarchic age, the intervening period of premonarchic Israel in Canaan is stamped by the experience of a people with sharply definable temporal-territorial and socio-cultural horizons. Also, unlike the patriarchal and Mosaic ages, but in common with the monarchic age, the intervening period of premonarchic Israel in Canaan is defined by the experience of a large association of peoples of diverse fortunes and cultural repertories who managed to become the one people Israel, dominat-ing for an extended period large areas of Transjordan and Canaan. The emphatic point is that the sociocultural synthesis of diverse peoples in a contiguous temporal-territorial setting, which was lacking in varying ways both in the pa-triarchal and the Mosaic periods, was integral to and original with premonarchic Israel in Canaan. The monarchy simply provided a new centralized political form, and in many respects an overlay, for Israel's already accomplished temporal-territorial and sociocultural identity. Unlike monarchic Israel, however, pre-monarchic Israel was not politically centralized, nor indeed was its political or-ganization differentiated from its social organization, so that Israel's initial unity and identity were achieved through a cultic-ideological, tribally structured cohe-sion. As a result, premonarchic Israel produced few, if any, documentary sources for reconstructing its history but passed on its traditions of the past, with historical data and implications chaotically embedded therein, within the framework of its important culturally unifying institution: the cult of Yahweh.

Consequently, although the premonarchic history of Israel can only be gotten at indirectly, it can be gotten at. The historical data can be ferreted out, can be compared and contrasted with the data for monarchic Israel and for surrounding peoples, and a probable reconstruction can be made. It will be a history richer in cultural and social matters than in chronological and biographical detail. At certain levels of historical reconstruction, the approximations and calculations for premonarchic Israel can be accurate, and especially so with respect to an analysis of how Yahwism arose and how it functioned for those premonarchic people. And, precisely where it will be fullest and most adequate, this history of premonarchic Israel will pass over into an account of the social system of premonarchic Israel.

Further supportive of the validity of a history of premonarchic Israel is the fact that Israel's origins are positioned in the midst of an ancient and highly developed arena of self-conscious civilization. There are broadly but sharply definable historical parameters and vectors in the total situation of Near Eastern history and culture which place Israel in an historic dynamic rather than in an apparently timeless, primitive cultural setting where no determinable historical boundaries and interactions can be grasped. If Israel was not just another instance of Near Eastern civilization, Israel was nonetheless an instance of a sociocultural entity which rose in reaction to and in interaction with the dominant forms of civilization. Its history of struggle to shape a kind of unity independent of political centralization and social stratification makes sense only in its interplay with the surrounding history of expanding and evolving forms of political and social domination. Israel chose a course of decentralizing, nonstratifying, essentially antipolitical development in deliberate contrast and opposition to its immediate neighbors and, in doing so, was propelled to a level of eventful struggle and inordinate self-consciousness which have all the marks of a striking historical consciousness. Therefore, while what we can say of the exact details of its origins may be frequently meager, what we can say will be of the order of history in its regard for spatio-temporal discreteness, since its subject is not a primitive people cut off from confrontation with advanced cultures and lacking in a vivid sense of change. To the contrary, its subject is a people facing advanced cultures, in fact spun off from those cultures, and achieving an adaptation that joins previously unjoined social sectors and cultural items as part of a larger experimental design for a socially egalitarian existence. And Israel manages to do this in the face of the most serious threats from powerful surrounding systems of domination determined to prevent its liberation.

All these facts and factors taken together make it plain that early Israel's history must begin with the formation of larger Yahwistic Israel in Canaan, for it is that distinctive development which gives us a twofold vantage point: from it we can *look back* at its Yahwistic precursor, the Moses group, at its earlier and smaller Elohistic forerunner, and also at the fragmented recollections of peoples who entered Israel either in the earlier Elohistic or in the later Yahwistic formations; and from it we can *look foward* to its markedly altered form under the monarchy.

6

Compendium of Historical Sources

What are the sources within which historical data regarding premonarchic Israel can be found? In presenting the following compendium of sources, I bypass for the moment the tangled literary problem of the large source strata identified cryptically in biblical scholarship by the sigla J, E, D, and P. This is done, in part, because I have no new proposals to make concerning the overall design of the literary source hypothesis, although I shall make some fresh proposals concerning one or another of the sub-sources which are best left to the appropriate contexts in the sections that follow. I accept the hypothesis of extensive literary strata, as progressively modified by subsequent work on oral tradition, form criticism, and tradition history. I associate myself very closely with the outlook of Albrecht Alt, Martin Noth, and Gerhard von Rad in accepting the literary-source framework as the necessary starting point for further inquiry. I differ from other scholars, including the three just mentioned, in one or another detail. In the comments with which I briefly annotate the compendium of sources, some references to the major source strata will be found. At certain points in the detailed argument in subsequent parts of this study I assess those judgments about literary sources which are germane to the historical or sociological discussion. In Part IV, for example, in treating the sources in Joshua and Judges, I explain my understanding of the Deuteronomic history (D) and its relation to the frequently conjectured extension of the J and E sources into Joshua and Judges.

Once the premise is granted that the larger sources dissolve into smaller sequences and units which must be assessed structurally and traditio-historically from case to case, the really important task for historical and sociological inquiry into premonarchic Israel becomes the form-critical and tradition-historical task. If one assumes, as I have already argued, that the J/E/D/P traditionists did not engage in fundamentally fresh historical research, our chief concern with their work becomes how their methods and aims must be taken into account in estimating the historical worth of what they have relayed to us. Have they omitted or altered the older traditions which principally concern us? That is necessarily an important factor in assessing the separate traditions, but it can be weighed from case to case without extensively reviewing the work of the traditionists as a totality, for which in fact another volume would be required. The criteria for source separation and the description of the contents and characteristics of the sources are available in countless biblical handbooks. Readers who are uninformed about biblical source analysis, or curious about some aspect of it, should consult those handbooks.[40]

Nor will I attempt to survey the entire enterprise, methodology, and results of form criticism. Its practical impact on my analysis will be evident to some extent from the start in the way I have grouped the sources in the compendium and in the evaluative annotations. The relation between the forms of tradition and their cultic and ideological functions will be extensively explored in Part III. But all the details and nuances of form criticism[41] and tradition history[42] will not be explored. For one thing, the flood of form-critical studies of biblical texts is swelling so rapidly that it would be impossible to report the conclusions of all such studies on all the sources we employ. I have tried to keep abreast of the output and to incorporate their pertinent results, but to turn this study into a complete report on the form-critical contributions would be pedantic in the exact sense of providing documentary overkill for points already established.

Even more significantly, form criticism has itself fallen into a rather narrow mold in which its interest in the conventional forms of speech has become highly technical and affectedly overrefined, to the impoverishment of form criticism's announced concern with "the place in life" of the forms. I contend that form criticism has not developed either a curiosity or a precision for dealing with the setting of the forms in any way equal to its minute dissection of forms, and I think the sterility of dissection is directly connected with the absence of a serious and refined sense of all that is connoted by the life-setting of a form.[43] In this study I want to break free of the stereotyped focus of much technical form criticism so as to lift its interests into a sociological dimension where the life-setting of the form can be examined in a more productive way than has generally been the case. This means in a sense bringing the broad cultural impulse in the mind of Old Testament form criticism's founder, Hermann Gunkel, up to date by informing it with a wider and more precise analytic sociological understanding.

In spite of the diverse conclusions of form criticism, which often give the impression of a hodgepodge of unrelated or contradictory phenomena, I believe there is a rather impressive operative consensus among scholars about the constant typical factors that control the conditions for the historical use of the traditions. Once the major premises of form criticism are granted, we are provided with highly sensitive measures not only for assessing whether historical data are preserved in the forms but also for estimating what kinds of data can be expected to occur in certain forms. One need not entertain highly rigid, almost mechanistic, attitudes about all biblical speech as conventional speech to realize the potential value of recognizing the parameters that formalized speech placed upon the development of biblical traditions. This can be of great assistance in tackling the delicate task of trying to work data from different form-settings into a single cohesive body of synthetic historical judgments. In fact, to erect historical judgments in disregard of the formal character of the sources is to court disaster.

These admittedly rather abstract remarks about form criticism as an aid to the historian are intended to alert and sensitize the reader to the fuller discussion in Parts III and IV and to the brief annotations in the source compendium which follows in II.6 1–17.

A word is in order concerning the wide spread of biblical books from which the sources in the compendium are drawn. If the biblical materials were self-conscious documented history, it would be natural to assume that the sources for pre-monarchic Israel would be grouped in one division of the account. We would look for them in Joshua and Judges and, in part, in the latter sections of Numbers and the beginning of I Samuel, i.e., in that segment of the biblical record which falls chronologically between Moses and Saul. By now we know that such an approach is mistaken. Cultic-ideological production of the traditions has created a unification of the traditions in which chronology is only one factor, and often the chronology by which the traditions are arranged is among the latest editorial features of the tradition. So we must reckon with the fact that not every tradition in Joshua and Judges will be of the same value, or even of any direct value, as a source for the formation of larger Israel; the traditions in those books will be of differing sorts and of differing values, and we must supply historical criteria in their evaluation. Some of them, on examination, may prove to be sources for monarchic Israel or for proto-Israelite groups. Likewise, we must reckon with the fact that traditions of historical value for premonarchic Israel have in some instances been lodged in temporally improper segments of the biblical story, notably in the books of Genesis through Deuteronomy.

The following compendium of the sources groups the materials in part by literary types and in part by thematic unities.[44] The accompanying annotations indicate what the groupings have in common in form and content, as well as the respects in which they are believed to be of historical value for our study. Within its brief compass, the lists and annotations are at least reasonably complete. At later points in the text, much fuller discussions of certain of the sources will be introduced; for example, as in the case of materials in Joshua and Judges examined in IV.17. By perusing the compendium with care the reader will have a synoptic view of the primary biblical data on which the remainder of this study is based.

6.1 Blessings, Songs, and Fable

Genesis 49:3–27†	Blessing of Jacob
Exodus 15:1–18, 21	Song at the Sea of Reeds; Song of Miriam
Numbers 10:35–36	Song of the Ark

---

†Chapter and verse divisions of the Bible are cited throughout this study according to the English versions. In a minority of instances where the Hebrew Massoretic Text (MT) departs from the English numbering, the Hebrew numbering will be indicated in parenthesis following the English numbering.

Numbers 21:14–15	Wahab in Suphah
Numbers 21:27–30	Taunt Song against Heshbon
*Numbers 23:7–10, 18–24; 24:3–9, 15–24	Oracles of Balaam
*Deuteronomy 32	Song of Moses
Deuteronomy 33	Blessing of Moses
Joshua 10:12b–13	Address to the Sun and Moon
Judges 5:1–31a	Song of Deborah
Judges 9:7–15	Jotham's Fable
I Samuel 2:1b–10a	Song of Hannah
*II Samuel 22//Psalm 18	Song of David
Psalm 68:1(2)–14(15)	Song of Victory over Enemy Kings
*Habakkuk 3	Prayer of Habakkuk

It is characteristic of many of these poetic compositions that they contain materials more ancient than the narrative contexts or poetic collections in which they are arranged and that their attribution to particular persons, such as to Jacob or to Moses or to Hannah, are formalistic and secondary. It is also characteristic that in poems composed of multiple self-contained units, notably the blessing catenas, some units are evidently much older than others. Occasionally the original poems have been altered in praise of the Israelite monarchy—certainly so in the Song of Hannah and possibly so in the Song at the Sea of Reeds. The Song of David presents a thorough monarchic working-up of materials which in many details derive from an earlier conceptual milieu. In varying degrees, the same is true of the Oracles of Balaam, the Song of Moses, and the Prayer of Habakkuk. The monarchic composition of songs in which the detectable premonarchic elements cannot be separated out by literary criticism, in contrast to earlier compositions with monarchic additions, is indicated in the above list by asterisks. Jotham's Fable provides a vivid early Israelite denigration of kingship couched in arboricultural metaphors. In fact the poems as a whole are rich in clues to premonarchic social organization, military practice, and economic modes of life.

6.2 Centralized Conquest Narratives

Joshua 2	Israelite spies visit Jericho and pledge Rahab's safety
Joshua 3—5:1	Israel crosses the Jordan River
Joshua 5:2–12	Israel observes circumcision and Passover at Gilgal
Joshua 5:13—15	Joshua meets "the commander of Yahweh's army"
Joshua 6	Capture and destruction of Jericho and the sparing of Rahab

Joshua 7	Defeat of Israel at Ai and punishment of Achan's violation of the ban on booty
Joshua 8	Capture and destruction of Ai
Joshua 10:1–15	Defeat of Amorite kings at Gibeon/ Beth-horon
Joshua 10:16–43	Execution of Amorite Kings and conquest of Judean cities
Joshua 11:1–15	Defeat of kings in Galilee and capture and destruction of Hazor

These stories of the conquest of Canaan by united Israel teem with historical difficulties so massive that the highly centralized picture of events they present is totally unconvincing. Nonetheless, in order to round out our collection of premonarchic sources, they are included because here and there the individual stories give some insight into actual processes and events and because they illustrate how traditions purporting to tell a continuous story are in fact materials gathered around a festival celebration of the conquest at Gilgal. While it is difficult to date the earliest stage of the Gilgal festival traditions, there are indications that it was premonarchic and thus provides some hints as to how the taking of the land was viewed toward the middle or close of the premonarchic period from a Benjaminite-Ephraimite perspective which became determinative for the centralized traditions of the Yahweh cult. Since Joshua 9 tells of a treaty with inhabitants of the land it is treated in another source category. On the other hand, the sparing of Rahab of Jericho is included here because the incident is interwoven as a sub-motif in the narrative of the spying out and conquest of Jericho. In Parts IV and V we shall direct our attention to the thicket of historical perplexities which Joshua 1—12 taken as a whole presents to the modern historian.

6.3 Localized Settlement "Annals"

Numbers 21:1–3	King of Arad defeated at Hormah
Numbers 32:34–38	Gad and Reuben build/rebuild towns in southern Transjordan//Numbers 21:21–35
Numbers 32:39, 41–42	Machir, Jair, and Nobah take East Manasseh
Joshua 10:6–11,15	Battle of Gibeon/Beth-horon in Benjamin
Joshua 11:5–10,11b,13	Battle of Merom in Naphtali
Joshua 13:13	(Manasseh?) fails to drive out Geshur and Maacath from Transjordan
Joshua 17:14–18	Joseph takes the central hill country as far as the Jezreel Valley
Joshua 19:47	Dan captures Leshem at the headwaters of the Jordan River
Judges 1:1–20	Judah, Simeon, Othniel, Kenites, and Caleb take the Southland

Judges 1:21	Benjamin fails to take Jerusalem
Judges 1:22–29	Joseph takes Bethel, but its component members Manasseh and Ephraim fail to drive out the Canaanites in fortified cities
Judges 1:30	Zebulun fails to drive out all the Canaanites
Judges 1:31–32	Asher fails to drive out all the Canaanites
Judges 1:33	Naphtali fails to drive out all the Canaanites
Judges 1:34–35	Dan fails to drive out all the Amorites, but Ephraim subjugates the Amorites
Judges 18:1b–2a,7–12, 27b–29	The Danite migration from south to north
Judges 20:18,31,35a,36	Intertribal skirmishes between Benjamin and Judah/Ephraim

In IV.17.3 I shall give arguments for believing that these traditions about individual tribal actions once constituted a corpus anchored in the interests of the twelve subdivisions of Israel which formed administrative districts in David's kingdom. Their purpose, as originally collected, was to define the separate identities and claims of the tribes in their covenant with David to form a single Israelite state. In its present form the source is badly fragmented and editorially expanded and revised. Yet it possesses value for showing how the settlement patterns of the respective tribes were viewed toward the end of the period of the settlement, and it supplements what we learn from other sources about the diversified histories of the individual sub-units of old Israel. I designate them loosely as "annals" because of their terse circumstantial style, but formally they lack the chronological specificity which political annals customarily display.

The annalistic materials incorporated into the elaborated traditions have been variously edited and subordinated to an all-Israelite perspective. Even the much valued list in Judges 1 has not escaped extensive modifications. I include among these annals two passages not usually associated with them, namely, brief reports of battles at Gibeon and at Merom. As edited, the original tribal names are deleted and the military action is credited to all Israel under Joshua. I suggest, however, that it was from such localized battle accounts that the Gilgal festival program, and then the traditionists E and D, worked up the schema of a unified campaign of all Israel under Joshua. Moreover, elements from such annals may be embedded in the account of Micah and the Danites in Judges 18 and in the prolix story of the intertribal sanction of Benjamin in Judges 20.

6.4 Inventory of Defeated Kings

| Joshua 12:9–24 | Thirty-one kings of Canaan defeated by Joshua |

When the framework attribution of these defeats to Joshua is removed, the list stands on its own feet as an ancient tally of city-states whose lords were deposed by Israel. That it is not simply a secondary summation of the Joshua narratives is evident in the fact that only fifteen of the thirty-one cities named are treated in the narratives (and of these, four cities are out of sequence with their order of appearance in the narratives). There are evident corruptions of the text at points, and it is difficult to say precisely how old the list may be. If it implies that all the cities named were taken over by Israel, the completed list would have to be no earlier than the time of David. If, however, it indicates only that the king was defeated in battle, or that he was deposed by his own subjects, or that, once defeated, his power was restricted to his own walled city, then the list may be from an earlier period. I hypothesize that the original list was premonarchic and that it was constructed on a conception that Israel overthrew city *rulers* rather than conquered or annihilated city *populations*. The list may have survived because, brought up to date, it served to round out a description of David's conquests; but as an actual roster of cities captured by David it is inaccuracte, since it includes many cities that had been Israelite long before David came to power—not to mention incomplete, since David took cities not included in the list. Nor does the proposal that it is an inventory of Solomonic fortified cities on important communication routes adequately account for the origins of the extant list.[45]

6.5 Inventory of Tribal Heads and Military Censuses

Numbers 1; 26   Moses takes two censuses of the "tribes" in the wilderness

The present position of the census inventories in the wilderness period is totally unhistorical, being the product of the late P narrative of Israel's beginnings. The form of the accounts is stamped by later experience with military censuses undertaken by kings, the first in Israel having been instituted by David against much opposition. The total of more than 600,000 arms-bearing males is ridiculously excessive, since that would yield a total population of at least 2,500,000, a figure far larger than the highest estimates for the most populous periods of ancient Israel under the late monarchy. I have included the inventories here because they contain terminology of group *officials* and of social organizational *divisions* with some claim to antiquity, as well as the recollection of a premonarchic tribal muster of troops.[46] They correctly connect the military organization of premonarchic Israel with its basic social organization. The late P traditionist seems to have had access to archaic data, which he recounts in labored and naive form, with little understanding of his materials, but which happily yield some information as to how the old social segmentation was arranged and how the fighting forces of premonarchic Israel were recruited.

6.6 Narratives of Military "Judges"

Judges 3:12–30	Ehud of Benjamin against Eglon of Moab, Ammon, and Amalek
Judges 4	Deborah of Ephraim and Barak of Naphtali against Canaanite city-state rulers of northern Canaan
Judges 6–8	Gideon of Manasseh against Midian
Judges 10:17—12:6	Jephthah of Gilead against Ammon

Preserved within the Deuteronomic framework of the Book of Judges are several vivid stories which tell of a tribal hero or heroine who gathered the forces of one or more "tribes" in order to drive out an invader or, in the case of Deborah and Barak, to crush an attack by local Canaanite city-state lords. Judges 4 gives the prose version of the battle against the Canaanite lords and Judges 5 celebrates the victory in poetry. The supposed campaign of Othniel of Judah against Cushan-rishathaim of Mesopotamia (Judg. 3:9b–11) is omitted, since it contains no circumstantial details and since the foreign king is not only otherwise unknown but is given the apparently capricious name "Cushan of twofold wickedness." In spite of the attempts to give the account a plausible historical setting,[47] it seems probable that it was fabricated by an editor in order to supply a major Judean judge. Moreover, I am aware of the complicated state of the Gideon and Jephthah traditions, layers of which were doubtless formulated only in monarchic times; nonetheless, I have included the entire accounts because on many items of historical and sociological interest I believe them to contain authentic reportage of premonarchic times.

6.7 Narratives of Military Virtuosi

Judges 3:31	Shamgar ben Anath against the Philistines
Judges 13–16	Samson of Dan against the Philistines

Although Samson is explicitly understood by the D editor as one of the "judges" and Shamgar is briefly presented as such by implication, it is striking that both men are pictured as fighting alone, and not at the head of the popular militia. In fact, Samson is even resented by the Judeans, who hand him over to the Philistines for retribution. The motifs of phenomenal strength, single-handed valor, brazen recklessness, and raucous pranksterism give these episodes a decidely folkloristic flavor. Even so, in their details of the daily life, in the apparent non-Israelite name of Shamgar, and in the dual roles of Samson as a physical prodigy and as a Nazirite, there is material evidently derived from premonarchic circles.

6.8 Narrative of an Upstart "King"

Judges 9
Abimelech of Manasseh forms a mixed Israelite-Shechemite princedom which soon collapses

Unlike the other judges with whom he is formally linked, Abimelech initiates an aggressive action rather than responds to an attack. His action consists of using his dual lineage as half-Manassite and half-Shechemite to impose a petty kingship or princedom on sections of the central hill country, including Shechem. The imposed rule lasts for only three years and is treated both by the original narrator and by the editor as "un-Israelite."

6.9 Notations about Nonmilitary "Judges"

Judges 10:1–2
Tola of Issachar holds office for twenty-three years

Judges 10:3–5
Jair of Gilead holds office for twenty-two years

Judges 12:7
Jephthah of Gilead holds office for six years

Judges 12:8–10
Ibzan of Bethlehem (Judah? Zebulun?) holds office for seven years

Judges 12:11–12
Elon of Zebulun holds office for ten years

Judges 12:13–15
Abdon of Pirathon in Ephraim holds office for eight years

The persons named in these brief, annalistic notes are said to have "judged" Israel for specified but irregular lengths of time, and in their sequential arrangement, this gives the impression that they functioned over all Israel successively. Unfortunately, neither the mechanisms of appointment nor the duties of office are given. In spite of the common use of the verb "to judge," these functionaries appear to have no connection with the military exploits of the so-called major judges, unless we harmonize the brief note about Jephthah with the long narrative about his victory over Ammon. It has been suggested that these men were "law proclaiming" officials in the intertribal Israelite league and thus held an office that was national in scope.[48] We shall attend briefly to this hypothesis in VII.31.2 (see notes 254–256 in particular) in conjunction with our critique of Noth's amphictyonic theory.

6.10 Narrative of a Tribal Relocation

Judges 17—18
Dan moves to Laish-Dan at the headwaters of the Jordan River and installs a Mosaic Levi-

tical priesthood "stolen" from a household in
Ephraim

Although the present form of the story is at least as late as 734 (cf. the reference
to the captivity of northern Israel in 18:30), its atmosphere and many of its details
concerning social organization and cult speak for a premonarchic origin. As it
stands, the narrative clearly serves the polemical purpose of discrediting the
northern Israelite state sanctuary at Dan, one of the two shrines erected by
Jeroboam I when he broke away from the southern Davidic dynasty.[49]

6.11 Narrative of Intertribal Sanction of an Offending Tribe

Judges 19—21   Intertribal sanction of Benjamin for an un-
                                  punished sexual crime followed by restitu-
                                  tion to full league membership

This narrative creates many misgivings as to its reliability for illuminating
premonarchic Israel. It is marked by a highly stylized conception of all Israel
punishing an offending tribal member, and it is composed of a number of motifs
and sub-plots which appear in other stories, such as the sexual crime of the
Sodomites (Gen. 19) and the capture of Ai (Josh. 8), most of which appear not to
be very ancient. Its sketch of the strategy and tactics of the sanctioning operation is
stereotyped throughout and is marred by serious internal contradictions. The
polemical thrust of this piece against Benjamin serves to discredit the home tribe
of Saul, Israel's first king. With all that said, the account exhibits some features,
such as the role of the Levites and the annual festival at Shiloh, which seem reliable
for premonarchic times. In any case, it is the one biblical passage that purports to
show the way the intertribal confederacy applied sanctions, and as such it was
drawn upon heavily by Martin Noth for his delineation of the early amphictyony
of Israel.[50] Thus, in VII.31.1 it will be imperative for us to assess its value for
reconstructing the constitutional arrangements of premonarchic Israel.

6.12 Narratives of Israel's Pre-Davidic Wars with the Philistines

I Samuel 4—7:2   Capture of the ark by the Philistines and its
                                  return to Israel
I Samuel 7:3–17   Israelite victory over the Philistines at Eben-
                                  ezer
I Samuel 13—14:46   Jonathan and Saul defeat and expel the Philis-
                                  tines from Benjamin

Here I have grouped a number of disparate narratives which indicate the
relations between Israel and the Philistines, who were the last group of people to
penetrate Canaan prior to the foundation of the monarchy and who posed an

unparalleled threat to the social system of old Israel. Of particular interest in these reports are the function of the ark in the wars of Israel and some occasional indications of the socioeconomic relations between Israel, on the one side, and the Philistines and older inhabitants of the land, on the other. Especially intriguing, if somewhat cryptic, is the scattered information on the relation between "Israelites" and "Hebrews." The account of the battle at Ebenezer has been heavily edited by the D traditionist, but ancient elements show through in spite of the drastic revision. The fortunes of the ark in Philistia and during its return to Israel are embroidered with legendary awe, but here too the cultic conceptions are pre-monarchic and carry us into the world of the old Israelite social system. The victories of Jonathan and Saul are described largely with historical sobriety, allowing of course for numerical exaggerations and sweeping summaries of victory.

6.13 Narratives of the Relations between Israel and Indigenous Populations

Genesis 14	Abraham, in league with Amorites of Mamre, is blessed by Melchizedek, king of Salem=Jerusalem
Genesis 23	Abraham buys the cave of Machpelah near Mamre from Ephron, the Hittite, as a burial place for Sarah
Genesis 26	Isaac in league with Abimelech, king of Gerar
Genesis 33:18—35:8	Jacob at Shechem: purchase of land, connubial covenant, attack and flight
Genesis 38	Judah intermarries with Canaanites from Adullam
Joshua 9	Joshua concludes treaty with four Hivite=Hurrian cities in Benjamin headed by Gibeon and incorporates them as cult attendants in the religion of Yahweh

Unquestionably there are perplexing problems of legendary form and of biases contributed by later writers and editors in all these accounts, not to mention the elusiveness of their historical contexts. But what is striking in them all is that they preserve memories, however distorted, of varying types of hostility, association, and accommodation between Israel (or proto-Israelites) and the native inhabitants of Canaan. They are of particular significance, in my judgment, for demonstrating that Israel's heterogeneity was partly a result of Canaanites who converted to its ranks and, furthermore, that considerable numbers of Canaanites adopted a friendly or at least neutral attitude toward Israel without actually becoming a part of Israel prior to the Davidic monarchy. This should not be taken to imply that "Canaanites" formed any simple ethnic or political bloc; in fact, to the contrary, it is our intention in this study to argue not only for the heterogeneity of Israelites but equally for the heterogeneity of Canaanites. The problem of the referents of "Canaanite" and "Israelite" in premonarchic times, and of their interaction, will be outlined in Part V and given extended analysis in Parts VIII and IX. Genesis 34 is of significance in assessing the pivotal role of the Levites as the priestly champions of Yahweh and in attempting to fill the major gap in our knowledge of Shechem in the period between the Tell el-Amarna letters and later Israelite dealings with Shechem as reported in Joshua 24 and Judges 9. Genesis 14 and 26 go back to a proto-Israelite stage when successors of the earlier Amarna 'apiru bands were growing stronger in southern Canaan. These highly informative texts will be taken up in detail at appropriate points in our continuing study.

6.14 Pastoral "Idylls"

Ruth 1—4:16	Family and peasant life in Bethlehem of Judah
I Samuel 1; 2:11–26	Family and religious life in Ephraim

Both of these traditional tales focus on women who seek the consolations and rewards of a pious trust in Yahweh as assurance of childbearing. It is obvious from the ending of the Book of Ruth that the completed work is no earlier than the time of David. The same seems likely for the stories about Hannah in I Samuel 1 and 2. Nevertheless, these pastoral tales of piety reflect social conditions and religious attitudes and practices which, if not actually formulated before the monarchy, are evident survivals from that age. For that reason I believe they may be used, with proper caution, as testimony concerning premonarchic Israel.

6.15 Territorial, Boundary, and City Lists

Joshua 13:6b—19:51	Joshua divides the land of Canaan among the twelve tribes by lot

This large bloc of geographical-territorial traditions, composed of three form-critically distinguishable types of descriptions, constitutes the literary recasting of records of the administrative district divisions in the kingdom of David. An extended analysis of these lists and an argument for their Davidic administrative provenance are presented in IV.17.2. Their value for premonarchic history is that they indicate the approximate distribution of the Israelite "tribes" at the close of the premonarchic era. For an accurate picture of tribal distribution over the land it is necessary, however, to subtract those territorial elements added to old Israel by David himself as a centralizing monarch.[51]

6.16 Theophanic and Covenant Texts

Exodus 19:3–8	Israel, through Moses' mediation, agrees to a covenant with Yahweh in which it accepts his sovereignty and agrees to do what he commands
Exodus 24:1–2, 9–11	Moses, the Levitical leaders, and seventy elders of Israel "behold" God on the mountain and eat and drink in his presence (a covenant meal?)
Exodus 24:3–8	Moses and young men of Israel officiate at a sacrifice in which the people covenant to obey the commands of Yahweh as written in "the book of the covenant" (the Covenant Code of Exodus 20:24—23:19) and announced in his "words" (the Decalogue of Exodus 20:1–17)
Exodus 34: 2–3, 5–10, 27–28	Yahweh declaims his sovereignty over Israel to Moses and announces his covenant "in accordance with these words" (the Decalogue of Exodus 34:11–26)
Deuteronomy 26:16–19	A two-sided covenant formula is given in which Israel declares that Yahweh is its God and Yahweh declares that Israel is his people
Joshua 24	At Shechem, Joshua receives converts to Yahwism in a covenant act in which the alternative choices of Yahweh, or the old clan gods, or the gods of Canaan are offered to the assembled peoples

These theophanic and covenant texts are included as sources for premonarchic Israel because they contain reflections of how the relations between Yahweh and Israel were conceived in early times. The early reflections are overgrown with later conceptions and are formulated in literary contexts which are the result of a long growth of the traditions, carrying well down into monarchic times. The signs of editorial revision are blatant, and we easily discern the difficulties of casting originally liturgical materials into quasi-narrative form.

The obstacles to identifying the life-settings of the underlying liturgical forms in Exodus and elsewhere, as well as in establishing an accurate literary-source analysis, are enormous. The original home of the material underlying these texts was the cult, and their "historicization"—i.e., their transformation into literary contexts as episodes in a narration of Israel's early history—has vastly complicated the task of recovering the original settings and meanings. While many of the literary and historical difficulties are as yet unresolved, it is possible to recover from these texts the outlines of early Israel's self-conception as a people distinctively related to its God and at the same time the outlines of Israel's social organization insofar as that is illuminated by its cultic ideology. Part III will be devoted to the cultic and ideological ground of the traditions and, among other types of traditions, will analyze the theophanic and covenant components in early Israel's cultic-ideological production. Parts X and XI will take up the relation between the covenant thought of early Israel and its social organization.

6.17 Apodictic and Casuistic Laws

Exodus 20:24–26	Altar law
Exodus 21:1–11	Slave laws
Exodus 21:12–17	Capital crimes
Exodus 21:18–36	Bodily injuries
Exodus 22:1–17	
(21:37—22:16 in MT)	Property offenses
Exodus 22:18(17)—31(30)	Religious offenses and duties
Exodus 23:1–9	Administration of justice
Exodus 23:10–19	Cultic instruction // Exodus 34:17–18, 21–25

The oldest collection of laws in the Hebrew Bible is found in the Covenant Code of Exodus 20:24—23:19, which requires simultaneous attention to closely related laws in the Decalogue of Exodus 34, in the Deuteronomic Code, and in the corpus of Priestly laws. Analysis clearly shows that the Covenant Code is a composite of many individual laws which were assembled in sub-collections before their inclusion in the present literary draft prepared for insertion in the narrative of Israel's constitution as a people at the sacred mountain Sinai-Horeb. The code is editorially linked to the covenant text of Exodus 24:3–8, which specifically refers to "the book of the covenant" as the content of Yahweh's instructions to his people. The setting for the formulation of the code in its extant state appears to have been a time under the monarchy, apparently in the northern kingdom, when the integrity of Israel's social system and legal community was threatened by alternative social structures resulting from monarchic centralization and a resurgence of Canaanite norms.[52] As a whole, however, the provisions make sense only as survivals of premonarchic times which are newly revived and reinforced in an effort at reform.

In the provisions of these early laws we encounter a range of matters concerning which premonarchic Israel adjudicated disputes; and, particularly for our sociological purposes, we gain some understanding of the focal cultic and socioeconomic interests of the community which had to be protected. Recognition of the differing forms and functions of these materials forces us to reexamine the sense in which they were "law," particularly since the so-called apodictic (categorical) and casuistic (case) laws seem to have operated in very different ways. The forms, functions, and contents of these "laws" sharpen our picture of Israel's social system. From the topics and terms of the instructions we are able to derive an actual socioeconomic content for Israel's understanding of "deliverance from bondage" or "national liberation."[53] This practical content is of inestimable value for constructing a sociology of Israel's religion, for it gives an unmistakable skeletal structure to the religion of Yahweh as the religion of a particular egalitarian social system. To worship Yahweh, to be an Israelite, meant above all else to practice a specific way of life in separation from and in overt opposition to time-honored established ways of life regarded throughout the ancient Near East as inevitable if not totally desirable.

This cursory survey of the biblical sources for our knowledge of premonarchic Israel indicates that they are composed of traditions of extraordinary variety in form and content, in levels of generality and specificity, in scope and tendency, and in purpose and spirit. The spatio-temporal lines of connection among these bodies of tradition, and even between specimens of the same type, are often less evident than their discreteness. They provide brightly colored bits of a mosaic which touch one another here and there and suggest intriguing patterns. Because sizable numbers of pieces are missing, however, the total design is far from patent. When the traditional canonical patterning of the biblical accounts tries to overcome this uncertainty by providing a kind of total design, it simply does not do justice to the oldest portions of the mosaic surviving in the traditions.

In the process of critically evaluating the traditional design of the sources, we must press steadily for a clearer understanding of the actual ground of unity for these diverse traditions within the distinctive social system of premonarchic Israel. To recover this ground of social unity we must examine the relation between the history of developing Israel and its cultic-ideological activity. We must, in short, extend literary and form-critical analysis of the texts in the dual but complementary directions of historical analysis and sociological analysis.

Part III

The Cultic-Ideological
Framework of the Sources

7

A Preliminary View

In the preceding parts we articulated the types and specimens of biblical tradition which form the source material for our inquiry into the history and sociology of premonarchic Israel. A necessary basic aspect of that task was the attempt to establish methodological controls for the historical use of the sources. We discovered that while the biblical traditions are heavily narrative and give every evidence of having been produced out of lively historical experience, they are not directly historical documents but rather quasi-historical communal products, reflecting both temporal distance from and cultic-ideological refraction of the typical data of documentary historiography.

We further identified certain pervasive tendencies or impulses within the traditions, such as the impulse to anachronize historical experience by retrojecting contemporary events and institutions into earlier temporal phases, a tendency that operates frequently in close and confusing association with an impulse toward the naive inclusion of older historical experience undifferentiated from the later historical experience. We observed also the impulse to form a comprehensive rationale for the whole body of traditions by formulating a canonical version of Israel's past, in which materials are formally phased into successive, but interconnected, eras: the patriarchal era, the Mosaic era, the settlement era. The anachronizing periodization of the traditions in the service of an approved standardized "history" is striking evidence of the tendency of the cult of early Israel to unify the diverse peoples of Israel by unifying their cultic practice and ideological outlook. It is this process of cultic-ideological stylization of the traditions that we want to examine in greater detail, to locate its significance for reconstructing the fundamental outlines both of the history and of the social system of early Israel.

Given the pervasive cultic-ideological shape of the early Israelite traditions, we must carefully examine the process by which the traditions were produced in order to gain a critical method for determining the early history of Israel. An analysis of the history of the production of Israelite traditions is the indispensable "bridging" method for passing from the literary accounts in the Hebrew Bible to a critical reconstruction of the history and social system of Israel. This is so because, as previously noted, a strictly literary-critical approach to the early sources carries us only back as far as the monarchy, since the earliest sizable, identifiable, continuous sources are not earlier than the time of David or Solomon. If we want to find out how the basic thematic structure and the "filler" materials of these later sources originated and developed in the period of Israel's origins, we have no alternative but to alter our perspective from a literary-historical axis to a form-functional and tradition-historical axis.

The form-functional and tradition-historical outlooks put before us a number of fascinating questions. Behind the later continuous literary sources, what can we discern of the processes and stages by which the individual traditions originated and agglomerated in ever enlarging sequences and in ever growing complexities of arrangement? What major themes and sub-themes became foci for attracting and agglomerating the traditions? What types of tradition circulated in the pre-monarchic period and what communal purposes of celebration or instruction did they serve? Can the thematic patterns of the traditions be related to the several types of tradition so as to uncover a coherent organic process of tradition formation in the cult? What impetuses and what activities in the nascent social system of Israel can explain the bewilderingly complex growth and stubborn retention of these traditions?

Clearly the answers to such questions are not to be found solely or even primarily in the documentary historical interests of early Israelite historians or story-tellers. The answers we seek are rather more diffuse and more concrete at the same time. They are more diffuse in the sense that we must look to general cultural, sociopolitical, and religious needs and impulses as the explanatory context for the traditions. They are more concrete in the sense that, once freed from positing self-conscious literary figures who take credit as "poets" or "authors" or "historians," we are able to focus on the communal processes by which the people Israel used traditions of many types and fortunes in an attempt to arrange itself into a viable social system forged out of diverse components. In denying the existence of independent literary figures in premonarchic Israel, we are not contending for the mystique of "collective authorship" but simply recognizing that the many individuals who helped to articulate the traditions did so under the sustained and sustaining pressure of communal needs and processes.

8

Israelite Religious Concepts as "Ideology"

The use of the terms "ideology" and "ideological" requires clarification.[54] The consensual constitutive concepts and attitudes of early Israel, which I choose to call "ideology," are more commonly in biblical studies called "religious ideas or beliefs," "religious thought or symbols," or "theology." I have no principled objections to such terms for particular purposes, provided that their denotations and connotations are carefully specified. Parts X and XI will examine systematically what is entailed in viewing the religion of Israel, including its ideational facets, according to sociological, genetic-historical, and theological perspectives or frames of reference. Only in some systematic frame of reference is it possible for any particular way of designating the constitutive ideas of early Israel to make sense.

At the moment I want only to indicate provisionally why, in this context, I have preferred the term "ideology" over all the others and what I mean by it as well as what I do not mean by it. This is particularly advisable because "ideology" is commonly perceived both as a value-laden and an affect-charged term, evoking connotations of conceptual rigidity or of deliberate or unconscious spuriousness. My primary reason for employing ideology for the constitutive ideas of early Israel is to use a term which deliberately sets *a methodological distance between sociological inquiry into Israel's religion and the more familiar historical and theological approaches to Israel's religion.*

Ideology denotes the fact that we are primarily looking at the systematic relationships between the religion of Israel and the wider Israelite social system, rather than at the genetic-historical development of the religion in its discrete forms or at a body of beliefs viewed either in their independence and internal coherence or as the foundation of later bodies of belief held by Jews or Christians. We shall, of course, necessarily give attention to aspects of the historical development of the religion, and we shall be concerned to see the relative independence and internal coherence of the religious ideas; but in both regards our focus is on how the historically developed and more or less internally coherent beliefs are systematically related to the fundamental social relations of the Israelites, including but by no means restricted to the cultic sphere of social relations. In short, we are taking as our field of study the widest conceivable coherence of the religious ideas within an entire system of social relations. Ideology serves as a useful cipher to describe religious ideas as integral aspects of total social systems.

Briefly put, when I refer to ideology in ancient Israel, I mean the *consensual religious ideas which were structurally embedded in and functionally correlated to other social phenomena within the larger social system,* and which served, in a more or less comprehensive manner, *to provide explanations or interpretations of the distinctive social relations and historical experience of Israel* and also *to define and energize the Israelite social system oppositionally or polemically over against other social systems.*

On the other hand, as I use the term ideology, it has nothing to say about the "truth" or "falsity" of the religious ideas. Nor does ideology imply any particular view about the genetic or causal relationship between the religious ideas and the social relations of Israel. Neither does the category of ideology entail any notions of the subjective states or processes by which ideology is entertained and perpetuated, either in the form of intuitive or unmediated subjective states of mind or in the form of rationalistic or intellectualistic constructs. Such additional connotations or implications of ideology will be reserved for fuller consideration in Parts X and XI, when we shall be in a position to consider them in the light of the results of our study. All that I am now comprehending as Israelite ideology is the religious beliefs as part of a system of social relations in which those beliefs serve explanatory and polemical functions intimately related to the specific social relations of the people who entertain the ideas. Ideology in this context is religious belief viewed from the angle of its social structure and function.

In what follows, tradition will be viewed as the communal production of ideology, intimately interwoven with the practices and institutions and values of the social system. The traditions of Israel project the ideological component of its experimental constitutional arrangements and its intense social struggle. The history of the production of Israel's traditions is one phase of the history of the formation of Israel's ideology in its unique form of a comprehensive system-wide commitment to Yahwism.

The very lushness and complexity of the traditions attest at once to the extraordinarily developed ideological bent of Israel. To note the astonishing "imaging" and "talkativeness" of early Israel, as compared with its neighbors, is already to note a seminal feature of liberated Israel. Although not given to philosophies or creeds, Israel had a pronounced predilection to render narrative, instructional, and poetic "accounts" and "rationales" of the liberation it had achieved and was achieving. By examining the form and scope of Israel's traditional talk about itself and its deity, in conjunction with its cultic practices, we are able to establish bench marks for the task of describing Israel's constitutional arrangements and its course of social struggle, both in the history of the Israelite settlement and in the structure of the early Israelite social system viewed typically and chronologically.

9

Israelite Religious Practices as "Cult"

Cult is one of those vexed jargon words in biblical studies. More often than not biblical scholars use the term without giving any clear content to it. For my part, I prefer the straightforward definition of Aubrey Johnson:

> . . . the term "cult" (or "cultus") may be and, indeed, should be used to include all those religious exercises which form the established means employed by any social group for (a) securing right relations with the realm of what is "sacred" or "holy," and (b) thus enjoying those benefits, including guidance in the various crises of life, which this realm is thought capable of bestowing upon mankind.[55]

This understanding of cult is congruent with a sociological understanding of the nature of religion. The affinities of Johnson's working definition with the efforts of Emile Durkheim to arrive at the fundamental operation of religion in all cultures, extrapolated from his study of the Australian aborigines, will be evident from the following:

> A religion is a unified system of beliefs and practices relative to sacred things, that is to say, things set apart and forbidden—beliefs and practices which unite into one single moral community called a Church, all those who adhere to them. The second element which thus finds a place in our definition is no less essential than the first; for by showing that the idea of religion is inseparable from that of the Church, it makes it clear that religion should be an eminently collective thing.[56]

Certain aspects of this understanding of cult need to be elaborated. In the first place, cult has to do with actions. Speculation about ultimate meanings which are not accompanied, in one way or another, by obligatory or customary actions is not a part of cult. Nevertheless, the cultic actions are always embedded in a nexus of belief and value. They always have to do with the "sacred" or "holy" realm of life as the source of wholeness of human existence for the community and for each of its members. Therefore, it may be posited that cult is always some body of prescribed actions which are intended to make available to the community, and to solidify within it, the power for wholeness which the community's beliefs and values locate in the realm of the sacred.

It seems pointless, at least in this context, to reopen the old argument as to whether beliefs and values precede actions, or vice versa. The distinctive thing about the cultic nexus is that it entails actions, values, and beliefs in an inseparable dialectical unity. We are barred from trying to isolate bare actions from abstract values and beliefs by the solid grounding of both in the functional unity of the social system as it is articulated in the cultic nexus. It is for this reason that I speak typically of the cultic-ideological horizon as a unity in spite of the permissible analytic distinction between the cult's "acts" and the ideology's "concepts." In positing the irrefragable unity of act and concept in the cultic totality I do not, however, accept the frequent implication of structural-functional interpreters that the cultic totality cannot be fruitfully analyzed historically-dialectically by noting its relation to the social system as both undergo change in altered cultural-material conditions and in interaction with other social systems.[57]

In the second place, the cultic actions are "established," joined in a given program with its own structure and sequence of elements. The form and meaning of any one action is located within the form and meaning of the whole. This is not to say that cult never changes, which is admittedly an impression sometimes given by structural-functional analyses. It is rather to say that cult seeks the "homeostasis" of a complex of acts and meanings which "hold up" (in the twofold sense of articulating and reinforcing) the agreed range of vital interests and values in a group. When the interests and values change, or when they are threatened, the cult will respond to the new balance of forces within the social system by adaptation or, in extremity, by collapse. Nevertheless, cult actions and meanings correlated to the social system do not change easily or without good reason. Normally the changes in cult observe a time-lag in comparison with technological change and alteration in social forms.

To stress the essentially social stabilizing character of cult may be misleading, however, without an adequate historical and comparative consideration of the cult in its social system. The vital interests and social relations articulated and reinforced by particular cults vary greatly in the respects and in the degree to which they are "reactionary" or "progressive" relative to earlier stages in the social system and relative to adjacent and historically antecedent social systems. Indeed, one of the notable aspects of Israelite cult is that its conserving instinct was in the service of forms of social life which were "mutant" and "progressive" by comparison with the cults and social systems of contiguous and historically antecedent peoples in that area of the ancient world. It is, therefore, logically necessary to distinguish between the stabilizing, conserving role of the cult *within a social system at any given moment* and the historical and comparative questions of the character of the social system served by the cult *within its developmental context,* both internally and within a network of juxtaposed or contending social systems.

In the third place, while cult is a body of "religious exercises," its location in an early historical society such as ancient Israel was considerably different structurally from the location of religion within a society highly differentiated institutionally, such as our own. There is, quite frankly, a difficulty for interpreters who live in a rationalized, compartmentalized, modern social system to project themselves into the more unified cultic world of primitive peoples or of ancient historical peoples such as the Israelites. On the average, a modern scientific-technological, politically differentiated, secular society has a religion both more highly rationalized within itself and more clearly differentiated from other aspects of life than is (or was) the case with primitive and ancient historical peoples. In other words, for us religion tends to be sharply discriminated within itself, via the subdivisions of theology, ethics, worship, etc., and religion is simultaneously more sharply distinguished from other spheres of life. Discriminations of the same sort in principle had begun to develop for many primitive and for all ancient historical peoples, but they were rudimentary by comparison with ours, and an underlying life-unity, an encompassing sense of the group's grounding in an inclusive system of interrelated natural objects and settings, divine beings and persons living and dead, was deep-going and foundational, supporting and overleaping all the societal and religious differentiations of act, institution, value, and belief.[58]

It is evident in the case of ancient Israel that differentiations both within the religion and between the religion and other aspects of the social system were observed, as compared for example with the situation of "primitives" untouched by contact with "civilization." There were different forms of Israelite cult and ideology, and they were not all neatly harmonized. Some were more highly articulated and more decisive for all Israel than were other forms which tended to be local peculiarities. The Yahweh cult had a structure that involved public occasions of "worship," formally analogous to services of worship in rationalized Western religion, but they were only roughly analogous. The public activities of the Yahweh cult were largely out-of-doors and drew the people together in the manner of "national holidays." They had a specialized language but allowed for many sub-languages, and they stimulated broadly instructional, intellectual, and cultural interest which knew no absolutely fixed boundaries vis-à-vis the other spheres of communal life. While there was an official Levitical priesthood in old Israel for particular aspects of the centralized cult, every adult male was capable of being a priest in the capacity of family head as occasion demanded. Furthermore, in the absence of any formal system of education, the transmission and elaboration of the cultural repertory was diffused and distributed among numerous role performances throughout the fabric of society.

Accordingly, while cult in ancient Israel had a powerful central, focusing and ordering function, it did not monopolize the customary spheres of daily life. Instead, it tended to stimulate focused reflection upon the origins and meanings of all sorts of historical and social experience in ancient Israel. There was, in short, vital two-way traffic between the systematizing action of the cult and the reflective action of tradition gathering and tradition production in the various sectors of Israelite society. In sum, the Israelite traditions, while shaped by a decisive Yahwistic perspective, are striking in their minimization of specifically "priestly" and "mythic" elements. The action of the deity, far from being restricted to narrowly religious concerns, is viewed typically as effective in the fortunes of the total community.

Noth has rightly called attention to the fact that as we move from the major formative themes and the overall ordering conceptions of the historical traditions to the individual stories and complexes of stories, we move increasingly out of the specialized cultic sphere as the province of the priest into the wider secular life of the people. Notable in these traditions is studied attention to the community's internal groupings and the circumstances of daily existence, as well as to Israel's interrelations with neighboring peoples:

> . . . when the Pentateuchal narrative was elaborated with individual materials, it emerged out of the cultic sphere within which the basic themes had been formulated and retold. Of course, to that contemporary reality of everyday life belonged also the element of the historically unique, insofar as the remembrance of this was and continued to remain alive, even without necessarily being connected with definite, visible evidence.[59]

Thus, we may speak of the central ordering and stimulating function of the cult in tradition building, while at the same time recognizing that the tradition formation which the cult set in process reached deep into the local roots of the people and drew upon the most common experiences and realities of secular life. Noth enlarges upon this paradoxical symbiosis of the cultic and the secular in the formation of tradition:

> Now, the fact that the Pentateuchal narrative in its detailed exposition abandoned the cultic sphere, in which the origins determinative of the structure of the whole were rooted, does not mean that it thereby became "profane." . . . the great acts of God toward "Israel" always remained the basis of the narrative content, even when the exposition moved out into small and individual matters. Nevertheless, in regard to the growth of the Pentateuch, the important fact stands that the narrative elaboration of the great cultically rooted Pentateuchal themes did not signify a mere further development of tendencies already present. Rather, their elaboration occurred in a broader and, if one prefers, flatter sense, in that it passed from the mouth of the priests or the worshipping community into the mouth of popular narrators.[60]

To be sure, the Yahwistic cult of Israel succeeded in fashioning a relatively homogeneous symbolism in which variegated historical and social experience was appropriated, condensed, and widely disseminated among the Israelite people, so much so that even when the public cult was not directly operative, its way of framing and interpreting national experience extended into large tracts of Israelite daily experience. Still, the variegated historical and social experience of Israelites contributed abundant striking, idiosyncratic details which cannot be simply deduced from the higher-order symbolism of the central cult. This is true both of traditions within the centralized history of the Pentateuch and of traditions outside of the Pentateuch. For example, the stories of the judges can hardly be understood as direct products of the cult in old Israel; yet the Yahweh who appears in the stories is recognizable as the Yahweh of the official cult, and to a considerable degree his relations with Israel are pictured in the stories with the underlying assumptions of the cult, and even at times by means of cultic language.

Of course such a complex view of the interrelation of cult and social life, of the activities of priests and popular narrators, does not solve all the problems of the growth of the traditions. In particular, it does not permit any simple typology of all the traditions into "priestly" and "popular" categories. Nor does it allow of an interpretation, which might be put upon Noth's analysis, that priests and popular narrators worked in temporal succession. Rather, it seems far more likely that they worked interactively, in varying sequences and combinations according to the tradition unit or complex in question. In quite a few traditions, priests and popular narrators alike have had a part to play. Furthermore, even the most cultic aspects of the tradition have a reference toward the secular life of Israel as a totality, and even the most popular aspects of the tradition are likely to be touched by traces or elements of cultic practice and conceptuality. Nevertheless, a nuanced understanding of the creative, but also tension-filled, interplay between cult and daily life prevents us from falling into simplistic, one-sided, rectilinear reconstructions of the growth of the traditions by keeping open the multidimensional and multidirectional interchange between cult and social life as displayed in the intricacies of the traditions.

10

Anatomy of the "Historical" Traditions

The early "historical" traditions of Israel form a great congeries of materials which can only be "cracked open" by using methods that are attuned to their cultic-ideological formation. Those methods are form criticism and tradition history. The present study does not pretend to any great originality in form criticism and tradition history per se, but will attempt to set "old facts in new relationships." The analysis that follows is deeply indebted in its fundamentals to the work of Martin Noth, whose monumental *A History of Pentateuchal Traditions* (1948) explored the early traditions with an incisiveness and grasp of their totality unexcelled among biblical scholars.[61]

While not alone in his analyses, sharing as he did with Gerhard von Rad and others in the methods and insights of the form-critical and historico-territorial approaches of Hermann Gunkel and Albrecht Alt, Noth preeminently succeeded in grasping the fundamental contours of the production of the stylized early Israelite traditions. Recapitulating much of Noth's argument, modifying it where advisable, I am attempting in this study to *begin* with the tantalizing enigmatic questions with which Noth's provocative analysis of the Pentateuchal traditions *ends.* I quote the final sentences of his *A History of Pentateuchal Traditions* in full:

> At the same time, every result of this kind yields new questions and new tasks. For the case at hand, it seems to me that the most important issue in this regard is the problem of what brought about the unity "Israel" and the common Israelite consciousness which constitutes the presupposition of the initial stages and the further development of the transmitted Pentateuchal narrative. For in view of all that has been said, this Israelite consciousness cannot be derived simply from a common history experienced by the twelve tribes before their occupation of the land, for such a history never existed. The problem is, further, how the events experienced by various individual groups that entered into this unity "Israel" came to be the commonly shared tradition and the decisive content of faith of the whole community. Here this problem can only be intimated, for a discussion of it would reach far beyond an investigation into the history of the traditions of the Pentateuch.[62]

So the distinction between Noth's tradition-historical study and my historical-sociological study is sharpened. Important as it is that we retrace much of the tradition-historical ground covered by Noth, what separates our respective undertakings is that Noth ends with the critical historical-sociological questions with which we begin and toward the answering of which we call his methods and conclusions into critical service. The historical-sociological "problem of what brought about the unity 'Israel' and the common Israelite consciousness," which he posed as the baffling and urgent consequence of his tradition-historical understanding, has *not* been addressed adequately by biblical scholars. Rather, insofar as it has been treated, it has been "answered" by theological fiat in a manner strikingly deficient in descriptive and analytic force. So we take as our challenge those closing queries of Noth concerning the empirical bases of that unity of Israel and of common Israelite consciousness which he felt compelled to posit in order to give scientific rationale and logical coherence to the astonishing growth of the traditions, a unity which in the last analysis he felt at a loss to account for simply within the frame of tradition history.

10.1 Structural Elements of the Traditions

What are the essential understandings of the cultic-ideological complex of traditions which form criticism and tradition history, particularly as formulated by Noth, have made available to us? These insights can be stated in a number of structural observations which move progressively from the totality of the complex of traditions toward their sub-parts, or vice versa, and which incessantly drive toward a correlation between the unity and diversity of the traditions, on the one hand, and the cult processes in their larger historical-social setting, on the other hand.

SMALL INDEPENDENT UNITS OF TRADITION. The extant early history of Israel is typically composed of small independent units of tradition (*literarische Einheiten* or *Einzelüberlieferungen*), chiefly narratives but including poems and laws, which either individually or—more often, gathered into sub-collections—were incorporated into the extended literary sources of J, E, D, and P. In this respect Noth accepted the fundamental analysis of Hermann Gunkel, the founder of Old Testament form criticism, who noted the concise, lapidary style of these units and further contended that they were frequently, if not invariably, tied to particular places, especially to sanctuaries. Both the original place-rootedness of the traditions and the related phenomenon of capsulating historical or typical experiences of groups in a story featuring one or a few persons are viewed by Gunkel and Noth as normally more dependable elements of the primary units than the connections of the stories with named persons, such as the patriarchs or Moses, who may in fact have been only secondarily introduced into the accounts. Such tradition-historical inferences about the reliability of the data reported in the tradition units are not as widely shared by scholars as the immediate analytic insight that the traditions are indeed divisible into relatively small units. Overall, however, the acceptance of the major analytic results of form criticism has given rise to a cautious, if not overtly sceptical, attitude toward the interconnections between units. As a consequence, the whole extended "plot line" of the history, which unfolds from Genesis through

Numbers [63] by means of the secondary arrangement of the primary units, has become freshly problematical.

BASIC THEMES. The small units, varied in form and subject matter, were selected and grouped and drawn into the body of traditions in affinity with a limited number of basic themes (*grundlegende Themen* or *Hauptthemen*). The basic themes were linked in a fixed order conceived as successive eras in the life of Israel: the period of Israel's prototypical ancestors or patriarchs, the bondage in Egypt and deliverance from Egypt, the wandering in the desert, the covenant-making and law-giving, and the occupation of Canaan. As Noth succinctly summarized the structural contours of the traditions: "The form was already given in the beginning of the history of the traditions in a small series of themes essential for the faith of the Israelite tribes."[64] Noth did not claim that all the basic themes arose at once, nor did he contend that they were of equal prominence. Neither was he denying that the small units could have existed as independent entities or complexes before they were caught up into one or another basic theme. In fact, it would not be inconsistent with Noth's analysis—although I am not aware that he discusses the point—to visualize the basic themes as originally prompted by the prior existence of independent stories with particular thematic tendencies.

Noth's point is that the origin of the historical traditions as a structured body must be located at that seminal moment when certain themes selected out and constellated certain tradition units or complexes as "materials" (*Stoffe*) which served as a "filling out" (*Auffüllung*) or "enrichment" (*Anreicherung*) of the themes. The process of tradition formation may thus be seen as interaction between the individual units, alone or grouped in complexes, and the basic themes. The existence of stories of a certain type or theme or spatio-temporal reference probably stimulated the development of basic themes in the first place. But the basic themes, once operative as ordering and phasing guidelines, attracted additional stories to themselves and encouraged the creation of further specimens. Moreover, stories of a more or less thematically neutral, or nondescript, type were drawn into the orbit of an appropriate basic theme and suitably shaped to elaborate that theme.

SUB-THEMES. It was clear to Noth that the formation of the Pentateuchal traditions was not simply a matter of a few basic themes gathering up a multitude of discrete stories. He recognized that there were many mediations in the process, by which individual units were grouped into sub-themes or subordinate themes (*Unterthemen*) before being taken up into a basic theme. Noth does not offer a full systematic discussion of this mediating structural reality; in fact, he seldom uses the term *sub-theme* but more often prefers "narrative materials" or "stories" or "complexes of traditions." He does, however, analyze the sub-themes and tries to suggest both their relative independence as sub-collections before they entered the total complex of traditions and the harmonizing process by which they were accommodated as aspects of one or another basic theme.

The sub-themes may be regarded from one point of view as potential basic themes that never developed sufficiently to occupy a primary place in the canonical sequence of basic themes. From another point of view they appear as alternative ways of stating a basic theme, or as a means of nuancing a basic theme, or as particular illustrative concretions of the theme. The organizing elements from sub-theme to sub-theme, as isolated by Noth, are extremely varied. At times the organizing element is a particular person, either associated with a locale or in his relations with another—e.g., Jacob at Shechem, Jacob in East Jordan, Isaac and Abraham. At times the sub-theme is an episodic recollection of groups settling in Canaan, such as the Transjordan tribes or Caleb in Hebron. At times it is a more general scheme or motif, such as the plague stories, or the struggle against hunger and enemies in the wilderness, or covenant and apostasy at Sinai. One of the sub-themes, Joseph and his brothers, has been elevated to a status of relative independence by serving as a bridge between the basic theme of the patriarchs and the basic theme of bondage in Egypt and deliverance from Egypt. Noth's fundamental point is that while these sub themes are extremely diverse in scope and character, each with its own independent traditional locus, they have found their way into the total historical traditions only by subordination to the basic themes, being recast in each instance so as to amplify and blend with a basic theme or to provide a transition between two basic themes.

Many questions arise concerning Noth's catchall category of sub-themes. In a sense a sub-theme is only a sub-theme *relative* to a basic theme that comprehends it and relative to individual units which it subtends. A sub-theme is accordingly a hypothetical constellation of separate traditions which was subordinated to a basic theme. Given the fact that the biblical traditionists make no notations of sub-themes by rubrics, and given the fact that Noth employed a stunning array of stylistic, structural, thematic, and historical arguments to isolate the sub-themes, it remains a debatable matter exactly how many such sub-themes are objectively discernible. Nor, in fact, does Noth wish to exclude that individual stories could find their way directly into the orbit of a basic theme without being organized in a sub-theme. In large measure Noth was characterizing the complex clustering and situating of the units according to narrower and wider, or more or less inclusive, frames of reference. It is a literary instance of the relativity of form and content when viewed structurally.

> The idea of a formal system of abstract structures is thereby transformed into that of the construction of a never completed whole, . . . incompleteness being a necessary consequence of the fact that there is no "terminal" or "absolute" form because any content is form relative to some inferior content and any form the content for some higher form.[65]

The complex of early Israelite historical traditions analyzed in terms of structure shows an ascending and descending inclusion of elements which are both form and content, depending upon whether they are viewed in terms of the elements they include or in terms of the elements that include them. A clause or sentence is a "form" relative to the words within it and a "content" relative to the tradition unit of which it is part. The individual tradition unit is a "form" relative to the sentences within it and a "content" relative to a cycle of units of which it is part. The cycle of units or sub-themes is a "form" relative to the individual units within it and a "content" relative to a basic theme.

Noth's endeavor to specify these mediating "forms" and "contents" as sub-themes is of heuristic value, logically correct and methodologically suggestive, even though his precise results are unfinished and challengeable at countless points.

HORIZONTAL LINKAGE. The vertical grouping and subtending of the traditions under the impulse of the basic themes is not the only form of "binding" in the tradition complex. Noth also called attention to instances of horizontal linkage by which sub-themes were bound to sub-themes and themes to themes in the emerging form of the traditions. He called these bonds "bracketings" (*Verklammerungen*) and the process he called "interweaving" (*Ineinanderwachsen*) or "blending" (*Verquickung*). Among the favored forms of horizontal bracketing were genealogies, by which originally separate figures were related familially—e.g., as father and son—as well as itineraries, by which the abrupt shift from the locale of one story to the locale of another story could be rationalized as episodes in a larger plot by means of the migration of the actors from place to place. Bracketing is often more subtle, as in the hypothesized displacement of traditions from one person to another, e.g., from Isaac to Abraham. Attempts to interlink the basic themes appear when a reference to an earlier or following theme is introduced in materials where it is strictly out of context but where it functions as a retrospective or prospective binding. An entire sub-theme, the Joseph story, serves to close the awkward gap between Jacob and his sons in Canaan and the Israelites in bondage in Egypt by offering an explanation of how Jacob and his family migrated to Egypt.

NOTION OF A UNITED ISRAEL. A fundamental ideological framework holds the basic themes, sub-themes, and stories together as frames and frames-within-frames, giving the incredible diversity of materials a pronounced unity in spite of all tendencies toward fragmentation and episodic formlessness. This fundamental ideological framework is the notion of a united Israel as *the people of Yahweh*.

> It is clear that the Pentateuch did not come into being by the summation of individual narratives, which, having been gradually accumulated from the sphere of all Israelite tribes and connected with one another in manifold ways, finally yielded by virtue of their combination an overall picture of a history or of a prehistory of all Israel. Rather, the all-Israelite scheme of the Pentateuchal tradition was presupposed from the very first and the individual materials, whatever their origin and prehistory, were at once given an all-Israelite orientation *in the very act* of being incorporated into the sphere of the Pentateuchal tradition.[66]

This ideological framework must be understood, moreover, as the conceptual counterpart of actual constitutional arrangements by which diverse peoples became a single self-conscious functioning social system called "Israel." Although the basic themes, sub-themes, and individual traditions were drawn variously from component members of united Israel, and while at points they reflect events and movements—as well as concepts—that are proto-Israelite and pre-Yahwistic, they have been brought together into the corpus of Israelite tradition on the principle that they tell of the fortunes of united Israel. Consequently, the production and agglomeration of these traditions must be understood as the *concrete self-conscious activity of the Israelite social system.* Noth is correct when he flatly asserts that "the origin of the Pentateuchal tradition presupposes the existence of the historical phenomenon 'Israel.' "[67]

It is less than adequate, therefore, simply to say that it was the basic themes that launched the process of tradition formation in ancient Israel, for such an observation limits itself too strictly to the literary phenomena. The only adequate way to state the matter is as follows: *the basic preconditions* for the formation of Israel's traditions were the deliberate arrangement of diverse peoples into the social system called "Israel" and their self-conception as "the people of Yahweh." *The formal mechanism* through which this deliberate arrangement of social relations and this self-conscious symbolic understanding triggered the growth of tradition was the articulation of basic themes within the cult, a process which symbolically capsulated the meaning-complex of Israel as the people of Yahweh in a story form susceptible of indefinite narrative elaboration. This is not to claim that all aspects of the Israelite social system were fully formed prior to the selection of the initial basic themes, much less that all the eventual members of Israel were included in the social system from the start. It is only to claim that there was a *systemic threshold of articulated social relations and self-consciousness which the people Israel had to attain before they could set in motion so highly structured and so symbolically dense a format as is evidenced in the basic structure of the historical traditions of the Pentateuch.*

CULT AS LIFE-SETTING OF THE TRADITIONS. Since we have already characterized the cult in ancient Israel, we need add only a word about the cult as the life-setting for the formation of the basic themes and the centralizing and cross-fertilizing tendencies in tradition formation which the themes set in motion. Noth is insistent that the basic themes were proclaimed and celebrated in the organized cult of united Israel. Given many features of the traditions which we shall explicate later in this chapter—and given the social systemic understanding stated above—this is an altogether tenable thesis. It was the cult, with its complex of religious exercises aimed at establishing and maintaining right relations with the realm of the sacred, i.e., the realm of Yahweh, which formed the institutional sub-set in the Israelite social system directly responsible for setting forth the nuclear themes around which the traditions gathered.

It is at once evident that this process of tradition formation was not a learned projection of a finished whole which any one person or group of persons sketched out so that they and others after them could execute it in predetermined detail. The proclamation of the themes in the cult was a communal speech-act, giving utterance to the self-consciousness of the people in their new existence. Such speech was discourse of a special kind, which we have called cultic-ideological. It was simple and concise speech, but speech not to be mistaken as a chronicle of events, or as archival information, or as casual conversation, or as description of technical processes. It was meaning-charged speech elucidating the identity of Israel, the terms of its constitution as a people, and the lines along which it could be perpetually renewed. It was speech that proclaimed the divine power in which the community was grounded. It was speech that addressed the community with its most fundamental obligations and reminded it of its most fundamental resources. And, as we shall see, it was even speech which allowed for the direct declamation of the divine word to the community. We must necessarily view the finished product of these early historical traditions, although rooted in cultic speech, as "unplanned" by any one person or group of persons within any single context, as in reality an organically developing whole laid down by deposits from many cultic and sociopolitical contexts and finally given circumscribed shaping by later traditionists known to us under the sigla J, E, D, and P.

The energizing and fructifying power of this cultic speech, centered on the basic themes and their elaboration, was enormous, but it was not at all autonomous speech that remained enmeshed within the cult. Our preceding discussion of cult has argued that there was a constant interplay between the cult and the wider social life. We may say that in the cult the distinctive social relations of Israel were celebrated and consolidated in symbolic speech and act. The cult gave the necessary symbolic articulation and concentration of energy, as well as the continuing framework, for disciplined tradition building. It did so, however, by transmitting the energy and symbolic categories of the cult and ideology of Yahweh into the many structures of social life and fructifying ever new tradition units which could be assimilated into the growing body of national tradition.

There is no reason to think, for example, that all the individual traditions were restricted to recitation in the cult, and every reason to think that many of them could and did lead a "double life," recited in the cult and recited in other social settings as part of the general cultural and intellectual heritage of Israel. In fact, some of the traditions may never have been recited in the centralized cult, although they were originally stimulated by and eventually assimilated to the basic themes of the cult in later compilations. The resulting complex of traditions is therefore not narrowly ritualistic, but so broadly reflective of the total range of Israelite social life that it stands in a position in ancient Israel comparable to that of a "national epic" among other peoples. And the deviation of Israel's traditions from the type of the national epic emerges not in any lack of comprehensiveness or heroic motifs but rather in the studied way that the whole people Israel, uneclipsed by its "heroes," stands in the foreground of the traditions with its vivid consciousness of being a new cultic-social reality in a world of cultic-social systems of a markedly different nature.

10.2 Sequential Articulation of the Traditions

Drawing upon the analysis of Noth—supplemented by the work of other scholars and my own research—I shall now briefly characterize the probable stages in the sequential linking up of the basic themes, their relation to the "filler" traditions, and the manner in which these sequentially linked themes developed into a canonical history of Israelite beginnings.

The basic themes of the Pentateuchal traditions seem not to have sprung up together at once. With Noth, we posit the initial linkage of two of the basic themes as the "twin pillars" of the tradition, i.e., Deliverance from Egypt and Leading into Canaan, to which the other themes were gradually added until the present basic form of the Pentateuch was reached. These other themes were introduced serially within the cult, as supplements to the two original themes, over a period of about 150 years as the major groupings of northern and southern "tribes" came together as segments within united Israel. When a new basic theme was introduced to the complex of tradition, it was not mechanically added as the last item in a sequence. Since the themes were narrative in form, possessing broadly temporal indicators, each new theme was inserted at the point in the sequence felt to be appropriate for articulating the proper order of events in the unfolding history of Israel. In one case, a basic theme—i.e., Guidance in the Wilderness—was "split apart" and another basic theme—i.e., Revelation at Sinai—was inserted into it. This is one clue to the peculiar status of the theme Revelation at Sinai, an eccentricity of the tradition which we shall examine closely at a later point in this discussion.

We may imagine the rise and sequential arrangement of themes in this way: the fundamental themes of Deliverance from Egypt and Leading into Canaan are related temporally as succeeding events, and they are related spatially as movement from a region of bondage to a region of freedom. While formally independent as structural elements, the two basic themes fuse into a conceptual whole which forms the minimal starting point for the cultic-ideological consciousness of Israel. Once given the temporal, spatial, and conceptual joining of these themes, it became easily possible to introduce additional themes without fundamentally altering the original schema. If we posit that the first Yahwists brought these twin basic themes into Canaan as their central acclamation of Yahweh's benevolent action on their behalf, it is natural to posit that in the course of time (especially as new groups joined in the worship of Yahweh), such themes would provoke further questions which could only be answered by the elaboration of additional themes. For example, the question "What were the circumstances of Israel's bondage in Egypt from which it required delivery?" gave birth to the elaboration of the conditions of bondage and, eventually, to the bridging of the stories of the prototypical fathers with the account of the descent into Egypt by Jacob and his sons. Or, the question "How did Israel get from Egypt to Canaan?" gave birth to the theme of Guidance in the Wilderness. Or the question "What were the fortunes of Israel before it was chosen by Yahweh in Egypt?" gave birth to the theme of the patriarchs conceived as the eponymous ancestors of all Israel.

The basic themes may thus be arranged according to the approximate order of their introduction into the standardized sequence, together with stipulation of their probable provenance, i.e., whether northern Israelite (N) or southern Israelite (S):

> Deliverance from Egypt (N) ⎫   introduced simultaneously to form
> Leading into Canaan (N)   ⎭   the fundamental frame
> Promise to Jacob (N)
> Promise to Abraham-Isaac (S)
> Guidance in the Wilderness (S)
> Revelation at Sinai (N)
> Joseph Story (N)—a "sub-theme" bridging two basic themes

The resulting standardized version of the basic themes produced this sequence in the recitation and, eventually, in the writing of the traditions:

> Promise to Abraham-Isaac
> Promise to Jacob
> Joseph Story
> Deliverance from Egypt
> Guidance in the Wilderness
> Revelation at Sinai (inserted into the preceding theme)
> Leading into Canaan

Within each basic theme, cycles or clusters of traditions frequently, but not invariably, form distinctive sub-themes incorporated as blocs of materials that develop facets of the basic themes. Among the distinguishable sub-themes and the basic themes into which they are set are the following:

> Abraham and Lot (basic theme of the Promise to Abraham)
> Jacob at Shechem / Jacob in Transjordan (basic theme of the Promise to Jacob)
> Egyptian plagues and Passover festival (basic theme of the Deliverance from Egypt)
> Thirst, hunger, and enemies in the desert / Murmuring of the people / Attack on Canaan from the south / Baal-peor and Balaam (basic theme of Guidance in the Wilderness)

The Mountain of God and the Midianites / Apostasy at the Mountain (basic
theme of the Revelation at Sinai)
Benjaminite conquest narratives (basic theme of the Leading into Canaan)

Close examination of the basic themes, sub-themes, and individual traditions
suggests that each had an original locus in particular sub-groups of Israel and that
each was attached to places and practices felt in one way or another to belong to
the realm of the sacred. The original loci of some traditions are much easier to
discern than the loci of other traditions. Enough of an original localized rootage
for the traditions is evident that we can legitimately hypothesize diffused decentralized cultic tendencies at work, which strove to retain the attachment of the
traditions to particular holy locations and to particular sub-units of the Israelite
people. This is the local cultic dimension of the centrifugal force operating among
the several "tribal" segments of Israel who, while wanting to attain greater unity,
also wanted to preserve their respective autonomies and cultural peculiarities.

Given these diffused and decentralized pre-Israelite tendencies, which unquestionably persisted within unified Israel to a marked degree (witness the stories of
the judges!), the achievement of the national Yahwistic cult in detaching these
traditions from their peculiar local associations and projecting them into a massive
all-Israelite cultural history is obviously of the first importance in estimating the
forces at work in producing a united Israel. Gerhard von Rad has claimed that this
work of detachment of the traditions from localized connections was primarily the
accomplishment of the first literary traditionist under the monarchy, the J
writer.[68] While the all-Israelite sublimation of the originally localized materials
came to a culmination in the work of the J writer, it must be insisted with Noth that
the process was decisively launched much earlier, at precisely the time when the
basic themes were taking shape and attracting the scattered traditions like so many
magnets. In fact, even more explicitly than Noth has done, it must be asserted that
the all-Israelite sublimation of the localized traditions via the standardized version
of the basic themes is one of the clearest clues we possess to the decisive beginning
point for the formation of Israel as a distinctive people in a distinctive social
system.

In the end, we must account for much of the curious lack of proportion and
harmonious progression within the Pentateuchal traditions by noting that they
represent a compromise formation in which centralizing and decentralizing tendencies met and triumphed in differing ways. The centralizing tendency of the
all-Israelite cult "won out" in that it provided the basic controlling structure within
which all the traditions had to fit and thereby gave the story of Israel its overriding
perspective. The decentralizing tendency of the localized pre-Israelite and autonomous Israelite segments "won out" in its demand that the all-Israelite unity
must preserve and safeguard the localized traditions by including them within the
official version. In a sense we may regard these incorporated localized traditions

as the precondition of proto-Israelite groups joining in the community of Israel or the precondition for members of Israel remaining in the community. It is to the centralizing tendency that we owe the spacious architectonic structure of early Israel's traditions, and it is to the decentralizing tendency that we owe the rich variegated texture and multilevel complexity of the content. Mere centralization could only have produced a skeleton of the present Pentateuch and mere de-centralization could only have produced a welter of disjointed accounts.

Yet in the joining of these forces the centralizing tendency was clearly the decisive and formative one in that only because of its impulse was it possible to gather and to preserve and to enrich the separate traditions by bringing them together in lively interplay within a common perspective. The tradition-historical process that produced early Israel's traditions is the close literary counterpart of the sociocultural process of compromise and sublimation by which Israel became a sum greater than any of its segments. In this manner we are able to discern a striking parallel between the complex unity of the cultic-ideological tradition and the complex unity of the social system which produced the tradition.

Such a reading of the contest between centralized and localized tendencies in tradition-building, and their resolution and synthesis, suggests that agreement was reached on the basic themes long before there was agreement on precisely which stories, or which version of agreed stories, should be included under the themes. Without a strong impulse to unity, the whole traditional structure could never have been initiated, and without steady progress toward greater unification, the traditional structure would have been in imminent danger of collapse. Equally, a premature and heavy-handed attempt to force all traditions into a rigid all-Israelite mold would have been no more than a cultural or political tour de force lacking support in the consciousness of the participating tribes. It would have barred the way to the very unity it sought to attain. A middle way was found by which the overarching unifying basic themes could be expanded and increased, incorporating the several tribal traditions at the same time that they were subordi-nated to the whole in the sense that the separate elements of the tradition became embroidery in the one great design of the story of Israel from the patriarchs to the settlement in Canaan. If we theorize that the Levitical priests were primarily responsible for the articulation of the basic themes in the cult, those cultic custo-dians of tradition were nonetheless obliged to make room for numerous "lay" contributions in the form of sub-themes and individual traditions.

11

Tradition Formation as Sociohistorical Symbolization

The relation between the standardizing, harmonizing pressure of the central cult and the diversified historical experience of the Israelite peoples, which was analyzed in the preceding section, brings to the fore the oft-repeated claim of biblical exegetes that Israel was uniquely "historical" in contrast to other peoples who were nature-oriented or myth-oriented. There is something accurate and important about this claim, and I shall assess it more fully in Parts X and XI, but it has not customarily been stated in an acceptable way.[69] It is correct to speak of the pronounced historical awareness of early Israel, but biblical scholars have hopelessly obscured the precise heuristic value of the insight by failing to distinguish the exact contours of this "historical consciousness." We have already observed that "history" is a protean term which requires that we indicate which of its many senses we have in mind when we use it in one context or another.

Earlier in our study we established one kind of vital distinction in employing the category "history." There is a fundamental distinction between a documentary, humanistic historical interest and method and a more diffuse popular cultural interest in tracing the origins of a people. The latter may be loosely described as "historical interest"; in its interest in origins it may contain the seeds of documentary, humanistic historical interest, but it is clearly of a different order methodologically and, in large measure, of a different order psychosocially. These two kinds of historical interest produce very different results. The one that we tend to credit as "real" historical inquiry employs rules of evidence. The other remains traditional and symbolic, of vital importance in grasping the central values and cultural perspectives of a people, but necessarily requiring examination according to homogeneous rules of evidence before its documentary historical value can be established.

But we must draw another distinction which the Israelite cult-based interest in origins lays bare. A fundamental distinction must be drawn between the historical awareness of a group with respect to experiences which it has directly undergone—however long ago in the past and however imperfectly the memories have survived, or with whatever transformations—and the historical awareness of a group with respect to its appropriation of another group's remembered experience as a symbolic statement about its own altogether discrete historical experiences. For example, the historical awareness of the Moses group concerning the deliverance from Egypt is of a different order than the historical awareness of "a

deliverance from Egypt" as cultivated by groups of Israelites who did not participate with the Moses group in the events remembered. Likewise, the historical
awareness of the Benjaminite group (or a wider Joseph group) concerning the
taking of the land, as recounted in the sub-stratum of Joshua 1—12, is of a
different order than the historical awareness of "leading into Canaan" as cultivated by groups of Israelites who did not participate in the Benjaminite/Josephite
campaigns but rather acquired their place in the land in separate actions.

We are asserting, therefore, that the historical awareness of early Israel was not
a homogeneous awareness drawn from a single common set of experiences
undergone by all Israelites, but rather a highly *composite* awareness consisting of
differing kinds of formal relations between the knower and the known, the
rememberer and the remembered. Limited sectors of various group experiences
were selected as definitive by those who had lived through them; and thereafter,
in a logically distinguishable step, those selected memories were cast in the form of
symbolic descriptions, or prototypes of experience, which became valid for interpreting the necessarily discrete experiences of other groups insofar as those
groups were a part of Israel. The past as lived-through experience, irretrievably
unreconstructable as soon as it elapses, is nevertheless retrieved and reconstructed selectively and focally in symbolic forms which affect both the course
and the perception of newly lived-through experience by providing interpretive
and motivational networks of meaning which dispose those sharing in the symbolic forms both to act and to evaluate events within a commonly shared range of
options.

At each of these stages of historical awareness a symbolic element enters in. In
the first stage, a group singles out particular aspects of its past lived experiences as
of unusual importance for its present self-understanding and thereby begins the
selective symbolization of its past. In the second stage, the already interpreted
experience of one group is extended to the experiences of other groups which,
although discrete, are felt to be analogous and capable of illumination when seen
through the symbolic categories that first arose in another lived historical context.
It is evident that in the passage from the first stage to the second *the symbolic element
in the historical awareness involved is enlarged or heightened.* The substantive alteration
of actual lived experiences increases proportionately, as we observed in II.4,
through the selective emphases of the traditions which delete, condense, introject,
transpose, join what was once separated, and separate what was once joined in
order to make edifying points for present needs.

It should be further stressed that *the degree of heightened symbolization entailed when
one group takes over the remembered history of another group varies greatly according to the
degree of correspondence between the two group histories.* For example, an Israelite
group that had either been victorious in or escaped from an encounter with

Egyptian troops in Canaan could appropriate the Moses group "deliverance from Egypt" theme with a considerably "lower degree" of symbolization than could an Israelite group whose encounter was with non-Egyptians; and it could do so with a much "lower degree" of symbolization than could an Israelite group which had no encounter with any enemy force during the time of its immigration into Canaan or its withdrawal from Canaanite society. This doubtless implies that the process of centralizing symbolization of the historical traditions proceeded very unevenly in early Israel and was as thoroughgoing as it was only because the associated tribes had to repel repeated military threats from Midianites, Ammonites, Moabites, Canaanites, and Philistines. In fact, the well-organized Philistine military machine, formally the client of the Egyptians, must have served to push even the most reluctant and hitherto "symbolically retarded" tribes into appreciating the direct relevance for them of all-Israelite basic theme "Deliverance from Egypt."

There is really no objection to saying that both these stages in the selective remembering of lived experiences demonstrate "historical awareness." In order to do justice to the fact that early Israel looked for its self-understanding in interpreted past experiences of social struggle rather than in hierarchically imposed mythic and political orders, it is useful to speak of Israel's "historical consciousness," although even here we should be more precise and speak of *Israel's historical consciousness of social struggle*. But the characterization cannot be made in such a way as to ignore the selective symbolic interpretation of the lived experiences, nor can it be made in such as way as to claim or to imply—as biblical scholars have often done—that this kind of historical consciousness is really not basically different from documented history of a humanistic stripe.

In short, the historico-symbolic appropriation of history characteristic of early Israel leaves us with the task of analyzing the processes involved in such historicizing symbolism, on the one hand, and the task of trying to uncover, insofar as we can, the underlying structure and detail of the lived experiences in a framework of documented history, on the other hand. Thus, there are sets of documentary-historical and historico-symbolic questions which must be combined in the analysis of each stage in the process of formulating and appropriating the group traditions:

Stage of Primary Group Symbolization

DOCUMENTARY-HISTORICAL QUESTION: What was the whole complex of lived experiences from which certain aspects were singled out by the experiencing group?

HISTORICO-SYMBOLIC QUESTION: Why were the selected aspects of such importance to the group and what patterns do they show for understanding the interests and traits of the group as articulated in its social structure?

Stage of Secondary or Extended Group Symbolization

DOCUMENTARY-HISTORICAL QUESTION: What can be known of the lived experiences of the appropriating group(s), particularly as they corresponded to and diverged from the lived experiences and symbolic memories of the primary group?

HISTORICO-SYMBOLIC QUESTION: Why were the symbolically interpreted experiences of the primary group of such importance for the appropriating group(s) and what patterns in this unifying symbolism throw light *both* on the overlapping and congruent interests and traits of jointly or successively appropriating groups, as they came to be articulated in a common societal and cultic-ideological constitutional framework, *and* on the divergent and optional interests and traits treated as nonprescriptive or inconsequential to the common constitution of the socio-religious whole?

If none of these crucial questions about tradition-symbolizing in old Israel can at present be answered with the fullness and exactitude we desire, they cannot even be partially answered unless they are properly formulated. Regrettably, biblical scholarship has generally failed even to formulate these questions in a precise and thoroughgoing manner; this failure is directly related to loose, formless invocations of the historicity *or* of the nonhistoricity of Israelite traditions. Moreover, only as the documentary-historical and historico-symbolic questions are asked in relation to one another can either be approached satisfactorily. It will be found that the presently attainable reconstructions of both the documentary and the symbolic "histories" of Israel are more or less adequate in differing respects. When compared, the results from one historical category can be used to suggest new theories or to estimate probabilities in old theories which customarily fall within the province of the other historical category. Consequently, the attempt of this study is to associate documentary inquiry and historico-symbolic analysis, without confusing them, in the context of the total Israelite social system.

Thus the tendency and ethos of these early traditions of Israel, so heavily narrative in form, is to articulate *prototypical symbolic assertions* of the actions of Israel's God Yahweh and the actions of Yahweh's people Israel so as to provide *a comprehensive and immediately appropriable set of common understandings for the community of united Israel.* These declamations or sets of common understandings in thematic narrative form reveal to us the critical centralizing ideological function of the cult.

Of course there were ritual and sacrificial activities in the early cult of Yahweh of a type similar to those practiced in the cults of other gods. But the specifically Israelite feature of the cult was the cementing of unity among disparate groups by means of corporate activities predicated upon a comprehensive ideology. The cult declaimed the prototypical actions of Israel and its god in a narrative form so condensed and synthesized from the collective experiences of the ingredient members of Israel that it formed a symbolic and dramatic framework that both expressed the consciousness of united Israel and evoked new dimensions and higher degrees of consciousness.

Because the nature of historico-symbolic processes is so often misunderstood, what was said in II.4 bears repeating, namely, that the refraction of history in the narrative traditions of early Israel is not a matter of careless recording and inattentive observation by aspiring historians who, by their own criteria, ought to have been more precise. It is, on the contrary, a matter of very selective recording and very specialized observation, not about some precisely described course of events experienced by a single group in common, but about *the way in which a range of diverse and yet broadly similar events among a spectrum of hitherto unrelated peoples could be viewed so as to affirm their cohesion as a people in transit from disunity to unity, from bondage to freedom, from being "no-people" to being "the people of Yahweh."* The traditions of early Israel emerge, therefore, as both the mirror reflection of, and the readily adaptive instrument toward, a growing unified consciousness and a unified social praxis within Israel. The result is a vast complex of traditions which synthesizes historical experience drawn from the many sub-histories of the component peoples of Israel and directs all these segmental sub-histories—deliberately conceptualized as one history—toward the cementing of a psychosocial and religio-national consciousness among all Israelites.

12

Cultic Actions and Cultic Traditions: Exodus-Settlement and Sinai Themes

We have argued that the salient themes of early Israelite tradition took shape and were recited as ideology in the cult of Yahweh. But is it possible to establish direct correlation between the component elements of the *cultic traditions* and the various kinds of *cultic actions*? To ascertain the extent to which the correlation of cultic traditions and cultic actions is possible we must examine the form-critical foundations of the early traditions, and in particular we must focus upon the structure and function of the basic nuclear themes.

12.1 Separation of Exodus-Settlement and Sinai Themes

The contemporary phase of form-critical study of the early historical traditions was launched by Gerhard von Rad's epochal inquiry, *The Form-Critical Problem of the Hexateuch* (1938), in which he called attention to the existence of certain liturgical compositions which contain highly stylized summaries of the chief narrative themes of the Pentateuch or Hexateuch.[70] He saw that these texts were not intended as factual summaries but as liturgies to be proclaimed, as articles of faith in narrative form. Von Rad called them "historical credos." Among the prime examples of the historical credo he singled out Deuteronomy 26:5b–9; Deuteronomy 6:20–24; Joshua 24:2b–13; and he further noted the free adaptation of such credos in the cult lyrics in I Samuel 12:8; Psalm 136; Exodus 15; Psalm 135. Von Rad claimed that the credo was a kind of Pentateuch, or as he preferred, Hexateuch *in nuce*.[71] He concluded that the compact examples were ancient and typical of the kind of cult liturgy which celebrated the basic themes of Israel's faith before they were elaborated with the rich growth of sub-themes and individual traditions.

His argument for the antiquity of the existing historical credos has not fared well; in fact, by available evidence they cannot certainly be traced back into the premonarchic period.[72] Yet they cannot easily be explained as late summaries of the literary complex of traditions, even of J or E, because they customarily omit certain of the themes which by the time of J and E had been incorporated in the larger traditional complex. We should probably understand the extant credos as relatively late surviving forms of a type that incorporated the basic themes on a normative model developed in premonarchic times. In fact, Noth's inventory of the basic themes by which the diverse traditions were organized provides just such a schematization, and this suggests that the schema was operative in the growth of the traditions. Thus we have good reason to believe that behind the late "baroque" forms of the credo which have survived there lay a premonarchic schema of stock historical themes that could be variously elaborated.[73]

Von Rad went on to observe that the historical credos omit reference to the Sinai theme altogether. In none of the credos, he contended, do the mountain of God and the covenant and the law-giving enter into the picture. Instead, he traced an entirely separate line of liturgical compositions in which Sinai occurs as the place of a theophany of Yahweh—e.g., Deuteronomy 33:2,4; Judges 5; Habakkuk 3. He noted that only in a late liturgy such as Nehemiah 9 do the themes of the historical credo and the Sinai tradition (vss.12–21) join together. From all this von Rad concluded that the historical credo with its focus on the exodus-settlement themes and the Sinai liturgy with its focus on theophany, covenant, and law-giving must derive from separate festival settings. He located the exodus-settlement themes in the festival of Weeks (barley harvest) at Gilgal, and he placed the Sinai theme in the festival of Tabernacles (grape and fruit harvest) at Shechem. The corollary of this hypothesis is that von Rad believed history, on the one side, and covenant and law, on the other, to have been totally separate streams of tradition until they were brought together for the first time by the J writer in the united monarchy.

It is not to be denied that von Rad has offered a valuable analysis of two different foci in the traditions, as well as an impressive rationale for their differences. In certain respects his analysis is indisputable. He tried to make sense of what had long been noted, namely, that in the present form of the traditions the whole complex of covenant and law at Sinai is very loosely and clumsily articulated with the narratives which move from the exodus through the wilderness toward Canaan. Likewise, Noth has emphasized the independence of the Revelation at Sinai theme and its dissonant position and form in the final sequence of basic themes. Von Rad suggested that we can best explain this peculiar literary hiatus if we assume that the two types of material, narrative and covenant/law, were originally anchored in totally separate festivals.

For my part, von Rad has demonstrated that some sort of tradition-historical and cultic separation of the two streams of tradition does underlie the literary hiatus, but I contest the adequacy of the particular explanation he offers. I am willing to concede that von Rad's hypothesis about originally disparate festival settings for the two types of tradition may correctly point back to the situation of the proto-Israelite peoples. For example, it is possible that the Levites brought only the exodus-settlement themes with them into Canaan and that some other member(s) of united Israel was (were) responsible for the introduction of the covenant theme and the law theme, either separately or in combination. Nonetheless, I contend that united Israel arose precisely at the confluence of those streams, at precisely the moment when the community affirmed theophany, covenant, and law in conjunction with narrative declamations of deliverance from Egypt and the leading into Canaan. For it is the conjunction of historical recollection and contemporary revelation, covenant and law-giving which normatively defines the religio-national community of Israel and corresponds to its emergence as a social system. The functional formation "Israel" was already a given for the J writer; he did not create it.

We have, however, moved somewhat ahead of our detailed assessment of von Rad's case. Here we must pay tribute to the tradition-historical work of Noth and of Artur Weiser[74] for a fuller rebuttal of von Rad's separation of the history and law streams prior to J. In what follows I have borrowed generously from Noth and Weiser, modifying and supplementing their work and drawing my own conceptual conclusions. Essentially what I should like to argue is that *the separation of the exodus-settlement (history) traditions from the theophany-covenant-law (Sinai) traditions was not a separation based on two entirely different conceptual worlds and two entirely separate festival programs* but rather *a separation based on a difference of function for the two sets of concepts and traditions within one and the same festival program, or at any rate within one ideologically and functionally cohesive schedule of festivals.*

We begin with the premise that the presupposition of the formulation of the tradition was the actual union of disparate peoples to form Israel. This is not to prejudge which of the eventual component peoples were included in the first step toward unity, nor is it to prejudge the precise form of the union. Those are questions yet to be considered. A further premise is that the essential form for embodying and expressing the union was the all-Israelite cult. By all-Israelite cult we mean the centralized, organized, communal exercises of celebration and instruction directed explicitly toward Yahweh, the God of united Israel, and subjectively or indirectly toward affirming and cementing the union of the people. To test von Rad's claim and to introduce my own alternative, it may be asked: What were the essential elements of cultic celebration and instruction for embodying and expressing the new-found unity of Israel?

Integral to the centralizing cultic program were these four elements:

Manifestation of the deity, by sight or sound or both, demonstrating and offering for acceptance his sovereignty over the community (Sinai theme, theophany sub-theme).

Constitution or reconstitution of the community as the people of the deity, including affirmation by the deity and affirmation by the people (Sinai theme, covenant sub-theme).

Recital of the actions of the deity on behalf of the people throughout their commonly portrayed history from the patriarchs to the settlement in Canaan (basic historical themes).

Declaration of the will of the deity for the community, defining how his sovereignty is to be expressed in the structure of communal interaction (Sinai theme, law sub-theme).

By noting the correspondence of these cultic elements with certain of the basic narrative themes (as indicated in the parentheses above), we observe that three of the four elements belong to what von Rad has characterized as the Sinai tradition (for Noth this is the Revelation at Sinai theme), while the fourth cultic element belongs to the exodus-settlement tradition (for Noth this includes all the remaining basic themes expanded from the original "twin pillars" of exodus and settlement). Von Rad wants to say that these two types of themes existed for two centuries prior to the monarchy in separate cult festivals. But if this were so, the apparent unity of the four cultic elements described above could not have belonged to the earliest foundation of Israel. In my view, it would have been conceptually and functionally impossible for Israel to have come into being apart from the intimate association of all four cultic elements embedded in a single ideological matrix. This means that the four *types* of materials in the traditions that correspond to the four cultic elements were of equal antiquity and of equal importance to the cultic foundation of early Israel. This, of course, is not to claim that *all* the extant biblical specimens of these types are of equal antiquity, nor is it to aver that the four types of materials were fully elaborated or written down at the same stage in the development of the traditions. Likewise, this assessment of the integral role of all four tradition types in the cultic foundation of Israel in no way passes judgment either on their age or on their importance within whatever *pre-Israelite* tradition context they may previously have been lodged.

Von Rad's analysis is not, however, so easily disposed of. If my argument for the foundational unity of exodus-settlement themes and theophany-covenant-law themes in the cult is to be sustained, it is necessary to deal with the tradition-historical situation which von Rad has uncovered: the exodus-settlement themes achieved a formal priority and separateness, and even a kind of predominance, in the traditions in comparison with which the theophany-covenant-law themes appear subordinated if not actually minimized. Put in another way, we must somehow explain why the Sinai sub-themes of theophany-covenant-law formed three-fourths of the basic cultic program, whereas they are crowded together in a single Sinai theme in the traditional history and awkwardly joined to the other, more "historical" themes. If the two types of themes, i.e., "history" and "theophany-covenant-law," grew out of original and integral cultic and ideological functions in ancient Israel, how are we to account for the massive disproportion between them, both in bulk and formal structure, in their extant form in the agglomerated traditions?

I propose to explain the discrepant developments of the historical themes and of the Sinai themes on the grounds that they functioned in formally different ways in the cult and that *this difference of function affected the timing, the scope, and the form of their incorporation into the complex of early Israelite tradition.* To clarify this functional difference in the cult it is necessary to examine the two sets of traditional themes from the viewpoint of their *temporal reference,* their *cultic context,* and their *immediate aim.* It will also be essential to describe more precisely what is meant by the sub-themes of theophany, covenant, and law.

12.2 Cultic Location of Exodus-Settlement Themes

The historical themes focused on exodus-settlement possessed a *past* temporal reference. They told of the things that Yahweh had done in the history of Israel. They were events of a past which could not be repeated as such; for any tradition to find its way into this recitation of Yahweh's deeds it had to be conceived as occurring within the "canonical" period extending from the patriarchs through the initial settlement in the land; i.e., it had to be representable as an event that took place no later than the lifetime of Joshua.

The primary cultic context of the recital of the historical themes was an *already constituted or reconstituted community,* looking back and consciously calling up what Yahweh had done in its past. The human subject of all the descriptions was none other than the same community gathered to perform the cultic actions, the recital of the historical themes being one such action. But the point of immediate importance is that the cultic action of reciting the historical themes is intelligible only if we posit that it was preceded by other cultic actions, namely, the manifestation of the deity to the community and the constitution or reconstitution of the community as the people of the deity. The integrity of united Israel on a pre-established foundation as the people of Yahweh is the ideological and cultic presupposition of the historical recitals. The historical recitals are sharp objectifications of a present consciousness rooted in constitutional arrangements in the community, a consciousness so keen and so insistent that it pushed its awareness of the communion of Yahweh and Israel into ever extended narrative accounts which drew larger and larger tracts of the people's past under the domination of that symbolizing consciousness.

The immediate aim of the recital of the historical themes was *to reinforce and to objectify the constitutional and ideological unity of the people* by providing them with a typology of the repeated delivering and guiding actions of the deity on the community's behalf. The historical recitals gave the people a fixed temporal structure for remembering what Yahweh can do by considering what he has done. Any particular instance of Yahweh's acting could be located within an unfolding story that issued in the contemporary flourishing community. The cultic celebration could avail itself of a growing repertory of themes, sub-themes, and narratives which served to intensify the belief that what Yahweh and his people had done in the past could be done again in spite of all adverse odds. Again, this immediate aim makes no sense unless the gathered community had already constituted or reconstituted itself as the people to whom the deity manifested himself.

In all regards, the *event-oriented* character of the recitations of basic themes of exodus-settlement, and their several enlargements and supplements, is not so much to be seen in its historical-descriptive form as in its *historico-symbolic substance and function.* The base of the collective remembering about the past is the present realized but imperfect unity of Israel striving for greater unity by viewing its several preceding sub-histories as varying instances of a movement toward unity under the tutelage of its patron deity. These "historical" themes and narratives make no sense viewed as careful chronological and territorial-geographical de-lineations of the actual stages leading to united Israel and to the cult of Yahweh. Indeed, so viewed, they are but mockeries of historiography. In short, they do not begin or end, nor at any point do they even approach, that kind of sketch which we as students of the religion of Israel would like to possess. They are one and all aetiologies of, and pedagogical stimulants to, the group consciousness of united Israel, in which the instinct to learn the disinterested and properly proportioned and nuanced past is totally swallowed up in the need to make the dramatically embellished past serve the urgencies of the present. Nonetheless, the form of this service to the present is an *historical form* in that it looks to the past and *objectifies the present meaning in terms of a definite recountable past.*

We may paraphrase both the intent and the substance of this historical recollec-tion as follows: "All that has gone before in Israel's experience, and thus in the experiences of all the groups who joined to become Israel, teaches us of the constant action of Yahweh to deliver us from threatening forces and to establish us securely as a thriving, independent people. Thus, our present urge to freedom and security, and our confidence that loyalty to Yahweh will assure us these boons, are amply guaranteed by the repeated instances in our past when he has proven wholly equal to the task of preserving us, even against seemingly overwhelming odds such as faced us when we broke free of our oppressors in Egypt and when we struggled to achieve a living space in Canaan." Such a paraphrase underlines the fact that the cult community operated on the principle that whatever belonged to the past of any group in Israel belonged to all Israel's past and that the import of all Israel's present could be read in the past of every group now joined in Israel. At the highest level of cultic-ideological generalization this meant that Yahweh, who held the contemporary community together under his sovereign will, had been at work in the history of every group who subsequently became Israelite so that those discrete histories could be rendered as stages in the singular history of Yahweh's formation of his one people.

12.3 Sinai Themes: Theophany; Covenant; Law

So much for the "historical" themes of the exodus-settlement complex of tradi-tions. What of those traditions which von Rad characterized as Sinaitic and which have to do with theophany, covenant, and law? To analyze this complex of themes accurately, we must make some principled distinctions, difficult as it often is to make clean separations in practice. For one thing, we must make a separation between theophany, covenant, and law as complexes of cult acts and recitations and their secondary connection with the basic themes of the narrative history of Israel, which occurred when they were grouped together as a basic theme and inserted in the traditional history as events which purportedly took place at Sinai-Horeb, the mountain of God in the wilderness. I find no evidence that von Rad makes this formal distinction, and in failing to do so he misses the opportunity to solve the dilemma he uncovered. In other words, we must distinguish between theophany, covenant, and law as *themes of the tradition* and theophany, covenant, and law as *structural elements of the cult.* Theophany, covenant, and law as formal cultic modes, with corresponding speech types, are logically separate from and temporally prior to their later transformation into a basic theme of the tradition under the rubric "Revelation at Sinai." We thus make a grave error if we confuse the absence of theophany, covenant, and law as narrative themes or sub-themes in the first stages of Israelite tradition with their presumed absence from the very same cult that produced the narrative themes. This vital distinction will be clarified subsequently in our discussion.

Furthermore, we must clarify what we mean by the structural modes of the cult denoted by theophany, covenant, and law.

THEOPHANY. By theophany we refer to the manifestation of a deity to a community such that he communicates directly within the cult experience his authority and his power to be the sovereign of the community. Reports of theophanies become literary products which are highly stylized, but they necessarily rest back upon underlying psychosocial and religio-national communal experiences which carried their own compelling authority. This is not to give any clear account of the elements that go into that sense of authority. We are not adjudging for the moment which of several factors may have been involved or decisive, factors such as awesome natural phenomena, individual or group ecstasy or mysticism, auspiciously overcome crises in the life of the group (such as military clashes), or priestly dramatics and indoctrination. The fact is that, as a result of whatever factors, the theophany is the base experience of religious authority in which the sovereignty of the deity becomes palpable. Yahweh's appearance to the cult community authenticates his right and his power to be the lord of the community. For the moment we stress only the formal mode of theophany. The cultic acts which projected the theophany and the speech forms which enshrined the theophany in the shape of literary survivals will be treated at a later point in our discussion.[75]

COVENANT. By covenant we refer inexactly and misleadingly to the formal structure of ordered relationships between the people and the deity who has manifested himself. A theophany by itself may be isolated and momentary, freakish and random; it may not rise much beyond an obscure sense that divinity or mystery is at work in some awesome happening. Theophany alone can never be the foundation of community, the basis for a social system. It is characteristic of the theophany in early Israel that it leads to compacting ties between deity and people, although, once the compacting ties are made, theophany can appear in other contexts to energize the people to utmost efforts, as in the conduct of war. The customary English term for describing the compacting ties between deity and people is "covenant," translating Hebrew $b^e rith$. The term is burdened with a history of speculation and debate, and the English word "covenant" is now either so archaic or used in such specialized legal and sentimental contexts as to be inadequate for our purposes. Still it is a convenient term, difficult to avoid, if only because alternative English terms are just as problematic. As long as we understand by "covenant" an ordered relationship, or a reciprocally but not necessarily symmetrically involving and limiting arrangement between parties, it is a useful term to employ.

In Israelite terms we may say that the covenant theme is present wherever Israel agrees to acknowledge the right and power of Yahweh to be its sovereign and thus to accept what he commands as constitutive of its life. Vital to this study is the further reality that the covenant is not simply an abstract religious concept, although it tends to become that in the course of Israelite experience. Covenant is also a cultic action which binds groups together; and at the same time, or in collateral actions, it is a sociopolitical action specifying the sovereignty which the compacting groups will recognize throughout the range of their collective sociopolitical life. Thereby covenant sets the structure and primary modes for interaction within the resulting social system. But these dimensions of covenant as a cultic action and as a sociopolitical action will be explicated in other contexts. Here we do no more than to establish the formal mode of covenanting.[76]

LAW. By law we refer to any specification of the will of the deity which is given to the community as an implementation of his sovereignty. As with covenant, the term "law" is laden with difficulties. As it stands, it implies much too legalistic and juridical a connotation in the case of early Israel. Law as jurisprudence existed in early Israel but only in rudimentary form, and the jurisprudence of early Israel was not simply coterminous with that divine instruction which stemmed from the cult. The divine instruction in the cult customarily appeared in the form of brief prohibitions or injunctions about ethical and cultic conduct. These prohibitions and injunctions carried important effects and implications for the day-to-day jurisprudence, but the relations between divine instruction and administration of justice were complex and often indirect.[77]

As now formulated, the complex of themes or sub-themes called Sinaitic by von Rad may be characterized as manifestation of divine right and power over the community, pledge of the people to acknowledge the divine right and power as the community's sovereignty, and implementation of the divine right and power in moral and cultic instructions. The themes are seen to possess an organic sequential connectedness, each proceeding out of the foregoing, altogether forming a unity of movement and a totality of conception which would be lost in the absence of any one of the elements. For how can a people pledge itself to a deity who has not authenticated himself? Or what possible significance can a divine manifestation possess that does not ask to be acknowledged? Or what can it mean to pledge oneself to a god who makes no concrete demands?

12.4 Cultic Location of Sinai Themes

In terms of the point of view of the theophany-covenant-law themes we note first of all that they possess a primary present temporal reference. They are conceptual modes and forms of praxis which the gathered cultic community *enacted in a definite program of events.* It is my contention that these modal actions were in the first instance totally contemporary constitutive and reconstitutive acts. Unlike the historical recitals, they did not involve the slightest distancing of the community from the present. The modal actions of theophany, covenant, and law were the forms for bringing into being a community which would have something to remember. Only secondarily, after the passage of decades, were these modal actions—which gave the basic structure to the early cult—objectified and lodged in the complex of historical traditions as though they had been events that occurred at Sinai. But the retrospective transformation of these modal actions in historical episodes in the course of time must not obscure *their primary and original contemporaneity* as modal action-word complexes to be performed whenever called for in the cult. It was typical of these modal actions to occur in an indefinitely expandable cultic present. They articulated the fundamental ideological structure of the group consciousness of united Israel: "We are a community to whom Yahweh is manifest, covenanted with Yahweh, instructed by Yahweh!" Only as the formative period receded farther into the past did it seem necessary to find a point in the recounting of historical narratives where theophany-covenant-law could be temporally fixed and objectively historicized as events in the migration of Israel from Egypt to Canaan.

The first clearly datable point for the historicizing of the cultic present of the modal actions was in the writing down of the extended sources during the monarchy. We can agree so far with von Rad that it is only as the past is viewed from an entirely new stage in the people's history that we find the firm linkage in the objectified traditions between exodus-settlement themes and theophany-covenant-law themes. But unlike von Rad, we go on to stress that prior to their linkage in the written traditions, the linkage had long existed in the cultic group consciousness and praxis of early Israel; and, furthermore, that it was only on the basis of such linkage that the historical actions of the deity could have been recited in the first place.

The cultic context of the modal actions of theophany-covenant-law is *contemporary united Israel acknowledging and regrounding the locus of sovereignty in its corporate life.* Here the focus is on the constitutional present, i.e., upon the group consciousness and communal structure taking shape as the ordering reality of contemporary existence. When we speak of "constituting" or "reconstituting" the corporate life of Israel, as we did in describing the covenantal component in the cult, we are alluding to the obvious historical judgment that at one point Israel as the cult community of Yahweh was *first* organized, whereas successive gatherings of the community (annually or every seven years?), were in a sense both repetitions and extensions of that first event. The first event and the successive events stood to one another formally in the relationship of primary constitution to secondary reconstitution or ratification.

Yet this is a misleading formulation if we do not also see that cultic thought has a tendency toward timelessness, not necessarily in the sense of the negation of time or the affirmation of eternity, but in the sense of a pregnant "timeliness," a meaning-filled and meaning-dispensing archetypal "gathered time," a cultic time interpenetrating with the archetypal time of Israel's social movement toward national liberation, heavy with the fatefulness of each new threat and each new deliverance. *Israel is brought near death and restored to life in each convergence and conjunction of cultic time and sociopolitical time.* This cultic "timeliness" is a symbolic organization of lived experience in which each new sociopolitical demand of time and space can find its place and thereby mobilize the energies of Israel to take appropriate action.

The cultic "timeliness" that gave organization to lived experience did not altogether flatten out the discreteness of each new combined cultic and sociopolitical moment. The content and quality of an earlier, even of the foundational, cultic moment tended to be continued, without a sharp sense of discontinuity, from one cultic context and from one sociopolitical context to another. The constitutional moment for old Israel lived on in each reconstituting moment with a peculiar vividness and in such a manner that the language employed in the various reconstitutions could speak with the freshness and with the finality of the first event. A further factor to be considered is that it is not strictly correct to posit only one constitutional moment for united Israel. As we have hinted and will more fully develop in following chapters, Israel seems to have been constituted by a series of stages, so that there was more than one "reconstituting" cultic assembly that was also "constitutional" in the sense that on that occasion new groups were brought within the communal framework of Israel and submitted themselves to Israel's god. Not only does this abiding "constitutional" force of the covenant renewal apply to those moments when new groups are brought into Israel. The same force persists throughout the history of the cult in the tendency to see each generation of Israelites as standing in a new and direct relationship to Yahweh, which is at the same time paradoxically a return to and a reassertion of the constitutional origins—a perspective advanced with exceptional forcefulness in the Book of Deuteronomy.

The immediate aim of the modal actions of theophany-covenant-law was to *resecure the foundations of the corporate life and to restate the norms for daily life*. If the aims of reciting the historical traditions were broadly didactic-inspirational and intellectual-cultural in a community already confident of its secure foundations, the aim of the theophany-covenant-law modal actions was *constitutional-normative* in the sense of realigning the community in its fundamental structure so that it could recollect the past and cope with its farthest-reaching present sociopolitical problems. The historical themes sought to encompass the many interests and experiences of the diverse Israelite peoples and to focus them upon the unifying allegiance to Yahweh, whereas the specific intent of the theophany-covenant-law modal actions was to relate the community directly to the realm of the sacred and to receive into the community the imprint of the sacred in the form of the divine instructions.

Put in another way, *the historical themes were what the people understood about Yahweh's activity in their previous experience, whereas the theophany-covenant-law modal actions were what the people did in Yahweh's presence to conform themselves to his sovereignty*. Thus, one of the things the people did was to receive once again the divine instructions which were to be implemented throughout the structure of the social system of Israel. Cultic action thereby concentrated all the energies of the society and at the same time constellated and released those social energies in a form that could return creatively to the many spheres, levels, and interfaces of the social system with bonding and mobilizing force.

When seen in this way, it is evident that the modal actions were not separable from the historical themes in other than a proximate functional way. In fact, it becomes clear that the complex of theophany-covenant-law within its context of present encounter between deity and people was the very heart of the cultic activity, and by comparison the historical retrospect was secondary. The modal actions formed the encompassing cultic-ideological substructure; the historical themes of the tradition were elaborated superstructure which in time, for the sake of completeness, expanded to include the original foundational modal actions in a historicized form as events at Sinai. The historical themes broadened and rationalized the outlook of a community which was previously established and re-established by the modal actions. In this way we can understand both the important peculiarities and the ultimate unity of the "subjective" modalities of cultic action and the "objectifying" narrative themes rooted in but extending beyond the cult toward an emerging independent status as an autonomous body of tradition.

I can imagine a cult in early Israel in which the deity appeared, compacted with the people, and instructed the people *without the recital of any historical retrospects.* I can also imagine a particular festival whose sole stated content was to celebrate historical retrospection, but only on the presupposition that it was a limited specific action by a people already compacted with and obedient to the deity whose actions were being recited. What I simply cannot imagine is a cult in early Israel in which the people merely recited past actions of the deity *without any present cultic-ideological rootage in theophany, covenant, and law.*[78] But it is this anomaly which von Rad seems to presuppose when he argues that a festival of historical retrospection occurred at Gilgal in which not only all the elements but, as I read him, even all the presuppositions of the "Sinaitic" cultic present were absent. In my opinion that reading of the cultic history would be tantamount to dissolving Israel as an historical entity, which would then have to be seen as the invention of the Yahwist traditionist. But that Israel existed in an articulated Yahwistic form well before the monarchy would be granted by von Rad; and, consequently, to do justice to the legitimate differentia which von Rad identified between the historical themes and the modal actions of the Sinai sub-themes, we must conclude that their difference lay in their varying structural locations in one unified cultic program and in their varying manners of incorporation into the growing complex of traditions.

13

Cultic Modalities and Narrative Themes: Substructure and Superstructure

Our analysis so far has been primarily structural-functional. We have seen that the matrix of the historical traditions of early Israel was immediately in the centralized cult in which the various forces for cohesion and diversification within the social system were constellated. The ordered relationships in the social system were dialectically related to the ordered actions of the cult and to the ordered agglomerations of tradition. We have further seen that the basic themes of the tradition were drawn in two fundamentally different ways from the life of the cult. One sort of basic theme was first created within the cult as a stylized recital of events, although it eventually came to have an extra-cultic life by means of numerous narrative elaborations. The other sort of basic theme was first a cultic action with accompanying words and acts which only secondarily was given a narrative form. This introduces the perspective of historical development in that the historical traditions emerged out of the matrix of the cult gradually and, stage by stage, grew in scope and complexity, eventually drawing all of the major modal actions of the centralized cult into the orbit of the traditions. It is necessary, therefore, to examine the progressive growth of the basic themes in a historical-developmental manner. I have supplied two charts which summarize my hypothesis concerning the development of the narrative themes out of the cultic modalities in two stages (see Charts 1 and 2, pp. 102–103). They should be consulted in connection with the following exposition, to which they are correlated by the sigla M for "cultic modalities" and T for "narrative themes."

13.1 Sociocultic Matrix of All Themes

How did the first distinctively narrative basic themes arise in the cult? Wherever the materials for the basic themes came from, their distinctive formation as declamations about all Israel must be subsumed under the generative activity of the all-Israelite cult. This was the cult in which (1) a theophany of the deity was staged, M^1; (2) a covenant with the deity was concluded, M^2; (3) historical thematic résumés of the past relations of deity and people were recited, M^3; and (4) cultic and moral instructions were delivered to the people by the deity, M^4. The growth of the historical traditions began in the cult in connection with the third structural element cited. Only the historical résumés were at first involved in the patterning into basic themes as crystallizing agents or frames for producing and gathering stories about Israel's past (T^{A-D}). The other structural elements of the cult —theophany (T^{E1}), covenant (T^{E2}), and law (T^{E3})—were only introduced into the structure of the basic theme as "historical" themes or sub-themes toward the middle or end of the premonarchic period, c. 1100–1050 B.C. Without the existence of the cult as the centralized organ of the social system of Israel, no basic themes would have developed at all, and there would have been no occasion for the agglomeration of disparate traditions of proto-Israelites into the harmonized tradition of united Israel. Thus, the narrative traditions in their inception, and in their formal structure and conceptualization, are fundamentally cultic products. The contrary impression, easily derivable from reading the present form of the traditions—namely, that the traditions laid down in their main outlines by Moses were accounts of events that occurred just as related before the cult was organized in Palestine—is in my view totally mistaken.

The formal ground of both cult and tradition in old Israel was the social system of Israelite people who emerged in late thirteenth-century Canaan. But in actual fact we cannot separate the cult from the social system historically, but only analytically. The social system itself can only be discerned as operative at that point when its most distinctive organ—the cult of Yahweh—was also operative. The very action by which the social system was set in motion was in fact the first action of the cult of Yahweh. Therefore, while the cult can be analytically separated from the social system in terms of its greater religious conceptual and institutional explicitness, the cult cannot be historically separated from the social system because cult is precisely that mode through which the peoples became conscious of themselves as forming a totality and through which the people took steps to constitute themselves as one social system whose sovereign and arbiter was Yahweh. The first covenant-concluding cultic assembly was "the founding convention" of Israel.

In arguing thus, I leave aside for the moment the nature of those predisposing conditions and preceding social arrangements of proto-Israelite peoples which admittedly lay behind and gave shape to the formation of the Israelite social system. To do justice to the total social system of Israel, it will be imperative later in our study to assess those preconditions and prearrangements, but for delineating the history of the tradition as it unfolded out of the cult, those pre-Israelite factors may be momentarily bracketed. We are simply establishing that for the tracing of the tradition history, the cult was the decisive generative institutional matrix within Israel.

Just how foundational the cult was for the tradition history becomes clear when we sum up the features of the main structural elements of the cult, paying particular attention to the specific acts and speech forms which accompanied the major segments of the primary all-Israelite cultic drama.

CHART 1

EARLY STAGE OF THE DEVELOPMENT OF NARRATIVE THEMES OUT OF THE ALL-ISRAELITE CULT MODALITIES C. 1200—1100 /1075 B.C.

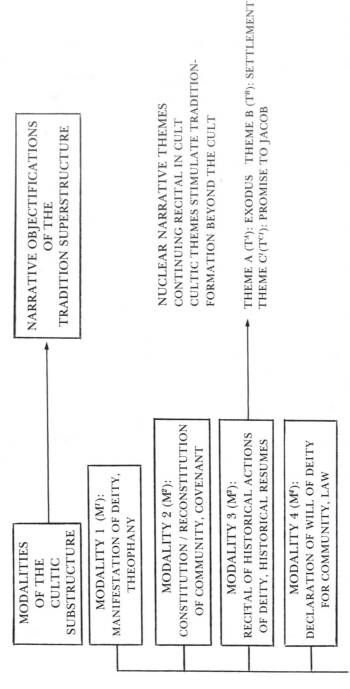

NARRATIVE OBJECTIFICATIONS OF THE TRADITION SUPERSTRUCTURE

MODALITIES OF THE CULTIC SUBSTRUCTURE

MODALITY 1 (M^1): MANIFESTATION OF DEITY, THEOPHANY

MODALITY 2 (M^2): CONSTITUTION / RECONSTITUTION OF COMMUNITY, COVENANT

MODALITY 3 (M^3): RECITAL OF HISTORICAL ACTIONS OF DEITY, HISTORICAL RESUMES

MODALITY 4 (M^4): DECLARATION OF WILL OF DEITY FOR COMMUNITY, LAW

NUCLEAR NARRATIVE THEMES CONTINUING RECITAL IN CULT CULTIC THEMES STIMULATE TRADITION-FORMATION BEYOND THE CULT

THEME A (T^A): EXODUS   THEME B (T^B): SETTLEMENT
THEME C' ($T^{C'}$): PROMISE TO JACOB

Appropriate word-declarations or liturgies for each modality re-cited within the cultic context. For $M^{1,2,4}$ (i.e., theophany, coven-ant, law), the words were repeated and developed solely in the cult context.

The words of M^3 (i.e., historical recitals) were objectified as narrative-traditions, now separable from the cult modality to the extent that they were repeatable outside the cult and subject to general cultural and intellectual reflection and expansion.

CHART 2

LATER STAGE OF THE DEVELOPMENT OF NARRATIVE THEMES OUT OF THE ALL-ISRAELITE CULT MODALITIES C. 1100 / 1075 — 1050 B.C.

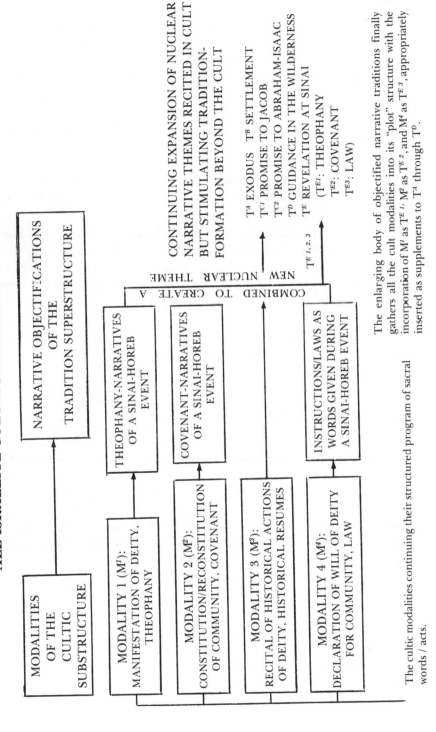

MODALITIES
OF THE
CULTIC
SUBSTRUCTURE

NARRATIVE OBJECTIFICATIONS
OF THE
TRADITION SUPERSTRUCTURE

MODALITY 1 (M^1):
MANIFESTATION OF DEITY,
THEOPHANY

THEOPHANY-NARRATIVES
OF A SINAI-HOREB
EVENT

MODALITY 2 (M^2):
CONSTITUTION/RECONSTITUTION
OF COMMUNITY, COVENANT

COVENANT-NARRATIVES
OF A SINAI-HOREB
EVENT

MODALITY 3 (M^3):
RECITAL OF HISTORICAL ACTIONS
OF DEITY, HISTORICAL RESUMÉS

MODALITY 4 (M^4):
DECLARATION OF WILL OF DEITY
FOR COMMUNITY, LAW

INSTRUCTIONS/LAWS AS
WORDS GIVEN DURING
A SINAI-HOREB EVENT

COMBINED TO CREATE A NEW NUCLEAR THEME

CONTINUING EXPANSION OF NUCLEAR
NARRATIVE THEMES RECITED IN CULT
BUT STIMULATING TRADITION-
FORMATION BEYOND THE CULT

T^A EXODUS T^B SETTLEMENT
T^{C1} PROMISE TO JACOB
T^{C2} PROMISE TO ABRAHAM-ISAAC
T^D GUIDANCE IN THE WILDERNESS
T^E REVELATION AT SINAI
   (T^{E1}: THEOPHANY
    T^{E2}: COVENANT
    T^{E3}: LAW)

$T^{E 1, 2, 3}$

The enlarging body of objectified narrative traditions finally
gathers all the cult modalities into its "plot" structure with the
incorporation of M^1 as T^{E1}, M^2 as T^{E2}, and M^4 as T^{E3}, appropriately
inserted as supplements to T^A through T^D.

The cultic modalities continuing their structured program of sacral
words / acts.

In the theophany (M^1) Yahweh appears to the cult community as the god with the power and the right to be its god. Corresponding to this offer of divine sovereignty over the community were liturgical pieces—whether oral or written is not critical in this context—i.e., more or less fixed pieces that gave rubrics for the officiants and the people and which contained dramatic statements of Yahweh's appearance to and claim upon the community. The liturgical pieces were doubtless accompanied by appropriate stage effects which used the senses to communicate the total presence of Yahweh in his awesome majesty. These fixed pieces probably varied in form from period to period and from place to place, and according to who was officiating; but the variations occurred within a determinate range, so that the critical desideratum of Yahweh's adequacy as a sovereign for Israel was asserted with dramatic cogency.

In the covenant (M^2) a compact is concluded between god and people in which Israel affirms the god Yahweh to be its god and Yahweh affirms the people Israel to be his people. This cultic action is tantamount to the investing of Yahweh with sovereignty over the group. Israel thereby pledges to observe the sovereign's demands upon the community as they become known through the appointed instruments of his sovereignty, i.e., through the institutions and offices of the social system and its cult. The covenant liturgical pieces give rubrics for the words and acts of the two parties to the compact, including the roles of the representatives of the people. Like the theophany pieces, the covenant pieces assumed a relatively fixed shape which could vary from place to place and from time to time, but which assured a clear conceptual assertion and practical implementation of the communal subjection to the divine sovereignty. The present variant and fragmented forms of the covenant pieces result in part from the original allowable variations in the exact form of executing the cultic modality and in part from the alteration of the cultically rooted program pieces into independent literary texts. Because the covenant was the central constitutional act of the cultic drama, it came to support a heavy conceptual overload of interpretation and reinterpretation. This practical and conceptual primacy of the covenant segment of the basic cult sequence is thus reflected in the extensive reshaping of the covenant texts to the point that they are among the most tangled literary units in the early traditions and among the most resistant to source analysis.

In the law (M^4) the concrete will of the sovereign for the proper operation of social system is articulated in the form of instructions directed to various aspects of social life and prominently including cultic activity. The basic form of the instruction rooted in the cult is the so-called apodictic or categorical law in the form of a brief prohibition or injunction. Apparently the first sets of these instructions were more cohesive in form and content than now appears, owing to their complicated literary editing.[79] In the process of editing they have been brought into association with the so-called casuistic law, and in many instances the two types are intermixed. The casuistic laws belong more properly to the sphere of general jurisprudence, but it is clear that cult and jurisprudence were not easily separated in old Israel and that there was a tendency for the dicta of the cultic apodictic laws to penetrate the realm of jurisprudence and to affect not only the range of items covered by case law but also the formulation of the case laws. The primary rootage of law in cultically declaimed instructions of the sovereign to the community set the conceptual pattern for conceiving all law within Israel as ultimately Yahweh's will.

These three structural elements of the basic cult (theophany, covenant, and law) form an inseparable triad linked on the one side with the social structure of the community and on the other with sets of programmatic actions and verbalizations which eventually became objectified in a body of quasi-historical traditions. This triad of cultic action lay at the foundation of the constitution and periodic renewal of the social system of Israel. To remove this cultic triad from our analysis, or to break it up into separate elements, would be to unhinge the Israelite social system, and thus to dissolve Israel as an historical phenomenon.

13.2 Historical Themes Emerge from the Cult

The recital of historical resumes (M^3), while emerging as an important action within the cultic drama, does not belong to the constitutional arrangement of Israel. It is a more secondary and reflective action in which the work of the sovereign in the past history of the people is recounted and traced in ever growing depth and complexity through a narrative speech form which constellates the episodes around sub-themes and basic nuclear themes T^{AE}. It is this cultic milieu for the thematically organized narratives which determines their fundamental all-Israelite conceptual framework. The narrative form of the historical résumés represents a stage of communal self-consciousness and objectification which the cultic modalities of theophany, covenant, and law did not attain for decades, indeed for a century or more (eventually in the form of T^E).

The theophany, covenant, and law modal actions (M^1; M^2; M^4) were experienced with such immediacy in the cult that they did not at once necessitate reflective formulation as items of the tradition which could be recited or read apart from their being acted out in the cultic ceremonies. Yet the immediacy of the cult stimulated reflection and objectification. In the experience of uniting Israel there was a strongly felt need for a cultic activity which did more than focus upon the immediate constitution and renewal of the community. There was an impulse to see the foreground of Israel's emerging unity in some background of historic depth. It was known to all the component peoples of Israel that, in spite of its recent mutation as a genuinely novel social system, the various peoples who joined their fortunes in Israel had prehistories of their own. There was a desire that these prehistories not be lost but that their peculiar features be preserved, yet preserved *systematically* in such a way that the peculiarities of each sub-history would affirm and solidify the unity of the whole.

While the flowering of unified Israel was recent, there was an urge to look for the ancient seeds from which it had germinated. The conceptual means for giving impetus and focus to this urge for historic depth was available in the fact that the cult of Yahweh had been brought into Canaan by the Moses group. Yahweh was a god with temporal precedence extending back beyond his adoption by unified Israel. Thus, the account of the relation between Yahweh and the Moses group could begin to fill out as the account of all Israel in its seed form. Given the impulse to trace the roots of newly formed Israel, coupled with the absence of documentary history concerning the Moses group, it was natural that no scrupulous or firmly controlled distinction was observed between the Moses group as proto-Israel or Israel in seed form, on the one hand, and the Moses group as simply an earlier stage of unified Israel, or Israel in its florescence, on the other hand. In fact, the lines of distinction were broken down, and it became normative to speak of all the tribes together in Egypt, in the wilderness, and in the entrance into Canaan in place of the more historically accurate specification of the Moses group, or the Levites, or the Joseph tribes, or whatever units we estimate to have been involved on the basis of a documentary-historical, probabilistic analysis.

In taking over the focal memories of the Moses group (perhaps already merged with the memories of a Kadesh group and/or of a Benjaminite or Joseph group) as the historic tap root for the Israelite community in Canaan, the story line was constructed around two pivotal memories: that the people had been delivered from Egypt (T^A) and that the people had been safely guided into Canaan, where it found a homeland (T^B). The basis was laid for ever enlarging rootages of unified Israel in the prehistories of proto-Israelite peoples, so that an underground system of proliferating roots could be developed comparable to the above-ground system of tribal branches united in the main trunk of Israel. Historical roots and contemporary branches could find their counterparts and, wherever the branches could be seen, roots could be analogized. And as the branches were appendages of one trunk, so the roots were offshoots of one tap root. The impulse to fill out the past story of Israel as a totality and with an amplitude equalling the rich articulation of its social segmentation was irresistible.

So firmly was the principle established that all prior experiences of any member of unified Israel were to be seen as experiences of all Israel that they were schematized insofar as possible as the experiences of the associated tribes from the bondage in Egypt to the occupation of the land. But there were limitations to continuing such a project of assimilating the discrete traditions. Some of the traditions were permeated by conditions and circumstances which were inconsistent with that unified picture. Specifically, some of the episodes concerned people who were not Yahwists (but rather worshippers of El), and the setting for the episodes was in or near Canaan. Such traditions implied either that they told of events *prior to* the unified history from Egypt to Canaan or of events *subsequent to* the unified history. Of the two temporal conceptions, the latter was clearly impossible to entertain, for it would burst apart the fundamental framework of united Israel if it were granted that after entering Canaan from Egypt the peoples were not unified as Yahwists.

It was possible, however, to conceive of a stage before Israel became a large association of peoples in Egypt; when it was a much smaller entity, an entity which could be represented as a large family whose sons became the progenitors of the later, greatly enlarged tribes (T^C). Some of the most glaring differences in the social forms of the people, in the population size, and in the religious ideas and practices embedded in the various traditions could be harmonized by grouping the stories into two successive periods: *the period when Israel was in Canaan as a large family and the period when Israel was in Egypt, in the wilderness, and returned to Canaan as an association of tribes.* In this manner, the pronounced contradictions and tensions in traditions which had Canaan as a common setting could be relaxed and harmonized by conceiving two different periods when Israel was in Canaan. The difficulty created by the tension between El and Yahweh worship could be relaxed and harmonized by interpreting El as another name for Yahweh.

The periodization of the traditions into two temporal phases—i.e., the patriarchal phase (T^C) and the exodus-settlement phase $(T^A; T^B; T^D)$—with two different social systems and two different sets of relations to the inhabitants of Canaan was not in itself sufficient. Within each period difficulties of continuity appeared.

The traditions felt to belong to the early temporal phases were not all homogeneous. They were clustered around more than one major figure and were connected with various parts of Canaan. The harmonizing device employed to resolve this difficulty was that of kinship linkage. Abraham (T^{C2}) became the father of Isaac and Isaac the father of Jacob (T^{C1}). Even then the problem of how the single large family or clan of a patriarch became the many tribes of Israel in Egypt demanded some resolution. To make plausible the "join" between the single family of the patriarchs and the tribes of Israel, Jacob was represented as the father of sons who became the tribal ancestors. To cope with the change of geographical setting from Canaan to Egypt, the Joseph story was interjected between the Jacob theme and the basic Deliverance from Egypt theme in order to explain how it happened that the sons of Jacob went into Egypt, where they were eventually enslaved, there to emerge no longer as individuals heading families but as their offspring, by now vastly increased as the tribes of Israel with their own leaders.

The traditions felt to belong to the later temporal phase were also not all homogeneous. A hiatus was felt in the experience of the people between their deliverance from Egypt and their entrance into Canaan, and so the basic theme of

Guidance in the Wilderness was developed (T^D), doubtless stimulated, as Noth has proposed, by the contacts of Israelites in the south of Canaan with the great Sinaitic wilderness through which tradition reported that their forebears had passed. The wilderness episodes functioned as a mirror image of the experience of unifying Israel in Canaan. The similarities keenly felt were that in both cases the community had experienced great initial success in deliverance from its enemies, but at the same time both communities were in a precarious position, requiring that they make new adaptations and struggle to master their environment and attain a secure hold upon a land they could call their own. Thus traditions about the wilderness experience of the Moses group, conceived as the unified tribes of Israel, stressed the larger guidance of Yahweh in bringing the people through all dangers, as well as detailing many kinds of struggle with nature, with hostile enemies, and with internal apostasy and rebellion—experiences reflective of analogous struggles within the unified people of Israel in Canaan.

I have explicated a certain internal logic for the growth of the narrative traditions which very likely did not find a corresponding straight line of development in the growth of the traditions. As indicated in III.10.2, I conjecture that following the formulation of the twin themes of Deliverance from Egypt (T^A) and Leading into Canaan (T^B), the Promise to Jacob (T^{C1}) next arose, and then the Promise to Abraham and Isaac (T^{C2}), which probably was preceded by an assimilation of two independent traditions in which Isaac was subordinated to Abraham. But the time span between the Promise to Jacob theme and the Promise to Abraham-Isaac theme was a matter of decades; for whereas the Jacob theme was from the north, the Abraham-Isaac theme was from the south and therefore did not enter the structure of the traditions produced in the cult as a basic theme until after Judah entered united Israel in the period 1100–1050 B.C. In that interim, Jacob had presumably already been linked with the tribes in Egypt by the genealogical scheme representing his sons as the ancestors of the tribe. When the Abraham-Isaac theme was added, in order to do justice to the previously unassimilated southern traditions, there was no place to insert the theme except before Jacob, who had by then become firmly understood as the immediate father of the associated tribes. The compromise was advantageous to both themes and to both the nothern and southern segments of united Israel: Jacob retained his honored position as the immediate father of Israel (indeed his other name was Israel; Gen. 32:28; 49:2), and Abraham achieved honor as the first of his people to receive the call and promise of Yahweh. The Guidance in the Wilderness theme (T^D) first crystallized with the entrance of Judah into Israel, when the imagination of Judeans, living close to the southern desert, came to play upon the vacuum that existed between deliverance from Egypt and entrance into the land. And it seems that the Joseph story (transition from T^{C1} to T^A) was last of all supplied to give a convincing transition from Canaan to Egypt.

In other words, the logic of growth and adjustment of the traditions was not simply an unfolding of structural necessities internal to the body of tradition but a logic that was influenced in large measure by the history of the unifying peoples, and especially by the circumstance of Judah's entrance into Israel at least a century after the founding of Israel. And, of course, in all this development I am distinguishing between the formation of basic themes in the unfolding traditional framework and the existence of the separate traditions which came to be constellated around those themes. I am not for a moment denying, for example, that some of the traditions about Abraham and Isaac long predated the moment when they were constellated as a nuclear theme and that, similarly, some of the traditions about the wilderness wandering long predated the moment when they too were constellated as a nuclear theme.

From the beginning, the historical résumés were paradoxically both rooted in the cult and capable of detachment from the cult. They were semi-independent cult products which, although they remained for a long time primarily within the aegis of the cult, were not restricted by being solely accounts for cultic celebrations. Their objectifying quasi-historical form, their thrust toward comprehending and systematically relating the origin stories of the people, gave the narrative traditions constellated by the basic themes a relative autonomy. They stimulated general cultural and intellectual concerns such as could easily lead on through progressive detachment from the cult to their literary embodiment in the great tradition sequences of J and E under the monarchy. Thus, unlike von Rad, I do not see the detachment of the narrative traditions from the cult as an abrupt accomplishment of the monarchy, although the monarchy brought a momentous final stage in the process, but as a latent tendency in the narrative forms from the very start which made of the traditions a general cultural and intellectual history as well as a cultic history.

The semi-independence of the historical narratives from the cult, as compared with the theophany, covenant, and law segments of cultic action, can be specified more precisely when we consider that, while they were in many cases prepared for cultic recitation, the historical narratives did not depend upon accompanying cultic action, as did the other kinds of cultic program pieces; and once a few traditions existed for cultic recitation, they could be adapted and added to for general story-telling without restriction to a formal all-Israelite cultic occasion. The theophany pieces, by contrast, could only be employed in company with a staged theophany. The covenant pieces could only be employed where a covenant was constituted or renewed. The cultic and sociopolitical instructions could only be employed where the community was being solemnly confronted with the sovereign will of Yahweh. All the theophanic, covenant, and instructional program pieces belonged for more than a century exclusively to the realm of the sacred as embodied in the all-Israelite cult.

It was otherwise with the quasi-historical narratives, for they could be employed outside as well as inside the centralized cult. They told stories which did not require accompanying cultic actions, although specific cultic actions may have been associated with them according to time and place, such as the probability that some of the patriarchal episodes were connected with a pilgrimage from Shechem to Bethel or that some of the conquest stories were connected with ceremonies at Gilgal, which enacted the deliverance from Egypt and the seizure of Canaan. But just because they told a story conceived as objectified in the past, they could be recited both within and without the cultic program. A general cultural and intellectual interest in origins would lead toward systematic reflection on and expansion of the narrative traditions, which could proceed apace in the intervals between the annual or septennial cultic renewals of the constitution of Israel. Such a tendency, growing out of but extending beyond the cult, would lead toward attempts to fix the history in greater detail in such a form as Noth has hypothesized as the common groundwork (or *Grundlage*) available to J and E.

13.3 Sinai Themes Emerge from the Cult

The distinction between theophany, covenant, and law traditions as liturgically circumscribed program pieces for the cult and the historical résumés as cultically originated, but increasingly autonomous cultural and intellectual products, does not tell the whole story by any means. The acceleration of such a broad cultural and intellectual enterprise inevitably began to have an effect upon the hitherto liturgically bound theophany, covenant, and law program pieces. At a point prior to the monarchy, which I take to have been around 1075–1050 B.C. and closely associated with the last major increment of membership to unified Israel, namely, the admission of Judah, those formerly liturgical pieces underwent a profound transformation. More properly, we should say they underwent a bifurcation. While the cult went on using them as program pieces for the stages of the renewal of Israel's constitutional arrangements (M^1; M^2; M^4), those very same program pieces were drastically revised and given a place within the great traditional narrative sequence (T^{E1}; T^{E2}; T^{E3}). The result was the insertion of an entirely new theme into the company of the previous body of themes; the theme of the Revelation at Sinai (T^E).

Why did this historicizing of the cultically embedded theophany, covenant, and law liturgical pieces take place? What were the methods employed and what were the results for the shape of the tradition complex and for the social system of Israel?

The reasons for the historicizing of previously cultic materials were doubtless highly complex. A major factor was the burgeoning growth of the historical résumés as basic theme after basic theme, transition after transition, tradition after tradition (individually and in clusters of sub-themes) enlarged the body of historicized tradition and gave it an approved, standardized, even proto-canonical form. Increasingly, this complex of traditions gained objective stature as an encyclopedic statement of the basic events and meanings of Israel's existence through time and space. As long as the complex of tradition was recognized as merely one functional branch of the total cult, the historical résumés need not have been complete. They did not have to tell about the basic constitutional arrangements which they presupposed and which were known to all Israelites as the cultic acts of theophany, covenant, and law-giving. But as the complex traditions built around the basic themes gained in cultural and intellectual autonomy, as they stood out from the cult while still retaining a connection with the cult—and especially as they began to be studied as independent testimonies to the past—the need was intensely felt for the story told to be more complete. It became urgent to correct the most glaring omission in that body of quasi-historical traditions, and that was *the lack of a narrative account of the introduction of theophany, covenant, and law-giving to Israel.* Where and when was Israel first formed as the people of Yahweh, i.e., as a covenanted and law-regulated community to whom Yahweh appeared?

Even so, it is hard to imagine that the pressure could have become urgent enough to historicize the cultic constitutional liturgies had not the cult itself, and the social system which it articulated with religious explicitness, undergone changes or faced crises or threats which impelled the community to carry through the historicizing of the entire cultic program. What changes, crises, or threats in the eleventh-century cult and social system of Israel may explain this process? One factor was a desire to lend authority to a standardized form of carrying out the theophany, covenant, and law-giving acts in the cult. Down to the middle of the eleventh-century there were probably several variant forms for observing these acts. But now that the first generation of Israelites who had participated in the original constitution of Israel were dead, even the cultic constitutional acts were beginning to be experienced as acts with historic depth. Should not these previously variant versions of the fundamental cultic acts be as standardized as the historical traditions? Moreover, when the members of Israel were all northerners, there were fewer difficulties of consensus than when, in the eleventh-century, the southern Judeans joined Israel. Israel was now composed of two peoples with decided regional and cultural differences, including dialectical differences in language. A more standardized cult program may have seemed necessary to facilitate the effective joining of these different elements in Israel.

Furthermore, the social system of unifying Israel had been able to repel all external threats from the Canaanite city-states and from the peoples who pressed into Canaan from the desert fringes. But by the middle of the eleventh-century a new threat rapidly appeared in the form of a Philistine city-state system more tightly organized politically and better equipped militarily than any previous enemy of Israel. It was imperative that the Israelite people be unified as never before, and precisely at a time when Israel had been demographically, territorially, and culturally expanded internally by the incorporation of Judah. Effective responses to internal and external strains were called for at the same time. The situation was critical: Could Israel, now more than a century removed from its initial formation and faced with a massive new body of "converts" and also confronted by an unprecedentedly strong foe, retain a viable functional cohesion?

Under the circumstances it is probable that efforts at standardization of the liturgical program pieces celebrating theophany, covenant, and law-giving were undertaken at this critical point in the mid-eleventh century and that, at the same time, the liturgical pieces were revised for inclusion within the historical résumé in the narrative form of a new basic theme (T^E). This last and probably rather hastily executed enlargement of the basic themes of the historical traditions was carried out in remarkable fashion. Previously every new basic theme added was allowed to stand independently and some transitional device was found for linking it to the adjacent theme or themes. The standardized sequence of basic themes was now so tightly arranged and so elaborated in content by the "filler" traditions that there was no satisfactory way to insert a new theme without upsetting the whole. It was obvious that the theophany, covenant, and law motifs could not be added to the whole complex as an addendum, for that would shatter the narrative structure of the entire edifice.

Moreover, these cultic themes were pivotal to the constitution of unified Israel. They must stand at a central point in the narrative, and they must be grounded at that point in the narrative where Yahweh breaks through as the novel deliverer of the associated tribes. Only one point in the sequence of themes would satisfy these requirements, namely, the period between the deliverance from Egypt and the entrance into Canaan. The result was that the basic theme of Guidance in the Wilderness (T^D) was split open, so to speak, and the Revelation at Sinai (T^E) was inserted, so that theophany (T^{E1}), covenant (T^{E2}), and law-giving (T^{E3}) were seen as the foundational events at which Moses officiated. Doubtless this move was dictated by the circumstance that the central cult of Yahwism in unified Israel was dominated by the Levitical descendants of those who lived through the experiences of the Moses group and claimed a lineal connection with Moses as their eponymous ancestor. Moreover, a number of very old liturgical texts picture Yahweh as originally at home in the southern desert in an area variously described as Sinai or Paran or Edom or Seir; hence, long before the theophany, covenant, and law motifs were set formally at Sinai during the wilderness wanderings of the people, there probably existed an implicit belief that the very first actualization of those cultic events took place among the Israelites who had escaped Egypt.

The attendant wound to the carefully articulated structure of the historical traditions is not in itself surprising, given this late and highly tendentious historicizing of elements that had so long been restricted to cultic acts and rubrics. The fact remains that liturgical pieces do not translate smoothly or effectively into narration. All commentators on the pseudo-narrative of the Revelation at Sinai have sensed the literary and historical difficulties in which it abounds. As they now stand, the "filler" traditions of the Revelation at Sinai theme are neither true liturgical pieces nor true narratives but a strange compound of aspects of both. The traces of liturgical action and speech are evident, but no original coherent cultic program survives. The old liturgical elements have been broken up and used again as steps in a purportedly continuous narrative, but it is a fabricated narrative shot through with lacunae and disjunctions.

An attempt to harmonize the tensions is made by periodizing the narrative so that some of the narrated cultic action takes place when the people first reach the mountain (Exod. 19—24), while the rest of the cultic action—presented as a re-establishing of the covenant—takes place after the community's apostasy to the golden calf shatters the first covenant (Exod. 32—34). However, even the two periodized sets of historicized cultic action are not internally coherent. The resultant hodgepodge strikes the reader as an ill-digested compendium of very imperfectly historicized liturgical speeches and rubrics. And because we cannot believe that Israelite traditionists were so grossly inept, it is highly probable that much of the structural incoherence is due to the official sanctity the various versions of the liturgical program pieces had acquired through long usage, so that it became impossible for the narrative traditionist to revise them by means of a single coherent perspective. Supremely within the body of the early Israelite traditions, the shape of the Revelation at Sinai traditions strikes us as a compromise formation.

The form of the historical traditions in old Israel which emerged at the time of the inclusion of the Revelation at Sinai theme, which Noth called the *Grundlage* or "common groundwork" of J and E, was probably much more simplified in its account of theophany (T^{E1}) and covenant (T^{E2}) than appears in the present extremely overloaded version of Exodus 19—24; 32—34. In spite of his trenchant probing of the basic themes, Noth does not attempt to specify their exact content within the common groundwork. Georg Fohrer, however, employing Noth's criterion that we should look for the groundwork in the structure and content common to J and E, suggests that the earliest form of the groundwork included under the Revelation at Sinai an account of the covenant which already contained the counterposed notions of Yahweh descending to the people and of Moses ascending the mountain to Yahweh.[80] He presumably refers to the oral substratum beneath the text of Exodus 19:2–25 which now stands as a fusion of J and E. Only at this point in the Sinai narrative do J and E overlap to form an interwoven narrative. Elsewhere the Sinai materials are set into the narrative in blocs, and this may imply that they were deviants from the old groundwork which were worked into the narrative at later times. This would not preclude their antiquity, for they could reflect traditions just as old as the groundwork but which, for one reason or another, were excluded from the groundwork. On the other hand, they can also be understood as later constructs intended to elaborate points or to correct omissions in the groundwork.

The form of the law sub-theme (T^{E3}) within the groundwork is even more difficult to determine, since it is generally recognized that the present form of the Covenant Code is no earlier than the ninth century and that the decalogues of Exodus 20 and 34 have been so revised that it is virtually impossible to isolate their premonarchic prototypes. Nevertheless, it is hard to believe that theophany and covenant alone could have formed the Sinai basic theme without some reference to law-giving. The clue to the difficulty probably lies in the distinctive form of apodictic law, which absolutely resists being cast into the form of a narrative. The apodictic law, which continued to be declaimed in the cult, entered the groundwork, but uncontrolled by narrative recasting, its content proved to be as variable as the content of the apodictic law declaimed in the continuing cult. When it came to writing down the apodictic laws, J and E chose the rather different versions current in their own circles. By contrast, the casuistic laws were not introduced to the basic theme of Revelation at Sinai until well into the monarchy, and it seems that this occurred for the first time in northern Israel in the ninth century in response to a deterioration of the socioeconomic situation brought on by the united monarchy and newly stimulated by the ominous centralizing monarchic policies of the Omrid dynasty.[81]

14

Uncentralized Traditions Resistant
to the Basic Themes

So far we have seen the extraordinary persistence of the cultic-ideological thrust toward the centralization of traditions within the framework of concatenated basic narrative themes, sub-themes, and individual units of tradition. It remains to consider some materials from this approximate period which were never successfully centralized, or were centralized in erratic ways. Within the uncentralized traditions we note two axes, a formal axis and a positional axis. As to form, we note that some of the traditions are basically liturgical pieces and some are basically narratives. As to position, we note that some of the traditions have been inserted arbitrarily into the sequence of basic themes without being centralized conceptually—i.e.; without being represented as the actions or the words of united Israel or after having arisen in a cultic context apart from the theophany-covenant-law modalities—while some of the traditions have been excluded from the sequence of themes and placed in the postcanonical phase of united Israel, i.e., in the period after Joshua. The formal and positional axes for grouping these uncentralized, or erratically centralized, traditions intersect in varying patterns from tradition to tradition.

There is, for example, a significant difference in the positional distribution of the liturgical and narrative traditions. Uncentralized liturgical and narrative units appear in a postcanonical position, but only uncentralized liturgical units appear in a canonical position. The reason for this difference seems to lie in the relative ease with which narratives can be revised and retrojectively historicized, in comparison with the much greater difficulty involved in revising liturgies. We have seen how poorly the task of historicizing the theophanic, covenant, and law sub-sets of the Sinai theme was carried out. Accordingly, individual narratives from sub-groups in Israel could find their way into the all-Israelite history with a minimum of revision, as long as they were felt to belong to the period preceding Joshua. In spite of the difficulty in historicizing liturgical pieces, the process was attempted in the case of theophanic, covenant, and law liturgies. So the question confronting us is this: Why were some liturgical pieces inserted separately in one of the basic themes other than Revelation at Sinai, or placed outside the basic themes altogether, instead of being grouped along with the theophanic, covenant, and law liturgical revisions under the Sinai theme? I have in mind here pieces such as the tribal blessings of Genesis 49 and Deuteronomy 33 and the songs of triumph in Exodus 15 and I Samuel 2.

14.1 Tribal Blessings

Let us first consider the tribal blessings.[82] It is apparent that the tribal blessings are of a different order of liturgical composition than are theophanic, covenantal, and legal program pieces. The latter were liturgical pieces for the constitutional arrangement of all Israel; they focused on the unifying acts by which the diverse peoples of Israel became and remained one people. The tribal blessings, by contrast, are in their very nature uncentralized. They are "all-Israelite" only in the secondary sense that they catalogue, when taken together, a series of blessings upon all the member groups of united Israel. But they are focused upon the member groups distributively as each is singled out in succession for particular statements of praise or condemnation. These half-jocular, half-serious blessing pronouncements probably had an origin in the separate tribes but came together in the centralized cult in the form of a catalogue of blessings declaimed by a speaker in the centralized cult and, in the case of Deuteronomy 33, supplied with an all-Israelite frame.[83] Their primary origin was decentralized and local, while their secondary appropriation was centralized and national. Yet, in a sense, the same was true of all the traditions of early Israel. What was distinctive about the blessings?

The essence of the blessing form, it if was to be used at all, was to preserve the individual blessings appropriate to each tribe. It would have been totally impossible to conflate them in the form of a general blessing upon all Israel, since the circumstantial references were applicable only to this or that single tribe. Applied to all Israel as an undifferentiated unity, they would have been meaningless and grotesque. Thus, these basically localized folk products were only partially modified by the centralizing Yahwistic cult, which had to make room for them in the same way that it had to make room for the distinctive local narrative traditions of the tribes. The difference was that the tribal blessings, as a result of their irreducibly uncentralized form, remained unassimilated by the centralizing thrust that won out in most of the traditions. These tribal blessings were known and remembered as early liturgical pieces, as ancient and authentic as any of the materials that were combined under the basic themes. Moreover, when all the discrete blessings were joined together, they encompassed all Israel. Therefore, they had to go into the body of all-Israelite canonical tradition in the pre-Joshua canonical era. The solution was to connect them either with the patriarchal or with the Mosaic age. The tribal blessings of Genesis 49 became the deathbed pronouncements of Jacob, the progenitor of the tribes of Israel. The tribal blessings of Deuteronomy 33 became the last pronouncements of Moses, the archetypal leader of the delivered and wandering Israelites before they reached Canaan. They are cast in the form of "prophetic" anticipations of the later fortunes of the tribes.

By contrast, a liturgical piece such as the Song of Deborah in Judges 5 is placed in a postcanonical position. This was unavoidable since the text explicitly refers to persons and events in Canaan following the death of Joshua. Judges 5, while poetic and celebrative, commemorates a specific historical event, a victory over a league of Canaanite city-states, which occurred about a century after Israel's initial formation in Canaan. The historical locus of this composition was so clearly defined that its postcanonical position in the tradition was assured.

There is a superficial resemblance between the tribal blessings and the song of triumph in Judges 5 in that the latter recounts and praises the contributions of the various tribes to the victory over the Canaanites and even employs some of the language of the blessing speech form. But the difference is decisive in that the tribal blessings have no single historical focus; they are not catalogues of what each tribe contributed to one centrally remembered event in Israel. By contrast, the song or hymn of triumph, of which Judges 5 is a conspicuous example, either celebrates some one clearly remembered historical victory or synthetically summarizes many such experiences into an ideal or prototypical victory. The Song of Deborah is an example of the focus on one remembered event. The Song at the Sea of Reeds in Exodus 15 is an example of a focus on a more distantly remembered complex of events in which the account has been stylized by language and concepts drawn from many subsequent experiences of conflict and victory. The Song of Hannah in I Samuel 2 is a collective song of the triumphs of Yahweh through Israel which possesses a national perspective but which synthesizes the triumphant process of the Israelite "conquest" as a kind of cross-section of all historical victories, without restricting the description to any one historical event such as the victory over the Egyptians at the Sea of Reeds or the victory over the Canaanites beside the Wadi Kishon. Exodus 15 and I Samuel 2 are "centralized" songs of triumph in the sense that they envision all Israel as an undifferentiated unity in the victories they celebrate. They are treated here as "erratically centralized" because of my contention that they were not composed as part of the historical résumés but were secondarily introduced to their present contexts and given historical settings associated with Miriam-Moses and Hannah.[84]

14.2 Hymns or Songs of Triumph

Songs of triumph or hymns of Yahweh's victories through Israel had a cultic context in the sense that they were vehicles for the community's celebration of its military achievements. According to the particular composition, they show now more and now less association with particular victories. To call them liturgies is not to judge precisely the extent of the direct and detailed historical reminiscences in any given specimen of the form. In the Song of Deborah there are obviously direct and detailed reminiscences. In the Song at the Sea of Reeds, the memories of what happened in the deliverance from Egypt are extremely formalistic. In the Song of Hannah there is no attempt to recollect a single victory, but rather an attempt to comprehend the fundamental form and import of all Israel's victories.

Of the various cultic modalities we have described, the song of triumph is most closely related to the theophany. Insofar as Yahweh is conceived as the ultimate victor in battle, the victory is a theophany or revelation of Yahweh. The victory of Israel is at the same time a concrete expression of Yahweh's sovereignty in Israel. The language of these songs conceives Yahweh as coming to the aid of Israel and as fighting in the battle. This is not to claim, however, that all the songs of triumph were developed within a theophanic cult act tied to the sequence theophany-covenant-law. Theophany was not only the first cultic action in the program of constitutional arrangement, commonly called the covenant or covenant renewal ceremony. Theophany also appears very prominently in the language of Israel's wars. The preparation of the army of Israel for war and the celebration of the people after battle provided another locus for theophanic cult action.

Von Rad has clarified the extent to which warfare in early Israel was a cultic act.[85] The songs of Yahweh's triumphs through Israel may well have had their origins in cultic actions which were specially arranged to prepare for war and to celebrate the close of the war. This is suggested by the obvious fact that the wars, especially since they were defensive wars, would not coincide conveniently with the regular festival calendar. In some cases they might, but in many cases the military exigencies would demand an emergency cultic assembly. From the admittedly rather late account of the initiation of Israelite "holy war" in Deuteronomy we see that the Levites had a central role in addressing, and perhaps also in convening, the troops before battle (Deut. 20:1–4). This representation seems congruent, moreover, with early monarchic accounts of the participation of the ark and its priests in the popular wars, e.g., in I Samuel 14; and, behind the late inflated form of Joshua 1—12, we probably can detect the same cultic dimension of warfare in premonarchic times, even though the ark may be a late feature in Joshua and is not mentioned at all in the Song of Deborah.

Assemblies for holy war were tied into the centralized cult in that the war was conceived as the war of all Israel and the personnel of the central cult officiated in the ceremonies of holy war. The assemblies for holy war, however, had the limited focus of empowering and legitimating the army for battle and, being subject to the vagaries of conflict, were irregularly scheduled as needed. The assembly to celebrate a victory would tend to draw most or all of the tribes, beyond the circle of those who directly fought the war, and the Song of Deborah goes out of its way to direct criticism to tribes who did not help in the battle but who were willing to share in the celebration.

Such cultic assemblies for holy war may be hypothesized as the locus both for the songs of triumph which reflected a particular victory and for songs of triumph which were prototypical in their formal descriptions of the characteristic way Yahweh enabled his people to defeat their enemies. Once such songs of triumph were in circulation, they could easily penetrate the scheduled centralized cult program, appearing as desired in connection with the theophany which introduced the covenant and law-giving, or, as in the case of the Song at the Sea of Reeds, becoming attached to the Passover festival and thus eventually to the basic theme of Deliverance from Egypt.

In any case, the songs of triumph have in common with the tribal blessings a certain independence from the centralized cult in the sense that they arose to meet quite specific needs for preserving the separate tribal identities, in the one case, and for waging effectual war, in the other case. The products shaped by these needs and adapted to the centralized cult were nonetheless relatively free-floating. They could be fitted into the total cult program in various ways and at various points in the festival schedule, but they could also continue an independent existence in local tribal celebrations and in the occasional preparations for war and celebrations after war. As with the tribal blessings, a place of attachment in the larger traditional sequences eventually had to be found for the songs of triumph.

Whereas the tribal blessings are put on the lips of prototypical fathers of all Israel, the songs of triumph are frequently placed on the lips of women, i.e., of mothers of all Israel. This practice probably reflects an ancient custom of female singers as the celebrants of war. A song of triumph which focused on the deliverance at the Sea of Reeds is put on the lips of Miriam, sister of Moses, in its abbreviated form (Exod. 15:21); as expanded, it is assigned to Moses and the Israelites (Exod. 15:1). A song of triumph recounting a victory over a league of Canaanite city-states is put on the lips of Deborah, a prophetess associated with the warrior Barak (Judges 5:1). And a song of triumph without any precise historical reminiscences, but which can be dated to the premonarchic national community by means of sociocultural analysis, subsequently taken over into personal piety as a description of the salvation of Yahweh in the life of a believer, is put on the lips of Hannah, mother of Samuel (or, in the original form of the tradition, perhaps the mother of Saul, Israel's first king; I Samuel 2:1). The transformation of the Song of Hannah from an original collective national reference to a personal pietistic reference is an instance of the so-called democratization of the cult, in which materials originally applied to the whole people or to its leaders are made available to the individual believer.[86]

14.3 Stories of "Judges": The Terminus of the Centralized Traditions

By far the greater bulk of the uncentralized traditions of premonarchic Israel fall, like the Song of Deborah and the Song of Hannah, in a postcanonical position. Not only are these postcanonical traditions—largely narrative, such as the stories in Judges—positioned chronologically after the death of Joshua, but no attempt is made to provide them with the veneer of an all-Israelite form, excluding of course the late Deuteronomic framework to the Book of Judges. They are stories of particular groups within Israel. There is no doubt that the groups appear as members of Israel and reflect the operative reality of Israel as a single social system, but the stories do not purport to be the accounts of what happened to all the Israelite people, in marked contrast to the stories which tell of the history from the patriarchs to the leading into the land. The stories in Judges specify when one or two or three "tribes" are involved, and they indicate precisely which ones are involved, even remarking at times when only sub-tribal groups or single individuals are acting. They also specify the locale of the events in some detail, and never is this locale the entire territory occupied by all the members of Israel. The one apparent exception is the story of the Benjaminite outrage in Judges 19—21, which has a character all its own and which will be examined in another context in our study.

Without going into detailed analysis of these postcanonical stories in Judges, since that will be the concern of later stages of our study, it is important to treat them in terms of their postcanonical placement and structure in comparison with the canonical placement and structure of the traditions which share the same narrative form. It is also pertinent to examine the question of the relation of these stories to the cult and to the wider lived experience of early Israel.

Within the basic themes and sub-motifs of the primary historical tradition, the typical individual unit of tradition was a narrative, precisely as was the typical unit of tradition in Judges. But a fundamental disjunction between the centralized and uncentralized bodies of narratives is apparent in their entirely different locations in the overall design of the traditions. This can be partly expressed as a *temporal disjunction*: The narratives of the basic themes extend from the prototypical ancestors, beginning with Abraham, through the life of Joshua; and with his death they abruptly end. In other words, the basic themes of the canonical historical résumés end with the leading into Canaan. The narratives of Judges relate incidents that occurred after the death of Joshua, even though they describe struggles to secure the land very similar to those described under the final canonical basic theme of the leading into Canaan. Even more crucially, however, the break between the canonical and the postcanonical narratives is a *conceptual disjunction*: The overriding determinative conception shaping all the narratives of the canonical phase is that of action by a united people over the whole of Canaan, operating as a mass, in which the tribal and other subdivisions are purely formalistic references. The determinative conception of the postcanonical phase, by contrast, is that of action by particular sub-groups of Israel within limited regions of Canaan, in which the subdivisions of the people are vitally intrinsic to the line of action.

It is by now demonstrable from our analysis of the actual beginnings of Israel that no undifferentiated unified Israel existed in the period from Abraham through Joshua and that this centralizing phenomenon of the historical traditions is a cultic-ideological retrojection. But *why does the formalistic all-Israelite retrojection stop with Joshua? And what do the centralized narratives about early Israel imply for the self-understanding and the cultic-ideological processes of the premonarchic age?* These are extraordinarily difficult questions, but I believe some tentative answers can at least be suggested.

We begin by noting that the basic themes of the historical traditions are, broadly speaking, aetiologies, or origin stories, detailing the major stages and the key events in the formation of Israel. According to their fundamental intent of objectifying and reinforcing the already experienced unity of newly formed Israel, we should expect them to close at that point where it was felt that the constitution of Israel was fully told, where the primary story was rounded out, where all the essential elements in the experience of united Israel were in some way touched upon in the rich variety of themes, sub-themes, and individual traditions of the canonical tradition. In temporal terms that cut-off point was Joshua, conceived as the successor of Moses who brought his master's work to completion. In conceptual terms that cut-off point was the leading into Canaan, at which point all Israel was securely established in its homeland. Basic themes could be added to the overall schema of the tradition as late as 1050 B.C. so long as they touched on central points in the constitution of Israel and so long as they could be given a place in the period ending with the death of Joshua.

It is necessary, however, that we understand this historico-symbolizing process of tradition stylization as one aspect only of the larger lived experience of the social system of Israel in Canaan between approximately 1250 and 1020 B.C., a system which included the centralized cult as well as the diverse sub-groups of Israelites articulated in segmented and cross-binding social arrangements. That lived experience embraced the wide-ranging reality of a newly mutant people carving out their own productive socioeconomic existence and developing their own historico-symbolic self-understanding. Crucial aspects of the struggle to become and persist as a functioning sociocultural unity were projected in the form of a stylized historical complex of tradition with fixed temporal and conceptual parameters. In other words, the cult and its historico-symbolic activity was intimately grounded in and correlated with the socioeconomic and national-cultural life of the whole people and thus with the material conditions of their existence.

The highly valuable studies of the cult of ancient Israel, which have vastly enriched our understanding of its traditions, have regrettably tended to abstract the cult from the total historical and social existence of Israel.[87] What we must stress, therefore, is that the lived experience of the new sociocultural entity Israel was both prior to and much broader than the particular project of constructing a stylized aetiological account of its beginnings. The socioeconomic and national-cultural concerns of Israel were not exclusively channeled into the cult, and while those concerns tended to find outlet in the cult, the tendency was only partially and unevenly realized. We have seen what difficulty the traditionists had in combining the semi-independent historical résumés with the cultically embedded modal actions of theophany, covenant, and law-giving.

Once the wider social context of early Israel is held in view, the work of the cult can be seen more realistically as a way of mediating between the chaotic conditions and circumstances of Israelite experience and the need for ordering the chaos institutionally and ideologically. Lines of connection bound the cultic actions and cultic traditions to all the forces and factors at work to pull Israel closer together and all the forces and factors at work to tear it apart or to obliterate it altogether. The continuing viability of the social system of Israel was the basic datum of the cult and its historico-symbolic work. The continuing activities within the social system of Israel found points of connection with the traditions as they were objectified conceptually and retrojected temporally into the unified traditional history. But the lived experience of Israel went on, continually preceding the cult and its traditions, posing ever new problems for communal resolution, which required not only adjustments in cult and ideology but also concrete forms of economic, social, and military-political action. Such a truism needs to be voiced because Israel's beginnings have been so "theologized" and "culticized" by inter-preters that Israel as a body of social actors in a concrete setting is repeatedly lost sight of in the rush to concentrate on its religious uniqueness. What Israel and its component members were severally experiencing could not be wholly exhausted or altogether anticipated either by the cult or by its salient work of historico-symbolic tradition building.

Specifically, this interrelation between cult and the wider social and historical experience of the people means that there always existed *a hiatus between what the traditions claimed and what the people experienced.* The traditions asserted the massive unity of early Israel, but the community knew very well from its contemporary experience that existing Israel was torn with inner divisions and tensions and repeatedly exposed to dangers from without. That the divisions and tensions could be overcome and the external dangers turned aside was the conviction and affirmation of the great centralized traditions, and as such they caught up the determined, self-conscious striving of the people with utmost authenticity. However, the conviction and affirmation of triumph were no substitute for coping with the actual divisions and dangers in the specific forms they took from generation to generation.

For this reason the Israelite urge to tell about its experience could not be cut off at some arbitrary point without attending consequences. *Did Israel really want to imply that Yahweh ended his great constitutional program for Israel with the death of*

Joshua? A too exclusive focus upon the centralized traditions would have the effect of giving an affirmative answer to that question. But the continuing experience of the people, and the continuing program of covenant renewal itself, fought against such a conclusion. The whole premise of the centralized tradition was that Israel as it now existed was brought into being by the actions of Yahweh in the events stretching from Abraham to Joshua. But what was the status of Israel in the present moment? Was it only a people remembering sacred times in the past? Obviously, as the temporal gap between Joshua and the contemporary confessing people widened, as generation followed generation, *it became urgent to "fill in" the postcanonical period, to demonstrate how Israel still lived on in all its vitality.* And it is the stories of the Book of Judges and some of those in I Samuel which, while no longer capable of being retrojected into the time before Joshua's death, could nonetheless express the continuing socioeconomic and national-cultural vitality of Israel.

The postcanonical stories are not products of the centralized cult of Israel which arbitrarily, and by now irreversibly, restricted its formation of narrative tradition with the cut-off point of Joshua. Nevertheless, the postcanonical stories are indebted to the cult, impregnated with many of its presuppositions, in part formed by its language, and cognizant in their own way of the vigorous reality of Israel as a mutant Yahweh-committed sociocultural entity. The postcanonical stories may be thought of as broadly cultic in that to tell these stories was to engage in a religous exercise aimed at establishing right relations with the sacred. But it is a cultic activity which has broken out of the centralized all-Israelite cult. In a sense, *the stories of Judges show us a culturally "laicized" consciousness of what it meant to be a part of premonarchic Israel,* a consciousness which we can check out against the more religiously explicit cult-ideological consciousness of the centralized traditions. Among other things, it is evident that this laicized consciousness felt no embarrassment in describing Israelite life in its rawest and bluntest terms. The crudity of personal and public morality in the stories of Judges, which most interpreters have explained by the mass apostasy of Israel from Yahweh following Joshua's death, is in my view rather to be "explained" by the frankness of the writers in reporting what they saw. I do not assume that Israel was morally more advanced under Joshua than it was under the judges. It is only the centralizing, moralizing intent of the unified historical traditions which give that impression at times.

Although uncentralized in the cultic-ideological sense we have described, it is evident that these stories reflect a general national consciousness of a directly experienced and deeply felt unity as a distinctive social system which broadly parallels the more explicit ideological assertions of the canonical schema. The two accounts of early Israel can be employed stereoptically to point toward their congruence in a circumscribed social system in a circumscribed historico-territorial space, *a social system rather more "ideally" and "typically" presented in the one case and rather more "realistically" and "concretely" disclosed in the other case.* The resulting picture is that of an integrated social system which, in the span of two or three generations, not only had become impressively functional but was still growing through continuous interaction between its contemporary lived experience and its reflective historico-symbolic traditions.

Because they are less cult-ideologically rationalized than the centralized traditions, *the stories of Judges are more explicit about the contradictory elements within the social system and the threats from without.* The divisions within Israel and the threats from without which are given a place in the centralized history are presented largely as admonitory statements of what should be avoided or as assurances that the worst obstacles to Israelite unity have been long surmounted. They are presented with a certain defensiveness, as an apologetic for the past or as a polemic against wrong tendencies in the present. By contrast, the divisions and dangers appear much more as facts of life in the stories of Judges, although even here, as in the story of Gideon, the tendency to moralize has arisen at points. On the whole, however, the stories of Judges seem to say: "This is the way things are. Our unity is basic and binding, so much so that we do not have to labor it, but it stands side by side with tensions and open conflict, and in each new generation we must cope with enemies who wish to annihilate us. It would be a great mistake to dwell so exclusively on past accomplishments that we fail to prepare ourselves for ever new struggles."

The impression I derive from these stories in their postcanonical placement and content is that so long as this kind of attentive engagement in the struggle of the present was alive, early Israel could read the vast assurance of the canonical history not as a finished story, giving security once and for all, but as a source of incentive and reinforcement to achieve in its own circumstances what its forebears had achieved in theirs. Whereas, according to the strict canons of documentary historiography, the canonical history was a deception, since things never occurred in the totally patterned manner that it claimed, this cult-ideological "deception" was accompanied by and nourished with realistic contemporary understanding and phenomenal energy directed at concrete action to preserve and extend the Israelite way of life. *Side by side with the claim of total unity stood stories of disunity and parochial achievement. This is why the "fiction" of the cult ideology must be seen in its vital dialectical interplay with the "reality" of the social system in the context of the historical struggles it faced.* As aids to an appreciation of the daily realities in old Israel, the stories of Judges are of incalculable value.

In this section I have explored the cultic-ideological roots and connections of most of the categories of sources for the history and sociology of premonarchic Israel which were listed and briefly annotated in II.6. I say "categories" because I have not examined every single specimen within each category, since the concern here is with formal principles. Moreover, some idiosyncratic specimens have been omitted or reserved for later treatment. And I say "most categories" because there have been some deletions dictated by the fact that the omitted categories will be considered in later sections. For example, the fragmentary settlement "annals" of Judges 1 and the territorial boundary and city lists of the tribes in Joshua 13—19 will be treated extensively in IV.17.2–3. With those qualifications of scope in view, I believe I have analyzed enough of the major categories and their representative specimens in their cultic-ideological matrix that the way is now cleared for a more direct attack upon the questions: Granted that Israel's historical traditions are largely refracted cultic-ideological products, how can they be used for getting at the actual lived experience of Israelites both in their successive development through time and space (history) and their typical organization and structure in a mutant social system (sociology)?

Part IV

The Tradition History and Composition of the Books of Joshua and Judges

15

Overview of Sources: Joshua and Judges

In the preceding two parts I have tried to set up parameters for the use of the earliest Israelite traditions in reconstructing the history and sociology of premonarchic Israel. It was demonstrated that the Israelite traditions are sources of a peculiar cultic-ideological kind whose points of intersection with the concerns of documented historiography are refracted and indirect. In establishing the fundamental reality of the cultic-ideological production of early Israelite traditions, I have further explored most of the major categories of sources and tried to show their immediate or derivative cultic anchorage and their interconnection with one another in the history of tradition. This has allowed us to uncover the primary constant factors that control the conditions for the historical use of these cultic-ideological and popular-cultural materials.

An adequate conceptual schema for understanding the cultic-ideological roots of the traditions necessitates a working method which distinguishes the various formal-structural units of tradition and their various functional contexts within and beyond the centralized cult. In addition, this working method aims both to detect the relation of the units of tradition to the lived experience of those who produced the tradition and to indicate the amenability of the traditions to analysis by the methods of documentary historiography.

We seek now to bring these formal principles of the cultic-ideological production of tradition to bear upon the segments of the tradition which purportedly tell the history of premonarchic Israel in Canaan, namely, the books of Joshua and Judges. In what light do the traditions of Joshua and Judges appear when examined within our schema and in terms of our working method? Moreover, the task of assessing the historical dimensions of Joshua and Judges requires also that we consider them as segments of larger literary contexts. To this point in our study, while granting the validity and importance of literary criticism, we have bracketed its concerns in favor of a focus on the cultic-ideological roots of the finished literary traditions. Now we must bring these two foci on the traditions, i.e., their cultic-ideological roots and their final literary formation, into dialogical relationship in order to grasp the full dimensions of the traditions as historical sources.

The procedure of this part will be to begin with a summary of the contents of the books of Joshua and Judges in order to display the range of forms included and to acquire a sense of the highly differentiated kinds and degrees of detail, as well as of the dominant tendencies and emphases, which characterize the several units and clusters of units. We shall then examine the overall literary contexts in which the books and their sub-units are placed, with particular attention to the way the Deuteronomic History makes use of the old basic themes of the primary historical tradition. The complexity and subtlety of the historical assessment required will be illustrated in the case of three major blocs of pre-Deuteronomic sources which have found their way into Joshua and Judges: the narratives of Joshua 1—12; the tribal allotment lists of Joshua 13—19; and the settlement "annals" of Judges 1. Finally, a sketch of the tradition history of Joshua and Judges will be offered, from their cultic-ideological roots to their terminal literary form, with particular attention to the larger historical and social settings in which the tradition-building process took place.

The summary of the contents of the two books will present the basic line of action or "plot" in précis form, with particular regard to geographical and historical data pertinent for reconstructing the early Israelite history. I have kept explanatory notes and interpretations to a minimum, even in the lists of tribal allotments where the densely packed historico-territorial items invite wide digressions. The summary of contents should be conceived as an introductory orientation to the later, fuller examination of selected types and segments of source materials, both in this part and in others to follow.

The primary sense units of the accounts in Joshua and Judges are summarized and marked by chapter and verse references in parentheses. These rough sense units of the summary should not be construed to imply either that the units are so homogeneous as to be indivisible into sub-sources or secondary accretions or that they are so self-contained as to lack all continuity in plot, form, or source from unit to unit. The internal and external articulation of the respective units can only emerge in the course of careful analysis. Where the editorial framework persists in very complicated relation to the sense units, the typographical indentation in the summaries is correspondingly more complex. This occurs chiefly at two points: in the summaries of the tribal allotments in Joshua and in the summaries of the stories of the judges. Endnotes at the relevant points will explain the format employed, including the special sigla used to identify tradition forms and editorial frames.

15.1 Contents of the Book of Joshua

Joshua is commanded to gather the people to possess the land and he in turn directs the officers to make military preparations (1:1–11).

Reuben, Gad, and Manasseh are to help their fellow tribesmen in taking territory west of the Jordan River, even though those tribes have already acquired their own holdings east of the river (1:12–18).

Jericho is visited by Israelite spies who are harbored by Rahab, a harlot, and return to Joshua with a recommendation to attack the city (2).

Israel crosses the Jordan River after its waters are stopped [by a landslide?], the ark being borne by the Levites. Stones for the twelve tribes are described as set up either in the middle of the river or in the camp and sanctuary at Gilgal (3—4; 5:1).

At Gilgal Joshua circumcises all the male Israelites who had been born in the wilderness since the first circumcision of Israelites in Egypt (5:2–9).

At Gilgal Israel keeps the Passover feast as the people switch over from eating the manna of the desert to eating the grain of the cultivated land (5:10–12).

Joshua is visited by "the commander of the army of Yahweh" in a kind of private theophany paralleling the theophany at the call of Moses (5:13–15).

Jericho is taken by encircling the city with the ark and blasting on trumpets until the walls collapse. The city and its people are destroyed, except for Rahab and her family (6).

Forbidden booty is secretly kept by Achan, instead of being destroyed in dedication to Yahweh, which results in the defeat of three thousand Israelites sent to take Ai in the hill country NW of Jericho. The offender is discovered by lot and stoned to death (7).

The Israelites are able to take Ai by a military stratagem in which they draw the defending army into open country and destroy it, after which the city and its people are destroyed (8:1–29).

Joshua builds an altar at Mt. Ebal (overlooking Shechem) in the central highlands, makes a copy of the law and reads it to the people (8:30–35).

Four Hivite=Horite/Hurrian cities in the central highlands W of Jericho and N of Jerusalem, consisting of Gibeon, the ringleader, Chephirah, Beeroth, and Kiriath-jearim, enter a pact with Israel to serve as cultic attendants at Yahwistic shrines. They accomplish this by the ruse that they are from a distant land and therefore need not be destroyed by the Israelites, who are committed to annihilating all Canaanites (9).

Jerusalem, abutting on the Hurrian cities and perhaps their sovereign by vassal treaty, leads a coalition including Hebron, Jarmuth, Lachish, and Eglon (all located S and SW of Jerusalem) against Gibeon in order to retaliate for its pact with Israel. Joshua hurries to Gibeon's defense from Gilgal by night, defeats the coalition in the pass at Beth-horon and pursues them into the shephelah (western foothills) of Judah. The defeated kings take refuge in a cave at Makkedah where they are found and killed by Joshua. Thereafter the cities of Makkedah, Libnah, Lachish, Eglon, Hebron, and Debir are captured and destroyed. Gezer's king and army are annihilated (10:1–39).

The foregoing campaign is summarized as a complete defeat of the inhabitants of southern Canaan from Kadesh-barnea and Gaza to Gibeon (10:40–43).

In Galilee, in the far north of the land, Hazor heads a coalition including the cities of Madon [or Merom?], Shimron, and Achshaph, as well as other unspecified cities, against Joshua. Their massed chariots are attacked by Joshua at the waters of Merom (probably NW of the Sea of Galilee) in a surprise move that routs the Canaanites. Hazor is captured and destroyed (11:1–15).

Five summaries of the conquest of Canaan are given:

Territory taken in W Jordan (11:16–20).

Anakim destroyed in southern Canaan (11:21–23).

Territory taken in E Jordan (12:1–6).

Thirty-one kings of W Jordan defeated by Joshua, identified only by cities with the formula "king of [name of city], one" (12:7–24).

Land in the Philistine plain, northern Phoenicia, and Lebanon yet to be taken (13:1–6a).

Joshua is commanded to allot the land to Israel[88] (13:6b, a note appended to the preceding summary list of land yet to be possessed).

Joshua is commanded to give land to 9½ tribes in W Jordan (13:7). Following a "flashback" to E Jordan land allotments, the W Jordan allotments proceed only as far as 2½ tribes (13:8—17:18):

A retrospect of the land Moses gave to 2½ tribes in E Jordan (13:8–33):

Reuben[L]: territory + cities (13:15–23).

Gad[L]: territory + cities (13:24–28).

Manasseh (half-tribe)[L]: territory + cities (13:29–31).

Joshua, Eleazar, the priest, and the tribal heads distribute land to 9½ tribes in W Jordan, the action apparently occurring at Gilgal (14—17):

Caleb[N]: presented to Joshua by the Judeans, he claims and receives a city in fulfillment of Moses' promise to him (14:6–15 // Josh. 15:13; Judg. 1:20).

Judah:

Boundaries[L] (15:1–12)

One city is given to Caleb and he captures a second[N] (15:13–19 // Josh. 14:13–14; Judg. 1:12–15, 20).

Cities[L] (15:20–63 // Judg. 1:21).

Ephraim:

Boundary of "the sons of Joseph"[L] (16:1–3).[89]

Boundaries[L] (16:5–10 // Judg. 1:29).

Manasseh:

Territory + cities[L] (17:1–6 // Num. 32:39–42).

Territory + cities + boundary (17:7–13 // Judg. 1:27–28).

Territory of "the sons of Joseph"[N] (17:14–18).

Joshua distributes land to seven tribes in W Jordan after an inventory is made of available territories, the action occurring at Shiloh (18—19:48):

Benjamin[L]: boundaries + cities (18:11–28).

Simeon[L]: cities (19:1–9).

Zebulun[L]: boundaries + cities (19:10–16).

Issachar[L]: cities (19:17–23).

Asher[L]: boundaries + cities (19:24–31).

Naphtali[L]: boundaries + cities (19:32–39).

Dan[LN]: cities + territory (in the region between Judah, Benjamin, and Ephraim) + summary of the tribe's relocation at the headwaters of the Jordan River (19:40–48 // Judg. 1:34–35a; 18:27b–29).

Joshua is given a city for his allotment and distribution of the land to the tribes is summarized. The summary in vs. 51 envisions Joshua and Eleazar and the tribal heads as having given land to all 9½ tribes in W Jordan by lot at Shiloh, thus combining the officials and number of tribes in 14:1–5 with the site of Shiloh in 18:1, 8, and 10. The summary thus ignores the substantive existence of 18:1–10 and the editorial frames of the seven-tribe distribution with the attendant claim that Judah, Ephraim, and Manasseh were separately awarded land at Gilgal and the remaining seven tribes were given land later by Joshua alone. The only awareness of the seven-tribe scheme of allotment is in the summary's retention of the allotment site at the tent of meeting in Shiloh (19:49–51).

The people of Israel designate six cities of refuge as places of legal asylum for the accused while murder charges against him are being weighed (20 // Num. 35:6–34; Deut. 4:41–43; 19:1–13).

Joshua, Eleazar, and the tribal heads at Shiloh order the people to set apart forty-eight cities for the landless Levites, approximately four from each tribe (21 // Num. 35:1–8).

The E Jordan tribes enroute home build a memorial altar at the Jordan River, which alarms the other tribes until the builders assure them that it is not intended for sacrifice and thus is no threat to the central Israelite sanctuary (22).

Joshua delivers a farewell address in which he warns against apostasy from Yahweh under threat of annihilation by the Canaanites left in the land (23).

A second address of Joshua at or near Shechem (in no sense a farewell) recites the saving deeds of Yahweh in the past and calls on the people to choose allegiance either to Yahweh, or to the gods of their father Terah (father of Abraham), or to the gods of the Amorites among whom they live. Joshua announces that he and his house (tribe?) are deciding in favor of Yahweh.

After a warning about the seriousness of the step and the terrible consequences of apostasy, Joshua leads the consenting tribes in an oath of fidelity to
Yahweh. The covenant is contracted with "statutes and ordinances" and a
stone of witness set up "under the oak in the sanctuary of Yahweh" (24:1–28).

The death and burial of Joshua and Eleazar are described, and the reinterment of
Joseph's bones in Shechem is recounted. As long as the elders who knew
Joshua lived, Israel was faithful to Yahweh (24:29–33).

15.2   Contents of the Book of Judges

"After the death of Joshua," Israel inquires of Yahweh as to which tribe shall
initiate the attack on Canaan. Judah is singled out and Simeon agrees to
accompany Judah, each helping the other to take possession of its allotment
(1:1–3; cf. 1:17).

Judah defeats ten thousand Canaanites/Perizzites at Bezek and mutilates their
king Adonibezek. Judah captures Jerusalem, kills its inhabitants, and sets it
afire. The hill country, Negeb (southland), and shephelah (western Judean
foothills) are attacked and Hebron is taken. Judah goes against Debir
(1:4–11).

Othniel takes Debir and Caleb gives him his daughter in marriage. She receives
"the upper and lower springs" [of Debir?] (1:12–15 // Josh. 15:15–19).

Kenites, in the company of Judeans, enter the Negeb from "the city of palms"
[Jericho? Tamar or Zoar S of the Dead Sea?] and settle near Arad "among the
people" or "among the Amalekites," cf. some LXX readings (1:16).

Simeon, with the help of Judah, takes Zephath-Hormah in the Negeb (1:17).

Judah takes Gaza, Ashkelon, and Ekron (1:18).

Judah takes the hill country but cannot take the plain since its people have chariots
(1:19).

Hebron is given to Caleb (1:20; cf. 1:10 // Josh. 14:13; 15:13–14).

Benjamin is unable to expel the Jebusites from Jerusalem (1:21 // Josh. 15:63).

The house (tribe?) of Joseph takes Luz-Bethel with the help of one of its citizens in
return for sparing him and his family (1:22–26).

Manasseh could not expel the populations of Beth-shean, Taanach, Dor, Ibleam,
and Megiddo, but later put them to forced labor (1:27–28 // Josh. 17:11–13).

Ephraim coult not expel the Gezerites but lived with them (1:29 // Josh. 16:10).

Zebulun could not expel the people of Kitron and Nahalol, but the Canaanites
living among them were put to forced labor (1:30).

Asher could not expel the people at Acco, Sidon, Ahlab, Achzib, Helbah, Aphek,
and Rehob, but lived among them (1:31–32).

Naphtali could not expel the people of Beth-shemesh and Beth-anath, but lived
among them and compelled them to forced labor (1:33).

Dan was hard pressed by the Amorites of the plain, who pushed Dan back into the
hills and persisted in occupying Har-heres, Aijalon, and Shaalbim, but the

house of Joseph mounted counter pressure on the Amorites and subjected
them to forced labor (1:34–35).

The Edomite border [reading "Edomite" with some LXX MSS in place of MT
"Amorite"] extends to the vicinity of the Ascent of Akrabbim and Sela at the
SE frontier of the land (1:36).

The angel of Yahweh, going up from Gilgal to Bochim [Bochim means "weeping,"
cf. the Oak of Weeping near Bethel in Gen. 35:8], tells the people that,
although Yahweh will not break his covenant with Israel, Israel has sinned by
making covenants with the Canaanites. Yahweh will not, therefore, drive out
all the Canaanites (2:1–5).

Israel remains faithful as long as Joshua and the elders of his period are alive. At
his death Joshua is buried in Timnath-heres [Timnath-serah in Josh. 19:50;
24:30] (2:6–10 // Josh. 24:29–31).

A new generation of Israelites turns from Yahweh to the Canaanite Baals (F1) and
thereby brings oppressors upon Israel (F2). When the people repent and call
for help (F3), Yahweh raises up "deliverers" [shōph^etîm, commonly translated
"judges"] who drive out the oppressors (F4) and bring relief or rest to Israel
for a time (F5).[90] In offering this rationale for the continued wars of occupation, the writer states two reasons for leaving the original inhabitants in the
land: to test the faithfulness of Israel to Yahweh and to train Israel in military
self-defense (2:11—3:6).

Othniel, Caleb's nephew and the conqueror of Debir, delivers Israel from
Cushan-rishathaim of Aram Naharaim, i.e., "Aram between the rivers"
[northern Mesopotamia?] (F1–5; 3:7–11).

Ehud, a Benjaminite, takes action against Eglon of Moab who has seized Jericho
and, with Ammonites and Amalekites, has pressed Benjamin and Ephraim
hard. Ehud delivers tribute to Eglon and assassinates him in secret. He flees to
W Jordan and calls out the levies of Benjamin and Ephraim to capture the
fords of the Jordan, cutting off the enemy at Jericho and annihilating him
(F1–5; 3:12–30).

Shamgar kills 600 Philistines with an oxgoad (F4; 3:31).

Deborah, an Ephraimite seeress, inspires Barak of Naphtali to assemble the forces
of Naphtali and Zebulun at Mt. Tabor to do battle against Jabin of Hazor,
"king of Canaan," whose commander Sisera leads 900 chariots against the
Galilean tribes. Ten thousand Israelites gather under Barak and Deborah at
Kedesh [probably modern Khirbet Qedish south of Tiberias rather then
Kedesh of Galilee north of Hazor]. They attack Sisera's forces in the plain by
sweeping down from Mt. Tabor and rout them toward Harosheth-ha-goiim
[probably not a city at all but "the wooded heights of the nations," i.e., the
forested hills of Galilee]. Sisera seeks refuge with Jael, wife of Heber the
Kenite, and is killed by her with a tent peg as he sleeps (F1–5; 4; 5:31b).

The Song of Deborah, a poetic celebration of the preceding battle, pictures Barak

and Deborah at the head of troops from six tribes (Ephraim, Benjamin,
Machir [Manasseh?] Zebulun, Issachar, Naphtali) and blames four tribes for
not joining in the muster (Gilead [Gad or E Manasseh?], Dan, Asher, Reuben).
The battle takes place along the Wadi Kishon in the vicinity of Taanach and
Megiddo. Sisera is killed by Jael after a drink in her tent. Jabin is unmentioned
(5:1–31a).

Midianite camel raiders plunder Israelite herds and flocks and graze over their
planted fields. A prophet sent by Yahweh announces the deity's saving deeds
in the past and reminds Israel of his prohibition against worshipping Amorite
gods, which has gone unheeded (F1–3; 6:1–10).

Gideon, a Manassite of Ophrah, rises to meet the threat of the camel raiders.
Gideon is called by a messenger of Yahweh who persuades the hesitant man to
accept a commission as Yahweh's deliverer by consuming the latter's offering
with fire. Under stealth of darkness, Gideon tears down the Canaanite cult
objects belonging to his father and builds an altar to Yahweh. The anger of the
populace is allayed by his father, who reminds them that if Baal is powerful he
will avenge the deed himself (F4; 6:11–32).

As the camel raiders spread into the Valley of Jezreel, Gideon openly declares his
leadership and rallies a force from Manasseh, Asher, Zebulun, and Naphtali
(F4; 6:33–35).

Gideon is reassured of his appointment by signs from Yahweh entailing the
appearance of dew, first on a piece of fleece on dry ground and then on the
ground around dry fleece (F4; 6:36–40).

The armies oppose one another across the valley, the Midianites by the hill of
Moreh and the Israelites at the spring of Harod. Yahweh instructs Gideon to
reduce his forces. From an original thirty-two thousand, Gideon chooses
three hundred who show military qualities in a test of their manner of
drinking water. By a combination of surprise, darkness, shouts, torches,
trumpets, and swords (?), Israel routs the encamped Midianites. The select
three hundred warriors, joined by a larger force, pursue the Midianites to the
Jordan River (F4; 7:1–23).

Gideon summons Ephraim to seize the Jordan crossing and the Ephraimites
capture and kill two Midianite princes. Most of the Midianites escape over the
Jordan and Gideon pursues them but is denied help by the leaders of Succoth
and Penuel. On the edge of the desert, the Midianites pause, thinking they
have reached safety. Gideon overtakes them, captures their two kings and kills
them in retaliation for their previous murder of his brothers. Enroute home,
Gideon takes retaliatory action against the rulers of Succoth and Penuel by
killing some and torturing others (F4; 7:24—8:21).

Gideon is offered kingship by "the men of Israel." He declines to rule since
Yahweh alone is ruler in Israel. He does, however, make an "ephod"

[presumably an image or emblem] from the gold jewelry taken from the Midianites and installs it in Ophrah as a cult object (F4–5; 8:22–28).

Gideon has seventy sons, including Abimelech by his concubine from Shechem. Gideon dies and is buried in Ophrah (8:29–32).

The Israelites worship Baal-berith and are faithless to Gideon's offspring (F1; 8:33–35).

Abimelech is presented anomalously, not as a deliverer of Israel, but as a gross example of the abusive office of kingship. He killed his brothers and was made king by the Shechemites at the sanctuary of Baal-berith. The fact that his father had earlier been asked to serve Israel as king and, considering that he lived away from Shechem at Arumah, it is highly probable that he had also been made king in at least the tribe of Manasseh. One surviving brother, Jotham, condemns Abimelech and the Shechemites in a fable that derides kingship. After three years, divisions develop between Abimelech and the Shechemites. Gaal leads a faction against the king. Open revolt at Shechem is quelled by Abimelech with great loss of life and physical destruction. In a related uprising in Thebez, Abimelech is killed and his kingdom aborted (9).

Tola of Issachar who lived in Ephraim "judged" Israel for twenty-three years (10:1–2).

Jair of Gilead "judged" Israel for twenty-two years (10:3–5).

Ammonites, in league with Philistines, oppress Israel, going so far as to harass Judah, Benjamin, and Ephraim in raids across the Jordan. Jephthah, an outcast from Gilead because he is a harlot's son, is summoned from Tob, where he had been a successful bandit leader, and asked by "the elders of Gilead" to lead them in war against the encroaching Ammonites. Jephthah agrees providing that they make him "head and leader over them," which they agree to do (F1–4; 10:6—11:11).

A diplomatic exchange between Jephthah's messengers and the king of Ammon goes as follows: Ammon claims that Israel took land by force, "from the Arnon to the Jabbok and to the Jordan," i.e., the southern section of Transjordan held by Israel, and should now return it to Ammon. Jephthah replies that Israel took no territory from Ammon but rather from Sihon, the Amorite. Furthermore, if Ammon had a claim to the region it should have done something about it earlier instead of waiting three hundred years to complain. Jephthah affirms that both Yahweh and Chemosh [note that the Moabite god and not the Ammonite god is mentioned] award land to their peoples; therefore, the contending claims over the same region must be settled by an extra-legal ordeal of war (11:12–27).

Ammon presses the war. Jephthah, passing through Gilead [Gad?] and Manasseh, meets and routs the Ammonites and pursues them from Aroer to Minnith and Abel-keramim (F 4: 11:28–29, 32–33).

Having previously vowed to make a human sacrifice if Yahweh will give him victory, Jephthah fulfills his vow on returning home by offering the first person to greet him, which turns out to be his only child, a daughter. Mourning her death becomes a four-day annual festival observed by "the daughters of Israel" (11:30–31, 34–40).

Ephraimites object to Jephthah that he did not rally them to fight against the Ammonites. Jephthah counters that he did summon them and they declined, or perhaps rather implies that they would have been of no help. An Ephraimite force comes to Jephthah at Zaphon, presumably his home city. He battles them, cuts off the retreating Ephraimites at the Jordan, and kills many of them (12:1–6).

Jephthah the Gileadite "judged" Israel for six years (12:7).

Ibzan of Bethlehem [of Judah or of Zebulun?] "judged" Israel for seven years (12:8–10).

Elon of Zebulun "judged" Israel for ten years (12:11–12).

Abdon of Ephraim "judged" Israel for eight years (12:13–15).

Israel suffers domination by the Philistines (F1–2; 13:1).

Samson, a Danite, is dedicated at birth as a Nazirite in response to the command of the messenger of Yahweh who appears to his childless parents (F4; 13:2–25).

Samson marries a Philistine woman from Timnah and at the wedding propounds a riddle which the groom's "companions" cannot unravel until his wife discloses the answer to them. In a rage at this betrayal of confidence, Samson kills thirty men of Ashkelon. When his father-in-law gives his bride to the best man, Samson burns the fields and orchards of the Philistines. They in turn kill the father-in-law and wife of Samson, for which he kills many Philistines. The Philistines respond with a punitive raid against Judean Lehi. The Judeans try to deliver Samson over to the Philistines, but he breaks his bonds and slays a thousand Philistines with an ass's jawbone. After the battle, he is marvelously supplied with water by Yahweh (F4; 14—15).

While he is visiting a harlot at Gaza, a trap is set for Samson, but he escapes in the night, carrying on his shoulders the city gate posts and doors, which he deposits on a hill top in the direction of Hebron (16:1–3).

Delilah, a Philistine woman from the Valley of Sorek, discovers that Samson's strength is in his hair because of his status as an unshaven Nazirite. When shaved, he is easily captured and blinded. As his hair grows back, his strength returns. In a last great burst of energy he pulls down the temple of the god Dagon at Gaza. Samson and his captors perish together in the collapsed ruins. He is buried in the family tomb (F4; 16:4–31).

Micah, an Ephraimite, makes a house shrine that contains carved and cast images, an ephod and teraphim. He hires an itinerant Levite from Bethlehem of Judah as his permanent priest. When the Danites are migrating from their first home in the shephelah to the headwaters of the Jordan, they carry off the priest and the cult objects, which they install in Laish-Dan after the city is captured. The priestly line founded by this Levite named Jonathan, a grandson of Moses, is said to have lasted "until the captivity of the land," presumably a reference to the seizure of this region of the northern kingdom by the Assyrians in 734 B.C. (17—18).

A Levite living in Ephraim takes a concubine in Bethlehem of Judah. While he is traveling with her they spend the night in Gibeah of Benjamin and she is raped and killed by the inhabitants. In revenge, all the other tribes attack Benjamin and so decimate the tribe that only 600 males survive. In a change of heart, the Benjaminites are given wives among the virgins spared when Jabesh-gilead is destroyed, because it failed to respond to the call to arms against Benjamin, and from among the virgins who dance in the vineyards in the annual harvest festival at Shiloh (19—21).

16

Deuteronomic History and the Old Basic Themes

Now that we have a bird's-eye view of the contents of Joshua and Judges, what literary-critical, form-critical, and tradition-historical observations are germane to the uses of the traditions for reconstructing the history of the settlement and formation of early Israel? We shall begin with what is most commonly agreed upon and work toward what is more widely disputed.

16.1 The Deuteronomic Version of Israel's Early History

Virtually everyone who carefully examines Joshua-Judges agrees that the present form of the books owes a great deal to the work of one or more editors and theological commentators who possessed a distinctive vocabulary and style and operated according to a definite recognizable set of moral-theological principles for interpreting the narratives, poems, and lists which he (or they) preserved in an artful arrangement. The language and outlook are pervasive in the Book of Deuteronomy, and since that book, in the main, can be dated in the latter part of the seventh century B.C., and since the same language and outlook have shaped the following books as far as Kings, which terminates with events in 561 B.C., we may reasonably assign the work of the "Deuteronomic" editor-commentator(s) of Joshua and Judges to the period between 621 and 550 B.C. More exactitude in our dating is dependent on whether we see at least two editions of Deuteronomy through Kings, in which case one was probably in Josiah's Judah of 621–609 B.C. and the other was in the Babylonian exile of approximately 561–550 B.C.[91]

Characteristic of the outlook of the Deuteronomic edition of Joshua and Judges is a cultic and theological view of the Israelite community as a people destined to occupy and hold Canaan provided only that it maintain its moral and cultic integrity.[92] That integrity is to be assured by absolute obedience to Yahweh as revealed in the law to be found in the collected stipulations of the Book of Deuteronomy. Among the critical provisions of the law are prohibition of all forms of Canaanite worship and a corresponding exclusive worship of Yahweh at an official central shrine (which for the Deuteronomic editor, writing after Josiah's reform in 621 B.C., means Jerusalem). The community of Israel, as the editor views it, was under command from Yahweh from the beginning to destroy all the Canaanites so that not a shred of their religion could survive to tempt Israel into sin. Therefore, his manner of setting forth the occupation of the land in the

Book of Joshua is to accent the features of military conquest and annihilation of the Canaanites.

In spite of his own predilections, the Deuteronomist had to come to terms with contrary evidence in his materials. When many of the traditions in his hand showed that in fact a total conquest never took place, at least not before the time of David, the editor supplied moral-theological rationalizations for the imperfect conquest: Yahweh will leave Canaanites in the land to punish Israel for its illicit contacts with the inhabitants and their gods, and specifically to test Israel's faithfulness (Judg. 2:21–22), or to train Israel in the arts of war (Judg. 3:1–2), or to preserve the environment against predatory wild beasts (Deut. 7:22; cf. Exod. 23:29). Whereas the notion of pantribal, total-territorial conquest aimed at insuring Israel's cultic purity controls the presentation of the material in Joshua, another sort of pan-Israelite outlook dominates Judges, namely, cycles of Israelite apostasies, foreign oppressions, Israelite returns to Yahweh, deliverances of Israel by "judges," and periods of rest for the land, i.e., the frame elements of the book of Judges (which we have designated in our survey of contents as F1–5; cf. note 90). Yahweh is pictured as directly at work in these events in reciprocal response to Israel's apostasy and to Israel's repentance; and, concomitantly, Israel is pictured as reciprocally responsive to the extremes of historical experience, faithful to Yahweh after each deliverance but complacently apostate as the interval of freedom from oppression lengthens, until another oppression awakens Israel's repentant recommitment to Yahweh.

These different types of pan-Israelite framework for Joshua and Judges allow the Deuteronomist to relate earlier stories which contradict his belief in a total conquest because he has succeeded, at least partially, in periodizing the events in such a way that two eras emerge: the era of Joshua when all Israel was faithful and almost succeeded in exterminating the Canaanites, and the following era of the judges, when Israel lapsed from Yahweh and allowed the Canaanites to regain their strength and to harass Israel and at the same time opened the way for desert-based raids by Midianites and intense pressure on the borders of the land by other recently settled peoples such as Ammonites, Moabites, and Philistines. The question for us is how this framing and periodizing work of the Deuteronomist compares to the earlier framing and periodizing of the old historical materials within the structure of the basic themes from the Promise to Abraham through the Leading into the Land.

The framing activity of the Deuteronomic traditionist in grouping and editorializing his materials must be seen in relation to the ancient cultic-ideological formation of the traditions he employed. Only in this way can we judge what is peculiar to D and what he shares in common with earlier traditionists. The Deuteronomist does not offer freshly researched data on Israel's beginnings, any more than did J or E, but rather takes up old materials, occasionally rewriting them, and presents them in certain perspectives. In this context, it also becomes of interest to try to determine which of these older materials had already appeared in one of the preceding large complexes of tradition and which were original to the D complex.

16.2 Deuteronomic Adaptation to the Moratorium on New Basic Themes

Martin Noth has claimed that the Deuteronomist was an author in a way that the Yahwist and Elohist traditionists were not.[93] He means by this that the overarching plan and structure of the work is the contribution of the individual D writer, who displayed considerable freedom and originality in the way he arranged his preexisting material. On the other hand, the overarching plan and structure of the J and E works was not the result of one person's activity but developed instead by stages within the cult via a series of incremental basic themes. The canonically arranged themes, with their "filler" sub-themes and traditions, achieved a relative fixity of outline in the *Grundlage* underlying J and E. The outline of the common groundwork of J and E was a form that came slowly into being, in a basically preliterary situation, without any single person or even any single generation having envisioned and constructed it as a whole. But when it had reached its fullest extent, as the precipitate of a long line of cultic-ideological productions, its laboriously built plan and structure had to be maintained. The literary ingenuity of a J or E could not change the standardized articulation of the basic themes, which lent the work its cohesion and perspective, although more or less freedom was exercised as to which "filler" materials would be included and how they would be slanted.

In my view, Noth is basically correct in this insight. To be sure, I am not persuaded of Noth's thesis that the Deuteronomic history from Deuteronomy through Kings is necessarily the work of one person. I tend to see it as having gone through at least two editions. Nor do I see the artfulness of the Deuteronomist in all the compositional details in which Noth traces it. I also depart from Noth in my understanding of the literary elaboration of the basic theme of Leading into Canaan, as will become clear later in this part. But one need not agree with all of Noth's views concerning the D "author" to grant his basic point that the Deuteronomist(s) gathered materials which, while fixed in their several units and complexes to one degree or another, still lacked a total plan, whereas the Yahwist and Elohist faced an already gathered body of materials with a total plan possessing normative status in the community, forbidding modifications of the themes, and limiting modifications of the contents of the themes. The implications of this basic contrast between the relative compositional freedom of D, on the one hand, and the relative compositional limitation of J and E, on the other, are far-reaching, including facets of the tradition building which Noth himself did not observe.

For one thing, this difference between D and J/E shows us that once the centralized cult of premonarchic Israel had produced its grand design of basic themes ending with the Leading into Canaan, no subsequent large-scale effort was made within the continuing cult to standardize and schematize the later history of Israel's fortunes in the land. For four centuries, from approximately 1050 B.C., when the common groundwork reached its developed form with all its basic themes included, down to the work of the Deuteronomist(s) in 621–550 B.C., the cult lacked the impetus to extend the basic themes or, more exactly, to prepare a second great complex of tradition showing how the history of Israel in the land should be understood in thematic sequence as the work of Yahweh. Of course, during this period, there were plentiful reports and interpretations of history, appearing in small narrative complexes and in the oracles of prophecy, but there was no grand thematically arranged narrative design encompassing the centuries of Israelite experience since the death of Joshua. Given the fantastic productivity of the early cult in spawning historical traditions in an integrated framework, why should the process have suddenly ceased?

The eclipse of large-scale tradition-building in the cult was in large measure due to the inability of the cult to adjust to the new circumstances of the monarchy. The cult had received its essential shape before the monarchy, at a time when all Israel was unified and increasing its scope through the progressive incorporation of new members, after which the divided history of the people in two states following the death of Solomon seemed reprehensible and retrograde, even conceptually incomprehensible. Much of the energy, moreover, had gone into the cult as an effective surrogate for explicitly political institutions. With the institution of hierarchical monarchy, the old cult of the associated tribes yielded its formerly primary position in the social system, its political functions increasingly pre-empted by the monarchy and its religious functions increasingly challenged by the new royal temple cult. Under the circumstances, the continuing centralized cult of Israel fell into a defensive and increasingly archaistic backwater, its cultural and intellectual energies waning.

In fact, the closest approach to a cultic celebration of the history of the monarchy was in the royal theology, which produced liturgical pieces for state occasions and temple festivities and which contained ideological formulations about the filial relation between Yahweh and the king. But this monarchic branch of the Israelite cult never succeeded in recounting the total history of Israel under its kings in a royal ideological framework. Only as the monarchy drew toward its end was such an attempt made, and even then the Deuteronomist, although using cultic materials, shaped his interpretive framework as a highly literary activity that stood apart from the cult, either by anticipating the demise of the cult (assuming a first edition about 609 B.C.) or having directly experienced its death (in the final edition about 550 B.C.).

The remarkable Court History or Succession History of David in II Samuel

9—20, I Kings 1—2 was perhaps stimulated by the incipient cult of royal theology, but its formulation is in no wise decisively cultic. Moreover, it ceases with the securing of the throne to Solomon, its aim having been only to record the struggle over the succession to David's office. Of course, if scholars are correct in believing that the Succession History was written early in Solomon's reign, its limited scope was inevitable. But the fact remains that no one took up the task of extending that account into a history of the Davidic dynasty (under the impulse of royal theology) or into a history of the divided monarchy (under the impulse of the older premonarchic covenant theology) until the Deuteronomic effort three centuries later. Such historical writing as did occur was either within the sphere of undigested court archival activity or within the sphere of lay groups inspired by prophets to view limited episodes or phases of the history critically, but even then it did not expand into a comprehensive history that surveyed and assessed the entire historical past, either from the death of Joshua or from the establishment of the monarchy.

It must be emphasized that I am not claiming the demise of the central cult during the monarchy. I think there is abundant evidence that cultic modal actions of theophany, covenant renewal, historical recitation, and law-giving continued throughout the history of the monarchy, although in attenuated form owing to an overall diminution of importance for the cult in the total social system. My claim is simply this: with the foundation of the monarchy, the centralized cult lost its creative force as the center for generating new comprehensive schemes for interpreting the history of Israel. Events since the death of Joshua were either surrendered by the cult to the interpretations of royal theology or subsumed under the old categories of the basic themes without serious regard for the major differences between the early intertribal history and social system and the contemporary monarchic history and social system.

The creative force of the centralized cult passed over into prophecy, and in prophecy it assumed another form, which drew formally on the old cultic frame and contents but subordinated all that it absorbed to an entirely new reality: the dialectic of judgment and grace as the theological implicate of the social and historical dialectic of contradictory forces which increasingly undermined the foundations of the community. Indeed, in the loss of will or capacity to conceive a comprehensive view of Israel's history more recent than the time of Joshua, we see most vividly the effective decline of the cult as Israel's central institutional organ. The old cult acts were repeated, without the sociopolitical centrality of premonarchic times, and they were as a consequence repeated with an increasing loss of connection between the cult acts and traditions, on the one side, and the contemporary, socially stratified and historically contradictory experience of the community, on the other side. In this light, Deuteronomy and the Deuteronomic history represent a bold but belated attempt to rejoin the divergent and incongruent sacral and secular histories.

The immediate implications of this reading of the role of the centralized cult under the monarchy for our understanding of the work of the Deuteronomist are of significance. The books of Joshua and Judges were not composed as separate books by D, however "naturally" they seem to break into separate entities, but as segments of one connected moral-theological critique of the history of Israel from Moses to the exile, comprising the extant books Deuteronomy through Kings. The segments of the connected history which in the course of transmission became the present "books" of Joshua and Judges are of particular interest to us, since they contain the line of demarcation in the temporal account where the Deuteronomist no longer had the frame of the old canonical basic themes to adhere to and where he had to move on to phases of the story for which he had to devise his own frame. It is highly instructive to see how he proceeded in the segment where he still had the last basic theme of Leading into the Land to guide him and how he proceeded once that theme was, so to speak, "used up."

The Deuteronomic work begins with Moses, but the astonishing thing is that, with slight exception (Deut. 34), the Book of Deuteronomy does not assume the form of a historical résumé but rather the form of direct address by Moses. On examination, this direct address shows itself to be the product of cultic preaching on the old basic themes. In Deuteronomy we get a clear picture of how the centralized cult, when it tried to renew itself in monarchic times, did so not by developing new themes, but by embroidering the old basic themes in sermons and hortatory addresses which aimed at closing the historical and social gap between ancient canonical Israel and contemporary monarchic Israel. It is evident, not only from the form of Deuteronomy as direct address but also from the many traces of liturgical rubrics that survive in it, that the centralized cult found innumerable ways of using the periodic covenant-renewal ceremony as an occasion for drawing together the old basic themes of the canonical historical résumés in a living cultic present that aimed to "re-form" present Israel, riddled as it was with contradictions, and to do so on the basis of a model of old Israel, organically unified and self-consistent. That it was a difficult and impossible task, given the lapse of time and the deepening contradictions in Israel's social system and historical position in the Near East, is evident, I think, from the intense moralizing tone of Deuteronomy and its passionate striving toward a total communal commitment which was rapidly fading away but, as the Deuteronomists saw it, hopefully still within practical reach.[94]

For our immediate purpose in discerning the tradition history of D, the key feature of the Deuteronomist's treatment of the Mosaic age is the fact that he did not undertake a fresh narrative. Clearly he was limited by the reality of the authentic narration of the period of Moses which already stood in the old canonical historical résumés, extant in their rather different versions as written by J and E, and perhaps by D's time already redacted together as a joint work. He could hardly replace that story had he wanted to, but he could have followed the course

of P, who chose to organize the account of J/E within his own chronological
framework and elaborate it here and there with materials expanding on the basic
social and religious institutions which were so important to the exilic or postexilic
milieu of the P writer. D, however, was well satisfied with the scope and detail of
the existing J and E versions of the early history. He preferred to capsulate the old
basic themes up to the land-taking by drawing out their moral-theological implications for the later monarchic history which he was the first to present in its grand
scope and its terrifying default. The cultic preaching on the old themes ideally
suited his purpose of assessing the later history of Israel in the light of the
programmatic meaning of the "Mosaic" constitution of old Israel. And so D built
up a great compendium of preached materials drawn from the cult, possibly
deriving in part from as early as the ninth and eighth centuries in northern Israel,
and then subsequently preserved in Judah and probably reused and modified in
the purified cult of Yahweh following the reformation of Josiah in 621 B.C.[95]

16.3 A Watershed between Joshua and Judges

When the Deuteronomist moved into the age of Joshua, however, he switched
from the mode of address into the mode of narration. This brings us to the thorny
question of the origin, form, and status of the so-called conquest narratives in
Joshua 1—12, an issue which is often simply posed as a literary-critical question
and which we shall also consider in that more restricted form in IV.17.1 and in
IV.18.1–2. But Joshua 1—12 also poses a cultic-ideological question as a problem
in tradition history. How are we to explain the sudden shift from the hortatory
address genre in which Deuteronomy presents all the other basic themes of the old
canonical history to the narrative genre of Joshua in which the terminal basic
theme of the Leading into Canaan is presented?

To approach this question properly we have to recall that the Pentateuch as it
stands contains practically no narrative units that fill out the basic theme of the
Leading into the Land. Only a few scraps of tradition at the end of Numbers
survive. On the other hand, the Pentateuch constantly projects and presupposes
the culmination of Israel's early history in the taking of the land. Why the basic
theme of Leading into Canaan—which with Noth we believe to have been one of
the two earliest supporting pillars of the historical tradition—should be so devoid
of narrative content in the Pentateuch is one of the most puzzling problems of
Pentateuchal literary criticism. A closer look at the Deuteronomist's narratives of
conquest will help us to approach more adequately the literary-critical question
about their antecedents and, more specifically, to throw light on the conjecture
that the Joshua "conquest" stories may once have been in the common groundwork and then taken up either into J or E, or perhaps into both.

The shift from a hortatory treatment of all the preceding basic themes of the old
canonical history to a narrative treatment of the final basic theme of Leading into

the Land was the Deuteronomist's way of underlining the occupation of the land as the most important of the basic themes for his purposes. Why Israel was in imminent danger of losing the land (if we posit a first edition around 609 B.C.), or had actually lost the land (from the angle of the final edition of 550 B.C.), was the urgent historico-theological enigma that D was addressing in his massive appraisal of the past. The plan of the work, therefore, called for singling out the basic theme of the Leading into Canaan for emphasis and amplification. That theme had already been prominent in Deuteronomy by anticipation. Moses is pictured in Deuteronomy as addressing Israel, just before his death, on the verge of the entrance into Canaan, and the national rewards and punishments conditional on Israel's response to the law are centrally described in terms of possession of the land or loss of the land.[96]

But the anticipation of land-taking and the contingency of land-holding tied to law observance in Deuteronomy were not sufficient for the Deuteronomist. He began his "history" by telling of the occupation of the land in narrative form. This may reflect in part the relative absence of hortatory materials in the cult associated with Joshua, although at least two hortatory addresses by Joshua are inserted in Joshua 23—24, the latter in the form of a covenant-renewal ceremony reflecting ancient premonarchic conditions. The primary motivation in highlighting the land-taking as a distinctive episode in history was the desire to drive home the message of Israel's overwhelming success in taking Canaan as its homeland. The land-taking was after all *a series of actions*, however schematized they had become in tradition, and it could be most vividly impressed upon the reader by recounting the military campaigns with all the circumstantial detail available. This would in turn prepare the way for the circumstantial narratives to follow in Judges, Samuel, and Kings.

What is at once arresting about the conquest narratives is that they are cast in the harmonizing centralized form in which all the narratives within the old basic themes were cast. The unified conceptualization of the conquest narratives is precisely the unified conceptualization of all the stories from Exodus and Numbers. The united tribes under a single commander carry out a total sweep of the land. As we have noted already, many aspects of the recounted narratives belie this unified conceptualization of events. Unless the Deuteronomist has wholly fabricated the stories of Joshua 1—12 in archaistic form, which is highly unlikely inasmuch as they lack his most distinctive stylistic features, *a centralizing conceptualization was already intrinsic to the conquest narratives before the Deuteronomist took them over and included them in his account.* Whatever the precise relation of these narratives to the preceding J and E sources (and we shall have more to say about that), the unified conceptualization of the conquest narratives of Joshua tells us something very important about their pre-D history: they stem from a stage of tradition production in which Israel was projected as an idealized unity; and since that idealized, unified projection of all Israel ceased with the last basic theme in the *Grundlage* in approximately 1050 B.C., it seems logical to conclude that an early formulation of these stories, although not all details in them nor necessarily the present articulation of units, goes back to that time.

How very different matters become once the Deuteronomist has reached the end of the final basic theme of the old canonical history. With the death of Joshua, he is on territory lacking the cultic-ideological maps that guided him previously, however much he substituted cunningly constructed cultic preaching for narrative illustration of the themes. As noted earlier in III.14.3, in the Book of Judges there are no narrative units that are cultically centralized, with the exception of the story in Judges 19—21, which we shall examine separately. Suddenly the formalistic façade of unified Israel drops away. We are dealing now with units of tradition which presuppose that the entity Israel was composed of sub-groups and that in the premonarchic period they acted with considerable autonomy, either individually or in varying combinations. We leave aside for now the question of whether the notations about nonmilitary "judges" in Judges 10 and 12 are evidence for a central office in old Israel. But even should that prove to be probable, the central office seems to have taken account of the separate component members of Israel, in that we must square the existence of such an office with the undoubted fact that the narratives proper tell of localized actions by varying numbers of sub-member groups in Israel, ranging from one to ten segments.

So sharp is this break between the conceptualization of the narratives before and after the death of Joshua, that some of the traditions about the original land-taking are placed illogically *after* Joshua's death in total defiance of the assumption that Joshua completed the land-taking. There seems to be only one plausible explanation of that temporal differentiation, namely, that the traditions about land-taking located in Judges 1 picture the tribes as taking possession of their land in separate military actions, actions which the centralized conception of the basic theme in the book of Joshua rules out. To the question of why D should have disturbed his scheme by including materials such as those in Judges 1 we shall return. As it now stands, Judges 1 confirms in the strongest possible way the manner in which the old basic themes determined the Deuteronomist's approach down to the point in his story where the themes cease, after which he felt at liberty to introduce accounts of military actions by separate tribes taking possession of the land or warding off enemies after the initial securing of the land.

It is, of course, obvious that the Deuteronomist intends the reader to treat the traditions of Judges in terms of the ideal moral-theological unity of Israel. This is clear in his following up the separate tribal occupation annals of Judges 1 with the heavy moral-theological summary and critique of Judges 2:1–5. It is equally clear in his editorial frame for the stories of the judges, which attempts to anchor the several stories as so many instances of one and the same all-Israelite process of apostasy, oppression, repentance, deliverance, and rest for the land. Without a doubt, the Deuteronomist himself sees all Israel acting in the separate episodes. Nevertheless, he did not attempt to revise the separate occupation annals and stories of judges so that they would resemble the centralized narratives of Joshua 1—12. That he could have done so had he desired is supported by his readiness to rewrite stories when he has a mind to do so, as illustrated more than once in Samuel and Kings. Paradoxically, it seems to have been his intense moral-theological passion which impelled him to let the annals and stories of Judges stand in largely unedited form because they vividly presented the bald, unvarnished weaknesses, divisions, and apostasies of the time. The stories buttressed in detail D's conviction that Israel backslid after the death of Joshua.

The realistically detailed stories of the judges had apparently developed in separate tribal locales and escaped obliteration because the old basic themes of the cult were not able to absorb and centralize them. The Deuteronomist took them over even though they tended to undercut his claim that Joshua had conquered the whole land because on balance, he regarded this dissonance as not offsetting the advantage of being able to use the stories to dramatically "document" his contention about Israel's departure from Yahweh after Joshua's death. With this interpretation, it then became possible to relax the dissonance between the centralized and uncentralized traditions: centralized traditions about Joshua and the twelve tribes acting in concert which reflect Israel's unity predicated on loyalty to Yahweh and uncentralized traditions about the judges and discrete tribes which reflect Israel's disunity stemming from her apostasy from Yahweh.

From the point of view of tradition history, we conclude that the fundamental periodization of the stories into temporal phases, featuring Joshua and the judges respectively, was a schema that D merely made *explicit*. Implicitly it reached as far back as the second generation of Israelites in Canaan, for at that time the centralizing narratives broke off with Joshua and all subsequent narratives about Israelite events were presented in terms of the discreteness of the sub-members, local leaders, and local sites involved. Naturally the intriguing question arises: Did those who first told and collected the stories of the judges share the later D's moral and theological abhorrence of the events related? Almost certainly they did not and, therefore, we must bracket the comprehensive Deuteronomic moral-theological critique in order to assess the stories in terms of the moral and theological prespectives they severally contain. When that is done, it will be found that the old stories are not devoid of judgments of praise and blame upon the actors and the events they relate; the point is that their criteria are the criteria of Israelites in the twelfth and eleventh centuries B.C. rather than the criteria of Israelites in the Deuteronomic reform movement of the seventh and sixth centuries B.C.

17

Pre-Deuteronomic Sources in Joshua and Judges

To return to the literary analysis, it is at once noticeable that several passages in Joshua and Judges are stamped with motifs and phraseology characteristic of the moral-theological perspective of Deuteronomy, notably Joshua 1; 8:30–35; 11:15–23; 21:43—22:6; 23; Judges 2:6—3:6, as well as the frames of the individual stories in Judges. Moreover, these distinctly Deuteronomic passages are positioned so that they serve as introductory and concluding editorial "clamps" which link together the more disparate traditions in between. And there is considerable difference of opinion over the extent of Deuteronomic editing in a number of other passages.

Our interest now focuses on the materials held together by the explicitly Deuteronomic editorial "clamps." At least in the Book of Joshua, the great majority of narrative materials seem to stem from an older northern cultic-theological milieu in which E was produced and to which the Elijah-Elisha stories and the prophet Hosea were also related. D's peculiar outlook and even much of his language is a distinctive elaboration of these old northern concepts. Thus, it is often very difficult to draw the line between what he has taken over untouched and what he has revised.

Can anything further be determined about the pre-Deuteronomic sources of Joshua and Judges? Were the materials in the Deuteronomist's possession already in the form of continuous sources or were they merely separate units? And, if they were continuous sources, can they be identified as continuations of the sources of the Pentateuch? Finally, should one or the other explanation be followed, what measurable consequences are there for our historical use of the traditions employed by D?

The evidence for the existence of pre-Deuteronomic continuous sources in Joshua and Judges is reasonably strong but by no means conclusive. The traces of parallel sources are clearest in stories such as the crossing of the Jordan River (Josh. 3—4), the capture of Jericho (Josh. 6), the Gideon episodes (Judg. 6—8), and the Jephthah story (Judg. 10:17—12:6). Sometimes these sources appear to be two in number, but in certain stories some critics have seen three sources.[97] The hypothesizing of sources, not only as parallel in particular accounts but as continuous from account to account, may also explain the presence of whole units which treat the same event or complex of events from different angles, such as the prose and poetic accounts of the battle against the Canaanites at the Wadi Kishon (Judges 4 and 5) and the two very different sets of literary modes and ideological conceptions expressed respectively in the conquest traditions of Joshua 1—12 and in the conquest traditions of Judges 1.

Nevertheless, if we suspect that such parallel and continuous sources may have existed for at least some segments of the account, it must be admitted that they are far more difficult to discern than in the case of the Pentateuchal sources. Why should this be so? The obscuring of the pre-Deuteronomic sources can be explained in part on the supposition that the Deuteronomic editor used a heavier selective and revisionist hand upon his materials than did the editor(s) of Genesis through Numbers. This is hardly an adequate explanation, however, since any revision undertaken by D seems to have assiduously avoided rewriting extensively in his own peculiar style. Another factor at work is the difficulty we have referred to in separating the D editor and his earlier E-family materials.

We have had to express so many qualifications about the matter that the question remains as to whether these hypothesized pre-Deuteronomic sources are really extensions of the Pentateuchal sources. In my opinion they probably are, although my judgment is based more on general tradition-historical considerations than on literary analysis.[98] The Pentateuchal sources themselves demand their culmination in a manner consistent with the contents of the pre-Deuteronomic materials in Joshua 1—12 and in Judges 1. By this I mean that the Pentateuchal sources repeatedly point forward to the settlement of Israel in Canaan. Without traditions of the taking of the land they are torsos. Of course we can posit that their endings were lost. If, however, the expected culminations of the Pentateuchal sources in accounts of the occupation of the land are anywhere to be found, they are certainly in Joshua and Judges.

Since I shall return to the question of the possible inclusion of the original endings of J and E in Joshua and Judges, for the moment I simply underline the previously established point that the conquest narratives of Joshua 1—12 were centralized before D took them over, and therefore they not only point backward to a time contemporary with the writing of J and E but even to the roots of the common groundwork of J and E in premonarchic times. When that fact is joined to the truncated form of extant J and E, the probability is very strong that either the conquest materials of J or E, or of both, have been preserved by D. But to make that more than a formal possibility it is necessary to offer more plausible tradition-historical explanations than have heretofore been advanced for the separation of the conquest narratives from the Pentateuch and their inclusion in the Deuteronomic history. This I shall try to do in IV.18.2.

But even as I urge the probability of continuous pre-Deuteronomic narratives, I must also assert that the hypothesis does not solve all the problems posed by the countervailing fragment hypothesis. It only removes them to a somewhat earlier point in the tradition-historical process. For when we talk about "sources" in Joshua and Judges we most definitely do not mean tightly knit, smoothly interconnected literary products with materials of one genre drawn from one single milieu. Such hypothesized sources are already in considerable measure generic "catchalls." Form criticism and tradition history continually direct our attention to the diverse units that have been joined in a source. When one looks intently at sets of narratives in Joshua and Judges, proper emphasis must be constantly placed on two features: (1) their tendency to be *united* by telling a more or less continuous story in two or three possibly parallel sources with certain overarching viewpoints seeming to link the episodes within each posited source; and (2) their tendency to be *fragmented* by the incorporation of diverse literary genres strung together by tenuous editorial linkages between units, which necessarily has the effect of disrupting temporal and thematic continuities.

The overall result is that the tendencies toward ideological and stylistic unity in the sources stand in constant tension with the discreteness and recalcitrance of the individual units. How much fragmentation can a supposed source permit before it is no longer a tenable unity? Finally, even if we allow some sizeable pre-Deuteronomic continuous sources in Joshua and Judges, it is hardly to be claimed that all of the individual units in those books can be related to one or another of the sources. It is necessary to supplement a provisional source hypothesis with a provisional fragment hypothesis. Obviously it is necessary to illustrate these generalities of judgment with some specific blocs of tradition, and we shall choose blocs that are of central importance for understanding the historical worth of what is related to us in Joshua and Judges.

17.1 Joshua 1—12

These narratives tell only in detail of the taking of the Canaanite highlands west of the Jordan by all Israel under Joshua. They give the formal impression of a total "conquest" of the land, but in actuality they tell only in great detail of the taking of a few cities and of two major battles with coalitions of Canaanite kings. The rest is itemized in summarizing narration or in lists. By far the greater part of the land, even of the highlands (not to mention the whole of Canaan), is not referred to at all in the stories but emerges only in occasional sweeping summary claims about the taking of the whole land.

From the stories themselves we get the impression of a couple of victories over opposing coalitions and a number of armed skirmishes and raids, the capture and destruction of a number of cities, but all occurring against a curiously unclear historical and territorial background. The occasional vivid details do not extend to a coherent temporal-territorial representation. The cohesion of the whole seems clearly to stem from the old cultic-ideological matrix. If we desire any kind of literary or historical analysis, we obviously must try to penetrate behind this cultic-ideological façade.

When we examine each unit by form criticism and by temporal-territorial analysis, we discover that the surface unity begins to break apart. We note especially that the locale of the chief episodes is almost exclusively in Benjaminite territory. Gilgal is so prominently featured that one is encouraged to believe that several of these sub-units, particularly those most fully developed, took shape in the milieu of the Benjaminite cult center at Gilgal, where a ceremony was enacted in a procession which crossed over the Jordan and marched around the ruins of Jericho, not far from the site of Gilgal itself.[99] It is further to be noted that the military accounts of precisely these Gilgal stories have a vague, stereotyped character without color and sharp detail and that the figure of Joshua lies rather loose to the accounts. Was he, in fact, originally involved in the incidents at all? By contrast, Joshua seems most securely linked to and defined by the battle at Gibeon and Beth-horon in Joshua 10, an area nearby his Ephraimite tribal home.[100]

When the consequences of that battle, however, are made to stretch out into the Judean hill country and lowlands and when Joshua is connected with the destruction of the far northern Galilean site of Hazor, his association with the accounts becomes suspiciously tenuous. This suspicion is all the more confirmed by the fact that certain conquests claimed for Joshua are elsewhere attributed to single tribes or clans, for example, in the case of Hebron (in Josh. 10:36–37, Hebron's capture is attributed to Joshua; in Judges 1:10, to Judah; in Judges 1:20 and Josh. 14:13–14; 15:13–14, to Caleb). The assumption that Joshua defeated the massed chariotry of the Canaanites at Merom near Hazor flies in the face of the gravest doubts about his association with the Galilean tribes, as well as the difficulty of determining the connection between the battle of Merom in Joshua 11 and the battle by the Wadi Kishon in Judge 4—5. Both are described as surprise victories over the chariotry of King Jabin of Hazor beside streams or springs. The sites of the two battles are some distance apart, and in Joshua's case Hazor is destroyed but in Barak's it is not. Sisera, as Jabin's general, appears in Judges 4 but is absent from Joshua 10, and Jabin himself is unmentioned in the song version of Judges 5.

As far as I can see, the historical incongruities between Joshua 11 and Judges 4—5 (as well as between Judges 4 and Judges 5) do not yield to source-analytic solution by grouping, for example, one strand in Joshua 11 with Judges 4 in one source and the other strand in Joshua 11 and Judges 5 in another source, or by assigning three sources distributed so as to account for discrepancies. We still encounter the difficulty of connecting up the regionally and temporally discrete or antagonistic elements of the battle traditions in these two or three hypothetical sources within a comprehensible historical-territorial nexus.[101]

Having raised the problem of the historical relation between the two Galilean battle-traditions in Joshua 11 and in Judges 4—5, let me simply report my own hypothesis. In my view the report of the destruction of Hazor in Joshua 11, following the defeat of a contingent of chariots at nearby Merom, refers to the late thirteenth-century seizure and destruction of the city which is attested in level XIII of the Hazor excavations.[102] I suggest that this is contained in an annalistic core to Joshua 11 in approximately vss. 5–10, 11b, 13, material which is similar in scope and style to the annalistic materials in Judges 1. I do not believe that Joshua had anything to do with the incident. It was probably an action by part of the later Israelite tribe of Naphtali, which challenged city-state rule in eastern upper Galilee. Jabin of Hazor may have been the name of the king, but the introductory depiction of a vast northern Canaanite coalition of kings against all Israel is apparently dictated by the desire to provide a symmetrical counterpart to the defeat of the southern Canaanite coalition in Joshua 10. As a result of this battle and the capture of Hazor, Naphtali (and perhaps other proto-Israelite groups) began to settle into upper Galilee, or, if they were already settled there, began to develop their own independent life unfettered by the feudal control of Hazor.

By contrast, the battle in Judges 4—5 is for control of the Valley of Esdraelon, which separates Samaria from Galilee, and it is a battle against a coalition of Canaanite kings on a large scale. Jabin is mistakenly introduced here in the prose account, as is shown by his absence from the poetic version and his grandiosely inaccurate title of "king of Canaan." The supposition that the Jabin of Judges 4 may be son or grandson of the Jabin of Joshua 11, who somehow managed to reoccupy Hazor, does not correspond to Canaanite customs of naming royalty and does no more than paper over an historical difficulty in clumsy fashion. Finally, I think it highly probable that the battle as reported in the traditions underlying Judges 4—5 influenced the confused way in which the older annalistic account of the earlier battle near Hazor was eventually worked into the account in Joshua 11.

From these brief examples, which are in principle no different from many others we could have chosen, it becomes clear how immensely complex and frankly problematic are the operations involved in translating the traditions of Joshua and Judges into historical discourse. Estimations of possible or probable sources at best merely help us to plot the contours of the historical problems a little more adequately. In no case can we reconstruct a source which carries back in a straight line to the original events of the occupation of the land articulated as a clearly ordered spatio-temporal totality. At most, certain vivid circumstantial details, or even a whole unit like the Song of Deborah, give us an opening into what took place. But even that detail or set of details becomes only one datum which must be laboriously combined with others to build up a larger historical context. The historical specification of the datum itself cannot be simply extended to other items in accounts, each of which must be examined in its context; and all the recoverable historical data together cannot be set with simple congruence into the eclectic spatio-temporal scheme which the cultic-ideological ground of the traditions has fashioned at great distance from the underlying lived experiences.

Thus, even this seemingly most coherent account of Israel's "conquest" of Canaan in Joshua 1—12 does not lessen our basic dialectical task of working back and forth between the cultic-ideological traditions and a laboriously built-up temporal-territorial framework which acknowledges that what appears now ostensibly as the coordinated action of all Israel is in fact a composite of numerous originally uncoordinated actions by proto-Israelites or by segments of united Israel. That we do not yield to what some defenders of a more conservative assessment of the historical value of the conquest stories have called "historical nihilism" is made clear in this undoubted confidence: behind the harmonized centralized accounts there is no doubt an actual, diversely rich fund of lived experiences whose reconstruction is only possible when we insist on the distinction between the original diversity and the traditional harmonization of the final reports. "Historical nihilism" in this context is a meaningless epithet.

Far from denying that there was an actual history of proto-Israelite and united Israelite peoples, we say that the only way of approximating accurate knowledge of that history is to realize that it was two histories: the history of the lived experiences of proto-Israelites and unified Israelites in their several separate courses and in their progressive stages of unification *and* the history of the development of their traditions as highly selective symbolic responses to and projections of that lived history, surviving as fossils or deposits within the final unity of the traditions. The dialectic in the various stages of the lived experiences and the dialectic in the various stages of tradition production must be grasped each in its own terms and, at the same time joined in the larger dialectic between the unfolding events and the unfolding traditions.

17.2 Joshua 13—19

We have noted in the summary of the contents of Joshua 13—19 that the complexities of the types of allotment descriptions and the editorial frames in which they are incorporated are difficult to represent schematically and to embrace within any single explanatory theory of compositional stages. We may, however, call attention to some of the salient characteristics of the lists and editorial frames. I think it is also possible to fix the historical period and even the immediate milieu to which most of the lists belonged in the first instance.

The descriptions of the tribal land grants or "inheritances"[103] from Yahweh by lot are of three formal types and include many composite examples:

1. *Territorial Lists,* either by the names of regions, or by descriptions of geographical extent employing the formula "from (place name) to (place name)."
2. *Boundary Inventories,* specified by describing the border as running through, along, or around settlements and natural features such as rivers, mountains, passes, stones, etc.

3. *City Lists,* often with numerical totals or sub-totals. Serious discrepancies
occur in several lists between the number of cities named and the
numerical total rounding out the list. This can best be explained by
the assumption that in the course of editing the lists have been
revised through deletion and expansion without corresponding
proper adjustments in the numerical totals.

A striking feature of the allotment descriptions is that in no case do the
boundaries, cities, or territories of a tribe appear to be given in their entirety.
Benjamin and Judah come nearest to being completely catalogued. The western
boundary and western settlements of Benjamin, however, appear to be missing,
and Judah lacks a list of cities for the central region between Jerusalem and
Beth-zur (this lack is made up in LXX). The city lists for the southernmost tribes
are fullest, while none at all survives for Ephraim. Boundaries, although not
always complete, are given in part for all tribes except for Simeon and Dan. The
omission of Simeon's boundaries is due to the reckoning of Simeon's territory
within Judah. Something similar seems true for Dan inasmuch as a close examination of the boundaries in the area where the tribes of Ephraim, Benjamin, and
Judah meet suggests that little, if any, territory was left over to accommodate the
Danite cities. Some borders between tribes are detailed twice, and occasionally no
boundaries are given for a tribal allotment but may be supplied from the border
descriptions of abutting tribes; e.g., for Issachar's northern and western boundaries, it is necessary to consult Naphtali's southern boundary and Zebulun's
eastern boundary. No information is given for relocated Dan except a note about
the capture of the city Leshem=Laish=Dan. This leaves the northeastern tribal
region ill-defined, since for Naphtali both the northern boundary and the eastern
boundary to the north of the Sea of Galilee are lacking.

In an attempt to identify the life-settings of the tribal allotments, a basic
distinction has been drawn between the boundary inventories and the city lists.
The city lists are taken to be administrative in intent and monarchic in date and are
placed at various periods under the monarchy ranging from the reign of David to
the reign of Josiah. The boundary delineations, however, are widely thought to
reflect the actual divisions of the tribes in the covenantal intertribal Yahwistic
community before the monarchy.[104] The city lists have been further distinguished: those from the south (Benjamin, Judah, Simeon, Dan) are fairly full
catalogues of place names sharply set off from the boundary accounts, whereas
those from the Galilean tribes are briefer, even fragmentary, and confusedly
mixed with boundary accounts. There is now considerable doubt that the Galilean
"city lists" were ever independent of the other topographical data, since it has been
argued with some persuasiveness that the boundary inventories were originally
only a sequence of place names later filled out with connecting verbs.[105] In the
south, the city lists are posited as provincial subdivisions of the kingdom of Judah.

The Simeonite city list is recognized as merged into Judah, whereas the Danite city list is increasingly excluded from connection with the Judean provincial scheme.

The debate presently centers on which period in the history of the kingdom of Judah (or in the united monarchy) is reflected in the southern city lists, both according to the boundaries of the kingdom which they assume and according to the presence or absence of particular cities.[106] This debate has tended to divert attention from the boundary lists as a whole, which most scholars continue to regard as premonarchic. It is precisely this hypothesized premonarchic provenance of the boundary lists that I want to examine. Following Z. Kallai, I think it can be shown that the boundary lists are not premonarchic but correspond with unusual exactness to everything we know about the territorial conditions in the late reign of David and the early reign of Solomon, i.e., prior to his administrative redivision of the kingdom.[107] The argument for the late Davidic–early Solomonic provenance of the allotment descriptions is composed of several strands, and I will only indicate its main outlines.

For one thing, the territory encompassed in the tribal grants in its outer limits corresponds very closely to the area encompassed by David's census (II Sam. 24:1–9) and by Solomon's administrative districts (I Kings 4:7–19). In addition, a series of internal features in the allotment lists converges on late Davidic–early Solomonic times as the only period that can explain them. The Israelite territory, within its outer limits, is conceived as solidly occupied, with no gaps in the contiguous tribal grants. This situation was only realized in David's time, following a politico-territorial organization of Israel as a sovereign state. Prior to David's reign, certain features of the allotment lists can only be accounted for as "utopian" sketches. That the "realist" interpretation of the allotment lists is necessary, in spite of gaps and obscurities in their surviving form, is made abundantly clear by little details that point convincingly to known circumstances of David's reign, or to Solomon's early reign at the latest. For example, the Canaanite fortresses in the Valley of Jezreel are in Manasseh's possession. Asher's holdings run up to Sidon in Phoenicia, which ceased to be the case once Solomon found it obligatory to sell Asherite cities to Tyre in return for gold. Gezer became Israelite only when Pharaoh gave it to Solomon as a dowry for his marriage to an Egyptian princess. The border description between Benjamin and Judah is meticulous in its specifications of the exact location of Jerusalem, which best suits a period after David had made the city his capital. Judah's northwestern frontier extends through Danite territory deep into northern Philistia, and can only be understood as reflective of the period after David had driven the Philistines into defensive positions in the immediate vicinity of their major cities.

These late Davidic–early Solomonic lists manifest an awareness of previous changes in tribal locations and adjustments in occupational patterns among the tribes, and in a sense they sometimes carry a history of tribal-territorial changes within them, but there is no evidence that tribal boundaries by precise geographical specification were projected prior to David's time. We know nothing of the supposed intertribal practice of delineating borders so as to insure territorial integrity. The tribes certainly understood where their occupational zones lay, but that they had strict conceptions of territorial sovereignty to be protected by fixed borders is dubious in the extreme. Of course, the laws of the premonarchic period show the greatest concern that land will not be alienated from a family or "clan"; they do not, however, put the matter in terms of territorial integrity but rather in terms of the right of patrimony of the extended social group. Each cultivator of the soil knew his own tribal and family affiliations and the boundaries of his own holdings; he had no need of politically drawn boundary documents to assist him. Nor does it seem possible to conjecture some context for an oral recitation of such detailed lists.

It is, in fact, virtually impossible to identify any viable life-setting for tribal boundary lists prior to the monarchy.[108] Similarly, there is no plausible premonarchic setting for city lists per se. Clan rosters of the type found in Numbers 26 may reflect a premonarchic muster of the Israelite army, and insofar as some of the clan names in that list are identical with city names in the Joshua lists, we might reasonably claim that the city lists of Joshua 13—19 grew out of the clan lists for the muster of the premonarchic army. On examination, however, it is apparent that many of the cities named were not Israelite until David's time. Thus, the lists as they stand are not old clan lists merely transformed into administrative city lists. This also raises the vexed question of the relation between social segmental names (clans, families) and place names (cities, towns), which will be considered in various contexts in Part VI. For the moment I merely contend that even if older clan rosters lie behind the present city lists, they have been thoroughly revised and now reflect a territorial political situation in the Davidic-Solomonic kingdom.

But can the boundary inventories and city lists be given any better explanation in the time of David than in the time of the intertribal association of old Israel? If we begin with David's census, the situation becomes clear at once, for it is only such a census that provides the inclusive conceptual framework for a territorial itemization such as we find in Joshua 13—19. The aim of the census was to organize the kingdom for military conscription, and perhaps also for taxation and the labor corvée. That being the case, the tedious listing of cities and towns and their environs was crucial for a complete assessment of human resources in the kingdom so that they could be appropriately organized for the economic and military support of the central government. Such was the meaning of the the city lists in their original state, although their true purpose is obscured by the sadly incomplete form in which they have survived.

We have explained the city lists as administrative records of a territorial division of David's state for purposes of mustering the army and collecting taxes in kind and in labor. But what about the boundary inventories and the general territorial descriptions? The reason for characterizing the exact scope of the administrative units apparently lies in the sudden incorporation into David's kingdom of Canaanite city-states and some Philistine territory over considerable stretches of the land where Israel as an intertribal premonarchic entity had never been able to extend control, particularly in the coastal plain and in the Valley of Esdraelon. Now the old Canaanite regions had to be brought into the kingdom of Israel. As we shall indicate more fully in VII.32.2, David chose to administer his kingdom internally along tribal lines. That meant in effect that all parts of the realm, including the formerly alien Canaanite city-states, had to be accepted into "tribes" for military and fiscal administration.

Hitherto the territories of the tribes were clear enough for all practical purposes. The conception of living space as administered space did not exist for the old tribes. Even when populations migrated, wherever they managed to establish roots and to cultivate or graze, the land of the region was theirs by right of use. The established kin relationships, real or fictitious, located each family and each clan or village in its proper tribal niche and provided for an organization of the militia. But the Canaanite populations of the plains had no such Israelite tribal identity. They were nothing at all in Israel's terms until David gave them an identity as members of this or that tribe. The only way to do that effectively was to demarcate tribes as living within firmly bounded areas. Each Canaanite city became part of some Israelite tribe by arbitrary assignment in the sense that the assignment was based on immediate territorial-political considerations rather than on a previous organic history. This process is still evident, for example, in the fictitious genealogies of Manassite "clans" (and alternatively or simultaneously "sons"/ "daughters") in Numbers 26:28–34 and in Joshua 17:1–6, which contain a number of recognizable Canaanite cities.

In the summary of Joshua 13—19 above, we commented briefly on the complex editorial frames in the tribal allotment traditions. The exact stages of editing in the pre-D phases of composition, the interaction of the frames on one another and on the lists and narratives which they encompass, have yet to be explained with entire satisfaction. This much is evident: as the text stands, two basically different phasings of the allotments are set side by side, each accompanied by differing representations of the officials involved and of the site of the allotment, with some effort to harmonize them in 19:51.

According to one editorial conception (14:1–5; cf. 13:7), after Moses had made 2½ tribal allotments in Transjordan, Joshua made tribal allotments to the remaining 9½ tribes in West Jordan. This yields the schema:

I

2½ tribes in Transjordan

&

II

9½ tribes in West Jordan

The officials presiding at the allotment are Eleazar, the priest, Joshua, and the tribal heads. However, 14:1a and 5 may be read as an allotment by the people themselves without reference to leaders, a construction supported by the people giving Joshua an allotment in 19:49. Moreover, since Joshua stands alone as the allotter in the second editorial frame, we may also hypothesize a development in the dramatis personae of 14:1–5 as follows:

> 1st stage: the people allot land among themselves by tribes
> 2nd stage: Joshua allots land by tribes
> 3rd stage: Eleazar, the priest, Joshua, and the tribal heads allot land
>   by tribes

On the surface it appears that the 9½ tribal allotments were determined at Gilgal (14:6), but this identification is secondary in that it occurs only in the introduction to the grant of Hebron to Caleb, a tradition unit (14:6–15) which otherwise stands apart from the tribal allotments in scope and form and links up most directly with Deuteronomy 1:19–40, which is in turn related to Numbers 13—14. We may conjecture that the development was as follows:

> 1st stage: site of the land allotment unnamed
> 2nd stage: Gilgal introduced as site of the land allotment, on the
>   assumption that Israel is still at its base camp of Gilgal, as cited
>   frequently in Joshua 1—12

The specification of the unnamed site as Gilgal probably was the work of D, who in inserting the Caleb narrative-allotment unit in its present position, juxtaposed Gilgal in vs. 6 with the anonymous location of the editorial frame in vss. 1–5.

According to the second editorial conception (18:1–10), after Moses had made 2½ tribal allotments in Transjordan, Joshua made the tribal allotments in West Jordan in two distinguishable actions: 2½ allotments to Judah, Ephraim, and West Manasseh, followed by 7 allotments to the remaining tribes determined after a survey of available land. This yields the schema:

I

2½ tribes in Transjordan

&

II

2½ tribes in West Jordan

&

III

7 tribes in West Jordan

The prior 2½ allotments to Judah and Joseph (Ephraim and Manasseh) are alluded to in the frame in such a way as to imply that the choice land was given to these tribes (or simply taken by them?), so that a fresh survey of the land becomes necessary in order to discover additional territories for the remaining seven tribes.

The location of the land division is Shiloh according to 18:1, 8, and 10. Since, however, vs. 6 leaves the place unnamed (note the twofold "here"), it is likely that Shiloh is a secondary intrusion for the purpose of identifying the place of land allocation as the central sanctuary where the tent of meeting was said to be located. In fact, vs. 1 begins as though Israel is gathering for the first time, thus ignoring the earlier 2½ tribe allotments which the frame seems to presuppose in vs. 5. It has even been suggested that "the camp" implies Gilgal (vs. 9; cf. 9:6; 10:6). We may, therefore, reconstruct the development of this editorial frame as follows:

1st stage: Joshua presides over the allotment at an unnamed place
2nd stage: Joshua presides over the allotment at the tent of meeting in Shiloh

Presumably D already possessed this editorial frame in its Shiloh form, which accorded well with another tradition he had at hand in I Samuel 2:22, according to which Eli's sons ministered as priests at the tent of meeting in Shiloh.

While it is instructive to identify possible lines of development within the editorial frames, it is not easy to reconstruct a tradition history of the overall growth of these framed traditions prior to their adoption by D. The tension between Gilgal and Shiloh, even though secondarily introduced, draws our attention to the prominence of the former in Joshua 1—12 and of the latter in the early chapters of I Samuel. The singling out of Judah and the Joseph tribes in the seven-tribe frame corresponds to their political importance, superior to that of all the other tribes, throughout Israel's history. The seven-tribe account of men sent by Joshua to survey the land and to write a description of its divisions reads like a clumsy retrojection of later census practices, and it may in fact be a memory of the original connection of these tribal allotment descriptions with the census and administrative divisions of David.

We can perhaps best account for the lamentable condition of the allotment descriptions in Joshua 13—19 on the theory that once they were no longer administratively current after Solomon's reorganization of the kingdom, they fell into abrupt disuse. Only later did learned collectors begin to gather them with an eye to including them in the traditions about the original division of the land among the tribes under Joshua. The work of these collectors shows up in the major editorial frames we have analyzed, either of which is very difficult to attribute to D. Any firm linguistic or conceptual criteria for identifying these editorial frames with J or E are lacking. P-type terminology in 14:1–5 and in 18:1–10 is not sufficient to argue for a revision under the influence of the later P source. It may, however, point to priestly circles of collectors of the sort who contributed to the later P source. The priestly provenance of the learned collectors of the tribal allotment materials is also suggested by the decided preference of these units for the P-type designation of "tribe" by the term *maṭṭeh* (in all instances apart from chapter 13) in place of the more common *shēveṭ*.[109]

In any event, the two editorial frames point to a pre-D collection of allotment accounts in at least two stages or in a single conflation of two recensions. The main conceptual issue at stake in the two versions was whether the tribes were to be viewed on a par in the equal distribution of land or whether Judah and Joseph (Ephraim and Manasseh) were to be singled out as of paramount importance. D retained both frames (or parts of both), their discrepant concepts harmonized imperfectly in 19:51. Further form-critical and tradition-historical research on these traditions is advisable. Thus far at least, it seems evident to me that the editorial frames do not constitute any firm ground for challenging the assignment of these lists to the political administrative world of the late Davidic–early Solomonic kingdom, from whence they were transferred rather clumsily to the premonarchic history in a far from coherent or complete form.

This has been a fairly long and complicated analysis and critique of Joshua 13—19; and even so, it has been far from complete. We have seen at any rate how the initial claim that the traditions of Joshua and Judges contain refracted history applies not alone to narratives but also to territorial-geographical lists. Yet the situation is different with the lists than with the narratives of Joshua 1—12. The factor of "temporal distance" means something rather different in the two cases. For the boundary lists we imagine hardly any distance in time between the described situation and the composition of the lists, once we grant them an actual administrative context in David's regime. The same would be true for the city lists of Judah and the other southern tribes, if they are taken to belong to a somewhat later period in the monarchy. So in the case of the lists we can "see through" them to an original stage of composition contemporary with the conditions they describe. Nonetheless, "temporal distance" remains in other ways as a major distorting factor.

The biggest confusion in the traditions is the editorial distortion resulting from their attribution to the time of Joshua. Substantive distortion has also occurred to the extent that major sections of the original adminstrative documents seem to have been lost or deleted. Also, narrative elements have been woven into the lists to provide continuity with the story being told in Joshua. All this means that we are lacking in an entirely satisfactory picture of the original contours of the administrative lists. Nonetheless, by putting aside the editorial sleight of hand by which the lists have been transported to a time two centuries earlier than their proper life-setting, we can recover them for historical reconstruction of parts of the administrative subdivisions of David's kingdom based on the old tribal system expanded to include Canaanite city-states on a territorial principle. Their value for determining the original settlement patterns of Israel, considerable as it is, must be limited to *the unevenly detailed view they give us of how the tribes were distributed in the land at the end of the settlement period.* Seen primarily as administrative documents, or remnants of such documents, from David's kingdom, the lists acquire their value for premonarchic times only insofar as *David constructed his administrative units on the basis of the tribal divisions of old Israel as they existed in his time.*

17.3 Judges 1—2:5

We turn our attention to a series of individual tribal occupation "annals" forming the entirety of the first chapter of Judges. The sub-units, sixteen in number, are clearly articulated pieces that are united around the theme of tribal occupation of land, sometimes described as successful and sometimes described in terms of failure. The "tribes" or segments of tribes in their order of appearance are: Judah and Simeon (vss. 1–3); Judah (4–11); Caleb and Othniel (12–15); Kenites (16); Simeon and Judah (17); Judah (18–19); Caleb (20); Benjamin (21); Joseph (22–26); Manasseh (27–28); Ephraim (29); Zebulun (30); Asher (31–32); Naphtali (33); Dan (34–35). As was noted in our earlier summary of contents, five of the sub-units are paralleled in whole or in part in Joshua. In addition, materials of the same general type, but without parallels in Judges 1, are represented in Numbers and Joshua: Machir, Jair, and Nobah take East Manasseh (Num. 32:39, 41–42); Israelites (originally East Manasseh?) fail to drive out Geshur and Maacath from Transjordan (Josh. 13:13); the Josephites take the hill country as far north as the Valley of Esdraelon (Josh. 17:14–18); the Danites capture Leshem (Josh. 19:47). I also suggest that the core of the accounts about the battle of Gibeon/Beth-horon (Josh. 10:6–11,15) and the battle at Merom (Josh. 11:5–10,11b, 13) are of a rather similar annalistic type and belong to the same stock of materials as Judges 1. Perhaps the references to Gadites and Reubenites building or rebuilding cities in southern Transjordan also belong to this stock of annalistic notations (Num. 32:34–38). Furthermore, the Danite migration may have been more fully described in the annals in what now appears as Judges 18:1b–2a, 7–12, 27b–29, and the fragments of an annalistic report of intertribal skirmishes between Benjamin, on the one side, and Judah and Ephraim, on the other, may still survive in Judges 20:18,31,35a,36 (see fuller discussion in VII.31.1 and especially in note 249).

While these terse descriptions of battles, of the capture of cities, of the occupation of regions and failures to expel inhabitants, and of the forced servitude of peoples are not technically annals in that they do not list events by years, they are annalistic in their terseness and specification of detail. In general they show what has been called "theological indifference." Most of all, they are barely touched by the notion that all Israel fought together as a united people to possess the land.

The position of this annalistic collection in relation to the bulk of Joshua-Judges is highly idiosyncratic.[110] The annalistic series pictures individual tribes conquering cities or failing to conquer cities which, according to the the Book of Joshua, have already been taken and distributed among the tribal holdings to which the people are peaceably dismissed (Josh. 21:43; 22:6). Joshua has given his farewell address, has died and been buried, and the series of Judges 1 opens with the temporal phrase: "after the death of Joshua. . . " The contradiction is so sharp that we naturally wonder what was in the mind of an editor when he inserted the section at this point. We have already called attention to the disjunctive periodization of the conquest events into the period before Joshua's death and the period after his death. How does this periodization function in the case of Judges 1, and what light does a close scrutiny of the annalistic series throw on the tradition-building process and on the historical usefulness of the data contained in the annals?

The primary motivation for segregating the sub-units of Judges 1 at a point after the death of Joshua is revealed in Judges 2:1–5. There it is said that Yahweh will not henceforth drive out all the Canaanites because Israel did not follow his command to refrain from all agreements with them and to extirpate the Canaanite religion. This perspective is congenial to the Deuteronomic overview from Deuteronomy through Kings, but it definitely had its origins in a view of the occupation independent of the dominant "united Israel under Joshua" concept of the centralized traditions in Joshua 1—12. It pictures Joshua as having died at Gilgal, and from there the people go up to Bochim (Bethel in LXX) to take the land, but with the clear understanding that they will be unable to conquer Canaan in its entirety. It seems not unreasonable to believe that the earliest stage of Judges 2:1–5—i.e., in its pre-Deuteronomic form—rounded out a version of the occupation of the land which lacked Joshua as the architect of victory and in which the tribes settled down separately and with very mixed success. Later, portions of that version were incorporated in Joshua and Judges, and Judges 2:1–5 was given a Deuteronomic veneer that explained Israel's failures, insofar as the Deuteronomist admitted them, as due to its infidelity to Yahweh's commands.

There is apparent significance for the writer of 2:1–5 in the fact that, according to Judges 1, the tribes who lived with Canaanites "*did not* drive them out" (vss. 27–33). The sense of 2:1–5 is that the tribes *refused* to expel the Canaanites, preferring to make covenants with them. It is quite clear, however, in the body of the annals that the Canaanites continued to live in tribal areas not because of Israel's refusal to drive them out, but because of *Israel's political-military weakness relative to certain of the Canaanite enclaves.* The Canaanites, possessing chariots (vs. 19), were formidable foes who "persisted in dwelling in that region" (vs. 27, cf. vs. 35), or, as I shall propose in the discussion of the Hebrew word *yōshēv* in IX.44.2, we should probably translate, "succeeded in continuing to rule in that region." In other words, the editor's belief in Israel's moral-theological failure of nerve is not even echoed, much less stated, in the contents of the annals he employs. Instead of rapprochements with the Canaanites, the Israelites struggled as best they could but were unable militarily to dislodge all the Canaanite city-state enclaves.[111]

By prefacing the annals with the note "after the death of Joshua," or by letting it stand in the sub-source he took over, the editor was able to make his moral point that Israel backslid, once the great leader of the conquest was gone. By placing the annals as a group prior to the stories of the judges he is able to explain why the tribes had to go on fighting to take territory supposedly already taken. In the process, of course, he disregards the historical incongruity that the occupation annals of Judges 1, taken by themselves do not presuppose prior conquests beyond a limited area, perhaps the base camp at Gilgal. But even this is far from certain (in spite of the note in 2:1; note that "the city of palms" in 1:16 may not be Jericho but may perhaps be Tamar or Zoar, south of the Dead Sea). The annals are not descriptions of mopping-up operations after earlier major conquests, nor are they accounts of battles that broke out in regions already settled. Judges 1 is clearly a fragmentary description of initial occupations of the land which has escaped to a considerable degree from the heavy hand of the pan-Israelite version of a total conquest under Joshua.

It appears, then, that Judges 1 and its cognate materials in Numbers and Joshua may contain material, and even describe an overall process, which is of potential importance for the historian of the land-taking. But is it a homogeneous source? How complete is it? Does it present an internally consistent picture of the settlement? What function did such traditions have in the community before they were taken up into Joshua-Judges? How close do they really come to the actual course of events in the settlement of the tribes? These questions can only be given tentative answers, but the answers seem adequate for certain historical conclusions.

Is Judges 1 a homogeneous source? As it stands, it certainly is not;[112] however, judging by the related fragments in Numbers and Joshua, it seems to have derived from a larger source, and the total shape of that source may have been considerably more cohesive than now appears. The lack of homogeneity in Judges 1 shows up in many ways. The segment 1:1–3 is shaped by the conception that the tribes consult together about their respective military moves and may persuade one another to work together at least in pairs. In other words, it implies that the tribes decide *collectively* how they will *severally* take their respective areas of occupation. Simeon agrees to help Judah and, in 1:17, Judah helps Simeon. Yet in the accounts of Judah's conquests, Simeon, after agreeing to help, does not appear at all. Not only is this notion of tribal collaboration imperfectly carried out in the case of Judah and Simeon, it is largely dropped thereafter. In fact, except for the taking of Bethel, the non-Judean annals say nothing at all about the conquests of the tribes, but only about their initial failures and the accommodations they had to make with the Canaanite populations until they were able to subject them to forced labor.

Moreover, the materials strung together to describe Judah's conquests are especially diverse and ill-fitting. Seizures of cities alternate abruptly with invasions and seizures of large areas. Judah "goes against" Debir, but it is Othniel who takes it and Caleb who grants it to Othniel. The result is brief snippets of separate actions rather than the account of a sequential campaign. They read like a collection of many kinds of actions attributed to Judah and its constituent elements (Calebites, Kenizzites, Kenites, Simeonites, Othnielites) in the course of its land-taking. It is, of course, possible that the parent source was similarly disordered, but it seems more likely that an editor, wanting to maximize the role of Judah, has inflated the section with every bit of information he could collect about the tribe without much regard for a unified picture.

Is the sketch of the occupation complete? Obviously it is not. Reuben, Gad, and Issachar are omitted. Besides the conquests of Judah and its related groups, only the conquest of Bethel by the house of Joseph is mentioned. For all the other tribes, we read only of their failures, even though these very "failures" imply that they had taken some territories contiguous with the Canaanite cities or regions which they could not for the time being possess. From the related passages in Numbers and Joshua we may reasonably conclude, however, that the parent source of Judges 1 had information about additional conquests, such as those of East Manasseh (Num. 32:39,41–42), of Benjamin/Ephraim (Josh. 10:6–11,15), of Naphtali (Josh. 11:5–10,11b,13), of Josephites (Josh. 17:14–18), and of Dan (Josh. 19:47; Judg. 18:1b–2a,7–12, 27b–29).

Indeed, if the terse report of the Gadite and Reubenite building or rebuilding of fourteen cities in southern Transjordan (Num. 32:34–38) is also to be attributed to the parent stock of annals, Issachar would then be the sole unmentioned tribe in the total reconstructed corpus of annals. The Reubenite cities are represented as largely enclosed within Gad, which extends to the south, north, and northwest. This is contrary to the conception of Joshua 13:15–28 (where Gad lies to the north and Reuben to the south) and, being somewhat less schematic, may accurately enshrine an old colonization tradition. Hesitancy about including Numbers 32:34–38 in the annals stock rests mainly on the lack of comparable prominence in the annals to the building or rebuilding of cities (but note the subsidiary allusion to city-building by a migrant from Bethel, Judges 1:26). Supportive of the inclusion of Numbers 32:34–38 in the annals is the report in Joshua 19:50 of the rebuilding and settling of Timnath-serah and the prolix account of the Danite capture of Laish in Judges 18:27b–29, which mentions rebuilding and settling the conquered city and may actually reflect an expanded alternative version of the Danite annal in Joshua 19:47. The incompleteness of tribal coverage in Judges 1 and the inordinate prominence of Judah seem to be linked to the editor's belief that compromise with the Canaanites was the endemic vice of the more northerly tribes and thus they were less successful in driving out the Canaanites than was Judah.

Granted the lack of homogeneity and completeness of coverage, is the account at least internally consistent in what it does report? It is consistent in showing the tribes settling one by one, with only immediately contiguous tribes aiding one another; e.g., Judah helps Simeon and Ephraim helps Dan. Even these references may be differently understood, however, since Simeon may here be understood as already subsumed under Judah (as are the Calebites and Kenites), and Ephraim may well be regarded as having subdued the Amorites only after Dan relocated in the north. Thus the limited and even problematic "pairing" of some tribes hardly undercuts the dominant theme of separate tribal action which runs throughout the series.

Moreover, there are many hiatuses and inconsistencies that cannot be resolved satisfactorily within the confines of the account, or even with the help of supplementary traditions that serve to fill out the hypothetical parent source. For instance, what is Judah doing fighting the Canaanites at Bezek, to the north of Shechem, when its territory is in the far south? Or is some other unknown Bezek intended? And doesn't the defeat of Adonibezek at Bezek suggest that one of the names is fabricated out of the other?[113] Why do the Judeans bring the captured king Adonibezek to Jerusalem when they have not yet captured that city—or was the maimed king brought there by his own subjects? Was Jerusalem indeed taken and burned long before David's time and subsequently reoccupied by Jebusites? If it was captured already by *Judah,* why is it said that *Benjamin* did not expel the Jebusites from Jerusalem? Do we not have here two different tribal claims on Jerusalem, one by Judah and the other by Benjamin? Did Judah as a whole or did Caleb alone drive out the three lords of Hebron, or is "Judah" in this case a cover term for one of its eventual components, Caleb? The same must be asked of the capture of Debir: Judah goes up against the city, but only Caleb and Othniel are involved in its seizure. If Judah could not occupy the coastal plain because its people had chariots, how is it possible that the tribe took Gaza, Ashkelon, and Ekron and their territories, i.e., among the chief fortresses in the plain? All in all, such difficulties do not encourage us to believe that we have here a comprehensive, self-consistent account of the conquest.

For the so-called negative occupation annals, the consistency is much greater in that they do not contradict one another concerning the cities that remain in Canaanite hands. They reveal a uniform condition throughout the central and northern tribes, namely, that Israelites and Canaanites had to live side by side for some time, one or the other sometimes having the advantage, until the Canaanites could finally be subjected totally. Yet this lack of outright contradiction does not make it any easier for the historian to know how to fit these accounts together in a reconstruction of the settlement. The lack of specification of regions and cities settled by these tribes puts decided limitations on what can be made of the presupposed limits of conquest. It will hardly do to assume that these tribes are thought of as occupying all the regions and cities not specifically exempted by the disclaimers.

Central to an assessment of the internal consistency of the account is the question of how these undated annalistic vignettes are to be related temporally. What is the temporal nexus between units and what is the temporal span within each unit? Since the opening promise of the passage to show some sequence in the actions of the tribes as a result of their joint consultation is unfulfilled, we must probably attribute that temporal feature to an editor and not to the source itself. We are left to conjecture in the light of other biblical traditions just what order, if any, can be given to the actions. There is a kind of spatial coherence in that the arrangement of the separate tribal pericopes moves from south to north, although Manasseh appears improperly before Ephraim in the spatial sequence. Dan climaxes the series probably because it is viewed as already relocated in the far north, in spite of the fact that the content of the unit describes its previous holdings in the south between Judah, Benjamin, and Ephraim.

Regrettably we conclude that the individual entries in the parent source appear not to have borne any overall schema that related them all temporally. Or if such a schema existed, it is now lost to us. Thus it is demonstrated that the perspective of the annals, while historico-territorial, is not sequentially historical. It offers us no more than some valuable fragmentary notations toward a reconstruction of the history of the Israelite settlement. It assures us that early Israel had distinct memories of individual tribal settlements, but it does not convey to us any patterns for coordinating the tribal occupations in an encompassing temporal frame which can simply replace the centralized frame of Joshua 1—12. Even so, we should not underestimate the significance of Judges 1 and related materials in fundamentally challenging the historical adequacy of the centralized frame. It provides us with valuable controls from within the traditions for working at the task of developing a spatio-temporal reconstruction of the settlement which will adequately treat all the biblical traditions pertaining to the land-taking.

Almost totally overlooked by commentators is the question of the temporal horizons within each of the smaller units of Judges 1. This question rises with particular urgency when we consider what is related in the "negative" occupation annals. For example, what period is referred to in the Manasseh annal by the phrase, "when Israel grew strong"? (vs. 28). Does this refer to a time after the victory over the Canaanites at Wadi Kishon (Judg. 4—5), after which the Canaanite cities nearby in the plain and on the coast were subjected to Israelite hegemony, even though they remained Canaanite? Or is it more plausibly a reference to

David's conquest of the Canaanite cities which were then incorporated in Israel and their inhabitants subjected to forced labor? Surely the latter is more probable, given the reference to "Israel" instead of Manasseh and given the fact that we have no independent testimony about premonarchic Israel enslaving or drafting Canaanites for labor.[114]

We note in Joshua 13:13 an additional "negative" occupation annal which is very similar to Judges 1:29–30 in form. It is evident that the general terms "Israelites" and "Israel" have displaced the original tribal name in this annal fragment. Since Geshur and Maacath were Aramean kingdoms in Bashan in northern Transjordan, it is highly probable that the original version of the annal referred to "Manassites" and "Manasseh," which is also supported by the context. Thus, Joshua 13:13 supplements the "negative" occupation annal concerning West Manasseh in Judges 1:27–28 with one concerning East Manasseh. If "when Israel grew strong" refers to Davidic rule, we see at once that this annal is a terse summary of a century or two of Manassite history vis-à-vis the Canaanite fortresses of the plain. It is equally clear that its present form cannot have been drawn up any earlier than the era of David. Much the same conclusions would have to be drawn for the annals concerning Zebulun and Naphtali.

But what then is to be made of those annals in the same form of a "negative" occupation account which do *not* refer to impressing the Canaanites into the corvée? Ephraim did not expel the Canaanites in Gezer but rather "lived among them" (vs. 29). Noticeably different is the parallel to this annal in Joshua 16:10 where it is stated that the Canaanites of Gezer "have become slaves to do forced labor." Likewise, the Canaanite inhabitants of cities in Asher live side by side with the Asherites and no allusion is made to their subjection to forced labor (vss. 31–32). Does this imply that when David conquered and incorporated the Canaanite cities into Israel he exempted some Canaanite cities, such as those in Ephraim and Asher, from the corvée? This is very improbable, not only on general considerations concerning David's policies but considering the twofold form of the Ephraim-Gezer annal in Judges 1:29 and in Joshua 16:10. Is it not more plausible to suggest that the Ephraim and Asher annals in Judges 1 simply have different temporal horizons than do the Manasseh, Zebulun, and Naphtali annals? These annals do not extend as far as the reign of David in their compass; they do not have in view the monarchic conquest, incorporation, and impressment into corvée of the Canaanite cities.

In the case of the Dan annal, do we not have an even more complex history telescoped within it? At least these stages in the Danite land-taking process seem referred to or presupposed: (1) the Danites are driven back into the hill country from the foothill settlements of Har-heres, Aijalon, and Shaalbim, which the Amorites occupy; (2) the Danites are forced to migrate northward, giving up all hope of winning back the lost area from the Amorites; (3) as Joseph (in this case

Ephraim is meant) grew stronger, it began to press upon the Amorites in the forementioned settlements and to retake some or all of them for Israel; (4) David's conquest enabled the Amorites in this region to be pressed into Israelite corvée service. In positing stage two, I assume that the position of the Dan annal at the end of the series, which proceeds as a whole from south to north, implies that the arranger of the annal read it as though Dan was already relocated in the far north. In positing stage three, I assume that it was Joseph (Ephraim) alone who retaliated against the Amorites without the aid of the Danites, who had already migrated. In distinguishing stages three and four, I assume, in the first place, that the pressure of Joseph (Ephraim) on Amorite settlements in the foothills must have been exerted much earlier than David's times, in fact prior to Philistine hegemony in that region (no later than 1050 B.C.?).[115] Secondly, I assume that the corvée impressment of the Amorites by Israel first began under David.

There are additional curiosities in the Dan annal which set it off from the other "negative" occupation annals. Whereas all the others present the Israelite tribes as the subject of the report and the Canaanites as the objects of Israelite action, the Dan annal presents the Amorites as the subject of action and the Israelites as the objects of Amorite action. It is thus the only one of the "negative" annals which represents the inhabitants of the land as taking the initiative in aggression. Moreover, we note that the non-Israelite inhabitants of Dan are called Amorites, whereas elsewhere in Judges 1 they are called Canaanites (but cf. in the annals of Num. 32:39 and Josh. 10:6). These divergences in form and language further reinforce the impression that very diverse kinds of materials have been drawn together in Judges 1 and that the temporal horizon of each unit must be assessed first of all on its own terms.

This leads us to ask if the original form of the annals may not have excluded all references to forced labor or corvée as the fate of the Canaanites, as is now the case only in the annals of Ephraim and Asher. Do we not have some ground for thinking that these "negative" annals were first shaped at a time prior to David's conquest of the Canaanite cities? And that when the culmination of the conquest in David's subjection of the Canaanites to corvée occurred, this remarkable finale to the conquest tended to creep into the annals in later revisions? And that the revising process was not carried through consistently, as witnessed by the survival of the earlier form of the Ephraim and Asher annals? Moreover, if we hypothesize that all the references to corvée are additions from Davidic times, should we not perhaps perceive in the variant wording of the early annals an assessment of the relative balance of power in regions where Israelites and Canaanites lived side by side? When it is said that Canaanites "lived among" the Ephraimites and Zebulunites and Geshur and Maacath "lived among" the East Manassites, this may express the relative preponderance of Israel in those tribal areas. Whereas, when it is said that the Asherites and the Naphtalites "lived among" the Canaanites, this may express the relative preponderance of Canaanite city-states in those tribal areas. A somewhat similar calculation of the balance of power in these regions could be intended if the verb translated "lived" actually means "ruled" in these contexts (cf. my discussion of *yōshēv* in IX.44.2).

Finally, what functions did such traditions perform? What was their setting? How did such a sizeable bloc of traditions manage to escape the pan-Israelite harmonization which has worked so powerfully throughout the Book of Joshua? Who collected and preserved such data? I believe that we must distinguish at least two functions and settings in the history of these traditions prior to their incorporation in Joshua-Judges.

We can get at the second of the two stages by noting the latest historical stage in Israel reflected in the annals as they now stand within the editorial frame. The prominence given to Judah, itself incorporating several southern groups, and the claims to subjection of the Canaanites to corvée throughout the center and north of the land, leave no doubt about the fact that this material in its extant form is no earlier than the Davidic monarchy. Only then was Judah fully formed and as important as Judges 1 pictures it. Only then were the Canaanites drafted by Israel for forced labor. Therefore, the setting of the materials in Judges 1 was a setting that already looked back upon the conquest as finished. From that perspective, the function of the materials seems to be to account for the very moderate initial successes of the tribes in the north as compared with Judah's greater success in the south. It seems tenable to assume that this southern source was a part of the J writer's account and that, in including these uncentralized conquest annals, he sought to supply a rationale for the slowness of the conquest and for the fact that it was eventually a Judean figure, David, who brought all Israel together in triumph over all its enemies.

But what of the earlier stage? How can we understand the function and setting of the parent source which the southern editor, presumably J, took over for his purposes? Once we remove the dominance of Judah and the theological explanation of the failure to drive out the Canaanites as editorial perspectives on Judges 1, what remains as a clue to the original function and setting of the separate traditions? The broad intent of the separate vignettes seems to be to catalogue some of the struggles that went into the accomplishment of the conquest. They answer the questions: What did the individual tribes contribute to the conquest? What striking successes and what peculiar difficulties did they have in their own regional efforts? They are a historicized counterpart to the tribal blessings.

In trying to identify the circle of origin more precisely, we also note the virtual absence of theological interest. Only in the Judah portions is theology involved, and there it may be due to the editor. The expression, "I [God] have given the land into his [Judah's] hand" (1:2) and "Yahweh gave the Canaanites and Perizzites into their hand" (1:4) are highly formalistic ways of describing success in battle. Otherwise, the traditions picture the occupation as solely the result of human action. No appeal is made to divine intervention, and no explanation of failure because of Israel's sin is introduced. Such an interpretation belongs solely to the editor of 2:1–5. The nearest approximation to a comprehensive theological explanation appears in the anecdotal confession of the defeated Adonibezek who says, "As I have done, so God has requited me" (1:7), but this is really no more than a very general statement about poetic justice. In the introduction to the Judah annals, the method of securing divine guidance is by oracle consultation, but this is a piece of reportage rather than a religious interpretation. Religious language and religious institutions appear so infrequently and in so matter-of-fact a way that we are struck by the entirely different mood that dominates the annals in contrast to the cultic religiosity of the traditions in Joshua 1—12.

If we try to move back to the stage before the southern editor gathered the annals into their present form, can we determine a setting and a function that are both sufficiently "untheological" and sufficiently explanatory of the impetus to develop and preserve such uncentralized materials? Apparently the locus for such matter-of-fact accounts of separate tribal conquests was at some point of serious friction between centralizing processes in Israel which tended to override and obscure diverse sub-histories, on the one hand, and local decentralized processes which struggled to keep distinctive sub-histories alive, on the other hand. Concretely, that point of friction was the one at which the several autonomous tribes of old Israel merged into the state of Israel under David's sovereignty. The centralization of politics in a government apparatus, and the resulting stimulus to unify the national traditions, aroused the defenses of the separate tribes to make sure that their respective interests and identities would be protected. Assuming the parent source behind Judges 1 and related annals in Numbers and Joshua to have possessed an integrity of its own—which the southern editor subsequently shaped and reworked for his own purposes—we must look for the source of its cohesion in a milieu where historico-territorial lists were being made as the basis of monarchic administration, lists such as now predominate in Joshua 13—19.

The purpose of this parent source behind Judges 1 was not, however, to facilitate administration; it was rather to set out a memorial of the contributions of the individual tribes in the formation of the monarchy, which strove to bring the conquest of the land to a culmination.[116] The pan-Israelite traditions of conquest in Joshua 1—12, were insufficient for the purpose because they did not discriminate the peculiar activities and fortunes of the tribes in their several regions. In this sense Judges 1 and its cognate materials formed a corrective to Joshua 1—12, but a corrective intended not for cultic recitation but for more explicitly political purposes: as a protocol of the historico-territorial integrity of the several tribes who mutually declared David as their king.

Accordingly, I propose to look for the specific setting of the parent source of Judges 1 in the circle of tribal officials who came together to make David king of united Israel. Of that event, II Samuel 5:3 reports: "So all the elders of Israel came to the king at Hebron; and King David made a covenant with them at Hebron before Yahweh, and they anointed David king over Israel." The annals drawn together at that time defined the tribal rights in historico-territorial form. In effect they delineated the respective power bases of the compacting tribes and fixed the historical claims of the various tribes to be full, free, and consenting covenant partners in the elevation of David as their leader. The annalistic form and the absence of theologizing are understandable on the theory that they were political in intent. They may have been deposited in state archives as a witness to the entrenched tribalism which compelled David to organize his administration on tribal-territorial lines and which in turn gave rise to the allotment lists of Joshua 13—19 as the administrative documents specifying the subdivisions of the new kingdom. Alternatively, or additionally, these summations of separate tribal achievements may have circulated in tribal assemblies under the encouragement of tribal leaders. In VII.32.2 I shall argue that this precise historic moment was the time when the twelve-tribe system was created in order to incarnate the strong tribal base of the new kingdom in schematic form.

Such an hypothesis goes some distance toward explaining how some of the excerpts of the parent source of Judges 1 also got into Numbers and Joshua. There may be some significance in the fact that the sequence of the tribes Asher-Naphtali-Dan in Judges 1 occurs in only one other place in the Old Testament, namely, in the ordering of the tribal allotment lists of Joshua 19. This may be a surviving trace of the original intention of the memorial source of Judges 1 to supplement the Davidic administrative tribal-territorial divisions of Joshua 13—19 by placing alongside the static administrative delineations historical accounts in compressed form of how each tribe came to occupy its territory. If the lists of Joshua 13—19 and the annals of Judges 1 were already associated in the political circles of the tribal officials, it becomes more understandable how some of the fragments of the annals have been taken over into the final editing of the tribal allotment lists in Joshua 13—19, albeit in very sporadic and truncated form.

Furthermore, the association of the tribal administrative dockets and the settlement annals in the same political milieu may also explain why an erratic fragment of a border list is presently appended to the annals in Judges 1:36. That it actually treats of the boundary of the Edomites instead of the Amorites is attested in some LXX manuscripts and corroborated by Joshua 15:1–4 and Numbers 34:3–5. A scribal slip has led to a "catch word" linkage between a fancied "Amorite" border and the Amorites mentioned in the Danite annal of 1:34–35. Rather than being purely arbitrary, however, such an association of the formally distinct boundary and annal tradition-types was facilitated by the existing connection in court circles of border lists and settlement annals, and is precisely the sort

of juxtaposition we also encounter more frequently in Joshua 13—19. It is remotely possible that the annal source contained a brief sketch of the outer
boundaries of the tribes and that what survives in Judges 1:36 is a fragment of the
southern boundary (cf. Num. 34:3–5), but the fragment is much too small for us to
be confident of this proposal.[117]

A conceivable objection to my proposal may be felt in the fact that for most of
the central and northern tribes, Judges 1 tells only of their failures rather than of
their successes. We must remember, however, that Judges 1 was tailored to a
pro-Judean point of view by the southern editor. In Numbers and Joshua are
several instances of annals which tell of the positive accomplishments of the
northern tribes: of the Josephites in West Jordan (Josh. 17:14–18), of Manasseh in
East Jordan (Num. 32:39,41–42; Josh. 13:13), of Benjamin and/or Ephraim (Josh.
10:6–11,15), and of Naphtali (Josh. 11:5–10,11b,13), and of Dan (Josh. 19:47),
and perhaps of Reuben and Gad (Num. 32:34–38). This suggests that the southern editor, perhaps J himself, cut out annals that would have had the effect of
eclipsing or at least equalling the military accomplishments of Judah. Such comprehensive but terse summations of each tribe's achievements in land-taking
corresponded to related compilations of tribal blessings and stories in Judges, all
of them examples of series of materials which are based on the distributive
autonomy and integrity of the separate tribes.

Still we are left with the fact that several of the extant annals do point out the
continuing existence of Canaanite cities within Israelite tribal areas. It may seem
wholly incongruous that annals which memorialize the bases of power in the
several tribes would have anything to say about the limitations on tribal achievement. How could such "admissions of failure" be helpful in securing tribal rights
against the central government of David? Here I think we have to recognize that
the Israelite tribes who covenanted together in Canaan did not intend to drive out
all Canaanites; or at least they were fully aware that they simply were in no position
to capture all of the fortified Canaanite cities. Their practical aim was to secure
independent zones of socioeconomic productivity free from political domination
by adjacent Canaanite city-states. Therefore, I do not believe that it was in itself a
sign of failure, nor even of theological dereliction, to recount that Canaanite
city-states still survived in Israel. Of course that suggestion of weakness and
dereliction shadows the present formulation of Judges 1, followed up as it is by the
moralizing of 2:1–5 and set within the overall moral-theological critique of D. But
the original point of the tribal elders in recounting the limited achievements could
well have been to underline the incredible tenacity of tribes which, unlike the less
exposed Judah, had to coexist for a long time in the very shadow of great and
powerful Canaanite city-states. Such coexistence could imply strength in apparent
weakness (cf., e.g., the metaphor of Issachar as a strong ass which bows to do
forced labor, Genesis 49:14–15). It could mean that the power of the Canaanite

strongholds over the rural and village areas taken by Israel was effectively neutralized and that, as Judges 4—5 indicate, the Canaanite cities were in some
instances virtual islands in a sea of Israelite resistance.

It is at this point that my earlier suggestion about a stage in the "negative" annals
which did not know of David's conquest of Canaan becomes especially pertinent.
When the tribal elders gathered to make David king over them, they had in mind
one chief project: to drive back the Philistines from the highlands permanently,
for since the death of Saul it was problematic whether a free Israel could continue
to exist in the face of the Philistine encroachment. In such a context, the older
Canaanite inhabitants of the land were not the primary enemy. Not only were they
no immediate threat, except as the Philistines might enlist them as allies against
Israel; it is even reported rather cryptically in I Samuel 7:14 that the Philistines
had the effect of driving the Israelites and the Canaanites together: "There was
peace also between Israel and the Amorites." The version of the annals as a
memorial of tribal historico-territorial rights, if drawn up at David's elevation to
leadership over all Israel, would not even have contemplated the *capture* of
specifically Canaanite cities (in contrast to those that had been taken over by the
invading Philistines), much less their *incorporation* into Israel or their *submission to
corvée*. Both the historical setting and the formal literary considerations agree in
suggesting that it was the southern editor who proleptically read the Davidic
policy of forced labor into the earlier histories of the tribes.

In terms of our analysis of the sources of Joshua-Judges for reconstructing the
Israelite settlement, we now see how limited even Judges 1 is for that purpose. It is
historical in form. It preserves memories in a more concrete and less harmonized
form than can be found elsewhere in the settlement traditions and in this respect
corresponds measurably to the concrete and uncentralized form of the tribal
blessings in Genesis 49 and Deuteronomy 33. But the focus and fulcrum of Judges
1, as it lies before us, is the Davidic monarchy, not only for the southern editor but
even for the tribal elders who we believe assembled the memorial source behind
Judges 1. From the monarchy this memorial source reached backward, with
greater or lesser fullness and with greater or lesser degrees of historical exactitude, to pull together what could be recollected of individual tribal settlements
and land-takings. The results are so meager not only because the full memorial
source has not survived editing but because its access to the history of the settlement and its impetus to record the settlement were both sharply circumscribed by
its setting. That setting, we repeat, did not call for a complete interconnected
account of the several tribal histories in all available detail; rather, it called for a
terse specification of the indigenous territorial strength of each of the tribes as
covenanting components in the founding of the monarchy of David.

18

Sociohistoric Sketch of Major Tradition Types

It remains to pull together the separate lines of tradition analysis we have explored by examining how the different tradition types in Joshua and Judges developed and interacted within the wider historical and social settings of Israel down to the time of the Deuteronomist. We shall look at the stages in the formation of the major corpora of traditions in Joshua-Judges, from their origins both cultic and political, down to their final incorporation in the great D literary history of Deuteronomy through Kings. In the process of this summary, we shall also offer tentative suggestions on the thorny matter of the relation between J/E and D in their various treatments of the older materials that eventually found their way into Joshua and Judges.

We have distinguished the following major blocs of traditions in Joshua and Judges that are relevant to the history of the conquest or settlement of Canaan by Israel:

A complex of centralized conquest stories giving the impression of a united Israelite seizure of the entire land of Canaan. On examination, however, the complex turns out to be a report of the seizure of Benjaminite territory, with attached references to a campaign in the foothills of Judah and another campaign against Hazor in northern Galilee (Joshua 1—12).

A complex of localized conquest annals reporting the taking of land by at least nine tribes (and perhaps by eleven) who fought alone (or at most in pairs), the descriptions in each case being either an account of occupation of land or a statement about cities or regions that were not (could not be?) wrested from the Canaanites. In the latter case, there is the attending assumption that the tribe named had taken areas adjacent to the unconquered Canaanites (Judges 1 and cognate traditions in Numbers and Joshua).

A complex of land allotment traditions composed of regions occupied, boundary inventories, and city lists for the respective tribes (omitting landless Levi) and purporting to survey the entire holdings of united Israel prior to the death of Joshua (Joshua 13—19).

A complex of localized stories of victories led by "judges" who headed various sub-groups of united Israel against their enemies, or fought alone (Shamgar and Samson?), in the period following the death of Joshua but before the rise of the monarchy (Judges 3—16 and cognate materials in I Samuel).

The rise and fortunes of these blocs of tradition will now be synthesized in accordance with the available cultic-ideological and literary-critical data.

18.1 Centralized Conquest Stories

The basis of the conquest complex in Joshua 1—12 was a localized account of the occupation of its territory by the tribe of Benjamin, probably with the help of the Joseph tribes and their Ephraimite leader Joshua. Whatever actual settlement history underlies the account, it took its present form around a cultic ceremony involving a procession across the Jordan and around Jericho, probably rooted in the sanctuary at Gilgal. This Benjaminite account became the skeleton for developing narratives which illustrated the last of the old canonical centralized cultic themes, namely, the Leading into Canaan; and, accordingly, the whole was developed so that it seemed to be an account of the conquest of all Canaan by united Israel. Because of the dominant centralized conception of conquest in this complex, it is reasonable to believe that an urform of expanded Benjaminite cultic legends already existed within the common groundwork that J and E had at hand when they prepared their written versions of the beginnings of Israel.

The centralized cult which shaped this narrative sequence was north Israelite, and its core was apparently developed at a time before even the Galilean tribes had joined united Israel; certainly before Judah joined the community of Yahwistic faith. The narrative sequence of the conquest was exclusively that of the Joseph tribes in central Canaan, telling as it did of a penetration into Canaan across the Jordan in the region north of Jerusalem. But this primary account of the Joseph tribes has been expanded by more circumstantial references to conquests in the Judean foothills and around Hebron, as well as in northern Galilee. These expansions are best explained as attempts to extend the original core of the conquest tradition so as to include references to later converts to united Israel in order to lend greater plausibility to the claim that a united conquest of all Israel was here attested. Whether this expansion had already occurred in the common groundwork preceding J and E or was undertaken later is uncertain, although I incline to the latter opinion.

While the old Benjaminite cult narratives, expanded by the Joseph tribes, early became the official centralized cult recital of the basic theme of land-taking, it was not a totally satisfactory fleshing out of the basic theme. In the case of all the earlier basic themes of the centralized traditions, a limited geographical locale was no difficulty. The experiences of a small family or band of people under the leadership of patriarchs were easily pictured as localized in this or that region of Canaan. It was assumed that the patriarchal group moved around; and so Abraham was connected primarily with Hebron, Isaac with Beersheba, and Jacob with Bethel, Shechem, and Penuel. The fortunes of the matured tribes as they fled Egypt, crossed the wilderness, and penetrated Transjordan likewise presented no insuperable problems of geographical locale. It was assumed that the tribes travelled together and the various places mentioned in the accounts were so many points on a connected itinerary from Egypt to Canaan.

With the entrance into Canaan, the geography of the conquest became an urgent matter. It was now far less convincing to represent the conquest of all the Canaanite highlands merely by telling about victories in Benjamin and adjacent areas. Tribes using the Benjaminite-Josephite conquest stories would very well know that their own unique histories of seizing and occupying the land were not directly referred to by those stories. The more distinctive memories of separate tribal-land seizures were of events sufficiently recent that the non-Josephite tribes could hardly be satisfied with a centralized version of the land-taking which focused so largely on the Benjaminite-Josephite campaigns. Nonetheless, the centralized cultic imprimatur on the official conquest stories was so decisive that the only accomodation made to all the other tribes was to graft onto the main stock of the narratives accounts of two thrusts by the Ephraimite Joshua, one into Judah and the other into Galilee.

This reading of the internal cult-communal tensions surrounding the amplification of the basic theme of land-taking illuminates the different ways in which J and E responded to the common groundwork version of the leading into the land. In my view Joshua 1–12 is largely E. Even where parallel sources show themselves, there are no sustained marks of J. Rather it appears that J refused to accept the groundwork's Josephite formulation of the narratives concerning the basic theme of land-taking. Instead he went his own way in substituting a body of localized land-taking accounts in which he gave Judah the prominent position, namely, the localized conquest annals of Judges 1. He could display this independence because the Davidic-Solomonic monarchy under which he wrote was based in Judah and he did not feel obligated to accept the Josephite domination of the received centralized tradition at this point. Instead, he drew on another source which called attention to the several separate tribal land-acquisitions, coordinated only in that there was collective consultation among the tribes as to the timing of their military campaigns (according to Judges 1:1–3).

When E wrote his version of the old canonical historical traditions, the monarchy had already divided into southern and northern branches. He operated within an independent northern kingdom, but he strove to shape the traditions so that they would express the fundamental cult-communal unity of all Israel in spite of its political rupture into two kingdoms. He aimed to show that the Davidic regime in the south was only a political episode in the one history of united Israel and that the true carriers of Yahwism had been overwhelmingly north Israelite. He adhered, therefore, to the old canonical version of the land-taking with its slanted Josephite cast. It is my suggestion that E first expanded the Josephite narrative so as to include the references to originally independent Galilean and

Judean campaigns, which he scrupulously attributed to the Ephraimite Joshua. By this "concession" to the far northern and southern tribes, E sought to assert the abiding cult-cummunal unity of all Israelites with its primary locus in the Joseph tribes. It is probable that in making these expansions, E drew in part upon the same fund of localized conquest annals that J had employed (e.g., in Joshua 10 and 11), but instead of accepting a localized framework which would have stressed the separate occupation histories of the tribes, he adhered to the old canonical centralized pattern. In extending the geographical scope of the recounted conquest, E maintained the conception of all the tribes at work in all the campaigns directed by the national leader Joshua.

18.2 Localized Settlement "Annals"

The basis of these annalistic summaries of individual tribal occupations of land was in the divergent sub-histories of the various member groups in Israel. It was precisely because of these peculiar sub-histories of land-taking that the various Israelite groups could collectively identify with the basic theme of land-taking. There was an element of commonality in all the actions: a socially and politically insurgent people had carved out living space of their own. But there were idiosyncratic features in the land-acquisition of each tribe, and these differences were glossed over in the centralized account so decisively stamped by Benjaminite and Josephite experience. The centralized cult converted one set of such recollections, concerning the achievements of Josephites and Benjaminites, into the standardized narrative-complex which fleshed out the basic theme. The remaining sub-histories, unable to penetrate the centralized account, survived nonetheless in the traditions of the separate tribes.

In the struggle to determine the authoritative version of the occupation of the land, the Joseph tribes asserted their dominance through the cultic-ideological production of an account in which their peculiar history of land-taking and their leader Joshua had the central place. Why should the Joseph tribes have been so dominating on this matter? Two factors seem to have been at work. One was the close link between the Joseph tribes and the Levites. This is often explained on the theory that the Levites and Joseph tribes were together in Egypt and entered Canaan together after the exodus.[118] The close link can be as well explained, however, by regarding the Joseph tribes as the first converts to Levitical Yahwism following the penetration of Canaan by the Levites. In these circumstances the Levites, who had so much to do with shaping the centralized traditions, gave priority to Josephite traditions as the most suitable vehicles for celebrating an all-Israelite conquest. A second factor, closely related to the first, was that the Josephite military campaigns in the territory north of Jerusalem were apparently the critical military catalyst that sparked the formation of Israel.[119] The tribal blessings preserve the memory of Josephite military prowess in those early days of the occupation (Gen. 49:23–24; Deut. 33:17). In a unique manner the land-taking by those one or two or three tribes (depending on whether we include Benjamin and whether we treat Joseph as one tribe or subdivided into Ephraim and Manasseh) was decisive in releasing a chain of events that energized all the tribes and brought them together as unified Israel. Therefore, the triumph of the Josephite narratives in the official account was not arbitrary but rooted in cultic, political, and military realities.

Still, the other tribes, while acknowledging the ascendancy of Joseph tribes and unwilling to dissolve the Israelite union, continued to cherish their own separate accounts of how they came into possession of their lands. These traditions lived in the various tribes as supplementary pieces which could be recited as correctives to the Josephite bias of the centralized traditions. And it is evident that the Joseph tribes themselves cultivated such traditions (e.g. Josh. 17:14–18; Judg. 1:22–28). Whether they were ever gathered together as a total "counter-program" to the centralized version of land-taking prior to the monarchy is not determinable, but, even as uncoordinated pieces, they served to keep alive alternate and more historically diversified ways of looking at Israel's settlement in Canaan.

An early gathering of the annals as a collection, which began their coordination and revision, was in the negotiations between the elders of the tribes and David at the foundation of his rule over all Israel. The tribes were jealous of their autonomy and fearful of autocratic rule by a monarch, even if, as seems likely, at the beginning David was installed merely as a lifelong commander-in-chief. Certain autocratic tendencies in Saul had been noted, and the elders did not wish to leave David unfettered. A collection of old tribal annals by these elders would strengthen their own resolve and would serve notice on David that he was only the leader of the old tribal league. Tribes who had earned their place in the Israelite community by such conquests and tenacious holding operations could better stand up against a leader who might overextend his claims.

The memorial source, setting on record the occupation histories of the tribes severally, was then taken up into the larger centralized history of early Israel by the J writer. Working out of the context of the united monarchy, the J traditionist was obligated, as Noth has convincingly argued, to repeat the canonical basic themes of the old cult. He was, however, unhappy with the canonical cult account of the land-taking, which was so patently a north Israelite account. In this he shared the misgivings which had originally prompted the preservation of parallel conquest annals. Knowing these old localized accounts in the form collected as a memorial addressed to the body of tribal elders who covenanted with David, J took them over for his purposes. In place of the substratum of what now appears as the narrative-complex of Joshua 1—12 worked up by E and passed on to D, J inserted the present Judges 1, which was condensed from a source considerably larger in scope, as indicated by the scattered cognate and parallel traditions in Numbers, Joshua, and the last chapters of Judges.

In substituting the localized conquest annals for the centralized conquest narratives, J accomplished two things: he undercut the north Israelite hegemony of the centralized conquest traditions, and he robbed the tribal elders of their use of the annalistic summaries as a bill of rights against the central monarchy. Since no intertribal covenant with Solomon is reported, it seems that the memorial source was already eclipsed in importance and value. J could safely revive it, while arranging the materials in such a way that Judah took the lead in the conquest and showed the greatest successes. The result was a southern-oriented, markedly truncated version of the memorial source. Subsequently, in part due to the work of E, portions of the J-edited conquest annals were worked into the centralized account in Numbers and Joshua.

Admittedly tentative as this proposal is, it throws light upon the baffling question: Why did the J/E/P version of the old canonical historical traditions in Genesis through Numbers almost completely lack narrative filler material concerning the basic theme of the Leading into Canaan? We have argued that J and E did not originally lack narrative materials concerning the theme of the land-taking; it was simply that they had different sets of materials. The conflict over what should be the proper form of the conquest narratives to elucidate the Israelite land-taking theme probably explains in large measure why the stories were lifted from J and E and worked into D.

The transfer of the land-taking narratives and annals from J and E into the D complex took place because the proper form of the basic theme of Leading into Canaan was so disputed by the two contradictory versions of J and E that D decided to take on the task of resolving the contradiction. The fall of the northern kingdom had eliminated the political rivalry of the two Israelite states and thus prompted the Deuteronomist to resolve the old historical conflict that was no longer a live political conflict. It is possible that the initial steps in the resolution were taken by an editor of J/E in the period between the fall of the north and the Deuteronomic history. I am uncertain of the existence of this editor as distinguishable from the editor of J/E/P. Even if there was a J/E editor preceding the J/E/P editor, that would not change the situation in principle. The Deuteronomic historian, with or without precedent, took over those two types of conquest accounts and arranged them in his narrative in a schematic way, reducing the tension between them by grouping the centralized narratives in the period before the death of Joshua. This feat was consonant with the Deuteronomist's aim of concentrating on the occupation of the land as the prologue to Israel's long history in Canaan down to the exile. By synthesizing the two conquest complexes with their separate cultic-political histories, he was able to close an old debate that was no longer necessary and, in the process, marshal all the surviving traditions about Israel's formation in the land within a set of comprehensive cultic-theological rubrics.

I am inclined to think, furthermore, that P found D's harmonization of the disparate conquest complexes of J and E so satisfying that he deleted entirely the J/E conquest stories from his own harmonization of J/E in Genesis through Numbers (except for the scraps in Numbers 32:34–38,39,41–42, which probably were retained because P visualized them as belonging to the Transjordan conquests, which he does recite). Alternatively, if J/E had been fused in an earlier edition, P simply deleted that segment of the story which overlapped with the D recension.

18.3 Land Allotment Traditions

As opposed to the other major blocs of tradition in Joshua-Judges, I have been unable to establish any certain premonarchic origin for the land allotment traditions. A possible old nucleus lay in clan rosters of the militia of the intertribal league which, as clans were identified with villages, laid the foundation for administrative city lists. Otherwise, there seems to have been no old cultic context for allotment traditions. If there was periodic reapportionment of land in old Israel, the reapportionments were all *within* tribes rather than *between* tribes. It is true that tribal settlement zones changed over the several decades before the monarchy and the composition of the tribal sub-units changed to some extent in that period. But in no instances that I can determine were the tribal land holdings a matter of conflict. The reported intertribal disputes in premonarchic Israel had to do with slights in warfare (Judg. 8:1–3; 12:1–6) or with real or alleged infractions of customary law (Josh. 22:7–34; Judg. 20:18,31,35a,36). There were quarrels and occasional open fighting between tribes on these points at issue, but there is no hard evidence that tribes fought one another over land or disputed over their territorial boundaries.

Consequently, a firm beginning for the allotment traditions is best assigned to the rise of the monarchy, when the tribal holdings as the natural concomitants of the socioeconomic components of premonarchic Israel were transformed into administrative districts in David's kingdom. The "tribes," newly delineated as territorially fixed entities, became the basis for consolidating previously Canaanite and Philistine regions and populations into the Israelite state. The "boundaries," which had once existed between tribes simply as the points where the people of one tribe lived contiguously with the people of another tribe, now became political dividers for designating the internal articulation of the centralized state apparatus.

This being the case, the tribal allotments never belonged to the old canonical traditions as filler materials for the basic theme of Leading into the Land. At most, the centralized basic theme of Leading into Canaan may have concluded with some general reference to the tribes taking their respective holdings. An early version of what now appears in the frameworks of the allotment lists in which

Joshua assigns the land by lot may have been included in the old canonical résumé. But if it was, the meaning of that "allotment" was simply the securing to each tribe of autonomous control over its land-holdings as assigned internally by family and "clan" divisions. It was a way of saying: All the tribes found a home in the land and settled down to a life of autonomous economic self-development based on their respective land-holdings.

I have suggested that the allotment lists of Joshua 13—19 are only a truncated revised form of the parent source, or sources, which I assume to have been administrative documents filed in the state archives at Jerusalem. Since I deny that they were a part of the filler material for the basic theme of Leading into Canaan, the question remains: At what stage was the present form of the material drawn from the state archives and retrojected into the period of Joshua?

Assuming the administrative prototypes of Joshua 13—19 to have been preserved in the state archives in Jerusalem, J could easily have had access to them. E, on the other hand, as a northerner, would not have had access to the state archives in Jerusalem. Presumably, however, any initial write-up of the allotment lists by J would have been available to E. He could perhaps also have come across copies of the originals surviving in the north from Davidic times, or even in use in the northern kingdom after the abolition of the Solomonic administrative system. An assumed southern editor of J/E or D himself could, like J, also have had access to the Jerusalem archives. A tentative reconstruction of the tradition history of Joshua 13—19 is as follows: after Solomon revised the administrative divisions of the kingdom, the administrative lists underlying Joshua 13—19 were nonfunctional. But while they were administratively defunct, except perhaps for a revival of some decades in the administration of the northern kingdom prior to Omri's centralization of power at Samaria, they did suggest to the literary traditionists a range of material which could describe the scope of the Israelite occupation. J may well have been the first to include the former administrative lists in his history in the altered form of allotment lists. If so, they stood prior to the conquest annals and described the areas which each tribe claimed for itself but which then had to be taken by force. It is possible that the reference to Joshua allotting the tribal land grants at Gilgal (Josh. 14:6) is a trace of the J framework of the allotment traditions. After the allotment, Joshua died at Gilgal, the tribes drew up a plan for the order of their attacks on their several assigned territories (Judg. 1:1–3), and only then did the people move up into the hill country, from Gilgal to Bochim near Bethel (Judg. 2:1). E took over the allotment tradition and worked it into his version of the conquest narratives, taking pains to reverse J's order. Whereas for J the sequence was allotment of land followed by localized conquest, for E the sequence was unified conquest followed by allotment of land. D "harmonized" the two variant versions of land-taking by letting the E conquest narrative and the J conquest annals stand, with the allotment lists placed between, the patent discrepancies being "rationalized" by claiming Joshua as the leader of the unified conquest (consonant with E), and the several tribes as independent conquerors of their own lands "after the death of Joshua" (consonant with J).

The disorder and incompleteness of the allotment lists reflects both the fact that the original political context of their parent administrative texts was soon lost and the fact that they underwent revision many times as they were variously handled by learned collectors and by J, E, and D. From the moment that the texts were projected as allotment lists rather than as administrative lists, the primary historico-territorial conditions of David's kingdom which produced the texts in the first place were speedily lost to memory. It is obvious, therefore, that even the most solid political documents can be employed by those who preserve and transmit them with very different purposes than were in the mind of those who wrote the original documents.

18.4 Localized Stories of Victories by "Judges"

The basis of these stories was the struggle of sub-groups in Israel to secure a firm hold on their land in the face of repeated threats from indigenous Canaanites and from extra-Canaanite enemies pressing in from the desert or from Transjordan and later, in the case of the Philistines, from the coastal plain. The stories escaped inclusion in the centralized cult, but they presuppose that cult in their assumption that Israel is a unity and in their saturation with old naive Yahwistic beliefs and practices. They do not, on the other hand, directly recount the action of the centralized cult, and in that sense are laicized and secular. Their focus is on the military defense of sub-sections of Israel and on internal political struggles. While they presuppose a unified entity Israel, we cannot determine from these stories the exact composition of Israel. The most complete roster of tribes is only loosely connected with the stories; in the song of triumph in Judges 5, ten Israelite segments are named, six of them actually having participated in the battle. In the stories proper, far fewer tribes are involved in the military campaigns. Nor do the stories portray anything other than the most arbitrary and formalistic chronological sequence. The origins of the stories were discrete, and the present ordering, whether by a pre-D editor or by D himself, shows no demonstrable connection with ancient tradition. Internally, some of the stories contain more exact chronological data, but they do not permit establishing firm temporal correlations between or among the stories.

How do the stories of the judges stand in relation to the conquest narratives and the conquest annals? They share at a very broad level in common historico-territorial and military interests. The differences, however, are pronounced. The stories of the judges are of course uncentralized, and thus clearly set off from Joshua 1—12; but that is also the case with Judges 1. In what way are the stories of the judges distinguishable from both kinds of conquest reports, other than the literary fact that they are grouped separately by the Deuteronomist?

The conquest reports are controlled by a basic concern with the question: How did Israel get its land in the first place? All reported spatio-temporal details are strictly subordinated to that question of the original tribal acquisitions of land. Even though the conquest annals are localized in their origins and retain a description of separate tribal actions, as soon as they became a collection they were, ironically, dominated by the very centralized notion of conquest which they intended to loosen up and diversify. Their reason for existence as a collection was to give an alternative account of the conquest to that offered in the centralized theme of Leading into Canaan. It is entirely otherwise with the stories of the judges. They did not arise in opposition to the centralized conquest narratives nor even as a supplement to them, and that means that they were not intended to be read as describing in more detail the events described generally in conquest narratives or annals. The generation of Israelites who first came into Canaan, who first formed the tribal confederacy, are nowhere in view in these stories of the judges. The basic concern is the query: How did Israel, once established as an entity in the land, maintain itself? The stories do not aim at giving a rounded account of all actions taken in Israel's defense, or of all internal struggles. They are selectively full or selectively terse by turns. While the result is to report activities by many of the tribes, they do not appear to have been written as a totality with a view to comprehensiveness in mind, as was the case conceptually both with the conquest narratives and the conquest annals.

The most distinctive thing about the stories of the judges, moreover, is their circumstantial military-political detail. They tell of battles and efforts at developing adequate leadership in the face of local and tribal divisiveness. These military-political features predominate even when aspects of the stories are shaped by cult theophany and legend (as in the Gideon story) and by folk motifs (as in the Samson story). The distinctive flavor of the stories can best be explained if we posit that they developed outside the primary centralized cult where the theophany, covenant, historical recital, and law-giving were celebrated. Their roots were more diversified. In part, their stimulus was in the occasional cultic activity of preparation for war and celebration after war (as is true also of the songs of triumph); and in part in local tribal settings where stories of particular recent events which fell temporally outside the scope of the basic themes were recited, in company perhaps with the tribal blessings. For with those blessings the stories in Judges share concreteness of locality, robustness of spirit, and even at times a coarse jocularity.

Finally, the stories of the judges show a more explicitly political concern with internal order than do the conquest traditions. D grasps this concern with internal order under the rubric of "judges." Admittedly, it is an extremely moot question as to exactly what D and his sources meant by "judges" who led battles (major judges) and "judges" who ruled over all Israel (minor judges), the two types appearing in markedly differing guises and functioning in very incompletely delineated historical contexts. But pending some conclusions about the office (s) of "judge" in old Israel, I should at least like to emphasize that the preoccupation of the D edition with "judges" seems to be an accurate clue as to the basic character of the stories. They are concerned in a rather chaotic and untheoretical way with how the members of Israel will select leaders to get the things done that have to be done without submitting to hierarchic and centralized rule. The conquest narratives, by contrast, are simply not interested in that question of internal leadership. Either Joshua does it all or the separate tribes are capable of taking care of matters on their own, with no attention to how leaders are chosen, or at what costs to the internal peace of the community. The stories of the judges, in their diversified and unsystematic ways, reflect a community very much involved in internal examination and experimentation in modes of leadership.

Apparently some of the stories were gathered in a sequence by a pre-D editor or traditionist.[120] The Samson stories stand apart from the preceding judges stories both in the hero's solo activity and in the folk motifs developed. The final two stories (Judg. 17—18, 19—21) do not tell of judges at all and have not even been brought within the pan-Israelite moral-theological framework of D, except in a very loose manner by the editorial note "in those days there was no king in Israel" (18:1; 19:1; 21:25). They can best be understood as a supplement to the judges stories, probably added in the final D edition. The last episode, that of the Benjaminite outrage, is the one episode in the book that is highly centralized; and it was apparently placed here to show that, in extremity, the unified action of all Israel could still be elicited.

Although there is some evidence for two or three sources in certain of the stories, there is no reason to believe that they are either J or E. I believe that they developed independently of J and E, in a manner similar to the complexes of Elijah and Elisha stories, which show stylistic affinities with E but are not on that account to be thought of as belonging to the E stratum. They had their home in localized tribal memories and recitals of events cherished for their demonstration of the vigor and autonomy of the tribes. Developed away from the monarchic centers, they reflected and buttressed the independent populist spirit of later Israelites who felt distant from or in outright conflict with the monarchy. The Deuteronomic historian found these stories eminently suitable to his overall view, somewhat naively it must be observed, since they unabashedly report beliefs and practices inconsistent with his late reformist understanding of Israelite religion. Whatever D could not countenance in the stories, he could understand as part of early Israel's inveterate "apostasy," of which it just as repeatedly "repented" so that, with each successive oppression, God could send a new judge to deliver the people.

In later sections of this study we shall analyze additional traditions of Joshua and Judges in connection with particular historical and sociological problems, but enough has been established to bear out our contention that Israel's conquest or settlement traditions, even where they are most closely in touch with lived experiences, are in fact refracted history—indeed, a collage of many histories. We have tried to give flesh and bone to that claim and to suggest in specific cases how a blend of literary-critical, form-critical, and tradition-historical methods is necessary in order to sort through the traditions for their historical pertinence. The modesty and tentativeness of the historical results for the Israelite settlement should be patent. Yet we have begun to gather sufficient data to encourage historical reconstruction, in spite of all the gaps, ambiguities, and caveats. We are beginning to form a picture of early Israel as a mutant social system taking form in the Canaanite highlands between 1250 and 1000 B.C. The fact is that some reconstructions of the settlement and formation of Israel are more consistent with the sources in toto than are others. To the task of explicating and evaluating the current models of the settlement we shall turn our attention in Part V.

PART V

Models of the Israelite Settlement in Canaan

19

A Preliminary View

We have initially surveyed and evaluated the biblical sources for premonarchic Israel, and more precisely, the traditions of Joshua and Judges concerning the Israelite occupation of Canaan. How is the evidence in those books concerning an Israelite "conquest" or "settlement" of Canaan to be construed? Three primary explanatory models have been proposed. It has been argued that Israel took Canaan by a massive, unified military conquest. Alternatively, it has been contended that Israel occupied Canaan by peaceful infiltration, treaty-making, and natural population growth. In contrast to both of these proposals, it has been more recently claimed that Israel was in fact that component of the native Canaanite populace which revolted against the city-state overlords and established its own sociopolitical order and religion.

For purposes of analysis we shall pose these as three distinct theoretical models. In actual fact they are seldom, if ever, held in absolute distinction from one another. Almost invariably, one model is advanced as primary with allowance for elements of validity in one or both of the other models. The conquest model is the oldest, and the one superficially most consonant with the traditional claims of the Bible as set forth in the centralized cultic-ideological schema. The immigration model has been the most widely championed view of critical biblical scholars since early in this century. The revolt model has only recently been advanced, and then only in such general terms that many questions raised by it have not been systematically examined. Initially our aim will be to state the models as sharply as possible as "pure types" and then to entertain the possibility that a more adequate model may require a new synthesis of elements from two, or even all three, of the current models.

Our method will be to describe the main outlines of each model without attempting to go into all the variants and nuances which particular advocates have introduced. Then we shall muster the chief evidence for and against the model. In doing so, attention will be paid to nonbiblical evidence, both material archaeological remains and extrabiblical literary and sociocultural data. Only after the analysis of all three models will we indicate how the narrow focus on methods of settlement must be enlarged to an examination of the formation of Israel's social system if a satisfactory settlement model is to be developed.

20

The Conquest Model

The conquest model of the Israelite occupation seems at first blush to be the one and only way of understanding Israel's sudden emergence in Canaan. It posits an invasion of Canaan from Transjordan toward the end of the thirteenth century B.C.[121] The twelve tribes of Israel are viewed as joined in a concerted campaign to conquer and to destroy the inhabitants of Canaan. The model conceives a total displacement of population, so that Israel, after annihilating the previous residents, was able to fill the vacuum with its own distinctive culture and religion. The conquest occurred within one generation—indeed, over the span of a few years—in three campaigns in the center, south, and north of Canaan. This aspect of the traditional biblical account is continuous with the view that Moses was leader of twelve-tribe Israel in the exodus and in the wilderness. The conquest ended with Israel dividing up the conquered territories into tribal homelands which were immediately occupied by the twelve tribes—excluding landless Levi, which was granted settlements among all the tribes.

Such a conception of total and rapid conquest was the earliest one to develop in Israel's own quasi-historical traditions. At least it was the conception that dominated the telling of the events of occupation in the Book of Joshua and in later biblical books which allude to, or presuppose, those events. In premonarchic times the conquest model became the official centralized model in Israelite circles, although not without dissent in the development of alternative localized traditions outside the centralized cult. A cursory reading of the Bible supports the conquest theory to such an extent that generations of readers never even considered another possibility. A typical biblical, centralized summary puts it succinctly: "So Joshua defeated the whole land, the hill country and the Negeb and the lowland and the slopes, and all their kings; he left none remaining, but utterly destroyed all that breathed, as the LORD God of Israel commanded" (Josh. 10:40). Nothing could seem more conclusive. Thus the solidest piece of evidence for the conquest model is its great antiquity, deeply rooted in the old Israelite traditions.

Another line of evidence for the conquest typology is the marked division running throughout the biblical tradition between Canaanite and Israelite. With few exceptions, Canaanite culture and religion are condemned and rejected by the most ancient Israelite sources. This sharp demarcation between Canaan and Israel, between Baal's sphere and Yahweh's sphere, appears to give credence to an original enmity between the two religiocultural and political worlds. In other words, it does not seem that the polarization of Canaan vs. Israel is merely a late traditional creation. The prophets accept it as a given datum of the tradition. Where did the polarization arise if not in an initial hostility between the two peoples, in a death struggle to possess the same land? If Israel entered the land peacefully and expanded by infiltration, treaty, and intermarriage, how can we possibly explain the utter rejection of all things Canaanite in Israel's traditions? And is it not still more absurd to conjecture that Israel was composed of former Canaanites in the face of the traditional Israelite adamancy against Canaan and all that it symbolized? A plain reading of the basic Israelite stance toward all things Canaanite seems to give additional weighty support to the explicit biblical accounts of a brief and decisive military victory over the Canaanites.

Since early in the twentieth century a whole new category of evidence has appeared to buttress the conquest theory, namely, the evidence of archaeology. Archaeology is the recovery of the material remains of the past, from which inferences are drawn about the culture and history of the people who left the remains. Archaeology speaks most directly of the culture as exhibited in foundations, walls, buildings, statues, cult objects, weapons, tools, ornamentation, metals, pottery, and bones. When we are fortunate, the remains may include written materials, even extended texts. But the ratio of written evidence to material evidence is normally low, and archaeology's contribution to the study of history is thus typically less direct than its contribution to the study of culture. The literary remains must be correlated with already existing literary sources if they are to become direct historical testimonies. Even so, the material remains at each site, in themselves historically mute, may be so coordinated and compared with remains of similar or related types in other places, that historical conclusions otherwise arrived at can be checked out and, in certain respects, even refined. The limits and appropriateness of this or that inference drawn from archaeology can only be judged in particular cases. The limitations of archaeology, frequently overlooked by the popular adulation accorded its sensational finds, will have to be borne in mind whenever we assess its pertinence for our study. For the moment it can be said that archaeology does contribute importantly to historical reconstruction, and on some points decisively, and therefore we must incorporate its conclusions in our analysis.[122]

Archaeological data said to support the conquest model are of two broad types: (1) evidence for widespread destruction of Canaanite cities in the approximate period when Israel is believed to have entered the land; and (2) evidence for a new and homogeneous type of occupation at some of the destroyed sites such that it can be connected with the Israelites.[123] In short, material evidence, which can sometimes be dated to within a very few years, argues for the cessation of Canaanite culture in large parts of Canaan in the period 1230–1200 B.C. and for the introduction of Israelite culture in the same areas immediately thereafter. That is the generalized claim. Let us view some of the details.

Ancient Near Eastern cities developed in successive levels of occupation on the same site. The artificial mounds (or tells) are excavated in layers which are dated primarily by a refined analysis of the evolution of pottery types, which in turn are dated in relation to inscriptional materials. Palestinian archaeology has excavated a number of mounds that may be identified with some degree of confidence as particular cities known to us from biblical and other ancient literary texts. Between layers of occupation it is often possible to distinguish traces of destruction in ashes and debris. These achievements of archaeological technique permit and even demand attempts to correlate the evidence from the mounds with the evidence from the Bible and other extant sources. That is the background from which archaeology contributes its part in answering the question: How did Israel come to control the land of Canaan?

A series of excavated mounds, identified as particular ancient cities with a high degree of probability, show evidence of having been extensively or totally destroyed during the late thirteenth and early twelfth centuries B.C.[124] These cities, are, from north to south, *Hazor* (Tell el-Qedaḥ), *Megiddo* (Tell el-Mutesellim), *Succoth* (Tell Deir 'Allā), *Bethel* (Beitîn), *Beth Shemesh* (Tell er-Remeileh), *Ashdod* (Esdûd), *Lachish* (Tell ed-Duweir), *Eglon* (Tell el-Ḥesî), and *Debir* or *Kiriath-Sepher* Tell Beit Mirsim or Khirbet Rabud).[125] Of these cities, four are specifically said to have been destroyed by Joshua: *Hazor* (Josh. 11:10–11), *Lachish* (Josh. 10:31–33), *Eglon* (Josh. 10:34–35), and *Debir* (Josh. 10:38–39), and a fifth city, *Bethel,* is said to have been taken by the house of Joseph (Judg. 1:22–26). It was tempting for biblical historians to conclude that here was independent material evidence for the validity of the biblical picture of Israel's conquest of the land.

The force of the archaeological support for conquest was further enhanced by certain negative evidence. Some cities which either are omitted from the accounts of the conquest—or are specifically said *not* to have been conquered by Joshua—have on excavation, shown no signs of destruction in the thirteenth century. For example, *Gibeon* (el-Jîb), which entered a client treaty relation with Israel (Josh. 9), showed no signs of destruction in the period. *Taanach* (Tell Taʻannak), not taken by Israel in Joshua's day (Judg. 1:27), was destroyed only about 1125 B.C. *Shechem* (Tell Balâṭah), whose capture is unmentioned—even though Joshua holds a tribal assembly within or near the city (Josh. 24)—reveals unbroken occupation, without physical disruption, from Late Bronze down to about 1100 B.C. *Jerusalem* (el-Quds), untaken by Israel until David's time (Josh. 15:63; II Sam. 5:6–9), insofar as limited excavations indicate, was not destroyed in the period and its Middle Bronze II walls survived to be used by David. *Beth-shean* (Tell el-Ḥuṣn), like Taanach unoccupied by Manasseh until much later (Judg. 1:27–28), continued to be an Egyptian administrative center down to about 1100 B.C. *Gezer* (Tell

Jezer), whose forces were defeated by Joshua in the field while the city's capture is pointedly unmentioned (Josh. 10:33), yields no trace of Late Bronze destruction.

All in all, supporters of the conquest model find a considerable combined corroboraton of the biblical account in the archaeological evidence about the cities conquered by Joshua and the cities not taken by him. They believe that the correlation of the archaeological and biblical textual evidence is sufficiently close at enough points to validate the traditional claim of a general Israelite conquest of Canaan. Obviously, however, the evidence about cities undestroyed in the period cuts against the grain of any literal acceptance of a total conquest theory. Already the archaeological evidence can be seen to point toward considerable modifications of the conquest model as it is set forth traditionally in the centralized biblical account.

Another kind of archaeological evidence, less dramatic and slower in accumulating, is given increasing credence. That is the evidence of the type and distribution of occupation in the layers following the thirteenth-century destructions. The evidence is not so widely spread as the signs of violent destruction, or at any rate it has not been so widely observed to date, but there are sufficient data for some interpreters to see significant patterns.[126] So far the reported evidence is concentrated at four sites: *Hazor, Succoth, Bethel,* and *Debir* (possibly also *Gezer* and *Ashdod*). In each instance, following virtually total destruction, unfortified and architecturally simple, even crude, settlements appear. At Hazor there were foundations of huts and tents, silos, and crude ovens. At Succoth, encampments appeared against the surviving Late Bronze walls, accompanied by storage pits. At Bethel, there was a complete break in building plans between the destroyed city and the new occupation, although the new structures were not so crude as those at Hazor and Succoth. At Debir, a small number of much simpler houses were built on the ashes of the destruction. *Beth-shemesh* in some ways also fits the pattern, although more use was made of surviving structures; the city wall was badly repaired and the new buildings were not well constructed, while silos and cisterns from the previous level were reused.

It is claimed that, taken together, this evidence points to a culturally less advanced population living in temporary encampments or in poorly constructed houses without fortifications. Assuming the new residents to have been the destroyers of the Late Bronze cities on whose ruins they settled, it is easy to see them as the technically impoverished, "semi-nomadic" Israelites.

To these settlements springing up on destroyed sites may also be added settlements emergent on previously unoccupied sites or at places where there had been long breaks in occupation during the Late Bronze Age. New settlements appeared in the twelfth century, or slightly earlier, at *Dor* (Khirbet el-Burj), *Gibeah* (Tell el Fûl), *Beersheba* (Tell es-Saba'), *Tell'Ēṭūn* (so far no convincing biblical identification, Noth thought it was Eglon), and *Tell Radanna* (SW of Bethel, possibly biblical

Beeroth or Ataroth-[adar]). Reoccupation of sites that had been deserted for some centuries occurred at *Shiloh* (Khirbet Seilûn), *Ai* (et-Tell), *Mizpah* (Tell en-Naṣbeh), *Beth-zur* (Kirbet eṭ-Ṭubeiqah), and *Tell Masos* (near Beersheba, possibly biblical Hormah) in the twelfth and eleventh centuries. The Iron I pottery at all these sites showed continuity with the pottery from the simple encampments at Hazor and Succoth and from the crude buildings of Bethel and Debir.

Now that a large inventory of Iron Age I pottery has been amassed, and its forms in relation to what preceded and followed have been traced, some archaeologists are attempting to characterize it as a whole and to try to draw cultural and historical conclusions. One such study proposes that while the major pottery forms are continuous from Late Bronze into Iron I, certain distinctions are apparent and argue for a distinct cultural break parallel to the architectural break. Among the features noted are (1) whereas Late Bronze pottery generally ranges from cream-color to white, sometimes with a greenish cast, Iron I has more color in the buff-brown and orange range; (2) whereas Late Bronze pottery is rather finely levigated, Iron I has diverse particles, which strongly suggests different kiln techniques; and (3) whereas Late Bronze pottery of the thirteenth century includes some imported wares, often imitations, in Iron I they disappear.[127] When these typological features are joined to the stratigraphic results—that is, when the new pottery forms are compared with the preceding destruction and the new settlement habits and structures—the material evidence is seen to support the hypothesis of a general Israelite conquest of Canaan.

These claims based on archaeology depend on an elaborate network of more or less demonstrable, and some undemonstrable, premises and inferences, including generous arguments from silence. Fairly widespread destruction of Canaanite cities occurred during the late thirteenth century and the early twelfth century. Settlements appeared at once on the ruins of some of the cities and, within a century, at long deserted cities and on new sites as well. The material culture, architecturally and ceramically, shows a degree of homogeneity. The people who made these settlements are not, however, identified inscriptionally or by any distinctive artistic or cultic objects. But who can they have been if not the Israelites? The Philistines are believed not to have come in force to Palestine before about 1150 B.C. On most of the sites, Philistine pottery is not in evidence before 1150 B.C. and, when it does appear, it is of a very different type than the pottery associated with the new settlements under discussion. No other people are known to have been on the move in Palestine at this time, so by a process of elimination it appears that the ruined Canaanite cities and the new settlements were alike the work of the invading Israelites.

The case for the conquest model seems sound enough, almost overpowering, but only as long as we select our evidence with suitable discrimination. When the whole body of biblical and extrabiblical data is examined, far-reaching objections to the conquest model arise.

In the first place, the biblical traditions do not monolithically support a conquest model. We have observed that there is a striking incongruity between the one-generation, pan-Israelite conception of the conquest expressed in the centralized editorial framework of Joshua, on the one hand, and the actual traditions marshalled to illustrate it, on the other hand. In fact, were it not for the editorial sledge-hammer assertions about a total conquest, the stories themselves easily give us a very different impression. The five major narratives about the conquest of the Canaanite territories report the following: (1) capture of Jericho (Josh. 6); (2) capture of Ai (Josh. 8); (3) client treaty with Gibeon, Chephirah, Beeroth, and Kiriath-jearim subordinated to Israel (Josh. 9); (4) capture of Makkedah, Libnah, Lachish, Eglon, Hebron, and Debir (Josh. 10); (5) capture of Hazor (Josh. 11). Far from being a comprehensive inventory of a general conquest, these narratives in actuality tell about military activity in no more than three tribal areas: items 1-3 above are in Benjamin; item 4 in Judah; and item 5 in Naphtali. There is a much more inclusive account in the list of thirty-one defeated kings who ruled in cities throughout the land from Arad in the Negeb to Kedesh north of Hazor (Josh. 12:7-24). Strictly speaking, however, the list states only that all these kings were defeated, not that their cities were captured or destroyed. In fact, the list includes cities which, after Joshua's death, were either taken by tribes acting separately (Bethel, Josh. 12:9; Judg. 1:22-26), or remained unconquered (Gezer, Taanach, Megiddo, Josh. 12:12, 21; Judg. 1:27, 29). Therefore, one is entitled to suspect that this list of kings did not, to begin with, purport to tell of captured cities; and, furthermore, that when it later was understood as an inventory of captured cities, it was constructed so as to attribute the victories to the archetypal conqueror Joshua.

If any further proof is needed of the incongruity between the centralized schema of total conquest and the substantive allusions to piecemeal conquests reflected in the traditions, we need only consider the so-called negative conquest lists, i.e., the inventories of territories and cities which are specifically said not to have been taken by Joshua. The utopian editorial frame dominates the accounts insofar as the overall form of the Book of Joshua assumes that the whole land was marked out for conquest and divided up for possession after victory, but the reality of a limited occupation obtrudes so starkly that it is amazing that so many Bible readers have managed to overlook the decided limits of the conquests actually described. This incongruity can be easily unnoticed because the "negative conquest lists" (except for Josh. 13:1-6a, which deals largely with extra-Palestinian territories) have been placed outside of the Joshua conquest narratives proper and included in the tribal boundary and city lists in Joshua 13—19 and in the first chapter of Judges. This has made it possible for the reader either to avoid the contradictions in the data or, if noticing them, to rationalize that Joshua did conquer most of the land, but that after his death Israelite power waned and Canaanites were able to stage a comeback. As we have noted, that rationalization seems to have been the explicit understanding of the Deuteronomic historian who shaped the final form of Joshua-Judges.

As a matter of fact, the equivocation in the biblical accounts, when read perceptively and as a whole, has resulted in most contemporary proponents of the conquest model adopting a sharply modified version of the model. What they tend to say is that Joshua led a group of tribes (not necessarily or even probably all twelve tribes) in a concerted attack which broke the resistance of the Canaanites in three swift campaigns: one in the center of the land at Jericho-Ai-Gibeon; a second in the Judean shephelah against Makkedah, Libnah, Lachish, Eglon, Hebron, and Debir (or at least some of those sites); and a third in Galilee against Hazor. These lightning attacks are thought to have broken Canaanite sovereignty over the mountainous regions of Galilee, Samaria, and Judah and left the Israelites free to consolidate and extend their holdings without serious opposition. At the same time, many proponents of the conquest model concede that the absence of reports about military action in the central regions of Ephraim and Manasseh, coupled with the assembly called by Joshua at Shechem (Josh. 24), probably shows that the center of the land was linked to Israel by peaceful entente (perhaps similar to the Gibeonite treaty) or by an amalgamation of the entering tribes with ethnically related peoples in that central highland region. Many conquest advocates are also willing to grant that certain conquests achieved by individual tribes or clans (e.g., Caleb's capture of Hebron, Josh. 14:13–15; 15:13–14; Judg. 1:20) have been attributed to Joshua in the course of consolidating and simplifying the traditions (Josh. 10:36–37).

In curtailing the scope of the conquest model, however, the extent and direction of the alterations begin in fact to alter the fundamental substance of the model's claim. Certainly Joshua as the unifying archetypical conqueror is not a very sharply defined figure; in himself he is not nearly as clearly etched as several of the judges. Is he, in fact, much more than the editorial cement joining loosely constructed and disparate narratives together under the illusion of a massive initial Israelite conquest? If his Ephraimite origin and burial at Timnath-serah in Ephraim are authentic memories, is it not possible that his role was chiefly connected with the Joseph tribes? If so, since no specifically Ephraimite or Manassite conquests are recorded under his leadership (with the possible exception of the battle at Beth-horon in Josh. 10), is it not likely that the real work of the Ephraimite Joshua is unrecorded in the battle accounts? In that event, is it not likely that the assembly he is said to have gathered at Shechem (Josh. 24) may in fact be much more truly his historical work than all the battles claimed for him?

Nonetheless, archaeology reports that there were fierce destructions of Canaanite cities at this time, and in some manner they must be accounted for. On closer examination, it turns out that there is as much—and maybe more—to be said *against* using the archaeological results to support the conquest model as there is in its favor.

To begin with, there is the gaping hole in the Joshua accounts created by the negative archaeological results from Jericho, Ai, and Gibeon. If Jericho stood at all in the late thirteenth century, it was apparently no more than a small unwalled settlement, or at most a fort.[128] Ai (et-Tell) was not occupied at the time and had not been occupied for centuries. No feasible alternative site for the biblical Ai has been located in a survey of the area around et-Tell.[129] Maybe the actual conquest of Bethel has been confused with Ai; but, if that is the case, we then have two different versions of how Bethel was taken, and they do not agree in details (Josh. 8:1–29; Judg. 1:22–26). No Late Bronze remains (other than some tomb pottery from the fourteenth and possibly early thirteenth centuries) have been found at Gibeon, raising questions about Joshua's purported treaty with the Gibeonites (Josh. 9).[130] Also, while the evidence from Hazor suits Joshua 11 very well, it also creates problems in Judges 4, where Hazor is still in the hands of a King Jabin. An outright harmonization of Joshua 11 and Judges 4 requires that Deborah and Barak predate Joshua or that Canaanites have returned in force to Hazor between the battles of Joshua 11 and Judges 4.

Such difficulties point up the necessity of cross-examining the archaeological data amassed to support the conquest model. There are at least three pertinent questions to be addressed to the archaeological data as interpreted by the conquest advocates: (1) Do we really know that it was the Israelites who conquered all the cities found destroyed in the thirteenth century? (2) how do these destructions compare in intensity, distribution, and number with destructions of the same or similar cities in the period before and after? and (3) if it was Israelites who destroyed all these cities, what is there from the material evidence which shows that they were destroyed in a coordinated campaign?

It is not easy for one who is not a trained archaeologist to venture an answer to these questions, and even archaeologists have difficulty doing so, given the incompleteness, imprecision, and ambiguity of the evidence. In fact, in order to attempt overall historical interpretations, the archaeologist must become an historian. Therefore, certain aspects of the rules of evidence employed by those who have used archaeological results for historical reconstruction may be legitimately examined by the historian.[131]

First, we must be completely clear that the conquerors of the Canaanite cities did not leave records revealing their identity, such as the steles that Near Eastern imperial conquerors sometimes erected. Also, there is nothing in the material evidence to tell us outright that they were Philistines, Egyptians, rival Canaanites or Canaanites in revolt, Israelites, or "semi-nomadic" raiders. The ruined occupation levels lie before us, but we must go elsewhere, namely to historical records, to hazard identifications. The Bible reports destruction of some of these cities but not of others; and with respect to some cities reported destroyed by the Israelites, the archaeological evidence is lacking or contradictory. Are we allowed to choose only those parts of the archaeological evidence that suit a "centralized" reading of the Bible—which is itself only one reading of the biblical evidence—or must we not remain inclusive and open and try to explore the possibility that some of the destructions were carried out by other peoples?

Probably the least likely among the proposed destroyers are the Philistines. Although there are many unanswered questions about Philistine origins, it is extremely doubtful that they came into Palestine in any force before 1150 B.C. Prior to that, they appear only as select mercenaries of the Egyptians.[132] But the Egyptians themselves are another matter. We know that the pharaohs of the nineteenth dynasty attempted to reassert historic dominion over Syria-Palestine. Seti I, Rameses II, and Merneptah carried out campaigns in Canaan. It is true that their itineraries of conquered cities tend to concentrate on the coastal regions and in the valleys, but it is probable that Merneptah (or an earlier pharaoh) had established a garrison at Nephtoah near Jerusalem.[133] Merneptah claims to have conquered Gezer and to have "destroyed Israel" (c. 1230–1220 B.C.).[134] When we examine the excavated cities destroyed in the thirteenth century, we note that, with the exception of Bethel and Debir, they are either in valleys or in the lowlands on the edge of the mountainous heartland west of the Jordan, within easy reach of Egyptian forces operating along the coastal road. Lacking a detailed account of Merneptah's campaign in Canaan, we are certainly not in a position to claim definitively that he destroyed any of the cities generally attributed to Israelite destruction. We are only saying that Egyptian destruction of one or more of those sites is a real archaeological and historical option.

Similar openness must be maintained to the possibility of destruction caused by internecine strife between Canaanite cities or by open revolt within cities. We know from the Amarna letters that the Canaanite cities were at one another's throats in the fourteenth century, and the response of Jerusalem and its allies to Gibeon's treaty with Israel shows that the same was true in the late thirteenth century (Josh. 10:1–5). Furthermore, Judges 9 reports what terrible destruction could be visited upon a city such as Shechem by civil war among its citizens, a destruction that may be the one identified by the excavators of the city as having occurred about 1100 B.C.[135] It has been claimed that the total destruction of Canaanite cities in the thirteenth century could not have been caused by revolting Canaanites because they would have wished to preserve the cities for themselves after they had overthrown their rulers.[136] Considering the destructive aftermath of the revolt against Abimelech, that does not seem a very cogent argument, and it does not accord with other revolts known from ancient history. To be sure, the rebels might prefer a minimum of destruction, but they also were ready to inflict the maximum destruction necessary to eliminate their oppressive rulers. In addition, since the fortified city was essentially the military-economic-political nerve center of the feudal institutions, any revolt that was antifeudal in intent might well deliberately aim at smashing the urban nerve center rather than taking it over. The proposal that Canaanites may have destroyed one another's cities, or that they may have been ruined in civil wars and revolts, is altogether consonant with the archaeological evidence. It remains for us to assess the historical and sociocultural evidence concerning intra-Canaanite conflicts, which we shall do in Parts VIII and IX.

The question about the relation between the thirteenth-century destructions and the destructions before and afterward is a logical one, but it is hard to find archaeologists who have approached the problem in this way. They have tended to focus on the archaeological data after reading the biblical text; they have, in short, adopted primarily an historian's stance toward the archaeological material. To be maximally helpful to the task of historical and cultural reconstruction, the archaeologists's stance might more logically be to locate the frequency and types of destruction over regions and throughout centuries, to attempt to develop a typology of destructions in a manner roughly analogous to the typology of ceramics. Obviously, the ceramics typology is possible because of the thousands upon thousands of pottery fragments (sherds), as well as a good number of whole specimens (normally from tombs), which reflect changes in forms and designs every decade or so. Many more ceramic articles were broken or deserted or entombed than were cities destroyed. Also, the techniques of military destruction, except where there are new types of fortification and siege warfare, do not change with anything like the frequency of change in pottery types. Apparently the period we are interested in did not see any marked technological changes in siege warfare between the arrival of the Hyksos in the eighteenth century B.C. and the penetration of the west by the Assyrians in the ninth century. In fact, the so-called glacis, the packed earth slope and revetment around fortified cities which appears in Palestine with the Hyksos, once thought to be military, is now regarded by some archaeologists as chiefly to prevent erosion of the walls.[137] Thus, I am fully aware that the controls for establishing a valid study of destruction frequencies and types are not so obviously at hand. Maybe, at this stage of archaeological development, it is an impossibility. Yet without it archaeologists have difficulty in giving us more precise evidence on the questions at hand, and are themselves as vulnerable and hypothetical in their historical reconstructions as are historians untrained in archaeology.

It should be stressed that archaeology is still a very young science, and Palestinian archaeology has had a remarkably small number of full-time practitioners. Many archaeologists have been biblical historians and literary critics or form critics by training and preference. Often with only limited funds, brief periods to dig, and little time to publish, it is not surprising that they have tended to focus on critical sites and pivotal historical problems from the standpoint of biblical studies. Only as the techniques of archaeology advance, and as more persons become full-time archaeologists, can we reasonably expect the kind of careful typological studies proposed here.

Another fruitful type of archaeological inquiry is the area study[138] which has so far been undertaken to some extent in survey fashion in the Negeb,[139] in Transjordan,[140] and in Galilee,[141] and more recently in the area around Ai.[142] The aim is to survey and/or sound all the sites in a given region so that they may be viewed contextually or ecologically. The results of such systematic area studies in depth should be of immense value for historical reconstruction in that an independent body of archaeological data could be queried in the search for patterns that might correlate with biblical and other historical textual data.

As to the last question we posed, it seems clear that nothing whatsoever in the archaeological evidence shows that the cities were all conquered in a coordinated campaign or series of campaigns, beyond the fact that they were destroyed within fifty, or perhaps twenty-five, years of one another in the late thirteenth and early twelfth centuries. But much can happen in twenty-five years that need not be attributed to a single historical agent. Any combination of Israelite, Egyptian, Canaanite, or other attackers could have destroyed many more than the score or so cities so far identified. Or, all of them could have been destroyed by Israelites operating as separate tribal entities or in combinations of two or three or more tribes. Even the fact that two cities as near to one another as Lachish and Tell Beit Mirsim were destroyed in the late thirteenth century does not compel us to posit a single attacker in the two instances. It is interesting that Lachish remained unoccupied after its destruction, whereas Tell Beit Mirsim was immediately resettled. This difference might be explained on the hypothesis that Lachish was destroyed by Merneptah but the Israelites failed to exploit the opportunity to settle it, perhaps because they regarded it as much too vulnerable to another pharaonic attack, whereas Tell Beit Mirsim, located higher in the hill country, captured by the Israelites, was settled because they felt relatively secure there.

The general typological picture of a culture intervening between extensive decline and destruction of Canaanite cities in the highlands and foothills, on the one hand, and the later arrival of the Philistines, on the other hand, does seem to bear considerable weight. Here archaeologists come into their own and offer a body of data undistorted by the need to support this or that historical theory. The evidence seems reasonably clear that a culturally distinct network of settlements spread over mountainous West Jordan from the late thirteenth century onward. Since it can hardly have been Philistine and since it clearly was not Egyptian, it is entirely logical to regard it as "Israelite."

The rub comes in giving greater specificity to this intervening culture called "Israelite." There simply is no one-to-one correspondence between "Israelite" as understood from the material-cultural evidence and "Israelite" as formulated by the centralized, cultic-ideological schema of Joshua. "Israelite" in the material-cultural sense does not mean twelve-tribe Israel. It does not even imply that the material-cultural remains belonged in all cases to groups who were members of a Yahwistic league of tribes. "Israelite" in the material-cultural sense suggested by archaeology might conceivably mean that its bearers were 'apiru/Hebrews or what we have called proto-Israelites. "Israelite" in the material-cultural sense might also mean some combination of rebellious Canaanite peoples and incoming Yahwists from which "Israel" in the centralized biblical sense began to take form. These and perhaps still other meanings of "Israelite" are all legitimate possibilities, archaeologically speaking. The archaeological typology of the period merely creates a setting and offers some preliminary parameters; it does not provide an immediate means for settling disputes between alternative historical reconstructions on which the material-cultural evidence throws no direct light. It gives us a significant field within which to explore and test possibilities, but the archaeological typology will have to be much more fully drawn before it can be a more precise tool. At the moment it simply does not give unalloyed or even predominant support to the conquest model.

As a self-sufficient explanation of the Israelite occupation of the land, the conquest model is a failure. On the literary-historical side, the biblical traditions are too fragmentary and contradictory to bear the interpretation put upon them by the centralized cult and by the editorial framework of Joshua. On the archaeological side, the data are too fragmentary and ambiguous, even contradictory, to permit the extravagant conquest claims made by some archaeologists and historians using archaeological data.

It may be said that biblical traditions and archaeological witnesses point to destruction of some Canaanite cities in the late thirteenth century. If the biblical data can be shown to be self-consistent, some aspects of the archaeological data, but not all, are consistent with the conclusion that Israelites captured these cities and settled on their ruins, but it is also possible that Egyptians and/or Canaanites destroyed some or all of the cities. And even if we accept a chastened conquest model for the destruction of a string of cities (e.g., Hazor, Succoth, Bethel, Beth-shemesh, Lachish, Eglon, Debir), that would only be a *limited* conquest theory and not a total conquest theory. And it is also quite within the biblical and archaeological evidence that if Israelites carried out the destructions, they did so not as a totally formed twelve-tribe unity but as proto-Israelite groups who only later became components of the biblical Israel, or, alternatively, as Israel in some early phase of its development before it was composed of all those who eventually entered into the union. Furthermore, as far as I can judge, archaeology to date has nothing to say on the question of whether the destroyers of cities were Canaanite "insiders" or invading "outsiders." What must be avoided is a facile circle of presumed confirmation of the conquest, built up from selective piecing together of biblical and archaeological features which seem to correspond, but in disregard of contradictory features and without respect for the tenuous nature both of the literary and of the archaeological data.

21

The Immigration Model

As critical study of the Bible succeeded in laying bare the units of biblical tradition and exposing their fragmented and contradictory nature as cultic-ideological products, first in a literary-critical focus on Judges 1 and then in an intensive form-critical and tradition-historical investigation of the entire range of "conquest" traditions, another view of how Israel entered Canaan began to gain advocacy. Here and there in the separate units of tradition could be seen traces of more peaceful occupation of the land, at least in the initial stages, and even of outright intermarriage and treaty-making with the Canaanite inhabitants. It was noted, for example, that the patriarchs lived for the most part in harmony with the resident population and that Judah is said to have intermarried with Canaanites (Gen. 38). The actual number of assaults on Canaanite cities described in the narratives of Joshua is small by comparison with the summary claims of a sweeping conquest. The territories excluded from the initial conquest, when added up, are so extensive that even the specific biblical claims themselves, when pieced together, do not amount to a total conquest.

In addition, the very polarization of Israelites and Canaanites posited in biblical tradition, often cited in support of the conquest model, may be seen as pointing in the opposite direction. Only if the Canaanites had *not* been displaced en masse could they have remained as a threat to Israel which had to be countered so vehemently. Later generations of Israelites are only interested in the polarization because the Canaanites had not been destroyed at the start. This may well suggest that an original more peaceful juxtaposition of immigrating Israelites and resident Canaanites became a rivalry only later. Or, as some have argued, with David's annexation of Canaanites into his empire, a cultural and religious struggle arose between the Canaanite and Israelite populations in his empire. Because Canaan was in effect politically absorbed into monarchic Israel, rather than militarily obliterated either by the incoming Israelites or by David, the intense Israelite-Canaanite polarization schema was developed as a weapon of Yahwism against syncretistic tendencies in the body of monarchic Israel.

The immigration model was developed in the late nineteenth and early twentieth centuries before significant technically accurate archaeological work was done in Palestine. As archaeological evidence has been accumulated, advocates of the immigration model, notably Martin Noth, have tended either to ignore it or to stress its muteness as an historical witness except as interpreted by literary materials.[143] They point, for example, to the shifting conclusions of archaeologists on such sites as Jericho and Ai; they believe that it was mistaken in the first place to think that archaeology could underpin the historicity of accounts which are clearly schematic and legendary. While those holding to the immigration model see a general cultural value in archaeological work, they minimize its importance for historical reconstruction and stress the disagreements among archaeologists themselves as to the historical implications of their discoveries. Sometimes the rebuttal of archaeology's historical value has been carried to absurd extremes by a circular argument as solipsistic and intractable as the circular reasoning of the extreme conquest theorists. The circle of logic runs something like this: since the occupation of Canaan by Israel was a priori peaceful, the destruction levels in late thirteenth- and early twelfth-century cities cannot have been carried out by Israelites. Their conclusion that Israelites *definitely did not* destroy this or that city seems as doctrinairely determined in some cases as the conclusion of traditionalists among the conquest theorists that Israelites *definitely did* destroy this or that city. In each case an initial hypothesis is set forth which, instead of being used to examine the archaelogical evidence, is used to select and cut the evidence along the exclusive lines of the hypothesis. Doctrinaire disregard of the actual ambiguous texture of the archaelogical evidence does not seem any more defensible for those rejecting the traditional conquest model than does doctrinaire credence in the service of those defending the conquest model.

Insofar as extrabiblical literary data are used to illuminate the immigration model, they tend to be administrative reports and cultural descriptions of the movements of supposed "semi-nomads" or diplomatic texts such as the Amarna letters telling of the *'apiru.* On the one hand, stress is laid on the normalcy of bedouin penetration into settled areas, at first in cyclical seasonal rhythms involving symbiotic agreements between herdsmen and farmers, and only later in fixed settlement on unoccupied land or by force of arms. It is sometimes assumed that the earliest Israelites to enter Canaan were of this seasonal nomadic type and that only much later, perhaps as reflected in the Book of Judges, did the immigrants become so numerous that they formed a threat to the Canaanite inhabitants. The extent of contact between the immigrating Israelites and the resident Canaanites is variously conceived by immigration theorists. Albrecht Alt's form of the model conceived the Israelites as entering empty space between the widely scattered Canaanite cities in the highlands. There the Israelites fell outside the jurisdiction of the city-states and developed for some time without significant contact with the natives.[144] Other immigration theorists see more contact and treaty relations between Israelites and Canaanites and even significant intermixture of the two populations.

On the other hand, a continuity is often underlined between the Israelites and the *'apiru* peoples who appear as social drifters throughout the Near East and specifically in Canaan in the late fifteenth and fourteenth centuries. Sometimes the *'apiru* attacked the established authorities, but more often they served them as mercenaries. If the *'apiru* of the Amarna letters entered Canaan in part by force of arms, their Israelite relatives in the thirteenth century probably did not have to employ force because they would have been welcomed by the earlier invaders. The absence of any biblical reference to battles in the center of the land, coupled with the prominence of Shechem as a city that collaborated with *'apiru* in the Amarna period and served as an assembly point for early Israel, seems to lend support to this view.

But precisely in summoning the "semi-nomad" concept or the *'apiru* concept, or both together, the immigration theorists often betray methodological shallowness. Exactly what relation should be seen between the bedouin concept and the *'apiru* concept, either in their own terms or as applied to early Israel, is seldom made clear. The very socioeconomic notion of nomadism or semi-nomadism has been very imprecisely and clumsily invoked by biblical scholars. What are the criteria for pastoral nomadism, and which of the people in and around Canaan meet the criteria? And the *'apiru*, while perhaps in some instances herdsmen, seem generally to have had a more varied and developed cultural repertory than that of pastoral nomads. Indeed, have the traits of animal husbandry and of migration, for whatever reasons, been too simply identified with pastoral nomadism? Should we manage to get our conceptions of semi-nomads and *'apiru* straightened out, and if it is granted that in some cases both groups used force, how is it that we can posit for the supposedly analogous Israelites solely a peaceful type of immigration into Canaan? Clearly, both the semi-nomad and *'apiru* analogues for early Israel require far more careful explication than they have yet received.[145]

One of the cardinal elements of the immigration model has been its stress upon uncoordinated movements of Israelites into Canaan from different directions and at different times. Once the editorial framework of the biblical traditions is challenged by literary criticism and its centralizing façade dissolved by form criticism, the diverse traditions become more prominent and it is possible to assemble an impressive array of indicators for an uncoordinated immigration of proto-Israelites in separate waves. There is evidence for one movement of Israelites directly from the Negeb into the mountains of Judah, in addition to the dominant editorial concept of penetration across the Jordan at Jericho-Gilgal. There are also clear references to colonization of Transjordan regions by Israelites who moved eastward across the Jordan after settling in the western highlands. It has also been claimed that the tribe of Asher is already referred to as resident in Galilee by Egyptian texts from the first part of the thirteenth century.

It has become virtually axiomatic for those holding the immigration model that if the exodus is historical, only a fraction of the eventual totality of Israelite tribes was involved in it. Indeed, this conception has won its way into the view of most advocates of the conquest model and is also taken for granted by the revolt model. But there is wide disagreement as to which tribes were involved in the exodus, as well as great variance in notions about the number, source, destination, and timing of the various separate immigrations and the relationships among them.[146] The most frequent view is that the Joseph tribes were the exodus tribes, i.e., Ephraim, Manasseh, and Benjamin. This is based in part on the supposed origin of the exodus-settlement and covenant traditions among those northern tribes, and in part on the prominence of the Joseph tribes throughout the premonarchic period. Others view Levi as the exodus tribe, either alone or in company with the Joseph tribes. This is grounded in the clear identification of Moses as a Levite and the considerable number of Egyptian names borne by Levites. It will be recalled from II.5.2 and IV.18.1–2 that I regard Levi as the Moses group and that I further explain the early salience of the Joseph tribes on the hypothesis that they were the first converts to Levitical Yahwism in Canaan.

A correlate of the hypothesis of uncoordinated waves of proto-Israelite immigration is the view that the twelve-tribe system did not precede the immigrations but was in fact the climax of the immigration process. Until 1930 it was generally believed among critical scholars that the twelve-tribe system was a late monarchic concept retrojected into the early history of Israel. But since Martin Noth's epochal study *Das System der zwölf Stämme Israels,* the twelve-tribe system has been widely seen as a development preceding the monarchy and holding a definitive institutional relationship to the cult of Yahwism. On this view Yahwism was in fact the religion of the intertribal league, now commonly called an "amphictyony" in analogy with the cultic leagues of city-states in ancient Greece and Italy. While the precise member tribes changed in the course of time (e.g., Levi dropping out; Joseph subdividing into Manasseh and Ephraim; Machir becoming Manasseh; Gilead becoming Gad), the number of twelve (or six, in earlier stages of development) was seen as fixed by the need to make cultic provisions for the central sanctuary on a rotating twelve-month basis. Shechem, Shiloh, Bethel, Gilgal, or Gibeon were variously seen as constituting this central cultic site. Noth, in order to explain both the composite nature of Judah and the fact that Judah was not in early communication with the northern tribes, posited a six-tribe league in the north and a six-tribe league in the south. The six members of the southern league were Calebites, Othnielites, Jerahmeelites, Kenites, Kenizzites, and Judeans who eventually came to form the single-tribe Judah, which entered the twelve-tribe league of all Israel as one member. The full twelve-tribe league thus came into existence prior to the time of Saul and David.[147]

By regarding the premonarchic tribal league—and particularly its collective cultic celebrations—as the life-setting for the early traditions of Israel, it was possible to explain their mixed and fragmentary character. The traditions are actually an amalgam of diverse materials drawn from the several ingredient members of the league and worked up in cultic recitations as enlargements of a series of basic themes demonstrating Yahweh's saving activity among his people Israel. The editorial framework of the accounts and the centralized façade of the stories presuppose the unified league, but the actual content of the stories reflects preceding conditions of separate tribes and locales prior to their unification. As a result, the complex literary traditions have to be viewed in somewhat the manner of occupation levels on a mound, or of geological deposits in rock and soil. The historical value of the accounts is fundamentally affected in all respects by the refraction and fragmentation of this tradition-historical process in which the traditions have been handed down, combined and recombined, and finally shaped by a concluding editorial hand. This is the combination of cultic-ideological and literary-editorial working methods typical of Israelite tradition which was set forth in considerable detail in Parts III and IV of this study, and applied particularly to materials in Joshua and Judges.

The immigration model stresses the great length of time involved in Israelite settlement, extending from the patriarchs to the time of David. It also stresses the environmental continuities between Israelites and other presumably semi-nomadic peoples and between Israelites and Canaanites. It tends to see the uniqueness of Israel not in the patriarchs or in Moses but either in the tribal league before the monarchy or in the religion of the prophets, although the latter view, very common in the early part of the twentieth century, is now in eclipse and doubtless discredited beyond recall.

As with the conquest model, the immigration model is sharply modified by many of its adherents. Thus, while the overall emphasis is on peaceful immigration, there is some allowance for military conflict, seen either in the form of a limited invasion by exodus or other Israelites or as a slowly accumulating crisis as the immigrating Israelites finally came into open conflict with the Canaanites. With respect to the entrance of the exodus tribes, the traditions of Joshua are thought to be vastly overlaid with legend; but, when criticized by the more sober accounts of Judges 1, they may reflect some seizure of land by force. This seizure, however, was undertaken only by one or a few exodus tribes, and their link-up with the other tribes was accomplished gradually in such actions as Joshua's covenant assembly at Shechem, impelled by the need for the various tribes to join their forces in self-defense against Canaanites and extra-Canaanite attackers.

As for objections to the immigration model, all the evidence that speaks for the conquest may be said to call the immigration model into question. At its baldest, the immigration theory presents a direct counterview to the centralized façade of the biblical accounts. The notion may be said to depend excessively on bits and pieces of materials drawn randomly from the text without regard to the overall biblical perspective. It may also be objected that so powerful a unity as that of the Israelite people could scarcely have resulted from such fragmented beginnings. Further, it seems to play down the Yahwistic tradition that Israel's god came from the desert and that he had constituted his people prior to their entrance to the land.

It is not difficult, in my view, to show that all these objections depend upon too naive a reading of the superficial form of the biblical account, but there is something to the objections to be borne in mind. They at least remind us that the immigration model is not perfectly obvious and that it too depends upon a selective reading of the evidence. In its own way, at least in some of its forms and tendencies, it may be a too neatly drawn counterview to that of the centralized tradition. It has been sketched to treat the facts, but necessarily in the adversary role of rebutting the excessive confidence in the harmonized tradition which characterized many conquest theorists. In the process the immigration model may have become much too one-sided and rigid. The modifications it has undergone and the tendency to combine it with elements from the conquest model suggest that a stage of unprofitable and simplistic opposition between the two conceptions may be ending and a new era of closer attention to the facts and a greater openness to new forms of theorizing may be emerging. This alteration of the context of debate has been particularly stimulated by the rise of the revolt model of the settlement which cuts across both earlier models and suggests a new configuration of interpretation transcending the stark antinomies of the simplistically opposed conquest and immigration models.

A further argument against the immigration model is the lack of agreement among its proponents. The diversity of counter-versions of the settlement of Canaan certainly does not prove the traditional account of the Bible to be correct, if only for the obvious reason that the Bible itself includes a number of contradictory testimonies. But it does show that we are still a long way from any solidly delineated account of what took place in the Israelite "conquest" or "settlement" of Canaan. Much of this disagreement stems from different points of emphasis depending in part on professional training and in part on temperament or philosophical stance. But probably the largest factor in the diversity of views is the nature of the evidence itself, for the historical deposits both in the biblical traditions and in the ancient mounds and literary texts are not all of one time or place or of one sort, and they are so far not wholly amenable to the constructions put upon them either by the latest editors of the Bible or by modern historians. There is a considerable mass of relevant evidence, but the interconnections among the data must still largely be supplied by inference and speculation.

22

The Revolt Model

We are not left simply to choose between the conquest and immigration models, or to combine them, for within the last decade another theoretical model of the settlement has emerged. Although it has yet to be as fully developed as the other two models, it does offer a serious third possibility. Whether it will prove to have the durability of the older models depends upon how it stands up to a more systematic analysis than it has yet received.[148] Indeed, it is part of my intention for this study to extend the systematic analysis of the revolt model beyond the present frontiers of biblical scholarship. In this context, I do no more than lay out the model, with supporting and opposing evidence, and suggest unanswered questions to be treated in subsequent sections, notably in Parts VIII and IX, where I shall focus on societal diachronics in the emergence of Israel.

The revolt model offers the intriguing proposal that we can account for much, if not for all, of what the Bible tells us of Israel's entrance into Canaan on the theory that Israel was in fact composed in considerable part of native Canaanites who revolted against their overlords and joined forces with a nuclear group of invaders and/or infiltrators from the desert. It is clear at once that in some respects the revolt model is allied to the preceding two models. It is allied to the conquest model insofar as, in its fullest presentation to date by Mendenhall, the catalyst to the rise of Israel is seen as deriving from a group of outsiders who entered Canaan with enthusiastic adherence to the deliverer god Yahweh and who supplied a militant stimulant to revolution among the native Canaanite underclasses. It is allied to the immigration model in that it does not make a sharp distinction between Canaanite and Israelite, or at any rate does not make it in the way the conquest model does, i.e., in terms of bitter, open conflict from the start between two clearly demarcated ethnic bodies. Furthermore, it stresses that the formation of later Israel resulted from the amalgam of many diverse groups with their own prehistories and ethnic backgrounds, all of whom poured their contributions into the common treasury of Israelite tradition.

The seminal novelty of the revolt model is its provision of a connecting link between the religious thrust of Yahwism and the socioeconomic and political realities of Canaan, a link which neither the conquest model nor the immigration model could offer other than in the most abstract ways. It proposes a way of accounting for the phenomenal rise of Yahwism, its indigenous roots and power to adapt, its astonishing growth and integrating inclusiveness. It suggests that the socioeconomic and political conditions of Canaan were ripe for just such a movement as Yahwism and that Yahwism must be understood as a peculiar development addressed to the life circumstances of underclass or marginal Canaanites. By offering a new way of looking at old problems, it has forced us to a fundamental rethinking of the settlement process and of the very structure of Israel and its Yahwistic cult. Just what does the revolt model claim and what does it offer for evidence of its claim?

The revolt model has two starting points: one is the decided and tenacious biblical core tradition about a group of slaves, delivered from Egypt and worshipping the god Yahweh, who eventually find their way securely into Canaan. The other starting point is the resistance of large segments of the ancient biblical traditions to simplistic inclusion within any conception that all Israel was composed of these former slaves from Egypt, on the one hand, or composed exclusively or even predominantly of diversly originated immigrants, on the other hand. It is impossible to do away with either of these two superficially contradictory sets of data. There is a sharp historico-religious focus on an outside Yahwistic group that entered Canaan, and there is an equally sharply drawn array of traditions about diverse peoples, including resident Canaanites, who subsequently or secondarily were drawn into the Yahwistic core group.

How can we account for these seemingly conflicting bodies of tradition? Normally, one or the other course is chosen: to opt for the massive conquest theory or to opt for the piecemeal immigration theory, or to attempt awkwardly to combine them. But so far the immigration theories have assumed that the Israelite elements which subsequently joined the Yahwistic league were almost totally extra-Canaanite groups—whether 'apiru adventurers or semi-nomadic Arameans, who like the Yahwistic exodus tribes, entered Canaan as wanderers in search of a home. Supposing, however, that we entertain the logical possibility of the conversion of substantial segments of the Canaanite population to Yahwism? Instead of looking around for obscure infiltrations and movements, why not turn to the resident population of the hill country of Canaan into which the exodus tribes entered? Suppose that it is not only true that most of the Canaanites were not *annihilated* but that many of them were *converted* to Yahwism?

But is this proposal more than a playful exploration of one merely formal logical possibility? Surely, if the immigration model strains our credulity at times, the revolt model positively boggles the mind. Nothing could seem more absurd on the face of it. That the Israelites left the Canaanites alone either by choice or by necessity we may accept, but that the Israelites were themselves composed of a majority—or even of a large minority—of Canaanites seems blatantly contrary both to the desert origins of Israelite Yahwism and to the biblical motif of Israelite-Canaanite polarization.

The background for the revolt model is the development of Canaanite city-states on a broadly "feudal" design, beginning in the Hyksos Age and extending throughout the Egyptian domination of Canaan during the eighteenth and nineteenth dynasties (c. 1570–1200 B.C.).[149] With the introduction of chariot warfare by the Hyksos, military technology began to modify social and political structures. To wage war required the necessary wealth, technology, and operating skill to create and sustain an effective chariot force and also to build strong enough fortifications (cyclopean walls and defensive slopes and revetments) to repulse an enemy's chariotry. This advance in warfare had the effect of concentrating population in or near well-fortified cities with a strong central government. It elevated a class of military warriors and bureaucrats and depressed the larger population in subservience to them. To build and support the enlarged military establishment, heavier taxation in kind became necessary and larger public building projects had to be undertaken with forced labor. The effect was to lay a heavier burden on the peasant population in that every increase in taxation in kind and in labor increased the tendency toward debtor serfdom. Indebted peasants, deprived of independent means of subsistence, were recruited as cultivators of large estates and compelled to serve the onerous demands of overlords from whom they had little prospect of escape. A larger percentage of the communal productive energy and wealth went into warfare and the centralized state.

This rough approximation to the medieval feudal system of Europe was presided over by the Egyptians, who exerted occasional direct and more frequent nominal hegemony over Canaan and Syria. The Egyptian aims were military-strategic and economic. Strategically, Egypt wished to retain Syria-Canaan as a protective buffer zone against foreign invasion. Economically, Egypt strove to draw on the trading wealth that passed through the network of routes in the Syria-Canaan corridor, as well as to obtain particular valuable natural products, such as timber from the mountains of Lebanon. Both goals could be served by establishing garrisons in the region and appointing Egyptian administrative officers to collect tribute from the native rulers, who were allowed to remain in the numerous city-states scattered over the corridor. From time to time pharaohs sallied forth with their armies to put down revolts and to "pacify" the region, thus restoring the flow of regular tribute to the Egyptian court and aborting independence movements in the buffer zone, as well as discouraging collaboration with outside powers such as the Hittites.

The resulting sociopolitical profile in Canaan consisted of a double layer of hierarchical structures: the native rulers subordinate to the pharoahs, and the native populations immediately subordinate to their rulers and indirectly to the Egyptians. When Egyptian control relaxed, the city-states gained room to maneuver, were able to omit the burdensome tribute, and were free to extend their own power at the expense of their neighbors. Such is the situation reflected in the

Amarna letters from the end of the fifteenth century and the first half of the fourteenth century B.C., written by Canaanite native rulers to the Egyptian court. But the freedom gained by the local rulers was not passed on to the lower strata of society. Taxation in kind and forced labor continued; the city-state, now relatively free of Egyptian interference, turned its resources toward inner feudal consolidation and toward aggrandizement at the expense of neighboring cities.

The level of royal and military bureaucratic consumption did not abate. It did not matter much for the fate of the peasant populace whether their labor went to pharaoh or to native prince; it was in either case an exaction that cost them bitterly. From the stance of the diplomatic correspondence, the whole struggle looks like a contest of city-states against Egypt and of city-state against city-state. The native princes are angling for preferential treatment from the pharaoh at the same time that they are acting as independently of Egypt as possible, each trying to secure himself against his neighbor's ambitions. The native rulers accuse one another of collaborating with the *'apiru,* a restive social element known from many references throughout the Near East.[150] The *'apiru* are even said to have succeeded in gaining and holding cities in the land—at least such is the inference if all the disturbances described in the Amarna letters are read exclusively as inter-city conflicts or conflicts between sovereign groups.

Who are the *'apiru*? The revolt model emphasizes the sociopolitical dimension of the term. While they work at many activities and seem to be ethnically mixed, the *'apiru* are characterized everywhere by their negative stance toward the existing social and political structures. Sometimes they work with and submit themselves to the powers that be, but they carry with them the aura of potential threat to the established order and seem ready to exploit any weaknesses in that order to their own advantage. It seems, in fact, from the colloquial and sarcastic usage of the term in the Amarna letters, that *'apiru* had come to be an epithet for any person or group in a negative stance toward some established authority who implemented that stance in socially disturbing action. Some interpreters of the Amarna letters regard *'apiru* as meaning in effect, "those who, like the *'apiru,* flout or contest authority." Thus, from the denotation of specific groups of mercenary or brigand outsiders, *'apiru* acquired the connotation of "insubordinates," "outlaws," "revolutionaries." This wider and looser connotative usage would explain, at least in part, the wide-ranging ambiguous, pejorative applications of the term. Native rulers accuse one another of having joined the *'apiru,* i.e., they have opposed Egyptian overlordship and they are seizing one another's territories. Anyone who threatens the established imperial-feudal order, no matter how high his station in that order, is acting like *'apiru*—indeed, *is 'apiru.*[151]

The revolt model conceives the turmoil in the Canaanite city-states as extending down into the lower levels of society. Rebellious serfs and restive free farmers were also acting the part of *'apiru*; in the confused situation created by the diminution of Egyptian control, these lower-class peoples revolted against those who exploited them. They might do this by removing particularly onerous native rulers directly, or they might join forces with another city-state which promised them better conditions. In other words, Canaanite society was not all of one piece. There were cracks and strains and outright disaffection, especially among the oppressed lower classes. They were looking for relief and seizing upon opportunities to better their lot, even though the measures chosen were largely ephemeral, since the basic feudal structures held fast.

When the exodus Israelites entered Canaan they encountered this stress-torn Canaanite society, which was in still further decline a century after the Amarna Age. Population in the hill country seems to have tapered off in the Late Bronze period, and the city-state units seem to have been reduced in number and size from the preceding century.[152] The advocates of a revolt model for Israelite origins picture these Israelite tribes as immediate allies of the Canaanite lower classes. Both groups shared a lower-class identity. The former slaves from Egypt, now autonomous, presented an immediate appeal to the restive serfs and the peasants of Canaan. The attraction of Israelite Yahwism for these oppressed Canaanites may be readily located in the central feature of the religion of the entering tribes: Yahwism celebrated the actuality of deliverance from sociopolitical bondage, and it promised continuing deliverance whenever Yahweh's autonomous people were threatened. The two groups coalesced. In the highlands, wherever they were strong enough, the combined exodus tribes and converted Canaanite lower classes threw off their overlords and formed "tribal" rule by elders in deliberate rejection of centralized political rule by imperial-feudal "kings." Taxation and corvée to support a large royal establishment were obliterated at one stroke wherever Israel prevailed. The Canaanite overlords in the plains were too weak to contest the revolt effectively in the hill country, and the symbiotic exodus Israelite/Canaanite lower class "conquest" went forward with measurable success.

What is the biblical evidence for this reading of affairs? Certainly the imaginative way in which the exodus and covenant symbolism is illuminated by such a theory is one piece of evidence. Why were these highly stylized and selected memories of such importance in early Israel? While brilliantly identifying the process by which the themes shaped the traditions, Noth was unable to offer an altogether plausible sociopolitical matrix for the development of Israelite tradition. The revolt model meets this deficiency most convincingly. The basic themes, sub-themes, and stories of the old tradition were symbolic precipitates of the sorts of experiences that all of the first generations of Yahwists had lived through, whether as outsiders or insiders vis-à-vis the Canaanite social system. The Canaanite "insiders," in overthrowing their rulers had, like the "outsiders" from Egypt, overthrown their "pharaoh"; and they had been delivered in their own "exodus."

This critical sociopolitical matrix for the origin of the cultic traditions goes a long way toward accounting for the care with which the main themes were selected and polished and also for the great mass of separate traditions clustered around them as diverse converted Canaanite peoples contributed their experiences to lend support to the praise of Yahweh and the unity of Israel. The religious traditions were so alive and so multiple because they presented in symbolic form the manifold but convergent social and political experiences of these early Yahwists. The coalescing Yahwists were astonishingly diverse ethnically and culturally, but they had common social and political experiences and were forging together a common life of mutual defense and self-development.

Specific textual support for the revolt model may be cited at several points in the traditions, even though the memory of the diverse origins of Israel quickly became subordinated to an emphasis upon its grand unity.

We begin with the Transjordanian traditions. Transjordanian Canaanite or Amorite converts to Israel may be asserted on the basis of Israelite adoption of an old Amorite taunt song against Heshbon contained in Numbers 21:27–30. This song tells of an attack on Heshbon from the north and is almost certainly the report of an Amorite attack on Moabite Heshbon rather than an exodus Israelite attack. Its inclusion in Israel's traditions may be understood as the contribution of Amorite converts to the Yahwistic literature.[153] Although I know of no one who has so argued, the inclusion of detailed lists of Edomite leaders in Israel's traditions (Gen. 36) might similarly be explained on the assumption that a sizeable number of Edomites became Israelites. It is also noteworthy that the display of the iron bedstead of the Amorite king, Og of Bashan, in the Ammonite city of Rabbath-Ammon (Deut. 3:11) may indicate that the victory over Og credited in the Bible to Israel was actually achieved by Ammonites, some of whom later defected to Israel and brought the memory of Og's defeat with them. It is also possible that Jair of the tribe of Manasseh is the same as Yauri, an Aramean group referred to by Assyrian kings, which may have been one of the diverse elements in Manasseh.

These latter two examples are of course not strictly of Canaanites, and may therefore be explained by the immigration model, but they are equally assimilable to a model of oppressed peoples in the region of Palestine who joined with the exodus Israelites. The revolt model seems more applicable since both the traditions about Og's bedstead and Jair's seizure of cities presuppose military activity rather than peaceful immigration.[154] Also, if the proposal is accepted that the Israelite tribe of Dan derived from the Sea Peoples known from Greek and Egyptian sources as the Denen or Danuna, who settled on the Palestinian coast north of the Philistines, we have a futher instance of the ethnically composite nonpastoral nomadic character of early Israel, if not direct evidence for the revolt theory.[155]

In the West Jordan region, we note the curious list of thirty-one Canaanite kings defeated by Israel. We have already claimed that the original form of the list did not envision the capture of cities so much as it pictured the overthrow of kings. Such a conception accords well with the hypothesis that at least some of those kings were overthrown by their own revolting populaces. Some of these very cities eventually appear as "clans" within the Israelite tribe of Manasseh. The report of the Israelite treaty with the Gibeonites may also be relevant to the revolt model. The present form of the story presents the treaty as a striking exception to the usual practice of annihilating Canaanites, and it pictures the Gibeonites as subordinated to the rank of cultic attendants. As the tradition stands, it serves a much later aetiological purpose of accounting for the survival of Gibeonite descendants as lower-order cultic attendants in monarchic and postexilic Israel. Behind the aetiological purpose, however, there stands the much older notion of how native elements in Canaan responded favorably to the exodus Israelites, even joining forces with them and depending upon the lightning-like guerrilla tactics which the Israelites developed to overcome the superior forces of the dominant city-states in the region. The immediate setting for the battle at Gibeon appears to have been the attempt of Jerusalem to reclaim sovereignty over the client cities, which it had lost when they collaborated with the exodus Israelites.

Also, the assembly at Shechem can be construed not unfairly as a great act of incorporation in which part of the Canaanite populace, purged of their oppressive kings, also threw off the Baal religion and/or their clan gods surviving from earlier cultural levels of experience, and accepted the god of the Israelites who had helped them in their victories. The emergence of Judah as a composite of many southern clans and tribes, including some by absorption of Canaanites, would also make sense on such a model. Issachar, described as one who "bowed his shoulder to bear, and became a slave at forced labor" (Gen. 49:15), may well refer to the highly vulnerable position of underclasses in the Valley of Jezreel and their forced subservience to nearby city-states, such as Beth-shean, Taanach, or Megiddo, until they grew strong enough to throw off their oppressors. It is not difficult to see Issachar as a "tribe" formed out of Canaanite serfs who threw off their masters with the help of already free Israelite tribes to their north in Galilee and to their south in Samaria.

It might also be added that the Israelite-Canaanite polarization concept can readily be understood on this model as a result of the tradition's shift of terminology. As soon as the Canaanite lower classes converted and left Baalism, they were no longer seen as Canaanites. Henceforth, the term "Canaanite" referred to the city-state hierarchical structure, with its ideologically supportive Baal religion, which continued in the cities of the plains and whose culture tended to creep back into Israel as the first-generation fervor abated. This occurred especially under David, when he incorporated whole Canaanite city-states into his empire which had previously never experienced a total Yahwistic religious and sociopolitical revolt.

Another strength of the revolt model is that it can deal with archaeological evidence for thirteenth-century destructions much more flexibly than the immigration or conquest models have tended to do. Destruction of cities by any of several agencies could easily fit within the model. Some cities may have been destroyed by invading Israelites. Others may have been destroyed by revolting Canaanite underclasses. Some may have been attacked by the Egyptians in punitive operations to quell the spreading revolt, such as is implied in Merneptah's "Israel stele." Still others may have suffered attacks by neighboring cities trying to take territory, or to overthrow a rival ruler, or to establish sovereignty over the entire city-state.

Moreover, the typological evidence for a distinctive early Iron Age culture falling between Late Bronze Canaanite and later Philistine culture would, in the view of the revolt theorists, attest to the developing Israelite and lower-class Canaanite symbiosis in a Yahwistic confederation. The fact that new kiln techniques seem to appear with Iron I may suggest that the potters were killed off or driven out with their Canaanite lords, so that the exodus Israelites and lower-class Canaanite Yahwists had to develop their own procedures in pottery-making. For the most part they followed familiar Late Bronze ceramic shapes, although new forms appear and there are differences in color preferences. The markedly lower incidence of imported wares reflects no doubt the cultural and economic divide between the Canaanite imperial-feudal system and the Israelite egalitarian social system. Moreover, discrepancies and lacunae between archaeological and biblical data, as in the cases of Jericho and Ai, are no difficulty for the revolt model since it shares with the immigration model the belief that the traditions are frequently inflated, transposed, or conflated in the process of their accommodation to the notion of a united Israel.

Objections to the revolt model are not hard to come by. It is countered that if the immigration model has trouble finding well-developed biblical evidence, all the more is that true of the revolt model. Almost all the specific biblical evidence so far cited may be explained as readily by the immigration model as by the revolt model. Perhaps the most persuasive bit of support is the Amorite-oriented taunt song against Heshbon, but that is a slender thread for hanging an entire model on. The Gibeonites are not pictured as being assimilated into the exodus tribes but are shown remaining a Hivite or Hurrian enclave within Israel even as late as the time of David. In Joshua's address to the Shechemite assembly he speaks of his audience's forefathers beyond the Euphrates, and when he mentions the gods of the Amorites this does not require, and may not even imply, that he is addressing Amorites or Canaanites. Furthermore, the rather detailed social and political cross-section of Shechem revealed in Judges 9 seems to presuppose the continued separation of at least some of the Israelite and Canaanite elements in the population of the highlands. Perhaps Joshua 9 and Judges 9 suggest not so much the assimilation of Canaanites into Israel as the coexistence of Israelites and certain friendly, or at least neutral, Canaanite cities. But were they friendly or nonhostile because of a common sociopolitical and religious perspective? Or were they at peace because the Canaanite cities such as Gibeon and Shechem saw that they were exposed to Israelite attack, could expect no substantial help from other Canaanite cities, and therefore reached an accomodation with Israel?

It has been further protested that the *'apiru* of the Amarna letters are hardly to be identified with lower-class Canaanites. They are said to be pictured as outside elements who have intruded into Canaan, and, by extension, the term is applied to city-states as hierarchical entities in battle with other city-states. The assumption of lower-class revolt in the events related in the Amarna correspondence does not rest upon unambiguous foundations. In fact, all of the *'apiru* references are re-solvable to actors in the internecine imperial-feudal struggles among the city-states and with Egypt. It is objected, therefore, that a social-class reading of the Amarna conflicts is vastly strained if not totally perverse.

It is also implied that the revolt model is at least in part a wishful retrojection from contemporary attention to social and political revolution. Presumably the real but hidden passion of the revolt model advocate is to ground his impulse to contemporary social justice in biblical injunctions, or at least in some romanticized ancient Israelite social religion. Or conceivably he is motivated to prove a Weberian instance of religious ideas in "elective affinity" with a social group that becomes their bearer, or to validate an implicit or explicit Marxist view of religion as the "projection" of social and economic forces. In any case, the taint of the revolt model is that it is felt to grow more out of the interpreter's immediate needs or out of his unexamined milieu than out of the biblical evidence itself.

Such an invocation of sociology of knowledge contains an important caution which, of course, applies equally to all theoretical modeling. One must similarly consider whether the conquest model has not been motivated oftentimes by a desire to confirm the truthfulness of the Bible, and it may also be asked if the immigration model has not been stimulated by modish but mistaken ways of reconstructing history and social evolution which did not first occur to the critic from reading the biblical data. Moreover, it could easily be retorted that those who cavalierly dismiss the revolt model may be so influenced by their fear of or distaste for contemporary social unrest that they refuse to look at the historical evidence concerning Israel's origins. But to point out the predisposing effects of the interpreter's social and cultural matrix toward one or another outlook on the material is not to settle matters; it is merely to call for more careful controls on these predispositions which will allow for close scrutiny of methods and conclusions. Theoretical adequacy—namely, the ability to account for the data over the widest range in the most coherent manner—is the only answer to the suspicion of contaminating presuppositions. While it is true that a current mood may lead to distorting reconstructions of the past, it is also true that a current temper of mind may be just the catalyst needed in order to see analogous tempers and forces at work in other times and places. Like may indeed fabricate like, but like may also discover like.

Personally I believe that there is ample evidence for the revolt model to make it a serious proposal; but in order for it to attain theoretical adequacy, it requires further elaboration and application, and even some modification. Certain of its claims require much closer examination and fuller demonstration, as, for example, the assertion that "a peasant's revolt" occurred in ancient Canaan, in fundamental continuity with the Amarna Age *'apiru* unrest. In particular, the model may have to be adjusted to the possibility that some Canaanite settlements were not so much polarized by the entering exodus tribes as neutralized, thus adopting a kind of live-and-let-live policy which Israel was willing or obligated to accept, at least down to the time when David overthrew the entire balance of power between Israelites and non-Yahwistic Canaanites.

23

Models of the Settlement and Models of the Social System

The models of the Israelite settlement in Canaan as they stand are inadequate as self-contained theoretical schemes. In varying respects and with varying adequacy they each point up aspects of the land-taking traditions that cannot be left out of account. It is by now clear that, in their current formulations, each of the models has been so modified that it is something of a composite of two or three models. We can only rather loosely speak of "conquest model" and "immigration model" and "revolt model" in order to indicate which mode of land-taking within a mix of modes receives the greatest emphasis. The critical test of any model is how adequately it will encompass and interrelate all types of pertinent evidence and not merely a few "preferred" types. Obviously, the adequate model of Israel's occupation of the land cannot simply be a composite of elements arbitrarily juxtaposed. It will have to be an integrated synthesis, i.e., it will have to show processually how groups of Israelites came to hold the land, severally as tribes and collectively as united Israel. But to do so, a settlement model will have to be set in a larger context than has been the practice to date.

A truly new synthetic settlement model will only emerge as the interpreter recognizes that the conflict over models of land-taking is in reality a much larger conflict over the proper understanding of Israel as a social system. This conflict has not surfaced in biblical studies with methodological clarity because of the reasons given in Part I for biblical scholarship's reluctance to adopt a sociological approach to early Israel. But the need for methodological clarity over the issue of Israel's social constitution is so urgent that it is difficult to imagine further significant progress even on the historical front until the scope and contours of the problem of Israel's social constitution are better formulated than at present. For the issue at stake is not simply the territorial-historical problem of how Israel took its land; e.g., the segments of Israel involved, the regions taken, the military or nonmilitary methods of occupation, etc., all the while being naively content with unexamined—or at best only partly examined—assumptions about the nature of Israelite society.

Behind these questions lurk the complementary questions: What was this formation of people called Israel which took land and whose social system took form as it took the land? And what were the shared goals and the bonding structures of Israel's social system in comparison with those of other social systems, both those from which it emerged and those against which it was counterposed? To put such questions is to recognize at once that they must be grappled with in a larger framework than that of questing for the details of the processes and spatio-temporal sequences of the land-taking, although the social questions obviously cannot be pursued in isolation from or in contradiction to the details of the settlement. In effect, I am claiming that a proper model of the settlement is not attainable apart from a proper model of the social system of the people who took the land, any more than it is attainable apart from a proper model of the cultic-ideological tradition production of that social system.

Up to now biblical studies have grappled with a model of the settlement and with a model of the cultic production of traditions, but there has been no adequate linkage of these two forms of inquiry within a larger analytic model of the social system involved in the twin processes of settlement and of tradition making. Only Noth can be said to have attempted such a larger model of the social system which tries to synthesize the range of form-critical, tradition-historical, and territorial-historical data available. In Part VII we shall note the decided inadequacies of his attempt. Mendenhall, in *The Tenth Generation,* offers an outline of the Israelite social system with far more explanatory potentiality than Noth's, but he has devoted almost no attention to the place of tradition production in the community and, in this respect, is less helpful than Noth. We have already indicated some of the ways in which an adequate model of the production of traditions requires a larger model of the Israelite social system. It is equally necessary to indicate some of the ways in which an adequate model of the land-taking requires a larger model of the Israelite social system, the point on which Mendenhall is far more pertinent and cogent than Noth. In doing so, we show how historical questions are insepara-bly intertwined with sociological questions in a study of Israel's origins, and at the same time we provide some of the perspectives necessary for a model of the social system of Israel to be proposed and developed in following sections.

We can perhaps best approach the points of intersection between models of the settlement and models of the social system of Israel by showing how the course of research into the problem of the settlement has gradually exposed the sociological dimensions of the problem.

The tradition-oriented conquest model scarcely raised any sociological ques-tions because it contained an implicit unexamined sociology of Israel. It assumed a twelve-tribe system composed of clans and families as sub-sets of each tribe which formed an unquestioned aspect of the miraculously formed religious community of Israel. Since the basis of the religious unity tended to be supernaturally posited, the concomitant social system of tribes shared the religious aura of sanctity and was not approached as a phenomenon requiring analysis and explanation. Loose and imprecise social and cultural indicators were identified, such as the absence of a king in early Israel and the prominence of wandering shepherds assumed to be nomads. This ill-examined impressionistic "sociology" was random and superficial and totally subordinated to the marvelous religious elements of the story. Such remains the case even for more recent, sophisticated versions of the conquest model; they tend to retain "the biblical faith" as an irreducible, unexplained core whose social base is irrelevant or inexplicable and scarcely provocative of social analytic curiosity. There is even a residue of this mystification in Mendenhall's use of "biblical tradition" and "the rule of God," surviving alongside and uncoordinated with his social scientific insights and methods.

With the introduction of the immigration model, sociological considerations were pushed a little farther toward the foreground. In recognizing that the twelve-tribe system was not part of the foundation of early Israel—as was commonly assumed by the immigrationists prior to Noth's startling counter-argument in 1930, more attention was focused on the diverse experiences and forms of life of the separate groups who became Israel. Although it first developed out of a literary-critical dissection of biblical sources, the immigration model gave impetus to and fitted well with form criticism and tradition history and quickly drew on their methods and results. But even with the stimulation of form-critical and tradition-historical approaches, the immigration model failed to develop a comprehensive and analytic social perspective. On the one side, the model tended to pick up on the traditional wandering-shepherds motif and to conceive the first Israelites as nomads in analogy with later Arab bedouins and at times with the 'apiru, widely assumed also to have been a migratory, thus nomadic people. On the other side, although attentive to the immediate cultic contexts for the various forms of the tradition, the model did not sufficiently expand the question of life-setting to encompass Israel's social and political system. A great hiatus remained between the rudimentary nomadic-'apiru perspective and the more fully developed cultic perspective. Because of the microcosmic focus on individual groups and traditions, no one seriously asked: How does the assumed nomadic and/or 'apiru background of Israel relate to and account for its cultic productions? Even when the nomadic background was further clarified by the recognition that Israel's nomadism was not the full nomadism of camel bedouins but rather the semi-nomadism of ass bedouins, the connection of this somewhat more socially informed semi-nomadic model with the cult activities and products was not adequately formulated or pursued.

Noth's vigorous and powerful defense of a twelve-tribe system at the very basis of Israel's premonarchic constitution introduced the potential for putting the question of the social system in more adequate form. Why was this potential unrealized? Of course, at the outset it must be stressed that Noth was in no sense returning to the old traditional conception of a fully formed twelve-tribe Israel stepping out of the desert into Canaan. The twelve-tribe system took shape emergently, as previously unrelated people joined together within it. But essentially it has to be realized that Noth's theory was not so much a theory about the full social system of Israel as it was a theory about its cultic system, whose social implications he only partially formulated and explored even less. As a form critic, Noth adhered to a fairly narrow focus on the lines of tradition production, with the result that his quest for the matrices of the traditions was basically in terms of specific cultic contexts in Israel. Although rejecting the supernaturalistic "explanation" of Israelite Yahwism, his own twelve-tribe cult theory tended to obfuscate the full range of social questions. Noth accepted, for example, without fresh justification, the pastoral nomadic model for early Israel, just as he accepted the immigration model of the settlement. The twelve-tribe cult seemed to appear out of nowhere, and its connections with the lived experiences and needs of the Israelites are only hinted at in his work. In a sense, "the cult" assumed for Noth the kind of mystifying function that "the revealing God" or "the biblical faith" held for many conquest theorists.

Given the sociological limitations of his analysis of the cultic system, it is hardly surprising that Noth's beginning on a wider model was not extended or enlarged or deepened by those influenced by him. The broad social-systemic issues remained frozen, as it were, in undeveloped seed-form within his work and are still awaiting a thaw that will allow them to germinate. That Noth and others who followed his methods did not break through to a fully sociological methodology for examining early Israel is no reflection on their intelligence or imagination, nor does it diminish their enormously valuable contributions to biblical studies. It shows rather the limits of the form-critical presuppositions and the tremendous anti-sociological weight of biblical scholarly tradition as a whole.

Max Weber, coming at early Israel from a sociological perspective in the second decade of the twentieth century, grasped the total structural issues more clearly and comprehensively than the biblical scholars whose basic work he depended on. Weber made his massive study of ancient Israel at a time when the immigration model was widely accepted by biblical scholars, and although he knew the work of early form critics such as Gunkel and Gressmann, the grounding of his analysis was still largely literary-critical rather than form-critical. Even so, he crudely anticipated some of the important form-critical and cultic-ideological insights of Alt, Noth, and von Rad. He gave the cult a large place in early Israel, even though he could not deal adequately with the discrete forms it took or the discrete traditions it produced. He further recognized the key role of the Levites in the premonarchic cult community. He boldly tried to sketch a model of the larger Israelite social system; however, lacking the means to discriminate accurately between the premonarchic and monarchic social systems of Israel, he failed in the end to provide the analytic clarity that could guide others in more detailed work.

With all the limitations imposed by the fact that he was not a technically trained biblical scholar and by the fact that form criticism was not yet sufficiently developed to give him some of the tools he needed to establish his thesis in detail, Weber saw that the critical question in early Israel's life was the question of the articulation of the member groups in the socioeconomic and religiopolitical entity Israel. His brief sections on the covenant and the confederacy contain such perceptive seminal insights as the following:

> ... we should consider the external forms in which this "theocratizing" of the Israelite social order was consummated and the driving forces of the process.[156]

> ... the peculiarity of the oathbound confederation in Israel consists in the first place in the extensive employment of the religious *berith* [i.e., covenant] as the actual (or construed) basis of the most varied legal and moral relations. Above all, Israel itself as a political community was conceived as an oathbound confederation.[157]

> The "covenant" concept was important for Israel because the ancient social structure of Israel in part rested essentially upon a contractually regulated permanent relationship of ... [Weber then lists the socioeconomic groups which he understood as constituent members in Israel]. An entire maze of such fraternal arrangements ... dominated the social and economic structure.[158]

It is not my intent at this point to assess the accomplishments and deficiencies in Weber's social reconstruction of early Israel in detail.[159] My point is to emphasize that, in spite of the undeveloped state of biblical studies in the first two decades of this century, it was possible for a macrosociologist conversant with biblical studies to make considerable strides in conceptualizing some aspects of early Israel's social system in comprehensive terms. What Noth might have accomplished had he possessed as much sociological understanding as Weber possessed biblical understanding, or what Weber might have achieved had he lived later and been able to draw upon more developed form-critical and tradition-historical results, are matters of speculation. Such an occasion for speculation nevertheless indicates the proportions of the unfinished task of a sociological analysis of early Israel.

The emergence of the revolt model within the last decade has exposed the social-structural question about early Israel even more glaringly than Noth's twelve-tribe cult theory. In introducing the model, Mendenhall showed that he had more in mind than describing the stages and processes of settlement. The fact that he prefaced his model with a discussion of nomadism and tribalism in relation to urban and rural modes of life in the ancient Near East makes the larger sociological backdrop of the model evident. The revolt model draws attention, however incompletely, to the question: What kind of people were these Israelites, i.e., what was their social system vis-à-vis the other social systems of their day? Mendenhall's summary of his argument catches up this sociological concern handily, even though it remains confusingly enmeshed in the more limited settlement question:

The fact is, and the present writer would regard it as a fact though not every detail can be "proven," that both the Amarna materials and the biblical events represent politically the same process: namely, the withdrawal, not physically and geographically, but politically and subjectively, of large population groups from any obligation to the existing political regimes, and therefore, the renunciation of any protection from those sources. In other words, there was no statistically important invasion of Palestine at the beginning of the twelve-tribe system of Israel. There was no radical displacement of population, there was no genocide, there was no large-scale driving out of population, only of royal administrators (of necessity!). In summary, there was no real conquest of Palestine at all; what happened instead may be termed, from the point of view of the secular historian interested only in socio-political processes, a peasant's revolt against the network of interlocking Canaanite city states.[160]

I understand the thrust of Mendenhall's position to be this: the question of the methods by which the land was taken must be subsumed under the wider question of the sociopolitical system of the land-takers and its oppositional stance to the Canaanite sociopolitical system. The "peasant's revolt" model is more broadly characterized as a "withdrawal" model. The clear implication is that the armed revolts that occurred took place within the context of a sociopolitical movement and that we will understand the military events and the demographic movements only as we understand the fuller sociopolitical movement. In fact, all doubt that such was Mendenhall's reading of the revolt model has been removed by the recent publication of his book *The Tenth Generation: The Origins of the Biblical Tradition,* in which he treats the question of Israel's social structure as fundamental for dealing with the historical issues of the settlement. In fact, in this later work, the social systemic analysis of early Israel so displaces the more limited question of the means of "conquest" that Mendenhall further explicates the "peasant revolt" model only in a very limited and indirect way as an aspect of tribal structure in post-Amarna Canaan. In particular, he does not deal with the transition from the Amarna *'apiru* to the early Israelites diachronically in much more detail than in the earlier essay.

The fact that Mendenhall sets the social systemic question in the center of the early Israelite field of action is of immense importance. For the first time in decades an Old Testament scholar has drawn deliberately and reflectively on anthropology and sociology in order to understand Israel's structure as a social totality. Even though he restricts himself largely to the work of Elman R. Service on primitive social organization, the theoretical framework proposed makes for a measurable methodological advance beyond previous attempts to understand Israelite society. Empirical and theoretical rigor within a tradition and body of anthropological-sociological inquiry is introduced as the *sine qua non* for the social study of early Israel. In this regard Mendenhall has set an important precedent of greater consequence than his particular conclusions and in spite of the tentativeness, the incompleteness, and even the error of certain of his conclusions.

The immense value of the revolt model lies in its insistence on a new way of looking at old data within a heuristic perspective that opens up fresh possibilities and opportunities for research and theory-building. Early Israel appears as a new social synthesis formed from peoples indigenous to previous social syntheses in and around Canaan. In trying to explicate that new social synthesis, Mendenhall has focused on the covenant with Yahweh as the social form which permitted the decentralized tribal social order to achieve unity and comprehensiveness in a community of tribes. The unity and comprehensiveness which the centralized state had achieved—but at a considerable social price—could now be assured in the absence of the state and, therefore, without the liability of those intolerable burdens which the state placed upon the populace.

The Tenth Generation is in large part a series of essays spelling out "the rule of Yahweh" through the covenant form from various perspectives and at various levels of social structure. Mendenhall shows that as the bond of the whole social system, the covenant instrumentality intersected with the practical need for a trans-tribalism which could provide solidarity without the oppression of the state and without the parochialism of the single tribe. By means of a typological comparison of state and tribe, he indicates how the early Israelite formation fits within the sociopolitical spectrum of ancient Near Eastern life. In short, he gives Israel "social plausibility" within its milieu by retrieving covenant from its restriction to cult and theology and explicating it as a social form for uniting communities in a network of agreed mechanisms to meet common needs. Much of his argument is properly given to rebutting in detail the notion that early Israel was an "ethnic" or "racial" entity.

There are difficulties with Mendenhall's view of the new social synthesis that was early Israel. He assumes that the covenant form was modelled on the suzerain-vassal treaty, but the suzerain-vassal analogue for Israel's covenant is not the only one available and, in my view, it is not the best. This might be considered a peripheral point, but in actuality this model of a suzerain-vassal covenant is closely implicated in the unsatisfactory way Mendenhall deals with political power in early Israel. He reads Israel's rejection of state power as tantamount to the rejection of sociopolitical power: "The starting point of politics is the concern for power, but the whole theme of early biblical history . . . is the rejection of power."[161] But what does it do toward clarifying a social system to say that it surrenders the monopoly of power to its deity? Clearly the tribal or trans-tribal social form in early Israel controlled and exercised power, and it is *the way in which early Israel distributed, mobilized, and rationalized power, and not its rejection of power, that we are seeking to determine*. This posited power renunciation of early Israel is a serious misreading to which I shall return in Parts X and XI (see in particular X.48.2).

Mendenhall's explication of early Israelite society is far from systematic. He shifts back and forth frequently between the microscopic and the macroscopic levels, between inductive and deductive arguments, and between internal description and cross-cultural comparison. Having struggled with the problem of organizing a sociology of Israel's religion, I am inclined to be lenient in my appraisal of the way a theorist chooses to arrange his study. In any case, however, there should be transitional signals and connectional formulations binding the theoretical work into a whole. Very often the reader must supply these links in Mendenhall's work. Frequently this can be done, but in many cases only after the book is completely read. In several instances the transitions and connections never become clear because they hover in ambiguity.

24

Social-Structural Analysis and Comparison: Prospect of Parts VI–IX

It is important to orderly analysis and effective theory-building to lay out the phenomena and the methods of approaching them as clearly as possible. It seems to me that Mendenhall's contribution can best be assessed, and further contributions most probably assured, if we first bend every effort to formulate what is to be studied and how. A theoretical model of early Israelite society entails two types of sociological problems which are formally separable but necessarily interlocking: the first entails the analysis and synthesis of Israel's internal structure at its several levels and in its various sectors; the second entails the characterization of Israel's social system as a whole in comparison and contrast with other social systems. Both types of problems have synchronic and diachronic dimensions. I shall now try to explicate these internal analytic and external comparative tasks, each viewed from synchronic and diachronic perspectives, and I shall do so with reference to what Mendenhall has provisionally treated as well as to what he has left untreated.

The analysis and synthesis of Israel's social structure asks: Who were the peoples who formed Israel and how were their segments arranged in a total network of interaction? Evidence for treating this question of the internal composition and synthetic structure of Israel is largely biblical and is drawn directly from the early traditions and indirectly from the implications of the process of tradition production which we examined in Part III. The biblical data must in turn be reflected upon in the context of the large body of data and theory we now possess as a consequence of anthropological field studies and theorizing about social organization. As already noted, Mendenhall has commendably taken the lead in drawing upon these social-scientific resources. He shows methodological self-consciousness about the problem of internal composition and structure when he explores the meaning of tribalism in the ancient Near East, as seen within a theory of "zones" of social organization, and briefly but cogently demonstrates that tribalism in that setting is not to be equated with pastoral nomadism. What is missing in *The Tenth Generation,* however, is a systematic penetration into the levels and sectors of social structure. Elements of such an inquiry are scattered through the book, but they are not concentrated in a step-by-step analysis with appropriate transitional signals and connectional formulations. While I shall be agreeing in many respects with what I take to be Mendenhall's implicit view of the inner working of Israelite society, I believe that the societal analysis/synthesis must be made more explicit in order to formulate testable theories.

For example, rejecting pastoral nomadic tribalism for early Israel, Mendenhall sets forth the Israelite tribe as a fictitious social construct in the service of religious, political, and and military solidarity. At the same time, he denies that Israelite tribes were "primitive," apparently on two grounds. First, he notes that the totality of Israelite society was a congeries of tribes and not a single tribe, but he does not deal with the fact that "primitive" tribes are sometimes confederacies of tribes, as in the case of the Iroquois "Five Nations." Second, and I think of more relevance to his denial of "primitiveness," he notes that Israelite tribalism was a "devolution or "winding down" (my terms) from Canaanite statism and not an ascent from simpler band organization or a transfer of desert tribalism into Canaan. This is a point of immense importance, calling for much more explication than Mendenhall has given it. Although suggesting that the tribe proper was not so important as other units in the social structure, Mendenhall does not set forth systematically the biblical data concerning "tribe," "clan," and "family." Only by such an undertaking can we hope to suggest how such "social fictions" actually operated.

And what is the whole of which the tribes are segments? For Mendenhall it is "the rule of God" through the covenant instrumentality, but what that meant in social-structural terms is only illustrated with respect to a few social items, chiefly in terms of legal and cultic practice. He approvingly cites Noth's theory of the twelve-tribe league in the essay, and in the recent book he seems to accept it by implication but without explication. We must ask, however, whether Noth's widely accepted amphictyonic theory speaks effectively, or indeed at all, to the issue of tribalism as a social fiction. In particular, does the normativeness of precisely *twelve* tribes bear the cultic-organizational weight that Noth gave it for pre-monarchic times? And, if it does not, how are we to understand the clustering of tribes in early Israel? Moreover, in abstracting a model from another society, has Noth actually bypassed the comparative task of relating the location of the amphictyony in Greek society as a whole to the location of the intertribal confederacy in Israelite society as a whole? Such an inquiry already propels us into the comparative study of societies.

The comparative view of Israel's social structure asks: What was the overall character of Israel's social system in comparison with other preceding and contemporary social systems? Such a comparison depends upon prior structural-functional analysis of the societies compared and includes such sub-systems as the forms of economic production, the kinship and residence patterns, the distribution of power, the cultic-ideological complex, etc., in order to construct a "picture" of the constitutional mix. But the critical factor is the comparison of social systems, not only with respect to each of the social sub-sets or sectors, but with respect to the resulting totalities. How structures and functions in different societal complexes are to be compared, whether in fact they are at all commensurable, is an issue of much dispute.[162] Certainly there has been an overabundance of crude and superficial cross-cultural comparison, but the defaults cannot abolish the desideratum of developing more adequate ways to compare and contrast. Mendenhall is methodologically aware of this problem when he indicates that Israel as a totality was sharply distinguishable from Canaanite "feudal" society as a totality. But because his characterization of Israelite society remains for the most part exceedingly general, a full range of comparison and contrast with Canaanite society is inhibited. Of course there are serious gaps in our knowledge of aspects of both Canaanite and early Israelite societies which make comparison difficult, but these comparative difficulties need to be brought out more systematically so that we will be clearer about the explanatory strength or weakness of our theory and thereby become aware of the kinds of research needed to test and improve theory.

It is evident that comparison of early Israel and other contemporary social systems entails a diachronic and interactional dimension. The social systems being compared were not static isolated entities; they developed internally and stood in varying relations to one another over the course of time. The relations between historical social systems can be studied either synchronically, as they faced one another at some representative or "typical" moment; or they can be studied diachronically, in succession through time. Where historical development can be reconstructed, even an adequate synchronic sketch depends upon tracing the temporal variables in their changing fortunes in order to strike a proper "average" or representative picture of the society. There may be considerable interchange between systems or very little interchange, and the interchange may be largely in one direction or the other as well as mutual. The interchange may be symmetrical, in that each system affects roughly comparable aspects of the other; or it may be asymmetrical, in that each system is differentially affected by the other. The systems may be geographically contiguous or distant; largely indifferent to one another, or in cooperative relations, or in competitive struggle for control of people, land, or resources. Furthermore, the systems may be viewed as "expanding" or "declining," either in terms of gain or loss in territory or in absolute numbers of persons within the system, or relative to other systems, or in terms of range and intensity of influence exerted on other systems, or in terms of complexity and versatility of cultural repertory vis-à-vis poverty and rigidity of cultural repertory.

Mendenhall grasps some of these diachronic interactional issues, but his own major focus, especially in *The Tenth Generation,* is on the massive synchronic contrast between the Canaanite mythic and statist form of society and the early Israelite covenantal and trans-tribal form of society. Mendenhall's seminal observation about the typological similarity of *'apiru* and early Israelites who "represent politically the same process" enables him to understand that the distinctive structure of Israelite society is oppositional and reactive toward Canaanite society. He does not, however, fill out the formal similarities and differences between *'apiru* and early Israelites sufficiently to propose an account of the transition from one to the other, or to construct a comparative profile of the way the *'apiru* and early Israelites stood respectively in relation to Canaanite society.

In pursuing the comparative approach to Israelite society a major methodological issue is how we are to decide which social systems should be compared with Israel's. This entails the vexed problem of determining the boundaries of social systems in relation to the boundaries of the various historic state, tribal, and other formations, which appear under various proper names and gentilics in the biblical and extrabiblical texts. Mendenhall has properly identified the Canaanite statist system as the dominant and definitive social system of the time, embracing considerable numbers of separate city-states of varying sizes and in varying coalitions. But do the *'apiru* of the Amarna period in Canaan form another such system? They appear rather more like a sub-sct of Canaanite "feudalism," or a deviant form of accommodation to this "feudalism"; but at the same time, insofar as they are seen as forerunners of early Israel, they may be viewed as another social system in embryo.

Mendenhall sees pastoral nomadism as yet another kind of social system, but he rightly indicates how doubtful it is that we can locate a genuine nomadic system in the immediate environment of Canaan contemporary with early Israel. He argues, and I believe correctly, that the transhumant, village-based, pastoral nomadism in Israel's environment was only a minor sub-set of village tribalism which was subordinated politically wherever possible by the Canaanite "feudal" system. Pastoral nomadism as a self-contained social system awaited the domestication of the camel, some time after the emergence of Israel, and even then it took much longer to develop fully than is commonly supposed. Consequently, at best we can only speak of transhumant pastoral elements within a larger social system in the thirteenth–eleventh centuries, organized either hierarchically around the city-state or tribally around village associations. Is there enough information about transhumant nomadic peoples who were predecessors or contemporaries of Israel (e.g., Amorites before being assimilated to Canaan, Shosu, Amalekites, Midianites, etc.) to permit us to compare and contrast them with the Israelite social system and with possible pastoral nomadic elements within Israel?

In short, what are the relative degrees of exactitude and completeness that can be attained in characterizing and comparing early Israel's social system with the social systems or sub-systems of Canaanite "feudalism," of the *'apiru* reactive formation, and of transhumant pastoralism? Evidently, in some instances our characterizations and comparisons will have to be at a fairly high level of abstraction, but we can at least plot the outlines of such comparative studies beyond the

patchy undertakings of Weber and Noth and the occasionally more scientifically
satisfying probes of Mendenhall. I am at least confident that we can rule out
some sociological misconceptions that are currently damaging to significant progress in the theoretical understanding of the considerable data we now possess. It
seems to me that Mendenhall has taken some very important first steps in this
regard.

In *The Tenth Generation* Mendenhall expands the roster of sociopolitical entities
which are relevant to early Israel, particularly the "Sea Peoples" (including the
Philistines) and Luwian, Hittite, Hurrian, and Hattic elements from Anatolia and
North Syria which, on the basis of name occurrences in Palestine, he believes to
have migrated southward in considerable numbers following the disintegration of
political structures in their more northerly homelands.[163] None of these peoples,
however, seems to have brought a distinctively new social structure; rather, they
appear to have insinuated themselves into ruling-class positions in the regnant
Canaanite "feudal" system, or else to have fallen into the position of subservient
peoples in that system. The case that Mendenhall makes for a sizable incursion of
north Syrian and Anatolian peoples into Canaan in the thirteenth–twelfth centuries may alter somewhat our way of viewing the relationship of Canaanite and
Israelite social systems, particularly with respect to the Amorite kingdoms of Og
and Sihon in Transjordan, but it does not, at least so far, introduce a basically new
social systemic factor.

Perhaps the most obscure peoples in the social environment of early Israel
continue to be the Ammonites, Moabites, and Edomites, in spite of the considerable information concerning them in biblical records during the monarchy. This
is an especially poignant deficiency since the origins of these Transjordanian
peoples are temporally coincident with Israel's emergence. Regrettably there is
little to propose about their social structure beyond a formulation of some possibilities which may, it is to be hoped, stimulate more intensive and systematic
study. Unfortunately, our sources on their beginnings remain meager in the
extreme. Whether the somewhat fuller archaeological record on them from finds
in the last two decades can now yield a plausible social reconstruction is not yet
clear to me. Certainly the filling of this gap in our knowledge of Israel's social
environment would be a most important control on our understandings of Israel's
formation. I shall return to a consideration of Ammonites, Moabites, and Edomites in VIII.38.

All of this leads to the nub of the question: What was the unifying principle of
the Israelite social system? How can we describe and account for the early Israelite
mutation without falling into the miasma of *sui generis* religious "explanations"
which in fact explain nothing, which are no more than tautologies, unassailable
because untestable? Mendenhall has gotten at that question by showing that not
only was Israel's social system constitutionally unlike the Canaanite social

system—which could be no more than an accidental and asymmetrical feature of it—but Israel's social system arose in direct opposition to the Canaanite system. In *The Tenth Generation* this theme is masterfully developed within the dialectic of cultural continuity and social systemic dichotomy between "Canaanite" and "Israelite." The novelty in the Israelite social system is "the religious movement and motivation" that "created a solidarity among a large group of pre-existent social units."[164] The "religious" covenant is in actuality a new social unity among "tribally affiliated families" whose common denominator was "deliverance from an intolerable political monopoly of force."[165]

I find myself in almost total agreement with Mendenhall on this point. The cult and ideology of Yahweh, the god of Israel, are at the nub of Israel's uniqueness. But the problem is to take the cult and ideology of Yahweh seriously as historical phenomena and to render them into their material equivalents and corollaries in the social system. What exactly was the "religious movement and motivation" of Yahwism? Can the motivation be rendered in terms of the basic life conditions of the "believers"? What was the material rootedness of "the movement"? What was the "solidarity" of Israel? In what aspects of life and through what modes in the social system was the solidarity expressed? What threatened the solidarity and how were the threats handled? What were "the pre-existent social units" which achieved solidarity in Israel? How were the older social units incorporated within the new solidarity of Israel? Who composed Israel and from what systems did its members break loose in order to enter Israel? The identity of Israelite, for so long pursued under sterile ethnic categories, can at last be approached in terms of social relations, in terms of the range and quality of human interaction. My chief quarrel with Mendenhall is that he does not pursue these questions far enough. In spite of all his concessions to the social rootedness of the religion of early Israel, he opts for philosophically idealist "explanations" of Israel, as illustrated in his totally unacceptable assumption that early Israel rejected power. *What we have to account for is that early Israel took power into its own hands at the same time that it attributed the source of power to Yahweh.*

In sum, it is essential that we devise a constructive model of the Israelite social system in its own right, firmly rooted in its material conditions, a model which delineates the major sub-systems and the segmented organizational divisions, as well as a model which grasps the integrating mechanisms and the solidifying rationale of the social whole. Such a model must incorporate the highly centralized and richly articulated religion of Yahweh, but it must do so *sociologically* by understanding the religion as a social phenomenon related to all the other social phenomena within the system. And it must do so without simplistic recourse to the tautological, philosophically idealist claim that because religion was central to the social system, it can be posited as the unmoved mover of the Israelite mutation.

Part VI

Models of the Social Structure (I):
All Israel; Tribes; Protective Associations;
Extended Families

25

A Preliminary View

Biblical scholars generally assume that Israel was internally articulated into "tribes," and that these tribes were subdivided into "clans," which were further subdivided into "families" or "fathers' houses." This inputed system of pyramided social building blocks is not, however, so obvious or unequivocal as it looks on the surface. It is frequently overlooked that the fullest schematization of the social units occurs in a relatively small number of biblical traditions which are judged to be among the latest in date and to evince tendencies toward patterning of data which were either not present or not so uniform in the earliest traditions. Consequently, it is necessary to probe behind the schematizations to see how far they correspond to the nomenclature and taxonomy of the internal groupings of Israel as reflected in the most ancient pertinent sources. As far as I am aware, that task has never been carried out in a thoroughgoing way.

Social structure also entails and implies social function. What functional roles did people perform as members of organized "tribes," "clans," and "fathers' houses," and how did the functions at the respective levels and units of organization intermesh to form a social whole? It is disconcerting to note that biblical scholars have been largely content to repeat the terms, as though it were obvious what they implied for social function. Frequently they are set forth without an awareness of the many possible forms of social organization to which they might refer, and thus without setting forth the criteria by which one form of social organization is claimed for Israel in preference to another. There has been a singular disregard of sociological and anthropological research on kinship and social organization. Where such studies have entered in, as in the work of W. R. Smith, J. Pedersen, and R. de Vaux, they have been very largely limited to scrutiny of Arab bedouins. Yet as soon as one turns to the wider social-scientific literature, it emerges that "family," "clan," and "tribe" are terms that have been applied to an amazingly varied array of kinship and sociopolitical arrangements. The specific terms really only make sense in some larger analytic system. I. J. Gelb, a student of ancient Mesopotamian society, comments helpfully on this point:

> The concept of *structure* means. . .that it is impossible to understand a part without relating it to the whole. This means that it is impossible to analyze and understand individual aspects of the society without placing them within the total framework of that society. Such terms, for instance, as "unfree" or "slave" are meaningless by themselves. They become meaningful only when constrasted with other terms involved in social stratification, such as "semi-free" and "free." *Structure involves completeness.*[166]

Reference to the sociological and anthropological research on kinship and social organization both facilitates the biblical scholar's task by opening up new and illuminating analytic methods and comparative materials and, at the same time, complicates it by requiring not only a closer look at the hard information on Israel's social structure but also a more disciplined clarification of the criteria by which Israel grouped certain social units under a given term. The most elementary attempts at translating the Hebrew terms into English open up a whole nest of problems. The terms are undefined to begin with, and the context may have little or nothing to say on the most basic matters of the scope, composition, and function of the entities named. Sometimes the same group is designated by different terms and sometimes the same term is applied to different levels of social organization. And over the entire enterprise hangs the thorny problem of properly discriminating variations in social organization according to time and place.

Very possibly we are dealing with more than one classificatory system, and it may be that only fragments of earlier systems have survived which, in their truncated states, can supply us no certain key as to the full outlines of the originals. In addition, the concept of "social system" itself must not be taken to imply an integration of groups as complete, for example, as the integration of parts in a mechanical system or as the integration of organs and sub-systems in a biological system. A social system does not develop with the externally designed and directed integration of a machine nor with the internally coherent unfolding of a biological organism. The "design" and correlation of parts in a social system are subject both to the vicissitudes of historical development and to the resistance or "incoherence" created by the fact that the system is composed of persons who are themselves complex separate systems whose total meaning cannot be reduced to univocal performance of roles in a social system. And, furthermore, each subsidiary set of patterns within the total social system presents resistance or incoherence which is never altogether overcome even in an optimally integrated social system. At best an analytic model of social organization will be "ideal typical" and not directly representational of the full range of variations and contradictions in the actual social structure.

In order to develop an analytic model of the structural-functional articulation of Israel's premonarchic social system, I shall attempt three things in this part: (1) to develop a model of the levels and functions of social organization drawn from the pertinent early Israelite traditions, supplemented as necessary by data from elsewhere in biblical reports (see Chart 5, on pp. 338 ff. for a summary of results); (2) to check and clarify this model by reference to anthropological and sociological research on tribal organization; and (3) to indicate some of the factors involved in theorizing about the priorities, directions, and sequences of interaction among the organizational levels in a diachronic model of the formation of the social system (see Charts 3 and 4, pp. 330–331).

26

The Comprehensive Social Entity

It is somewhat surprising that there is no unequivocal organizational term for the social system of united Israel which is comparable in precision or frequency to the terms used to designate subdivisions within the system. Given the sociopolitical implications of Israel's *bᵉrīth*, "covenant," as noted in III. 12.3, and since the early sources contain instances of the political and military sense of *bᵉrīth* as "league" or "alliance"—e.g., Amorites of Mamre as *baʿᵃlē bᵉrīth ʾavrām*, "lords allied with Abram" (Gen. 14:13)—it is logical to expect that some such organizational term should have been applied to Israel as a whole, possibly *bᵉnē bᵉrīth*, "covenanters," or *ʾᵃnshē bᵉrīth*, "covenanted equals," or *ʿam bᵉrīth*, "a people formed by covenant," or *ʿammē bᵉrīth*, "peoples in covenant," or even *bᵉrīth- ʾaḥēm*, "covenant of brothers" (applied apparently to a treaty of amity between states in Amos 1:9). In place of the more common *bᵉrīth*, the root *ḥbr*, "to unite, be joined" (with sociopolitical use in Gen. 14:3; II Chron. 20:35,37) might have been expected, in a noun form such as *ḥever, ḥevrāh,* or *ḥāvēr,* meaning "association" or "union" (cf. *ḥᵃvērīm* for all the men of Israel "united, gathered, or massed as one man," Judg. 20:11).

That no such comprehensive technical organizational word for Israel appears in the sources has been a cause of some embarrassment to those who envision early Israel as a counterpart to the Greek–Old Latin amphictyony or sacral league.[167] We can at least conclude that if such a term (or terms) was once in use, it never succeeded in crowding out the proper names and the more loosely descriptive common nouns that we meet in the traditions as the characteristic way of designating the social entirety.

26.1 Israel / Israelites

A survey of the sources for old Israel reveals that the preferred, in fact the conventional, way of identifying the social totality was the proper name "Israel," which stands alone or in the expanded form *bᵉnē* Israel, "Israelites" (literally, "sons of Israel" or "descendants of Israel," i.e., "those belonging to or stemming from Israel.") The Hebrew language frequently describes the members of a collectivity with the term *bānīm*, "sons." The root reference of "sons" to biological descent becomes an extended metaphor for describing clusters of persons according to certain common functions or traits. Likeness or joint participation is represented as common descent (cf., in U.S. colonial history, "the Sons of Liberty"). There is a pronounced tendency in Israel to characterize social groupings, including those on the largest scale, as kinship groups descended from eponymous ancestors whose members are therefore kinsmen. So entangled are the literal and metaphorical uses of kinship language and imagery that it is sometimes impossible to separate them or to know when a writer wishes to be understood literally and when he wishes to be credited with metaphorical adroitness.[168]

Accordingly, the expression $b^e n\bar{e}$ Israel was readily accommodated to the pseudo-genealogical scheme of common descent from the single ancestor Jacob, who is also secondarily called Israel. This scheme is explicitly developed in the birth legends of the sons of Jacob (Gen. 29:31—30:24; 35:16–20). The sequence of transformations between eponymous ancestor and all Israelites runs like this: the sons of the eponymous all-Israelite ancestor Jacob become in turn the eponymous heads of the several tribes from whom are descended all present tribal members who collectively compose the "sons of Israel=Israelites" living at any one time. Just as the proper name Israel could be transferred into the genealogical scheme as the other name for Jacob, so the name Jacob, used for the hypothesized common ancestor, could be applied likewise to the social entirety. "Jacob" as the name of the whole people of Israel is restricted to a few poetic contexts in the early sources, although later it came to have considerable currency in the northern kingdom. Jacob, in its collective metaphorical use drawn from a "founding" figure, stands to Israel in somewhat the same relation that the personification "Columbia" stands to the United States of America. Whether Jacob ever referred to a sub-group taken into Israel, of which the patriarch became a personification, as some have thought, is not determinable from the existing information. Also deserving mention is Jeshurun, "the upright one," applied four times to the people of Israel in poetic settings (Deut. 32:15; 33:5,26; Isa. 44:2). It was presumably a very old term of endearment formed as a word play on Israel and stressing the ethical distinctiveness of the community.[169]

In many idiomatic contexts, "Israel" and "Israelites" are directly interchangeable, so that stylistics came to play a large part in the preference for one or the other. Examples of idioms in the early sources which contain interchangeable uses of Israel/Israelites are the following: "to give into the hand of Israel/the Israelites," "to make peace with Israel/the Israelites," "to judge Israel/the Israelites," and "the land/territory of Israel/the Israelites." There are, nevertheless, discernible overall differences in the nuances and connotations of the terms which make one or the other more suitable, or even obligatory, in given contexts. The use of "Israel" can serve to point up the unity, the completeness, and the peculiar identity of the community as a collectivity, whereas "Israelites" can serve to describe the people distributively as actors in a particular historical horizon.

For example, the deity is repeatedly called "Yahweh, the God of Israel," but never "Yahweh, the God of the Israelites." Here the emphasis is upon the conceptual totality of the community under its single sovereign. When leaders are described, it is almost always as "elders of Israel" or "commanders of Israel" ("The chief men of the Israelites" [Exod. 24:11] and "young men of the Israelites" [Exod. 24:5] are exceptional). Here the stress falls on the conceptual totality of a bounded organized community which delegates authority to its officials. Also, the frequent construction "in Israel" (e.g., "peasantry in Israel" [Judg. 5:7,11]; "a mother in Israel" [Judg. 5:7]; "all in Israel able to go forth to war" [Num. 1:3,45; 26:2]; "no sustenance in Israel" [Judg. 6:4]; "a/the custom in Israel" [Judg. 11:39; Ruth 4:7]; "there was no king in Israel" [Judg. 17:6; 18:1; 19:1; 21:25]; "folly and/or wantonness in Israel" [Gen. 34:7; Judg. 20:6]; "this great victory in Israel" [I Sam. 14:45]) attests to the primacy of the term "Israel" as the conventional way to denote the widest social system and thus to underscore the typical unity of the social relations in force within the system.

On the other hand, "Israelites" is entirely absent from poetry (possibly Exodus 19:3 and 6 are exceptions), whereas it is particularly favored in accounts of historical actions, such as battles, migrations, negotiations, etc. It occurs often in Joshua 1—12 and in Judges 3—21, generously intermixed with "Israel." Some of the connotative differentia between the two terms are evidenced in the predilection for the use of "Israel" in contexts where the people are addressed or referred to in their historic connection with Yahweh (especially in the speeches of God, of Joshua, and of Gideon in which moral-theological assertions are prominent), in accounts of the routing of the enemy, when a story is summed up or climaxed, and where the inclusiveness of the actors is emphasized (note the frequency of "all Israel"). Otherwise, the agents of action in these stories are often called "Israelites," connoting the severalty of the individuals or groups acting within the totality of "Israel."[170]

26.2 People / The People

Another frequent designation for the social entirety of Israel is *'am*, "people." As frequently observed, *'am* is decidedly preferred for Israel to *gōy*, commonly translated "nation." We may accept the rough distinction widely proposed between *'am* as a chiefly social and cultural term and *gōy* as a chiefly political term, particularly referring to states, although the terms are not used with absolute rigor and there are specialized sub-meanings for certain uses (see the discussion concerning Exodus 15:1–18 in IX.44.2). Numbers 23:9 aptly epitomizes the sense of distinction with which Israel is called an *'am:* "Lo, a people dwelling apart, not reckoning itself among the nations [*gōyim*]." In fact, Israel is called a *gōy* in only a small number of early passages. The self-conscious use of *gōy* in Exodus 19:6 in parallel with *mamlākāh*, "kingdom," displays a sophisticated and ironic redefinition of both terms when applied to Israel: "You shall be to me a priestly 'kingdom' and a holy 'nation.' " The peculiarity of Israel consists in its being a "kingdom" and a "nation" totally unlike the politically centralized kingdoms and nations (cf. also Deut. 26:18).

Israel is most often simply called *hā'ām,* "the people." More precisely, the peculiarity of the Israelite people is that it is *'am-Yahweh,* "the people of Yahweh" (Judg. 5:11, 13; I Sam. 2:24), which implies the full formulation "Israel, the people of Yahweh," as the correlative obverse of "Yahweh, the God of Israel" (Judg. 5:3,5; 11:23; Josh. 24:2,23). This is expressed in frequent occurrences of "his people," "your people," and "my people," wherein the subject of the possessive pronoun is Yahweh. Also, Israelite leaders are often called "heads of the people" or "elders of the people." Many uses specify "the people" as the entire community, or that portion assembled, acting in agreement and with authority, especially in making covenant and in deciding for war (Judg. 5:2; 21:2,15; I Sam. 4:4; 14:45; Exod. 19:8; 24:3,7; Josh. 24:16,21,24). "All the people" occurs several times as the equivalent of "all Israel." That "the people" also designated a community of legal jurisdiction is clear from expressions in the Covenant Code: "You shall not curse a ruler of your people" (Exod. 22:28 [27]), and "the poor of your people" (Exod. 23:11). In many instances "the people" are distinguished from the leaders, such as Moses and the Aaronite priests, or Joshua, or Saul and Jonathan, but the leaders characteristically secure the consent of the people for their actions or serve as mediators or presiding officers at deliberations or actions of the whole people. On occasion, the people act on their own initiative against the decision of a leader.

Not all uses of "the people," however, have the entirety of Israel as their evident reference. In Joshua 3—4 and 6, for example, in the account of the crossing of the Jordan and the fall of Jericho, *hā'ām* means "the laity" who are assigned appropriate places and roles in the line of march distinguished from those of "the priests." In one segment of the report of the capture of Ai, "the people" refers respectively to the two groups of Israelite troops who divide to form an ambush (Josh. 8:5,9–10,20). In fact, "the people" throughout many historical contexts has a strong military coloring, accenting the community in arms (oftentimes alternating with *'anshē* Israel, "men of Israel" or "Israelite citizens in arms") and could be paraphrased as "the militia" or "citizen levy." Some of the more limited meanings of "the people" will be discussed in the treatment of Exodus 15:1–18 in IX.44.2.

26.3 Congregation / Assembly

Another class of terms for comprehending Israel designates the body of members in a *qāhāl,* "assembly," or in an *'ēdāh,* "congregation." "The congregation" or the *'adath bʻnē* Israel, "the Israelite congregation," appears in the census accounts Numbers 1 and 26, in the story of the covenant with the Hivite/Hurrian cities in Joshua 9, and in the report of the outrage at Gibeah in Judges 19—21. Considering that it is a favorite term of the later P writings for the religious community (the traditionist of Numbers 1 and 26), that Joshua 9 is shaped by a late cultic interest in the Gibeonites as temple servants, and that Judges 19—21 presents a veritable collage of communal terms in baroque profusion, it remains questionable whether *'edāh* was a term used in premonarchic Israel for the popular assembly, although some scholars have made a plausible case for it.[171]

The *qāhāl*, "assembly," on the other hand, appears in the ancient poetry of Deuteronomy 33:4 in the form *q^{e}hillath* Jacob as the communal setting for law-giving (cf. Josh. 8:35) "when the heads of the people were gathered, all the tribes of Israel together" (33:5). Micah 2:5 refers, perhaps archaistically, to the *q^{e}hal* Yahweh in which the communal lands are divided by lot. In the gathering of Israelites to consider sanction against Benjamin, it is said that "they presented themselves in the assembly of the people of God" (Judg. 20:2; "in assembly to Yahweh" in 21:5,8). The "appearing before Yahweh" of all males three times in the year for festivals, mentioned in early laws, is presumably another form of the Israelite assembly, although it does not follow that the gatherings were at any single sanctuary and thus multiple regional gatherings may be meant (Exod. 23:17; 34:23–24).

Although the total number of references to "the assembly" in demonstrably or probably early sources is not great, the impression is strong that the body of free-and-equal males gathered for stated cultic celebrations, for periodic redistribution of land, and for exceptional deliberations on matters of war and of internal dispute. However, even in its technical usage for the assembled Israelites, empowered to exercise authority, it cannot be said that *q^{e}hal/q^{e}hillath* Israel was used comprehensively to designate the entire social system. Aside from its infrequent occurrence, the denotation is not so much "the assembly which is Israel" as "Israel in assembly." The *qāhāl* is, as it were, an instrument by which Israelites come together to reach collective decisions and to carry out ceremonial activities. The profile of the functions of the early assembly, sketchy as it is, points to tribes voluntarily in session ("ceremonial," "legislative," "executive," or "judicial" by turn) but retaining their respective autonomies.

26.4 The Tribes of Israel

The expression *shivṭē* Israel, "the tribes of Israel," may be the nearest approximation to a technical organizational term for the total Israelite society.[172] There are contexts in which it appears to have the sense of "the associated tribes composing Israel" or "confederated Israel." For example, Dan is called "one of the tribes of Israel" (Gen 49:16), and the assembled people with their heads are said to constitute "all the tribes of Israel together" (Deut. 33:5). We also meet the formulation: "according to the number of the tribes of the Israelites" (Josh. 4:5,8), and in a psalm, difficult to date but probably preserving very ancient terminology, we encounter *shivṭē* Yah, "the tribe of Yah(weh)" (Ps. 122:4), which reminds us of "Israel, the people of Yahweh." Also, in my view among the oldest elements in the late expanded narrative of Judges 21 is a series of idioms expressing the pleroma of Israel as a totality of tribes which cannot tolerate the loss of any one of its associated members (see discussion below in VI.27.4).

On balance, however, the relative infrequency of *shivṭē* Israel makes it doubtful that it was ever the customary way of referring to the social entirety. Even if we conjecture that it was once more widely used, eventually being replaced by the simpler "Israel" or "Israelites," it is notable that the term does not contain a distinctive common noun for the highest level of communal organization, comparable to the specificity of the Greek term "amphictyony" for an association of cities in a sacral league. To denote the most comprehensive level of organization, *shivṭē* Israel resorts to a plural form of the technical term for the primary subdivision in Israel. The comparable linguistic formation for a Greek sacral league would have been to speak of "the cities of Hellas." This relatively weak term accurately reflected the organizational looseness of the wider nonstatist unity of Israel as *an association of tribes,* a social system which apparently did not feel the need for a highly distinctive organizational term precisely because its structural life was articulated in a decentralized tribal arrangement.

We have discussed the terminology for the comprehensive social structure of early Israel sufficiently to provide a backdrop for the analysis of the subdivisions of the system. Further discussion of the overall form of the Israelite society, whether as a cultic "amphictyony" or as a military league, is reserved for Part VII, in which Noth's model of the Israelite social system will be critically analyzed and the outlines of an alternative suggested. In the meantime, characterizations of the subsidiary levels of social organization will be advanced in the following pages.

Primary Subdivisions of the Social Structure

27.1 *Shēveṭ* / *Maṭṭeh* = **Tribe**

Israel is divided into a number of units each of which may be called a *shēveṭ* (*shevāṭîm*, plural; *shivṭē* in plural constructions preceding a noun) or a *maṭṭeh* (*maṭṭōth*, plural). *Shēveṭ* is by far the most commonly used term in our sources. *Maṭṭeh* is typical of a smaller number of Priestly traditions which display a serious effort at systematization of the social organizational terminology. From the fact that both terms are applied to the same named divisions, there can be little doubt that, at least in almost all cases, they are alternative terms for the same social groupings (cf., e.g., the use of *shēveṭ* and *maṭṭeh* together in Num. 36:3). It is further noteworthy that both terms are used in a literal sense to refer to a "rod" or "staff" conceived as a weapon, an implement, or a ceremonial object, which includes military and political denotations of "staff" and "scepter." The force of the term as applied to a social unit apparently emphasizes the group's autonomy and potency in military self-defense and in political self-rule (cf. the Latin *fasces*, a bundle of rods bound together around an ax, carried before magistrates of ancient Rome as an emblem of authority).[173]

The several *shevāṭîm* can be viewed as distributive parts of one larger entity, as in the term "*shivṭē* Israel," normally translated as "the tribes of Israel," or in the expression "*shivṭē* Yah" (Ps. 122:4), "the tribes of Yah(weh)." Each *shēveṭ* has its own proper name (Reuben, Simeon, Judah, etc.), but it is a *shēveṭ* only by virtue of being one of the *shivṭē* Israel. Through its participation in Israel, the *shēveṭ* has standing as one of the primary segments of the whole people, and it shares jointly in that status equally with all the other *shivṭē* Israel. The precise number and names of the *shivṭē* Israel at the various stages of early history has been a subject of immense research and controversy, and the issue must be considered when we turn to Noth's amphictyonic model. But formally prior to that tangled set of issues, it is essential to establish that the widest community of Israel was subdivided into parts on the same general organizational level, each with equal status as a primary segment of one people. This proposition does not, however, imply that the *shevāṭîm* were demographically equal in size, nor does it imply that the *shevāṭîm* occupied regions of similar territorial extent, nor does it imply that all the *shevāṭîm* came into existence simultaneously or by the same process, nor does it imply that the several *shevāṭîm* were created or controlled by a central political organ in Israel.

It is also apparent that although *shēveṭ* and *maṭṭeh* were the appropriate general terms for the primary subdivisions of Israel, they were not invariably used when a subdivision was named. In fact, the subdivisions are referred to by name alone far more frequently than they are designated by a technical organizational term. For example, the early poem describing the victory of Deborah and Barak over the Canaanites can recount the activities of the subdivisions of Israel in vivid circumstantial detail without once characterizing a single one of them as a *shēveṭ* or *maṭṭeh*; indeed, only one sub-unit is given a generic term: Zebulun is an *'am,* "a people" (Judg. 5:18). It appears that in customary speech the technical terms were not required (we commonly say New York or California instead of the State of New York and the State of California).

The technical terms tend to appear with greater regularity when the point at issue is to describe how a person was selected out of the entire community, either for a particular office or for criminal punishment. They appear with greatest frequency, and often with a serious effort at rational systematization, when a comprehensive list is given (of blessings, or of territorial holdings, or of censuses, or of officers) in which both the parity and the severalty of the *shᵉvāṭīm* as articulated parts of all Israel come to the fore. It would be unwarranted, I believe, to assume that the technical terms were unknown to those who neglect to use them when referring to the subdivisions by proper names. The technical terms occur randomly enough in early texts to indicate that they were well known. The point seems to be that in most contexts their use was merely optional, while in some specialized contexts they were felt to be appropriate and even obligatory insofar as the writer strove by means of his chosen genre to give a synopsis of the social structure in accordance with the data available to him and according to his best lights.

Just as Israel can be termed *bᵉnē* Israel, so any *shēveṭ* in Israel can be analogously termed, e.g., *bᵉnē* Judah, *bᵉnē* Benjamin, *bᵉnē* Dan, etc. The plain meaning in such cases is simply "Judahites," "Benjaminites," and "Danites," but again the biological rootage of the metaphorically employed *bānīm* contributes to the conceptualization of all members of the *shēveṭ* as descendants from the eponymous ancestor whose name is identical with the name of the *shēveṭ*. This is simply a further refinement of the scheme of Jacob-Israel as the progenitor of all Israelites, in that each of Jacob-Israel's sons is the progenitor of all members of the *shēveṭ* named after him. This notion is spelled out not only in the pseudo-genealogies but also in the report that after the capture of Leshem, the Danites "called Leshem, Dan, after the name of their father [i.e., ancestor] Dan" (Josh. 19:47).

27.2 People / House = Tribe

A primary subdivision in Israel may also be called an *'am,* "a people," just as all Israel is an *'am,* e.g., Joseph claims to be "a numerous *'am*" (Josh. 17:14–17),

"Zebulun is an *'am*" (Judg. 5:18), and possibly we should also read "the people Gilead" (Judg. 10:18, deleting *sārē* from MT).

The referent of the name Gilead is an extremely vexed question which we can hardly hope to settle here, but some indication of the ambiguous range of geographical and sociopolitical meanings for Gilead may be useful to our subsequent discussion about tribal territoriality.[174] Predominantly in the biblical traditions, Gilead is a region, the rugged hill country in East Jordan, stretching roughly between the Wadi Yarmuk on the north and the Wadi Arnon on the south and bisected by the Wadi Jabbok. In the Song of Deborah it occurs as the name of one of the major fighting entities of Israel, among whom Gad, by contrast, is conspicuously absent. An obvious first thought is that Gad is simply a shortened form of Gilead, but the different etymologies of the two names do not permit that linguistic solution of the problem. As a region, Gilead is sometimes credited to Manasseh and sometimes to Gad.

In the Jephthah story, the term gives every indication of being a sociopolitical entity. As in the Song of Deborah, the expected Gad does not appear. Jephthah is said to have "passed through Gilead and Manasseh" (Judg. 11:29), which strongly suggests that the narrator conceives Gilead as a major subdivision in Israel on a par with Manasseh. In fact, Manasseh's holdings east of the Jordan covered the northern portions of the hill country of Gilead. Gilead is said to be "a people" with its own "elders," able to empower Jephthah as its "head and leader." A sociopolitical referent for the name Gilead is further supported by a reference in Numbers 36:1 to the heads of families of one of the "clan" subdivisions among the *bᵉnē* Gilead, i.e., Gileadites. The conclusion seems solid that at one period in early Israel the major group or *shēveṭ* in Transjordan located to the south of Manasseh was known as Gilead and that subsequently it became known as Gad. How that might have come about will be considered when we examine the principle of tribal territoriality.

A primary subdivision in Israel may also be designated a *bayith*, "a house," e.g., *bēth* Joseph, "house of Joseph" (Judg. 1:22, 35). The status of Joseph as one of the primary subdivisions in Israel is clouded by the fact that Joseph comprehends two subdivisions, namely, Ephraim and Manasseh, represented as his "sons." The anomaly may be understood tradition-historically as a result of the tradition's impetus to maintain the fiction that Israel was composed of precisely twelve *shᵉvāṭîm*, no more and no less. Thus, in some forms of the tribal system, Joseph stood as one *shēveṭ* (when eleven other *shᵉvāṭîm* were calculated), whereas in other forms of the tribal system Ephraim and Manasseh stood as two *shᵉvāṭîm* (when only ten other *shᵉvāṭîm* were calculated). This can produce curious "joins" between the two systems, as in Numbers 26, where the full inventory of the *mishpāḥōth/bᵉnē* Manasseh and the full inventory of the *mishpāḥōth/bᵉnē* Ephraim are preceded by a skeletal reference to "the *bᵉnē* Joseph according to their *mishpāḥōth:* Manasseh and

Ephraim" (26:28). The carefully wrought twelve-tribe symmetry of the census passage is thus disturbed by the inclusion of Joseph, which means that thirteen tribes are actually listed.

While granting that tradition-historical stylization was a factor in the way Joseph and Ephraim/Manasseh have developed as alternatives in the tribal rosters, we may nonetheless argue that the later stylization reflects an actual historic bifurcation of one large group (Joseph) into two autonomous groups (Ephraim and Manasseh), who remembered their original unity. This hypothesis is supported by the tradition in Joshua 17:14–18. The sub-history of tribal bifurcation was mirrored in the "father-sons" extended biological metaphorical scheme and employed as a unit of variable magnitude for adjusting twelve-tribe reckonings in various forms of the traditions. I assume, therefore, that at an early stage in the formation of Israel, there was a *shevet* called Joseph, and that it was this unit which is also called a *bayith*.

Although *bayith*, especially in the form *bēth-'āv*, "father's house," is most frequently used for a tertiary subdivision in Israel, it could be appropriately applied to a primary subdivision, just as it could be extended to a dynasty or to an entire kingdom composed of many formerly independent *shevāṭīm*. A *bayith* is more than a building, "a house" or a dwelling for a social unit, "a home"; it is a social organism which is "built up" through procreation and adoptions, "a household." Insofar as the *shevāṭīm* were represented as bodies of descendants from eponymous sons of Jacob, it was entirely natural to conceive them metaphorically as *bāṭīm*, "houses." In fact, it seems probable to me that in Ruth 4:11 the reference to "Rachel and Leah who together built up the house of Israel" contains a double meaning which incorporates the *bayith* as the immediate household of the ancestor Jacob and the wider *bayith* of the people of Israel descended from its ancestor. This intended double meaning is delivered by the phrase *bēth* Israel, using the less preferred proper name for the patriarchal ancestor (Israel in place of Jacob) because it was the highly preferred proper name for the whole people.

Moreover, there is a reference by Joshua to his *bayith* in Joshua 24:15 which may be a reference to his *shēvet*. Joshua is an Ephraimite and, in the context of the address to the assembly at Shechem, he is inviting the gathered peoples to enter covenant with Yahweh. He challenges them, "choose today whom you will serve, but as for me and my *bayith* we will serve Yahweh" (24:15). The setting of a great public assembly does not favor the common interpretation that by *bayith* Joshua simply means his own household. Since he is from the very subdivision of Israel which is also called *bēth* Joseph, it is probable that he refers either to *bēth* Joseph as his *bayith* (if the bifurcation has not yet occurred) or to *bēth* Ephraim as his *bayith* (if the bifurcation has occurred.) Furthermore, it is difficult to think that Joshua could have spoken with much authority if he represented only the commitment of his own family to Yahweh, whereas the authority represented by the backing of an entire *shēveṭ* (either Joseph or Ephraim) would have been more commensurate with his public appeal and with the positive response he evoked from the assembled peoples.

27.3 *Mishpāḥāh* = Tribe

Seemingly more curious is the use of the term *mishpāḥāh* for a primary subdivision, since this noun is normally restricted to secondary subdivisions in Israel and, among them, at times to units smaller than a single city or town. In the Samson stories, the hero's father is said to be from the town of Zorah of the Danite *mishpāḥāh* (Judg. 13:2). In the account of Micah and the Danites, Dan is again called a *mishpāḥāh* (Judg. 18:2), and Judah is likewise termed a *mishpāḥāh* (Judg. 17:7). There are, however, textual difficulties in both the last two citations.

Not only is *mishpaḥath* Judah lacking in one (Syriac), and possibly two (LXX[B]), of the versions, but the phrase's appositional connection in the passage is awkward, for the whole clause reads, "And there was a young man of Bethlehem of Judah, from the *mishpāḥāth* Judah, and he was a Levite" (17:7a). But if it is a late insertion it is odd that the less common term *mishpāḥāh* has been employed for Judah instead of the more common *shēveṭ*. Possibly it was intended as an appositional explanation for Bethlehem, namely, "belonging to a *mishpāḥāh* of Judah," but, had that been the intention, we would expect the specific name of the *mishpāḥāh*, especially since Judah was already mentioned earlier in the verse.

The originality of the designation of Judah as a *mishpāḥāh* is broadly supported by the specification of the Danites as a *mishpāḥāh* in the same story, although here too a textual uncertainty exists. The MT reads it as a singular, "And the Danites sent from their *mishpāḥāh* five men of substance (or standing), from Zorah and from Eshtaol, drawn from their total male population" (18:2). Both LXX and Targum have understood this as a plural, "from their [the Danites'] *mishpāḥōth*." Since no change is involved in the consonantal text, either understanding could have been read in the original text. If a singular was intended by the author, he obviously understood *mishpāḥāh* as a designation of all the Danites, comparable to *shēveṭ* in inclusiveness. If a plural was intended, on the other hand, he was referring to the *mishpāḥōth* as subdivisions of Dan. The question that the Danites put to the Levite throws some light on the problem, but not unambiguously, "Is it better for you to be a priest to the house of one man, or to be a priest to a *shēveṭ* and to a *mishpāḥāh* in Israel?" (18:19). Our first instinct is to read this as a reference to two entities in a whole-part relationship, i.e., the *mishpāḥāh* included in the *shēveṭ*, but in Hebrew the construction is perfectly fitting as a hendiadys, i.e., a reference to the same entity by means of two terms. That this is the probable meaning is supported by 18:30, where it is stated that Jonathan and his sons were priests to the whole *shēveṭ* of Dan and not merely to some segment within Dan. Accordingly, it seems best to read *mishpāḥāh* instead of *mishpāḥōth* in 18:2 and to acknowledge that in this story *shēvet* and *mishpāḥāh* are used interchangeably for a major entity in Israel.

Why does this story, and the Samson story as well, employ a term for Dan which normally refers to a segment of a *shēvet*? A possible explanation lies in the extreme plight to which Dan had been reduced because of its exposed position in the foothills abutting the coastal plain. Judges 1:34 reports that "the Amorites pressed the *bᵉnē* Dan back into the hill country, for they did not permit them to come down to the plain." Only the intervention of *bēth* Joseph (probably Ephraim) kept this region from being taken over altogether by the Canaanites in the plain, and perhaps this intervention did not occur until after most or all of the Danites had either moved to the headwaters of the Jordan or merged with other tribes. The pressure of the immigrating Philistines on the adjacent Danites is reflected in the tales of the virtuoso Samson. Although I would not overly press the point, because of the very schematic character of Numbers 26, it may be significant that in the enumerations of *mishpāḥōth* according to the *maṭṭōth*, only one *mishpāḥāh* is credited to Dan (vss. 42–43). For all the other *maṭṭōth* the numbers of *mishpāḥōth* range from three to eight, supplemented in many instances by a number of sons not specifically said to have formed *mishpāḥōth*. In the case of Dan, only the *mishpāḥāh* of Shuham is named (Hushim in Gen. 46:23). This is curious, since the formal pattern of the list is maintained, with the resulting oddity that the introduction and conclusion of the Danite entry speak of "their *mishpāḥōth*" and even of "the *mishpāḥōth* of the Shuhamites."

The paucity of Danite *mishpāḥōth* in Numbers 26 may of course be due to an accident of transmission, but the fact that P had so little internal data on Dan may well reflect the declining historical fortunes of the *shēvet*. First the Canaanite and then the Philistine military pressure on Dan reduced the *shēvet*'s population and its internal cohesion. The migration of Dan to the far north probably further disrupted its internal organization and may actually have led to the reorganization of the survivors from the remnants of originally separate *mishpāḥōth* into one *mishpāḥāh* which was virtually coterminous with the *shēvet*. The Danite warriors who move to the north are six hundred in number, and from all that we can judge of the account they are pictured as the total number of surviving arms-bearing Danites.

It is of course possible that not all the Danites migrated, but there is no clear indication that they continued as an integral autonomous group in the foothills where they originally tried to locate. By the time of the boundary lists of Joshua, the regions of Ephraim and Judah are so defined that little room is left for the Danites. Any Danites who remained in their old home region apparently joined with other adjacent *shᵉvātīm* and lost their specific identity as Danites. One indeed wonders if the main body of Danites has not already left the foothills by the time of Samson, for he gathers no military force around himself there and when he needs protection from the Philistines he flees into Judah. Furthermore, no boundaries are given for the relocated tribe of Dan. For all practical purposes its domain was coterminous with the city of Dan and its environs. Dan was a vastly diminished entity that only formally compared with the major *shᵉvāṭīm* of Israel and its migration would probably have been lost to memory altogether had not traditionists been interested in explaining the origins of the important northern sanctuary of Dan. In the beginning the sanctuary's importance was enhanced by the fact that its Levitical priest was Jonathan, grandson of Moses.[175] Later its importance was magnified when Jeroboam, the first ruler of the northern king-dom, made Dan into one of his two major border sanctuaries.

The circumstances of Dan's history thus go some distance toward explaining how terms that possessed a certain elusiveness to begin with could be applied interchangeably to a people whose internal structure had been badly strained, if not altogether pulverized. Dan was technically and formally a *shēveṭ*, one of the major autonomous groups involved in the early formation of Israel, but it was reduced in its social substance to little more than a sub-section of a usual *shēveṭ*, i.e., to a *mishpāḥāh*.

27.4 *Shēveṭ* = A Tribal Subdivision?

A possible anomaly of a different sort occurs at two points where sub-units within a customary *shēveṭ* appear to be called *shᵉvāṭīm*. This is the opposite of the fore-going anomalous class of usages: whereas there a usual term for secondary subdivisions in Israel, namely *mishpāḥāh*, is used for a primary subdivision, in this instance a usual term for a primary subdivision in Israel, namely *shēveṭ*, appears to be used for secondary subdivisions.

The two eccentric usages of *shēveṭ* occur in the story of the Benjaminite outrage. One is in Judges 20:12, where it is said that "the *shivṭē* Israel sent men though all the *shivṭē* Benjamin." Where we expect Benjamin to be called a *shēveṭ*, the text speaks of Benjamin as composed of two or more *shᵉvāṭīm*. The versions have corrected this plural to the singular, "the *shēveṭ* Benjamin," probably not because they had a different Hebrew text but because it seemed like an obvious slip on the part of the writer. The error, involving only one letter, could easily have been the result of inadvertently repeating the plural from the immediately preceding phrase, "*shivṭē* Israel." Or "*shivṭē* Benjamin" may have risen from an original "*bᵉnē* Benjamin." Some such textual correction seems the best solution for the difficulty.

The second usage of *shēveṭ* for a tribal sub-unit cannot be so easily dismissed. When the Israelites inquire as to whether all Israel responded to the muster against Benjamin, they ask, "Which one of the *shivṭē* Israel did not come up to Yahweh at Mizpah?" (Judg. 21:8) The culprit is discovered to be Jabesh-gilead in Transjordan. Now the most natural sense in which the Hebrew of 21:8 is to be read is that the Israelites were inquiring about *shᵉvāṭīm* as totalities and not about persons or cities within *sheᵛāṭīm*. The earlier form of the question in 21:5 is less exact and can be rendered, "Who [i.e., which persons or groups] from the *shivṭē* Israel did not come up in the assembly of Yahweh?" But the addition of *'eḥād,* emphasizing "which *one* of the *shivṭē* Israel" (vs. 8) seems purposefully precise in its specification that Jabesh-gilead was a *shēveṭ* in Israel.

Given the grotesque historical blunders of which Judges 19—21 is capable, it is difficult to know how to evaluate this use of *shēveṭ* for a city in Israel. Since the *sheᵛāṭīm* composing Israel are not distinguished by name in this story, we do not know how the author conceived the roster of tribes. It is remotely possible that he reckoned Jabesh-gilead as the equivalent of the tribe of Gilead or Gad, but this seems far-fetched, since there is no surviving hint anywhere else in the traditions of such an identification. Furthermore, if the author meant it literally, he at once lands himself in a further difficulty, namely, that in order to save one *shēveṭ* in Israel, i.e., Benjamin, he describes the obliteration of another *shēveṭ*, i.e., Jabesh-gilead! Normally such shocking inconsistencies would wholly discredit the originality of the term *shēveṭ*, but since the story is laden with many other incongruities, it is just possible that the traditionist relates a very old occasional usage of *shēveṭ* for a secondary subdivision and that he repeats it without harmonizing the usage with his overwhelming preference for *shēveṭ* as one of the primary subdivisions. Such a shaky foundation for this eccentric usage of *shēveṭ* does not provide much confidence, however, for believing it to be authentic usage, and it is best attributed to the clumsiness of the traditionist.

One other feature of the tendentious story of the Benjaminite outrage bears comment. In Judges 21 we find several statements embedded which emphasize the unity of the *shivṭē* Israel and the absolute necessity of preserving the segments of Israel in their totality. Four times the point is made and in each case with an exceedingly strong verb or noun. Benjamin's defeat means that "a *shēveṭ* is lacking in Israel" (vs. 3), "a *shēveṭ* is cut off from Israel" (vs. 6), or that "a breach in the *shivṭē* Israel" (vs. 15) has been made. To forestall the definitive loss of Benjamin, its survivors must be given wives so that it can re-form itself, "that a *shēveṭ* be not blotted out from Israel" (vs. 17). Now if this remarkably intense sentiment, repeated and artfully elaborated, is detached from its artificial context, we can recognize it as a very ancient basic concern in premonarchic Israel. The contrived circumstance that this loss of a segment of Israel resulted from military action by eleven Israelite tribes attacking one Israelite tribe does not bear serious historical scrutiny. We have seen in the Jephthah story that Israelites sometimes fought one another, but there is no other account beside Judges 19—21 of a whole segment of Israel being virtually wiped out by fellow Israelites. That feature of the tradition is attributable to its fierce anti-Benjaminite animus, which also shows up in the denigration of Jabesh-gilead, a city closely connected with the Benjaminite Saul.

But the ideology of the wholeness of the *shivṭē* Israel as "members one of another" is all the more noteworthy since it rises in contradiction to the supposed action against Benjamin and serves in the end to temper the predominantly anti-Benjaminite spirit of the account. That ideology seems anciently rooted and independent of the historical fabrications surrounding it. Segments of old Israel were repeatedly faced with the threat of annihilation, and it was only through cooperation among the tribes that total disaster was averted for this or that *shēvet.* What is here purportedly said of Benjamin as the result of a fanciful all-Israelite onslaught against it is nonetheless historically very pertinent to many of the *shevāṭīm* in Israel. It would apply to greatly weakened Dan, pushed back into the southern foothills and finally migrating to the north. It would fit Issachar, bending low under Canaanite forced labor in the Valley of Esdraelon. It would correspond to the plight of Reuben and Gad in East Jordan, suffering decline to the point that we seldom hear of them in the later history. It would illuminate the lot of Simeon, which finally had to take refuge within Judah; and it would suit Benjamin proper after its forces under Saul met such crushing defeat by the Philistines at Gilboa. Famine and disease may well have had similar effects upon Israelite groups. My point is that this theme of all Israel taking action to prevent the loss of any segment is authentic for old Israel, however devious and distorted its literary and historical formulation in Judges 19—21. The vivid language of the above-cited formulations about the threat of the loss of a *shēvet* to Israel stands out from the clumsy, verbose style of the story and suggests that these may well be ancient idiomatic, even proverbial sayings. Mutual help among the segments of ancient Israel was a foundation of its early existence, and though proffered inconsistently, it was this solidarity in aid which gave concrete social reality to the unity of Israel. In short, *shevāṭīm* were not only autonomous sociopolitical and military units; they were segmental members of larger Israel, ideologically committed to aid one another whenever the autonomy and integrity of a single tribe were threatened.

27.5 *Shēvet* as a Territorial and Organizational Unit

The *shevāṭīm* in Israel are territorial groupings as well as primary organizational units. As there is an *'erets* Israel, "land of Israel," so there is an *'erets* Benjamin, "land of Benjamin," or an *'erets* Judah, "land of Judah." By territorial groupings in premonarchic Israel I do not mean what is implied by the allotment lists of Joshua 13—19, which were administrative lists for the kingdom of David and the early kingdom of Solomon. For old Israel a territorial grouping was not a bounded administered space, controlled by a centralized government, but rather a territory within which the *shēvet* lived, the settlements and fields which it occupied and cultivated and grazed, and the natural resources of the region which it exploited. This concept depends in large measure on anthropological delineations of tribal society and will require further explication. For the moment we may simply emphasize that the *sheᵛāṭīm* were not entities distributed horizontally in the land occupied by Israelites, so that members of all or many of the *sheᵛāṭīm* characteristically lived together; they were social entities vertically distributed in the land, so that their members lived contiguously and controlled an entire region.

Vertical distribution of the *sheᵛāṭīm* is the "ideal typical" base from which we should start for the conditions in old Israel. With the monarchy, the factors of political centralization, social stratification, speculative commerce, urban growth, and wars and famine eroded the foundations of the system of vertical distribution of the tribes, and increasingly the tribes were horizontally distributed. Vertical and horizontal distributions of tribal members were mixed together. In rural areas and small towns, the *shēveṭ* as an encompassing systemic social unit remained relatively strong. In the larger cities and in the countryside controlled by the crown or speculative landlords, the *shēveṭ* was attenuated to little more than a regional or traditional concept and the actual functioning systemic realities were the state and class stratification. The *shēveṭ* (and the *mishpāḥāh* in particular) was less and less a viable protective social unit as persons from many *sheᵛāṭīm* were thrown together in new social and political structures with which the un-centralized organization of the *shēveṭ* could not cope.

Yet even for earliest Israel we should not present the ideal type of the vertically distributed *shēveṭ* in too rigid a way. We do not mean to imply, for example, that the region of the *shēveṭ* was unchanging in scope or even in general location. (Dan moved a great distance from the southwest frontier of Israel to the far northeast frontier; Manasseh, and probably Ephraim as well, spread over the Jordan into the highlands of Gilead, etc.) Nor should we imply that the population of each *shēveṭ* was hermetically sealed off from the populations of all the other *sheᵛāṭīm*, for there is evidence that members of one *shēveṭ* sometimes lived in the recognized territory of another *shēveṭ* as a result of special circumstances. Levitical priests itinerated throughout the landed *sheᵛāṭīm*. Members of one *shēveṭ* made pilgrimages to sanctuaries located in another *shēveṭ* and the great festivals mixed people together from many, and on occasion perhaps from all the *sheᵛāṭīm*. Organization for war frequently brought members of contiguous *sheᵛāṭīm* together, and in great emergencies most or all of them fought together for the collective defense.

In fact, far from being "frozen" geographically or demographically, it is clear that the *sheᵛāṭīm* developed over time and space, with both the component members and the territory occupied undergoing change, sometimes of a pronounced nature. We have seen this to be true in the case of the migration of Dan from the southern shephelah to the headwaters of the Jordan. We have noted also the probable bifurcation of Joseph into Ephraim and Manasseh. The history underlying the bifurcation is sketched in Joshua 17:14–18, where it is suggested that Joseph was at first concentrated in the highlands of southern Samaria and that it eventually spread into the highlands and broader valleys of northern Samaria as far as the Valley of Esdraelon. This wider distribution of Joseph led to regional and agricultural diversification of the people which was significant enough to create two distinguishable social entities corresponding to the southern region, namely Ephraim, and to the northern region, namely Manasseh.

We earlier hypothesized that the *shēveṭ* in Transjordan lying immediately to the south of the Manassite settlement was known as Gilead at first and later as Gad. It is generally granted by historians of the settlement that Manassites colonized northern Transjordan from their prior base in West Jordan, thus creating the so-called half-tribes of Manasseh on either side of the Jordan.[176] It has also been claimed, on the basis of some scattered biblical clues, that Reuben once lived in West Jordan but, unlike Manasseh, lost its foothold there altogether and moved in its entirety to Transjordan.[177] On still slighter specific grounds, but by analogy with Manasseh and Reuben, it has been suggested that Gad too was at first settled in West Jordan and only subsequently moved to Transjordan.[178] In this way it would be possible to explain the change of name from Gilead to Gad, the migrants having brought their name with them. However, we then have to account for a discontinuity in Israelite population between the group known as Gilead in the Song of Deborah and the Jephthah stories and the group known as Gad, unless we can explain the change of names by some other means than by major population change.

Perhaps the change is better explained by the assumption that Gilead was at first the sole Israelite *shēveṭ* in Transjordan and was named for the mountainous heights that stretched north and south of the Jabbok River. When, however, Manassite colonization north of the Jabbok and the entrance of Reuben in the south resulted in three *shevāṭim* occupying portions of Gilead, and with the expansion of tribal Gilead away from geographical Gilead and into Moab, it became appropriate to change the name of the original *shevet*. Whether the name Gad derived from elements who crossed from West Jordan to join the old Gilead or from some entirely unknown source, the name was perhaps chosen because it was similar enough in sound to the former group name of Gilead to make it acceptable to common usage.

But in this context, more important than the name change from Gilead to Gad is the evidence of Israelite population movements which resulted in shifting areas of tribal settlement and in changes in the composition of the tribal populations.[179] In fact, memories of heated disputes among the tribes over the Transjordan colonization are transmitted in Judges 12:1–6, where Ephraim deprecates the Gileadites as "fugitives" or "refugees" of Ephraim. This may imply a specifically Ephraimite migration to Transjordan, which may incidentally account for the curious place name "the forest of Ephraim" for an area in Transjordan (II Sam. 18:6). In any case, enough has been said about the Transjordan tribes, joined with similar information from the tribes west of the Jordan, to validate the point that the *sh*ᵉ*vāṭīm* were far from being static entities with absolutely fixed boundaries and with unbroken demographic continuity.

That the *shēveṭ* was both a primary unit of social organization and a territorial grouping is corroborated by a wide range of biblical evidence. David, for instance, found the social and territorial groupings of the *sh*ᵉ*vāṭīm* a ready-made basis for administrative divisions in his kingdom. In Judges the *sh*ᵉ*vāṭīm* are represented as concentrated demographically and acting militarily within regions that correspond approximately to the tribal territorial heartland regions embraced in Joshua 13—19, but not with regard to the exact boundaries meticulously recorded there. Moreover, it was a standard practice in ancient Israel to identify settlements by their locations in a particular *shēveṭ*, e.g., Gibeah of Benjamin or Bethlehem of Judah, and when persons identified themselves under David's monarchy, they were asked, "From what *city* are you?," to which they answered, "Your servant is of such and such a *shēveṭ* in Israel" (II Sam. 15:2–3). This is apparently an ellipsis for the full reply, "of such and such a *city* of such and such a *shēveṭ*," e.g., from Kedesh of Naphtali or from Bethel of Ephraim, etc.

Nonetheless, it is equally clear from the surviving data about the peculiar sub-histories of the *sh*ᵉ*vāṭīm* that the existence of a general organizational level of primary subdivisions in Israel must not be construed as a neat "cookie cutter" device that was arbitrarily imposed. The system of the *sh*ᵉ*vāṭīm* was rather more like a summing up of basic organizational units determined by a range of variable factors involving demography, agricultural mix, territory, and historical circumstances, which joined in varying proportions in the concrete formations of individual *sh*ᵉ*vāṭīm*.[180]

28

Secondary Subdivisions of the Social Structure

A secondary subdivision of the people Israel is normally termed either a *mishpāḥāh (mishpāḥōth,* plural; *mishpaḥath* in singular constructions preceding a noun) or *'eleph ('ªlāphīm,* plural; *'alphē* in plural constructions preceding a noun). *Mishpāḥāh* is by far the most frequent term, whereas *'eleph* appears in a few ancient texts, in which it seems that *'eleph* and *mishpāḥāh* refer either to the same social unit or to the same general level of organization. In Priestly census lists, however, such as Numbers 1 and 26, *mishpāḥāh* and *'eleph,* although associated, are not simply interchangeable. In fact, *'eleph* has a distinctive military organizational meaning which is unfortunately obscured by the Priestly traditionist's misreading of *'eleph* as the number "one thousand."

28.1 *Mishpāḥāh* = Protective Association of Families

We have already noted a very few instances where *mishpāḥāh* is used for a primary subdivision of the people, equivalent to a *shēveṭ.* In the great majority of cases, however, *mishpāḥāh* is either directly referred to in context as a social unit smaller than a *shēveṭ,* often clearly included within a *shēveṭ,* or is so described as to indicate that it is conceived as a social unit smaller than a *shēveṭ.* On the other hand, *mishpāḥāh* designates an entity larger than a *bēth-'āv;* and where the two appear together in a single context, the *mishpāḥāh* is inclusive of the *bēth-'āv.*

What is a *mishpāḥāh?* The noun is derived from a verb with the meaning of "to pour out" or "to shed," apparently having water, blood, and/or semen in mind.[181] The social solidarity implied in the root accords with the information we have on who composed a *mishpāḥāh* and what its social functions were. A *mishpāḥāh* is composed of "kinsmen" (not implying common descent as such but basically a community of shared interests) and the organization of the *mishpāḥāh* has certain definite functions for protecting the solidarity of its members. It also has military functions, a point to which we shall return when we examine the term *'eleph.* Furthermore, all available evidence suggests that the *mishpāḥāh* lived together in the same village or neighborhood, a matter of great importance for plotting the location of the *mishpāḥāh* in a general anthropological typology of social organizational forms. The ambiguous intermediate position of the *mishpāḥāh* is expressed in the equivocation of the English translators who sometimes prefer "clan" and sometimes "family" (in the sense of extended or larger family). It is better to keep the meaning more open, however, and so we shall translate *mishpāḥāh* by the more neutral, and structurally more accurate, term "protective association of extended families."

The textual data on the *mishpāḥāh* are considerable. When Abimelech, son of Gideon by a Shechemite concubine, seeks aid in establishing himself as king in Shechem he goes "to all the *mishpāḥāh* of his mother's *bēth-'āv*" (Judg. 9:1). Shimei ben Gera is "a man of the *mishpāḥāh* of *bēth* Saul" (II Sam. 16:5). Rahab's *bēth-'āv*, "father's house," in Jericho is spared from annihilation by the Israelites because she had befriended and collaborated with the spies who scouted the city (Josh. 2:12–13,18;6:25), but the social unit to which Rahab belonged is also described once as a *mishpāḥāh*: "and they brought out Rahab, and her father and mother and brother and all who belonged to her, and all her *mishpāḥāh* [reading singular with LXX, Syriac, and Vulgate instead of MT plural] and set them outside the camp of Israel" (Josh. 6:23). In the other references, "all who belong to her" (or "to them," i.e., to her father and mother and siblings) are understood as forming a *bēth-'āv*, but in 6:23 the *bēth-'āv* is expanded to a *mishpāḥāh*. Since *mishpāḥāh* has not occurred earlier in the Rahab traditions, it is probable that it is a secondary feature added to emphasize the considerable size of the Rahab group. Even so, the addition attests to the interlock between *bēth-'āv* and *mishpāḥāh*, the latter being a larger association of *bēth-'āvōth*, for it would have been pointless to include *mishpāḥāh* if it simply was a synonym for the members of the *bēth-'āv*, i.e., her father and mother and brothers.

The implication of the foregoing references is that the *mishpāḥāh* is a larger unit encompassing the *bēth-'āv*. This is brought out explicitly in two passages, from E and D traditions respectively, which describe a systematic search of the Israelite people in order to locate, in the one case, an offender who is to be punished (Josh. 7) and, in the other case, Yahweh's designate as the king of Israel (I Sam. 10:17–27).

Joshua 7 tells of the search for the Israelite who violated the ban against taking booty from Jericho. The search narrative is articulated in two sections: first a command by Yahweh declaring the oracular procedure for ascertaining the criminal and, second, an account of the implementation of the procedure. The command states:

> You shall be brought near by your *shᵉvāṭīm* and the *shēveṭ* which Yahweh takes shall draw near by *mishpāḥōth*, and the *mishpāḥāh* which Yahweh takes shall draw near by *bātīm* and the *bayith* which Yahweh takes shall draw near man by man (7:14).

The implementation of the command is reported as follows:

> So Joshua . . . brought Israel near by its *shᵉvāṭīm* and the *shēveṭ* of Judah was taken, and he brought near the *mishpāḥōth* [reading plural with some Hebrew MSS and LXX] of Judah and the *mishpāḥāh* of Zerah was taken; and he brought near the *mishpāḥāh* of Zerah, and Zabdi was taken, and he brought near his [i.e., Zabdi's, or LXX, Zimri's] *bayith* man by man, and Achan the son of Carmi, son of Zabdi, son of Zerah, of the *maṭṭeh* of Judah was taken (7:16–18).

The conception here is schematically clear: The *shēveṭ* of Judah (or *maṭṭeh*, which is omitted in LXX^*BA*) is composed of several *mishpāḥōth*, one of them being the *mishpaḥath* Zerah. The *mishpaḥath* Zerah is composed of *bātīm*, one of which is *bēth* Zabdi (or Zimri). *Bēth* Zabdi is represented as consisting of at least four generations: Zabdi–Carmi–Achan–Achan's unnamed sons and daughters. Zerah appears among the *mishpāḥōth* in Numbers 26:20 belonging to Judah and is apparently additionally reckoned to Simeon (Num. 26:13), the *shēveṭ* which was absorbed into Judah before the monarchy.

In I Samuel 10:17–27, a schematic search is reported in order to single out by oracular lot the one who is to be king over Israel. The twofold articulation of Joshua 7 recurs, except that the command is given in incomplete form and the terms of the command and its reported implementation do not entirely correspond. Samuel declares:

Present yourselves before Yahweh by your *sheᵛāṭīm* and by your *ᵃlāphīm!*

The narrative reports:

Samuel brought near all the *shivṭē* Israel and the *shēveṭ* Benjamin was taken. He brought near the *shēveṭ* Benjamin by its *mishpāḥōth*, and the *mishpāḥāh* of the Matrites [perhaps Bichrites, cf. Gen. 46:21: I Sam. 9:1; II Sam. 20:1; I Chron. 7:6,8] was taken. And he brought near the *mishpāḥāh* of the Matrites [Bichrites?] man by man (with LXX), and Saul the son of Kish was taken (10:20–21).

As in Joshua 7 we observe a stage-by-state sifting of the people by the oracular lot in which there is a progressive narrowing of candidates, until the king designate is finally reached by the process of elimination. The stages are, however, not threefold, since the *bēth-ᵓāv* is not mentioned (although probably implied by the identification of Saul as *ben* Kish). Except for the most inclusive term *shēveṭ*, the terms of the command and of the narrative report are asymmetrical. *'Eleph* in the command is replaced by *mishpāḥāh* in the execution of the command.

Saul is here said to be of the *mishpāḥāh* of Matrites. This name appears nowhere else in the Old Testament and is conspicuously absent from Kish's genealogy in I Sam. 9:1. Some have suggested replacing Matri with Bichri. Becher is listed as a son of Benjamin in Genesis 46:21 and in I Chronicles 7:6,8. The name Becorath appears in the genealogy of Kish (I Sam. 9:1) and the Benjaminite Sheba is called *ben* (i.e., "son of") Bichri (II Sam. 20:1). The substitution of Bichri for Matri has some appeal, but there is no manuscript support and the last two references noted create difficulties. If Bichri (II Sam. 20:1) and Becorath (I Sam. 9:1) refer to the same person or social unit (*mishpāḥāh*), they do not correlate generationally. Becorath is three generations prior to Kish (and four to Saul), whereas Bichri is only one generation prior to Sheba. Since Sheba and Saul are at least contemporaries, and more likely in successive generations, Sheba being the younger, Sheba *ben* Bichri would have to be read as a gentilic meaning, "Sheba the Bichrite" rather than literally, "Sheba, biological son of Becher." Indeed, the form Bichri, rather than Becher, suggests a gentilic interpretation. But to harmonize Bichri and Becorath, on the assumption that they designate the same *mishpāḥāh*, runs into the difficulty that Becorath in Kish's genealogy is followed by yet another name, Aphiah; if, however, Becorath really stands for the name of the *mishpāḥāh*, we should expect it to end the series of names as the most inclusive social unit within Benjamin to which Kish belonged. All in all, it seems best to retain Matri in I Samuel 10:21 as the name of Saul's *mishpāḥāh* in spite of the solitariness of the reference and our resulting inability to draw social correlations between it and other information about Saul's kin.

Another type of narrative throws some light on *mishpāḥāh*, and that is the genre in which a person chosen for some public honor offers social demurrers protesting his unfitness to be so honored. The objections are so conventionally formulated that they seem to have belonged to an accepted etiquette of modesty and protestation which had to be indulged in no matter how eager the person may actually have been to accept the honored position.

For example, in I Samuel 9, when Samuel first broaches the kingship to Saul, he says: "And for whom is all that is desirable in Israel? Is it not for you and for all your *bēth-'āv*?" (9:20), to which Saul responds: "Am I not a Benjaminite, from the least of the *shivṭe* Israel? And is not my *mishpāḥāh* the weakest of all the *mishpāḥōth* of my *shēveṭ* Benjamin?" [repointing MT, which now reads "*shivṭē* Benjamin"; Targum, Vulgate read "*shēveṭ* of Benjamin"] (9:21). The *bēth-'āv*, "father's house," referred to by Samuel is not mentioned in Saul's reply. It is doubtful, however, that the narrator intends *bēth-'āv* and *mishpāḥāh* to be interchangeable. Rather it appears that Saul responds at once with the customary references to the larger kin solidarity to which his *bayith* belongs, and he objects that it is inappropriate for such a weak *mishpāḥāh* to have one of its *bēth-'āvōth* so highly honored. This reading of the conversation is supported by the exchange between Saul and David when the former, as king, offers his elder daughter Merab to the latter, as one of his military commanders (I Sam. 18:17–19). David's protestation insists, "Who am I and who is my *ḥay*, the *mishpāḥāh* of my father in Israel, that I should be son-in-law to the king?" (18:18). In this instance, where the honor is not even a public office but a privileged marriage tie, David too responds not with a reference to his *bēth-'āv* but to the larger entity, "the *mishpāḥāh* of my father in Israel," which is understood not in the sense of "the *mishpāḥāh* headed by my father" but rather in the sense of "the *mishpāḥāh* in Israel to which my father and his *bayith* belong."

But what is the *ḥay* to which David refers in conjunction with the *mishpāḥāh*? Arguing on the principle of the originality of the more difficult reading, it is likely that the rare form *ḥay* [repointing MT *ḥayyīm*, which incorrectly understood David to be saying, "What is my life?"] was original to the text and *mishpaḥath-'āvī* was added to explain the obscure *ḥay*. This is the sole occurrence of *ḥay* as a masculine noun, but the feminine *ḥayyāh* as a term for a unit of military organization occurs in II Samuel 23:13, "and a *ḥayyāh* of Philistines was encamped in the valley of Rephaim." *Ḥayyāh* may also be used similarly in II Samuel 23:11 and Psalm 68:10 (11), but syntax and context in both cases are so problematic as to warrant leaving these verses out of our account. The term in I Samuel 18:18 as commonly understood is "kinsfolk," but that a specific social unit is intended is suggested by the explanatory *mishpaḥath-'āvī*, by parallel demurrers of Saul in I Samuel 9 and Gideon in Judges 6, and by the reference to the Philistine *ḥayyāh* as a fighting unit.

W. Robertson Smith noted that *ḥayyāh/ḥay* are cognate with an Arabic word *ḥayy* denoting a group of families united by blood-ties which moved and acted together, forming a unit smaller than a tribe but larger than a single family.[182] It would of course be inexcusably simplistic to transfer everything known about the group in Arabia to ancient Israel merely on the strength of the linguistic cognates. The Arabian evidence, however, does strengthen the supposition that the *ḥay/ḥayyāh* was a social unit in old Israel. It is possibly significant that the two Old Testament uses of *ḥay/ḥayyāh* for a social unit occur in military contexts from the time of Saul and David. A Philistine fighting unit is called a *ḥayyāh*, and David speaks of his *ḥay* in Israel in a context where he is offered reward and encouragement for his military leadership against the Philistines. The term may thus have been restricted to military organization and dropped out of usage altogether when the more common *'eleph* become current in military parlance. Alternatively, *ḥay/ḥayyāh* may once have had a wider social denotation but managed to survive only in military organization and then only briefly in the early monarchy.

To complete our examination of the demurrer narratives, we call attention to Judges 6:14–15 in which Yahweh says to Gideon, "Go in this might of yours and deliver Israel from the hand of Midian; do not I send you?", to which Gideon responds in the familiar manner of a demurrer, "Pray, Lord, how can I deliver Israel? Behold, my *'eleph* is the weakest in Manasseh, and I am the least in my *bēth-'āv*." Clearly, *'eleph* here occupies the position filled by *mishpāḥāh* in the other demurrer speeches. The most probable explanation of the preference for *'eleph* in this context is that the Gideon narratives go on to make frequent references to the *'alāphīm* as fighting elements in the war against Midian. The stereotyped modesty and repetitious formalism of all these demurrer speeches means that we cannot take seriously the claim that in all these cases the social unit or the person deprecated were in fact generally recognized as "weak" or "inferior." They are simply stylized, socially mandated self-deprecations.

Before we turn to an analysis of *'eleph* for a secondary subdivision in old Israel, we can get a somewhat more detailed conception of the scope and functions of the *mishpāḥāh*, particularly by examining what is said about the *mishpāḥāh* in the Book of Ruth and some related passages in Leviticus and Numbers.

In a sense the entire Book of Ruth is an explication in popular form of the function of the *mishpāḥāh*. Regrettably the narrative form pays little attention to explaining the social forms and functions that underlie the action, with the exception of a brief note on the customary and contractual meaning of "drawing off the sandal" (4:7). The general plot is well known. It concerns a decimated family of "Ephrathites from Bethlehem" (1:2) who, in order to escape famine, lived for some time in Moab. At the death of Elimelech, the head of the family, and of his two sons, Elimelech's widow Naomi and Mahlon's widow, the Moabitess Ruth, return from Moab to Bethlehem. There they meet Boaz, who is described as follows: "Now Naomi had a *mōda'* [preferring Q over K in MT] of her husband's, a man of wealth, of the *mishpāḥāh* of Elimelech, whose name was Boaz" (2:1). *Mōda'*, from the verb "to know," may be rendered as "a known kinsman," which is further defined as one who belonged to the same *mishpāḥāh* as Elimelech.

Naomi further explains Boaz's social position to Ruth: "The man is *qārōv* to us; he is one of our *gō'alīm*" (2:20). When Ruth remarks on her overtures to Boaz, she tells him "You are a *gō'ēl*," to which Boaz replies with personal appreciation but with the further clarification, "It is true that I am a *gō'ēl*. There is, however, a *gō'ēl* more *qārōv* than I" (3:12). How are the terms *qārōv* and *gō'ēl* to be understood in this context? *Qārōv* is the common Hebrew adjective for "near" or "close" and is applied to proximity of person, place, or time. Here the meaning is obviously of person, i.e., Boaz is a "near relative" of Naomi and Ruth, but he also knows of a man who is a "nearer relative" than himself. *Gō'ēl*, a participle functioning as a noun, derives from *gā'al*, "to buy back" or "to restore" the property, person, or honor of someone, specifically by fulfilling the role of *gō'ēl*, "kinsman protector," on behalf of someone with a prescribed social claim to merit the activation of the practice or institution of the *ge'ullāh*, "kin protection" or "kin restoration." It is permissible to speak of the *gō'ēl* as "redeemer" provided that the English term is shorn of all later and secondary allusions to moral or spiritual salvation.[183]

The joining of *qārōv* and *gō'ēl* in Boaz's reply to Ruth indicates that the primary criterion of "nearness" is Boaz's eligibility to perform the role of protector or restorer of his and Elimelech's *mishpāḥāh* by marrying Ruth and siring a son who will continue the line of the threatened *bēth-'āv* of Elimelech. As the story later makes it clear, this also involves paying off the debt on a small piece of land that belongs to Elimelech's line (as least that seems the most likely interpretation).[184] Thus to serve as a *gō'ēl* means in this instance to be the "protector" or "restorer" of the *bēth-'āv* of Elimelech by assuring the deceased a continuing line of male heirs and a piece of land to sustain the *bēth-'āv*. Boaz acknowledges that he is a potential *gō'ēl* on behalf of Elimelech and thus also of Naomi and Ruth; but he also indicates that he is not first in the line of potential *gō'alīm*. He knows of one who has the first option on the role of *gō'ēl*; and, as the story develops, Boaz is only free to marry Ruth when the man with the first option declines on the grounds that to marry Ruth and pay off the debt on the plot of ground would jeopardize his own patrimony.

What is it that constitutes the eligibility of Boaz and of the unnamed nearer relative to serve as *gō'ēl* for the *bēth-'āv* of Elimelech? They are clearly not of the immediate house of Elimelech, for all males of that house have perished. What constitutes their eligibility is that they are members of the same *mishpāḥāh* as was Elimelech, i.e., their *bēth-'āvōth* are grouped together in a larger *mishpāḥāh* to which Elimelech's *bēth-'āv* belonged. But the role of *gō'ēl* is not equally open to all male members of the *mishpāḥāh* simultaneously. Eligibility to act as *gō'ēl* follows a prescribed order according to degrees of nearness to and distance from the kinsman to be restored. The story of Ruth tells us nothing in detail about this order of eligibility to act the *gō'ēl* and the evidence for reconstructing any order is meager and rendered particularly confusing by the several functions which are embraced in the Old Testament under the work of the *gō'ēl*.

The various functions of the *gō'ēl* in old Israel are as follows: (1) to raise up a male heir for a deceased family head; (2) to buy up or buy back property so that it remains in or returns to the social group; (3) to purchase the release of a group member who has fallen into debt slavery, or to pay off his debt so that he does not fall into debt slavery; (4) to avenge the death of a member of the group. In the story of Ruth, the first two functions are involved, although the provision of a male heir receives primary attention and the purchase of the property as a motif is not well integrated and developed in the account. The raising up of a son for the deceased so that his line may continue is attested in the levirate law of Deuteronomy 25:5–10, which provides that in instances where brothers live together, the surviving brother will marry the deceased's widow and raise a male heir for him. Boaz is obviously not acting on the basis of this law, since he was not a brother of Elimelech. Nor does the limited levirate law envision any line of eligibility, even among brothers (e.g., from eldest brother on in order of age), since it speaks only of a situation where two brothers live together. If the work of the *gō'ēl* were restricted in the Bible to the levirate marriage as described in Deuteronomy 25, we would have to be suspicious of the whole conception of *gō'ēl* as it is attributed to Boaz. But since *gō'ēl* embraces many functions, it is altogether plausible that the levirate law of Deuteronomy 25 is an attenuated form of a once more general obligation of a *mishpāḥāh* through the agency of the *gō'ēl* to keep all of its member *bēth-'āvōth* alive and functioning through an emergency form of marriage. Indeed, strictly speaking, the levirate of Deuteronomy 25 was unnecessary to preserve the line of the *bēth-'āv*, since the surviving brother's sons would retain the grandfather's name and inherit the property of the *bēth-'āv* through their father. The levirate actually only provides for the continuation of the personal name of the deceased brother. Deuteronomy 25: 5–10 might then be understood as a last surviving shred of that older practice which was obligatory on an entire *mishpāḥāh* and which could by the Deuteronomist's time only be enforced at most in cases where biological brothers still lived together and had close personal ties. Even so, it is clear from the form of the legislation that even the limited practice could not be uniformly enforced.

Only in the Priestly materials do we find information on the order of succession in filling the *gō'ēl* role, or rather in filling one of the *gō'ēl's* several roles, and such data must be used with the caution that we are not certain how far back into old Israel they actually carry. Apart, perhaps, from the extremely questionable provision for release of debt in the year of Jubilee, the laws on the *gō'ēl* in the Holiness Code of Leviticus seem to reflect old conditions. They prescribe that if an Israelite has to sell himself into debt slavery, "one of his brothers may redeem him, or his uncle, or his cousin may redeem him, or one of *she'ēr besārō mimmishpahto* may redeem him" (Lev. 25:48–49). The Hebrew phrase means literally, "one of the bodily flesh belonging to his *mishpāḥāh*," i.e., a fellow member of his *mishpāḥāh*. Three degrees in the order of obligation or eligibility to act as the restorer of the enslaved man are specified. First option falls to the biological brothers. Second option falls to the uncle. Third option falls to the cousin. Nothing is said about an order of priority within each category, e.g., when there is more than one brother, uncle, or cousin. Nor is it clear how uncles and cousins are counted. Are they paternal uncles or maternal uncles or both? Are they parallel cousins (children of siblings of the same sex), or are they cross cousins (children of siblings of the opposite sex), or are both included? Beyond these three degrees in the performance of the redemption role the law does not go. Whether it means that the traditionist knew of no further degrees or simply broke off the fuller series, either to save space or because further degrees in the series were not often reached in practice, it is impossible to say. He simply gathers up all other eligibilities to perform as *gō'ēl* of the enslaved debtor under the rubric, "any fellow member of his *mishpāḥāh*." From this remark it is clear that P understood the *mishpāḥāh* to be the widest social unit that had the obligation to do *gō'ēl* service for any of its needy members.

On the hypothesis that the same or similar order of degrees of obligation or eligibility may have applied to other *gō'ēl* functions beside delivering an enslaved debtor, we may ask how Boaz's situation compares to what is described in Leviticus 25:48–49. He is not the brother, and probably he is neither an uncle nor a cousin to Elimelech, since we would expect so close a relationship to have occasioned some comment in the text. Apparently he was an instance of "one of the fellow members of the *mishpāḥāh*" of Elimelech. Perhaps the unnamed *gō'ēl* who declined his right and deferred to Boaz was an uncle or cousin of Elimelech, since the absence of comment on the relationship would correspond to the literary convention by which he remains unnamed, but I see no positive reason for assuming that he was so near a relative of Elimelech. The only thing we know is that he was "nearer" to Elimelech than was Boaz.

Another tradition from P is of pertinence, namely, the provision for inheritance by daughters, which is given a narrative connection in Numbers 27 through a ruling on behalf of the inheritance of Zelophehad of Manasseh, who died in the wilderness without having fathered any sons. The daughters protest, "Why should the name of our father be taken away from his *mishpāhāh*, because he had no son? Give us a possession among our father's brethren" (Num. 27:4). The ruling then follows that a man who has no sons may pass on his inheritance to his daughters. If he has no daughters, the inheritance passes to his brothers. If he has no brothers, it passes to paternal uncles. Finally, *sh*ᵉ*ērō haq-qārōv 'ēlāv mimmish-pahtō*, "the nearest relative of his *mishpāhāh*" (vs.11), may inherit in the absence of paternal uncles. As in Leviticus 25, where distinctions stop with cousins, we see a merging of all further degrees of kinship into one indistinguishable mass.

The *gō'ēl* function is not directly referred to in this account, and the sense in which the deceased's line was actually preserved by these rules of inheritance is hard to visualize. The inheritance by the daughters of the deceased allows the continuation of the man's name and his possessions, so long as the daughters live, but the daughters themselves do not perform a service that directly guarantees *gᵉ'ullāh* in perpetuity. We can imagine a way in which they might have actively worked to restore their father's *bēth-'āv*, e.g., after marriage, by giving their first-born son to the line of their father so that his house might continue independently. We know nothing, however, of such a practice; very likely the prohibition against incest would block the way to a scheme where a daughter became the mother of her own father's child. But in the absence of male heirs in the father's line, what would become of his name and inheritance when the daughter married or when she died?

The additional story and ruling about Zelophehad's daughters in Numbers 36:1–12 reflects the difficulties that would follow upon trying to ensure the continuity of a *bēth-'āv* through the device of a daughter's inheritance. Since there is some evidence that women could hold property independently of their husbands, there might be no formal difficulty in a woman being incorporated into her husband's house while simultaneously retaining property that she cared for in her father's name. But what would happen at her death? Would not the property then revert, by means of the degrees of inheritance cited in Numbers 27, to some member of the deceased man's *mishpāhāh*? Presumably the background of Numbers 36 entails some clash between the right of the inheriting daughter to pass on the property at her death to someone in the *mishpāhāh* of her father and the right of her husband or of his *mishpāhāh* to claim the property of the wife even though she administered it during her lifetime in the name of her father.

Numbers 36 is further confused by applying the problem of female inheritance and marriage arrangements to the organizational level of the *matteh* (preferred here by P, but *shivtē bᵉnē* Israel occurs once, vs.3), whereas the problem of female inheritance in Numbers 27 is dealt with at the organizational level of the *mishpāḥāh.* There is no certain way of resolving the complex of difficulties raised here, but some probes and suggestions can be made. There are indications in Numbers 36:1–12 which strongly suggest that the original form of this tradition did not apply to the tribal level of organization at all but, like Numbers 27, adhered to the organizational level of the *mishpāḥāh.* For example, the officials who bring the difficulty for an all-Israelite ruling are heads of a *mishpāḥāh,* or possibly of several *mishpāḥōth* in the single tribe of Manasseh. Furthermore, although the description of the problem speaks primarily of marriages between persons from different *maṭṭōth,* there are three references in the text to the *mishpāḥāh.* For instance, "Let them [i.e., the inheriting daughters] marry whom they think best; only, they shall marry within *mishpahath maṭṭeh ʾªvīhen* [reading with many Heb. MSS and Samaritan pentateuch instead of MT *ʾªvihem*]" (36:6). If the prohibition concerns intertribal marriage, there is no reason at all for the text to include *mishpāḥāh,* i.e., "they shall marry within a *mishpāḥāh* of the tribe of their father." And the same is true of the more generalized form of the ruling, "And every daughter who possesses an inheritance in any tribe of the people of Israel, shall be wife to one of *mishpahath maṭṭeh ʾaviha*" (36:8), i.e., "shall be wife to a man from a *mishpāḥāh* of the tribe of her father."

If, however, the original involved *mishpāḥāh,* and *maṭṭeh* is an insertion [note that LXX omits *maṭṭeh* in vs. 8], the sense is plain. And by deleting *maṭṭeh* from vs. 12, the original *mishpāḥāh* locus of the passage is clearly summarized: "They were married into a *mishpāḥāh* [reading singular with one Heb. MS, LXX, Vulgate in place of MT plural] of the Manassites of Joseph, and their inheritance was retained in the *mishpāḥāh* of their father." Thus, I think it probable that the original ruling in vss. 5 and 8 was simply this: let the inheriting daughters marry within the same *mishpāḥāh* to which their father belonged. The expansion of the ruling into an intertribal affair is apparently due to an imaginative exercise by the P traditionist as he tries to envision the disruption in the year of Jubilee when the *inherited* land of the daughters would pass into control of their husbands' tribes, in contradistinction to *sold* land which would return to the original owners (36:3–4).

On this interpretation of Numbers 36, the two passages may be correlated to give the following picture: by inheriting from her father in the absence of a male heir, the daughter can keep alive his name and *bēth-ʾāv* through the cultivation of his land as long as she lives. She could continue to do so legally even though she was married. Practical difficulties would arise, however, if through marriage she had to move a great distance away from her father's land. If the land was of any size, she could not cultivate it alone, but would depend upon the cooperation of her husband and his household. The surest way to facilitate the daughter's maintenance of the father's estate was for her to marry someone from her father's *mishpāḥāh.* This would insure that she would continue to live near her father's estate, and it would insure the sympathetic assistance of her husband, because not only was he from the same *mishpāḥāh* as her father, but, upon her death, if there were no eligible relatives to act as *gō'ēl* for her father's *bēth-'āv*, the estate would devolve to the husband or, if he died first, to the estate of his *bēth-'āv*. Thus, the *bēth-'āv* of the deceased man without male heir was kept intact formally during the lifetime of his daughter, and, at her death, it either devolved to an eligible near relative acting as *gō'ēl*, or the total substance inhering in the estate was kept alive through its incorporation into another *bēth-'āv* of the same *mishpāḥāh*. This reconstruction, while unconfirmed in all respects by the spotty data, renders plausible the attention given to inheriting daughters in old Israel. While we do not read elsewhere in the Old Testament that daughters frequently inherited, given the incidence of male deaths in warfare and of sterility, the fate of family heads without male heirs must have been an urgent matter requiring solutions that would serve the various interests of the persons and social units affected.

While the details are far from adequate for a full reconstruction, and while the details we have do not always agree (perhaps because they refer to different practices according to time and place and according to the constructs of later traditionists), we do possess at least a cross-sectional view of the function of the *mishpāḥāh* in old Israel. From passages we have examined, the *mishpāḥāh* stands out as a protective association of families which operated to preserve the minimal conditions for the integrity of each of its member families by extending mutual help as needed to supply male heirs, to keep or recover land, to rescue members from debt slavery, and to avenge murder. These functions were all restorative in that they were emergency means to restore the normal autonomous basis of a member family, and they were all actions that devolved upon the *mishpāḥāh* only when the *bēth-'āv* was unable to act on its own behalf. The very existence of such a protective association gave vital reassurance to Israelite families, while the overt action of the protective association was always an exceptional measure of the last resort.

28.2 Size of the *Mishpāḥāh*

How large was the *mishpāḥāh*? According to the census of Numbers 26, the number of *mishpāḥōth* per tribe ranged from one in Dan to eight in Manasseh, yielding a total of 57 *mishpāḥōth*, or an average of 4.75 *mishpāḥōth* per *shēvet/matteh*. The census totals are too fantastic to be credible, not only for the wilderness period but for any period in ancient Israel. As we shall shortly see, however, the P traditionist has unwittingly preserved numbers which, when properly interpreted, are modest reports of the size of the military muster in premonarchic times. Numbers 26 is intriguing for its combination of ancient materials in a labored and artificial framework. That he accurately recorded here the average number of *mishpāḥōth* per *shēvet* in old Israel is not one of the virtues with which we can credit the traditionist of Numbers 26. A comparison of this list with the list of

Genesis 46:8–26 (partially paralleled in Exodus 6:14–15), where the *mishpāḥōth* of Numbers 26 appear only as *bānīm*, "sons," of the tribal ancestors, shows that these compendia of tribal sub-units were variable both as to the names and numbers of subdivisions within each tribe.

The names of the *mishpāḥōth* in Numbers 26 form a puzzling mishmash apparently drawn from diverse sources. Some of them are well-known legendary figures whose roles in the narrative traditions are sometimes commented on by the traditionist. Many more are found only in this list, or only here and by repetition in Chronicles. Some are place names. Hepher, Hoglah, Shechem, Shemida, and Tirzah are recognized cities in Manasseh, and Shimron was a city in Zebulun (here credited to Issachar). Hezron, appearing both in Reuben and Judah, may be the site Hezron near Kadesh-Barnea or Kerioth-hezron in southern Judah. Elon of Zebulun may be Aijalon. Gilead of Manasseh is the mountainous region of Transjordan that early gave its name to a *shēveṭ* in an area later inhabited in part by the *shēveṭ* Gad. Now if there were only eight *mishpāḥōth* in all Manasseh, and at least five of these were coterminous with single cities and their environs, it would appear that many regions of Manasseh are left unaccounted for. Moreover, the apparent census list is actually constructed as a pseudo-genealogy (cf. Gen. 46:8–26) in which each named entry is both a "son" of one of the eponymous tribal fathers and himself the "father" of a social collectivity called a *mishpāḥāh*. This pseudo-genealogy is unevenly developed, so that in most cases all the *mishpāḥōth* of a given *maṭṭeh* are conceived as siblings in one generation, whereas in the cases of Judah, Ephraim, Benjamin, and Asher a two-generational scheme is introduced (i.e., some of the *mishpāḥōth* are grandsons of the eponymous tribal fathers) and for Manasseh a three-generational scheme is given. Occasionally, the list lapses altogether into a genealogical mode and entries are simply called "sons" or "daughters" without any designation of them as *mishpāḥōth*.

Thus, the inventories of Numbers 26 vacillate erratically between representing a family tree and an inventory of social units. In this they share much in common with other biblical traditions that purport to be genealogies or official lists. My own feeling is that the relatively small number of *mishpāḥōth* in Numbers 26 results in part from the limited traditions available to P and in part from his concern to picture what he does report under a genealogical guise. In that event, he may have omitted the names of *mishpāḥōth* he did not recognize as elements in the traditional genealogical schemes. Or, even more likely, the names of many *mishpāḥōth* simply disappeared when they lost their original social protective and military functions. Before a more conclusive evaluation of Numbers 26 could be made, it would be necessary to make an exhaustive comparison between its entries and those in the many other "genealogical" and official lists, including comparable material in Chronicles.

The Book of Ruth throws some inadvertent light on the size of the *mishpāḥāh* and for that reason may be all the more valuable as a bit of information that has escaped the revision of late traditionists. Elimelech and his family are said to be "Ephrathites from Bethlehem" (1:2). The gentilic form also appears in I Samuel 17:12 where it is said that "David was the son of an Ephrathite of Bethlehem in Judah." The place name appears as the nearest settlement to Rachel's tomb, "and she was buried on the way to Ephrath," to which the explanatory gloss has been added, "that is, Bethlehem" (Gen. 35:19). Ruth 4:11 also names the place, "May you [Boaz] prosper in Ephrathah and be renowned in Bethlehem." Finally, in Micah 5:2(1) an awkwardly worded oracle declares: "But you, O Bethlehem Ephrathah, who are little to be among the 'alphē Judah, from you shall come forth for me one who is to be ruler in Israel." (Note the late prophetic retention of the conventional demurrer formula!)

All the citations associate Ephrathah with Bethlehem. They also make it clear that Ephrathah was not simply an alternate name for Bethlehem, comparable to Laish-Dan or Bethel-Luz. Ephrathah appears as a place in its own right, near to Bethlehem, and encompassable within Bethlehem conceived as the city and its environs. All these features are satisfied by the supposition that Ephrathah was a village or rural neighborhood adjacent to Bethlehem, possibly lying to the south in the direction of Tekoa (I Chron. 2:24). Furthermore, it seems a reasonable assumption that the region known as Ephrathah was inhabited by a single *mishpāhāh* and that when Elimelech's family members are called "Ephrathites" it means more than that they lived in Ephrathah; it means that they were of the protective association of families known as *mishpahath* Ephrati (comparable to Saul's *mishpahath* Matri, or possibly *mishpahath* Bichri). Micah still remembers that Ephrathah was counted "among the 'alphē Judah" (*'eleph* here replacing the more common *mishpāhāh*), a memory probably kept alive by the prominence of the *'eleph* of David. The proposal that the *mishpahath* Ephrati of Elimelech and Boaz inhabited a sub-section of larger Bethlehem fits well with the general conception of the story. If the entirety of Bethlehem was one *mishpāhāh* or only a part of a still more widely dispersed *mishpāhāh* (as would appear to be the case if we follow Numbers 26:19–22 in believing that there were only five *mishpāhōth* in all Judah), then the singling out of Boaz as "known kinsman" of *mishpahath* Elimelech is foolish. If all Bethlehemites were from the same *mishpāhāh* as Elimelech, then all Bethlehemites would have been "known kinsmen" of Elimelech. The excitement and suspense of the story depends upon the fact that only some Bethlehemites are of Elimelech's *mishpāhāh*.

The conclusion is that in larger settlements there was more than one *mishpāhāh*. We have no population information on Bethlehem that would permit further calculations. The concomitant of this suggestion is that probably many smaller settlements were joined in a single *mishpāhāh*. The situation would vary depending on the size of settlements, population growth and decline, natural terrain, and the seriousness of the communal crises which would tend to strengthen the protective family associations by repeated calls upon their service. In my judgment the conception of a *mishpāḥāh* in Numbers 26 is extremely attenuated, since in monarchic times the social and military functions of the *mishpāḥāh* were greatly weakened and the term tended to be applied either archaically to fabled names from genealogies of the past or administratively to cities or regions which functioned as governmental units under the monarchy. On the other hand, Numbers 26 does relate directly authentic information about the old military functions of the *'eleph*, and so we must keep open the possibility that many of the otherwise unfamiliar names it has retained as *mishpāḥōth* derive from ancient times, although the inventory is necessarily incomplete.

28.3 *'Eleph = Mishpāḥāh* in Arms

So far our analysis of the secondary subdivisions in old Israel has focused on the social functions reported in contexts where *mishpāḥāh* is the technical term for a protective association of families. In addition, the same secondary level of organization in old Israel served a military function which is denoted by the technical term *'eleph*. It is to be noted that while *mishpāḥāh* and *'eleph* are used frequently in social organizational contexts, they seldom appear together in the same context; where they do occasionally appear together, however, we find the necessary key for understanding their organizational interconnection as well as their connotative differences.

In the large majority of usages, *mishpāḥāh* is the term for a secondary level of social organization. By contrast, in the majority of occurrences of *'eleph*, it is the numeral "one thousand." In the uses of the numeral there is a decided bias toward its employment in military contexts, so that a frequent meaning of *'eleph* turns out to be "a military unit of one thousand men." It was typical of military organization under the Israelite monarchy to arrange the troops in units of tens, fifties, hundreds, and thousands (cf. the apparently artificial application of this military organization to juridical organization and its retrojection into the wilderness in Exodus 18:13–27). Under the monarchy *sar-'eleph* appears as the commander of a one-thousand-man military unit. Consequently, even in the latest biblical uses of *'eleph* in military contexts, it may not simply refer to one thousand men in a distributive or cumulative numerical sense, but may designate a specific military unit composed of one thousand men.

This necessarily leads us to ask: Was the *'eleph* a military unit in premonarchic Israel, and was it at that time composed of one thousand men? Further, since *'eleph* and *mishpāḥāh* both refer to the secondary level of social organization and are actually associated in the census traditions of Numbers 1 and 26, and also in the account of the choice of Saul by lot in I Samuel 10:17–27, what was the relationship between the *'eleph* and the *mishpāḥāh* in early Israel? I anticipate my conclusions as follows: *'eleph* was a military unit in old Israel, but it did not contain one thousand men, nor indeed any fixed number, but rather a very much smaller but variable number of men actually mustered or promised for muster by a *mishpāḥāh* in order to supply a round number of troops from the *shēveṭ* for all-Israelite wars. In some premonarchic texts, *'eleph* refers to this mustered unit of fighting men from a *mishpāḥāh*, but the term may also refer to the larger social unit from which the fighting unit is drawn; when it is so used, *'eleph* designates the same social unit as *mishpāḥāh*. Although *mishpāḥāh* and *'eleph* at times refer to the same social unit, these terms carry different connotations. *Mishpāḥāh* connotes the social and economic protective functions of the unit. Moreover, while the social protective activities imply the functional autonomy of the *mishpāḥāh* in that the group can act on behalf of needy *bēth-'āvōth* without the necessary aid of other *mishpāḥōth*, the military protective functions of the *'eleph* cannot be carried out by any single *'eleph*. *'Eleph* entails a larger interlocking military organization, since an *'eleph* cannot fight effectively alone but must be united with the other *'ᵃlāphīm* of the *shēveṭ* and, beyond that, with the *'ᵃlāphīm* of all the *shivṭē* Israel or with as many of them as can be mobilized for a particular war.

This understanding depends upon the incisive interpretation of the census lists in Numbers 1 and 26 developed by George Mendenhall, who established convincingly that the P traditionists (and the Chronicler also in I Chronicles 12:23–40) passed on precise and modest premonarchic military enumerations which they themselves no longer properly understood.[185] The traditionists understood the military unit of the *'eleph* in the framework of the monarchic military organization with which they were familiar; i.e., in their view an *'eleph* was a fighting unit of one thousand men. Thus, in summing up the numbers in Numbers 1 and 26, they understood that the army of Israel was composed of slightly more than 600,000 warriors. Attempts to see these figures as belonging to David's census are unsatisfactory, since the total population would have been between three and five million, far in excess of the most generous population estimates for the most populous period under the monarchy (perhaps an optimum of one million in the mid-eighth century B.C.).[186]

Mendenhall tried to see what sense could be made of the lists if they were detached from the presuppositions of monarchic military organization in Israel and viewed instead in the context of how armies are organized and mustered either in the absence of centralized political power or in situations where the central power has to conscript from relatively autonomous smaller social units. He was able to gather information from ancient Greece and Rome, from early Japan and China, and from Mari, Ugarit, and Alalakh in the ancient Near East. These data showed that "tribally" organized peoples customarily supplied small units of fighting men from existing social units, which were then organized into tactical units to carry out a wider strategy either under leaders designated by the contributing units or under professional officers appointed by the monarchy which held sovereignty over the units. He noted that *'eleph* (or *'allūph*) in premonarchic texts and its counterpart in a list from Ugarit, corroborated by the military muster procedures of the kingdom of Mari, did not originally denote a unit of a certain size but rather an organized group under its leader. This led him to construe premonarchic *'eleph* not as a large fighting unit but as a small conscripted unit of men who were variously absorbed into the actual fighting units of the army. *'Eleph* as a tactical fighting unit of one thousand men was a secondary and more sophisticated development owing to political centralization from David's reign on.

When this insight was applied to Numbers 1 and 26, the lists—although obviously much revised in format—became intelligible records of premonarchic military organization. In particular the numbers shrank dramatically to proportions that suited ancient Israel and fell in the same range of magnitude as those given in the kingdom of Mari. The army musters are grouped by tribe and follow a formal pattern, although the kinds of itemizations and details differ from Numbers 1 to Numbers 26: the *mishpāḥōth* of the *maṭṭeh* are either simply referred to en masse (Num. 1) or are listed by names (Num. 26), and the total of fighting men in each tribe is stated. For example, "the number of the *maṭṭeh* of Ephraim was forty *'ᵃlāphīm* five hundred" (1:33). The P traditionist, and most biblical exegetes before Mendenhall, understood this to mean, "the total number of warriors of the *maṭṭeh* of Ephraim was forty thousand, five hundred (40,500)." Compiling all the tribal entries yielded an army of 603,550! Mendenhall suggested, to the contrary, that the numerical citations are not simple sums of men but composites, i.e., the first element is the unit number and the second element is the total of fighting men for the tribe. Far from claiming, therefore, that there were 40,500 warriors in E-phraim, the claim of the old enumeration used by P was this, "the number of troops of the *maṭṭeh* of Ephraim was forty units (i.e., *'ᵃlāphīm*) constituting a total of five hundred men."

By recognizing that *'eleph* in the old lists was not used for a predetermined unit of one thousand men, or simply as the numeral for one thousand, but rather for a variable unit whose average size is to be determined from the summary figure of men, the fighting force of Ephraim, as an example, was reduced by more than eighty times, from 40,500 to 500 men. Similarly, the total for all Israel could then be read: "So the whole number of the people of Israel, by their *bēth-'āvōth*, from twenty years old and upward, every man able to go forth to war in Israel—their whole number was 603 units (i.e., *'ᵃlāphīm*) constituting 5,500 men" (1:46). Actually, the tribal entries of units add up to only 598, but this slight discrepancy in the P total does not affect the basic mode of interpretation, since it remains a difficulty in any mode of interpretation. The enumerations in Numbers 26 vary considerably in particular tribal entries, but overall the results are close to the total of Numbers 1, namely 596 units constituting 5,730 men (26:51). Again, the total of the *'ᵃlāphīm* is incorrect, i.e., 601 units. Since P is normally so careful with numbers, these discrepant totals may be due to adjustments in some of the tribal entries in the early stage of transmission which were not subsequently adjusted in the totals, a phenomenon related to the inaccurate totals for cities in the tribal allotment lists of Joshua 13–19.

Numbers 1 reports, therefore, a situation at some point in the premonarchic federation of *shivṭē = (maṭṭōth)* Israel when they collectively committed themselves to field an army of 5,500 men mustered by small quotas from the secondary organizational units, averaging almost fifty *'ᵃlāphīm* per tribe, with each *'eleph* averaging a little more than nine men per unit. The averages for Numbers 26 vary only fractionally from those of Numbers 1. Also, in both lists the totals of each tribe round out to units of a hundred (except for Reuben in 26:7, which has 730 in MT and 750 in LXX). By contrast, the numbers of the *'ᵃlāphīm* are unschematic, suggesting no evidence of tendentious patterning. Moreover, the totals of *'ᵃlāphīm* for the respective tribes vary considerably, both from tribe to tribe within each list (e.g., 32 for Manasseh and 74 for Judah in Numbers 1; 22 for Simeon and 76 for Judah in Numbers 26) and between the two lists in the respective entries for the same tribe (e.g., 59 for Simeon in Numbers 1 shrink to 22 in Numbers 26; 32 for Manasseh in Numbers 1 increase to 52 in Numbers 26).

Mendenhall concluded that the two lists reflect two different historical situations not far removed from one another in time, Numbers 26 probably being later, since it reflects a tendency toward slightly larger units. His brief suggestions about dating contain little that is compelling apart from the genealogy in Ruth 4:17–22, which would place the officer over Judah, Nahshon ben Amminadab (Num. 1:7), in the approximate period 1125–1100 B.C. We have already seen reason to question the scope and integrity of the names of the *mishpāḥōth* in Numbers 26, and much the same is true of the names of the tribal officials in Numbers 1:5–15. However, taken together, the modesty of the numbers interpreted as composite sums of units and of men, the grouping of the tribal contingents into hundreds which vary in total from tribe to tribe, and the unstylized numbers for the *'ᵃlāphīm* in each tribe—all these features seem to reflect authentic information which can only make sense under a premonarchic military organization in which *mishpāḥōth/'ᵃlāphīm* contributed small quotas of warriors who were integrated into larger tribal tactical units.

I also concur with Mendenhall in believing that the tribal totals contributed by *'ᵃlāphīm* did not constitute the total fighting force of the *shēveṭ* but only the commonly agreed quota of the *shēveṭ* to the national wars. They constituted minimal obligations which could be exceeded in great emergencies and doubtless were exceeded by the tribes most directly threatened in particular wars. A tribe threatened with military attack could call for troops from the other tribes according to the agreed quotas. Of course, as the Song of Deborah makes especially clear, tribes did not always deliver the quotas. Although there were no physical sanctions for such a failure, there were religious sanctions. A tribe that failed to deliver the quota was guilty of having failed to come to the aid of Yahweh and his people.

Although Mendenhall does not deal with the relations between the *'eleph* and the *mishpāḥāh*, it is my judgment that the *mishpāḥāh* conceived from the standpoint of its military function was also called an *'eleph*. If that is accepted as a working hypothesis, it can be seen that an average of just over nine men from each *mishpāḥāh* would not have been an onerous number to supply. A large *bēth-'āv* might easily have that many men of military age; and a *mishpāḥāh* composed of several, even scores, of *bēth-'āvōth* would only be mustering a minority of its manpower in order to meet its pledged share of the tribal quota. Able-bodied men would be left to cultivate the land, tend the flocks, and defend the tribal home-ground. For example, Jesse had eight sons, only three of whom (the eldest) answered Saul's muster to fight the Philistines. Although David, as the youngest, is pictured as ineligible for military service, it is probable, given Jesse's advanced age, that the remaining four sons were eligible but not needed to fill the quota of their *mishpāḥāh/'eleph* (I Sam. 17:12–14).

If it is conjectured that *mishpāḥāh* and *'eleph* (in the extended sense of the social unit from which the military unit of the same name was drawn) refer to the same organizational entity, we have at least the outlines of an answer to our earlier question about the approximate number of *'ªlāphīm* per *shēvet*. The lists of Numbers 1 and 26 yield an average of about fifty *'ªlāphīm* per tribe, ranging from a low of twenty-two for Simeon to a high of seventy-six for Judah. In this light, when Judges 5:8 says, "Was shield or spear to be seen among forty *'ªlāphīm* in Israel?", it is probably simply saying, "Was any *shēvet* in Israel well armed?" (i.e., compared to the heavy infantry and chariots of the Canaanites). Certainly an average of fifty *mishpāḥōth* per *shēvet* is a much more credible figure than the one to eight *mishpāḥōth* per tribe named in the list of Numbers 26. Our interpretation entails of course that the P traditionist, not knowing that an *'eleph* was a small unit in the old source he employed and mistakenly construing it as the numeral "one thousand," did not realize he was giving an entirely insufficient number of names for the actual *mishpāḥōth* in old Israel. I assume that the old list, in giving the units and number of men, did not name the units, and thus the form of the list in Numbers 1, which only speaks of the *mishpāḥōth* collectively without naming any, corresponds more closely to the form of the old military roster than does Numbers 26.

This implies that P derived his names for the *mishpāḥōth* from elsewhere, a probability enhanced by their lack of homogeneity. As earlier noted, they appear to be drawn from more than one source, including prominent names from old stories and genealogies and city names from territorial-historical lists. Since a majority of the names are otherwise unknown, P may well have had some reliable ancient information about premonarchic *mishpāḥōth* which is otherwise lost to us.

Since less than one-tenth of the enumerated 596 mishpāḥōth/'ᵃlāphīm of Numbers 26 are given by name, it is obvious how incomplete P's information was. Thus, for example, alongside the named mishpāḥōth of Judah (Shelah, Perez, Zerah, Hezron, and Hamul), there were, on my interpretation, another 71 mishpāḥōth which must have included mishpaḥath Ephrati, and perhaps also mishpāḥōth with the names of Jerahmeelite, Kenite, Kenizzite, Calebite, and Othnielite and perhaps others which now appear as proper names in the traditions about Judah in Genesis 38 and in I Chronicles 2:3–55. The pseudo-genealogies in Chronicles have scarcely been examined with serious sociological intent, but any further elaboration and testing of the hypothesis here advanced will require close attention to them.

The sorts of detailed probes necessary to test the hypothesis may be illustrated in the case of the mishpaḥath Ephrati, to which Elimelech, Boaz, and David belonged, and which appears in I Samuel 17:17–18 in the form of an 'eleph from Bethlehem in which David's brothers serve under the national army commanded by Saul in the Philistine war. The present form of the story envisions this 'eleph as a unit of one thousand men led by a sar-'eleph. David is pictured as taking provisions for his three brothers and for the commander of the thousand, but not for the remaining nine hundred and some troops which one person could not possibly provision in any event. It is unlikely, however, that Saul had departed from the older military organization so far as to organize thousand-man fighting units. The actual situation seems rather to have been this: David brings food for the entire 'eleph mobilized from mishpaḥath Ephrati in the region of Bethlehem. An ephah of grain, ten loaves, and ten cheeses are ample to supply the entire unit which, according to the figures of Numbers 1 and 26, consisted on the average of from six to nine men, of whom three, the brothers of David, were from the bēth-'āv of Jesse. This story may be read as challenging Mendenhall's claim that the 'eleph was never a tactical unit; however, since the account is given a monarchic military veneer and since the military organization is not directly described, it is possible that the 'eleph of mishpaḥath Ephrati is integrated with other 'ᵃlāphīm in a larger force (although still involving only scores of men) and that the officer of this larger tactical unit is here referred to by the later monarchic sar 'eleph.

Mendenhall's hypothesis about the premonarchic 'eleph, supplemented with my proposal that mishpāḥāh and 'eleph refer to the same organizational jurisdiction, throws light on the story of Gideon, which provides some of the fullest materials concerning the old 'eleph. The hero's self-deprecation as one from "the weakest 'eleph" in Israel and "the least in my bēth-'āv" (Judg. 6:15) is supplemented by the information that his father is Joash, an Abiezrite (6:11), that he lives in Ophrah-of-the-Abiezrites (6:24), and that he first mustered his own Abiezrites for battle before he called out all Manasseh (6:34; cf. 8:2). Now (Ab)iezer is named as a mishpāḥāh in Manasseh (Num. 26:30; cf. Josh. 17:2). The practical equation of the 'eleph of Gideon with the mishpāḥāh of Abiezer, which inhabited Ophrah and to which Gideon's *bēth-'āv* belongs, seems assured. In the muster and deployment of the Israelite forces in Judges 7:2–8, exegetes have been hard put to explain the reduction from 32,000 to 10,000 to 300 men. Beginning from 7:3, we find a total of 32 *'ᵃlāphīm* which correspond exactly to the 32 *'ᵃlāphīm* for Manasseh in Num. 1:35 (but not to the 52 *'ᵃlāphīm* of Manasseh in 26:34). Our interpretation sees a direct equation between these 32 *'ᵃlāphīm* and the 300 men of 7:7,16;8:4. The fact that 300 men are mustered instead of the 200 in Numbers 1:35 may be accounted for by the immediate threat which the Manassites felt in the penetration of the Midianites into their territory in the Valley of Esdraelon (but again 300 is far below the total of 700 for Manasseh in Num. 26:34). Apparently the monarchic traditionist responsible for editing the story understood *'ᵃlāphīm* as thousands and felt he needed to explain how 32,000 men were reduced to 300. The story of the 300, vindicating their eligibility for the strike force by lapping water "as a dog laps," may well have had an independent existence, for it shows us something of the skills which the guerrilla-like warriors of Israel had to develop against superior enemy forces. The story is included precisely at its present point in the tradition, however, in order to supply an explanation for the sudden trimming of Gideon's massive army.

The muster that Gideon initiated is summarized in Judges 6:33–35. It occurred in three stages; first, Gideon musters his own *mishpāhāh/'eleph* of the Abiezrites. He can do this in person because the Abiezrites live in a compact region, including Ophrah, but not necessarily limited to that settlement. In the second stage he sends messengers throughout Manasseh. In the third stage he sends messengers to Asher, Zebulun, and Naphtali. Except for Issachar, these were the tribes most immediately affected by the Midianite razzia. Issachar may be omitted because Midian was occupying and blockading most of Issachar's territory. From this summary, it is often assumed that the 32 *'ᵃlāphīm* represent the fighting forces of the four tribes named. We have seen, however, that the 32 *'ᵃlāphīm* correspond so neatly to the 32 *'ᵃlāphīm* of Manasseh in Numbers 1:35, that we should attempt some reading of events which sees the 32 *'ᵃlāphīm* of 300 men as exclusively Manassite. This reading may be provided by Judges 7:23, "And the men of Israel were called out from Naphtali and from Asher and from all Manasseh, and they pursued after Midian," followed by an extension of the muster to Ephraim, summoning that tribe to cut off the line of Midian's retreat by seizing the fords of the Jordan. This suggests that only Manasseh was involved in the attack of the 300 on the Midianite camp and that the other tribes joined in the pursuit only after the enemy had been routed by Manasseh.

28.4 Nonmilitary Uses of *'Eleph*

That *mishpāḥāh* and *'eleph* can be used interchangeably as terms for the same unit of social organization in old Israel is shown in I Samuel 10:17–27, where Samuel commands: "Present yourselves before Yahweh by your $sh^ev\bar{a}tim$ and by your $^{'a}l\bar{a}ph\bar{\iota}m$!" (10:19), but the actual election of Saul proceeds by lot from the $sh^ev\bar{a}tim$ to the $mishp\bar{a}h\bar{o}th$ (10:20–21). In I Samuel 23:19–24 Saul, who has been futilely pursuing David from one hiding place to another, tells the loyal Ziphites to make sure of David's whereabouts, "and if he is in the land I will search him out among all the $'alph\bar{e}$ Judah" (23:23). As a direct reference to the mustered fighting units this makes no sense since the army is still under Saul's command and David has fled to live the life of a renegade freebooter. As a reference, however, to the sub-regions of Judah occupied by the seventy-odd $mishp\bar{a}h\bar{o}th$ Judah, it stresses the diversified character of the Judean populace and terrain in whose "lurking places" David has successfully eluded Saul.

The wider usage of $'eleph$ (or $'all\bar{u}ph$) for a social unit is attested in two prophetic texts. An eighth-century prophecy in Zechariah 9:1–8 declares that the Philistine city of Ashdod shall be purified of its evil "and shall be like an $'all\bar{u}ph$ in Judah" and Ekron "shall be like the Jebusites" (9:7). Many exegetes have proposed changing $'all\bar{u}ph$ to $'eleph$ on the assumption that $'all\bar{u}ph$ always means a leader or officer of an $'eleph,$ but the change is unnecessary inasmuch as $'all\bar{u}ph$ in other contexts seems to refer to a group rather than a person (cf. the $'all\bar{u}ph\bar{e}$ Edom and the $'all\bar{u}ph\bar{e}$ Hori in Genesis 36:15–30). At any rate, the parallel with Jebusites, whom David incorporated as a separate body of citizens after he made their city of Jerusalem into his capital, indicates that an $'all\bar{u}ph$ in Judah was here understood as an encompassing social entity and not a military unit. On the other hand, in the much later Zechariah 12:5–6, the $'all\bar{u}ph\bar{e}$ Judah appear in an explicitly militaristic eschatological passage in which it is said that "I [Yahweh] will make the $'all\bar{u}ph\bar{e}$ Judah like a blazing pot . . . a flaming torch, and they shall devour to the right and to the left all the peoples round about." Here the $^{'a}l\bar{a}ph\bar{\iota}m/'alluphim$ as the unified fighting force of Judah comes to the fore. The $'alph\bar{e}$ Judah in Micah 5:2 (1) echoes the narratives of search for a royal leader which we earlier examined, including the demurrer motif, and it is thus noteworthy that $'alph\bar{e}$ Judah occurs rather than $mishp\bar{a}h\bar{o}th$ Judah. Perhaps $^{'a}l\bar{a}ph\bar{\iota}m$ is preferred because, since the leader expected is of the line of David, the militaristic traditions of the Davidic dynasty are accented. This occurrence of $'alph\bar{e}$ Judah seems to me to incorporate both organizational meanings with deliberate inclusive ambiguity: $^{'a}l\bar{a}ph\bar{\iota}m$ as social units equivalent to the $mishp\bar{a}h\bar{o}th$ and $^{'a}l\bar{a}ph\bar{\iota}m$ as the mustered units of troops for the national wars.

There is some evidence that the actual line of development in the social organizational uses of $'eleph/'all\bar{u}ph$ was the opposite of that implied by the preponderant military weight of the term in Old Testament texts. The root verb $'\bar{a}laph$ (illuminated by known cognates in Akkadian and Arabic) has the meaning "to cleave to, to become familiar with," and there are a number of occurrences of the noun $'all\bar{u}ph$ in the sense of a close relative or friend, and even of a marriage partner. Micah 7:5 parallels the $'all\bar{u}ph$ with the $r\bar{e}a',$ "intimate" or "neighbor," in the context of *'anshē bēthō*, "the men of his house." Psalm 55:14 parallels *'allūph* with the *mᵉyuddāʿ* (cf. *kᵉthiv* of Ruth 2:1), "familiar" or "known kinsman." Jeremiah 3:4 and Proverbs 2:17 speak of the husband as the *'allūph nᵉʿūrīm*, "partner [or intimate] of one's youth," i.e., a man to whom a woman has been married since her youth.

Since none of these usages of *'allūph* is demonstrably earlier than the seventh century B.C., it is easy to assume that they represent a secondary extension of the monarchic military term. But is such a secondary extension from military to intimate social contexts really plausible? The opposite development seems much the more intelligible. With the monarchy, *'eleph/'allūph* as a military unit drawn from a *mishpāḥāh/'eleph* was eclipsed by *'eleph* as a fighting unit of one thousand men. In other words, the military unit of the *'eleph* was decisively severed from its former social base in the *mishpāḥāh* social unit, the old protective association of families. It is not probable that *'allūph* would be applied for the first time to persons standing in close social, and even intimate marital, relations to one another in a period when the major referent of the term was no longer social but rather military.

It is more probable that in old Israel *'eleph/'allūph* was a common term for the secondary subdivision of the social system, that fellow members of the *'eleph* by birth or marriage were sometimes called *'alluphīm ('alluphōth?)*, and that, by extension, the small units of men contributed by the *'eleph* as a social unit became known by the same name. With *'eleph* acquiring a specialized military meaning, *mishpāḥāh* began to develop as the preferred term when speaking of the secondary social division in Israel and, with the monarchic alteration of the form and function of the military *'eleph,* the term dropped completely out of use in everyday speech with respect to the social unit, while *mishpāḥāh* remained as the appropriate social term. Thereafter, *'eleph/'allūph* for the social unit, and *'allūph* for members of the social unit by blood or marriage, survived only in archaizing poetic contexts. While this is no more than a tentative hypothesis, it does offer a plausible reconstruction which makes sense both of the equivalencies between *mishpāḥāh* and *'eleph* and of their increasing divergence as a result of historical permutations in the social and military organization of Israel.

28.5 *'Eleph* and *Rᵉvāvāh* in Archaic Poetry

There are four formulaic occurrences of *'ᵃlāphīm* in conjunction or in parallelism with *rᵉvāvāh* (plural, *rᵉvāvōth;* in plural constructions preceding a noun, *rivᵉvōth*), normally understood as "ten thousand" or "myriad," in poetic contexts which are either premonarchic or which though monarchic in their present form, retain archaic language and concepts. These poetic constructions are terse in expression and often syntactically ambiguous, since the compressed and elliptic style may well omit prepositions and other syntactic elements which would normally appear in a prose text. I shall briefly introduce the expressions and then discuss the parallel terms.

A blessing pronounced upon Rebekah as an eponoymous ancestress of Israel declares:

> O our sister! Grow into countless thousands! (*'alphē rᵉvāvāh*)
> May your offspring possess the settlements of their enemies!
> (Gen. 24:60)

A cultic exclamation accompanied the action of carrying forth the ark into battle and the action of returning the ark after battle. It is in the form of an address to the ark as the embodied and effective presence of Yahweh:

> Arise, O Yahweh!
> May your enemies be scattered, and your foes flee before you!
> Return, O Yahweh of the countless thousands of Israel! (*rivᵉvōth*
>   *'alphē* Israel). (Num. 10:35–36)

A collection of tribal blessings in Deuteronomy 33 is given a hymnic frame which includes in its introduction a description of Yahweh coming forth from the desert into Canaan leading the assembled *shᵉvāṭīm* in battle and giving the communal instructions. The difficult Hebrew text reads literally:

> Yahweh came forth from Sinai,
>   and dawned from Seir upon them
> he shone forth from Mount Paran,
>   he came from the holy ten thousands (*rivᵉvōth qōdesh*),
> fire flashing at them from his right. (Deut. 33:2)

The versions, however, reflect different readings of the Hebrew text in the next to the last line. Targum Onkelos and Jonathan, and the Vulgate, read: " . . . and with him [Yahweh] were the consecrated ten thousands." LXX speaks here of "the myriads of Kadesh," which suggests that the Hebrew text it used may have read Meribath-Kadesh (instead of *rivᵉvōth qōdesh*), referring thereby to the place name, "the waters of Meribath-Kadesh" (Num. 27:14; Deut. 32:51; cf. Num. 20:13).

In the blessing on Joseph, in the same collection of tribal sayings, that aggressive tribe is described as a wild ox:

> In his majesty (like) a first-born bull,
>   his horns those of a wild ox
>   with which he will gore peoples
>   and push them to the ends of the earth—
>   such are the ten thousands of Ephraim (*rivᵉvōth* Ephraim)
>   and such are the thousands of Manasseh (*'alphē* Manasseh).
> (Deut. 33:17)

Psalm 68:17(18) is a textually corrupt and stylistically eclectic liturgy that attained its present form under the monarchy, as is clear from its locus in the sanctuary at

Jerusalem. However, it is shot through with archaic language and conceptions of the old theophany of Yahweh in the premonarchic wars. In my opinion the essential shape of vss. 1 (2)–14(15) was developed in the old pre-Davidic cult. Verses 11 (12)–14(15) recount an ancient victory of Yahweh and his people over kings at Zalmon. If Bashan in vs. 15 (16) defines the location of Zalmon in Transjordan, it is probably a reference to the victory over Og and Sihon (Num. 21:21–35). But since the one clear geographical specification of Zalmon identifies it as a mountain in the vicinity of Shechem (Judg. 9:48), the psalm probably refers to an otherwise unrecorded victory over Canaanite kings near Shechem (see my discussion in IX.44.2).

The MT goes on to describe a theophany of the deity with military imagery:

> The chariots of God are twice ten thousand (dual, *ribbōthayim*),
>   thousands on thousands (*'alphe shin'ān*)
> The Lord is among them, Sinai is in the sanctuary. (Ps. 68:17 [18])

With the help of the versions the text may be corrected to read:

> The chariotry of God are the twice ten thousand,
>   the roaring thousands (*'alphē shā'ōn*)
> The Lord came from Sinai in holiness.

In order to avoid premature narrowing of the meaning of *'ªlāphīm* and *rªvāvōth* in these passages, I have simply translated them by the general terms "thousands" and "ten thousands." It is apparent, however, that all these old poetic pieces are explicitly military in context. The action of Yahweh revealed in the theophany is a military blow of Israel's forces against the enemies. Or rather, the blow that Yahweh delivers in his self-revelation is at one and the same instant the blow delivered by Israel's militia against the enemy. The world of premonarchic theophanic military imagery in all these liturgies demands that we approach the meanings of *'ªlāphīm* and *rªvāvōth* in more precisely premonarchic social and military terms.

The senses in which *'ªlāphīm* is used are clearest: *'ªlāphīm* as the military units contributed by the *mishpāhōth*, and as a plural noun collectively summarizing the fighting forces of Israel (or of a *shēvet* in Israel), appears in the attribution of deity as "Yahweh of the countless *'alphē* Israel" (Num. 10:36), in the identification of the horns of a wild ox that gores peoples with "the *'alphē* Manasseh" (Deut. 33:17), and also in "the thousands of *'ªlāphīm*" (MT) or "the roaring *'ªlāphīm*" (corrected text) in Psalm 68:17(18). If MT is followed as the original, the phrase in the psalm may well be a clumsy gloss on the dual form of *rªvāvōth*. Even so, such a gloss would attest to an early interpreter's military understanding of *'ªlāphīm*, although it might cease to be a premonarchic datum.

Since Genesis 24:60 has in view not only the defeat of the enemies but the occupation of their settlements, it is probable that "the countless *'ᵃlāphīm*" alludes, as in Micah 5:2(1), both to the collective military forces of Israel and to the social units, i.e., the *mishpāḥōth,* from which the militia are drawn and which will settle down in the locations wrested from the foe.

The association of *'ᵃlāphīm* with *rᵉvāvāh/rᵉvāvōth* in all these old liturgical passages calls for special attention. In the first place, there is no clear evidence from any biblical source that there was ever a unit of ten thousand men in Israelite military organization analogous, for example, to the Greek "myriad." In the descriptions of the army under the monarchy, the term appears at most to signify a collection of ten *'ᵃlāphīm,* and even then the point is their aggregate number and not their coordination as a larger tactical force. But if the *'eleph* in old Israel was a small number of men contributed by an *'eleph/mishpāḥāh,* what was a *rᵉvāvāh* under such conditions? If *rᵉvāvāh* did not have any rootage in military organization but was used only as a numeral to refer to aggregations of *'ᵃlāphīm* as monarchic units of one thousand men each, why was *rᵉvāvāh* used in close connection with *'eleph* in old Israelite military settings?

A tentative suggestion is that *rᵉvāvāh* was not originally a term for "ten thousand," any more than *'eleph* was originally a term for "one thousand." As its root *rāvav,* "to become many, to multiply" suggests, it meant "a multitude." The term offered itself as a way of designating the massed body of *'ᵃlāphīm,* stressing their numerical strength when joined together. Poetic parallelism encouraged the use of *rᵉvāvōth* as a counterpart to *'ᵃlāphīm.* Thus, when Deuteronomy 33:17 says, "such are the *rivᵉvōth* Ephraim, and such are the *'alphē* Manasseh," there is no reason to believe that Ephraim's militia was organized in any different units than Manasseh's militia. The two terms are typical poetic parallel members which, taken together, give this essential meaning: "such are the massed forces of the *'ᵃlāphīm* of Ephraim and the *'ᵃlāphīm* of Manasseh." With this understanding of *rᵉvāvāh/rᵉvāvōth,* we can render the construct forms in which it appears with *'ᵃlāphīm* by the adjective, "countless," e.g., in Genesis 24:60, "countless armed protective associations of families *('alphē rᵉvāvāh)*" and in Numbers 10:36, "the countless armed units drawn from the protective associations of families of Israel *(rivᵉvōth ' alphē* Israel)." Obviously for a united force of five or six thousand men, "countless" is a poetic hyperbole, but one which connotes forcefully the unified strength of the militia.

If we follow MT in the problematic line containing *rivᵉvōth* in Deuteronomy 33:2, we read, "he [Yahweh] came from the holy multitudes *(rivᵉvōth qōdesh)*." This suggests that the *rᵉvāvōth* may once have referred to the heavenly hosts surrounding Yahweh. This sort of *double-entendre* for a term, involving both mythological and military meanings, has a close parallel in the Hebrew term *tsāvā'* (plural, *tsᵉvā'ōth*), which refers to the "army" or "massed hosts" of Israel and also to the heavenly hosts surrounding Yahweh, as in the divine title, *Yahweh-tsᵉvā'ōth,*

"Yahweh of hosts." This notion corresponds very well to the close identification between Yahweh's revelatory appearance and Israel's collective action in war, an identification which runs throughout the cultic theophanic ideology of oldest Israel. Indeed, Yahweh's revelation is precisely his victorious prosecution of war by means of the instrumentality of Israel's forces. While the possible parallel between *revāvāh* and *tsāvā'* is attractive, there are no other texts clearly denoting the *revāvōth* as heavenly hosts (unless Psalm 68:17(18) is so construed) and the text of Deuteronomy 33:2 is very problematic. Thus, I can no more than propose the possibility that *revāvāh* as a "multitude" applied to the Israelite army was derived from its prior technical use for the heavenly host surrounding Yahweh.

28.6 Religious Functions of the *Mishpāḥāh* / *'Eleph*

Virtually the entirety of our information about the *mishpāḥāh/'eleph* concerns its socioeconomic and military protective functions. There is, however, one datum which elucidates the religious function of this level of social organization. When David and Jonathan are fabricating an excuse to give Saul for David's absence from the king's feast, David advises Jonathan to tell his father:

> David implored me for permission to hasten to Bethlehem, his city, for there is an annual sacrificial feast there for all the *mishpāḥāh*. (I Sam. 20:6)

When Jonathan offers the excuse to his father, he says:

> David implored me for permission (to hasten?) to Bethlehem. He said, "Release me, I beg, for our *mishpāḥāh* holds a sacrificial feast in the city, and my brother has ordered me to be there. So now, if I have found favor in your eyes, let me slip away and join my brothers." (I Sam. 20:28–29)

Even though this is a fabricated excuse, we may take it as a highly reliable allusion to one function of the *mishpāḥāh* in old Israel, for the obvious reason that the excuse would only have been plausible if Saul knew that such feasts were conducted by *mishpāḥōth* as a regular feature of Israelite life. When Saul explodes with rage upon hearing Jonathan's explanation of David's absence, it is not because he finds the specific reason implausible but because he is not prepared to accept any excuse, given his deepening suspicions of David's designs on the throne. That Jonathan now offers an excuse on David's behalf further enrages Saul, for it confirms his growing awareness that his own son is in collusion with David.

We may conclude, then, that the *mishpāḥāh* normally held a yearly feast which all of its members attended, including, whenever possible, those who were no longer living at home. The obligation to return home for the yearly feast of the *mishpāḥāh* was so urgent that it could take precedence over other duties, even those of fealty to the king. If the MT singular, "my brother has ordered me to be there" is accurate (some versions of LXX have the plural), the eldest brother seems to have had the duty of summoning his *bēth-'āv* to the *mishpāḥāh's* celebration. Whether this was true of all *mishpāḥōth*, or simply devolved on the eldest brother in the *bēth-'āv* at the father's death, is not clear.

We read of a yearly festival to Yahweh at Shiloh in Judges 21:19 and of the yearly pilgrimage of Elkanah and his family to Shiloh in I Samuel 1:3, but no convincing correlations between these festivals (or festival, if they in fact allude to the same event) and the feast of a *mishpāḥāh* can be drawn. The tradition unit I Samuel 1—3 is so much under the influence of the notion that Eli is the priest over all Israel, and the portrayal of the holy place that of a temple for all Israel, that it is impossible to assess whether a feast by a *mishpāḥāh* underlies the later form of the story. As it stands, we see only the *bēth-'āv* of Elkanah, who is from Ramathaim, "the two heights," in Ephraim. The last element in the full place name, Ramathaim-zophim is probably a scribal misreading for "Zuphite(s)," since Zuph is listed as an ancestor of Samuel in I Chronicles 6:26(11), 35(20). It is possible that the reference is to *mishpahath* Zuphi, which inhabited the site of Ramathaim. The locations advanced for Ramathaim are all a good many miles to the west of Shiloh, and thus it seems improbable that Shiloh ever lay within the region where Elkanah's *mishpāḥāh* lived. Possibly, in instances where important holy places lay within the tribe of a *mishpāḥāh*, the members journeyed there to observe their annual feast, but with no more than I Samuel 1 to base it on, such a possibility would be highly conjectural.

The annual feast at Shiloh as described in Judges 21 is apparently a festival of the grape harvest, since the daughters of the city dance in the vineyards. Nothing is said of the identity of those who come to the festival. The limitation of the dancers to Shilonite women might accord with a local feast conducted by the *mishpāḥāh* of Shiloh or by one of the *mishpāḥōth* of Shiloh. However, this limitation of the dancers may be due rather to the assignment of the cultic role to those who live near the holy place. Alternatively it may be a feature we owe to the traditionist of Judges 19—21, who assumed that all the Israelites are gathered in battle against Benjamin and thus could hardly allow the representation of the festival as involving more than the immediate citizens of Shiloh. In fact, the exclusive focus on the Shilonite women may be the traditionist's way of resolving an apparent contradiction. How could the Shilonites be conducting a festival when they were supposedly warring against Benjamin? The traditionist's answer was that the men were absent, but the women carried on the festival. In conclusion the texts about the festival(s) at Shiloh are so scanty on some points and so idiosyncratic on others that we cannot identify the Shilonite festivities with the feast of the *mishpāḥāh*.

Nonetheless, even without confirmation from any other source, the religious role of the *mishpāḥāh* attested in I Samuel 20 is clearly etched. The season of the year is not indicated; we hear only that it was at the time of a new moon (vss. 5,18,24,27). Conceivably the occasion was a harvest festival, such as might follow the gleaning in the fields described in the Book of Ruth, either during the early and late spring grain harvests or during the fall grape harvest. Perhaps all the *mishpāḥōth* in a region where the same crop was harvested at the same time would observe the feast at the same time. The details of the festival, beyond the sacrifice and attending meal, are unstated, although it is likely that stories about important members of the *mishpāḥāh,* such as the story of Ruth, were recited. Possibly even the larger themes of the centralized cult were also recited, particularly if Levitical priests well-versed in those traditions were immediately available to take part. When we put the possibilities in such terms, the question of the boundaries between the feasts of the *mishpāḥōth* and the regularly observed all-Israelite festivals is posed, since on the above interpretation it could reasonably be inferred (although by no means required) that the festival of the *mishpāḥāh* annually, at a time of the new moon, was a preliminary stage in one of the all-Isralite festivals such as Tabernacles (cf. Num. 29:1, where "first day of the month" means the time of the new moon.)[187] There are no available immediate answers to that question, which must be held in abeyance as a matter for further research. All that I Samuel 20 clearly tells us is that the *mishpāḥāh* in Israel was in the habit of observing an annual feast which was of such importance to the social entity that every effort was made to have all living members in attendance.

28.7 'Ammīm and Pᵉlaggōth = Tribal Subdivisions?

Finally, there are two possible references to secondary subdivisions in old Israel which appear idiosyncratically in Judges 5. In a textually disturbed context, Benjamin is addressed as entering the battle "with your *'ammīm*" (5:14), probably to be understood as "kinsmen," but the exact denotation eludes us, for it may mean "in company with your kinsmen," i.e., Ephraim just mentioned, or it may mean "according to your kin groupings," i.e., organized by Benjaminite *ᵃlāphīm.* The other intragroup reference is to "the *pᵉlaggōth* Reuben" (5:15–16). The verb *pālag* and the nouns formed from it bear the primary sense of division into streams or channels of water. Since the context concerns the internal indecisiveness of Reuben in joining the battle, the *pᵉlaggōth* may refer to "factions" within Reuben, i.e., those who wanted to answer the intertribal muster and those who wanted to hold back, without any indication that the factions corresponded to familiar social entities. On the other hand, a noun from the same root, *pᵉluggāh,* is used in II Chronicles 35:5 to designate "divisions" of priests who are to minister as representatives of the *bēth hā-'āvōth,* "the fathers' houses," of the laity. This late usage in Chronicles may be an archaism reflecting an ancient association of *pᵉluggōth* or *pᵉlaggōth* with social subdivisions, possibly the *bēth-'āvōth* but more likely the *mishpāḥōth,* since both P and the Chronicler frequently blur and interchange the categories of the *mishpāḥāh* and the *bēth-'āv.* In both instances in Judges 5, the atypical expressions permit no more than a conjecture that they may refer to social subdivisions within a *shēvet.*

Tertiary Subdivisions of the Social Structure

29.1 *Bayith | Bēth-'āv* = Extended Family

In the course of examining the levels of organization represented by *sheᵛāṭīm/maṭṭōth* and by *mishpāḥōth/ᵃlāphīm,* it has become clear that the third level of organization in old Israel was that of the *bayith* or *bēth-'āv,* "the household" or "father's house." It will be unnecessary to repeat the citations already given. Instead we shall try to indicate the scope, structure, and function of the *bēth-'āv* and also to clarify some of the confusions that arise from the tendency of the tradition to genealogize the relations between larger groups in Israel by the scheme of pseudo-kinship, which expresses affinity through the rubric of common ancestry. It will be seen that this tendency has had the effect of confusing an actual *bēth-'āv* as a living group or as a lineage within a living group, on the one hand, with the *bēth-'āv* as a schematic social fiction, on the other hand.

The *bēth-'āv* is an extended family. It is composed of two or more nuclear families and optimally comprises all the generations living at any one time in a given lineage, which means that as many as five generations of Israelites might be encompassed in a single *bēth-'āv.* In making this calculation, I take into account the early age of marriage in the ancient Near East and assume a twenty-year spacing between the generations.

The *bēth-'āv* is primarily a living group. It includes members with affinal ties, i.e., by marriage, and it excludes some members with consanguinous ties, i.e., by birth, namely, those who leave the group to marry into other *bēth-'āvōth* or who separate by choice or circumstance in order to live elsewhere. Thus, the *bēth-'āv* is a compromise formation involving kinship and residence. A *bēth-'āv* customarily includes the family head and his wife (or wives), their sons and unmarried daughters, the sons's wives and children, and so on, as far as the biological and affinal links extended generationally. Attrition would occur through deaths, marriages out of the group, and separation of members to start new living groups. Addition would occur through births, marriages into the group, and incorporation of outsiders through adoption or the assimilation of *gērīm,* "resident aliens." Although no biblical figures are given, a thriving *bēth-'āv* might easily comprise from fifty to one hundred persons, depending upon the economic support base and the freedom of the community from external threats.

The decimation of Elimelech's house, the infertility of Hannah, the deaths of several of Judah's sons, the plight of Zelophehad's daughters—these and other reports—indicate that *bēth-'āvōth* in Israel were often reduced to near extinction, and at such times the vital defensive measures of the larger *mishpāḥāh* in their behalf had to be invoked. Obviously famine and war would tend to reduce the size of the *bēth-'āv* and, conversely, plentiful harvests and communal peace would tend to increase its size. Proof of the blessing of Yahweh is constantly expressed by the triad of human fertility, agricultural bounty, and sociopolitical peace. That these terms of Israelite well-being are so emphatically intoned means paradoxically that they were the precarious preconditions of communal survival, which had to be renewed again and again in defiance of the whims of nature and the devastations of war.

The extremity to which a *bēth-'āv* might be reduced is vividly illustrated in the hard legal case which the wise woman of Tekoa brings to David at Joab's instigation. That it is a fictitious incident, solely intended to trap the king into self-condemnation for his treatment of Absalom, does not detract from its lifelikeness. Indeed, David found the case altogether convincing as the sort of plight into which a *bēth-'āv* in Israel might fall under exceptional circumstances. The woman laments:

> Alas, I am a widow; my husband is dead. And your handmaid had two sons, and they quarreled with one another in the field; there was no one to part them, and one struck the other and killed him. And now the whole *mishpāḥāh* has risen against your handmaid, and they say, "Give up the man who struck his brother, that we may kill him for the life of his brother whom he slew"; and so they would destroy the heir also. Thus they would quench my coal which is left, and leave to my husband neither name nor remnant upon the face of the earth. (II Samuel 14:5–7)

The predicament is that of a family in which the two sons were either not married or had no sons of their own to carry on the *bēth-'āv*, and presumably had no daughters to inherit in the manner prescribed in Numbers 27:1–11 and 36:1–12. The larger *mishpāḥāh* steps in to invoke the right of blood revenge. The punishment of fratricide threatens to extinguish the *bēth-'āv* altogether. The woman's story may imply that the *mishpāḥāh* was more punitive than helpful to one of its own *bātīm*, in that it was inconsistent in invoking blood revenge while making no offer of emergency marriage to provide the widow with a husband. The story, however, may imply that the widow is past childbearing, and if the two sons were unmarried, there would in fact be no woman to bear an heir to the family head. Extreme and ironic in its complications though the story may be, it illustrates the fragility of the *bēth-'āv*, which might as easily decline and perish as expand and prosper.

In the expression *bēth-'āv*, the "father" is the oldest living male of the lineage, his position devolving at his death upon his eldest son in the living group. The line of succession might be challenged. Jephthah, born of a prostitute and apparently the oldest son of his father, was expelled from the household by his legitimate younger brothers, who declared, "You shall not inherit in our *bēth-'āv*, for you are the son of another woman" (Judges 11:2). In the true *bēth-'āv*, in contrast to a larger social unity conceived fictitiously as a *bayith* or *bēth-'āv* (such as a tribe or a dynasty), there is no permanent name for the *bayith*. It is simply the *bayith* of the current family head, who is comprehended in the impersonal term "father," in contrast to the *bayith* of an eponymous founding ancestor, e.g., the tribe of *bēth* Joseph or the dynasty of *bēth* David.

We observed that in Joshua 7, the *bayith* to which Achan belongs is described as embracing four generations: Zabdi, Carmi, Achan, and Achan's sons and daughters. It is instructive, I think, that the text does not speak of *bēth* Zabdi (although it earlier speaks of *shēvet* Judah and *mishpahath* Zarhi, i.e., the *mishpāḥāh* of Zerah). Although one MS of LXX offers "*bēth* Zabdi," the following "and he brought near his *bayith*" rather conclusively argues that LXX added *bēth* Zabdi simply to provide symmetry to all the social organizational terms in the passage. The account thus pictures Zabdi, Carmi, Achan, and his offspring as living together in one household. Nevertheless, while Zabdi is the current "father," because he is the oldest male in the lineage, it is not permanently his house in the way that a *mishpāḥāh* or a *shēvet* remained permanently stamped with the name of its presumed founder. The "father" of a *bēth-'āv* as a living group was not its founder but only its head pro tem, and this position would pass to his descendants in his lineage. The *bēth-'āv* was thus the functional living unit gathered around a family head at any given moment, and it was, in a narrower and more definable sense, the lineage—i.e., all the biological descendants of a known common ancestor (distinguished from a fictitious ancestor), thus distinguishable from members of the living group who participated by marriage or by adoption or by incorporation.

29.2 *Bēth-'āv* as Metaphor for *Mishpāḥāh*

When biblical commentators on Israelite social organization claim fluidity and blurring in the designations *mishpāḥāh* and *bēth-'āv*, they are usually being too uncritical toward the pseudo-kinship attributions of the traditions. The pseudo-kinship claim is indeed a confusing habit of mind, and it is far from easy to follow the various ways in which the fictitious attributions are worked out from tradition to tradition. The basic practice is that the traditionist uses the solid scheme of the known traceable lineage within a *bēth-'āv* as a device for representing the ties between much larger social groups whose actual blood ties were far too complex and too poorly known, and too much at odds with the simplistic lineage scheme, to be remotely capable of representation in this way. As a result, the same persons may be designated as members of a lineage proper, on the one hand, and as themselves the heads (eponyms) or members of fictitious lineages by which *mishpāḥōth* or *sheᵛātīm* are arranged in a pattern of pseudo-kinship. The family tree becomes a table of related groups while still purporting to be a family tree.

A striking example is the very different conceptualizations in the treatments of Tola and Puah (or Puvah) of Issachar in Judges and in Numbers. Tola is one of the so-called minor judges, the son of Puah, in Judges 10:1. These names appear, however, in Numbers 26:23 as two of the four *mishpāḥōth* of Issachar. Here is a blatant instance of the interchangeability of persons and social groups in the Israelite traditions. In the list of the "minor judges," Tola and Puah are individuals, son and father. In the census list of Numbers 26, Tola and Puvah are "sons" of Issachar, but their individuality is absorbed in their eponymous function as progenitors of *mishpaḥath* Tolaite and *mishpaḥath* Punite. Furthermore, in Judges, Puah and Tola are of successive generations, father and son, whereas in Numbers they are brothers, the sons of Issachar. The two representations yield very different social organizational designs. In Judges, the scope of the representation is of two persons, Puah and Tola, in successive generations within a single *bēth-'āv*. In Numbers, the scope of the representation is of the entire body of Issachar viewed synchronically, within which Tola and Puvah are two *mishpāḥōth* forming one-half of the total *maṭṭeh,* called Issachar.

It seems to me, given the exceptional nature of the names linked together in the same tribe in both contexts, we must explain this anomaly in one of three ways:(1) Puah and Tola were persons related as father and son who, because of their prominence in Issachar, were used eponymously by the P traditionist in order to invent names for *mishpāḥōth* in that tribe which never actually existed;(2) Puah and Tola were the names of *mishpāḥōth* in the first place and the traditionist of Judges 10:1 has personified them fictitiously as individuals;(3) a middle way might be found by hypothesizing that Puah and Tola were important persons whose names were actually taken over as gentilics by two Israelite *mishpāḥōth* who were henceforth called the Punites and the Tolaites. Since Puah and Tola are represented as father and son in one *bēth-'āv,* this would have been possible, it seems to me, only as the result of a major expansion or reorganization within Issachar, since it is not easy to imagine how two different *mishpāḥōth* drew their names from the same *bēth-'āv.* A variant of this view might argue that though actual persons, Puah and Tola were first linked as father and son in Judges 10:1, after the *mishpāḥōth* bearing their names had formed, and that this linkage of the two ancestors was intended to strengthen the ties between the *mishpāḥōth.*

29.3 *Bēth-'āv* as Metaphor for *Shēveṭ / Maṭṭeh*

The confusion that notions of pseudo-kinship introduced into the biblical data on social organization is well illustrated in P's use of *bēth-'āv* to refer to a *maṭṭeh.* This emerges sharply in the account of the Aaronite rod that bore almonds (Num. 17:1 [16]–11[26]). Moses is told:

> Speak to the Israelites, and get from them rods (*maṭṭeh maṭṭeh*), one for each father's house (*bēth-'āv*), from all their leaders (*nᵉsī'ēhem*) according to their fathers' houses (*bēth'ᵃvōthām*), twelve rods (*maṭṭoth*). . . .there shall be one rod for the head of each father's house (*rō'sh bēth'ᵃvōthām*). (17:2[17]–3[18])

With the specification of twelve rods, there is no doubt that the *bēth-'āv* is here understood as the major sub-unit of Israel, equivalent to a *maṭṭeh*. The immediate reason for this usage is evident. Since the traditionist uses *maṭṭeh* as a rod, it would have been gauche to employ his preferred term for the major social unit in Israel, namely, the identical word *maṭṭeh*. By using *maṭṭeh* for rod, every occurrence of that word necessarily carries the overtones of its most frequent meaning as tribe. The reader would perceive *maṭṭeh* in this context as meaning "tribal rod."

But why was *bēth-'āv* preferred over *mishpāḥāh* as the synonym for *maṭṭeh*? P was certainly aware that in old Israelite social organization a *mishpāḥāh* was a larger unit than a *bēth-'āv*. His introduction to the census totals of Numbers 1 states: "Take a census of all the congregation of the Israelites, according to their *mishpāḥōth*, according to their *bēth-'āvōth*" (1:2). And in the totals for each *maṭṭeh*, the formula runs:

> Of the *bᵉnē*-(name of the tribe), their registrations according to their *mishpāḥōth*, according to their *bēth-'āvōth*, by the total of names, head by head, every male from twenty years and upward, all who were able to go forth to war—the enrollments of the *maṭṭeh* of (name of the tribe) were (total number of fighting men). (1:20 and *passim*)

In the introduction of the names of the tribal heads in Numbers 1, however, another much larger referent for *bēth-'āv* emerges: "Associated with you [Moses] shall be a man from each *maṭṭeh*, each one being the head of his *bēth-'āv*" (1:4). Taken by itself, this might be taken to mean that each tribal officer is to be selected from those who are heads of households. Subsequent verses make it clear, however, that *bēth-'āv* is here understood as a synonym for the *maṭṭeh*:

> These were the ones selected from the congregation, the leaders (*nᵉsī'īm*) of the ancestral tribes (*maṭṭōth ᵃvōthām*), the heads (*rō'shē*) of the fighting contingents of Israel (*'alphē* Israel). (1:16)

Of interest in this summary are two features:(1) the survival of the term *'ᵃlāphīm* for the old military units drawn from the *mishpāḥōth*, in contrast to P's otherwise prevailing assumption that the term means military units by thousands; and(2) the designation *maṭṭōth ᵃvōthām* providing a clear link between the *bēth-'āv* and the *maṭṭeh*, revealing as it does that the P traditionist thinks of even the large social unit of the *maṭṭeh* as a kind of "*bēth-'āv*" writ large. And the identification of *bēth-'āv* with *maṭṭeh* is clinched by the summary to the entire list: "Those are the enrollments recorded by Moses and Aaron and by the leaders of Israel (*nᵉsī'ē* Israel), twelve men, one man to each *bēth-'āv*" (1:44).

Clearly the conceptual ground for using *bēth-'āv* in the extended sense of a *maṭṭeh* was the scheme of pseudo-kinship, according to which each *maṭṭeh* was conceived as a very large lineage on analogy with the lineage of the *bēth-'āv*. This set up a tension in identifying the "head" or "father" of the *maṭṭeh* conceived as a *bēth-'āv*. According to the total scope of the tribal pedigrees, the true "fathers" of the *maṭṭōth* were none other than the twelve sons of Jacob. Thus, the "father" of Reuben would be Reuben the eponymous ancestor-founder of the group. But in the true *bēth-'āv* as a functional living group, the "father" was the living male "head" of the household. The historical setting of the census list in the wilderness presupposed, however, that the twelve sons of Jacob were dead and that the current "leaders" or "heads" of the tribes were not the same as the founding "fathers" of the tribes. Thus, while Reuben is the "father" of *maṭṭeh* Reuben, the present "head" of *maṭṭeh* Reuben is Elizur ben Shedeur (1:5), and so on for each *maṭṭeh*. A double representation results: the eponymous ancestor is the proto-typical head of the *maṭṭeh*, but the operational head is a prominent living member of the *maṭṭeh*. Yet no genealogy is given to show the line from Reuben to Elizur.

A similar tension in the representation of the heads of the *bēth-'āvōth* conceived as *maṭṭōth* underlies Numbers 17:1(16)–11(26). The tension is ignored by the traditionist in that he only names one tribe and one head, i.e., Aaron as the "head" of the *bēth-'āv* of Levi (or *bēth* Levi, 17:8 (23). Scholars differ as to whether Levi is here included among the twelve *bēth-'āvōth* with their rods or is counted separately to form thirteen in all. The focus of the tradition upon the exclusive rights of the Levites to priestly office leaves the other *bēth-'āvōth/maṭṭōth* so much in the background that they are not even named, nor are their heads named. But in spite of these major differences between Numbers 17 and the census enumerations of Numbers 1, the agreement of the two in representing *maṭṭōth* as *bēth-'āvōth* is emphatic. Just as certain is the fact that the P traditionist, while projecting the formal comparability between the strict lineage of a *bēth-'āv* and the metaphorical lineage of a *maṭṭeh,* is unable to fill out the tribal lineage with much detail or with convincing genealogical linkages. In spite of some efforts to extend the names of the *mishpāḥōth* in Numbers 26 over as many as three generations in the case of Manasseh, the lists for the most part remain synchronic maps of supposed contemporary component groups within the tribes rather than diachronic sketches of lineages extending over generations. Accordingly, even the P traditionist—with all his zeal for compiling ancient lore—is unable to employ the device of pseudo-kinship in any consistent and thorough way to bring order into the ancient traditions about social organization. His failure reflects the fact that the larger social units of the *mishpāḥāh* and the *maṭṭeh* never were true lineages but, instead, enlarged composites of lineages in residential and regional groupings whose various pseudo-identifications with ancestral founders were sociopolitical affirmations of unity and not biologically demonstrable links.

29.4 Residency Patterns and Economy of the *Bayith* / *Bēth-'āv*

Since the term *bayith* is used for a building in which people live as well as for the basic living group proper, it may seem a logical inference that the *bēth-'āv* inhabited a single building. Doubtless this was the case when a *bēth-'āv* was small, but for a large *bēth-'āv*, even for an average-sized one including scores of persons, we must rather envision a cluster of dwelling units. It is evident from archaeological remains that, with the exception of palaces and the homes of the upper class in large cities or administrative centers, the average Israelite dwelling was modest in size.[188]

In fact, the story of Micah in Judges 17—18 offers an instructive picture of the distribution of the dwelling units in *bēth* Micah located in the hill country of Ephraim. Micah is head of a *bayith* which includes his widowed mother (who interestingly has property of her own in the form of eleven hundred pieces of silver), and at least two and probably more sons. One of Micah's sons serves as priest for the family shrine until a Levite, Jonathan, grandson of Moses (cf. 18:30), who had been a *gēr* in Bethlehem of Judah, comes to live as a *gēr* with Micah, "and the young man became his priest and a member of *bēth* Micah" (17:12). Since these members of the *bēth-'āv* are mentioned only in connection with their relevance to the plot, Micah's household doubtless had many additional members unnoted in the story. Since his son was old enough to serve as priest, it is probable that the son was married and may have had children of his own. In short, counting the widowed mother we can easily project four generations living together in Micah's household.

As to the physical living arrangements of *bēth* Micah, we find explicit references to a number of buildings. When the five men who first scouted the land for the Danites bring their tribesmen to Micah's household, they say to them, "Do you know that in these houses there are an ephod, a teraphim, a graven image, and a molten image?" (18:14). The young Levite has his own dwelling: ". . .and they came to the house of the Levite youth of Micah's household" (18:15). When the abduction of the Levite and the theft of the cultic objects is discovered, "the men who were in the houses comprising (*'asher 'im*) the household of Micah were called out, and they overtook the Danites" (18:22). This reading is preferable to the usual, "the men who were in the houses next to Micah's house" (i.e., implying them to be from other *bēth-'āvōth*), because the Danites warn Micah to break off the pursuit, "lest you lose your life and the lives of your household" (18:25). In a word, the representation of Judges 17—18 is of a small unwalled village in which Micah's *bēth-'āv* occupies several adjacent buildings, although not necessarily the entire village. The reference to "the gate" (18:16–17), where the six hundred Danites wait while the five scouts enter, is not to a city gate; either the gate of the courtyard in Micah's home is meant, or it is an anachronistic reference to the family shrine conceived as though it were a sizable temple.

The *bēth-'āv* was the basic economic unit in the Israelite social system. It formed a self-sufficient unit in the sense that it produced the basic means of subsistence for all its members and consumed all, or nearly all, of what it produced. Beyond sexual division of labor (and even this is not clear), there was almost no significant division of labor within a *bēth-'āv*. Simple wooden implements and utilitarian pottery were made for family use by a member of the household. Specialization in crafts, however, is unknown in premonarchic texts, except for the Kenite metallurgists. Only for metal tools and weapons was it necessary to rely on outsiders, such as the Kenites for copper and, later on, the Philistines for iron.

The typical agricultural *bēth-'āv*, such as Gideon's (Judges 6), grew grains and fruits, and practiced limited animal husbandry, owning some sheep and goats and a few cattle. The staple crops were barley and wheat, wine and olive oil, which were produced alone or in combinations depending on the variable climate and soil from region to region. A pastoral *bēth-'āv*, such as Nabal's (I Sam. 25), bred large herds of sheep and goats, probably practiced some agriculture, and, through barter, was able to secure whatever additional foodstuffs were needed. Specialization in commerce is unattested in the early sources. Such barter as existed was marginal to the *bēth-'āv*'s primary cycle of production and consumption. Surplus was used mainly for storage as a guarantee against the devastating famines that might strike at any time, sometimes lasting two or three years in a row.

Whenever the self-sufficiency of a *bēth-'āv* was threatened, the *mishpāḥāh* stood by to offer relief. It was incumbent on Israelites to advance loans in kind to needy *bēth-'āvôth* without charging interest, and this practice of mutual aid probably fell first to the *mishpāḥāh* to which the needy *bēth-'āv* belonged. But since famines would tend to incapacitate whole *mishpāḥôth* and even whole *shevāṭīm* in the same climatic zone, the obligations of mutual aid extended in principle as far as the boundaries of Israelite social organization. The Israelite *bēth-'āv* had one great advantage in its struggle with nature which the small farmers of Canaanite society did not have. The Israelite *bēth-'āv* was economically autonomous in the sense that it did not owe any of its produce to higher authorities in the form of the payments in kind which so heavily burdened the subjects of the feudal Canaanite city-states. The surplus production of the Israelite small farmer and herdsman was not given over to or shared with any centralized political apparatus. Of course this autonomy was qualified by the obligation to extend aid to another *bēth-'āv* in need, but this was more a matter of reciprocal exchange than of commercial transaction. Whatever was given out would in time return. If the recipient *bēth-'āv* was decimated and could not reciprocate, the unreciprocated *bēth-'āv* could count on help as needed from yet another *bēth-'āv*.

30

Israelite Tribalism: Anthropological and Sociological Commentary

It is not easy to find a satisfactory term to describe the social structure of ancient Israel. "Tribalism" may after all be the most apt term, but the concept can be reclaimed for use in biblical studies only if we set aside almost everything previously written on the subject by biblical scholars, as well as much that has been written in the social sciences.[189] Mendenhall put his finger on the flaw when he emphatically rebutted the facile identification of tribalism with pastoral nomadism. The slightest acquaintance with anthropological studies should have alerted biblical scholars to this grievous misjudgment. After W. R. Smith and J. Wellhausen studied the applicability of bedouin tribalism to early Israelite tribalism, so headlong was the retreat away from any further sustained anthropological and sociological studies of Israel that biblical study has been almost totally divorced from the social sciences for half a century.

The early brief contact between anthropology and Old Testament studies, followed by a sharp and continuing break, produced a curious contradiction in the body of accepted assumptions about early Israel. While biblical scholars almost unanimously renounced the appropriateness of the later Arab bedouins as close analogues to the Israelites in the evolutionary scale, they uncritically retained Smith's and Wellhausen's larger presupposition that the Israelites were pastoral nomads prior to their settlement in Canaan. This presupposition was derived from the "tribal" terminology for social organization in the Bible and from the assumption that migration is identical with pastoral nomadism. That some of the Israelites migrated into Canaan from elsewhere is certain, and migrating peoples may very loosely be called "nomads," at least during the time of their movement. But peoples of very different socioeconomic types have been pushed into migration, and the mere fact of their migration tells us absolutely nothing about their culture or mode of economic production. An increasingly refined understanding of ancient Near Eastern nomadism has thrown the whole issue of Israelite "nomadism" into confusion. As full camel nomadism has been recognized as emergent in the Near East only after 1200 B.C.,[190] and as a more adequate account of "tribal" life among subjects of the kingdom of Mari has become clear,[191] the foundations on which Israel's "pastoral nomadism" was posited have been steadily

293

washed away. There probably were some pastoral nomads in early Israel, but the entire matter must be approached *de novo* and with a discriminating use of anthropological and sociological tools.

Since I shall return to the question of the nomadic model for early Israel in VIII.39, I will only anticipate here that the overwhelming body of evidence for early Israel shows its tribally organized peoples to have been settled agriculturalists who also practiced animal husbandry. Such evidence as there is for pastoral nomadism fits best with a transhumant form of pastoralism. Transhumant pastoralism is characteristic of a settled community in which large herds are sent out seasonally to distant preferred pasture lands under the care of herdsmen specialists. The so-called nomadism of the Rechabites or Kenites is best explained on the hypothesis that they were peripatetic metallurgists,[192] which serves to emphasize that other occupations besides the breeding of large herds may require people to move around. Exactly what form of socioeconomic life was practiced by the proto-Israelites who migrated through the wilderness from Egypt to Canaan must be further investigated, but it cannot be accepted that their migration is prima facie evidence that they were pastoral nomads. We shall see that, on the contrary, there are a number of indications in the traditions which suggest otherwise.

30.1 What Is a Tribe?

In order to establish controls for examining early Israelite tribalism, it is essential that we explore current anthropological theory about tribalism. Now that ethnology has collected a remarkable array of information about social structure among hundreds of human societies and cultural evolutionists have begun to plot some regularities in the development of different forms of society, there has been a phenomenal burst of energy in the direction of characterizing "tribal society." Despite all the variations and novelties from society to society, a large number of social systems tend to exhibit similar structural features that can be broadly typified as "tribal." Marshall Sahlins points to the challenges and the difficulties in trying to typify a tribal mode of life so as to do empirical justice to discreteness as well as to commonality:

> So what I am about to do—which is to formulate a generalized design of tribal culture—is plainly hazardous and perhaps futile. But such is the magic of the sociologist's "ideal type" that, founded as it is on actual or pretended ignorance of the empirical diversity, inadequate as it is as a representation of complex realities, primitive as it may be as an intellectual procedure, it can yield remarkable insights into the particular case. I think the general model of tribal culture suggested here helps one understand particular tribes—at least a fair number of them.[193]

While there are still many disputes and uncertainties in details, anthropological theorists of tribal society are developing a considerable consensus about "a generalized design of tribal culture." Turning away from earlier pseudo-historical speculations about such matters as the totemistic origins of tribes, they attempt rather a more circumspect and better-rounded theoretical design induced from the empirical data of specific societies.

What is it, then, that typifies tribal society? One simplistic answer that only leads in circles is to say that a tribal society is a society organized in tribes. This is, of course, no answer at all but only a rephrasing of the question, which now becomes: What is it that characterizes a society organized in tribes? The snare in the rephrased question is that it tends to block the way to a proper methodology because it rather naively assumes that we know what a tribe is, and that wherever we see it present we know that the society is tribal. The *tribus* in early Latin history was "a third part" of the people, i.e., one of the three segments of the Roman patriciate which supposedly exhibited common descent and complete political autonomy. When we say that a society is organized by tribes we presumably mean that it possesses social units which exhibit the actual or presumed traits of the Latin *tribus*.[194] That the model of "tribe" is selective should be evident, for example, in the fact that the threefoldness of the Latin tribes has never been taken as one of the criteria of a tribal society. The "tribe" is not a fixed entity that we can locate in ancient Rome, or anywhere else; an empirical touchstone by which we can judge whether any other social entity is or is not a "tribe." "Tribe" is an ideal type characterized by a cluster of traits which is heuristically useful in analyzing specific societies. Consequently, we may expect to find degrees of tribalism depending on how fully the traits are exhibited from case to case.[195]

Another confusion resulting from focusing at the start on tribes as social building blocks is that we tend to miss the fact that tribal society is a system in which the whole inheres in and determines the parts. It is only in terms of their structure and function in the larger whole that we are able to make any sort of intelligent judgment about whether social units within the whole exhibit certain ideal typical traits of tribalism. The discernment of a social whole as a system is something very different from aggregating a number of separately defined parts. This reality calls for a special attention to the boundaries of the system and to the specific constellations of social interaction within the system. System implies completeness or, at least, a striving for completeness, a meaningful functional whole.

One of the holistic traits of tribal society is that the body of persons in it, arranged in separate living groups, are bound together with various cross-ties which constitute a network of identifications and activities among the people that reach out beyond the borders of the individual living groups. The pairing of nuclear families or the clustering of extended families by residency are cross-cut by other kinds of groupings which bring people together around specific meanings and activities which are not the function of residency, but rather the function of kinship, age, skill, initiation, or any other of a number of foci for pulling people together or for establishing a sense of affinity with others outside the immediate living group or neighborhood. Morton Fried summarizes this tribal network as

> a boundable system of relationships whose armatures, the devices connecting the members of the component polar bands, are sodalities, cross-cutting associations devoted to kinship affiliations, age-grades, secret societies, ritual congregations, and ceremonial parties.[196]

In developing a typological profile of tribal society it has been impossible to avoid evolutionary considerations. After the bold but somewhat premature efforts at grand cultural evolutionary theories in the last half of the nineteenth century, anthropology fell back upon more careful empirical field-work in order to amass data as a basis for more cautious and substantial theory. Increasingly this mass of data has forced the old evolutionary questions into the foreground and demonstrated that the great evolutionary theorists were not wrong in their instincts but rather limited by the paucity of data and hamstrung by too simple models. No one now doubts that social forms develop over time and in stages of complexity and that there are some regularities involved in the process. The question becomes: What are the regularities occurring in typical sequences which underlie the processes of social development?

Developmentally it is clear that the tribal network is a social form that grows out of a preceding stage now generally called "band society" in which the smaller living groups cooperate in joint activities at times, usually ceremonial and religious, and separate to live and work independently, in hunting and/or gathering, at other times. What distinguishes the band from the tribe organizationally is that it lacks the interconnective tissue of cross-cutting group identities and activities. The band of course recognizes itself as a whole, but band activities are either carried on by the band as a whole when it is together or independently by each smaller living group when apart. The simplicity of the loosely aggregated parts in band organization permits the extension of the band only so far. Beyond a point the band must either fission and become two bands or it must move on to develop the intergroup, cross-cutting ties which can give the whole body suppleness and coherence. When the band fissions there are merely more bands at the same organizational level. When the band develops the cross-cutting instrumentalities, it moves to another organizational level; it becomes a tribe.[197]

While the band society is typical of hunting and gathering economies, the tribal society is characteristic of agricultural societies. The population sizes show a definite increase from normally fewer than one hundred persons in the band to as many as several thousand in a tribe. This increase in size is a function both of the more sophisticated tribal bonding devices and of the increased level of economic productivity. Actually there is a considerable range of ecological adaptations among tribal societies, involving "slash-and-burn" agriculture, intensive or plow agriculture, pastoral nomadism, equestrian hunting and, occasionally, hunting, fishing, and gathering in exceptional environments where there is an abundant supply of wild food. The more complex cooperative skills and work routines involved in these ecologies, as contrasted with hunting and gathering in marginal environments, call forth social forms more complex than the band, forms which assure a larger and more finely calibrated functional integrity commensurate with the more sophisticated and productive economy.[198]

If the band society marks off the zone of social organization which logically and developmentally *precedes* the tribal society, the state (and its antecedent, the chiefdom) marks off the zone of social organization which logically and developmentally *follows* the tribal society. This typological social-evolutionary assessment is, of course, not to be construed as a rigid description of an iron law of evolutionary stages through which every society must pass. It entails no claim that every observed tribal society was once a band society or that every tribal society will evolve into a chiefdom or state. And it does not deny the important factor of interaction between societies in shaping the pace and form of evolutionary development. Instead, it identifies levels of social organization which tend to move toward greater complexity in conjunction with factors such as economic production, modes of communication, and quality and extent of interaction with other societies. Consequently, if the tribal society is characterized by cross-cutting groups which bind it together more coherently and subtly than the band society is held together, the tribal society at the same time lacks the specialization of political office and centralization of political power which provides the state such marked organizational advantages for coercing and channeling human energies for economic and military ends.

Viewed in such a broad design of social forms, premonarchic Israel was clearly tribal in character. Israel's economy was a form of intensive rain agriculture with animal husbandry, an economy that capitalized on the recent introduction into the highlands of Canaan of iron implements for clearing and plowing the land, the invention of slaked lime plaster for constructing watertight cisterns to hold reserve water through the annual dry season, and the art of rock terracing to hold and channel water and to control soil erosion against the fickleness of too little or too much rainfall. The members of Israelite society were arranged not only in large extended residence groups, forming relatively self-contained socio-economic units and political equals, but also in cross-cutting sodalities or sodality equivalents. Among these cross-cutting groups were the protective associations of extended families, the citizen army, the ritual congregation, the Levites (landless and distributed among the tribes), and probably also the itinerant Kenites/Rechabites.

On the other hand, Israel was not yet a state, which it became fully only under David. Tendencies toward the chiefdom and monarchy are clearly evidenced in

Saul and even earlier in some of the diverse functionaries called obscurely "judges," notably Gideon and Abimelech, and perhaps also in some of the so-called minor judges such as Ibzan. At its founding Israel had no specialized political offices rooted in a superordinate sovereignty, and it resisted such institutions and offices strenuously even after reluctantly resorting to the military advantages they offered in the face of the mounting Philistine threat, which was itself a powerful and effective regrouping and tightening of sociopolitical formations from the preceding era of Egyptian imperialism and Canaanite quasi-feudalism.

The defining feature of politics in old Israel was that political functions were diffused throughout the social structure or focused in temporary ad hoc role assignments or "seizures." While the details of Israel's social structure, and especially of its "offices," are as yet unrecoverable in many respects, so that we do not possess the fully rounded cross-section we desire, all available evidence supports consistently the view that early Israel was tribal with fiercely resisted tendencies toward the chiefdom. We are also able to establish beyond any shadow of doubt that this political feature of Israelite tribalism was not derived from pastoral nomadism but was securely rooted in a form of agricultural tribalism for which there are ample parallels in ethnography.

30.2 Cross-Cutting Associations: The Exogamous Clan

Now we must inquire into the types of cross-cutting sodalities or sodality equivalents which comprised the ligaments or armatures uniting the extended families (bēth-'āvōth) in early Israel. Probably the single most frequent and significant sodality in tribal societies is the "clan" (sometimes called the "gens" or the "sib"). It was the enduring contribution of Lewis H. Morgan to anthropological theory to have discovered the exogamous clan or gens organization, with its corollary classificatory kinship system for defining social interaction, as the critical cross-cutting and bonding mechanism in many tribal societies.[199] Morgan found the clan on five continents as the primary social unit among peoples who had attained horticulture (hoe or digging-stick farming and domestication of animals) but had not yet advanced to large-scale irrigation agriculture or to extensive stock breeding.

Two or more clans are found in each tribe or village. Each person belongs to a clan by birth, and this identity defines his/her relation to other persons in the society. Decisive for understanding the clan is a grasp of its absolutely exogamous nature; i.e., it is forbidden to marry any other member of one's clan, even though that clan member might be from the remotest region of the tribe; and it is correspondingly permitted to marry persons close at hand in the village or living group, even cross-cousins, provided that they are of another clan, and respecting only the prevalent incest taboos. Prior to this discovery, anthropologists made erroneous constructs of the social organization of tribes on the assumption that whole tribes were exogamous. The map of tribal society is fundamentally altered once it becomes clear that two or more subgroups within the society are exogamous and form complementary relationships to one another, but that the society or tribe as a whole is endogamous.

The clan is neither a residential unit nor a single work group, although work groups are often organized on the basis of clan affiliation. The clan is a social entity cross-cutting the residential group and comprehending various work groups constellated around the economic holdings of the clan. The difficulty in keeping terms and structures clear is increased by the fact that some anthropologists use "sib" for the extensive cross-cutting unilineal descent group (which the majority call the "clan"), while reserving "clan" for the coresidential body of sib members together with their spouses in which particular biological families are included. Members of two or more clans are always found in a single family. Because of the unyielding requirement of exogamy, every union of a man and a woman brings two clans together. The clan is reckoned either through the mother (matrilineality) or through the father (patrilineality), or sometimes by a mixed or bilateral method.

Morgan was convinced that all clans were at one time matrilineal and only became patrilineal as technology advanced and economic goods increased and were concentrated as surpluses to the point where men seized control from the women. Many of his reconstructions and interpretations of this process are now seen to be highly speculative, awaiting more evidence, or simply in outright error. Nevertheless, his main contention is still an arguable one, and need not rest solely on his more doubtful and discredited arguments. Indeed, the thrust of his account of clan evolution does not even stand or fall upon the argument for an original matrilineality. Underlying the question of matrilineality is Morgan's insight into the clan as a democratizing leveling mechanism for sharing and supervising communal wealth, a mechanism which gradually gives way in higher civilization to the expropriative mechanisms of private property and the state. Even on the strict point of the priority of matrilineality, Morgan's claim still possesses considerable credibility. Although a majority of clans observed by nineteenth- and twentieth-century ethnologists are patrilineal, there is evidence that some of these societies have become patrilineal following an earlier matrilineal or bilateral form and that the pressure of patriarchally organized higher civilization has been a major impetus toward the adoption of patrilineality among simpler societies.[200] It is at any rate clear that the matrilineal clan is a common form but that the clan device also functions in patrilineal form and in bilateral forms, and that, whatever the method of kin reckoning, it preserves a form of economic democracy fundamentally unlike that of politicized societies in which the state, the patriarchal family, and private property distribute economic surpluses in arbitrary and grossly unequal fashion.

In spite of the continuing dispute over the possible originality of one or another manner of reckoning the clan line, it is abundantly clear that the clan is a distinctive and dominant ingredient of all those tribal societies in which it can be identified. Membership in a clan determines one's place in the society, whom one marries, to whom one owes duties and who owes duties in return, as well as one's share in the social product of labor. It is in the clan that the title to economic goods lies. Beyond a small supply of personal articles of clothing, adornment, tools, and weaponry, property is vested in the clan and passed on intact as a collectivity through the acknowledged line. Thus, husband and wife are separately incorporated into two clan systems which define their fullest social identity, support their physical existence, and exact their deepest loyalties.

Property, chiefly in fields or in herds, remains vested in the clan and is supervised by the oldest male or oldest female members of the resident branch of the clan. Work forces that cultivate the fields, prepare and store food and other necessities, or tend the herds are often organized along clan lines, although there is great variability in the composition and patterning of the work units from society to society, depending on factors such as patrilocality or matrilocality in residence, distance between intermarrying residential communities, and sexual division of labor. In a *matrilineal* tribe, for example, married men will frequently help their sisters to work the fields and care for the herds of their mother's clan, while their own wives will work alongside their brothers in the service of their mother's clan. In a *patrilineal* tribe that is not yet organized by patriarchal families, married women will frequently assist their brothers in the work of their father's clan, while their own husbands will work side by side with their sisters in the daily economy of their father's clan. In short, the organization of work along the lines of clan holdings is often the dominant principle, greatly reducing the scope of work carried on along the lines of affinal or residence groupings.

Parenting functions are also profoundly affected by the clan organization. In a *matrilineal* system, the maternal uncle of the child will often assume or share many of the paternal roles that we associate with the biological father, while the biological father serves as a social father to his sister's child. Although the "surrogate mother" form of clan-based parenting is perhaps less common than the "surrogate father" form, in a *patrilineal* system, the paternal aunt of a child may assume or share many of the maternal roles that we associate with the biological mother, while the biological mother serves as a social mother to her brother's child. Naturally, the incidence of such extensions of parenting roles beyond the biological parents is either facilitated or discouraged by the distance between the residential lineages which typically intermarry. In general we observe that parent functions are rather widely shared compared to the situation in a nuclear family and are distributed along clan lines. The parenting arrangements may assume manifold quirks and permutations, and those we have briefly identified are merely some of the most common forms for illustrative purposes.

Of critical consequence for the overall societal structure is the fact that, in a clan-organized society, the family is decisively subordinated and circumscribed by the clan. Families constellate through marriage and birth and dissolve through divorce and death, while the clan structure goes on in functional perpetuity. In fact, divorce is normally rather easily executed in the clan society; and while there is some clan pressure to preserve unions, they can be dissolved without catastrophic consequences either to the social fabric or to the persons involved. The family is totally without a substantial independent base of power and remains overshadowed by the clan, which limits and supports the family in all its functions. Indeed, the family looks like the clan's reproductive agency, so located in relation to the clan that it performs its limited functions without threatening the ever-renewed power base of the clan. Families may be influential, as when they contain forceful personalities; but they are radically excluded from holding the basic means of production, and they are unable to confer rights and duties that frame the major forms of interaction in the society. The family in the true clan system is the circumscribed instrument for biological reproduction, whereby the dominant clans meet and mix and replenish themselves, but in this meeting and mixing and replenishment the clan defines and implements the economic and socializing priorities of society.

30.3 Did Early Israel Possess the Exogamous Clan?

With this ideal-typical profile of a clan in mind, and without attempting to trace all the variants and idiosyncrasies that it assumes from society to society, we may properly ask: Did the clan exist in early Israel? In the face of the recurrent and tenacious uncritical assumption that the *mishpāḥāh/'eleph* in old Israel was a "clan," I submit that it is by now crystal clear that Israel did *not* have the clan system of organization. It had a middle-range or secondary level of social organization called the *mishpāḥāh/'eleph,* but this social unit was no clan. The crucial test in this regard is, of course, whether the *mishpāḥāh* was exogamous, i.e., did the Israelite have to marry outside his or her *mishpāḥāh*? Correlatively, do we find evidence that members of different *mishpāḥōth* were linked in a single *bēth-'āv* and correspondingly distributed horizontally through the *shēveṭ*? I shall now indicate my reasons for answering these questions with a firm negative.

Since there is no complete corpus of marriage law in the Old Testament, it is not a conclusive answer to our questions to report that no laws speak of clan exogamy. If all of the law corpora in their present forms are monarchic in origin, we may concede that clan exogamy could have been practiced in premonarchic times, and then lapsed before the laws were formulated or collected and revised. We might even argue that clan exogamy was so traditionally ingrained in practice that it did not require explicit mention in laws. So we must examine what little information there is from the laws, including those concerning inadmissible marriages between kin and those concerning inheritance by daughters, in order to see if the data are consistent or inconsistent with clan exogamy, or simply neutral toward it. And because of the fragmentary state of the laws, we must also examine pre-monarchic narratives which may inadvertently reveal the presence or absence of the clan system. We shall be especially attentive for phenomena which are not reconcilable with a clan system. The study of the marriage practices and kin patterns of old Israel has been a vexed subject ever since W. R. Smith tried to explain them by means of an original matrilineal totemic clan surviving partially into biblical times.[201] While, for many reasons, his broad interpretation has been conclusively demolished, alternative patterns have been difficult to reconstruct, particularly given the incomplete and occasional—even random—nature of the biblical data on marriage and kinship. In my view, however, enough can be established from early texts to show conclusively that there is no substance to the view that ancient Israel was organized on an exogamous clan basis.

In Leviticus 18:6–18; 20:11–12 and Deuteronomy 27:20,22–23 appear incest taboos and/or impediments to marriage according to degrees of relationship between categories of kin based on blood (consanguinity) and on marriage (affinity). Whether the proscriptions are prohibitions of sexual intercourse or bars to marriage, or both at the same time, has been much disputed. K. Elliger and J. R. Porter have made a plausible case for Leviticus 18:6–18 constituting a set of incest taboos within an extended residential family viewed from the perspective of the male head of the family.[202] More difficult to accept is their further claim that marriage is not at issue because a good number of marriages described in the Old Testament openly violate the prohibitions. In some societies, classes of kin prohibited from marriage may be permitted sexual intercourse, but the reverse is not attested, to my knowledge—namely, that classes of kin under an incest taboo may legitimate their relationship by marriage.[203] It seems to me more probable that Old Testament instances of marriages between classes of kin proscribed in these laws are to be explained as unsanctioned violations of law or, more probably, as variant practices at different times and in different circles in Israel. In other words, the prohibitions against incest/marriage described in Leviticus and Deuteronomy were not in force throughout all Israel at all times, or were not at any rate uniformly sanctioned.

On either interpretation, however, I think the taboos give rather telling evidence against the alleged presence of the exogamous clan in the sector of early Israel responsible for this legislation. If it is the intention to give a complete list of prohibited liaisons and/or marriages between kin, or at least to encompass the most common or crucial forbidden ties, then it is at once striking that cousins are omitted (not to mention the probably accidental omission of daughters). If Israel observed clan exogamy, we should have expected the inclusion of cousins, for under that system some cousin marriages are permitted, and may even be favored or prescribed, while other cousin marriages are forbidden, depending on the lineal reckoning of clan membership in vogue. One would expect all ambiguity as to which cousins could marry to be removed by a taboo list which otherwise shows such scrupulosity. It could, of course, be argued that "you shall not uncover the nakedness of anyone belonging to your *mishpāḥāh* (clan)" was a blanket prohibition so totally taken for granted by the community that it need not be expressed. That interpretation, however, is fatally flawed by the redundancy of specifying particular prohibited relations which would per force fall under such an unexpressed general prohibition based on clan exogamy. If Israel had a patrilineal exogamous clan, why is it necessary to forbid incest/marriage with a sister who is your father's daughter (Lev. 18:9), with a grandchild who is your son's daughter (18:10), and with a paternal aunt (18:12)—liaisons already emphatically prohibited under the laws of patrilineal clan exogamy? Since the center or "ego" of the taboo list is a male, a matrilineal exogamous clan seems out of the question; but even if we should conjecture that traces of an original matrilineal exogamous clan have been overlaid by patrilineal revision, then the need for prohibition of specific liaisons on the maternal side corresponding to those mentioned above on the paternal side would be totally gratuitous. Moreover, a matrilineal exogamous clan arrangement would also necessitate specification of forbidden cousin marriages.

If the taboos are intended to encompass liaisons forbidden by the exogamous clan, they omit crucial forbidden relationships, and are thus *incomplete*. If, on the other hand, liaisons forbidden by exogamous clan organization are presupposed by the formulator, the lists unaccountably specify some relationships which would have been most obviously covered by exogamous clan laws, and are therefore *redundant*. On any reading of the incest/marriage taboos in Leviticus and Deuteronomy, it seems impossible to reconcile them with the practice of clan exogamy. Since, however, we have allowed that the jurisdiction of these prohibitions never extended to all Israel throughout its history, the possibility remains open that clan exogamy was practiced at some time in some sector within Israel. The taboos might be explainable, for example, on the hypothesis that they were formulated *after* the breakup of clan exogamy, with the intent of specifying a limited number of liaisons, formerly proscribed by clan exogamy, which ought still to be prohibited, along with others not based on clan exogamy.

In fact, the negative testimony on the exogamous clan uncovered in the incest/marriage taboos is confirmed by the negative evidence from other biblical laws. If I am correct that the original form of Numbers 36:1–12 directed the daughter inheriting from her father to marry within her *mishpāḥāh* (rather than within her *maṭṭeh*), we confront an absolute inconsistency and total rupture with the true clan system. Moreover, the entire emphasis in biblical rules of inheritance is on the *bēth-'āv* as the instrument of possession rather than on the larger *mishpāḥāh,* which merely serves to intervene on behalf of severely threatened *bēth-'āvōth*. Even when we allow for *bēth-'āv* sometimes being used metaphorically for *mishpāḥāh,* it stretches credulity to try to reconstruct the *bēth-'āv* on the model of a typical far-flung, exogamous clan, if only for the simple reason that no term would then be left in biblical Hebrew to designate the residential family.

The results of examining biblical laws at the points where they come closest to dealing with an hypothesized exogamous clan system in old Israel are, to put it most charitably, that they yield no evidence on the point, and, more exactly, that they actually show or strongly imply that members of the same *mishpāḥāh* were marriageable partners. When to this evidence is added the primacy of the residential family as the locus for inheritance in a manner inconsistent with the primacy of the clan investiture of property, we are justified in concluding that incest, eligibility for marriage, and property inheritance in old Israel proceded on bases entirely other than the exogamous clan. If a clan system existed in old Israel, it was not in force at the time or in the milieu of these laws. At this point it becomes necessary to supplement our inquiry with data in narratives.

In the accounts of marriages in narratives with some claim to premonarchic provenance, or to the retention of premonarchic influences, the marriage of cousins reckoned patrilineally is fairly common. In a true patrilineal clan system the marriage of cousins on the father's side (or of a man to his patrilineal niece) would be absolutely forbidden, thus categorically prohibiting the marriages of Isaac to Rebekah (Gen. 24:15), Jacob to Leah and Rachel (Gen. 29:10,29), Esau to Mahalath (Gen. 28:9), Zelophehad's daughters to his brothers' sons (Num. 36:11), Othniel to Achsah (Josh. 15:16–17; Judg. 1:12–13), Rehoboam to Maacah (I Kings 14:31; 15:2), and Eleazar's daughters to his brother Kish's sons (I Chron. 23:22). We should perhaps leave out of account royal marriages, since they were often multiple and involved foreign alliances and thus may not have been representative of general Israelite practice. At any rate, this is a sizable body of evidence which does not appear to be resolvable by positing matrilineal exogamy or by the hypothesis of numerous violations of or exceptions to patrilineal exogamy.

Now the consistent reckoning of the line in *bēth-'āv* through the male head makes it almost certain that if any clan is implied in these marriages it is a patrilineal clan. It is also axiomatic that the above listed marriages of cousin to cousin and of uncle to niece render null and void any possibility of a patrilineal clan structure lying in the background of these passages. If we attempt to hypothesize a matrilineal clan organization, we run totally counter to the overwhelming weight of biblical reckoning of patrilineage and patrimony in the *bēth-'āv*. The patrilineal and patrimonial context is starkly underlined by the passage in Numbers 36:1–12 where the breach in the male line requires exceptional provision for a daughter to inherit from her father. In the juxtaposition of such irreconcilable social features, one or the other must give way. Obviously what must give way is the otherwise ungrounded hypothesis of clan exogamy in old

Israel. The body of references to the marriage of cousins and of men to their nieces, on the father's side, in a context which is blatantly patrilineal and patrimonial, counts conclusively against the existence of exogamous clans in the social milieu of the Israelite traditionists who passed on the accounts.

The supposed existence of matrilocal residence in early Israel (and by inference of the matrilineal clan) resting on Samson's marriage to the woman of Timnah (Judg. 14—15:8) is of no validity. It has been claimed that Samson's marriage to the Philistine woman is evidence for the practice of a man living with the clan of his bride or of visiting his bride periodically in her home, called *beena* marriage by anthropologists, from a Ceylonese custom, and *erebu* or *ṣadiqa* (including a temporary *mot'a* type) marriage in the ancient Near East, from supposed allusions to such practices among the Assyrians and the bedouin Arabs.[204] Even if the practice is attested in Samson's case, it would not necessarily entail Israelite matrilineality (after all, Samson is rebuked for his irregular liaison with the Philistine woman). It might at most only tell us something about Philistine matrilineality. Concerning the conjectured *beena/erebu/ṣadiqa (mot'a)* marriage, it must be countered that nothing is said about a fixed practice of the husband living with or visiting his wife periodically by way of explaining Samson's behavior. The marriage of Samson to the woman is disrupted by events, the groom storms off in anger, and, upon returning one day, discovers that his wife has been given to another man. This hardly attests to the supposed custom, either among Israelites or among Philistines. Further alleged instances of the groom living with his bride's family (the case of Jacob with Laban; Gen. 29:1–30) or visiting the bride in her home (the case of Gideon and his Shechemite concubine; Judg. 8:31;9:1) do not stand examination. Jacob's residency results from his seeking asylum with Laban, and having paid for his wives in labor, he leaves Laban's company (Gen. 30:25—31:50).[205] Gideon's liaison with the Shechemite woman is with a concubine and not with a full wife. As far as I can determine, none of these passages has any bearing on clan exogamy and matrilineality in early Israel.[206]

Of much greater pertinence to our question is the report that the minor judge Ibzan of Bethlehem (probably in Zebulun) "had thirty sons; and thirty daughters he sent [i.e., gave in marriage] outside, and thirty daughters he brought in from outside for his sons" (Judg. 12:9). But "outside" what? The English translations notwithstanding, the Hebrew text does *not* say. The RSV and JB remedy the omission by gratuitously supplying "outside his clan" and the JPS renders "from abroad." Since the ancient narrator failed to specify his meaning more exactly, we can only indicate some possibilities and record some preferences.

Among the social entities which may be the referent of "outside" in Judges 12:9, I see the following possibilities: the *shēveṭ* or *mishpāḥāh/'eleph* (primary or secondary level of social organization); the *bēth-'āv* (tertiary level of social organization); Israel as an entirety (the most inclusive level of social organization). If the meaning is outside the *shēveṭ* or *mishpāḥāh* (or possibly outside Bethlehem as the locale of Ibzan's *mishpāḥāh*), the note may refer to an exceptionally wide network of marriage alliances, in contrast to the normal situation in which marriages were generally made between members of the same *mishpāḥāh* or neighborhood or between members of the same *shēveṭ*. If the meaning is outside the *bēth-'āv* of Ibzan, the note may be understood as calling attention to either of two departures from usual practice. In the one case, it may emphasize that Ibzan enforced a consistently patrilocal residency rule. All of his daughters went to live in the *bēth-'āvōth* of their husbands and all of the brides taken by his sons came to live in the *bēth-'āv* Ibzan. This would imply that in the annotator's circle, matrilocal residence was required, customary, or frequent. In the other case, it may emphasize that Ibzan strictly enforced incest taboos within his *bēth-'āv*. This would assume that the large number of sons and daughters meant that Ibzan had several wives and that, under such circumstances, the marriage of his sons and daughters by different wives would have been customary. It would also assume that Ibzan forbade his offspring who were half-sisters and half-brothers to intermarry and thus had no recourse but to send the daughters outside the *bēth-'āv* and bring in wives for his sons. If the meaning is outside Israel altogether, the note may be understood to refer to the pretensions of Ibzan in contracting marriages with foreigners for diplomatic purposes. This would imply either that the custom was favored in Israel at this time or that Ibzan broke precedence in countenancing on a large scale what Gideon and Samson only undertook modestly and with evident general disfavor.

Now in assessing these several possible interpretations, I agree with Noth that the formulaic use of thirty sons and/or daughters for Jair (Judg. 10:4), Ibzan (Judg. 12:9), and Abdon (Judg. 12:14; although here the thirty are grandsons and his sons are forty in number) should be looked upon with some suspicion. I am myself inclined to look upon it as a virtual equivalent of the general adjective "many." The status and prosperity of Ibzan are certainly stressed by the notation, and this should perhaps caution us against pressing for very precise sociological presuppositions. But I also concur with Noth in believing these notes, even if additions to the original, to have been ancient, for they do not serve any obvious tendentious function nor betray any late sociological constructs. While opaque, they are probably premonarchic and merit our attempt to judge the probable social organizational situation that is presupposed.[207]

What are the probabilities in the various lines of logical possibility proposed above? The interpretation that the intermarriages arranged by Ibzan were with non-Israelites is unsupportable on general grounds. Ancient Israel, prior to David, with the disastrous exception of Abimelech, did not aspire to conquer other peoples or to intermarry with them in the game of power politics. The status of Gideon's Shechemite woman as a concubine does not argue for the political nature of the arrangement, and Samson's choice of a Timnite woman arises from his unstable whims. Even if we are not to think of anything so grandiose as thirty actual foreign alliances through marriage, if all of Ibzan's many daughters married foreigners it would have meant a reaching for political power on his part concerning which we have no independent information. Considering the attention given the upstart Abimelech, it is difficult to believe that had Ibzan been a man of such ambition beyond the accepted frame of Israelite society, he could have escaped more explicit commentary in the biblical text.

The suggestion that the reference is to marriages contracted outside Ibzan's *bēth-'āv* is too strained. The likelihood that the stress is on Ibzan's insistence on patrilocal residence is diminished drastically by the fact that patrilocal residency was the norm in Israel and thus Ibzan's practice should have occasioned no special comment. Given the probability that most Israelite men, both in premonarchic and in monarchic times, did not have many wives, and that marriages between half-brothers and half-sisters are not often attested, we are probably right in thinking that marriage outside the *bēth-'āv* was the normal practice. In that case, there would have been little point to noting Ibzan's adherence to custom. Only if Ibzan, as a man of wealth and power, is here contrasted with foreign royalty who may have encouraged the marriages of half-brothers and half-sisters, can we make plausible sense of the remark, but such an interpretation is refined and probably oversubtle in addition to lacking any direct evidence.

This leaves us with the probability that the allusion is to marriages contracted beyond the customary social field for such arrangements, i.e., outside Ibzan's *shēvet*, or his *mishpāḥāh*/*eleph*, or his town of Bethlehem. This understanding fits most comfortably with the general intent of the notations to stress the status and wealth of the minor judges. The annotator apparently wanted to show that Ibzan solidified his leadership by giving his daughters to men in segments of Israel farther afield than marriages usually reached and that he in turn drew into his household women from these more distant segments. If the framework of the minor judges entries is taken seriously as an original, at least pre-Deuteronomic, claim to the function of these men throughout all Israel, then the annotator may well mean that the daughters were sent outside his tribe of Zebulun and his sons' wives were similarly secured outside his own tribal bounds. In this way Ibzan fortified his status as a leader by building affinal networks with other tribes.

Whatever the precise social organizational presupposition of Judges 12:9 (and the matter remains problematic), it is at least clear that nothing in the description of the marriages, not even in the use of the term "outside," argues that rules of clan exogamy are in mind. That daughters should marry out and wives be brought in is an extremely general formula which would, of course, broadly accord with a patrilineal exogamous clan pattern, as also with a matrilineal exogamous clan pattern practicing patrilocal residence. Since, however, no mention is made of those with whom the daughters and sons could permissably marry, the basic desideratum of the clan system is altogether ignored. Again, as we have seen elsewhere, the exogamous clan can be found in Judges 12:9 only by importing it from outside the text.

Recently, the Assyriologist J. Renger has reported traces of exogamous clan organization among presumed semi-nomadic Amorites in the vicinity of Sippar in Mesopotamia in the second millennium b.c.[208] I am in no position to evaluate his reading of the cuneiform texts as witnesses to ancient Mesopotamian social organization, but I have some rejoinders to his hypothesis that patrilineal exogamy was attested among the biblical patriarchs.

On the basis of Genesis 11:27–30; 22:23; 24:29; 25:20; 29:10,12, Renger reconstructs lineages which "marry out" by giving daughters as wives in this pattern: The Haran lineage gives Milcah to the Nahor lineage and the Nahor lineage gives Sarah (her kin connection has to be attributed by analogy), Rebekah, and Leah-Rachel to the Abraham lineage.[209] In each case the woman marries one generation up, i.e., the wife is pictured as the niece of her husband. Since, however, in Genesis 24:29 and 25:20 Laban is said to be the brother of Rebekah rather than her father, Renger allows that the original scheme may have mated people of the same generation, i.e., the husband and wife were cousins. This latter alternative appears to him as "a supplementary fictitious genealogy, remote from the facts of the case."[210] He identifies this unlikely scheme as an "indirect exchange" of wives in which the Abraham lineage receives wives from the Nahor lineage, the Nahor lineage receives wives from the Haran lineage, and the circle of exchange is closed by the Haran lineage receiving wives from the Abraham lineage. (In actuality, I see no reason why this circular indirect exchange of wives is not equally applicable, or inapplicable, to his preferred hypothesis of an uncle-niece marriage, since in both instances the wives move in one direction only and in neither case is the circle actually closed by a report of the Haran lineage receiving wives from the Abraham lineage.)

This hypothesis of exogamous lineages among the patriarchs ignores a thicket of difficulties. It has to assume that Sarah is Nahor's daughter, and it acknowledges that sometimes Laban is Rebekah's father and sometimes Rebekah's brother. It cites only three instances of "marrying out" (Milcah, Rebekah, and Leah-Rachel) and posits a fourth by analogy (Sarah). Not only is this a small sample, but it runs up against the difficult question of the sort of descent traced in the patriarchal genealogies. Is it actually a lineage descent by known links from a common ancestor? Is it a lineage descent in which intervening generations have been accidentally or purposely elided? Is it an artifically constructed lineage created by fusing originally independent figures into one line? Is it gross kinship phrasing intended to express the relationship of groups by means of descent language? In other words, were Abraham, Nahor, and Haran actually brothers and Abraham, Isaac, and Jacob actually father, son, and grandson? Or, were they related by common descent but farther removed than now appears because of the elision of branch lines or of intervening generations, so that what results is a "telescoped lineage"? Or, were they individuals from entirely separate historico-social contexts who have been fused in a "fictitious lineage"? Or, were they never individuals at all but simply group personifications?

While not discussing these critical preconditions of interpretation, Renger seems to want matters two ways, i.e., sometimes the genealogies in Genesis are of actual descent lineages and sometimes they are fictitious or eponymous. At least that is the only way in which his hypothesis could be correct. For the construction of his exogamous hypothesis he takes the reported kin relations at face value, but only up to a point, for he arbitrarily cuts off the kin relations in the upper generational direction beyond Abraham, Nahor, and Haran. He uses the fact that the latter three are designated "brothers" in order to posit them as coequal heads of lineages, but he ignores the fact that if they are indeed "brothers," then they are also "sons" of the one "father" Terah. The disregard of Terah, however, is vital to Renger's argument, because if Terah's status is integral to the same stage or level of the genealogy as the kin relations of his descendants, the result is that the genealogies he uses cannot possibly be explained as witnesses to patrilineal exogamy. This follows, in short, from the fact that all of the offspring of Abraham, Nahor, and Haran would be fellow clan members who trace common descent from Terah and would be ineligible to intermarry.

Although Renger is unaccountably silent on this point, one can readily conceive reasons for severing the Abraham-Nahor-Haran lineages and the Abraham-Isaac-Jacob succession from Terah, treating the former as instances of known links and the latter as a fictitious eponym introduced at a subsequent stage in the tradition. After all, Terah is a shadowy figure of whom little is reported, possibly no more than a transitional device for getting the better-known patriarchs from Mesopotamia/Haran to Palestine. But precisely this dissection of the descent lines exposes the problematics of any use of these genealogies for reconstructing actual social practice in kinship and marriage. If Terah is problematic as a known link in lineage descent, and even as a cipher for a clan embracing lineages, so too are the patriarchs problematic as lineage heads. If little is said of Terah, the same is true of Nahor and Haran. The probability of Abraham, Isaac, and Jacob having been linked secondarily in the traditions, or at least of collateral lines and intervening generations having dropped out, is exceedingly high, as Noth's analysis of the pentateuchal traditions indicates.

Possibly Renger's proposal of patrilineal exogamy among the biblical patriarchs can be rescued by arguing that at some stage in the patriarchal traditions, even if as late as P, the traditionist put together his kinship data in a manner which shows that he at least understood them exogamously—either because he had some good ancient tradition or because clan exogamy was practiced in his own milieu. Even this assumption is dubious in the extreme, precisely because the kin relations reported are so small a fragment that, at most, they allow for the possibility of lineage or clan exogamy but do not in any sense require it. To be sure, these fragments are consistent with a pattern of indirect exchange of wives; but they are not fully evidential for that practice, since the exchange circle is not closed in any of the few instances of wife-giving detailed. The traditionist may simply have viewed the Abraham, Nahor, and Haran social units as such small entities that they had to marry out merely to observe the normal incest/marriage prohibitions within the family (of the sort reported in Leviticus 18 and discussed above). Within our own marriage and kin system (called by anthropologists an "Eskimo" system), which altogether lacks exogamy by gross social units such as the clan, two or more families may prefer to intermarry over generations for social and economic reasons entirely unrelated to rules of clan exogamy. Moreover, the one-directionality of the wife-giving in Renger's examples may after all be the function of the intense narrowing down upon Abraham's line, so that the movement of wives toward his line only looks like indirect exchange of wives. As far as I can see, there is nothing to rule out that Abraham's lineage may have given wives back to the Nahor lineage in direct exchange. Or, instead of either giving wives to the Haran lineage in order to close an indirect exchange circle or giving them to the Nahor lineage in direct exchange, the Abraham lineage may have given wives to some entirely unnamed lineage.

Additional problems could be raised, but the essential obstacle to the acceptance of Renger's hypothesis of patrilineal exogamy among the patriarchs is that we are removed from the social milieu of the patriarchs and/or the patriarchal circles by such a long chain of tradition, in which nonkin factors played the decisive role, that we simply do not have a large homogeneous assemblage of known kinship links in any sense analogous to the data a field anthropologist can gather. It may be that some of the patriarchs, or their circles, or the later traditionists practiced exogamy by gross social units, but the scraps of information which may be so interpreted do not prove it or even unambiguously suggest it. The final form of the tradition, which makes the patriarchs all members of one kin group by descent, militates emphatically against clan exogamy, since patriarchal group members are said to intermarry with persons clearly descended from the same common ancestor according to the genealogies taken at face value as recording known links.

Finally, in our consideration of narrative evidence on clan exogamy, we come to Genesis 34:16, which tells of a proposed connubium between the Israelites and the city of Shechem. This verse was first cited by E. B. Tylor as a kind of classic statement of exogamy viewed as "the simple practical alternative between marrying-out and being killed out,"[211] and it has been cited approvingly since then by anthropologists, most recently to my knowledge by R. Fox.[212] The men of Shechem first proposed that wives be exchanged between the two groups and that the Israelites settle down in the region of the city and carry on agriculture and trade. The Israelites responded: "Then we will give our daughters to you, and we will take your daughters to ourselves, and we will dwell with you and become one people." This text and its exogamous interpretation confront us with the same range of problems as Renger's proposal about the patriarchs. From what original social milieu, either in the patriarchal environment or in later Israel, does this tradition derive? What is the organizational level of the social units which are proposed as wife-exchangers? What does this general description of inter-marriage actually say or imply in the way of group exogamy?

In the older source hypotheses, Genesis 34:16 was almost unanimously assigned to the P source, although more recent analyses have retreated from that judgment (e.g., O. Eissfeldt and G. Fohrer find no P material in Genesis 34). But even if the account is as late as the P collection in the sixth–fifth centuries B.C., that in itself is no final word on its value for sociological purposes. For the sake of argument, I set aside the enormous difficulties in identifying the sources and clarifying the circumstances related in Genesis 34, and I imagine that the text may indeed carry us back into a historico-social setting in which either a small group of proto-Israelites or a larger assemblage of Israelite tribes was considering a modus vivendi with Shechem which was to include intermarriage.[213] (For the moment I leave aside the fact that the connubium was never established because the Israel-ites reneged on it, for it can be argued that the mere fact that such an arrangement appears in the tradition means at least that it was a familiar one and that possibly Israel was related by connubium with other groups.)

What does Genesis 34:16 in context actually tell us? It tells us only that Shechem-ites and Israelites began to reach agreement on an alliance that was to include the exchange of wives. It does *not* tell us that a presupposition for the proposed wife-exchange was that Israelites and/or Shechemites could not marry among themselves and thus were obliged to get wives from outside. It does *not* tell us that the wives to be exchanged between the groups constituted all or most of the marriage arrangements to be made by Israelites and Shechemites, thereby ex-cluding or sharply reducing intragroup marriages or intermarriage with other groups. In other words, since we do not know the actual scope demographically or the internal social structure of the two contracting entities in Genesis 34, it is we the readers who have to try out various hypotheses to see how "clan exogamous" they look on close examination. The results are not reassuring.

If, for example, "Israel" in Genesis 34 was actually only a relatively small social group (still proto-Israelite), the connubium formula might be read—especially noting the phrase "we will become one people"—as alluding to an early attempt to meld together two groups of people in one tribal formation as complementary moieties. We might in that case be witnessing an initial act by which a member of later Israel (Manasseh or a section of Manasseh?) was formed by two originally separate groups that become segments practicing exogamy and thus exchanging wives. Granted that the formation was not carried through according to Genesis 34, it could at least be construed that connubium covenant was a means by which some peoples did come together as tribal entities within Israel, the tribes being built up by exogamous clans.

If, on the other hand, we imagine (as the final state of the text does), that many Israelite tribes are present and that this is an "external" arrangement between autonomous entities, a matter of intertribal "foreign policy," we could say that Israel developed, or sought to develop, peaceful relations with some surrounding peoples by connubium covenant. But would a tribal organization (Israel) and a city organization (Shechem) be likely to enter into such an exogamous connubium? Would a large assemblage of tribes be able to get enough wives from one city for an exclusive connubium if exogamy forbade marriage of Israelites to fellow Israelites? Besides, as I understand anthropological evidence, whole tribes are not exogamous; it is clans within a tribe which are exogamous and take wives from and give wives to other exogamous clans, the tribe as a whole remaining endogamous (although marriages may be allowed or prescribed outside the tribe in certain cases). Thus, the more large-scale the Israelite partner in the proposed connubium is conceived to have been, the more likely it becomes that the group already would have worked out marriage patterns, exogamous or otherwise (that cannot be known from the text), among its member units, and thus the more peripheral the connubium with Shechem would become as a wife-exchange mechanism and the more it would look like an alliance sealed with limited inter-marriage bearing no correlation whatsoever with exogamy rules. Maybe the difficulties can be eased by conceiving the proposed connubium as an arrangement involving only a single clan or group of clans (of Manasseh?) located in the vicinity of Shechem. In that way a possible symmetrical, exogamously based exchange of wives could be made plausible, but that still fails to deal with the issue of whether a city would be interested in or capable of wholesale exogamy.

The farther our analysis and speculation about alternatives runs, the more evident it becomes that even if Genesis 34:16 goes back to early times, the difficulties of perceiving its exact context, the parties involved, and the mechanisms posited, are insuperably opposed to any reasonable confidence that Genesis 34 shows the existence of exogamous clans in early Israel. My guess is that if the anthropologists who have been fond of quoting the verse to illustrate the exogamous exchange of wives between groups were to sit down with the biblical text for a few hours and study it, in its total range and in all its nuances, they would not be so sure about it either. I doubt that anthropologists would be ready to posit exogamous unilineal descent groups among the Kariera, the Hopi, or the Tallensi if they had been compelled to rely on composite texts which contained only disjointed and indirect kinship data. Maybe Genesis 34:16, when put together with other biblical texts, does attest clan exogamy in some segments of early Israel. I welcome any informed effort to demonstrate it. So far I don't see that anyone has. As we shall note shortly, L. H. Morgan, the father of kinship study in anthropology, tried to find the exogamous clan in early Israel and could do so only by means of a scantily documented analogical hypothesis.

In summary, not only do the narrative texts we have examined fail to give any firm indications of the presence of the exogamous clan, either patrilineal or matrilineal, in ancient Israel, but the effect of several of the texts is to prove rather conclusively that the exogamous clan did not exist in the social spheres in which they were formulated and passed on.

Another factor of importance in concluding that ancient Israel lacked the exogamous clan is the absence of kin terminology which would distinguish the two sides of the house by special terms for relatives in the father's clan and relatives in the mother's clan. Such terminology is very richly and profusely developed in most clan-organized societies. As D. Jacobson has noted:

> . . . the fact that Semitic languages generally make no linguistic distinctions between father's brother and mother's brother; between father's sister and mother's sister, and between children of these relatives, contradicts this theory of primitive exogamy; for in the practice of exogamy, the brothers [and sisters] of the father must always belong to a clan different from that of the brothers [and sisters] of the mother. . .[214]

Moreover, there is always a clear distinction in Hebrew between lineal relatives in one's own house and relatives in a corresponding position in a collateral line; e.g., Hebrew, like English, never groups together terminologically father with father's brother or sister with father's brother's daughter. By contrast, the classificatory terminology of clan societies partly or wholly blurs the distinction between lineal and collateral relatives, commonly in the bifurcate merging or Iroquois terminology which groups father and father's brother under the same term and mother and mother's sister under the same term.[215] Without pretending to have mastered the intricacies of classificatory kinship systems, I can at any rate report that so far I find no signs of such systems in the early Israelite terms for kin.

In an attempt to explain the "feel" of the classificatory system of clan exogamy, Ernest L. Schusky remarks:

> All kinship systems face the problem of excluding some relatives while including others. . . . Most peoples have solved the "exclusion problem" by including only relatives who have a common ancestor and who can trace ascent to that person entirely through one sex. When ascent is through males, or *ancestors,* the group is said to be *agnatic;* where ascent is through females, or *ancestresses,* the group is *uterine.* In either case what emerges is a unilineal descent group. Such a system is difficult for Americans to comprehend. Relatives on the mother's side are of a different type from those on the father's side. The idea of descent itself is quite different from our own, where we think of mothers and fathers each contributing one half to our life.[216]

And, reminding us that a kinship system is an arbitrary social construct which selects and patterns only a limited number of all possible relationships, Ina C. Brown summarizes:

> All these patterns will make more sense if we remember that there is a difference in a set of genealogical relations and a kinship system. All peoples have essentially the same genealogical relations, but what is important in human societies is not genealogical relations as such but the way they are defined by the particular society. The kinship system consists of the real or assumed genealogical relationships recognized by the society and, as we have seen, not only can the actual genealogical relationships be defined in various ways but fictional relationships can be assumed.[217]

Put in a very crude way, one of the simplest indices that clan exogamy is lacking in old Israel is the general facility with which an American reader can make sense of the kin terms in the Bible. They are very similar to the kin terms of American society. By contrast, the kin terms of a much simpler society which is clan-organized will present kinship patterns which are completely foreign to American experience. That simple test is an indicator of how great is the gap between the facile attribution of the exogamous clan to Israel and the plain evidence of the Hebrew terms for kin.

Finally, we shall take into account that the one who first recognized and delineated the exogamous clan, namely Lewis H. Morgan, believed that the exogamous clan was present in ancient Israel. In this instance, however, he shows great uneasiness about the slimness and ambiguity of the evidence and, in the end, pleads a uniqueness for Israel's social system which he is unable to understand. It is striking that Morgan wrote only five pages on the Israelite clan in his *Ancient Society,* in marked contrast to the reams of data he was able to offer for other societies he treated.[218]

With respect to evidence from marriage practices, he was able to cite only four instances which he thought attested the matrilineal clan or gentilic structure in Israel:(1) Rebekah's bride-purchase was arranged with her brother and mother and not with her father (Gen. 24:15,28–9,53);(2) Abraham married his half-sister Sarah (Gen. 20:12);(3) Nahor married his niece, the daughter of his brother (Gen. 11:27,29);(4) Amram married his aunt, the sister of his father (Exod. 6:20). Morgan admits that these incidents do not prove the existence of the matrilineal clan in Israel, but he claims that they accord well with it and are most logically explained by it. Each of these departures from usual practice, however, may be easily explained in other ways. Rebekah's father, Bethuel, is dead and her brother represents the male family head. Half-sisters and half-brothers are known to marry in societies other than clan-organized societies. Nahor's and Amram's idiosyncratic marriages simply reflect greater latitude in admissible marriages to kin than those reflected in the incest impediments of the later law codes—e.g., marriage to an aunt is prohibited in Leviticus 18:14.

Furthermore, in an inconsistent manner Morgan sometimes cites the *mishpāḥāh* as the clan and sometimes the *bēth-'āv*. His evidence in either case is not more solid than the observation that since Israel was not yet advanced to a political society, it must have been tribal and therefore possessed the *sine qua non* of tribal society at that stage, as he saw it, namely, the matrilineal clan. Yet his confusion as to how the *bēth-'āv, mishpāḥāh,* and *shēveṭ* should be functionally construed is revealed in his admission that "very few particulars are given respecting the rights, privileges and obligations of the members of these bodies of consanguinei."[219] In observing, as we have, the remarkably schematic metaphorical extension of the kinship pattern to the ultimate levels of Israelite organization, at least as they are traditionally represented, Morgan concluded with honest bafflement:

> Human experience furnishes no parallel of the growth of gentes and phratries precisely in this way. The account must be explained as a classification of existing consanguine groups, according to the knowledge preserved by tradition, in doing which minor obstacles were overcome by legislative constraint.[220]

Here Morgan briefly introduces, by way of accounting for the arbitrary and fictitious kinship constructs of Israel, the factors of tradition and legal constraint, but there the matter is rested. Either he lacked the patience or lacked the facility in biblical studies—or both—to pursue the questions. It can at least be said that he was aware of the flimsiness of his basis for positing an Israelite matrilineal clan. Indeed, to read Morgan's remarks carefully is to underscore the dubiousness of the argument for the existence of any form of the exogamous clan in ancient Israel.

The conclusion is therefore emphatic that there is no solid evidence for, and much damaging evidence against, the theory that early Israel was exogamously clan-organized. And it is precisely for this reason that I have consistently refused to translate *mishpāḥāh* as "clan" and have preferred "protective association of extended families." The old Israelite *mishpāḥāh* was not a unilineal descent group practicing exogamy and cross-cutting the residential family units. It was not the primary social unit in ancient Israel for conferring duties or titles or for holding and transmitting communal property. The *bēth-'āv,* or extended family, constructed along patrilineal and patriarchal lines of authority, was the primary socioeconomic unit.

30.4 *Mishpāḥāh / 'Eleph* as a Clan Equivalent

With all that said, it is clear that the *mishpāḥāh* was nonetheless a social entity of major importance. We have already delineated its salient functions, namely, to protect the socioeconomic integrity of *bēth-'āvōth* threatened with diminution or extinction and to organize troops for the tribal levy. It was organized, not as a cross-cutting sodality, but as an aggregated cluster of *bēth-'āvōth,* all of whose members had mutual obligations to extend the assistance of their own *bēth-'āvōth* to any needy *bēth-'āv* within the *mishpāḥāh,* and to arrange among themselves how they would muster and field a quota of fighting men as required for the tribal and national levy. In other words, the obligation of the *shēvet* to protect all its members was implemented through local or regional groupings of families with primary and direct responsibilities for one another's welfare.

The *mishpāḥāh* did not intersect with and impinge upon the family, reducing it to primarily biological reproductive functions, but it heightened and brought to prominence the centrality of the family and was in fact itself fundamentally a collective of families for specific purposes. Instead of qualifying the power and importance of the family, as a clan would necessarily do, the protective association of families maximized and guarded the integrity and viability of the member families. When seen in this light, it is apparent that the *mishpāḥāh* was a com- promise adaptive formation which provided the social fabric with some of the bonding virtues of the true clan while carefully avoiding any restrictions upon the family's primacy or any taking over of the family's affirmative roles. The *mishpāḥāh* was obviously without the preponderant socioeconomic power of the genuine clan. It held no property of its own, serving simply but crucially to preserve the several collective properties of the *bēth-'āvōth* which constituted the *mishpāḥāh.* Rather than being the constitutive social unit, the *mishpāḥāh* was a level of organization for banding the constitutive social units of the *bēth-'āvōth* into strong mutual aid groups large enough to overcome the inherent weakness of totally separate extended families. And since the *mishpāḥāh* was an aggregation of extended families, it had a vital regional or neighborhood character which might be coextensive with a rural neighborhood, a cluster of small settlements, a single settlement and environs, or a segment of a large settlement. Thus rooted in a territory or region, the *mishpāḥāh* was altogether differently organized than a clan distributed throughout a tribe or throughout several associated tribes.

While not a cross-cutting sodality in organization, the *mishpāḥāh* was neverthe- less a sodality equivalent in its functions. In the sense that the *mishpāḥāh* obligated and facilitated interaction between *bēth-'āvōth* in various forms of mutual aid and even, in last resort, took into itself the inheritance and survivors of decimated *bēth-'āvōth* by incorporating them in surviving households of the *mishpāḥāh,* it had a critical bonding function in the society functionally comparable to the perform- ance of the clan sodality. The difference between the two operationally lay in the fact that the *mishpāḥāh* accomplished its ends by a far looser organizational mode than did the true clan. Lacking the positive power to subordinate the family to itself, it had the reserve power to sustain the family in its vulnerable autonomy. As a brotherhood of families, the *mishpāḥāh* helped to define sub-communities in old Israel, and in its ceremonial religious functions—about which we know so little—probably developed forms of tradition and celebration which gave all the members a sense of identity larger than that of the *bēth-'āv* but not yet so inclusive as the identity of the entire *shēvet*.

By contrast with a band society, either functioning separately in its scattered families or jointly in its gathered totality, the *bēth-'āvōth* of Israel lived together and assigned tasks to aggregations of families which divided and shared among all the associated families the risks of their several separate struggles. All this occurred in a middle zone of social interaction below the level of the tribal collectivity and mediating between the *bēth-'āv* and the *shēvet*. In the crucial matter of military organization, the *bēth-'āvōth* of Israel surrendered their prerogative of self-defense to an association of families who could muster the needed troops in a manner which would least jeopardize the ongoing economic life of the families and which would produce fighting men who, being accustomed to intimate interaction in a circumscribed social sphere, could fight side by side with high spirit and confidence in one another.

I am aware that this functional analysis of the bonding functions of the *mishpāḥāh*—comparable in certain respects to the true clan's functions but quite separate from the clan in its organization and self-limitation—may well have given the impression of a totally free and arbitrary design, as though the Israelites chose this form in a theoretical vacuum. Such would be a mistaken impression. Only by supplementing functional analysis with an historical-cultural perspective can we adequately grasp the dynamics of the Israelite development. We cannot divest the origins of Israel from the world in which it took shape and from the human and social materials which contributed both the content and the metabolism of Israel's idiosyncratic system.

Although the point will be fully developed and explored subsequently (e.g., in VI.30.7–8 and in VII.33.1–2), I must briefly insist that the specific form of the *mishpāḥāh*, as also of the *bēth-'āv* and the *shēvet* and all other sodalities or sodality equivalents in Israel, was a social mechanism emergent within the parameters of a cultural developmental process in late Bronze and early Iron Age Canaan. The nonappearance of the true clan in early Israel is not to be explained, therefore, on the assumption that the clan was well known to the people of Israel and was for good reasons rejected. Nor is it to be explained on the assumption that Israel was in a position to hypothesize the sophisticated clan structure as a viable possibility, finally to reject it in favor of the *mishpāḥāh*. Widespread as it is, the exogamous clan is fairly firmly connected with a specific range of ecological niches. So far as I am able to judge, the clan, with its accompanying economic conditions, had virtually if not totally disappeared from the political and cultural world of thirteenth-century Canaan centuries before Israel's formation. For it must not be forgotten that Israel emerged in a region with a long tradition of fully politicized social forms.

Moreover, even if the exogamous clan had survived here and there in attenuated form in or adjacent to Canaan, it may be seriously doubted that so subtle and complexly organized a social entity could have been reconstructed in the relatively few decades in which the diverse Israelite peoples were forced to experiment in forms of collective action which retained their decentralized autonomies. Indeed, just how the clan system develops in a society has never been observed as it happened, and the various explanations of anthropological theorists are highly conjectural. It does seem that such a development required long association among peoples in relatively stable conditions—a longer period and more stable conditions than the Israelites enjoyed before they had to take rapid defensive action against the surrounding politicized societies.

A range of nonpolitical adaptive social devices were within Israel's reach, but the probably long-defunct clan with its incredible interlocking complexity was hardly one of the live options. Nevertheless, at least some of the impulses which produced and preserved the exogamous clan were revived in the people who formed Israel, precisely in that Israel as a social innovator moved away from political centralization and social stratification toward forms of association which sought to secure economic equality in the community. Such was also the basic intent of the clan form. In the broad similarities and profound differences between the Israelite *mishpāhāh* and the exogamous clan lies a key for unlocking the distinctiveness of Israel's social system as a curious mutation in Near Eastern culture, as a socioeconomic and cultural leap forward which was at the same time paradoxically a strategic retreat or withdrawal from levels of sociopolitical organization which elsewhere in the Near East were taken for granted as the essential concomitants of high human civilization. Israel tried to go culturally "higher" by going sociopolitically "lower." In order to go "higher" in serving communal needs with just distribution of goods and power, Israel believed that it was necessary to cancel out and reverse centralized organizational forms then regnant in society. Yet within this range of genuinely exercised revolutionary freedom, there were determining parameters, and there is every reason to believe that the exogamous clan lay well outside those parameters in thirteenth-century Canaan.

30.5 Other Cross-Cutting Associations in Israelite Tribes

My contention is that the *mishpāhāh,* while not an exogamous clan and thus not strictly a cross-cutting sodality, was nonetheless functionally a bonding ligature or armature which served to integrate Hebrew society and which operated within a broadly tribal model as contrasted with band-like social atomism and state-like centralization and stratification. Very briefly I shall also indicate some of the other major bonding mechanisms in Israelite society that specify its tribal character. Each of these groupings will be more fully developed in following contexts. In this context my sole purpose is to indicate the bonding functions of these groupings in a tribal societal design.

We have already touched upon the army by way of the *mishpāḥāh*'s duty to supply quotas of troops for the levy. In one dimension, to study the army in terms of social structure is to study the military function of the *mishpāḥāh/'eleph*, but not exclusively so, since the army was arranged and fought by tribal contingents. While the socioeconomic functions of the *mishpāḥāh* were directed "downwards" to the member *bēth-'āvōth*, the military function of the *mishpāḥāh* was directed "upwards" toward the level of tribal coordination. These few additional remarks on the army will attempt to point out the vertical bonding effect of military organization upon the social whole.

Israel's army was a citizen militia and not a standing professional army of full-time Israelite experts or of mercenaries. Yet Israel was called upon to face the professional armies of the Canaanite city-states, and perhaps also professional armies fielded by intruders into Canaan, although we know little about the military organization of Midianites, Ammonites, and Moabites. Clearly the highly professional Philistine military machine proved to be more than the Israelite militia could cope with, and it was this threat above all which moved Israel rapidly through the chiefdom to the monarchic form of political organization. From the beginning Israel was called upon to develop a tough, resourceful, and disciplined fighting force well beyond the level of individual heroic raiding and ritual skirmishes typical of the band society and of many tribal societies as well. In short, Israel's fighting tribes were unequally opposed from the start by fighting states.

Being unpracticed in and unequipped for the conventional warfare of the day, and specifically lacking the composite bow and the chariot, Israel's army had to counter the superior numbers and firepower of the enemy with disciplined guerrilla tactics, which took every advantage of terrain, surprise, ruse, and mobility and which relied upon civilian cover among a supportive population. Loose band organization cannot supply such military skill or provide such an integration of military and civilian activities in sustained struggles against politically centralized opponents. While the battles and campaigns of early Israel were modest by our military standards, they did demand the mustering of hundreds, often thousands, of fighting men who could coordinate and sustain their energies over considerable periods of time. Although we have no record that all the tribal levies ever fought together in one single coordinated action prior to the time of Saul, it is clear from the Book of Judges that many battles were fought in which two or more tribes cooperated, and it is just as evident that the survival of Israel hung upon the success of these coordinated efforts.

Consequently, while the army was not a closed sodality, such as among the military age groups of the Masai of East Africa,[221] it was one regularized form of organization which drew people together from clusters of *mishpāḥōth* and fielded them as tribal units which were committed to work together, even across tribal lines, as the vital precondition for military victory. The mustering of the troops out of the basic social units was a primary factor in the morale and cooperative skill of Israel's army, and the flow of cooperative military experience back into the social units, as the warriors returned home, inevitably served to heighten a sense of community and to give deep experiential meaning to the cultic-ideological celebrations of Yahweh's victories on behalf of his people Israel.

Among the sodalities or associations which Sahlins notes as characteristic bonding devices in tribal society are "ritual congregations" and "ceremonial parties." All the adult males formed a ritual congregation in ancient Israel. By intertribal agreement, ritual and moral laws were "imposed" upon all its members and ultimately the whole society felt their effect. Through affiliation in a pantribal body of Yahwists and through the centralization of Yahwism cultically and ideologically, there was a strong tendency toward standardizing religious thought and practice throughout Israel. The binding regulatory function of the ritual congregation of Israel upon the whole social system should not be underestimated.

The focus and instrument of this tendency toward standardization of religious thought and practice was in the Levitical priesthood, which functioned as a teaching association with instructional as well as ceremonial responsibilities. Instead of being concentrated in one region and formed as a territorial shēveṭ alongside the secular sheᵛāṭīm, the Levites were distributed throughout Israel. In spite of the obscurities of Levitical origins, it seems conclusive that they were the primary bearers of Yahwism in premonarchic times and that they were the single most important explicitly religious sodality in old Israel. In saying this, of course, we do not take as normative of Levitical organization and function all that is attributed to them in the Priestly accounts, for an overreliance on these accounts unduly accents the ceremonial activities of the Levites at the expense of their instructional activities in decisively shaping the traditions and laws. It is the impress of the Levitical mind and practice which has stamped the cultic-ideological centralized traditions. It is also these same Levites who stimulated the citizenry of Israel to take arms on behalf of Yahweh and to fight with the confidence that Yahweh, who had delivered his people from Egypt, would deliver them anew from all oppressors in Canaan.

This not not the place to plumb the problematics of Levitical history.[222] It is well known that according to some biblical traditions, it appears that Levi was once a compact secular tribe. Whatever the exact form and meaning of Levi's earliest existence as a secular tribe, the foundation of the peculiar Israelite social system was laid when Levi became the specialized bearers and functionaries of Yahwistic tradition and were arranged in a cross-cutting sodality that permeated and bonded the discrete tribes into one worshipping, militant, tradition-building and law-formulating community.

A final possible cross-cutting bond in old Israel was the peripatetic craftsmen known as the Kenites. They are described as very anciently connected with Israel. Indeed, Moses is said to have married among them and to have received counsel from them in the arts of wilderness survival (Judg. 1:16; cf. Exod. 2:15b–22; 3:1; 4:18–20; 18:1–5; Num. 10:29–32). While the Kenites are not prominently described, there are brief but substantial traditions of their entrance into Canaan with Judah, and they are reported to have been living not only in the far south of Judah but in lower Galilee as well (Judg. 1:16; 4:11,17; I Sam. 15:6; 27:10; 30:29). The Rechabites (Jer. 35; cf. II Kings 10:15–27) are directly linked with the Kenites (I Chron. 2:55) and are associated with Irnahash, probably "copper city," and with the Kenizzite craftsmen (I Chron. 4:12–14; reading "Rechab" in vs. 12 with LXX instead of MT "Recah"). These Kenites/Rechabites are best understood on typological analogy with other groups of travelling metallurgists, and the Rechabites may have been chariot builders, at least in monarchic times.[223] Some of these smiths may have become assimilated into the tribe of Judah, but others remained sufficiently apart from the tribal formations as to stand on friendly terms with the Canaanites (Judg. 4:17). However, precisely such friendly relations were turned to Israelite advantage when the trusting Canaanite general Sisera was killed by a Kenite woman in whose tent he had sought asylum (Judg. 4:17–22; 5:24–27). In IX.45.3 I propose to interpret Kenites/Rechabites as metal-working guilds in protective treaty relations with Israel.

All in all, the Kenites/Rechabites appear as an occupationally specialized group which stood somewhat apart in Israelite society, could do business with Canaanites and Israelites, but were also fierce Yahwists and in decisive cultural and sociopolitical matters were counted as a part of Israel. Although nothing is said of it, we can reasonably hypothesize that their skill in metallurgy was important in supplying Israel with copper (and iron?) tools and weapons. The later Philistine monopoly on iron (I Sam. 13:19–21), which apparently cut off the Kenites from a supply of the metal and presumably from knowledge of how to work it, was a critical threat to the survival of Israel. In fact, a strict reading of the note that "no smith was to be found throughout all the land of Israel" (I Sam. 13:19) implies that the Philistines had driven away or isolated the Kenites from the main body of Israelites in a deliberate campaign to render Israel technologically subservient to Philistia. It is of no small significance that this one identifiable specialized craft sodality in Israel showed no inclination toward ranking or stratification. The Kenites' peripatetic life and loyal Yahwism were functions of their renunciation of all claims to special privilege or power in Israel.

30.6 Israelite Tribal Segmentation and Diffusion of Political Functions

In describing the tribal society typologically as a flowering out of the band society, we have seen some of the tribe's formal features: increase in demographic size, control over an enlarging agricultural or pastoral surplus, and social bonding through cross-cutting associations. To these features should be added two others: segmentation of the tribal units and diffusion or temporary assignment of political functions.

Segmented tribes are composed of two or more primary segments which are structurally and functionally equivalent and also politically equal.[224] In Israelite terms, the basic units of the *bēth-'āvōth* were largely self-sufficient socioeconomic entities, formally on a par. Through the protective association of families in *mishpāḥōth*, another level of organization was built up, but again each *mishpāḥāh* was on a par with all the others. The same equivalence in structure and function and the same political equality carried on to the largest member entities in Israel, i.e., the *shevāṭīm*. The principle of segmentation carried through to the very highest or most inclusive level of organization, resulting in a confederation of equal tribes. Equivalence in organization and equality in formal power typified the *shevāṭīm*, even though the actual size and effective power of the individual *shevāṭīm* varied greatly over time, the gap between the stronger and weaker widening markedly as a result of differences of fortune in war and in economic production.

Political functions followed the lines and limitations of the segmentation in organization. Through bodies of elders drawn from the *bēth-'āvōth* and *mishpāḥōth*, village and regional decisions were made, and this process was carried to the level of a council of elders for the entire *shēveṭ*. The network of elders diffused political authority so as to ensure the adequate participation of all *bēth-'āvōth* and *mishpāḥōth* in critical tribal decisions. Whether there existed a regular body of elders drawn from all the tribes in Israel is unclear,[225] but, given the fact that covenant linkages among tribes would have required joint decision by elders from different tribes, it seems very likely that modes for intertribal consultations by the elders were developed. This question is intertwined with the question of whether there existed a central office over all Israel in the form of a "judge" or otherwise.

If the elders embodied the regularized diffusion of political functions in the social system, there was also a need for temporary assignments of political and military leadership in crisis situations. It is such draft assignments that the stories of the "judges" relate. For the moment we leave aside the complicated issue of the distinctions between major and minor judges. We note rather how these assignments carried a built-in tendency for strong leaders to usurp more than their share of assigned power and, particularly, to try to pass on their power to their sons (or, conversely, for their sons to try to claim or extend their power). Such is the struggle reflected in the Gideon and Abimelech stories, and such may well be the import of the brief notations about the wealth and rank of some of the minor judges. In this way the chiefdom attempted to make inroads in egalitarian Israel, but not very successfully before the time of Saul.

Why did the chiefdom have such difficulty in taking root in early Israel, considering the examples of political centralization and social stratification in the environs and considering Israel's dire need for military coordination? Obviously the chiefdom ran directly counter to the basic thrust of Israel toward locating power in equivalent and equal extended families. Ranking privileges which typify tribes with chiefdoms were fiercely resisted in Israel and the claims of certain families to greater wealth and honor than others ran against the grain of the egalitarian leveling mechanisms guarded by the protective family associations. The concentration of economic surplus in particular families was checked and retarded by the obligation to share with other families through mutual aid. Furthermore, since Israel's economy throughout the premonarchic period remained agricultural and pastoral, the opportunity for strong families to monopolize the economy through trade or craft specialization was minimized. The metallurgical specialists, the Kenites, stood apart from the families as a peripatetic sodality intensely committed to Yahwistic egalitarianism. All in all, the chiefdom was effectively restrained in early Israel until the military exigencies posed by the Philistines triggered the dramatic inrush of the chiefdom under Saul and its rapid escalation into a centralized monarchy under David and Solomon.

A further factor which probably worked against the rise of the chiefdom in early Israel was the ecological distribution of major food sources. A primary function of the chiefdom is the regularized redistribution of resources.[226] The need for a redistribution system is particularly urgent in societies dependent on a variety of food sources which are geographically balkanized. While Israel cultivated a considerable range of food sources, these tended to be available over sufficient portions of the land that in each region a fair mix of the major food types was normally at hand. For example, although wheat and barley grew best in particular zones, one or the other of these staple crops could be raised in most Israelite regions. The same was true of the other staples, such as olive oil, grapes, and animal herds. For this reason, the typical bēth-'āv was relatively self-sufficient and in no great need of a system-wide redistribution scheme with a central clearing-house administered by a chief. Local reciprocal exchanges of different food types were generally adequate to meet Israelite needs.

30.7 The Historical Peculiarity of Israelite Tribalism

What the gross typological-evolutionary scale of band, tribe, and state does not provide of course is a finely calibrated historical understanding of specific societies. The historical locus of early Israel is of decisive importance for understanding the unique mix of factors and tendencies at work in its social-organizational evolution. In commenting on the absence of the exogamous clan in Israel we noted that this was probably both the function of the loss of an exogamous clan tradition in Canaan and the function of an urgent need to improvise in noncentralized social bonding among a people who did not have the time to work out an elaborate clan system.

The insights of Morton Fried concerning tribal formations as "secondary phenomena" are pertinent for understanding Israel's peculiar tribalism, granting all the while that Fried's position is adjudged extreme by most anthropologists when applied to all tribal societies. Fried points out that many tribes are known to us in colonial situations where the external pressure of more highly organized and dominant civilizations leads to administrative synthesis and consolidation of the society internally, so that it comes to present the form of a tribe to those who control the society. He cites the Makah of Washington State, the Tonga of Northern Rhodesia, and the Chiga of Uganda.

> Most tribes seem to be secondary phenomena in a very specific sense. They may well be the product of processes stimulated by the appearance of relatively highly organized societies amidst other societies which are organized much more simply. If this can be demonstrated, tribalism can be viewed as a reaction to the formation of a complex political structure rather than a necessary preliminary stage in its evolution.[227]

Fried notes that this is probably not a development peculiar to European colonialism, since "the Roman, the Chinese, and other expanding state societies had grasped the essentials of divide and rule."[228] If we modify his "most tribes" to "some tribes" or "many tribes," Fried's insight may be taken seriously as an indication of the way the centralized state may intrude on simpler societies and force them into certain social forms. But surely Fried does not mean to imply that these simpler societies were entirely indisposed to the tribal direction in which the more organized societies pushed them. It would be stretching his case ridiculously far to claim that segmentation and the exogamous clan were imposed by colonial powers. These elements of tribalism must be closely connected with economic production. Fried himself admits the pertinence of Elman Service's contention that the tribal organization extends the peace group and enhances military effectiveness in a world of competing bands and tribes, quite apart from and prior to the entrance of state societies on the scene.[229]

Under the circumstances, Fried's model must be altered considerably to apply to Israel. This can be done if we not only allow that colonial centralized states can shape tribalism within a subject people, hardening and skewing elements already present, but if we also posit that elements of the population within or adjacent to a centralized state may withdraw from it or rebel against it and develop less centralized social forms both as constructive alternatives to the state and as defensive mechanisms against the state. What these two versions of the social-organizational effect of opposed centralized and uncentralized societies have in common is the conflicting juxtaposition of societies at different organizational levels and the decisive organizational effect of the stronger and more complex party upon the weaker and less complex party.

In specifically Israelite terms, we must view its tribalism as a form chosen by people who consciously rejected Canaanite centralization of power and deliberately aimed to defend their own uncentralized system against the effort of Canaanite society to crush the budding movement. Israel's tribalism was an autonomous project which tried to roll back the zone of political centralization in Canaan, to claim territory and peoples for an egalitarian mode of agricultural and pastoral life. Unquestionably there were significant antecedent forms of struggle and modes of organization which fed into Israelite tribalism, which we shall examine closely in Parts VIII and IX, but in terms of demographic size, organizational novelty, and political effectiveness there was a far greater qualitative leap from pre-Israelite to Israelite tribalism than there was from pre-colonial to post colonial tribalism among the Makahs, Tongas, or Chigas. The sum of these qualitative differences suggests that we should speak of Israel's adaptive tribalism as a "retribalization" movement.

All the evidence for early Israel points to its tribalism as a self-constructed instrument of resistance and of decentralized self-rule rather than tribalism as an administrative structure imposed by Canaanite rulers in order to govern proto-Israelite or Israelite subjects. Seen from the perspective of Canaanite society, Israel was not a resistant colonial underling to be subdued, but a foreign growth in its own body politic to be cut out. Seen from Israel's perspective, its tribalism was not a continuous ancient development to be preserved and extended, although lines of continuity with its past were affirmed (cf. the patriarchal stories), but a freshly constructed instrument for "cracking open" the centralized and stratified monopoly appropriation of natural and human resources of which the people forming Israel were an essential part prior to their act of revolt. Israel's tribalism was a politically conscious and deliberate social revolution and, more loosely, a civil war in that it divided and counterposed peoples who had previously been organized within Canaanite city states.

At this point, however, it is necessary to introduce a complicating factor in the sociopolitical dynamics of Israelite origins, for it is the omission of this factor from Mendenhall's model that contributes to the air of unreality many critics have detected in his hypothesis of a "peasant revolt." I refer to the fact that in virtually all such revolutions and civil wars the polarization of the populace is far from complete, especially in the early stages of conflict. There is evidence that a sizable part of the Canaanite populace was "caught in the middle," staying neutral as long as possible and only reluctantly gravitating toward one side or the other when forced to do so by the logic of events. In IX.45.2 we shall have more to say of these Canaanite "neutrals" whose active support or tacit cooperation was sought by the contending parties in an effort "to win the hearts and minds of the people."

The implications of this concrete sociohistorical understanding of Israel's leap to tribalism are enormous. It means that our image of Israel's formation cannot be that of a continuous line of cultural evolution upwards from the band society to tribal forms of segmentation and sodality formation, nor can our image be that of a spill-over or eruption of pastoral nomadism from the desert into the settled land. Our image of Israel's formation must be that of a profound discontinuity in the hierarchic feudal social fabric of Canaan, a rupture from within centralized society. This rupture was accomplished by an alliance of peoples who withdrew directly from the Canaanite system with other peoples who, beyond the centralized system's immediate reach in the hinterland of Canaan, refused the customary path of being drawn into that system and accommodating themselves to it.

In terms of Fried's typology, Canaan did not make an "appearance" in a long-developed or latent tribal society called Israel. To the contrary, Israel, with a mutant sophisticated tribal mode of organization, made an "appearance" within the social system and territorial domain of Canaan. The people who came to be Israelites countered what they experienced as the systemic aggression of centralized society by a concrete, coordinated, symbolically unified, social-revolutionary action of aggressive self-defense. Appropriating the land and economic modes of production, this body of people organized its production, distribution, and consumption along essentially egalitarian lines. The specific historic rise of old Israel was thus a conscious improvisational reversion to egalitarian social organization that displaced hierarchic social organization over a large area previously either directly or indirectly dominated by Canaanite centralization and stratification for centuries.

These conclusions about the distinctive "retribalization" formation of early Israel impel me to call attention to rather similar observations by G. E. Mendenhall on the cultural break involved in the rise of Israel, for which he suggests an analogue in early Greek society following the break-up of the Minoan and Mycenean societies. While he has not explored the model and its analogues systematically, Mendenhall's suggestions have high priority for future research in order to acquire a better idea of "retribalization" as a phenomenon in the social history of the ancient Near East and of the eastern Mediterranean world. Mendenhall's remarks are deserving of quotation in full:

> In the past, the discontinuity from the Lower Bronze Age to the Iron Age has been explained on the basis of a hypothetical change or displacement of population: the Israelites displaced the Canaanites in part, the Phoenicians displaced the Canaanites elsewhere; the Arameans displaced still more, and so on down the line. All of these ideas are now untenable. If the Phoenicians are merely the continuation of Canaanite culture, with considerable changes of course, the Israelites also represent such a continuation with a change of a more radical sort (particularly in the religious and social system). As revealed by excavations, certainly it is true that there are only minimal differences between the two in material culture and those differences are most readily explained as functions of the differences in the social, economic, and religious structure of the ancient Israelites.[230]

> . . . particularly in ancient Israel, there was a systematic, ethically and religiously based, conscious rejection of many cultural traits of the Late Bronze Age urban and

imperial cultures. There is a vast difference between a society that has never known "civilization" and one that—partly through a deliberate choice and partly through circumstances beyond its control—has reverted to a culture of farmers and shepherds. The same thing occurred in the Greek cultures after the collapse of the Minoan-Mycenean Empires.[231]

> . . . reconstructing the picture will be possible at all only by a systematic rejection of the idea that the formative period of Israel represents a totally new culture unrelated to anything in the past. The old idea of one ethnic group's moving in to displace or destroy a predecessor which then promptly disappears is based upon most unsophisticated notions that cannot be too thoroughly repudiated. Such an interpretation is related to the original function of flood stories in many cultures; a way to explain a gap resulting from failure of historical memory or due to a period of accelerated social change.[232]

In the context of the eclectic formation of intertribal Israel which I have been elucidating in this study, Mendenhall's provocative remarks bear close attention and careful testing by detailed research. He has the temerity to state that our explanatory models of early Israel have been scarcely more scientifically accurate than ancient flood stories! On the other hand, a counter-theory such as Mendenhall proposes is not proven true merely because the old theories are failures. Hard questions must be asked and relentlessly pursued in a more systematic and thorough manner than Mendenhall himself has chosen to do. Among the critical questions are these: How did the post-Minoan, post-Mycenean period in Greece actually compare with the situation in Late Bronze–Early Iron Canaan? To what extent was early Israel's formation a result of "deliberate choice" and to what extent the result of "circumstances beyond its control"? In what respects and for what reasons did the Israelite "radical" mutation in Canaan vary from the Phoenician and Aramean "moderate" mutations? And, a question to which I shall return in Parts X and XI, can we actually say that Israel's break with Canaan was "ethically and religiously *based*" (italics mine) or should we more properly speak of Israel's break with previous Canaanite social organization as being ethically and religiously *expressed*? In my judgment, if Mendenhall's work contained no other values, it would be significant for its posing of these methodologically crucial issues.

30.8 The Formation of Israelite Tribal Structure: "Bottom-Up" vs. "Top-Down" Models

With an initial understanding of Israel's socially revolutionary tribalism in mind, we may briefly explore the developmental dynamics in such a tribalizing or "retribalizing" society. Tribal societies may be viewed as built up from below, aggregating smaller units until the total sociocultural autonomous unit is reached, or they may be viewed as differentiated internally from above, by the functional segmentation and articulation of the parts. There is value in each perspective, although neither alone altogether accounts for the peculiar development of tribalism, for it would be possible to offer an embracing explanatory account only if ethnologists could have observed a tribe coming into being over a lengthy period of time and at very close range. To my knowledge, no such account of tribal origins exists. Furthermore, even if we did possess such an account of tribal genetics, we should have to allow for peculiar factors in the genetic dynamics of Israelite tribal formation. Nevertheless, some value is found in exploring the limited insight into the developmental dynamics of tribalism provided by these models.

It seems wisest to view "bottom-up" and "top-down" analyses as complementary approaches to a single process in which complicated forces are working in both directions simultaneously. Sahlins is doubtless correct in stressing the important comprehensive framing function of the whole system, all the more so since so much anthropological research has been devoted, especially in kinship study, to "a worm's-eye view of 'the system' " as seen by "the all-purpose universal 'ego.' "[233] In some way a large group of people, facing a common stimulus or crisis, find a common experience of identity in a common mode of social interaction. This frame of reference, bracketing a common experience and need, sets organizational and behavioral guidelines for the smallest social units within the emerging society. The smaller units are profoundly shaped from above, even though this dimension of "aboveness" cannot be expressed as centralized power or a thoroughly worked out social plan. In ancient Israel it was most probably the covenant linkage of groups which provided the initial societal frame of reference. This explicit covenant mechanism doubtless sets off early Israel in a measure of self-conscious deliberation far beyond the more tacit mode by which many tribal societies grope their way into being.

The larger frame of reference, however, is very skeletal. For tribal societies it is neither monolithic nor fully projected. Because it is politically uncentralized, it has to unfold by a series of adjustments, accommodations, and experiments in social coordination. The small units of the society, given pointers and conditions by the larger frame, react upon the frame and determine the range within which it can operate. Since no centralized administration legislates or decrees the precise boundaries of the units, or imposes leadership, the smaller units develop along lines stamped with local peculiarities. Units at the same general level of organization will vary considerably demographically and geographically in size, and will retain organizational and behavioral peculiarities not specifically excluded by the societal frame. Since the societal frame is worked out by consent, or at least by majority agreement, there being no centralized organs of coercion, the leadership of the smaller units becomes critical for the success of the tribal project. The elasticity and resourcefulness of the social whole, its capacity to withdraw from unproductive experiments and to project new developmental directions, are finally dependent upon the leadership diffused through the segmented social members. Precarious is the process by which these local initiatives relate to one another in the general societal frame, proceeding along roughly congruent lines.[234] Obviously, the stimulus or crisis provoking such a development must be broad and sustained if a whole system is to arise by this cumbersome process of trial-and-error through the constant reciprocal distancing and bonding of the forms and functions of the segmented parts.

In the meeting of the lines of energy from the bottom up and the top down, the sodalities are formed. The sodality focuses the emerging unity of the people and constellates it organizationally by drawing members from various lower-level social units, so as to supplement the primary functions of the segmented units with specialized sodality functions which create interstitial "horizontal" networks binding the "vertical" tribal segments. Simultaneously, the sodality respects the autonomy of all the social segments, by sharing its members with all the other social units in which they remain grounded and by renouncing all claims to general power beyond the specific function which the sodality serves. It is the ingenious task of the cross-cutting association to interweave with the segmented social units so that the social fabric achieves a warp and woof which knit it together, a fabric in which no single thread is dominant but all are securely interwoven.

The two ways of analyzing the developmental dynamics of tribalism in Israel are here represented in chart form (Charts 3 and 4, pp. 330–331). Since the intent is to show the organizational modes, rather than to indicate the number of units at each level of organization, I have for simplicity's sake limited the number of units at each level of organization below the level of the confederacy of Israel. Obviously the number of *sh^evāṭîm* can be expanded to ten or twelve, the number of *mishpāḥôth* to approximately fifty per *shēveṭ*, and the number of *bēth-'āvôth* to approximately eight or ten per *mishpāḥāh*, all within the same organizational scheme.

It is obvious from constructing and exploring the explanatory possibilities of such schematizations that they imply a logical purity and consistency in social organization which rarely exist in practice and that each analytic model entails notable explanatory gaps in accounting for movement from one level of social organization to another. I shall discuss some of these difficulties as they specifically apply to early Israel.

The bottom-up model, strictly adhered to, would have us believe that lower-level steps in organization can be taken without regard for higher-level aims and models. It suggests that a social system is merely aggregative of its parts. It ignores the larger context in which geographical, economic, and military pressures at the boundaries of the nascent system are shaping responses to stimuli and crises at all levels. The critical problems with which social organizations at the tribal level are coping are trans-familial, confronting the whole people and demanding organization beyond the family level. The larger stimulus and response involving the whole people implies movement toward organization at more than one level at

CHART 3

Israel's Societal Formation on a Bottom-Up Model

B = *beth-'āv*   M = *mishpāhāh/'eleph*   S = *shēvet/maṭṭeh*

C = confederacy of all Israel

Autonomous EXTENDED FAMILIES group themselves into local PROTECTIVE ASSOCIATIONS to
give mutual socioeconomic aid and to levy troops

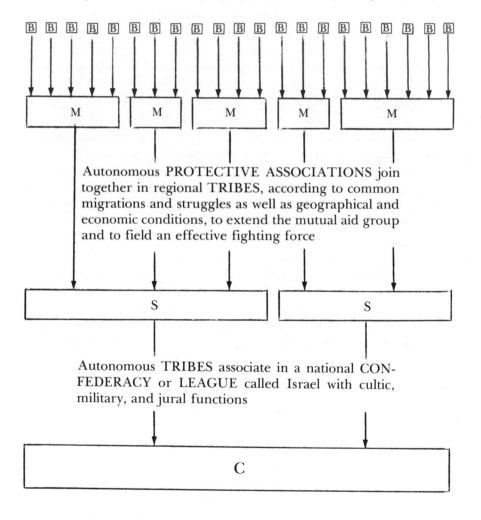

Autonomous PROTECTIVE ASSOCIATIONS join
together in regional TRIBES, according to common
migrations and struggles as well as geographical and
economic conditions, to extend the mutual aid group
and to field an effective fighting force

Autonomous TRIBES associate in a national CON-
FEDERACY or LEAGUE called Israel with cultic,
military, and jural functions

The final encompassing confederacy is co-terminous
with the social system and is the RESULT or END
PRODUCT of aggregated or pyramided smaller units.

CHART 4

Israel's Societal Formation on a Top-Down Model

C = confederacy of all Israel   S = *shēveṭ/maṭṭeh*   M = *mishpāhāh/ʾeleph*

B = *beth-ʾāv*

An unorganized or variously organized body of people commit themselves to a CONFEDERACY or LEAGUE called Israel with cultic, military, and jural functions

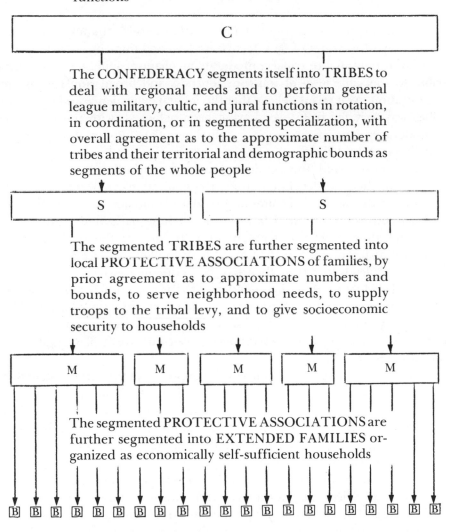

The CONFEDERACY segments itself into TRIBES to deal with regional needs and to perform general league military, cultic, and jural functions in rotation, in coordination, or in segmented specialization, with overall agreement as to the approximate number of tribes and their territorial and demographic bounds as segments of the whole people

The segmented TRIBES are further segmented into local PROTECTIVE ASSOCIATIONS of families, by prior agreement as to approximate numbers and bounds, to serve neighborhood needs, to supply troops to the tribal levy, and to give socioeconomic security to households

The segmented PROTECTIVE ASSOCIATIONS are further segmented into EXTENDED FAMILIES organized as economically self-sufficient households

The final sub-division within the social system is the RESULT or END PRODUCT of differentiated or segmented larger units.

once, such that a whole is being formed not of separate aggregated, prestructured parts but of pliant, adaptable constellations of functional energy which modify and adjust in relation to one another as functions are redistributed.

In the case of Israel it seems necessary to conjecture that the movement was not simply diachronically from lower to higher organization but synchronically and dialectically at several levels at once. For example, I do not see how the *bēth-'āv* and the *mishpāḥāh* could have been solidified short of a certain level of larger group consciousness and practice. Specifically, the *bēth-'āv* and *mishpāḥāh* alone give no satisfactory solution to military needs. It was necessary for a considerable number of regional family associations to band together in order to muster a sufficiently large body of warriors to be effective under conditions of warfare in Canaan. Moreover, only an intertribal confederate mechanism could have brought many tribes to the same level of self-consciousness and broad similarity in internal organization. As it was, I believe that the factual equivalence and equality of the tribes was very far from ever having been achieved, with the result that the confederacy cannot be projected as a final negotiated union of fully formed and equally powerful tribes.

On the other hand, the top-down model, strictly adhered to, would have us believe that the lower-level steps in social organization can be serially unfolded *de novo* out of the higher-level aims and models. It implies that a social system is a well-formed blueprint, an elaborate whole whose parts flow readily one from the other in symmetrical segmentation. It ignores the problem of social-organizational continuity in all human life. It implies a social *tabula rasa* on which people completely torn from their past can write their own social destiny without any bondage to the past. It does not deal with the transitional gap between the old social system and the new. Either it seems to say that the system leaps full-blown into history or it implies that the system could function over some time merely at higher levels, leaving unanswered how people could live at all without lower-level social forms of some sort.

In the case of Israel, it seems necessary to posit that the social system was not a totally arbitrary creation that was free to control all the ingredient peoples, organizing them along the lines of theoretically agreed principles. Proto-Israelites were already living in social forms. Various kinds of resistance to or incongruence with Canaanite centralization and stratification had long existed in Canaan. Particular local and regional struggles developed associations of peoples at levels comparable to the *mishpāḥāh* and the *shēveṭ*. These local and regional struggles and the bonding devices they developed were internal stimuli to a search for still higher levels of organization and proximate models for what a confederacy might become. The covenanting together of tribes shows that social entities had vested interests and that they compromised and experimented in a form of association that could preserve the several interests and autonomies of those entities. If I am correct, Israel's Yahwistic confederacy was not the first such effort at a coalition of antifeudal forces in Canaan. Insofar as members of Yahwistic Israel had been members of earlier coalitions, they brought that coalition experience with them, even though it probably attested more to failure than to success. The form in which the historical social-revolutionary movement of ancient Israel emerged was not in terms of an undifferentiated mass of rebellious individuals free to construct a society as they wished, but in the form of a coalition or alliance of resisting and rebellious groups who, in order to advance their resistance and rebellion to the level of historical success, had to balance and interweave their respective identities and social forms in a painfully built-up whole.

Obviously, then, early Israel developed through a mutually interpenetrating process of coalescing and accommodating groups and of higher-level organizational leaps and experiments that in turn reacted on the forms of organization brought into the coalition, strengthening some forms, weeding out others, and tending all the while toward standardization of organization without ever fully attaining it. A further evidence of the absolute necessity of uniting bottom-up and top-down perspectives on the dynamics of Israel's social structure is the key role of the cross-cutting sodality in which energies originating at the bottom and framing perspectives originating at the top met and interacted, thereby throwing out connective lines of human interaction to overcome the inherent centrifugal force of segmented social units which lacked centralized authority. For Israel these bonding sodalities were the protective associations of families, the army organization, the ritual congregation and Levitical priesthood, and, to a lesser extent and in a still largely undiscerned manner, the Kenite metallurgists.

I am inclined to agree with Munch that the "tribe" was the last social entity in Israel to reach a relatively fixed form and that it was of less social organizational significance than the *bēth-'āv* and the *mishpāḥāh*, although I do not concur in his blurring of the distinction between *bēth-'āv* and *mishpāḥāh*.[235] We should, therefore, stress the "bottom-up" model of social-structural development in the sense that the tribe was a slowly, or at least erratically, developed fusion of smaller groups. The development of tribal consciousness and identity was markedly uneven, with some "tribes" reaching much higher levels of self-consciousness and more tightly knit organization than others.

Yet the "top-down" model properly accents the priority of a broad community of consciousness and of a shared social fate among smaller groups which created the precondition for the banding of those smaller groups into regionally definable tribes. For this reason we should not assume that the original confederating social units were comparable in their scope and in their formal organization. The label "tribe" apparently masks great differences along a wide spectrum of regional organization above the *mishpāḥāh* level. "Tribe" is, in fact, a term used in many of the biblical traditions with a certain anachronizing tendency retrojected from the structural formalism of the twelve-tribe system once the state under Saul and David had already arisen.

Very instructive in this connection are the observations about the tribal migrations, and especially the claims about the transfer of protective associations and extended families from one tribal sphere to another, which Aharoni has assembled.[236] Not to be forgotten are the geographical-topographical and techno-economic factors in the definition and sharpening of tribal identities. Apparently the extended families and the protective associations of extended families were capable of great resilience in forming and re-forming "tribes," and this gave to early Israel adaptive advantages for expansion and survival as compared with the rigid, top-heavy, overorganized political centralism of the Canaanite city-state system.

30.9 Pseudo-Genealogies as Political and Cultural Ideology

Some final comments on the cultural and political functions of the descent ideology of old Israel are in order. In Israel all levels of social organization, as we have observed, are represented formally as unilineal descent groups from a common ancestor. Only the extended family, however, could in fact trace its lineage to a known common ancestor. At all other levels the kinship links were fictitiously projected by means of mythical or assumed patrilineal ancestry. L. H. Morgan offhandedly attributed Israel's pronounced tendency toward fictitious kinship patterning to "tradition" and "legal constraint." M. Sahlins has helpfully enlarged on the historico-political significance of the habit of employing kinship models to express the shared or sought-for unity of social groups:

> . . . "descent" in major residential groups is a political ideology and not a mere rule of personal affiliation. It is a way of phrasing political alignments and making political differentiations. It is a charter of group rights and an expression of group solidarity. And quite beyond relating man to man within the group, the descent ideology makes connections at a higher level: it stipulates the group's relation, or lack of relation, to other groups.
>
> The ideology of descent, then, is no simple expression of group composition or direct recognition of existing practices of personal affiliation. It is quite capable of reinterpreting contradictions of membership in its own terms. . . . This capacity of major descent groups to override their own internal discrepancies is one very good reason for choosing to describe the tribal kinship organization from the top down. The greater groups are not the smaller writ large; it is rather the other way around. The "primary" groups and relationships are shaped by their incorporation in a larger system of a certain type.
>
> As a political arrangement, furthermore, this larger system has its own dialectic even as it has its own functional context. The issues transcend such domestic concerns as who associates with whom. They have to do with the continuity of the community in a tribe of communities, and with the persistence of the tribe in a world of tribes. Here too, and here decisively, are disputes joined, battles fought, alliances pledged,

and cooperation effected. The principles of higher organization are forged by selective forces in play at this level.[237]

With this systemic understanding of the sociopolitical functions of descent ideology as a backdrop, it may be possible to bring further theoretical clarity to the astute observations of Malamat concerning biblical genealogies viewed in the light of anthropological studies of kinship systems.[238] In practice Malamat sees the difference between genealogies and pseudo-genealogies, but his typology does not sufficiently illuminate the differences between them. He distinguishes between "vertical" genealogies that trace a lineage over generations and "horizontal" genealogies that give a panoramic view of the relations among several groups of people conceived as branches of a single stock who ultimately have a single common ancestor. He rightly points out that these latter schemes represent ancestors as "points of segmentation," "nodal points" or "nodal eponyms," from which many people in more than one group can trace their descent collaterally.[239]

It is questionable whether a "vertical"/"horizontal" classificatory scheme brings the needed theoretical clarity to the two modes of genealogizing. Both modes are in fact "vertical" (i.e., cross-generational and diachronic) in that they express a succession of direct links, known or asserted, from generation to generation. The "horizontal" genealogies are not without cross-generational depth; their distinguishing feature is their fullness at the bottom, i.e., their cross-sectional elaboration of relations within the generation viewed as contemporary by the genealogist. Moreover, both modes are "horizontal" in character. Even the "vertical" genealogy, adhering closely to a single line, enters the "horizontal" domain whenever the descent is traced back beyond a point that can be empirically controlled (as in the upper generations of the Babylonian, Assyrian, and Israelite royal genealogies with which Malamat illustrates "vertical" genealogies).[240] By this I mean that the single line being traced eventually either links up with a network of "nodal eponyms" (as in the case of the Israelite royal lineages) or ties into a sequence of names which are identifiable as personified social collectivities, even though they do not "branch" nodally (as in the Babylonian and Assyrian royal genealogies).

There are social organizational implications to the fondness of Israel for horizontally elaborated genealogies which Malamat observes. The "synchronic spread" of many biblical genealogies is due, I think, to the tribal egalitarian need to relate all groups in the society to higher-order "nodal" explanations, whereas in the statist societies of the ancient Near East it was enough to give the king or the dynasty a primordial ancestry, because all his subjects as a "loyal family" would then be genealogically legitimated as subjects through his legitimacy as king. These hierarchic societies had no great social need for a "genealogical panorama" of the contemporary populace; the social need for symbolic unity was concentrated in the office of the king, which provided an enduring "imperial panorama" accompanied by appropriate administrative articulation of the people within the operative political system. Of course, the king's narrow line of descent was linked up with older, upper-generational, broad-ranging pseudo-genealogies to show that he was truly sprung from the ancient legitimating charters either of premonarchic times or of a time before his dynasty was established. Since no ultimate social power resided in the populace, it was enough that they should participate vicariously in the honor of the royal genealogy. Since for Israel the ultimate social power lay with the populace, the basic framework genealogies of Israelite tradition are pseudo-genealogies of the articulation of the sub-groups within the society. "Top-heavy" Near Eastern hierarchic genealogies give way to "bottom-dense" Israelite egalitarian genealogies.

It seems to me that the distinction for which Malamat is reaching is the distinction between a genealogy and a pseudo-genealogy, between a map of known kin connections and a rationalization of social relationships by alleged kinship. The *genealogy* proper formulates the cross-generational and synchronic relatedness of people *within* temporal and demographic horizons in which such relatedness can be empirically established. The *pseudo-genealogy* (or fictitious or metaphorical genealogy) formulates the cross-generational and synchronic relatedness of people *beyond* empirically controllable horizons. Sometimes this loss of control occurs because of great time depth, and thus the lower-generational genealogy merges into an upper-generational pseudo-genealogy. Sometimes this loss of control occurs because composite demographic entities are the genealogical units (families, tribes, nations) personified as persons, and in such cases the entire cross-generational sequence of links is metaphorical and the total scheme is a pseudo-genealogy.

Another way to view this typology is to consider what question the genealogist is asking, consciously or unconsciously. He may be asking one or more of the following: Who are the actual known ancestors of individual X? This is a question about the socially significant biological ancestors by which identity is established and social rights and duties determined. Or, over and above the demonstrable socially significant biological ancestry of X, what are his imputed connections with earlier generations of traditionally important personages? Or, apart from what is known about the socially significant biological ancestry of individuals within group Y, what are the upper-generational connections of this group as a whole—i.e., where does it come from, and how is it related to earlier generations of traditionally important personages or groups? Moreover, what is the relationship between group Y and group Z, or what are the relationships among any number of groups which are joined presently in some common functional grouping? Granted that the precise magnitudes of the genealogical units in biblical traditions are often not easily determinable; nevertheless, the *sine qua non* of any progress in the study of biblical genealogies is to make the most accurate determination possible. I have argued earlier, with respect to Renger's hypothesis about patrilineal exogamy among the patriarchs and with respect to alleged exogamy in the Israelite-Shechemite connubium of Genesis 34, that existing theories of clan exogamy have failed to establish convincingly that the organizational level they posit is in fact the same level dealt with in the biblical data they cite.

Of course, in trying to formulate the genealogist's questions, we recognize that he may not have been able to distinguish between a person and a collective personification or eponym in every instance, especially once his genealogical range had moved backward some generations. Yet it is our task as social scientists to make sense of the genealogist's activity, not only in terms of the distinctions he was conscious of, but in terms of those distinctions in his social behavior and social reasoning that we are able to make on the basis of systematic inquiry into the phenomena in a comparative context. I shall have more to say about the tension and priority between the social subject's own interpretation of his behavior and the social observer's interpretation of his behavior when I discuss "emic" and "etic" approaches to sociology and anthropology in X.50.3 (and see notes 558, 564, and 566.) The preceding typology suggests at least the basis for encouraging research strategies that will penetrate further into the thicket of biblical genealogies in the direction that Malamat's valuable initial thrust has opened up.[241]

If the cultural and political formulation of pseudo-genealogies or descent metaphors was developed to an extreme by early Israel, we readily see that this prolix ideology was addressed to the pressing need for rationalizing (i.e., explaining, regularizing, and bonding) the complicated interrelations of communities in a tribal community, of tribal communities in a confederate world of tribes, and of the whole vis-à-vis the constant threat of politically centralized societies to crush the emergent egalitarian social movement. The elaborateness of Israel's descent ideology and the vehemence with which it was advanced are direct correlates of the fragmented separate sub-histories of proto-Israelites, i.e., of socially uprooted people seeking ideological roots for newly designed, comprehensive and cooperative intergroup relations.

CHART 5

A SUMMARY SCHEMATIZATION OF EARLY ISRAEL'S SOCIAL STRUCTURE

HIGHEST ORGANIZATIONAL LEVEL: ISRAEL, a *CONFEDERACY* or *LEAGUE* of TRIBES *

The widest societal and culture-bearing unit of associated egalitarian Yahwistic tribes (*shevāṭīm*)

Fundamental traits or conditions of membership in the confederacy:

1) Exclusive devotion to the cult, the ritual, the moral instructions, and the ideology of Yahweh
2) Commitment to economic egalitarianism as reflected in the socioeconomic laws
3) Readiness to marshal military opposition to Canaanite, Philistine, and other threatening peoples
4) Sub-articulation into autonomous segmentary divisions by *shevāṭīm, mishpāḥōth,* and *bēth-ʾāvōth*
5) Recognition of and cooperation with the cross-tribal sodalities, which implemented various of the above, cross-cutting societal interaction patterns: the protective associations of extended families, the army organization, the ritual congregation, the Levitical priesthood, the Kenites

Functions of the Confederacy

1) Cultic celebration and production of ideology

2) Propagation of cultic and moral categorical law in the centralized cult and projection of a jural matrix for religious sanctioning of institutional behavior enforced through case law

Organs of the Confederacy

// Assembly of adult males from all the tribes gathered for periodic re-enactment of the covenant (annually? every seven years?)

Levitical priesthood: ceremonial and tradition-building activities

// Assembly of adult males gathered for periodic recitation of categorical laws (annually? every seven years?)

Levitical priesthood: ceremonial and instructional functions [Assembly of tribal representatives to collate and standardize case laws?

and/or

An all-Israel judge to collate and standardize case law and to adjudicate cases referred from the tribes?]†

†Entries set off by brackets are elements of the Israelite social structure regarded as possibly or probably present but as yet undemonstrated.

---

*On highest organizational level, see Chapters 25–26, 30–33.

3) Military self-defense through cooperating tribal levies

    // Assembly of adult males mustered for war from two or more cooperating tribes

    Levitical priesthood: summoners to war and bearers of the sacred ark in battle

    Judges as the drafted or voluntary leaders for particular campaigns who coordinate the military forces of the cooperating tribes

    [Assembly of tribal representatives to decide for war or peace?]

PRIMARY ORGANIZATIONAL SEGMENTS: *TRIBES (shēvet/maṭṭeh)* *

The tribe is an autonomous association of segmented extended families (*bēth-'āvōth*) grouped in village/neighborhood protective associations (*mishpāḥōth*), averaging about 50 per tribe, functionally interlocking through inter-marriage, practices of mutual aid, common worship, and a levy of troops.

Factors shaping the peculiar identities and the demographic and geographical boundaries of the tribes:

1) Common experiences of migration, oppression, and military struggle, especially against Canaanite city-states and the Philistine league

2) Territorial contiguity or separation owing to terrain, forests, and belts or enclaves of Canaanite city-states

3) Distinctive combinations of agricultural/pastoral pursuits and distinctive combinations in the basic bread-wine-oil agricultural pattern, based on different soils and rainfalls, which produced distinguishable "natural regions" (cf. D. Baly, "The Wheat and the Barley, the Oil and the Wine," *Geographical Companion to the Bible*, 1963, pp. 60–77).

Functions of the Tribe

Organs of the Tribe

1) Cultic celebration and production of regional tribal traditions

    // Tribal assembly of adult males at stated feasts (three times yearly?)

    Levitical priesthood cross-cutting and functioning within the tribal cult

2) Military self-defense through a tribal levy

    // Tribal assembly of adult males mustered for war

    Levitical priesthood cross-cutting and functioning within the framework of holy war

    Assembly of tribal elders to decide for war or peace

---

*On primary organizational level, see Chapters 27 and 30.

3) Intermarriage within the tribe preferred but not obligatory

[4] Jural community to decide cases referred from local courts?]

[5] Mutual socioeconomic aid for extended families and protective associations of families weakened by drought, disease, or war?]

// Arrangements between heads of extended families within the tribe

// [Assembly of tribal elders as a court of appeal for cases referred from secondary level of social organization?]

// [Assembly of tribal elders to recommend allocation of surpluses to needy segments of the tribe?]

SECONDARY ORGANIZATIONAL SEGMENTS: *PROTECTIVE ASSOCIATIONS* of EXTENDED FAMILIES (*mishpāḥāh/'eleph*)*

The protective association is a cluster of extended families (*bēth-'āvōth*) living in the same or nearby villages, rural neighborhood, or section of a large settlement, providing socioeconomic mutual aid for its constituent families, contributing troop quotas to the tribal levy, and indirectly serving alone or in concert with other adjacent *mishpāḥōth* to provide a local jural community.

Functions of the Protective Association	*Organs of the Protective Association*
1) Mutual economic aid for constituent extended families	// Extended families acting alone or in concert through their respective heads
2) Military self-defense through contribution of a troop quota to the tribal levy	// Extended families cooperating through their heads to determine their allotments to the military quota of their protective association
3) Cultic celebration and possibly production of local traditions	// Extended family heads acting as lay priests [Levitical priesthood when available?]
4) Jural community for enforcing case laws consonant with a developing tribal and confederate consensus regarding normative behavior in Israel	// Heads of extended families forming a village or local body of elders, drawn from a single protective association or from adjacent protective associations
5) Inter-marriage among extended families in the same protective association preferred and at times obligatory	// Arrangements between heads of extended families in the same protective association

*On secondary organizational segments, see chapters 28 and 30.

TERTIARY ORGANIZATIONAL SEGMENTS: *EXTENDED FAMILIES* or *HOUSEHOLDS* (*bêth-'āv*) *

The extended family is a primary residential and productive socioeconomic unit of two or more generations, grouped patrilocally, including wives, sons, and unmarried daughters of some or of all male descendants of the family head. It is a compromise formation involving kinship and residence which includes some affinal members (e.g., wives brought into the family) and excludes some consanguinous members (e.g., daughters married out to other families; brothers or sons or grandsons who break off to form their own extended families). Kinship is reckoned patrilineally and residence determined patrilocally.

Functions of the Extended Family:

1) Reproduction through marriage in accord with existing incest taboos but not according to exogamous clan divisions
2) Basic unit of economic production, largely self-sufficient in the production, distribution, consumption, and storage of agricultural and pastoral products
3) Military self-defense by supplying warriors for the tribal levy through a quota raised by the protective association to which the family belongs
4) Education and social control inculcating the basic all-Israelite obligations and ideological convictions reached at the tribal and inter-tribal levels of organization
5) Cultic celebration, such as observance of Passover

---

*On tertiary organizational segments, see Chapters 29 and 30.

Part VII

Models of the Social Structure (II):
All Israel, Amphictyony or
Confederacy?

31

The Prevailing Amphictyonic Model:
Critique and Rebuttal

Our inquiry to this point has established that the inclusive social system of old Israel was an organization of autonomous social entities built around the extended family as the prime socioeconomic unit but extending to higher levels of organization in the form of protective associations of families and in the form of tribal units. We have observed that the basic economic, social, political, military, and religious functions of the system were diffused throughout these units in varying patterns, so that no hierarchical leadership or social stratification existed—or, where they sought to appear, they were radically resisted. At the same time it is clear that the associated tribes formed a bounded, distinctive social system with cultural, socioeconomic, political, and religious facets.

When a system is more inclusive than a single tribe, but is not a political society, how is its unity to be expressed and named? How is the overall social system of old Israel to be characterized? As we have seen, there was no single Hebrew term that unambiguously served to designate this overall system organizationally, other than the proper name Israel and, less commonly, "the tribes of Israel." Among the terms commonly used to characterize associations of tribes are "confederacy," when the stress is on political cooperation, and "league," when the stress is on military cooperation. Neither term, however, is well-developed typologically, and both are more loosely descriptive than prescriptively analytic. Perhaps the most exact and least confusing term for the inclusive social system of old Israel would be "a protective association of tribes," on analogy with the *mishpahah* as a protective association of extended families. For the moment we shall work with the handy term "confederacy," recognizing that its precise structure remains to be specified and clarified.

Since Martin Noth's epochal study on the twelve-tribe system,[242] it has been widely assumed that the Israelite confederacy was of a very specific organizational type whose closest analogues lay in religious confederacies of the Mediterranean world among the Greeks, Old Latins, and Etruscans. Noth felt that he had conclusively demonstrated the emergence in Canaan, shortly after the settlement of the exodus tribes, of a full-blown twelve-tribe confederacy organized around a covenant with Yahweh in support of a central shrine. Noth and others have devoted much energy to relating that confederacy and its member tribes to patriarchal and exodus/Sinai traditions, as well as to the conquest-settlement traditions in Joshua and Judges.[243] In particular, numerous inquiries have tried to establish the roster of member tribes within the welter of variant tribal lists preserved in the Old Testament.[244] Working within a posited twelve-tribe scheme, two basic versions of the membership have been identified: one containing Levi and Joseph; the other omitting Levi and subdividing Joseph into Ephraim and Manasseh. The former is regarded as earlier; the latter is viewed as a later adjustment to the historic realities of Levi's eclipse as a secular tribe and the bifurcation of Joseph into two strong tribes in the central highlands.

Within the twelve-tribe scheme, in both of its principal forms, appear the sub-groups of the Leah tribes (Reuben, Simeon, Levi [replaced by Gad in the "later" version], Judah, Issachar, Zebulun), represented in tradition as sons of Jacob by his wife Leah, and the Rachel tribes (Ephraim, Manasseh [both included as Joseph in the "earlier" version]), and Benjamin, represented as sons of Jacob (or grandsons) by his wife Rachel. The remaining tribal members (Dan, Naphtali, Gad [in the "earlier" version], Asher), represented as sons of Jacob by his wives' handmaidens and thus often called "concubine tribes," are not so clearly defined a group and show the greatest variation in the order of their appearance in tribal lists.

It is often asserted, in agreement with Noth, that the fixed order of the Leah tribes at the head of the tribal lists, which survives into later times—even when three of the Leah tribes were no longer significant historical factors—is evidence of an earlier six-tribe confederacy in the central highlands which was incorporated in the twelve-tribe confederacy spearheaded by the incoming Rachel or exodus tribes.[245] It is also widely held that Judah was itself the result of an amalgamation of a six-tribe confederacy into a single entity (including lesser Judah, Simeon, Othniel, Caleb, Jerahmeel, and Kenites).[246] The amalgamation of the Rachel tribes with the Leah and concubine tribes, already settled in Canaan for some time, produced the twelve-tribe league that became the biblical "Israel." Proponents of the twelve-tribe confederacy differ in their estimates of the historical worth of the traditions concerning the preconfederate period. Some give credence to an historical Moses among the exodus tribes, while others do not. Virtually all, however, stress the importance of the exodus-settlement traditions (and some would include the Sinai traditions) as the bond for uniting the tribes in their common struggle.

The elements of this reconstruction of the twelve-tribe confederacy, largely dependent on Noth's basic work, are complex and more or less convincing from point to point. The difficulties and objections are considerable, and we shall introduce them serially as we proceed with our analysis. Let it be said, however, at the start that the illuminative power of the confederacy model of Israel's origins is particularly evident in the way it has managed to explain the coming together of ethnically and culturally related groups in a firm institutional religious framework. The institutional framework of the Yahwistic cult community has been employed to explain cultic practices, the creation and preservation of the chief narrative themes and the traditions clustered around them, and the rather different lines of development of two types of Israelite laws: the specifically Yahwistic categorical or apodictic laws and the more general Canaanite-derived case laws. The twelve-tribe confederate model has served to encompass and connect a wide range of cultic, literary, and legal phenomena contained in the biblical traditions. Moreover, it has offered a tangible beginning point for Yahwism as a distinctive phenomenon in Israel prior to the monarchy, has gone some distance in accounting for the unity of Israel on a prepolitical basis, and has helped to sharpen the distinction between premonarchic and monarchic forms of Israelite organization as systems in tension or contradiction. The success of the scheme is apparent in its ability to do justice both to the evidence for the many separate ethnic, cultural, and religious ingredients that contributed to the mix of Israel and to the evidence for a radical break with the ancient world which Israel constituted in its remarkable cohesion in spite of the absence of centralized political ties.

In fact so remarkable has been the twelve-tribe confederate model's explanatory power on general historical, cultic, literary, and religious levels that the full form of the model as proposed by Noth has frequently been accepted without careful scrutiny of his detailed argument. Furthermore, as the first model offering this comprehensive explanatory power, it was readily adopted by many scholars who did not sufficiently consider whether the virtues of Noth's confederate model might be better represented by a rather different form of the model, i.e., one that does not settle for Noth's assumption that Israel's confederacy was a religious league of a Greek–Old Latin–Etruscan "amphictyonic" type. In short, the values of Noth's comprehensive understanding of early Israel were too readily extended to the details of his reconstruction and to a rather too facile endorsement of organizational correspondence between Israel's confederacy and the Mediterranean religious leagues.

It will perhaps by now be clear why I have avoided describing the twelve-tribe system as an *amphictyony,* which was the term Noth proposed, following up the analogy which earlier scholars had briefly suggested.[247] Amphictyony was the Greek name for an association of tribes or city-states in a single cult at a central shrine which is reported from Greece and Italy before the Hellenic and Roman worlds had any single overarching political rule. The Greek *amphiktuonia* is generally understood to have derived from *amphiktiones,* "inhabitants of the neighboring district" or "dwellers around" (i.e., in this instance, "around" the common sanctuary). Now in the broadest sense the analogy is suggestive in that both in

Greece and Italy, on the one hand, and in Israel, on the other, we observe politically autonomous units bound together by common religious ties involving specific cult practices. Noth, however, carried the analogy further to ascribe certain specific features both to the Mediterranean and to the Israelite "amphictyonies." These supposed definitive features bear close reexamination. And even more seriously, Noth failed to question the varying structural and functional positions of the religious confederation in the two different social systems.

In short, Noth drew a series of parallels on questionable points, while overlooking the macrosystemic entities he was comparing. The result has been considerable confusion over a few much-debated points coupled with almost total avoidance of the issue of the comparability of the two social phenomena both intrasystemically and intersystemically. Both Noth's claims about correspondences in details and his failure to compare the respective societal complexes must be dealt with before any more satisfactory model of Israel's confederacy can be proposed. By avoiding the term *amphictyony* for early Israel, I am expressing in advance my conviction that the peculiar traits of the Mediterranean amphictyony are not demonstrable in old Israel. At the same time unlike most of Noth's critics, I am agreeing with him in seeing old Israel as a well-articulated association of tribes united by common religious ties, in what I shall for the present continue to call loosely a confederacy.

Specifically, Noth identified three traits of an amphictyony in Israel about which the biblical records are either silent or obscure: (1) a central shrine; (2) a body of amphictyonic officers delegated from the member tribes; (3) a fixed twelve-tribe membership.

31.1 Central Shrine

Noth thought that the original central shrine was at Shechem where the confederacy was first given its twelve-tribe form (Josh. 24; cf. Deut. 11:29–30; 27:1–14; Josh. 8:30–35). At the close of the period of the judges, and thus at the threshold of the monarchy, the central shrine was Shiloh (I Sam. 1:3; 4:1–4; cf. Josh. 18:1; Judg. 21:19). In the interim, it apparently was located for a time at Bethel (Judg. 20:18, 26–28; 21:2; Gen. 35:1–8) and then for a time at Gilgal (Josh. 3—4). The reason for the departure from Shechem may have been the disturbances attending Abimelech's brief rule over that city (Judg. 9). By analogy with the customary Greek amphictyonic pattern, there should have been only one central shrine. Its transfer from one site to another is not an insuperable obstacle to the analogy, however, since the city-states confederated around the shrine of Apollo at Delphi had earlier been organized (or, more properly, their antecedents had been organized) as tribes around the Demeter shrine at Anthela, and for some time it seems that the amphictyony observed the two cults at the two locations.

The difficulty in the biblical data is not simply with the transfer of the central shrine from site to site but with the very question of the existence of a central shrine. No doubt Shechem, Bethel, Gilgal, and Shiloh were important cultic centers, but the biblical citations do not require the interpretation that they served successively as the definitive national shrine. Of course Noth did not deny that many other tribally important cultic centers existed alongside the national shrine. The centralized cult of Yahweh, however, is not simply equatable with the cult peculiar to any one single center or even to a single center moved about among the tribes. By contrast, an amphictyony was intrinsically bound to a particular shrine. The same intrinsic connection between Israel and any one or any succession of shrines cannot be demonstrated. Doubtless the all-Israelite assembly or its representatives met in worship at central points, but Yahweh was not a deity whose cult in Israel was restricted to a single center or series of centers, and the Israelite priesthood was not a priesthood that was attached in the first instance to a single center or series of centers. Thus, the issue of the central shrine is not simply the matter of whether there was one national place of cultic observance. The issue is whether a single cultic center was structurally constituent of the Israelite confederacy in the way the amphictyonic cult site was structurally constituent of an amphictyony. In my view, the two forms of centralized cult were different; so different, in fact, that Israel's centralized cult is not directly analogous with a Mediterranean amphictyonic cult.

The highly stylized story of the rape and murder of the Levite's concubine in Judges 19—21, which Noth refers to as an authentic tradition attesting the amphictyony,[248] mentions intertribal consultations and/or cultic celebrations not at *one* location alone but at *three*: (1) the tribes "assembled as one man to Yahweh at Mizpah" (20:1); (2) they "went up to Bethel and inquired of God" as to which tribe should initiate the attack on Benjamin (20:18); and (3) they recommended that the decimated Benjaminites find wives among the maidens at "the yearly feast of Yahweh at Shiloh" (21:16–21). By ignoring the other two sites, the mention of Shiloh may be taken to refer to the amphictyonic shrine at which all the tribes worshipped Yahweh annually. But the passage in question does not say that all the tribes worshipped there; in fact, the women to be captured are simply "daughters of Shiloh," i.e., Ephraimite inhabitants of the city only. As a matter of fact, an explanatory comment identifies Bethel as the place where the ark was located "in those days" (20:27), which Noth understands as the amphictyonic center. The people assemble to Yahweh at Mizpah (20:1), however, in a manner suggesting a cultic gathering.

Since the account gives a very stylized portrait of the confederate members acting in concert against an offending member, the mention of three cultic sites does not strengthen the impression of a definitively central shrine. Of course, it might be argued that the impression of three central shrines is a result of editorial expansion and that originally only one site was named in Judges 19—21, but I see no way to recover this "original" form of the tradition with any degree of certainty.[249] To be sure, nothing in this account precludes the possibility that the original confederation formed at Shechem (according to one way of reading Joshua 24). Nor am I in any sense denying that centralized—i.e., standardized, system-wide—cultic practices and traditions were developed by the Levitical priesthood (as described in Part III). The point is that the cult of Yahweh was not the cult of a single obligatory site and the priesthood of Yahweh was not the priesthood attached to a single obligatory site.

31.2 Amphictyonic Council

As to the existence of an intertribal body of delegates from the tribes which served as an amphictyonic council, there is absolutely no proof. The references to tribal leaders, sometimes in the form of lists of names given one-word technical rubrics (*n^esī'īm; ro'shīm; sārīm* or *shōph^etīm*), or compound technical rubrics (*n^esī'ē maṭṭōth ^avōthām; ro'shē 'alphē* Israel), show only that the tribes had leaders and that on occasion they consulted together. These leaders are not pictured as forming an official body such as the Greek *synedrion* or *koinon,* or as being appointed representatives to such a body, or as meeting together in any regular manner to take responsibility for the shrine, or as taking votes on matters of policy. And even if it must be conjectured that there was some regularized way for tribal heads to consult and make decisions, it does not follow that such a mechanism was analogous to a body of delegates responsible for a shrine, as was the case with an amphictyonic council.

In fact, our knowledge of the offices and functions of the amphictyonic council in Greece and Italy is far from adequate. It is limited almost totally to inscriptions from Delphi and literary comments about the Delphic institution, and these are fullest only for a rather late stage in the life of the Delphic amphictyony, i.e., fourth–second centuries B.C.[250] Two types of council delegates are referred to: *pylagoroi,* "those gathering together at Pylae," and *hieromnemones,* "those mindful of sacred things." The *pylagoroi* appear to have been the sole deputies when the amphictyony was at first gathered around Pylae (Thermopylae) and the shrine of Demeter at Anthela, while the *hieromnemones* appear to have been added when the amphictyony expanded to encompass the eventually much more important shrine of Apollo at Delphi.

The separation of functions between the two sets of deputies cannot be certainly established, and there is some suggestion that, in voting, the two kinds of officers representing each member city-state deliberated together and cast a single vote. Their functions, whether singly or collectively, included (1) the administration of finances (e.g., the receipt of subscriptions from the faithful for the establishment and upkeep of shrines, memorials, athletic facilities, roads, etc., and of revenues from rents on houses and farms belonging to the shrine; the seizure of debts, the confiscation of criminals' property, the receipt of proceeds from flocks, of interest on loans from the shrine treasury, etc.); (2) limited legislative functions (e.g., declaration of sacred truce to permit pilgrimage and sacrifice, waiver of tolls on pilgrims, summoning and supervision of the Pythian Games, decrees against plundering the shrines and cultivating sacred land—infractions could be punished by fines, which were often ignored); and (3) limited judicial functions (e.g., adjudicating matters involving individuals or states or serving as a court of arbitration—but these functions seem to have been sparingly exercised). Many of the duties of the amphictyonic officers in the council were delegated to lesser bodies (e.g., handling and auditing the monies, supervising rentals, the letting of contracts for workmen, the preparation of plans for rebuilding destroyed temples, etc.).

The two classes of amphictyonic officers were chosen by various methods and for varying terms of office within each member state. Owing to expanding membership in the important Delphic amphictyony, the original twelve amphictyons could only be maintained over centuries by assigning one voting membership to two city-states, leaving it to the deputies from those city-states to determine how the vote should be cast. It is obvious that the two sets of amphictyonic officers and the idiosyncrasies of appointment, as well as the sharing of more than one city-state in a single voting membership, are features so peculiar to the dual cult origins of the Pylaean-Delphic amphictyony and its growing political-symbolic importance in later Greek history that we cannot legitimately attribute the same features to other amphictyonies in the absence of information about their councils of deputies.[251]

In old Israel there is no recognizable technical term for amphictyonic delegates analogous to the Delphic *pylogoroi* or *hieromenmones*. The effort of Noth to demonstrate that the *nᵉsi'im* were such delegates is not convincing.[252] While no single conception of the role of the *nᵉsi'im* is altogether satisfying, they are more adequately conceived as tribal heads than as delegates to a council with responsibility for maintaining the shrine, discharging its financial affairs, etc.[253] Nor is it at all clear that Noth's identification of the minor judges with an all-Israelite office fits within the amphictyonic design.[254] Noth correctly argues that they did not have priestly functions, which were reserved to the Levites, and in this respect there is broad correspondence with the amphictyonic officers, who left all directly cultic activities in the hands of the Pylaean and Delphic priesthoods. But when Noth suggests that the minor judges were in fact proclaimers and interpreters of the categorical or apodictic law, we can find no parallel in the Greek amphictyony.[255] The one all-amphictyonic officer at Delphi was the titular head of the council, or president, which office was always exercised by the Thessalians. He called the meetings of the councils, presided over them, and commanded the amphictyonic army when it was necessary, although the actual fielding of an amphictyonic armed force appears to have been very infrequent and largely ineffective.[256] The president of the amphictyonic council is not pictured as the declaimer of decrees, and the sum total of special decrees given out by the council, pertaining largely to protection of the cult and mitigation of warfare among the amphictyons, is more restricted in jurisdiction and less integral to the foundations of the member states than the apodictic law of Israel, which Noth assigns to the office of the minor judge.

Admittedly the exact role of the minor judges is so disputed a point that it is difficult to get enough control on the position to make any kind of comparison with the Greek amphictyonic officers. But within the range of possible under-standings, and specifically with reference to Noth's identification of the minor judge as law-proclaimer, the parallels with Greek amphictyonic officers are so inexact as to be totally unconvincing. This points up rather cogently the fact that the amphictyonic entity in Greece was in no significant sense a legal community, whereas the confederate entity of Israel was a primary legal community. Whether Noth is right or wrong about the minor judge being a law-proclaimer, we have uncovered one of the indicators of the fundamentally different structural and functional location of the Greek or Italian amphictyony in the larger society, on the one hand, and the structural and functional location of the Israelite confeder-acy in the Israelite social system, on the other.

31.3 Twelve Amphictyonic Members

Less frequently criticized has been Noth's linkage of the Greek and Italian am-phictyonies with the Israelite confederacy on the basis of their division into twelve members. The "twelve tribes" are sometimes referred to in a summary way in narration, although less frequently than one might suppose, considering the fact that the lists of the tribes contain, for the most part, exactly twelve units. Noth correctly emphasized that the number twelve is so established that changing historical realities are forced to accommodate to it. Tribes may come and go, change their names, amalgamate or subdivide, but the twelve-tribe system en-dures. In short, no one can deny the prominence of the twelve-tribe pattern. The real questions are these: When did the definitive segmentation into twelve con-federate members arise? Was this twelve-foldness integral to the foundation of the confederacy in old Israel? Exactly why was twelve the chosen number?

Noth addressed these questions and gave firm and apparently solidly documented answers. He claimed that the twelve-tribe system arose at Shechem soon after the entrance of the exodus or Rachel tribes into Canaan. Precisely twelve tribes were involved, in Noth's view, because that was the prescribed number of members necessary to an amphictyony in order to maintain the central shrine on rotation throughout twelve months of the year. The same result could be assured by six members maintaining the shrine for two months each annually.

Noth found twelve to be the characteristic number of members in the Mediterranean amphictyonies. The number of tribes affiliating in Israel was so far in excess of six that the larger number of twelve became obligatory. Furthermore, Noth cited associations of twelve tribes among Israel's neighbors, first noted by Ewald, namely, the Ishmaelites (Gen. 17:20; 25:13–16), the Arameans (Gen. 22:20–24), and the Edomites (Gen. 36:10–14), as well as six Arab tribes (Gen. 25:1–4), and perhaps in the original form of the text, six Horite tribes (Gen. 36:20–28).[257]

The evidence that Noth amassed was so impressive that it has not been carefully evaluated by many scholars who have enthusiastically accepted Noth's conclusions. In the Mediterranean amphictyonies, twelve does not hold the absolutely dominant position that Noth claimed for it. It is true that the best-known of the amphictyonies, the Pylaean-Delphic amphictyony, originally had twelve participating tribes and later twelve participating city-states. Likewise, ancient historians report that some of the Etruscan, as well as pre-Roman, Latin amphictyonies had twelve-member formations. On the other hand, the amphictyony around the Poseidon shrine at Calauria is reported to have had only seven members. Also, the Latin amphictyony with its center at the Jupiter Latiaris temple on Mons Albanus was composed of thirty members. That the number of amphictyonic members could change is evident in Augustus' expansion (from twenty-four to thirty) and redistribution of the council votes so that new entities, such as the newly founded city of Nicopolis, could be included in the Delphic amphictyony without dropping former members (although some were merged under larger groupings). Moreover, Augustus expanded the Etruscan amphictyons of the goddess Voltumna at Veslinii from twelve to fifteen.[258] Of course the imperial intrusions of Augustus into the amphictyonic structure are late and need not be decisive for the formative and thriving periods of amphictyonic organization.

It should also be pointed out that apart from the fairly full information on the Delphic amphictyony, we know about the others only sketchily from brief descriptions by historians. These historians show a propensity to perceive and interpret the less well-known amphictyonies by reference to the better-known Delphic amphictyony. It is, therefore, not unlikely that they have at times attributed a twelvefold division to these lesser-known associations for which they did not have firm evidence. Indicative of this tendency to read the other amphictyonies in the light of the Delphic formation is the probability that the very name "amphictyony" for such a formation of tribes or city-states was drawn from Delphi and extended to other formations felt to be similar in kind.[259] While twelve is the most common number for the participating units in an amphictyony, I see no evidence that twelvefold (or sixfold) membership was a precondition for the formation and operation of an amphictyony.

As to the Near Eastern twelve-tribe amphictyonies posited by Noth on the basis of the pseudo-genealogies in Genesis, they are purely the products of conjectural imagination. The six Arab sons of Keturah (Gen. 25:1–4) are merely named in a straightforward table without any attention being called to the number and without any claims that they stand for formally related groups, although clearly Midian among them gives the table an ethnic significance. Also, the table is not simply a list of six sons but runs on to name ten second- and third-generation offspring (in groups of two, three, and five), which is hardly amenable to an amphictyonic interpretation of the list. Likewise, the Aramean sons of Nahor (Gen. 22:20–24) form a pseudo-genealogical register, with eight sons by his wife and four by his concubine. Again there is no attention called to the twelve, and, while some of the names have clearly ethnic reference, no claim is made about any type of intertribal union. The claim that there are twelve Edomite eponyms in Genesis 36:10–14 is mistaken, since fifteen names appear, five as the sons of Esau and ten as his grandsons (nine if the grandson by a concubine is omitted). The most explicit analogy is that of the Ishmaelite "twelve princes according to their tribes" (17:20; 25:13–16). These twelve tribes are not, however, described as forming a confederation for cultic purposes or, in fact, for any purposes.[260] The use by P of the rare term *'ummāh* for "tribe" or "people" with reference to Ishmaelites/Midianites both here and in Numbers 25:15 may retain an old memory of the social organization of these peoples. However, the use of *nāśī'* for the tribal "prince" or "head" is the general and problematic term we have discussed above and does not inspire confidence about its precision. The rubric about the "twelve princes" need be nothing more than the P writer's superficial observation, motivated by Israel's twelve-tribe scheme, which he imposed on the Ishmaelite units. The numbers of Ishmaelite *'ummōth* in his list may in fact have been twelve; on the other hand, he may have chosen to cut or expand the units in order to yield precisely twelve.

Moreover, Noth's insistence that there was a cultic necessity for an amphictyony to consist of exactly six or twelve members is not successfully argued. His assumption that the amphictyonies had to be composed of six or twelve units in order to maintain the shrine on a monthly or two-monthly rota is supported by a reference to Solomon's division of the kingdom into twelve administrative districts to supply the court for one month each year (I Kings 4:7).[261] This comes with some surprise, since Noth is at such pains to stress that the amphictyony in Israel is an old premonarchic institution. Accordingly, we hardly expect him to seek a clue to the rationale for its numerical composition from so late a source and especially from such a totally different institutional context. Presumably, Noth means to argue that the Solomonic administrative division into twelve is a late reflection of the same principle at work in the amphictyonic cult division into twelve parts. At this point Noth cites H. Ewald[262] for the origin of the proposal, and he also notes that Emil Szanto applied the same explanation of a monthly rota for support of the shrine to the Greek amphictyony.[263] An examination of both authors cited by

Noth shows that they offer no independent evidence for the notion. In particular, Szanto simply refers to a possible (but undemonstrated) monthly rota explanation for the twelve-member Israelite confederacy and assumes that a similar purpose obtained in the twelve-member Greek amphictyony. Noth also cites H. Buergel as connecting the practice of a rota for cultic support of shrines with astral phenomena, e.g., the signs of the zodiac.[264]

The net effect of the Ewald-Szanto-Noth hypothesis about the cultic need for precisely six or twelve amphictyonic members is exceedingly weak. The proponents set forth no evidence from the Mediterranean amphictyonies to show that their members did in fact maintain the central shrine on this basis, and their evidence for Israel is drawn from a later practice of monarchic administration. My examination of the literature on the amphictyonies, including an alleged Sumerian example, has uncovered no support for the notion.[265] To the contrary, as I read the inscriptions from the Delphic amphictyony, the prevailing practice was for the member states of the amphictyony to discharge their duties toward the shrine through the common council and its officers without any indication of the delegation of monthly assignments to particular members.[266] Perhaps a more thorough investigation of this question will turn up additional evidence, but to date the rota argument as an explanation of six or twelve amphictyonic members appears to be a piece of hypothetical circular reasoning which moves airily back and forth between Greece and Israel without being grounded securely in evidence from either society.

As to the proposal that twelve has astral connections, it is difficult to see that establishing the point would have any direct bearing on the cultic rota hypothesis. There is a certain plausibility to the suggestion that twelve is a number connoting· totality and wholeness and that this is reflected in the division of the heavens into twelve parts.[267] It is not clear, however, whether this sense of totality derives from astral phenomena or whether it is simply illustrated in astral phenomena; and, whichever proves to be the case, there is no demonstrated link between the astral significance of twelve and the necessity of organizing a monthly rota to support a shrine.

In actual fact, Noth has moved from the frequent, but not exclusive, occurrence of twelve tribes or city-states in Greek and Italian amphictyonies to the claim that six or twelve members were required. And from there he has moved to the claim that where six or twelve eponyms occur in Near Eastern lists we have a similar obligatorily composed amphictyony. His logical links lack supporting empirical evidence. An amphictyony is something more specific than a cluster of ethnically or politically related groups numbering six or twelve, and it is clear from the Mediterranean world that the amphictyony did not always consist of six or twelve members. The amphictyony is a specific religious insitutional arrangement, and such arrangements are not demonstrated in the biblical passages Noth cites. In fact, B. C. Rahtjen has observed that the only Syro-Palestinian parallel to the amphictyony is among the Philistines, who may have formed such a union around the Dagon shrine, first in Gaza and later in Ashdod. He notes that the Philistines were themselves Aegean in origin but that their amphictyony consisted of *five* city-states, not six or twelve.[268] Whether Rahtjen has really demonstrated a Philistine amphictyony is doubtful, but he has shown that a case for an amphictyony of Philistines is more cogent than a case for an amphictyony of Israelites, notwithstanding the absence of six or twelve Philistine members.

When we come to an examination of the religious union of Israelite peoples, we must be able to find something more specific than twelve tribes to be convinced that an amphictyony is in question, and it must be something more than a fixed order of tribes in lists. In fact, what we discover is that the tribes of Israel are referred to as twelve in number in contexts which are either certainly or probably monarchic or later in origin. There is not a single occurrence of the term "the twelve tribes (of Israel)" in a text that is indisputably premonarchic. That arouses our suspicion and curiosity at once, so that when we encounter the tribal lists in the form of blessings, genealogical accounts, lists of officials, census enumerations, and encampment layouts we appropriately ask: Is there anything in the lists which suggests more than a cluster of related tribal units? Is there any sign of specifically amphictyonic features, such as a central shrine or amphictyonic delegates? And if the lists entail some comprehensive religious organization, does it necessarily follow the amphictyonic pattern? And, whatever its nature, did this religious organization entail twelve parts from its inception? Noth answered in the positive to all these questions, whereas I would answer positively only to the first question. There was a premonarchic religious union of the tribes of Israel, but it was not a union of twelve tribes and it was not an amphictyonic union. The twelve-tribe framework of the tribal lists is better understood as a retrojection from a life-setting entirely other than the pre-Davidic confederacy, and at no stage of the confederacy, premonarchic or monarchic, did it constitute itself organizationally as an amphictyony.

31.4 Limited Merit of the Model

It appears then that the twelve-tribe amphictyonic model is an erroneous over-refinement of some suggestive analogies between Greek/Italian amphictyonies and the Israelite religious confederation. It begins from a real enough fact: the undoubted association of Israelite tribes in a common religious institutional and ideological framework in premonarchic times. Finding the same broadly analogous situation in ancient Greece and Italy, it then transfers the detailed features of the classical institution of amphictyony into the Israelite setting. From the hypothetical Israelite amphictyony it undertakes to explain ambiguous or neutral biblical data as features of the conjectured model. *Nᵉsī'îm* become amphictyonic delegates and the minor *shōph^eṭîm* become law proclaimers and interpreters of the amphictyony. Important cultic centers become official central shrines. References to twelve units in Israel and to twelve (or six) units among some of its neighbors become proof of an amphictyonic form of association. A heuristic model that is useful, as long as it compares and contrasts what is actually known at first hand about the two types of unions, becomes dogmatically inhibiting and distorting when it overreaches itself and insists on correspondences when none are known to exist, ignores evidence that is not amenable to the model, and ends up by using the more fully described example from another culture to "reconstruct" the less fully described example in Israel.

Consequently, a starting point for ascertaining the history of tribal relations in ancient Israel must be a setting aside of the tyranny of the amphictyonic model, freeing us to use it where it is applicable but insisting that our first responsibility is to account for the data in Israel itself. Such an approach means that we are no longer intent on straining to find faint or fancied reflections of amphictyonic traits by scouring the biblical texts. We turn rather to a balanced delineation of what the traditions present. In particular, we do not have to make the focal point of our inquiry the question about precisely which twelve tribes were in confederation in which periods. We can get at that question by trying to locate the context of the twelve-tribe notion.

32

An Alternative Explanation of "the Twelve-Tribe System"

Since we have challenged a fundamental article of most current reconstructions of the early Israelite period, it is appropriate that we go on to give at least a preliminary answer to those questions which we believe the twelve-tribe amphictyonic model has not correctly answered, or has answered only inadequately. The key question is this: From what period does the twelve-tribe system derive?

32.1 Alleged Normativeness of Twelve Tribes before the Monarchy

We have agreed with Noth that the twelve-tribe motif is a prominent one in the Old Testament. But we must qualify that observation immediately on examining the references to the pattern contextually. We may anticipate the results by stating that there is no uncontested pre-Davidic reference to the twelve tribes, and in any case the few problematic references do not speak for a strict amphictyonic interpretation of twelve tribes.

The references to the twelve tribes as a totality and the enumeration of twelve tribal units occur in three types of traditions: (1) references in narratives; (2) references in descriptions of cultic activities or appointments; (3) references in lists of tribal officers, genealogies, census figures, etc. The lists usually entail twelve tribes, but not invariably so, and the tribes named vary within certain limits and occur with some variability in sequence. While some of the lists are as early as the united monarchy, and certainly contain data from the premonarchic period, absolutely nothing in the traditional twelvefoldness of the units points compellingly to a normative pre-Davidic origin. Even though we have shown, for example, that Numbers 1 and 26 refer to the muster of troops by *'alāphīm* in old Israel, the present arrangement of the muster lists in twelve tribes is not necessarily as old as the contents of the lists and shows no primitive rootage in a prior twelve-tribe system. The lists merely indicate rootage in some form of premonarchic intertribal association and not specifically in a union of twelve tribes. This is borne out as well in the poetic blessings of Jacob and Moses, which clearly are dissoluble into individual units that have been arbitrarily strung together, and not always on a strict twelvefold scheme (cf. Deut. 33:13,17,18). Neither the tribal lists nor the tribal blessings contain any direct evidence for a premonarchic twelvefold tribal pattern, since, in every instance, the twelvefold framework is detachable from the older contents.

The descriptions of cultic acts or the construction of cultic objects in the number of twelve, either explicitly or implicitly referring to the twelve tribes, are found in Priestly, Deuteronomic, or Chronistic passages which do not confidently reach back beyond the monarchic tradition of the twelve tribes and thus do not rest securely upon any independent historical evidence. All these references can be understood without difficulty as adoptions of a twelve-tribe tradition that arose no earlier than the monarchy.

Of course all three types of twelve-tribe enumerations may be explained as late surviving memories of a premonarchic scheme. But they do not in themselves compel such an interpretation, which would be probable only if we could find some firm basis for the twelve-tribe scheme in data directly from the settlement period. When we examine the narrative references which might derive from premonarchic times we are struck by the paucity of references to the twelve tribes. We list them in biblical order: the twelve sons of Jacob (Gen. 29:31—30:24; 35:16–26; 42:13, 32; J/E with P summary, 35:22b–26); the twelve pillars at Sinai-Horeb (Exod. 24:4; E?); the muster of 12,000 troops, a thousand per tribe, for the war against Midian (Num. 31:1–6; P); the prophesying of seventy elders plus Eldad and Medad, i.e., seventy-two elders [composed of six from each tribe?] (Num. 11:16–30; J/E); the sending out of twelve scouts from twelve tribes to reconnoiter the land (Deut. 1:23); twelve pillars for the twelve tribes taken from the Jordan and set up either in the river bed or at Gilgal (Josh. 3:12; 4:3–4,8–9,20; E?); and twelve dismembered parts of the concubine's body sent throughout Israel to summon the tribes to punish Benjamin (Judg. 19:29; E?). That, so far as I can see, is the full corpus of possibly authentic premonarchic references to the twelve tribes operating as a normative collectivity.

We may safely set aside the P and D references as insubstantial for our historical question because they contain nothing that cannot be explained as reflections of later belief. The same may be said of the references in Numbers 11, Joshua 3—4 and Judges 19, all of which operate under the conception of the whole of Israel acting together either to prophesy, or to conquer the land, or to punish an intertribal crime. In all these cases the twelveness is not a feature that adheres strongly to some ancient feature in the story. The allusions to 12,000 troops (twelve mustered 'ᵃlāphīm), twelve scouts, seventy-two elders (twelve times six), twelve stones, and twelve parts of a corpse have a self-conscious, adventitious character in each case, merely attaching themselves to the stories in a formalistic and schematic manner. The twelveness in no instance illuminates some distinctive feature of the structure or activities of the tribes so that they can be viewed in either their individuality or their organizational relatedness.

It may be objected that just such a distinctive feature occurs in the version of the twelve stone pillars which has them set up at Gilgal (Josh. 4:20). Now it is likely from the context that at some time in Israel's history twelve such stones did stand at Gilgal, but there is nothing to prove that they stood there before the monarchy or that, if they did, they were explained as symbols of the twelve tribes at so early a date. Judging from the way the site of Gilgal operates as a cultic center and as a base camp for the Israelites in the traditions of Joshua 1—12, it is highly probable that Gilgal came to have a confederation-wide significance in Israel. It is even possible that before the monarchy a number of stones representing the tribes stood at Gilgal. That the stones were twelve in number does not, however, inhere necessarily in the story. They might have been, for example, ten stones to correspond to the tribes named in the Song of Deborah.

We are left, then, with two texts. The genealogical narrative of Jacob's sons, born of two wives and their handmaidens, openly presents an aetiology for the twelve tribes of Israel. The names listed are the names according to one form of the tradition, namely, that form which includes Levi and undifferentiated Joseph as tribes. But it cannot be shown that this highly elaborated account is the basis for the Levi-Joseph version of the twelve tribes; or, more exactly, it cannot be demonstrated that it goes back to a situation before the monarchy when precisely the twelve named tribes were joined in a religious union. The story's playfulness with etymologies and its arrangement of the births to contribute suspense to the unfolding plot, so that Joseph and Benjamin come last, indicate that this is a schematic device derived from an already existing Levi-Joseph tribal arrangement which is not demonstrably earlier than the united monarchy, when the Yahwist wrote down the earliest strand in the account. Noth himself comments on this passage as follows:

> Tradition-historically it is a late passage, hardly the subject matter of living narrative at all. Contentwise, it is constructed by distributing certain groups of sons to certain mothers on the basis of the history of the tribes. . .As a consequence it is very artificial in structure.[269]

Although I cannot find that he does so, Noth might reasonably have argued that since the passage contains J and E elements, it belonged to the common foundation of traditions (G) which lay back of J and E and, therefore, the twelvefold tribal pattern inheres in that premonarchic time. I am perfectly willing to grant that a tradition of articulating tribes as sons of Jacob was premonarchic. What I am challenging is the premonarchic origin of this precise twelve-son structure of the tradition. That structure is not anchored in specifically premonarchic conditions any more convincingly than is the twelve-tribal scheme of the various lists we have surveyed. G may very well have contained the motif of representing the tribes as sons of Jacob, but there is no indication that G contained the motif in a twelvefold form.

Finally, among the narratives, the twelve pillars set up at the foot of the mountain in E's account of the covenant at Horeb (Exod. 24:4) makes perhaps the strongest claim to a premonarchic origin. It is widely held that we have here a form of the covenant celebration among the tribes observed at some northern sanctuary, perhaps at Shechem. The participation of lay males in the ceremony and the casting of the blood on altar and people give credence to the view that the passage reflects a premonarchic ritual. Nonetheless, it is striking that the twelve stone pillars play no further visible role in the account. Nothing is written on them, nor is the sacrificial blood applied to them, nor are they said to have witnessed the covenant. The twelve stone pillars appear totally uncoordinated with the flow of ritual action. In Joshua 24, which may fairly be ascribed in its core to premonarchic northern Israel, the analogous ceremony has only *one*, not twelve stones, and it is given the specific function of witness to the terms of the covenant. The presence of the single stone in Joshua 24 suggests that one or more stone pillars may have been mentioned in Exodus 24, but that this element was altered by a monarchic traditionist who specified twelve stones. When that alteration was introduced, the pillars lost their original ritual contextual meaning and the traditionist was unable to tie them into the sequence of ritual activity. Conceivably the twelve stones of Exodus 24:4 were connected with known ritual practice at some date (note the twelve stones at Gilgal); but, as in Joshua 4:19–20, nothing firmly attaches the practice to premonarchic times, and their inclusion at Horeb runs against the continuity and cohesion of the covenant-concluding actions there described.[270]

All in all, these narrative references to the purported operation of the twelve-tribe scheme in premonarchic Israel are pale and formalistic. Not one of them carries us into the unquestioned world of premonarchic Israel. Every one of them can be explained as a retrojection. In the narratives of Judges 3—16 and the early source of Samuel, where we might expect to learn something about the twelve-tribe arrangement, the sources are silent.

We have seen that all the references to a premonarchic origin of the twelve-tribe system are suspect and perfectly intelligible as later editorial retrojections into the period. Yet, if the rootage of the twelve-tribe scheme is monarchic, a further oddity of the tradition strikes us: namely, the remarkably small number of narrative references in later Israel to the twelve tribes. Ahijah the Shilonite designates Jeroboam king of the north by the symbolic action of tearing a cloak into twelve pieces to represent the tribes (I Kings 11:29–31). Elijah, in what is widely taken as a later intrusion in the story, uses twelve stones to make an altar representative of all Israel (I Kings 18:31–32a). Ezekiel charts a reconstructed land with twelve tribes (Ezek. 47:13; 48:1–7,23–29). Elsewhere, the many references to "the tribes (of Israel)" are unqualified by the number "twelve." Indeed, we are led to wonder: What can have been the setting and meaning of a twelve-tribe scheme which was able to affect so profoundly the traditional formulation of the tribes in all kinds of lists but has left so few traces in narration, either in premonarchic or in monarchic times?

32.2 Levi Omitted: Twelve Tribes as David's Administrative Districts

The whole traditional superstructure of the twelve-tribe scheme must have a resting place and a foundation in the social organization of Israel. Had we only the rather meager narrative allusions to twelve tribes we might not have thought the scheme of much importance; in fact, we would hardly be able to speak of a twelve-tribe "scheme" at all. It is the use of the twelve-tribe motif in ritual descriptions and in tribal lists which shows that it was a scheme with some very specific historical context and function. Yet the memory of the twelve-tribe scheme's historical origin seems rather effectively effaced from the Old Testament. Still, we do have something to go on. We can narrow the range within which the conception must necessarily have arisen. The *terminus a quo* is the rise of the monarchy. That we have already shown. The *terminus ad quem* must be the division of the kingdom. That is simply enough demonstrated by the fact that the twelve tribes represent the totality of the two kingdoms and, unless it is a sheer product of fancy whose purpose was entirely capricious, the scheme must have been grounded in a setting when all the tribes were conscious of their unity and when to refer to the twelve tribes would have been to refer to a functioning organizational totality. That, of course, was precisely what advocates of the early amphictyony argued and claimed to have shown. We have argued that their proposed milieu is wrong, but their fundamental claim that the twelve-tribe scheme arose as the conceptual correlate of an actual social organizational stage in Israel's life remains correct. We can now assert that the historical origin of the twelve-tribe scheme which the amphictyonic proponents saw in the premonarchic tribal amphictyony actually belonged to the period of the united monarchy.

I further contend that the twelve-tribe scheme arose with the unification of the tribes as a political entity and that the function of the twelve-tribe scheme was practically and theoretically a political function. The major tribal elements for composing such a twelve-tribe scheme were historically at hand as members of Israel. "The tribes of Israel" had long been related religiously in the cult of Yahweh. They had spoken a common language, shared similar socioeconomic institutions, developed a common legal community, cooperated in warfare. But those tribes had been without formally distinguished political unity prior to the monarchy, and they were not an amphictyony requiring that they consist of a specific number of tribes, neither more nor less. They had never thought of themselves as necessarily twelve in number. For most of Israel's premonarchic history, the confederating tribes had been fewer than twelve (e.g., the Song of Deborah represents the tribes as ten in number). As the monarchy took shape, I assume that the tribes had by then attained the number of twelve. But in reaching the figure of twelve, the confederacy did not impose a limit to further membership. I assume that had other groups existed who wished to join Israel, they would not have been barred on the grounds that the confederation of Israel could consist of only twelve tribes. The historical situation on the verge of the monarchy was simply this: twelve tribes, unfettered by amphictyonic preconditions about their exact number, happened to compose the confederacy of Israelite peoples. It was the sudden introduction of monarchic institutions which recast the twelve-tribe confederation into a fixed twelve-tribe scheme.

The hypothesis I propose is as follows: 1. The twelve-tribe scheme was originated by David for administrative purposes in order to recruit the citizen army or militia, and possibly also to raise taxes and to impose the corvée. 2. The twelve-tribe scheme, while not the most rational administrative arrangement, served the important socioreligious transitional function of solidifying David's kingdom on the foundation of the tribal entities of the old Yahwistic association of Israelite peoples. 3. We can explain the different forms in which the twelve-tribe membership is retrojected into early traditions by the shifting relations between these two somewhat disparate functions, namely, the administrative and the symbolic, especially as their intermixture and balance changed radically once the scheme ceased to exist for administrative purposes, which was the case after Solomon reorganized the kingdom on other lines. I shall now attempt to explicate the three aspects of the hypothesis and to offer evidence in their support.

We begin with the fact that King David took a census (II Sam. 24:1–9).[271] Censuses always have the practical aim of registering a population for taxation or draft. David had a highly effective army composed of a core of regular professional troops (partly his own men and partly foreign mercenaries) which could be expanded, as needed, by a muster of the citizen militia. Although II Samuel 24 is silent about the administrative arrangements which followed on the census, I Chronicles 27 gives detailed accounts of two administrative systems. These systems are normally dismissed as imaginative elaborations of conditions in Solomonic or Josianic times.[272] There is no question but that they have been preserved poorly and that the Chronicler himself no longer had any clear conception of the systems he was reporting. It seems to me, however, that Yigael Yadin has correctly discerned within them the outlines of David's military administration and, I may add from my own study, the origin of the twelve-tribe scheme in ancient Israel.[273]

I Chronicles 27:1–15 describes a citizen army composed in monthly aggregations of 24,000, each with a different commander drawn from among the crack members of the career army. The system does not refer to the tribes, except for occasional identifications of the origins of the commanders (e.g., 27:10,12,14). The conception of these verses is so ill-suited to our usual interpretations of the united monarchy that it has usually been set aside as sheer fantasy. Admittedly the numbers are dubiously high (if *'eleph* is "thousand," yielding a total army of 288,000 men) or dubiously low (if *'eleph* is the old muster by *mishpāhāh*). But the method of organizing the militia is a plausible one, as Yadin has suggested, especially in that it steers a middle course between organizing the militia strictly by tribes or strictly by national units in which individuals from all tribes are indiscriminately mixed.

The third option, illustrated by this passage, was to organize the army in twelve reserve formations, on call for one month each year, and composed of permanent units drawn from the tribes, joined in such a way as to yield national units of about equal size, and containing a mixture of the various kinds of weapons and skills for which particular tribes were known—e.g., Benjaminite slingers, Ephraimite archers, etc. Each tribe raised its own quotas for the militia and determined which units would serve in which months. It also supplied officers for its subsidiary units. The national staff, composed of David's "thirty," orchestrated the militia units by assigning elements from the various tribes in accord with tactical needs. The staff also supplied the top commanders for forging the tribal units into wholes and coordinating the militia with the standing career army. On this understanding of the system, the numbers do not appear so excessive, since the twenty-four thousand-man reserve force was drawn from all the tribes as expanded and reconstituted by David in order to incorporate the conquered Canaanite populace.

This system drew on the advantages of both the tribal and national systems while minimizing or eliminating their disadvantages. The tribal system of mustering troops invited feelings of discrimination and unequal treatment, as is abundantly clear in the premonarchic traditions (Judg. 5:16–17; 8:1; 12:1). Under the old system, tribes were tempted to compare their own performance or the demands made upon them favorably or unfavorably with those of the other tribes. It made for tribal divisiveness. It also made for imbalance both in the size of contingents and in fighting styles and strengths of respective tribes. On the other hand, a national call-up of individuals randomly mixed together would have resulted in units poorly trained and badly integrated for instant service. It would be a good organization "on paper," but unpracticed and cumbersome in the field.

A national system of rotating monthly units, composed of permanent tribal sub-units, combined according to overall strategic and tactical needs, reduced the sense of discrimination against particular tribes and also provided units of fighting men who were well-trained and integrated for instant action. It is just such a system that I Chronicles 27:1–15 reflects.

Such a system could function smoothly only if there was a steady tribal supply of units of troops according to quotas agreed on in advance. It is this internal recruitment system, tribe by tribe, which is alluded to in I Chronicles 27:16–22.

The roster of tribes is not directly reflective of the united monarchy nor indeed of any period in Israelite history. It follows the scheme of twelve tribal entities, but the twelve listed are formed by including Levi, West Manasseh, and East Manasseh as full tribes, while omitting Gad and Asher. The deletions of Gad and Asher might be explained as purely arbitrary on the assumption that those tribes occurred last in the order of tribes preferred by the Chronicler (cf. I Chron. 2:1–3). This does not, however, explain the extraordinary reckoning of the two parts of Manasseh as occupying two positions in the roster of twelve tribes. More probable is the hypothesis that the Chronicler here constructs the twelve "tribes" so as to include six Leah tribes and six Rachel tribes in order to picture the two sections of Israel as equally represented in the unity of David's kingdom. To accomplish this feat, two Leah tribes had to be dropped. Levi was retained because of the tradition of its armed militancy. Gad and Asher were omitted as the last two Leah tribes on the list. Also, the Rachel tribes had to be "filled out" by including the two "concubine tribes" of Naphtali and Dan and by artificially counting West Manasseh and East Manasseh as two of the twelve tribes. Just as P often retains premonarchic data alongside later artificial constructions, so here the Chronicler has retained the account of an authentic tribal muster for the national army under David but has set forth an idiosyncratic version of the tribal entities.[274]

The Chronicler speaks of the "commanders of the tribes of Israel" (*sārē shivṭē* Israel, I Chron. 27:22; one officer is called a "prince" or "leader," *nāgîd*, 27:16). Reading this pericope in relation to the preceding one, and noting the references to registering for military service (27:1,23), the officers named may be seen as those in charge of organizing and delivering as required the tribal musters for the national units on a monthly rotation. Few of the officers are otherwise known to us in biblical tradition. Eliab (27:18, reading with LXX, cf. I Chron. 2:13), David's brother, heads the Judean muster. Jaasiel, son of Abner of the house of Saul, heads the Benjaminite muster (27:21). The Iddo ben Zechariah who is in charge of East Manasseh in the land of Gilead may be the father of Ahinadab, who was Solomon's district officer in the same region at Mahanaim (27:21; cf. I Kings 4:14). Possibly the Hashabiah ben Kemuel listed over the Levites is identical with Hashabiah the Hebronite who, with 1,700 of "his brethren," had charge of "the worship of Yahweh and the service of the king" in West Jordan (27:17; cf. I Chron. 26:30).

It is also probable that the officers listed as "over the tribes" were not only for purposes of tribal military muster but also for taxation in kind and for supply of men for corvée service. It is to this division of the tribes by David into administrative sub-units of his kingdom that the "tribal allotments" of Joshua 13—19 largely refer. We have seen that the main outlines of the tribal boundaries there described fit David's period very well. Of course, Joshua 13—19 does not stand in the precise form of a docket from David's time. It betrays severe editorial reworking: unevenness in detail, gaping omissions, conflation of data, fusion of styles, and accommodation to the narrative context of the settlement period. It is not by any means a simple or complete totality, but its most distinctive historico-territorial features locate it securely in the tribally drawn administrative subdivisions of David's kingdom.

My hypothesis assumes that the roster of the twelve tribes in the form David gave it followed this sequence: Reuben, Simeon, Gad, Judah, Issachar, Zebulun, Ephraim, Manasseh (or Manasseh, Ephraim), Benjamin, Dan, Asher, Naphtali, i.e., the form we know from Numbers 1 and 26. These "tribes" were viable traditional entities which had retained their distinctiveness, although they certainly must have varied markedly in their population sizes, socioeconomic styles of life, and politico-military strength. I assume that they were the actual total of self-consciously distinct tribes in Israel in David's time. They were made to correspond to the number of months into which the militia would be divided for reserve service, even though this meant including tribes which were weak and on the verge of extinction as autonomous social entities. The declining tribes were "revived" as coequal administrative units. Had David's taxation program been heavy, the socioeconomic disproportion in these tribal districts would have been subversive of his administrative intent. Beyond possible limited use of the corvée, it may be doubted that David imposed any direct taxation on the tribes. His crown estates and tribute from conquered areas in Transjordan and Syria were sufficient to meet his rather modest needs by comparison with Solomon's later extravagancies. The inequity in population and surplus wealth from tribe to tribe would not have been a serious problem for military organization as long as the army was formed by monthly reserve units in which tribal contingents were intermixed on a proportional basis. This would serve to explain why traditionally important but territorially limited tribes such as Benjamin, and demographically depleted or virtually socially defunct tribal groups such as Reuben and Simeon, could be included along with the large tribes of Ephraim, Manasseh, and Judah.

In other words, David made the best administrative use he could of subdivisions of his kingdom which were in fact traditional and tribal. For military purposes it was acceptable because the tribal components of the militia, although recruited tribally, were organized for battle on a nontribal basis. Taxes in kind and corvée were not so extensive that the demographically and economically inequitable tribal subdivisions were impossible to manage. Yet the basically improvisational character of the tribal administrative arrangement for the new kingdom was such that it could hardly cope with vast new administrative functions. In fact, the arrangement barely outlasted the reign of David. Solomon was simply forced to redistrict his kingdom on fundamentally different lines once he decided to support a lavish court apparatus through direct contributions from the several districts.

We have proposed that the tribal members of David's administrative sub-units were those listed in Numbers 1 and 26, namely, excluding Levi and replacing Joseph with Ephraim and Manasseh. I have already contended that the lists in Numbers retain accurate memories of old Israelite tribal musters by *'ªlāphīm*, with some incomplete and heterogeneous recollections of the names of some of the *mishpāhōth/'ªlāphīm*. The twelve-tribe structure of the lists, however, gives no similar indication of being premonarchic. If I am correct that the accretion of tribes to the confederacy of Israel had reached the total of twelve at the verge of the monarchy, it remains a possibility that Saul, by mustering and coordinating a national army from the tribes, took the step which prompted David to make those same twelve tribes the basic administrative units of his kingdom.

Whether Saul took such a first step in conceptualizing a twelve-tribe united militia depends in part on how one reads the strange account in II Samuel 2:12–17 of the ritualistic battle conducted by young men from the forces of the house of Saul and the forces of David: "Then they arose and passed over by number, twelve for Benjamin and Ishbosheth the son of Saul, and twelve of the servants of David" (vs. 15).[275] If this is a ritual combat in which the participants represent the whole armies in microcosm, the fact that they are twelve in number may point to the articulation of Israel's militia in twelve parts. Since the incident occurs prior to David's installation as king over all Israel, we may conclude that the twelvefold segmentation of Israel's army may indeed have been introduced by Saul. Still, the suspicion cannot be suppressed that twelve in this account may be a later traditionist's insertion in the light of David's full-blown tribal administrative organization. But even if we grant the possibility that Saul took the first step in launching the twelve-tribe system, it was a modest one at best. It was David, in that case, who took over the twelve-tribe militia system from Saul, solidified it by means of a census, sketched the boundaries, totally reshaped the manner of calling up and composing the military units, and, as we shall argue shortly, probably also invited tribal representatives to participate in the Jerusalem cult of the relocated ark.

32.3 Levi Included: Weakened Functions of the Twelve-Tribe System after Solomon's Administrative Reorganization

My hypothesis further posits that the second major form of tribal reckoning, the form Noth and most others have taken to be the original one, was in fact secondary in development. I refer of course to the enumeration: Reuben, Simeon, Levi, Judah, Issachar, Zebulun, Joseph, Benjamin, Asher, Gad, Dan, Naphtali. As long as one believes that the tribal roster reflects actual membership in a premonarchic amphictyony, it is altogether logical to regard the roster including Levi and Joseph as an early one. Later on, Levi is not counted as one of the landed tribes and Joseph is not a functioning entity but has been totally replaced by its subdivision into Ephraim and Manasseh. On such a theory, the only place for this sort of amphictyonic tribal roster must have been in the early stages of the confederacy. But once the amphictyonic model is set aside, we have, I believe, a completely satisfactory way of locating this seemingly erratic, rootless scheme in its own proper milieu. The milieu of the "Levi-Joseph" tribal roster is the period in Solomon's reign when the twelve-tribe system had lost its administrative political function as assigned by David, i.e., when its chief purpose had become one of cultural-national conceptualization and, to a lesser degree, one of circumscribed religious cultic activity.

The watershed development for the twelve-tribe scheme was Solomon's reorganization of the kingdom on lines that were no longer primarily tribal and that explicitly dropped the tribal designations for the administrative districts, except in a minority of cases where the tribal lines accorded with demographic and socioeconomic administrative equity (I Kings 4:7–19).[276] David's concessions to tribal sentiments were replaced by Solomon's administrative structure proceeding along the lines of demonstrated bureaucratic rationality. The new districts of Solomon were responsible, through their crown-appointed officers, for support of the court on monthly rotation. They were also the means for gathering the corvée. Both taxation in kind and enforced service to the crown were heavily imposed by Solomon to maintain his opulent building program. Although nothing is said of it directly, it may be assumed that the army muster was raised according to the new districts. The key added factor in Solomon's arrangement was his appointment of officers who operated in the districts by direct command from his court.

Centralization of economic and military control of the populace meant that a fundamental conceptual change had occurred between David's view of his kingdom and Solomon's view of his. David, whether by choice or necessity, conceived of his kingdom as *coordinating* the economic and military contributions of the several traditional tribal entities in Israel, even though they were necessarily expanded and modified to include the new territorial conception of Israel. Although Canaanite entities, previously foreign to the Israelite confederacy, were assimilated into the administrative structure, they were included insofar as possible as elements within the tribal scheme. Solomon saw the inconsistency of this approach, probably from the bitter experience of being unable to control taxes and troops as he wished. Solomon, therefore, deliberately conceived of his kingdom as *imposing* economic and military requirements on the populace conceived as royal subjects whose Israelite or Canaanite backgrounds were immaterial to the dynastic claims he made upon them. This is another way of saying that with Solomon the hierarchic claim of Near Eastern monarchy emerged so decisively that he drew the administrative consequences and centralized his control over the peoples. This is not to say that traditional tribal conceptions were altogether lost on a national level. In a moment we shall attempt to discern the forms they took. It is to say, however, that for the immediate administrative purposes of Solomon's kingdom, the traditional tribal entities ceased to have any substantive significance. The two chief powers of the state, to tax in kind or in service and to raise an army, were now no longer exercised by the tribal apparatus. The reasons for which David had devised the twelve-tribe system ceased to exist. As a purely administrative measure, that system lapsed.

This confronts us with the question: If the twelve-tribe system orginated as a political administrative device, why did it survive its abandonment for that purpose?

The answer lies in the second part of our claim about David's creation of the twelve-tribe system. We saw that David did not simply cut the scheme out of whole cloth. His originality was to supply twelvefoldness (possibly anticipated by Saul) and the centralized political and religious focal point at Jerusalem. David did not, however, fabricate the tribal entities; they were preexistent, and he manipulated them within a certain range, as when he incorporated conquered or compliant Canaanite territories into the tribal framework. David's twelve-tribe scheme was thus an acknowledgement of the socioreligious base of his kingdom. His fantastic success, in spite of revolts in his later reign, seems to have lain not only in his power to conquer enemies and to centralize power but equally in his capacity to concede the socioreligious tribal base of his power by honoring a considerable measure of local administrative autonomy within the several tribal districts.

Furthermore, it is reasonable to speculate about further functions of the twelve-tribe system in David's reign. David was not only administrative and military head of Israel. In his elevation to the office of king, he also became the juridical and religious head of Israel. It is clear, both from the contrived legal appeal of the woman of Tekoa to David (II Sam. 14:1–20) and from the base of Absalom's revolt among citizens who felt a legal default on David's part (II Sam. 15:1–6), that the king held the titular office of chief justice of the realm. This meant that David had to see to it that justice was done in the land. It did not require him to create a whole new system of courts and to appoint judges at every level. Silence on this matter suggests that he acknowledged the de facto operation of tribal justice as de jure for his kingdom. In fact, such an understanding was probably one of the terms of covenant by which the tribal elders designated David as king in Israel. He did not have to collect a precedent-code of law under royal aegis, since Israel's laws were already operative as intertribal confederate law.[277] Legal disputes involving royal officers and crown land were perhaps dealt with by special provisions, but the judgment and execution apparently remained within the jurisdiction of the tribal legal system. Wherever applicable, offenders were handed over to justice in their respective tribes. Perhaps only the citizens of Jerusalem, not assigned to any single tribe, and foreigners in royal service had to be treated in some extratribal legal framework. The king himself entered directly into the judicial scene only when some particularly aggravated case for which no precedents existed, or where two valid principles of law were in direct conflict, required that he do so. We can imagine that he would seek to minimize such cases and that in practice the tribal legal system was expanded to deal with all possible cases within his kingdom. First Chronicles 23:4 may correctly recall that some Levites were appointed as judges by David, conceivably in connection with their settlement in Levitical cities at key points on the border or in regions heavily Canaanite in population, but this feature of the tradition is of questionable antiquity.

Similarly, in the case of his titular role as chief priest, David showed that he could properly preside at the transfer of the ark to his new political center of Jerusalem. We need no theories of the divinity of the king to explain such a royal initiative in Israel. Sacrifice was a wholly proper function of any family head according to the narrative accounts for early Israel. David as head of his people could make cultic arrangements for his people subject only to their consent, which he seems to have secured by making certain that the foci of religion in his kingdom would be the well-known and beloved cultic objects and practices from the tribal past: the ark, the tent, the ephod, and the bronze serpent.[278]

No doubt much of the reason for David's success in reconstellating the cult at Jerusalem was that no amphictyony in the strict sense had existed in Israel. There was no single obligatory tribal center that Jerusalem had to fight to replace. There were many centers, and Jerusalem could be introduced as merely another such center, albeit an increasingly crucial one as a result of royal patronage and concentration of national cult objects. Further, the old cultic centers were not abolished by David. His act of cultic concentration on Jerusalem did not appear as a deliberate displacement of existing worship at other places but as a supplement. The great festivals continued to be observed at many points throughout the land at the same time they were observed in Jerusalem; indeed, some of the festivals important to the tribal centers may not at first have been observed at all in Jerusalem. The distinctive thing about the Jerusalem celebration was that it was consciously nationalized, and by association with the royal political center of the land, its cult attained increasing stature. To the Jerusalem cult we can well imagine that all the tribes sent representatives, and it is very likely that in David's twelve-tribe system we have a formal framework for the participation of the tribal representatives in Jerusalem cultic festivities, a reality which formed the basis for all later retrojections of a twelve-tribe cult into the settlement and wilderness periods.

Of Solomon's judicial system we know next to nothing. Presumably he continued David's procedures, since little was to be gained by trying to uproot the longstanding tribal system of justice. Second Chronicles 19:5–10 tells of Jehoshaphat appointing judges "in the land in all the fortified cities of Judah, city by city," and in Jerusalem he designated certain priests and family heads as adjudicators in difficult cases. If this is an accurate memory, it seems to imply that such direct royal control of the judicial system was an innovation.[279] Even then, the wording permits the interpretation that the appointees were only assigned in the more recently established or fortified cities of Judah and thus supplemented rather than replaced tribal justice. It appears, then, that the centralization Solomon undertook in economic and military affairs did not extend to the judicial system. Here the tribes continued to function, but their twelveness was not important in this regard and in practice judgment was rendered by local bodies of elders for the most part. Since the tribes were apparently not contributing judicial officers to an appellate system of courts, exact jurisdictions were left to local custom. The sharp administrative delineation of tribes necessary for central governmental taxation and military muster was not demanded by the generally decentralized judicial autonomy of the tribes.

The one point at which the twelvefoldness of the tribes, conceived as a functional totality, might have been important after Solomon's administrative reorganization may have been in the continuation of tribal representation in the Jerusalem cult. Yet here we get the impression that Solomon in building a temple transformed the Jerusalem cult from that of the nationalization of intertribal Yahwism to that of a private royal celebration of the dynastic deity. The ark of Yahweh, symbol of the intertribal faith, was swallowed up in an opulent royal chapel and effectively hidden from the view of the celebrating assembly. It is not likely under the circumstances that tribal representation of the sort consistent with David's cultic intent continued in the Solomonic cult, or at any rate with the same significance. It may have straggled on as a formality, but already the tribal entities were feeling a less direct stake in Solomon's regime than they had felt in David's. Thus, the centralizing program of Solomon in taking direct royal control of taxation and army muster, plus maximizing the corvée, was complemented by his appropriation of the Jerusalem cult as a royal cult. The end result was the virtual emasculation of the twelve-tribe system as David had conceived and employed it when he was obliged to come to terms with the strong tribal socioreligious foundations of his kingdom.

We must look to the events surrounding the break-up of the united kingdom for an answer to the question: Why did the twelve-tribe scheme survive at all, once it had outlived its administrative purposes? The answer seems to lie in the way it came to serve the need for continuing expression of the unity of Israel under Yahweh in the face of political and social divisiveness. Ahijah the Shilonite was still able to think of the constituency of Israel under the rubric of twelve tribes when he symbolically assigned ten tribes to Jeroboam and granted two to David's line. But once the split occurred, the twelveness of the tribal system was effectively ruptured as a practical administrative measure. The twelve-tribe system could survive henceforth only as a traditional conception for all Israel or in an attenuated or altered form as a proxy format in cultic organization.

When Jeroboam drove the Levites out of the north (II Chron. 11:13–15; 13:9), he did so because he identified them correctly as instruments of the Davidic dynasty. Since the Chronicler's remark is set in an exceedingly antinorthern context, we should perhaps read it to mean that Jeroboam's purge was not of all Levites but only of all those whose loyalty to his new regime was lacking or in doubt (cf. I Kings 12:31; 13:33).[280] That Jeroboam clearly intended to continue, indeed to restore a pure form (i.e., a pre-Jerusalemite form) of the cult of Yahweh, indicates that he retained some priestly continuity with the older Yahwism. Very probably the division was made in large measure along the lines of those Levites who had long been in the north (e.g., at the shrine of Dan) and those who had been newly established there under David and Solomon. At any rate, a large body of Levites was expelled from the north on the grounds that they formed a fifth column of a decided pro-Davidic stamp.

Once driven out of the north and confined to Judah and parts of Benjamin, the Levites were in a problematic position. Their firm lodgement in the royal scheme of David and Solomon was shattered, and they now had to fall back to greatly reduced significance in a truncated southern kingdom. Previously they had no practical place to fill in the twelve-tribe system as a scheme of administrative districts. They were not taxed in kind or in service, and they did not fight as part of the general militia. They were an arm of the royal state useful for consolidating a far-flung kingdom by wedding the old Yahwistic confederate ideology to the Davidic state. But now the twelve-tribe scheme was otiose in all the senses for which it had been established by David. Even its attenuated function in the cult required establishment on some other basis. No more would the representatives of the ten tribes of the north come to Jerusalem to celebrate the feasts and to symbolize the unity of tribal Israel under the political aegis of a southern dynasty.

The twelve-tribe system was converted totally into a traditional concept which expressed the original and ideal unity of all Yahwists. Whether the sundered tribes, two in the south and ten in the north, served any practical administrative functions in the respective kingdoms is another matter, which I do not intend to pursue at this point. However, if they did, it was necessarily as the two southern tribes and/or as the ten northern tribes and not as the united twelve tribes of all Israel. The utmost the twelve-tribe concept could do politically was to express the claim of David's dynasty to the rebellious north. With each passing year's failure to reconquer or to woo the northern tribes, even that political claim faded further into the background. Only for Josiah could it once again have viable political meaning, and then only for two decades at most.

Some remnant of the former cultic celebration involving twelve tribal representatives in Jerusalem may have survived. In place of the actual twelve-tribe representatives gathered at the ark in David's reign or present in the outer court of Solomon's temple, proxy representatives may have been appointed to symbolize the religious unity of all Israel. One psalm refers to tribes in a cultic procession at the temple and may be a survival of this proxy cult of the twelve tribes in the post-Solomonic Jerusalem temple (Ps. 68:24[25]–27[28]).[281] Without naming any specific tribes, Psalm 122 speaks of Jerusalem, "to which the tribes go up, the tribes of Yah, as was decreed for Israel, to give thanks to the name of Yahweh" (vs. 4). Whether the psalm refers directly to the living unity of intertribal worship at Jerusalem under David or Solomon, or points back to that reality as a normative concept now dead in practice or observed only by proxy, the basic conception of an inclusive participation by the tribes in the Jerusalem cult is strongly advanced.

The real force of the twelve-tribe notion from Rehoboam onwards was in its conceptualization of Israel's encompassing unity as a community of Yahwists, north and south. But once it became a traditional expression of that religious unity, chiefly entertained in the south—which alone lived with the hope of politically reuniting all Yahwists—the twelve-tribe roster of David's creation was immediately recognized as inaccurate. If it intended to designate the totality of Israel, David's version of the twelve tribes had one glaring omission. *It did not include Levi.* As an administrative instrument, the twelve-tribe roster without Levi was an accurate reflection of that tribe's separate status. As a religious concept, a twelve-tribe roster without Levi was a gross misrepresentation of that group's tremendous importance to Yahwism. Therefore, it became imperative to introduce Levi to the schema, where it was inserted in a position among the Leah tribes. The linkage of Simeon and Levi in the tribal blessing of Genesis 49:5–7 was the basis for retrojecting the same pair of tribes awkwardly and inconsistently into the narrative of Genesis 34:25,30 (cf. note 213). It is not clear whether the Simeon-Levi coupling in Genesis 49:5–7 predated or antedated the revision of the twelve-tribe system so as to include Levi. The notion that Levi was once a nonpriestly and landed tribe is based largely on the erroneous insertion of Simeon-Levi into Genesis 34. By itself, Genesis 49:5–7 in no way necessitates that the Levi there condemned for its violence was a nonpriestly tribe.

The listing of Levi in a twelve-tribe sequence was introduced after the Davidic system lapsed and after the system was transformed from a practical political to a religious symbolic function. The inclusion of Levi in the twelve-tribe roster makes no claim about Levi as a secular landed tribe comparable to the other tribes, any more than does Genesis 49:5–7. Levi's inclusion as one of "the twelve" rounds out the traditional religious totality of Yahwists comprising Israel.

Yet to insert Levi in the twelve-tribe conceptual scheme meant that it was no longer twelve tribes but *thirteen*, an awkwardly uneven number and one that militated against the accustomed enumeration since David's time. Levi's claim was unimpeachable, but what tribe could now be omitted? Since we posit that the "Levi-Joseph" version of the twelve tribes is Judahite in origin and later than the division of the united kingdom in its fixed form, although it may well have begun

to take shape at any time after Solomon's administrative reorganization, it is easy
to reply: any tribe could have been omitted other than those in the southern
kingdom, i.e., other than Judah, Simeon, and possibly Benjamin. But to omit any
tribe arbitrarily would have been to strike a blow at the completeness which the
concept aimed to express. Therefore, the logical recourse was to conflate two
tribes, but to do so in such a way that both of the tribes would be represented in a
tertium quid.

The way this was done was to fix upon the memory that the largest and most
important tribes of the north, Manasseh and Ephraim, had originally been one
before they so spread over the central highlands, and even into Transjordan, that
they became separate entities. They were known once to have been the single
tribe, "Joseph." This tradition seems to have had a sound basis, going well back
beyond the novelistic schema of the Genesis account which pictures Joseph as the
father of Ephraim and Manasseh. It is directly alluded to, as we have seen, in the
premonarchic narrative of Joshua 17:14–18 (where "Ephraim and Manasseh" in
vs. 17 is secondary and anachronistic) and also in the poetic blessing of Genesis
49:22–26 and apparently also in the original form of Deuteronomy 33:13–17. We
may also note "the house of Joseph" in Judges 1:22,35. Therefore, without doing
violence to the traditional memories, a method was found for including Levi and
retaining the twelvefold structure of the tribal roster.

32.4 Summary and Synthesis

With this kind of understanding of the origin and development of the twelve-tribe
system, it becomes possible to understand the variety of traditions about the exact
identities and proper ordering of the twelve tribes. All these traditions can be
understood either as versions of David's twelve-tribe administrative system or as
versions of the post-Solomonic twelve-tribe traditional religious concept. The
major narrative traditions of J/E were taking shape just as the twelve-tribe system
as a basis for administration was originating and then undergoing transformation
into a symbolic construct. These developments are reflected in different ways in
the various traditional tribal lists that have survived. We can also understand why
the twelve-tribe motif is sparsely expressed in narrative, both before and after
David's time. It is not mentioned in any text known to be pre-Davidic because the
system as such did not exist, even though the tribal members of Israel were filling
out to an eventual total of twelve by the time of Saul and David. It is not mentioned
often in narrative from David's time onward, because it was not a living functional
system administratively for longer than thirty-five or forty years. Early in
Solomon's reign the system was rooted out of its setting in political administration
and thereafter had to be treated in other ways. The administrative twelve-tribe
system was already dysfunctional by the time the court historian of David's reign
and the Yahwist wrote, assuming them both to have written after Solomon's
reorganization of administration.

David's experiment in monarchic administration based on tribal divisions had served an important consolidating, transitional function. When Solomon felt the need for more sophisticated administration, and was confident of the power to carry out a thorough administrative reorganization, David's transitional scheme was abolished in one stroke. No records of the tribal district officers, analogous to those for Solomon's newly created districts, survived from David's time, and that was obviously because there never had been such officers appointed by the crown. The district heads were the tribal heads who undertook, as part of their pact with David at Hebron, to meet agreed quotas of militia. The tension between David's impulse to organize his kingdom tightly from the top and his desire to give scope to the tribes is reflected in the dispute over the census, which is reported not to have been fully carried through (I Chronicles 21:6 says that not only Levi but Benjamin was omitted, and II Samuel 24:3–4 recounts Joab's strong objections to taking a census). Behind these reports probably lies a compromise decision of David simply to levy quotas on all the tribes, leaving it to them to meet the quotas in any way they saw fit. He had to settle for a system in which the tribes policed their own contributions to the crown in return for the security which David's centralized power offered them militarily. Once Solomon struck out on the course of direct administrative control of his provinces, David's compromise solution was forgotten and with it the original locus of the twelve-tribe system. The way was open to generalize the twelve-tribe system and to employ it in the traditions as an encompassing conception read back into the earliest days of Israel's history. It became equivalent to talking about the unity of the Israelite people from Moses onwards, and it could even be retrojected into the grand genealogical design of the twelve sons of Jacob.

Nevertheless, traces of the administrative function of the system survived. We have seen that one such survival appears in the docket(s) of tribal administrative boundaries and cities which gave content to the tribal allotments in Joshua 13—19. Those allotments comprise one instance where a list cast in the twelve-tribe framework carries us directly into the original setting of the twelve-tribe system. Another, although in far sketchier and confused form, is the list of the tribal officers responsible for the monthly muster of troops for David's reserve militia as preserved in I Chronicles 27:16–22. As far as I can judge, all the other lists, especially those retrojected into the premonarchic period, use the twelve-tribe system anachronistically. This usage was rooted in the sound memory that old Israel had formed an intertribal confederacy, but it involved the mistaken belief that the twelve-member version of that confederacy from which David's system was congealed had also obtained throughout earlier times—indeed, in the traditionists' view, from Moses onwards. So, we must constantly distinguish between the twelve-tribe formula that frames these lists and the frequent authentic materials within them attesting to features of the old confederacy.

33

Greek Amphictyony and Israelite Confederacy: Structural-Functional and Sociohistorical Comparisons

This part began with an explication of Noth's amphictyonic model of old Israel and a rebuttal of its appropriateness at any other than the most general levels of organizational analysis. It was seen that the actual and supposed distinctive traits of the amphictyony are not demonstrable in old Israel. Next, in an aside to the main line of argument, I tried to show how the twelve-tribe scheme, on which Noth based much of his case, can be explained along entirely different lines. There remains the task of assessing the overall structural-functional positions of the Greek amphictyony and of the Israelite confederacy in their respective societies. The basic structural-functional analysis must be supplemented by historical understanding of the trajectories of development in Greek and Israelite societies as a whole.

I begin by summarizing certain comparative and contrasting traits of the two confederate designs that have been developed with greater or lesser fullness in the preceding discussion:

Comparable Traits of the Greek Amphictyony and the Israelite Confederacy:
* Each is an association of autonomous political units.
* Each supports a common religious cult as the framework of the association.

Traits of the Greek Amphictyony Lacking in the Israelite Confederacy:
* A single (or dual) central shrine and cult is the constitutive feature of the association.
* Membership in the common cult permits innumerable other city-state public cultic commitments.
* An amphictyonic council composed of delegates appointed by each member unit is responsible for the upkeep and protection of the central shrine.
* Amphictyonic members are city-states and not tribes (except for the early Pylaean amphictyony and possibly some of the Old Italian amphictyonies).

Traits of the Israelite Confederacy Lacking in the Greek Amphictyony:
* The confederacy functions as the primary legal community.
* The confederacy coordinates the national military organization.

* The confederacy is committed to a single national deity whose cult is observed at many shrines.

* The confederate organization is a national societal organization encompassing and subsuming *all members* of the society and *all sub-groups* within the society.

Trait Claimed for the Amphictyony but Undemonstrated either for the Greek Amphictyony or for Its Supposed Israelite Counterpart:

* The supposed obligatoriness of precisely six or twelve members in order to maintain the amphictyonic cult on a monthly rota is as yet unproven.

When one surveys this summary result of the comparison of the amphictyony and the Israelite confederacy, it becomes clear that the comparability holds on only two points, namely, the formal likeness of associated autonomous political units and the formal likeness of primary definition of the association in terms of a common religious cult. When, however, these formal similarities are qualified by all the traits present in the one confederate form but absent in the other, this conclusion stands out: *Precisely the general formal similarities between amphictyony and Israelite confederacy involve quite different confederating elements arranged in quite different ways in relation to the overall social systems.* The net result is that the formal similarities tend to diminish as decisive cross-cultural criteria because of the structural-functional dissimilarities of the two confederate forms in their respective total societal settings.

We can best set forth the fundamental contextual discontinuities between amphictyony and Israelite confederacy by offering two tables, (see Charts 6 and 7, pp. 378–381), one of the amphictyony in Hellenic society and the other of the confederacy in Israelite society.

On the basis of the comparison and contrast of traits in the Greek amphictyony and in the Israelite confederacy and their systemic implications when the Greek and Israelite societies are seen as evolving totalities, two major conclusions can be drawn about the fundamental inapplicability of the amphictyonic model to old Israel.

33.1 Structural Levels and Scope of the Entities Compared

The Israelite confederacy comprehends the whole of society, whereas the Greek amphictyony is one very circumscribed form of social organization within a much larger society.

The coalition or confederacy known as "Israel," "Israelites," or "tribes of Israel" was coextensive with Israelite consciousness and culture and embraced all the forms of segmented and cross-cutting social organization. That one of the formal likenesses between the Greek amphictyony and the Israelite confederacy happened to be the central organizational role of a common cult has proven to be much too facile a basis of comparison in two fundamental respects.

First, the comparison ignores the fact that, within the Greek amphictyony proper, the cultic activity was virtually all-consuming, leaving many other social

CHART 6

THE AMPHICTYONY SUBSUMED WITHIN GREEK SOCIETY

HELLENIC CULTURE AND SOCIETY

organized by city-states (with some surviving but diminishing tribal states) variously interconnected by means of military leagues, federal unions, and cultic amphictyonies

THE HELLENIC AMPHICTYONY as a circumscribed cultic community with limited legislative, jural, and military functions, as in the two following examples:

12 member city-states (=CS), with other possible
and actual confederate connections, join together in

7 member city-states (=CS), with other possible
and actual confederate connections, join together in

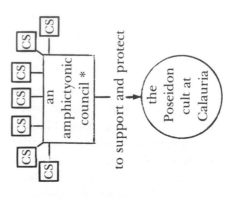

No formal connecting or comprehending links between the Delphic and Calaurian city-states, amphictyonic councils, or cults

CS CS CS CS CS CS CS CS CS CS CS CS

an amphictyonic council

to support and protect → the Apollo cult at Delphi

an amphictyonic council *

to support and protect → the Poseidon cult at Calauria

by discharging the cult's financial affairs, limited legislative decrees, limited adjudication and arbitration, and occasional military action

AMPHICTYONIES SUBSUMED AS ONE AMONG MANY CONFEDERATE FORMS WITHIN THE WIDER HELLENIC SOCIETY

1) Several amphictyonies existed contemporaneously in Hellenic society in accord with the national polytheistic cultic and ideological framework.

2) Participation of a city-state in an amphictyonic cult did not preclude devotion, either of the city-state as a whole or of its individual citizens, to the cults of other gods.

3) Amphictyonies existed not only contemporaneously with one another but contemporaneously with other confederate instrumentalities, such as the military league and the federal union, which involved varying constellations of city-states in convergent and divergent memberships, and which permitted the same city-state to belong to two or more different confederate groupings at the same time.

4) City-states could and did stand apart from any or all confederate affiliations at any given moment, and they could and did change their affiliations in accordance with their own perceptions of self-interest.

by discharging the cult's financial affairs, limited legislative decrees, limited adjudication and arbitration, and occasional military action

---

*The construct of an amphictyonic council and its duties for the Calaurian amphictyony is supplied from the Delphic amphictyony, since we do not have direct information on these matters except for the cult of Apollo at Delphi.

CHART 7

THE ISRAELITE CONFEDERACY COEXTENSIVE WITH ISRAELITE SOCIETY

ISRAELITE CULTURE AND SOCIETY

articulated by extended families, protective associations of families, and tribes cooperating in a common cultic, military, and jural community tending toward standardization of ideology and coordination of action

without rivalry from any other confederate instrumentalities

THE ISRAELITE CONFEDERACY is coextensive with the Israelite culture and society in that it comprehends all ideology and all action in the social system, while distributing power to undertake various forms of social action to the different levels of organization subsumed within the total confederacy, and it does so in lieu of any centralized political power, either in the confederacy as a whole or in its tribal segments.

THE ISRAELITE CONFEDERACY AS A COMMON CULTIC, MILITARY, AND JURAL COMMUNITY

OF INTERACTION WITH SEGMENTED ORGANIZATION

into

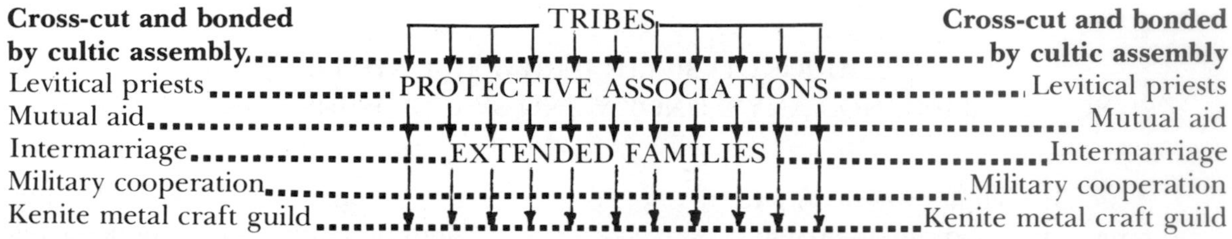

TRIBES

PROTECTIVE ASSOCIATIONS

EXTENDED FAMILIES

Cross-cut and bonded
by cultic assembly,
Levitical priests
Mutual aid
Intermarriage
Military cooperation
Kenite metal craft guild

Cross-cut and bonded
by cultic assembly
Levitical priests
Mutual aid
Intermarriage
Military cooperation
Kenite metal craft guild

All Israelites were within this confederacy of segmented tribal and sub-tribal members—a common cultic, military, and jural community—the Israelite social system. All those not within this confederate communal system were non-Israelites, i.e., "Canaanites," "Egyptians," "Midianites," "Ammonites," "Moabites," "Edomites," etc.

THE ONE CONFEDERACY (contra the many amphictyonies) WITH ITS SEVERAL MODES OF OPERATION (contra the many uncoordinated Hellenic confederate forms) IS COEXTENSIVE WITH THE ISRAELITE CULTURE AND SOCIETY

1) Only one confederacy existed as "Israel," even though it may have subsumed earlier confederacies in its formation and in subsequent increments of membership.

2) Participation of a tribe in "Israel" absolutely excluded from the start any other tribal cult than that of Yahweh, permitting only the continuation of pre-Israelite tribal cult elements which could be reinterpreted and reshaped as Yahwistic cult elements.

3) So far as we can see, the tribal needs for coordinated belief and action were all met within the one embracing confederate framework, so that in Israel all member tribes were joined in a cultic-military-jural communal continuum which left no place for separate uncoordinated, confederate groupings to meet varying sets of needs. To be joined in Israel was to belong to a single system which addressed all dimensions of socioeconomic, military-political, and cultural-religious life.

4) A tribe in Israel had no freedom to stand apart from the confederacy. To be Israelite was to be in the confederate system. A tribe might be lax in its participation, but the formal constitutive obligation to act in and through the common cultic, military, and jural community was absolutely foundational to the Israelite system.

functions to the spheres of the separate city-state members and of other confederate instrumentalities. It has been overlooked, even by so astute an analyst as Noth,
that to acknowledge military and jural functions of the Israelite confederacy fully
as important as its cultic functions, is in reality to recognize that the confederacy
operated over a total range of social-systemic responsibility far in excess of the
jurisdiction of the Delphic amphictyony at its apogee of influence.

In saying this, I intend to make clear that I do not go so far in my criticism of
Noth as to dismantle an overarching confederate structure for old Israel, in the
way, for example, that R. Smend does when he insists that the military league for
holy war and the cultic covenant community were two entirely separate institutional systems which only merged just before the rise of the Israelite kingdom.[282]
Nor can I follow A. D. H. Mayes who, after a trenchant critique and rejection of
Noth's amphictyony theory, goes still further in denying any definitive social-
structural unity embracing all the Israelite tribes (whether cultic, military, or
sociopolitical) prior to Saul's military actions which permitted Judah to join with
the other tribes.[283] For Mayes the sole ground of unity was worship of Yahweh,
which had been spread among northern and southern tribes by two groups
branching off from Kadesh in the presettlement period. There are valid objections lodged by Smend and Mayes to the usual ways of conceiving Israel's confederate unity. In sum, however, I do not find that Smend sustains his case for a
complete dichotomy between holy war and tribal confederacy, nor do I see that
Mayes, after cogently demolishing the amphictyonic version of confederacy, has
offered adequate grounds for explaining the unity of Israelite consciousness and
practice in the period before Saul. In fact, once we recognize that an amphictyony
is only one eccentric form among countless confederate forms, the objections of
Smend and Mayes largely evaporate as evidence against confederacy as such. With
these and other critics of the amphictyony, I agree on the inappropriateness of the
amphictyonic model as a comprehensive societal model for early Israel. Nevertheless, a social-structural bond, more encompassing than separate sub-alliances for
warfare and for cult and more precise than widely diffused belief in Yahweh, is
necessary to account for the emergent unity of premonarchic Israel under the
turbulent and hostile conditions of Late Bronze–Early Iron Canaan.

Secondly, the comparison between the Greek and Israelite common cults ignores the fact that, vis-à-vis all the national and cultic activities of the society, the
narrowly focused cultic commitment of the Greek amphictyony was exceedingly
circumscribed and partial; it made absolutely no claim to be the sole city-state cult
of the participating member, much less the one definitive national cult. By sharp
contrast, the Yahwistic cult of Israel's confederacy was both inclusively national
and deliberately, even vehemently, exclusive of any other national or tribal or
local cult. The multiple forms of Israelite cult all had to be justified and assimilated
as modes of worship of the single deity. Moreover, it needs to be emphasized that
the considerable versatility of the Israelite cult in adapting forms from the cults of

proto-Israelite deities was decisively controlled by the initial purgative, intensely puritanical drive of Yahwism to exclude all those religious concepts and lavish ceremonial practices which served to represent the deity as the guarantor of centralized oppressive politics and thus a support for self-propagating elites.

Put in another way, the amphictyony in Greece merely represented one way in which groups of already formed cultural and political entities expressed one out of many religious interests and commitments and served thereby at least some of their numerous political aims. For Israel, on the other hand, the cult of its deity was from the start sole and exclusive in intent and grew increasingly so in concept and in practice. Moreover, for Israel the very autonomy of the several member tribes was coterminous with the confederate cultic union. The cohesion and viability of Israelite culture and independent polity were predicated upon the union of the tribes in its cultic, military, jural, and socioeconomic dimensions. In the most literal sense we can say that the Israelite confederacy was the frame for Israelite culture and society. Such a claim in the case of the Greek amphictyony would be absurd. The most that could be said is that some groups of Dorian and pre-Dorian tribes, such as those associated with Pylae in earlier forms of the Delphic amphictyony, may have developed regional consciousness, culture, and political strength through their primitive amphictyony. But we should have to know much more about the obscure beginnings of the Pylaean amphictyony to be at all sure of such a guess.[284] On the larger scale, there is simply no evidence whatsoever that pan-Hellenic culture and society stemmed from or grew up alongside some early comprehensive intertribal amphictyony.

The primary constitutional character of the confederacy in Israel, vis-à-vis the secondary or tertiary role of the Greek amphictyony, can be summed up in this manner: If we were to strip away analytically the cultic, military, socioeconomic, and jural structure of the Israelite confederacy, Israel would simply fall apart into autonomous tribes without any discernible defining relationships among them and without any distinguishable consciousness or culture. If we were to strip away analytically the Greek amphictyonic structure, all its member city-states (or tribes insofar as we can discern them) would continue their own social and political identities without serious disturbance, and they would continue to exhibit a general Hellenic consciousness and culture. Such a radical negative analytic exercise speaks volumes for the fundamental structural discontinuity between Israelite confederacy and Greek amphictyony.

33.2 Organizational Zones of the Entities Compared

The Israelite confederacy was a consciously contrived surrogate state for its peoples, indeed a veritable "anti-state," whereas the Greek amphictyony was a limited way for autonomous city-states to achieve certain specific purposes.

Old Israel before the monarchy was a stateless society. It organized in social revolt against Near Eastern kingship, and it boldly strove to achieve the cultic,

military, socioeconomic, and jural coordination of a new society without recourse
to the socioeconomically repressive institutions of central government and social
stratification. The confederating tribes were embarked on a critical undertaking
on unfamiliar ground, and the very survival of all the component peoples hung
upon the success of the coordinating and unifying ties plaited from many
socioeconomic, cultic, military, and jural strands.

In amphictyonic Greece, political centralization had already arrived by the time
we have any clear view of the amphictyony. J. A. O. Larsen, in describing the
different confederate forms in ancient Greece, points out that in parts of Greece
the older Dorian tribal organization survived for some time, untouched by or
resistant to urbanism, and reliant on popular assemblies of all men under arms or
on councils of nobles, sometimes introducing the chiefdom. Some of these tribes
were federated into what he calls "tribal ethnic states."[285] Larsen is not entirely
clear here in his typology for the state, since he sometimes implies a state in the
absence of chiefdom. In sum, he seems to point to a boundary-line situation in
terms of the zones of social organization we earlier reviewed; i.e., these Dorian
tribal organizations represent the tail-end of decentralized tribalism in Greece
giving way to urbanization and monarchy or oligarchy.

For our purposes, what is decisive is that we have no indications of the amphictyony functioning as the framework for constellating tribal organization. Of
course, I concede that this may be a sheer accident of tradition. We do know that
the Pylaen amphictyony was originally organized at a tribal level, but how intrinsic
that organization was to the overall adjustment of social organization among its
members we have not the faintest idea. Doubtless that is a subject calling for
further research; but on the basis of what classical scholars have been able to tell us
thus far, we have no reason to attribute a constitutional sociopolitical role to the
early tribal amphictyony in Greece. Indeed, we cannot even find evidence that the
amphictyony was widely distributed in tribal Greece. In this regard, the Pylaean
amphictyony still appears highly erratic.

When the amphictyony appeared in historical times in Greece, it was by no
means a primary factor in shaping Hellenic consciousness, culture, social organization, or political structure. It did perform certain cultural and political functions
of at least secondary importance, particularly in later political machinations
among the various city-states and in the implementation of imperial designs (both
by Greek city-states and by outside powers such as Macedon and Rome), but these
developments of the amphictyony appear adventitiously against the ground of the
already separately existing amphictyonic cults and the already formed city-states
with their pan-Hellenic mentality and culture. In fact, some of the later so-called
amphictyonies, such as the Delian league and the Panionion, were such peculiar
political formations that they seem only tenuously connected with the amphictyonies of mainland Greece. Athens manipulated the Delian league as an instru-

ment of its imperialistic maritime trade, and the Panionion was a kind of cultural fraternity for the Ionian colonists in western Asia Minor. The more one studies the various organizational specimens lumped together under "amphictyony," the more suspicion grows that the scholars have yet to make a sophisticated, fine-grained analysis that will adequately uncover their varieties in structure and function as viewed over the long range of Greek history. So far as I can determine, no one has made a careful structural, typological study of Greek amphictyonies analogous to Larsen's study of the Greek federal unions. Perhaps because of the still more limited Old Latin and Etruscan sources, a similar analysis of the Italian amphictyonies is even less in prospect.

While Noth used the best sources on the amphictyony available to him in 1930, neither those sources nor Noth himself gave sufficient attention to the relation between the amphictyony and other confederate instrumentalities in ancient Greece. From his discussion, one would never know that the most characteristic associations of Greek city-states were not amphictyonies but military leagues (symmachies), tribal or ethnic states (ethnoi), and federal unions (sympolities). How much more analytically precise matters become when we see that the confederacy of Israel not only carried out some cultic and instructional functions which might be compared with those of amphictyonies, it also carried out military, socioeconomic, and political functions (although in decentralized forms), which might bear comparison with those of symmachies, ethnoi, and sympolities. Indeed, far more plausible than the exclusive use of the amphictyonic model for Israel might be the suggestion that Israel was something more like a symmachy or military league of autonomous tribes (ethnoi) with a common religion. To state matters in such a way is not, of course, to offer a serious comparative model but merely to indicate that the range of functions involved in the Israelite confederacy extended well beyond those performed in an amphictyony. In overlooking the various confederate forms and functions in ancient Greece, Noth was led farther and farther into a much too simplistic cross-societal comparison.

It is of critical importance for cross-societal comparisons with Israel to give adequate weight to the fact that Israel's confederacy represented not only a *noncentralized* form of polity but an *anticentralized* form of polity, a distinct rupture with prevailing Near Eastern centralized polities. Both against its own immediate backdrop and in comparison with other tribal societies, Israel presents the highly visible profile of a "break" or "mutation" in social organizational terms. Of course, Israel "evolved" out of preexistent human and sociocultural materials, but its evolution was markedly abrupt, revolutionary, and totalistic. The historical leap forward in old Israel was possible only because a total set of newly defined institutional relationships among peoples was set in motion. The association "Israel" exhibited a *comprehensiveness* and a *structural impulse* involving a whole people which neither the amphictyony nor any other confederate form possessed for the Greeks. The amphictyony was structurally subordinate and, in the form we know it, temporally late as a religious and political development. For Israel, the confederate framework was coterminous with and constitutive of Israel's emergence culturally, religiously, socioeconomically, and militarily. For the Greek amphictyony to have occupied the place that the confederacy occupied in Israel it would have had to form the framework for a major antipolitical break initiated by all or most of the Dorians, focused on and energized by the cult of some deity identified with the liberation of the people. There were Greek agrarian protests against centralized society's expropriation of the debtor peasants, such as Hesiod reflects, but none of them seems to have been rooted in or influenced by amphictyonic cults.

For all the reasons cited, the amphictyony is not a proper model to apply to Israel's overall confederate design, nor is it even the appropriate model to apply to the cultic aspects of the confederacy, since the details of cultic organization and the structural-functional location of the cult in the two societies are so different. Nonetheless every serious cross-societal comparison has its values, even when the investigator draws the wrong conclusions. Noth introduced a method and rigor of inquiry which lifted the study of Israelite origins into a cross-societal perspective with an explicitness matched only by the earlier cross-societal treatment of Israel and Arab bedouinism.[286] In comparing the two cross-societal studies, it becomes evident that Noth's methodology was considerably more discriminating than was W. R. Smith's and J. Wellhausen's. In fact, my critique rests to a large extent upon Noth's methods and some of his criteria, but with differing conclusions. I have been able to state these differing conclusions sharply because I have insisted on raising the question of the total societal setting of the compared elements to a much greater prominence than Noth gave it. This was possible because of the insights afforded by macrosociological analysis,[287] a field in which Noth showed little interest, although it would have helped him immensely in his undertaking.

In spite of all these demurrers, Noth's undertaking has been of immense heuristic value. It has helped us to conceive the questions to be asked in other cross-societal comparisons with old Israel. Furthermore, given the kinds of criticisms raised in this evaluation of the amphictyonic model, there seems great need for a return to a closer study of the Greek/Italian amphictyonies, a field which currently seems almost totally neglected among classical scholars. As old information is sifted anew, and perhaps as new information comes to light, still greater precision in employing the amphictyonic comparison with Israel may be possible. In the end, some aspects of Noth's analysis may prove to be better grounded than now appears to be the case. In my opinion, however, startling new finds in ancient Greece or in ancient Israel would be necessary in order to resuscitate the Greek amphictyony as a viable model for the Israelite confederacy.

Parts VIII—XI
Diachronic-Comparative Social Structure
Sociology of Religion vs. Biblical Theology

Part VIII

Comparative Social Systems
and Economic Modes:
The Sociohistoric Matrices of
Liberated Israel

34

A Preliminary View

In the last three parts a profile of Israel's social system was begun by pursuing three lines of analysis: a sketch of prevalent models for the Israelite settlement-formation in Canaan (Part V), an examination of the internal articulation and segmentation at four levels of Israelite social structure (Part VI), and a comparison of the overall social system of Israel with the proposed analogue of the amphictyony in Greece (Part VII). The result has been the emerging cross-section of Israel as an egalitarian, extended-family, segmentary tribal society with an agricultural-pastoral economic base.

The Israelite society was characterized by profound resistance and opposition to the forms of political domination and social stratification that had become normative in the chief cultural and political centers of the ancient Near East. There was a definite sociohistorical intent to the organizational segmentation of Israel's intertribal order into structurally and functionally equivalent and politically equal entities forming extended families, protective associations of families, and tribes in an overarching intertribal confederacy. The same sociohistorical intent guided the mutual cooperation of these pyramided social segments in cross-cutting bonding associations and activities, such as the cultic assembly of adult males, the Levitical priesthood, mutual economic aid, intermarriage, military levy, and the Kenite metal craft guild. *Together, the societal segmentation and inter-group bonding of early Israel were adaptively related to the fundamental aims of these segmented but cooperating people to escape imperialism and feudalism imposed by outside powers and to prevent the rise of feudal domination within their own society.*

So heavily have we emphasized this anti-imperialist and anti-feudal bias of old Israel, thereby staking out its distinctively oppositional and egalitarian character, that it becomes essential to our characterization of the early Israelite social system to counterpose it against the designs of Egyptian empire and of Canaanite feudal society. We have already laid the foundation of our sketch of this opposed dominant society in our brief summary of the revolt model of Israel's settlement (in V. 22) in which we described the Canaanite city-state feudal order as it developed under Egyptian hegemony from about the middle of the eighteenth century B.C., when the Hyksos imposed their rule on Canaan and moved on to become the masters of Egypt. Although the Hyksos rulers were later expelled from both Egypt and Canaan, the Hyksos feudal pattern continued as the normative political and socioeconomic structure of Canaan.

Although we possess archaeological data and historical texts concerning the Egyptian-Canaanite imperial-feudal blend spread over several centuries from about 2000 B.C. to about 1200 B.C., the Archimedean point for our analysis of Canaanite society is the diplomatic correspondence from the Amarna Age (c. 1410–1350 B.C.).[288] There is a richness and fullness to the documentation, even though the specifically social organizational data are relatively meager in comparison with the political and military data. Certain projections about social organization in the period can be hypothesized on the basis of north Syrian texts from Ugarit[289] and Alalakh,[290] which offer a somewhat fuller account of social organization in an area which shared at least some cultural continuities with southerly Canaan. The value of the Amarna texts is that they picture the political situation in the precise area in which Israel arose somewhat more than a century later.

In this part of our study, we shall consider first the Egyptian imperial hegemony over Canaan, the indigenous Canaanite feudal system, the functional interlock between the two, and the specific adaptation to feudalism made by a sub-element of the populace known as 'apiru, a social grouping which constituted a significant antecedent to and, in my view, one direct line of connection with early Israel. With the Egyptian-Canaanite-'apiru sociopolitical complex in mind, we shall then show how the Philistines functioned basically as operatives within that preestablished complex. Possible sociopolitical models for Ammon, Moab, and Edom in the thirteenth through the eleventh centuries will be briefly explored. The persistent model of early Israel as a pastoral nomadic society will be sharply criticized and drastically reformulated. Finally, appropriate models or social "morphemes" will be proposed in a cross-cutting grid of complementarity and opposition in order to locate the synchronically fragmented but diachronically converging social segments of Canaan whose conjunction eventuated in the sociopolitical formation of early Israel.

35

Egyptian Imperialism and Canaanite Feudalism:
The Amarna Age Interlock

The background to the development of Amarna imperialism/feudalism is complex and only sporadically and asymmetrically documented. The Egyptian Middle Kingdom (c. 2052–1786 B.C.) extended nominal control over Syria-Palestine. Its interests during the period were mainly in trade and the extraction of natural resources. Since there was no major political opposition from the east, Egypt was not greatly challenged to develop its loose political and military suzerainty in the region into a tighter system of imperial control. The Egyptian Story of Sinuhe[291] and the Execration Texts[292] give some valuable information on the populace in Canaan during the Egyptian Middle Kingdom.

35.1 Hyksos and Canaanite "Feudalism"

By all accounts, it was the entrance of the Hyksos into Syro-Palestine which introduced a tighter system of city-state social stratification and exploitative control over the surrounding countryside of a sort which can be broadly characterized as "feudal." Students of feudalism point out that its strictest and most elaborate form was developed in medieval Europe, and even there it appeared only in its "purest" form in northern France in the eleventh and twelfth centuries A.D. In the vacuum left by the collapse of the Roman Empire and the decline of the Merovingian and Carolingian kingdoms, as well as by the attrition of international trade, a remarkably closed and self-contained system of tenurial and personal relationships developed between lord and vassal. The feudal system, by means of the grant of land in return for service, built up a network of economic, social, and political dependencies. In its full European form, feudalism developed intricate procedures of homage, tenant service, wardship, marriage, reliefs, aids, escheat, and forfeiture. By comparison with this fully developed feudalism, some scholars prefer to speak of the less fully developed but similar systems elsewhere as possessing "feudal tendencies."[293] In this context, in order to avoid clumsy circumlocutions, we shall speak of Canaanite feudalism, while remaining fully aware that it arose from peculiar Near Eastern developments and did not exhibit all the detailed features of European feudalism. What marks the Canaanite system as feudal is its bonding by a network of regional dependencies with tenurial ties which locked a majority of the populace on the land.

In the section on settlement models (V.22) we alluded to the new developments in military technology which the Hyksos brought into Syro-Palestine and Egypt in the eighteenth century B.C. While there are now some second thoughts about the proper interpretation of the massive walls and revetments around Hyksos Age cities,[294] the hypothesis that it was the Hyksos who brought chariot warfare into the region remains intact. This military advance seems to have been the primary factor in stimulating the growth of the feudal system. Chariot warfare required: (1) strongly fortified cities which could dominate their hinterlands; and (2) concentrations of wealth, artisan skill, and military agility in order to develop and maintain chariot forces.

This twofold requirement concentrated populations within or near fortified cities in which a militarized upper class was able to expropriate increasing shares of the general productivity. The militarized upper class was related symbiotically to a local dynast who coordinated political and economic life. The dynast in turn depended upon the loyalty of the militarized vassals who were given grants of land on which serfs worked to support the centralized superstructure. This process apparently diminished vastly the power of assemblies of free citizens and councils of elders or nobility who had once held considerable stature,[295] and the very existence of a class of formally "free" peasants (ḫupshu) was seriously threatened. The data are very sketchy on these matters, but it seems that the revolution in military technology brought a new class of warrior-specialists into power at the expense of former hereditary nobility and free peasants.[296] The extent of the deprivation of the latter groups remains uncertain, but the dominant picture of the Amarna texts is that of so much internecine fighting, at such heavy expense to all parties, that economic erosion of the affluent classes and rapid swelling of the impoverished classes seems a plausible reading of the sketchy evidence.

A brief word about the Hyksos is in order, particularly since they have been improperly explained in many biblical studies. The misleading point of departure was the claim of the Hellenistic Egyptian historian Manetho that Hyksos meant "shepherd kings." From this erroneous etymology scholars frequently fantasized a nomadic Semitic people, and some of them went so far as to equate the Hyksos with the Hebrews and to view the descent of Joseph and his brothers into Egypt as part of the invasion of Egypt by the Hyksos. Most biblical scholars, without controlling all the data, nonetheless recognized the flimsy and incongruous basis of the identification, if only because Joseph and his brothers—whatever favor they found in Egypt—certainly did not come as conquerors.

It is now known that Manetho's "Hyksos" is in fact a rendering of an old Egyptian term meaning "rulers of foreign lands." Since the Hyksos adopted the Egyptian language once they became the rulers of Egypt, we know of their language mainly through transliterated personal names. They appear to have been an ethnically composite people, since Semitic, Hurrian, and Indo-European elements occur among the personal names. That they introduced chariot warfare and presided over a process of urban growth, political centralization, and feudal stratification altogether discredits the notion that they were pastoral nomads. Increasingly it is felt that the Hyksos were part of a widespread migration of Hurrian peoples, presided over by an Indo-European ruling class, which spread over the upper part of the fertile crescent in the early second millennium B.C. and extended eastward beyond the Tigris River and southward through Syria and Palestine. Hyksos itself is primarily a political identification for those migrants who succeeded in penetrating Egypt and establishing pharaonic dynasties during a period of marked political decline following the Middle Kingdom.[297]

The feudal development in Canaan thus appears as the result of markedly different conditions than those obtaining in medieval Europe. Feudalism in Syria-Palestine was precipitated by advances in military technology introduced by the influx of an ethnically mixed ruling class. Feudalism in Canaan was characterized by the concentration of the populace in and around cities and the subordination of the countryside to the city. Finally, Canaanite feudalism occurred in a context of hegemony by the Egyptian imperium and in a situation of international trade which made of Canaan an emporium for the exchange of goods from all parts of the ancient Near East. Thus, whereas feudalism in Europe represented a more stagnant and socioeconomically retarded system compared to preceding periods, feudalism in Canaan occurred in a setting of general cultural advance, even though the "advance" was very unevenly shared by the general populace.[298]

These striking differences in the location of European and Canaanite feudalism in the evolutionary scales on the two continents compel great caution in interpreting the lesser-known Canaanite feudalism in terms of the better-known European feudalism.[299] Nonetheless, the similarities are evident, including the fact that the basic feudal units, articulated as city-states in Canaan, were autonomous and highly competitive, their only firm linkage lying in the overarching Egyptian imperial control which was, in its very nature, often exceedingly nominal. An inverse ratio existed between Egyptian suzerainty and Canaanite autonomy: the stronger the Egyptian presence, the weaker the assertions of Canaanite independence and the more "harmonious" the picture of political affairs; the weaker the Egyptian presence, the more virulent the competitive assertions of the multitudinous Canaanite autonomies and the more "disruptive" the appearance of political life.

It is evident that in spite of the political friction between Egypt and Canaan, the systems of Egyptian imperialism and of Canaanite feudalism were joined in a mutually dependent interlock. Each depended in important ways upon the existence of the other. Egypt developed no highly integrated administrative system for dominating its empire, of the sort the Assyrians and Persians were later to introduce.[300] Egypt learned to rely upon native princes for exercising local rule and delivering the necessary services and tribute to the imperial master. It was highly advantageous that these local princes should be numerous and competitive toward one another, since the fragmentation and dispersal of their power vis-à-vis the Egyptian power tended to minimize the dangers of revolt. From the viewpoint of the Canaanite city-state princes, the Egyptian presence was a stabilizing factor which kept the general populace and its various restive factions in line and at the same time served as a guarantee against aggrandizement by other city-state princes. Furthermore, a stabilizing Egyptian political and military presence fostered a favorable climate for inter-city trade, so vital a factor in maintaining a high level of culture and luxury for the privileged upper classes. Obviously there were weaknesses in the interlock, since the areas of shared common interests between Egyptian and Canaanite were far less extensive than the official propaganda claimed. Egypt would have preferred more direct control of Canaan and Canaan would have preferred complete independence from Egypt but neither had the realistic prospect of imposing its maximal desires and neither had effective models for fully "going it alone." The Amarna correspondence reflects the intimate interlock between the two systems, but it also shows the growing strains and the contradictory interests of Egyptians and Canaanites.

35.2 Egyptian-Canaanite Dominion: Temporal and Territorial Horizons

I shall now offer a generalized design of the various levels and dimensions of the interlocking Egyptian imperial and Canaanite feudal systems, with particular attention to the nature of the stresses within the overall symbiotic relations, in part those between Egyptians and their Canaanite vassals but mainly those between the Canaanite ruling class and other segments of the Canaanite social order. The discussion will increasingly focus on the 'apiru as the most strikingly disruptive force in the system.

Obviously, such a cross-sectional design must bear in mind that the Amarna texts are as yet only imperfectly understood, both because of their occasional character as letters and because of the numerous Canaanite terms and idioms that the scribes employed. While they are written mostly in Akkadian, it is a form of that language permeated by the Canaanite dialect of the scribes. Furthermore, the texts represent the various regions of Canaan in a highly uneven manner. Cities such as Byblos, Megiddo, Shechem, and Jerusalem are documented with scores of letters, while others are unmentioned or alluded to only in letters from another city. Also, the place of origin of some of the letters is unknown.

It is important to recognize that the extent to which the Egyptians effectively controlled their Canaanite empire and the extent to which the ruling classes dominated their respective city-states varied considerably from period to period and from region to region. We can in fact establish two horizons for characterizing the differentials in extent of effective domination by ruling elites, one a temporal horizon and the other a territorial horizon:

TEMPORAL HORIZON. Maximal Egyptian domination is to be posited for the first half of the eighteenth dynasty with its acme in the reign of Thutmose III (c. 1490–1436), following which the Amarna period represents a steadily declining, although never altogether relinquished, exercise of Egyptian domination over Canaan, connected with Egypt's growing absorption in internal affairs.

A corollary maximal Canaanite ruling-class domination over the populace is to be posited in the first half of the eighteenth dynasty, following which the Amarna period represents a weakening of Canaanite ruling-class domination, undermined by inter-city strife and internal revolts. But two qualifications are necessary. First, the internecine city strife also had a counter-effect of strengthening elites in some cities in the short term, even though the overall long-range effect was to undermine the system of elite control. Secondly, the city-state feudal system did not weaken at the same pace or to as great an extent as the Egyptian imperial domination, since weakening or termination of Egyptian expropriation did not automatically end the infrastructure of feudal expropriation by native elites.

TERRITORIAL HORIZON. Maximal Egyptian domination was normally exerted over the regions of Canaan most directly accessible to Egyptian armies and most profitable to Egyptian imperial needs, namely, in the coastal plains, the lateral valleys, and parts of the Jordan Valley. By contrast, the hill country east and west of the Jordan experienced minimal or sporadic Egyptian domination and in some periods escaped with no more than formal or nominal Egyptian claims of suzerainty.

Maximal Canaanite ruling-class domination over the populace was exercised in cities of the plains and valleys, whereas cities in the highlands, although apparently organized by elites, were less effective in extending control over their hinterlands. The correlated differentials in Egyptian and Canaanite elite control according to regions were functions of a complex set of variables affecting accessibility and profitability to overlords. Specifically historico-territorial factors were at work. The city-states in the productive plains and valleys were close together, with the result that rural populations were easily dominated by urban elites.

The city-states in the highlands were farther apart. Population was much sparser in the hills than in the plains and valleys because of the difficulty of cultivating a thicketed and forested region with bronze tools and with an undependable water supply. Trade was inhibited by the rough terrain and the region's relative remoteness from the main coastal and valley communication arteries. It was always possible for groups resisting domination by the highland city-state elites to withdraw into relatively inaccessible areas and to escape direct control. It was just such hilly regions that served as base areas for the Amarna *'apiru* and for the later Israelites.[301]

35.3 Egyptian-Canaanite Dominion: Internal Dynamics

With the conditioning of perspective provided by these variable but correlated temporal and territorial horizons on Egyptian-Canaanite domination, we offer the following sketch of the dominant system in ideal-typical form. In doing so, account is taken of historical development and of problematic features, as well as documentation on the *'apiru* and the nature of the strains within the overall system.[302]

DYNASTS AND GOVERNORS. The Canaanite city-states were headed by native dynasts (sing. *ḫazannu)* and loosely integrated into the Egyptian empire by the oversight of Egyptian commissioners or governors (sing. *rabiṣu)* who had regional responsibility for a number of city-states.

TWO LEVELS OF ELITES. The chain of authority in control by elites operated on two levels: (1) the pharaoh granted the city-state as a fief to the dynast in return for goods and services; (2) the dynast granted lands and their usufruct to local aristocrats in return for their goods and services. Possibly there also existed independent crown land, held by the pharaoh or by the dynast or by both, although the evidence on this point is unclear.

GOODS AND SERVICES PLEDGED. The return of imperial-feudal goods and services was as follows: (1) the dynast provided the pharaoh with metals, craft products, timber, agricultural produce to supply Egyptian troops, harbors and garrisons for Egyptian use. He barracked Egyptian troops, and, as needed, supplied local troops to assist the Egyptians in punitive campaigns; (2) the aristocrat provided the dynast with such professional military service as a chariot-warrior, a body of troops in his charge, agricultural produce as "rent" on land, and probably also the corvée labor of his serfs.

SUBORDINATED SOCIOPOLITICAL GROUPS. This chain of authority, with its interlocking system of grants and services, depressed a considerable part of the populace into serfdom and pushed technically "free" elements of the populace into increasing powerlessness. We hear of peasants not wholly assimilated to the feudal system (*ḫupshu).* There are references also to "the people" (assembly of free citizens?), and "the council" (council of leading citizens, nobles, elders?). The materials about these groups are so sporadic and terse that it is impossible to judge whether they were given some formal status within the dominant system, and, if so, whether the assemblies and councils were more than "rubber stamp" bodies. Nor is it possible to say whether such groups were represented in all or most of the city-states. What does seem clear is that such social and political weight as they had was used to shift relative power balances within the system rather than to challenge the imperial-feudal system in a fundamental way.

COMPLIANCE OR REBELLION AGAINST EGYPT. City-states either complied with their obligations to the pharaoh or revolted, either in a general coordinated plan (as in the time of Thutmose III), or individually (as in the Amarna Age), or with the stimulus and support of another major power (as became increasingly the case with the Hittite intervention in Syria in the latter part of the fourteenth century and in the thirteenth century).

COMPLIANCE OR REBELLION AGAINST DYNASTS. The populations of the city-states either complied with their obligations to the local dynast, willingly or reluctantly, or rebelled against him. Uprisings might involve one or more of the following potentially disturbing segments of the populace: relatives of the dynast, feudal aristocrats, the people as more or less free citizenry (with such organizational assemblies or councils as may have existed), 'apiru bands, "free" peasants, or serfs. The descriptions in the Amarna letters allow us to identify at least some of the rebel elements, but often the terms are very general or are ambiguously used, particularly in the case of the label 'apiru. Uprisings might be restricted to the city state populace or might be aided and abetted by dynasts in rival city-states.

INTER-CITY AGGRANDIZEMENTS. Dynasts freely seized territory from one another, and thus secured or lost feudal or crown estates, whenever Egypt was too weak to impose a "freeze" on inter-city rivalries. These inter-city aggrandizements were formal violations of the Egyptian imperium in that they disturbed the status quo. Only if they led to a diminution in imperial tribute, however, were the Egyptians likely to be greatly concerned. Probably in many cases the aggrandizing dynast continued to return his feudal services to Egypt. The exact relation between the inter-city struggles and the patterns of loyalty to or defection from Egypt is greatly obscured by the political dissembling that permeates the Amarna correspondence. Egypt was still strong enough in Canaan that every Canaanite dynast wanted to appear as the loyal servant of the pharaoh while stigmatizing his rival fellow dynasts as rebels against the pharaoh. The sentiments and motives, and even some of the reported events, recorded in the Amarna letters must be read with a generous grain of salt.

CITY-STATE EMPLOYMENT OF 'APIRU TROOPS. Dynasts made use of 'apiru troops in their armies, and this is true both for dynasts identified as Egyptian loyalists and for dynasts identified as Egyptian defectors. 'Apiru is used in the Amarna letters with a number of denotations and connotations. When these references are studied in relation to references to 'apiru (or the equivalent SA.GAZ) from throughout the fertile crescent, the primary specific denotation for Amarna Canaan 'apiru is as mercenary troops and as brigands. The kinds of relations between dynasts and 'apiru groups appear to have been threefold: (1) 'apiru mercenaries employed to serve as auxiliary infantry; (2) 'apiru brigands encouraged and/or supplied by a dynast to harass an enemy dynast in paramilitary operations: (3) 'apiru groups settled on lands as client but semi-independent forces, possibly conceived as a feudal grant entailing reciprocal military service.

One of the aims of territorial aggrandizement may have been to secure new lands for settling 'apiru as militarized enclaves and buffers.

FORMS OF INTER-CITY CONFLICT. Rebellions against authority within the city-states were often encouraged by dynasts in other city-states who saw therein an opportunity to weaken rival states and to seize control over their territory. Rival dynasts thus played upon the social unrest in their opponent's domain. They were eager to pit the rival dynast against those in the upper echelons of power (or those who thought they should be included), such as the dynast's relatives (especially brothers), princes, and feudal aristocrats. They were equally ready to capitalize on the resentments of those who suffered under the feudal order, or who had been pushed aside by it, such as the peasant serfs, the semi-free farmers (ḫupshu), remnants of the free citizenry with their assemblies and councils as a political tradition resistant to feudalism, and the 'apiru. The latter, although at times collaborative with feudal dynasts and lords, stood to profit greatly from an overall weakening of the feudal system.

IMPERIAL-FEUDAL DISINTEGRATION. The above-described strains and conflicts in the Egyptian-Canaanite imperial-feudal symbiosis fit most securely within an imperial-feudal system that was undergoing slow but progressive internal disintegration. This was in full process over the entire region, but in the Amarna Age it was far from having reached the point of total breakdown.[303] The disintegration of the imperial control of Egypt was in fact very much farther advanced than that of the feudal system in Canaan. While the peoples of Canaan in this period show a steady convergence of consciousness on the desirability and possibility of weakening the Egyptian imperial grip, they do not show a corresponding convergence of consciousness on the desirability and possibility of reorganizing their socio-economic and political existence on nonfeudal lines. When the Egyptian imperium is conceived as eliminated, the result is a plethora of city-state dynasts competing for dominance and of aspirants within each city-state striving to gain control. These are the articulate social forces at work in the Amarna Age, whatever the inarticulate strivings of segments of the population to be rid of the whole heavy burden of feudalism.

35.4 Alleged 'Apiru Revolt against Egyptian-Canaanite Dominion

The caution that we can discern no consciously conceived and organized counter-system, or even any articulate movement against the system, is of great importance in assessing the 'apiru of Amarna Canaan in terms of their continuities and discontinuities with early Israel. The lower-class unrest in Amarna Canaan had not yet taken the form of a consciously conceived and explicitly organized movement of the disaffected with coordinated expression that reached across the city-state boundaries. The preconditions for such a conscious nonstratified, widely coordinated movement were building and perhaps find their fullest expression in a letter of Rib-Addi of Byblos to the pharaoh (EA 74) in which he recounts the propaganda used by his opponent, Abdi-Ashirta of Amurru.[304] Yet, even here, the sociopolitical references are too obscure, and the co-opting aims of Abdi-Ashirta too obvious, to provide solid ground for believing that Abdi-Ashirta was gathering and leading a consciously anti-feudal lower-class movement.[305] Nonetheless, that such social restiveness was at hand to be co-opted by warring feudal factions is itself a significant datum. For this also implies that a reservoir of social restiveness was available for mobilization on explicitly anti-feudal lines, provided that a viable organizational and ideological model could be found and provided that the political security of Canaan should continue to deteriorate.

I shall now attempt to explicate the last point above somewhat more fully as the context for discussing the 'apiru, since it is abundantly clear that for our purposes it is absolutely essential not only to understand the specific data about the 'apiru but, above all, to discern if possible their location within the total societal system, both cross-sectionally in relation to the other social actors and longitudinally in terms of the trajectory along which the total system was moving.

As far as I can determine from the Amarna letters, the leaders most frequently identified as 'apiru, or as collaborative with the 'apiru (e.g., Abdi-Ashirta and Aziru of Amurru; Labaya and his sons from Shechem; Milkilu of Gezer; Tagi from an unnamed city, etc.)[306] are not depicted as representatives of a nonstratified, anti-feudal sociopolitical movement. Their essentially statist ethos and practices show up well-marked features: They are dynasts like all the other ḫazannūtu, i.e., fathers and sons rule in succession unless interrupted by a coup from within or a defeat from without (EA 117:33, 35–39; 250:4–55; 253:11–17; 289:5–10, 25–26). They possess chariot forces and thus depend on feudally pledged professional military forces (EA 87:18–24; 197:2–5, 7–12). They pay tribute to Egypt, even though reluctantly (EA 254:10–15). They take peace oaths not to disturb the imperial status quo in Canaan (EA 252:10–11). They supply troops to Egypt for local campaigns (EA 195:24–32; cf. 189 verso: 9–18). They observe noninterference with Egyptian trade (EA 255:8–25). One dynast actually turns over his son to the Egyptians because he has associated (plotted?) with the 'apiru (EA 254:31–37).

Of course it is admittedly possible, and even inherently likely, that with respect to some of these claims made by supposed 'apiru dynasts, they are actually dissembling, i.e., denying what they have done or merely complying in part in order to cover up their deeper conspiratorial actions. Some points, however, are not easily explainable by deception, since they touch on the fundamental internal organization of the rebellious government or army. For example, the references to the principle of dynastic rule and to the use of chariot forces seem to serve no purpose of deception or intrigue, and it is difficult to conceive of a genuinely anti-statist leader delivering his son voluntarily to the Egyptians as a hostage.

It is particularly striking that Abdi-Ashirta, whose propaganda pitch to the dominated segments of the population in the area around Byblos which he sought to conquer might incline us to think of him as a leader of an egalitarian movement, actually founded a dynasty which soon became vassal to the Hittites. Granted that Aziru's submission to the Hittite empire was undertaken with a measure of compulsion; nonetheless, the historical introduction to the treaty of Suppiluliumas and Aziru[307] pictures Aziru as taking the lead in establishing friendly relations with the Hittites, while other lands much closer to the Hittite homeland were still hostile toward the Hittite intruder. W. Helck points out the intriguing fact that Abdi-Ashirta and Ba'aluja, his son who succeeded him, bore Semitic names, whereas his second son to reign, Aziru, and the following six rulers (as far as the line can be traced), bore recognizably Hurrian names.[308] This seems to imply that Abdi-Ashirta regarded it as politic (assuming that it was he who named his son Aziru from the start) to identify his line with the Indo-European/Hurrian stratum whose princely families carried royal claims. This act may be understood as an assertion of sociopolitical pretensions which were in the end more basic to the man and his program than the pseudo-egalitarian rhetoric with which he urged Rib-Addi's subjects to revolt and come over to his side. At most, the impression of widespread revolt, conveyed both by Rib-Addi's alarm and by the quoted propaganda of Abdi-Ashirta, suggests the nucleus of a broad anti-Egyptian alliance of the sort that had rallied to Megiddo against Thutmose III a century before. Yet, in a letter from the pharaoh to Aziru chiding him for his hostility toward Rib-Addi, the Egyptian does not seem to regard Aziru as the real center of intrigue in southern Syria, but rather a certain "man of Kadesh" (Etakkama?; EA 162:15–29), who is elsewhere charged with treason by four princes of the region in separate (but commonly dictated?) letters to the pharaoh (EA 174—176; 363).[309]

In my judgment, the named dynasts, although often stigmatized as 'apiru or accused of collaborating with 'apiru, were not fundamentally challenging the feudal order. They were seeking greater elbow room for themselves by loosening the Egyptian imperial grip and by seeking advantages at the expense of their neighbors. But appeals such as those made by Abdi-Ashirta to the subject peoples of another city-state, when read in the light of the hysteria marking the Amarna references to the 'apiru, strongly indicate that these dynasts made effective tactical use of lower-class resentments against the feudal order. The trick was to exploit the resentments of subjects against rival dynasts, while transferring and redirecting their energies toward allegiance to the new dynast. Thus, when a rebel sought to grasp the throne within his own city-state, or when one king sought to overthrow or take over the territory of another king, he deliberately stirred up and capitalized upon the general discontent and opposition toward the authority who was his prime personal target of attack. Implicitly or explicitly, the new contender for power claimed that his rule would offer an improvement in the subjects' conditions. We easily recognize that this hope was so often disappointed that subjects grew cynical; nonetheless, even the hope of marginal improvement spurred many an uprising and many an inter-city state conflict.

36

The *'Apiru* Adaptation in Amarna Canaan

While there is growing consensus that *'apiru* and Hebrew are linguistically related,[310] there is no certainty as to the language (NW Semitic, Hurrian, etc.) or the verbal root from which the sociopolitical technical term was originally drawn. Our grasp of the sort of social group(s) called *'apiru* must depend on categorization and comparison of the traits of *'apiru* attested in numerous texts widely distributed over the ancient world in the period 2000 to 1200 B.C.[311] The distinguishing generic trait of the *'apiru* turns out to be sociopolitical rather than ethnic or economic, although there are economic features that follow systematically from the dominant sociopolitical factor.[312] *'Apiru* cannot be characterized as ethnically homogeneous in any one location, much less throughout all the regions where they appear. Nor are the *'apiru* engaged in any single economic activity throughout the Near East, although in particular locales there is often a tendency toward one or another form of economic specialization.

The one trait that best comprehends all the *'apiru* appears to be that of the *outsider status* they occupy vis-à-vis the regnant social and political order. The term "outlaw" conveniently catches the double nuance of the *'apiru* as those who stand recognizably outside the prevailing order, both as "fugitives" or "refugees" who *flee from the dominant order* and as "robbers" or "rebels" who *prey upon or threaten the dominant order*. But "outlaw," except as broadly redefined, tends to miss the many grades and variations of adaptation of which the *'apiru* "outsiders" were capable vis-à-vis the dominant social order. While standing distinguishably apart from the existing order, they also relied upon it insofar as their livelihood was dependent upon the wider society, for which they often worked either as individual "contract laborers" or as hired groups of soldiers, agricultural laborers, or construction gangs.

It seems advisable to maintain a distinction between the individual occupations of *'apiru* before they departed from the prevailing order and the occupations they engaged in as hired laborers or mercenaries once they became members of *'apiru* communities. For example, in the Alalakh texts from fifteenth-century northern Syria, settlements of *'apiru* are recorded in forty-three places, where they appear as state-supported warriors. In a few instances the former occupations of *'apiru* are listed. They include a thief, a slave or servant, priests, and even what appears to be an ex-governor or ex-dynast *(hazannu)*.[313] How the past experiences and

401

skills of the individual 'apiru would be deployed as a member of an 'apiru community, if at all, seems to have depended in part upon the particular services in which the 'apiru band to which he attached himself had come to specialize and in part upon the kinds of services which the ruling classes in the area were in need of hiring.

In Amarna Canaan, the 'apiru appear mainly, perhaps exclusively, as military mercenaries or as renegade robbers. This picture of their occupations, it must be admitted, may be slanted by the diplomatic correspondence in which they are mentioned. Since Egyptian texts refer to 'apiru as vintners, stone cutters and haulers, and temple servants (as well as in the role of auxiliary infantry), and since these same 'apiru were reportedly captured in various military campaigns in Syria-Palestine,[314] it is altogether possible that the 'apiru of Canaan engaged in a wider variety of economic activities than appears in the Amarna letters. The prominence of their military or freebooting activity may be a skewing effect of the Amarna texts with their political-military bias. In terms of their primary reported involvement in Canaanite society, 'apiru operated as armed groups semi-independent of the feudal structure, available for hire as auxiliary troops or resourceful in carrying on freebooting, either on their own or at the instigation of one city-state against another.

The 'apiru appear in the context of struggle between the feudal city-states, being enlisted as auxiliaries in the service of one city-state against another and in some instances even settled on land, doubtless partly in payment for their services and partly as a way of keeping a close watch on their activities. Their well-organized skill in banditry was a career they could practice on their own, directed at whatever targets were at hand, or it could be subsidized by one city-state against another as a form of paramilitary harassment. Because they were armed bands, only loosely integrated into the general society, the 'apiru constituted an uncertain factor which every dynast had to watch, even as he employed them. So far as we can see, however, these bands by themselves could not and did not overthrow dynasts. The aristocratic chariot forces held the upper hand militarily. But in the contest of city-states, the 'apiru could tip the balance of power one way or another.

The extent to which the 'apiru of Canaan were skilled as charioteers is a matter of some dispute. EA 87 (from Rib-Addi of Byblos to Amanappa, high Egyptian official) states that "Batruna went over to him [i.e., to Abdi-Ashirta]. And (now) a SA.GAZ[315] army and chariots are stationed in [its] midst, and they do not move from the gate opening of Gubla [i.e., Byblos]."[316] This is sometimes understood to mean that the SA.GAZ/'apiru army had a chariot contingent, but the simplest sense of the passage is that the SA.GAZ were infantry who were supplemented by a chariot force provided by Abdi-Ashirta. EA 197 (from Biryawaza, royal deputy in Ube near Damascus, to the Egyptian king) seems much more explicit on first reading:

Your servant was/is in the land of A [bi (=Ube) . . .]. Its horses and its chariots [*they have given*] to the SA.GAZ; they have not g[*iven them*] to the king, my lord. When Biridashwa saw this deed, he stirred up the city of Yanuamma against me and closed the gate behind me. Then he took chariots from Ashtarte and gave them to the SA.GAZ; he did not give them to the king, my lord. And Arzawiya went to Qadesh and took the army of Aziru. He seized Shaddu and gave it to the SA.GAZ; he did not give it to the king, my lord. See! Itatkama has caused the loss of the land of Qadesh, and behold, Arzawiya with Biridashwa have caused the loss of Abi.[317]

The plain sense of the text appears to be that horses and chariots from Ube and chariots from Ashtarte were given to the SA.GAZ/*'apiru*, along with the town of Shaddu. There is, however, ground for suspecting that the formula "to give to the SA.GAZ/*'apiru*" may here be used in the broad sense in which the idiom occurs in many letters, i.e., as a general reference to surrender of land and populace to a hostile city-state. In that case, the expression may mean that the chariots were given to the rebel, i.e., anti-Egyptian, side (as defined by Biryawaza) without any intent of specifying that SA.GAZ/*'apiru*, in the strict sense of mercenary components of the rebel army, were outfitted with horses and chariots. That is the extent of our knowledge about possible *'apiru* chariotry in Canaan.

In the Alalakh census lists of armed SA.GAZ/*'apiru* there is more precise information. AT 180 refers to two charioteers among 29 men, AT 182 mentions 7 charioteers among 29 men, and AT 183 and AT 226 speak of 80 charioteers among 1,436 men.[318] Thus, while the great majority of armed *'apiru* at Alalakh were infantry, a significant minority were charioteers. Given the general social disdain in which *'apiru* appear to have been held, and the fact that they are listed separately from the upper classes, it is doubtful that these Alalakh *'apiru* charioteers were members of the military elite. It is probably more accurate to think of them as former feudal aristocrats, *maryannu*, who, as fugitives from other city-states, brought their skills in chariotry to Alalakh and were hired to drive chariots owned by local aristocrats. The *'apiru* captives from Canaan who are mentioned in Egypt, however, are never associated with chariots; when they are described as warriors, they are infantrymen and clearly distinguished from the *maryannu* chariot-warriors.

Our conclusion is that the *'apiru* of Canaan were overwhelmingly armed infantry. Insofar as some of their recruits may formerly have been skilled in chariotry, they could on occasion operate chariots, but it is not at all certain that they did so in Amarna Canaan. There is no reason whatsoever to believe that they formed large enough chariot units to be any match for the professional aristocracy of the city-states. Their military effect consisted in their adroitness in combat in rough terrain and in the extra punch they could deliver as auxiliaries to the elite chariotry and the local infantry. In Canaan the *'apiru* warriors probably had learned to specialize in guerrilla-like tactics, and by shifting their services to each new arena of hostilities they had the great advantage of more or less continuous battle experience, compared with more lackluster local infantry who would have to be drawn periodically off the land in order to mount campaigns of offense or defense. Thus, the reputation of the 'apiru mercenaries seems not to have resided in their equipment or in their superior firepower, but in their hardiness, versatility, and ready availability as full-time professional fighters.

It is obvious, however, that the strict sense of SA.GAZ/'apiru does not account for many, probably not even for a majority, of the references to them in the Amarna letters. Two social characteristics of the 'apiru contributed to a wider and looser pejorative usage of the term with meanings such as "outlaws," "traitors," "conspirators," "enemies." For one thing, the 'apiru were regularly hired or encouraged by city-state dynasts to fight for them or to harass other city-state dynasts. Very likely a dynast would most often hire 'apiru auxiliaries when he was mounting an attack against another dynast. The activation of units of 'apiru would be a warning signal that a local dynast was planning aggression. It was, therefore, an obvious extension of the term to label the dynast who hired the auxiliaries as "chief of the 'apiru" or "GAZ-man." Secondly, the 'apiru, by standing apart from the social order with a measure of independence, were conceived as an incipient threat to city-states which were under stress from within and attack from without. It was known that the 'apiru bands were recruited from discontented and deprived fugitives of the social order. In stable times, the 'apiru could be contained and their services employed to the mutual advantage of the ruling class and of the 'apiru themselves. But they were also clearly perceived as a restless, volatile, threatening element. Thus, any person or group perceived as threatening the stability or vital interests of a person in authority could easily be viewed as "acting the part of an 'outlaw,' " as indeed an 'apiru, rather analogous to the pejorative and hysterical use of the epithet "Communist" for any person threatening capitalist societies. At times all limits on the use of the term seem to have burst, and the writers of the Amarna letters savagely label anyone who opposed and threatened them as traitorous, conspiratorial, reprobate, rebellious 'apiru—or, in effect, 'apiru fellow travelers.

Not only are city-dynasts opposed to a correspondent often called 'apiru, or identified with 'apiru, but even an Egyptian commissioner in EA 286 can be reprimanded with the accusatory question, "Why do you favor the 'apiru but hate the governors [i.e., local dynasts]?"[319] Moreover, the rebellious underlings in a city-state, who give no evidence of having been previously organized as 'apiru, can be so stigmatized when they attempt to throw off feudal authority. In EA 271, Milkilu of Gezer implores the pharaoh, "Let the king, my lord, rescue his land from the hand of the SA.GAZ. If not, let the king send chariots to take us, that our servants not smite us."[320] And in EA 288, ER-Heba of Jerusalem exclaims, "See! Zimrida—the town(smen) of Lachish have smitten him, servants who have become 'apiru."[321] The term translated "servants" in both these letters, ardūtu, may also be rendered "slaves"; it does not tell us the specific form of servitude or obligation. The fact that these *ardūtu* are equated with "townsmen of Lachish" (lit., Lachishites) may in fact suggest that the term is a broad label for feudal subjects, equivalent to "citizens subject to the dynastic ruler." In rebelling against authority by murdering Zimrida, these people of Lachish have rejected the feudal obligation under which they stood. They have "become *'apiru*" by rejecting and over-throwing established feudal authority. There is no sign, however, that these rebellious Lachishites then withdrew from the city as fugitives to join existing *'apiru* bands or to form a band of their own. Their assassination of Zimrida was apparently successful and the rebels held the town, so that when the same letter says "the *'apiru* capture the cities of the king," the seizure of Lachish by feudal subjects within the city, rather than by *'apiru* mercenaries from without, seems to be conceived by ER-Heba as an *'apiru* action. Nor is there any indication that after the revolt Lachish was organized nonfeudally. Here the *'apiru* designation refers to a conspiratorial rebellious state of mind and mode of action rather than to a specific social formation known beforehand as *'apiru* or even subsequently organized as *'apiru*.

Yet the tendency to tar all opponents with the *'apiru* brush may well bear in many cases, if not in all, some connection with a concrete sociopolitical reality. It is plausible that city-states were expanding their control over their neighbors, not only by making use of *'apiru* auxiliaries and bandits, but also by settling them in their own undeveloped territories or in captured territories. Indeed, the settling of *'apiru* in conquered territories may have been one of the chief means of payment for their services, since the cost would not have had to come out of the resources of the hiring dynast. At the same time, the potentially troublesome *'apiru* could be removed some distance from the capital city and their threat to the dynast thereby decreased. For example, in EA 287 ER-Heba charges that "this deed is the deed of Milkilu [of Gezer] and the deed of the sons of Labaya [of Shechem] who have given the land of the king to the *'apiru*."[322] Greenberg notes that in EA 289, ER-Heba puts this land seizure in another way, "See! Milkilu never parts from the sons of Labaya and from the sons of Arzaya in order to acquire the land of the king for themselves,"[323] which leads him to suggest that these two claims can best be reconciled if we understand "giving the land to the *'apiru*" in either of two possible senses,

> as giving them a free hand to do as they pleased in the land, or as assigning them quarters in various localities. (Similarly Achish, king of Gath, assigned the city of Ziklag to his Israelite renegade retainers; note that in I Sam. 27:6 the verb *natān* [i.e., "to give"] is used exactly as *nadnu* here.)[324]

Thus, to summarize, the term *'apiru* in the Amarna letters ranges variously, from (1) an original denotative reference to circumscribed bands of armed "out-siders" loosely related to the feudal system as auxiliaries or brigands, through

✗ (2) extended application to those in the city-state system who use these bands, and (3) finally to loose metaphorical applications to all those who threaten a dynast, including his own subjects, an opposing dynast and his forces, or an Egyptian official. I believe it is a methodological error to attribute the conscious organized unity of the primary 'apiru bands to the looser senses of the term. And it is equally erroneous to assume a unity of consciousness and explicit anti-feudal strategy among all 'apiru bands. Deserving of closer attention is the question of whether some of the apparently metaphorical applications of 'apiru may in fact be more literally based, such as the identification of a ruler as 'apiru because he settled 'apiru in captured territory or the identification of Lachishites as 'apiru, not merely because they acted rebelliously against authority, but also possibly because they were inspired or led by 'apiru mercenaries. The texts that provoke these questions, however, are so terse and cryptic that for the present no confident answer can be given.

I have gone to some pains to indicate the range and ambiguity of data about the Canaanite 'apiru in order to underline my earlier claim that, in spite of all the restiveness in Amarna Canaan, we meet no clear articulation of an egalitarian social movement that directly challenged the feudal system of Canaan. The seeming severity of this conclusion, however, should be carefully qualified or conditioned in the following ways:

TREND TOWARD IMPERIAL-FEUDAL DECLINE. Whatever the lack of conscious intent to overthrow feudalism and whatever the absence of an organized alternative to feudalism, it is certainly true that the cumulative attacks and counterattacks among the city-states, criss-crossed as they were with internal power struggles and complicated by varying loyalty-defection patterns toward Egypt, seriously ate at the foundations of the Egyptian imperium, which in turn eroded the supports of the city-state feudal structure. This deterioration of the imperial-feudal interlock tended to strengthen whatever residue of free-citizen populism survived in the cities and to enlarge the freedom and power of the 'apiru bands and of the village-based agricultural/pastoral communities (more about this 'apiru-peasant cooperation below). As centralized power weakened, those resisting it had more "breathing space," and a favorable climate was developed for the later emergence of a consciously organized social egalitarian movement.

TREND TOWARD 'APIRU CONSOLIDATION. The 'apiru bands were not strong enough to unsettle the old order by themselves. This was in large measure because in the Amarna Age they showed no signs of operating as a united force but remained splintered in their support of various feudal states or factions. As combined circumstances led to the gradual decline of centralized Egyptian and city-state power, however, the relative independence of armed and organized 'apiru bands tended to weigh as an increasingly important power factor, especially in those hilly regions where centralized power was "thinnest" in its territorial coverage. About 1310 B.C. Seti I tells of deploying the Egyptian army against 'apiru who were operating out of a base in the mountains in the vicinity of Beth-shean.[325] 'Apiru grown stronger relative to declining feudal power and weakened Egyptian control could disrupt and plunder trade, seize crops, and occupy land, without feeling any obligation to render service to dynasts too weak to coerce them. Such seems to have been the trajectory along which the precariously balanced feudal system moved during the century following the Amarna Age, a period known to us from regrettably few Egyptian sources and thus one whose sociopolitical developments must be reconstructed largely by extrapolation forward and backward from better-documented periods.

'APIRU-PEASANT COOPERATION. We are left to conjecture about the possibility of these 'apiru bands providing nuclei for an anti-feudal social order in those regions of Palestine where Egyptian and city-state power had receded in the post-Amarna Age. We have already noted that 'apiru bands were regularly fed by a stream of fugitives fleeing the established order. Doubtless the degree of "openness" of 'apiru communities to newcomers varied considerably, depending upon the demographic composition and economic marginality of the 'apiru group, as well as on the skills that the newcomers brought. The destitute who gathered out of Israel to join David as freebooters indicate how an 'apiru group could recruit and assimilate large numbers of newcomers around a strong band leader (I Sam. 22:1). As the Canaanite cities weakened, they lost their grip on some regions while tightening it on others. To escape taxation in kind and corvée, peasants would rebel, remaining in place if possible, fleeing if necessary. To make up for the loss of human and natural resources, the cities would have to increase the burden they placed upon those who remained under their control. This in turn would increase the flow of fugitives. An enlarged flow of newcomers to the existing 'apiru bands would reach a point where the assimilation of newcomers was no longer possible. New "outlaw" communities would form, composed of nuclei of refugees from the same city, village, or former status. They would be primarily dependent on their own resourcefulness, but 'apiru groups of longer standing provided them with counsel and adaptive models of social, military, and economic organization.

Whether the expanding bands and communities of escapees from Canaanite feudalism characteristically or uniformly called themselves 'apiru is a moot point. In fact, since all the references to 'apiru in the Near East are by officials in the dominant order, we do not know how extensively, if at all, people in that social stratum accepted the term 'apiru for themselves, even in more stable situations than post-Amarna Canaan. As entire "outlaw" communities sprang up, without any previous 'apiru tradition, they may have resisted employing a term so freighted with negative judgment by the society they had abandoned. If "Hebrews" as a self-designation of the Israelites is an equivalent to 'apiru, the decided limitation of the name to very restricted contexts (e.g., in talking to foreigners) may indicate an aversion to the label *'apiru* among many of the rebels as they broke loose from feudal dependence.

Moreover, as Mendenhall has stressed, this "withdrawal" from Canaanite feudalism must not be seen solely as physical flight. The "withdrawal" entailed the strengthening of the village agricultural/pastoral complex against the urban-dominated latifundist-agricultural and trading complex.[326] Groups "withdrawing" would not necessarily flee from their homes. In fact, resistance on their familiar home ground would have been the preference of the rebels. Depending on the defensibility of the location, the attrition of central power, the local self-organization, the availability of *'apiru* allies, and other such factors, the village units could develop autonomy on their home ground. If forced out, they could fall back into more inaccessible areas and begin the reconstruction of their former economy and social organization, with such alterations as changes in natural environment or political-military exigencies required, drawing as needed on the growing fund of *'apiru* experience in making such adaptations.

In other words, I am suggesting that the line between *'apiru* as organized military and brigand bands and the village agriculturalists and pastoralists was probably a rather indistinct one in many cases, becoming less and less distinct as central authority crumbled. In certain respects, once relieved of Canaanite feudal domination, the two ideal types would tend to move toward one another. *'Apiru,* no longer receiving regular supplies from a dynast, would tend to settle and cultivate land as their own. Villagers, openly or covertly resistant to the authorities, would tend to develop local defense measures. Each group had something to learn from the other. At some hypothetical point in this expansion and slow convergence of nonfeudally organized peoples, the preconditions for a wider unity developed. In such a setting early Israel took its rise.

LACK OF ANTI-FEUDAL SOURCES. Finally, we must also remember that what we know about the Amarna Age developments comes exclusively from the dynasts and ruling circles in control of the city-states, or from the Egyptian court. We do not have material from the *'apiru* bands or from the serfs or semi-free peasants. As we have noted, we are not even certain that *'apiru* was a term used by the people so labelled by the established order. Both *'apiru* and depressed peasants and pastoralists may have been much more anti-feudal than we now have any way of knowing. The content of their daily experience was such as to have ingrained in them the hardships and injustices of the feudal system, but how widely they generalized from that experience, how articulate they were in their grievances and acts of protestation, and how united they felt themselves to be with others in similar situations remain unknown. At any rate, the reported conduct of the rebellious and warring victims of feudalism in the Amarna texts does not indicate an explicit anti-feudal consciousness and strategy of action. Helpful at this point is an analysis such as Eric Hobsbawm's treatment of robbers as an ideal type (actually a series of types), in which he delineates the many levels of sociopolitical consciousness and practice among organized robbers, ranging from the random indulgence of self-interest to very explicit revolutionary consciousness.[327]

That a large measure of anti-feudal sentiment existed among some of these groups is suggested by the kind of social revolutionary propaganda Abdi-Ashirta manipulated for his own Machiavellian purposes. But it is only in the literature of early Israel that the revolutionary consciousness of the Canaanite underclasses finds an articulate voice. Only with early Israel did the diffuse anti-feudal sentiment of Canaan become a highly charged cultural, socioeconomic, and military-political revolution. But it may also be true that we would be able to detect signs of the gathering revolutionary consciousness at earlier points had we any direct testimonies from the pre-Israelite lower classes in Canaan. Egalitarian social-revolutionary consciousness—as distinct from ruling-class appropriation of aspects of egalitarian sentiment—first receives full literate expression in the Near East with early Israel. That in itself is of great significance: the underclasses of Canaan who joined in early Israel decided that writing was too valuable a tool to be left to the ruling class; they seized upon the alphabetic script as a simple instrument of expression that could serve an egalitarian community instead of aiding a ruling elite to control and manipulate the populace.

37

Philistines as Heirs of Egyptian-Canaanite Dominion

The Philistine settlement on the southwest coastal plain of Canaan, from Gaza in the south to Joppa in the north and inland to the foothills of the central mountain range, began shortly after 1200 B.C. and culminated in 1050–1000 B.C. in a direct contest of arms with Israel for the control of Canaan. Thanks to extrabiblical texts and archaeological finds, the Philistines are now better understood culturally and militarily than they were as recently as twenty-five years ago.[328] However, the Philistine social and political organization, and particularly the transitional stages from their initial settlement to their assertion of sovereignty over all Palestine, are still very imperfectly known. Enough is reconstructable to establish with assurance that the Philistines emerged in Canaan as the heirs of Egyptian imperialism and of Canaanite city-state feudalism. What remains uncertain, for want of detailed information, is the precise manner in which preceding Egyptian/Canaanite elements of sociopolitical organization were juxtaposed with newly introduced Philistine elements of sociopolitical organization to produce a fresh and formidable historic force in Palestine.

37.1 Philistine Dominion in Canaan

There is a growing consensus that the appearance of the Philistines on the southwest coastal plain of Canaan can best be explained on the theory that they were installed there as protégés and vassals by the Egyptians in order to buttress declining Egyptian imperial control over that region. The Philistines were one of the "Sea Peoples" who had been displaced from the Aegean-Anatolian regions (the Philistines having migrated perhaps from Crete or, even more probably, from Lycia in Asia Minor, and perhaps before that from Illyria or Etruria). With their allies, they attempted to invade the Nile Delta during the reign of Rameses III (some time in the first three decades of the twelfth century). They were blocked in this attempt, but not long afterwards archaeological data show these very Philistines to have been serving as mercenaries for the Egyptians in the Nile Delta, in Nubia, and in southwest Canaan as well.

During the twelfth century Egyptian imperial control over Canaan declined to zero; simultaneously the Philistine grip upon Canaan increased steadily to fill the power vacuum. It was precisely the old Egyptian administrative district in southwest Canaan, where Ashkelon and Gaza were located, that was both the last toehold of the Egyptian Asiatic Empire and the strategic base of the flourishing Philistines. This synchronization of Egyptian withdrawal and Philistine expansion seems best explained not on the theory that the Philistines forcefully ejected the Egyptians from the start, or that the Philistines entered a region evacuated by the Egyptians, but rather on the theory that the Philistine establishment in Canaan "took place under acknowledgement of Egyptian sovereignty and with Egyptian sanction, or at least with Egyptian toleration."[329] As Egyptian sovereignty over Canaan crumbled away in the following decades, the Philistines became the successors to defaulted Egyptian claims of sovereignty. This would have been a particularly logical historical development if we grant, as seems most plausible, that these same Philistines had been originally permitted to enter the region as military, and probably also as administrative, overseers of the Egyptian imperial apparatus by vassal or mercenary arrangement.

On the other side, it appears that the city-state structure of the southwest coastal plain of Canaan was not fundamentally disturbed by the entrance of the Philistines. The sociopolitical subdivision of the land into city-states, which had persisted throughout the Egyptian imperium in Canaan over centuries of time, continued in what was to become Philistia. Ashkelon, Ashdod and Gaza, on or near the coast, were ancient cities whose independence as units within the empire remained intact. Further inland, Ekron and Gath were apparently built after the Philistine settlement to insure military and commercial control of the approaches to the hill country of Judah. Greater certainty about the early history of Ekron and Gath continues to be frustrated by a lack of consensus in identifying the actual sites of these cities.[330] The Philistines, with Egyptian concurrence, not only made no attempt to disrupt the old city-state pattern but even contributed to its extension inland on the coastal plain. It is commonly assumed, on the basis of biblical data such as I Samuel 6:17–18a, that the frequently mentioned "lords of the Philistines" were the direct rulers of the five major city-states of Ashkelon, Ashdod, Gaza, Ekron, and Gath, although this longstanding interpretation is now properly questioned. In any event, the initial accommodation of the Philistines to the older city-state divisions was perpetuated even after the Egyptian withdrawal from Asia. Accordingly, not only did the Philistines fall heir to the succession of Egyptian empire but they also fell heir to the old internal Canaanite subdivisions by city-states and incorporated those city-state entities as a mode of their hegemony, just as the Egyptians before them had done.

The leaders of the Philistines are referred to characteristically in the Bible by the term s^erānīm, "lords" or "military aristocrats," always in the plural as a collective body acting in concert. The term is plausibly related to the Greek tyrannos; but, since it is suspected that tyrannos is a loan from Lydian or Phrygian (and is sometimes compared with the Etruscan turan, "lady"), the Philistine seren may derive finally from Anatolia (or Etruria?).[331] The fact that this is one of a small number of technical words known to have survived the wholesale Philistine adoption of Canaanite speech strongly suggests that a collective aristocratic military leadership characterized the Philistines before they settled in Canaan. We are completely in the dark as to whether such coordinated leadership was operative in their original homeland or was an adaptive device developed during their migrations to insure survival. Further support for the hypothesis of the presettlement origin of the Philistine military aristocracy is the fact that we know of no such sustained collective leadership among the older Canaanite city-states which, even when faced with extreme external threats, had been capable only of episodic alliances markedly unstable in their membership and longevity.

It has been customary to conceive of the Philistine lords as installed in the five major city-states as feudal lords who replaced the former Canaanite rulers. Our source of information on this matter is the Israelite historical writings, which sometimes speak of the Philistine lords as five in number, although in several instances their number is unspecified. Only in I Samuel 6:18a is the five-member body of s^{e}rānīm expressly equated with the five major cities of the Philistines, and then only by a rather clumsy circumlocution with an appositional expression which leaves the matter in some doubt. After it is said that the five golden tumors, fashioned as a guilt offering to Yahweh, correspond to the five cities ("one for Ashdod, one for Gaza, one for Ashkelon, one for Gath, one for Ekron," vs. 17), it is further stated that the golden mice were "according to the number of all the cities of the Philistines belonging to (or connected with) the five lords, ranging from fortified cities to unwalled villages" (vs. 18a). The position of this note in the narrative, the stylistic opening ("these are the golden tumors" without immediate antecedent [vs. 17]), the obvious attempt to elaborate on 6:4, and the ambiguous appositional construction of the final phrase all attest to vss. 17–18a as a learned secondary expansion. Granted that a secondary notation may contain reliable historical information, there is sufficient ambiguity in this case to construe the relation of the lords to the cities in either of two ways: (1) it may be construed that there were as many golden mice as there were cities owned by the five lords, including a considerable number of walled cities and unwalled villages, which would obviously be many more than five in number; or (2) it may be construed that the five familiar cities of the Philistines are identified respectively with the five lords, the phrase "ranging from fortified cities to unwalled villages" referring to the entirety of the region controlled from each of the five major cities. Given the larger context of the notation, it is probable that the latter sense is the one intended, but even such a determination does not settle the matter because the exact sense of the prepositional connection between cities and lords is indeterminate. In what sense do the cities "belong to" the lords?

On close analysis, the assumption that the five lords of the Philistines ruled directly over the five city-states is by no means conclusive, resting as it does on rather slim foundations in the biblical materials. On the basis of the distinction between the Philistine *s^erānîm* and Achish, king of Gath, in I Samuel 29, H. Kassis has contended that Gath was ruled dually by a native Canaanite king, Achish, who was in turn subject to the Philistine *s^erānîm*.[332] Although Kassis does not extend the proposal of dual rule to the other Philistine cities, he does note that in I Samuel 29:2 it is reported that "the Philistine *s^erānîm* were passing on by hundreds and thousands." This enumeration of the *s^erānîm* in the magnitude of hundreds and thousands, coupled with passages which give no indication of number, may imply that they were "a class of charioteers who manipulated and controlled the land that came to bear their name."[333] It would in my view be more accurate to speak of a class of military professionals, since as a whole the Philistine warriors were not restricted to chariots. Also, it is noteworthy that certain of the *s^erānîm* are singled out as "commanders" or "princes" (I Sam. 29:3–4).

It seems to me worth exploring the hypothesis that the dual rule posited for Gath was also typical of the other Philistine cities. On such an hypothesis each city will have possessed its own local petty ruler who was subordinate to the collective authority of the military aristocracy. Certain of these *s^erānîm* will have formed the military high command, and either they or another group of *s^erānîm* will have been assigned to administrative oversight of the vassal kings in the five major cities. Such an organization, essentially that of a military ruling elite with particular members assigned specific military and administrative leadership roles, helps to explain why *s^erānîm* are described as a collectivity in close cooperation, whereas their number is only sporadically indicated. When no number is stated, or when hundreds and thousands are reported in one instance, the reference is to the collectivity of military aristocrats encompassing all the professional warriors conceived as self-governing and unitedly dominant over the respective city-states in the total realm. When "five *s^erānîm*" are specified, the reference is to the "commanders" or "princes" with special military and/or administrative functions which were articulated according to the five major city-state subdivisions of the Philistine state.

Moreover, the hypothesis of dual rule in which a Philistine military aristocracy was superimposed on Canaanite vassal kings in the major cities corresponds closely to the situation of Egyptian rule over Canaan. The pharaoh never ruled directly over the city-states. Instead, Egyptian commissioners supervised regions of the empire, but internal affairs were the jurisdiction of the native vassal-kings. Proceeding on the assumption that the Philistines had been admitted to Canaan as the agents of Egyptian imperial rule and were, therefore, predisposed to follow previous Egyptian imperial policies, we should not be surprised to find the Philistines exercising their sovereignty through indirect oversight rather than through direct rule over the city-states. At the same time, we cannot underestimate the major new element supplied by the Philistines, namely, a remarkably well disciplined and cohesive ruling military aristocracy in comparison with which the bureaucratically organized foreign service of the Egyptian empire was diffuse, poorly coordinated with the army, deficient in morale, and relatively ineffectual.

37.2 The Philistine Challenge to Early Israel

We begin to see the contours of the great organizational strength of the Philistines, even though we lack much detail. Internally, as a body of mercenaries and administrators serving the Egyptian empire in Canaan, they had a ready-made organization seasoned by years of testing in warfare and self-rule during their long migrations. This hardy organization, increasingly rooted in a Canaanite habitat in contrast to the ill-adapted colonial intrusion of Egyptian rule, provided continuity and stability which made them surer masters of those parts of Canaan they controlled than the Egyptians had ever been, except for brief periods under the most energetic pharaohs. Obviously Egypt was the stronger power in terms of total human, economic, and military resources, but Egypt had the great disadvantage of having to operate from a base separated from Canaan by the Sinai desert. Egypt had learned to depend upon periodic military campaigns into Asia to terrorize the opposition into compliance, but for the sustenance of the empire the lines of communication and resupply from the Nile to Canaan were long and precarious. Moreover, the line of pharaonic succession had not always been smoothly maintained. Internecine court fights in Egypt, as well as periodic tendencies toward absorption with domestic affairs, had contributed to an erratic imperial policy which aborted efforts at systematic exploitation of the Canaanite provinces. Also, the garrisons of Egyptian troops stationed at points in Canaan were thinly spread and manned by troops who did not regard Canaan as their home. The Philistines, by contrast, were concentrated in a well-provisioned and strategically defensible area, and they soon came to regard Canaan as their home. They ardently adopted Canaanite culture in most regards, remaining distinguished chiefly by their extraordinary military-political guild structure. The Philistines could thus feel themselves to be far more "Canaanite" and could represent themselves to their subjects as far more "Canaanite" than could the Egyptians. It is evident that on geographic strategic grounds and on military-political organizational grounds the Philistines posed a challenge to Israel far more serious than single or allied Canaanite city-states and even more serious than the Egyptian empire itself in the attenuated form in which pharaonic rule affected the Canaanite highlands.

Another major factor in Philistine strength was its superb military technology. Much has been written on this subject in recent years, [334] and I shall only draw summary conclusions relevant for our examination of the adaptive advantages enjoyed by the Philistines. We know that the Philistines had chariots. Unlike the *maryannu* charioteer aristocracy which in previous centuries had come to hold great military and political power in the various Canaanite city-states, the Philistines fielded a more diversified array of forces, including heavily armed infantry, some of whom were of great physical stature. Probably through their contact with the Hittites in Anatolia and northern Syria, the Philistines had acquired skill in iron-working and were able to deploy iron weapons with devastating effect. The Bible reports that the Philistines asserted their hegemony over the Israelites by denying them knowledge and practice of iron smithing, thereby preventing their access to iron weapons (I Sam. 13:19–22). In fact, the Israelites had to take their iron agricultural implements to the Philistines for sharpening. The technological leap from bronze-working to iron-working is a measurable one. Compared to bronze, iron demands more complicated sets of favorable conditions and precise techniques in working the metal into tools and weapons.[335] Israel had acquired iron tools and implements for clearing and cultivating the highlands, but not many iron weapons had come into its hands as a result of the iron monopoly of the Philistines. Nor did Israel have diplomatic relations with Syrian states by means of which it could gain access to Hittite iron technology or come into possession of iron weapons through foreign trade. Apparently the bronze-working Kenites, allied to Israel, either had not begun to experiment with iron-working techniques or had not enjoyed any success in such endeavors. In any case, the Philistines cut short all advance toward iron technology and weaponry in Israel.

By confronting Israel's bronze military technology with an iron military technology in the hands of disciplined professional warriors, the Philistines strove to cancel out the Israelite advantage of mountainous terrain and to deny Israel its hitherto marked success in the tactics of guerrilla warfare. Previously, the Canaanite city-states had been heavily dependent on chariots and composite bows,[336] which were not well adapted to warfare in the thicketed ravines of the hill country where Israel normally chose to fight.[337] By contrast, the Philistines had better trained and equipped heavy infantry, who could challenge an enemy to single combat with sword and spear (I Sam. 17; II Sam. 21: 15–22), or who could form "strike forces" capable of hard-hitting raids into Israelite territory (I Sam. 13:17–18; 14:15).[338] By challenging Israelite guerrilla tactics on their own level, the Philistines managed to penetrate into the highlands north and south of Jerusalem and to establish outposts or garrisons (I Sam. 10:5; 13:3–4,23; 14:1,4, 6,11,15; I Chron. 11:16). One of their large fortified structures may be attested from excavations at Gibeah.[339] Owing, therefore, to a remarkable convergence of mutually reinforcing factors—unified military and political organization, flexible repertory of tactics and weaponry, a secure home base within easy striking distance of the hill country, and a monopoly on iron—the Philistines were able to gain the upper hand over Israel in a seesaw struggle which precipitated the rapid emergence of the institution of monarchy in Israel as the only recourse if this unprecedented threat was to be met.

Yet the reality of Philistine power does not at once explain why they were so intent on dominating the highlands occupied by Israel. The Philistine moves against Israel were hardly in direct self-defense, for the Israelites were not engaged in open attacks upon their cities. Nor were the Philistines in need of new territory to settle a rapidly expanding population. Relative to the total population of the coastal plain in which they settled, the Philistines were a decided minority. This facilitated their speedy adoption of Canaanite language and culture, but there is no evidence for notable population growth which would have pressured the Philistines to advance into the hill country. Why, then, were the Philistines so ardently committed to the domination of Israel?

One commanding reason was the need for the Philistines to protect their trading empire. They controlled several strong positions in the coastal plain north of Philistia, in the lateral Valley of Esdraelon and in the northern Jordan Valley, but these strong points were insufficient to extend adequate protection to the caravans of their clients in Transjordan.[340] As long as Israel was in control of the highlands on either side of the Jordan, the Philistine trade hegemony was precarious. Although I am unaware of any direct evidence, it is probable in my view that Israel raided the trade routes in Transjordan and in the Jordan Valley over which Philistine-controlled commerce regularly moved—just as Israel had formerly raided the Canaanite caravans. Moreover, being predominantly warriors and traders, the Philistines depended upon their subjects for agricultural support. The plain of Philistia was a fertile grain-growing region, but as the Philistine commercial empire expanded, the coastal agricultural base was probably insufficient to produce large surpluses of grain and oil, so necessary as trading commodities to offer in return for the more exotic products not indigenous to Canaan. Consequently, the Philistines set out to conquer Israel

> with the intention of establishing their overlordship along the lines of the former dynasty of the Pharaohs, and with the practical aim of exploiting the husbandry and agriculture of the mountain regions by exacting tribute. They would be a ruling military class; the Israelites and Canaanites would be their subjects and produce the food—this is how the Philistines would have liked to see the distribution of functions throughout Palestine.[341]

When the aims of Philistine hegemony over Israel are seen in the context of political economy, it is evident that in resisting such hegemony Israel was fighting for its survival as an egalitarian, self-determining, socioeconomic system. The handing over of her agricultural and pastoral surpluses to Philistia would have meant not only the end of formal independence for the tribes but also impoverishment for the predominantly peasant-herdsmen populace of Israel. Philistine hegemony would also have opened the way for conscription of Israelite troops as auxiliary forces under Philistine command and for drafting of Israelite manpower for state labor, either on building projects or in servitude on feudally organized agricultural estates. This would have signalled Israel's integration into the imperial-feudal grid system of social relations, with the rapid eclipse or attenuation of her own autonomous institutions.

The fate of subjection to Philistia would have been for Israel a virtual return to bondage in Egypt. In resisting the Philistines, all the rich, highly charged symbolism of the centralized cultic traditions about deliverance from Egypt and possession of the land was available to mobilize the fighting spirit of the people (cf. III.11). And it was precisely this grave threat from the Philistines that gave the final stimulus to the development of the centralized traditions, cementing them ever more firmly into the superstructure of Israelite society and imbedding them ever more deeply in the public consciousness of Israel. However, far more than rich symbolism and a will to resist were called for. Somehow the superior organization and technology of the enemy had to be neutralized, and it was of course this fundamental desideratum that elicited the forced experiments in more centralized leadership under Saul and David, experiments which proved to be highly successful in blunting the Philistine hegemonic drive and in confining the Philistines to their former coastal homeland.

37.3 Philistine–Israelite–Canaanite Triangular Relations

It would be a deficiency in our method of study, however, to restrict our view of the struggle in Canaan during the eleventh century to the Philistine and Israelite antagonists. We must also take into account the Canaanite populations which had not been absorbed into Israel and which, to greater or lesser degrees, were still beyond the control of the Philistines. In the southwest coastal plain the Canaanites had come under Philistine hegemony when these Sea People were installed there by the Egyptians; the Canaanites continued as Philistine subjects when Egyptian suzerainty passed into Philistine hands. As Philistine control reached up the coastal plain, across the Valley of Esdraelon and into the northern Jordan Valley, more and more Canaanite city-states felt its effect. Although our information is meager, by extrapolation from known Philistine policy we can conclude that wherever possible they subjected the Canaanites and exacted tribute from them. And even apart from the extent of political control exercised by the Philistines over these Canaanite entities, which probably varied from region to region, we must recognize that the lucrative trade that had prospered the major Canaanite cities in the great valleys now passed more and more into the hands of the Philistines. Unquestionably this meant a decline in the prosperity of the Canaanite cities; or, in circumstances where the level of prosperity was maintained, the Canaanite city-states were at any rate compelled to give up larger shares of commercial wealth to the Philistine masters, so that the Philistine overlords prospered at a faster rate than did their Canaanite vassals.

It has been argued, chiefly on linguistic grounds, that the cryptic Shamgar ben

Anath, credited with slaying six hundred Philistines with an ox-goad, was in fact a Canaanite (Judg. 3:31; 5:6).[342] Of course, what is not clear from the scraps of information in Judges is whether Shamgar was operating as the representative of one of the Canaanite cities that opposed the Philistines or whether he was merely an individual adventurer who joined the Israelite cause. In either case, he illustrates vividly that not only Israelites but Canaanites as well were threatened by the encroachment of the Philistines. This perception of political forces in eleventh-century Canaan is further reinforced by a brief comment in I Samuel 7 in connection with the much disputed account of Samuel's victory over the Philistines: "There was peace also between Israel and the Amorites" (vs. 14b). This occurs in an E-type traditional context where "Amorite" refers in a general way to the indigenous populace of Canaan. Now this is so general a remark as to cover a wide spectrum of possible relations between the two peoples, ranging all the way from mere cessation of conflict to the actual contracting of alliances of varying scope. There is no independent evidence of such alliances, and we do not read of the forces of Canaanite city-states joining with Israelite forces against the Philistines. Yet even if we put a minimal construction on the circumstances summarized in I Samuel 7:14b, it is patent that a cessation of Canaanite hostilities against Israel would have been a great boon, releasing Israelite forces to concentrate exclusively on the Philistine invaders. Moreover, a truce between Canaanite city-states not dominated by Philistia and the Israelites signalled an important shift in political sympathies, for it meant that the still independent Canaanites recognized the Philistines as a far greater threat to themselves than the traditional Israelite enemies. This was certainly a realistic assessment on the part of the Canaanites, not only because of the superior Philistine organization and technology but also because of the overt expansionist policy of the Philistines in contrast with the long-prevailing defensive stance of Israel.

We need not exaggerate the Canaanite change of mind. It could be construed as little more than a forced diversion of their attention from trying to dislodge the Israelites from the hill country because they were compelled to cope with the Philistine political, military, and economic encroachment upon their spheres of dominion and influence. Nevertheless, those who have a common enemy have common interests even if they maintain other very different and opposed interests as well. In such circumstances, Canaanite city-states would have been indirect beneficiaries of Israelite successes in resisting or driving back the Philistines, and vice versa. Accordingly, we can see a convergence of anti-Philistine interests which brought Canaanites and Israelites closer together after two centuries of diverging and clashing interests. David's success in incorporating the surviving old Canaanite city-states into his kingdom after the defeat of the Philistines must be seen in this context. The records are blank on the details of that incorporation, but it is consistent with the conditions we have just described that these Canaanite entities would have been greatly relieved to be delivered of the Philistine threat, and that at least in many instances, they would have tended to look upon Davidic rule as a means to safeguard their vital interests once they were incorporated into one or another of the tribal subdivisions of David's kingdom. It need scarcely be said that in the early reign of David these Canaanites had no inkling of the despotism which was to become Solomon's hallmark in dealing with his subjects.

The Canaanite-Israelite-Philistine triangular relations were further complicated by the presence of 'apiru who continued to operate symbiotically with organized city-states in Canaan. While considerable numbers of 'apiru became a part of Israel, the tribes of Israel did not spread over the entirety of Canaan. For that reason it is to be expected that wherever the imperial-feudal pattern held firm in Canaan, 'apiru continued to function as mercenary bands in the city-states. This reading of developments is borne out by some cursory details about "Hebrews" in I Samuel 13—14. These details have troubled interpreters to the extent that they have resorted to unnecessary textual and exegetical contortions to avoid the evident meanings of what is said. I shall quote these allusions to "Hebrews" and, in brackets, indicate the sense in which each of them is to be understood. Afterward the asserted equations for Hebrews will be defended against contrary interpretations.

I Samuel 13:3–7a: Jonathan defeated the garrison of the Philistines which was at Geba (Gibeah?); and the Philistines heard of it. And Saul blew the trumpet throughout all the land, saying, "Let the Hebrews ['*ivrim* = '*apiru*] hear!" And all Israel heard it said that Saul had defeated the garrison of the Philistines, and also that Israel had become odious to the Philistines. And the people were called out to join Saul at Gilgal. And the Philistines mustered to fight with Israel; . . . they came up and encamped in Michmash, to the east of Beth-aven. When the men of Israel saw that they were in a critical situation (for the people were hard pressed), the people hid themselves in caves and in holes and in rocks and in tombs and in cisterns, and [whereas?] the Hebrews ['*ivrim*=*apiru*] crossed over the Jordan to the land of Gad and Gilead.

I Samuel 13:19–20: Now there was no smith to be found throughout all the land of Israel; for the Philistines said, "Lest the Hebrews ['*ivrim* = Israelites] make themselves swords and spears"; but every one of the Israelites went down to the Philistines to sharpen his plowshare, his mattock, his axe, or his sickle.

I Samuel 14:11–12: So both of them [Jonathan and his armor bearer] showed themselves to the garrison of the Philistines; and the Philistines said, "Look, Hebrews ['*ivrim* = Israelites] are coming out of the holes where they have hid themselves." And the men of the garrison hailed Jonathan and his armor-bearer, and said, "Come up to us, and we will show you a thing." And Jonathan said to his armor-bearer, "Come up after me; for Yahweh has given them into the hand of Israel."

I Samuel 14:21–23a: Now the Hebrews ['*ivrim* = '*apiru*] who had been with the Philistines before that time and who had gone up with them into the camp, even they also turned to be with the Israelites who were with Saul and Jonathan. Likewise, when all the men of Israel who had hid themselves in the hill country of Ephraim heard that the Philistines were fleeing they too followed hard after them in battle. So Yahweh delivered Israel that day.

In these excerpts, "Hebrews" is used in two senses by two sets of speakers: in one sense it is the term used by the Philistines for the Israelites, whereas in the other sense it is a term used by the Israelites (either by a speaker in the narrative or by the narrator) for a group not equatable with Israel which fought with the Philistines but was won over to the Israelites after Jonathan's rout of the Philistines. All interpreters agree as to the presence of the first sense in I Samuel 13—14, but a majority deny a second sense, or, if granting it of necessity in 14:21, they do not know what to make of it and fail to see the same meaning of "Hebrews" in 13:3 and 13:7, nor are they able to establish an adequate sociopolitical link between the two senses of "Hebrew."

This blindness toward the double meanings of Hebrew in I Samuel 13—14 follows from the inability of interpreters to believe that any groups other than Israelites could have been called Hebrews. Accordingly, all occurrences of 'ivrîm are made into Philistine statements about the Israelites—or, in one instance, into a narrator's accommodation to Philistine usage. This sleight of hand is adroitly performed. Beginning with the undisputed Hebrew-Israelite equation in 13:19 and 14:11, the same equation is found in 13:3 by emending the text, along the line of LXX, and transposing phrases with the resultant reading:

> Jonathan defeated the garrison of the Philistines which was at Geba, and the Philistines heard of it and proclaimed, "The Hebrews have revolted!" And Saul blew the trumpet throughout all the land, and all Israel heard it and said, "Saul has defeated the garrison of the Philistines."[343]

In 13:7, "Hebrews" is stricken from the text, usually on the assumption that the original reading was a verb form describing how the men of Israel "passed over" the Jordan,[344] but sometimes on the conjecture that the original was 'am rav, "a great crowd,"[345] which would similarly refer to some of the Israelites. The final reference to 'ivrîm in 14:21 is taken to refer to a group of Israelites who had defected to the Philistines but who were won back by Saul's and Jonathan's striking victory. If the matter is discussed at all, the defecting and returning Israelites are said to be called "Hebrews" in keeping with Philistine convention.

The weakness of this univocal understanding of Hebrew as Israelite is that it does not consider a sociopolitical meaning for Hebrew as a viable alternative to the traditionally accepted ethnic meaning. As a result it forces all occurrences of "Hebrews" into the same ethnic mold and, even though it gets rid of two of the troublesome references by textual emendation, its treatment of the recalcitrant "Hebrews" in 14:21 is highly strained. On the other hand, if we take into account the sociopolitical 'apiru type previously discussed, it is possible to establish a sociopolitical meaning for "Hebrews" which encompasses both of the senses identified in I Samuel 13—14.

It is noteworthy that those called Hebrews by the Philistines are consistently called Israel or Israelites by the Israelite speakers and narrator. This can hardly be attributed to the late Deuteronomist traditionist who edited the narrative, for to him "Hebrew" was simply an ethnicon for Israelite. There is every reason to believe that the original narrator was close enough to the events to remember accurately that the Philistines did indeed regularly refer to his people as "Hebrews." Only one explanation of this linguistic practice is plausible. The Philistines employed this opprobrious term in order to express their claims of hegemony over the Israelites. They refused to recognize the people of the highlands as a separate autonomous sociopolitical entity; they saw in them only rebellious subordinates whose proper place was within the imperial-feudal system as subjects of the Philistine overlords.

> A certain degree of haughtiness can be discerned in the application of this term by the Philistines—from their point of view quite understandable, as the Israelites were their subordinates for some time by then, and was [sic] even disarmed (I Sam. 4:9; 13:19). The same preventive measure was applied by the Egyptian Pharaoh to the *'ibrīm* then subordinate to him (Ex. 1:15f.) . . . For the Philistines then, the Israelites are *'ibrīm* because they regard them as their servants and subordinates.[346]

In so labelling the Israelites, the Philistines did not have to coin a term. They simply adopted a common Canaanite term. Since *'apiru,* as political dependents and mercenary auxiliaries, still served Canaanite city-states and Philistine *s^erānīm* alike, it was a label at hand for the Philistines to attach to a people they were intent on keeping subordinate to their rule. The continuing existence of non-Israelite *'apiru* was, however, not in itself a sufficient reason for calling Israelites "Hebrews." After all, the Israelites composed a large congeries of tribes including tens if not hundreds of thousands of people, and extending over a large contiguous area of the highlands. Furthermore, the Philistine intent was to requisition the agricultural surpluses of the Israelites and to impress Israelite manpower as needed into Philistine state projects. The Philistines confronted the Israelites in a manner more analogous to their confrontation of a Canaanite city-state or group of city-states than in a manner analogous to one city-state among others vying for the services of outlaws who might become their mercenaries. So there must have been additional factors which led the Philistines to select the rather restricted, and in some ways anomalous, term *'apiru* /Hebrews to designate the Israelites.

One of these additional factors was probably the respect that the Philistines had for the Israelite soldiery. Of course, they did not regard the Israelites as a match for their superior weapons and organization, but they did perceive them as very tough fighters whose service as lightly armed infantry auxiliaries and as raiders would be very useful. The Philistines already employed hired bodies of auxiliaries, including '*apiru* from Canaanite city-states, and it was therefore appropriate to extend the same term to the Israelites.

Still, we have not fully accounted for the contemptuous overtones of the Philistine epithet "Hebrews" as directed at Israelites. This is best explained by a continuous living tradition of contempt toward '*apiru*, passed along from the Amarna imperial-feudal establishment to the Philistines when they inherited that establishment from the Egyptians. The term '*apiru* still carried wider pejorative auras of meaning which aptly branded the Israelites as arch-rebels against the imperial-feudal order. Israel recognized neither imperial nor feudal masters. It must have come early to the attention of Philistines that Israelites alone in Canaan refused on principle to be ruled by others or to rule themselves according to the long-canonized system of political hierarchy. They saw at once the sizable agricultural and manpower resources that would be theirs if they could subject the Israelite "outlaw" society. They would not concede the pretension of autonomy contained in the name "Israel" by deigning to use it. Thus the contempt conveyed in the epithet '*apiru*/Hebrew expressed Philistine frustration and apprehension that the '*apiru* project of becoming relatively independent of the imperial-feudal establishment had been carried through to successful revolution by the Hebrews/Israelites. It was the Philistine intention to wipe out that revolution and to return the mass of Israelites to the status of '*apiru* captives of war, analogous to the '*apiru* in Egypt. Having done so, they might then select the best Israelite warriors for more privileged status as mercenary auxiliaries.

So it seems that there was a mixture of meanings, a mélange of nuances, in the Philistine epithet "Hebrews." Israelites were "Hebrews" in that, like the '*apiru* at large, they were viewed by the Philistines as subordinates in the overall imperial-feudal system. Israelites were "Hebrews" in that they gave promise of being good auxiliary troops in the best '*apiru* tradition. Israelites were "Hebrews" in that they had become the supremely successful rebels against the imperial-feudal system. Israelites were "Hebrews" in that, with sufficient force, they could be reduced to state slavery as the Egyptians had done to their '*apiru* captives.

When the sociopolitical basis of the Philistine use of '*apiru*/Hebrews for the Israelites is grasped, we can more readily make sense of the other occurrences of '*ivrīm* in I Samuel 13—14 which allude to an armed body (or bodies) independent of the Israelites.

The touchstone for this understanding is 14:21 where an armed group called "Hebrews," who had been in the Philistine camp, is said to have switched its loyalty to the Israelites under Saul and Jonathan. There is no way of seeing "Hebrews" and "Israelites" in this context as simply interchangeable terms for the same group. "Hebrews" is here used as a differentiating term, either for non-Israelites or for some Israelites viewed in a particular way. In either case, the differentiation entailed is a sociopolitical one. In other words, we must apply our previous determination that 'apiru is a sociopolitical "outlaw" category with military sub-specialization in the Canaanite setting. If the "Hebrews" of 14:21 are non-Israelites, they are to be seen as a professional military band offering their services first to the Philistines and later, when the balance of power shifted to the Israelites, switching their support to the latter. If the "Hebrews" of 14:21 are Israelites, the only reason for differentiating them with this term would be that they were an armed band of Israelites who had given their services as 'apiru to the Philistines but returned to the Israelite side when the battle went decisively against the Philistines. In that case, the Israelite 'apiru engaged in a fight with their own people would have been in the situation that David and his band narrowly avoided when, contrary to the wish of Achish of Gath, the Philistine s⁽ᵉ⁾rānīm disqualified David and his troops from fighting against Saul at Gilboa (I Samuel 29).

A similar sociopolitical understanding of "Hebrews" in 13:3 is evident. In spite of the awkwardness of the Hebrew text, perhaps stemming from confusion among the later traditionists once the original sociological context for 'apiru/Hebrews was lost to their view, there is no real satisfaction to be gained by the frequent emendation of the text we referred to above. The LXX of 13:3 is not less clumsy than MT, and the transposition of phrases in order to iron out difficulties by shifting the speaker of the exclamation, "The Hebrews have revolted!" from Saul to the Philistines is wholly conjectural. In fact, the impulse to emend the text starts from the inability of scholars to accept "the name *Hebrews* in Saul's mouth, which cannot be correct."[347] To those interpreters it "cannot be correct," of course, because elsewhere in context the Israelites call themselves only Israelites, and most scholars do not consider that "Hebrews" may be sociopolitical nomenclature referring variously to Israelites and non-Israelites who fill the appropriate 'apiru/Hebrew role.

Actually, what is said of the "Hebrews" in 13:3 fits well with what is said of them in 14:21. The sound of the trumpet is a military signal. "Let the Hebrews hear!" is more properly to be translated, "Let the Hebrews listen / pay attention / obey!" This is Saul's appeal to the "third force" of 'apiru warriors, who have served the Philistines but should now be warned or inspired by the Israelite victory to withdraw their support from the Philistines and come over to Israel—precisely as they eventually did, according to 14:21. The two verses fit comfortably together, and they do so whether "Hebrews" are non-Israelite mercenary 'apiru or whether they are a band of Israelites who gave 'apiru service to the Philistines.

The "Hebrews" in 13:7 present a difficulty not easily overcome on any view of the identity of the Hebrews in I Samuel 13—14. The consonantal change in the Hebrew text required to get the LXX's "and they passed over Jordan" (subject, "the people," or, by implication, "some of the people"), which eliminates "Hebrews" altogether, corrects a kind of textural error that is common enough and, at the same time, eliminates the problem of relating the "Hebrews" of 13:7 to those of 13:3 and 14:21. In the end this may be the proper course, but there is one feature held in common by 13:7 and 14:21 which gives me pause and which suggests that "Hebrews" in 13:7 may indeed be original. I refer to the fact that 14:21 distinguishes a group of Hebrews from the Israelites who hid themselves in West Jordan and that precisely the same pairing appears in 13:6–7 where Hebrews who fled over the Jordan are set off from Israelites who hid themselves in West Jordan.

There can hardly be any doubt that the Israelites who hide themselves in 13:7 are the same Israelites who come out of hiding in 14:21. Should it not at least be seriously considered that the Hebrews who come over to the support of Israel in 14:21 are the Hebrews who fled over the Jordan in 13:7, or, at least, that they are an armed band analogous to those in 13:7? If, however, the 'apiru/Hebrews of 13:3,7 and 14:21 are conceived as Israelites or non-Israelites fighting with the Philistines, but who later align with the Israelites, it is virtually impossible to make sense of their flight across the Jordan in 13:7. I say this because the hiding of many Israelites and the flight of the Hebrews in 13:6–7 is occasioned by the large muster of Philistine troops who strike panic among the forces of Saul. If these Hebrews were at the time still a part of the Philistine force, there would be no explanation of their flight except desertion. According to 14:21 the desertion to Israel came only after the Philistines were faring badly in the fight. Thus, the Hebrews of 13:7 can only be seen as former fighters with the Philistines on the assumption that this early in the action some of them deserted the Philistines—i.e., before the larger desertion of 14:21—and on the further assumption that, once they had deserted, instead of standing firm with Saul, they fled in panic. This is not a plausible reconstruction of events. If "Hebrews" is to be retained in 13:7, they would have to be understood as a group of Israelites who, though they customarily gave 'apiru service, were not supporting the Philistines in the present campaign but were within Saul's army. They would be like the Hebrews of 13:3 and 14:21 in that they regularly offered themselves in 'apiru service, but they would be unlike the Hebrews of 13:3 and 14:21 in that they had not given their services to the Philistines in this campaign but had remained loyal to Saul. All in all, this is so precious an argument that I am not prepared to urge it decisively against the rather simpler recourse of deleting "Hebrews" in 13:7. For the moment, I would only argue that there is at least one way in which Hebrews can be retained in 13:7 in a manner that is sociopolitically plausible and conceivably resolvable within the framework of the narrative events.

While a sociopolitical understanding of 'apiru/Hebrews does not quite resolve all difficulties in the terse reports of I Samuel 13—14, it brings far more illumination to the events there described than does the ethnic understanding of the terms. It not only renders plausible the different senses of "Hebrews" when used, on the one hand, by the Philistines for all Israelites as their subjects and, on the other hand, by the Israelite speaker or narrator to designate Israelite or non-Israelite elements giving *'apiru* service. It also shows that not all combatants were firmly locked into the Philistine or Israelite camps; some wavered between the two opposing forces. A factor in the eventual victory of Philistines or Israelites was to be their relative success in enlisting the support of these uncommitted groups. From I Samuel 13—14 I have been unable to determine whether the "Hebrews" in 13:3 and 14:21 (and 13:7 if that reference to Hebrews is tentatively retained) were Israelites or non-Israelites. If "Hebrews" is retained in 13:7, the balance of evidence points toward Israelite *'apiru*/Hebrews, but we have seen that any firm conclusion about 13:7 is dubious. If it is objected that Israelites could not be conceived as giving *'apiru* service, especially to the Philistines, we must remember that David and his band offered just such service to Achish of Gath only a little later than the events of I Samuel 13—14. If the Hebrews of 13:7, and perhaps also of 13:3 and 14:21, were Israelites, then we should have to imagine that Saul had alienated some Israelites at an early point in his career as leader of united Israel. While I know of no independent evidence on this point, his later falling-out with David, which prompted David and his band to give *'apiru* service to Philistines, makes the hypothesis of earlier analogues to the Saul–David rift altogether plausible.

38

Ammon, Moab, and Edom: Societal Problematics

To complete our inventory of the sociopolitical complex in which early Israel arose, we must look briefly at the Ammonite, Moabite, and Edomite neighbors of Israel who developed as national states ruled by kings in the area east of the Jordan River at approximately the same time as Israel arose in West Jordan and in the highlands of East Jordan abutting on Ammon and Moab. Our information concerning these peoples in the period before the monarchy, and thus in their formative stages, is shockingly sparse. There are archaeological data, and although these have increased impressively in recent years, they are still meager by comparison with the archaeological data for the area west of the Jordan.[348] Egyptian, and later Assyrian, records refer sporadically to these peoples. There are so far no legible or certainly decipherable writings deriving from these peoples in the thirteenth through the eleventh centuries, although inscriptional material is beginning to fill out our knowledge of the Ammonites contemporary with the Israelite monarchy. The Old Testament remains our primary source of information for the premonarchic history of the Transjordanian peoples. The secondary literature concerning them is unusually sparse on studies of the Ammonites, Moabites, and Edomites in their own right as sociocultural wholes, tending rather toward technical reports on archaeological finds and concentration on points of contact between them and Israel.[349]

The question that concerns us is the delineation of the sociopolitical forms of these Transjordanian peoples, as they varied from and as they corresponded to the sociopolitical forms of early Israel. Unfortunately, our "answer" to this question must be exceedingly general, and at this stage of limited knowledge, can be little more than a sketch of hypotheses that fuller research will have to bear out or correct.

A useful beginning point is the suggestion of A. Alt that Israel, Philistia, Ammon, Moab, Edom, and the Aramean states should be seen together as instances of "national states" organized according to the principle of peoplehood. These "national states" arose in and near Canaan after 1300 B.C. following centuries of dominance by "territorial states," mainly city-states organized according to the principle of place or region. Since Alt described the "national states" typologically far more explicitly than any other biblical interpreter, I quote from him at some length:

A few generations after the end of the Egyptian rule the political map of Palestine is completely changed; there were hardly more than half a dozen separate states in the country, including the area east of Jordan, which comes into the light of history for the first time . . . the new states were all named after tribes and peoples who had played no part in the earlier history of the country, and indeed had only just settled there—Philistines, Israelites, Judeans, Edomites, Moabites, Ammonites, Arameans. And the naming of the states after their people also betrays a national consciousness which the earlier political formations, and the city-states in particular, never had and because of their structures could not have.

There is a very close connection between the national element in the make-up of the new states in Palestine, and the extent of their territory: they extend at least as far as men have settled who belong to the same people or tribe. . . . the new states were by no means restricted to the mountains [as in the case of Israel], but also brought under their rule the areas where previously the system of city-states had prevailed. It will be worth while first to take a closer look at the final state of the transformation, the swallowing-up of the city-principalities by the new larger states, since this clearly implies a most fundamental change in the territorial situation.

The encounter with the city-state system understandably took different forms and led to different results, according to whether a new community was built from the beginning on land that belonged to the old city-states, or whether it advanced on to their domains at a later stage. The typical example of the first case is that of the Philistines in the coastal plains.[350]

Before quoting further from Alt, let me at once exclude Philistia from his typology. The entire drift of my previous analysis, and indeed I believe the entire drift of Alt's own analysis of the Philistines, militates against conceiving them as a "nation state." While the term Philistia, drawn from the people, was applied to the coastal plain where they first settled, it was not a term extended to the entire region they dominated. It seems perfectly clear that the Philistines proper remained a minority ruling class superimposed on Canaanites and Israelites, one which finds its nearest analogy in continuity with the Egyptian empire rather than in any significant way corresponding to the other "national states" named by Alt.

In subsequent discussion, Alt does not deal with the nation states of Ammon, Moab, and Edom in their own integrity. Only in connection with one distinguishing feature of the early Israelite monarchy does he offer sufficient analysis to allow us to grasp what he conceives to have been the correspondence in constitutive principles between early Israel and the Transjordanian states. What he does have to say is instructive:

The real parallels to the internal structure of the young Israelite nation-state are to be found elsewhere [than in Philistia or Canaan]: not in the plains of the west, where city-states, their origins far back in time, pursue their individual and widely divergent courses, but in the highlands to the east, on the far side of the Jordan, among those people in which the Israelites, in spite of their national consciousness, saw their closest relatives, and which from all appearances came only a few generations before the Israelites to occupy land and form states in the border areas of the settled agricultural regions near the Syrian-Arabian desert. . . . It becomes quite evident that their kingdoms were just as far removed from the Canaanite pattern as was the kingdom of Israel in its original form.

The kingdom of Israel came on the scene as one of the last of this series of closely similar political structures, and so played its own part in the sweeping change in the political map of Palestine which came to its conclusion in the tenth century B.C. From the purely chronological point of view, one might consider the much later development of the Israelite state as a mere imitation of the long-established nation-states east of Jordan. But it is intrinsically improbable that the connection can be explained in such a mechanical way. In both cases we are dealing with related peoples, who were led from their common desert home by a similar route into the various parts of the civilized region of Palestine. If, as far as we can see, all these nations show in the formulation of the state traces of the same creative principle in operation, and if this is in fact a principle which was unknown to the previous inhabitants of the territory in which their new states were set up, then we should be able to recognize with greater confidence the consequences of a tendency which was common to all the new intruders, and which sooner or later, and according to individual circumstances, brought into being the same type of national structure, without one nation having to learn from the others. The special case of the considerably later development of the Israelite state can be adequately explained by the fact that the Israelites were thrust far deeper into the area influenced by the ancient and completely dissimilar city-states of Palestine, and consequently had far less scope for the fulfillment of their political tendencies than their cousins east of the Jordan near the desert border.[351]

It is necessary to pause here and to repudiate totally the notion of the nomadic origins of these nation-states. To speak of their "common desert home" is to speak in the face of all present evidence to the contrary and to purport an explanation of origins which in fact explains nothing. The full evidence for the rejection of the hypothesis of nomadic origins, not only for Israel but for the Transjordanian peoples as well, is presented in VIII. 39 below. Once this correction is made in Alt's analysis, it may be allowed to stand as an exceedingly useful way of formulating the problem of continuity and discontinuity between Israel, on the one hand, and Ammon, Moab, and Edom on the other. Alt's more detailed analysis of the continuity between Israel and the Transjordanian states may now be quoted:

> Everything that has been said previously about the peculiar development of earlier Israelite institutions, and the adoption of contemporary Philistine forms in the make-up of the Israelite kingdom, becomes extremely significant when we consider its distinctive features; for of course it is not to be supposed that all these elements played an identical part in the development of the kingdoms east of Jordan, and every disparity in the underlying causes at work necessarily resulted in a corresponding disparity in the resultant national structure. . . . there was still one important feature found only in the kingdoms east of the Jordan. Apart from the national principle on which their structure was based they were all without exception organized in a monarchy, yet we find that their kingdoms do not always appear to have had the hereditary form which was universal among the Canaanites, and which we can also presume to have existed among the Philistines and the other Aegean peoples in Palestine.

On the contrary, in the only place in the Old Testament where the preservation of an authentic list of kings allows us to trace the development back to a very early period, in fact, perhaps, as far as the first formation of a national state, i.e., in the case of the Edomites, we also discover the remarkable fact that the title of "king" was quite regularly passed on, for many generations, to men of completely different origins and that there is never any recognizable attempt to establish a dynasty; it was only after David's suppression of their kingdom that the Edomites in their struggle for emancipation gave allegiance to a successor of the former king. Elsewhere among the Ammonites and the Moabites we find the son's accession to his father's throne in isolated cases, but this also occurs only at the time of David or later; so one may well ask whether dynastic continuity in a monarchy in these kingdoms was likewise a secondary development and replaced a more flexible form similar to that in Edom. But even if we accept that before the birth of the kingdom of Israel the dynastic form of monarchy had already been introduced into some of the states east of the Jordan, the list of Edomite kings still provides convincing evidence against the view that we should assume that this form existed throughout this group of peoples from the very beginning.[352]

How are we to assess this typology in the light of our previous analysis of sociopolitical formations in Israel's milieu? Once the outmoded and useless hypothesis of nomadic origins is discarded, we can perceive in Alt's typology an affinity among several peoples over against the existing imperial-feudal, sociopolitical formations. The origins of Israel, Ammon, Moab, and Edom fall apparently within the same broad category of anti-imperial and anti-feudal sociopolitical formations. They are alike indebted for their emergence to the decline of Egyptian control of Canaan and to the relative weakness of the city-states. What is so carelessly and inappropriately called "nomadic" in their origins is the solid factor of tribal-egalitarian organization. With the retreat and collapse of centralized political authority over much of Canaan, peoples who had long been resident in the area and peoples newly arrived by migration (not by evolution from the lower cultural stage of nomadism), were able to rule themselves according to less centralized, more egalitarian forms of sociopolitical organization. In this sense, Israel, Ammon, Moab, and Edom appear to have been united in a common sociopolitical typology.

Yet the biblical evidence shows not only that Israel was closely related to Ammon, Moab, and Edom but also that they diverged sharply, so that as early as the time of the judges Israel was at war with Ammon and Moab—not to mention the repeated conflicts between all the Transjordanian states and Israel, both as a united monarchy and in its later subdivision into the kingdoms of Israel and Judah. From the evidence available, it appears that the Transjordanian peoples moved more rapidly into a form of *centralized* political leadership than did the Israelites. Alt is correct in emphasizing the probability that the Transjordanian centralized political leadership was not hereditary kingship at the start. According to biblical accounts, however, Ammon (Judg. 11:13–14,28), Moab (Num.22–24;

Judg. 3:12–30), and Edom (Gen. 36) had kings before Israel. It is explicitly stated that the Edomite kings "reigned in the land of Edom before any king reigned over the Israelites" (Gen. 36:31).

Alt is also correct in stressing that we have no way of knowing at exactly what time these peoples changed over to hereditary kingship. We must necessarily be suspicious of biblical references to "kings" among these people. An anachronizing use of the term from the tenth–ninth centuries may well be at work. It is likely that those Edomite leaders called "kings" in Genesis 36 should in fact be designated "chiefs" or if the Canaanite term for king had been adopted by then, it should be understood in a much different sense: namely, as a title for the tribal chief who served in rotation as the head of the association of tribes or, even more modestly, as a leader in a restricted region of Edom.[353] On the other hand, Eglon of Moab conducts himself toward Israel like an hereditary king. He exacts tribute from Israel. This suggests a problem in constructing and applying the typology of hereditary kingship. On analogy with Canaan, we conceive of hereditary kingship as implying full control over a feudal establishment and full exercise of state taxation and draft of citizen labor. We also assume that, in the absence of Egyptian overlordship, a native king could exact tribute from a subject people. It is, however, not to be excluded that rulers selected in rotation from various groups within a political formation, as in Genesis 36, could already have begun to exercise strong centralized leadership in the appropriation of domestic and foreign resources.

What is striking, in my opinion, is a point that Alt passes over very quickly. I refer to his remark that "the Israelites were thrust far deeper into the area influenced by the ancient and completely dissimilar city-states of Palestine, and consequently had far less scope for the fulfillment of their political tendencies than their cousins east of the Jordan near the desert border." If we take this remark seriously, the implication should be as follows: Israel, closer to the Canaanite city-states, should have resorted to kingship much earlier than the Transjordanian states which were protected from Canaanite interference by the cleft of the Jordan Valley and the Arabah. Instead, exactly the opposite occurred. Israel avoided monarchic institutions longer than any other of these related peoples.

In my opinion this discrepancy can only be explained if we grant that early Israel consciously developed a tribal-egalitarian sociopolitical organization, well integrated with its Yahwistic religious organization and symbolism, whereas the Transjordanian peoples had no such social strategy for remaining independent of the centralized state. At this stage of our knowledge, it is largely a matter of conjecture as to why this should have been so. Particularly intriguing is the question: Why did not Ammon, Moab, and Edom join in the confederation of Israel? Our knowledge of these people is far too meager to give any more than a shrewd, and perhaps wide-of-the-mark, guess to such a question. This much is clearly reported in biblical traditions: the Yahwist catalytic agents of Israel who passed through Transjordan on the way from Egypt to Canaan did not fight with Ammon, Moab, and Edom, and one tradition reports that both Moab and Edom sold provisions gladly to the Exodus Yahwists (Deut. 2:28–29). On the other hand, the Exodus Yahwists did not convert the people of Ammon, Moab, and Edom to their cult, or at any rate did not convert them en masse or even in the majority.

Part of the reason for the failure of Ammon, Moab, and Edom to join these Yahwists may lie in the fact that the Levitical Yahwists who came through their region were not yet the broad-based alliance of Israelite people which eventually formed west of the Jordan. These Yahwists may have seemed too small in number and too exclusive in their claims to be appealing to the Transjordanian peoples. Yet, if Mendenhall is correct in his claim that Amorites from the kingdoms of Og and Sihon converted to Israel in conjunction with the overthrow of their leaders,[354] the reason for Ammonite, Moabite, and Edomite reluctance may lie elsewhere. It may be that they were so far on the road to hereditary kingship, even at this time, that they could not risk the egalitarian form of life exhibited by the Levitical Yahwists. The Amorite kingdom of Sihon had made inroads on the Moabites, and perhaps the Ammonites as well, but once that kingdom was overthrown, by a combination of Levitical Yahwists and rebellious peoples within the kingdom of Sihon, the Moabites and Ammonites seem to have felt safe and satisfied in maintaining their own autonomy, or, as recent studies tend to indicate, they may have been pressured by Midianite suzerainty.

We have already indicated one piece of information which may suggest that some Ammonites came over to the Yahwists at this time, and it is clear from the story of Ruth that some Moabites joined Israel, although on what scale we cannot say (cf. I. Sam. 22:3–4). Moreover, the lodging of the Edomite lists of "chiefs/kings" (Gen. 36) within Israelite traditions may plausibly be accounted for by the entrance of a segment of the Edomite populace into Israel (cf. Doeg the Edomite; I Sam. 21:7 [8] 22:18,22). In any event, the elitist leadership of Ammon, Moab, and Edom won out and managed to retain most of their subjects in the face of the counter-current to join in a wider conferteration of tribally organized peoples united in the worship of Yahweh.

Possibly we should look to the role of the Midianites in Transjordan in the late thirteenth and twelfth centuries as a decisive factor in hastening and strengthening monarchic institutions in that region. As we have noted, the traditions about Moses generally show a close and friendly relation between Israel and Midian. However, when the Israelite trek through Transjordan is recounted, Midianites appear in a belligerent posture toward Israel: Midianite leaders collaborate with the king of Moab in summoning Balaam to curse Israel (Num. 22:4,7), a Midianite woman who brought plague to the Israelite camp is killed by a zealous priest

(Num. 25:6–9, 14–15), and a major campaign against Midian is launched by Israel (Num. 25:16–18; 31). Later, of course, Midianites penetrate west of the Jordan and are driven out by Gideon (Judg. 6—8).

What are we to make of these seemingly contradictory traditions of Midianite friendliness and intimacy toward Israel followed by Midianite belligerency toward Israel? Numbers 25 and 31 may reflect the end of a period of loose association or friendly coexistence between Israel and Midian (and also Moab) in the lower Jordan Valley at Shittim. The close ties appear to have been sharply broken by an epidemic (bubonic plague?) that forced Israel to reject the cult of Baal-peor, as the culturally acceptable way to avert the plague, in favor of strict adherence to the cult of Yahweh. In these Midianite traditions in Numbers it is noteworthy that camels do not appear, contrary to the situation among the Midianites in the time of Gideon. Doubtless these are confused and polemically inflated accounts of growing conflict and eventual open warfare between Midian and Israel which preceded the Gideon war. There are reasons, however, to believe that the Midianites were exercising a protectorate over Transjordan in the interests of developing a trading empire similar to the much later Nabatean empire in the same region. At various times the Midianites controlled Edom and Moab (Gen. 36:35), and probably also Ammon and the Amorite kingdom of Sihon (Josh. 13:21).[355]

Israel, in overthrowing Sihon, would in that case have been opposing the interests of Midian. It was vital to the Midianites to control the major north-south "King's Highway" which ran through Ammon, Moab, and Edom. They therefore had a direct stake in keeping friendly clients in power in those areas. The absorption of Ammon, Moab, and Edom into Israel would have dashed the Midianite strategy of commercial empire inasmuch as Israel had no elite leadership interested in trading in luxury goods to be shared with Midianite "protectors." We can hypothesize a contest between Midian and Israel over the form of sociopolitical organization which was to prevail in Ammon, Moab, and Edom. Midian, by conquest and support of sympathetic native leaders, sought to install statist rule supportive of its commercial interests. Israel, eschewing conquest, sought to ally with egalitarian elements in the resistance struggle against Midian and local elites. In the end the resistance forces were not strong enough to prevail, possibly owing in large measure to the difficulties of sustaining guerrilla warfare on the open Moabite plateau and on the plains of Ammon and Edom which merge into the desert. Whereas Israel succeeded in ousting statist control from northern Transjordan (the kingdoms of Og and Sihon), it did not succeed in doing so in southern Transjordan (Ammon, Moab, and Edom). It may, however, have been precisely in connection with the struggles against Midian in the late thirteenth and twelfth centuries that some sectors of the Ammonite, Moabite, and Edomite peoples, defeated on their home territory, fled into Israel and were absorbed as Israelite groups.

Admittedly, this reconstruction of the Midianite factor in the differentiated developments of Israel and of Ammon, Moab, and Edom is highly conjectural. It is put forth, however, as an hypothesis for further research to verify, falsify, or modify.

I have tried to stress that our knowledge of the Ammonites, Moabites, and Edomites is grossly rudimentary. Given that limitation, it seems to me that Alt's broad typology holds true, namely, that Israel was formed out of populations very similar to those who formed Ammon, Moab, and Edom. This becomes especially striking if we surrender the nebulous and mistaken nomadic hypothesis of the origins of these peoples. Mendenhall, in particular, has recently assembled telling evidence for the origins of many of the Israelite and Transjordanian peoples in northern Syria and Anatolia.[356] If we combine this evidence with the breakdown of the imperial-feudal system in Canaan, we tentatively conclude that the sorts of peoples who formed Israel, Ammon, Moab, and Edom were very similar in ethnic mixture and in socioeconomic background. 'Apiru and other discontented elements from Canaan contributed to these populaces. Groups forced to migrate from Anatolia and Syria, with the disruption and collapse of the Hittite Empire, pressed southward and joined in the "national states" forming east and west of the Jordan. A majority of these peoples opted quickly for a version of kingship, at first headed by a leader who was "first among equals" and then increasingly by a leader in hereditary succession. Only Israel developed a staunch tribal-egalitarian mode of organization buttressed by a novel religious organization and conceptuality. The Israelite tribal-egalitarian revolution against centralized statism did not extend to its widest potential. Related peoples such as Ammon, Moab, and Edom chose not to join in the risky experiment of Israelite antistatism, although perhaps only *after* a struggle in which the balance was tipped toward monarchic rule by the intervention of the Midianites. Israel was firmly bounded before its egalitarian revolution could spread to the maximum, and at the same time its own fate was sealed. It could put off transmutation into a form of centralized statism for two centuries, but it was only a matter of time before it too would succumb to the pattern it had revolted against.

Obviously the above sociopolitical typology of early Ammon, Moab, and Edom is no more than a beginning, greatly lacking in descriptive and explanatory power because of the deficiency of empirical data and the relative inattentiveness of biblical scholars to these Transjordanian peoples. One basic feature of the typology is that Israel and the Transjordanian peoples belonged together in their beginnings in a broad sociopolitical field, distinguishable from previous and contemporary city-state structures in West Jordan and in the "kingdoms" of Og and Sihon in Transjordan. Another basic feature of the typology is that Ammon, Moab, and Edom became monarchic states more rapidly, or at least took initial steps toward monarchy more quickly than did Israel. Moreover, we discover no certain evidence that the Transjordanian peoples attempted to form a broad intertribal association analogous to Israel.[357]

But this typology only sets very broad parameters and gives urgent pointers as to needed research. We clearly need to know more about the specific conditions and circumstances of the Ammonite, Moabite, and Edomite formations to be able to theorize adequately as to why the common origins of Israel and the Transjordanians gave way to diverging sociopolitical institutions at varying paces of change. Yet to be determined is the extent to which segments of the populace of Ammon, Moab, and Edom did in fact join early Israel. It seems evident that a better understanding of the origins of Ammon, Moab, and Edom will throw important light on Israelite origins, serving as an independent control on theories developed primarily at present from Amarna Canaanite and early Israelite sources.

The Pastoral Nomadic Model for Early Israel: Critique and Radical Revision

39.1 Regnant Theory of Israelite Pastoral Nomadism

A perspective shared by virtually all commentators on Israelite origins prior to 1960 was the scheme of early Israel as a pastoral nomadic people who penetrated Canaan from the desert, and who, in the course of settling down on the land, underwent massive transition to an agricultural economy and, more slowly and unevenly, moved through village organization toward urbanization. Both those who accepted the conquest model of the settlement and those who preferred the immigration model of the settlement were alike in positing for Israel an original socioeconomic base of pastoral nomadism and an original or transitional territorial base in the desert steppes to the south and east of Canaan.

The issues dividing conquest and immigration theorists had little or nothing to do with the socioeconomic mode or territorial origins of the first Israelites; the disputes rather raged over the methods and timing of Israel's entrance into and mastery over Canaan. Did the pastoral nomads who came from the desert arrive as a unified mass or in various smaller groupings which only united after entering the land? Did the pastoral nomads come as military conquerors, or did they infiltrate peacefully and only gradually gain the power to overthrow Canaanite enemies? Naturally, the varying answers to these questions about the means of Israel's acquisition of the land affected how the theorists conceived the process of Israelite nomadic acculturation to settled life, but they did not alter the basic presupposition: Israelites came as pastoral nomads from the desert steppes. Even those who have more recently challenged sharply an Old Testament "nomadic ideal" as a positive cultural and religious norm have generally not doubted that the first Israelites were pastoral nomads; what they have doubted is that later sedentary Israelites idealized the nomadic way of life practiced by their ancestors.

The revolt model of the Israelite formation in Canaan broke flatly with a comprehensive pastoral nomadic explanation for early Israel.[358] Unfortunately, critics of Mendenhall's "peasant revolt" model have paid almost no attention to the historical and cultural foundations of his rejection of early Israelite nomadism. This neglect followed in large part from the fact that Mendenhall based his critique on the still unpublished research into ancient Near Eastern pastoral nomadism at Mari which was carried out by one of his students, John T. Luke.[359] The recent critique of early Israelite nomadism draws upon a greatly refined understanding of pastoral nomadism achieved in the last several decades in ethnological and ecological studies. Slowly the results have been applied to the demographic, socioeconomic, and political conditions of the ancient Near East. Bit by bit, but still in a diffuse and indirect manner, word of the altered perception of pastoral nomadism is filtering into Old Testament studies and awakening doubts and second thoughts.

Anyone who becomes informed concerning the new data and theories will see at once that it is utterly impossible to retain the hypothesis of original Israelite nomadism in anything like the form it has enjoyed for a century. The notion that replenishment of populations and initiation of cultural and political changes in the historical civilizations of the ancient Near East can be accounted for by the Arabian desert as a fertile spawning ground from which pastoral nomads flowed in streams, or flooded in waves, into the settled zone has come under fundamental attack. To employ pastoral nomadism as an explanatory model for early Israel is to go wrong from the start.

In order to understand the critique of pastoral nomadism as an explanatory theory in ancient Near Eastern cultural and historical studies, and especially in the case of Israel, it becomes necessary to grasp pastoral nomadism as a socioeconomic type in its relationships to other socioeconomic types and to take account of the great variety of ways in which the typical traits of pastoral nomadism have been combined in particular instances. Most biblical scholars lack such a comprehensive analysis of pastoral nomadism, either as a general type or as a particular formation in the ancient Near East, and have thus been at the mercy of the old uncritical constructs of nomadism with their faulty perceptions about the relation between pastoral nomads and settled peoples. For example, it is now widely thought that the hypothesis of early Israelite nomadism can be resuscitated by regarding the Israelites as *semi*-nomads. The discovery that the camel or horse nomadism so typical of large parts of the Middle East today was not in fact developed until after 1200 B.C. was initially a blow to the nomadic dogma. Advocates of Israelite pastoral nomadism, however, soon adjusted their scheme to speak of ass nomads as "semi-nomads" or "half-nomads." The result was a puzzling and uncritical juxtaposition of empirical observations about "semi-nomads" unrelated to the surviving unrevised structural and developmental assumptions based on the older model of "full nomadism."

The matter in dispute is not whether pastoral nomadism existed in the ancient Near East. It is agreed by all parties that it did, although not in the manner popularly imagined. The issues have to do with the forms, functions, locales, incidences, population size, and overall significance of pastoral nomadism in that time and place, and especially in the formation of early Israel. It is possible to grant that some, even many, early Israelites were pastoral nomads of one sort or another and still conclude that the regnant pastoral nomadic model for early Israel and the sweeping historical and cultural inferences drawn from it are fundamentally in error.

39.2 Pastoral Nomadism in the Ancient Near East

Pastoral Nomadism as a Socioeconomic Mode

What is pastoral nomadism? It is a socioeconomic mode of life based on intensive domestication of livestock which requires a regular movement of the animals and their breeders (a movement which is neither aimless nor boundless) in a seasonal cycle dictated by the need for pasturage and water. Worldwide, pastoral nomadism has involved these domesticated stocks: reindeer, sheep, goats, cattle, yaks, horses, asses, and camels. In some cases there is maximum specialization in one animal stock. More often there is a mix of two or more of the animal stocks. When pastoral nomadic communities are studied comparatively, we discover a wide range in the densities of the human and animal populations and an equally wide range in the ratios between human population density and animal population density.[360] Pastoral nomadism develops a close symbiosis between man and animal, so intimate and comprehensive that their respective behaviors and attitudes are changed. I leave aside the modifications in the animals, pointing only to the profound effects upon herdsmen in diet, housing, forms of property, social organization, etc., which result from dependence upon the exploitation of the stock as "living farms, or factories on the hoof."[361]

Because of the specialized ecological niche in which pastoral nomadism is sustained, with the attendant rather dramatic effects on the forms of socioeconomic life, it is easy to misconstrue the distinctiveness of the pastoral nomadic mode of life as though it were a totally independent self-contained whole, thereby overlooking the many ties by which pastoral nomadism is connected with other socioeconomic modes of life. Here we shall restrict our attention to the arid and semi-arid zone of the transcontinental dry belt of central and southwest Asia and North Africa.[362]

Given his primary needs for pasturage and water, the pastoral nomad is linked to the settled zone. The prevailing pattern in the Near East is that the winter rains of this region allow the herdsmen to move out into the steppes to graze their flocks and herds, whereas in the summer dry season they must move back into close proximity with the settled zone in order to find pasturage and water. A less frequent pattern consists of upland or mountain grazing in the spring or summer. Nomads must, therefore, reach agreements with the settled peoples as to grazing and water rights. The common practice is for the pastoral nomad to graze his stock in the stubble of harvested fields. The advantage to the agriculturalist is that the animals fertilize his fields for the coming season. Along with this exchange of services there is exchange of pastoral and agricultural products. By some means, the pastoral nomad must acquire agricultural products, which he may do by barter, by exacting tribute, by himself engaging in agriculture, or by raiding.

More must be said about engagement of nomads in agriculture and in raiding as two types of interaction between the settled and nomadic zones. Actually, raiding is more frequently carried on between nomadic groups than directed against fully settled peoples. Its chief object is to enlarge flocks or herds and to secure the territorial and status "boundaries" of the respective groups. Chronic raiding of the settled zone is not an invariable feature of pastoral nomadism. Where the pastoral nomads are strong enough, they are likely to establish political dominance and impose tribute on the agricultural settlements. As to engagement in agriculture, some pastoral nomads do not farm at all. They may consider it irreligious or uncouth and thus depend wholly on barter, tribute, or raiding.

Many pastoral nomads do engage in agriculture, however, or we may say somewhat more appropriately that pastoral nomadism and agriculture are often carried on within the same human community and frequently are engaged in by the same persons. This is especially true in situations where the animals bred by the pastoralists are no different than those bred by animal husbandry within the farming villages. Such was the setting in the ancient Near East in the period of Israel's emergence. Sheep, goats, and asses were peculiar to the pastoral nomads only in numbers bred, which necessitated the annual movements to take advantage of winter steppe pasturage or of summer upland pasturage. Since it was necessary to return the animals for half the year from the steppe to the settled zone and to depend upon grazing in field stubble and watering at springs, wells, and perennial streams, it was altogether natural that many pastoral nomads were also farmers. There would be an advantage to the pastoral nomad in retaining the ownership of fields, which he could exploit doubly, through the cultivation of crops and through the summer grazing of his animals.

The actual forms that the simultaneous mix of farming and pastoral nomadism have assumed in one community are numerous. For example, some pastoral nomads own fields in the arable zone which are farmed for them. Others plant their fields before departing for the steppe and harvest them on their return. In some cases, herding specialists in the farming community take large flocks and herds out into the steppe, while most of the people remain sedentary. In still other instances, the community is divided into sedentary farming and nomadic pastoral segments, such as the modern 'Agêdât on the middle Euphrates. In summer the whole community of the 'Agêdât lives in villages and hamlets along the river in tents, huts, and mud houses. In winter the pastoral segments take the flocks into the steppes north and south of the river, returning to join in summer harvest, chiefly of grain raised by irrigation. The flocks then graze the field stubble.[363] It is abundantly clear, therefore, that agriculture and pastoral nomadism are by no means mutually exclusive but are often combined in the same human community in manifold forms. The full implicatons of this undoubted socioeconomic fact have yet to be applied historically and sociologically to pastoral nomadism in the environment of early Israel.

Pastoral Nomadism Distinguished from Migration and from Other Forms of Nomadism

It is essential to make distinctions between nomadism proper and migration, on the one hand, and between pastoral nomadism and other forms of nomadism or itineracy, on the other hand.

Nomadism is to be understood as regular movement in necessary conjunction with a particular socioeconomic mode of life that is often culturally reinforced. Migration is to be understood as any irregular or occasional movement of a group necessitated by natural or historical factors external to the intrinsic socioeconomic mode of life. Peoples are *nomadic* when they move about in the normal and regular exercise of their mode of production, this movement sometimes being reinforced by a cultural tradition that makes a virtue of their margination in relation to settled peoples. Peoples are *migratory* when wars or political unrest and oppression, or when change of climate or disease, force them to leave one region and go to another, quite apart from what their mode of production or cultural traditions may be. As a result of migratory uprooting, peoples may make adaptations from a nomadic to a sedentary or from a sedentary to a nomadic socioeconomic and cultural existence. Thus, in spite of superficial resemblances between nomadism and migration, both in principle and in practice the distinction between the two is completely clear.

Moreover, it should be equally obvious that not all nomadism is pastoral nomadism. Strangely enough, however, many writers on the subject of nomadism do not acknowledge the distinction at all, or else form judgments in practical ignorance of it. We must therefore underline the point that nomadism is the genus and pastoral nomadism only one of several nomadic species.

Another species of the nomadic genus is hunting-and-gathering nomadism. While this had ceased to be a major, independent socioeconomic mode in the ancient Near East, hunting and gathering as forms of supplementary food-getting did not cease altogether in historic times. The life of the hunter or gatherer on the steppes or in the hills is reflected here and there in ancient Near Eastern literature and in the Bible itself. Customarily, such allusions to hunting, as in the cases of Nimrod (Gen. 10:8–9), Ishmael (Gen. 21:20–21), and Esau (Gen. 25:27–28; 27:1–4), either have been naively understood as direct references to pastoral nomadism or have been construed as literary relics of a long defunct hunting-gathering society. To my knowledge there is no direct attestation in Near Eastern records of any communities remaining either exclusively or primarily at a hunting-and-gathering stage, but it is evident that hunting and gathering continued to be viable activities in pastoral and agricultural communities alike, since the staple products of field and flock could be periodically or sporadically supplemented by game and wild foods.

Furthermore, it is insufficiently stressed that certain occupations in the ancient Near East were essentially nomadic or itinerant, or frequently so, without being necessarily pastoral. Tinkers travelled in the sale of their wares. At times metal craftsmen moved camp to secure metal and fuel for smelting. Some merchants regularly travelled to oversee the transport of their goods, to sell them in distant locations, or to arrange business deals. Caravaneers habitually traversed the trading routes. Given the great distances over which international trade moved in the ancient Near East, the mercantile forms of nomadism involved sizable numbers of people for long periods of time.

There is, of course, the question of whether tinkers, craftsmen, merchants, and caravaneers travelled as social communities or as family units, or whether the practitioner of the skill or trade journeyed alone, leaving his settled community and family for greater or lesser periods of time. I am not aware that this question has been carefully studied for the ancient Near East, but evidence from elsewhere suggests that in some cases the social units involved in craft and trade nomadism were fairly large living groups which were in fact complete communities, such as the travelling gypsies. In such circumstances, the whole family or community was engaged in a type of economic specialization by which it serviced other larger communities as travelling "guilds." In such instances, the primary economic specialization in a skill or trade tends to be incompatible with the intensive breeding of animals, although craft and caravaneering specializations may at times be auxiliary activities of small groups within larger pastoral nomadic communities. It has been proposed with plausibility that the Kenites/Rechabites within early Israel were a nomadic community specializing in metal crafts.[364]

Overall it is perhaps advisable to speak of such travelling occupational specialists as itinerant rather than nomadic, especially where they do not move as families or communities. Yet, for our purposes, we bring them into association with pastoral nomadism because references to these itinerant craft and trade specialists in ancient Near Eastern texts have often been uncritically accepted as references to pastoral nomads.

In this connection it is instructive to comment on the occurrence of the tent as an index of pastoral nomadism.[365] The mere mention of tents in ancient Near Eastern or biblical texts is commonly understood as an unambiguous trait of pastoral nomadism. The contention can easily be demonstrated to be erroneous. All the nomadic or itinerant craft and trade specializations named above frequently, although not invariably, employed tents. For that matter, even pastoral nomads were not restricted to tents but often lived for varying periods in grass or wood huts, in mud houses, with wind screens, or in caves. Moreover, there were certain activities of settled communities in which the tent was often used. For example, armies on expedition customarily lived in tents, as did royal hunting parties. Agriculturalists who had considerable wealth in livestock, or who suffered a shortage of suitable building materials, occasionally lived in tents. It was also not uncommon for cultivators of the soil, especially where fields were widely spread, to spend part of the year in huts or tents, particularly during harvest, in order to hasten the crop-gathering and to keep thieves and wild animals from stealing or damaging their yield. It is apparent that the tent can only be taken as indicative of pastoral nomadism when there are other less ambiguous traits associated with it.

Pastoral Nomadism Follows Agriculture and Animal Husbandry: Historical and Cultural Implications

Recognition of the manifold forms of pastoral nomadism in relation to farming leads on to the larger issue of the developmental relationship between agriculture and pastoralism as the context of the specific conditions for the emergence of pastoral nomadism in the ancient Near East. On the basis of nineteenth-century cultural developmental schemes, it is still widely taken for granted that domestication of animals preceded the domestication of plants and that we are to think of early man in the ancient Near East as having been first a pastoral nomad and having evolved later into a farmer. Moreover, in a cultural version of "ontogeny recapitulates phylogeny," it is often assumed that each historic movement of pastoral nomads into the settled zone represents "progress" or "advance" toward sedentary agriculture in recapitulation of the hypothesized original emergence of agriculture out of pastoralism. Thus, Israel is pictured as emerging out of its "primitive" nomadic womb in the desert and reaching its "civilized" agricultural maturity in Canaan.[366]

It is now overwhelmingly argued by prehistorians and ethnologists that the underlying developmental conception in this scheme is grossly mistaken. Neolithic plant domestication and agricultural village life first developed in the grassy uplands along the foothills rimming the outer edge of the Tigris-Euphrates basin and then spread into the river valleys as the complexities of irrigation and transport were mastered.[367] The neolithic communities moved from general food-collecting to incipient cultivation and domestication of plants to primary village farming and finally to towns and cities without any evidence of a transitional pastoral nomadic stage.[368] C. A. Reed finds that goats were domesticated in the agricultural village setting before 6000 B.C. and sheep by about 5000 B.C.[369]

The historical and cultural implications of the developmental priority of agriculture over pastoralism in the ancient Near East are far-reaching and pivotal to the critique of the regnant pastoral nomadic model as it has served to explain early Israel's origins. Sabatino Moscati, articulating the long prevailing but now outmoded view of the temporal and cultural priority of pastoral nomadism, summarizes the developmental process in historic times in a manner basically similar to William Robertson Smith's reconstruction more than half a century earlier. Even allowing for a reticence to speak at all about a prehistoric "original home" for Semites and a recognition that it was ass nomadism rather than camel nomadism prior to the twelfth century B.C., Moscati continues to operate with the older assumptions:

> Let us now consider the historical movements of population within the area, and their relations with one another, and ask ourselves whether, in these movements, it is possible to identify a constant direction or a predominant law. The answer is immediately evident: there is a direction of movement constantly repeated throughout the centuries, namely, movement from the centre towards the outskirts, from the Arabian desert towards the surrounding regions.[370]

But what was "immediately evident" to Moscati is now seen as the last stand of a rapidly crumbling developmental scheme. J. T. Luke succinctly poses the new understanding in all its diametrical opposition to the preceding view:

> Early Mesopotamian culture evolved *toward* the steppe and desert, not out of the desert to the town. As a relatively late rather than an early phase of this process, pastoralism based on sheep and goats—the animals which remain primary for the Near Eastern village today—developed from the agricultural village.[371]

The upshot of this entirely altered developmental perspective on pastoral nomadism in the ancient Near East is that pastoral nomadism must now be seen as a culturally and socioeconomically late marginal development. It was a specialized offshoot and adaptation of the agricultural-pastoral village community. The specialization occurred in the form of concentration on stock breeding adapted to the ecological niche of the semi-arid steppe and, to a lesser degree, to the ecological niche of uplands and mountains. This means that pastoral nomadism spread outward *into* the semi-arid steppe *from* the settled agricultural zone. It emphatically did not first arise in the desert and then give birth to agriculture. Furthermore, it is highly doubtful that we can characterize any of the later major movements of population in the historic period (e.g., Akkadians, Amorites, Arameans) as mass invasions or incursions of nomads into the settled region. In addition to the already cited, searching rebuttal of the Mari nomads as invaders from the desert presented by J. T. Luke, A. Haldar has examined the entire range of evidence on the socioeconomic status and origins of the Amorites—including their involvement in metallurgy and merchant caravaneering—and has conclusively demolished the foundations of the hypothesis that the Amorites were pastoral nomads from the desert.[372]

The representation of "land-hungry" nomads lurking in large numbers on the fringes of the sown land, waiting for the chance to break in and dispossess the agriculturalists, is a parody on a minor motif of nomadism torn out of context and used as a general formula for explaining the origins of historic shifts of power in the ancient Near East. The formula succeeds in reducing cultural and political complexities to an ethnic-cultural formalism on the pattern: desert/nomadism= prior/culturally lower; sown land/agriculture=later/culturally higher. The formula tends to explain cultural and political shifts within the higher formations primarily, if not solely, as the result of eruptions from the lower formations into the higher.

This is not to deny that there were cases of pastoral nomads giving up their way of life and settling down. Nor is it to say that pastoral nomads never fought sedentary peoples. It is to say rather that the movement flowed in the other direction just as freely, farmers taking up pastoral nomadism; and it is to say that the attacks of pastoral nomads on other pastoral nomads were more frequent than their attacks on settled peoples, and that when pastoral nomads did fight the settled peoples, it was characteristically in resistance to encroachments of the state upon the nomadic community.

This is not to overlook the undoubted fact that, under suitable inducements, there were nomads who hastened to adopt the statist form of rule in order to impose tribute or to coerce subject peoples into commercial collaboration, as was the case with the Nabateans in Graeco-Roman times and apparently also with the Midianites in Transjordan in early Israelite times. Both what we know of the origins of nomadism and what we know of its operations in historic times lead us to this conclusion: the movement of pastoral nomads to settled life was more a return than an advance, and the attacks of pastoral nomads on settled peoples were more a matter of internecine strife in an agricultural-pastoral mixed economy, or of aggressions and resistance struggles centering on statist rule and the control of trade, than attempts at annihilation or conquest by cultural outsiders.

Furthermore, current estimates of the nomadic population of the Near East project approximately ten percent of the total population, a figure that seems limited by the inability of the desert steppe to support intensive occupation. No historical factors imply any larger proportion of pastoral nomads in antiquity. It is altogether doubtful that pastoral nomads were numerically capable of the penetrations and conquests of the higher civilizations with which they are credited, especially when their notorious difficulties in uniting for concerted action are taken into account. In addition, now that the earlier theory of a periodic desiccation of the desert as providing the impulse to invade the sown land has been effectively eliminated on climatological grounds, no naturally grounded impulse to move in a united mass against the settled region can be posited.

Moreover, the zone in the Arabian desert that could sustain small-cattle nomadism was limited to the area receiving between 250 and 100 mm. of rainfall per year. Areas receiving more than 250 mm. became agricultural regions, and areas receiving less than 100 mm. did not offer sufficient grazing to sustain flocks. This meant in effect that the Hamad, or Syrian Desert, lying in a rough half-circle on the inner flank of the fertile crescent (to the north of a line extending approximately from Damascus to Mari) was the only part of the interior desert available to pastoral nomadism prior to domestication of the camel—and in fact this semi-arid steppe extended on to the north and east, across the plain between the upper Tigris and Euphrates rivers. The drier interior of northern Arabia, the Nafud, was inhabitable only at oases and crossable only by well-provisioned and watered caravans keeping to the routes linking the oases. This area, according to the older nomadic "original home" thesis, should have constituted the heartland of ancient Near Eastern nomadism from which the pastoralists flooded into the fertile crescent; but it was just this region that was virtually uninhabited before wide use of the camel for transport, and even then could not sustain a sizable population.

Finally, the supposition of sudden massive moves of pastoral nomads toward settled areas which they eagerly covet depends in considerable measure on a misreading of the dramatic diminution of nomadism in the Middle East under the pace of modernization, which has altered aspects of the economic and cultural life of the steppe irreversibly. At least two things are overlooked in comparing modern and ancient conditions. One is that modern technology and attendant inflation of land values cannot be credited for ancient times; and the other is that, more often than not, the pastoral nomad today resists being settled or resettled by the central goverment. In fact, this hostility of pastoral nomads toward the planned programming of central authorities gives us a clue to the ancient situation: the disruption so often read as the offensive penetration of the pastoral nomad into the settled zone in order to seize land was in fact more a matter of defensive counter-measures against governmental authorities who were attempting to encroach upon farmers and pastoral nomads alike, particularly with the intent of subjecting them to burdensome taxation in kind, or to resented military service or draft labor. This greatly neglected political factor in pastoral nomadism will be developed more fully as we proceed.

Transhumant Pastoralism: Winter Steppe and Spring/Summer Upland Grazing

Many commentators on ancient Near Eastern or biblical pastoral nomadism speak of transhumant nomadism. Considerable unclarity exists concerning transhumant (literally "across ground") nomadism, since it appears to be used both in a broader and a narrower sense.

In the broader sense transhumance refers to all pastoral nomadism in which there is a seasonal movement of livestock to regions of different climate. As such, it tends to be a virtual tautology for pastoral nomadism per se—at least in those areas, such as the Near East, where such a movement is inevitable in the light of the alternating dry and wet seasons. It is in this sense that "transhumance" is used by most students of the ancient Near East and of the Bible, often interchangeably with the expression "semi-nomadism," where semi-nomadism refers to sedentation during the summer season and nomadism during the winter season.

The terminological intersection gets extremely confused at this point, importing all sorts of unexamined agendas, owing to at least two other senses in which "semi-nomadism" is used, not always with adequate explanation by the writer. Semi-nomadism is also used to refer to small-cattle (sheep/goat) or ass nomadism, as distinguished from full nomadism or camel nomadism. In this case "semi" is often also taken to mean "less fully developed" or "less independent of the settled zone," or both; and "full" is taken to mean "more fully developed" or "more independent of the settled zone," or both. Yet again semi-nomadism is employed with the implication that those who are nomadic during part of the year and sedentary during the other part of the year are former full nomads in transition from a continuous nomadic life to complete sedentariness. Those who use the expression in this way, at least in biblical studies, very rarely make this one-directional evolutionary understanding explicit, but its operational force is frequently made clear by the context in which a mass of roving nomads are presupposed as falling into greater and greater dependence upon the settled peoples, becoming more and more attracted by the taste for settled life, and finally moving in to take over coveted farm lands. Needless to say, our entire previous discussion calls all of these overriding assumptions into question. Let us see, then, if we can bring some understanding to transhumant nomadism which does not rely upon imported developmental schemes.

There is a narrower sense in which transhumant pastoralism is employed, and that is to refer to a form of intensive herd or flock breeding by communities which are primarily agricultural, have developed their crop cultivation intensively, and may even be advanced industrial societies. Pastoral role functions are restricted to a relatively small number of herdsmen-specialists who accompany the flocks and herds to seasonal pasturage, usually without their families. This form of transhumant nomadism has been well known to Western observers in the high mountain regions of southern Europe, notably in Spain and in Switzerland and Austria, where advantage is taken of the well-watered summer upland and mountain pasturage. Obviously the predominantly agricultural and industrial mixed economies of these European countries cannot possibly be called "pastoral nomadic." We speak rather of a limited pastoral nomadic sub-specialization restricted to a small percentage of the populace who are gone with the stock for a relatively short summer trek. This form of transhumant pastoralism is not confined, however, to Europe; it extends through the upland and high-mountain regions of the Caucasus and of southwestern and central Asia as far as Tibet.[373] It occurs in pastoral communities where agriculture is neither so productive nor so technologically developed as in western Europe and where most of the population is involved in the summer upland trek, as in central Iran.[374] In other instances, as among the Masai of East Africa, it is practiced by only a few of the herdsmen among a people who themselves engage directly in no cultivation but depend upon tributary peoples to provide them with agricultural products.[375]

It appears that the well-known European form of transhumant pastoralism has led to an overly close connection between two traits which happen to be associated in that environment but are by no means always found together among other transhumant pastoralists. In other words, in Europe the hyperspecialization of agriculture and industry is associated with limited sub-specialization in summer upland and mountain grazing. When we survey the great spectrum of pastoral nomadic ecological communities, it becomes clear that summer upland and mountain grazing is a variable determined by the specific natural environment, and that its occurrence does not depend upon intensive agriculture. Moreover, transhumant pastoralism is not limited to the ecological niche of summer upland or mountain grazing. Accordingly, we should view transhumant pastoralism as involving movement of greater or lesser segments of the community between two or more different ecological zones which vary in type according to the region. Sometimes this will entail winter steppe grazing and sometimes it will entail summer upland grazing, and possibly both occur together. Sometimes it will involve all or most of the community and sometimes only a few herder-specialists. Sometimes it will be associated with intensive agriculture, sometimes with marginal agriculture, and sometimes with no agriculture at all.

In the semi-arid region of the Near East in and around Canaan, the most common form of transhumant pastoralism was winter steppe grazing. However, where the coastal range extends down through Syria and Palestine, offering some snowy heights and well-watered ranges facing the sea, the conditions for summer, or late spring, upland and mountain grazing are not altogether absent. In my judgment, although the data are very terse, some features of biblical accounts of pastoralism may best be understood in that mode, such as the sons of Jacob taking their flocks from Hebron to the region of Dothan and Shechem (Gen. 37:12–17), Absalom from Judah shearing sheep in Baal-hazor of Ephraim (II Sam. 13:23), and Judah shearing his sheep at Timnah in the shephelah (Gen. 38:12–13).

This form of late spring/summer grazing which moved not toward the desert but toward the plains, uplands, and mountains facing the sea, seems to have been developed in later Israel as a form of royal or aristocratic monopoly in herds and flocks which were kept in the most prosperous regions. Amos remarks that the women of Samaria are "cows of Bashan," and from other uses of this expression we gather that the rich grazed their herds on this tableland to the east of the Sea of Galilee (Amos 4:1; Ps. 22:12[13]; Ezek. 39:18). The Chronicler tells of persons appointed as "stewards of King David's property," which included herds in Sharon, herds in the valleys, camels, she-asses, and flocks (I Chron. 27:29–31). King Uzziah is said to have owned herds in the shephelah and in the plain (II Chron. 26:10), and King Hezekiah is credited with flocks and sheepfolds and with herds and cattle stalls (II Chron. 32:27–29). That many of these locations were in the plains or low hills along the western escarpment of the highlands reflects the fact that the winter rains seeping into the limestone hills found outlets in perennial springs which watered the western plains well into the summer. Of course, in monarchic times the breeding and grazing of these large herds and flocks was in fact a form of animal husbandry, "nomadic" only insofar as it involved itinerancy for the herdsmen-specialists. Nevertheless, the monopolization of summer upland-and-plains grazing by the urbanized upper classes and the court appears to rest upon an older form of transhumant pastoralism which existed side by side with the more frequently observed winter steppe pastoralism.

The above suggestions about summer upland transhumant pastoralism in early Israel are very tentative, both because of the meager biblical evidence and because I am not aware that the various forms of transhumant pastoralism, other than winter steppe grazing, have been well studied in the case of the ancient Near East. The kind of summer upland-and-plains grazing here posited for ancient Canaan could easily have been combined with winter steppe grazing. A key variable in the relation between summer upland and winter steppe forms of transhumant pastoralism is certainly the factor of political control. The well-watered plains, uplands, and mountains of Canaan were relatively close to the major population and governmental centers, at least by comparison with the semi-arid steppes farther south and east. If we assume that, all things being equal, the transhumant pastoralist preferred the sea-oriented grazing grounds to the desert-oriented grazing grounds, things generally were *not* equal politically speaking.

The harsh reality of centralized political domination in Canaan would tend to push pastoral nomads toward the steppes, even when they preferred the lusher pasturage scattered through the settled zone. Another variable is the effect of the winter climate in Canaan on the use of the plains and uplands for year-round grazing. Winters in Canaan are not so severe as in most of the upland and mountain ranges of the better-known transhumant communities. This is the function of lower elevations and of proximity to the sea. Flocks and herds could be left out during much of the winter, except for occasional severe storms. Since deep freezing seldom occurs, pasturage would generally be available year round. This increased the attractiveness of the plains, uplands, and mountains as permanent pasturage, which would tend toward monopolization of these regions by the ruling classes, leaving the steppes to be claimed by the more socially and economically marginated peoples. While the subject calls for much further research, it appears to me that summer upland transhumance was one variation of pastoral nomadism which tended to be quickly appropriated by centrally controlled animal husbandry in Canaan, primarily because the best pasturage was within easy reach of city-state control and was dominated by the ruling classes, who were already committed to intensive agriculture on feudal-style estates.

39.3 Evidence for Early Israelite Pastoral Nomadism

Pastoral Nomadism in Pre-Israelite and Early Israelite Canaan:
Ecological and Political Aspects

We are now in a position to formulate a sketch of the pastoral nomadic parameters in the area of Canaan immediately prior to and coincident with Israel's formation as a people. We may safely exclude camel nomadism from our purview, since the camel-riding Midianites who struck at Israel in the time of Gideon, about a century after Israel's initial formation, appear to have been the first full nomads known to us in the ancient Near Eastern sources (Judg. 6:1–6). If the early Israelites were pastoral nomads, their economy was based on sheep, goats, and asses, a marginal sub-specialization within the basically well-developed animal husbandry practiced by the intensive agriculturalists of the fertile crescent. In the areas of Canaan toward the south and east (i.e., along the margin of the arable land as fixed largely by rainfall patterns), the normal intermixture of agricultural and pastoral components in one economy was skewed in the direction of a heavy pastoral component, which either made use of the well-watered pasturage in the heavier-rainfall zone or turned toward transhumant exploitation of the semi-arid steppes beyond the cultivable boundary. I have argued above that climatological and political factors tended to close off the year-round plain and upland pastures to those living a marginated existence, with the probable result that summer upland transhumance tended to be absorbed into a form of ruling-class monopolized animal husbandry, leaving the less hospitable southern and eastern steppes to the dominated or marginated peoples.

It is completely clear that all of the pastoralists of the area at this time were fully familiar with agriculture and that most of them are to be viewed as engaging in some form of agriculture. Where they did no farming at all, the pastoral nomads depended on some accommodation with settled communities for summer pasturage, watering facilities, and agricultural products. We are justified, I believe, in regarding pastoral nomadism in ancient Canaan as a subsidiary offshoot of the agricultural village, an offshoot marked by its transhumant specialization in sheep- goat- and ass-breeding. We may flatly state that there was no notion of an absolute dichotomy between cultivating land and breeding flocks and herds requiring transhumant movement.

No such notion existed because climate and terrain and political circumstance combined to make the coexistence and combination of agricultural and pastoral pursuits, in varying ways, altogether viable and frequently necessary for considerable numbers of people. Given the erratic rainfall averages over the whole area from year to year and the peculiar regional variations in rainfall according to altitude and distance from the sea, combined with the absence of any large-scale irrigation possibilities, agriculture throughout Canaan was always precarious —and especially so toward the south and east. Total dependence on crops could be disastrous. It is true that lack of water strikes both at crops and at animals. But with the animals there were certain safety margins not built into the cultivation of crops. Animals could move about and take advantage of watering and grazing opportunities over wide areas. Moreover, the animal products were available to help tide the famine-stricken farmer over a difficult year. They gave meat and milk products and some of the necessities of shelter and clothing. Of course, in a prolonged drought the pastoral and agricultural components of the economy could alike fail. But the mix of crops and animals provided a better chance for survival than sole reliance on crops. In fact, the hardiness of sheep, goats, and asses suited them ideally to the steppes which stretched beyond the agricultural zone, so much so that exploitation of the otherwise wasted winter growth of the steppes by grazing animals must have been a very early, completely logical extension of animal husbandry.

In my view it is impossible to understand pastoral nomadism in the ancient Near East, and especially in Canaan, without an appreciation of the political factors at work in its development and expression. At the time of Israel's appearance, centralized government had existed in the ancient Near East for at least two thousand years and probably for a great deal longer. Centralized authority was more or less solidly based in the most prosperous regions of the fertile crescent, operating out of urban centers and extending control into the countryside in the form of taxation in kind and in forced military service and draft labor. Often, as in Amarna Canaan, centralized government was in fact a host of competing jurisdictions in the form of city-states struggling to extend their control at one another's expense, over which competing imperial powers or a single imperial power (Egypt in the case of Amarna Canaan) sought to impose superordinate control for the purposes of raking off the rich economic surpluses and securing military and mercantile control over the communication routes.

On this way of looking at the political situation in the ancient Near East, the city stands over against the countryside; the centralizing and stratified monarchic and aristocratic classes stand at variance with the peasant and pastoral populations. Whether the rural population engaged primarily in farming, or primarily in stock-breeding, or in some combination of the two, all of them shared much more in common than they did with the urban elites.[376] To be sure, the rural populations might reluctantly concede that obligations to the central authority were inevitable—or even at times worth the gain in security, if the exactions were held to a tolerable limit or if the alternative of subjection to a still more onerous power from without was thereby forestalled. The point is that the countryside did not accept this domination by the city unquestioningly. Farmers and pastoralists of the underclasses expressed a general undercurrent of resentment toward the political elites and practiced a cold calculation of benefits given and benefits gained, always with a sharp eye to the possibilities for noncompliance or for open revolt.

As a general rule, it was in the countryside that lay at the greatest distance from the urban centers and main communication lines, which included the least prosperous and the most inaccessible regions, where resistance to the central authorities could be most effectively conducted and where, on occasion, open revolt could succeed.[377] Pastoral nomadism in such a political climate of precarious and resisted domination of the countryside by the city-states must be seen as more than an economic adaptation to the steppe. It is also viewable in part as a form of political resistance. The rural segments of the populace, under pressure from the dominant urban centers, could relieve that pressure by moving toward pastoral specialization. Movable flocks and herds were less easily taxed than real property. The periodic trek over the steppe carried the nomads beyond the normal reach of the police power of the state and made impressment into the army less likely. Nomads who moved over regions that lay between two conflicting central authorities could parlay advantages by playing one authority against the other. In short, there were possibilities in pastoral nomadism for relative political independence vis-à-vis the state in comparison with the farmer wholly tied to his land.[378]

The political component in pastoral nomadism has been observed in modern Palestine:

> Occasionally village folk took to Beduin life to evade conscription, or to flee from tribute, taxes, blackmail, debts or drought. Sometimes too, criminals might turn Beduin, having perforce left their villages after committing murder or other crimes. Tribal tradition frequently has it that a certain tribe or family is of non-nomadic origin and at a certain time has gone over to the Beduin way of life.[379]

Movement of the pastoral nomads back to a more fully agricultural life may similarly be viewed in a political framework. As the political pressure from the settled zone declined with the decay of central authority, some nomadic groups would return to sedentariness. Thus in the marginal zone of Canaan (notably along its eastern and southern flanks), the combination of and oscillation between agriculture and pastoralism, between sedentariness and nomadism, is to be seen primarily as a unified development within a single area, unified economically and ecologically by the close juxtaposition of conditions favorable to agriculture and to pastoral nomadism and unified politically by the attempt of the central authorities to dominate the agricultural-pastoral village and by the resistance of the village complex, which could take the form of pastoral nomadic "tactical retreat." The pastoral steppe zone on the east and south of Canaan thus formed both an ecologically specialized outrunner of the settled zone and a hinterland for political asylum and regrouping available to those who found life in the settled zone no longer tolerable. In all basic respects the pastoral nomadic ecological zone and its political horizon were fundamentally bound up with the strains and stresses within the settled, politically centralized zone.

Evidence for the Patriarchs as Pastoral Nomads

In estimating the socioeconomic status of the persons and groups reflected in Israel's patriarchal traditions (Gen. 12—50), it is essential to keep in mind the distinction we have made between nomadism as regular, occupationally conditioned movement, whether pastoral or otherwise, and migration as irregular movement provoked by unsettled political conditions or by disturbances in the natural environment.

The patriarchal stories of early Israel tell of many movements of Abraham and Lot, of Isaac, of Jacob and Esau, and of Joseph and his brothers. These movements are pictured as originating in upper Mesopotamia (and perhaps ultimately in lower Mesopotamia), ranging back and forth across Canaan and Transjordan, and finally ending in a descent into Egypt. The accounts are edited in such a way as to give the appearance of a continuous line of action involving one group over several generations. As a result of form-critical studies, it has long been recognized that these traditions must be treated individually both in regard to their origins and in regard to their contents. They stem from different traditional circles; and just as it is inadmissable to refer the descriptions in the traditions to a single historical entity, it is inadmissable to assume a homogeneous socioeconomic mode for all of the peoples described therein.

When the editorial schema of one long migration from Mesopotamia through Canaan to Egypt is dissolved, there remain embedded in the several traditions reports of movements which cannot be easily reduced to any single type. Some of the data suggest circumstances typical of transhumant seasonal treks. On the other hand, most of the movements are described with reference to circumstances of famine, intermarriage, pilgrimage, or inter-group conflict, factors which tend to be better understood as evidence of migration than of nomadism. This may well be due to the dominant conception by which the scattered accounts were absorbed into the central Israelite traditions after the formation of united Israel. The conception is that of migration as preparation for a religious destiny. Israel, in its early patriarchal phase, is viewed as fated to roam over a land that it could not yet possess. Such a tendentious conception, applied ex post facto from a later time when the land was possessed, certainly did nothing to encourage a very accurate retention of information concerning the actual socioeconomic status of the proto-Israelites who are the subject of the patriarchal stories. It is consequently highly gratuitous to believe that these stories picture the wandering of the patriarchs as functions of their underdevelopment as pastoral nomadic peoples. Only a closer analysis of the modes of production mentioned in the stories may help us to determine the socioeconomic realities behind the motif of migration as preparation for a religious destiny.

When we search behind the façade of the anachronistic patriarchal migratory schema, the socioeconomic data generally taken to indicate pastoral nomadism turn out to be far from lucid or compelling. There are traits, such as the sizable flocks and herds, which accord with pastoral nomadism. That these traits, however, exhibit a form of pastoral nomadism which set off these proto-Israelites from others living in the same regions of Canaan at the time is by no means evident. The basic "at homeness" of the patriarchal communities in rural Canaan is emphasized by the prominent agricultural component in the socioeconomic descriptions. Abraham and Lot (Gen. 12:16; 13:5; 20:14; 21:27; 24:35), Isaac (Gen. 26:14), and Jacob (32:5,7,15) have oxen or cattle and in the Near East these bovines were bred only in the settled zone. Abraham buys part of a field near Hebron to bury his dead (Gen. 23). He sacrifices a heifer, a turtledove, and a pigeon (Gen. 15:9), and he offers his guests bread, cakes made from meal, and a calf (Gen. 18:1–8). Isaac sows and reaps plentifully in the vicinity of Gerar (Gen. 26:12–14); and, as he drinks wine with his meat, Isaac blesses Jacob with promises of abundant grain and wine (Gen. 27:25–29). Jacob boils pottage of lentils (Gen. 25:29–34), and he gives forty cows and ten bulls to Esau (Gen. 32:15). Reuben gathers mandrakes "in the days of wheat harvest" (Gen. 30:14), Joseph dreams of binding sheaves (Gen. 37:5–8), and Jacob sends balm, honey, gum, myrrh (or labdanum?), pistachio nuts, and almonds to Joseph in Egypt (Gen. 43:11).

Now I submit that this is a very considerable body of evidence that the patriarchal communities practiced diversified and intensive agriculture. I am well aware that some or all of these features might be dismissed as anachronisms from a later agricultural stage of Israel's life. However, to strip them away would not uncover any undisputed primitive, pastoral nomadic core. As a matter of fact, it would be just as logical—indeed even more so—to assume that pastoral nomadic traits in the patriarchal stories are anachronisms to embroider the motif of migration as a preparation for religious destiny. It seems to me that the anachronizing possibilities cancel one another out and leave us with no methodological alternative but to interpret the socioeconomic evidence in the several traditions as they stand.

Accordingly, the socioeconomic data permit the interpretation that some or all of the patriarchal groups were transhumant pastoralists. It is clear, however, that they practiced diversified and intensive agriculture, and there is no certain indication that the entire community was engaged in transhumance. In fact, some of the information (cf. Gen. 37:12–17; 38:12–13) suggests that only segments of certain groups were engaged in transhumant pastoralism. Finally, there is absolutely nothing in the socioeconomic details of the traditions that argues for the recent intrusion of these patriarchal communities into Canaan, implying that they are "in transition" to settled life. The patriarchal communities are not represented as markedly different in their agricultural-pastoral mix from other peoples in Canaan; and, in instances where they are in opposition to the "native" Canaanites, it is not pictured as friction between farmers and herdsmen competing for differentiated use of the same living space. The opposition is political conflict, as witnessed by the fact that the patriarchal opponents are not rural but urban Canaanites. It must be concluded, therefore, that transhumant pastoralism is no necessary correlate of, and no sufficient socioeconomic explanation for, the data presented in the traditional motif of the patriarchal migrations as preparations for religious destiny.

Evidence for Exodus Proto-Israelites as Pastoral Nomads: Biblical Data and the Shosu

Tradition pictures the Israelites as wanderers in the wilderness enroute from Egypt to Canaan. Virtually all scholars have assumed that this is bona fide proof of the pastoral nomadism of early Israel. Unfortunately, the socioeconomic data on the Exodus Israelites are as sketchy and uncoordinated as the socioeconomic data in the patriarchal accounts. This much is clear: the wandering in the wilderness is not represented as a regular seasonal movement but as a major displacement from one place of settlement to another. It is commonly assumed that only because they were pastoral nomads could the Israelites make their successful trek across the Sinai desert. There is apparently a measure of truth in that claim, but it must be sharply modified and clarified afresh by a closer look at the evidence.

The Exodus Israelites are described as stock-breeders in Goshen, a region of Egypt along the frontier between the Nile Delta and the Sinai Peninsula. The legends of Moses' connections with Midian in eastern Sinai and the mention that the God of Israel was to be worshipped at a location three days' journey into Sinai suggest that at least some of the Israelite community regularly moved out into the Sinai steppe in transhumant herding. The reports that detail their domesticated animals are surprisingly meager, and particularly those embedded in the legislation attached to the Sinai events must be treated cautiously since they reflect naive retrojections of later agricultural conditions in Canaan into the archetypically conceived desert period of Israel's origins. Furthermore, while there is a rich Hebrew vocabulary for domesticated animals, some of the generic terms commonly translated "cattle" are used inclusively for sheep and goats, or "small cattle," as well as for bovines. For example, *bᵉhēmāh* and *miqneh* are often used in this inclusive sense. In some cases *bᵉhēmāh* is a class term for all domesticated animals in contrast to *ḥayyāh* as a class term for all wild animals. The use of *miqneh* is sometimes extended to all kinds of possessions or acquisitions in wealth. On the other hand, *bāqār* is normally, if not exclusively, restricted to large cattle, i.e., oxen and cows. Even apart from the problematics of biblical terminology for domesticated animals, it has been observed, in connection with the relation between the Beirut and zeboid types of cattle in the ancient Near East, that "the history of cattle in Bible times needs much intensified study."[380]

Even if, however, we set aside all references to bovines in the Sinaitic legislation and in the P materials, there remains a considerable body of references to oxen or large cattle in J/E narratives, which strongly imply that the Israelites in Egypt were understood to have been sufficiently tied to the soil to have bovine herds. Jacob in Egypt has both small cattle and large cattle (Gen. 45:10; 46:32; 47:1), although one passage implies that at least some of the herds he kept belonged to the pharaoh (Gen. 47:6). If, with Noth, we set aside the Joseph novella as one of the latest bridging devices in the Pentateuch, there are still ample references of the same sort in Exodus. Moses requests that the Israelites be allowed to make a pilgrimage to worship Yahweh accompanied by their small and large cattle (Exod. 10:9,24). At the crossing of the sea, the fleeing people take their flocks of sheep and goats and their herds of large cattle (Exod. 12:32,38), which are again alluded to in the wilderness (Num. 11:22; 20:4,8,11). Moreover, the complaining Israelites recall a diet in Egypt including fish, cucumbers, melons, leeks, onions, and garlic, which suggests that they had been fishermen and small gardeners (Num. 11:5,22). The Israelites also take eagerly to eating the manna, which is described as a bread substitute, "like coriander seed" (Num. 11:7–9). Although we should like much fuller information, we can at least say that the socioeconomic data on the Exodus Israelites are in no way specifically pastoral nomadic and, in fact, contain items that tell against an exclusively pastoral nomadic reconstruction of the community.

The problems of socioeconomic survival for the Israelites in the Sinai wilderness were assuredly enormous. They were neither a small, well-provisioned travel party nor were they camel nomads adapted to fairly rapid movement over inhospitable and arid regions. We shall not enter into the still vexed question of the route of the Exodus, although I tend to prefer the view that they moved eastward along the main coastal route toward Canaan for some distance before striking out toward Kadesh in the interior.[381] According to the traditions, although they were attacked by Amalekites, the major communal obstacles in the wilderness were environmental. They had to make their way from oasis to oasis (apart from Kadesh none of these locations can be identified with any certainty), while trying to preserve as many of their animals as possible for a dependable supply of dairy products and wool for shelter and clothing, as well as occasional meat and hides.

The impression given is of an eclectic community which as a totality was not familiar with the wilderness and not accustomed to living there. According to tradition, the leader Moses had spent long years in Sinai, living among the Midianites. It is these very people who "serve as eyes" for Israel, advising them as to "how to encamp in the wilderness" (Num. 10:31). Even so, the food supply ran dangerously low and the people had to learn how to survive on a makeshift diet, including quail blown in from the sea and a bread substitute of "manna" (Heb. "what is it?"), possibly an edible excretion of scale insects deposited on tamarisk bushes.[382] The implication is that most, if not all, of the animals they started out with from Egypt perished in the wilderness or had to be eaten for food. Water was a constant deficiency, and apparently only as they found their way to the multiple springs around Kadesh were they able to establish a viable existence.

The tradition that the whole generation of those who left Egypt died in the wilderness, except for a favored few leaders, may well reflect the severe losses from starvation, thirst, and exposure which overtook not only animals but people as well. There are also highly colored reports of dissension in the decimated ranks and of contests for leadership so furious that the greatly regarded Moses was known not to have reached Canaan with his people. Although the traditions moralize the premature death of Moses exclusively as a divine rejection, it is probable that they attest to dissatisfactions with his leadership so great that he was deposed, banished, or killed during the intense intra-communal struggles for power.

Looking back at the Egyptian matrix of Israelite origins, there is of course the now famous report that Israelites were forced into helping to build Pithom and Raamses, the store cities that Rameses II erected in the eastern delta to serve his imperial ambitions in Palestine and Syria (Exod. 1:11), and this is generalized in summary form to state that their lives were made bitter "with hard service, in mortar and brick, and in all kinds of work in the field" (Exod. 1:13). If one assumes that the Israelites who left Egypt were a homogeneous group, we could conceivably hypothesize their condition as follows: they were a people settled in the irrigated region of Goshen, where they gardened, fished, and grazed flocks and herds, their sheep and goats being taken into the steppe during the winter rains. Being under Egyptian tutelage, they were forced into draft labor when the pharaoh embarked on large building projects in the area related to a revived Asiatic imperial policy and, moreover, they were obliged to work the pharaonic fields.

But the homogeneity of the Israelite community cannot be taken for granted. It is more probable that the "Israelites" who left Egypt together were a loose assemblage of people holding in common only the fact that they were lower classes oppressed by the Egyptian crown who sought relief under opportune leadership and were only gradually welded together in the cult of Yahweh. Such an interpretation is hinted at by comments in the traditions that "a mixed multitude ('ērev rav) also went up with them" (Exod. 12:38) when Israel set out from Raamses to

Succoth, and that "the riffraff (*hā'saphsuph*) that was among them" (Num. 11:4) agitated against Moses because of the lack of food. The rare word *'asaphsuph* suggests a motley assortment of undisciplined camp followers, an aggregation of persons which has not yet become a community. Of course, the traditions attempt to distinguish between the main body of Israelites and the mixed followers, but that is what we should expect from the centralized tradition. It is rather remarkable that these solid allusions to heterogeneity survived as authentic memories of the conglomerate origins of those who banded together in flight from Egypt, not as a pre-existent community but as those whose intolerable conditions of oppression drove them in the direction of a community yet-to-be.

Given the probability of heterogeneous origins for the Exodus Israelites, the various socioeconomic data cropping up here and there in the traditions may in fact belong to different segments of the proto-Israelites who joined in withdrawal from Egypt. Some may have been fully agricultural and others transhumant pastoralists, while still others were fishermen. Those impressed into building projects may well have totally lost contact with their earlier agricultural or pastoral pursuits, having become wards of the state. The means by which these groups entered Egypt varied with circumstance. Probably many had entered the delta region as part of the normal movement of transhumant pastoralists. Others were probably uprooted from their former homes by famine and driven into whatever accommodations they could make in Egypt. Still others were doubtless captives of war from the pharaoh's Asiatic campaigns who were brought into the region to build the store cities and to cultivate the crown estates.

A large majority of these peoples would have been militarized, either as *'apiru* troops taken as captives or as Shosu plunderers seized by the Egyptians. The deepening incursion of pharaonic control into the Delta during the Nineteenth Dynasty sparked widespread resistance among the hitherto separate groups of displaced Asiatics and set the stage for them to join together in a break for freedom. What appears to have formed the axis of emerging unity for these socioeconomically diversified peoples was their common fate of increasing incorporation into the pharaonic state economy, so that whatever their precise backgrounds and means of production, they were jointly subjected to increasing political control, regimentation, and depressment as a reservoir of "coolie" labor on whose bent backs the pharaoh could march to his Asiatic victories.

Of particular pertinence to this assessment of the contention that the early Israelites were pastoral nomads are the Shosu mentioned by the Egyptians as their foes throughout the vast region east of the Delta and extending as far as Edom on the east and northward into Palestine. There has been surprisingly little systematic attention to the Shosu, either in their own right or in their connections with the early Israelites. Since Shosu is normally translated "Bedouin," these people deserve a closer examination.

In a thorough study of the more than fifty Egyptian documentary references to the Shosu, extending from 1500 to 1150 B.C., Raphael Giveon concludes that they were pastoral nomads.[383] The evidence he cites consists of a few texts that show the Shosu bringing their flocks or herds to watering points under Egyptian control,[384] but the observations are so cursory that we do not know either the exact animals bred or in what number, and it is not certain whether these are instances of transhumant pastoralism or of extraordinary migrations. That Giveon is somewhat uneasy about the slimness of the data is reflected in his comment that the pharaohs speak so much of pillage of Shosu goods and destruction of the Shosu countryside that it is difficult to regard the land of the Shosu as desert.[385] His misgiving is well advised since the Shosu are found over a vast region ranging from the Sinai as far east as Edom and northward into southern Syria. They are often involved in fighting on behalf of cities in Canaan, either as the inhabitants of those cities, or as mercenaries in their employ, or as confederates of the urban dwellers. Where places are specifically located in "the land of the Shosu," the heartland appears to have been southern Edom, where an upthrust of mountains makes for a moderately well-watered region suitable for limited agriculture.

When it comes to characterizing the social life of the Shosu, Giveon is again reduced to sparse evidence. He points out that the Shosu are never said to have a "king" but always "a great one" or "chief." He also observes that the Shosu, as well as the Libyans, are said to have the *mhwt*, a term that denotes a unit of social organization based on kinship. The range of meanings for *mhwt*, from "near relative" through "family" and "clan" to "tribe" and even "people," does not permit exactitude in characterizing the social organization of the Shosu.[386] For independent evidence concerning distinctive subdivisions among the Shosu, Giveon can only cite the variations in coiffures in the pictorial representations which he suggests were distinctive marks of particular subdivisions among the Shosu.

As a matter of fact, Giveon has done little more than to show that the Shosu were not organized in a statist form of politics and that a broad "tribal" designation suits them. From this fact he has appeared to find tacit corroboration of their pastoral nomadic condition of life. We have earlier observed that the anthropological evidence is overwhelmingly clear, however, that tribalism is not restricted to any one socioeconomic mode but occurs as a form of social organization throughout a spectrum of socioeconomic modes, including pastoral nomadism; hunting, fishing, and gathering; equestrian hunting; forest or slash-and-burn agriculture; and intensive agriculture.[387] In fact, where the Shosu appear most vividly in the Egyptian texts, they are marauders and brigands who spring ambuscades on travellers through the pass at Megiddo and in the mountainous regions of southern Lebanon.[388]

When Giveon contrasts the Shosu and the Sea Peoples (including Philistines) as confederacies with chiefs, on the one hand, and Hittites and Amorites as monarchies with kings, on the other hand, he inadvertently discloses that the "tribalism" of the Shosu refers to a nonstatist social organization and not to any necessary socioeconomic mode such as pastoral nomadism. The Philistines were certainly not pastoral nomads. Taking into account that their movement into Palestine was part of an historic migration, we cannot properly call the Philistines nomads at all. In attempting to penetrate Egypt and the Syro-Palestinian coastlands, the Sea Peoples were not engaging in the conduct of their normal occupations, except perhaps to the degree that they had adapted themselves as roving mercenaries. Basically, the Sea Peoples were seeking a new home after having been displaced from their former locales somewhere in the islands of the Aegean or in western Asia Minor.

Finally, Giveon concludes that the etymology of Shosu is not from an Egyptian word "to roam," as commonly assumed, but from a Semitic root, cognate to Hebrew *shāsas*=*shāsāh,* "to plunder,"[389] The usual English translation of Shosu as "Bedouin" in the Egyptian texts gives an unjustified socioeconomic skewing of the term, not only because Bedouin is generally reserved for camel nomads but because the primary reference of the term is to "pillagers" or "plunderers" rather than to pastoral nomads of any sort.

What were the relations among Shosu, *'apiru,* and Exodus Israelites in the thirteenth century B.C.? The Egyptian categorization of Shosu refers to people not primarily, and perhaps even not at all, according to their homogeneous socioeconomic condition but according to their disturbing military-political effects as plundering and warring elements who upset the imperial status quo in Syria-Palestine. That certain Shosu are shown in guerrilla or bandit activities similar to some *'apiru* and the *ḥabati,* or "brigands,"[390] whereas *'apiru* are distinguished from Shosu, at least in the booty list of Amenhophis II,[391] implies that in some circles there were criteria for representing peoples as Shosu in addition to their plundering. At the moment we can only speculate about these criteria. Perhaps one of these criteria was the original cohesion of the Shosu as a tribally organized people in southern Edom. As the term Shosu came to be used, however, it seems to have developed into a wide-ranging term, a virtual epithet, so that the crude basis of the distinction between *'apiru* and Shosu may simply have been that *'apiru* were believed to have been groups composed of outlaw or refugee elements from politically centralized communities who did not have a native region of their own, whereas the Shosu were perceived as having a continuous tribal—i.e., politically decentralized—social organization, with a known or supposed land base.

Giveon is impressed by the twofold geographical and temporal conjunctions of Shosu and Exodus Israelites: both were identified with southern Edom (Seir/Paran) and both were in the eastern Delta region of Egypt during the reigns of Rameses II and Merneptah. He concludes that the Exodus Israelites may very well have been Shosu, or that at least some Shosu may have been included among the proto-Israelites.[392] The first of his alternatives oversteps the evidence, but the second is attractive as a working explanation for one of the motley components in Israelite origins. In this context it should be stressed, however, that even if all the Exodus Israelites were Shosu, their pastoral nomadic status is not thereby demonstrated. Insofar as we allow for others, such as 'apiru, in the Israelite mix, their pastoral nomadic status becomes all the more questionable. It is possible that the Midianite allies of the Exodus Israelites were included by the Egyptians in the term Shosu, which invites the hypothesis that the reason the Midianites and Exodus Israelites recognized collaborative interests was that among the Israelites were Shosu who were originally from Midian. This may be the sociopolitical reality presently masked in the form of legends about Moses' flight to Midian and his intermarriage with the Midianites. The extrabiblical data on the Shosu thus incline us toward the probability that Shosu were involved in the mixed Israelite origins, but those data do not speak unambiguously for the Shosu as pastoral nomads. In this connection it should not be overlooked that there is evidence for viewing the Kenite sub-section of the Midianites as smiths and thus occupational itinerants rather than pastoral nomads.

In my view much the most striking feature of a comprehensive search of the data on the Shosu is their militarization. Not only the hypothetical 'apiru component of Israel but also the hypothetical Shosu component of Israel emerges as highly militarized with a long history of plunder and warfare against the Egyptians. Moreover, neither the militarism of the Shosu nor the militarism of the 'apiru is pictured as a foreign invasion by cultural outsiders; instead they are presented as elements of strain and conflict in a chaotic sociopolitical struggle indigenous to Syria-Palestine. In this regard, the Exodus Israelites fall comfortably and logically into the discernible framework of sociopolitical conflict at the heart of Syro-Palestinian society.

39.4 Summary and Prospect: Pastoral Nomadism as a Minor Socioeconomic Component in Israelite Tribalism

We have concentrated on the biblical traditions about early Israel prior to the so-called conquest of Canaan, for it is here that the strongest case for the pastoral nomadic origins of the Israelite people has been thought to rest.[393] In the sense that there is evidence that some of the proto-Israelites had large flocks bred under the conditions of transhumant pastoralism, we concur that it is probable that pastoral nomadism was *one* socioeconomic mode of life represented in early Israel. We observed, however, that mixed with the evidence pointing toward two forms of transhumant pastoralism (winter steppe and spring/summer upland grazing) there is abundant attestation to the fact that these pastoralists lived among the settled peoples of Canaan and Egypt and that they themselves practiced diversified forms of intensive agriculture and raised bovine herds.

What must henceforth be strongly contested are the cultural and historical inferences so widely drawn from the limited evidence for pastoral nomadism in early Israel, inferences either totally unfounded or highly questionable. Neither the movements of "patriarchal" proto-Israelite groups into Canaan and into Egypt nor the movements of proto-Israelite groups from Egypt into Canaan may be legitimately understood as military attacks or expropriative infiltrations based on cultural hostility of pastoral nomads toward settled peoples or upon covetousness toward their lands. The relationships of the early Israelites with the indigenous peoples run a range from cooperation to open hostility, following along the lines of social-structural tension and conflict within the society. In other words, the relationships between Israelites and other groups are not understandable in terms of Israelite pastoral nomadic status versus Canaanite/Egyptian sedentary agricultural status but rather in terms of Israelite organized opposition to Canaanite/Egyptian centralized political authorities and modes of economic expropriation. This Israelite opposition to statism and economic oppression is an especially sharp and successful instance of the general Near Eastern opposition of tribalism to statism.

There were obviously many distinctive features of Israelite tribalism at the peculiar juncture of forces in thirteenth-twelfth century Canaan, but those distinctive elements can only be appreciated and rightly interpreted when we first grant that Israel arose at an intersection or conjunction of social forces which we can clearly identify as widely operative in the ancient Near East. Within that wider social matrix, it can be plainly seen that the pastoral nomadic Israelites shared with the agricultural Israelites a common resentment toward and a common resistance against the exploitative domination of Canaanite feudalism and Egyptian imperialism at whose hands they suffered alike. A defining feature of the Israelite movement for liberation was that it was not "ghettoized" as a pastoral nomadic movement but represented an effective combination of pastoralists and agriculturalists who managed to subordinate their differences in a unified effort to strike at the source of their common misery. The Israelite movement sought to eliminate the feudal and imperial power organizations from an area in which the communal members could pursue their variegated patterns of farming and herding in autonomous conditions free from crushing taxation and impressment into building projects and wars in which they stood to gain nothing for themselves.

So, while conceding a limited measure of truth to the older hypothesis in the sense that some Israelites were transhumant pastoralists, I offer the following theoretical formulation which sets circumscribed Israelite transhumant pastoralism in its proper context, thereby fundamentally altering and diminishing the cultural and historical significance previously assigned to it:

1. In the total mix of proto-Israelite peoples, as reflected in the patriarchal and Mosaic traditions, *transhumant pastoralism was a subsidiary sub-specialization within the dominant socioeconomic mode of production, namely, intensive agriculture.*

2. The transhumant pastoralism of the patriarchal and Mosaic traditions is best perceived *as a sub-specialization altogether indigenous to Syro-Palestine and in no way a*

culturally foreign intrusion from outside the area. The population movements indirectly represented in the patriarchal travels and in the wandering of the Exodus Israelites are movements within the culture zone or between regions in that zone.

3. The transhumant pastoral element in early Israel *did not embody a distinctive monolithic cultural or social organization distinct from the Syro-Palestinian peoples who lived in the countryside, nor did it represent a lower stage of cultural and social evolution than did the Syro-Palestinian peoples in the rural areas.* They all belonged loosely to a "tribal zone" of social organization.

4. The transhumant pastoral element in early Israel *did not project a unified military attack against settled Syro-Palestinian peoples, nor a more covert infiltration, with the intent of annihilating or displacing the natives so as to take over their agricultural means of production,* thereby "advancing" from a lower cultural level of pastoral nomadism to a higher cultural level of intensive agriculture.

5. *Israelite tribalism as a socioeconomic, political, and religio-cultic form of social organization was in no sense ever a peculiarly pastoral nomadic phenomenon.* Israelite tribalism belonged to the sphere of rural resistance to political domination, a sphere that included the agricultural village and the pastoral nomadic sub-specialization within the village or closely related to the village. The transhumant pastoralists of early Israel were aligned with agriculturalists in a common sociopolitical and ideological perspective which united the resisting countryside (sown land and steppe) in all its converging egalitarian socioeconomic dimensions against the walled city with its hierarchic and stratified organization of human social life for the advantages of an elite at the cost of the many.

I shall now briefly elaborate on the tribal/statist analytic model proposed in the preceding paragraph. In order to clear the air of entrenched misconceptions, it must be flatly stated that the basic division and tension in the ancient Near East at the time of Israel's emergence was not a division and tension between sedentariness and semi-nomadism, between settled zone and desert or steppe. At most, the division between sedentariness and semi-nomadism was secondary, or even tertiary; it was, in fact, not a "division" assuming conflicting interests but merely a relative distinction within a basic continuum. In the main, the relations between the settled areas and the steppe were more socioeconomically cooperative than hostile. The zone where agriculture was possible and the adjoining regions where only grazing was possible, and then only during part of the year, were ecologically distinguishable zones to be sure, but they were ultimately integrated within a larger framework of demographic, economic, cultural, and political symbiosis.

The social reality is that the basic division and tension, the crucial conflict of interests, in the ancient Near Eastern society during Israel's appearance was between the city and the countryside. The "city" and the "countryside" as analytic types may be respectively characterized by antithetical traits in the following simplified and schematic manner:

"City"	*"Countryside"*
urbanism	village life
maximal division of labor	minimal division of labor
social stratification	tendency toward class leveling
imposed quasi-feudal social relations	contractual or kin egalitarian social relations
political hierarchy	diffused and limited self-government
military imperialism	noncooperation and military self-defense
latifundist agriculture	agriculture by autonomous peasants
commercialism	barter trade
concentration of surplus wealth in a sociopolitical elite	direct and equal consumption of wealth by the immediate producers of wealth

The analysis indicates that the basic division was not between agriculture and pastoralism in Syro-Palestine, but between(1) centralized and elitist-controlled latifundist agriculture, animal husbandry, pastoralism and/or commercialism subservient to political domination by the city-state, or comparable statist formation, on the one side, and (2) agriculture, animal husbandry, pastoralism, and direct-use trade by autonomous peasants and herdsmen in a nonstatist and egalitarian community, on the other side.

For purposes of analysis, the above sets of traits are formulated as diametrical opposites. The actual historical and social configurations in this generally identifiable conflict naturally varied greatly according to time and place, and in each instance the precise configurations, including the degree to which the above-type traits were operative, must be established by careful research. Particular Syro-Palestinian formations were more or less exemplary instances of "city" or "countryside" models. Our categorization of these formations must proceed on the basis of careful research that properly nuances in each case the extent of our factual knowledge. In this way the ascriptions of sociopolitical models will be kept free of abstract dogmatism and susceptible to refinement, correction, or discard, as the advance in our understanding warrants. Such sociopolitical models are, however, more than expendable luxuries; they are heuristic devices for pointing and sharpening research, alerting us to relevant data and potentially significant correlations which otherwise can easily elude our attention.

Let me illustrate with the example of the Midianites, who pose an intriguing historical case in the light of our assessment of the pros and cons of Israelite pastoral nomadism. I shall assume, from what is said of them in the Moses and Gideon traditions, that the Midianites included major pastoral nomadic components, although not necessarily exclusively so (witness the Kenite/Rechabite smiths who are subsumed under Midian, not to mention Mendenhall's proposal that the very name Midian is of Hittite-Luwian origin). According to my tentative reconstruction in VIII.38, the Midianites of Transjordan embarked on the building of a trade empire in the thirteenth and twelfth centuries. This project obliged them to try to impose control over a large area buffering the north-south trade route between Damascus and the Gulf of Aqabah. On the basis of the fragmentary evidence, the Transjordanian Midianites can be provisionally characterized as exhibiting the "city" statist traits of social stratification, imposed quasi-feudal social relations, political hierarchy, military imperialism, commercialism, and concentration of surplus wealth in an elite. The mechanisms by which this trade empire was built and administered remain for the moment shadowy, but the above traits can be used as directives for further research in an effort to clarify the forms of control that Midianites seem to have exercised over a wide region. On the other hand, to my knowledge, we know nothing of their urbanization (where in fact was the Midianite capital or base?), of their division of labor, or of latifundist agriculture among people subject to them. In further research, these "absent" traits should be watched for, since the inventory of "city" statism traits appearing in Midian will help us to reconstruct the Midianite empire or protectorate in all its historical "eccentricity" and "atypicality."

As to the implications for Israelite pastoral nomadism, what is striking about Transjordanian Midian is that a bold, and at least briefly successful, effort at commercial empire is altogether consistent with a continuing pastoral nomadic socioeconomic population base, as further illustrated by the later Nabateans. In other words, pastoral nomadism, while essentially tribal and egalitarian in its foundations, is capable under the appropriate historical conditions of providing an elite that dominates other peoples, especially in the formation of a trading empire, as it were, "stealing a card from the deck" of city-state societies. However, when we compare Transjordanian Midian with early Israel, there is no ground at all for believing that Israel was composed of such an elite core of pastoral nomads dominating a trade-oriented confederacy trying to beat the Canaanite city-states at their own game.

The value of the above analytic model is that it delivers us from an atomistic description of discrete socioeconomic modes and sets us on the search for the specific constellation of social, economic, and political forces assembled and interacting in early Israel in conjunction with the corresponding constellations ranged against Israel. In my judgment the key variables in discriminating Israelite society from Canaanite/Egyptian/Transjordanian Midianite society, and in determining their interrelationships, will prove to be *political domination* vs. *political decentralization* and *social stratification* vs. *social egalitarianism,* rather than the simplistic and erroneously invoked variables of agriculture vs. pastoralism or of sedentariness vs. nomadism.

40

Socioeconomic Morphemes in Canaan: Coexistence and Opposition

The problem of the socioeconomic composition of early Israel is really a question in two parts: 1. What were the means of subsistence on which early Israelites depended? and 2. Under what social and political relations were the means of subsistence carried on? Or, put in another way, who decided about the production, distribution, and consumption of the basic goods for sustaining life? We study the political economy of early Israel in order to locate its point of departure from Canaanite society, the direction in which it developed, and the social distance empirically separating "Israelite" from "Canaanite."

The answer to the first question is by now clear: agriculture, including supplemental animal husbandry, was the primary means of subsistence in early Israel, with transhumant pastoralism as a significant secondary means of subsistence. Moreover, the ecological conditions and the economic forms of life were such that agriculture and pastoralism were joined as symbiotic means of subsistence, either through the same persons practicing both or through specialization in one or the other by different parts of the population.

The answer to the second question is that the social and political relations in Israel determining what was to be produced and how it was to be distributed and consumed were egalitarian. Those who worked the land, bred the herds, engaged in crafts, and presided over the religious cult were to receive the fruit of their respective labor. The social relations in large extended families were coterminous with the basic productive and consumptive units. The wider social units (protective associations of families, various cross-cutting associations, tribes and the confederacy of tribes) secured the autonomy of the many family productive-consumptive units. The security offered by the larger units was both *internal*, through measures of mutual economic aid, and *external*, through the formation of a citizen militia serving to repel attempts by the urban or other statist feudal-imperial centers of power to subject Israel to their control. The retention and consumption of wealth by the producers of the wealth were unencumbered by any social stratification or political authority that could claim a share of the wealth. There was no taxation, no corvée, and no drafted army in early Israel.

In a system so constructed, there was no fundamental division or hostility

464

between farmers, herders, and craftsmen (such as the Kenite-Rechabite metallurgists), since each economic specialization, however different, shared with the others a common interest in enjoying the fruits of its labor unfettered by urban feudal-imperial domination. This is not to deny that there were important differences in technique, mode of life, and outlook among the different kinds of producers in Israel, differences that created tensions and required constant negotiation and adjustment. It is to say that what held these different kinds of producers together was more important than what separated them. They were separated by technically different forms of production, but they were united in that they all practiced forms of *free* production in the countryside in deliberate contrast and opposition to the hierarchically controlled and exploited production dominated by statist power centers.

In early Israel the basis of cooperation ruled out in advance that any type of producer should seek to establish a hegemony over the others, neither farmer over herdsman and craftsman, nor herdsman over farmer and craftsman, nor craftsman over farmer and herdsman, nor—to anticipate—priest over farmer, herdsman, and craftsman. Each type of free producer had its own peculiar demographic-environmental, techno-economic, and social-structural weight and locus, but neither prestige of priests, nor numerical superiority of farmers, nor mobility of semi-nomadic herdsmen, nor arcane skill of craftsmen was invoked as a rationale for the producers of any one type to extract wealth from the other types of producers by imposing political domination upon them. Nor, finally, did there arise a warrior patrician class to dominate Israelite society.[394]

40.1 Complementary Morphemes: Agriculture and Transhumant Pastoralism

The coexistence of agriculturalist and pastoralist, of settler and semi-nomad, of town and tribe in a single community has been recently characterized as socioeconomic *dimorphism,* drawing on a term coined by French ethnologists. In his probing study of the Mari "nomads," J. T. Luke quotes from the work of C. H. Charles on the modern 'Agêdât semi-nomads of the middle Euphrates:

> The 'Agêdât are not properly to be called either semi-nomads or semi-sedentaries. They are at the same time nomads and sedentaries. They are a people of "double morphology," according to the classic formulation by which our eminent teacher, M. Mauss . . . has first characterized the social condition of the Eskimo tribes. Each of the two forms of life is in reality characterized by one technique: that of the pastoral life for the nomadic form; for the sedentary form that of irrigation.[395]

It is evident that "dimorphism" can be used to stress the two different sets of techniques, of interrelated work procedures, by which agriculture and nomadic pastoralism are carried on respectively in one community. Of course the exact combinations of work procedures employed in the techno-economic morphemes of agriculture and transhumant pastoralism vary considerably from region to region even today, and doubtless they varied as greatly from community to community in the ancient Near East and in early Israel. For example, the irrigation agriculture of the 'Agêdât has no certain counterpart in the environmental conditions of Canaan. The point is that in economically dimorphic communities, the two differing sets of techniques, however varied within themselves and in their relations and ratios to one another in the total populace, coexist and dovetail with surprising persistence and harmony, many members of the community being proficient in both techniques.

"Dimorphism," however, can be used in a more extended sense to refer beyond the coexistence of economic techniques to the coexistence of two differing sets of living arrangements and of social and political relations, which M. Rowton describes as the social morphemes of "the town" and "the tribe." Rowton distinguishes tentatively among six basic categories of dimorphic society in the ancient Near East:

(i)   The fully settled tribe which retains tribal institutions and traditions.

(ii) The semi-nomadic tribe which reverts to a nomadic mode of life for a few months each year.

(iii) A tribe, part of which is settled, part nomadic.

(iv) A region in which tribe and town, though distinct, are in close interaction.

(v)   A village which pays taxes and tribute, both to a provincial town and to a nomadic tribe; undoubtedly a factor in the tendency of the peasants to desert the countryside.

(vi) A band composed of the socially uprooted, whether from tribe or town; so the ḫapiru in the Bronze Age.[396]

This is an extremely useful exploratory categorization of dimorphism which we can take up and modify in the light of our previous determinations. Regrettably, Rowton does not undertake a radical evaluation of pastoral nomadism in the ancient Near East,[397] so that in spite of the value of his study of dimorphism, it is at times encumbered by the impression that tribalism was an exclusive and pure feature of pastoral nomadism and that, wherever we encounter tribalism in the settled zone, it is in the last analysis always to be viewed as a survival or carryover from pastoral nomadism. The controlling bias of this conception shows through in the above typology in the verbs "retains" and "reverts." We can, however, adjust his observations to take account of this common methodological error. Also, while Rowton implies, especially in his category (v) above, that dimorphism must be understood politically as well as socioeconomically, he does not offer a clear and developed characterization of the contrary pole to be set against tribalism. This is related to his unclarity about nomadism. Since he tends to equate tribalism with pastoral nomadism, the opposite pole to tribalism tends to be understood by him as sedentariness, i.e., settled existence in a town or city.

It is clear, however, from what we have said above, that tribalism is not restricted to pastoral nomadism but is perfectly consistent with village life. Thus, the polar element of the "town" needs clarification by distinguishing between the town in two senses: (1) the town as a form of sedentary life distinguished by the contiguous residency of many families made necessary by the economic means of subsistence requisite for intensive agriculture; and (2) the town as a form of social life which tends, under the circumstances of the highly politicized ancient Near East, to be drawn into the orbit of political centralization and social stratification. This means that we must adjust and elaborate our model of the dimorphic relation between agriculture and pastoralism, between town and tribe, to the historical-political realities posed by the hyperdevelopment of the feudal-imperial state in the ancient Near East.

Whereas in many societies the town or village is perfectly compatible with egalitarian or ranking social relations (because the society as a whole has no state or social stratification), in the ancient Near East the town was constantly subject to the powerful statist and stratifying pressures of the urban center. In effect then, to make full and apt use of Rowton's categories, we have to develop two types of morphism for our analysis. We accept the *"dimorphemes" of agriculture and transhumant pastoralism as polar economic components of the settled area.* But we also posit the *"antimorphemes" of city and countryside as two contrasting and clashing forms of sociopolitical life.* The "antimorpheme" of the countryside represents an egalitarian blend of the "dimorphemes" of agriculture and transhumant pastoralism, perennially resistant to the incursion of the city into its domain. The "antimorpheme" of the city represents an intrusive centralization of power and expropriation of the produce of the rural "dimorphemes" in order to sustain the basically parasitic life of the urban center.

40.2 Antagonistic Morphemes: Urban Statism and Rural Tribalism

This double dimorphism identifies two persisting tensions in the countryside: the tension between agriculture and pastoral nomadism and the tension between egalitarian and hierarchic/stratified social forms. These tensions, however, are very different in their nature, scope, and implications. The tension between agriculture and pastoral nomadism is relative and subordinate to a deeper unity in a common predilection of farmers and herdsmen for egalitarian social life. It can be said that there is no necessary "contradiction" in the dimorphism of agriculture and transhumant pastoralism. Not only can persons engage in both means of subsistence and coexist peacefully in contiguous areas without either means of livelihood depriving or threatening the other means, but these means of subsistence by their nature tend strongly to complementarity in the same community. By contrast, the tension between egalitarian social life anchored in the countryside and hierarchic/stratified social life anchored in the urban centers is deep-going and fundamentally antagonistic. Because the urban center is politically and militarily the more powerful it tends to extend its sway into the countryside as far as it can penetrate. The village touched by an urban center becomes the center of contest, the battleground between egalitarian and hierarchic/stratified forms of community.

By contrast with the farming-herding dimorphemes, which is merely a tension and not a necessary social contradiction, the city-countryside dimorphemes exhibit a fundamental social contradiction. This social contradiction takes the form of a critical struggle in which the morpheme of the city, in order to carry out its vital functions, must inevitably impose demands upon the countryside which threaten the very means of subsistence of farmers and herdsmen. The respective vital needs of city and countryside cannot be mutually realized, for the one must always gain ground at the expense of the other. In order to maintain hierarchic rulers and affluent social strata, the city must expropriate a large part of the surplus of the rural producers; and, furthermore, it must recruit the rural population for its building projects and its armies and to replenish the urban populace, which is repeatedly decimated by the crowded, unsanitary conditions of city life. The city must subordinate and expropriate the countryside in order to survive. In direct opposition, the countryside must either throw off or materially reduce the demands of the city if its people are to fulfill their vital interests in autonomous production, distribution, and consumption.

The stronger the power of the urban center, the more total its control and the more it succeeds in isolating and fragmenting the potential mass resistance of the countryside by breaking up the villages into administrative units and by encouraging the farmers and the herdsmen to oppose one another, to regard their different economic modes as the basis for an enduring and irresolvable enmity. The urban center in particular tries to brand the pastoral nomadic and all restive migrant elements of the countryside (e.g. 'apiru) as the enemies of "law and order" and to convince the village farmers that their best interests lie in paying their taxes in kind and in service in order to gain "protection" from the threatening semi-nomads and migrants. On the other hand, when the urban center weakens and when, correlatively, the tacit resistance of the countryside becomes articulate and organized, the many diverse peoples, who have previously allowed themselves to be divided and weakened by the central power, perceive that they have a common enemy. Their mutual interests in banding together in order to gain control over the distribution and consumption of what they produce—however different their respective means of subsistence—tend to unite them in opposition to the urban center. Often they fail to hold the central power at bay or to overthrow the central power. It is difficult for any coalition against the city to maintain itself with adequate organizational unity. Sometimes they gain provisional success, and their oppression by the urban center is relaxed. Sometimes they overthrow the central power or their resistance allows another central power to overthrow the immediate oppressor. When another power takes over the city, or even when the countryside itself overthrows the central power, the tenacity of the hierarchic and stratified forms of sociopolitical life is so great that the formerly egalitarian-minded victims tend to slip into the city-dictated roles as a new group of oppressors.

A seemingly endless contest goes on between countryside and city, often through sullen, unorganized resistance, sometimes in open revolt, occasionally in unified and victorious struggle—only to have the dominant power of the hierarchic/stratified forms typified by the city reassert themselves, the former victims rapidly becoming new oppressors of yet other victims. Luke sums up this process of struggle aptly and notes why it is that historians looking at the ancient records often miss the significance, and sometimes even the presence of this struggle:

> The success of the urban political center in the Near East in attempting to extend authority over village-pastoral groups, is rarely complete. The further removed in distance or accessibility a given village or pastoral group may be, the less its gain in terms of protection and exchange, and the less its enthusiasm for submission. Since there is always this delicate nature to certain areas of government, the possibility of "withdrawal" is always present, relative only to the performance and power of the urban center. Furthermore, the very factors which enrich the city and its elite threaten the village. If the economic and manpower drain on the village-pastoral groups is increased, the urban center may appear enhanced to the outsider, including the historian, but since these pressures may easily become oppressive they create, at the same time, the conditions in which "withdrawal" may be expected. Therefore, the ability to maintain constituency was equally important to the ancient urban center as its position in broader patterns of conflict or alliance with similar cities and states.[398]

The city's ability to maintain constituency was always more or less problematic. In order to maintain its accustomed level of consumption and luxury and to steel itself against the threats of competing urban centers, the city had to treat its constituency in the hinterland as a support base to be drained and manipulated at will and as necessary, being obliged only to leave that minimum of resources necessary for the countryside to replenish itself as supplier of agricultural and pastoral products and of draft and military manpower. And in this regard, the impositions of the city-state upon the countryside tended to become economically counterproductive and eventually self-defeating. In particular, the more the city drew upon rural manpower to fight in its wars and to erect its monumental structures and fortifications, the more the rural agricultural-pastoral productivity was endangered by a loss in dependable labor to work the fields, orchards, and vineyards and to tend the herds. The mounting demands for various kinds of services laid on the countryside thus became contradictory of one another, since the effective delivery of agricultural and pastoral surpluses to the city militated against the effective delivery of draft labor and army service, and vice versa.

Now it is my contention that when we speak of tribalism in the ancient Near East at this time we are referring to the form of social organization in the countryside which had not been, indeed could not be, altogether replaced by hierarchy and stratification. To be sure, the villages and the provincial towns, in particular, often had their feudal lords and administrative officers sent in by the city or recruited from the local populace. There was a superficial lower-level duplication in the countryside of the central hierarchic and stratified sociopolitical forms, but those engaging in these local offices remained a small part of the rural populace thinly spread over large areas. For the hierarchy and upper strata to function economically they had to remain a small percentage of the populace, no more than five to ten percent of the total populace, heavily concentrated in the cities.[399]

In Part VI, tribalism as the zone of social organization between band and statist societies was characterized by the following primary traits:

CROSS-CUTTING ASSOCIATIONS. The tribe is a type of human community bonded by means of cross-cutting associations that link residential groups in varying patterns of cooperation through kinship affiliations, age-grades, secret societies, ritual congregations, ceremonial parties, and military societies.

INCREASED SIZE AND ECONOMIC COMPLEXITY. The sophisticated bonding of the community permits the "tribe" to be much larger than the "band," and it corresponds to increasingly complex work relations in the means of subsistence and to an enlarged agricultural and/or pastoral surplus (or, in other cases, to a surplus of fish, game or wild fruits, nuts or berries, or to a surplus of crafted articles).

EQUIVALENCE AND EQUALITY OF SEGMENTED PARTS. The tribal community is composed of segmented parts that are structurally and functionally equivalent and politically equal, at least in principle if not always in practice. The several segments corporately, and their members severally, enjoy approximately equal access to the basic economic resources. Moreover, associated tribes can federate as equivalent and equal segments of a larger confederacy.

DECENTRALIZED SOCIOPOLITICAL LEADERSHIP. Corresponding to its egalitarian socioeconomic structure, the tribal community "rules" itself by the diffusion of political functions throughout the social organization or by the temporary assignment of political roles. The egalitarian traits of tribes may be increasingly qualified as the institution of "chiefdom" develops in order to facilitate the circulation of goods.

In this typology of tribal traits, the mode of residency may be extremely variable and will depend upon a combination of ecological, economic, and military-political factors. Tribalism will as often appear among people living in concentrated villages as among those in scattered encampments. Equally, the means of subsistence may vary, providing only that their collective exercise yields a marked increase in economic surplus attainable only by the cooperation of social labor in complex work processes within a larger bonded community. The surplus is as often in agriculture as in domesticated herds, and it may entail hunting, fishing, and gathering in environmental conditions where the available "uncultivated" surpluses are so plentiful that they match or exceed the productivity of intensive agriculture and pastoralism.[400]

With all this in mind, I think we can now correct the dimorphic model of Rowton in which he rather too simply associates and opposes the complexities of "town" and "tribe." Town and tribe, in the ancient Near Eastern setting that concerns us here, are not simple opposites. Ancient Near Easterners did not advance from hunting-and-gathering nomadism, through pastoral nomadism, through village agriculture, to urbanism. That conception is wrong in its ordering, in the first place, since pastoral nomadism was no more than a specialized offshoot of village agriculture. Moreover, such socioeconomic stages did not replace one another in simple succession, each new form totally replacing the preceding form—a point which I believe Rowton would concede along with virtually all other cultural historians of the ancient Near East. Most significantly in this context, however, the social forms appropriate to each socioeconomic mode are not to be allocated as Rowton, depending uncritically on older scholarly canons, tends to do.

The assumption of many scholars, and the implication in Rowton in spite of the counter-evidence he helpfully points to, is that tribalism belongs uniquely to the pastoral nomadic phase. The implication is that with the coming of agriculture and the village, tribalism fades and the territorial rather than the kin principle of human organization arises. With territorialism goes the trend toward hierarchy and stratification. We are now in a position to see what is wrong in this typology. If pastoral nomadism is a subdevelopment of village agriculture, and ecological specialization of animal husbandry, then it is erroneous to look to pastoral nomadism as the locus for the development of the tribe. The tribe must belong to village agriculture as the mode of social organization developed in neolithic times when hunting and gathering bands learned to domesticate plants and animals, and thus as a social morpheme continued in varying forms among farmer and herder specialists, including transhumant pastoralists, within the dominant agricultural horizon.

The further implication of this understanding is that village residency per se does not weaken or contradict tribalism. The mere fact that farmers live together in concentrated settlements is not in any way antipathetic to the distinctive traits of the tribe. Thus, if we imagine a group of transhumant nomads who settle down to full farming, we do not posit any necessary accompanying abandonment of tribalism in the broad sense. Their particular form of tribalism will indeed alter, but the fundamental traits of the tribal form of organization—cross-cutting bonding, increase of populace and assured economic surplus, segmentation of parts, and diffused or temporary political functions—are quite adequate to meeting the conditions of village farming. In fact, such village farming permits a richer exploitation of tribal organizational possibilities than does pastoral nomadism, especially in the elaboration of cross-cutting bonds, the expansion of population, and the maximization of economic surpluses.

Nevertheless, Rowton correctly points to a contradiction which he describes under the rubrics of "town" and "tribe." In actual fact the villages and towns of the ancient Near East did not easily sustain an effective tribal form of organization. By introducing our second set of dimorphemes, the "antimorphemes" of city and countryside, we see why this was so. The reason was that the stage of urbanism in the ancient Near East had been reached millennia prior to the rise of Israel. Political hierarchy and social stratification had developed to a high degree around the fertile crescent, and everywhere the original tribal social organization of the countryside was overlaid and penetrated by the statist organization emanating from the politically dominant city-states and empires. Consequently, Rowton does not point to an absolute dichotomy between "town" and "tribe," for precisely his analysis wants to show that they existed as complementary "dimorphemes."

His point is better made by noting that what is opposed to the tribe is not the town per se but the *imposition of the sociopolitical morpheme of the "city" upon the town/village/encampment which are by tradition strongholds of the sociopolitical morpheme of the "tribe."* Within the village or town itself, the tribe and the city are in uneasy juxtaposition, in constant tension, and often in open conflict. The village or town participates, even though unequally from case to case, in the spheres of the two "antimorphemes": the town as "countryside," on the one hand, is the residential concentration of tribally oriented equal producers; but the town as "city," on the other hand, is the lowest echelon of an administrative chain of command centered in the city and reaching into the rural populace in order to rationalize it by appropriating its labor and the products of its labor to sustain the nonproductive ruling class. The villager and the semi-nomadic camp dweller are divided beings. Their human instincts as producers and their persisting "underground" tradition is tribal, but they face the insistent authority of the city-state encroaching upon them. That authority they must submit to, find an advantageous accommodation to, or overthrow. In submitting to the city, they violate the basic tribal desideratum of autonomous control of production by the producers. In maneuvering a compromise, they adroitly employ their tribal strength to mitigate the worst features of statism. In overthrowing authority, they usually reject an immediate, intolerable form of statism. However, they have difficulty in maintaining tribalism as a viable form of organization once they control the apparatus of the city-state; for instead of destroying it altogether, they tend to adopt it as their own, thus sooner or later assimilating to the very statism they formerly deplored as its victims.

In all their struggles against the city-state, those who operate as tribalists have the deep-seated and chronic problem of effective unity. The very traits that make tribalism so suited to large-scale cooperation among equal producers are precisely the traits that enfeeble unified opposition against oppression. The inarticulate traditional socialism of the tribe does not easily pass over into a form of explicit revolutionary socialism, i.e., a form of resistance which can demolish the apparatus of the state once it has broken free from it. The problem of transition from tribalism of town and village to a tribalism able to cope with the city was not effectively solved until Israel arose. The real transitional hiatus between tribalism and hierarchy/stratification was not between the nomadic encampment and the village/town but between village/town/encampment and the city. Israel had its own way of coping with the transitional problem, with the means by which inarticulate tribal socialism could be extended to a wider area of the Near East as a dominant mode of life without succumbing to revived hierarchy and stratification. Israel's solution was markedly successful in the short term (for about two-hundred years), but in the long run proved inadequate (with the challenge of Philistine imperialism, Israelite egalitarianism gave way to a native monarchy). Nevertheless, one thing that clearly distinguished Israel's emergence was the explicitness with which it faced the problem of turning a rebellion against specific grievances into a total social revolution. There had been many rebellions, and Israel's way was prepared by this endemic urge to rebellion; but Israel proper took root and grew by virtue of its ideological and organizational success in generalizing and consolidating diffuse grievances and local rebellions into a sustained, coordinated social revolutionary movement and potent strike force.

41

Post-Amarna Antistatist Social Sectors: Convergence and Fragmentation

In this part we have focused on the ʽapiru and the pastoral nomads as the socioeconomic groups most frequently proposed for comprehending the origins of Israel. We discovered that the only way to reach an adequate understanding of these socioeconomic types is to view them in relation to the total socioeconomic and political system in Canaan. The ʽapiru and pastoral nomads can only be understood within the interlock of Egyptian imperialism and Canaanite feudalism, as that interlock sought to dominate an economy of intensive agriculture. It became clear that the nomadic pastoralism of the Canaanite world was not a major autonomous way of life intruding into Canaan from an independent desert base. We concluded that the pastoral sub-specialization of Canaanite agriculture is best characterized as transhumant pastoralism.

As a result of our systemic inquiry into social dimorphemes and antimorphemes, we have begun to note points of convergence in the sociopolitical form and tendency of the ʽapiru and of the transhumant pastoralists. Simultaneously we have detected differences in socioeconomic origins and in particular, differences in their social locations within the dominant system, which underline the fact that the points of convergence did not lead smoothly or directly to combined action. We must, therefore, look more closely at the persisting lines of convergence and the stubborn tendencies toward fragmentation which characterized not only the ʽapiru and the transhumant pastoralists but also the Shosu and the ḫupshu or peasants of the Canaanite world. We shall begin by examining the convergences and divergences between ʽapiru and transhumant pastoralists, gradually enlarging our analysis to include the Shosu and ḫupshu.

41.1 Toward an Antistatist Coalition: Lines of Convergence

Both ʽapiru and pastoral nomads in Canaan are basically comprehensible as elements within the Canaanite social world rather than as intrusions from without. The conflicts between ʽapiru and pastoral nomads, on the one hand, and resident Canaanites, on the other hand, were not the conflicts of invaders and defenders of land. They were rather conflicts over social organization and the appropriation of economic production between different segments of the population in Canaan, conflicts which arose intrasystemically.

Both 'apiru and pastoral nomads were broadly united by a "tribal" form of social organization in opposition to the structurally dominant "statist" form of social organization. 'Apiru and pastoral nomads were themselves members of the Canaanite social world who opposed not all Canaanites, but Canaanite rulers and aristocrats and necessarily all those supporting the rulers and aristocrats. 'Apiru and tribal pastoralists, although unquestionably different in many details, were joined in an egalitarian conception of autonomous economic and political life which sought wherever possible to ameliorate or to overthrow the domination of "statism" and its specific oppression through taxation in kind, draft labor, and forced military service.

'Apiru and pastoral nomads cannot be properly appraised as "tribalists," or differentiated as particular socioeconomic sub-types, apart from their relation to another socioeconomic component of Canaan, namely, the peasants. In principle the peasants were "tribal" in their sympathies and orientation. Owing to their settled mode of life and extensive incorporation into the feudal system throughout much of Canaan, the peasants as a whole, however, were more fully integrated into the Egyptian-Canaanite dominant system than were 'apiru and pastoral nomads. Still, the peasant integration into Canaanite feudalism was uneven and incomplete. In many areas they could and did resist the encroachment of the city expropriation of their labor. In addition, we have come to see that the pastoral nomads of this time were either in fact partial agriculturalists or worked symbiotically with agriculturalists. In those terms, the pastoral nomads of Canaan may be viewed as a specialized form of animal husbandry rooted in the settled zone but extending out adaptively into the steppes. Pastoral nomadism was thus a form of episodic retreat from statist domination available to peasants, especially to those living along the margins of Canaan where mountain or steppe pasturage was readily accessible. In effect, we are saying that not only was there a broad "tribal" convergence between 'apiru and pastoral nomads, but there was also a broad "tribal" convergence among 'apiru, pastoral nomads, and peasants.

The social morphemes which best comprehend the interrelations, both in terms of commonality and in terms of differentiation, among 'apiru, pastoral nomads, and peasants are *the antimorphemes of "city" and "countryside"* (to identify the contending poles territorially), or, otherwise described, *the antimorphemes of "state" and "tribe"* (to identify the contending poles socioeconomically and politically). The fundamental tension running steadily throughout Late Bronze and Early Iron Canaan, breaking into open conflict from time to time, was the tension between urban-based statism and rural-oriented tribalism. We remind the reader that by tribalism we refer to the broad criteria of social organization previously developed and not to any one specific trait, such as the presence of the exogamous clan. We also remind the reader that we do not assume that this tribalism was a uniform homogeneous, continuing tradition of social organization, since it had been so radically challenged and broken into by statism during the preceding centuries and millennia. On the contrary, with the help of Fried's analysis of tribalism as an imposition by intrusive statism,[401] we think of this Canaanite tribalism as a defensive reaction that finally, with Israel's rise, became a counteroffensive employing the surviving tribal forms in fresh strategic and tactical formations to resist and to overthrow the encroaching statism. Thus, it is vitally important to apply ethnological data about tribalism judiciously to Late Bronze and Iron Age Canaan, inasmuch as the historic juncture between statism and tribalism, partially as a synthesis and partially as a running conflict, has complicated the social forces at work and given them their unique composition and dynamic.

The common convergence of 'apiru, *pastoral nomads, and peasants* can be identified by their constellation around the antimorpheme of rural tribalism. All three groups had basic interests in preserving their autonomy that brought them into conflict with the city-state, thereby creating the objective conditions for episodic or more enduring cooperative action with one another.

41.2 Inhibited Coalition-Building: Fragmented Group Interests

On the other hand, *the differentiations among* 'apiru, *pastoral nomads, and peasants and the obstacles to their joining in unified action* can be explained by the variations in their relationships to the city, by the specific economic modes they followed, as well as by the forms of struggle available to them. These differentia which frustrated common action will now be explored.

The *'apiru* seem largely to have stemmed directly from the cities, or from the countryside under urban control, forming bands by the accretion of refugees from the city-state system. In Canaan they turned to banditry and to mercenary soldiery. We may view them as a kind of occupational guild; but unlike disarmed guilds directly supported by the state, they were in a structural position of incipient insurgency against the statist social order. Unable to overthrow the system as a whole, and unable or unwilling to migrate elsewhere, they took advantage of the contradictory situation in which the imperial-feudal structure, although holding firm as a totality, was riddled with strife among its various city-state components and between its imperial overlay and its colonial sub-units. In such circumstances the *'apiru* developed the art of mercenary warfare that made them indispensable to the very system they despised and allowed them the ironic pleasure of legitimately striking back at the system through their normal occupational activity as soldiers. One way of perceiving the weakness of the overall system is the dependence of the city-states on the *'apiru* whose militarization they had to legitimate because they severally depended on mercenary aid, even though the more extended the *'apiru* military activity became, the closer the total system drew toward dissolution.

The transhumant pastoralists were specialized practitioners of animal husbandry who had moved out from a farming base to engage at least half the year in large-scale herding. The factors impelling them to do so were a shifting mixture of economics and politics. Supplementing the agricultural base of the economy as a whole by exploitation of the seasonal grazing land was a steady attraction, but the relative freedom from the city-state's most oppressive actions was also a major stimulus to pastoral nomadism. Unlike the *'apiru*, who had to break decisively with their previous mode of life and who generally did so as individuals or small companies, transhumant pastoralists merely developed more intensively a side of settled production with which they were already familiar, while continuing to live for part of the year in their former full-time homes, and operating as social entities more or less continuous demographically and organizationally with their previous full-time sedentary social existence.

This is not to deny that important adaptations took place in the movement from sedentary agriculture and animal husbandry to transhumant pastoralism. It is to stress that the movement between full-time agriculture and pastoral nomadism was never so decisive a rupture as was the movement from the city or countryside into membership in an *'apiru* band. There was always the possibility of a way back into sedentariness for the pastoral nomad. For the *'apiru* there was no easy way back into the order of society. For these reasons, we might conjecture that the oppositional consciousness of the transhumant pastoralist against the state was probably not so fully developed as the oppositional consciousness of the *'apiru*.

The economic modes of *'apiru* and pastoral nomads were strikingly different. Pastoral nomads were herders in an intensive form of animal breeding that profoundly shaped their form of life, tying them closely to the movements of the herds, which required constant direction and care. The *'apiru* in Canaan were, by contrast, specialists in infantry warfare, and perhaps a few of them in chariot warfare. If the impression of their frequent engagement in internecine city-state struggle is at all to be trusted, it is difficult to believe that they had much time for agriculture and animal husbandry on a self-supporting scale. In fact, references in the Amarna correspondence to provisioning the *'apiru* probably indicate that their pay freed them from the need for intensive cultivation of land. That they were at times settled in particular regions is hinted at in the Amarna letters, and it is not to be excluded that the *'apiru* women and children, and the men themselves when not on campaigns, engaged in some agriculture and kept some animals. The point is that they were not dependent on plant cultivation or animal husbandry for their means of subsistence, or at most these means were supplemental. They were free to fight when needed on short notice, and thus had a great advantage over the full-time peasants who, in leaving their land to fight, could easily jeopardize agricultural production.

The numerous references in Egyptian documents to Shosu fighting against the Egyptians, and occasionally in later times as mercenaries for the Egyptians, are sometimes compared with the similar role of the Sutu, a militarized people commonly but inconclusively identified as Syrian bedouin. In the Amarna period, Sutu are reported to have been in the ranks of the Egyptian ioyalist troops of Biryawaza of Ube (EA 195.29). These references raise the question of the extent to which pastoral nomads in Syria-Canaan were militarized at this time. We have already noted the precariousness of the simplistic identification of Shosu as pastoral nomads which has been uncritically fostered by translating the term unambiguously as "bedouins." The small-cattle nomad raids and skirmishes more than he conducts sustained war. His livelihood is in his flocks, which he must constantly tend. It is totally improbable in my view that the extent and intensity of warfare attributed to the Shosu by the Egyptians could have been carried out by an exclusively pastoral nomadic people, i.e., by a people in which the whole community moved in transhumance throughout half of the year. In my view the Shosu who fought against the Egyptians must have been a people from communities in which a large part of the populace was engaged in sedentary agriculture. Since Shosu means "plunderers" rather than "nomads," according to the most probable etymology, and since they were spread over such considerable regions— appearing even as highways brigands in northern Palestine and southern Syria —I am inclined to think that many of the groups called Shosu were not pastoral nomadic at all, or had no more than a minor part of their populace engaged in transhumant pastoralism.

The question naturally arises, however, if we allow that some pastoral nomads were militarized and engaged in warfare with or against the Egyptians, just how they are to be distinguished from the 'apiru. A broad geographical distinction is possible in that the center of gravity for Shosu distribution is in southern Palestine, northern Sinai, and Edom, whereas the center of gravity for 'apiru is in southern Syria and northern Palestine. Although his remarks are not fully elucidated, Helck regards 'apiru and Shosu as regional variants of the same sorts of immigrating groups, the 'apiru to the north of the Dead Sea and the Shosu to the south.[402] We leave aside for the moment his gratuitous assumption that 'apiru and Shosu represent recent incursions from outside Canaan, which Helck bases largely on an Egyptian text referring to "foreigners . . . who come in flight from their lands" to threaten an unspecified part of the empire,[403] a text which in my view is just as logically understood on the 'apiru model of persons taking flight from cities within the empire. The difficulty with Helck's assumption that 'apiru and Shosu are basically the same groups, according to northern and southern regional differentiations, is that the proposed boundary between the two groups does not hold with any definitiveness. Shosu are identified throughout all of Canaan as far north as Kadesh, and 'apiru appear as far south as later Judah in southern Palestine. On the other hand, that 'apiru and Shosu were viewed as distinct groups by the Egyptians is evident from Amenhophis II's booty list in which 'apiru captives and Shosu captives are separately itemized side by side.

My proposal for linking and differentiating 'apiru and Shosu is as follows: 'apiru and Shosu were alike in that they were definable continuing (as opposed to ad hoc) militarized groups, imperfectly integrated into the feudal system and posing a threat to the Egyptians and to particular city-states in Canaan. They were alike in that they were similarly caught up in the cross-currents of shifting coalitions and counter-coalitions involving Egypt and the city-states. Being groups extensively distributed, 'apiru and Shosu were variable power factors that could appear from point to point, now aligned with one city and now with another, depending upon the immediately perceived mutual interests of the city-states and of the semi-independent militarized groups. Most of the time both 'apiru and Shosu appear on the side of Canaanite city-states that are antagonistic to Egypt in the sense that they are disturbing the status quo of the Egyptian imperium, even though they are not always directly engaged with Egyptian forces.

As to differentiating criteria between 'apiru and Shosu, I suggest that they were socioeconomic with a secondary geographical factor. The 'apiru were recently formed, or constantly augmented, communities of persons who withdrew as "outlaws" from the urban-dominated feudal society and, composed in guild-like enclaves, came to specialize in mercenary soldiery which compelled them to live in virtually complete economic dependence on the society they had withdrawn from. Regarding the Shosu we have little pertinent socioeconomic information, but I propose a tentative typology to differentiate them from 'apiru. The Shosu were continuing self-supporting communities of persons engaged in an agricultural and pastoral mixed economy, some of whom were pastoral nomads. The territorial base of the Shosu at some remove from the urban centers and their partial pastoral nomadism preserved them from being as fully integrated into agricultural feudalism as were the peasants who lived in the more densely populated plains where the city-states were situated close to one another and effectively controlled the countryside. This relative freedom from urban statism meant that Shosu often had to develop self-defense measures against other groups (in one Egyptian text Shosu are described as fighting one another) and their forces could not be as readily drafted by the urban centers as could the peasants on the feudal latifundia. Perhaps in return for bartered goods or for an agreement by the city-state not to interfere excessively in their internal affairs, these Shosu would agree to offer their troops as auxiliaries for the city-states. Whereas 'apiru appear to have been almost totally dependent upon their military specialization in order to receive in exchange the means of subsistence, the Shosu appear as self-subsisting communities with self-defense forces which could not always be well controlled by the city-states and thus appear, especially to the Egyptians, as a threatening entity which could be compared to the volatile 'apiru.

The geographical differentiation, by itself insufficient to account for the differences between 'apiru and Shosu, is nonetheless a secondary factor closely correlated with the socioeconomic differentia. The 'apiru, dependent as mercenaries on the very city-states they withdrew from, had to remain near the city-states if their services were to be relevant. Thus, the 'apiru appear typically in the vicinity of the major city-states throughout Canaan, from Hebron northward. The Shosu, as self-subsisting agricultural and pastoral communities which remained relatively free from urban statism were—in reverse of the 'apiru—to be found mainly to the south and east of the main Canaanite settlements. In fact, their primary identifiable locus was in southern Edom, a region well suited to mixed agriculture and pastoral nomadism. Neither our textual nor our archaeological knowledge of Edom is well developed, but it seems that at this time no major city-states existed there which were capable of dominating the Shosu. In Edom they were free to develop their own form of village tribalism.

The Edomite Shosu thus stood out in the minds of Egyptians as a strikingly "pure" concentration of the kinds of groups of imperfectly feudalized agricultural-pastoral communities which existed here and there throughout Canaan. Highway brigands, whose function appears in no way different from that of 'apiru engaged in the same business, were called Shosu, it seems, when they were recognized as coming from such self-subsistent communities and as not having formed military guilds of the 'apiru type. Thus we may view the groups mentioned in Amenophis II's booty list[404] as follows: city-state dynasts, brothers of dynasts, 'apiru infantry mercenaries, Shosu infantry auxiliaries, Neges=Nukhashshe infantry auxiliaries from northern Syria, and Kharu=Horites/Hurrians, who probably included both the maryannu, or aristocratic charioteers, and the drafted peasant infantry of the feudal latifundia of Canaan.

41.3 Inhibited Position of the Depressed Peasant Majority

Finally, in our review of the "tribal" sectors of Canaan we come now in more detail to the peasants. We begin by recognizing that the agriculturalists, although more or less fully integrated into the feudal system, were basically alienated from the statist form of social organization for the obvious reason that their labor was expropriated or threatened with expropriation by that system. This feudal expropriation gave the peasants little in return. Obviously the socioeconomic type of peasant overlaps with the socioeconomic type of pastoral nomad, for the repeatedly disclosed situation of the Canaanite pastoral nomad was that he was a transhumant pastoralist who also cultivated land or made arrangements with the cultivators of land. We can, however, formulate a continuum for peasant existence on which one extreme is the mixed peasant-transhumant nomad distant from the urban center, and the other extreme is the fully sedentary peasant working on feudal latifundia under the direct control of the urban aristocracy. Accompanying the former extreme position was a relatively high consciousness of autonomy and a relatively successful struggle to remain free of the most blatant forms of urban oppression. Accompanying the latter extreme position was a low consciousness of autonomy, even dumb resignation to a seemingly inexorable fate, and a lack of viable means for collective struggle against the directly experienced expropriation of labor by the city-state system. This is, of course, only a schematization which in historical reality was departed from and variegated in innumerable ways. For example, relatively autonomous agricultural-pastoral communities on a frontier might agree to considerable statist control as an assurance against attack by some neighboring group. And when internecine struggle between city-states upset the balance of power, internal coups might activate the hopes and even the collaboration of the most feudalized peasants, or briefly break the grip of the aristocracy so that numbers of peasants could desert to the enemy or flee to the remoter countryside. By developing a broad analytic framework that suggests those circumstances under which peasants might be more or less compliant with, or more or less rebellious toward, city-state domination, we are able to see the historic "exceptions" as lawfully shaped by the peculiar conjunctions of typical forces.

The peasant segment of the Canaanite populace is most commonly referred to by the term *hupshu,* which has a Hebrew cognate, *hopshī.* In addition to the Amarna letters and the Old Testament, references to the *hupshu* are found in the Assyrian law-code, Late Assyrian texts, an Ugaritic text, and the Alalakh tablets. Regrettably, no single reference gives an absolutely clear account of the status of the *hupshu,* but, viewed compositely, the allusions to *hupshu* do permit of some narrowing of possibilities in describing the social location of the great mass of the peasant population. The *hupshu* were the tillers of the land on behalf of the royal or aristocratic owners. The extent of their personal freedom and the sense in which they owned houses, tools, animals, etc., is far from evident in the texts. They are distinguished from slaves. In Alalakh they formed one part of the *sabe name,* probably to be understood as "the rural population," in which the *hanyahena,* "craftsmen," are also included. They are said to own cattle, agricultural implements, houses and even vineyards, but in the same list detailing their holdings the caption reads: "localities belonging to the king."[405]

Albright conceives the *hupshu* as "serfs or peons,"[406] but Mendelsohn emphasizes that the *hupshu* were not bound to a particular grant of land in the way that feudal serfs were bound, and he prefers to think of them on analogy with the Roman *colonus* (pl. *coloni*), who constituted a class of free-born tenant farmers.[407] In any case, they were subject to forced labor and military service,[408] and we must be careful not to give too much weight to the "free-born" status of the *hupshu.* If the stress is on their distinction from slaves, as with *hopshī* generally in the Old Testament,[409] the term may be said to have a somewhat favorable connotation. The total range of evidence shows, however, that the "freedom" of the *hupshu* was more a legal technicality than a social reality. Bluntly put, they were "free" of owning land and controlling their product. Through a confiscation of land by the crown, the granting of estates to aristocrats, and the expropriation of land in default of payment on debts at onerous interest rates, the agricultural holdings controlled from the city center tended to concentrate in the hands of a small class of landlords who used the state apparatus to dispose of the labor and the labor product of the great majority of the rural populace as they saw fit.

If the *colonus* analogy for the *ḫupshu* is apt, they were legally free to leave the estate. Insofar, however, as the agricultural latifundia grew in number and size, casting more and more free farmers into economic bondage, this formal freedom to seek another "employer" became increasingly hollow and meaningless. For the vast majority of the *ḫupshu* there was no place to go; it was literally a case of submission to the landlord or starvation. In this decisive socioeconomic sense, the *ḫupshu* were bound to the land and to the *métayage* system.[410] The census lists from Alalakh show that the ratio of *hupshu* to other social elements was approximately five to one, and we may take that figure (for want of any closer data) as a broad indicator that the great majority of the Canaanite populace was similarly composed of peasants without actual free holdings, whatever their precise legal status.

As individuals, the most that *ḫupshu* could hope for was some lightening of economic burdens through the extraction of favors from landlords. By extraordinary work performance, a few favored *ḫupshu* might gain the privilege of cultivating small private holdings. Some may have worked as day laborers on more than one estate. In the unsettled conditions of Amarna Canaan, the lot of the *ḫupshu* was notoriously vulnerable.

All the Amarna allusions to *ḫupshu* occur in the voluminous correspondence of Rib-addi of Byblos. As the enemy pressed against a city, the rural homes of the *ḫupshu* bore the brunt of the attack and their families were forced to flee to the walled city, while the men themselves faced impressment into military service (EA 81:33–41; 85:11–15). Within the besieged city, provisions were eventually depleted, and we can be reasonably sure that the lowly *ḫupshu* were among the first to feel the pangs of starvation (EA 85:8–19; 114:54–60; 118:22–23). In their desperation, the *ḫupshu* might desert to other cities where they had reason to expect more plentiful provisions (EA 125:25–30). Rib-addi laments that his *ḫupshu* have actually deserted to the sons of Abdi-Ashirta and that "when the *ḫupshu* desert, then the GAZ will seize the city" (EA 118:36–39). In the Rib-addi correspondence, there is an unmistakable convergence of external and internal threatening forces: the besieging enemy is strengthened by the restive, undependable *ḫupshu* before whom the king even fears for his life (EA 77:36–37; 117:90–95; 130:36–42). Rib-addi wonders, in a more than rhetorical manner, whether he needs protection primarily against his external foes or against his unruly *ḫupshu* (EA 112:10–15). The GAZ/ʿapiru may also in this context be understood, not simply as a label of opprobrium for the sons of Abdi-Ashirta, but for particular mercenary elements employed by them.

One letter from Biridiya of Megiddo to the pharaoh throws light on the feudal-imperial organization of agricultural labor in Canaan (EA 365).[411] The dynast of Megiddo boasts that he has cultivated fields in Shunem by furnishing corvée workers (the Akkadian word *ma-as-sà* is cognate with Hebrew *mas,* "servitude" or "forced labor gang," cf. Gen. 49:15: *mas 'ōvēd,* "forced laborer"). Biridiya reports that he has drawn the impressed laborers from Megiddo and from two other towns in his realm. He complains that other city dynasts have failed to provide corvée workers. The impression of the letter is that pharaonic crown lands were under the charge of local dynasts, who had to cultivate them by exacting corvée duty from peasants shifted from their regular labor on local latifundia. Although the term is not used in this letter, the corvée workers cited were doubtless from among the peasant populace known as *ḥupshu.*

Of the socioeconomic types we are examining as components of the antimorpheme of the tribally oriented countryside, the peasants were those in the most advanced state of integration into the antimorpheme of the urban state. Most of them had lost, and the remainder were under threat of losing, their free holdings, and the technical freedom of person which they still held was of slight benefit in the face of the massive expropriation of their labor by the *métayage* system of state-dominated agriculture. The coping devices of the *'apiru* as military specialists and of the transhumant pastoralists as herdsmen adapted to long periods of survival on the steppes were not directly available to peasants who had lost control over their means of subsistence and were tightly held within the city-state system. To rebel successfully they would have to either drive out the urban officials and defend their villages and fields or flee and attempt to set up farming in more remote, and probably less hospitable, conditions. Under the circumstances, hard-pressed but confused and dispirited, it is understandable that they often looked upon a neighboring city-state which was attacking their own city-state as a possible lesser of two evils.

We have shown that the line between peasant and pastoral nomad was not an absolute one. Still, not all peasants shared equally in accessibility to or actual practice of transhumant herding. The peasant who was also a pastoral nomad, or the peasant who was most likely to become a pastoral nomad, was not the peasant most closely controlled by the *métayage* system in the densely populated and compact city-states of the plains. The peasant who was, or who could become, a pastoral nomad was the peasant in the hill country and along the eastern and southern margins of Canaan, where the arable land imperceptibly shaded off into the steppes. Similarly, we should not draw an absolute line between peasant and *'apiru.* Among the recruits to the *'apiru* military bands and robber gangs were not only those who had fled from the major urban centers but also peasants. Particularly those peasants who had become experienced soldiers in the course of repeated military service for the crown could easily make the transition to mercenary soldiery. Although they might fight for the same dynasts as before, they now fought with a certain pride of craft and with a deep self-interest, for their communal autonomy depended on their indispensability to the rival dynasts.

Nonetheless, we can readily imagine obstacles to the mass withdrawal of peasants into *'apiru* bands. The obstacle from the side of the restive peasant would be both objective and subjective. Under surveillance by officials and guards, it was not easy to escape, but probably the greatest impediment was the peasant's uncertainty of succeeding on his own. Where could he flee? If alone, how could he find land and till it? Or, if he dared to conspire with others to flee, would not the escape plan be discovered? And how was he to make contact with an *'apiru* band? Since *'apiru* bands were engaged on all sides in the inter-city struggles, some of them might at the very moment be engaged for or against his own city-state. Could he trust *'apiru* bands to receive him? The obstacles from the side of the *'apiru* bands would be both objective and subjective as well. Could the band afford to take in another recruit, another person to be fed and trained? In a sense, one can say that the success of the *'apiru* adaptive deviation from the feudal sytem depended on there not being too many *'apiru*! Was the newcomer in fact an agent of the city-state feigning flight but actually sent to spy? Consequently, in spite of the objective common interest of *'apiru* and peasants in collaboration, the structure of the system that provoked the inter-city wars also militated against widespread cooperation between them.

41.4 Summary and Synthesis

We synthesize the results of this section as follows: Social tension and struggle within Canaan in the fourteenth and the first half of the thirteenth century was in a stage of converging class interests among *'apiru,* transhumant pastoralists, Shosu, and peasants in the sense that they were each carrying on struggles for their own autonomy and survival which brought them into repeated friction and collision with the same ruling-class enemies. These were struggles which could only be successfully culminated for each group to the degree that they were successfully culminated for all groups. These converging struggles, however, had not reached the level of a common consciousness of the fundamentally congruent interests—indeed the critical structural interdependence—of the several groups, and of the absolute necessity for a united front and a joint strategy if they were ever to break loose from imperial-feudal domination.

Another way to put this matter is to say that the struggles of the several segments of the underclass populace of Canaan were still being waged within the divisive ideological and organizational limits of the very city-state framework which they protested against. The most advanced form of struggle, waged by the *'apiru,* was flawed by the fact that it had to depend upon selling military services to one or another city-state, services necessarily used from time to time against struggling peasants and transhumant pastoralists, who were forced to fight for their over-lords and whose unwalled villages, fields, and pastures were often devastated by the military campaigns. In fighting one another, the "tribal" groups strengthened their common enemy. There was as yet no clear conception of unity in struggle and no widely shared instrument of action which could break through the city-state divisions and unite the underclasses in many or all city-states so as to break apart the entire system of domination from within.

It was precisely that inner-societal strategic vision and tactical unity which Israel introduced. The social struggle for tribally organized self-rule in Amarna and post-Amarna Canaan is thus to be sharply phased according to its pre-Israelite and Israelite stages. Prior to Israel, the lines of convergence among broadly congruent "tribal" social groups were constantly stymied by the fragmentation of the groups within the dominant system, a system which astutely employed its tight organization at the top to separate and to splinter restive groups at the bottom and on the fringes. In Israel, the lines of convergence met and transcended the previous fragmentation; and in the resulting combination of forces, the dominant system was ruptured from within, its hierarchic rule in dozens of separate city-states faced with the egalitarian unity of former subjects joined together across all the old dividing lines. With the appearance of Israel, the Canaanite "tribe" at last found an ideological base and an organizational mode for successfully challenging the Canaanite "state."

Part IX

A New Egalitarian Canaanite Society:
Liberated Israel vis-à-vis Indigenous Peoples

42

Revolutionary Israel: An Expanded Coalition
of Antistatist Social Sectors

Our basic approach in the preceding part has been to make a synchronic typological cross-cut of the sociopolitical structure of Amarna Canaan, in which we have noted a persisting diachronic movement toward increasing disintegration of the overall feudal-imperial interlock, a movement which has as its terminal horizon the emergence of early Israel as the antithesis of the feudal-imperial Canaanite system. In preceding chapters we have developed the materials and concepts for conceiving the Israelite egalitarian system in twelfth–eleventh century Canaan. We shall now draw together a descriptive sketch of early Israel's social system, both as the culmination of and as a mutation upon those lines of social tension and contradiction which were converging in Amarna Canaan and tending toward the dissolution of a system which could finally no longer contain the glaring contradictions. We shall then be in a position to offer some tentative hypotheses about the relatively obscure transitional stage between the Amarna era and the emergence of Israel; namely, the century or more from 1350 to 1250 or 1225 B.C.

In the case of Yahwistic Israel we see fully formed precisely the marks of a conscious, organized, broad-scale social egalitarian movement which were lacking amidst all the Amarna unrest. In Israel, antifeudal sentiment and protest has become antifeudal and pro-egalitarian ideology and social organization. Not only does Israel challenge Egyptian imperialism, it rejects city-state feudalism as well, and does so by linking up exploited peoples across the boundaries of the old city-state divisions. A class *in* itself, hitherto a congeries of separately struggling segments of the populace, has become a class *for* itself. More precisely, how are we to characterize the Israelite community vis-à-vis the *'apiru,* peasant, and pastoral nomadic peoples of Amarna Canaan?

UNITARY CULTURE AND SOCIAL ORDER. In spite of its own inner tensions, Israel—as compared with Amarna Canaan—is clearly one community in conception and one community in practice: socially, economically, politically, militarily, and religiously. The single-cult community with its loyalty to Yahweh is closely correlated with a set of similar egalitarian social relations, a similar range of economic activities involving a primary specialization in agriculture within an agricultural-pastoral mix, similar ways of governing society by the diffusion of political organization through the social structure, and similar ways of organizing weaponry, strategy, and tactics in a citizen militia. We observe, then, precisely the kind of embracing unitary culture and social order in early Israel that was lacking as a bond or framework for 'apiru, peasants, and pastoral nomads a century or more earlier.

UNITARY CULT AND IDEOLOGY. The religious cult and ideology of Yahwism are potent organizational and symbolic forces in establishing and reinforcing the social, economic, political, and military arrangements normative for community. The Levitical priesthood, the bearers of Yahwism, form an intellectual and organizational cadre of leadership which cuts across and penetrates the several autonomous social segments, binding them together for actions based on common sentiment. Not only is Israel characterized by a range of coexisting sets of social, political, military, and religious traits, but these aspects of the total social system interpenetrate and reinforce one another, and are exhibited in leaders who carry out functions in one or more of the dimensions of the total social system according to limited assignments of power appropriate to each task.

A NEW "OUTLAW" MAJORITY. It is apparent that early Israel was partially in continuity with the Amarna 'apiru; but, it must be stressed, only in part. Like the 'apiru, Israel stood apart from the feudal system, but whereas the 'apiru were only semi-independent and were in fact ultimately dependent on the feudal system for a livelihood, Israel broke totally free of feudalism and extended its "outlaw" system over an entire region and an entire people, so that "outlawry" became "inlawry," the basis of a new order. The appropriation of the economic product by the producers themselves in egalitarian social relationships, which the old order necessarily rejected as illegitimate, was newly legitimated by a mutant people under a mutant deity. The 'apiru remained an outlaw minority who could be accommodated by the system; Israel became a newly validated majority which broke the system apart wherever it gained control. In the 'apiru we see unassimilated pockets of people skillfully working the larger feudal system in which they are outweighed politically and militarily; in Israel we see an antifeudal way of life which has become an entire counter-society, politically and militarily autonomous.

AN ECLECTIC COALITION. Nonetheless, the massive alteration in the scope and political strength of the antifeudal social movement visible in the transition from Amarna to early Israelite Canaan does not entirely answer the question of the transitional relationship between 'apiru and Israelite. The alteration does not tell us whether or not it was the old Amarna 'apiru who managed to flower into Yahwistic Israel. In my view, some but not all of the descendants of the Palestinian Amarna Age 'apiru entered into early Israel; and at the same time some, but by no means all, of early Israel was composed of former 'apiru. In other words, *early Israel's uniqueness may be understood socially in terms of its success in bringing together the diverse underclasses which the declining feudal-imperial system had until that time been able to keep separated.* Early Israel was composed not only of former 'apiru bands but also of peasant and transhumant pastoral populations who had been more or less integrated into city-state feudalism, more so in the urban-controlled latifundia and less so in the highlands and marginal areas where agricultural-pastoral villages struggled with some limited success to keep a measure of autonomy. Among those who entered Israel in the thirteenth–twelfth centuries, indeed those who formed its ideological and organizational spearhead, were congeries of 'apiru and mixed agriculturalists and pastoralists, some of whom had fled from Egypt. *Consequently, Israel is most appropriately conceived as an eclectic composite in which various underclass and outlaw elements of society joined their diffused antifeudal experiences, sentiments, and interests, thereby forming a single movement that, through trial and error, became an effective autonomous social system.*

The original Yahwistic proponents who fled Egypt were eclectically composed in reaction to Egyptian statism in its domestic guise of forced labor. The later full formation of Israel, drawing underclasses from all over Canaan, was an enlarged version of essentially the same process of eclectic social composition, this time in reaction to Canaanite feudalism and to the remnants of Egyptian imperialism in Canaan. This eclecticism of converging, but in many ways diverse, social elements posed a precarious unity which can in no way be accounted for in terms of prior ethnic or cultural factors. Only the long process of social struggle in Canaan, which step by step induced an agonizingly slow emergence of common consciousness among the oppressed peoples, can account for the integration and focus of the new community of Israel. Israel's vehement and tenacious identity as one people under one God has its indisputable axis around an antifeudal egalitarian social commitment.

EGALITARIANISM TAKES THE OFFENSIVE. In view of the preceding analysis, I grant that the rise of Israel could be understood as a greatly expanded 'apiru movement. We could view Israel as a community in which not merely a few people but the entire populace has become 'apiru, particularly in the sense that the 'apiru band commitment to military specialization has become characteristic of the entire Israelite citizen army en masse. But in offering such a proposal, we see at once its inaptness, for the reason that the very essence of the 'apiru status, wherever it appears in the ancient Near East, is that it is defined as "outlawry" in terms of some judging established community; and as a way of life, 'apiru existence is no more than an adaptation to the dominant system. Wherever the 'apiru have become an autonomous majority, they are no longer 'apiru. Even if the military skills of 'apiru and early Israelites represent a continuum of tradition, the context of the exercise of those skills is fundamentally different. The 'apiru fights for others as mercenary; the Israelite fights for himself. If the 'apiru also fights for himself in the sense that by fighting for others he maintains his self-serving adaptation to the established order, the Israelite faces no such contradiction inasmuch as he fights only for himself and not for any other master.

Consequently, while up to a certain point in the transition from Amarna Canaan to early Israel, the *'apiru* movement may be said to have grown by the accretion of peasants and pastoralists breaking away from the city-states, at a certain point the *'apiru* movement emerges into a new autonomous movement. The defensive *'apiru* stance passes over into the offensive Israelite stance. The crucial turning-point can be defined in many ways. Above all, however, it is that stage where the way to freedom is no longer defined as adopting a particular socioeconomic mode of mercenary soldiery or brigandage, but the way to freedom is understood as the unified action of many kinds of socioeconomic producers. Otherwise stated, the point where the *'apiru* movement becomes the proto-Israelite, and then the fully Israelite, movement is that point where the community no longer defines itself solely by opposition to the Canaanite city-state but, more importantly, by advocacy and enactment of the new egalitarian relations it practices, relations operationally broad and adaptive enough to include former *'apiru,* peasants, and pastoral nomads in a self-conscious social-systemic unity.[412]

When and where was the point reached that the underclasses in Canaan began to achieve a positive revolutionary movement which brought diverse socioeconomic groups together in a common organization and ideology? Was it only for the first time when the proto-Israelites from Egypt entered Canaan at the end of the thirteenth century? In my opinion there must have been an earlier moment of proto-Israelite unity which prepared the underclasses of the Canaanite highlands for the propitious entrance of the Yahwistic proto-Israelites. This earlier moment of unified revolutionary consciousness formed the transition between Amarna Age social struggle and the rise of Yahwistic Israel.

43

The Path through Elohistic Israel to Yahwistic Israel

We have seen that from 1350 B.C. on there was a continuing decline of Egyptian imperial control in Palestine and a weakening of the city-state feudal order. The relative strength of antifeudal elements in the populace, notably the *'apiru*, increased, even if we were to assume no growth in their absolute numbers, which seems unlikely. The growing power of the *'apiru* is evidenced in the campaign that Seti I waged against the *'apiru* who were based in the mountains around Beth-shean, formerly one of the most impregnable Egyptian garrisons in Canaan.[413] From the side of Israelite origins, it has long been recognized that components of Israel were already in the land of Canaan prior to the entrance of the Exodus tribe or tribes. Who were these pre-Yahwistic proto-Israelites? What was it that united them prior to their organization as Yahwists?

In Genesis the patriarchs are pictured as leaders of semi-autonomous socioeconomic groups engaged in agriculture and in animal husbandry (and in limited transhumant pastoralism) and who live in treaty relations with Canaanite cities at Mamre-Hebron, Jerusalem, and Gerar in the south of Palestine.[414] In Genesis 14, there is presupposed an *'apiru*/Hebrew band which can field 318 armed men for battle in league with its allies from Mamre-Hebron and which also has treaty relations with Melchizedek, "a covenanted king,"[415] possibly of Jerusalem. In Genesis 26, another such band is presupposed in the territory of Gerar, at first near to the city, then driven some distance away, and finally in a treaty relationship with the city. It seems clear that these bands practice agricultural-pastoral subsistence and are militarized. The account in Genesis 14, in particular, makes it look as though the city-states are subordinate to the *'apiru* band, but this seems to be the function of anachronizing Israelite tradition, which makes of Abraham an epic figure who foreshadows David's empire.[416]

It is a feasible conjecture that these proto-Israelite groups were in formal subordination to the city-states for which they fought, but by virtue of the importance of the military service they had to offer, they often became important and powerful beyond their size. They stood outside the city-state structure and were broadly "tribal" in structure. It is, of course, problematic whether these accounts give us a homogeneous picture of a single community or whether they represent composites distilled through a long traditional history. Their location toward the south of the land and their apparently stable communal continuity suggest groups of the type lumped together by the Egyptians as Shosu. Genesis 14:13, however, calls Abraham an *'ivri* = *'apiru*. There is no corresponding point in the Israelite traditions where the familiar Hebrew term *shōsim*, "plunderers," is applied to the Israelites in the sense of the Egyptian Shosu, although Israelites are said to have " plundered" (*way-yāshōssū*) the Philistine camp (I Sam. 17:53). Perhaps what is reflected here in the south of Canaan is the growing strength of the *'apiru* communities, to the point that they have their own agricultural and pastoral holdings and do not have to depend upon direct provision from the city-states for whom they fight. The significant point is this: if we subtract Yahwism (which these groups have not yet adopted) and if we remove a larger inclusive tribal structure (since only relatively small communities are described), the Hebrew bands of Genesis 14 and 26 are in clear typological continuity with *'apiru* groups, and perhaps also with Shosu groups. They are militarized, nonfeudally organized groups, engaging in farming and herding, standing outside of the urban network while at the same time serving it as mercenaries or auxiliaries.

Our next question is this: prior to the entrance into Canaan of the Yahwistic proto-Israelites from Egypt, did any of these *'apiru* (Shosu?) groups enter into a larger union? I take up this question by first of all noting the anomaly that the Yahwistic association of tribes took the name of Israel. Regrettably no clear etymology has yet been established for the first element in this name,[417] but the last element leaves no room for doubt. It is the common generic divine name, "el." Surely this is a curiosity. Given the overwhelming importance of Yahweh as the proper name of Israel's god, we should have expected the divine name Yahweh, probably in the short form Yah, to have appeared in the people's name, yielding "Israyah," or the like. The simplest explanation of this anomaly, I believe, is that Israel must have been a pre-Yahwistic entity larger than any one of the tribes which eventually entered Yahwistic Israel, for there is not the slightest hint in biblical tradition that Israel was ever the name of a single tribal entity.[418] Now it is pertinent that Noth explains the peculiarities of development in the tribal lists by hypothesizing an early amphictyony of middle-Palestinian tribes in which the Leah tribes, including Simeon and Reuben who later virtually disappear, played a prominent part.[419] It will be recalled that I do not accept Noth's hypothesis of an Israelite amphictyony, but the fact remains that, on whatever hypothesis, the fixed priority and order of the Leah tribes in traditional lists has to be reckoned with. It is therefore a reasonable conjecture that the separate *'apiru* bands, grown more numerous and powerful in the highlands and contributing to the breaking away of peasant settlements from the city-states, made efforts at joining together in an El-worshipping association (probably near Shechem). The deity of this association was apparently El Elohe Israel, i.e., "El, the God of Israel."[420]

I have no concrete proposal concerning the source of the name Israel, but the hypothesis that Israel was the name of a *pre-Yahwistic* union of Canaanite peoples does help to explain why the later *Yahwistic* union of tribes possessed the anomalous name of Isra*el*. It adopted that name because an earlier association of Canaanite underclasses had employed it and it was the single comprehensive term available with adequate historical associations to communicate the intent of Yahwistic Israel to be an egalitarian social order. Such a union, probably falling within the period 1325–1250 B.C., expressed the growing consciousness of the antifeudal movement as a powerful social movement in its own right, able to cooperate in the search for new forms of liberated social organization and a cult appropriate to such aims. In this context, it is probable that Genesis 34 (minus its interpolated references to Simeon and Levi in vss. 25, 30) gives a composite account of two or more contacts between proto-Israelites and Shechemites during the events in the formation of Elohistic Israel.[421] Noteworthy here is the equation "sons of Jacob/Jacobites" = "Israel" (34:7), together with Jacob's deity "El Elohe Israel" (33:20), a connection further epitomized in the renaming of Jacob as Israel (32:28[27]).

In the eventual full formation of Yahwistic Israel, we can provisionally distinguish those features that carried over from the older Elohistic Israel and those that were new infusions.

Foundational elements of Elohistic Israel retained in Yahwistic Israel:

MILITARIZATION. A strong tradition of military skill, notably in irregular and guerilla warfare, provided coordination among many segmented military bands that lacked a formal command structure. The fighting tradition of the Exodus Yahwists was able to combine with an already tested and experienced military organization among underclass Canaanites.

DECENTRALIZED SOCIOPOLITICAL COOPERATION. Segmentary social units, of a broadly "band-like" or "tribal" character, clustered together in a community of perceived interests that facilitated coordinated actions while excluding hierarchic leadership or formal unity. The joint military cooperation found a counterpart in a growing socioeconomic infrastructure that could be utilized and ignited by the infusion of the Yahwistic cult and ideology.

COMMON CULT. The several segmented social units embraced a common religious identity through a cult of the deity El. Allegiance to the common cult probably allowed simultaneously for collateral cults connected with groups, natural and social functions, and places—of the sort reflected in the patriarchal accounts. In any case, the devotion to El was sufficiently strong that the new deity Yahweh retained El(ohim) as an alternate name.

COMMON NAME. The several cooperating social units, while retaining their distinctive names, selected the overarching name "Israel" to identify their coalition. The name "Israel" seems not to have been identified with any single member group but to have decisively expressed a societal sum greater than a mere total of tribal parts. So entrenched was the use of "Israel" for the underclass coalition in

Canaan that the later Yahwistic reconstitution of the coalition simply adopted the old name.

New elements in the reorganized coalition of Yahwistic Israel:

INCREASE AND DIVERSIFICATION OF MEMBER GROUPS. Yahwistic Israel represented an organizational leap forward by virtue of an increase in the number, socioeconomic types, and previous historical experiences of the groups entering the community. In particular, the coalition expanded to include a larger proportion of peasants emboldened to break away from city-states by now less and less able to take effective punitive action against defectors. Only as sizable numbers of the great Canaanite peasant majority were won over to Israel could the coalition be said to speak for a truly representative body of people. Sheer growth in numbers and stimulation through cross-fertilization of skills and experience strengthened the coalition both internally and externally.

REVOLUTIONARY CADRES. Whatever their actual numbers, the Exodus proto-Israelites, who had broken away from the grip of the Egyptian empire and survived a trek through the desert, became a powerful catalyst in energizing and guiding the broad coalition of underclass Canaanites. Their experience became exemplary for all Israel, fundamentally shaping, as we noted in Part III, the entire format of the Israelite traditions. Organized as the priestly militarized Levites, spread throughout the tribes, they became intellectual and military-political cadres significantly leavening the whole coalition. The Exodus-Levitical infusion of energy and leadership emboldened the coalition to overcome the defeat it seems to have suffered somewhat earlier at the hands of Pharaoh Merneptah, as reported on his so-called Israel stele.[422]

COMMON CULT OF YAHWEH = EL. The Exodus Levites introduced the cult of Yahweh to Israel, not strictly as a substitute for El, but as a deity who could absorb valued El attributes and functions as aspects of his own comprehensive adequacy for meeting coalition needs, particularly for symbolizing, defining, and defending the locus of sovereignty within a diffuse egalitarian community. The impetus for Canaanite underclasses to turn to a totally, or largely, strange deity was apparently the result of factors both negative and positive. Negatively, there was disappointment and frustration with El as a deity for validating an antifeudal social order, inasmuch as El had come to be so largely appropriated as the high father god of the very feudal city-states that Israel was challenging head-on. Positively, there was the overwhelming, demonstrated, military and cultic-ideological appeal of the Levites in convincing the coalition that Yahweh, who had defeated Egypt on its home ground, could defend an enlarged anti-imperial and antifeudal order in Canaan.

In sum, then, I am arguing that the descendants of the Amarna Age 'apiru gained strength in the Palestinian highlands, at first as separate bands, increasingly as models for peasants to emulate, then as a cultic-sociopolitical-military association of previously separate groups (Elohistic Israel), and finally as a greatly expanded association of former *'apiru*, Shosu, peasants, and transhumant pastoralists from Canaan and Egypt under the same name Israel, but with a new religious identity of Yahwism. This should begin to make clear *the senses in which Israel was both continuous with the earlier* 'apiru *and at the same time discontinuous.* It was continuous in that highland *'apiru* probably formed the greater part of Elohistic Israel which in turn entered Yahwistic Israel, contributing their wealth of experience in social struggle against the city-states of Canaan. It was discontinuous in that not all Palestinian *'apiru* joined in Élohistic or in Yahwistic Israel, in that the *'apiru* mode of minority deviation gave way to a mode of comprehensive legitimated divergence from Canaanite feudalism, and in that Yahwistic Israel encompassed a very much larger and more socioeconomically variegated—not to mention regionally differentiated—association of peoples than did Elohistic Israel.

44

Canaanite Belligerents vis-à-vis Liberated Israel

44.1 Alleged Enemies of Israel: Canaan/Canaanite(s) and Other Terms

We shall now test out our general model of the Israelite sociopolitical system vis-à-vis the regnant Egyptian imperial/Canaanite feudal sociopolitical system by examining biblical textual data which give varying degrees and kinds of specification to the abstract catch-all terms: "the enemies" or "the adversaries" of Yahweh and Israel.

In biblical scholarship it has become conventional to speak of the land occupied by Israel as "Canaan" and its people as "Canaanites." We have followed this convention in speaking of "the Canaanite feudal system" or of "Amarna Canaan," and even of "the Canaanites," although the Amarna corpus itself contains only twelve occurrences of "Canaan" and but one of "Canaanite." It comes as some surprise, therefore, to discover that the biblical traditions are by no means agreed in their references to the region that the Israelites came to control, and even less agreed in their choice of names for the previous inhabitants. Alternative terms for the same areas and peoples, as well as major differences in the referents of the same term according to context, are frequent in the Old Testament. But in this respect, the Bible reflects historical reality in a manner analogous to the extrabiblical sources. Lacking a strong independent, indigenous, political cohesion and representing such a mixture of demographic and cultural elements, Syria-Palestine did not develop a single, clearly defined pattern of regional, political, and ethnic terms comparable to those which reached a certain standardization in Egypt and Mesopotamia (although even there, of course, variations and obscurities existed, especially in ethnic designations as each major political and population change required adjustments in terminology).

The major complexity in the biblical traditions is that they represent so many stages in agglomerated and reinterpreted territorial-political and demographic references that it is extremely difficult to unravel the usages of the terms according to their respective original contexts. In this respect, the extrabiblical texts give us a somewhat more controlled account of terminology in given historical horizons. There is frequently a greater "temporal distance," as well as "ideological distance," between the biblical terms for indigenous peoples and their referents than between the comparable terms and their referents in extrabiblical texts, since those texts did not form a part of a developing canon of religious writings. By analyzing the extrabiblical usages according to a combined historico-territorial and religio-ideological developmental grid, it is possible to see, with varying degrees of clarity, how generally accepted contemporary usages have been taken over into biblical usages and frequently modified according to inner-Israelite idiosyncrasies.[423]

In recent years scholars have come to certain general conclusions about the origins and application of the terms "Canaan" and "Canaanite." By about the fifteenth century B.C., an Akkadian term *kinaḫḫu,* "reddish purple," probably in Hurrianized form, came to be applied to a treasured dye from the Mediterranean murex shell, and to the expensive cloth colored by the dye, as also to the region where the dyeing industry and trade was centered, i.e., the north Syrian coast later known as Phoenicia: thus, Canaan or "land of the purple dye/d goods." Furthermore, *kinaḫḫu* came to serve as a designation for the Phoenician merchants or traders: thus, Canaanites as "merchants selling dyed cloths," and, on occasion by extension, for all the inhabitants of the region: thus Canaanites as "people living in the land of the merchants selling dyed cloths." While Canaan tended to refer mainly to the coastal area north of Acco, it was at times expanded to include the Palestinian coast south of Acco, and even the interior of Syria and Palestine, thus becoming virtually identical with the large Egyptian Asiatic province of Syria.[424]

Elements of this terminological history correspond to the biblical usage of Canaan and Canaanite. A few texts overtly employ the primary mercantile meaning, i.e., the Canaanite is a trader (Isa. 23:8; Prov. 31:24; Zeph. 1:11; Zech. 11:7,11). For the most part, however, Canaan and Canaanites seem to designate a region or its inhabitants. When we take into account, however, that pejorative references to peoples as enemies of Yahweh and Israel often retain a socioeconomic dimension, we get the distinct impression that the term "Canaanite" carries in some instances, if not a specifically mercantile reference, at least an upper-class overtone alluding to royalty or aristocracy. This impression will require our further investigation below. At times (especially in the J stratum), "Canaanites" is the preferred term for all the inhabitants of Palestine west of the Jordan River, those east of the Jordan being called "Amorites." At other times (especially in the E and D strata), the Canaanites are omitted or restricted to the coastal plains and the Jordan Valley, "Amorites" serving as the more inclusive term for the general population of Palestine or for those living in the hills. Obviously this difference in biblical usage corresponds roughly to the extended and restricted usages in extrabiblical sources.

In apparent awareness of the lack of any single normative term for the region and its peoples, the Old Testament also frequently speaks of a cluster of peoples in the area west of the Jordan. The fullest customary form of this "table of peoples" (which is often abbreviated) includes Canaanites, Amorites, Jebusites, Hivites, Hittites, Girgashites, and Perizzites. The seven terms appear in no invariable order, so I have listed them somewhat arbitrarily in terms of their prominence in the biblical accounts. In every case we either lack independent knowledge about the people referred to or face difficulties in conceptualizing their presence in Israelite territory, whether in terms of their location, their composition, or their relation to extrabiblical people of the same name. A brief comment on each term is in order.

Of the Girgashites and Perizzites we know nothing substantial. The Jebusites are the pre-Israelite inhabitants of Jerusalem. The Hivites, in western Benjamin, Shechem, and the northern fringes of the land, are generally taken to be the Hurrians, the name having been changed in Hebrew to avoid confusion with the Horites (cave-dwellers?), the original occupants of Edom.[425] The presence of Hurrians in Palestine is perfectly plausible in the light of the general movement of those peoples southward through Syria during the early second millennium, a movement which can be traced in the large number of Hurrian names in the Amarna letters. The Hittites in Canaan are localized around Hebron, Beersheba, and Bethel, and probably also at Jerusalem and in the vicinity of Kedesh in Galilee. These Hittites are not easily related either to the Anatolian Hittites or to the north Syrian neo-Hittite states. The Palestinian "Hittites" in the Old Testament are sometimes interpreted as a misreading for "Hivites/Hurrians." More often the term is seen as an anachronism from an earlier date when Hittite kingdoms controlled parts of Canaan. It is possible, however, that the allusion is to resident Hittite traders or government officials in the service of local city-states. It has also been suggested that survivors of the overthrow of the Hittite Empire by the Sea Peoples migrated southward into Canaan in considerable numbers. The problem of these Palestinian Hittites will be discussed more fully in IX.45.1 in connection with Judges 1:22–26.

"Amorites" we have seen to be the term applied at times to the general populace of the land, or of the highlands when associated with restriction of Canaanites to the coastal plain and Jordan Valley. In a more localized sense, however, it refers either to the rulers or to the populace of the kingdoms of Og and Sihon in Transjordan. Sumero-Akkadian texts spanning the period 2300–1600 B.C. refer to the area extending westward from the Euphrates River as far as the Mediterranean as *Amurru* (Sumerian MAR.TU). "The people of Amurru" are alluded to only in southern Mesopotamian texts of the Akkadian and Ur III periods prior to 2000 B.C. However, groups with the same language are found spread over northern Mesopotamia well into the eighteenth century B.C., and it is generally believed that Amorite-speakers entered Canaan c. 2100–1900 B.C. In fourteenth-thirteenth century Syro-Palestine, an area located in the mountains and along the coast of present-day northern Lebanon, was known as the kingdom of Amurru. The relation of this kingdom to earlier usages of Amurru and to biblical usages of Amorite is unclear. It is still much disputed whether the language of the Amorites was the direct predecessor of Canaanite-Hebrew or of Aramaic, or was rather an early development without direct ties to any of the later, better attested Northwest Semitic tongues.

In any case, we observe a striking discontinuity between all extrabiblical usages of Amorite and the biblical usages. In the Bible there is no geographical term Amor, comparable to Akkadian *Amurru* or parallel to Canaan. There is no known connection between the Syrian kingdom of Amurru and the Amorite kingdoms of Sihon and Og in Transjordan. Even if one were to hypothesize that a ruling class, fleeing the turbulent kingdom of Amurru in the Amarna Age, founded kingdoms of the same name in Transjordan, the theory yields no explanation of why the Israelites should have extended the term Amorites to the general populace of West Jordan.[426]

From the correlation of biblical and extrabiblical references to the land and its inhabitants we get no satisfactory unified picture. Certain usages are made understandable, as in the case of Canaan/Canaanites and Hurrians. Other usages, although we have considerable extrabiblical data, remain problematic, as with the Amorites and Hittites. Still others, lacking extrabiblical information altogether, remain obscure, such as Jebusites, Perizzites, and Girgashites. Even for those terms which are most fully documented extrabiblically, it becomes clear that their biblical use is uncorrelated to any single commonly harmonized set of terms. No such harmonized terms for Syro-Palestine existed outside of Israel, and Israel did not succeed in providing—apparently did not even try to provide—its own harmonized vocabulary. There appear to have been a number of temporally and regionally discrete Israelite nomenclatures which were never worked out systematically.

We seem to be on safe ground in claiming that the inhabitants of the land Israel was to take had no prior single ethnic or national consciousness, nor indeed even a series of recognizable identities that corresponded univocally to "Canaanite," "Amorite," "Hurrian," or "Hittite." The most localizable term, Jebusite, denominated only the people of Jerusalem, and how they understood themselves beyond their common residence in Jerusalem completely escapes us. Indeed Adonizedek, king of Jerusalem, who headed a league of five cities against Israel, is simply described as one of "the five kings of the Amorites" (Josh. 10:5). Furthermore, the political aggregations in the area were not large enough, nor their self-identities strong and distinctive enough, to provide a harmonized set of political identities. With the emergence of Israel, Philistia, the Transjordanian states of Ammon, Moab, Edom, and the Aramean states of Syria, national entities appear in which the consciousness of being a single people, shared by insiders and recognized by outsiders, began to provide a stable set of geopolitical terms for the area. The politically fragmented but culturally and ethnically more homogenized Canaan into which Israel was born offered a plethora of terms, used at various times and places and with various ranges of meaning, a pastiche of historical-territorial and gentilic names. Israel took up these names and modified them in ways which we can sometimes grasp rather clearly but which at other times remain completely opaque to us.

Even so, what does this variegated nonharmonistic terminology imply for the identification of the actual enemies of Yahwistic Israel? It certainly means that we must look beyond and behind the nominal labels for regions and peoples in an effort to identify the constellations of persons whom Israel opposed. It means that we cannot simply take up these terms, either as synonyms for all the inhabitants of the land or as a deliberately cumulative inventory of the subdivisions of the total populace—as though they single out a monolithic target for an intrusive nomadic or migratory people, or even for an internally revolting people, to annihilate or to expel or to subjugate. Nothing in the nomenclature of "the people of Canaan" corresponds to the view that one entire people is viewed as replacing another entire people. The great uncertainty in the applications of the proper names of the enemies of Israel means that those names by themselves do not provide us with any clear conception of the enemy or any clear corresponding conception of Israel's mode of settlement or of Israel's social system. It is true that such objectifying names can be, and generally have been, taken as evidence of the total hostility and opposition between all the preceding inhabitants of Canaan, by whatever names designated, and the entirely separate people of Israel who entered Canaan as outsiders, whether as invaders or immigrants. Indeed, this view gained an early currency in Israel's own traditions. It should be clear by now, from all that we have unearthed earlier in our study, that there simply are no cogent socioeconomic, political, or cultural grounds for conceptualizing Israel as a major intrusion into Canaan. Israel was a mutation of major proportions *within* Canaan, and its mutant reality as a social system must not be confused with a monolithic ethnic identity, a monolithic socioeconomic pastoral nomadic identity, or a monolithic religious identity as if, somehow, Israel's mutational significance could be accounted for by seeing it as an entirely separate people of non-Canaanite heredity coming out of the desert, professing an utterly supernatural deity, self-contained and complete. In my opinion, all the evidence tells against the notion of Israel as a pre-set monolithic entity and all the evidence tells in favor of Israel's eclectic, synthetic emergence at the vortex of Canaanite civilization. The formalistic proper names of its enemies are best understood as surviving, variously developed and variously applied labels for sociopolitical collectivities in the jumbled world of Canaan in which Israel arose and out of which segments of Israel itself were composed.

The explanatory possibilities of this synthetic model of Israel as a social formation composed eclectically of previous Canaanite anti-statist groups can be developed in several ways. For one thing, we can test the model by looking more closely at the earliest Israelite texts, especially the poetry, with pointed questions in mind: Who are identified as the enemies of Yahweh and Israel and to what extent do these enemies correspond to or depart from the gentilic nomenclature and the regional names we have just surveyed? Moreover, we can ask of these early sources: Who among the peoples of the land are *not* pictured as Israel's enemies, either because they are reported to have been exempted from attack or because they appear as allies or neutrals? Finally, can certain silences in the biblical traditions concerning segments of the indigenous Canaanite population be explained as indirect evidence of their incorporation into Israel?

44.2 Actual Enemies of Israel in Early Poetry and Related Texts

Our method in pursuing this intriguing issue will be to itemize the stated enemies of Yahweh and Israel in several early poetic sources, to ascertain the explicit or implicit grounds of the belligerency, and to compare and summarize the data on the enemies in their compositional contexts and in pertinent related materials.

Judges 5: Song of Deborah

kings (*mᵉlākīm*) [vs. 3, and possibly vs. 6]
rulers (*rōzᵉnīm*) [vs. 3]
caravans/military campaigns = expeditions (*'ōrᵉḥōth*) [vs. 6]
warriors (*gibbōrīm*) [vss. 13,23]
kings of Canaan (*malkē kᵉna'an*) [vs. 19]
horses (*sūs* and *'abbīrīm*) [vs. 22]
Sisera, a king from upper Galilee or an army commander (*sar-tsāvā'*) [vss. 26,28,30; cf. 4:2,7]
chariots (*rekev* and *markāvōth*) [vs. 28; cf. 4:3,7,13,15–16]

The kings of Canaan are the primary enemy singled out in this song of triumph. In a battle near the Wadi Kishon, in the lateral valley between the sea and the Jordan River which separates Samaria to the south from Galilee to the north, Israel has routed the massed chariots of Canaanite city-states: nine-hundred chariots according to the prose account (4:3)!

We do not know the exact number nor the precise identities of all the Canaanite coalition partners in this battle. In the song, the kings are unnumbered and unnamed, unless Sisera is viewed as a king (which seems probable), whereas in the prose version all the Canaanite forces are said to belong to Jabin, grandiosely and inaccurately called "king of Canaan" (4:2,23–24), an office, of course, that simply never existed in balkanized ancient Canaan. In fact, the Israelite account itself punctures this inflated notion of Jabin's role by once referring to him more modestly as "king of Hazor" (4:17). In the prose report, Sisera is described as the commander of Jabin's forces who "lives," or, perhaps, "exercises authority" in Harosheth-ha-goiim, a name best referred, not to a city, but to a region: "the wooded heights of Upper Galilee" (4:2).⁴²⁷ A plausible explanation of the disparities and omissions in the identification of the Canaanite leaders might argue that Jabin of Hazor is singled out in Judges 4 because, given the position of Hazor as a Canaanite enclave within Israelite eastern Upper Galilee, he was the most immediately threatening of the coalition kings, whereas Sisera, possibly king in a city in central or western Upper Galilee, is singled out in Judges 5 because he took an active part in the battle and was dramatically slain by Jael. The other coalition kings may not have fought in person or, if they did so, managed to escape.

It is at any rate a coalition of dynasts from Canaanite city-states in and around the great northern lateral valley which poses a unified threat to Israel and which is decisively crushed in the battle. It is likewise these defeated dynasts, and others like them (the "kings" and "rulers" of vs. 3), whom the song of triumph ironically and derisively addresses in a celebration of the victory of Yahweh and his people.

Previous interpreters of the Song of Deborah have consistently misread both the text and the sociohistorical circumstances of vss. 6–7. The word repointed *'ōreḥōth* in vs. 6 is generally understood as "caravans" of the Israelites which "have ceased" (*ḥādelū*), in parallel with the peasantry of vs. 7 who "have ceased" (here the verb appears in two forms: *ḥādelū* and *ḥādēllū*). At the same time it has been sensed that this gives a very problematic and obscure meaning in vs. 7. If caravans "have ceased to operate," in what sense have the peasants "ceased"? Have the peasants "ceased" trading or traveling, or have they "ceased" cultivating their fields, or have they "ceased to exist" or, metaphorically, "grown faint"? Neither the customary uses of the verb *ḥādal*, nor the syntax, nor the linguistic context, nor the historical setting, nor all these factors taken together, have been able to give an intelligible explanation of "the peasantry have ceased in Israel." Nevertheless, exegetes have persisted in believing that these lines describe the plight of Israel before the battle, its caravans driven from the highways and its peasants hardpressed and demoralized, if not actually destroyed, by the Canaanite armies. This reconstruction of the situation behind vss. 6–7a is a sheer figment of the imagination.

The key to unlocking the tangled text and to setting right the misconceived historical situation is along the philological lines initiated by D. Winton Thomas and P. Calderone, and extended by Marvin L. Chaney in philological, literary-exegetical, and sociohistorical detail.⁴²⁸ These scholars have convincingly demonstrated that there were in fact two *ḥādal* roots:(1) the familiar and more frequent *ḥādal*, "to cease," and (2) a second root *ḥādal*, "to grow fat or plump," for which there is an Arabic cognate with the meaning "to grow plump or fleshy." The sharp distinction to be drawn between the two roots is signalled by the Massoretic pointing of the second root as a stative verb and by the unusual dot (or daghesh) placed in the third consonant in one of its two occurrences in Judges 5:7 and in the single occurrence in I Samuel 2:5.

Recognition of a second *ḥādal* root clears up many philological, syntactic, and exegetical difficulties. By way of illustration, if *ḥādellū* in I Samuel 2:5 is construed as heretofore to mean "have ceased," the verse is either nonsense or requires speculative completion of the meaning:

> Those who were full have hired themselves out for bread,
> while those who were hungry have ceased. . . [but "have
> ceased" from what or in what respect?]

Just as we are unable to say in what particulars the peasantry of Judges 5:7 "have ceased," so we have no idea as to the respect in which the formerly hungry in I Samuel 2:5 "have ceased." Have they "ceased" hiring themselves out as day-laborers, as the formerly "full" or well-fed people now have to do? Have they "ceased" from some other activity which is unexpressed because a word has fallen out of the text? Is a tautology expressed to the effect that "those who were hungry have ceased (to be hungry)"? Have the hungry "ceased (to exist)"? The last possibility mentioned seems excluded by the context, while all the other possibilities named, although consistent with the context, pose formidable textual or syntactical difficulties.

If, however, *ḥādellū* in I Samuel 2:5 means "have grown fat" (and the following *'ad* is read as "booty"), the poetic parallelism falls into congruence with the other "reversals of fortune" described in the poetic series of I Samuel 2:4–5, while all the philological, syntactical, and textual difficulties evaporate:

> Those who were full have hired themselves out for bread,
> while those who were hungry have grown fat on booty.
> [Or, as NAB handily renders the last line: "while the hungry
> batten on spoil"]

Applying our newly acquired knowledge that *ḥādal* appears in a second sense, we can now interpret Judges 5:6–7 as artfully posing a word play on the two different *ḥādal* roots with ironically juxtaposed meanings:

> . . .caravans/campaigns [of the Canaanites] ceased,
> travelers [or, possibly, "kings" following LXX[4]] kept to the
> byways;
> they went by winding detours.
> The peasantry grew fat,
> In Israel they grew fat on booty
> When you arose, O Deborah,
> When you arose, a mother in Israel!

The sociohistorical implications of this rendering of the much-disputed lines are far-reaching. The ironic clash between *ḥādal* as "to cease" and *ḥādal* as "to grow fat" underscores the sharply contrasted subjects: Canaanite imperial ventures, whether viewed as caravans or military campaigns (or possibly as both encompassed in the translation "expeditions"), are counterposed to Israel's egalitarian peasant army, the former having "ceased" while the latter "grow fat on booty" from the plundered caravans and military stores.

The recognition that the caravans, including probably both commercial expeditions and military supply trains, are actually those of the Canaanite city-states follows from the socioeconomic logic of the times quite as readily as from the two contrasted meanings of ḥādal. Although caravan trade by private speculators flourished in the ancient Near East from early historical times, after 1500 B.C. such trade passed increasingly under the monopoly of the state.[429] Moreover, all we have learned of the retribalizing Israelites militates decisively against our viewing them as engaged in trade in luxury goods (e.g., fine cloths, metals, ivories) and skilled weaponry (e.g., chariots and composite bows), precisely the articles that made up the bulk of trade in this period. Such "trading" as Israelites engaged in at this time consisted of local exchanges of agricultural goods and simple craft products within a narrow circle of producers and exchangers, transactions which did not speculate in middleman profits and did not require hauling goods in quantity over long distances. The generations of biblical interpreters who have believed they saw Israelite caravans in Judges 5:6 were unaccountably oblivious of the categoric premonarchic Israelite rejection of the economics and ideology of state-monopolized trade or of commercial speculation by professional merchants.

When the long-misconceived vss. 6–7 of the Song of Deborah are read as above, they reinforce the entirety of the composition as an eloquent testimony to the growing strength of Israel, newly emboldened to interrupt the flow of inter-city trade and to drive the city-state armies from their most advantaged terrain in the great plains, which they once commanded. The urban centers were increasingly isolated from one another and placed on the defensive against the Israelite "peasantry" (peʾrāzōn, "rural populace," vss. 7,11). No longer confined to the hill country, the insurgent peasants began to penetrate farther and farther into the plains and to disrupt the agricultural, commercial, and military operations of the city-states. Of course, here too, lacking an adequate socioeconomic calculus, many interpreters have conjured up wholly imaginary objections to the song's depiction of an Israelite "peasantry," a topic to be expanded by the discussion of the Israelite countryside in IX.46. Security on the main routes deteriorated and pack trains laden with luxury goods, agricultural surpluses, and military supplies became vulnerable targets of plunder for the advancing Israelites. The loot was appropriated for the needs of the free producers of Israel, who did not think of this action as "stealing," but rather viewed it as the rightful reappropriation of wealth that had been extracted by kings, aristocrats, landowners, and merchants from the raw labor of the lower classes. Israel saw itself as legitimately reclaiming what belonged to Yahweh and to the oppressed whom he upheld.

The references to Israel "growing fat" on booty (Judg. 5:7; I Sam. 2:5), or "devouring" captured goods (e.g., Gen. 49:27), raise the hermeneutical issue of how literally such expressions should be taken. Is it to be understood that what was captured was actually edible, such as grain and other staples in transit or in military camps or depots? No doubt such was often the case. However, the bulk of the captured luxury goods, and especially the metals, does not accord with a literal interpretation of "eating" booty. Probably we should posit a metaphorical sense of "feasting upon" the plunder as a nutritional source for building up the emaciated socioeconomic body of Israel, a general notion which seems also to lie behind the imagery of Zebulun and Issachar "sucking affluence. . .and hoarded treasures" (Deut. 33:19b). Yet, even in the case of nonedible valuables seized by Israel, it is perhaps not to be ruled out that one of the uses to which these valuables were put was to buy up food staples—when they could not be simply taken by force—as communal protection against crop failure due to lack of rain or blight. I shall return to this question of the Israelite uses of the valued objects seized from the enemy farther along in this chapter when I analyze the sociological setting of "holy war" and the *ḥērēm*.

To round out this specification of Israel's enemies in the Song of Deborah, a summary look at the leadership nomenclature and the inventory of weaponry referred to shows dramatically that, unlike its opponents, Israel has no kings or overlords and no horses or chariots. It is even asserted that Israel lacks the advanced infantry weapons of "shield" (*māgēn*) and "spear" (*romah*) [vs. 8; cf. I Sam. 13:22]. In the song, Israel's troops are not even called "warriors" (*gibbōrīm*), which became a stock term under the monarchy), no doubt because they did not possess the standardized heavy infantry equipment of the Canaanite forces. They were at best "irregulars," or even "guerrillas." The terms that do appear for the Israelite military functionaries ([*m*ᵉ]*ḥōqᵉqīm*, "commanders" [?], vss. 9,14; *mōshᵉkīm bᵉshēvet sōphēr*, "wielders of the scribal staff" = "musterers" or "recruiters" [?], vs. 14) and for the celebrants of the victory (*mᵉḥatsᵉtsīm*, "musicians" or "bards" [?], vs. 11) are not customary nomenclature for military and ceremonial personnel during the Israelite monarchy, nor do they correspond to the nomenclature for functionaries in the Cananite statist system.

In short, we confidently conclude that the poem projects two decisively different worlds of social organization, the hierarchic pitted against the egalitarian, "the city" against "the countryside," two worlds that confront one another in two entirely different military structures: a professional army equipped to the hilt with the most advanced weaponry facing a citizen army, modestly and irregularly armed, charged with extraordinary élan and infused with tactical flexibility and cunning.

Exodus 15:1–18: Song at the Sea

horse (*sūs*) and his rider (*rōkᵉvō*) [vs. 1]
pharaoh's chariots *(markᵉvōth par'ōh)* [vs. 4]

pharaoh's army (ḥēlō) [vs. 4]
pharaoh's picked officers, or the flower of his officers (mivḥar shālishāv) [vs. 4]
nations or peoples ('ammīm) [vs. 14]
inhabitants or rulers of Philistia (yōshᵉvē pᵉleshet) [v. 14]
chieftains of Edom ('allūphē ᵉdōm) [v. 15]
leaders [lit. "rams"] of Moab ('ēlē mō'āv) [v. 15]
inhabitants or rulers of Canaan (yōshᵉvē kᵉna'ān) [v.15]

In my earlier description of the Song of Miriam (in III.14.2), I characterized it as an uncentralized liturgical piece that eventually found its way into the centralized canonical history. I further stated that it harks back to a distantly remembered complex of events—namely, the delivery from Egypt, stylized in language and concepts shaped by subsequent experiences of conflict and victory in Canaan. Thus, I take it that the references to the pharaoh and his armed forces are prototypical of similar lords and their armies in Canaan and vicinity. In fact, by following a stylized narrative sequence (exodus-wandering-entering into the land), the poem moves in its specification of the enemy from initial focus on the pharaoh to a focus on the rulers of Canaan and Philistia, and of Moab and Edom. All are of one piece in their roles as actual or potential enemies of Israel.

In their thorough linguistic and textual study of the poem, F. M. Cross and D. N. Freedman[430] have correctly characterized it as archaic rather than archaistic; i.e., it belongs to the premonarchic conceptual world, with the possible exception of vss. 16b–18. Even these verses, however, may be read, in keeping with Cross and Freedman, as stylized references to Yahweh's cosmic rule firmly based in Canaan, references which—although borrowed from Canaanite myth—do not imply that the Solomonic temple has been built. Cross and Freedman are probably also correct in believing that if the references to Philistia, Edom, and Moab are to be given precise historical context, the time of formulation should be located in the twelfth or eleventh century B.C. My own estimate is that the song probably stems from the late twelfth century, when the Philistines were well entrenched on the coastal plain; when Edom and Moab were taking shape as Transjordanian states (although at least Edom was still led by "chieftains" instead of, as later, by "kings") and beginning to threaten Israel (cf. Eglon of Moab in Judges 3:12–30); and when the deliverance from Egypt was still vividly recalled in tradition, although none who had lived through the Exodus was still alive and the event was increasingly seen as the prototypical liberative experience of Israelites, whatever their peculiar backgrounds.

Furthermore, Cross and Freedman correctly emphasize that in spite of the clichéd speech, the chief antagonists of the song are not mythological beings but the historical entities of Egypt (and other comparable peoples) and Israel, albeit with Yahweh's powerful help:

the sea remains "the sea"; it is never Rahab or Yamm, "Sea" [i.e., primordial chaos]. The opposition is a human host, historical armies, horses and chariots. . . ."mere" men, horses and chariots are thrown into the sea, where they sink. . .we have "history" shaped by familiar clichés, motifs, and literary styles. . .It is a historical conflict; the enemy is Israel's historically-limited foe. Pharaoh is a tough opponent, but there is not the slightest hint that he is the Enemy, the symbol of cosmic chaos, dissolution, or death.[431]

I think it should be emphasized that, in large measure, the "clichés, motifs, and literary styles" of the poem serve to present the pharaoh as the prototypical political oppressor, exemplary of other political oppressors well-known to Israel in its own land, oppressors who can expect a like fate with the pharaoh. Thus, while agreeing with Cross and Freedman that the pharaoh is not "the Enemy, the symbol of cosmic chaos, dissolution, or death," I contend that he is perceived as *the* historico-political Enemy, the epitome of those oppressive rulers which the imperial-feudal systems of Near Eastern statist society necessarily produce and which Israel and her God just as necessarily must oppose and defeat.

As in the Song of Deborah, we hear of the king and his army, especially of the horses and chariots. The term translated "picked officers" is literally "his choice third men." The *shālīsh* is probably to be explained as the third man in a chariot, understood as the officer in command. The meaning may be, therefore, "his crack chariot officers."

Of particular interest is the cluster of prospective enemies in and around Canaan introduced by the broad term *'ammīm,* usually translated "peoples." The common generic terms for socio-political entities in Hebrew are: (1) *'am,* which, over most of its range of meanings, corresponds roughly with "people" in the sense of those bound together by cultural, ethnic, or social ties, and (2) *gōy,* which, over most of its range of meanings, corresponds roughly with "nation" in the sense of those bound together politically, normally in a state but also in a tribal form of self-rule. The distinction may be loosely thought of as the one commonly made in the social sciences, following Hegel, between civil society and the state.

E. Speiser has helpfully identified some of the distinguishing features in the usage of the two terms.[432] Yet, considering that altogether the terms are used more than 2,300 times in the Old Testament, it cannot be said that Speiser's inquiry, nor any inquiry known to me for that matter, is adequate, particularly in establishing the points of overlap or conjunction between the two terms and the possible specialized sub-meanings of the terms. Speiser, for example, dismisses "a small number of passages in which *'am* and *gōy* are interchangeable" with the remark that they are "relatively late and due in the main to stylistic variation or poetic parallelism."[433]

Based on a cursory examination of psalms with a fair claim to being early pre-exilic, or even from the united monarchy, I do not find Speiser's summary judgment about the relative lateness of the equivalence of *'am* and *gōy* to be satisfactory. It seems to me, for example, that in many of the "royal" and "enthronement" psalms, '*am* and '*ammīm* refer to political entities (e.g., Ps. 2:1; 45:5[6], 12[13], 17[18]; 97:6; 99:1–2). "Princes/nobles of the peoples" (*nᵉdīvē* '*ammīm*) appear as the politicized *gōyim* who "gather as the '*am* of the God of Abraham" (Ps. 47:8[9–9[10]]). Moreover, '*ammīm* are paralleled with *mamlᵉkōth*, "kingdoms," an even more explicitly statist term than *gōyim* (Ps. 102:22[23]). Especially pertinent is the reference to Israel "wandering from *goy* to *goy*, from one *mamlākāh* to another '*am*" (Ps. 105:13). In contrast to the more general *gōy*, *mamlākāh* is the stronger and more precise term for a monarchically organized state, and the psalmist—anomalously in terms of Speiser's schematization—introduces '*am* as a synonym for *mamlākāh*. Poetic parallelism in no way accounts for the usage, since it would have been the normal practice to repeat *mamlākāh* in the second poetic member in parallel with the repetition of *goy* in the preceding member.

Although the enormous dimensions of the task of examining more than two thousand occurrences of these terms prevent me from undertaking at the moment an extended and thorough study of '*am* and *gōy*, it is clear that Speiser and others have paid insufficient attention to the possibility of quite specialized social-organizational meanings of '*am* in certain biblical contexts. I mention only two technical classes of meaning which are cited by BDB in the 1906 Hebrew-English Lexicon based on the Hebrew-German Lexicon of Gesenius and Buhl.[434]

Firstly, BDB alludes to a special meaning of *hā* '*ām* as a collective singular for "retainers, followers," frequently followed by preposition and noun or pronoun: "*hā*'*ām* with x." Of the examples given, I find those referring to *hā*'*ām* attached to Lot (Gen. 14:16), to Jacob (Gen. 23:7[8]; 35:6), and to Esau (Gen. 33:15), most amenable to that interpretation; in these contexts *hā*'*ām* is an '*apiru*-like band of retainers around a prominent leader. By no means all of BDB's "examples" are equally convincing. Jeremiah 41:13–14 is inappropriately cited, since *hā*'*ām* with Ishmael is actually a group of captives from Mizpah, including soldiers, women, children, and eunuchs (cf. vs. 16). Also, when Gideon speaks of "*hā*'*ām* who follow me" he seems to be referring to the armed men from his *mishpāḥāh* or *shēveṭ* (Judg. 8:5). BDB's citation of II Samuel 15:17 concerning "all *hā*'*ām*" who followed David in his flight from Jerusalem is problematic because of the uncertainty of the Text. Moreover, BDB's listing of *hā*'*ām* in Judges 3:18 as an instance of "retainers/followers" overlooks yet another specialized meaning: "And when Ehud had finished presenting the tribute [to Eglon, king of Moab], he sent away *hā*'*ām* that carried the tribute." Here it appears that *hā*'*ām* means "the delegation."

Secondly, BDB refers to a class of occurrences in which *hā*'*ām* denotes "people bearing arms," for which I Samuel 11:11 and I Kings 20:10, plus Judges 8:5 mentioned above, are good examples. Having pointed out some specialized sociopolitical meanings for "people" or "the people," we cannot simply rest with the common assumption that the term is always merely a loose designation for social, ethnic, or cultural collectivities without precise organizational specification.

Let us now look at the more delimiting nomenclature for collectivities introduced in Exodus 15:14–15 by the caption '*ammīm,* "nations" or "peoples." The clearer of the four terms are those for Edom and Moab. The '*allūphē* Edom call to mind our discussion of the '*eleph*/'*allūph* in early Israel (cf. VI.28.3–5). The use of '*allūph* in the Edomite and Horite "genealogies" of Genesis 36:15–30,40–42 hovers ambiguously between a reference to the social segments in Edom and a reference to the leaders of those segments, and perhaps intentionally so in order to carry the *double entendre* of individuality and collectivity which we have seen to be characteristic of the biblical pseudo-genealogies. The fact, however, that the list of Edomite '*allūphīm* is accompanied by a list of Edomite kings (Gen. 36:31–39) indicates that an editor (if not the original compiler of the '*allūphē* Edom list) wished to accent the denotation of '*allūph* as a leader.

In Exodus 15:15, '*allūphē* Edom stands in poetic parallel with '*ēlē* Moab, an association that strengthens the interpretation of '*allūph* as a leader or chieftain. Derived from a root meaning "to be in front, precede, lead," the noun '*ayil* normally means "ram" (leader of the flock?). In addition, there is a technical architectural meaning of "pilaster" (that which projects from a building or façade). In Exodus 15:15 the usage is metaphorical for leaders of the Moabite community (analogous to rams as leaders of flocks?), and is paralleled by three usages of '*ēlīm* in Ezekiel and one in II Kings. In Ezekiel 17:13, "the leaders of the land (of Judah)" are specified in context as the king (*melek*) and his princes (*sārīm*), and in II Kings 24:15 (in Q), "the leaders of the land" are listed in addition to Jehoiachin, the king's mother, the king's wives, and his officials (*sārīsīm*). In Ezekiel 31:11 it is declared that "the leaders of the nations" (unnamed but amplified by "foreigners") will cut down the great cedar which symbolizes the Egyptian pharaonic state, and in Ezekiel 32, the deceased "mighty leaders" or "warrior leaders" (vs. 21), apparently from Assyria, Elam, Meshech, Tubal, Edom, and Sidon [Phoenicia?] (cf. vss. 22–30), will greet the pharaoh and his army as the descend into the underworld (vss. 19–21,31–32). Thus, the evidence points to '*allūphē* Edom and '*ēlē* Moab as Edomite and Moabite leaders. In the case of Edom, the choice of '*allūphīm* strongly implies that the poem does not view Edom as a monarchy (which it became prior to Israel's adoption of monarchy, cf. Genesis 36:31), but the same cannot be said with assurance about Moab on the basis of the choice of '*ēlīm,* since three, and possibly all four, of the parallel usages of the term cited above indicate that it could refer to kings and their officials. Our earlier discussion of the problematics in tracing the introduction of kingship among the Transjordanian peoples is relevant at this point (cf. VIII.38).

The terms for the leaders of Edom and Moab are enclosed within two other terms whose parallel status is made evident by their sharing the same plural participle form *yōsh^eⁿvē* X (from *yāshav*, "to sit," or more generally, "to dwell"). The "X" represents a proper noun, in the one case Philistia and in the other Canaan. Anticipating my treatment of *yōshēv/yōsh^eⁿvīm* as having the sense of "rulers" in this and other similar contexts, rather than the more commonly construed "inhabitants," I point out that these four items of nomenclature in vss. 14–15, introduced by *'ammīm,* form a symmetrical chiastic structure literarily, territorially, and sociopolitically as shown in Figure 1.

FIGURE 1

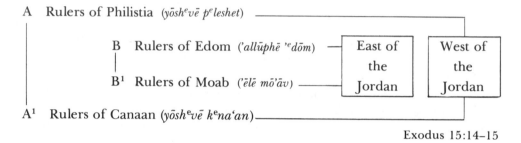

A   Rulers of Philistia (*yōsh^eⁿvē p^eⁿleshet*)

    B   Rulers of Edom (*'allūphē 'eⁿdōm*) ── East of the Jordan │ West of the Jordan

    B¹ Rulers of Moab (*'ēlē mō'āv*)

A¹ Rulers of Canaan (*yōsh^eⁿvē k^eⁿna'an*)

Exodus 15:14–15

Yōshēv *as "Ruler, Authority"*

Throughout the Hebrew Bible, *yōsh^eⁿvīm* is normally translated as "inhabitants" or "residents," i.e., those who live together in a place, and there is no doubt that many, indeed a large majority, of its occurrences are properly translated in that manner. There is, however a strong case to be made for a more specialized political structural meaning of the term in some contexts. So far as I am aware, only three textual studies have argued for rendering *yōsh^eⁿvīm* in certain cases as "rulers" or "lords." In the Song of Deborah, a strophe concerns Meroz, an otherwise unknown place:

> Curse Meroz, says the angel of Yahweh,
>   curse bitterly its inhabitants (*yōsh^eⁿvehā*),
> because they came not to the help of Yahweh,
>   to the help of Yahweh against the mighty. (Judg. 5:23)

Albrecht Alt, in the course of giving what remains the most plausible unraveling of the Meroz conundrum, has this to say about the term translated "its inhabitants":

> That the poet of the Song of Deborah precisely in company with Meroz makes special mention of its "inhabitants," makes perfectly good sense; the expression here, as in many passages of the Old Testament, designates the proprietors and lords of the aristocratically composed Canaanite polity, on whom political leadership fell and who were obligated, therefore, with political responsibility.[435]

That is the extent of Alt's observation. He gives no footnote and cites none of the "many passages" which he claims also contain *yōsh^evīm* as "proprietors and lords." Nor does he indicate by what development the common verb *yāshav*, "to sit, dwell," came to have this upper-class political nuance when used participially in construct with a place name. Eugen Täubler, in summarizing Alt's argument, observes that apparently Alt understood *yōsh^eveha* in the sense of *yōshev 'al-ham-mishpāṭ*, "he who sits in judgment," i.e., presides in adjudication (Isa. 28:6), or *(yōshev 'al-kisse' ham-m^elūkah*, "he who sits upon the royal throne," i.e., exercises royal authority (I Kings 1:46; 2:12).[436]

Cross and Freedman in their study of the Song of Miriam comment far more fully on *yōsh^eve* Philistia/Canaan, and they do so in a manner closely paralleling Alt's observation on *yōsh^eve* Meroz.[437] They construe *yōsh^evīm* as "reigning princes," which, following Albright, they regard as applicable to Canaan but not to Philistia. They see the derivation of this meaning from the idiom *yōshev 'al hak-kisse'*, "he who sits on or occupies the throne," i.e., the king (cf. in biblical Hebrew, *yōshev hak-k^eruvīm*, "he who sits enthroned on the cherubim," with reference to Yahweh on his heavenly throne, and in Akkadian *ašibūt kussi*, "he who occupies the throne"). They find the idiomatic biblical usage strongly attested in Amos 1:5,8:

> I will cut off the ruler *(yōshev)* from the Valley of Aven
>   and him that holds the scepter from Beth-eden.
>
> I will cut off the ruler *(yōshev)* from Ashdod
>   and him that holds the scepter from Ashkelon.

Obviously the proper counterpart to "scepter-holder" in the second poetic member of each verse is "throne-sitter" in the first poetic member. Both idioms refer to the king or executive authority of the state. Cross and Freedman also refer to Lamentations 4:12:

> The kings of the earth *(malkē 'erets)* did not believe
>   nor did any of the rulers of the world *(yōsh^eve tevel)*
> That foe or enemy could breach the gates of Jerusalem.

They summarize this peculiar development of *yāshav* as follows:

> ... technical usage seems to have produced a development in the meaning of the root *yšb* in special idioms from "sitting" on a throne to being a "throne-sitter," i.e., a king, and finally to the virtually denominative use of the verb and its derivatives with the meaning "rule."[438]

For the finite verb in the sense of "to rule," they refer to Zechariah 9:5–6. Although they do not offer a translation or discussion, I conclude that they intend this sort of rendering:

> The king shall perish from Gaza;
>   Ashkelon shall not be ruled (*lō' tēshēv*);
> A bastard shall rule (*w^eyashav*) in Ashdod;
>   and I will make an end to the pride of Philistia.

This gives a far more symmetrical set of poetic members, all referring to the disintegration of political leadership in Philistine cities, than does the common rendering, as in RSV:

> The king shall perish from Gaza;
>   Ashkelon shall be uninhabited;
> A mongrel people shall dwell in Ashdod;
>   and I will make an end of the pride of Philistia.

The proposal to read the verb *yashav* in this oracle in the sense of "to rule" accords with and aptly rounds out my contention that the "bastard" *(mamzēr)* of Ashdod is a person and not a bastardized, i.e., ethnically mongrelized, people; and, moreover, that this "bastard" or upstart ruler is identifiable in the local politics of late eighth-century Ashdod:

> ... decisive is the statement that "a bastard *(mamzēr)* shall dwell [I would now translate "shall rule"] in Ashdod" (vs. 6). The only other biblical use of this term refers to a person (Deut. 23:2) rather than to a whole people and syntactically there is no reason to believe that it means "a bastard or mongrel people" on the model of Nehemiah 13:23–24, as the RSV understands it. In fact the parallelism requires that the *mamzēr* of Ashdod be analogous to the *melek* ("king") of Gaza. Rather, this doubtless refers to Iamani, who seized the throne in Ashdod and fomented a revolt against Assyria which was suppressed in 711. Whether or not Iamani was a Greek, the Assyrian record says emphatically that he was "without claim to the throne," and it is apparently in this sense of political illegitimacy that he is called "bastard." Such a figurative political use of the term is far less forced than that which applies it to culturally or religiously mixed populations.[439]

In my judgment, Cross and Freedman have provided an intelligible explanation of the idiomatic development of *yōshēv* as "ruler," corresponding closely with Alt's unexplicated assertion of a similar if not identical meaning. Furthermore, they have noted a few convincing biblical instances of this usage. My chief dissent from their explanation is that I do not limit the "sitting" to the rule of kings, a point that will become clearer in the investigation to follow. Restricting myself largely to the participial form, I should like first to offer several examples of the same usage which are rendered highly probable by specific contextual features. Some of the strongest attestations to *yōshēv* as ruler occur in prophetic books, partly because of the abundant poetic parallelism and partly because of the fuller descriptions of the *yōsh^evīm* which their oracles on occasion supply, but there are a few demonstrable cases for the premonarchic period as well. I shall group the examples so as to proceed from the more certain to the less certain cases, and conclude by focusing on problematic usages of *yōshēv/yōshᵉvīm* in certain premonarchic texts which I find freshly illuminated by the enlarging body of demonstrated idiomatic usages of *yashav* for the exercise of political authority.

YŌSHĒV AS "RULER" IN PROPHETIC TEXTS

Isaiah 9:8[7]–10[9]

> The Lord has sent against Jacob a word,
>   and it will light upon Israel;
> and all the people will know,
>   Ephraim and the ruling class of Samaria (*yōshēv shōmrōn*)
>   who say in pride and in arrogance of heart:
> "The bricks have fallen,
>   but we will build with dressed stones:
> the sycamores have been cut down,
>   but we will put cedars in their place."

The identification of *yōshēv shōmrōn* as the ruling class of Samaria is supported by the quotation which the prophet attributes to them. The capital city of Samaria and other cities of the realm have been attacked by the Assyrians and have suffered severe damage, but the *yōshēv shōmrōn* boast that they will rebuild with dressed stones and cedar timbers. Only the outer fortifications and the large and opulent buildings in the governmental palace-complex, where the king and aristocrats lived, were built with these fine materials—as is made absolutely clear for Samaria by the excavations carried out at that site[440]—and it would be only the ruling class who had the authority and the means to make such boasts (cf. "the proud crown of the drunkards of Ephraim," i.e., the debauched upper class and their lackey priests and prophets, Isaiah 28:1–8).

Isaiah 10:13–14a

> "By the strength of my hand I have done it [the Assyrian king
>   speaking]
>   and by my wisdom, for I have understanding;
> I have removed the boundaries of the peoples (*hā'ammīm*)
>   and have plundered their treasures;
>   like a bull I have brought down rulers (*yōshᵉvīm*).
> My hand has found like a nest
>   the wealth of the peoples (*hā'ammīm*)."

This is evidently a case where *'ammīm* are political collectivities, i.e., the various sovereignties which opposed the Assyrian imperial advance into Syria-Palestine. As the RSV correctly translates, the *yōshᵉvīm* are not indiscriminately the "inhabitants" of the conquered lands but, more exactly, their "rulers," i.e., "those sitting on thrones" who had to be overthrown, their royal treasuries plundered, and their domains incorporated into Assyrian provinces ("I have removed the boundaries of the peoples").

Isaiah 20:3–6

"As my servant Isaiah [Yahweh speaking] has walked naked and barefoot for three years as a sign and portent against Egypt and Ethiopia, so shall the king of Assyria lead away the Egyptians captives and the Ethiopians exiles, both young and old, naked and barefoot, with rearends uncovered, to the shame of Egypt. Then they shall be dismayed and confounded because of Ethiopia their hope and of Egypt their boast. And Philistine-Phoenician vassal kings [yōshēv hā'ī haz-zeh, literally, "rulers of this coastland"] will say in that day, 'Behold, this is what has happened to those in whom we hoped and to whom we fled for help to be delivered from the king of Assyria! And we, how shall we escape?' "

We may leave aside the complicated and confusing editorializing that the passage has undergone and also the complex historical details of the uprising.[441] For our immediate purpose, the identity of yōshēv hā'ī haz-zeh is unmistakable. They are collectively the pledged vassals of Assyria who rule over the old Philistine cities, notably Ashdod and Gath, which were prominent in the revolt of 715–711 B.C. against Assyria, as well as other vassal kings in the city-states extending northward into the Phoenician "coastland" who entertained ideas of revolt. Hezekiah of Judah was tempted to join in the revolt and in fact may have done so, if only briefly and half-heartedly.[442] Isaiah delivers a solemn warning to Hezekiah that if he conspires with the rebels, he too will be among the hapless vassal kings whose false reliance on Egyptian aid will be thoroughly exposed when they suffer the stinging retaliation of defeat and deportation by Sargon's army. Although long delayed by involvements elsewhere, Sargon did eventually crush the defection in two campaigns into Palestine.

Isaiah 23:2–3

In a scathing oracle against the mercantile city-states of Phoenicia, Isaiah declares:

> Be silent, O rulers of the Phoenician coastland (yōsh^{e}vē'ī; cf. 23:6),
>   O merchants of Sidon,
> whose agents travel over the sea,
>   and over great oceans,
> whose revenue is the grain of Egypt, [Shihor, a rare term for the Nile]
>   O you who have become the merchant of the nations!

The subordinate clauses following "O merchants of Sidon" are translated from a restored text, partially with the help of LXX, but even the textual uncertainty fails to obscure the clarity with which yōsh^{e}vē 'ī are identified by the prophet with the merchant princes of the Phoenician cities, whose agents crisscross the Mediterranean and who carry on a brisk grain trade with Egypt. In biblical usage, Sidonians are sometimes referred to for Phoenicians in general (Deut. 3:9; Judg. 3:3; I Kings 16:31), and, in fact, it is evident both from the superscription to the oracle ("concerning Tyre") and the references in 23:5,8 that the city of Tyre is as prominent in the poem as is Sidon proper. In this same oracle, it is said of Tyre that "its merchants were princes, its dealers in dyed stuffs [lit., "Canaanites"] were the honored ones of the earth" (23:8). That the prophet here employs the restricted sense of Canaanite as the virtual equivalent of Phoenicia is confirmed by 23:11:

> He [Yahweh of hosts] has stretched out his hand over the sea,
>> he has shaken the kingdoms;
> Yahweh has commanded concerning Canaan [Phoenicia!]
>> the destruction of its fortresses.

Jeremiah 12:4

In one of his confessional laments, Jeremiah cries out:

> How long will the land mourn,
>> and the grass of every field wither?
> Because of the wickedness of those who rule in it (yōsheᵛē bāh)
>> beasts and birds are swept away,
>> because they say, "He will not see what we are up to!"

Although many commentators have regarded all but the last line of this unit as intrusive from some other context, because it is thought illogically to introduce drought, I can find no conclusive grounds for excluding it. Actually, it strengthens the case for the prophet's appeal to God to destroy the wicked, whose success he presupposes in the stark questions:

> Why does the way of the wicked prosper?
>> Why do all who are treacherous thrive? (12:1)

The prosperous wicked should be destroyed because they are bringing drought upon the entire land so that all people, indeed even animal and bird life, suffer (cf. 9:10[9]; 14:5–6). While the poetic language is indirect, there is every reason to believe that the successful rich here referred to are the king, probably Jehoiakin, and his officials, who were consistently contemptuous of the prophet and his message; who, urged on by the priestly and prophetic opponents of Jeremiah, had been ready to put him to death (chap. 26); and who destroyed the scroll containing Jeremiah's word in a display of open hostility and rejection (chap. 36). It is these royal and aristocratic leaders who constitute the party of treachery and who must be singled out for punishment if Yahweh's justice is to prevail in the land.

Jeremiah 25

The original textual and literary structure is highly problematic, as is made abundantly clear by the different recension in LXX, which inserts following 25:13a the foreign oracles located in chaps. 46–51 of MT. I suggest, however, that the consistent specification of kings and rulers as those who are to drink the cup of

Yahweh's wrath (cf. 25:17–26), strengthens the case for reading in 25:9: "I will bring them [i.e., Nebuchadnezzar and his armies] against this land [Judah] and its rulers (yōsh^{e}vehā)," and in 25:29: "You [i.e., the foreign nations] shall not go unpunished, for I am summoning a sword against all the rulers of the earth (yōsh^{e}vē hā'ārets)."

A similar nuance attaches to a series of allusions to yōsh^{e}vē Babylon in Jeremiah 50:35; 51:1,12,24,35, for wherever the general descriptions of destruction and punishment are given precision, it is the king of Babylon and his diviners, princes, administrators, commanders and armies, ensconced in the fortified city, that are firmly in view (50:18,26,35–38; 51:3,20–23,30–32,46,56–58).

Ezekiel 11:14–15

And the word of Yahweh came to me: "Son of man, your brothers, your fellow exiles, the whole house of Israel, are those of whom the rulers of Jerusalem (yōsh^{e}vē Jerusalem) have said: 'They have gone far from Yahweh; to us it [i.e., "the city," glossed in Hebrew with "the land"] is given for a possession.' "

If we accept that this unit belongs to the admittedly confused sub-collection of chaps. 8—11, and thus is to be dated c. 591 B.C. (cf. 8:1), the yōsh^{e}vē Jerusalem should be identified with the pro-Babylonian officials who were installed along with Zedekiah at the time of the deportation of Jehoiachin and those upper-class elements who had supported the revolt against Babylon. Eichrodt's attempt to lift this passage out of its present context and associate it with a superficially similar expression in 33:24–29 is not convincing,[443] since what is at issue in chap. 33 is not an antagonism between Jews still in Jerusalem and Jews in exile prior to the final deportation of 587, but rather the depleted condition of those remaining after 587 in Palestine. The yōsh^{e}vē Jerusalem in Ezekiel 11:15 may be more explicitly equated with twenty-five men headed by "the princes of the people" (sārē hā'ām) Jaazaniah and Pelatiah (11:1; cf. 8:16), who appear to be pro-Babylonian supporters of Zedekiah, perhaps even a council of state, who by slavish adherence to Babylonian culture and religion (cf. Babylonian sun worship, 8:16–18) hope to secure themselves as the permanent official replacements for the deported and detained retinue of Jehoiachin. Eichrodt comments on this body of officials as follows:

> . . .in them we are to see no mere leaders of political parties, but ministers of state, who preside over a "council with full governmental authority" (Herrmann) whose numbers and composition are such as to be known even to the exiles. The verses which follow show that there is no limit to the powers which this college takes to itself, and that we will not be mistaken if we regard it as a sort of "national council" which had gained control by the social and political revolution that followed upon the first exile of 598. The Babylonian overlords had allowed or perhaps even authorized their seizure of power, and under the protection of king Zedekiah they had to a very large extent taken over the executive power.[444]

Ezekiel does not further develop the identity or fate of these *yōsh^evē* Jerusalem, but, in company with Jeremiah, he insists that all political factions in Jerusalem will in the end suffer a like fate of deportation and that the real sources of renewal and future leadership in Israel will emerge from the Jews carried into exile.

Micah 6:12

> Its [i.e., the city's] rich men are full of violence;
>> its upper classes (*yōsh^evēhā*) speak falsehood,
>> and their tongues frame deceit.

Although this parallelism of "rich men" and *yōsh^evīm* occurs in a notoriously difficult oracle, the linkage of terms supports a rendering of the latter as "upper classes" or "leaders." The rich men are at least in part described as crafty, dishonest merchants in the preceding verse. But if this oracle belongs to Micah (and there is no decisive argument against his authorship), the great concern of this prophet with the expropriation of the fields of the poor (cf. 2:1–5) probably also lies behind the indictment of the "treasures of wickedness" (6:10). Both the immediate context and the larger emphases of Micah militate against regarding *yōsh^evīm* as the common people, as is implausibly claimed by some commentators:

> While violence was predicated only of the rich, deceit is charged against all without discrimination. This is practically saying that all are equally bad; the poor would be as oppressive as the rich had they but the power. Trickery which is possible for all is confined to no special class.[445]

On the contrary, of all the prophets, Micah is most insistent in targeting the source of evil in the urban upper classes. "The rich men" full of violence and "the upper classes" practiced in deceit are synonymous parallelisms. The falsehood and deceit refer either to false weights and measures of the merchants or to the falsified legal processes by which commercial claims of foreclosure on loans at exorbitant interest take precedence over the right of an Israelite to retain his land. If the fraudulent legalities used to expedite and justify the economic deprivation are included, *yōsh^evīm* here may encompass the judges who collaborate in foreclosures on the peasants' land (cf. Amos 5:10–13, and note also the phrase *yōshēv'al ham-mishpāṭ*, "the one who sits in judgment," Isa. 28:6).

YŌSHĒV AS "RULER" IN HISTORICAL TEXTS

Against the backdrop of several contextually supported usages of *yōshēv/yōsh^evīm* as "rulers" or "leaders," I now turn to passages from Genesis, Joshua, and Judges in which similar usage of the participle (and occasionally of the finite verb) is arguable. Some of these passages have already been discussed; it will only be necessary to comment on the features strictly supportive of the idiomatic meaning of *yāshav* under examination.

Genesis 34:30

After Simeon and Levi kill the Shechemites in violation of treaty agreements Jacob says to his sons:

> You have brought trouble on me by making me odious to the rulers of the land (*yōshēv hā'ārets*), to the Canaanites and Perizzites, for I am so few in number that they will muster in coalition against me and attack me and I shall be destroyed, I and my house. (Gen. 34:30)

This reading emphasizes that it was the rulers of Shechem, pictured as Hamor and his son Shechem (cf. *b^enē* Hamor, "Hamorites," Gen. 33:19), who were discredited by the Israelite breach of amity, for it was they who had persuaded their townsmen to enter the agreement with Jacob in good faith. Jacob recognizes that the rulers of other cities will now hesitate to risk comparable treachery from Israel, and moreover they will be encouraged to form a united front against him. Genesis 34 seems to be operating on two sociohistorical planes: one level conceives the Jacob group as an *'apiru*-like militarized band, whereas the other level retrojects a conception of all Israel in embryonic form and seems intent on slanting the account so that the perfidy of Simeon and Levi is underscored to account for the later fortunes of those tribes. The proto-Israelite *'apiru* sociohistorical plane is determinative in 34:30, for here it is assumed that the Jacob group is small, without allies, and in no position to make frontal attacks on the Canaanite system. Therefore, it depends for survival on making arrangements with city-states which are as advantageous as possible. The objection to the treaty violation by Simeon and Levi is strategic and tactical rather than ethical. If the Jacob group comes to be known as an untrustworthy treaty partner, it will be unable to negotiate with city-states and will become the object of punitive action by the ruling classes acting in united self-interest. By contrast, Genesis 49:5–7 harks back to the events underlying Genesis 34 in a more ethically judgmental manner and condemns the "violence," "anger," and "wantonness" of the action. In any case, the apprehension expressed by Jacob is not against the populace en masse but against the rulers whose good faith in negotiations was betrayed and who have the power to retaliate militarily.

Genesis 36:20–21

One of the Edomite lists of rulers begins with the heading: "these are the sons of Seir, the Horite, the rulers of the land (*yōsh^evē hā'ārets*)" (Gen. 36:20). The several genealogical lists of Genesis 36 concerning Edom are divided between those with familial representation (vss. 1–5,9–14) and those with a wider sociopolitical representation (vss. 15–43). The second class of genealogies is in turn divided between those attesting a chieftainship and those attesting a monarchy. A further distinction is made between the chiefs of Edom and the chiefs of the Horites, the earlier population of the land dispossessed by the Edomites according to Deuteronomy 2:12,22. The Horite superscription occurs in doublet form:

> These are the sons of Seir the Horite, the rulers of the land
> (*yōshᵉvē hā'ārets*). [36:20]
> These are the chiefs of the Horites (*'allūphē hāḥōrī*), the sons
> of Seir in the land of Edom. [36:21]

The effect of this juxtaposition is to equate *yōshᵉvīm* with *'allūphīm*, in a manner analogous to Exodus 15:14, with the difference that in this case the same leaders are designated by alternate terms.

Joshua 2:9–11a, 24

Rahab of Jericho says to the Israelite scouts:

> I know that Yahweh has given you the land, and that the fear of you has fallen on us and that all the rulers of the land (*yōshᵉvē hā'ārets*) have grown faint-hearted (*nāmōgū*) before you. For we have heard how Yahweh dried up the waters of the Sea of Reeds before you when you came out of Egypt, and what you did to the two kings of the Amorites that were beyond the Jordan, to Sihon and Og, whom you totally destroyed. And as soon as we heard it, our hearts melted (*yimmas*), and there was no further fighting spirit left in any man, because of you. (Josh. 2:9–11a)

The scouts report back to Joshua:

> Indeed Yahweh has given all the land into our hands, for in fact all the rulers of the land (*yōshᵉvē hā'ārets*) are faint-hearted (*namogu*) because of us. (Josh. 2:24)

That the allusion here is to the authorities in the Canaanite city-states rather than to the populace in general is made probable by the reference to the destruction of the Amorite kings, Sihon and Og, as well as by the similar language used in 5:1 for the reaction of kings to the Israelite crossing of the Jordan: "When all the kings of the Amorites that were beyond the Jordan to the west, and all the kings of the Canaanites that were by the sea, heard that Yahweh had dried up the waters of the Jordan for the people of Israel until they had crossed over, their hearts melted (*yimmas*) and there was no longer any fighting spirit in them because of the people of Israel."

Joshua 7:8–9

After the initial defeat of Israel at Ai, Joshua cries out:

> O Yahweh, what can I say, when Israel has turned its back before its enemies! For the Canaanites and all the rulers of the land (*yōshᵉvē hā'ārets*) will hear about it, and will surround us, and obliterate our movement [literally, "our name"] from the land. How will you uphold your greatness in that case?

Again the horizon is fundamentally military and political. Once it is known that Israel can be bested by a single city-state such as Ai, the kings will gather their armies and annihilate the Israelite social base in West Jordan.

Joshua 9

When the rulers of Gibeon (*yōshᵉvē* Gibeon) heard what Joshua had done to Jericho and to Ai, they disguised themselves [in worn-out clothing and gear and with stale provisions]. . . .and they went to Joshua in the camp at Gilgal. . . . The men of Israel said to the Hurrians, "Maybe you are nearby rulers (*b*ᵉ*qirbī yōshēv*); in that case how can we possibly make a treaty with you?" (Josh. 9:3, 6–7)

The Hurrian delegation to Israel goes on to explain itself:

> "Our elders (*z*ᵉ*qēnēnū*) and all the rulers of our land (*yōsh*ᵉ*vē 'artsēnū*; rulers of all four Hurrian cities?, cf. 9:17) said to us, 'Take provisions in hand for the mission. Go to meet them [the Israelites] and say to them, "We are your servants (*av*ᵉ*dēkem*; dependents in treaty); come now, make a treaty with us." ' " (9:11)

The treaty is concluded; shortly thereafter the Israelites discover that the Hurrians are from nearby cities, and the Hurrians explain why they "tricked" Israel into a treaty with them:

> Three days after having made the treaty with them, they [the Israelites] learned that they [their Hurrian treaty partners] were neighboring rulers (*q*ᵉ*rōvim hem 'ēlāv ūv*ᵉ*qirbō hēm yōsh*ᵉ*vīm*, i.e., "they were near neighbors and rulers in their very midst"). . . .they [the Hurrians] replied to Joshua, "Because it was related to your servants for certain that Yahweh your God had instructed his servant Moses to give you all the land, and to destroy all the rulers of the land (*yōsh*ᵉ*vē hā'ārets*) before you; that is why we feared greatly for our lives and decided on this course of action." (9:16,24)

The story of the Gibeonite-Israelite treaty is one of the most baffling traditions in early Israel.[446] It contains at least two unreconciled historical perspectives:(1) an explanation of how certain Hurrian cities in western Benjamin (Gibeon, Chephirah, Beeroth, and Kiriath-jearim) were spared the general destruction of Canaanites and how at least the Gibeonites came to be low-ranking cult attendants at an Israelite sanctuary, either in Gibeon itself or at Gilgal, and still later in the Jerusalem temple;(2) an undoubtedly much older tradition about how the Hurrian cities entered into treaty relations with Israel, relations implying Israel's superior role as protector but by no means entailing servitude or subjugation for the Hurrians. If, in fact, a cultic role was assigned to the Hurrian partners in the treaty, it was a privileged one at the beginning. In the late re-write of the tradition, the treaty is an embarrassing anomaly to be explained as a duplicitous exception (the Hurrians lied about their true identity!). In the older tradition, the treaty is a recognized and accepted mode of accommodation between the Israelite tribes and cooperative Canaanite cities.

Especially puzzling is the deceptive masquerading of the men of Gibeon as residents of a far country. The late historical horizon overlays the earlier in such a way that the deception motif is manipulated to explain why the Israelites concluded a treaty with Canaanites in total defiance of the Deuteronomic injunction to destroy all the Canaanites (cf. Deut. 20:10–18). Normally, commentators dismiss the deception motif as no part of the original events;[447] it is thought to have been introduced only as a device to excuse Israel's lapse of conduct in concluding a forbidden treaty. However, the original circumstances are better understood and the basis for the later distortion of the tradition more fully accounted for, if we assume that the deception was integral to the oldest tradition, but that it was deception of a very different sort than the late revision imagined. The Hurrian deception was directed toward the surrounding aggressive city-states, with which the four cities broke rank when they went over to Israel's side.

That there was indeed a treaty between Gibeon and Israel is entirely verified by a report from the time of David (II Sam. 21:1–14), and it is further attested by a still earlier account of the action taken by five Canaanite city-states against Gibeon as soon as they learned of the treaty (Josh. 10:1–5). Even though this witness to an ancient Gibeonite-Israelite treaty in Joshua 10 has been superficially harmonized to accord with Joshua 9, an underlying independent tradition is evident.

It is pertinent that neither report makes mention of a king in Gibeon, or in any of the Hurrian cities. In Joshua 10:2 it is somewhat ambiguously noted that Gibeon was "like one of the royal cities" (*kᵉʾahath ʿārē ham-mamlākāh*), an expression understood by Noth to mean, "like one of the cities with [the institution of] kingship."[448] The explanatory note appears to mean that Gibeon was comparable to a royal city in size (in fact larger than Ai—in area or in population, or in both?) and in strength (being highly militarized; "all its men were warriors"), even though Gibeon did *not* have a monarchic form of government.

Observing the surprise and alarm of the king of Jerusalem when he discovers that the treaty between Gibeon and Israel was arranged "under his nose," we may hypothesize that the reported pretense and ruse on the part of Gibeon was directed toward adjacent royal city-states, in particular Jerusalem, to whom Gibeon very likely stood in a dependent position. In that event, when the authorities of Gibeon sought a modus operandi with Israel, their action necessarily ruptured their existing ties with Jerusalem, and possibly other nearby cities. For this reason we can understand why the negotiating delegation slipped out of Gibeon disguised as travel-weary commoners and surreptitiously made for the Israelite base camp at Gilgal. Seen in this light, the secretiveness of the Gibeonite-Israelite contact is similar to the secretiveness of the contact between Rahab and the Israelite spies at Jericho, and to the meeting between the informer from Bethel and the Israelite forces closing in on that city. The great difference, of course, is that the Gibeonites who made contact with Israel did so under unanimous, or at least majority, instruction from their people. Their secretiveness was not intended to keep the contact with Israel hidden from their own people but to conceal it from the rulers of nearby royal cities, who might impede or block the treaty overture were they to learn of it in advance. Since Gibeon and the other Hurrian cities approached Israel as a bloc, their successful negotiation of a treaty was a major coup for the Israelite tribes, since it was now unnecessary for Israel to take military action against those cities.

With such a conception of the original circumstances of the treaty, the rendering of *yōshēv/yōshᵉvīm* in Joshua 9 as "rulers" or "authorities" makes considerable sense. To be sure, it is challengeable whether there is sufficient coherence in the story to believe that the original terms for the Hurrian leaders have survived the late revision of the passage, particularly since the characterization of the Israelite negotiators oscillates erratically between Joshua, the men of Israel, and the princes or leaders of the congregation.[449] I think there can be little doubt that the late reviser of the story understood *yōshᵉvīm* throughout in the customary, less political sense of "inhabitants" or "residents." What we want to find out is precisely whether it is possible to go behind the perspective of the revision to an earlier historical plane that still possesses some integrity.

One of the ways to probe the extent of the coherence of an earlier report, embedded and overlaid in a revised story such as Joshua 9, is to examine the semantic range of words according to criteria of internal and external consistency. It is therefore worth exploring what coherence the early treaty with the Hurrians might be given if the *yōshᵉvīm* are understood here as we have clearly established them to be in many other contexts—i.e., as "authorities" or "rulers" rather than simply "inhabitants." So construed, the authorities of Gibeon constitute the actual negotiating party (9:3), but they approach Israel under mandate from the elders and authorities of all the Hurrian cities (9:11). It is, of course, perplexing that four Hurrian cities are referred to and named only in 9:17. The concentration on Gibeon may be explained in part by its leading role among the four cities and in part by the late traditional selective interest in the cult attendants who came from Gibeon. Actually, mention of a flight of the people of Beeroth to Gittaim (II Sam. 4:3) may be viewed as the result of Saul's treaty-violating attacks on the Gibeonites (II Sam. 21:1–2), thereby indirectly attesting that Beeroth as well as Gibeon was in treaty with Israel.

In the negotiating maneuvers which unfold in Joshua 9, the actual suspicion which the Israelites entertain regarding the Hurrians is not that they *live* nearby (that is a late intrusion dictated by the Deuteronomic command to annihilate all Canaanites), but rather that the Hurrians *rule* or *exercise authority* in nearby cities and are thus potential enemies who may be trying to beguile Israel into letting down its defenses. The Israelite negotiators must proceed with extreme caution. Eventually, the Israelite fears are allayed, not by assurances that the Hurrians are from a far country (a manifest absurdity that is once again recognizable as a later rationalization of the broken Deuteronomic command), but rather by Israel's becoming thoroughly convinced that the negotiators really do represent cities that are determined to be delivered of customary city-state dominion and wish to collaborate with the retribalization movement of Israel. Accordingly, the Israelite visit to the four Hurrian cities (vs. 17) was not an angry response to their partners' treachery, but a tour of inspection to satisfy themselves that the negotiating party which had come to Gilgal did in fact fully represent the true situation and intent of the populace of the four cities. The present sequence of events being by no means wholly trustworthy, it is likely that this confirmatory Israelite visit to the Hurrian cities *preceded* rather than followed the conclusion of the treaty.

An objection to translating *yōshēv/yōshᵉvīm* in Joshua 9 in this manner is the questionableness of a narrator referring to Hurrian leaders as "rulers," since these men give up royal aspirations and prerogatives upon entering the protective treaty with intertribal Israel. The usage could, of course, be seen as mere convention, following the frequent habit of referring to leaders of Canaanite city-states as *yōshᵉvīm*. On the other hand, there is perhaps a more precise and deliberate reason for the narrator speaking of Hurrian "rulers." If the Hurrian cities were dependents of Jerusalem, as we have seen to be strongly implied by 10:1–2, the *yōshᵉvīm* label would appropriately refer to the leaders in the dependent cities who functioned under contractual vassal obligations to the suzerain Jerusalem. They were leaders through whom Jerusalem "ruled" the vassal cities. Whether voluntarily or involuntarily, these leaders filled their prescribed roles until they saw in the growing strength of Israel an opportunity to be free of control by Jerusalem. The reported initiative and alacrity shown by the *yōshᵉvīm* in approaching Israel suggests that they had been less than whole-hearted vassal officials on Jerusalem's behalf, a very understandable attitude on the probability that the "rulers," while pledged to Jerusalem, were natives of the subject cities. It thus emerges that the Hurrian "rulers" were not like the other Canaanite rulers; they were ready to accept Israelite predominance and to join forces with Israel against the domination of the highlands by imperial and feudal control systems.

This reconstruction of the leadership situation, within the special circumstances of the Hurrian cities and prompted by construing *yōshᵉvīm* as "rulers/authorities," is admittedly conjectural, since it requires filling in gaps in our knowledge and positing a coherent early historical horizon in a text where few commentators have been able to establish a coherent early tradition. I do not feel the same degree of certainty about the specifics of my Hurrian leadership analysis that I feel with respect to the larger reconstruction of the status of the Hurrians vis-à-vis Jerusalem and Israel. It remains possible that some or all of the occurrences of *yōshēv/yōshᵉvīm* were introduced only by the late reviser of the story. If, however, all or most of these occurrences of the participle belong to the older account I believe they must be understood as "rulers/authorities," for only on this reading are we able to obtain a coherent (if still far from complete) picture of the offices and roles of leadership in the Hurrian cities that entered treaty with Israel.

Joshua 10:6

When the coalition of Amorite kings besieges Gibeon, the city calls upon its Israelite protectors for aid:

And the Gibeonites sent to Joshua at the camp in Gilgal, saying "Do not relax your hands from your servants; come up to us quickly, and rescue us, and help us; for all the kings of the Amorites who rule the hill country (*yōsh^evē hāhār*) are mustered against us."

The political idiomatic rendering of *yōsh^evē hāhār* is made probable by the context in which Gibeon is attacked because it has created a fissure in the unified anti-Israelite policy of the Amorite kings who assert dominion over the hill country, including suzerainty over the kingless Hurrian cities at least to the extent of reserving the right to veto objectionable external relations.

Joshua 12:2–5

The "table of kings" defeated by Joshua is prefaced with a summary of kings in Transjordan:

Sihon, king of the Amorites, who ruled (*hay-yōshēv*) at Heshbon, and held sway (*mōshēl*) from Aroer. . .to. . . , and Og, king of Bashan, one of the remnant of the Rephaim, who ruled (*hay-yōshēv*) at Ashtaroth and Edrei and held sway (*mōshēl*) over Mt. Hermon and Salecah and all Bashan to. . .

The point in using *hay-yōshēv* is not the residence of the kings per se so much as it is their seat of governance as an administrative center, a differentiation made abundantly clear in these parallel verses: "Sihon, the king of the Amorites, who reigned (*mālak*) in Heshbon" (13:10,21) and "Og, who reigned (*mālak*) in Ashtaroth and in Edrei" (13:12). Indeed, the notion is that of a king "ruling from" an administrative center, his control extending outward territorially to a recognized perimeter (cf. the full text of Joshua 12:2–5 for the reported perimeters of the kingdoms of Og and Sihon).

Joshua 17:16

When Joshua tells the Josephites to move northward and clear land in the central highlands, they reply:

The hill country is not sufficient for us; yet all the Canaanites who dominate the region of the plain (*hay-yōshēv b^e'erets-hā'ēmeq*) have iron chariots, both those in Bethshean and its villages and those in the Valley of Jezreel.

The introduction of the fearsome chariots suggests not only that *hay-yōshēv* should be construed politically but that the emphasis is upon the overwhelmingly firm control of the plain of Esdraelon by the Canaanite chariot-warrior ruling classes, which prevents Israel from spreading at will into their fertile domains.

Judges 1:9–11a,17,19,21,27–35

Having already expatiated at some length on the form-critical, literary, and socio-historical contents and contexts of the settlement annals in Judges 1

(IV.17.3), I shall here apply the demonstrated political sense of *yōshēv/yōsheʿvīm* in translation and then draw out some of the implications for our total conceptualization of the annals sequence.

> After that, the Judahites went down to battle the Canaanites ruling (*yōshēv*) the hill country and the Negeb and the Shephelah [western foothills]. So Judah went against the Canaanites ruling (*hay-yōshēv*) at Hebron. . . and they defeated Sheshai and Ahiman and Talmai. They went from there against the rulers of Debir (*yōsheʿvē* Debir). . . .[Judg. 1:9–11a] Then Judah went with Simeon his brother and defeated the Canaanites ruling (*yōshēv*) Zephath. . . [1:17] So Yahweh was with Judah, and he possessed the hill country, but he was not able to drive out the rulers of the coastal plain (*yōsheʿvē hāʿēmeq*) because they had iron chariots. . . . [1:19]
>
> The Benjaminites did not drive out the Jebusites ruling (*yōshēv*) Jerusalem, with the consequence that the Jebusites have lived (*way-yēshev*) alongside the Benjaminites in Jerusalem to this day. . . [1:21]
>
> Manasseh did not drive out Beth-shean and its villages, or Taanach and its villages, or the rulers of Dor (*yōshēv* Dor; some MSS *yōsheʿvē* Dor) and its villages or the rulers of Ibleam (*yōsheʿvē* Ibleam) and its villages or the rulers of Megiddo (*yōsheʿvē* Megiddo) and its villages; in that region the Canaanites succeeded in continuing to rule (*lāsheveth*). When Israel grew strong, it subjected the Canaanites to forced labor, but did not drive them out altogether.
>
> Ephraim did not drive out the Canaanites ruling (*hay-yōshēv*) in Gezer, with the consequence that the Canaanites lived (*way-yēshev*) in their midst in Gezer.
>
> Zebulun did not drive out the rulers of Kitron (*yōsheʿvē* Kitron), or the rulers of Nahalol (*yōsheʿvē* Nahalol), with the consequence that the Canaanites lived (*way-yēshev*) in their midst until they were subjected to forced labor.
>
> Asher did not drive out the rulers of Acco (*yōsheʿvē* Acco), or the rulers of Sidon (*yōsheʿvē* Sidon), or of Ahlab, or of Achzib, or of Helbah, or of Aphik, or of Rehob, with the consequence that the Asherites lived (*way-yēshev*) among the Canaanites who ruled the region (*yōsheʿvē hāʾārets;* some MSS read *yōshēv hāʾārets*), for they did not drive them out.
>
> Naphtali did not drive out the rulers of Beth-shemesh (*yōsheʿvē* Beth-shemesh), or the rulers of Beth-anath (*yōsheʿvē* Beth-anath), with the consequence that they lived (*way-yēshev*) among the Canaanites who ruled the region (*yōsheʿvē hāʾārets;* some MSS read *yōshēv hāʾārets*), but [nevertheless? eventually?] the rulers of Beth-shemesh (*yōsheʿvē* Beth-shemesh) and of Beth-anath were subjected to forced labor on their [i.e., Naphtali's] behalf.
>
> The Amorites pressed the Danites back into the hill country, for they did not allow them to descend to the plain. The Amorites succeeded in continuing to rule (*lāsheveth*) over Har-heres, over Aijalon, and over Shaalbim, but (in time) the hand of the house of Joseph weighed heavily on them and they were subjected to forced labor. [1:27–35]

It will be noted that throughout this collection of settlement "annals" I have translated both the participle (conceived sometimes as a common noun and sometimes as a verbal noun) and the infinitive with the meaning of "rule"; whereas I have left the finite verb with the meaning of "live, dwell." Against the background of demonstrated frequent occurrences of the participial form of *yāshav* as a political administrative idiom, the consistent application of that meaning in Judges 1, precisely in a context where we might expect a political administrative meaning, yields a coherent picture congruent with the existence of varying temporal horizons within the several units as described earlier (IV.17.3). The issue in these "annals" is *not so much who lives in cities and regions as who exercises control over cities and regions.* It is not a matter of driving out all inhabitants but of expelling kings and rulers, of abolishing royal-aristocratic-feudal control, and only as the final temporal horizon of some of the units—determined by the entirely different framework of Israel's own royal policies under David-Solomon—is the entire Canaanite population viewed as subject to forced labor.

Naturally there was a residential correlative to the primary political administrative axis of the reports in Judges 1. The dynamics of residency, however, flowed from the nature of the sociopolitical struggle. Where Israel could not drive out the rulers and their administrative apparatus extending into the countryside (notably in the case of the strong cities in the plain north of Manasseh with their networks of village control and in the case of the centrally controlled villages in the foothills of the Danite territory), it became difficult for Israelite communities to take root or to persist. Since to be "Israelite" was to be in a community of free producers, unfettered by urban political control, it was essential to avoid or to pull back from regions where the rulers of the city-states could effectively assert their control. Israelite abandonment of, or Israelite persistence in, precarious and disputed positions depended on a careful calculus of local conditions. For example, we do not hear of Manassites dwelling among the Canaanites in the plain dominated by Beth-shean, Taanach, Dor, Ibleam and Megiddo, since geopolitics so greatly favored the hierarchic rulers in that area. On the other hand, in Zebulun, Asher, and Naphtali the Israelites are pictured as settled into pockets in the general vicinity of the dominant city-states, a situation made tenable by defensible mountainous and forested terrain and by the fluctuating fortunes of the city-states and their varying degrees of aggressiveness toward or inclination to accept, however begrudgingly, the developing Israelite antifeudal movement.

Judges 4:2

And Yahweh sold them into the hand of Jabin, king of Canaan, who reigned (*mālak*) in Hazor; and the commander of his army was Sisera, and he exercised authority (*yōshēv*) in the wooded heights of Galilee (*ḥᵃrōsheth hag-goyīm*).

This notation about the enemies of Deborah and Barak is understandable in two possible ways: (1) according to the conception that Jabin rules over the entire region and Sisera is his general, the latter is said to have "exercised authority" in northern Galilee, i.e., the area especially infested by the Israelites and from which they swept down on the caravan trade to plunder it; or (2) according to underlying tradition which sees Jabin as king solely of Hazor (cf. 4:17), Sisera may be viewed as another king who joined in coalition with Jabin against Israel. While the latter is a conjecture based on fragments, it finds some support in the text of the Song of Deborah, where Jabin is unmentioned, but may have been included in "the Canaanite kings" of 5:19, and where Sisera dominates the action in a manner consistent with the view that he was not only a commander of the army but one of the kings in the Canaanite coalition.

Judges 5:23

> Curse Meroz, says the angel of Yahweh,
>   curse bitterly its rulers (*yōsheₑvēhā*),
> because they came not to the help of Yahweh,
>   to the help of Yahweh against the warriors.

This translation follows the lead of Alt in seeing *yōsheₑvîm* in Meroz as a collective group of "proprietors or lords." Instead of "inhabitants (of the city)" as a feeble repetition of Meroz, *yōsheₑvēhā* denotes the leadership responsible for refusing to enter the battle on Israel's behalf. This interpretation is strengthened by the sub-units of the poem which precede and follow the Meroz strophe, for each refers to high leadership: the kings of Canaan in 5:19–22 and Sisera, commander of the coalition army and perhaps a king in his own right, in 5:24–31. If, with Alt, we tentatively hypothesize (largely for want of a better solution) that Meroz was an independent city in treaty with Machir/Manasseh, and lying close to the site of the battle near Taanach,[450] *yōsheₑvē* Meroz finds a parallel in *yōsheₑvē* Ibleam and *yōsheₑvē* Megiddo (Judg. 1:27) in the same general vicinity along the southwestern edge of the great plain on which the battle of Judges 4—5 was fought.

Judges 9:41

> And Abimelech ruled (*way-yēshev*) at Arumah; and Zebul [i.e., Abimelech's governor (*sar*) in Shechem] expelled Gaal and his kinsmen/political supporters ['*aḥîm* may be relatives by descent or "brothers" by political commitment] from ruling (*mish-sheveth*) in Schechem.

Since the whole context is a struggle over who is to control Shechem, Gaal having led an insurrection against Abimelech's rule which was put down by Abimelech's troops, the above rendering of the root *yāshav* seems far more apt than as a mere allusion to where the king lived. Of course, the two meanings of the root are not exclusive in the passage, since Arumah is "the seat" of Abimelech's rule and the expulsion of Gaal from his leadership of the insurrection also entailed his expulsion from the city. I offer this interpretation with tentativeness, however, since it involves the finite verb form for which the only clear support I can find is in Zechariah 9:5–6, cited by Cross and Freedman.

Judges 18:7

Then the five men [i.e., the Danite scouts] departed, and came to Laish, and saw the people who were in its midst, ruling confidently (*yōsheveth lāveṭaḥ*), in the manner of the Sidonians, quiet and secure, lacking nothing [reading *maḥsōr kol-*, cf. vs. 10] that is in the earth, possessing wealth (?), far removed from the Sidonians and having nothing to do with Aram [reading *'ªrām* with several of the versions in place of MT *'ādām*, "(any) man"].

There are grave textual difficulties in this description of the mode of life in Laish, including an anomalous feminine form *yosheveth* with the masculine noun *'am* (perhaps the subject was originally the feminine noun *'īr*, "city"). It is true that a majority of the biblical usages of the idiom *yōshev lāveṭaḥ* yield the sense of "dwelling securely" (also, with *shāqēn*, "to lie down"), and such a sense is admittedly intelligible here. On the other hand, the full description implies the economic and political independence of Laish from its nearest large neighbors, Sidon and Aram (=Damascus?); and in my judgment there are at least four other usages of the idiom *yoshev lavetah* in which the context favors the sense, "ruling confidently": Isaiah 47:8 (of the daughter of Babylon, with an effective word play on *yāshav* both as "to rule" and "to sit"); Jeremiah 49:31 ("concerning Kedar and the unwalled kingdoms"); Zephaniah 2:15 (of Nineveh); and I Samuel 12:11 (of Israel in the time of judges, contrasted with its later clamor for a king). An extremely literal reading of the apparently corrupt text in Judges 18:7, replaced in the above translation by "lacking nothing that is in the earth, possessing wealth," may be interpreted as an explicit claim that the people of Laish had no king: "For there was none in the land possessing authority who might put them to shame in anything" (as in RV and ASV, and in modified form in NEB). If, however, MT is rendered more paraphrastically (as, for example, by R. G. Boling: "without any-one perverting anything in the territory or usurping coercive power"), the point made may be less an observation about the internal political structure of Laish than a reference to its independence from interference, limitations, or support by treaty relations with other city-states.[451] This would mean that in attacking Laish, the Danites had no reason to worry about intervention or retaliation from Sidon or Damascus.

Summary and Implications for Moral-Theological Critiques of Conquest Israelites

While it has been impossible within the limits of this study to examine systemati-cally all occurrences of *yāshav* in detail (according to BDB there are 1,090 in the Hebrew Bible), the following conclusions are warranted concerning one technical political shade of meaning for that verbal root:

1. There is a significant incidence of *yashav*, primarily in participial form, proceeding along the lines of an ellipsis of the idiom "sitting on the throne" (and of

related idioms such as "sitting in judgment"), in which it has the sense of a common noun, "ruler/leader" or of a verbal noun, "ruling/filling an office/exercising authority."

2. The idiomatic usage of *yāshav* for communal leadership is applied directly to Israelite leaders (eight times in our examples), as well as twice to leaders of cities in league with Israel (Meroz and Gibeon), but it shows a decided preponderance of applications to non-Israelite political entities (more than fifty times in our examples). Of the eight applications to Israelite leaders, only one attaches to a pre-monarchic figure, namely, the severely condemned upstart, "king" Abimelech.

3. The idiomatic political use of *yāshav* by itself (i.e., without adverbial qualifiers, as in the phrases "he who sits on the throne" or "he who sits in judgment") either directly denotes, or strongly connotes, a pejorative meaning. The *yōshēv* (sing.) or *yōsheᵛvīm* (pl.) are very largely the object of Israel's opposition and attack insofar as they are non-Israelite rulers, or they are the object of severe criticism and threatened punishment insofar as they are Israelite rulers. The term, therefore, has the unmistakable coloration of "ruling abusively" or "ruling oppressively," and at times even the sense of "ruling illegitimately." I can find only a few instances of what appear to be neutral uses of the term in the sense of lacking a negative value judgment. Two such "neutral" references can be explained by the fact that the "rulers" in question are not in direct contact with Israel: the *yōsheᵛvīm* overthrown by the king of Assyria (Isa. 10:13) and the *yōsheᵛvīm* who headed the Horites in Edom (Gen. 36:20). The *yōsheᵛvīm* of cities in alliance with Israel (Meroz and Gibeon) are a special case, perhaps simply being allowed to bear the customary epithet for Canaanite kings, not without a measure of irony. On the other hand, the *yōsheᵛvīm* of Gibeon and the Hurrian cities in league with Israel may in fact carry the technical meaning of "vassal officials" appointed by the suzerain Jerusalem to rule its dependent cities.

4. The scope of leadership referred to by *yāshav*, "to rule," is wider than kingship proper, although in a few contexts *yāshav* is paralleled by *mālak*, "to reign," and this in spite of the supposed primary derivation of the verbal meaning from the idiom "to sit on the throne." This is explained, I think, by the fact that it was not only kings who "sat" in the exercise of office. All manner of political officials "sat" in council and, similarly, judges "sat in the gate." In its scope of reference, *yōshev/yōsheᵛvīm* as "rulers/leaders" is at times comparable to *rō'sh/ro'shīm* as "heads/leaders," even though the bias of the former is more strongly toward the highest leadership, normally the king. Surveying the many examples we have cited, we note that a *yōshēv* may be a king, a prince, a military commander, a judge, or simply a leader or official of unspecified position or rank. Moreover, he may not even be a person with formal authorization or claim "to rule," but simply someone who exerts effective power over the community, such as an abusive merchant or land-grabber.

5. The plural *yōsheᵛvīm* is used in a majority of instances, and there are contexts

where *yōshēv* is a collective singular designating members of a single class of leadership. When referring to the leaders of a single city-state or kingdom, the plural or collective singular often appears to denote a college or council of leaders of the same rank or function; however, many of these usages may also be understood as a lumping together of leaders in various branches of communal life in a comprehensive manner with the approximate meaning of "the authorities" or "the powers that be."

When referring to the leaders of a region which we otherwise know to have been divided into several political sovereignties, such as Canaan with its independent city-states, the plural views all the heads of state in those several political units as a collectivity sharing similar values, attitudes, policies, or strategies. Therefore, while I incline to view most of the enemy leaders called *yōshēv/yōsh^evīm* in the premonarchic sources as kings or princes, I do not agree with Cross and Freedman in restricting the meaning of the term to "reigning princes." The functional import of the general designation is something like this: *yōshēv/yōsh^evīm* are leaders in the imperial-feudal statist system of social organization, with primary reference to enemy kings but embracing other functionaries in the statist system. As Israel developed statist sociopolitical organization of its own, the term was increasingly applied to Israelite functionaries in the state apparatus and, on occasion, referred to persons of power in the upper socioeconomic strata irrespective of their holding political office.

Finally, with respect to the political meaning of *yāshav*, I want to point out how different a shape certain moral-theological critical passages on the conquest assume when that meaning is taken into account. I refer in particular to two passages (Exod. 23:20–33 and Judg. 2:1–5) which have two features in common: (1) the motif of "the messenger of Yahweh" as the forerunner or motive power by which Israel is "brought up" from Egypt and "brought into" Canaan; and (2) solemn warnings against forming alliances with the Canaanites. There are signs of extended rhetorical elaboration in these passages, some of which may be due to the Deuteronomic editor. On the other hand, they contain features which are in no way attributable to D, such as the motif of the messenger of Yahweh and the itinerary of Israel from Gilgal to Bochim/Bethel, cf. Judg. 2:1. The fact that both units are attached as summations or codas to older materials, namely, the Covenant Code in Exodus and the fragmentary settlement "annals" in Judges, has prompted most commentators to see J or E materials in them, or a J/E composite. If *yāshav* is understood as "rule" in these contexts, the heavy emphasis on avoidance of ties with the Canaanites takes on a predominantly political, rather than ethnic, cast. Even the animus against Canaanite gods becomes an animus against the gods of the Canaanite rulers who stand in systemic opposition to Yahweh, the god of the egalitarian Israelites. We quote the longer of the two texts first:

> Behold, I send a messenger before you, to guard you on the way and to bring you to the place I have prepared. Pay attention to him and obey his voice; do not rebel

against him, for he will not pardon your transgression; for my power is in him. But if you truly obey his voice and do all that I say, then I will be an enemy to your enemies and an adversary to your adversaries.

When my messenger goes before you, and brings you into the Amorites, and the Hittites, and the Perizzites, and the Canaanites, and the Hivites, and the Jebusites, and I blot them out, you shall not worship their gods, nor serve them, nor do according to their works, but you shall totally overthrow them and break their pillars in pieces. You shall serve Yahweh your God, and I will bless your bread and your water; and I will take sickness away from the midst of you. None shall miscarry or be barren in your land; I will fulfill the number of your days. I will send my terror before you, and will throw into confusion all the people against whom you shall come, and I will make all your enemies turn tail before you, and I will send hornets [figure for military attack or plague?] before you, which shall drive out Hivite, Canaanite, and Hittite before you. I will not drive them out from before you in a single year, lest the land become desolate and the wild beasts increase to your hurt. Little by little I will drive them out before you, until you are increased and possess the land. . . [omitting vs. 31a, giving the boundaries of the Davidic kingdom]; for I will deliver the rulers of the land (*yōshᵉvē hā'ārets*) into your hand, and you shall drive them out before you. You shall make no treaty/covenant with them or with their gods. They shall not survive (*yeshᵉvu,* or "rule" [?], or possibly a *double entendre,* "survive in a position of authority" [?]) in your land, lest they make you sin against me; for if you serve their gods, it will surely be a snare to you. (Exod. 23:20–33)[452]

It is noticeable that in Deuteronomy 7, where many of the themes of Exodus 23:20–33 are taken up and expanded rhetorically and theologically, the political dimension of the Israelite-Canaanite antagonism is forcefully underlined even in so late a homiletical amplification of the themes. For example, the conventional table of seven peoples in the land is introduced with the characterization of "many nations" (*gōyīm rabbīm;* 7:1), i.e., political structures which are to be remorselessly smashed. In the section that closely parallels the "conquest-by-slow stages" motif in Exodus 23:28–30, the *gōyīm* are even more specifically delineated as political collectivities headed by kings who are singled out as the objects of Israel's destruction:

Moreover, Yahweh your God will send hornets among them, until those who survive and hide themselves from you are destroyed. You shall not be in dread of them; for Yahweh your God is in the midst of you, a great and terrible God. Yahweh your God will clear out these nations (*gōyīm*) before you little by little: you may not finish them off quickly, lest the wild beasts increase to your harm. But Yahweh your God will give them over to you, and throw them into great confusion, until they are destroyed. Indeed, he will give their kings into your hand, and you shall exterminate their memory from under heaven. When you destroy them, not one of them shall be able to withstand you. (Deut. 7:20–24).

The phrase "he will give their kings into your hand" (*wᵉnāthan malkēhem bᵉyādekā*) in Deuteronomy 7:24 parallels the phrase "I will give into your hand the rulers of the land" (*'ettēn bᵉyedᵉkem'ēth yōshᵉvē hā'ārets*) in Exodus 23:31b. And in the third "hornet" passage in the Old Testament, we read:

. . .the lords of Jericho (*ba'alē y^erīhō*) fought against you [omitting the table of seven nations as a gloss, although it is pertinent that the glossator associates these gentilic terms with "the lords of Jericho"] and I gave them into your hand. And I sent the hornet before you which drove out the two kings of the Amorites before you [presumably Sihon and Og, although the reference is out of sequence (cf. vs. 8) and the LXX reads "twelve kings"]. (Josh. 24:11–12).

Finally, Judges 2:1–3 declares:

> And the messenger of Yahweh went up from Gilgal to Bochim (LXX Bethel), and he said, "I brought you up from Egypt, and brought you into the land which I swore to give to your fathers. I said 'I will never break my treaty/covenant with you, and you shall make no treaty/covenant with the rulers of the land (*yōsh^evē hā'ārets*); you shall break down their altars.' But you have not obeyed my command. What is this you have done? Consequently, I now declare that I will not drive them out before you; but they shall become adversaries [reading *tsārīm* with several versions instead of MT *tsiddīm*], and their gods shall be a snare to you."

Taking this body of traditions together, we get the following picture: Israel is to drive out her enemies and not to make treaty with them. The significance of the prohibitions against cult borrowings is in part that political treaties were solemnized by cultic ritual, but the larger, controlling reality is that cultic and sociopolitical systems formed complementary wholes. To worship the Canaanite gods would entail adopting the Canaanite polity of petty monarchy and social stratification. The enemies are variously identified as *gōyīm*, *'ammīm*, *m^elākīm*, *b^e'ālīm*, and *yōsh^evīm*. The first two terms specify the enemy political collectivities and the last three single out the enemy hierarchical leadership, but together they form a body of statist terms in a framework of political-cultic antagonism which the later tendency to conceive the antagonism as ethnic-religious has not been able to efface.

I Samuel 2:1b–10a: Song of Hannah

The so-called Song of Hannah is recognized by virtually all commentators as having originated independently of its present narrative setting. It is generally understood as a hymn, reappropriated in its present setting as an individual thanksgiving song with hymnic elements. In its final form as an independent composition, prior to its insertion in I Samuel 2, the poem was altered to culminate in an assurance of divine support for Yahweh's "king" and "anointed one" (2:10b).[453] With this alteration, the "I" speaker of vs. 1 was presumably regarded as the king himself. The original body of the psalm, however (2:1b–10a), recites the action of Yahweh in reversing the fortunes of his friends and enemies, and the people whom Yahweh exalts are not pictured as having a king but as replacing kings. The language and imagery accord well with premonarchic conditions and show affinities with poems acknowledged to be premonarchic (cf., e.g., *ḥādēllū*, "to grow fat," in 2:5 and in Judges 5:7).[454]

The poem is best conceived as a premonarchic hymn which was later expanded for use in the royal cult. The "I" of 2:1 was originally either the collectivized community or the singer who initiated the hymn in worship (cf. Judg. 5:2). That fragments or blocs of psalm material were recast in fresh contexts is a well-known phenomenon; in fact, there is an instance of portions of this hymn being reworked in yet another version (cf. Psalm 113:7–9). Interestingly, Psalm 113 is a congregational hymn without explicit allusion to the Israelite kingship. Possibly the textually questionable "with the nobles of his people" (113:8) includes a roundabout reference to the monarchic establishment, but that is insufficient to locate in the hymn any distinctive features of royal ideology.

The identification of Yahweh's enemies in I Samuel 2:1b–10a is accompanied contrapuntally by the identification of his faithful. The key to the structural and conceptual articulation of the hymn is the scheme of "reversal of fortune"[455] which is enunciated in 2:4–5 and, in varying ways, is carried through to the end of the composition. The series of reversals of fortune in 2:4–5 may be generalized according to the formula: the one(s) who had good fortune, NOW (x) have bad fortune, WHEREAS (X) the one(s) who had bad fortune, NOW (x) have good fortune. In this formulation, the rubrics "(x)" and "(X)" symbolize the reversals of fortune seen from two different but complementary points of view. The twofold "NOW(x)" punctuates the fact that *the two social categories of persons have experienced dramatic total reversals of fortune.* The single "WHEREAS (X)," which links and hinges the two described groups, punctuates the fact that *the contrasted groups have actually changed positions on the scale of fortunes,* i.e., those once at the top are now at the bottom and those formerly at the bottom are now at the top. A full paraphrastic rendering of 2:4–5 is shown in Figure 2.

The reversal of fortune scheme continues in 2:6–8, but is elaborated differently by focusing on the *source* of the kinds of radical societal changes just described. It is Yahweh, God of Israel, who is the great reverser of fortune in life and in death (Sheol=underworld), in poverty and in plenty (Figure 3).

At the end of the sequence on Yahweh as reverser of fortunes, attention shifts entirely to those whose bad fortune is turned into good fortune by the divine action:

> "He [Yahweh] raises up the poor from the dust,
>   from the dump pile lifts the destitute;
> In order to give them a place with nobles,
>   and assign them sovereign authority [lit., 'a seat of honor']."

The culmination of these descriptions of juxtaposed reversed fortunes hails the elevation of the poor and destitute to the status of communal leaders and to the full exercise of sovereign self-rule. The poem concludes in vss. 9–10a with rather diffuse contrasting terms about Yahweh guarding "his faithful/pledged one"

FIGURE 2

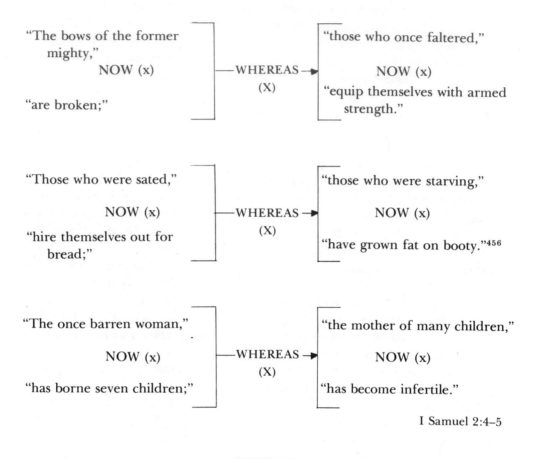

"The bows of the former mighty,"
          NOW (x)

"are broken;"

——WHEREAS→
    (X)

"those who once faltered,"

          NOW (x)

"equip themselves with armed strength."

"Those who were sated,"

          NOW (x)

"hire themselves out for bread;"

——WHEREAS→
    (X)

"those who were starving,"

          NOW (x)

"have grown fat on booty."[456]

"The once barren woman,"

          NOW (x)

"has borne seven children;"

——WHEREAS→
    (X)

"the mother of many children,"

          NOW (x)

"has become infertile."

I Samuel 2:4–5

FIGURE 3

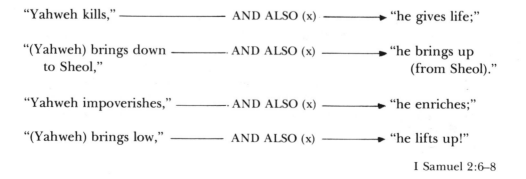

"Yahweh kills," ———— AND ALSO (x) ————→ "he gives life;"

"(Yahweh) brings down to Sheol," ———— AND ALSO (x) ————→ "he brings up (from Sheol)."

"Yahweh impoverishes," ———— AND ALSO (x) ————→ "he enriches;"

"(Yahweh) brings low," ———— AND ALSO (x) ————→ "he lifts up!"

I Samuel 2:6–8

(*ḥªsīdāv*) and cutting off "the wicked" (*rªshā'īm*) who are finally termed "his opponents/contenders/challengers" (*mªrīvāv*, reading with Q).

Within what sociopolitical model are we to construe the conditions underlying the hymn? Who are the social actors alluded to, and what forms of conflicting social relations are made the subject of liturgical celebration? There are, I believe, three possible models:

A MODEL OF INTERNAL SOCIAL MOBILITY. We may understand the poem to mean that individual poor in Israel are able to rise to the top echelons of leadership because of Yahweh's intervention. The social categories of professional soldiers and demilitarized populace (2:4), of a gorged elite and a starving poor (2:5a), of a well-fed and fertile upper class and of a depleted, infertile country folk (2:5b)—and the striking shift in their balance of power—do not support the notion that the poem merely cites striking exceptional cases of Israelites of lowly background who "made it big." Moreover, "the poor" and "the destitute" (2:8a) are collective singulars, and it is they as whole classes of people who will rank with nobles and rule themselves. It is true, however, that the more individualistic model of internal social mobility tended to creep into the reading of the psalm following the monarchy, as is especially clear in the editorial decision to place the song on the lips of Hannah, a pious "barren woman" whose son Samuel became the leader of his people.

A MODEL OF SOCIETAL ATTAINMENT OF KINGSHIP. We may construe the hymn to mean that Israel, formerly downtrodden and weak, has at long last gained the upper hand by replacing the monarchs of Canaan with its own king. That was, of course, the sense in which the hymn was understood in the royal cult when references to Yahweh's "king" and "anointed one" were appended to it (2:10b). As with the preceding model, however, it does not accord with the details of the reversals of fortune described. In the liturgical products of the royal cult, it is the agency of the king by which Yahweh brings his benefits to the people and destroys the enemies. In I Samuel 2:1b–10a there are no such royal traits; in fact, no king is present. Yahweh alone acts on behalf of his people, and their highest honor is not to be led by a king but to share among themselves the power that kings arrogate to themselves.

A MODEL OF SOCIETAL OVERTHROW OF KINGSHIP. In this framework of interpretation, the hymn celebrates Israel's rise from the sociopolitical dregs of Canaan to the point where it has challenged and overthrown the seats of Canaanite power. The only "king" in view is Yahweh; and his "challengers," the Canaanite authorities, are "broken in pieces; the High God thunders against them in heaven" (vs. 10a). Meanwhile, on earth, the armed forces of Canaan have been broken before the constantly renewed peasant army of Israel. The lucrative feudal monopoly on the land and its products has been abolished and the Israelite peasants now are amply fed while the former owners of the land have become day laborers in order to survive. The population growth rate has been radically altered, falling off in the depleted Canaanite cities but rising in the economically strengthened Israelite countryside. From the "dump pile" Israel has risen to take over thrones, not in order to install kings of her own, but to overthrow elitist rule in favor of self-rule by the community. The dump pile (*'ashpōth*; vs. 8) is a vivid image for the lower-class refuse of society, for it is the place outside the city walls where garbage and trash were piled and burned, a place of gathering for the homeless and outcast; in short, the "dump pile" was the social locus of the city lying at the extreme opposite of the social locus of the "seat of honor." Lamentations 4:5 shows the reversal of fortune in the opposite direction, i.e., from palace to dump pile:

> Those who ate dainties are desolate in the streets.
> Those who were brought up in royal purple embrace dump piles.

Such, in my view, are the sociopolitical parameters in which the somewhat elusive poetry of "a place with nobles" and "a seat of honor" are to be read. Had this high point of the hymn been intended to describe Israel's establishment of monarchy, there are simple direct ways in which it could have been stated. Instead, the hymn avoids saying that a king was chosen or installed in Israel or that the rejuvenated poor of Israel formed a kingdom. What I think the rather circuitous political language alludes to politically is Israel's highly effective cancellation of the power of Canaanite kingship. Political imagery is used because it was a political event in that one set of power relations was abrogated and another put in force. The Israelite poor *replaced* the former system of rule, and not merely the former rulers. Israel did not "take over" the office of kingship by immediately appointing its own king; it flatly rejected kingship. But the Israelite rejection of kingship was not self-abnegation, either in the form of inner spiritual withdrawal or in the form of reluctant accommodation to kingship. Israel seized hold of ("inherited") kingship by asserting a valid claim to the sovereign power that the "throne" represented and Israel thereby preempted the former sphere of royal sovereignty as its own rightful jurisdiction under the tutelage of Yahweh.

There is apparent deliberation in the choice of the term "nobles" (*nᵉdīvīm*) in the climactic phrase "in order to give them a place with nobles." For the most part this is a term preferred by wisdom tradition (it appears several times in Job and Proverbs). It may refer to kings, or officials surrounding kings, but it has a wider reference, colored by its verbal root *nādav*, "to incite, impel" and, in one stem, "to volunteer" or "make free-will offerings." It carries the connotation of "generous," "outgoing," "taking the lead," in somewhat the same manner as the adjectives "princely" and "noble" in English. From the distribution of the noun, we might at first glance conclude that it was a relatively late term, which militates against a premonarchic date for the hymn. However, on the strength of two undisputed early uses (one of the noun and another of the verb), it seems clear that *nādav/nᵉdīvīm* was an old poetic expression for "leaders" which has survived as a poetic archaism in many late passages.

In Judges 5:2, we read, "Because the people volunteered themselves (*hith-naddēv*), bless Yahweh!" or, perhaps better, "Because the people answered the call to arms with alacrity, bless Yahweh!"[457] This clearly refers to the readiness with which the citizen militia of several of the tribes responded to the call to do battle with the Canaanite coalition. It is thought by many commentators that the parallel poetic member should be read, "Because the leaders took the lead in Israel (*biphᵉrō'a pᵉrā'ōth*)," following cognate words in Arabic. Because this would be the only biblical occurrence of the root (possibly also Deuteronomy 32:42), and because there is another root with the same consonants which would give the meaning, "because [or when] locks were worn loose in Israel" (apparently referring to a vow by warriors to let their hair grow long, cf. the Nazirites, Numbers 6:5),[458] the meaning of the poetic member corresponding to *hithnaddēv* remains in dispute. On either interpretation, however, it is clear that the verse praised the spontaneity and enthusiasm of the citizens in arms in their spirited response to the call to battle.

The one other premonarchic use of the noun *nᵉdīvīm* (besides I Samuel 2:8) is in the Song of the Well in Numbers 21:18:

> Spring forth, O well! Sing to it!
> the well which the chiefs/princes (*sārīm*) dug,
> which the nobles of the people (*nᵉdīvē hā'ām*) uncovered
> with the scepter, with their own staves.

In spite of the labored attempt of the biblical traditionist to give this poem a setting in the trek of Israel and Moses through Transjordan,

> it is scarcely a historical poem, but belongs rather to a particular class of popular poetry, of which, unfortunately, very few Hebrew examples survive. Such poetry consisted especially of short snatches sung in honour of the vine at time of vintage, or of wells and springs, and even, as Ewald. . .put it, "of popular songs accompanying the alternate strokes of hard labour."[459]

It is not necessary, for our immediate purposes, to explore all the facets of the text. What interests us is the attestation to the term *nᵉdīvīm* for Israelite leaders in this very old song, parallel with the much more common *sārīm*. The *nᵉdīvīm/sārīm* are the tribal leaders who participate at least ceremonially with their rods or staves, and perhaps also in the actual physical labor, in the opening or reopening of wells. Whether *nādīv* ever was a technical term for a particular office is uncertain; the root from which it is derived, plus the way it is used in the later wisdom tradition, suggests that it may always—at least in Israel—have been a generalized honorific for all those Israelite leaders who distinguished themselves by "taking the lead," i.e., by their initiative, generosity of spirit, and readiness to set an example for their people.

I suggest that with respect to $n^e d\bar{\imath}v\bar{\imath}m$ in I Samuel 2:8, two results of our brief inquiry into the term are pertinent: (1) $n\bar{a}d\bar{\imath}v$ was a solidly established term for Israelite leaders in premonarchic times; (2) from the surviving occurrences of the terms, no specific technical leadership function can be identified; instead, given the poetic contexts in which it is exclusively employed and given the uses of the verb ("to volunteer, to respond to the call of battle") and of the adjective ("willing"), it seems that $n\bar{a}d\bar{\imath}v/n^e d\bar{\imath}v\bar{\imath}m$ was a positively charged, quasi-poetic designation of leaders roughly comparable to the English term "worthies" for exemplary leaders.

In conclusion, the body of the hymn in I Samuel 2:2b–10a speaks from and about the premonarchic egalitarian community of Israel. Those formerly ruled and deprived in all the basic areas of their existence are now self-ruled, abundantly provisioned, prolifically reproduced, and socially fulfilled. The enemies of Yahweh in this song are not evil fellow Israelites, nor Canaanite or other kings dispossessed by Israel's king, but Canaanite kings dispossessed by the depressed egalitarian community of Israel before it had any kings of its own.

Genesis 49: Blessing of Jacob

horse and rider ($s\bar{u}s/r\bar{o}k^e v\bar{o}$) [vs. 17]
raiding party or strike force ($g^e d\bar{u}d$) [vs. 19]
archers ($ba^{\alpha}l\bar{e} \ hitsts\bar{\imath}m$) [vs. 23]

In these vivid impressionistic tribal blessings there are some details which make clear the nature of the enemy. The horse and its rider which Dan attacks, like a viper biting at the animal's heels, refers almost certainly to horse-drawn chariots, although it is possible that mounted scouts are referred to. The likely first impression that cavalry are intended is improbable, since it is now well documented that cavalry units were only introduced effectively into the Near East by the Assyrians in the eighth–ninth centuries.[460] The military use of the horse was restricted for centuries to the chariot and to occasional scouting units. It is highly probable that "horse and his rider" here is a collective singular for a chariot force, exactly as in the Song at the Sea (cf. Exod. 15:1). Dan's "biting at the heels" of the chariot horses suggests harassing action of a guerrilla nature rather than direct frontal engagement. Since Dan was absent from the battle recounted in the Song of Deborah, some other encounter with enemy chariotry is implied, perhaps in the skirmishing over Dan's attempt to occupy the foothills around Har-heres, Aijalon, and Shaalbim (cf. Judg. 1:34–35).

"Raiders shall raid Gad" ($g\bar{a}d/g^e d\bar{u}d/g^e g\bar{u}denn\bar{u}$, vs. 19) as a deliberate word play on the tribal name alerts us to considerable caution in taking the terms of the description too literally. Nonetheless, the $g^e d\bar{u}d$ is a familiar word in military and paramilitary parlance. While in post-exilic usage it came to refer to a divisional unit within the army, in earlier times it has the connotation of "a raiding party" or "a strike force," implying a quick surprise attack.[461] It is characteristic of biblical commentators' frequent loose and uninformed invocation of nomadic categories that H.-J. Zobel, for example, leaps to the conclusion that this verse shows Gad to have been a semi-nomadic people, "which explains why he with his holdings in cattle was exposed to constant robberies on the part of bedouin neighbors."[462] In reality, while the band of camel-riding Amalekites that attacked David's camp in the Negeb is called a $g^e d\bar{u}d$ (I Sam. 30:8,15,23), elsewhere the term is applied to troops from Aram-Damascus (I Kings 11:24; II Kings 5:2) and from Moab (II Kings 13:20–21), to armed groups of Chaldeans, Arameans, Moabites, and Ammonites mustered by Nebuchadnezzar (II Kings 24:2, where the meaning may well be "irregular troops"), and even to Israelite bands headed by two captains from Beeroth, the Hivite city in Benjamin (II Sam. 4:2). None of these references implies semi-nomadic cattle-raiding. What they do imply is that the units called $g^e d\bar{u}d\bar{\imath}m$ are much smaller than the total military forces from which they are drawn, or which they supplement, and that they carry out their attacks swiftly and by surprise, so as to avoid contact with the main force of the enemy. Thus the "raiding parties" which engage Gad and against whom he in turn "raids," assuming the tribe's location in Transjordan, may just as well have been forces sent out from Moab or Ammon or from a Canaanite city as from semi-nomads, such as Amalekites or Midianites.

The allusions in both the Dan and Gad sayings to attacking the enemies' "heels" suggest the guerrilla tactics of striking at an enemy's vulnerable rear, but this in no sense limits the military tactics implied to semi-nomads. Conventional armies often did the same, and the technological imbalance of weaponry, heavily weighted against Israel in its wars with the Canaanite city-states, required that it capitalize on every ruse and stratagem possible to take maximum advantage of its assets of mobility and surprise.

In the blessing of Joseph the picture is rather different than in the cases of Dan and Gad. The impression is that of fixed battle, archers against archers, in which Joseph, at first hard-pressed, managed to stand its ground and drive off the enemy. Archers ($ba^{ca}l\bar{e}/hitsts\bar{\imath}m$) were the mainstay of the military forces of the Canaanite city-states, as reported repeatedly in the Amarna correspondence. There were chariot archers and infantry archers, but the context here gives no clue as to the presence or absence of chariots. The mention that "Joseph's bow stayed taut" (vs. 24) recalls the cryptic statement of Jacob to Joseph: "And I have given you one mountain slope [shekem, identical with the Manassite city Shechem] more than your brothers, which I took from the hand of the Amorites with my sword and with my bow" (Gen. 48:22). There is not enough detail in Genesis 49:23–24 to say whether it refers to the battle by the Kishon (Judg. 5), or to an original Josephite seizure of land around Shechem (as asserted in Gen. 48:22) and perhaps attested elsewhere (Ps. 68:11[12]–14[15], but hardly in Gen. 34), or to some other unrecorded incident, or merely to a composite image projecting the notorious alacrity and toughness of the warriors of Ephraim and Manasseh.[463] We can at least set aside Wellhausen's assumption that the archers are Arameans from Damascus in monarchic times[464] and Gunkel's gratuitous claim that they were nomads (probably Midianites) because, on the strength of Ishmael's expertise with a bow (Gen. 21:12), he regards archery as a nomadic characteristic.[465] In this assumption, Gunkel overlooked that Ishmael's cunning with the bow was mainly in hunting (cf. Gen. 27:3) and that archers had become the primary shock troops of all Near Eastern armies by this time and were in no way distinctive of nomads—nor, for that matter, had the bow originated with nomads.

Two other features of the enemy are expressed in Genesis 49 in such oblique form that their meaning must be drawn out by implication. In the one case Issachar is described as a "sturdy ass" that "bowed his shoulder to the burden, and became a slave at forced labor" (vss. 14a–15b; JPS renders the sense effectively: "and became a toiling serf"). When this biblical verse is coupled with Amarna letter 365 describing just such corvée labor on crown lands in Shunem in what was later Issacharite territory,[466] we can readily see that part of this tribe's history had been to serve as serfs or tenant farmers within the Canaanite feudal system. The picture is of a group that persisted stubbornly in a region where it was threatened with extinction by corvée labor practices. Like the hardy ass with which it is compared, Issachar "bore its burdens" until it managed to escape impressment into Canaanite city-state service. The commendation in the blessing is of Issachar's hardihood and not of the practice of forced labor, which is implicitly condemned. The blessing consequently gives us an indirect testimony to the enemy of Issachar as the crown land administrators and aristocratic feudators who deprived the peasants of their freedom. In order to come into its own as an Israelite tribe, to be able to join with Zebulun in "sucking the affluence of the seas and the hidden treasures of the sand" (Deut. 33:18–19), Issachar had to stand up to these imperial and feudal land-holders and break free of them.

The other indirect reference to the enemy of Israel is the statement that Simeon and Levi "in their anger slay men, and at their pleasure hamstring oxen [or bulls; shōr, vs.6b]."[467] The practice of cutting the tendons in horses' legs is attributed to Joshua at Hazor (Josh. 11:6,9) and to the early David in his battle with the Arameans of Zobah (II Sam. 8:4). The reason is clearly given in the remarks that Joshua also burned the chariots and that David saved one hundred horses, either as replacements for his own chariots or, more likely, to equip the captured Aramean chariots newly incorporated into his army. Crippling the horses rendered them unsuitable for chariot warfare, and it was only haltingly under David that Israel began to make use of chariots. Earlier, horses were of no use to Israel and in fact represented a threat. Hamstringing horses and burning chariots were defensive measures against the hated and feared superior weaponry of the enemy. On the other hand, hamstringing of other animals is not attested except in this "blessing" on Simeon and Levi, which is actually a severe condemnation of the two tribes. Doubtless this rebuke of Simeon and Levi bears some connection with the tradition telling of their reprehensible attack on the Shechemites (Gen. 34). The connection is hardly a direct reminiscence, however, since in that account the animals are not harmed (and in one strand of the story they are taken by the Israelites, cf. vs. 28–29). While there is no way to define the historical situation implied, or to know for a fact that Simeon and Levi did hamstring oxen, we may take the remark as a clue to the difference in attitude in old Israel toward horses, which were war animals, and toward oxen (or bulls), which were draft animals in agriculture. It was just as reprehensible to kill valuable farm animals as to kill men "in anger" (without just cause?).

Sociological Setting of "Holy War" and Ḥērem

The notion fostered by Deuteronomists that Israel destroyed all the inhabitants and their possessions in Canaanite cities has greatly distorted our understanding of the "conquest" by forcing our perceptions of the text into one mold. The instruction on treatment of captured cities in Deuteronomy 20:10–18 expressly states that everything alive in a Canaanite city is to be destroyed (and material goods as well?), in contrast to non-Canaanite cities ("the cities which are very far from you") in which the women, children, cattle, and goods may be spared.

Where details are given in the narratives of Joshua and Samuel, there is considerable inconsistency in the application of the ḥērem ("utter destruction," "devotion to the ban," "anathema").[468] In Jericho, everything was destroyed (6:21), except for the family of Rahab spared by previous oath (6:22–23,25; cf. 2:12–14,17–21) and precious metals reserved for the deity (6:24). The latter exemption was of course disturbed by Achan, who kept aside silver and gold for himself, as well as a fine garment (7:20–21). In Ai, however, the cattle and goods were spared by Israel (8:27). In the formalistic recital of the destruction of the cities in the shephelah and Judean highlands (10:28–39), it is said that the people were killed (are animals included in nephesh, i.e., "every living thing" or "every living person"?), but concerning the goods there is silence. In Hazor, and the cities in league with it, cattle and goods are taken as booty, while the horses are hamstrung (11:9,14). (On my interpretation, however, there is an older annalistic core in Joshua 11 which speaks only of the killing of the king and the hamstringing of horses.) While Saul was condemned for taking livestock and goods from the Amalekites (I Sam. 15:9,14–15,21), against the same enemy David felt free to take animals and other valuables (I Sam. 27:8–9; 30:20). (Of course David [or the narrator] may not have regarded an Israelite as obligated to ḥērem rules while conducting raids in the service of the Philistines.) There are, in fact, many other instances of inconsistency and contradiction in the application of the ban against persons, animals, and objects captured.

In an earlier study, my own explanation of these inconsistencies was to posit the destruction of captives and booty in accord with an optional vow before battle:

> One can go some distance in explaining the biblical data if one assumes that *herem* was in fact always imposed in fulfillment of a vow, as is plainly stated in Numbers 21:1–3. The vow before battle will have stated explicitly who and what would be destroyed in dedication to the deity and this will have varied from case to case. The increasing scope of the *ḥērem*: men, women, children, domestic animals, goods, will have corresponded to the religious devotion of the warriors and to the passion with which they sought victory. Perhaps in a majority of battles no *herem* vow was thought necessary. If such is the case, Deuteronomy takes the most severe form of the vow and treats it as normative for all of Israel's wars in Canaan.[469]

Provided that it is given greater socioeconomic precision, this "vow hypothesis" works plausibly well for captives and goods destroyed, but further attention needs to be given to *ḥērem* as the practice of setting aside booty for special uses, as is the case with captured metals.

Attempts have been made to assemble instances of the *ḥērem* from among other peoples. With one striking exception, these "parallels" are imprecise and of modest value. The ninth-century Moabite Stone tells of a Moabite king delivering thousands of captured Israelites to the *ḥērem*, as well as dedicating captured Israelite cultic equipment to his own deity.[470] The idioms and concepts concerning Mesha's "consecration" of Israelite captives and cult objects to Ashtar-Chemosh show remarkable correspondence with aspects of the biblical *ḥērem*. Especially noteworthy is the fact that the great majority of *ḥērem* parallels cited by scholars such as W. R. Smith, F. Schwally, and F.-M. Abel are taken either from nonnomadic tribal societies, such as American Indians and Germanic tribes, or from statist societies in the ancient Near East, such as Egypt and Assyria, or from the Graeco-Roman world.[471] The distribution of these "parallels" according to patterns of sociopolitical organization is oddly incongruent with the recurrent generalization made by scholars that the Israelite *ḥērem* and related war practices (such as ambush and feigned flight, single combat, use of spies) are rooted in pastoral nomadic military organization.[472]

The citation of Arabic materials to demonstrate that the *ḥērem* was of bedouin origin is notable for its carelessness of observation and perverseness of inference. Sometimes the Islamic "holy war," or *jihad*, is naively equated with biblical *ḥērem*, and both with pastoral nomadism. For one thing, this disregards the fact that Islamic *jihad* was directed either at the conversion of pagan peoples or at the subjection of Christians and Jews to poll and land taxes under Moslem rule.[473] There is no evidence that tribal Israel was trying to convert Canaanites to a new religion or that it aimed at imposing imperial rule on Canaanites. In addition, there is reason to believe that one of the aims of the Islamic *jihad* was to control blood-revenge and divisive raiding among pastoral nomadic converts to Islam who did not readily unify in a larger brotherhood.[474]

Thus, insofar as there may be some very general correspondences between "holy war" in Islam and in early Israel, it is by no means evident that these correspondences exhibit qualities of bedouin life in distinction from other socioeconomic sectors that came together respectively in Israel and in Islam. For example, in W. R. Smith's references to warfare in Israel and in the "primitive" Semitic world, which he posits by using bedouin sources, there is but one comparative note on *ḥērem.* The examples he gives, with the exception of a dubious parallel cited by C. M. Doughty, are drawn from nonnomadic peoples such as the Assyrians.[475] In fact, as far as I can determine, the Arabic word cognate to *ḥērem* in Hebrew, although plentifully used for sacred or prohibited areas or actions, is never applied to treatment of war booty. In addition, a ritual slaughter of captives or destruction of booty is not attested anywhere among the allegedly nomadic peoples mentioned in the Bible, either among the Amalekites and Midianites or among the various peoples of Arabia referred to in the pseudo-genealogies of Genesis and in prophetic oracles.

In recent years A. Malamat has proposed a formal similarity between some aspects of the biblical *ḥērem* and the observance of religious and royal taboos in the treatment of troop musters and distribution of booty at Mari.[476] When Malamat concludes, however, that these Mari parallels attest "the very old legal practices current among the West Semitic tribes, substantially of semi-nomadic existence, hundreds of years before the Israelite conquest of Canaan,"[477] it is difficult to see how this "semi-nomadic" attribution follows from anything he has found in the texts. On the contrary, it seems no more than an assumption that since, according to the prevailing view advanced by J.-R. Kupper,[478] the Amorites were once semi-nomads and the Amorites founded the kingdom of Mari, the *ḥērem* parallels in Mari must be of semi-nomadic origin. However, the recent work of J. T. Luke and A. Haldar has convincingly demolished the conception of Mari/Amorite tribalism as a pastoral nomadic incursion from the desert,[479] just as the prehistorians R. Braidwood, C. A. Reed, and J. Mellaart have shown pastoral nomadism to have been a sub-specialization of animal husbandry that moved out of the sown area in the ancient Near East and made particular environmental and economic adaptations to the steppe zone.[480]

The tribalists at Mari are engaged in a political contest with the administrative apparatus of the state, seeking to avoid its taxing and drafting powers, striving for an accommodation that will leave them with a large measure of self-rule. The state answers back with military ordinances ideologically undergirded. Tribal elements that will not fully mobilize their manpower for state service and who countenance private booty-taking unapproved by the crown are stigmatized as "eating the *asakku* of god and/or king." These restive tribalists are viewed in the texts as "poachers" on the state domain.

For example, one text cited by Malamat extends the sacred prohibition to heads of the supposedly semi-nomadic Yaminites who are responsible for mustering troop quotas for the royal army: "Any 'mukhtar' [village or tribal chief; *sugāgum*] whose troops are not mustered in full, who leaves out (even) one man, has eaten the king's *asakku*" [*asakku* apparently referring to a magical plant].[481] The general sense of the idiom seems to be "to intrude or trespass on the prerogatives of constituted authority." In the Mari texts this constituted authority is the king or the god, or both together. In another text, a tribal chief finds that one of the men in his command has violated the state-sanctioned assignment of booty by taking some objects for himself, including two bronze kettles, silver and gold (the parallel to Achan in Joshua 7 is obvious).[482]

A close reading of the texts simply does not support the view that the taboo sanctions concerning troop musters and captured booty were native with the marginal, "semi-nomadic" peoples impressed into the king's army. The *ḥērem* sanctions at Mari are rather instruments of the central authority to assure its social control over the less politicized peoples in the kingdom. It is precisely the tribal, rurally based subjects, the alleged pastoral nomads, who are most careless in observing the sanctioned military behavior, and it is the state administration that is pressing for stricter observance and firmer sanctions.

Although I am dissenting from Malamat's contention that the *ḥērem*-related practices at Mari were pastoral nomadic, the importance of his substantive study should not be overlooked. Malamat has disclosed the fact that at Mari the military taboo sanctions were directly associated with the office and person of the king, as well as with the gods. It should be further noted that both the *ḥērem* of the Moabite Stone and the proscription against "eating the *asakku* of god and/or king" of the Mari texts are ideologically framed sanctions administered by the state authorities. Also, while admitting the aptness of the Mari parallels to biblical *ḥērem* in some limited regards, it should also be noted that the Mari evidence does not touch on the murder of captives and that the punishment for infractions cited seems to be a fine.

In sum, when all the parallels to *ḥērem* that have been proposed are taken together, it appears that the general—and admittedly loose—criterion of religious sanction for consigning captives and booty to execution, destruction, or designation for special use is as often attested in statist war practices as in tribal war practices. If we include in our criterion the slaughter of large parts of the population, the practice is *much more often* exhibited in statist societies than in tribal societies.[483] Moreover, *ḥērem*-like war practices that do appear in tribal societies are emphatically not limited to pastoral nomadic tribal societies.

The veil of the Deuteronomic *ḥērem* dogma is pierced often enough to see that early Israel took the captured booty with zest, but also with a socioeconomic purpose. The purpose was not to destroy wantonly or to feast gluttonously. Naturally the threatened Canaanite establishment, then as always with elitist rule, hoped to brand the Israelite revolutionaries with the stigma of anarchy and self-indulgence. The Israelite socioeconomic program was, however, carefully thought through and well organized, and it seems to have appealed to a great majority of the populace in the highlands and probably far beyond. That program was first of all to push back the zone of Canaanite city-state control, in order to be permanently rid of the oppressive taxation, corvée, and military draft. Secondly, the Israelite socioeconomic program required a viable autonomous social order based on equality of access to basic resources so that no one lived off the surpluses produced by others.

In the light of this revolutionary Israelite socioeconomic program, the biblical *ḥērem* dogma may indeed preserve distorted recollections of an original sociohistorical situation. Given the aims and methods of the Israelite revolution, everyone and everything captured in the struggle had to be wisely disposed of in terms of the overall strengthening of the insurgents' social design. Kings and their agents or supporters—officials, commanders, landlords, merchants, artisans of luxury goods, priests—all these would be killed or expelled, or suitably converted to accept a more modest nonelitist role in Israelite society. All other Canaanites had a legitimate place in Israel as previously exploited lower classes or as unwilling former accomplices in the old elitist order who had no alternative until the Israelite revolution began to make headway.

Criteria that applied to people captured also applied to goods captured, with necessary modifications. For instance, the notion that whole flocks and herds were killed off is deserving of more careful evaluation. Animals are, after all, nonpolitical. Slaughtering animals, or allowing them to die off, is conceivable if they were species that the Israelites did not know how to breed, or if they were peculiarly serviceable to the Canaanite city-states and thus of potential harm to Israel. It is noteworthy that Joshua and David are said to have hamstrung captured horses for the good reason that they wished to deny the enemy horses for chariot warfare. (Thus, the contrast in the treatment of oxen and horses noted in the preceding section of this chapter.) The animal booty was treated in these two instances with socioeconomic selectivity: *horses* were destroyed because they belonged to an alien war technology and could not be profitably used by their captors, whereas *oxen* were kept because they nourished the free peasant by cultivating and fertilizing his fields, carrying loads, and providing occasional meat.

In this connection, it is of interest to note that one of the most frequent reasons given for the decline of agriculture in the Mediterranean area is the over-grazing caused by goats. Although I have not observed any biblical data on this point, it is certainly pertinent to raise the question: Was a program to control the goat population one of the factors in Israel's successful revival of agriculture in the highlands?

Finally, the treatment of metals under the *ḥērem* is of particular interest. In the state society of ancient Canaan, metals were monopolized by the central authorities. The metals were worked by smiths and artisans, and the products were circulated by merchants who funneled them into royal and upper-class hands at a healthy profit. Fortified palaces, arsenals, and temples were customary repositories of metals, either in their pure form or as crafted articles. Gold and silver circulated or were stored as ingots or bars, as smaller pieces of uniform size, or as rings, pendants, or bracelets. They were valued both for their aesthetic qualitites as jewelry, art objects, and furnishings and for their durability and convenience as a store of value and a medium of exchange for purchasing goods and services (cf. Judg. 9:4). Copper and iron, the sturdier and less frequently hoarded "household metals," were shaped into vessels, utensils, tools, and weapons.[484]

The imposition of *ḥērem* at Jericho exempts both classes of metal from destruction. Gold and silver, as well as copper and iron articles, are to be assigned to the treasury, storehouse, or arsenal ['*ōtsar*] of Yahweh (6:19,24; omitting "house" in the latter verse as a probable late reference to the Jerusalem temple). Achan is said to have taken for himself two hundred pieces of silver and a "tongue" (bar?) of gold worth fifty smaller gold pieces (7:21). After a battle in which kings and armies are scattered in the vicinity of Shechem/Mt. Zalmon, the Israelite women dividing the spoil come upon the statue or figurine of a dove with wings of gold and silver (Psalm 68:13[14]). Gideon takes the gold earrings, and the decorations from the camels and robes of the Midianite kings, and makes a cult object (Judg. 8:24–27), as does Micah with two hundred pieces of silver belonging to his mother (Judg. 17:1–5). To be sure, both of these acts elicit judgmental editorial comment or inference, but the factual accounts of the manufacture of the metallic cultic objects are not at all derogatory, in my opinion.

What uses did early Israelites have for metals? Copper and iron tools were immediately put to use, and the same was true of copper and iron weapons—up to the level of military technology that Israel was prepared to assimilate in terms of its egalitarian societal organization and nonprofessional army. The iron chariots, as we have noted, were slow in entering the Israelite army, and doubtless the same was true of the intricately constructed composite bow. There appears to have been some resistance to ostentatious jewelry. In one case Gideon melts it down and in another case Jacob is said to have buried it under a sacred tree (Judg. 8:27; Gen. 35:4). There was always the option of melting down offensive or nonfunctional objects and reusing the metals, or of setting them aside until some better use could be found for them. Israel at least had coppersmiths in the person of the Rechabites, and probably also ironsmiths, except during the period when the Philistines enforced a ban on ironsmithing in Israel. Micah was able to find a silversmith to make cult objects from silver pieces.

What did it mean that metals went into the treasury of Yahweh or that metals were *ḥērem* to Yahweh? It could be understood to mean, as the D writer(s) seems to have construed it, that the metal was totally withdrawn from use and put in a sacred area (such as a deposit under a sacred tree) where the cache was neutralized against all use. Or it could be viewed as a source of support for priests, who exchanged metals from time to time for life necessities. Or it might have reference to melting down the metals and making objects for use in the Yahweh cult.

On the other hand, what lies behind the schematic *ḥērem* may not have been the withdrawing of articles from use but the withdrawal of articles from random private accumulation and speculation in profit. That metals were *ḥērem* to Yahweh could be understood to mean that they were put into a common pool for various purposes, such as cult objects, support of priests, distribution of tools and weapons as needed, and perhaps also other social purposes such as buying staple foods in time of famine, securing ransom to recover or retain land and people threatened with confiscation or debt slavery, and perhaps even to ransom war captives.

It is doubtful that the treasury of Yahweh mentioned in the Jericho *ḥērem* story was any single storehouse, since the singular in this passage is probably a function of the highly centralized twelve-tribe system imposed on the traditions. More likely a number of depots in different regions are implied, some perhaps at shrines guarded by Levites, and possibly even deposits in individual *mishpāḥōth* and *bēth-'āvōth*. On this proposal, metals were *ḥērem*, not because they were to be unused, but because they were to be distributed according to a just plan in which all participated and in which metal reserves were held for emergencies. Various biblical texts speak of the proper distribution of spoil to the fighters, to the community at large, and to the priests (e.g., Num. 31:25–54; I Sam. 30:21–31). Contrary to the practice under the monarchy, the tribal Israelite leaders did not have the right to possess all the booty, although others might voluntarily make a special gift of their shares of the spoil to a leader, as was done for Gideon, who promptly turned the fund of metals into a cult object.

The above ways of conceiving the *ḥērem* as applied to metals accord both with the flexible manner in which metals are handled in the texts and with the archaeological and sociocultural desiderata which show that Israel did appropriate metal technology from the beginning, although in a manner consonant with its egalitarian level of socioeconomic organization—which meant that military technology advanced slowly and that smithing in luxury items, as well as commerce in metal goods, were proscribed or severely limited.

The point in sketching such a range and pattern of approaches to the realities underlying the schematic Deuteronomic *ḥērem* is to illustrate how socioeconomic models can facilitate a fresh analysis of old questions, providing a point of triangulation on matters that remain stubbornly resistant to solution solely by inner biblical analysis or even by the accumulation of parallels lacking a critical theoretical framework.

Much additional work has to be done to test and refine the hypothesis proposed, namely, that behind the *ḥērem* lie selective expulsion and annihilation of kings and upper classes and the selective expropriation of resources such as metals—all with the aim of buttressing the egalitarian mechanisms of Israelite society and providing a solid, renewable support base for the peasant economy. Whatever the detailed outcome of further research, such a proposal is already more coherent and testable than vague invocations of pastoral nomadic background, not to mention endeavors to explain *ḥērem* solely by religious ideology or psychologistic taboo theories.

Psalm 68:1(2)–14(15): Victory Near Shechem

> kings of the armies (*malkē tseⁱvā'ōth*) [vs. 12(13)]
> kings (*meⁱlākīm*) [vs. 14(15)]

This psalm has long been recognized as containing ancient materials, although its overall structure remains a matter of much conjecture.[485] In my view, vss. 1(2)–14(15) constitute a whole very similar in character to other theophanic victory hymns such as Judges 5, Habakkuk 3, and the framework of Deuteronomy 33. The composition is especially rich in elaboration of the motif of God's defense of the powerless Israelites, with explicit mention of "orphans" (*yethōmīm*), "widows" ('*almānōth*), the "homeless" (*yehūdīm*), "prisoners" ('*asīrīm*), and the "poor" ('*ānī*) (vss. 5[6]-6[7], 10[11]), forming a kind of inventory of the low-order sociopolitical status of early Israelites. The reference to rain is expanded beyond the normal clichés of a theophany (vs. 8[9] into an actual declamation about the abundant rain that restores the land (vs.9[10]), suggesting that the text was recited at some stage of its development during the autumnal festival in anticipation of the beginning of the rainy season.[486]

The hymn culminates in a brief impressionistic account of a victory over kings at Zalmon (vss. 11[12]–14[15]). While the meaning of each of the words in the strophe is reasonably clear (except for the doubtful "sheepfolds" (?) [*sheⁱphattāyim*], perhaps from Judges 5:16), the syntax is dubious at points, and thus the reconstruction of the Israelite participants in the event is problematic. We are given glimpses of the fleeing kings pursued by the Israelite army, of a troop of Israelite maidens bringing the good news of the victory (*meⁱvasseⁱrōth*), and of the women at home dividing the spoil (*neⁱwath bayith*), including such choice items as a carved or cast dove overlaid with silver and gold. The lack of interconnections among these vignettes, coupled with the absence of any tribal or personal names, would ordinarily incline the reader to see this as an ideal-typical portrait of Israel's many victories in taking the land, or perhaps a very truncated version of the victory celebrated in the Song of Deborah,[487] except for one striking detail—namely, the reference to Zalmon as the site of the battle.

Zalmon is identified in Judges 9:48 as a mountain near enough to Shechem for

Abimelech and his men to have gone there to gather brushwood to build a fire against the stronghold of the city. The identification of the Zalmon of the psalm as a mountain is strengthened by the reference to snow having fallen on it at the time of the battle. Moreover, the editor who followed the hymn with an apostrophe to the mountain of Bashan seems also to have recognized that Zalmon was a mountain, although the existence of a Mt. Zalmon in Bashan is unknown and the suggestion of some exegetes that the kings referred to in the hymn are Og and Sihon seems quite unfounded. From all appearances, vss. 15(16)–35(36) constitute an entirely separate unit or units, oriented around the temple mountain in monarchic times. This battle at Zalmon cannot, on the other hand, be associated with Abimelech's destruction of Shechem, for the only "king" involved in that battle was Abimelech himself, his enemies having been the rebellious citizens of Shechem who had tired of his petty rule. Nowhere in Israelite tradition is Abimelech's action in aspiring to kingship and in quelling the revolt shown as bearing divine approval, and still less is it regarded as one of the "saving wars" led by a bona fide Israelitae "savior-judge." The narrator's judgment in Judges 9.56–57 is that Abimelech and his Shechemite co-conspirators were alike guilty in the murder of Gideon's sons, and therefore the collapse of Abimelech's brief reign was a requital for their sin. In fact, Abimelech was remembered only as a byword for an ignominious death (cf. II Sam. 11:21). Nor can Psalm 68:11(12)–14(15) be a reference to the battle by the Kishon, for Mt. Zalmon near Shechem was far removed from that locale. The fact remains that the notation "when the Almighty scattered kings there, snow fell on Zalmon" reads like a piece of ancient reportage, especially memorable because a rare snow storm accompanied, or even triggered the onset of, the battle and probably worked to the advantage of the Israelite guerrilla fighters (cf. II Sam. 23:20 for a snowfall to mark an event, and II Sam. 5:24 for a natural phenomenon to signal the auspicious moment to launch an attack).

It is well known that in Joshua there is no account of a battle in the mid-section of the land, between Ai on the south and Hazor on the north, even though certain kings in that area are listed in the inventory of the rulers conquered by Joshua, including the kings of Tappuah and Tirzah, but not of Shechem (Josh. 12:7–24). On the other hand, Israel was able to gather in a great assembly at Shechem which was called to incorporate additional peoples into the Israelite community (Josh. 24). This would have been possible only after the city-state of Shechem had been neutralized to the extent that the egalitarian Israelites were free to gather at the holy place outside of the walled city of Shechem without fear of harassment or challenge by the urban center so close at hand. The presupposed "neutralization" of the city-state of Shechem was probably a defeat administered by the Joseph tribes and attested in the fragmentary saying of Jacob to Joseph: "And I have given to you one mountain slope (i.e., one Shechem, Heb. sh^ekem = shoulder, slope) more than your brothers, which I took from the hand of the Amorites with my sword and with my bow" (Gen. 48:22), and is probably also alluded to in the echoes of a fierce battle of Josephite and enemy archers (Gen. 49:23–24). Nonetheless, Shechem was not at once taken into Israel. In Abimelech's time it had no king, but it had its own council of leading citizens, and it followed the worship of Baalberith, i.e., Baal of the Covenant. Following the disaster of Abimelech's attempted kingship, the people of urban Shechem were in time drawn into the tribe of Manasseh as Israelites, although perhaps not until the early reign of David.

From this curiously twofold body of evidence, which pictures Shechem as a separate entity within Israel but not threatening Israel, I conclude the following: the Joseph tribes defeated the king of Shechem and his allies in a battle near Shechem, smashed the royal-aristocratic feudal apparatus, and opened up the northern highlands to free-holding by the peasants of Manasseh. Shechem itself, however, chose not to enter the Israelite confederacy at the great assembly recounted in Joshua 24, for reasons we cannot specify. At the same time, partly because they had no choice, and perhaps partly because they actually preferred their condition without the burden of kingship, the Shechemite populace lived at peace with Israel. The exact relations between the two communities before Shechem was finally absorbed into Israel are not known, but its position may fairly be described as that of a friendly neutral. Indeed, we should probably distinguish between former subjects of Shechem who lived on the agricultural latifundia in the vicinity and early became part of Manasseh, and the urban populace that remained apart from Israel and was allowed to coexist with Israel down to David's time, once the city was shorn of all power to dominate the countryside and exploit its wealth.

Joshua 10:16–43: Aftermath of the Battle at Gibeon

In this survey of the enemies of Israel and Yahweh, I have so far used the early poetry as a point of entrance into the premonarchic world and also as a point of reference to an examination of some related prose data. At the close I want to refer to a composite account in Joshua which further elucidates the nature of the enemy in early Israel. Joshua 10:16–43 is noteworthy because it stands out from its later Deuteronomic mold in emphasizing that the royal-aristocratic establishment was what Israel opposed and not the populace in its entirety.

The report of the aftermath of the battle at Gibeon is far from forming a single unified composition.[488] Not only are there two references to Joshua and all Israel returning to the camp at Gilgal (vss. 15,43), but vss. 16–27 (the account of the execution of the kings) and 28–43 (capture and destruction of cities in Judah) are different in style and represent different historical horizons in many respects, in spite of their common focus on enemy kings in Judah. The two accounts are commonly harmonized by supposing that following the defeat and execution of the allied kings, Joshua moved on to "mop up" by capturing and destroying their cities. Unquestionably that is the D editor's intent in grouping the materials as he has, or in accepting a still earlier grouping, but the lack of homogeneity between vss. 16–27 and vss. 28–43 is evident on closer inspection.

The captured and destroyed cities are as follows: Makkedah, Libnah, Lachish, Eglon, Hebron, Debir. The kings of Lachish, Eglon, and Hebron were among the five allied rulers who fought the preceding battle. Jerusalem is omitted, even though its king was killed, presumably because of the tradition that it was not taken until the time of David. (But was its king Adonizedek [10:1,3] the same as Adonibezek in Judges 1:5, who was taken to Jerusalem after he was mutilated? And what are we to make of the report in Judges 1:8 that the Judeans attacked Jerusalem and set it afire?) Jarmuth is omitted, for no apparent reason, even though its king was among the enemy coalitionists (10:3,5,23). Presumably the D traditionist had no independent account of Jarmuth's capture. Libnah and Debir are included, although unmentioned in the battle at Gibeon/Beth-horon. Such omissions and expansions would not in themselves tell decisively against the unity of the accounts. More telling is the description of the treatment accorded Hebron: "They assaulted it, and took it, and smote it with the edge of the sword, and its king and its towns, and every person in it"; for it is a notation without knowledge of the preceding account of the slaying of the king of Hebron at Makkedah (vss. 23,26). By contrast, mention of the kings of Lachish and Eglon are lacking in vss. 31–32, 34–35. In my view the D editor was responsible for this lapse of memory in failing to delete from this independent account the mention of Hebron's king, which became flatly contradictory once the passage was inserted after the originally separate report of the king's execution at Makkedah. Moreover, the kings of Makkedah and Libnah were said to have been disposed of in the same manner as the king of Jericho, obviously meaning "killed," even though there is no reference to the special fate of the king of Jericho in Joshua 6. This means that only in Lachish and Eglon are kings unmentioned, suggesting that the D editor deleted them while failing to do so in the case of Hebron. Then there is the interesting reference to Horam of Gezer who led an army to help Lachish but was routed; no attack on Gezer itself is recounted, correctly reflecting the fact that Gezer remained an independent Canaanite city until the Pharaoh gave it to Solomon as a dowry.

Evidently, then, the D editor has drawn vss. 28–43 from a source unconnected with vss. 16–27 and, joining them together, has created a transition between the battle at Gibeon and the expedition against a string of Judean cities. He was at the same time responsible for introducing Joshua as the subject of all the assaults on the Judean cities, whereas originally, as in Judges 1, Joshua was not mentioned at all. Even though it is kings and their armies which stand out prominently as the objects of all the assaults, except for the doctored Lachish and Eglon episodes, the

Deuteronomic formula of total destruction of all the inhabitants inconsistently suffuses the descriptions with a lack of reality.

By contrast, the action of vss. 16–27 is solely against the kings and their armies. Joshua strives for a conclusive victory by trying to prevent the enemy forces from scattering to the safety of their cities. Nonetheless some escape, and it was probably this detail that suggested to the editor the advisability of following up with the string of assaulted Judean cities. The actual culmination of the battle, however, was the ceremonial enactment of victory over the kings and their execution. The Israelite officers are summoned and told to put their feet upon the bowed necks of the captured kings. Then Joshua solemnly intones: "Do not be afraid or dismayed; be strong and of good courage; for thus Yahweh will do to all your enemies against whom you fight" (10:25). The kings are then executed and hung from trees until burial at sundown.

The rounding out of the battle at Gibeon forms a clear picture. The enemies are the kings who contest Gibeon's alliance with Israel and whose forces are decimated. In the battle the kings' forces are necessarily the enemy to be defeated. Once that is accomplished, the kings are eliminated. Only if new kings should arise in the cities from which the dead kings came, would it be necessary to attack the cities, but the story does not consider that eventuality. The following recital of the Judean cities attacked in succession also originally singled out kings and did not conceive of those cities as bereft of kings who had already been killed by the Israelites. Thus, where the same cities appear in the two blocs of tradition (Lachish, Eglon, Hebron), the accounts of the overcoming of those cities are conceptual doublets: in the one case the cities are conceived as overcome when their kings are defeated and captured in battle outside the walled fortresses; in the other case the cities are conceived as overcome when the kings are defeated while defending their cities (this assumes, of course, that the original references to the kings of Lachish and Eglon were omitted by the editor).

My point is not to claim that the account of the five named Amorite cities in league is historically accurate *in toto,* either in the names of cities and kings or in the events detailed. I am not, therefore, claiming that those particular five cities were all taken in one blow by defeating their kings in coalition, in contrast to their having been taken one by one, as the subsequent account reports. My point is that, in spite of the two different historical horizons in the traditions about the aftermath of the battle of Gibeon, when separately examined they attest a common early emphasis upon the kings and their armies as the enemies of Israel and not the populace of the cities *in toto.* Both accounts are extremely patterned, highly legendary in their stylization, but they show that the sociopolitical situation they are ideologizing was a confrontation between Israel and the royal aristocratic statist system of rule centered in the cities.

45

Canaanite Converts, Neutrals, and Allies
vis-à-vis Liberated Israel

The model I am proposing for early Israel as a tribal synthesis of eclectic societal elements indigenous to Syria-Palestine hypothesizes the conjunction of antistatist groups in emergent Israel, groups which had been previously integrated in varying ways and degrees in the Canaanite city-state system. In IX.44.2 I have tried to show that in text after text the enemy is equatable with the Canaanite rulers and their military-political functionaries rather than with the Canaanite populace as a whole.

But further questions arise: Who among the peoples of the land are represented as *not* being the enemies of Israel, either in the sense that they are said to have been exempted from attack by Israel or did not initiate attack against Israel, or in the sense that they appear in some positive supportive relationship to Israel? According to the proposed model of the early Israelite formation, it is among precisely such groups that we ought to look for indications of the types of societal groups that became Israelites and the processes by which they made the transition from incorporation in the city-state system to incorporation in the tribal system of Israel. By applying the sociological analytic developed in preceding chapters, a close examination of these groups in their textual settings may enable us to see at least the outlines of some of the processes by which "Canaanites" became "Israelites."

Our discussion need not start *de novo*. In V.22 we offered a provisional model of Israel's formation as a peasant's revolt. In VIII.41 the convergence and absorption of '*apiru,* peasants, and transhumant pastoralists in the formation of Israel was argued. In IX.43 a two-stage transition from Amarna Canaan, first to Elohistic Israel and then to Yahwistic Israel, was proposed. Moreover, partial answers to the above questions are scattered through preceding parts of this study in the elucidation of particular biblical texts. It will not be necessary, therefore, to reexamine textual ground already explored. It is advisable, however, to draw together the results of these textual studies where pertinent and to supplement them by analysis of additional texts. This will be done by setting forth a tentative typology of the various nonhostile or nonoppositional modes of Canaanite response to Israel, modes that include *conversion* (incorporation into Israel), *neutrality* (nonintervention in the internal affairs of Israel and noncooperation in hostile actions against Israel by other parties), and *alliance* (under protection of Israel and giving support to Israel while maintaining formal independence).

45.1 Conversion: The Local Populace Becomes Israel

As to the mode of Canaanite "conversion" to Israel, I have in mind situations wherein city-state rulers and upper classes are overthrown, thereby freeing elements of the city-state populace to incorporate in the burgeoning alternative social system of Israel.

Subjects of the Amorite Sihon

Here I cite the evidence, admittedly indirect, that subjects of the kingdoms of Sihon and Og in Transjordan participated in the overthrow of their leaders (see V.22). The most probable way to explain the appearance in the corpus of Israelite traditions of the Taunt Song against Heshbon celebrating Sihon's victory over Moab (Num. 21:27–30) is to infer that some of Sihon's insubordinate subjects became Israelites (of the tribe of Reuben?). Likewise, it may be inferred that rebel subjects of Og who captured his iron bed entered the Ammonite kingdom where the iron bed was deposited in Rabbath-Ammon, and still later some of them became Israelites (Deut. 3:11).

There are two explicit biblical reports of residents of cities under pressure by Israel collaborating with Israelite spies and of the subsequent inclusion of these collaborators and their social groups into Israelite society. I refer to Rahab of Jericho (Josh. 2; 6:22–25) and an unnamed man of Bethel (Judg. 1:22–26). The striking similarities in the collaboration-conversion process in the two cases have seldom been noted, chiefly because the relocation of the man of Bethel within Israel has been consistently overlooked by interpreters.

The Rahab Group in Jericho

It has been pointed out by J. A. Soggin that the Rahab story presupposes an actual armed struggle and the capture of the city by a ruse rather than by the miraculous collapse of the walls as the climax of a ritual procession around the city.[489] Only if the Israelite spies anticipate a fight, and thus the need to improve their prospects by finding allies within the city, is there any point at all to their risky liaison with Rahab. As to the motivation for Rahab's collaboration with the spies, the text offers a confessional statement by the woman in which she identifies with the paralyzing fear of the Yahwistic Israelite invasion that has fallen on the rulers of Jericho. The historical basis of this high rhetoric is that Rahab is convinced that the Israelites have the power to take the city, and she is willing to help them provided she is assured of safety for herself and her kin. But was fear her only, or even her primary, motive in siding with Israel? Much hinges on Rahab's social position as a harlot. To be sure, it may be that she operated an inn, and thus it was logical that the spies should have gone immediately to her quarters.[490] But while that may explain the contact from the Israelite side, it hardly explains the ready welcome she gave them and the dispatch and aplomb with which she hid them, diverted the searchers, and finally directed the spies safely back to the Israelite camp. The account gives the decided impression that the spies knew of Rahab in advance and that she was prepared for them and had even worked out contingency plans to assure their escape as part of a larger plan for seizing Jericho. This would be especially probable if we think of the Israelites as having been in the vicinity for some time and, in fact, as including rural subjects of the city, rebels by night and "loyal subjects" by day who were in constant communication with, or had direct access to, the city.

Sociological Setting of Prostitution

As a matter of fact, Rahab's susceptibility to participating in a conspiracy to overthrow the city's ruling class is understandable when we note that in the typical ancient city harlots formed one of several groups of occupational outcasts whose services were greatly desired but who, because of their demeaning work and the social taboos, codes, and conventions which they breached, bore a scapegoating stigma and worked under decided disabilities. Among the familiar types of outcasts in ancient cities, as noted by G. Sjoberg, were slaves, leatherworkers, butchers, barbers, midwives, prostitutes, entertainers, lepers, and merchants (varying from culture to culture according to the economics and according to particular taboos, codes, and conventions in vogue).[491] Sjoberg further notes the hypocritical and cynical symbiotic relationship between the ruling class and the outcasts:

> . . . to sustain its power and authority, the upper class seeks to ostracize persons who pose a threat to the status quo. It is because elements of the society—including the elite—require the performance of certain despised, or "defiling," activities that some persons are permitted to pursue these, all the while removed beyond the pale of respectability. The result: the upper class "has its cake and eats it too." . . . all non-industrial cities harbor prostitutes; but as long as these are socially isolated they do not disrupt the normal male-female relations or the family system: hence their clients can "sin" respectably.[492]

It is probable, therefore, that Rahab had social-class reasons for resenting the ruling class in Jericho and for gambling on an improvement in her lot by siding with the rebel movement.[493] The fact that she is represented as living with her father's bēth-'āv may mean that she was pushed into harlotry in order to support her family. Apparently this was a form of economic pressure that Israel itself experienced, although perhaps only later under the monarchy, as implied by the injunction: "Do not profane your daughter by making her a harlot" (Lev. 19:29).

In typical Israelite narrative style, the story adheres strictly to the main issue, which is the circumstances of the seizure of Jericho. Thus, there is no inkling as to whether Rahab continued her social role as a harlot once her household was absorbed into Israel. Such laws as the above (see also Lev. 21:7,9) make it clear that harlotry existed in pre-exilic Israel, but all the legal stipulations may refer to monarchic conditions. Jephthah was the son of a harlot (Judg. 11:1), but it is not clear that his mother was an Israelitess. Tamar resorts to the temporary ruse of harlotry in order to be impregnated by her father-in-law, who had willfully refused to give her a husband to raise up sons to her deceased husband's name (Gen. 38). Whether the town of Enaim, at whose entrance Tamar posed as a harlot, was as yet Israelite is not clear from the account (vss. 13–14,21). Insofar, however, as harlotry is an offshoot of economic necessity, it can be conjectured that the overall effect of the egalitarian Israelite system was to reduce its incidence dramatically because extended families became autonomous productive units in which all the members, women included, were provided for without resort to selling their bodies, either as debtor slaves or as prostitutes.

Interestingly, the report about Rahab ends with the observation that "Joshua saved alive Rahab the harlot, and her father's *bēth-'āv* and all who belonged to her, and she has lived in Israel to this day" (6:25). The temporal setting of "this day" is unknown, and need not even presuppose that Rahab herself was still alive but only that her *bēth-'āv* still existed in Israel. We cannot, of course, rely in any way on the accuracy of an historical Israelite attack upon Jericho, given the negative archaeological data concerning the city previously mentioned. Nevertheless, the traditionist believed that Jericho was taken by Israel, and he goes on to note that a curse was pronounced on anyone who should rebuild it. According to I Kings 16:34, it was not until the reign of Ahab in the mid-ninth century that Jericho was rebuilt. Consequently, the traditionist presupposes that while Rahab and her *bēth-'āv* were taken into Israel, they did not continue to live in the destroyed and uninhabited city of Jericho. Without hinging our sociological reconstruction on the specific connection with Jericho, it is clear that the tradition presupposes known conditions in which that part of the population of a destroyed city which was converted to Israel was transplanted to another region. Assuming that Rahab's household was economically depressed we may imagine that the entire household (and perhaps an even larger group as implied in the rather awkwardly added *mishpāḥōth* in 6:23) was established on lands in the vicinity of the city which had formerly been held by the crown or the aristocracy, and thereupon Rahab's group joined the free peasantry of Israel. The detail of the story concerning the stalks of flax spread on the roof of Rahab's house (Josh. 2:6) implies that her household was already engaged in agriculture, probably as tenant farmers with small holdings near the city, or perhaps as suppliers of linen workers, or themselves linen workers such as those at Judean Beth-ashbea (I Chron. 4:21).

The Informer and His mishpāhāh at Bethel/Luz

Although considerably briefer, the account of the taking of Bethel in Judges 1:22–26 exhibits many formal parallels to the account of Rahab at Jericho: Israelite spies approach the city; a resident of the city cooperates with them so that they gain entrance to the city by surprise; the collaborator and his social group are spared, and, leaving the destroyed city, they settle elsewhere in Israel. The collaborator is in this instance a man, unnamed and unidentified by social position or occupation. While the terse narration indicates no previous familiarity between spies and collaborator, neither does it rule out the possibility. And while the incident could be understood as coerced collaboration under threat of death, the idiom "we will deal kindly with you" ('āsīnū 'imm^ekā hesed, 1:24) favors a mutually acceptable agreement, exactly as the same idiom does in the case of the spies and Rahab (cf. Josh. 2:12,14).

It is said that "the man went to the land of the Hittites ('erets hahittîm) and built a city, and called its name Luz; that is its name to this day" (1:26). Most exegetes have taken for granted that this refers to Syria as the region formerly claimed by the Hittite empire. In a confusing territorial description in Joshua 1:4, it does appear that 'erets hahittîm is in Syria, and this may also be the sense of the original text in II Samuel 24:6 when restored from the Lucianic LXX, i.e., "toward Kadesh in the land of the Hittites." Yet this understanding is untenable for three reasons: 1. No city by the name of Luz is known to have existed in Syria; on the contrary, in biblical tradition Luz is exclusively applied to Bethel itself, or to another settlement nearby Bethel. 2. The notation "that is its name to this day" is of a class of etiological comments throughout early biblical narratives which always refer to continuing phenomena in Israel but never to phenomena located outside of Israel (the reference to the survival of Og's iron bed in Rabbath-Ammon is only an apparent exception, since it indicates that former Ammonites who became Israelites brought the tradition with them). 3. No plausible reason is given for the man of Bethel and his social group to remove themselves entirely from Israel. Like Rahab, the man of Bethel has the solemn pledge of the Israelites to deal kindly with him. Only perhaps on the theory that the man was a trader or official from Syria, serving at the pleasure of the king of Bethel, can we account for his desire to return to his homeland now that the royalty and aristocracy of Bethel have been annihilated. But this is improbable for two reasons. In the first place, the man is not alone but has a large social group around him (his mishpāhāh), so large in fact that together they can build a town or city. It is difficult to imagine a foreign servant in Bethel having so large a family or company of retainers. A further objection, though not so decisive, is that a person so closely dependent on the royal establishment in Bethel would hardly be a collaborator with the Israelites, since he stood to lose his privileged occupational status with the overthrow of hierarchic government in Bethel.

The contexts in the two accounts point clearly to comparability between Rahab's relocation within Israel but outside Jericho and the man of Bethel's relocation within Israel but outside Bethel. While Luz is used in the traditions as an earlier or an alternate name for Bethel, there is one bit of evidence that during at least one period (in Davidic-Solomonic times?) Luz was a place in the near vicinity of Bethel but not simply identical with Bethel. I refer to the boundary description of the Josephites, which states that the border "then proceeded from Bethel to Luz" (Josh. 16:2). All things considered, I believe that the most intelligible reconstruction of events is that the man and his group moved a short distance west of the destroyed city of Bethel and founded another settlement. Possibly the use of the term *mishpāḥāh* for the man's group—as we have seen, a normally larger association of peoples than the *bēth-'āv* which predominates in the Rahab account—indicates that in fact these Israelite sympathizers represented a large percentage of the former inhabitants of Bethel, even a majority. We may further speculate that the destruction of Bethel necessary to overthrow the royal establishment was so extensive that the large group who had collaborated with Israel were unable to find living quarters in the buildings still standing. Under the circumstances it was simpler to move a short distance away and build a new settlement than to attempt to raise the ruins of Bethel proper.

On this theory the characterization of the land around Bethel as "the land of the Hittites" admittedly is awkward, but it is by no means impossible. In IX.44.1 we noted that biblical traditions refer to Hittites who are said to be living in the vicinity of Hebron (Gen. 23) and Beersheba (Gen. 26:34), and the same may be implied for Jerusalem (on the basis of Ezek. 16:3,45). A more general reference appears in Numbers 13:29: "the Hitties, the Jebusites, and the Amorites live [or rule?] in the hill country" (in contrast to Amalekites in the Negeb and Canaanites by the sea and along the Jordan), and also in Joshua 11:3 (with the addition of the Perizzites). It is also probable, in my view, that the phrase "toward Kadesh in the land of the Hittites" in David's census itinerary (II Sam. 24:6) refers not to Kadesh on the Orontes (much too far to the north) but to Kadesh in Galilee; if so, an Israelite region is here actually called "the land of the Hittites."

The sense in which these peoples in Canaan are called "Hittites" remains an enigma, and it has been proposed that some or all of the references should be changed from "Hittites" to "Hurrians" (requiring a change of only one consonant in the Hebrew text). I. J. Gelb notes that all the names of Hittites in the Hebrew Bible, with possibly one exception, are Semitic, from which he concludes: "Thus it is clear that the Hittites living in Palestine, no matter what the memory or tradition of their ethnic background might have been, represented a group of people fully assimilated to the surrounding Semitic population."[494] It should be noted in this connection that Genesis 36:2 subsumes Elon the Hittite under the general rubric of "Canaanites." Recently, G. E. Mendenhall has assembled linguistic data that in his view argue strongly, if not conclusively, for a sizable influx of Hittites and other northern peoples into Palestine attendant on the invasion of the Sea Peoples in the thirteenth-twelfth centuries B.C.[495] Consequently, whatever its exact meaning may be, there is no insurmountable objection—given the entire context of Judges 1:22–26—to regarding "the land of the Hittites" as the neighborhood of Bethel where the collaborators from that city resettled in a newly built location called Luz.

Adullam and Cities in the Judean Foothills

Although we lack any account of the capture of Adullam, it is stated that the king of Adullam was overthrown by Israel (Josh. 12:15) and in Genesis 38 we encounter Judah in intimate relations with Adullamites, extending as far as intermarriage. Judah has a $r\bar{e}'a$ ("friend" or "associate"), Hirah the Adullamite (perhaps the local leader following the defeat of the king?), by whose mediation Judah marries the daughter of a Canaanite from Adullam. So far the story can be read merely as an account of relations between individuals, but it quickly becomes clear that at another level, larger intergroup relations within the tribe of Judah are referred to. The "sons" born of the union (Er, Onan, Shelah), as well as the sons born of the curiously contrived union of Judah with his daughter-in-law Tamar (Perez, Zerah), appear in the census list of Numbers 26, where three of them are described as mishpāḥōth in Judah (26:19–22; Er and Onan are apparently not identified with mishpāḥōth because of their early and inauspicious deaths, cf. Gen. 38:7–10 where it is stated that "Yahweh slew" both of them). Moreover, according to I Chronicles 4:21–22, Shelah's sons are said to have been "fathers" of towns in the Judean shephelah in an area extending to the west and southwest of Adullam: Lecah (Lachish?), Mareshah, Beth-ashbea, and perhaps also Achzib (as in Josh. 15:44, in place of Cozeba; cf. Chezib in Gen. 38:5). Interestingly, at Beth-ashbea are said to be "mishpāḥōth of the house (bayith) of linen workers" (4:21). Since the Chronicler is purportedly giving traditions from the time of David, or earlier (cf. the narrator's note: "these are ancient records," 4:22), it may not be implausible to assume that this village of linen workers was brought into the Israelite formation of Judah in premonarchic times. The social-structural terms in this case may have specialized economic organizational meanings appropriate to the craft described; tentatively, I suggest this translation: "associations (mishpāḥōth) of the linen workers' guild (bayith) in Beth-ashbea."

In the Jericho and Bethel traditions, the focus is on the destruction of the cities by collaboration with insiders, and the destruction is so devastating that the populace won over to Israel has to relocate elsewhere, but of the reorganization of these converts in Israel we are given no information. In the Adullam traditions, on the contrary, there is no story of destruction, only a notation that its king was defeated. The city seems to be standing undisturbed on its original site, but of course this does not necessarily mean that Adullam escaped destruction by attack or uprising; it only means that occupation of the city was not interrupted for long. Given the fact that the Adullamite father-in-law of Judah is called "a Canaanite" (Gen. 38:2; and his daughter "a Canaanitess" in I Chron. 2:3), I assume that the former subjects of the king of Adullam continued to live in the city after his deposition. Moreover, we can perhaps discern some aspects of the reorganization of the Canaanite converts to Israel. Since Hirah the Adullamite, Judah's "friend," is the one with whom Judah first makes contact when he seeks to arrange a marriage with a young woman of the city, we may regard Hirah as the chief elder, or one of the elders, at the head of Adullam, since the overthrow of its king. Hirah is also shown accompanying Judah to a sheepshearing in Timnah, which suggests that herders from the Judah group and from Adullam worked together in this operation. It is through the agency of Hirah that Judah sends the kid he had promised in payment to the harlot, whom he did not recognize as his own daughter-in-law.

In Genesis 38 Judah remains an individual, without delineation of the inner structure or activities of the Israelite group which he clearly embodies as indicated both by his name and by the ways he relates to the Adullamite community. The only clue is the opening statement that "Judah went down from his brothers," which appears to be a linkage of the incident with the locale of Hebron (37:14) in the novella of Joseph and his brothers whose continuity is awkwardly interrupted by the insertion of the story about Judah and Tamar. In going from Hebron northwest to Adullam, a journey of about ten miles, there is a descent in altitude. The highlands around Hebron was the region long identified with Abraham, one of the 'ivrī='apiru forerunners of Israel, and Hebron was one of the early centers of Israelite strength (Judg. 1:10,20). We may, I think, read the story in group sociohistorical terms with the understanding that Judah and his community represent one of the first Israelite groups in the southern highlands, whereas Hirah and the Adullamite community represent one of the more recent Israelite groups, which is accented by one of its members being called a Canaanite. Between these groups there are regular arrangements for economic cooperation and provisions for intermarriage. In the account Judah stands for a leader of his group and Hirah stands for a leader of his group, the contacts between the two communities being channeled through the respective leaders. In every way, the "older" Hebron group and the "newer" Adullamites appear as two sub-communities within one larger Israelite community.[496]

The inclusion of Lecah, Mareshah, Beth-ashbea, and Achzib as related communities in the Judean shephelah within the pseudo-genealogical scheme for Judah in I Chronicles 4:21–22, and specifically their attachment to Shelah, son of the union of a man from the Hebron group and a woman from the Adullamite group, points to the probability that these communities in the general vicinity of Adullam were also incorporated into Israel after the overthrow of the Adullamite king who had previously exercised control over them. One of these communities is described as a settlement devoted to the production of linen cloth, especially desirable for summer clothing because of its coolness. While the level of craftsmanship in Israelite territories unquestionably suffered a decline with the loss of patronage by a royal-aristocratic leisured class, this will have been chiefly the case for crafts that produced luxuries such as jewelry, ivories, ointments, etc. In the turmoil of Israelite attacks and uprisings from city to city, many craftsmen were killed or fled. But apparently others, especially those engaged in producing basic articles for the daily needs of the general populace, such as the linen workers of Beth-ashbea, not only survived but were taken into the formation of Israel.

45.2 Neutrality: The Local Populace Remains Outside Israel

As to the mode of Canaanite "neutrality" toward Israel, I have in mind situations wherein city-state rulers and upper classes are overthrown, sometimes in battle in the open country, after which the city continues an autonomous existence vis-à-vis Israel for an indeterminate period—while relinquishing all claims to feudal control of its environing countryside, as well as all rights to support other city-states in hostile action against Israel.

Shechem

As I understand the early biblical traditions about the important city of Shechem, located in the heart of the territory of the powerful Joseph tribes, its status from the emergence of Israel until well after the time of Abimelech, i.e., from approximately 1250–1225 B.C. until some time in the eleventh century, and perhaps as late as the reign of David, was that of a neutral Canaanite city as described above.

According to Psalm 68:11 (12)–14(15) and Genesis 48:22, as I have interpreted them in the preceding chapter, Shechem was neutralized as a military and political threat to Israel soon after the entrance of the Exodus Yahwists into the area. There is no archaeological evidence of the destruction of the city at that time, nor do the traditions tell of a direct attack on the city (Genesis 34 refers to an earlier 'apiru or proto-Israelite contact with Shechem, and even the attack described did not leave the assailants in permanent control of the city). Consequently, the neutralization of Shechem seems to have occurred by the defeat of its king in league with other kings (analogous to the city-state coalitions led by Jerusalem [Josh. 10] and by Hazor [Josh. 11]).

Shechem continued to be formally independent of the Israelite tribes, at least such is the most coherent way of interpreting the account of Abimelech's short-lived attempt at a dual monarchy encompassing Canaanite Shechem and Israelite

Manasseh, or at least sectors of that tribe (Judg. 9).[497] Shechem lacked a king, but it had a collective leadership of important citizens called ba'alē Shechem, "lords" or "masters" of Shechem (9:2,6,18,20). The city was not committed to the cult of Yahweh but followed the worship of Baal-berith, "Baal of the Covenant," who was worshipped at a temple that formed part of the fortified governmental complex with a tower. This complex was known as Beth-millo, or "filled-in quarter," i.e., a structure or complex of structures built on an artificial platform of stamped earth (9:4,6,20,27,46–49). The Beth-millo has been uncovered in archaeological excavation of the city.[498]

On the other hand, Joshua 24 tells of a major assembly of peoples at or near Shechem in which they were challenged by Joshua to choose either Yahweh or the tribalized "gods your fathers served" or the city-state "gods of the Amorites" (vss. 14–15). In my judgment, this assembly followed on the defeat of the coalition of kings defending the sovereignty of royal Shechem and of other hierarchically governed cities in the central highlands, namely, the region that was to become the domain of Ephraim and Manasseh. I agree with those interpreters who see in Joshua 24, in spite of its later revisions and expansions, an original historical reference to the formation of a strong Yahwistic Israelite intertribal association constituted of a group coming from Egypt and groups that had been resident in the land, some of the latter having earlier formed an association around the cult of El under the name of Israel.[499]

The view that Shechem proper remained a neutral Canaanite city in the midst of Israel for up to two centuries depends on distinguishing between the holy place *inside* the central fortified complex of Shechem and the holy place located some distance *outside* the walled city. The topography of the cultic sites at Shechem is more than a little confused in the biblical traditions, particularly since there appear to have been sacred trees (oaks or terebinths?) located at both holy places.[500] It is, therefore, necessary to marshal the evidence in defense of two sites, one *an Israelite holy place sacred to Yahweh outside the city* and the other *a Canaanite holy place sacred to Baal inside the city.*

At the culmination of the assembly at Shechem, Joshua is said to have erected a great stone "under the sacred tree [hā'allāh; an error for hā'ēlāh?] in the sanctuary of Yahweh" (Josh. 24:26). An ancient, premonarchic cultic site at Shechem is mentioned (or, as I argue, two sites are mentioned) in considerable specificity in seven biblical passages (Gen. 12:6; 33:18b–20; 35:4; Deut. 11:30; Josh. 24:26; Judg. 9:6,37). All but one of the descriptions refer to a sacred tree(s) at the holy spot(s). The sacred tree of the soothsayers ('ēlōn; Judg. 9:37) is certainly outside the city and is probably the same as Abraham's sacred tree of instruction ('ēlōn; Gen. 12:6; also Deut. 11:30?). Conceivably this is the same as Jacob's "sacred tree which was near Shechem" (hā'ēlāh 'ªsher 'im shᵉkem; Gen. 35:4), especially if it is to be associated with the altar built by the patriarch on the plot of land he bought *adjacent* to the city (Gen. 33:18b–20). In spite of the form-critically detected hiatuses between the units in the Jacob cycle of stories, the probability is high that Genesis 33:20 and 35:4 refer to one and the same holy place.

Returning to Joshua 24, we observe that Joshua's stone is erected under a sacred tree in a Yahweh "sanctuary," but this *miqdāsh* was by no means necessarily an enclosed structure and there is no reason whatsoever to identify it with the temple of Baal-berith within the city. In fact, the only way it could be so identified is to assume that the Baal temple was reconsecrated for Yahweh worship by Joshua and that, subsequently, it lapsed once again into Baal worship, as evidenced in the story of Abimelech. It is much more plausible, given all the data, that the Yahweh-sanctified tree was outside the walls of Shechem and had previous sacred associations among the peoples who formed the Yahweh loyalists under the leadership of Joshua and his "house."

In fact, the account of Jacob collecting and burying "all the foreign gods that they [his household and all who were with him] had, and the rings that were in their ears . . . under the sacred tree which was near Shechem" (Gen. 35:4) has a striking formal similarity with aspects of the account in Joshua 24: both are reports of assemblies at sacred trees near Shechem where new deities were adopted and foreign gods were renounced.[501] The major and decisive difference between the two events is that Jacob calls the people to accept *his personal or "clan" God*, "who answered me in the day of my distress and has been with me wherever I have gone" (Gen. 35:3), whereas Joshua calls the people to accept *the intertribal God of the whole people Israel, i.e., Yahweh*, "who brought us up from Egypt, out of the state of slavery, . . . preserved us in all our journeys, . . . and drove out before us all the peoples, the Amorites who ruled in the land" (Josh. 24:17–18). In the one case it is a gathering of El-worshippers around the eponymous Jacob, while in the other case it is Israel confederating as a Yahwistic community. It is altogether likely that Genesis 35:1–4 alludes back to the creation of Elohistic Israel. Because that earlier commitment to an Israelite association took place in the highlands where the Joseph tribes settled as the champions of Yahweh, it has been described proleptically in Genesis 35:1–4 in terms of the later Josephite-dominated assembly detailed in Joshua 24.

The correctness of the distinction between the two holy places inside and outside Shechem is made conclusive once Judges 9:6 is properly translated. Abimelech is said to have been made king "beside the sacred tree [*ēlōn*] of the *mutstsāv* in Shechem." This unusual word is normally corrected to the far more common *matstsēvāh*, "pillar." Thus corrected, the text is thrown into connection with the great stone raised by Joshua under the sacred tree (Josh. 24:26), and, on that connection, exegetes proceed to locate the site of Joshua's assembly inside the city at the same holy spot where Abimelech was made king. The textual correction in Judges 9:6 is unnecessary, however, since in Isaiah 29:3, the offending *mutstsāv* occurs in poetic parallel with a word for siegeworks and appears to mean something like "palisade" or "embankment." Accordingly, we should read Judges 9:6 as follows: "by the sacred tree of the embankment [not pillar] in Shechem," thus locating Abimelech's investiture as king at a sacred tree in the precinct of Baal-berith in the fortified temple-palace complex of Beth-millo, and at the same time sharply separating the site from the Yahweh holy place and sacred tree beyond the city walls where stood a stone pillar commemorating the assembly of tribes under Joshua. When the text of Judges 9:6 is so clarified, insuring a firm demarcation between the sites of Judges 9:6 and of Joshua 24:26, the last remaining argument for locating the Israelite holy place inside the city of Shechem falls to the ground.[502]

Returning to the connection between the Israelite assembly near Shechem and the posited neutrality of the city of Shechem, it is necessary to stress the difference between the general Deuteronomic assumptions of the larger source in which Joshua 24 is set and the peculiar contrary presuppositions of the old underlying tradition in Joshua 24. The wider Deuteronomic assumption of a total conquest takes for granted that all the Cannanites have either been wiped out or hermetically sealed off from Israel. The report of the assembly, however, bears ancient features which either state or imply conditions at odds with the D traditionist's outlook. This can easily be seen by comparing Joshua 24 with its Deuteronomic parallel in Joshua 23 which relates a "final speech" of Joshua. The view that Joshua 24 is basically E source and that it has been supplemented at points with a second source, likely J, has considerable plausibility. There are indications of "doublet-like" literary and conceptual phenomena, and neither source is evidently Deuteronomic. Joshua 24 is pre-Deuteronomic but not homogeneous, having been reshaped in the light of the continuing liturgical practice of celebrating the covenant renewal.[503] Nevertheless, the text retains memories of pre-monarchic cult forms and recollections of an epochal event foundational for Israel as a whole. Form-critically, Joshua 24 shows a fusion of the Exodus-Settlement traditions and the Sinai covenant-and-law cultic modalities (III.12–13). The peculiar fusion of the traditions and the cultic modalities is not traceable to D bias, nor can it be wholly accounted for by the E traditionist's shaping of the material so as to warn solemnly against the apostasy that was a grave threat in his ninth-century northern Israelite milieu. For an adequate explanation of the form we are driven back to a distinctive socio-cultic organizational assembly summoned at, or close to, the beginning of Israel's formation in Canaan as a wider Yahwistic community.

The central novelty in Joshua 24, which shatters the typical cult proclamation framework, is simply this: many or all of the participants "choose" Yahweh for the first time after freely considering the option of "choosing," or more properly of retaining, other gods. The caption to the passage identifies the congregants as "all the tribes of Israel," but this can only make sense as a proleptic usage of the phrase.

The meaning is as follows: all those who were to *become* the tribes of Yahwistic Israel as a result of the covenant at Shechem gathered together to negotiate and make the fateful decision for or against a union of tribes in the new cult. They were not the tribes of Yahwistic Israel beforehand, although some of the congregants were probably members of Elohistic Israel. The obverse of this is the conclusion that not all the congregants necessarily entered Yahwistic Israel. Of course, the account does not tell us of any who declined; it is intent only on emphasizing that many groups assembled did renounce both the "clan" gods and the city-state gods in favor of Yahweh. If we look at the event in terms of the proposed model of Shechemite neutrality, I think it probable that Shechemites were present at the assembly but that they were among those who declined to enter Israel. At the same time, there was probably a division in the populace of the former city-state of Shechem which previously, under its now deposed petty king, had laid claim to a large region of the central hill country. The rural populace once dominated by Shechem was now free to enter into Israel as members of the tribe of Manasseh, while the city of Shechem proper remained separate from the organization and ideology of Israel. The city continued Baal worship and had its own form of self-rule. Shechem retained no more than the immediate fields surrounding the city as an agricultural support base for the populace, but its former feudal powers to extract human and material resources from its hinterland were surrendered *in toto*.

Other Cities in Manasseh

Although we lack traditions for other cities in the central highlands on the same scale as those for Shechem, it is probable that other Canaanite cities in Manasseh besides Shechem were also independent neutrals vis-à-vis Israel, their rule restricted to the walled settlement and the adjacent fields.

For example, it is reported that the kings of Hepher and Tirzah were defeated by Joshua (Josh.12:17,24). Also, according to the Davidic-Solomonic tribal lists (Josh. 17:2–3), these cities were reckoned as *mishpāḥôth* in Manasseh. Admittedly, the independent neutrality of Hepher and Tirzah for some time prior to their incorporation in Israel is not demonstrated from the terse data cited, since the same data could be explained by a conversion of the populations of those cities to Israel immediately upon the overthrow of their kings, or even by the assumption that the deposition of the kings referred to did not occur until the time of David. I am merely suggesting that what is clearly documented in the case of Shechem could also have been the case in other cities in Manasseh about which we know too little to be certain. For example, the city of Thebez, attacked by Abimelech after his suppression of the revolt in Shechem presumably because it too was involved in the insurrection (Judg. 9:50–55), was conceivably likewise an independent neutral city-state which Abimelech had brought under his rule along with Shechem.

Cities in Upper Galilee

The possibility that Shechem was not alone in its status of independent neutrality may also be indicated by the observation that "none of the cities that stood on mounds did Israel burn, except Hazor only" (Josh. 11:13). As a literal summary for all Israel, the claim is sharply contradicted by reports such as Judges 1:8 for Jerusalem and Judges 18:27 for Dan. If we grant, as I have argued, that an original local settlement annal underlies this part of the account, we may rather see Joshua 11:13 as an allusion only to the conditions of Israelite assumption of power in northern Galilee. Aharoni's archaeological survey of upper Galilee has found a considerable number of premonarchic settlements that were probably Israelite.[504] If we read the notation regionally to the effect that "none of the cities that stood on mounds in upper Galilee did Israel burn, except Hazor only," the apparently measurable Israelite settlement over upper Galilee could then be explained by the continuing coexistence of Israelite settlements side by side with Canaanite cities that had defeated their kings in local uprisings or whose kings had been defeated in the Battle of Merom by an army of Israelites (Josh. 11).

Jerusalem

The reported premonarchic contacts of Israel with Jerusalem are relatively few, and there is no scholarly consensus about the temporal order, the historical reliability, or the import of these rather obscurely reported events. In Genesis 14:18–20 Abraham is said to have met Melchizedek, priest-king of Salem, in a ceremonial meal after battle. The phrase "king of Salem" probably originally meant "a covenanted king" (see note 415). There is little doubt, however, that by the time of the monarchy this was understood as "king of (Jeru)salem." In Joshua 10, Jerusalem is ruled by Adonizedek, who leads a five-city coalition against Gibeon and Israel and is defeated and killed. In Judges 1:1–8, a king named Adonibezek is defeated by Israel, carried to Jerusalem where he dies, and the city itself is captured and set on fire and its populace killed. Judges 1:21 and Josh. 15:63 pointedly state, on the other hand, that the indigenous populace of Jebusites remained securely in control of Jerusalem. In Judges 19, a Levite travelling northward from Bethlehem with his concubine and male servant passes by Jerusalem as night falls. The servant suggests that they spend the night there, but the Levite replies: "We will not turn aside into a foreign city ('ir nokrī [yyāh?]) which is not an affiliated member of Israel" (vs 12). The travel party continues on its way and spends the night in Gibeath of Benjamin.

Without undertaking a fresh and thorough historical and literary examination of all these passages,[505] we can at least note the range of probabilities in any reconstruction of the sociopolitical status of Jerusalem vis-à-vis Israel prior to the Israelite seizure of the city by David (II Sam. 5:6–9). We may speak of a maximalist and a minimalist view of the pre-Israelite Jerusalemite traditions. The maximalist view regards all of the above passages as in fact pertaining to Jerusalem. Salem in Genesis 14:17 is taken as a shortened form of Jerusalem and the name of the ruler Melchizedek, formed with the root zdk (tsdk), "to be righteous," is compared with the name of the king of Jerusalem in Joshua 10, i.e., Adonizedek. In Judges 1:1–8 Adonibezek is understood as a corruption of Adonizedek of Jerusalem who was brought home to die after his defeat in battle by Judah. Some of the maximalist interpretations even allow that Jerusalem was attacked and partially destroyed before David captured it, but that either the Israelites withdrew and allowed the Jebusites to return to the city or else only some part of the city was taken, perhaps the citadel or lower city, leaving the rest in Jebusite hands.

The minimalist view, on the other hand, denies that either Genesis 14 or Judges 1:1–7 had any original connection with Jerusalem. In the former passage, Salem is doubted as a proper name in context, zdk (tsdk) is noted as a rather common element in compound names and in no sense peculiar to Jerusalem, and Jerusalem is seen as an inexplicable shift of scene ill-fitting the preceding focus on Sodom and Hebron. In the latter passage, Adonibezek as a misreading for Adonizedek is rejected since, among other difficulties, it leaves us with two discrepant accounts of how that king met his fate (cf. Josh. 10:1–5, 22–27 and Judg. 1:6–7). Moreover, the report in Judges 1:8 of Jerusalem's capture and destruction, entirely at odds with Judges 1:21, is viewed as an editorial consequence of the false association of Adonibezek with Jerusalem.

In this cursory review of the parameters of interpretation, I have given only some of the most frequent arguments without going into all details or attempting to show the complex and idiosyncratic views of particular scholars. My own inclinations are decisively toward a minimalist view; insofar as Jerusalem is present in Genesis 14, it looks as though it serves a monarchic apologetic function; and insofar as Jerusalem is present in Judges 1:1–8, it is due to an attempt to make sense of the hazy figure of Adonibezek long after there was any clear information about his original geopolitical point of attachment.

What I would like to stress, however, is that on either of these general lines of interpretation of the premonarchic Jerusalemite traditions, the position of Jerusalem vis-à-vis Israel is much the same in sociopolitical typological terms: Jerusalem was one of the Canaanite city-states that at first vehemently resisted the rise of Israel in the highlands. It suffered defeat at the hands of Israel and was hemmed in by Judean settlements to its immediate south and Benjaminite settlements to its immediate north, all the while keeping its populace intact and maintaining its autonomy (apparently without a king) until David took the city and made it the capital of the Israelite state. If Jerusalem is regarded as integral to Genesis 14, an earlier stage is added in which Abraham and his 'apiru band were in alliance with the city. If Jerusalem is accepted in Judges 1:1–8, the defeat of

Jerusalemite forces in the field was followed up by an attack on the city which, however, did not have lasting effects, since the Jebusites continued to exercise self-rule until David ended their independence. On either outlook, the exact fate of the king of Jerusalem defeated by Israel is problematic. According to Judges 1:7, he died of his battle wounds and/or mutilation in Jerusalem. According to Joshua 10:22–27, he was killed at the cave of Makkedah in the Judean foothills after his capture. Even if we discount Judges 1:7 as a late editorial confusion, the identity of the kings slain at the cave of Makkedah is open to some question. Noth thinks, for example, that instead of the five kings of the Gibeonite campaign (Josh. 10:1–15), the older form of the tradition told how the kings of the cities named in Joshua 10:29–32,34–39 were executed by the Israelites at Makkedah, and, in that case, the king of Jerusalem was not among them.[506]

In any event, all the evidence points to an idependent Jerusalem existing as an enclave in a heavily settled Israelite area right up to the moment of its capture by David. Moreover, after the Adonizedek-led coalition against Gibeon was frustrated, Jerusalem does not appear as an aggressive city trying to attack and expel Israelites from its region, nor does it appear as a beleaguered city, itself under pressure by the Israelites (unless one assumes that the attack of Judges 1:8 was historical and that it is not a doublet of the defeat of Adonizedek recounted in Joshua 10, but occurred between Adonizedek's defeat and David's capture of Jerusalem). The fact that Israelite settlements virtually surrounded Jerusalem on the north, west, and south (Gibeah, Nephtoah, Manahath, Bethlehem) indicates that Israel freely controlled the former environs of Jerusalem to within a few miles of the city. This could only have been possible if Jerusalem's previous sway over the countryside (reflected in the Amarna letters and in Joshua 10) had been neutralized. The Levite, travelling from Bethlehem to Gibeah (Judg. 19:10–15), passes unworried within sight of Jerusalem. His servant regards it as natural for an Israelite to stop there. The priest declines to enter the city, not because he is afraid, but simply because it is not a part of Israel and he prefers to travel on to the first Israelite settlement only a few miles to the north.

All the evidence suggests that, once the king of Jerusalem was defeated in battle (and probably also killed) by Israel, apparently in the late thirteenth or early twelfth century, he was not replaced by another monarch. The impression is rather of either a formal or a de facto recognition of the dominance of intertribal Israel in the region and of a live-and-let-live policy between both parties. According to my view of Israelite origins, Judah proper did not become a part of the intertribal Israelite confederation before the period 1100–1050 B.C. On this understanding, Jerusalem was situated between the intertribal formation of Israel to the north (Benjamin being its immediate neighbor) and proto-Israelite Judah to the south for a century or more before Judah was admitted to the Israelite confederacy. Possibly the report of an attack upon Jerusalem in Judges 1:8 is a fragment of proto-Israelite Judean or Simeonite history which was poorly coordinated with the other Israelite traditions about contact with Jerusalem. Because Adonibezek remains such a shadowy figure, it is difficult to pursue such an hypothesis fruitfully.

In any event, it is noticeable that when David takes the city there is no mention of a Jebusite king ruling in Jerusalem (II Sam. 5:6–9). The resistance David encounters from the Jebusites may be understood as their strenuous objection to his breaking the state of neutrality which had prevailed between the city and its proto-Israelite and Israelite environs for more than a century. Moreover, David's willingness to leave the Jebusite population intact within the city, even after it became the capital of his kingdom, probably reflects the preceding state of truce between Jerusalem and Israel/Judah. David acted unilaterally to violate the status quo between Jerusalem and Israel, but he did not wholly abolish it, for he retained the Jebusites in their former home, even through this put them in the administrative heart of his new Israelite kingdom.

The consequence of the preceding discussion of Canaanite "neutrality" toward Israel is that the usual antinomy in conceptualizing the settlement, namely, to assume either that a city was captured or that it held out under its established royal leadership, needs to be modified. One qualification is the outright conversion of the entire populace to Israelite society and religion, excluding of course the resistant deposed or executed leaders and their agents. A second qualification, here proposed chiefly on the evidence from Shechem and Jerusalem, is that a city might lose its king and be "defeudalized" by the impact of the Israelite uprising, but still remain unabsorbed in the wider Israelite movement for some time. With this hypothesis in mind it should be possible to review the traditions of the settlement with a more sensitive and finely calibrated spectrum of Canaanite responses to Israel in mind.

45.3 Alliance: The Local Populace Enters Protective Treaty Relations with Israel

As to the mode of Canaanite "alliance" with Israel, I have in mind situations wherein city-states entered direct treaty relations with Israel which put them under special obligation and provided them special protection; these were apparently cities that stood in the shadow of stronger nearby city-states from whose onerous claims they sought to escape by entering the Israelite protectorate.

Gibeon and the Hivite/Hurrian Cities

The clearest example of Canaanite allies of Israel is the status of Gibeon and the Hivite-Hurrian cities that took the initiative in approaching Israel and arranging a treaty (Josh. 9). Of course, the actual provisions of that treaty are sadly obscured by the late traditionist's interest in using the incident to offer an aetiology for the much later participation of "Gibeonites" in the temple cult as second- or third-class attendants. Joshua 9—10 makes no mention of kings in the cities that contract treaty with Israel. On the other hand, the immediate intervention of a league of cities headed by Jerusalem suggests that the Hurrian cities in Benjamin were under the sovereignty of Jerusalem until they dared to invoke Israel's counter-protection.

When we combine Joshua 9—10 with the traditions about Saul and the Gibeonites (II Sam. 4:1–3; 21:1–14), we derive the following skeletal picture of the treaty connection between Israel and the four Hurrian cities: the Gibeonites entered into the worship of Yahweh, which means that there was no place in Gibeon for the worship of Baal such as was continued in the neutral Shechem. Although II Samuel 21:2 sharply separates the Gibeonites from Israel ("who were not of the people of Israel, but of the remnant of the Amorites"), Gibeonites themselves speak of their right to "a place in the territory of Israel" (II Sam. 21:5), and they fluently invoke the sanctions of Yahweh on the house of Saul for having violated the covenant between Israel and Gibeon.

Also, it seems that a Canaanite city entering treaty relations with Israel committed itself to military defense of Israel. To be sure, Joshua 10 represents Gibeon in an entirely passive position, the object of attack by Jerusalem and its allies and the suppliant of military assistance from Israel. The passivity of Gibeon is the function of the magnification of Yahweh and Israel and is no trustworthy guide to the orginal treaty. The fact that Gibeon could call on Israelite military aid implies that the treaty stipulated reciprocal defense obligation, requiring that when Israel was attacked, Gibeon and the Hurrian cities were expected to come to its assistance. According to Joshua 10:2, Israel acquired an enviable military ally when it made treaty with Gibeon, for the latter was able to field an army more impressive than that of some royal cities such as Ai. Presumably the Gibeonite troops had been kept in readiness for use as auxiliary forces by their Jerusalemite suzerain. Adonizedek of Jerusalem, knowing at first hand the military prowess of his vassal Gibeon, felt secure in attacking the city only when he had mustered forces from the allied cities of Hebron, Jarmuth, Lachish, and Eglon (Josh. 10:3–5).

The assumption of a mutual defense clause in the treaty between Israel and the Hurrian cities seems further supported by the inclusion of those cities in the cult of Yahweh. To be a worshipper of Yahweh meant commitment to the common social project of Israel and thus willingness to come to the aid of Yahweh whenever Israel was under attack. That these Hurrian cities in Benjamin were not simply the recipients of Israelite military aid is corroborated by the report that two men of Beeroth, one of the four cities in question, were captains of raiding parties in the service of Ishbaal, son of Saul (II Sam. 4:2–3). Of course, it is not obvious that we can draw a direct line of connection between the military activity of Beerothites before the monarchy and Beerothites during the monarchy. The fact, however, that these captains were serving under Ishbaal, and thus very likely earlier under Saul—i.e., prior to the major military reorganization under David—heightens the probability that they represented continuity with a premonarchic tradition of military service rendered to Israel by Beerothites.

Meroz

In the context of a model of Canaanite cities as "allies" of Israel, Alt's proposal that Meroz in Judges 5:23 was a Canaanite city in Manasseh takes on particular interest. If with Alt we imagine it to have been a city close to the site of the battle and thus under the geopolitical domination of one of the large fortified cities on the edge of the plain of Esdraelon (such as Jokneam, Megiddo, Taanach, or Ibleam),[507] Meroz's situation suggests parallels with the position of Gibeon, Chephirah, Beeroth, and Kireath-Jearim vis-à-vis Jerusalem. Assuming that Meroz threw off royal rule under the stimulus of the Israelite uprising, we can imagine the danger in which it stood from the nearby heavily centralized Canaanite city-states that continued to oppose Israel. The only recourse for Meroz, if it wished to capitalize on its new-found freedom from onerous royal control, was to invoke the protection of Israel by treaty arrangements. The wording of Judges 5:23, with its vehement curse of Meroz for failing to live up to its commitment, implies that Meroz had entered into the cult of Yahweh, or at the very least that the treaty with Israel had involved the sanctions of Yahweh. But at the last minute Meroz had reneged in its commitment to send troops to the battle. Its leaders (yōsh^{e}vīm) may have gotten "cold feet" in the face of the massed chariot force which the Canaanite allies mustered against Israel.

Succoth and Penuel

Succoth and Penuel were Transjordanian cities on or near the Wadi Jabbok, apparently located in the territory of Gad (cf. Josh. 13:27). The noncooperation of the leaders of these cities with Gideon against the Midianites (Judg. 8:4–17) has been noted as analogous to the earlier refusal of the Gileadites/Gadites to respond to the war against the Canaanite kings led by Barak and Deborah (Judg. 5:17). There is, I think, a more plausible explanation of the behavior of the men of Succoth and Penuel and of Gideon in his reaction to their rebuff.

The key to a more discriminating view of the incident is found in noting what it was that Gideon demanded of the cities which they refused to give him. Gideon did *not* ask Succoth and Penuel to join in the battle, in itself surprising had they been Israelite settlements, since their locations along the Jabbok acquainted them at first hand with the terrain through which the elusive Midianites had hurried as they retreated eastward. Instead of making appeals for manpower, Gideon asks only that his hungry troops be given food. The leaders of Succoth and Penuel derisively reject the request, for they have little confidence that Gideon will be able to overtake the Midianites, much less to defeat them. Mistakenly, as events turn out, they fail to anticipate that Gideon will not only make short shrift of the Midianites but will speedily return to punish the recalcitrant leaders in Succoth and Penuel. Indeed, Gideon's reprisal by executing the offending officials, including torture in the case of the leaders of Succoth, was extreme—even unparalleled—against those who had taken no agressive actions toward his forces.

If, on the other hand, Succoth and Penuel were Canaanite cities in a protective alliance with Israel, both Gideon's request and his indignant reprisal at its rejection become more understandable. According to my analysis in the cases of Gibeon and Meroz, Canaanite cities in protective alliance with Israel were bound by a mutual defense pact. In this instance, Gideon does not ask for armed assistance, perhaps in part because he already has sufficient support from other Israelite tribes (cf. Judg. 7:23–25), but perhaps also because of prior evidence leading him to question the dependability of the allies in Succoth and Penuel. Had those cities been double-dealing by taking sides with the Midianites as long as the latter held the upper hand in Transjordan?

In any case, Gideon asks for what is even more urgent than additional troops, namely, food so that his weary men can take up hot pursuit of the camel-riding Midianites. When the officials of Succoth and Penuel haughtily refuse his request for a measure of help less than he could rightly demand of allies (and possibly already suspicious of their loyalty), Gideon is particularly incensed. The leaders of the allied cities have reneged on the treaty terms. They have in fact given aid and comfort to the fleeing Midianites by refusing to provision the Israelite forces. Gideon's swift avowal of punishment on the spot, and his prompt administration thereof after "finishing off" the Midianites, may be understood as a determination to impose sanction on faithless treaty partners. Even so, Gideon does not appear to destroy either the cities or their inhabitants indiscriminately. He takes great care to single out only the responsible officials. "The men of Penuel" (Judg. 8:17) are equal in rank to "the men of Succoth" (Judg. 8:8), who are further specified as seventy-seven "officials and elders" (Judg. 8:6,14). The demolition of the tower in Penuel doubtless ensued when the officials fled there to escape Gideon's retribution (vs. 17). The story does not tell us enough to judge whether the protective alliance with Succoth and Penuel was considered null and void following its violation, with the result that the cities were either thrust outside the Israelite protective network or incorporated directly into Israel, or whether the protective alliance was renewed with newly appointed local leaders.

There are additional indications that Succoth and Penuel may properly be construed as Canaanite city-states in alliance with Israel. Although the mere reference to the local leaders as "officials" (sārīm) and "elders" (zᵉqēnīm) does not distinguish them as Canaanites, both of these terms are elsewhere applied to leaders in Canaanite or other non-Israelite cities or regimes (cf. Num. 22:7,14;

Jer. 48:7 [of Moab]; Josh. 9:11 [of Gibeon]; Judges 9:30 [of Shechem]; II Sam. 10:3 [of Ammon]; Ezek. 27:9 [of Byblos]). What, then, are the probabilities from a wider historical context that Succoth and Penuel were either Canaanite or Israelite cities at this period? It is noteworthy that prior to the monarchy, when Solomon had the temple vessels cast at Succoth (I Kings 7:46; II Chron. 4:17) and Jeroboam refurbished Penuel as a temporary or alternate capital of his kingdom (I Kings 12:25), neither city had any prominence in Israelite history apart from the incident in Judges 8. The mentions in the Jacob stories are tangential, in fact little more than word plays on Succoth ("booths") as the place where Jacob made shelters for his animals (Gen. 33:17) and on Peniel = Penuel = "the face of El" as the place where Jacob glimpsed the face of God as he wrestled with an assailant (Gen. 32:30 [31]). Neither allusion gives much reason for thinking that there were Israelite settlements at Succoth and Penuel in premonarchic times, although they may reflect the association of proto-Israelite "Jacob" groups with the Jabbok region.

Further supporting the Canaanite status, at least of Penuel, is Y. Aharoni's observation about the tower at Penuel, which Gideon demolished:

> We do not know who the inhabitants of these towns [Succoth and Penuel] were, but the reference to a tower at Penuel, which brings to mind the tower of Shechem, strongly suggests that it belonged to a Canaanite enclave in the Gad-Gilead region like the one at nearby Zaphon which had been absorbed by Gad.[508]

Aharoni is not more precise as to what he understands the status of "a Canaanite enclave" to have been, or what it meant for such an enclave to have been "absorbed" into an Israelite tribe. He also inclines to the belief that Succoth was Israelite, on the far from convincing reasoning that *only* its leaders were punished by Gideon, whereas a careful comparison of Judges 8:6,8,14,17 discloses that it was likewise *only* the leaders of Penuel who were slain.

Regrettably there is little direct light thrown on the status of Succoth by the intriguing finds at Tel Deir 'Alla, including a Late Bronze Age sanctuary and ruins of furnaces and metal slag dating on into the Iron Age.[509] The identification of the mound as Succoth is far from assured; the excavator believes that the site was primarily a regional metallurgical and cultic center with a strictly seasonal population, and he prefers to locate Succoth proper on one of the several as yet unexcavated mounds in the well-watered vicinity of Tell Deir 'Alla.[510] Indeed, the dramatic destruction of the sanctuary in the first part of the twelfth century was caused, not by military attack, but by an earthquake and fire. Although the reoccupation shows a lower cultural level, there is nothing to distinguish it as "Canaanite" or "Israelite" within the terms of the sociopolitical paradigms we are exploring.

All in all, there seem to be reasonable grounds for hypothesizing that Succoth and Penuel, once freed from the domain of Sihon the Amorite ruler (cf. Josh. 13:27), declined to enter Israel as full members but concluded protective treaty arrangements with Israel, or with the surrounding tribe(s) of Gad and possibly Machir=Manasseh. Incidentally, in none of the passages attesting Canaanite city-states as protective allies of Israel is there firm evidence to distinguish whether the alliances were contracted between the city-states and the entire Israelite confederacy or between the city-states and one or more adjacent tribe(s). Positing, as I do, that the protective treaties were mutual defense pacts, it seems to me most probable that the Israelite endorsement of a protective alliance will have been participated in by representatives of all the tribes, even though the initiative and negotiating of terms in any given treaty may have fallen to the tribe in closest contact with the Canaanite partner.

As interpreted here, Succoth and Penuel still enjoyed the status of Canaanite allies of Israel in the time of Gideon. When they coldly violated their duties under the treaty, the city leaders were dealt severe punishment by death, in a manner analogous to the retribution heaped on Saul's family for his violation of the similar treaty with Gibeon (II Sam. 21:1–14). Being reciprocal pacts, both parties were subject to sanctions, and the execution of Saul's sons shows that Israel was not exempt from the treaty sanctions even though it was the stronger and superior party.

For how long did Succoth and Penuel continue as Canaanite cities in protective treaty with Israel? Nothing further is said about the two cities until Succoth is listed among the holdings of Gad in the allotment inventory of Joshua 13:27. In general we have seen that the allotment lists describe the approximate holdings of the tribes at the time David was elevated as king over all Israel (IV.17.3), revised, however, to include Canaanite territories incorporated into the several tribes functioning as administrative units of David's kingdom. Thus, it is not possible to determine definitively whether the occurrence of Succoth in Joshua 13:27 means that it had become a fully Israelite city by the time of David or whether it means that Succoth, along with all the other Canaanite cities within his kingdom, was for the first time absorbed into Israel by David. Nor should too much be made of the absence of Penuel from the allotment lists, since the coverage of cities in these inventories is far from complete. In any event, David's incorporation of all the Canaanite cities into his kingdom swept away the peculiar arrangements of Israel with Canaanite cities that stood either as independent neutrals or as quasi-independent allies within the intertribal sociopolitical order of Israel. How the previous status of the Canaanite cities, whether as belligerents, neutrals, or allies, affected the manner in which they were consolidated socially and administratively is not apparent because of the lack of direct information about David's program of incorporation.

A closer determination of the timing and circumstances of Succoth's entrance into Israel might be possible if we knew how it reacted to the growing Philistine penetration into the northern Jordan Valley from 1050 b.c. onward. There must have been considerable pressure on Succoth, vulnerably located at the point where the Wadi Jabbok debouches into the Jordan Valley, in contrast to Penuel, better protected in the hill country to the east, to take a firm decision for capitulation to the Philistines or to seek the greater protection that full incorporation into Israel would offer. By the time of the Philistine defeat of Saul, it is most likely that the Philistines came into complete control of Succoth, if not before. Whether prior to that debacle, in order to stave off the Philistine menace, Succoth had directly entered Israel, we have no way of judging other than to admit the possibility on one interpretation of Joshua 13:27. The probabilities are that the settlements of Succoth and Penuel were among those allied Canaanite cities standing formally outside Israel either until the Philistine threat undermined their independence or until David's spectacular victories marked them for consolidation into the new Israelite state.

Kenites / Rechabites

There are aspects of the fragmentary traditions about the Kenites/Rechabites that seem best explained on the hypothesis that a treaty of alliance was in effect between them and the Israelites. The Midianites were at first on friendly terms with Israel during the wilderness wanderings—until conflict broke out between them over the control of Transjordan as the Midianites tried to establish and maintain hegemony over a lucrative trading empire in that region. On the other hand, the Kenites/Rechabites, represented as a sub-group of the Midianites, are pictured in consistently close association with Israel in an unbroken line of friendship undisturbed by Israelite-Midianite warfare.

Also to be noted is the considerable evidence that the Kenites/Rechabites were metal craftsmen whose life-traits—previously thought to speak for their pastoral nomadic status—tend rather in the direction of craft itinerancy or of semi-permanent settlement among other peoples as craft specialists. For purposes of this analysis, Kenites and Rechabites will be treated as a homogeneous group, although the traditions are elusive about the precise relation between them. From all appearances, Rechabites were a sub-group of Kenites who came to prominence during the monarchy and may have been specialists in chariot-making. As to their distribution in Israel, Kenites enter the Negeb around Arad with Judah and settle down among the Judeans (Judg. 1:16). Heber the Kenite separates from his fellows and sets up his trade in lower Galilee (Judg. 4:11). Kenites are living among the Amalekites in the Negeb (I Sam. 15:6–7). During the monarchy, Rechabites are found in Samaria (II Kings 10:15–27) and in the vicinity of Jerusalem, within whose walls they seek protection during the Neo-Babylonian invasion of Judah (Jer. 35:1–11).

In recent years it has been argued with persuasion that Exodus 18 describes, and other texts presuppose, a formal treaty of friendship between Israelites and Kenites.[511] The assumption of such a mutual defense alliance illuminates certain traditions that otherwise merely imply nepotism based on the intermarriage ties between Moses and Jethro and their descendants. If Israelites and Kenites shared in a mutual defense alliance, it is understandable that Jael the Kenitess killed Sisera the Canaanite, since in that event the specific treaty terms with Israel took precedence over the general rule of hospitality to a stranger in one's home (Judg. 4:11–22; 5:24–27). An Israelite-Kenite treaty of alliance would also explain Saul's warning to the Kenites who lived among the Amalekites that he was about to attack the Amalekites. This advance notice to the Kenites gave them time to separate themselves from their hosts so that they would not suffer harm from the Israelite attack (I Sam. 15:6–7). It is not likely that Saul would have issued such an early warning merely as a personal or family favor, since the maneuver risked "tipping off" the Amalekites that an attack was impending, whereas the heavy obligation of an alliance treaty weighing on Saul could not easily be evaded. This point is less than decisive of course, if only because it was Saul who violated Israel's treaty with Gibeon (II Sam. 21:1–14).

Certain anomalies in the Israelite-Kenite relationship resist easy categorization, however. Exodus 18 anchors the treaty during Israel's wilderness wanderings when it was arranged between Moses and his father-in-law, the Midianite-Kenite Jethro. If that is historically accurate, and the Kenites were already in league with the exodus Yahwists, their relationship does not correspond closely to the other alliances described or hypothesized above, namely, alliances between Israel and Canaanite city-states. On the other hand, one pentateuchal tradition insists that even though Moses strongly urged Jethro to accompany Israel as it moved on to Canaan, Jethro emphatically declined (Num. 10:29–32). This may be understood as the tradition's oblique way of saying that the Kenites associated with Israel in the land of Canaan were not from the desert after all, but first compacted with Israel within the land itself. It would not be at all surprising if Israelite traditionists, noting that both the Kenites and Moses' father-in-law were Midianites, have retrojected the Israelite-Kenite treaty into the archetypal wilderness period, thereby conceiving it as a compact entered by the eponymous Moses and Jethro. The tendency to conceive the Kenites eponymously and to genealogize their affinity with Israel is given another form in the ancestral figure of Cain, "a fugitive and wanderer," from whose line spring tent-dwelling cattle breeders, musicians and, through Tubal-cain, forgers of instruments in bronze and iron (Gen. 4:14–22). Unfortunately, the English spelling "Cain" obscures the fact that in Hebrew *qayin* is both the collectivity of Kenites (also in the gentilic form *qēnī*) and the proper name of Cain = Kenite.

From cognate Semitic terms we can establish that the term Kenite refers to a "metal worker" or "smith." This suggests that the primary principle of organization among the Kenites was occupational specialization and that the tendency of biblical tradition to derive the Kenites from the eponymns Jethro or Cain (and in the case of the Rechabites from J[eh]onadab ben Rechab or from Rechab himself) is a way of phrasing guild solidarities and relationships in kinship language. This in turn opens up the possibility that guilds of metal workers scattered over Canaan were brought into a treaty relationship with Israel, thereby becoming Yahwists, receiving a protected status under Israel and offering their services to Israel. More conjecturally, several of the confusions and discrepancies in Kenite traditions might be explained if we were to assume: (1) a treaty with a group of metal workers at an early stage in Israelite history, perhaps initiated by the exodus Moses group; and (2) a continuing entrance of Canaanite metal-working Kenites (= "smiths") into the same formal treaty relationship with Israel. The fact that Kenites were actually congeries of variously originated metal workers would account for the alternate ways in which biblical traditions try to genealogize the relationships among them.

The notion of Kenites as variously originated and specializing metal workers may also illuminate their wide distribution in Israel and the apparent variety in their residency and itinerancy patterns. Kenites are most frequently mentioned in sections of the Negeb or southern Judah, but they appear also in Samaria and lower Galilee. There are said to be "cities of the Kenites" in the Negeb (I Sam. 30:29), and Kenites are mentioned in conjunction with settlements at Hammath (I Chron. 2:55), Irnahash, "copper city" (I Chron. 4:12; reading "Rechab" in place of "Recah") and Zanoah (Josh. 15:56–57). On the other hand, Heber the Kenite seems to have lived in the countryside beside a prominent oak tree (Judg. 4:11). The Rechabite community that sought refuge in Jerusalem is called a "house," presided over by Jaazaniah, but the size of its membership and its former place of residence are unspecified. Viewed socioeconomically, metallurgical skills can be practiced in settlements given over wholly to that craft, or in sections of larger towns and cities with mixed craft specializations, or at any point in the countryside with access to raw materials or to customers, depending on whether the craftsman is at the moment making metal articles or selling and mending them as a tinker, or both. The apparent range in the living conditions of the biblical Kenites corresponds to the range in the living and working conditions of smiths.

Apparently the Kenites were not themselves militarized. Instead of military services or food provisions that allies such as Gibeon, Meroz, Succoth, and Penuel owed to Israel, Kenites were able to substitute the highly prized metal farming implements, household tools, and weapons. These smiths depended on those among whom they lived both for protection and for food. Because they were not restricted to a single city or region, but moved in pursuit of their craft, Kenites could be found among non-Israelite peoples. Even though they remained in treaty with Israel, they could do business with outsiders provided their services to foreigners did not harm Israel. This may explain the fact that Saul advised the Kenites to separate from the Amalekites but did not call upon the Kenites to join in the attack against Amalek. The hypothesis that the Kenites were nonmilitarized and free to serve non-Israelites, as long as the Israelite-Kenite treaty of alliance was honored, also throws light on the report that "there was peace between Jabin king of Hazor and the house of Heber the Kenite" (Judg. 4:17). This may mean that Heber was under contract to make metal goods for Hazor. When Hazor spearheaded a military league against Israel, Heber and his wife Jael were forced to chose between one loyalty and another by the turn of fate that brought Sisera to their tent. Because Heber was a nonmilitarized craftsman he was not expected to fight in the battle, either by the Canaanites or by Israel. His wife Jael, however, became a voluntary "combatant" when the enemy leader entered her tent and presented her with a golden opportunity to kill him.

The above remarks do not speak directly for or against the hypothesis that it was the Kenites who contributed the belief in Yahweh to Israel as a whole, nor do they depend upon that theory.[512] Insofar, however, as I have proposed a possible formal comparability between Israel's alliances with Gibeon, Meroz, Succoth, and Penuel and Israel's alliance with the Kenites, it may be said that the conception is not so much that of Kenite religion spreading to Israel as it is the conception of Kenites coming into relation with a superior partner and accepting the cult of Israel. Nevertheless, if there was a pre-settlement treaty of exodus proto-Israelites with Kenites (and I am not at all certain of this), it remains a possibility that Yahwism did come to Israel via the Kenites. There is still the difficulty that the texts thought by some enthusiasts to speak tellingly for the Kenite origin of Yahwism (e.g., Exod. 18) are by no means conclusive or even probable evidence for that reading of Yahwistic origins.

45.4 Summary and Implications: Status of
Non-Israelite Cities in the Israelite Highlands

The fact that Canaanite cities struggling to be free of domination by their stronger neighbors, or to throw off their own oppressive rulers, should turn to Israel for support bespeaks a massive shift in the balance of power in Canaan, or at any rate in the highlands of Canaan. As much as anything in the traditions, this client relationship of particular cities (or of guilds such as the Kenites) to Israel shows how far Israel had progressed beyond the resourceful but marginal adaptation of the 'apiru to the oppressive Canaanite sociopolitical conditions. It was no longer a situation where small groups of oppressed peoples worked out diverse survival modes and techniques that ultimately bowed to the superior power of the hierarchical power system. Now whole cities and occupational groups could stand up to their kings and to neighboring kings, eliminate them or neutralize their control, and find support in a broad coalition of tribal groups unified in their determination to overthrow oppression. If our delineation of the "alliance" mode of Canaanite response to Israel is accurate, it was possible for city-states to enter the protective coalition of Israel without totally surrendering the social forms peculiar to each urban center.[513] There was leeway for transitional responses, for groups that had been traumatized and stultified by royal-aristocratic institutions to find their way slowly and by stages into full membership in Israel.

Our study has, of course, made it abundantly clear that the fealty of Canaanite allies to Israel was not massively unshaken, any more than the willingness of Israelite tribes to come to one another's defense was uniformly sustained. Faced with the Canaanite chariots, the leaders of Meroz reneged on their obligation to join the battle at the summons of Barak and Deborah, and thereby earned for themselves a vehement curse in the victory song. In doubt of Gideon's strength in Transjordan and probably also under counter-pressure from the Midianites, the leaders of Succoth and Penuel declined even to provision Israelite forces. Nor, in fact, did the Israelite tribes always honor the protective treaties from their side, any more than those tribes were able always to overcome friction or avoid fighting among themselves. The treachery of Saul toward the loyal Gibeonites is sordid evidence of the reality of broken treaties on Israel's part, not to mention the cunning advantage that Abimelech took of the Shechemites in thrusting them farther back into oppressive hierarchic government than they had bargained for when this renegade Israelite broke definitively, and calamitously for himself, with the Israelite antimonarchic sociopolitical union.

Even when we acknowledge that there were breaches of protective alliance from both sides, the network of treaty relations between Israel and its Canaanite allies, coupled with the neutralization of other Canaanite cities, must be judged as largely effective in securing a nonexploitative framework for the cities and in providing buffers for Israel against the remaining hostile city-states, just as the overall collaboration of Israelite tribes managed to surmount the debilitating effects of indifference, rivalry, and occasional open conflict. The general effectiveness of such loose confederacies and alliance networks, in spite of frequent divisive counter-incidents, is well attested among other peoples at somewhat similar levels of sociopolitical organization.

We may cite, by way of example, the Iroquois Five Nations Confederacy of upper New York (eventually Six Nations when remnants of the Tuscaroras of North Carolina joined the league about 1710 A.D.)[514] It is less often realized that the core confederacy of the Iroquois, expanded by conquest, offer of sanctuary, and adoption mechanisms, reached out in a much wider network of protective alliances with additional tribes extending southward into Pennsylvania, northward into Canada, and westward into Ohio. The socially intricate and territorially extensive network of Iroquois ties, accomplished entirely in the absence of state organization, was a remarkable adaptive formation which gave the Iroquois far more resiliency and endurance against the encroaching French, Dutch, English, and Americans than any other eastern tribes were able to muster. While by no means analogous to the Iroquois league in all respects, the Israelite confederate achievement was similar to the Iroquois undertaking in being no easily arranged or smoothly maintained monolithic unity, either among the member tribes or with their Canaanite allies; but it was, like the Iroquois league, a functionally effective unity for some two centuries or more, steadily assisted by the developing Yahwistic culture and by grim reminders of the dangers of relapse into subjugation by hierarchic states always ready to take advantage of the slightest faltering in Israelite intertribal and treaty ties.

With such evidence of varying Canaanite modes of response to Israel, we begin to appreciate that there were many alternatives to the total destruction of enemy cities. Since the enemies of Israel were the city-state leaders with their imperial-feudal claims over entire territories, once that leadership was overthrown and any further revival of such leadership prevented, the cities might relate themselves to Israel in ways that differed according to local conditions. Much depended upon how extensively a city was destroyed in the uprising of the populace, or in the attack by Israelites from outside the city, or in the chain effect of an attack that triggered revolt or lent support to revolt already underway. We have seen evidence that some of the kings were defeated in battle in the open country, and thus their cities may have been spared destruction altogether. A badly destroyed city might not be worth rebuilding. The value of walled cities as fixed fortifications was not so great for early Israel, since it depended greatly on mobile guerrilla warfare. Houses that remain standing might be occupied, or temporary structures built from the ruins of the former city. In many instances the populace dispersed into smaller rural settlements or built a replacement for the destroyed site not far away.

The essential thing from Israel's point of view was to abolish the expropriative reign of the cities over the countryside. With that accomplished, there were options for the city populace to incorporate directly into Israel, to enter treaty relations while remaining quasi-independent, and even to continue outside the cult and social system of Israel altogether as long as the city populace did not try to impose control on Israelites or to give aid to other city-states threatening Israel. In any case, the life of these cities was profoundly affected by the Israelite revolution, no matter what their precise form of accommodation to Israel. The city no longer held the upper hand over the countryside. Now unable to preempt the wealth of the rural areas and to impress the rural populace into its interminable wars with other cities, or to build its fortifications and palaces, the city declined markedly in opulence and ceased to have the great attraction it formerly had as a place to get rich, or at least to live comfortably, by currying the favor of kings and aristocrats.

Those cities that did not enter the Israelite confederation doubtless soon discovered that their opportunities for high living were sharply reduced, and increasingly they had to come to economic terms with Israel, which controlled the greater part of the agricultural wealth of their environs and with whom they would have to deal if they were to survive. The luxury trades in the cities declined, for there was no longer a rich leisured class to support them. Other trades, serving basic needs—such as weaving, dyeing, and pottery-making—would have a demand in the rural Israelite populace, and on this basis the cities could barter their crafted goods in return for grain, wine, and oil from the peasants.

We are not speaking of those city-states that retained the kingship and were so positioned that they could maintain a feudal grip on the countryside around them (notably the great fortresses along the Valley of Esdraelon); they did not enter Israel until compelled by David's conquests. We speak rather of those cities in the highlands such as Shechem, divested of royal rule and feudal holdings by the Israelite revolution. Although such cities would have some advantages in enjoying general Israelite protection without having to contribute auxiliaries to the citizen militia of Israel, the indirect protection of the Israelite presence was not so reliable as the protection afforded by membership in Israel or by specific treaty relations. The growing threat of the Philistines probably induced several such cities to relinquish their independence and to join Israel, or at least to enter into treaty relations with Israel. Moreover, the immense socioeconomic advantages of the "tribal" support system of mutual aid must have been very attractive to cities which now had to operate on a reduced economic base. In times of famine they would feel the pinch acutely, and only as full members of Israel could they expect to lay claim to the fraternal assistance provided by the tribal network of *mishpāḥōth* and *sheʿvātīm*.

46

The Israelite Countryside: Heartland of the Yahwistic Socioeconomic Revolution

Omitted so far from this typology of Canaanite responses to revolutionary Israel are the depressed peasants in the countryside whom I posit as having formed the large majority in the ranks of the Israelite movement. The absence of open references to them in the narratives of Joshua is altogether consistent with the dominant centralizing view of the cultic-ideological traditions, which assumes that *all* the Israelites attacking Canaanite cities had come out of Egypt and over the Jordan in a single migration. As a result, there is a curious hiatus in the sociopolitical contours of the Joshua conquest traditions: the countryside proper is virtually absent from view, evidently uninhabited either by Israelites or by Canaanites and pertinent only as the locale of battles, not as the base of a peasant population. It is not as though the biblical accounts picture the rural populace as subject to the Canaanites or as in willing solidarity with them; the rural populace is simply ignored. It is the cities with their royal bastions and exploitative apparatuses that are the consistent targets of attack, and it is monolithic Israel, entirely sprung from Egypt, that is the consistent agency of assault upon the cities.

Clearly, however, in the light of all that we have seen about Amarna and post-Amarna Canaan, and given the incontestable evidence that early Israel was overwhelmingly an agricultural people (*not* mainly a pastoral nomadic people and *not* mainly a craft-industrial or trading people), this "invisible countryside" can only be explained in one way: the centralized tradition obscures the massive and eloquent presence of the countryside in the rising tide of Israelite power.

The *destination* of the conquest action was the smashing of the city-state system of domination over the countryside; correspondingly, the *origin* of this assault was not a region outside of Canaan but rather the countryside of the Canaanite uplands coordinated in revolt against the city-states. To be sure, a major segment of the countryside had come from Egypt via Transjordan and/or the Negeb, but it had come as a revolutionary catalyst, renewing and vastly expanding in Yahwist form the earlier Elohistic Israelite coalition of restive *'apiru*, peasants, and transhumant pastoralists intent on breaking the grip of the city-state system. The Yahwists from Egypt did not arrive in Canaan as pastoral nomads aspiring to take over as the latest operators of the city-state system, or as pastoral nomads intent on

584

establishing a hegemony over regional agriculture and trade so as to rake off profit from the continuing royal-aristocratic monopoly of economic production in the city-states tributary to them.[515]

The egalitarian program of early Israel and the general course of the growth of Israelite power in upland Canaan are sociopolitically intelligible only on the hypothesis that coalescing groups of 'apiru, Shosu, peasants, and transhumant pastoralists, spearheaded by the militarized and articulate escapees from Egypt, moved as a rural coalition against the cities and, wherever possible, formed allies in those cities whose inhabitants assisted in the overthrow of the hated regimes. Moreover, although the countryside is recessive, indeed virtually "invisible," in the narratives of Joshua, it is strikingly present in the early poetry and to a large extent in the stories of Judges. It is *Yahweh's "peasantry in Israel"* that has disrupted the inter-city trade network of Canaan by striking a mortal blow at the north Palestinian coalition of kings (Judg. 5:7,11).[516] It is the blessings of *agrarian fertility* that are repeatedly invoked as the characteristic shape of the good life in early Israel (Gen. 49:11–12, 14–15,20,22,25–26; Num. 24:6–7a; Deut. 32:13–14; 33:13 16,24,28; Judg. 9:8–15; I Sam. 2:5; Psalm 68:9–10[10–11]; Hab. 3:17).

Once the processes of Israelite formation in Canaan lying behind the stories of Joshua and Judges are seen, despite all differences of form and perspective, to constitute a basic continuum, the largely rural agricultural composition of the peoples described in the stories of Judges, Ruth, and I Samuel becomes telling evidence for *Canaanite peasants as constituent members of the new Israelite community from its very foundation* (Judg. 3:26–27 [reading $s^e\bar{\imath}r\bar{a}h$ as "wooded hill country"]; 4:2, 13, 16 [$h^aros heth\ hag\text{-}g\bar{o}yim$ = "the wooded heights of the nations," i.e., Upper Galilee]; 6:2–4,11,19,25; 7:13–14,24; 8:2; 9:8–15; 11:26,34,37–40; 13:9,19; 15:1,5 [a description of Philistine wheat fields and olive orchards also applicable to Israelite agriculture in the adjacent shephelah]; 17:1; 18:7–10; 19:18–21; 21:19–21; Ruth; I Sam. 1:1, 24–25; 6:13–15,18b; 7:1; 8:14–17; 9:11–13; 10:3–4; 11:5–7; 12:17–18; 13:20–21; 16:20; 17:17–18; 23:1; 25:2,11,18).

In sociological tradition there are well-worn objections that peasants are too individualistic and traditionally inhibited to be effective revolutionary agents. Their periodic frustrated uprisings against authority are often described as un-coordinated and ephemeral, and thus abortive and ill-fated. This assessment derives in part from the early Marxian assumption that only the industrial pro-letariat could be the effective agent of socialist revolution, and in part from the historically illustrated ideal-typical studies of M. Weber, who concluded that it was mainly mobile skilled artisans and merchants of the cities, rather than peasants, who have been the bearers of new social and political forces and ideas.[517] It is clear, however, contrary to this judgment, that a number of twentieth-century social and political revolutions have been either spearheaded by or significantly participated in by peasants. Eric R. Wolf's study of these modern peasant revolts has isolated some of the specific conditions which can combine to turn traditional peasants into revolutionary peasants. Most, if not all, of the conditions contributory to a cohesive and effective revolutionary peasantry cited by Wolf appear to have been present in thirteen- to eleventh-century B.C. Canaan.[518]

Thus, at the end of our survey of the relations between Israelites and Canaanites in the eclectic formation of early Israel, we return to the greatly abused terms "Canaan" and "Canaanite(s)." We have seen that the terms are variously employed in old Israel for socioeconomic categories such as aristocratic merchants, for smaller or larger regions of the south Syrian corridor, for peoples living in those regions, and for the feudal forms of society and government dominant in those regions. Our detailed examination of these usages discloses no final harmonization in the biblical traditions. The referents of "Canaan/Canaanite(s)" are often value-neutral, so that we cannot even generalize that early Israel viewed "the Canaanite" per se as the enemy. We understand that this was so in part because, in Israel's environment, "Canaan" was not a standardized univocal place name, and "Canaanite" was not a standardized univocal gentilic denoting persons according to some single regional, political, or socioeconomic identity. We also now see that this "confusion" or "ambiguity" over the referents of "Canaan/Canaanite(s)" was more importantly a consequence of the fact that early Israel at its foundation, and for many decades thereafter, simply did not define its enemy as a region or as an entire people. To have done so would have been unthinkable, a gross simplism, since Israel arose from the very land and out of the very people to whom the terms "Canaan/Canaanite(s)" were variously applied.

In concluding this phase of the study, we must be completely clear on the results. Stated as an ideal type, *Israel's enemy was a sociopolitical system to be abolished: the imperial-feudal hierarchic state.* More concretely stated, *Israel's enemies were particular persons in various socioeconomic and political groupings who profited from the hierarchic system as rulers or as agents of the system* at various levels and in various sectors of its operation. When Israel used the cipher "Canaan/Canaanite(s)" to designate those enemies, precise socioeconomic and political groupings and functionaries within the hierarchic system were meant: "Canaanite kings," "Canaanite armies," "Canaanite merchants," "Canaanite landowners and overseers," "Canaanite city-state officials," and "Canaanite gods and cults and their priestly functionaries." "Canaanite(s)" as an epithet for Israel's enemy was not a term for an entire region and an entire populace, nor was it a term for a particular ethnic group distinguishable from an Israelite ethnic group, nor was it a term for a body of language speakers distinguishable from the language speakers of Israel (in any other than a regional dialectical manner or in terms of differences in vocabulary and style based on class distinctions).

Even when we include the Canaanite religion as an object of Israelite scorn and hostility, we must take pains to emphasize that *it was the political-cultic complex as a totality that was abhorred and opposed,* i.e., not the gods and cults as autonomous mistaken "religious" beliefs and practices, but the gods and cults as distorted "ideological" and "functional" counterparts and buttresses of socioeconomic and political oppression. In the next phase of our study I shall explore some of the ramifications and implications of this understanding of Israelite-Canaanite "religious" conflict for an adequate sociology of old Israelite religion. So far the conclusion is patent: as a pejorative expressive of what early Israel wholeheartedly opposed and struggled to overthrow, "Canaanite(s)" refers to a hierarchic socioeconomic and political system (or system set) peopled by kings, administrators, armies, monopoly merchants, feudal landlords and overseers, deities and priests—in short, a system and a set of roles and functions—ideologically justified and energized by certain beliefs about gods and by cult acts resolutely geared to solidify the system and to extend the system as far as the forces of its ideas, its armed might, and its administrative apparatus could be made to reach.

Part X

The Religion of the New Egalitarian Society: Idealist, Structural-Functional, and Historical Cultural-Material Models

47

A Preliminary View

It is my intent in this part of the study to examine Yahwism as a dimension or plane of social organization and ideology in old Israel. I shall try to specify the major inter-ties and correlations between the general Israelite social system and its explicitly religious sub-system. These systematic interconnections between religion and society will be set forth initially in a model of structural-functional interdependence. I shall argue, however, that a multidirectional, synchronic, structural-functional model must be supplemented by—or, more properly, extended into—an historical comparative model in order to deal adequately with the emergence of Israel's social system and to account for the peculiarity of its religion. Particular attention will be paid to research imperatives concerning cultural-material data needed in order to develop an informed and nuanced conception of the social-struggle base of early Yahwism.

In the course of explicating these models of the religion-society nexus it will be necessary to hold conversation with interpretations on two fronts. On the one side, I shall address the philosophical and religious idealism through which most scholarly analysts of early Israel view their subject matter. As exemplars of this general perspective, I have chosen John Bright, George Mendenhall, and Georg Fohrer, three historians of early Israel who have gone a considerable distance in delineating the social dimensions of premonarchic Israel, and who represent in the last analysis three rather typical forms of what I call "non-theory" or "anti-theory" when it comes to synthesizing and interpreting results. On the other side, I shall address the partly convergent and partly contradictory perspectives of those sociologies of religion that have attempted systematic theorizing about the relation of religion to society. This brings us to Emile Durkheim, Max Weber, and Karl Marx, in that order, not only as major analysts of the religion-society nexus but as initiators of continuing streams of sociological tradition that to date have been only infrequently and unmethodically applied to a study of the religion of ancient Israel.

591

48

Religious Idealism: Yahwism as an Autonomous Self-Generative "Faith"

48.1 Israelite Religion Severed from Israelite Society

In the second edition of his *A History of Israel,* John Bright has gone a long way toward adopting Mendenhall's proposal for a "peasant revolt" or "withdrawal" model of the Hebrew conquest.[519] It is, therefore, of more than passing interest to note what conclusions, if any, he draws for an interpretation of the religion of early Israel from his understanding of the conquest as "an inside job." It turns out that he has drawn no conclusions of any substance, but has instead continued to advance an unrevised view of Yahwism which sees it as a "faith" starkly contrasted with the history of Israel as a course of events otherwise of little significance except for the religious interpretation given them. In this stance, Bright is not at all exceptional, for his idealist understanding of the religion of Yahwism can be duplicated at random from scores, even hundreds, of works in Old Testament theology and history. I single out Bright for illustrative purposes, in part because his statements are succinctly typical of numerous other scholars, and in part because in view of his having so largely come to see the origins of Israel in a social revolution, one expects from him a rather different reading of a religion born in such circumstances of social upheaval.

Bright's view of the religion of early Israel, and its relation to Israel's social origins, is summed up as follows:

> . . . we have seen how Israel took possession of her land and began her life as a people there. This was in itself an occurrence in no way unique, and one that history would scarcely have noticed, had not these newcomers brought with them a faith quite without parallel in the ancient world. No history of Israel can proceed without some consideration of that faith, for it was this alone which set Israel off from her environment and made her the distinctive and creative phenomenon that she was.[520]

This argument may be construed to contain four terms:

1. The way Israel took over the land and began her life was in no way different from the experience of other Near Eastern peoples.

2. The religion of Israel, by contrast, was totally without parallel in the ancient world.

3. History would have taken hardly any notice of Israel except for her religion, a proposition that may mean at least two things:

    a. Contemporaries of Israel and Israelites themselves would not have thought of Israel as unusual except for her religion.

    b. Later peoples would not have remembered Israel except for her religion.

4. The religion of Israel was the only aspect of her life that set her off from her environment and made her unique and creative. In one sense this is a summation of the first three terms, but it may also be construed as a generalization which not only eliminates the manner of settlement or conquest as distinctive of Israel but further eliminates all other possible "nonreligious" features or traits, or combination thereof, as demarcating Israel from her environment.

I shall respond to each of these judgments in the light of the social-revolutionary understanding of Israel's origins that Bright accepts from Mendenhall, as well as with elaborations of that understanding developed in this study:

ISRAEL'S "ORDINARY" SOCIOPOLITICAL ORIGINS. The way Israel took over the land and began her life was in no way unique, Bright claims. From one who has just articulated the conquest as a social revolution against the feudal city-state system, this is a strange non sequitur. What other instances do we possess from the ancient Near East of the underclasses from a feudal society overthrowing their lords and living in an egalitarian social system over a wide area of formerly feudalized land for two centuries before becoming a monarchy? I am aware of none. Other "new societies" in the ancient Near East took over the existing state apparatuses and controlled them via a change of personnel, often with modifications in form; or else, arising in periods of indigenous political decline or exhaustion, these "new societies" developed state apparatuses of their own in all essentials as centralized and hierarchic as those of their predecessors. To be sure, elsewhere in the ancient Near East we know of religious innovations (such as Atonism in Egypt) [521] and of social reforms (introduced, undoubtedly because of pressures from below, by kings such as Urukagina of Lagash in early Mesopotamia),[522] as well as of periodic release from debts by royal decree (in early Mesopotamia);[523] but none of these can be discerned as a direct movement from the underclasses that broke through the existing state structure and social stratification in order to create a comprehensive alternatively structured, sovereign community.

Israel's sociopolitical egalitarian mode of life, involving an entire populace of formerly oppressed peoples, was unique in its explicitness and in its spatio-temporal effectiveness. Admittedly, two centuries is not a long period in terms of the millennia of ancient Near Eastern history, but the relevant point in my view is that we do not know of any other egalitarian structure that came into autonomous existence in historic times in that region. Obviously the base of the Israelite social revolution lay in the social unrest running as an undercurrent through the ancient

Near East, surfacing only indirectly in literature and official documents that reflect the viewpoint of the rulers rather than of the ruled. Indeed, it was the concentrating and heightening in early Israel of forms of social conflict elsewhere diffused in the Near East that gives the necessary field of evidence for forming an historical-dialectical, causal and comparative model of Israel's religion. This "concentration" and "heightening" of social conflict in early Israel is evident in the fact that only there, to our knowledge, did an egalitarian tribal life wrest control from imperial-feudal hands and succeed in establishing a sustained *vocal* alternative social order. In the case of Israel alone in the ancient Near East did the struggle of the antimorphemes of urban statism and egalitarian countryside issue for a time in such a clear and decisive provisional victory of the countryside over the city.

I conclude, therefore, that the first term in Bright's evaluation of early Israel is mistaken in that it does not credit the novelty of the egalitarian social revolution which he himself earlier describes as an historian.

ISRAEL'S "EXTRAORDINARY" RELIGION. The religion of Israel, on the other hand, was totally without parallel in the ancient world. Bright isolates the "faith" of Israel from the process and context of Israel's formation as a society. The "faith" was without parallel, while the process of national formation was in no way unique. This implies that Israel's religion was separable from its actions as a people in coming together and carving out a living space and a style of life. Such a separation is not merely questionable; it is absolutely contradictory to the intimate union of religion and the social order in early Israel. The Israelite social revolution and Israelite Yahwism constituted an inseparable whole from which no nonsocial, nonrevolutionary, or solely "religious" elements can be isolated even for purposes of analytic convenience. Of course, one can focus on the explicitly religious dimensions of ideology and cult in early Israel, but in doing so there is no way of avoiding the fact that one is analyzing the ideology and cult of a social revolution.

In sum, it is agreed with Bright that Israel's religion was innovative in the ancient world in significant ways. What was innovative about that religion, however, was precisely its character and status as the religion of an egalitarian social revolution. Bright offers an untenable distinction: the social revolution of early Israel was not at all unique, but the religion of that social revolution was unparalleled. I believe that the evidence supports a totally different reading: the social revolution of early Israel was innovatively distinctive in the ancient world; and as the ideology and cult of that social revolution, Israel's religion was also innovatively distinctive.

In place of the grossly misleading terms "unparalleled" and "unique"—which, if taken literally, claim that distinctively shaped Israelite cultural items have absolutely no continuity and comparability with cultural items of environing peoples—I suggest that we speak more modestly of Israel's innovative distinctiveness. Whatever our exact terms, I think that what we must emphasize is the emergent novelty of cultural items or configurations in Israel without in any way denying continuity or comparability in socioreligious items between Israel and other peoples. In fact, without positing a unitary cultural field in which Israel can be located, no science of ancient Israelite society or religion is possible. Lawful statements about the socioreligious system of early Israel, including the controlled identification of what is innovatively distinctive in Israel, necessitate a body of wider cultural data whose established regularities can be systematically compared with Israelite regularities to see where they converge and where they diverge. In fact, precisely because most students of early Israel have neglected the continuity and comparability of cultural data provided by sociological and anthropological methodologies, they have finally been unable either convincingly to locate what is distinctive in Israel or to propose lawful causal statements about the emergence and growth of Israel's innovative configurations.

ISRAEL'S LACK OF HISTORICAL NOTEWORTHINESS. History would have taken hardly any notice of Israel except for her religion. I shall examine that judgment in the two possible senses it may carry.

First, contemporaries of Israel and Israelites themselves would not have thought Israel unusual except for her religion. This implies that the only distinction early Israelites recognized in themselves was that they believed in Yahweh and practiced his cult, and that the only distinction their contemporaries recognized was that the Israelites had a religious outlook and practice different from their own. Everything that we have discovered about the origin of Israel in its sociopolitical formation in Canaan militates against such an interpretation.

Early Israelites recognized themselves as a distinct social formation banded together in egalitarian tribal coalition from which imperialism and feudalism were to be categorically excluded. They experienced their own distinction as social actors who expelled alien authorities and struggled to prevent the development of centralized authority within their own community. They experienced this distinction in the form of belief in a deity who assured their success in this social enterprise. They expressed this distinction in cultic practices which were of a piece with the entire continuity of their revolutionary social action. They "took notice" of themselves as effective social actors supported and assured by their God.

Similarly, Israel's contemporaries recognized the distinction of early Israel as a community that challenged them to abandon the imperial-feudal system of domination. Early Israel did not invite them to a comparison of the merits of this or that set of beliefs or cultic practices. Israel took direct action in overthrowing the system of domination with the power of a mass movement. Yahwism was an integral part of that mass action. Rulers and personnel in the alien system could resist and be killed or driven out, or they could desert to the egalitarian system of

Israel, or they could take flight to other regions. The underclasses dominated by the old system could fight for their former rulers, or they could join the uprising of Israel, or they could flee to other regions. But the basic dynamics were the dynamics of sociopolitical polarization and revolutionary armed strength. We have seen that this sharp polarization was tempered at times by treaties or accommodations which recognized neutrals, but the *sine qua non* of neutrality vis-à-vis Israel was that the parties must relinquish attempts at imposing domination on Israel and must not aid and abet other city-states against Israel.

Had these contemporaries of Israel in Canaan been asked what they noticed about Israel, it would certainly not have elicited this kind of reply: "We notice that Israel has a very unusual belief in God and a strange set of cultic practices. Some of us are convinced by those beliefs and practices and have adopted them. Others of us just can't accept them as true, or at least as right for us. The rest of us are thinking the matter over but haven't decided yet. Except for their strange religion, the Israelites are like us in every way. When we become Israelites, we just change religions; otherwise, we remain the same." It is difficult to formulate such a reply without caricaturing it.

We know very well what these contemporaries "noticed" in Israel, namely, a major disturbance of the enclosed city-state sociopolitical order in Canaan. A socially conscious version of what her contemporaries "noticed" about Israel would go something like this: "We notice that Israel is a total community that confronts and challenges us to join in its way of living. To do this we have to relinquish voluntarily or involuntarily the old forms of sociopolitical domination, including the old religious ideologies. Israel calls us to a new form of social relations which destroys class privileges. For those of us enjoying class privileges there is nothing but the prospect of loss as Israel grows stronger. For those of us who have been exploited by the privileged classes there is the uncertain promise of a better life in the Israelite alternative. Others of us, neither at the top nor at the bottom of the social order, enjoying both advantages and frustrations as agents of class rule, are torn in our responses to Israel. All of us in the old feudal social order respond to Israel and her religion in terms of perceived threat or promise to our whole existence in society."

Secondly, later peoples would not have remembered Israel except for her religion. This is a more difficult proposition to evaluate, since it easily leads into profitless "second guessing" based on formulating alternative models of how history might have developed if certain variables had been altered. If Bright means to point out that we now remember the social revolution of early Israel chiefly because it was enshrined in the religious ideology and traditions of a continuing community that outlasted the initial social revolution, he is obviously correct. One conceivable implication of this proposition is that perhaps somewhere in the ancient Near East there was another egalitarian social revolution that succeeded for a time, but because it soon failed and no continuing religious or sociopolitical community preserved records of it, subsequent history has no memory of it. In any case, there may be special reasons for certain aspects of a social system being singled out as important in retrospect. It cannot be taken for granted that the religion of Israel had the same significance relative to the total social system at its inception that it had in later Israel and in Judaism and Christianity. That Israelites, Jews, or Christians "remember" only the religion of early Israel as important or distinctive is simply one datum, and not the decisive one, in coming to an understanding of the place of Yahwism in early Israel.

In fact, what later generations remember about an earlier society is often very misleading as testimony for a faithful reconstruction of that society. In the case at issue, it is evident that the original status of Yahwism as the ideology and cult of a social revolution has tended to be eclipsed, and at times deliberately suppressed, because of the different social situations in which the continuing communities of synagogues and churches have passed on the ideology and traditions of the Old Testament, which were originally developed in a very different social situation. Once the initial social-revolutionary experience of Israel was submerged in its own monarchy, a course of development was set in train wherein the Yahwistic ideology and traditions were increasingly seen as a self-contained body of beliefs and practices separable from any particular kind of social order. This process of detaching the religion from its social base was already well under way in monarchic Israel, and it was vastly accelerated in later Judaism and Christianity.

On the other hand, it is also true that the memory of the Israelite religion as the religion of oppressed peoples making a social revolution has survived in synagogue and church, springing to life from time to time when new revolutionary social conditions appear. And it is furthermore true that as scientific study of the origins of Israel penetrates more and more closely to the circumstances and dynamics of Yahwism's emergence, the integral social-revolutionary character of Yahwism comes more clearly to light and thereby once again challenges the synagogues and churches with the disturbing implications and consequences of claiming continuity with a religion sprung from such roots.

Therefore, as a description of what later history, chiefly through Jewish and Christian bodies, has for the most part remembered about early Israel, Bright's statement bears considerable truth. What it overlooks is the underground memory of that religion as a revolutionary social ideology, a memory periodically noted by segments within the higher religions and by secular rebels and revolutionaries brought up on Jewish and Christian traditions. What it also fails to note is that as historical memory is increasingly informed by scientific scrutiny of Israelite origins, the full socioeconomic and political tangibility of what is being remembered in the religion of Israel comes more and more to the surface of consciousness.

The conclusion then, is that Bright is totally wrong about the original historical noteworthiness of Israel being solely in its religion, and he is only half right, and deceptively so, in describing later historical memories of Israel as related solely to the distinctive religion of Israel.

ISRAEL'S CREATIVITY SOLELY RELIGIOUS. The religion of Israel was the only aspect of her life that set her off from her environment and made her unique and creative. If this is intended by Bright to generalize beyond the social revolution as being "in no way unique" in order to deny all other nonreligious uniqueness to Israel, this claim should be emphatically challenged. Certain areas of material culture, such as the technological advances of iron tools and slaked lime plaster for cisterns, as well as the art of rock terracing, need to be reexamined in relation to Israelite "uniqueness" and "creativity."[524] The same is true concerning the invention of the alphabet, which took place in the general Canaanite culture field during the centuries prior to the rise of Israel. The relation between the alphabet and the forms of Israelite literature needs exploration. In literary production Israel showed astonishing creativity in polishing and perfecting, if not in actually "inventing," multiple forms and styles of expression that were put to the service of egalitarian communal needs. The older hieroglyphic and syllabic scripts with their complex burden on the memory were well suited to imperial-feudal monopoly, whereas the alphabetic script contributed to a democratization of language and thus to the celebration of a people and its deity in a new social system.[525]

An adequate causal and comparative model of the early Israelite social system will have to take such wider cultural developments into account, especially in their conjunction and combination in early Israel. It really will not do to say that only in religion was Israel unique and creative, when, in fact, her literature shows innovation and when certain configurations of culture in that geographical region, including technological advances, may have been preconditions or contributors to the signal religious elements of Israelite life. This problem will have to be looked at more fully later (X.51).

I only want to emphasize how useless it is to make sweeping denials of the "uniqueness" of Israel apart from its religion, for this merely compounds the misconstruction of separating religion from the social revolution that was early Israel. It leads us to look solipsistically only at those aspects of Israel which are traditionally defined as unique and cuts us loose from the total cultural base on which even the most novel religion is erected. The result is the distribution of Israelite culture into two categories: religious culture, oriented narrowly and explicitly around Yahwism, and the rest of culture in which Israel is like all the other peoples. This removes incentives and inhibits methods for viewing Israelite culture in terms of its many levels or planes in dynamic causal interaction. When we obscure the unitary nature of the culture of early Israel as the culture of a liberated underclass newly organized in an egalitarian social system, we simply further augment the age-old ecclesiastical and dogmatic picture of an active mighty God and a passive dependent people, thereby cutting the synergistic unity of people and deity, suppressing from consciousness the vitality and energy of a people in permanent revolution in major "nonreligious" aspects of its existence as well as in the more strictly "religious" sectors.

48.2 Israelite Society Derived from Israelite Religion

George Mendenhall, who first proposed the revolt model of the Israelite settlement and whose recent *The Tenth Generation* has advanced our thinking about early Israel as an anti-statist transtribal movement, has been much less persuasive in his theorizing about the sociology of early Israel's religion.[526] In fact, in place of sociological theory to explicate Yahwism he relies largely on old uncritical remnants of philosophical and religious idealism. Since he has helpfully identified elements of the sociopolitical dynamics of Israel vis-à-vis empire and city-state, one expects Mendenhall to focus on the religious aspects of the transtribal way of handling power developed in Israel as a theoretical issue of the first magnitude calling for a theory of the sociology of Israel's religion as innovative and heuristically promising as his hypothesis of the social-revolutionary origins of Israel.

Instead, Mendenhall curiously chooses to deny that Yahwism had anything to do with political power, except in a negative, exclusionary manner: Yahwism embodied and enjoined the rejection of political power. Amidst the inexactitude of his invocation of Yahwistic "rejection of power," one thing becomes completely clear: by this idealist short circuit, Mendenhall avoids grappling with a sociology of Israel's religion commensurate with the rigor of his observations about the eclectic revolutionary social formation of Israel.

On analyzing Mendenhall's "non-theory" about the relation of Yahwism to the wider Israelite society, the following lines of reasoning seem basic:

REJECTION OF POWER. Early Israel's anti-statism is equatable with the rejection of power, since Israel's God was regarded by the people as the source of all power in place of the claims made by the hierarchic state. In Mendenhall's view, this proposition removes Israel's religion not merely from the sphere of centralized politics but from the sphere of politics, the exercise of power, in any form.

NONPOLITICAL ETHICAL NORMS. In place of politics, Israel's anti-statism is equatable with the voluntary communal acceptance (through the covenant form) of "ethical norms" grounded in the revelation and authority of Israel's God. The covenantal social order provided Israel with a nonpolitical basis for necessary communal order.

ISRAELITE RELIGION NONPROJECTIVE. The result of this combination of equations and contrasts is to picture the religions of Near Eastern societies as projections of the power interests of the Near Eastern states. It does not, however, occur to

Mendenhall to consider the correlative hypothesis: that the religion of Israel was a projection of the power interests of its tribal egalitarian society. Whereas he clearly sees statist religion as a self-serving projection, Mendenhall inconsistently, and without reasoned justification, posits Israelite transtribal religion as a reality beyond all projections, as itself the ground of reverse projections and insertions into socioreligious history. In other words, Yahwism enters into history from the transcendent realm of the Idea (the revealing God) and goes to work unfolding itself with no more than token debt to its environment.

Consequently, Israel is seen by Mendenhall as a society in which religion and ethics are separate from and, in decisive ways, above politics and the power struggle. It is this separation of religion and ethics from politics and this logical and procedural priority of religion and ethics over politics that distinguish Israel from its environment. Instead of a new form of politics, Israel abolishes politics. The paradigm seems to run like this: Whereas in the Near Eastern world at large, centralized politics determine social order and religion, in Israel religion determines an ethical social order that not only excludes centralized politics—i.e., the state—but makes all uses of human power optional or immaterial to social order.

It should be evident that this sharp theoretical separation of spheres is discordant with the very close correlation of Israelite tribal society and Israelite religion that Mendenhall himself has empirically identified as an historian and as an observer of social phenomena. In particular, it flies in the face of the very anthropological and sociological data and categories Mendenhall has summoned to assist him in his analysis of early Israel. Accordingly, Mendenhall's assumptions can be challenged and refuted as follows:

REDISTRIBUTION OF POWER. Anti-statism in tribal organizational form is never a rejection of power, but rather the rejection (or the nonattainment) of particular forms of political power organized and excercised hierarchically. In place of centralized power in the state, the tribal or intertribal (Mendenhall's transtribal) community distributes power on a more egalitarian design. The institutionalization of a rough socioeconomic equality within the tribe means that many aspects and incidents of internal order are dealt with by social persuasion, compromise, and consensus in place of the state's more pervasive resort to force. The tribe, therefore, looks more "pacific" or "noncoercive" than the state—and in important respects it is—but the tribe, like the state, retains a monopoly on the use of force and does not hesitate, at decisive points, to use physical force against its own members and against threatening outsiders.

Specifically in Israel's case, its fundamental need was to muster adequate decentralized power for the community to come into existence in the first place and thereafter to survive in the midst of hostile centralized states. We can properly speak of a different distribution of power and a more diffused and restricted use of power in ancient Israel, but we cannot speak of an Israelite rejection of power.

Israel enforced capital punishment and Israel fought fiercely against its enemies. Wherever a society establishes and defends its sovereignty, by whatever symbolics that sovereignty is expressed, politics is present. That is true of tribal and intertribal communities, and it was true of early Israel.

ETHICAL NORMS ARE POLITICAL. Tribally organized societies characteristically have ethical concepts and norms which are given support by religious tradition and sanction without being for that reason "apolitical" or "antipolitical." Rather, these ethical concepts and norms set forth certain "anti-hierarchic" models of political behavior showing how the good leader will exercise the power that the community grants to him even as it limits the grant to specific ends and means. In Israel's case, the ethical norms of Yahwism, far from being ahistorical and antipolitical generalities, speak directly and adamantly to the problem of how the community is to be organized internally so as to channel nonabusive power toward the necessary ends of communal viability.

YAHWISM AS PROJECTIVE AS ANY NEAR EASTERN RELIGION. If the religion that accompanies and justifies and energizes statism is a projection of power interests, there is every reason to believe that the religion that accompanies and justifies and energizes tribalism or intertribalism is also a projection of power interests. Instead of a crude formula of projection for religion supporting statism and a denial of projection in any form for religion supporting tribalism, it is more logical to look for adequately nuanced formulae of projection for both forms of religion.

To be sure, the two sets of power interests represented in statism and tribalism are at sharp variance with one another, structurally different and often in open conflict in historical settings. Yet to grant that the religion of the state serves the interests of the state, but to deny that the religion of the tribe or of the intertribal confederacy serves the interests of the tribe or the intertribal community, is to desert sociological method at a decisive juncture. What reason can there be for this retreat from scientific method into an asocial and ahistorical vacuum unless it is the unchallenged survival of philosophical idealism that sees religion and ethics, especially those for which the observer feels an affinity, as somehow *sui generis* and self-generative? Where idealist infinite regression replaces scientific method we cannot have a sociology of religion, no matter how astute the observations about particular interfaces between society and religion.

ISRAELITE RELIGION VALIDATES POWER. Finally, if there is after all something empirically distinctive about Yahwistic religion that removes it alone among intertribal/transtribal religions from the realm of practical politics, Mendenhall has not made clear what it is. Indeed, his examples of the application of the Israelite "rule of God" to some of Israel's social institutions (such as the limitation and control of private vengeance)[527] show how intimately Yahwism was bound up with establishing norms and procedures for the uses of power. I am prepared to grant with Mendenhall that there are many distinctive features of Israelite religion, but not a single one of them justifies the conclusion that Yahwism was separate from, or prior to, the power interests and the social struggles of the Israelite people. Not one of these Israelite religious innovations is made any more secure in history or given any fuller elucidation by appeals to idealist interventions in the sociohistorical process.

I have cited Mendenhall's failure at a sociology of Israel's religion precisely because I am so greatly indebted to his empirical work as an historian and to his probes in sociological modeling of the Israelite community. His failure to undertake the final stages of functional and causal-comparative social theorizing about early Israel as a socioreligious totality shows dramatically that careful description of the social bases of Israel's revolutionary emergence in the ancient Near East does not necessarily lead to clarifying theory. Whereas Bright limits himself to a distinctive Israelite religion, restricting Mendenhall's sociological observations to the revolt model of the Israelite formation, Mendenhall advances our understanding another step by insisting on a distinctive Israelite society, even though this distinctive society remains suspended in thin air. Unfortunately, Mendenhall's arbitrary extrapolation of a distinctive Israelite social movement from a distinctive Israelite religion via the medium of "ethical norms" employs no sociological method and offers no theory to bridge the various social processes and historical movements and to articulate the religious (cultic-ideological) dimension or plane.

For Mendenhall the relativizing and decentralizing of power in the Israelite community, which he has grasped and elucidated more forcefully than any other historian of early Israel, turns out to be a spontaneous epiphenomenon of "power-rejecting" religion and ethics that cannot be further theorized about. At this point Mendenhall is no advance on generations of biblical historians; indeed, he represents a step backward from the integrative, quasi-sociological synthesis of Martin Noth. In spite of all the evidence that he has uncovered to the contrary, for Mendenhall the religion of Yahweh is not an intrinsically social reality but a suprahistorical Idea that from time to time takes social forms and has social effects. In the last analysis, for Mendenhall as for Bright, Yahwism is an unmoved mover of people and events, and neither deities nor philosophic first principles viewed as uncaused causes, rather than as the ideas of human beings, have any place in the historical dialectic of social evolution. As long as we stay in the framework of idealism, there can be no sociology of religion for the simple reason that no lawful statements can be made about social phenomena, religion included, if they cannot be correlated and causally examined.

48.3 Social Influences on "Nonessential" Features of Israelite Religion

Claiming that questions of the influence of religion on the social structure of Israel (e.g., law, kingship, Deuteronomic Reform) have been often discussed, whereas "the reverse process—the influence of the social situation and of social forces on the religion—has been little observed to date," Georg Fohrer undertakes to show the religious consequences of three major social formations in ancient Israel.[528] First, he argues that the primitive nomadic society had religious effects in the conception of the deity connected with the group instead of a place, in the promises of possession of land and many progeny, in the Passover, in the cultic objects of tent and ark, and in forbidden intra-clan marriages. Secondly, he states that the changeover of Israel from pastoralism to agriculture and urbanism had religious effects in the expansion of Yahweh's domain as a God of rain and fecundity, in the development of a wisdom model of conduct for the privileged and educated upper clases, and in the intermixing of Canaanite and Yahwistic people and religion. Thirdly, the shift from barter to a money economy and the concentration of landed wealth in a few hands, accompanied by the legal deprivation and economic dispossession of the majority of Israelites, had religious effects in the elaboration of a high ideal of kingship as the guarantor of social justice and in the incisive prophetic condemnations of a corrupt, unjust society.

Considering all I have had to say about the baselessness of the nomadic mirage as an explanatory model for Israelite origins, I need say little about Fohrer's first category of social effects on religion. If we understand the zone of social structure to which he alludes to be tribalism rather than nomadism, the pertinence of many of his observations can be retained, although, as I argued in VI.30.3, the incest/marriage taboos do not attest the exogamous clan in early Israel. The religious effects of the major social shifts to agriculture and urban life and thence to an accelerating socioeconomic stratification of the populace noted by Fohrer are largely phenomena that others have previously observed. Fohrer brings additional insight mainly on the wisdom model of conduct for the upper classes and on the inflation of the ideal of royal justice. Of course, what Fohrer describes as the shift from pastoralism to agriculture is in my view the shift from tribally organized agriculture to state-dominated agriculture with an increasing component of urban-based trade and light industry. At any rate, the sketch of the religious effects of social-structural change offered by Fohrer is fairly conventional and represents in the main a summary of commonly held views.

SOCIETY-RELIGION INTER-TIES. What is of greater interest is Fohrer's brief attempt to reflect theoretically on the developmental inter-ties between society and religion. I quote the more reflective theoretical portions of his essay:

> By no means everything in the early Israelite religion and in the Mosaic faith in Yahweh is derivable from social structure and explainable by it. Only individual structural elements, arrangements, and cultic features are determined by the social structure. Untouched thereby are the fundamental features of the personal element and the correlation between God and man. These features represent direct and underived essential marks of the faith.[529]

Thereby [i.e., by the expansion of Yahweh's domain to include rain and fertility] the worship of Yahweh was exalted to an urgent desire of the Israelite peasant; it corresponded to the social structure of his life.[530]

The attempt of Nietzsche to interpret the position of the prophets, as of the whole conception of the Old Testament, as a slave revolt misses the mark. The prophets were no representatives of slaves; rather they represented the legal right of the weak derived from God and on the basis of faith. They asserted the imperishable divine right of those deprived of their rights. Therefore they needed no political or colorful emotional derivation for their critique and their demands, but only reference to the divine will. . . . So little do the prophets explain themselves sociologically in any case that the causes of their historical appearance in economic and social conditions, in the social structure, or even in a class war connected with it, lie closed. To be sure the prophets have taken a position with respect to the conditions of their time, but therein is to be found nothing of the ground or motive of their behavior. They did not arise from a proletariat, but rather from the circles of landowners or from the upper class. Nor did they live in conflict with their "class," which drove them to the side of the "proletariat."[531]

This pastiche of assertions, denials, and demurrers about the social shaping of Israel's religion, which can only be characterized as sociological "anti-theory," is curious indeed from one who purportedly seeks to show broad-ranging systematic social influences on the religion. Like all idealist interpreters of religion, Fohrer wants to be able to toy with social influences on religion without facing up to the social formation of religion in a fundamental way. The social-structural influence on religion has to do only with "details," while "essentials" of religion are "untouched." Elements of the religion which are "personal," or which treat the divine-human correlation, are the essential matters in Yahwism, and such things are not social in their origin or fundamentally affected by social developments. There are no overall patterns, systematic dependencies, or socioreligious behavioral regularities in the interplay of society and religion. Religion is influenced by society repeatedly and heavily, but not "essentially" and not lawfully.

The result of Fohrer's atheoretical stance is an endlessly expanding assemblage of discrete social-religious inter-ties which, however much they mount up, prove nothing because they are held to embody no generalizable regularities. At any given point, the religion of Israel may assume a certain shape and be appealing to Israelites because "it corresponded to the social structure" of someone's life, e.g., the peasant. Nevertheless, the religion retains an inner ahistorical, asocial integrity all its own which can never be penetrated and illuminated by the unfolding designs of the societal matrix of the religion. In fact, religion has no social matrix; at most it has a detachable social frame. Social comment on religion is admissible, even advisable, since it helps us to explain the alterations in the religion's outer forms. By contrast, a fundamental analysis of religion precisely as a social phenomenon whose regularities are explored in correlation with wider societal regularities is excluded in advance, studiously ignoring the pressure for systemic social explanation of religion constantly being built up by the accumulated empirical observations. The "social influences" that Fohrer gives with one hand are just as promptly snatched away with the other hand.

SOCIOLOGY OF PROPHECY. The explanatory poverty of an approach which talks about "social influences" that do not influence "religious essences" comes to its fullest expression in Fohrer's remarks on the prophets. Whether he has properly understood Nietzsche's view of the prophets I shall leave aside. Basically his argument is this: because the prophets don't explain themselves sociologically, we can't either. We must simply take their word for the totally religious basis of their outlook and activity. Fohrer, along with numerous other Old Testament interpreters who are fond of the same line of thought, fails to see the absurdity of his position for scientific study of ancient Israel. If Fohrer is right on this point, it follows that all of his own scientific inquiry into ancient Israel has been in vain. So the prophets do not explain themselves sociologically? Well, neither do they explain themselves literarily, historically, or religiously according to all the criteria and methods of humanistic study which Fohrer feels obligated to employ if he is to understand the prophets.

For example, the biblical writers did not analyze their work in terms of literary criticism, form criticism, and tradition history, but that does not prevent Fohrer from using such scientific methods to understand their methods of composition. Nor did the biblical actors and biblical traditionists reflect on history through modern historiographic categories, but that does not impede Fohrer from employing historiographic tools to understand what occurred in biblical times. Similarly, biblical personages did not reflect on "social influences" that shaped or motivated their life, but that does not discourage Fohrer from commenting on a whole array of such influences on the formulation of biblical religious practice and thought. Suddenly, however, when it comes to a theoretical wrap-up of the import of the sociological method, Fohrer conjures up a forbidden area into which sociology cannot profitably enter. One species of modern scientific methodology is abruptly denied its theoretical fruits because the biblical subjects would not have been at home in sociological theory.

Obviously it would be another matter if Fohrer had carefully examined the social-structural location of prophecy (or of other religious phenomena) and concluded that the evidence did not establish any dependable socioreligious correlations capable of generalization. Instead, his "analysis" consists of remarking that the prophets were not "proletarians," and that is supposed to dispose of sociological data—as if it were not common sociological knowledge that the ideological and organizational leaders of lower-class movements are often from other classes altogether, and as if the prophets could not be understood sociologically unless they were involved in an explicit organized "proletarian" movement, naively asssuming that the only time sociological categories are relevant is when there is an openly revolutionary situation in society.

FAILURE OF SOCIOLOGICAL NERVE. All in all, Fohrer's undertaking, useful in empirical details, is theoretically weak. Because of his assumption of the nomadic beginnings of Israel, the original socioreligious revolution of early Israel which I have reconstructed in this study escapes him entirely. He sees no fundamental patterned socioreligious regularities at work in the rise of Israel, just as he sees none developing subsequently. Fohrer leaves us with a disjointed bundle of discrete "influences" that do not really influence but only channel a religion that is perpetually prior to and beyond society, indeed beyond all explanation as a human phenomenon. Religion proceeds along a self-set course; at most, social factors push it somewhat in one direction or another, mold the form in which it will appear, but the religion obeys an inner genetic code made up of personal, prophetic, and divine-human interrelational elements.

Fohrer's apparent concession to the social influences on religion is highly deceptive and methodologically meaningless. Bright and Mendenhall are more consistent. Bright separates the religion methodologically from the society. Mendenhall brings them together in order to posit the extrapolation of the society from the religion. Fohrer wants to have empirical social influences on religion without facing up to the explanatory significance of the lines of social force which he cannot avoid delineating insofar as he faithfully notes one influence after another. I do not regard this failure as some personal perversity of Fohrer's. In fact, I take the trouble to analyze the contradictions of his position because they are the contradictions of a majority of those who have purported to deal with social influences on Israel's religion. The social commentator pursues his study up to the point that he has to summarize and generalize the results. All at once he backs off from the logical consequences of his detailed observations. This is so extraordinary an abandonment of scientific method just as it is about to pay off that we naturally wonder why it happens so often.

It seems to me that there may be two basic reasons for the failure of sociological nerve among biblical scholars. For one thing, being for the most part less familiar with social-scientific method than with the methods of the humanities, biblical scholars may be uncertain as to how to theorize on what they have discovered in their studies of social phenomena. Feeling the need to reach general conclusions of some sort to round out their studies, they tend to fall back upon religio-historical generalizations which imply or insist that there are no valid general sociological conclusions. In the second place, biblical scholars may feel that to admit systematic social influences on religion is to deny the creativity and impor-tance of religion, or, in the extreme, to invalidate the religion which, in one way or another, they may regard as valid for themselves. Such fears have by now gener-ally been allayed with regard to literary, historical, and religiohistorical methods, but they persist with regard to sociological methods. Somehow a "core" of "untouched" religiosity must be spared the sociological analytic knife. The bugaboo of "reductionism," if not named, lurks in the background.

In fact, I have no basis for judging specific factors operative in Fohrer's withdrawal from theory, since his essay does not reflect methodologically on the scholar's stance vis-à-vis his biblical-sociological subject matter. In this too Fohrer is typical of the sort of lacuna in theoretical reflectiveness that constitutes so deep a problem in much "sociological" study of ancient Israel. Characteristically, when the scholar abandons social-scientific method, there is no explicit reflection on the tendency to back away from the logical conclusions of the method previously pursued. The hesitant scholar seldom says, "I deny the possibility of theoretical conclusions because I am not sure how to formulate them," or, "I deny the possibility of theoretical conclusions because I am uncomfortable with the possible consequences for my previous methods of study or for my religious stance or philosophy of life." In no sense does this observation attribute bad faith or deliberate deception to such scholars. In many instances, I suspect, scholarly reservations about sociological theory are not explicitly framed because they still lie half-formed below the level of operational consciousness.

In the remainder of this part of the study, and in the next, I shall pursue the logic of a sociology of Israel's religion with a view to flushing out these unexamined and unadmitted taboos and inhibitions about sociological study of ancient Israel. Unless this is done, rigorous consistent methodology will constantly be aborted and deflected by sentiments and obsessions that the scholar can neither throw off nor openly embrace, simply because they remain fully or partially hidden from awareness.

49

Structural Functionalism: Mutual Reinforcement of Yahwism and Social Egalitarianism

In place of the vagaries of nonmethodical idealism, which either severs Israelite religion from Israelite society (as with Bright), or arbitrarily derives Israelite society from Israelite religion (as with Mendenhall), or establishes social-structural influences that merely affect the surface form and not the deep substance of Israelite religion (as with Fohrer), the subject requires: (1) a method that will plot *the correlations between Israelite society and Israelite religion;* (2) a method that will mandate *the clarification of causal relationships according to laws of probability;* and (3) a method that will facilitate *the comparative differentiation of the Israelite religion-society complex in a field of other religion-society complexes, both historically and typically.*

Whether in fact there exists such a method, or assembly of methods, is presently the subject of intense inquiry and debate in the social sciences. The inquiry is admittedly still in its youthful stages, but clearly it must be undertaken resolutely, even if cautiously, in the case of ancient Israel if we are to have anything to offer in place of the vacuous unscientific nostrums of idealism as applied so generously but so unproductively to the subject matter.

49.1 Structural-Functional Societal Models

The initial phase of the task belongs to the method that has been employed in structural-functional anthropology. Granted its severe limitations, some of which we must comment on, this method helps us to plot a "map" of the religion of Israel and the society of Israel as systemic totalities with regular correlations between the respective totalities and between and among various items in the social and religious repertories. Such a method assumes that although distinguishable from other aspects of the social system by its explicit symbolism, religion belongs to the total field of social relations, and that the religion may be seen either as a sub-set of the entire social network or as a particular symbolic code articulating the whole network, and perhaps most properly as both. As with all patterns of social interaction, religion is seen to serve interests, meet needs, and perform functions which stand in coherent relationships to the other elements of the societal whole. The functional approach operates with the assumption that it is possible to establish at least some of the interlocking and mutually supportive functions of social and

608

religious items in old Israel among an abundance of activities which at first glance seem merely random, unconnected, or even outright contradictory.

Within the general assumptions and correlative procedures of functional modeling there are several notions of what "function" actually is in a social system.[532] In the course of advancing and interpreting a functional model of Israelite Yahwism in its societal network, I shall examine the major notions of function as they apply to my proposed model. As a start, it seems to me that the basic usage of "function" is for *the relation of dependence or interdependence between two or more variable factors in a field of social action.* This means that changes in one variable will be seen to produce changes in the other variable. When the identified influence is in one direction we speak of "dependence"; when it is mutual we speak of "interdependence," although the interchange of effect need not be symmetrical in quantity or quality.

Sometimes a functional dependence is expressible in quantitative terms, as in population growth or in divorce or suicide rates. Sometimes the functional dependence is not quantitatively measurable, either because data are lacking or because the relationship is at a level which cannot be, or has not yet been, put into a mode of quantification. Whether all functional relationships are ultimately quantifiable is a matter of continuing dispute among functionalists. At any rate, where quantification is not possible of attainment (or has not yet been attained), the functional dependence has to be hypothesized as a correlative weakening, strengthening, or alteration in the dependent variable resulting from changes in the independent variable—as, for example, in the contention that when Israelite tribalism was weakened or strengthened or altered, Yahwism was weakened or strengthened or altered.

When we formulate a functional proposition of this sort, we say that Yahwism is a function of Israelite tribalism, i.e., Yahwism is dependably related to Israelite tribalism. A reverse functional dependence might be formulated with Israelite tribalism as the function of Yahwism. Or, the two might be held together in a statement of functional interdependence. The extent to which a functional model offers a predictable or retrodictable relationship is much disputed. Many functionalists are so little interested in change over any extended period that they do not think of the test of prediction or retrodiction of change as pertinent to a functional model. Others believe that unless a functional model can point out regularities in change, past and future, it possesses minimal explanatory value. This is a central issue to which I shall return in the course of my analysis of the Israelite society-religion nexus.

It is legitimate to see a social variable as having more than one function, i.e., as being in dependable relationship with more than one other variable. Yahwism, for example, may be seen not only as the function of Israelite tribalism but also as the function of military conflict or the function of an articulate intelligentsia, etc.

Unless, however, functionalism is to be more than a sophisticated way of piling up all kinds of unrelated and unweighed connections between social items, functional theory will be adequate to the degree that it brings logical systematization and simplification into the discerned relations of variables. For example, if it is granted that Yahwism is dependably related to social egalitarianism *and* to military conflict *and* to the presence of an articulate intelligentsia, it is logical to try to reduce this plurality of functions either by showing how one function in fact subsumes the other functions as special instances of the encompassing function, or by showing that all the functions cited have a higher-order factor in common which can be expressed by a more inclusive functional formulation.

Very often, however, functional models have presented considerable numbers of functions which do not clearly articulate in any hierarchic pattern or in which, due to unconcern about the change factor or to lack of information about change in the system, there is no convincing way of rendering a configuration of associated social items into a formulation that indicates which item or items have priority or dominance. However, even if functional dependencies cannot be altogether rationalized, a model will prove its adequacy to the degree that it can show the extent of the regularity (in quantity and/or quality) with which one functional dependence is "interrupted" or "qualified" by another functional dependence. This amounts to showing how the "all other things being equal" qualifier in the statement of any functional dependence is regularly altered by some other functional dependence.

Since functional models of societies have been so largely applied to "primitive" peoples whose development over time is often virtually unknown, functionalism has been a victim of "temporal nihilism," of a kind of obliviousness to—at times even an irrational antipathy toward or a curt dismissal of—the significance of societal development. In spite of structural-functional anthropology's general acquiescence in an "atemporal" field of operation, I shall argue strenuously in what follows that any meaningful functional model involves a time perspective, however short by choice or however hypothetical by necessity, since the only way we can finally identify significant relations among items in a social system is to detect regular changes in the quality or quantity of the interacting elements.

Insofar as functional models admit no time factor whatsoever, they fail to be explanatory of social phenomena and must be regarded as no more than assemblages of associated social items whose posited significance still awaits demonstration. Insofar as old Israel has been studied in a loosely structural-functional manner, I regret to conclude that the "maps" offered have been little more than collections of purportedly major social and religious items whose interconnections have not been established precisely because regularities in synchronic metabolism and in the configurations and directions of social change have not been proposed or tested. It seems to me that even the fantastically erudite study of ancient

Judaism by Max Weber, impressive as it is in many ways, must be included in this negative assessment.

In all this it ought to be obvious, although practitioners and critics of functional models of society often seem to have forgotten it, that any statement of function as the relation of dependence or interdependence between two or more variable factors in a social inventory is a highly selective abstractive operation. It represents one way of viewing the phenomena in context, and to be even proximately adequate it has to try to set the phenomena in the largest possible relevant context. In functional modeling, the larger the field of modeling, i.e., the more social items encompassed, the more likely it is that some relevant items (perhaps even crucial items) will be omitted and the more likely it is that irrelevant items will be included which are either not at all germane to an explanation of the phenomena or have a very subsidiary role to play.

A functional model is not justified because it is the only way to view the interplay of social items in a total system; it is justified by its ability to show that a particular set of relations among items is the most important one for determining the unitary operation of the system, particular aspects of or states within the system, and the direction of movement in the system.[533] Thus, functional models are never to be taken as photographs (they never attempt to include everything), but as highly selective dimensional models that trace significant relationships and are necessarily open to cross-questioning and reformulation. A functional model is not a societal inventory but an analytic design which focuses on the critical life-sustaining metabolism of the social system. Accordingly, merely to compile an indeterminate number of social items observed in ancient Israel is not to give a functional model. Only when we have specified which of the innumerable items are axial—i.e., most significant for determining the structural totality of the system, or of some aspect or state of the system—and thus which items when changed will bring change in the total system, will we have offered a functional model. Obviously this is an enormous challenge, fraught with endless possibilities of error and misemphasis, but nothing less than this undertaking is worthy of the scientific impulse to render a sociology of the religion of early Israel that is more than a descriptive tautology.

49.2 Mono-Yahwism as the Function of Sociopolitical Equality

With this background concerning the goal and the methods of functionalism, as well as its merits and limits, I now propose that *mono-Yahwism was the function of sociopolitical egalitarianism in premonarchic Israel.* I here employ "mono-Yahwism," as proposed by T. C. Vriezen, to specify the innovative, nonphilosophical, practical monotheism of early Israel.[534] To begin with, this functional proposition means that mono-Yahwism is viewed as dependably related to sociopolitical egalitarianism in the sense that any strengthening or weakening or alteration in

Israel's sociopolitical egalitarianism enhanced the probability of a strengthening, weakening, or alteration in Israelite mono-Yahwism. The functional relationship between Yahwism and communal egalitarianism has additional meanings in my opinion, including a reverse or reciprocal dependence of sociopolitical egalitarianism on Yahwism. These further meanings will be introduced later in our analysis.

For the moment I concentrate on the way Yahwism's structure and fortunes were tied to the structure and fortunes of egalitarian tribalism. This is particularly crucial because it is precisely this "earthy" dependence of Israelite religion on Israelite social forms which idealism resists, even as it makes vague concessions to "the historical character" or "the social relevance" of Israelite faith. In X.50.4 I show why the functional dependence of Yahwism on Israelite egalitarianism, when all is said and done, is the basic functional and causal reality in a sociology of Israel's religion. So far idealists have had the field when it comes to "explaining" early Israel. Their "nonexplanations" can be exposed only by offering an analytic/synthetic model which traces the lineaments of the metabolism of the Israelite socioreligious system and goes on to explore the historico-social "genetic code" which is responsible for this metabolism.

Surprisingly little functional modeling has been attempted with reference to a sociology of Israel's religion. It seems to me, for instance, that Weber's efforts were actually premodular in the sense that he suggested the lines along which a number of functional models of early Israel might be developed. Later we shall see the attempt of one sociologist in the Durkheimian tradition to establish a functional model for early Israelite monotheism.[535] What follows is an initial mapping of a functional model which tries to lay out a structure of the religion-society nexus in old Israel with the deliberate intention of inviting criticism and refinement, and without going into all the details which the enterprise might eventually require.

To begin with, the proposition that mono-Yahwism was the function of Israelite sociopolitical egalitarianism is a highly complex proposition with two composite terms involving sub-sets or clusters of factors grouped under mono-Yahwism and under sociopolitical egalitarianism respectively. It is advisable, therefore, to break down or to unpack the two cluster terms into their constituent parts and to indicate at least the most crucial dependable relations between sub-terms as well as between the composite terms as wholes.

Sociopolitical egalitarianism typifies the Israelite social system composed of a number of sub-factors or common denominators that represent various sectors or planes of the total system:

TERRITORY. The society inhabited a more or less contiguous territory of marginally to plentifully productive and strategically defensible uplands and steppes, together with some enclosed valleys, stretching from west to east between the

Mediterranean coastal plain and the north Arabian desert, and from south to north between the Sinai desert and the Litani River.

LANGUAGE. The society used a common spoken and written language, consisting of at least two, and possibly more, dialects of a Northwest Semitic language (Canaanite/Hebrew/Phoenician) that had been in use for some centuries by the indigenous population and that continued to be used by Israelites and non-Israelites in the area for some centuries thereafter.[536]

MEANS OF PRODUCTION. The society was primarily engaged in rain agriculture (chiefly grain, oil, and wine) with a sizable supplementary pastoral economy (bovine herds and small cattle, i.e., sheep and goats) in a basically rural and small-town environment, and practiced some crafts providing tools, household articles, and clothing.

SOCIOECONOMIC ORGANIZATION. Ownership of the basic means of production (land, herds, and flocks) was vested in extended families (the primary residential and production units) that were sub-clustered into protective associations, backed by tribes, and charged with implementing measures to inhibit social stratification: prohibition against sale of land outside the family, prohibition of interest on loans, limitation on debtor servitude, periodic redistribution of land holdings, and obligations of mutual economic aid to prevent the destitution or demise of extended families, etc.

POLICY-MAKING. Determination of public policy was by assemblies of "citizens" (probably largely males) and by heads of families, protective associations, and tribes in various combinations and jurisdictions, assuring the decentralization and diffusion of power, with local and regional units reserving rights of veto or nonparticipation in contested public decisions, and with certain "charismatic" leadership roles open to women as well as to men.

NORMS AND RULES. The society was guided by a body of customary and quasi-legal norms and rules enforced by social pressure and by elders from the several levels of social organization serving as judges, and also by teaching priests (Levites) and occasional "charismatics" or mantics.

MILITARY ORGANIZATION. The society fielded a citizen army, its units based on pseudo-kinship lines, that could be summoned to the defense of the interests of any sub-group in Israel, whenever those interests were perceived as the interests of all Israel—a matter to be determined from case to case through the proper channels for approving public policy.

Sociopolitical egalitarianism, in sum, designates a self-governing association of economically self-sufficient free farmers and herdsmen constituting a single class of peoples with common ownership of the means of production vested in large families. These traits of sociopolitical egalitarianism in Israel set it off sharply as a social system from the hierarchic centralized rule of the city-states in the same general area, from which Israel broke away, and against which Israel carried on a constant social struggle that frequently erupted in open warfare. Especially characteristic of this sociopolitical egalitarianism was its paradoxical combination of political decentralization, on the one hand, and of sociocultural cohesiveness, on the other hand. Such a system depended greatly on consensual understanding of and commitment to common interests, requiring, as it were, the ancient tribal equivalent of "an enlightened and publicly active citizenry."

Mono-Yahwism typifies the explicitly religious symbol and action sub-system, or the cultic-ideological dimension or plane, of general Israelite society composed of a number of sub-factors or common denominators that represent various sectors or planes of the sub-system:

A SINGLE GOD. Yahweh, while conceived as the sole sovereign of the land in which Israel lived, was not defined primarily with reference to place, either the land as a totality or particular locations within it, but with reference to his rule over a people.

A GOD BOTH OLD AND NEW. The deity was conceived as different from and opposed to the gods of the land (in his identity as Yahweh over against the Canaanite Baal), but at the same time he was paradoxically regarded as continuous with certain deities or with aspects of certain deities of the land (in his identity as El).

A GOD SUBORDINATING NATURE TO SOCIAL EQUALITY. The deity was regarded as controlling the processes of agriculture, animal husbandry, and human fecundity—processes which were, however, subordinated to the creation and maintenance of an egalitarian social order of farmers and herdsmen who were entitled to participate equally in the production and consumption of natural goods.

LIMITED PRIESTHOOD. The cult was led by a teaching and quasi-military priesthood distributed among the major social groupings but lacking in political power except as its views were persuasive to those groupings, and whose support through endowments of land and sacrificial offerings consumed a relatively small part of "the gross national product" in comparison with the priestly establishments of surrounding peoples.

SANCTIONS FOR POLITICAL EQUALITY. Deity and cult supported conceptually and institutionally the popular equality of all males as members of extended families, an equality evident both in the cult assembly proper and in all segments of communal life in which the ultimate symbolic attribution of sovereignty and leadership was reserved to the deity, with the result that all communal leadership roles were conceived either as temporary task assignments or, if hereditary, as sharply limited in function and scope.

SANCTIONS FOR ECONOMIC EQUALITY. The deity "revealed" in cult traditions and instructions supported conceptually and institutionally the right of access of all communal members to the basic resources of land, herds, and flocks through the established extended families and protective associations of extended families,

while prohibiting individual and group economic speculation and aggrandizement.

SANCTIONS FOR COLLECTIVE SELF-DEFENSE. The deity and cult passionately advocated the collective self-defense of the egalitarian community against imperial-
feudal incursions by means of the so-called holy war, i.e., a war to preserve the
egalitarian social constitution of Israel and to insure that none of Israel's constituent members be lost to the imperial-feudal counter-systems.

SANCTIONS AGAINST RELIGIOUS MYSTIFICATIONS. The deity and cult suppressed
all forms of sexual mystification, ancestor worship, and speculation about life
after death in favor of sexuality as a societal ingredient and a studied concentration on developing the entire community of living Israelites in its total range of
existence as the highest good.

Such formulations of the sub-factors or common denominators in the respective structures of mono-Yahwism and sociopolitical egalitarianism—which could
easily be expanded and refined—present a rich field of correlations with numerous functional interlocks between the religion and the society. Yahweh's symbolic
roles and the cultic and sociopolitical instructions developed as divine
law refer precisely to the pivotal structural features of the community and serve
to strengthen those axial features against system-disrupting counter-tendencies.

In Israel *as a cult community,* Yahweh is the sole jealous *patron deity* working
against divisiveness and waywardness in the ranks of his worshippers. In Israel *as a
popular army,* Yahweh is *commander-in-chief,* "a man of war," arousing the faint-
hearted and solidifying common military efforts. In Israel *as a customary and
quasi-legal community,* Yahweh is *arbitrator and judge* pressing toward standardized
practices in securing the integrity of the egalitarian community. In Israel *as a polity
or realm of self-rule,* Yahweh is the ultimate and sole *sovereign,* the surrogate king,
who guarantees the diffusion and decentralization of power within the several
sovereign groups of the community. All of the symbols of Yahweh in his various
guises refer with positive reinforcement to socioeconomic desiderata in the community and to the assurance that power will be used in ways that preserve the
system externally and internally.

The loosely federated egalitarian tribalism of Israel was symbolized and institutionalized at the most comprehensive level by a common cultic-ideological
allegiance to mono-Yahwism. When viewed in a functional model, i.e., when
Yahwism is seen in terms of socially expressible and effect-producing activity, it is
obvious that Yahwism was more than a single specialized sub-system in old Israel.
It was a pervasive social force with a central position in the structure of the socially
converging but politically decentralized people who formed Israel. Yahwism as a
social force was operative at precisely those critical points of common structural
interest where the monarchic and aristocratic institutions of the Near East normally functioned to give hierarchic order and cohesion to societies—at the cost,

however, of an enormous repression of human energies and values in the larger part of the populace. It was precisely social order achieved by general repression that Israel strove to resist at all costs and over against which it hoped to build an alternative social order that would be functional for the whole of the populace.

One way of viewing the relationships of religion and society in old Israel is to recognize in Yahwism an experimental conceptual-institutional alternative to repressive human authorities. In Israel the element of experimental calculation is reflected in the people's free choice of the covenant relationship with the deity. Thus, while in explicitly cultic terms the demands of Yahwism were strict and excessive compared to the demands of official Canaanite religion, the actual social empirical situation was that the "tolerant" Canaanite cult justified the centralized political rape of human and natural resources and energies by a small elite, whereas the "strict" Israelite cult justified the development and enjoyment of human and natural resources and energies by the entire populace. Yahweh, in appearing to demand much more than Canaanite gods, actually gave back to his worshippers the benefits and potentialities of productive human life which a small Canaanite minority had arrogated to itself under the symbolic approval of hierarchic polytheism.

Accordingly, my functional proposition that mono-Yahwism was dependably related to communal egalitarianism leads us to see that mono-Yahwism, far from being an eccentric cultic compartment of Israel's life or an arbitrary ornament on the main body of society, was in fact of critical significance as an axial, form-giving, and energy-releasing reality in literary and intellectual culture, in economics, in social organization, in military affairs, and in self-government. Naturally such an insight suggests not only that mono-Yahwism was a function of sociopolitical egalitarianism but that, in some senses at least, sociopolitical egalitarianism was a function of mono-Yahwism. To this way of enlarging the proposition, by identifying *interdependent* relations between society and religion, we shall return after additional, more precise formulations of the dependence of mono-Yahwism on sociopolitical egalitarianism.

Having laid out what I view as the important factors or common denominators in mono-Yahwism and in Israelite egalitarianism, a somewhat fuller and more discriminating formulation of the proposition of the functional dependence of the former on the latter can now be given: The belief in Yahweh as the sole God of Israel who motivates and sanctions a particular system of social interaction, coupled with the cult's minimal command of political power and minimal consumption of communal wealth, *was dependably related* to the rise and maintenance of sociopolitical egalitarianism in ancient Israel with its structural features of extended family ownership of the means of production, mutual-aid measures for keeping the extended families on an approximate par in production and consumption, and the dispersal of social, political, and religious power among the structural sub-units.

The claims involved in this functional proposition are twofold and may be explicated positively and negatively as follows:

SOCIOECONOMIC EQUALITY FACILITATES RELIGIOUS EQUALITY. For one thing, the dependable relatedness of mono-Yahwism to sociopolitical egalitarianism, stated positively, means that the fundamental intention of Israel to limit the exercise of power by any one person or group within the intertribal system, in order to insure egalitarianism in production and consumption of goods as well as in public policy-making among all the constituent members, *enhanced the probability* that the community would adopt or, as necessary, create a religion that did not usurp communal resources or communal power but rather legitimated the egalitarian impulse.

The same functional dependence, stated negatively, means that had Israel been unconcerned with economic egalitarianism and the diffusion of communal power roles, i.e., had it developed social stratification and kingship or oligarchy at its inception, *the probability is enhanced* that it would have adopted a religion that was politically dominating and whose cult made large claims upon communal resources.

SOCIOECONOMIC UNITY FACILITATES RELIGIOUS EXCLUSIVENESS. In the second place, the dependable relatedness of mono-Yahwism to sociopolitical egalitarianism, stated positively, means that the necessity of the groups uniting in Israel to seek a degree of cultural, sociopolitical, and military unity sufficient to protect themselves against Canaanite, Egyptian, and Philistine domination, *enhanced the probability* that, having from the outset rejected political centralization and social stratification, the community would adopt or, as necessary, create a religion with strong traits of exclusivity and with social norm-sanctioning measures adequate to help form Israel into a cultic, military, customary-legal, and cultural whole in the absence of structural hierarchy and stratification to accomplish that end.

The same functional dependence, stated negatively, means that had Israel not been threatened by Canaanite, Egyptian, and Philistine domination, so that its tendencies toward egalitarianism and decentralization could have had freer play without fear of being stamped out at any moment, *the probability is enhanced* that Israel would not have adopted or created a religion that made such severe exclusive demands and imposed such insistent sanctions on social behavoir.

RELIGIOUS NOVELTY AND THE CONTRADICTION BETWEEN EQUALITY AND SURVIVAL. What I think is being stated in the foregoing rather formalistic double equation is that the decisive factor in Israel's having developed the novelty of mono-Yahwism, instead of adhering to El or to the gods of the fathers or to some other preexistent cult in the region, was *the acute necessity of creatively resolving the potentially destructive contradiction between two fundamental needs: the need for the peoples who formed Israel to be internally egalitarian, and the need for this internally egalitarian system to defend itself against encroachment and destruction by neighboring hierarchic and stratified social systems.* The potentially destructive contradiction lay in the sobering reality that unless strenuous innovative steps were taken, the maximizing of internal egalitarianism would leave the system open to obliteration by rival systems from without, on the one hand; while the maximizing of internal unity to defend the system externally would encourage the inner-systemic development of hierarchy and stratification that would undermine the egalitarian system from within, on the other hand. To establish and maintain socioeconomic and political egalitarianism, *Israel had to struggle simultaneously against contrary social systems externally and against contrary social tendencies internally.*

Mono-Yahwism, as I visualize its relation to this set of finely balanced social dynamics, contributed pointedly and decisively to the achievement of internal unity and stability on an egalitarian basis. Mono-Yahwism was, in short, a delicately balanced, innovative, cultic-ideological instrument for selectively strengthening both egalitarianism in social relations and an effective united front against enemies in minimally contradictory or antagonistic ways. Another way of stating the functional relationship is to observe that mono-Yahwism as symbol and cult was strong precisely where the decentralized community was most vulnerable—i.e., in historically rooted and culturally unifying forms—whereas mono-Yahwism as symbol and cult was nondemanding precisely where the decentralized community was most jealous of its rights—i.e., in direct command over the production and consumption of goods and in the self-rule of the community through diffused and limited power roles.

49.3 Sociopolitical Equality as the Function of Mono-Yahwism

So far in my functional sketch I have restricted myself to examining the probable effects on the religious factors that would result from varying the sociopolitical factors in early Israel. Now I wish to examine the reverse situation, namely, that material alterations in mono-Yahwism would have had predictable effects on communal egalitarianism. If it turns out that not only is mono-Yahwism dependably related to sociopolitical egalitarianism, but that likewise sociopolitical egalitarianism is dependably related to mono-Yahwism, we will be able to speak of the two social-systemic entities as interdependently or reciprocally related as functions one of the other. We shall then have to ponder exactly what such a proposition means beyond a brute juxtaposition of two sets of functions.

Taking into account the foregoing formulation of the dependable relation of mono-Yahwism to sociopolitical egalitarianism, I now propose a corresponding reciprocal formulation of Israelite tribal egalitarianism as a function of mono-Yahwism: The rise and maintenance of a viable Israelite egalitarian social system with its structural features of extended-family ownership of the means of production, mutual aid measures for keeping the extended families on an approximate par in production and consumption, and the dispersal of social, military, political, and religious power among the structural sub-units, *was dependably related* to the innovative conceptual-institutional projection of Yahweh as the sole God of Israel, who motivates and sanctions the desired system of social relations by means of a cult with minimal command of political power and minimal consumption of communal wealth.

The claims involved in this functional proposition are twofold and may be explicated positively and negatively as follows:

RELIGIOUS EXCLUSIVENESS FACILITATES SOCIOPOLITICAL UNITY. In the first place, the dependable relatedness of tribal egalitarianism to mono-Yahwism, stated positively, means that the innovative formation of mono-Yahwism, as a set of concepts and institutions making severe exclusivist demands and offering powerful motivations for egalitarian social behavior, *enhanced the probability* that the decentralized, heterogeneous constituent members of Israel would achieve cultural unity and collective self-defense without losing the desired egalitarian social structure.

The same functional dependence, stated negatively, means that had the religious cult adopted by Israel lacked Yahwism's intensely exclusivist conceptual and institutional character, *the probability is enhanced* that the sought-after unity, identity, and collective self-defense of the heterogeneous peoples would have been unattainable.

RELIGIOUS EQUALITY FACILITATES SOCIOECONOMIC EQUALITY. In the second place, the dependable relatedness of tribal egalitarianism to mono-Yahwism, stated positively, means that the innovative formation of an exclusivist Yahwistic cult, which was relatively nonconsumptive of communal wealth and whose leaders had no explicit political power, *enhanced the probability* that the tendency of Israel to limit the exercise of power by any group within the intertribal confederacy, and the parallel tendency to insure basic resources equally to all extended families, would be structurally implemented.

The same functional dependence, stated negatively, means that had the religious cult adopted by Israel consumed large amounts of the community's economic resources, and had its leadership possessed political power, *the probability is enhanced* that the community would have been frustrated in its basic goals of assuring socioeconomic egalitarianism and diffused, decentralized political leadership.

The concept of "function" used in the above formulations is the relationship of dependence or interdependence between two or more variable social factors. As previously intimated, however, there are other meanings of "function," and some of them are clearly involved in the way I have stated and explicated the dependable relatedness of mono-Yahwism to tribal egalitarianism, and vice versa. Function, for example, may also refer to *the utility of a social item in meeting a need or needs.* This view of function is operative when I state that the belief in Yahweh as the motivator and sanctioner of the social system, together with his cult's minimal demands on resources and on political power, met the two potentially contradictory communal needs for cultural identity and unified self-defense against rival systems, on the one hand, and for egalitarianism and self-rule, on the other hand. Obviously such "needs" are cultural products rather than biological necessities, and it must be granted that functional theorists have been notoriously obscure in explaining the "needs" of social "organisms."

Function may also refer to *the maintenance of a particular state or condition within a particular social system.* Accordingly, we may say that the Yahwistic motivations and sanctions of the social system, joined with the cult's minimal demands on communal wealth and power, contributed to the maintenance of a state of effective balance between cultural and military unity, on the one side, and tribal egalitarianism and self-rule, on the other side, within the ongoing system of intertribal association. The same meaning of function can be referred to the maintenance of a state of maximal unity in tension with maximal egalitarianism within the sub-units of the intertribal association, as described in VI.27–29, e.g., within the tribe, or within the protective association, or within the extended family—provided, of course, that we know enough about the inner workings of these sub-units to delineate the maintenance function hypothesized.

Function may also have the meaning of *consequences for a system resulting from the way in which variable factors in the system act upon one another.* Sometimes the attribution of "consequences" is the result of experimental manipulation in which we methodically remove one factor, or posit it as changed in some way, and then estimate the results for other factors or for the system as a whole. "Experimental manipulation" in this instance does not, of course, refer to laboratory tests but to disciplined exercises in estimating sociohistorical probabilities. Where the object of study is a social system whose change over time has not been observed, as is frequently the case with nonliterate societies, this experimental manipulation of dependable relations in order to project consequences is as far as the analyst can go, although use can be profitably made of supposedly analogous situations in other societies in which changes have been observed.

At other times, however, something may be known about the development of the society, as when literary sources or archaeological data are available or observers have been able to report on a society over a long time span. The more social-change information is available on a society, the more functionalism as the modeling of consequences raises questions of societal development and, at its extreme, questions of the origin and demise of societies. In facing such issues we have reached the boundaries of functional models, and we must look beyond them for a way of introducing diachronic and causal dimensions into social models. Precisely this boundary-situation is apparent in a functional model of old Israelite religion-in-society, inasmuch as we have some knowledge of the origins and development of the Israelite social system and of the Yahweh cult. Indeed, the foregoing functional model strongly implies various causal possibilities for Israelite social phenomena as the matrix of Yahwistic religion. These possibilities, extrapolated from the functional model, are sufficiently vague and potentially contradictory that causal questions must not be left to ambiguity and to the whimsical preferences of interpreters.

50

Historical Cultural Materialism: Yahwism as the Symbolization of Egalitarian Social Struggle

So far our modeling of the inter-ties between mono-Yahwism and Israelite egalitarianism has remained within the framework of the functional interdependence of sub-sets or planes in a hypothetically unitary social system. At the point, however, where reciprocal or interdependent functions are recognized as feeding back and forth between Yahwism and the egalitarian social system, questions arise which functionalism is not equipped to treat. While advantageous for discerning the overall dynamics and interlocking workings of a society in cross-section, a functional model is finally inadequate to deal with processual sequences and with social causation. In positing the functional interdependence of all or many of the elements and tendencies of a social system, functionalism tends to assume their interchangeability within a more or less fixed metabolic state in the system. All the elements or aspects of the social system are so many forms of the system's "expressive totality," each element simply mirroring or echoing the indivisible whole (a point of view brilliantly applied to ancient Israel in the first volume of Johannes Pedersen's *Israel: Its Life and Culture,* 1926. From this perspective on a social system, there is no methodological leverage for determining the formative priorities of one or another of the elements, or of the interactions among elements, in giving rise to the system and in bringing about change within the system.

The provisional strength of the functional model of societal unity-amid-diversity is that it astutely circumvents premature or data-less speculation about cause and effect in social process. It does this by a methodological suspension of the diachronic and genetic plane, or at least by a rigorous subordination of the diachronic/genetic concern to the synchronic/metabolic concern. However, "suspension" or "subordination" is not "annulment" or "annihilation." Functionalism on its own grounds gives rise to precisely those issues of processual development which it initially suspends, i.e., to questions about the origins of a system (which once did not exist and eventually will no longer exist), about change within a system (as long as it does exist), and about the impact of systems one upon another (since no system is an island). System qua system is a formal analytic that slows

622

down the flow of process in order to abstract what is typical of the society's mode of operation, but the life of the social actors within any system so analyzed is in flux, one network of lived relationships passing away and another coming into being (however slow or rapid the process may be), while contemporary systems act and react on one another in the varying responses and adaptations of the historically positioned social actors.

Accordingly, the functional interdependence of Yahwism and tribal egalitarianism stands out in skeletal abstraction as a symmetrical relationship which, so long as we stay within the functional presuppositions, permits of giving no priority to one factor-set or the other. The functional model delineates how neatly the religion and the social order dovetail together, interlocking and supporting one another, and how neither can be imagined in the mature system without the other. To be sure, hypothetical time spans, or observed time spans of relatively short duration, are implied in the logical operations by which factors are varied in order to trace the resulting functional changes viewed as consequences. The limited diachronic span in a functional model does not, however, provide a wide enough horizon to examine change factors satisfactorily, i.e., with sufficient controls. The functional cross-sectional analysis, defensible as a first-stage operation, encourages an illusion of systemic stability and insularity in the absence of a trajectory of long-term change within the system and lacking comparative study of trajectories of change in two or more societies.

When pressed, functionalists will grant that societies develop over time, and they are likely to concede that it would be extremely valuable to know how this happens. The point is that they do not believe any method exists for identifying the regularities in social development and change. They are in a position where they look at the layering of societies as a geologist might look at the "layering" of the earth's surface in the absence of any way of knowing how the layering had come about. Descriptive analysis of the observed layering of the earth is better than nothing, but geology as a science becomes significant only as it succeeds in explaining the temporal process of layering. Similarly, a science of society is still collecting information about societal layering until it can offer explanation of the history of that layering.

We know that social systems do not appear full-blown. They develop through a selecting out of social structural elements in response to basic factors in the wider natural and social environment. We sense that some elements or features of the social system arise earlier than others, or at least that some elements or features of the system are more dominant than others in that they have an axial directive role in the development of the system. The crucial question is this: Do the undoubted changes in societies over time, the transitions from one system of social life to another, proceed according to regularities, i.e, according to lawful behavior, which it is the task of a science of society to discover and articulate?

This is the broad backdrop in social-change theory against which we place our concern with the origins of Yahwism and of Israelite tribal egalitarianism. Three major approaches to questions about the regularities in the relation of social and religious elements in a system of human interaction are connected with the perspectives, methods, and conclusions of the theoretical sociologists Emile Durkheim, Max Weber, and Karl Marx. I shall attempt to apply to premonarchic Israel their respective approaches to the religion-society nexus, even though only Weber intensively studied the specific circumstances of Israelite development.

It may seem at the start of our discussion that this exploration of the accomplishments and limits of theorizing about the society-religion nexus viewed diachronically and causally is beside the point at issue, namely, concrete understanding of the particular religion-in-society of early Israel. In fact, my contention is that the shallow social-theoretical context in which Israel's early religion has been customarily viewed has guaranteed a methodological blockage which persistently frustrates the formulation and testing of hypotheses that could convincingly replace the idealist nonhypotheses presently dominating the field with something better than sweeping assertions of crude material determinism.

50.1 Durkheim: Collective Representations

Durkheim's approach is the least diachronic among those of the three social theorists in question and is, in one sense, merely a theoretical underpinning for structural-functional models which take little or no account of development or of cause-effect relations in societies. It seems to me that Durkheim's perspective is important, however, not only because his views have informed a good deal of valuable but incomplete sociological-anthropological modeling but because he did perceptively put his finger on a peculiar core connection between society and religion which some of his intellectual heirs have tried to refine in a direction that takes cause-effect questions into account.

It was Durkheim's view that in religion people adopt an attitude of reverence and submission toward the revered sacred objects that is exactly analogous to the attitude of reverence and submission concurrently adopted toward "social facts," i.e., toward the givenness of human social solidarity.[537] "The idea of society is the soul of religion."[538] Primal solidarity produces "collective representations" in the form of religious notions that objectify the underlying human drive (or drift) toward cohesion and order in the social system. This seminal insight, however, is of no help in accounting for the specific forms that religion takes in relation to society. It describes only "the ever-present causes upon which the most essential forms of religious thought and practice depend."[539] Durkheim offered no controls over the variations in religion, and thus, with his approach, we are unable to understand why any particular form of religion arises. We are left with a static identification of the underlying, ultimately psychic, dependence of religious representation on social solidarity, but the hypothesized social solidarity is a vast abstraction subsuming all particular societies. It says little more than this: because people are inveterately social, they are inveterately religious.

When pressed to its foundations, Durkheim's conception is one more version of idealism. Society emerges out of the group mind and objectifies itself symbolically in religion. There will always be intimate connections between religion and society, but the particular concretions and combinations of society and religion, their phenomenal origins and sequences, are neither of much interest nor capable of explanation in strict Durkheimian terms. The variabilities of social phenomena and the variabilities of religious phenomena are jointly subsumed under a kind of instinct toward sociality unavailable to scientific analysis.

Nonetheless credit must be given Durkheim for what was more an intuition than a demonstrated conclusion, namely, that the human attitude of veneration and respect toward the sacred symbols is parallel to and somehow systematically congruent with the human attitude of veneration and respect toward moral authority and toward society. The religious symbols have social facts as their true referents. The murkiness of his approach and its final frustration as a mode of scientific analysis follow from his claim that the social facts are not the empirically observed relations among people in particular societies but are inaccessible intuitions and impulses toward human solidarity whose manner of mediating particular societies and religion is simply inexplicable.

Guy Swanson took up Durkheim's main theme of society as dominant over individuals, creating supportive solidarity enduring beyond individual lifetimes and symbolically mirrored in the collective representations of religion. As an empirical sociologist, however, Swanson was interested to know why collective representations take the form of spirits who become unified and personified beings, rather than remaining mere impulses or forces, and, in particular, whether it is possible to specify more exactly which aspects of societies are venerated analogously with religious objects.[540] Swanson hypothesizes that spirits as religious objects are "organized clusters of purposes" analogous with distinctive enduring purposes of particular social groups extending across generations.[541] Such sovereign groups, i.e., groups with original and independent jurisdictions over some sphere of life, provide the conditions from which a concept of spirit originates. Put in another way, the supernatural spirit world is like a society of sovereign groups in that it embodies purposes and potentialities and pervades the inner life and the outer experience of individuals. In polytheism, deities correspond to the constitutional structure of various intra-societal groups; they influence events or processes which particularly concern those groups; and they reflect in their coexistence as multiple deities the coexistence of multiple groups in society.

For our purposes, Swanson's further attention to the origins of monotheism is of particular interest. He understands "monotheism" as any belief in a high god, dominant above all others in a society, even though other deities exist for particular jurisdictions or clienteles. His hypothesis is that belief in a high god as orderer of all, or at least of the most significant experiences and events, will arise in a society with "at least three types of [sovereign] groups arranged in a hierarchy."[542] The point is that the high god as coordinator or nerve center of the supernatural world corresponds to social mechanisms for coordinating and ranking purposive decision-making in human groups structured by fairly complex internal layering or differentiated into sub-groups.

So far it would be easy to dismiss Swanson's hypotheses as pure speculation. What distinguishes his work, however, is an attempt to offer statistical support for the hypotheses by drawing codified comparative data from fifty societies represented in Murdock's World Ethnographic Sample.[543] Among his sample societies for monotheism is ancient Israel in the time of the judges, which falls precisely within the period of our study. Swanson's results indicate a highly positive correlation between the presence in a society of three or more sovereign groups whose claims are mediated hierarchically and the presence in that same society of belief in a high god as the prime orderer of experiences and events. In terms of probability calculations, the co-presence in societies of hierarchically arranged sovereign groups and of monotheism occurs far more often than can be credited to chance. So far as he has gone, Swanson appears to have narrowed Durkheim's intuition in the direction of greater precision, and particularly to have shown how it is possible to form and test hypotheses growing out of the Durkheimian intuitions about religion.

What is strikingly non-Durkheimian, however, is Swanson's empirical specification of "social facts." Whereas for Durkheim the social facts were not to be seen in any particular society, nor in all of them together, but rather in some deep structure in the collective human mind, for Swanson the social facts are particular constitutional arrangements of societies which have been observed and recorded and can be grouped in their quantitative and qualitative variability to establish correlations with religious variables. In place of universal collective representations of the social mind in religious dress, Swanson establishes that variable social arrangements of certain types occur in systematic correlation with variable religious representations of certain types. Instead of invoking an inaccessible group mind, Swanson formulates general propositions about the society-religion nexus in terms of descriptions of the frequency with which these variable sets of religious and social phenomena go together in a large sample of known societies.

It seems to me that this shift puts Swanson well beyond Durkheim in the direction of an historical-dialectical model. In wiping away the mystifying residue of idealism in Durkheim, Swanson shows that nothing is gained by positing social facts and their collective representations embedded in the group mind as supposed sources of all particular religions and societies. Such an hypothesis is so vague as to explain everything and nothing, inasmuch as the group mind, severed from mediations in empirical phenomena, cannot be verified or falsified. Instead, within the great range of known societies there are forms of religion which have a conceptual and functional verisimilitude to forms of social organization, especially to the forms in which human purposes are concretized and adjusted to one another. Although Swanson does not say so, it seems evident that he has broken out of the idealist circle of Durkheim of frankly propounding that socially embodied and often conflictive human purposes are the "causes" or "occasions" of the religious veneration of spirits and high gods.

When Swanson's hypothesis that monotheism is precipitated by the emergence of hierarchically ordered sovereign groups is related to my own model of early Israelite Yahwism and social egalitarianism, a certain congruence appears which in turn provokes further questions. My model presents a systematic correlation between *paradoxical egalitarian needs* for cultural and military unity *and* for political decentralization and *paradoxical religious elements* of an exclusive and intense religiosity *and* of a politically powerless priesthood requiring low-level consumption of surpluses by the cult. My model falls within the general area of sociopolitical organization which Swanson identifies as decisive for the emergence of monotheism. It could be said, for example, that the exclusive and intense religion of Yahweh as the sole God in Israel arose in a society with sovereign groups striving to adjust their several claims to authority in such a manner that the whole social system could survive. Yahweh conceived as the ultimate agent of order and purpose corresponds symbolically to the struggles of the Israelite peoples for unifying order and purpose that would permit many lower orders and lower purposes to exist within its framework. Furthermore, if my model is offered as an instance of Swanson's hypothesis about monotheism, it means that the circular functional interdependence of Yahwism and egalitarianism would be broken through in such a way that the infinite regress of the two terms would come to rest in sociopolitical egalitarianism as the "cause" of Yahwism. But before my functional model can be confidently equated with Swanson's conclusions, it would be necessary to have a clearer understanding of what he means by sovereign groups "arranged in a hierarchy." I shall return to this point in X.50.3.

50.2 Weber: Elective Affinity and Co-Determination

Max Weber's treatment of the religion-society nexus in premonarchic Israel must be viewed as a part of his overall inquiry into the relation between religion and economics in historical societies, beginning with modern Europe and extending to China, India, and ancient Israel. He viewed changing social relations and changing religious forms as reciprocally influential, although the selective force of particular religions in contributing to particular forms of economics was his prime focus. This lifelong interest in tracing how religion affects the course of socioeconomic development can easily be lost sight of in the labyrinthine detail of his studies of particular societies such as ancient Israel.[544]

Weber's work is eminently diachronic, as, for instance, in his overview of Israelite social and religious history from its beginnings through early post-exilic times.[545] He exhibits a persistent analytic interest in singling out the field of interrelated socioeconomic and religious forces. Yet so much the historian does he remain that Weber does not really propose a functional model of how the social and religious forces were interconnected at any one time or how the patterns of interconnections shifted over the course of time. From the wealth of analytic detail, chronologically arranged, a synthetic model or paradigm of the relative input of socioeconomics and religion toward societal change does not emerge. Instead, the enterprise is dominated throughout by "ideal-typical" categories of the sort that are set forth and illustrated from many historical settings in his collected essays and in his *Sociology of Religion.*[546]

In the work of Weber there is a formal level of ideal-typical sociological categories which he can invoke as conceptual tools for analyzing sets of relations in particular societies on the empirical data level. In between these two levels, however, there is a noticeable vacuum in functional and genetic models which, had Weber supplied them, could have shown how he constellated the social forms in particular societies on the basis of his ideal-typical analytic units. This explains in part why it is so difficult to formulate what Weber actually intends to say about the religion of Israel in its social setting.

As a result, Weber's approach to social change is ambiguous. Increasingly in his study he emphasized a long-term trend in Western society toward rationalization in its various forms of economic capitalization, bureaucratic specialization and routinization, and intellectual categorization. Along various historical routes, he traced the impact of Judaism and Protestantism in contributing to this rationalization of the human social world. He insisted that religious phenomena exercised a powerful influence on social existence, as for instance in the remarkable theodicy or religious justification of the history of early Israel carried out by the Hebrew prophets. This prophetic achievement gave the Jewish people rational categories for making sense out of their confused history, and it had the effect of selecting out certain lines of social behavior and excluding others. The one line of Jewish social behavior that interested Weber most, in the light of his earlier study of the relation of Calvinism to European capitalism, was the prohibition of loans at interest to fellow Jews which had the two-sided effect of excluding Jews from direct capitalist development while giving them a subsidiary role in capitalism as a money-lending status group.

The obverse inquiry into the effect of social forces on religion did not engage

Weber's full attention, although it is absolutely clear from the way he describes historical societies, as well as from his overall theory of social causation, that he took it for granted that the distinctive lineaments of historic religions were shaped by the distinctive social settings in which they developed. Among these social forces Weber also included geographical, techno-environmental, and economic factors. Nonetheless, these factors, either in their own right or in their combined impact on religion, did not receive his sustained attention, either in detail or in theoretical reflection. His occasional cultural-material observations about early Israel, for example, were thrown out succinctly and left largely unintegrated with the religion-society interaction he preferred to accent.

In the end, Weber did not offer more than a very loosely designed field of social causation. He saw that social relations, rooted in particular natural and techno-environmental settings, did shape religion. He saw that religion acquired sufficient independent force to act upon the social order and to shape it in one direction or another. When it came to articulating this two-way flow of causation in human affairs, he spoke of the "elective affinity" of certain kinds of religion for certain kinds of social relations and vice versa, or he noted the "co-determination" of religious and social factors, a term intended to circumvent what he regarded as the impoverished one-directionality of the Marxian claim that social relations and religious ideas were determined by the economic base. The formula of "elective affinity" or "co-determination" was, however, less a model of social change than it was a statement of the problem.

What method for inquiring into social causation should follow from such a formulation? The methodological directive remains so general as to be mainly a stance or a perspective on the scope of inquiry. The conclusion is: look for the way religion affects society and for the way society affects religion, and pay attention to those points of congruence and intersection where religious ideation and valuation, on the one hand, and social needs and values, on the other, are jointly concretized in the interests of particular social groups. This broad methodological directive did not lead the diachronically oriented Weber to fill the gap between his abstracted ideal types and his rich historical data with functional or genetic models of "elective affinity" or "co-determination" in given societies, with the consequence that Weber carried the problem of social causation only as far as a functional model of the sort I have developed for early Israel. In his view, cause-effect interactions occur throughout a society and over time in varying ways between religious and social dimensions of the society, but he did not venture to say according to what priorities or in what sequences.

When it came to giving more precision to this general approach to social causation, Weber offered the notion of certain classes or groups within society as the bearers or carriers of certain religious ideas.[547] At this point, two of Weber's most important ideal-typical categories served to demarcate the process of convergence by which specific social groups and specific religious phenomena were drawn together. The two categories were "charisma" and "routinization." Out of any number of religious formations which have their roots in the minds and experiences of unusual personalities (who are qualified for leadership neither by hereditary succession nor by bureaucratic appointment), only those will become socially concretized or routinized which attract social groups strong enough to determine the future development of society. This is so decisive a formulation for Weber that it actually supplies a hidden bias to his supposed neutrality on the question of social causation, for what the charismatic origin of religion does is to remove the question of the causes of religion from the social equation. Religion enters into social causation only at the point where some group is attracted to and takes up the cause of a religion whose origin we know nothing about from a social point of view.

In Weber's approach, this notion of "asocial" or "supersocial" sources of religion operates both at the beginning and throughout the course of historic religions. For ancient Israel it would apply equally to the origins of Yahwism with Moses and to the redirection of Yahwism by the prophets. The "founders" or "reformers" of religion retain their inner mystery; it is only after they have launched their beliefs into the social stream that we can begin to trace causes and effects, selective adaptations and selective sloughings-off of this or that aspect of religion or socioeconomics. Thus, there remains in Weber's outlook the idealist "escape hatch" of the great personalities as the mysterious sources of religions which are later adapted into a social routine. In such a formulation of the religion-society nexus there is no way of penetrating to the social matrix in which the religious innovators themselves are formed in order to establish what regularities in the religion-society nexus tend to give rise to such religious innovations. An artificial division results between a pure presocial religion of epic personalities and a mixed, diluted, selected social religion suitable to the interests of classes and status groups.

To my mind, however, we must come to terms with Moses and the prophets, as with all religious innovators, as propagandists for a religion already formed or forming in a given social field, and thus from the start a thoroughly mixed, diluted, and selected religion.

As to particular elements in Weber's premodular sketch of the premonarchic Israelite religion-society nexus, I would concur with him on several vital points: the eclecticism both of the religion and the society of Israel; the important role of the Levitical priesthood and of the covenant mode of thought and action for giving unity to Israel's eclectic pluralism; the significance of Yahweh as a god of battle for energizing loosely organized Israelites to face external threats; the margin of freedom for socioreligious experimentation that Palestine provided as against the more economically productive and politically dominated Tigris-Euphrates and Nile heartlands, etc.

The most conspicuous weakness in Weber's analysis was his overrating of the military function of Yahwism at the expense of the social egalitarian function of Yahwism. Although there are observations in *Ancient Judaism* that point in the direction of Israel as a peculiar social order of mixed peasants and herdsmen, particularly when he comments on the covenant, these tendencies are vitiated by his positing of an early Israelite urban patrician class analogous to the Canaanite urban patrician class. This prevents Weber from establishing the most distinctive structural and ideological feature of Israelite society, namely, its deliberate and vigorously sustained break with political hierarchy and social stratification. The result of this misconstruction is to enfeeble the social-structural dimensions of his analysis of the social location of prophecy and to encourage psychologizing of the prophets as interiorized mystics and lonely innovators.

50.3 Marx: Lawfully Interacting and Evolving Inter-Human Totalities

This brings us finally to Marx, who hypothesized that at the root of all social organization and mental ideation, including religion, is the way human beings within nature act upon nature to produce their means of subsistence and thereby fashion their own social nature. As the modes of acting upon nature (technology and cooperative forms of labor) change over time, the ways people associate with and control, or are controlled by, one another (social and political organization), as well as the ways they think about themselves in nature and in society (religion and philosophy), also change correlatively.

Premises and Methods

A passage from *The German Ideology* lays out the basic perspective of historical cultural materialism in a form relatively free of obfuscating jargon:

> The premises from which we begin are not arbitrary ones, not dogmas, but real premises from which abstraction can only be made in the imagination. They are the real individuals, their activity and the material conditions under which they live, both those which they find already existing and those produced by their activity. These premises can thus be verified in a purely empirical way.
>
> The first premise of all human history is, of course, the existence of living human individuals. Thus the first fact to be established is the physical organization of these individuals and their consequent relation to the rest of nature. . . . The writing of history must always set out from these natural bases and their modification in the course of history through the action of men.
>
> Men can be distinguished from animals by consciousness, by religion or anything else you like. They themselves begin to distinguish themselves from animals as soon as they begin to *produce* their means of subsistence, a step which is conditioned by their actual physical organization. By producing their means of subsistence men are indirectly producing their actual material life.
>
> The way in which men produce their means of subsistence depends first of all on the nature of the actual means of subsistence they find in existence and have to reproduce. This mode of production must not be considered simply as being the

production of the physical existence of the individuals. Rather it is a definite form of activity of these individuals, a definite form of expressing their life, a definite *mode of life* on their part. As individuals express their life, so they are. What they are, therefore, coincides with their production, both with *what* they produce and with *how* they produce. The nature of individuals thus depends on the material conditions determining their production.[548]

According to Marx, there has been a distinctive trend in the developing modes of production = forms of activity = modes of life. Overall, changing modes of production have brought about increased population and new forms of intercourse among people that take shape according to the division of labor, i.e., according to the differentiated ways in which people participate in the modes of production and the differentials in their appropriation of what is produced. From this, Marx analyzed certain typical epochs in Western history characterized by the systems of tribal ownership, ancient communal and state ownership, feudal or estate property, and capitalism. Each of these epochs was characterized not only by a mode of production in the sense of techniques, materials, and human labor power (forces of production), but simultaneously by a mode of production in the sense of forms of activity in distinctive social and political relations with other producers (relations of production).

He then goes on to discuss the need for empirical observation of the relation of the social and political modes to the material conditions in every society to be studied.

> The fact is, therefore, that definite individuals who are productively active in a definite way enter into these definite social and political relations. Empirical observations must in each separate instance bring out empirically, and without any mystification and speculation, the connection of the social and political structure with production. The social structure and the State are continually evolving out of the life-process of definite individuals, but of individuals, not as they may appear in their own or other people's imagination, but as they *really* are: i.e., as they operate, produce materially, and hence as they work under definite material limits, presuppositions and conditions independent of their will.[549]

It should be underscored, given the constant misrepresentation of the meaning of materialism in Marxian method, that "definite material limits" include not only the techniques and materials of production but the forms of cooperative activity in production which are necessarily social forms.

Marx then notes the function of ideation and consciousness in this process of production as a definite form of activity:

> The production of ideas, of conceptions, of consciousness, is at first directly interwoven with the material activity and the material intercourse of men, the language of real life. Conceiving, thinking, the mental intercourse of men, appear at this stage as the direct efflux of their material behavior. The same applies to mental production as expressed in the language of politics, laws, morality, religion, metaphysics, etc., of a people. Men are the producers of their conceptions, ideas, etc.—real, active men, as

they are conditioned by a definite development of their productive forces and of the intercourse corresponding to these, up to its furthest forms. Consciousness can never be anything else than conscious existence, and the existence of men is their actual life-process. If in all ideology men and their circumstances appear upside-down as in a *camera obscura*, this phenomenon arises just as much from their historical life-process as the inversion of objects on the retina does from their physical life-process.[550]

In summing up this closely interconnected set of premises and methodological directives, Marx reiterates forcefully the comprehensive rigor of his intention to derive all human phenomena from the way people interact in mutual and reciprocal association to produce the means of subsistence:

> We do not set out from what men say, imagine, conceive, nor from men as narrated, thought of, imagined, conceived, in order to arrive at men in the flesh. We set out from real, active men, and on the basis of their real life-process we demonstrate the development of the ideological reflexes and echoes of this life-process . . . Morality, religion, metaphysics, all the rest of ideology and their corresponding forms of consciousness, thus no longer retain the semblance of independence. They have no history, no development; but men, developing their material production and their material intercourse, alter, along with this their real existence, their thinking and the products of their thinking. Life is not determined by consciousness, but consciousness by life. In the first method of approach the starting point is consciousness taken as the living individual; in the second method, which conforms to real life, it is the real living individuals themselves, and consciousness is considered solely as *their* consciousness.
>
> This method of approach is not devoid of premises. It starts out from the real premises and does not abandon them for a moment. Its premises are men, not in any fantastic isolation and rigidity, but in their actual, empirically perceptible process of development under definite conditions. As soon as this active life-process is described, history ceases to be a collection of dead facts as it is with the empiricists (themselves still abstract), or an imagined activity of imagined subjects, as with the idealists.[551]

I have quoted extensively from what is surely one of the clearest and most compact statements of the Marxian historical cultural-material method of approach to social and religious phenomena because I hold it to be the most coherent and promising understanding for developing research strategies in the social sciences. It provides a framework within which to include structural-functional models as stepping stones in the analytic task of determining how social evolution occurs. Insofar as this techno-environmental hypothesis can be demonstrated as an accurate account of what has happened in the human past, it should also be important for projecting future developments. I leave all questions of the future out of account, however, because they are not immediately germane to an understanding of the sociology of Israel's early religion and because it is vital for scientific inquiry to distinguish between Marx's method and the lengthening political storm in which his ideas have been embroiled since he first propounded them more than one hundred years ago. In fact, Marx may have been largely correct about social evolution and largely wrong about the precise steps to change in the immediate future. As a matter of fact, the precision of his "predictions" is often misconceived, since his main concern with the future was to uncover the crucial tendencies of present toward future. In adopting Marx's fertile perspective for scientific research into social phenomena we are not obligated to adopt without further examination his specific projections for the future, nor are we tied to any particular sociopolitical program described as Marxian.

Marx warns us against taking up his hypothesis as the occasion for more speculation. He calls for "empirical observation in each separate instance" of the connections between the social and political structure and the forces and relations of production, and, to follow out his logic, the connections between religious ideas and practices, on the one hand, and social and political structures in their techno-economic matrix, on the other hand. If we thus focus on empirical observation, we will, for example, look into the occurrence and distribution of religious phenomena in relation to social and political forms and to the modes of production, and we will try to establish—over the range of data which we can empirically control—whether there is a demonstrated constellation of these phenomena and whether they can best be explained on the hypothesis that changes in the forms of production (including techniques and modes of cooperative labor) lead correlatively to changes in social and political forms and to changes in ideas, including religious ideas.

Contrary to superficial dismissals of the Marxian hypothesis, it is not invalidated by observations such as Weber's that religion exercises counter-influences on society and production.[552] Nor is the Marxian hypothesis invalidated by its failure to find connections as predicted in every societal instance. The historical cultural-material hypothesis will be invalidated if the counter-influences of religion or ideas in general on social relations and production can be shown to be either purely arbitrary or voluntaristic (e.g., as the function of strong will or belief), or if religion and ideas in general can be shown to be inclusively explanatory of the regular appearance of particular forms of social relations and production. Likewise, the historical cultural-material hypothesis will be invalidated if the connections among factors identified by Marx as regularities are statistically reducible to mere chance. In any of these regards, the hypothesis will be exposed as having no diagnostic or prognostic legitimacy. Scientific tests of the hypothesis are called for rather than the persisting abundance of mindless dismissals of the hypothesis because it is too comprehensive or because it threatens or embarrasses the social or philosophical stance of the critic.

What we ask after all of an adequate hypothesis in social sciences is not that it prove itself in all imaginable detail or that the factors it isolates as predominant in certain regards operate to the total exclusion of all other factors. What we ask is that it be more adequate in its explanations of social-change phenomena than any other hypothesis dealing with the same data. This includes recognition of what the hypothesis actually explains, what it does not purport to explain, and what it has not yet explained (although it is striving in that direction). Accordingly, when a theory says that, all other things being equal, an x-complex of natural and human factors will lead to a y-complex of social changes, we regard it as a valid operational theory if the posited sequences of preceding factors and consequent changes do in fact occur more regularly than the sequences posited by other theories. Moreover, if a theory establishes such regularities in social change, we regard it as a successful provisional rebuttal of anti-theorists who claim either that no social change occurs or that social change is purely arbitrary.

Critics of the historical cultural-material hypothesis are sound insofar as they challenge the use of that hypothesis as a dogma or as a simple formula producing instantly patent results wherever applied. The hypothesis has no other justification than as a scientific method, and it must stand or fall on how accurately and amply it illuminates the evidence. Now the evidence, or the subject matter, of the hypothesis is the stuff of human history itself, the endless succession of variously arranged human interactions with nature and of person with person in definite social forms. Therefore, every application of the hypothesis is a complex operation that must take into account the specific conjunctions and trajectories of the phenomena, not as one would wish them to be, but as they are actually observed to be at work.

Somewhat differently stated, the historical cultural-material hypothesis must be flexible and fine-grained enough not only to establish the main lines of social development but also to achieve increasing refinement in penetrating the initial opacity of historical contexts in which the phenomena are never twice combined in precisely the same way in all respects. Far from being a dogma or a finished formula, the historical cultural method is a scientific-field theory, or even a meta-field theory (since it embraces data from so many disciplines), that is still in its infancy—its potentialities but modestly realized and, like all theories of the human mind, capable of misunderstanding and abuse.

Marx himself gave surprisingly little attention to empirical observations about religion, and Engels and other Marxians only a little more attention.[553] For the cultural-material hypothesis to be properly tested in its full range, enormous amounts of empirical work remain to be undertaken, in the course of which the Marxian hypothesis about social change may be overthrown altogether, or what is even more likely, may be expanded to include accounts of the various forms of complex mediation between and among the different levels of social life. Such modifications and refinements can go on indefinitely within the cultural-material evolutionary framework, which will remain intact in its fundamental force so long as empirical evidence verifies that the material conditions of production, expressed in concrete social activity organized around forces and relations of production, retain the fundamental initiating role in social change.

Origin and Destiny of Religion

One approach to "the origin of religion" is excluded if we follow the historical cultural-material directive. The hypothesis gives us no basis for speculation about the prehistorical rise of religion predicated on psychological reconstructions of primitive man or on conjectured primal happenings, in the manner of Freud's positing of the deity as the return of the slain father. To be sure, Marx assumed that in prehistoric times, before the rise of class relations as a social form to control the means of production, there was no religion. At present this claim is untestable, and it may never be testable. There are promising developments in archaeology, in conjunction with anthropology, which have begun to develop "a sociology of material remains," i.e., ways of drawing conclusions about the social relations of those who made the material artifacts of the past.[554] So far attempts at "a theology of material remains" have been grossly amateurish, amounting to little more than speculations about belief in spirits or survival of the dead.[555]

Strictly speaking, an historical cultural-material method at this point simply says: Over the range of empirical data for human societies that we can control, religion appears as a type of cultural expression in various forms correlative to various congeries of material conditions. Thus, assuming that the same conditions observed in known societies hold good in situations still beyond our empirical observation (in prehistoric times or in historic societies for which we lack data), we hypothesize that the observed relation of religion to material conditions also holds good in those as yet unobserved contexts. The methodological point is that we do not pull a theory of the origin of religion out of thin air and then impose it on observed religions. We form a theory of religion based on observed religions in their social contexts and then extrapolate to unobserved religions. This extrapolation is distinguished from the verified body of theory by the fact that we await further data which it may be hoped new methods of recovering the past can bring to us.

The religion Marx empirically observed was mostly modern European, in both Jewish and Christian forms. In keeping with the above methodological discussion, it seems to me that his confidence that religion will disappear under new forms of social relations in the future is a concrete function of the religious sublimations he knew best. If, as he thought, religion is chiefly or exclusively a form of class justification and of class struggle (whether employed by the dominators or by the dominated), it follows logically that with the disappearance of class struggle, religion will also disappear. If, however, it turns out that religion is a more pervasive form of consciousness that cannot be restricted to any of the known religions, or to all of them taken together, and is further separable from beliefs in gods as personal beings or as invisible forces, it may be that its origins are anterior to social stratification in a form of ideation which tries to grasp the synthetic human experience of the interpenetrating mode of production, network of social relations, and elaborated cultural products *as a coherent but changing, even fragile, totality.* If that possibility is admissible to a cultural-materialist orientation, religious consciousness in which people did not alienate their selfhood may at one time in prehistory have preceded the distorted sublimations that accompanied class divisions. If so, such religious consciousness (comparable to the attributes of "socialist consciousness" or of "religious naturalism") might continue indefinitely into the future.[556]

Of course, a religious consciousness differentiated from belief in the dogmatic content and observance of the liturgy of any particular religion is sufficiently unlike religion as we know it to raise the question of the appropriateness of labeling it as "religion," or even as "religious consciousness." The essential feature of such a consciousness of the whole context of human life would be the exclusion of all nonmaterial reality as the religious object, i.e., the exclusion of gods and spirits as nonhuman or superhuman beings. Whether such a stage of "religion" can ever be directly verified for prehistoric humans seems highly dubious, since its hypothesized absence of specific sublimated religious objects seems to imply that we should not expect to find any material evidence of such a consciousness in cult regalia or in iconography, unless of course certain artistic products of prehistoric peoples constitute such evidence.

Another class of evidence is the growing body of persons who count themselves either as atheists or as agnostics, or whose experience and interpretation of the traditional religious traditions and dogmas is moving steadily in the direction of evacuating them of any objective—i.e., of any nonhuman or superhuman— content. Insofar as, over extended time and in various contexts, this phenomenon of rejection or diminution of religious content can be correlated to social and political forms and to the forces and relations of production, it may become possible to test Marx's cultural-material version of religion. What I am pointing out is that the Marxian view of religion cannot be settled by merely reaffirming or denying its truth, but only by extended scientific research and by the future unfolding of human life in changing social relations.

Researched Regularities in Social and Religious Change

Since for American scholars, until very recent years, Marxian social research has seemed to be no more than elaboration of sterile dogma or the brandishing of weapons in political combat, it is of some surprise to discover the extent to which Marxian methodology has in fact been applied by Western scholars, although often in disguise because of the fear of social rejection and at times because scholars did not recognize the intellectual roots of the method they were employing. Marvin Harris, in the first history of anthropological theory to appear in English in thirty years, traces some of the acknowledged and unacknowledged debt to Marx expressed in anthropological research over the last generation or two.[557] This debt shows up in sustained efforts to get anthropological research and theory off the dead center of historical-particularist, culture-and-personality, structural-functional, and ethno-linguistic approaches to society. Instead of merely classifying data or restating problems of social causation tautologically, there are new strategies aimed at discovering the laws of social behavior and of social evolution (what are termed the "nomothetic revival" and "etics").[558]

Identifying himself with cultural materialism, in broad company with Leslie White, Gordon Childe, and Julian Steward, Harris formulates a cultural-materialist theory for guiding research strategy which is remarkably like Marx's statement cited above, minus rhetorical flourishes:

> I believe that the analogue of the Darwinian strategy in the realm of sociocultural phenomena is the principle of techno-environmental and techno-economic determinism. This principle holds that similar technologies applied to similar environments tend to produce similar arrangements of labor in production and distribution, and that these in turn call forth similar kinds of social groupings, which justify and coordinate their activities by means of similar systems of values and beliefs. Translated into research strategy, the principle of techno-environmental, techno-economic determinism assigns priority to the study of the material conditions of sociocultural life, much as the principle of natural selection assigns priority to the study of differential reproductive success.[559]

Harris further reports on some of the successes of the application of the cultural-materialist approach to social phenomena which idealist strategies of various stripes have failed to penetrate.[560]

I will not tarry to debate whether Harris also makes sense when he rejects the dialetical aspect of Marx's method as excess harmful baggage carried over from Hegel. Harris has a point if dialectics refers, as he supposes, only to catastrophic change, since he wants to take slower, cumulative change into account; but, unless I am badly mistaken, dialectics for Marx referred to the dynamic interaction of all levels of the social system and to the altogether different qualities and quantities in the actions and reactions of social phenomena according to how they are related to other social phenomena over time. Such variations in quality and quantity would embrace catastrophic and cumulative change.[561] If I read Harris rightly, he too is committed to dialectics in this sense; it appears rather that Harris is trying to avoid political controversy in the choice of a cultural-materialist research strategy and has therefore rejected a term frequently clouded with crude politicized meanings.

Certainly one of the cultural-materialist studies cited by Harris which should be of great interest to biblical scholars is the work of Robert Mc.C. Adams on ancient

Mesopotamian and Meso-American urban civilizations. Adams sums up his study of these two strikingly parallel but independent developments as follows:

> What seems overwhelmingly most important about these differences [between Mesopotamia and Meso-America] is how small they bulk even in aggregate, when considered against the mass of similarities in form and process. In short, the parallels in the Mesopotamian and Mexican "careers to statehood," in the forms that institutions ultimately assumed as well as in the processes leading to them, suggest that both instances are most significantly characterized by a common core of regularly occurring features. We discover anew that social behavior conforms not merely to laws but to a limited number of such laws, which perhaps has always been taken for granted in the case of cultural subsystems (e.g., kinship) and among "primitives" (e.g., hunting bands). Not merely as an abstract article of faith but as a valid starting point for detailed, empirical analysis, it applies equally well to some of the most complex and creative of human societies.[562]

Adams strikes precisely the note that is required as historical cultural materialism emerges from its entanglement in the cold war to wider acceptance as a valid and enormously promising approach, whose possibilities have been barely explored compared to the overuse of other methods which have gotten us very little distance in explaining social phenomena. Adams' reference to lawful social behavior, within surprisingly tight cultural-material parameters, "not merely as an abstract article of faith but as a valid starting point for detailed, empirical analysis," points succinctly to Marx's confidence in his method as a scientific method. But why not add: Not *at all* as an abstract article of faith, but as a guiding hypothesis to be changed by enrichment, alteration, and if need be by discard, as the evidence indicates?

How, then, would an historical cultural-materialist strategy deal with the emergence of Yahwism in ancient Israel? Oddly enough, the purportedly Durkheimian hypothesis of Guy Swanson about the association of monotheism with sovereign groups in a hierarchical arrangement appears to have some promise for a cultural-materialist approach to Yahwism. In this connection it is of note that Swanson thought the results of his inquiry to be a refutation of any "compensatory" view of religion.[563] Apparently Swanson attributed to Marx the theory that when men were hungry they invented gods to console them or to induce nature to increase the food supply. Since Swanson found that the societies with developed beliefs in single dominant deities were generally societies with ample agricultural surpluses, he was confident that he had shown Marx to be wrong. On the contrary, however, Marx recognized that religious "compensation" (which is not his word) occurred with indirection and subtlety and did not depend at all upon there being a natural scarcity of goods but rather on the available goods being monopolized in certain ways by certain groups so that some in the society were deprived while others were enriched. Marx stressed the "masking" or "mystifying" function of religion in giving ideological justification to those power relations by which some dominated the means of production at the expense of others.

One might reasonably expect, therefore, in keeping with Swanson's discovery that monotheism is associated with efforts to mediate the purposes of sovereign groups in a society, that some forms of unifying purpose are articulated religiously by picturing the god's supremacy as the legitimation of the supremacy of the society's overarching resolution of the struggle among contending internal sub-groups. In this manner the social stress and conflict entailed in reconciling the highly differentiated qualities and quantities of "local" sovereignties were eased by positing these arrangements as the determination of a superhuman will taking precedence over the desires and preferences of individual actors in the society. This explanation of religion, and especially of beliefs in single high gods with pronounced personalities and wills, is related to supernatural sanctions for morality (an aspect of religion also treated by Swanson), which buttress loyalty to a particular set of social arrangements. It is noticeable how often in such societies blasphemy and treason are closely connected: to blaspheme the god(s) is to undermine society, and to attack the social order is to dishonor and disobey the god(s).

Such an understanding of religion throws light on the high-energy intensity and gravity of religion which, even though it is concerned with "holy" matters set apart from daily life, is in fact directed toward the preservation of a social order always in danger of becoming unbalanced. It should be emphasized that an historical cultural-materialist account of religion as the mystifying validation of social order does not necessitate the attribution of hypocrisy or deceit to the social actors who entertain the religious beliefs, not even to those at the top of the society who profit most from religion's social-security function. In reality, the beliefs are generally held with sincerity and often with the deep emotional investment of "conviction." After all, the religious mystification long precedes the consciousness of the individual social actors at any moment in time.

The truth is that, short of scientific method people have no means of penetrating to the origins of the religious disguise which to their minds looks like transparent truth. Here applies the wisdom of Marx's insight that no science of society can ever be constructed by naively beginning (or naively ending!) with what people think about themselves as social beings:

> The social structure and the State are continually evolving out of the life-process of definite individuals, but of individuals, not as they may appear in their own or other people's imagination, but as they *really* are, i.e., as they operate, produce materially, and hence as they work under definite material limits, presuppositions and conditions independent of their will.[564]

Mystified by its past and mystifying in its present, religion becomes one of the definite material limits, passed along from generation to generation, that molds all its participants into more or less sincere believers in what is, after all, the upside-down (Marx's *camera obscura)* image of their accepted social world.

Swanson's study, however, leaves too many aspects of the societal complex lightly touched upon to be an entirely convincing cultural-materialist study. In his coding of the societies from Murdock's World Ethnographic Sample, there are a number of items that fall within or are closely connected with the cultural-material base in production (e.g., principal source of food, amount of food produced, forms of property, debts, social classes determined by differences in wealth, etc.). But the codification is sufficiently cryptic that, in the end, it is not possible to tell exactly, for example, how Swanson intends to correlate the social relations of sovereign groups to the techno-environmental and techno-economic base.

Indeed, even in terms of the specification of sovereign groups as hierarchically arranged, the criteria of hierarchic arrangement are none too clear. At first glance, the reader assumes that Swanson refers to political centralization in the state. However, a perusal of his societal samples casts grave doubt on this interpretation, since many of the coded societies seem to have been no more than rank societies and possibly even egalitarian societies. Thus, it is much more probable that Swanson means by "hierarchy" any agreed-upon adjustment of respective jurisdictions by sovereign groups in a society, with the result that some jurisdictions will be "wider" or "higher" than others according to criteria of numbers of persons affected, range of social behavior affected, and principles of precedence when two jurisdictions make contrary claims.

When the social relations correlated to monotheism are left in that much ambiguity, it is clear that Swanson's study must be treated as no more than a very limited pointer in cultural-materialist directions. An adequate cultural-material strategy for enlarging upon Swanson's undertaking would have to do more than justify its sample of societies on the basis of representativeness of regions and noncontamination by historic religions. The sample would have to reflect representativeness of the zones of social organization in the scale of social evolution as developed by Steward, Service, Sahlins, Fried, and others: band, tribe, chiefdom, state.[565] To do this adequately it would be necessary to go back to the sources on each society. In any case, Swanson, true to his Durkheimian orientation, does not think it important to arrange the societies sampled for the religious item of monotheism according to their incidence in the several zones of social organization, or to determine where the societies sampled for various other religious items beside monotheism distribute themselves comparatively within the zones of social organization. In sum, it appears that Swanson barely broke out of the Durkheimian circle of social facts and collective representations embedded in the collective mind; his empiricism does not properly capitalize on the cultural-material possibilities hinted at.

Meanwhile, significant applications of far more careful and systematic methods of cultural materialism to primitive societies have been undertaken by the French anthropologists Claude Meillassoux and Emmanuel Terray in their work on the Guro of the Ivory Coast.[566] They have attempted to analyze precisely the means of subsistence, the forms of cooperation in work, the social relations of production, distribution, and consumption, and the relation of all these basal economic factors to superstructural factors such as the kinship system. Interrelations of social phenomena and their determinations by the way production is organized and its results shared are carefully broken down into analytic units. These efforts at greater methodological precision in the study of production in primitive societies are exemplary of the sort of work to be undertaken in additional societies. Provisional as their achievements are (they do not treat religion, for example), and as lively and heated as are their differences (especially over the exact characterization of the means of production), Meillassoux and Terray have already opened lines of research which are able to do what the static formalism of Levi-Strauss's "order of orders" and the structural-functionalist's "expressive totality" have been unable to do: to indicate what elements in society are "dominant" or "basal" in the sense of exhibiting priority in the initiation of social change; and, of equal importance, in what combination of elements and along what trajectories the change occurs.

50.4 Priority of Cultural-Material Conditions and Social Struggle: Yahwism as a Societal "Feedback" Servomechanism

Given the foregoing understandings of historical cultural materialism as an hypothesis about social development and as a framework for social research, I shall now translate the model of Yahwist/tribal egalitarian functional interdependence into a model of Israelite socioreligious development which can serve as the basis for further research strategies along the lines of cultural-material premises.

A Movement for Social Equality Subtends Yahwism

The closed, noncausal model of the functional interchangeability of religion and society in ancient Israel can be rendered into a developmentally open historical cultural-materialist hypothesis which states the priority of Israelite social relations over Yahwist religion in the intitiation of cultural innovation and in the stabilization of the new cultural network. This formulation moves beyond the noncommittal "expressive totality" of a functionally described society in which the identification of variables as independent and dependent is strictly equivocal, because the functional method offers no basis or tools for analyzing change sequences and for weighing variably the different sectors and items of social life according to their importance in moving the system along certain lines of development.

A cultural-materialist version of my functional model states: (1) that social-egalitarian relations (rooted, of course, in the constant production and reproduction of the material conditions of existence) among proto-Israelites and Israelites provided the "leading edge" (initiating motive and energy) in bringing the Yahwist religious innovation into being, and (2) that within this flow of social relations into religious symbolization, the Yahwist religion powerfully sustained the foundational egalitarian social relations. Thus a cultural-materialist model need not exclude, and would in fact be simplistic in excluding, the reciprocal and reinforcing impact of Yahwism on the primary social relations rooted in production. Ample room is present for semi-independent religious initiatives, not on the Weberian model of unlawful oscillatory exchanges of initiative between social relations and religion, but on the model of fundamental initiative lying in the social relations from which the variously elaborated religious developments "feed back" toward the strengthening or the weakening, the maintaining or the altering, of the given stream of social relations. In other words, Yahwism, possessed of forceful and richly elaborated religious contents, works as "a feedback loop" within the larger parameters of a controlling system of social relations rooted in production.

There are a number of lines of historical evidence drawn from data and models in earlier chapters which support this hypothesis. I shall briefly focus the most important of these lines of historical reasoning upon the cultural-material hypothesis of Israelite origins:

EGALITARIAN ORIGINS OF YAHWISM. The religion of Yahweh appeared from the start exclusively as the religion of socially egalitarian peoples. It is not known to have had any other kind of social base prior to its adoption or innovation by Israel. If we assume, as is most probable, that Yahwism had a prehistory in the proto-Israelite Moses group, everything that we know of the Moses group confirms that it was socially egalitarian in reaction to hierarchic and stratified social relations. Endeavors to trace elements of Yahwism to pre-Mosaic roots, either in biblical traditions or in extrabiblical sources, are so hypothetical, and the elements traced are themselves so disengaged from any larger pattern, as to yield no firm picture of an autonomous religion or of a corresponding socioeconomic base for the sought-after pre-Mosaic religious roots.

PROTO-ISRAELITE SOCIAL RELATIONS. Contrary to the absence of connections between Yahwism and its presumed religious precursors or sources, the prehistory of the social relations of early Israel is somewhat better known. Lines of convergence among various social groups in pre-Israelite Canaan ('apiru, Shosu, depressed peasants, transhumant pastoralists) had been gathering force for two centuries prior to the formation of Israel. Straining at the sociopolitically layered and regionally balkanized structures of the dominant Egypto-Canaanite order, these converging social groups moved steadily (which is not to say smoothly or always at the same rate of speed everywhere) in the direction of intertribal social egalitarianism. The intertribal social egalitarianism of early Israel possesses, therefore, an historical and social backdrop that removes its innovativeness from the realm of sheer arbitrariness.

PROTO-ISRAELITE RELIGION(S). The proper perspective on the innovativeness of Yahwism is not to grasp after the straws of the pre-Israelite origins of this or that feature of Yahwism, or to see Yahwism as a resurfacing sublimation of Egyptian monotheism (Atonism), but to pay attention to the religions of the peoples who were converging socially toward the formation of Israel. While these precursors of Israelite social rebellion were non-Yahwists, they were not lacking forms of religion by which they validated their social existence. When the innovative social relations of Israel emerged sharply into the Canaanite world they were articulated in religious form. It seems reasonable to conclude, by analogy, that the pre-Yahwistic social rebellion of underclass Canaanites also had religious articulations, even if they were more muted and uncoordinated than in the case of Yahwistic Israel.

Regrettably we know little about the religious ideas and practices of the socially restive Canaanite groups which would differentiate their cults and ideologies from the better-known versions of Canaanite religion promulgated by the city-state elites. The methodological point is to formulate the inquiry differently than in the past efforts to reconstruct the origins of the formal elements that went into Yahwism viewed as a self-contained religious entity. The study of the religion of Yahwism must be placed within an inquiry into the religious forms of the social groups that converged toward Israel and emerged at last as Israel. Previous studies of Canaanite religion and of pre-Yahwistic religious survivals in early Israel, such as the titles and cults of the gods of the fathers and of El who were eventually conflated with Yahweh, are all to the good.[567] The religious data, however, must be set within the framework of social-egalitarian tendencies, movements, and systems against the larger hierarchic and stratified background of Canaanite society. In particular we need to give more attention to El as the central, if not sole, deity of a pre-Yahwistic intertribal egalitarian formation with the very name Israel which preceded, and in some respects anticipated, the later Yahwistic intertribal formation of Israel as the people of Yahweh.[568]

A TOTAL SOCIETY–NOT A NEW RELIGION. The lines of evidence brought forth in previous chapters point conclusively to earliest Israel as eclectically composed of various social groups (and survivors of groups) with differentiated prior histories, sociopolitical fortunes, and religious affiliations. The point of conjunction for these groups was not the introduction of a new religion per se as an alternative to other religions. The point of conjunction was rather a new set of social relations with appropriate religious counterparts as an aspect of the new social relations or as a symbolic phrasing of the new social relations. The world of Canaanite polytheism would have had no difficulty in including another god, and it could even have allowed for a god to be exclusively worshipped by a particular group. What the Canaanite world, given its hierarchic social formation, could not allow was that these religious elaborations should have a corresponding social base that would directly undermine the social base of Canaanite hierarchy and stratification. The novelty and threat of early Israel was not the introduction of new religious ideas and practices as such but the conjunction of previously separated and contradictory social groups in a united and mutually supportive network of egalitarian relations.

The cultural-materialist priority of the social relations over the religious formations, even in an instance where notoriety has attached to the religious formations because of their abiding impact on later religions, is attested in the biblical tradition by the recognition that the ancestors of Israel struggled toward social-egalitarian existence with the help of older religious forms, such as the gods of the fathers and El, before they realized their objective more fully as an intertribal association with a Yahweh cult and ideology. When the inverted image of the society-religion nexus is turned right side up, we can identify the continuity of the social struggle with its adaptive selecting out of various religious forms, leading finally to Yahwism.

In an historical cultural-material framework, the continuity of the struggle toward social egalitarianism can be identified in the biblical traditions under the guise of a religious philosophy of history according to which Yahweh of united Israel was present under other names and modes of action in the prehistory of the peoples who entered Yahwistic Israel. The cultural-material directive is to press the religious data back to their social base. In short, the proper phrasing and nuancing of hypotheses and the proper pointing of research strategies is to move away from studying the independent or abstracted history of religious ideas and practices, merely because that is the way the Yahwistic cult and ideology viewed matters, and to move toward the study of the religious phenomena in ancient Israel and its environs as concrete forms of expression for concrete social relations anchored to the forces and relations of production.

Yahwism Legitimates and Empowers a Movement for Social Equality

Since the cultural-materialist assertion of the initiating and sustaining primordial status of social relations over religious formations has been and will continue to be fiercely resisted by idealist theoreticians, we must dwell in more detail on the reasons for saying that the admission of Yahwism's functional selectivity in enforcing social-egalitarian relations neither demonstrates the priority of religion over social relations nor corroborates the evasive Weberian co-determinacy of religion and social relations. There is an orderliness to social evolution, such as that noted so cogently by Adams with respect to urban Mesopotamia and Meso-America, which leads us to try to locate the fundamental structures of lawful social behavior. Social forms have arisen and changed according to regularities which belie the contention that ideas in men's heads have been responsible for their introduction and development—and this includes the idea that the gods give men their ideas.

Nor does it make sense to call off the search for the social-change regularities by saying with Weber that *sometimes* socioeconomic forms take the lead in change and *sometimes* religious forms take the lead. Even if that observation contains a certain rough prescientific truth, this capricious "sometimes" does not deal with the phenomena scientifically, unless it can show according to what regularities various sectors of society take the lead in social development. Lawful social behavior certainly does not mean rigid homogeneous behavior; else how could social change have come about? Laws of society will certainly uncover many sectors and levels of behavior with varying jurisdictions and temporal ranges, acting and interacting within the conditions set by the whole system. Laws of society aim at formulating the constants in social relations with sufficient clarity that the range of variation in social change can be explained as logical mediations of the constants.

With such an understanding of the rationale for the continued search for the laws of society, let us look more closely at how we can trace the lawful behavior of Yahwism as a crucial feedback loop within a social system whose basic parameters are set by the social relations grounded in material conditions.

YAHWISM AS CRUCIAL FACILITATOR OF SOCIAL EQUALITY. We recognize the peculiarity of the Yahwistic feedback loop in Israelite egalitarianism when we give due weight to the developmental reality that the Yahwistic cult and ideology validated and motivated egalitarian social relations to so great an extent that it proved to be the single most significant servomechanism for the society. My initially functional model formulated Yahwism's projection of a single demanding, norm-sanctioning and behavior-motivating deity and his peculiarly nonconsumptive and politically unobtrusive cult as factors of significant, indeed decisive, effect in maintaining the desired social relations. When that functional model is phrased in terms of the model of a communication system, we see that the basic units of the system are modes for processing information structured according to certain ends. If we posit early Israel as an egalitarian social-action system, the symbolic projection of Yahwism appears as a servomechanism which served to feed "information" back into the social relations and thereby enabled the system constantly to "correct" itself. Yahwism thus appears as a symbolic facilitator of the kind of social interaction which the system prized highly and whose regular occurrence was the condition of the system's continuance.[569]

In other words, the interdependence of tribal egalitarianism and Yahwism— when phrased as a communication system whose information consists of "measuring" and "reporting" adherence to or departure from egalitarian social relations rooted in forces and relations of production—points us toward an understanding of Yahwism as a particular mechanism for organizing social information and for symbolically objectifying it in such a way that maximal system-building behavior-input from all the social actors is encouraged. Although the communication-system analogy for human interaction systems is not altogether apt, since it lacks a genetic dimension as well as positing a loop closed to all external disturbance, it does offer a theoretical understanding of how prominent idea-formations, which appear to be *sui generis* and even massively dominant in a society, are in fact subordinate to the entire system, similar to feedback loops as servomechanisms. The feedback loop has no independent status as a "cause" of the system, but is rather itself "caused" by the requirement of the system for certain ways of organizing information so that the system can monitor and adjust itself. Correspondingly, the historical cultural-material hypothesis is that Yahwism is derivable from the social system as a whole and meaningful only in the frame of reference and realm of discourse provided by the social relations of which it was a particular form of symbolic expression.

IDEOLOGY OF SOCIAL EQUALITY: ONE GOD–ONE PEOPLE. It may further be said that social relations of a certain type require an ideological formation commensurate with them. To say this is not to imply that the ideology is required to bring the system into being, in the sense that a preexisting idea or configuration of ideas leads to its realization in actual social relations. It is to say something very different, namely, that ideology or symbolic projections of actual human beings in a definite configuration of social relations, once they reach a certain level of objectification, can and do serve to solidify, motivate, and extend the primary social relations within the limits of the total techno-environmental, economic, and sociopolitical field. Consequently, the introduction of a new philosophy or religion is not to be construed as an unlawful exception to the material-social conditions of life, but rather as a definite sign that a breach or polarity has occurred in the material-social conditions; as evidence that society, so to speak, is pulling in two or more directions and, therefore, new and competitive projective symbolisms have arisen to legitimate and solidify the forces in struggle.

When religion is thus hypothesized as the symbolic side of social struggle, it may be said of Yahwism that at a certain point in the widening and deepening struggle of social groups antagonistic toward the dominant Canaanite system and converging toward one another, the consciousness of struggle in the shaping of concrete egalitarian social relations crystallized in the ideology of Yahwism. This construction of the rise of Yahwism in no way denies, but rather implies, that elements used to form the new ideological configuration were drawn from preexistent sources. Put in such terms, the ideology of Yahwism has more in common with Canaanite religion in terms of its formal structure as projective ideology than is usually admitted, for this similarity in formal structure allows for endless difference in detail and even for the fundamental novelty of "standing Canaanite religion on its head" just as Israelite society was engaged in "standing Canaanite society on its head."

It cannot escape our attention that, instead of the many gods, Israel projected one God, in symbolic complementarity with the determined way in which, in place of the many strata of Canaanite society, Israel projected a strataless society, which is to say: one indivisible God for one indivisible people. The cultural-material hypothesis begins with the assumption that Yahwism as the symbolic side of Israelite social relations had no existence whatsoever independent of the thoughts of these particular socially egalitarian Israelite people. Scientifically, which means concretely and actually, Yahwism was the symbolic work of an intense and bitter social struggle, as all ideas and practices are the work of people in given social relations which evolve over time.

Lest this cultural-material reduction seem to deprive Yahwism of its admittedly immense significance, even if that significance has been erroneously construed time and again, let it be emphatically repeated that the feedback effect of Yahwism within the social-egalitarian formation of Israel was of such importance as a servomechanism that only as the social actors were able to produce just such innovative ideas of "transcending" sources of social energy were they able to "clinch" the social relations of equality in an enduring pattern over some two centuries of time.

However, the cultural-material reduction holds firm, for the cultural-material reduction is a resolution of apparently patternless phenomena into regular mediations of the empirical relations of actual human beings "reduced" to the fundamental structural simplicities of human existence. The idealist or supernatural reduction, on the other hand, is a referral of patternless phenomena to inaccessible causes which are equally patternless. They do no more than justify the abandonment of explanation.[570] Thus the chimera of the upside-down *camera obscura,* or of the illusion of the feedback loop that precedes and fashions the communication system. If we are committed to scientific method, to building methodically on what we already know (and of course "knowing" means not that we grasp objects in themselves but that we perceive their predictable and retrodictable relationships and can make use of that understanding for human purposes), we must consistently and relentlessly return to history and to society (which are, after all, the same reality seen from two different perspectives) as the experience of actual individuals in association. With respect to Israelite Yahwism, we begin to "know" it when we ascertain that only the attainment by actual individuals of a certain form of social relations under the historical conditions of thirteenth–eleventh century Canaan could have produced the content and the form of the religion of Yahwism.

"GREAT MEN" AND "CHARISMATIC" NON-THEORIES OF YAHWISM. If, as a last line of defense, resort is had to "great men" theories of history, or to more subtle "charismatic" hypotheses, in order to exclude Moses or the Moses group from the social-evolutionary process and thus from the social production of religion, we are simply once more on the same untenable ground as when we try to exempt Israel as a whole from the social production of its religion. Moses or the Moses group cannot be bracketed out of the continuum of social evolution. The sharp objectification of Yahwism was in any case not a conception that Moses or his group received as passive receptacles of ideas; it was a conception within *his* or *their* human consciousness. Moreover, it was not a conception flowing from them as contextless initiators of new ideas but the determinate conception of persons formed in definite social relations, i.e., the concrete expression of their socially produced human consciousness. Idealist accounts of religion do not become one whit more convincing when they point to extraordinary religious "founders," for whether they are a mass, a smaller group, or single individuals, people are social beings, including the most "charismatic" and innovative among them.

51

A Program of Historical Cultural-Material Research into Early Israel

Identification of social relations as the initiating source of religion does not, of course, constitute the whole or even the heart of cultural materialism, for we must then go on to ground the social relations in particular techno-environmental and techno-economic foundations. We have done so to the degree that we have recognized the agricultural small-peasant productive basis of Israelite life and in the measure that we have called attention to the way Yahwism furthered the independent agricultural production of Israel—not only positively by the norms of socially egalitarian reciprocity it endorsed, but negatively as well by relinquishing customary excessive religious claims to the populace's economic surplus. It should be evident, however, that a cultural-material model for early Israel, with its concrete material base fully in view, has not been sufficiently deepened and developed in an economic and environmental direction. In the present work, this insufficiency is due in considerable degree to my own lack of specific training and experience in those disciplines and skills vital to assembling the data for analysis of the economic and cultural-material foundations of old Israel. Moreover, those who have done most to study the relevant material have generally lacked a sustained and coherent research strategy capable of relating their findings to testable social-developmental hypotheses. This methodological poverty applies both to specialists in biblical studies and to specialists in Near Eastern studies.

51.1 An Economic and Cultural-Material Inventory

If we are to extend and deepen an historical cultural-materialist hypothesis of the social and religious development of Israel, the following kinds of economic and cultural-material information are needed regarding early Israel in comparative context with its neighbors and in terms of temporal trajectories:

FORCES OF PRODUCTION. What were the forces of production in early Israel, including raw materials (mineral, plant, and animal), environmental conditions and climate, physical condition of the human laborers, tools, the simple and complex work processes involved in the transformation of each of the relevant raw materials into the products to be distributed and consumed? From the composite results there will emerge a concrete account of *the actual material base of the society, both in its raw state and in its cultural transformation* into consumable products.

RELATIONS OF PRODUCTION. What were the relations of production in early Israel, with particular attention to: (1) the forms of cooperation among the producers in keeping with the respective requirements of the predominant processes of production, e.g., effects on residential patterns, seasonal work cycles, etc.; and (2) the ways of appropriating and distributing what was produced, e.g., "ownership" or "use rights," distribution of decision-making powers, etc.? The forms of cooperation and appropriation may in fact be characterized according to number of people, duration, sex and age differentiation, direct or indirect reciprocity, structure of interaction, etc., and from the composite result will emerge a concrete picture of *the division of labor* and of *the specific networks of human interaction* rooted in the ways Israelites organized themselves to produce and to appropriate their material subsistence.

POPULATION AND ECONOMIC GEOGRAPHY. What was the size and distribution of population characterized not only according to its regional location and growth curve, but also according to the populace's common and differentiated participation in the processes and relations of production? From the combined results will emerge a picture of the *variable mixtures of forces and relations of production* according to *the different geographical regions* in diachronic dimension and according to *the approximate numbers or proportions of the populace engaged in them.*

Moreover, the familiar and vital discipline of historical geography, long an adjunct of biblical study, must be deepened and specialized to include techno-environmental studies and economic geography whereby a bridge between economics and social relations will be more firmly established than at present. Among the items to be clarified are: sources of raw materials, distances (if any) from sources of materials to processing sites, land fertility and effect of soil types on the mixture of forces and relations of production, impact of technological innovations on population size and distribution and on sociocultural innovations, material factors facilitating or inhibiting the storage, circulation, and distribution of products, and all manner of *topographical, geological, hydrological, climatological, and other natural factors entailed in the shaping of the total Israelite mix of forces and relations of production,* both in its typical totality and in its regional variations, as well as in its changing dynamics over time.

This brief inventory of types of techno-environmental and techno-economic information needed for an adequate testing of a cultural-materialist hypothesis of social change in ancient Israel will necessarily be extended in the pursuit of detailed research strategies.[571] Similar specifications can be drawn for the information needed concerning the social and political forms and the ideational forms of religion in order to correlate them with the forces and relations of production.[572] Some of this latter task has been carried out in an initial schematic way in earlier chapters of this work. Enough has been said to show that our work is barely begun in the requisite direction, and it is by now clear that a great range of expertise in many disciplines previously considered marginal or irrelevant to biblical studies will have to be drawn into the enterprise. My undertaking in this study has been informed by a gross hypothesis of the predominance of agriculture in ancient Israel and of the location of the primary relations of production in the extended family. Given the erratic attention of biblical scholars and Near Eastern specialists to such questions, it was as far as I could personally carry the hypothesis at this stage. Nonetheless, our information on the material culture of early Israel is not so meager as the absence of systematic, testable, cultural-materialist hypotheses of social change in Israel implies.

51.2 Historico-Territorial and Topological Studies

For example, A. Alt's historico-territorial method, by paying attention to the correlation of topography and political units in ancient Palestine over extended time spans in which variables could be controlled, was able to introduce significant proto-sociological perspectives for treating geographical and historical data which had hitherto been approached atomistically.[573] Alt formulated conceptual categories for Canaanite society and Israelite society in a frame of development spanning Amarna Canaan, tribal Israel, and monarchic Israel. Even though Alt's conceptual categories are somewhat impressionistic and greatly in need of refinement, resting at times on minimal statistical support and only vaguely informed by sociological method, and even though in my view he is sometimes badly mistaken (e.g., in his reliance on the concept of nomadic Israel acculturating to settled agricultural life), the fact remains that Alt time and again provides an excellent starting point for extending the cultural-materialist study of early Israel more rigorously by more exacting methods of data-gathering and by better-informed social theory.

M. B. Rowton has continued this historico-territorial method by trying to correlate the literary evidence on the distribution of the *'apiru* with what he calls the topology of the upland regions of Syro-Palestine composed largely of thicketed and precipitous hills.[574] More recently, Rowton has launched a series of articles which will attempt to deal programmatically with the different forms of nomadism in the ancient Near East (which he terms broadly "enclosed" and "external" nomadism).[575] As I understand his initial conclusions about nomadism, they are congruent with my own analysis, and his attempt to relate the work of Near Eastern specialists to the work of ethnologists is precisely what is needed if we are to have the analytic categories and the data necessary for constructing social-developmental hypotheses and not merely compiling information and hazarding occasional unsystematic guesses about what the mountain of information actually means for historical and social understanding.

Alt and Rowton show a basic concern for a disciplined analytic breakdown of geographical and historical phenomena and their interpenetration in "topology";[576] they even admit broadly socioeconomic data to their field of interest. Still, they have not penetrated to the simplest units of cultural-material life, starting with the forces and relations of production conceived as definite applications of techniques in definite work processes according to definite forms of social cooperation in labor, and with definite patterns, in the social appropriation of the labor product.

For a systematic cultural-material methodology, the work of Marx in analyzing the precise units in the forces and relations of production in nineteenth-century capitalism is exemplary. His *Capital* makes informative reading from the point of view of how to construct cultural-material research strategies. Examples closer to our subject, in that they deal with pre-capitalist or noncapitalist society, are the forementioned works of Meillassoux and Terray on the Guro of the Ivory Coast. As a matter of fact, in the preceding techno-environmental and economic inventory for early Israel, I have followed in rough outline Terray's summary of the steps in determining the material base of a society.[577]

Naturally the same qualification attaches to the cultural-material reconstruction of early Israel that attached to the historical reconstruction: we are dependent in large measure on the accident by which ancient texts have survived. Even here, however, it is doubtful that the textual survivals are altogether accidental. At least the types of texts that have survived are likely to reflect fairly accurately the function of written texts in early Israelite society. At any rate, patchy or lopsided sources are no valid reason for shirking social-developmental model-building. Only as some model of the society evolving over time is developed and tested and refined does it become possible to "correct" our superficial impressions of that society based solely on tallying up quantities of material or textual remains. In the case of early Israel we desperately need to process, to analyze, and to conceptualize the data that are available. In doing so, there is every prospect that we shall increasingly become aware of additional data embedded unnoticed in long-published texts and material objects. Above all, we need hypotheses that develop a cultural-material framework with its own nexuses and blank spaces and growing edges able to point directions in research by establishing priorities and by suggesting points of greatest potential yield.

51.3 Biblical Archaeology and "the New Archaeology"

Cultural-material hypotheses can richly inform the work of archaeologists, whose contributions to the task of societal explanation have been and will continue to be enormous.[578] In this respect, the so-called new archaeology, especially productive in Amer-Indian studies, can prove highly instructive and stimulative for Near Eastern and Palestinian archaeologists. So-called biblical archaeologists in particular have tended to apply an analytic frame to their work dictated largely by the format and concerns of biblical historical traditions, as we observed in Part V with respect to the Israelite "conquest" of Canaan. That is certainly one legitimate frame, but a basic contention in this work has been that study of the highly cultic-ideological frame of biblical history will remain incestuous and sterile until it is set in wider cultural and social-developmental frames. In cutting loose from the restricted frame of biblical history, without of course relinquishing archaeology's continuing contribution to historical studies, Palestinian archaeologists need not be consigned to the ignominy of "pot collecting." As it is, archaeologists worthy of the name are no mere pot collectors; they use ceramics as one index to cultural change. Solid archaeological work on ceramics can yield grounds for what has even been called "a sociology of pottery," i.e., for probing into the social forms of the people who made the ceramics.[579]

Archaeologists should of course remain autonomous in following the internally developing rules of the archaeological game, and they should be rightly resistant to historians or social theorists who press them to skew the material evidence one way or another to corroborate theories. Nevertheless, the data to be studied and the applicable methodological rules within any discipline tend to change not only through internal development but through interchange with other cognate disciplines. The archaeologist's eye is a selective human eye. Archaeologists will be vastly better observers if they are critically aware of theoretical frames operative in their scholarly world and if they realize that what they find and interpret will contribute measurably to testing hypotheses about cultural and social phenomena.[580]

51.4 Population Size and Distribution

The distance we have to go in collecting the materials and forming the conceptual units of cultural-material analysis for early Israel is well illustrated by the challenge of determining the population size and distribution. It is somewhat surprising that our information on population in ancient Israel rests on nothing more solid than some rough calculations by a few scholars, beginning with W. F. Albright, who extrapolated loosely from estimates of the number of persons living at excavated sites, census totals reported in biblical texts, and rough comparisons with population totals for modern Palestine. The biblical census figures appear in problematic historical contexts, so that we are uncertain about the actual periods from which they derive. Moreover, in accordance with well-known tendencies toward enlargement of numbers, it is evident that these enumerations have suffered extravagant inflation (in part, as we observed in VI.28.3, because the original social organizational meaning of 'eleph ceased to be understood in monarchic times and was mistakenly construed to mean "one thousand" in premonarchic lists).

Of course there is no point to complaining that earlier scholars made rough estimates of the population size of ancient Israel. Indeed, we have every reason to be grateful for their preliminary guesses inasmuch as they have at least focused attention on the problem. I am simply deploring the failure of their genera- tions—and of ours to date—to take up the task in a rigorous way worthy of the subject and the tools available for its pursuit in a proper research strategy. As far as I know, no one with specific training in demography has taken up the question. Before we conclude that the population of ancient Israel is unknowable, we need to apply existing demographic methodology to the problem. In the end we may still have to settle for a broad approximation, and conceivably that approximation may confirm some of the previous crude estimates, but it will be a conclusion more soundly reached and one that can be refined as the study of demographics improves or as new data on ancient Israel become available.[581]

51.5 Technological Factors:
Iron and Waterproof Plaster—Terracing and Irrigation Systems

Two technological advances in particular have been singled out by biblical ar- chaeologists and historians as significantly contributory to the successful Israelite settlement in the hill country.[582] I refer to the introduction of iron and to the invention of slaked lime plaster for waterproofing cisterns. It is thought that together these innovations created the material conditions for an increase of productivity in intensive agriculture and for a corresponding increase in popula- tion. Yet these innovations and their effects, singly and in combination, have hardly received the scrutiny they merit. Their effects as forces of production on the relations of production and on social and political forms, not to mention religion, have not been explored in a systematic way. Furthermore, these two technological innovations are too readily abstracted out of a network of other technological factors which can alone render a plausible cultural-material account of Israel's rise.

Briefly, the posited effects of these technological innovations worked as follows. Iron, introduced into Canaan from Anatolia in the thirteenth or early twelfth century, proved to be a far stronger metal than the previously used bronze. Weapon for weapon, armies equipped with iron chariots, spears, swords, and daggers acquired greatly increased striking power over opponents equipped with equivalent weapons in bronze. The military impact of iron technology within Israel was minimal before the united monarchy because whatever iron weapons for foot soldiers Israel may have managed to capture or acquire by trade—or even by iron smithing on its own—were always less numerous than the city-states possessed and were not sufficient to overbalance the Canaanite monopoly on chariotry. On the other hand, iron in Israelite techno-economics had a great and immediate impact. Iron axes enabled more rapid and thorough clearing of land, while iron ploughs, mattocks, spades, sledges, etc., meant that more land could be cultivated per unit of human labor with larger surpluses. At about the same time, a successful method for waterproofing the highly porous, rock-cut cisterns of the hill country opened up entire new areas for settlement, in that the populace was no longer exclusively dependent on locating near springs.

In the Canaanite highlands where Israel formed, these two innovations apparently worked hand-in-hand to bring under settlement and cultivation extensive areas that had previously been either wooded or thicketed, or whose soil had been resistant to ploughing and cultivating with bronze technology, or that had simply been too distant from springs to sustain the permanent settlement of cultivators. The twin technological innovations collaborated in cumulative effects: land cleared and cultivated with iron tools could be more intensively used by a populace that could now settle more widely with the help of an independent water supply collected in reliable cisterns which, in turn, were now more easily cut into the rock with the stronger iron tools. The consequence of this development was to diversify settlement over wider areas in small self-supporting village units and to stimulate a cumulative "development spiral." More and more of the empty countryside was occupied as a better-fed populace multiplied and more intensive agriculture reclaimed inhospitable areas. The sociopolitical effect was to weaken the already tenuous dominance of the city-states in the hill country and to secure the material base for a more or less continuous chain of egalitarian rural communities.

The waterproof cisterns had begun to appear in Canaan in pre-Amarna times, but they sharply accelerated after 1200 B.C.—in part because they could be more readily hewn out with the newly introduced iron tools[583] and in part because the aggressive Israelite peoples were intent on making maximum use of the means available to them in their struggle for economic and political autonomy. Customarily, however, discussion of the waterproof cisterns has overlooked certain critical questions. Cisterns that store water for agricultural use require a collection and dispersal system; the larger the area watered, the more elaborate this system must be. Rain-fed systems will remain precarious in comparison to more reliable spring-fed systems. Can the spread and intensification of settlement and cultivation be at all reconstructed in the Israelite highlands without looking at entire water systems rather than isolating one feature of such systems? I shall return to this important point.

So far the archaeological evidence on the early Israelite use of iron has been rather sketchily observed and recorded.[584] In fact, until recent years the direct evidence seemed to consist of a single iron plough tip from Saul's Gibeah. Additional evidence is now appearing. Finds of iron objects have been concentrated in and along the edge of the plains in certainly or probably non-Israelite regions. The relative paucity of iron finds in premonarchic Israel may be due in part to the dispersal of the populace in many small settlements which have been little excavated until of late,[585] and in part to careful husbanding of the precious iron tools by the Israelites who probably made every effort not to leave them behind when they moved or were driven from settlements. Moreover, iron was a metal seldom discarded by peasants who did not have easy access to trade. As old tools wore out, the iron would be reused to forge new tools. Also, small particles of disintegrated iron, previously undetected (or at least unrecorded), are now being reported on excavated sites from the premonarchic period.

Such observations and speculations point toward the advisability of a fresh examination of the archaeological evidence on early Israelite use of iron.[586] For the moment, there seems to be no valid reason for revising the view that the introduction of iron to agricultural production, together with a more dependable water supply, facilitated Israelite growth in population and in economic productivity. But how rapid was this growth and how can it be measured? It may turn out, for instance, that iron technology made its way rather more gradually into early Israel than previously thought. Perhaps we have to distinguish between a relatively slow increase in population and productivity throughout the twelfth century followed by a more rapidly accelerating growth curve in the eleventh century.

Vital for our cultural-material concerns are the questions that Palestinian archaeologists and historians have not generally considered. First, there are questions about the exact impact of iron tools as a productive force on the processes and relations of production. What increase in efficiency is introduced by iron tools over bronze tools? Can this be calculated in terms of work output per unit of labor invested and in terms of increase of crop yields and consumption of foods? Were some plants cultivated only for the first time with the introduction of iron in conjunction with a better water supply? Which crops benefited most directly from the technological shift to iron? On first thought, it appears that crops requiring yearly ploughing and sowing of fields, such as grains and vegetables—rather than those grown on trees and vines, such as olives and grapes—were the immediate beneficiaries of improved farming tools. A large-scale increase in wheat and barley cultivation in the highlands will have been of critical importance in supplying the food staples that heretofore were cultivable on a large scale only in the feudally dominated estates of the plains. Israelites-to-be, fleeing from their onerous role as laborers in the quasi-feudal system, were enabled to form the material base for a separate economy and an autonomous society only as they found a way to replace the feudally extracted grain surpluses with grain surpluses extracted by free and equal labor.

A cultural-material study of iron in early Israel will therefore seek more precise information to determine whether the increase in agricultural productivity in the highlands, especially in the staple grain crops and in vegetables, was for the first time attainable with iron tools. If this can be demonstrated, we will have a material basis for understanding why Israel formed when it did. Taking into account the sociohistorical dimensions of Israel's emergence treated in Parts VIII and IX, we would then be able to say that prior to the introduction of iron tools the restive,

feudally dominated groups in Canaan who had been straining toward autonomous "retribalized" life had been unable to develop an adequate material base in a
surplus grain economy in the only region of the country open to them for political
and military reasons, namely, in the highlands. The gathering potentialities
for a new social order were activated once a techno-environmental and techno-
economic base was realizable in the mountainous hinterland.

We also want to know how the forms of cooperation in work were affected by
the adoption of an iron technology. Was the difference only in the efficiency of
implements and in productivity levels, or did changes occur in the size of work
groups and in the organization of the labor processes? Did production continue
within the framework of the residential family, enlarged only as the families
themselves enlarged through propagation and absorption of converts or refugees? Or did the enlargement of cultivated areas and the work routines necessitated by iron technology lead to new ways of organizing the production tasks? Did
new cooperative forms of labor reach across extended-family lines, e.g., in mul-
tifamily ploughing and harvesting? Did the growth of surpluses in regionally
specialized crops lead to an increase in barter trade of surpluses between these
variously specializing regions?

Questions also arise about the technological foundations of the extended family, which I have argued was the primary socioeconomic unit in early Israel
(VI.28–29). Did this productive unit of society and economy have its material
rootage in a specific level of intensive agriculture attainable only for the first time
in the highlands with the use of iron tools? Is the Israelite extended family a
collective surrogate for the feudal labor battalion? If such a hunch can be given
empirical content based on detailed information about the forces and relations of
production in transition from a bronze to an iron technology, we can bring the
resulting analysis to bear upon social causation in the successful emergence of
tribally organized, extended-family social relations in early Israel. To carry out
this analysis adequately it will be necessary to examine the ancient evidence in
relation to analogous technological and social transitions that have been observed
and studied at first hand during the last century or two. Anthropology and
social-organizational and evolutionary theory become the indispensable analytic
and comparative tools for this kind of reconstruction of ancient socioeconomic
history.

It would, however, be a grave error to restrict research to the few cultural-
material factors so far accented in biblical archaeological and cultural studies.
Additional factors, joined with long-recognized factors in systemic interaction, are
coming to light. In addition to iron and waterproof cisterns, there is renewed and
deepened attention both to the rock terraces that facilitated agriculture on hill-
sides and in wadi beds and to the waterworks (tunnels, aqueducts, reservoirs) that
made small-scale irrigation feasible in many regions of the hill country.[587] Draw-

ing upon the work of researchers such as Z. Ron[588] and L. Stager,[589] C. H. J. de Geus[590] has recently stressed the immense potential value of studying local systems of "terraces, irrigation-works, roads and settlements . . . built according to a design."[591] So vital was cultivable and well-watered soil that everything else was built around the contingencies of soil and water; settlements and roads, for example, tended to be situated on higher ground not readily suited to irrigated cultivation.

De Geus shares with other recent researchers the belief that relative dates can be assigned to terrace and irrigation systems, either on the basis of ceramic sherds and coins washed into the rock walls or by means of datable structures that cut into older terraces and waterworks. He also recommends exploring the possibility that pollen analysis of bog-formations under springs and pools may tell us something both about the original vegetation that was cleared in order to build the terrace and irrigation systems and about the plants cultivated in its place. In the vicinity of Jerusalem, Herodian repairs of older water systems have been found, and part of the Gihon irrigation installation at Jerusalem must precede Hezekiah's tunnel (c. 700 B.C.). Terraces from as far back as approximately 1500 B.C. have been located in Galilee. De Geus thus gives formulation to the growing possibilities in viewing terrace systems and water systems as interrelated features of entire agricultural complexes that can be dated approximately and described as functional totalities.[592]

Furthermore, de Geus sketches the possible "payoffs" from reconstructing such ancient agricultural complexes. They may tell us a great deal about the specific conjunctions of technology and environment that made possible the extensive settlement and cultivation of the highlands. In his judgment, these integral irrigation and terrace systems, fanning out from walled or unwalled settlements, imply a large measure of political and military security. One implication of his observation is that the emergence of the Israelite intertribal confederacy was an emphatic precondition for the successful functioning of a large number of such agricultural complexes spread over the hill country. Only if the autonomous local and regional entities could be free of internecine strife and class plunder, and only if they could unite in a common front against enemies from without, was there any prospect of the "free space" needed to reclaim the hill country for agriculture practiced by an egalitarian community.

Perhaps the hitherto baffling question of population density, distribution, and growth can be approached in a fresh way by calculating the approximate number of people that could have been supported by the reconstructed agricultural complexes. It will be necessary to examine demographic data drawn from similar agricultural environments with similar social organization to which we still have access in various parts of the world. De Geus also notes the likelihood that features of social organization may be ascertainable, at least indirectly, through a careful study of the terrace and water systems, although he goes no farther than to note the observed fact that even today in Palestine some communities have a common pool and in other communities each family has its own pool.[593]

The general results of such a cultural-material investigation, no longer limited to single technological factors but embracing a functioning system of production, appear far more congruent with a socioeconomic interpretation of early Israel than with the hitherto prevailing ethnic conceptions. De Geus puts it this way:

> It could be asked whether it is necessary to give this phenomenon [the early Israelite irrigation-terrace systems around village settlements] an "ethnic" explanation. So far, archaeology has failed to make the Israelites "visible" as a new ethnic group in those settlements. In my opinion this change of the pattern of settlement should also be connected with the coming of the Iron Age. It was then that large-scale terracing of mountain slopes began, followed by new settlements. The also changing political conditions made it possible to live and work in many small settlements scattered all over the country. It was the terraces which made agriculture possible on the slopes where other conditions, such as temperature and rainfall, were much more favorable than in the plains and riverbeds.[594]

51.6 The Socioeconomic Shift from Amarna to Israelite Canaan: A Provisional Historical Cultural-Material Hypothesis

Pulling together the exceedingly incomplete picture that we presently possess of cultural-material conditions attending the rise of Israel, the outlines of a provisional hypothesis about how the "great leap forward" from Amarna to Israelite Canaan came about can at least be hazarded as a basis for further inquiry.

By the end of the Amarna age, centuries of politically centralized and socially stratified collective life in Syro-Palestinian conditions had pulverized the older tribal forms of life, or had driven them so far to the periphery of public life that nowhere did they provide a viable base for an autonomous sovereign community. *'Apiru* bands were troublesome symptoms of strain in the dominant system, but their "tribal" character is dubious and they remained divided from one another and from other discontented social groups. The mass of the populace was organized for economic production from the top down. Families as such were not productive units on the large estates. Where small farmers continued outside the big estates, they suffered the expropriation of their surpluses and struggled to survive in isolation from any mutual help within a community of free and cooperative producers.

If such expropriative relations of production were to be overthrown and replaced by other relations, an "opening" in the dominant system had to occur at some vulnerable point. Not only must the old system be perceived as "unrewarding," but some actual concrete alternative must be available. New social relations could arise only on a material base by means of new productive forces that secured the life needs of the producers at least as effectively as the old social relations. We may conceive of the various thrusts toward freedom among pre-Israelite groups in Canaan as attempts to find such materially sufficient alternatives. Apparently those most successful in the struggle were the *'apiru,* but they succeeded not primarily as food producers but as sellers of needed professional services for which they could secure the means of subsistence in return; or, as unstable political conditions permitted, they took to brigandage and freebooting. Transhumant pastoral segments of the populace could move periodically toward the less controlled steppe fringes of Canaan and secure relative freedom.

But if there was to be a major new socioeconomic system in Canaan, it would have to be constructed on the material base of agriculture, since that was the massively predominant mode of production. Peasants, however, comprising the great majority of the Canaanite populace, were largely paralyzed by their socioeconomic position. They were unable to find nonagricultural alternatives to their feudally determined lot. They did not possess military, craft, or religious-mantic skills as a bargaining point. They did not have large flocks or herds of their own. They were locked into feudal estates. Even if formally independent, the peasants were separated from one another and overwhelmed by state-controlled agriculture. Technical freedom of person in itself provided no economically realistic alternative by which to exercise a hollow "freedom" to leave lords and masters. Only as this vast peasant majority found a way to seize the means of production it knew how to operate could there be any chance of a major overturn of the dominant imperial-feudal system in Canaan. That is, of course, precisely what happened with the uprising of the people called Israel. But can we say anything more about that process in terms of its material conditions?

As Amarna Canaan declined politically, and as economic hardship fell disproportionately on the countryside as the supplier of the cities, groups of peasants broke away from their feudal fate. Those who stayed in the plains and tried to cultivate the land detached from state control were at once exposed to reseizure by their former masters or by other acquisitive city-state lords and aristocrats striving desperately to retain their material base. Those who fled to the hills faced the difficulty of cultivating thicketed and rocky soil with the too soft bronze tools and in the face of a fickle water supply. They faced great difficulties in sustaining a level of subsistence commensurate even with their meager subsistence level under Canaanite domination. It was a dubious and frustrating venture to trade off former oppressions and assured minimal subsistence in return for personal freedom and uncertain, possibly insufficient, subsistence levels. We can readily project a high rate of failure in such efforts to erect a bronze-based agricultural tribal society in the highlands. In order to succeed, the renegades needed to gather enough people, well enough fed and housed, skilled enough in the new methods required by upland agriculture (including the construction of terraces and water systems), to be able to extend mutual aid to one another, to absorb and encourage newcomers, and finally to defend themselves collectively against the constant efforts of the politically declining Canaanite city-states to reassert their control over the upstarts and over that portion of the means of production which the rebels had "stolen" from them. It was a long, "uphill" struggle, and Elohistic Israel, which preceded Yahwistic Israel in the central highlands, represented the most successful effort prior to the breakthrough of biblical Israel.

In such a situation, the convergence of technological innovations tailored to the hill-country environment tipped the balance of material conditions in favor of a sustained growth in intensive agriculture throughout large stretches of the highlands. As the requisite level of material subsistence was reached, dissidents from all over Canaan were drawn to the new possibilities. On arrival, they found that the means of production in relatively small-scale but intensive agriculture were well suited to middle-sized cooperative work groups (the extended families), and not at all necessitating the assembling of large work forces on a feudal scale. They also found that they could care for their own defense needs without paying the heavy price of taxation and drafted labor to the state. Thus a vital equation in the mix of factors attending Israel's "breakthrough" was the reality that these small-scale intensive agriculturalists were not producing the greater part of their surpluses to support a voracious leisured class. What they produced they consumed or bartered, and thus the critical question for them—once having expelled or eluded the dominating leisured class—was to organize forces and relations of production that could secure them a stable and advancing subsistence level. The subsistence level had to be consistent not only with physical survival (bodily nourishment to continue to work and to repel the dominating classes trying to "recapture" them) but also with the development of social relations among equals and with the increasing cultivation of an independent symbolic culture making use of the "popular" alphabetic script in the articulation of a new religion (the development of strong internal leadership and interhuman responsibility while preventing elites from seizing unequal shares of goods or powers).

What have we gained by this hypothesis? It is to be hoped that we have gained a clearer sense of the vital interaction between material conditions and the "higher" social and religious structures. In place of geography, climate, economics, etc., treated as separate prolegomena or as mere "background," we have begun to see how all that was specifically Israelite, extending to the "highest" reaches of its Yahwistic faith, was the expression of a total interpenetration of material and socioreligious factors in one single system. Furthermore, the hypothesis illustrates the point that historical cultural-material hypotheses of social organizational and ideological causation are real hypotheses. By that I mean that they are testable. They can be falsified or verified by probability calculations. In the process of developing research strategies to test the hypotheses, other technological innovations and other techno-environmental factors will doubtless have to be included in the reformulation and extension of ever more precise and comprehensive historical cultural-material hypotheses. As only one example, what foods were cultivated and in what distribution patterns,[595] and what light does such information throw on the forms of cooperative labor and on social organization and ideology? Likewise, new conjunctions and contradictory relations between material conditions and socioreligious structures, as also among the various social and religious structures themselves, will doubtless have to be delineated. Consequently, an inquiry that begins with "the material conditions" as its object opens out, by the very nature of the human system under examination, into "the social, cultural, and religious formations," which attain a relative distinctiveness in their own spheres while remaining intimately and irretrievably bound to their historical material matrix.

Such empirical examinations of the factors making for social change in the Canaanite-Israelite milieu contrast strikingly with the "nonhypotheses" now holding the field. By far the greater number of these nonhypotheses are idealist "explanations" of early Israel that merely restate tautologically the singularity of Israel as an irregular, uncaused religious phenomenon (see especially my discussion in X. 48). From time to time, on the other hand, there have arisen suggestions of the determination of Israel's novelty by singular geographical, economic, or psychological conditions, one of the more popular of these notions being the theory that the monotony of the desert produced monotheism.[596] These too are "nonhypotheses," their simplistic ahistorical materialism or psychologism failing both to specify the material base of Israel in analytic detail and to indicate the forms of mediation between variables in a systemic process.

The superiority of historical cultural-material approaches to social causation in early Israel will become evident only as research strategies are applied to the early Israelite culture domain comparable in rigor and thoroughness to those that have been applied to societies by way of the disciplines of ethnology and political economy. Idealist and mechanistic-materialist hypotheses about early Israel, as about all else, can only be grappled with by philosophical debates. Historical cultural-material hypotheses about early Israel, as about all else, can be falsified or verified, and, if verified partially or within limited ranges, can be reformulated or complexified so as to offer the prospect of increased explanatory power. A *science* of the sociology of Israel's religion demands and welcomes such historical cultural-material clarifications as the only firm basis on which it can proceed.

Part XI

Biblical Theology or
Biblical Sociology?

On Affirming and Defining the "Uniqueness" of Israel

52.1 Biblical Theology: An Attempt to Mediate the Clash between Historical and Theological Methods

My intention in this final section of the study is to explore the relation between biblical-sociological method and biblical-theological method. The end that I have in view is a social hermeneutic of the Bible that will be both scientifically and religiously cogent. The point of departure for this inquiry is "Biblical Theology," a loosely articulated movement that dominated biblical studies for close to half a century. Biblical theology arose in the wake of World War I on the European continent, spread slowly to England and the United States, was transmitted throughout the non-Western Christian world via the ecumenical movement, reached its apogee in the 1950s, and has been in slow but continuous decline over the last decade—without as yet having given way to an alternative consensus.

This development in biblical studies was roughly paralleled by an uneasy hegemony of neo-orthodoxy (Barth) and existentialism (Bultmann) in theological studies, the breakdown of which has similarly failed to issue in any commanding theological alternative focus or foci. Contemporary systematic reflection on the "ideas" or on the "faith" of the Bible is as confused and contradictory as contemporary systematic reflection in the broader fields of Christian and Jewish theology. At present we flounder in a multitude of biblical and theological methods and conclusions which are uneasily juxtaposed or stalemated, partly overlapping or converging and partly divergent or antagonistic, often combined eclectically in the same thinker as they are intermixed chaotically in the general religious-intellectual environment.

In this critical interim period of religious thought about the Bible, the present study can be no more than a provisional assessment of some of the principal features of biblical theology viewed as a congeries of tendencies and as an episodic synthesis (one cannot speak of "method" or "school" in any precise sense) that sought to express the internal unity-in-diversity and the comparative uniqueness-in-environmental continuity of ancient Israelite faith. The thrust of the brief assessment will be to suggest that the good intentions of biblical theology were thwarted at every turn by its failure to treat the religion of Israel as a social phenomenon. By contrast, I shall attempt to show that at least certain of the assertions of the biblical theology movement can be more coherently and convincingly expressed in a sociological theory of religion concerned with how religious symbols function for social beings within an historical cultural-material perspective of human development.

I do not present a new theology so much as the preconditions for a new theological method which would employ the biblical records as ideological products and instruments of the social formation of Israel. The modesty of the undertaking does not derive only from the limitations of space, which preclude full development of an alternative to biblical theology. Of even more decisive limiting import is the fact that my study has been devoted to the sociology of Israel's *premonarchic* religion. Obviously the larger part of the biblical records reflects markedly different Israelite social forms, with accumulating complexities and contradictions, during the later monarchic, exilic, and postexilic eras. My attention has been deliberately and scrupulously given to the initial formation of Israel as an egalitarian social system with a religious servomechanism. Since that egalitarian social system subsequently underwent drastic changes (both in internal organization and in its relation to other social and political systems in the ancient world), with corresponding transformations in the accompanying religious ideology, it is obvious that any adequate replacement for "biblical theology" will have to deal with the whole range of the history of Israelite religion viewed systematically in its changing social nexus.

With that limitation acknowledged, it will nonetheless be clear from the way I relate Israelite religion to its social base during the first two centuries of Israel's existence, that there follow certain consequences with far-reaching implications for systematic reflection on Israelite religious symbolism and organization in *all* periods of Israel's life. This permits the sketch of an alternative method to biblical theology, even though the empirical content is restricted in this analysis to the opening phase of Israelite praxis and ideology.

I shall assume that it is unnecessary to rehearse the major tenets or tendencies of biblical theology, since they are so well known. Not only are they reflected in a vast advocatory literature[597] in which two or three generations of seminarians, churchmen, and scholars in religion have been tutored; they are also the object of an increasingly critical literature,[598] now that it is generally sensed that biblical theology has reached its high watermark and is ebbing steadily, and probably irreversibly—because both its explanatory power in synthesizing biblical phenomena and its function as a bridge to general theology are seen as ever more problematic and fragile.

It is sufficient for my purposes to emphasize what seems to have been the underlying aim, the central achievement, and the basis of popular appeal of biblical theology, namely, its harmonization of the scientifically grasped historical discreteness of biblical data with a tenacious hold upon the religious uniqueness of biblical thought in such a way that each element in the mixture seemed to enhance and to reinforce the other. For some decades biblical theology validated the "human" and the "divine" dimensions of biblical religion in an intellectually and religiously satisfying manner by audaciously making a virtue out of contradictory and incommensurable methods so that their mutual indigestibility became a necessary "paradox." The very same religious phenomena in ancient Israel could be seen simultaneously and stereoptically as part of the tissue of religio-historical phenomena continuous with the culture of the ancient Near East *and* as a locus for the superordinate and unique "acts of God" or for "revelation as encounter." On the other hand, neither method of viewing the phenomena could be reduced to, or intelligibly combined with, the other method.

The decline of this biblical-theological synthesis has come largely from the recognition that the bridge it threw across the chasm between the historical and the theological, between what was common and what was unique in ancient Israel, was more a hope or a poetic gesture than it was a well-forged methodological link. The former impressive consensus around biblical theology is increasingly viewed not so much as a resolution of history and theology in a viable method but rather as a temporary truce in the ongoing conflict between the two planes, a moment of surcease and consolidation preparatory to further battle about to be joined.

Profound ecclesial needs for a pause in the struggle between advocates of history and advocates of theology were deeply at work to impose and to sustain this momentary biblical-theological truce in the warfare of methodologies. The supposed consensus, which was really a decision not to press radical inquiry, was rooted in a psychosocial need to give credibility to the actual coexistence of historical and theological interests and methods whose interrelations could not be resolved in a higher unity with the available intellectual and religious resources, whether from the older orthodoxy and liberalism or from the more recent neo-orthodoxy and existentialism. Moreover, in the United States at least, biblical theology served to temper the fundamentalist-modernist theological dispute and power struggle, which threatened to tear apart major Protestant denominations,[599] a tempering which proved of only brief avail as social unrest in the 1960s and 1970s has reopened the conflict in the churches on a more pragmatic and tactical rather than intellectual and theological front.

One of the accomplishments of biblical theology was to uncover a basic structure of the biblical faith conceived both as a stance toward life and as a developing body of traditional thought and practice which set off ancient Israel from all its neighbors and which flowed on, with modification, into the life of the synagogue and early church. There can be little doubt that this analytic work on the structure of Israelite faith was extraordinarily productive and has contributed tools and conceptual units of enduring value.[600] What has been thrown more and more into doubt is that this structure of Israelite faith is in fact so distinctive of Israel as has been claimed, or, if in some sense it is distinctive, that it really offers any substantial basis for contemporary religious thought.

52.2 The Common Theology of the Ancient Near East

Shortly after the appearance in 1950 of the first edition of *Ancient Near Eastern Texts Related to the Old Testament* (ed. J. A. Pritchard), Morton Smith published an article which received little attention in that heyday of biblical theology but which, from our perspective, can be viewed as significantly prophetic.[601] Smith set as his task "to try to state in outline just how the theological material in that collection [of ancient Near Eastern texts] is relevant to the theological material in the Old Testament." For "theological material" Smith restricted his study to texts, particularly prayers, "which describe a god (or gods) and his (or their) actions."[602] In short, Smith found a commonly patterned structure of belief articulated in the cults of the major deities throughout the ancient Near East, a structure of belief in which Israel participated just as thoroughly as Israel participated in the general cultural environment.

The elements that Smith identified in the common structure of ancient Near Eastern belief were the following: 1. One god is singled out from others for highest worship. 2. The effectiveness of this god is affirmed in history, nature, and morality (legal and civil). 3. The god is represented by symbols of power such as sun, bull, father, king. 4. The god is just and merciful; he punishes offenders against his will and rewards those compliant with his will. 5. The relationship of the god to the worshipping people is "essentially contractual," i.e., there is a direct relation between obedience and disobedience to the god and the fortunes of the people. 6. There are everywhere "prophets," i.e., those who understand the state of the relationship between the god and the people and who announce appropriate punishments and rewards.

In his concluding brief remarks about the significance of Israel's participation in a general ancient Near Eastern "pattern for major deity," Smith surmised that the common theology probably developed independently in each culture since "the uniformity of the results. . . can be explained better by postulating relatively uniform causes, i.e., social, psychological, and rhetorical patterns, rather than accidents of historical transmission."[603] He does not deny the presence of cultural borrowing but, in view of the gross overuse of that hypothesis in Old Testament studies, he cautions that "it is only when the texts are parallel in some peculiar, accidental detail, something which *cannot* be explained as a possible product of natural development, that the parallelism can be taken as *proving* literary connection."[604] The general drift of Smith's position is clear, although his formulation contains a number of extremely ambiguous and problematic terms that are not adequately defined, e.g., "causes," "accidental detail," "natural development," and "literary connection." To mention only one ambiguity, is the only kind of cultural borrowing via the medium of "literary connection"? Smith also notes that "the knowledge of this general pattern should serve as a guide in Old Testament studies. . . by making clear the peculiarities of the Old Testament, the points which need special explanation—for instance, Yahweh's abnormal jealousy and the almost complete neglect of the underworld."[605]

Morton Smith's temperate delineation of a common Near Eastern theology, carefully qualified against mechanistic procrustean inferences, was little heeded at the time. The field of discussion tended to be preempted by extreme claims in two directions. On the one side were those who posited pervasive underlying Near Eastern patterns of "myth and ritual" (emphasized among Scandinavian scholars and by S. H. Hooke in England) or of cyclical motifs of "protology and eschatology" (argued by the German scholars H. Gunkel and H. Gressmann).[606] These patterns were projected on ancient Israel by rather freely filling out the large gaps in biblical traditions, not simply with details, but with entire structural designs drawn purportedly from other religions in Israel's environment. Against this methodologically hazardous undertaking, "biblical theologians" not unexpectedly reacted by virtually denying all commonality in religious patterning between Israel and its neighbors, generously employing watchwords such as "the historicity" of biblical religion and "the historical revelation" of biblical faith.

In such a confrontation there was no methodological meeting-point, no common language, no way of proceeding to the formulation of testable hypotheses. In short, there was little taste for what Smith attempted in an initial cursory manner, namely, to examine Near Eastern and Israelite theological materials with a view to determining what commonalities were actually expressed in the texts, leaving open for the moment the question of whether these commonalities were due to independent parallel development or to cultural diffusion, or to some combination of the two processes, and thereby providing a sound basis for recognizing the distinctive features or emphases of Israelite religion.

52.3 Common Ancient Near Eastern Concepts of Divine Action in History

A more thematically and illustratively detailed comparative study by Bertil Albrektson sets out to examine the pivotal claim of the biblical theology movement that Old Testament theology views history as the medium of revelation in contrast to nature or the word as the characteristic means of revelation elsewhere in the ancient Near East.[607] After an analysis of Old Testament, Sumerian, Akkadian, Assyrian, Old and Neo-Babylonian, Hittite, Moabite, and Canaanite Amarna texts, Albrektson concludes soberly that Israel's uniqueness clearly did not lie in different attitudes about history. He conducts his inquiry by examining six of the most common ways of formulating the alleged uniqueness of Israelite religious thought about history. In each formulation he finds that the assertion of Israelite uniqueness is mistaken, for where Israelite distinctiveness emerges, it always has to do with something else besides the formal conception of divine revelation in history.

Albrektson's results in summary are as follows:

THE SPHERE OF DIVINE ACTIVITY. The Near Eastern gods and Israel's god are alike active not only in nature (the elements, catastrophes, agriculture, etc.) but equally in history (military and political affairs).

HISTORICAL EVENTS AS DIVINE ACTIONS. Historical events (mostly past but in some instances future as well) are actions of the gods, either in the sense that acts of men are directed or empowered by the gods, or, more directly, that the human acts are seen as the actual acts of the gods.

> The idea of historical events as divine actions is not restricted to a certain type of texts. Just as they come from the most different periods of ancient Mesopotamian history, so they represent the most different categories: historical texts, hymns, prayers and rituals. . . . This belief that the gods act in history, which can be found in abundance in Mesopotamian texts, seems to have been common to the whole ancient Near East [there follow examples from Hittite and Mitannian texts].[608]

KINGSHIP AND DIVINE RULE IN HISTORY. The king is the agent or representative (deputy, vice-regent, governor) of the gods through whom they act in historical events. The kings' decisions and victories are the gods' decisions and victories, and rebellions against kings are rebellions against the gods. Sometimes, however, royal bad fortunes are explained by the kings' failures to obey the gods. This same view of the divine rule through the king appears in Israel, but not uniformly, since "there is hardly such a thing as *the* Hebrew view of kingship: rather we must reckon with different attitudes in different circles of Hebrew society."[609]

THE DIVINE WORD AND THE COURSE OF EVENTS. The word(s) of the god(s) is (are) active in human affairs, decisively affecting or even effecting military and political events. It is frequently said that something happens "at the word, order, or command of" a god. Sometimes this word is an oracle or omen in advance of or in conjunction with events but at other times this "word" is detected in some natural or human event that could not be (or was not) anticipated. Sometimes the word of the god is described in a morally causal way. Sometimes the word of the god is connected with belief in "fixing the fates" or "decreeing the destinies" of men and nations. Single incidents or whole chains of events can be attributed to the word(s) of deity.

> . . . to the peoples of the ancient Near East the word of the god was a mighty and terrifying power which could prove effective in all spheres of life, a dynamic force

bringing about the death or victories of kings as well as the growth or withering of the crops. The power of the divine word knows no bounds; its effects can be traced in nature and history alike. The ancient Israelites knew this: Sumerians and Babylonians, Assyrians and Hittites knew it as well.[610]

THE DIVINE PLAN IN HISTORY. In Israel and in the ancient Near East there is a similar belief that the god acts purposefully in what he does, but this is in no sense identical with the notion of a fixed divine plan for all of history. There are chains of events in which gods act with limited goals, but these do not resolve into any single divine plan anywhere in the ancient Near East, Israel included. Only in late Jewish apocalyptic is there a comprehensive, deterministic view of history. In the earlier period, the Mesopotamian notion of "the tablets of destiny" or "the fixing of destinies" actually offers a more explicit concept of a divine plan than any pre-apocalyptic expression in Israel. Moreover, the widely alleged non-Israelite "cyclical" conception of history is a gross misrepresentation of the facts. Near Eastern views of history were "undulatory" in the sense of identifying the rising and falling fortunes of kings and empires, but not "cyclical" in the sense of a precise pattern of events repeating themselves in the same order. To be sure, in Israel the deity is singular and monopolizes power, thus dominating history with particular insistence, but this is rather a different conception of God than a different conception of history. Israel and its neighbors alike "know the idea of purposeful divine action toward a definite goal in history,"[611] but they do not know of a comprehensive, detailed, and all-determining plan for history.

HISTORICAL EVENTS AS DIVINE REVELATIONS. It is an inaccurate schematic to say that the biblical view of revelation is active, concrete, and realistic, whereas elsewhere in the ancient Near East revelation is static, abstract, and intellectualistic. The fact is that elements both of concrete activity and of intellectual reflection and summation characterize views of revelation in Israel and among its neighbors. As to what is revealed about the god in history, only two things emerge consistently in Israel and in its religious environs: (1) the god is powerful, can and does control events; (2) the god is angry or merciful, judges or saves, and often does so on the basis of morality. Human defeats and reversals are regularly interpreted as the judgment of a god. In contrast to a great wealth in the *means* of revelation, the actual *content* of revelation is meager and abstract: "they all [Old Testament and ancient Near Eastern documents] speak of a great variety of historical events interpreted as divine acts in history, and these manifold events are all held to reveal the same few things: the power, mercy or wrath of the god."[612]

In view of his trenchant, and I believe largely correct, refutation of the facile differentiation of Israel from its religious environment by the category of revelatory history, we are interested to discover what Albrektson has to say about the proper basis for differentiating Israel's religion. He cites two basic differentia: one concerning the prominence of historical events as divine manifestations in the cult and a second concerning the large role played by the word of God which interprets events in anticipation:

HISTORICAL EVENTS AS DIVINE MANIFESTATIONS IN THE CULT. There is a shift in emphasis from the Ugaritic, or north Canaanite, cultic texts (where there is no mention of explicit activity of the gods in historical events), and even from Mesopotamian cultic texts (where there is a certain attention to the activity of the gods in historical events), to Israelite cultic texts in which divine manifestations in historical events are prominent.

> It would seem that the idea of historical events as divine manifestations has marked the Israelite cult in a way that lacks real parallels among Israel's neighbors. . . .it appears evident that the deity's saving acts in history are nowhere afforded so central a position in the cult as in Israel. . . .The distinctiveness is not, however, found in the conception as such but in its relative importance, its capacity for influencing the cult.[613]

Albrektson comments also on the way in which cult tends to turn historical events into timeless mythical symbols, even in Israel, and to such an extent that we can only say that within the historical-mythical tension that runs throughout the ancient Near East there is a relative strengthening of the historical pole in ancient Israel.

THE DIVINE WORD INTERPRETS EVENTS IN ADVANCE. Since historical events by themselves are mute or ambiguous, other media of revelation must give further information both as to the purpose or intention of the god in acting as he does and as to the appropriate human responses to these events. "Something must be given in addition to the events: the *word* of revelation, which may be about history but cannot be simply deduced from history."[614] Such words are especially plentiful in the Old Testament and ought not to be called, as they often carelessly are called, "revelation *in* history" but rather "a revelation *about* history." This means that "Israel's knowledge of God's purposes in history is not obtained through history but through the divine word about history."[615]

After exploring the interrelation of event and word as revelatory media, and showing some of the complex ways they are related (particularly in Old Testament historiography and prophecy), Albrektson closes with some vague and impressionistic comments about the content of Old Testament revelation being "in several respects unique." This is clarified only by the further statement that in the words of Yahweh "we learn about Yahweh's purposes and intentions, his true nature and the innermost thoughts of his heart, his gifts and his claims, which make him different from all the other gods of the ancient Near East."[616] This assertion is disappointingly imprecise and unexplicated, especially when set against the author's painstaking analysis of mistaken conceptions of Israel's religious uniqueness.

Naturally we want to know of Albrektson just what it is that the words of Yahweh tell us of "his true nature and the innermost thoughts of his heart" that is different, after all, from the basic content of revelation in terms of the power, wrath, and mercy of the deity previously advanced by him as a framework comprehending ancient Near Eastern and Israelite deities. What are the specific "gifts" and "claims" of Yahweh? Here we reasonably expect some attention to the promises of the deity, to the thanksgivings of the people, or to the instructions of the law. Or, conceivably, Albrektson has in mind two points about Israel's religious distinctiveness noted in his earlier exposition, namely, the demanding singularity of Israel's god and the fact that Israel was far from unanimous in seeing the king as the agent of divine revelation. Presumably, because these ideas would carry him far beyond his attention to the theme of divine revelation in history, Albrektson fails to make any further reference to them. In actual fact we are left with the objective analytic result that Albrektson has found the differentia of Israelite religion in two shifts of emphasis within the general structure of ancient Near Eastern belief in divine revelation in history. In Israel historical events as divine manifestations occupy a much larger place in the cult and the divine word more frequently interprets events in advance than is true elsewhere in the religions of the ancient Near East.

53

Common High-God Paradigms:
Ancient Near Eastern and Early Israelite

It seems to me that the analyses by Smith and Albrektson, while differing somewhat in the texts examined and in the scope of the themes examined, tend to converge in their identification of a general structure of belief in the ancient Near East in which Israel as a Near Eastern people fully participated. "Common theology" (Smith's term) may be too grandiose a term for this structure of belief, perhaps wrongly implying a degree and form of systematic thinking that only developed much later under the impact of Greek philosophy. Nevertheless, both analyses have made clear that the elements of belief in the ancient Near East, far from being random and quixotic, were interrelated and tended to form a structured whole, and at least in a rudimentary sense it is permissible to call this a theological foundation for the more highly rationalized formal theologies of later Judaism and paganism.

It seems to me that for two reasons Morton Smith's typology provides the more adequate general framework, even though he did not develop it to the same extent as Albrektson developed the points he studied. For one thing Smith is consciously trying to encompass and articulate the basic structure of belief, whereas Albrektson focuses his attention precisely on one leading, if highly complex and far-reaching, element within a general structure, i.e., historical events as divine manifestations. Secondly, Smith aims at trying to state a structure of belief that comprehends all ancient Near Eastern religions, including Israel's religion, whereas Albrektson's dominant concern is to work backward, so to speak, from the asserted uniqueness of Israel's religion on certain points to its conjunction with and departure from ancient Near Eastern religion as a whole. The end result is that Albrektson, like Smith, is led to put great stress upon a common pattern of belief. Methodologically, however, it is far better to begin by establishing commonality prior to demarcating differentiation. By spelling out the presuppositions and filling out the logical operations and links involved in the Smith-Albrektson typology, I think it is possible to articulate a sketch of the common Near Eastern symbolic structure of religion that is explicitly inclusive of ancient Israelite religion. In keeping with the time frame of this study, I am limiting ancient Israelite religion to the premonarchic period: In the following typological characterization of ancient Near Eastern/premonarchic Israelite religion, I employ the six trait categories proposed by Smith, nuanced as appropriate with Albrektson's observations and articulated according to my own understanding.

THE HIGH GOD INDIVIDUATED AND ELEVATED. The comprehensive generative or engendering power "behind," "beneath," "above," or "within" natural and human phenomena, symbolized as primordial divinity, was concretized and individuated in the form of specific high gods, personal beings, any one of whom could be accorded the highest position according to time, place, and function.

THE HIGH GOD ACTIVE IN THE WORLD. The individuated high god was regarded as effectually at work in nature, in history, and in the social order, although the sphere of activity of any single god might be limited to or concentrated mainly upon one sector of phenomena. While the root power of the high god transcended morality, it tended to find expression in a moral order in which the god sanctioned legal and administrative organs of society.

THE HIGH GOD CONCEIVED BY NATURAL AND HUMAN ANALOGIES. The nature and action modes of the high god were conceived by analogies drawn from the natural world, from history, and from society. The analogical conceptualization of the god occurred in titles, in iconic symbols, in accounts of the activities of the god among people and with other gods, and in expressions of the feelings and expectations of worshippers. The most common analogical domains were the natural elements (water, fire, earth), atmospheric and meteorological phenomena (wind, air-breath, storm), topographical features (sea, river, spring, mountain), heavenly bodies (sun, moon, stars), animals and plants (bull, lion, grain, tree), familial roles (father, mother, husband, wife, sister, brother), and sociopolitical roles (warrior, judge, prince, princess, king, queen). By examining the natural and human phenomena that offer the analogies for representing the high gods, we note precisely those dimensions of human experience in which deity was typically involved and effectual.

THE HIGH GOD AS POWERFUL, JUST, AND MERCIFUL. The way the god is involved and active in nature, history, and society follows certain modal manifestations of power, justice, and mercy. The god is experienced as *power* to unleash nature or to restrain it; to motivate and enable people to act effectively or to endure the action of others as necessary. The god is experienced as *justice* to punish the misuses of human power and to reward the proper uses of human power. The god is experienced as *mercy* to cancel out the misuses of human power; even to repair the catastrophes of nature, so that ever-renewed historical and social life is assured. The power, justice, and mercy of the god are not restricted to isolated momentary manifestations but become manifest in chains of events rooted in the larger context of past, present, and future. It is precisely this primordial potency that marks off divine power, justice, and mercy from their human derivatives and counterparts. There is a "going beyond" in the divine power, justice, and mercy that humans can never fully exhaust in the present or entirely anticipate in the future.

THE HIGH GOD IN BOND WITH A PEOPLE OR A REGION. The high god stands in a special relationship with a people, which normally is a national or territorial group (nation, region, city), but may also include a familial, lineage, tribal or intertribal group, or an occupational or social group based on division of labor (soldiers, merchants, priests, craftsmen), or a functional group with shifting membership (the diseased, pregnant women, travellers). While the bond between god and people is often primordial, in the sense of being assumed from antiquity or from creation instead of having been fixed at an historical moment by agreement, the relationship tends to be reciprocal, even contractual, in the sense that god and people know what to expect of one another and the god frequently imposes sanctions on the people when they fail in their obligations. The people have no sanctions to level against a god, but they do have the recourse of choosing an entirely new god (often the god of conquerors or the god of a region or city newly prominent as a political capital) or of downgrading the importance of the offending god in the total mix of gods to be honored.

THE HIGH GOD INTERPRETED BY HUMAN REPRESENTATIVES. The proper understanding of the current state of the relationship between god and people is committed to interpreters of the deity who have recognized social roles fixed variously according to traditional, bureaucratic, or charismatic modes of authority (to use M. Weber's ideal types)[617] within social organizations of egalitarian, rank, or stratified structure (to use M. Fried's ideal types).[618] The people look to these interpreters for an up-to-date reading of their relationship to the god and for a calculus of appropriate actions on their part to avoid punishments and to secure rewards. "Punishments" and "rewards" are moral-religious code-concepts for concrete gains or losses in the natural, historical, and social domains (e.g., health or disease, good or poor crops, adequate rain or famine/flood, military victory or defeat, presence or absence of strong leadership, independence or collapse of a regime or social order, loyalty to or revolt against a regime, ability or inability of a regime to perpetuate itself, general socioeconomic prosperity or deprivation for segments of society, etc.). Especially in times of social conflict and political turmoil, when a great deal is at stake in the gain/loss=reward/punishment calculus, it often happens that the interpreters of the god will disagree among themselves as to the state of the divine-human relationship and recommend differing, even diametrically opposed, courses of action.

54

Differentiated High-God Paradigms:
The Early Israelite Mutations

When the common structure of ancient Near Eastern theology is formulated as above, we immediately detect points where Israelite religion stands out as a highly idiosyncratic version of the common theological pattern. It is important for our inquiry to identify these idiosyncratic features against the backdrop of the common pattern. The tendency in the study of Israelite religion vis-à-vis ancient Near Eastern religion has been either to give Israelite religion short shrift or to blow it out of all recognizable proportions. Studies such as Smith's and Albrektson's, while acknowledging and briefly mentioning the peculiarity of certain Israelite religious phenomena, have tended to give insufficient attention to them. On the other hand, scholars within the biblical theology movement, in their eagerness to isolate the distinctive elements of Israelite belief, have usually ignored the common Near Eastern framework and have consequently expressed the Israelite religious idiosyncrasies in so rootless and contextless a manner as to lose the controls necessary for scientific analysis of phenomena and for constructing precise continuity-discontinuity paradigms.

Within each of the categories of common ancient Near Eastern–Israelite theology explicated above, I shall now try to state the structural peculiarities of premonarchic Israelite religion precisely as mutant developments of the general ancient Near Eastern theological pattern.[619]

THE SOLE HIGH GOD USURPS THE ENTIRE SACRED DOMAIN. The tendency in the ancient Near East toward individuating primordial deity in the form of high gods and according to one of them peculiar honor, congruent with time, place, and function, was carried through in Israel with unusual rigor and consistency to the point of exclusive recognition of one deity in the life of the people. It is too rationalistic an understanding of this process to call it "monotheism" or "henotheism," and it binds the process too narrowly to the cult to call it "monolatry." The radical exclusivity of Yahweh in Israel has been characterized as "practical monotheism" or "incipient monotheism," but both terms tend to emphasize a more fully rationalized monotheism as the teleological goal and norm of the earliest belief. I prefer the somewhat awkward neologism *mono-Yahwism*, which serves to stress the radical exclusivity of Yahweh in Israel's earliest belief without simply assimilating it to later monotheism and without regarding it merely as a crude forerunner of full monotheism.[620]

The precise term we choose for the hyperindividuation of Yahweh is less important than as exact a delineation as possible of the radical exclusivity of God in early Israel, including the rhetorical modes of expression, the domains of application, and the specific behavior prescribed or prohibited by the deity. Further attention must also be given to whether the clear subordination and assimilation to Yahweh of other Semitic names and epithets for deity allowed, at least in the beginnings, for a measure of independent operation of minor regional or group-associated gods in spheres not specifically preempted by Yahweh. This delineation of Israelite mono-Yahwism must discriminate the way it moves within the ancient Near East individuated high-god pattern, with its tendency toward selective elevation of one god over others, and the way it diverges from and goes beyond the general high-god pattern by positing a sole deity, not merely as a functional tendency or as a cultural-political preference, but in radical superses-sion. Yahweh's usurpation of the entire sacred domain consists in his sole and exclusive right to be recognized as the effective force in all matters decisive to the constitution and functional continuity of the social entity Israel. Such a delinea-tion must also carefully exclude from the depiction of early Israelite mono-Yahwism all features that arose only later under the aegis of royal, prophetic, wisdom, apocalyptic, or rabbinic theologies, even though those later monotheistic developments can be viewed as elaborations or systematizations of features in the earliest mono-Yahwism.

THE SOLE HIGH GOD ALONE ACTIVE IN THE WORLD. In spite of the tendency to magnify selectively the position of one or another god within any single society or culture field in the ancient Near East, the net effect of the involvement of more than one god in the life of the world was to diversify, fragment, and disperse the activities of the gods in nature, history, and society. By contrast, Israel's exclusive devotion to one deity prompted a more integrated and coherent assertion of the divine activity in all (or in most) domains of existence without rival. Albrektson remarks on this contrast between a tendency toward magnifying one god among the many and the recognition of one god in place of the many:

> It goes without saying that the idea of a divine purpose in history must be rather differently conceived in a polytheistic religion and in the Old Testament. Hebrew monotheism naturally does not allow of any ideas of rival plans and conflicting divine aims, but strongly enhances the tendency to a unitary perspective of history. But this is ultimately not so much a different understanding of history as a different concep-tion of the deity; the basic difference concerns the idea of God and the possible difference in the view of the divine purpose in history is only a corollary.[621]

Leaving aside the question-begging word "naturally," it seems to me that Albrekt-son has rightly grasped the important logical connection between the positing of a sole ultimate actor in all phenomena of decisive importance to a community and the tendency to see all phenomena in a more unitary manner.

Of course the unity of the phenomenal world as the arena of the sole divine actor must not be overstated by way of a naive retrojection of later monotheistic dogma. In premonarchic Yahwism there were domains of worldly experience not directly penetrated by Yahweh, such as the realm of the dead and the realm of heterosexual intercourse. Even at that time, however, so far as can be seen, no other deity was officially allowed a status in those realms avoided by Yahweh. The spheres which Yahweh did not directly enter had no independent status: the dead were dead and were not to be lavishly memorialized, worshipped, or communicated with, and heterosexual intercourse had no mystical powers for making contact with the deity or for inducing fertility of the earth.

It is equally true, however, that the spheres of death and of heterosexual intercourse were not negated in the sense of being repressed from consciousness. Instead, these spheres were integrated into larger domains in which Yahweh did have a role to play, in such a way as to acknowledge the existence of death and sexuality, while simultaneously depriving both phenomena of the magico-religious potency which they often had in other Near Eastern religions. For example, it was not denied that people die or have sexual intercourse; the question was rather how these admitted actualities were to be related to the rest of reality, i.e., what structural location they were to have in socioreligious praxis and ideology. Accordingly, Israel's deity is said to be the one who "slays and makes alive, brings down to Sheol [the underworld] and raises up" (I Sam. 2:6), a formulation which is to be understood not as resurrection of the dead but as revival of the sick and dying by snatching them from the brink of death. Once dead, that was the end of it for the deceased and for the living survivors, but Israel's god could keep people from premature or untimely death. Similarly, Israel's deity promises "blessings of the breasts and of the womb" (Gen. 49:25), in parallel with the bounties of agricultural fertility, so that heterosexual intercourse is set within the framework of the self-sufficient extended family continually reproducing itself in human progeny. Sex was a functional aspect of a wider historical socioeconomic process.

While Yahweh's activity in the many spheres of human life is formally duplicated by the activities of the gods within the ancient Near Eastern religious systems, a measurably "tighter" structural coherence, both in praxis and ideology, results from the sustained, unrelenting attribution of all these spheres and modes of action to a single effectual deity rather than to several deities, even though some one of the multiplicity of deities might under certain circumstances become by far the most important deity. There is both a formal continuity and a qualitative leap in the movement from "the activities of the gods" to "the activity of God." The formal continuity is expressed in the categories of "individuated deity" and "divine action," while the qualitative departure is contained in the concentration of multiple divine activities into "the activity of one divine actor" and in "the hyperindividuation of the deity" expressible by the difference between "gods/gods" (including even "the highest God") and "God/the one God."

Radical Israelite devotion to a sole deity encouraged the tendency to look for coherence in the chains of events or processes in nature, history, and society as it also encouraged symbolic reflection on *the* activity of *the* one God in the midst of that God's many-faceted activities. A movement in early Israelite thought toward discerning comprehensiveness and coherence in the divine purposes and activities and in worldly phenomena is discernible, even though we are rightly cautioned by Albrektson not to view this tendency in terms of an alleged single divine plan. Without a doubt, the ancient Near Eastern common theology both expressed and searched after coherence in human experience, but in Israel the testimonies to and the quests for coherence were given still higher priority and more developed systematic means of expression in the symbolism of mono-Yahwism.

THE SOLE HIGH GOD CONCEIVED BY EGALITARIAN SOCIOPOLITICAL ANALOGIES. The panoply of domains from which titles and imagery of the deity are drawn throughout the ancient Near East is the same basic repertory that Israel draws upon. In Israel, however, there is a decided diminution of analogies from nature and an emphatic concentration of the analogies in the historical and social domains, with particular focus on the deity as leader, ruler, and defender of his people. Yahweh as the proper name of the god of Israel accents the active role of the deity as warrior-leader in bringing a distinctive intertribal society into being and defending it against external attack. But that this Yahweh is equated with El, is in fact commonly titled *Yahweh 'Elōhē Yisrā'ēl* (Yahweh, the God of Israel), places the historico-social initiating action of the god against the backdrop of his general primordial role as the might one, the creator of all that is, the fatherly leader and ruler of human communities.

It is probable that the proper name Yahweh rose as an epithet of El, in the form *'ēl zū* (or *dū*) *yahwī ṣaba'ōt*, "El who creates the (armed)hosts," which contained the *double entendre* of the armed hosts of heaven and the armed hosts of Israel.[622] The causative verb *yahwī* became the proper name Yahweh as the historico-social action of El in bringing the mutant Israelite intertribal society into being was singled out as the primary function of deity. Accordingly, Yahweh uses the natural elements (stars, sun and moon, rain, hail, and wind) as "heavenly hosts" which accompany and support his "earthly hosts," i.e., the citizen army of the Israelite tribes. The other major domain of nature in which Israel's god is involved is in the securing of agricultural and pastoral bounty, but instead of the natural phenomena that continually reproduce themselves being treated as mystical or magical bonds with deity, these phenomena are conceived as the material base for sustaining the intertribal order through the productivity of the extended-family units.

Titles, epithets, and images avoided or seldom used for Israel's god, although common elsewhere in the ancient Near East, become instructive for grasping the peculiar structural ordering of experience which the religion of Yahweh sanctioned. No single epithet for the deity occurs with anything like the regularity of the names Yahweh and El (ohim), singly or in combination. A series of sociopolitical epithets may be used to designate Yahweh-El (ohim), for example, as king (*melek*), sir or honored one (*'ādōn*), shepherd (*rō'eh*), judge (*shōphēṭ* or *dayyān*), father (*'av*), warrior (*'īsh milḥāmāh* or *gibbōr*), and even master or owner (*ba'al*). But these epithets are used sparingly and reticently, probably because of various negative connotations already firmly rooted in Canaanite sociopolitical and religious praxis and ideology—connotations which Israel struggled to purge from its own conception of deity or at least to limit sharply in usage.

It is noteworthy that Yahweh is not closely identified with the natural elements or with topographical features, although the title El Shaddai (Mighty El or El of the Mountain) contains the faint recollection of West Semitic *ṭdw/ṭdy* as "mountain."[623] The frequent imagery of storm phenomena, in which Yahweh is depicted as coming amid dark clouds, flashing lightning, and rain (to the extent that he may even be called "rider on the clouds," Ps. 68:4[5], cf. Isa. 19:1; or "rider in the sky," Deut. 33:26), is always associated with his powerful manifestation as warrior god at the head of his fighting people. Likewise, the heavenly bodies are described as working on behalf of the victory of Israel. There is no indication, however, that this imagery was rooted in Israelite cults of fire worship or of the worship of the heavenly bodies.

In some circles, the god may have been called "the bull of Jacob" (Gen. 49:24; Ps. 132:2,5; Isa. 49:26; 60:16, and "the bull of Israel," Isa. 1:24, i.e., if in these verses *'avir*, "Mighty One," is read as *'abbīr*). This may be the name of a proto-Israelite deity transferred to Yahweh. That the bull or calf was used in early monarchic worship to represent the attendant or pedestal of the divine throne may imply that even in premonarchic times the great strength of the bull could be used to express the strength of Yahweh. There is no foundation, however, to the belief that the bull statue actually represented Yahweh, or any other god, for this interpretation (expressed in the golden calf incident) is a later Judean polemic against Jeroboam's break from Jerusalem when he set up a royal Yahweh cult in Dan and Bethel independent of Jerusalem. Thus, Yahweh was not tauromorphic, either in premonarchic praxis and ideology or in the northern national cult established by Jeroboam. Nor is Israel's god imaged by means of plants or trees with their ample potentialities for expressing the mystical-magical powers of fertility at work in the life-sustaining grains, vegetables, and fruits.

From inanimate nature, only one epithet occurs with any frequency, and that is

Yahweh as "rock" (*tsur*; Deut. 32:4,15,18,30–31,37; I Sam. 2:2; II Sam. 22:3,32,47 //Ps. 18:2[3], 31[32], 46[47]), "crag" (*sela'*; II Sam. 22:2 // Ps. 18:2[3], or "stone" (*'even*; Gen. 49:24; I Sam. 7:12, Yahweh = "the stone of [military] help," i.e. Ebenezer [?]). These epithets, however, give no ground for thinking that the standing stone (*matstsēvāh*) was an actual embodiment of deity, although it probably served as a symbolic and didactic pointer to Yahweh.[624] What is implied in calling Yahweh "rock," "crag" or "stone" is reference to his role as the sure support and protector of his people—i.e., as a rock provides the foundation and material for solid building, shade from the scorching summer sun, and a hiding place for the guerrilla fighter.[625]

In this connection, the prohibition against representing Yahweh by any physical image is probably to be thought of as coterminous with the rise of Yahwism. Admittedly there is difficulty in conceiving exactly what this prohibition entailed.[626] Apparently the early resistance to picturing deity was not a blanket prohibition on all iconic symbolism. In this respect, the freedom with which many Jews later on included visual symbolism (although I think never direct representations of deity) in the mosaic floors of synagogues appears to be a truer clue to the original latitude of the Yahwistic prohibition against idols than the puritanical position of some later Jews against all pictorial representations.[627] At any rate, the ark carried in battle, as a kind of portable throne base of Yahweh, had no statue of Yahwèh set up on it or in it. Nevertheless, as a highly venerated palladium, the ark generated superstitious awe (I Sam. 4—7:2, especially 6:19–20; II Sam. 6:1–19), as did apparently a bronze serpent that was traced back to Moses (II Kings 18:4).

Archaeological evidence from the excavation of Israelite sites in this period has found no iconography of male deity. On the other hand, there is a high occurrence of goddess iconography in the form of crude statuettes and amulets apparently worn by women to induce pregnancy. While this sort of popular magic was probably discouraged by official Yahwism, it was perhaps never viewed as a serious infringement of the iconic prohibition since there was no danger of confusing a goddess with Israel's deity, who is normally conceived in *male* imagery.

The issue of Yahweh's "masculinity," thrust to the fore by a vigorous women's movement within the church and synagogue, is not easily to be resolved. Philologically, there is no question but that the pronoun references to Yahweh and the verbs of which Yahweh is subject are masculine throughout the traditions. Moreover, the dominant metaphors and similes for deity are male societal roles. The intriguing hypothesis that Elohim as a name for the singular Israelite deity (its plural form usually interpreted as a "plural of majesty" with something like the meaning "God of gods" or "incomparable God") actually alludes to a composite of male and female divine powers is a conjecture worth further research— particularly since no explanation of the usage has been entirely satisfactory. The evidence adduced to date, however, is unconvincing.[628]

If Yahweh developed out of an appositional title for El, it may be said that

Yahweh merely followed "cultural drift" in retaining the gender of the old Canaanite deity. In an historical sense, therefore, it is appropriate to refer to Yahweh as *he*. On the other hand, as Israel reflected on the gender of the deity it was not in sexual-biological categories but rather in terms of the indivisibility and completeness of the deity. Yahweh has no consort and does not sire Israelite "sons" and "daughters" but creates a people by adoption. If we try to state the indivisibility and completeness of Israel's deity in sexual terms, we might more nearly describe Yahweh as hermaphrodite than as either male or female.

Nevertheless, Yahweh's asexuality was apparently *not* invoked to challenge or to shatter male dominance in the Israelite society as a whole—in the decisive way, for example, that class dominance was challenged and shattered by Yahweh's liberating action. The overthrow of class dominion in early Israel had the indirect effect of improving the status of women relative to their status in Canaanite society, but there was no frontal assault in Israel on several forms of feminine subordination. We are greatly in need of further research into the relation between the role of woman in early Israel and the apparent paradox of the sexually undifferentiated but societally gender-typed deity.[629] Thus, I deliberately pose the problem for research and reflection by referring henceforth to Yahweh as "he."

Dominating all this terminology and imagery of the deity is the notion of Yahweh as the god of the people rather than as the god of a *city* or the god of a *holy place* or the god of *natural processes*. The Israelite deity gives land to the people, accepts worship at holy places, guides natural processes, but is preeminently and exclusively the leader-defender of a people organized as an intertribal social order. It seems that it is primarily from the historico-social struggle of a sovereign intertribal community that the major analogies for conceiving Yahweh are drawn. The analogical symbolism applied to deity is a way of characterizing the locus of sovereignty in the decentralized intertribal social order.

THE SOLE HIGH GOD COHERENTLY MANIFEST IN POWER, JUSTICE, AND MERCY. One of the most important dimensions of the common Near Eastern theology which Smith and Albrektson identified is the far-reaching commonality and astonishing formal simplicity of the content of the divine revelation. Yahweh is altogether like the other gods of the ancient Near East in that "he" manifests power, justice, and mercy in all "his" many deeds and words. This typological clarification cuts through all the obfuscating verbiage of biblical theology about the alleged special character of the Israelite notion of divine revelation in history. Not only is the medium of divine action much the same in the ancient Near East and in Israel, but what is revealed is much the same in the two instances. Through all the many varieties of revelation according to medium, time, place, and circumstance, only a relatively few things are revealed. What do we actually know about the gods of the ancient Near East and the God of ancient Israel? We know that they are powerful, create existing and potentially new situations, act justly to reward and to punish, and extend their mercy when humans have reached the limits of their resources.

While it is important to stress that the *content* of Yahweh's manifestation is basically the same as the content of the manifestation of other deities, it must also be emphasized that Yahweh's powerful, just, and merciful dealings with humankind, taken as a sum total, are considerably different in *structure* from the formally comparable dealings of other ancient Near Eastern gods. The structural alteration in the divine manifestations to Israel is in part a function of *the singularity of the divine manifestor* and in part a function of the object of the manifestation, namely, *the singularity of the social entity Israel.* I shall here deal briefly with the effect of the singularity of the divine manifestor, and reserve the effect of the singularity of the people to the following subheading.

The fact that there is but one God in Israel means that all manifestations of divine power, justice, and mercy are manifestations of a single purposive divine agent. While Albrektson is correct in denying that all that happens is reduced to a single comprehensive divine plan (apart perhaps from some versions of late Jewish apocalyptic thought), it is nonetheless true that, in all those aspects of nature, history, and society where Yahweh does manifest "himself" purposefully, there is a tendency to emphasize the dependability and coherence of the manifestations in their several discrete chains of events and processes. Yahweh is a faithful, reliable, and consistent deity. Of course similar things are said of other gods, but, to the extent that Yahweh eliminates all other divine agents from the effective world of "his" operation, the impetus toward a greater conceptual unification and rationalization of the divine attributes and purposes is exhibited in Israel. In other words, all other things being equal, the exclusivity of Yahwism would more often and more urgently stimulate questions about the relation between one divine manifestation and another than would the shifting and only partially developed tendency toward elevating one god above others in the ancient Near Eastern general theological pattern.

The trend toward unification and rationalization of the divine manifestations in early Israel does not reach the stage of highly systematic reflection, although there are formulaic assertions that go some distance toward stating the interrelations of the divine attributes revealed in the various manifestations. For example, the liturgical acclamation of Exodus 34:6–7 affirms the just punishments of Yahweh as logically coherent expressions of steadfast mercy. Yet the tension between the divine mercy and justice is far from fully explicated even in this quasi-rationalization of the divine ways. It does not, for instance, explain the basis for the distinction between the iniquity which Yahweh "forgives" and the iniquity of the fathers which Yahweh "visits upon the children" as far as three or four generations. Are some sins forgivable and others unforgivable? Or, are the same wrongdoings involved in both cases, with the distinction that those persisted in are to be punished? The most that is asserted is that Yahweh is acting true to "his" nature when forgiving sin and when punishing sin.

The characteristic way that Israel expressed the unification and rationalization of divine manifestatiaons is to be understood. In Israel, however, the fact that Yahweh's deliverance of the people from bondage and their establishment in a liberated existence in Canaan. The separate tradition units and cycles encompass large series of phenomena and events, thereby filling out the great themes of the centralized history of Israel's beginnings. Together these chains of phenomena and events constitute an immense history of divine manifestations through which Yahweh has secured the liberation of the people. The sequential linkage of events is informed by a sense of consistency of purpose and coherence of result extending over generations. Thus, for example, the ambiguity about forgivable and unforgivable sins noted in the liturgical formulation of Exodus 34:6–7 finds various "answers" in the way that Yahweh is represented as forgiving and punishing sins in the course of "his" generations-long dealings with Israel. In the several accounts of forgiven or punished sins, the Israelite hearer/reader could note the nature of the wrongdoing, the extent of its public or social effect, the attitude of the wrongdoer, and the measures taken by Yahweh to deal with the wrongdoing. In the cultic-ideological centralized history, as in liturgical acclamations, the one constant element amid all the tactical variations in Yahweh's dealings with the people is the singularity of the divine manifestor. Amid all the diverse manifestations of divine power, justice, and mercy Israel experiences one purposive will.

In the ancient Near East, various aspects of power, justice, and mercy can be exhibited in one or another deity, emphasizing now this or now that attribute or activity and even uniting them momentarily in one deity in formal analogy with Yahweh, without necessarily bringing to the fore the question of how the sum total of divine manifestations are to be understood. In Israel, however, the fact that these manifestations exhibit the attributes and purposes of a single god pushes the question of the coherence of what is revealed farther into the foreground of communal consciousness. On the one hand, this means a heightened sense within the Israelite society of being confronted by a consistently purposing and revealing god; and on the other hand it means that serious problems of theological comprehension and of communal praxis and self-understanding are provoked in Israel when there is a prolonged absence of divine manifestations where they are expected, or when natural and historico-social developments unexpectedly contradict the understood purposes and attributes of deity. This opens the road to that consuming passion for theodicy, for justifying the ways of deity, which Weber identified as one of the primary characteristics of ancient Israelite thought.[630] Although such challenges to and strains within the coherent manifestations of deity were felt in premonarchic times (notably in the Philistine crisis), they did not reach critical proportions as long as the intertribal order was freely developing and functioning viably. Only under the monarchy, with its major shifts and dislocations in social and political evolution, did the coherence of the divine manifestations become so dangerously problematic as to threaten the dissolution of Yahwistic praxis and ideology.

THE SOLE HIGH GOD IN BOND WITH AN EGALITARIAN PEOPLE. Among the several types of social groups and territorial entities with which ancient Near Eastern gods had special bonds, the unit with which the god of Israel was in bond was of a very specific and limited type. Yahweh is consistently represented as the God of Israel, and our study has shown that the name "Israel" in the premonarchic period regularly signifies a body of people organized in a comprehensive intertribal social order. Failure to analyze properly the historico-social emergence of Israel as a kind of "retribalization" rift within Canaanite society has led to gross misunderstandings of the entity Israel as the covenant partner of Yahweh, and consequently to gross misreadings of the nature of Israel's God. Since the primary manifestation of Yahweh is Israel itself, any misconstruction of Israel entails a misconstruction of Yahweh.

Yahweh was not in bond with a land, a region, or a city. Although there are a few traces in tradition that some Israelites felt they could not worship Yahweh if they were removed from the land occupied by Israel in Canaan (I Sam. 26:19; cf. Ruth 2:12; II Kings 5:17), it is striking that Israel's god is never called "the God of Canaan," or "the God of the land of Israel," or "the God of the land of Judah" (or of any other tribe), or "the God of Shechem" (or of any other city).

Yahweh was not in bond with a people joined by actual genealogical links. While the interrelationships of the groups joined together in intertribal Israel are expressed by means of genealogies, this is easily recognizable as the well-known phenomenon of giving pseudo-kinship symbolic phrasing to complicated couplings and linkages of large heterogeneous social groups. The people with whom Yahweh was in bond did not have a common biologically traceable descent, or even a unified prehistory, but were a composite people whose new-found unity was expressed, in spite of their heterogeneous origins, by means of the sociopolitical artifice of "the family tree."

Yahweh was not in bond with an occupational group through whom "he" was then secondarily linked to Israel at large. It is possible that the origin of the name Yahweh (probably as a verbal epithet for El, "he who creates") was among an occupational group; however, by the time of the formation of Israel as an intertribal entity, Yahweh was the god of the whole social system. It is true that the Levitical priests formed a kind of intellectual leadership cadre within the body of Israel, but they were servants of the whole people, and the tie of Yahweh is first of all with Israel and only secondarily with Levites as functionaries of the total Israelite system. It is also true that Yahweh was especially close to the citizen army when it went out to battle; however, since this was not a professional army, but the people bearing arms from time to time as necessary, there was no basis in military division of labor for creating Yahwism as a military cult in the sense that Mithraism was a military cult in the Roman Empire. It is further true that Yahweh was fiercely and tenaciously worshipped by the Kenites/Rechabites, who were metal craftsmen, but they did not form a privileged caste within Israel. Yahweh was no Israelite Vulcan.

It is true, moreover, that Yahweh was intimately associated with certain functional groupings of the populace with fluid membership (e.g., with the diseased, the barren, the famished, the orphan, the widow, the slave, etc.), but was not so associated because "he" was the god of a cult solely devoted to succoring those who had fallen into a physical or social plight. Yahweh was no Israelite Aesclepius. Yahweh was closely identified with these shifting distressed sub-groupings as signal instances of those within the larger society who were vulnerable to deprivation and death, and "he" came to their help as the god of the whole people Israel. Indeed, it was precisely the will of Yahweh that there should be a social system in which such suffering and disempowerment would be hastily alleviated and rectified, not so much by charitable deeds to individuals, as by assuring the ongoing stability of a functionally effective egalitarian social system.[631]

THE SOLE HIGH GOD INTERPRETED BY EGALITARIAN FUNCTIONARIES. The principle that the high god's activity in nature, history, and society is explained to the community by authenticated speakers is exhibited throughout the ancient Near East. The peculiar feature in early Israel is that the speaker for Yahweh has a defined social role within a nonstatist intertribal order rather than as a functionary in a centralized statist order. While it is possible that in the literature of the ancient Near East some testimonies to prestatist or tribal religion subsumed within the politically dominated culture that religions survive, as far as I have been able to determine, the high gods of the ancient Near East apart from Yahweh are always adjuncts of politicized societies. Ideas of gods have everywhere come to terms with centralized governments and with social stratification; accordingly, the gods are supramundane authenticators of the political and social order in which a minority of the members of the society dominate the majority. Only in the case of earliest Israel do we have a clearly articulated "national," i.e., culturally comprehensive, religious system wherein the interpreters of the deity do not recognize a central government or the division of society into privileged and nonprivileged strata.

In II.5.2 it was noted that Moses functions in the early traditions of Israel as a cipher for many leadership roles in the community. It is significant, however, in my judgment, that these functions and offices are consistently depicted as nonstatist, if not actually antistatist. The covenant is between Yahweh and Israel, and even when one account speaks of "a covenant with you [Moses] and with Israel" (Exod. 34:27), it does not represent Moses in anything other than the role of go-between. The mechanism for articulating the will of Yahweh in the community is a mechanism of diffused leadership roles. Elders apply the current understandings of the law to cases requiring adjudication and make consensus decisions for war and peace. Priests teach the contemporary interpretation of the instructions of the deity. Military leaders emerge to command the forces of one or more of the tribes in defense of the intertribal order. By the time of the Philistine crisis, prophets appear who stir up the people to defend Israel against its most danger- ous enemy to date. There was probably even a priestly or lay figure who played the mediator role of Moses in cultic-ideological covenant-renewal ceremonies.

All of these leadership types tended to be validated in terms of Mosaic legitima- tion, but none of them was authoritarian in a statist or bureaucratic sense. Each of these leadership roles was one or another form of traditional or charismatic authority. Even the so-called charismatic military "judge," sometimes described as a whimsical arbitrary element in the tribal order (often as evidence of "super- natural" intervention in Israel), fits comfortably within intertribal leadership of "the big man" type, i.e., the person who has a legitimate ad hoc function delimited by existing forms of traditional leadership. In fact, it is often overlooked in discussions of the supposedly free-wheeling "charismatic" judges that most of them begin their "judging" either on the basis of some traditionally sanctioned office they already hold (Ehud as head of a delegation carrying tribute to Moab, Deborah as a prophetess to whom Israelites come "for judgment," Samson as a Nazirite) or on the basis of a direct charge by those occupying traditionally sanctioned offices (Barak summoned by Deborah, Jephthah appointed by the elders of Gilead).

The later prophets of Israel fall within the monarchic period entirely, and thus not strictly within the period of this typology of early Israelite religion. It should be noted, however, that these later prophets owed little to statist and bureaucratic sociopolitical order except by way of critical reaction, for their own roots and conceptions were predominantly in a continuing traditional-charismatic tribal tradition and constituency with which the bureaucratic monarchy and social stratification stood in tension. Of course, there were accommodations of prophecy to the monarchic order, notably in the office of the cultic prophet,[632] and even certain of the so-called great prophets were probably economically supported by royalty and allowed at least a quasi-official role in the court apparatus. The detailed defense and illustration of these generalizations about later prophecy require empirical evidence and theoretical analyses far beyond the parameters of this study.

Admittedly a convincing map of the forms and jurisdictions of premonarchic leadership has yet to be drawn, since controversy continues to swirl around the various offices alluded to in the early traditions. What is clear, however, is that when the total body of premonarchic traditions is added up they indicate an impressive consensus among the decentralized tribal functionaries (however their roles are eventually to be defined) concerning the status of the relation be- tween Yahweh and Israel. In one way or another they spoke of the urgency of strengthening the intertribal system internally and externally. In practice this meant maximizing those institutions and forms of social relations which increased the cooperative autonomy of extended families and protective associations of families. It also meant maximizing intertribal military cooperation to turn back every assault against the sovereignty of the intertribal system over the highlands of Canaan. The speakers for Yahweh in the premonarchic period declared that the covenanted intertribal order of Israel should be strengthened and sustained by a unifying cultic-ideological practice and tradition and by social and military institutions of mutual aid in which communal leadership was widely diffused so as to prevent hierarchic authoritarian tendencies from taking root.

55

Socioeconomic Demythologization
of Israelite Yahwism

With the foregoing ancient Near Eastern–early Israelite paradigms of religious continuity and discontinuity in mind, it is clear that biblical theology was correct in asserting that Israel was religiously distinctive. The weakness in the biblical-theology paradigms of Israel's "uniqueness' was that they were formulations of religious idealism which failed to root the religious organization and ideology of early Israel in its distinctive social-constitutional framework. The intent of biblical theology to characterize the distinctiveness of early Israel is better served by depicting the religion of Yahweh as the symbolic bonding dimension of a synthetic egalitarian, intertribal counter-society, originating within and breaking off from hierarchic, stratified Canaanite society. All of the primary aspects of the religion of Israel, including its most idiosyncratic elements, hitherto viewed autonomously in the theological tradition, can be viewed more intelligibly in a socially organic manner that "demythologizes" them into functions and expressions of socio-economic and communal-cultural existence instead of into states of existential or mystical consciousness.

In brief, the chief articles of Yahwistic faith may be socioeconomically "de-mythologized" as follows: "Yahweh" is the historically concretized, primordial power to establish and sustain social equality in the face of counter-oppression from without and against provincial and nonegalitarian tendencies from within the society. "The Chosen People" is the distinctive self-consciousness of a society of equals created in the intertribal order and demarcated from a primarily centralized and stratified surrounding world. "Covenant" is the bonding of de-centralized social groups in a larger society of equals committed to cooperation without authoritarian leadership and a way of symbolizing the locus of sovereignty in such a society of equals. "Eschatology," or hope for the future, is the sustained commitment of fellow tribesmen to a society of equals with the confidence and determination that this way of life can prevail against great environmental odds.

Some of the most striking features of Israelite religion, which biblical theology sought to emphasize, can be lucidly articulated as aspects of the proposition advanced in Part X that Yahwism was the function of communal egalitarianism

692

and, in particular, that Yahwism was a servomechanism to reinforce the social system:

YAHWEH'S EXCLUSIVITY AND ABNORMAL JEALOUSY. Yahweh is unlike the other gods of the ancient Near East as Israel's egalitarian intertribal order is unlike the other ancient Near Eastern social systems. Yahweh forbids other gods in Israel as Israel forbids other systems of communal organization within its intertribal order. The social-organizational exclusionary principle in Israel finds its counterpart in a symbolic-ideological exclusionary principle in the imagery of deity.

Biblical theology returned again and again to the questions: What was the uniqueness of Israel's God? What were the basis and import of Israel's consciousness of being a chosen people? The answers were never satisfying in that they failed to relate the religious beliefs to the larger life of Israel as a social entity. A sociology of Israel's religion can establish coherent patterns between the religious anomalies and the social anomalies. As to the uniqueness of Yahweh, it lay not in the fact that "he" was personal, or that "he" was powerful, or that "he" was judgmental, or that "he" was merciful, or even that "he" acted in history. Yahweh's uniqueness lay in the fact that "he" was the symbol of a single-minded pursuit of an egalitarian tribal social system, a symbol drawn out of a common pool of ancient Near Eastern belief in individuated high gods, but appropriately refined and altered to fit the distance that lay between ancient Near Eastern society and Israelite society. Yahweh "transcended" Israel as the symbol of Israel's "transcendence" over ancient Near Eastern society, not in the sense that Israelite society was "more spiritual" or "more religious" or "more sophisticated," but in the sense that Israel created deliberate organizational distance between itself and the prevailing social systems. Yahweh stood for the primordial power in historical development for people to go beyond what is visibly realized at any given stage of historico-social development. In short, Yahweh was so different from the other gods because "he" was the god of such a different people.

Only a sociological approach to the notion of the chosen people can give it credibility and rescue it from absurdity. Other approaches, however ingenious, lose their way in mystifications, invoking idealist and supernatural notions of divine favoritism toward one people for no discoverable reason, or else appealing to ethical or metaphysical attributes possessed by a superior gifted people. The end result of such nonsociological interpretations of "chosen people" is either irrelevant supernaturalism or exclusivist racism, or both together. What was "different" about Israel is very clear to a dispassionate sociological analysis and does not have to be conjured out of the unknown transcendent or from the hidden folk soul. Israel *thought* it was different because it *was* different: it constituted an egalitarian social system in the midst of stratified societies, a system which congealed diverse peoples and functioned viably in the Canaanite highlands for at least two centuries. When the religious symbols of Yahweh and chosen people are broken down to their sociological base, it turns out to be the "distancing" or "transcending" power of a retribalizing community amid the "civilized," politically centralized ancient Near East. Yahweh and the chosen people are extreme innovative expressions in ancient Near Eastern religion parallel to and consonant with Israelite retribalization as an innovative expression in ancient Near Eastern social evolution.

YAHWEH'S PURPOSIVE NEGLECT OF THE UNDERWORLD. We have already commented on the peculiar aversion of early Yahwism to the domain of the dead. From the viewpoint of a sociology of religion, it may be said that Yahweh disregarded death as Israel disregarded death. To those who gathered together to form Israel, the risk of death as retribalized equals was preferable to the security of continued half-life in Canaanite society as part of the disprivileged underclasses. Yahweh forbade communication with the dead as Israel forbade the socially enervating and economically draining preoccupation with ancestor worship and memorialization of the dead, practices that were ways of securing loyalty to the sociopolitical status quo. This may well have been a direct reaction to Egyptian preoccupation with death and to Egyptian monopolization of communal resources for the cult of the dead, which not only made a decidedly negative impression on the Moses group but probably continued to confront Israel among the upper classes in Canaan.

Unfortunately we have only sketchy knowledge of the extent and precise forms of the cult of the dead in Canaan, although the early Israelite prohibitions against the cult of the dead indicate clearly that it was practiced in Canaan. By renouncing the grip of the dead upon the living, Yahwism struck a blow at the ideological supports of stratified society and at the same time released the economic products for direct consumption by the living instead of wasting them in sacrifices and memorials to the dead. For one thing is clear in the ancient Near Eastern cult of the dead: the lavish expenditures on that cult did not jeopardize the living standards of the ruling class. The ruling class continued to enjoy its luxury and opulence; the mystifying ideology of the hierarchic state merely allowed the ruling class to expropriate a larger surplus wealth from the populace that could in turn be squandered in self-indulgent efforts to assure immortality. In short, the Israelite uprising in Canaan had the double effect of abolishing in one stroke both the ruling class and the ideological specters of the dead that buttressed class rule.

YAHWEH'S REJECTION OF SEXUAL COMMODITY FETISHISM. Just as Israel rejected the fetishism of death with its reinforcement of class rule, so it rejected the fetishism of sex with its reinforcement of class rule. Fertility rites and concepts in ancient Near Eastern religion saw the human and divine worlds united in a bisexuality that extended from crops and herds and flocks through human pairing to the innumerable divine couplings of gods and goddesses with their consorts. This sexualization of natural and social reality tended to concentrate human energies in microcosmic imitations of the divine energies. The sexual symbols were monopolized by priesthoods and political elites, so that celebration of the sexualization of reality was celebration of the ruling system. While much more study of the sexual cults needs to be undertaken in order to determine their precise social locus, the general evidence points to the celebration of sex as a ruling-class luxury analogous to ruling-class celebration of the continued potency of the dead. Meanwhile, common prostitution was left mainly to the lower classes, economic deprivation driving women into the occupation.

When Israel broke with the sociopolitical monopoly of city-state feudalism and imperialism, it also rejected the sexual fetishism by which people were integrated into the hierarchic social order. Heterosexuality was reduced to an empirical phenomenon in the reproduction of society, but the locus of the divine in the society was not in the reproductive process but in the arrangement of social relations culturally produced and reproduced. While the matter calls for further research, I have already indicated in my analysis of the Rahab story the high probability that the integration of women into self-sufficient extended families in early Israel brought about a sharp reduction, if not actual eradication, of common prostitution in the society. The socioeconomic system for the reproduction of life along humane cultural lines rather than the mystically imbued, value-laden, biological reproductive process was primary for ancient Israel. The effect of the retribalization process in Israel was to recover sex as an empirical human phenomenon, restoring a unity which had split dualistically into either a mystical glorification of sex or an economically compelled degradation or dehumanization of sex, both of which served very well the interests of a ruling class.

LIMITED SOCIOECONOMIC DEMANDS OF THE PRIESTHOOD. Although I have not pursued a detailed study of the sociological import of the early Israelite priesthood, it is clear to me that the priestly establishment prior to the monarchy was a modest affair.[633] The Levitical priesthood was primarily a teaching order with responsibility for shaping the centralized cultic celebrations, and according to some traditions, it had paramilitary functions to perform.

The priesthood among Near Eastern peoples was closely tied to the ruling and aristocratic circles and tended to have disposal of a considerable share of the economic surplus. In Egypt, under the New Kingdom, the priesthood came to own or to control immense amounts of land.[634] Public sacrifices in the ancient Near East consumed considerable quantities of agricultural and pastoral products, and these sacrifices tended to be symbolic accompaniments of the delivery of economic surpluses from the general populace into the keeping and control of the ruling classes. As in all other economic matters, we can be sure that this priestly consumption of wealth did not cut into the ruling-class living standards but was regularly taken out of the share of communal production that the common people might otherwise have consumed. Our knowledge of priestly practice in the immediate Canaanite environment of Israel is not very detailed, but in broad outline the Canaanite priestly involvement in the sociopolitical order seems to have followed the general ancient Near Eastern pattern.

By contrast, in Israel the priesthood was landless in the sense that the Levites, dispersed throughout the tribes, were granted use-holdings but could not sell these holdings or amass additional holdings. Sacrifice was a limited part of the cultic celebrations; in fact, it appears that any male family head could preside at sacrifice without the presence of a priest. In short, the Levitical priesthood of early Israel was granted such powers as the covenanting tribes chose to give it, and those powers were so hedged about as to preserve the autonomy of the several tribes and to prevent the priesthood from gaining authoritarian control over the intertribal order. All in all, as we noted in Part X, a relatively small portion of the gross national product of liberated Israel went to explicitly religious sacrificial and cultic consumption. Yahweh owned all but demanded less economic investment and expenditure from worshippers than was customary in the monarchic-imperial cults of the ancient Near East. This is a dramatic instance of Yahwism's function as a social servomechanism—i.e., as a facilitator of chosen societal ends—since Yahweh's massive symbolic power was marshalled to prevent the old familiar game plan of political manipulation of religion in order to extract surplus wealth from the general populace.

PROMINENCE OF YAHWISTIC "POPULAR" HISTORIOGRAPHY. The well-developed traditions of the deeds of God among and through the people correspond to the historic sociological mutation of Israel as a community of actors working out new egalitarian forms of social existence without the burden of hierarchical leadership and fixed cosmic political structures. Since all Israelites were potential actors in Israel's struggles, the whole community was stimulated to produce traditions that could be joined in a great communal sequence of traditions.

By "popular" historiography I mean the recounting of a history involving the whole populace directly, and not by proxy as in royal historiography. Smith and Albrektson have shown convincingly that it is typical for ancient Near Eastern gods to perform mighty deeds. The differentiating criterion in Israel is that Yahweh's deeds are conceived as stages in the liberation of a whole people within the recent historic past. Elsewhere in the ancient Near East the gods are active chiefly in the deeds of kings, dynasties, ruling classes, city-states, and national entities which are assumed to have rootage in a distant past.

The content of the divine action is formally the same in Israel and in the ancient Near East—i.e., the god saves or punishes by natural, political, and military forces—but the sociopolitical scope and structure of Yahwistic saving deeds are very different. Yahweh "acts" both *for a people* and *through a people,* instead of for and through kings and dynasties and centralized political entities, which are assumed to represent the welfare of their subjects. Moreover, Yahweh "acts" for and through *a whole people simultaneously acting on its own behalf* to "birth" a novel retribalized social creation. These saving actions of Yahweh and Israel were moving, as it were, against the grain of customary praxis and ideology in the ancient Near East at the same time that they employed the religious high-god categories widely developed in the ancient Near East. In Israel the object of the divine activity is an entire people struggling to unify and defend a living space on the organizational principle of equal access to the basic resources for all members.[635]

"History" for Israel was not the story of elitist leaders nor the elaboration of pre-existing hierarchical religious and sociopolitical patterns. "History" for Israel was the activity of a whole people, a popular movement of extended families in protective associations and tribes, realizing itself in an open-ended venture of "covenant" linkage among its segments and with the divine source of its social energy. "History" thus took place in Israel as the experience of the genuinely new, which a human community discovers when it attempts a novel fusion of social praxis and ideology by throwing off inner fears and outer oppressors. We may loosely paraphrase this perception of God-on-behalf-of-"his"-people in an Israel-ite Yahwistic slogan: Yahweh is the spirit of the people, which is greater than the Canaanite's technology and elitism! All power to Yahweh and to "his" people! "Is anything to hard [or impossible] for Yahweh?" (Gen. 18:14; cf. Jer. 32:17,27; Deut. 30:11–14).

This explication of the popular historiographic aspect of early Yahwism can be rounded out by citing and commenting on a provocative observation by Martin Buber:

> He [the *malk*-type leader god exemplified by Yahweh] is not, as the French school of the sociology of religion wishes to conceive of this sort of thing [presumably he refers to E. Durkheim], the personified spirit of the community, but he represents the power which transcends it, happens to it, which *changes* it, even historicizes it; a power which in a formative hour drives it on to do the unaccustomed and untraditional, in a feud-overcoming gathering together of all clans as a single tribe, of all tribes as a single people.[636]

It seems to me that Buber has put his finger on the Achilles' heel of Durkheim's religious "collective representations" as symbols of the community in its simple givenness, as a kind of passive projection or mirror reflection of group feeling. But, as we have seen, there is another kind of sociology of religion based on an historical cultural-material hypothesis of social evolution that does justice to Buber's perception that the *malk*-type leader god, best represented by Yahweh "is not the personified spirit of the community, but. . .represents the power which transcends it, happens to it, which *changes* it." Such a sociology of religion (as I have tried to formulate in Part X) recognizes that it is not the mere givenness of society that projects a god image of the Yahweh type, but it is the tensions within

the onward-moving social process, the breaks and leaps, the struggles and mutations in the "distancing" process that occurs when a new social formation comes
into being and people are "stretched" to realize new possibilities of social interaction.

YAHWISTIC SALVATION PARADIGMS: MODES OF ENGAGING HISTORY AS THE SPHERE
OF SOCIAL STRUGGLE. Albrektson, as we noted, has singled out the prominence of
saving historical events in Israel's cultic recitations and enactments. He contrasts
this historical dimension with a tendency of the cult to revert to "timeless repose."
The undoubted tension in the Israelite cult referred to can be put in a somewhat
different way when we view it as a correlate of social praxis. It appears that the
extraordinary power of the exodus-conquest paradigms in early Israel was precisely their capacity to give symbolic meaning to a broad range of historic experiences of liberation and retribalization among the many social segments of Canaan
joined in Israel.

"Deliverance from Egypt" typified all sorts of "escapes" from Canaanite, Egyptian, Philistine, and Transjordanian political-military domination. "Conquest of
the Land," under the rubric of united Israel directed by Joshua, typified the way
in which the strivings for autonomous socioeconomic existence among several
converging proto-Israelite social sectors were realized by their unification as
segments in an intertribal social system. As long as such liberating and retribalizing actions were actually occurring—which was the case right up to the establishment of the monarchy—the cultic paradigms were live and "historical," resistant
to "timeless repose." The proper and immediate referent of the Pentateu-
chal/Hexateuchal traditional paradigms was one and the same: contemporary
liberated and retribalized Israel in Canaan.[637]

Only as such liberation and retribalization was frustrated and in major respects
cut short by the social evolution of Israel into a centralized state with internal social
stratification did the paradigms of the cult begin to lose their historical power and
lapse toward archaism and timelessness. In this context, "timelessness" is not
mystical transcendence or cyclical thought but the attrition of contemporary social
experience comparable to the social struggle in early retribalizing Israel which
first gave birth to the powerful, thematically concatenated symbolism of Yahwism
in the intertribal cult. As with other centrally politicized ancient Near Eastern
peoples, monarchic Israel began to live vicariously and by proxy on the exploits
and glory of its kings. Nevertheless, the notion that a whole people makes history
was not altogether extinguished under the Israelite monarchy.

Insofar as the historical paradigms continued to have power, it was because the
older social base of tribalism did survive under the monarchy in various accommodations to and struggles against the new hierarchic order. In these accommodations and struggles, the later prophetic movement was born. Social and religious forces were unleashed by which Yahwistic communities were able to survive

the eventual downfall of the independent Israelite states. These later developments are beyond the purview of this study, but I believe they can be traced as logical social developments from the foundational period of intertribal Yahwism.

An adequate sociological analysis of the monarchic and exilic/postexilic developments in Israel will require at least two detailed inquiries: first, to establish to what extent the older egalitarian social order managed to survive in partial manifestations under the monarchy and, thus, the degree to which Israelite monarchy was limited and modified by the persistence of an egalitarian social praxis and ideology; secondly, to determine to what extent both the politically disenfranchised Yahwistic community of the exiles and the semi-autonomous, postexilic, restored Yahwistic community were typologically related to the foregoing premonarchic and submonarchic social egalitarianism. In other words, both the internal social structure and its external relations with other social entities must be examined systematically throughout the history of biblical Israel if we are to determine the empirical meaning of "Israel" in all its stages of social evolution.[638]

It may be said, then, that this study is only the first stage in a continuing project. It has established the empirical social identity of Israel at its inception, and it has suggested a method and program for extending the study to the whole history of Israel. It appears that the earliest paradigms born of social struggle were expressions of the Israelite effort to overcome the intertribal community's precarious and problematic existence as a people without the kind of "proper" cosmic hierarchic charter possessed by politicized ancient Near Eastern peoples. From the start, Israel lived with a covenant charter which put optimum value on a people in egalitarian relations under one sovereign divine power.

Not only did those earliest paradigms become decisive for the subsequent course of Israelite religion; they also continued to thrive among social sectors of the populace within monarchic Israel. Those social sectors, displaced from a determinative position within the hierarchic, stratified social order, were nonetheless possessed of the powerful weapons of the canonical religious paradigms of liberation and retribalization. They were able to produce that extraordinarily self-critical Israelite prophetic movement which aided the survivors of the wreckage of the Israelite states in later times to form various kinds of truncated quasi-tribalized social forms in dispersed communities as well as in a restored Palestinian community. Just as I have tried to trace the earliest Yahwism as a function of the distinctive social praxis and ideology of emergent Israel, the later Yahwistic elaborations will have to be traced as the functions of ever-changing social praxis and ideology as they underwent complexification over time.

56

The Key to Israel's Religion: Idealism or Historical Cultural Materialism?

It is by no means a simple task to plot the intersection between biblical theology and biblical sociology. It does seem, however, that certain conclusions flow from viewing mono-Yahwism as the function of intertribal egalitarianism within the context of ancient Near Eastern–early Israelite religious continuity and discontinuity.

56.1 Yahwism as the Symbolic Expression of the Israelite Socioeconomic Revolution

Our study has demonstrated that the correlate and referent of early Israelite god symbolism was the heterogeneous, classless, decentralized association of tribes conceived as a brotherhood—and at least in larger measure than in Canaanite society, as a sisterhood—of social, economic, and political equals, and as a society striving for cultural meanings and purposes in the absence of clear precedents.

Israel's emergence exhibited a conjunction between an attempt to introduce a change in social relations at a certain *plateau stage in social evolution* in the ancient Near East and an attempt to introduce a change in religious perception and practice at a certain *plateau stage in religious evolution* in the ancient Near East. For at least two millennia the monarchic-imperial, socially stratified mode of life had held dominance in the ancient Near East accompanied by sociopolitically reinforcing theologies of individuated high gods. Israel "cut back" on the sociopolitical mode by attempting to decentralize and destratify social relations, and did so in tandem with a "stepped up," reinforced theology of a super-individuated sole deity who dramatically covenanted with a radically new, retribalized social order.

A radical social experiment birthed a radical theology without which it could not have succeeded as well as it did. If the Yahweh symbolism was essential to the emergence of Israel, it must not be overlooked (as biblical theologians generally do) that the Yahwistic religion was the praxis and ideology of an actual social community. The focus of all that hyperdeveloped religious symbolism was the social relations of a people. In Israel there emerged a continuity of successive and overlapping sets or series of social relations in which were developed a social-symbolic tradition acutely aware of Israel's "transhistorical" status, i.e., an aware-

700

ness of both the highly vulnerable change factor in all social relations and the persisting human significance of striving to construct free and self-correcting social systems.

In our attempt to position the socioreligious nexus of mono-Yahwism and egalitarian Israelite society within the context of a larger contemporary understanding of religion, it is necessary to take our cue from the methodological insight that religion is the function of social relations rooted in cultural-material conditions of life. This entails *a rejection of forms of theology that separate religion from theology and that abstract religious beliefs from the socially situated locus of the religious believers.* The uniqueness of the Israelite religious perception lay in its discovery through social struggle that the concrete conditions of human existence are modifiable rather than immutable conditions.

The cosmic religiopolitical charters of social life elsewhere in the ancient Near East mirrored and legitimated submission to the stratified world of class inequality, to the dependence of the many on the few for physical sustenance and for human identity. The covenant charter of early Israel mirrored and legitimated commitment in struggle toward the intentional "destratification" of the human world, to the elevation of all Israelites to the status of free producers— both of their physical lives and their religiocultural identities. Israel both "took back" a world and "freshly filled" a world with the realities and meanings of free and equal human beings. The covenant charter thus attests the enormous power of a social movement embracing the interests and identities of an entire populace that no longer waits to be given its due and its meaning from an elite.

Precisely here a profound warning enters our considerations. The weakness of the religious symbolism, when left unreduced to social struggle in actual material conditions, is that it can seem to overstate sheer willfulness, to enunciate no more than a pious truism that "all things are possible," to resolve the contingencies of every moment of struggle in history to the abstraction of "an all-powerful God." *The power of the religious symbolism in early Israel was precisely its integration within and penetration of a total struggle situation,* so that it articulated a willfulness informed by the situation, illuminating a route for those divided Canaanite underclasses to follow as, step by step, they realized "the impossible possibility" of free communal life in hierarchic Canaan.

There is but one way in which those ancient religious symbols can be employed today in anything like their full range and power, and that is *in a situation of social struggle where people are attempting a breakthrough toward a freer and fuller life based on equality and communal self-possession.* Even then it is a risky business to "summon up" powerful symbolism out of a distant past unless the symbol users are very self-conscious of their choices and applications, and fully aware of how their social struggle is both like and unlike the social struggle of the architects of the symbols.

In any case, the changefulness of the human experience includes both self-

absorbed and self-initiated change dialectically interacting within parameters set
by the unfolding material-cultural conditions. In my judgment, it is this persistent
mutant social base to Israelite religious praxis and ideology, deeply rooted in a
movement for equality, that preserves the valid insights biblical theology was
groping to express, while simultaneously freeing us from the mystifying idealistic
and supernaturalistic dregs of biblical theology.

56.2 Israel's Election: Socioreligious Actualities vs. Theological Puzzles

I take it, therefore, that the old theological conundrum about Israel's special
election through divine choice can at last be seen for what it is.[639] What it
represents is an absolutizing of an experiential social reality into dogmatic general
claims as the special property of a group. It is an instance of the objectification and
reification of an actual reality into such a form and context that it becomes an
embalmed relic and grosteque parody of the original truth.

We can see the truth in the claim well enough: Israel alone in the ancient Near
East, or at least to such a degree and with such self-consciousness, welded an
autonomous egalitarian social, economic, and political life out of heterogeneous
struggling groups which managed to thrive for two centuries. This objective social
situation surrounding the rise of Yahwism means that the notions of chosen
people and divine election were not simply an especially excessive instance of
national arrogance. The "excessiveness" of the Israelite religious claim corresponds to the "excessiveness" of the objective Israelite break with surrounding
social organization.

So far so good. Had the religion which accompanied the social achievement
died out when Israel became a monarchy, or somewhat later when it lost political
independence, the problem of the divine election of Israel would never have
arisen in the form of an endeavor to justify Israelite particularism by recourse to
various subterfuges and rationalizations. Divine election of Israel arose as "a
theological problem" only when the form of life that gave birth to the belief ceased
to be dominant in Israel, whereas Yahwism itself—suitably revised and adapted
and expanded—lived on as a religious cult and ideology under social conditions
that no longer corresponded to the social conditions obtaining in earliest Israel.

Put in another way, divine election could only be a question when the actual
reality of total social-systemic liberation and retribalization in old Israel had
passed away. When Israel no longer was Israel in its former sense, it began to lose
the capacity to see the wholeness involved in the unity of liberated life and the cult
of Yahweh. What had been an integral function of social life became an alienated
product incongruent with later social contexts. Yahweh became a mystery, "his"
choice of Israel arbitrary, so that only the willful divine love toward Israel could
explain the otherwise inexplicable rise and persistence of this Yahwistic tradition.
A socioreligious union of praxis and ideology became a fetishistic intellecutal-
theological puzzle.[640]

We may say, accordingly, that the theological puzzles about divine revelation and the election of Israel are only puzzles for a religion that has already changed its character and lost its original unity of social praxis and ideology. Yet Jews and Christians go on speculating about those puzzles because they are stock items in the received religious tradition. The theological puzzles have become independent intellectual games to be played out with a fairly standardized set of strategies and tactics.

The only way out of the impasse is to fix our attention on the relation between the persisting theological game patterns and the social conditions in which they are played from age to age, including our own social contexts. It is insufficient and untenable merely to conceive of the task of religious communities to be the intellectual elaboration and refinement of the received game traditions. Once we are able to understand religious traditions as functions of material conditions of life and the social relations rooted in those conditions, we are obligated precisely as religious persons to subject the received traditions to a thoroughgoing analysis of their social content and to take responsibility for religious reconstruction appropriate to the social content of our own experience. There is no imaginable way that this can be done without social conflict within the community itself, since every effort of a community (especially of a religious community) to become self-conscious about its social position will be attended by deep resistance insofar as every community tends to overlook its contingent character and to feed upon various myths of its enduring legitimacy as a faithful reflection of the timeless transcendent.

56.3 On Being Religious: In Ancient Israel and in the Present Social and Intellectual Climate

In the effort to do theology by reflecting back upon the social base which produces religious symbolism, our social understanding of religious praxis and ideology puts us in a peculiar relationship to early Israel. From one point of view, we can ask what it meant "to be religious" in terms of the original unitary reality of intertribal Yahwism. That is, how would we look upon religion if we were to look upon it after the manner of ancient premonarchic Israel? Possibly the answer is that we would not look upon it as religion at all, by which I mean that we would not see "religion" the way we now see it, i.e., as a sharply separate body of beliefs and practices already existing as a fixed traditional quantum to which we somehow have to relate our other ideas and practices.

To be religious, in the sense that the early Yahwists were religious, would not be to have a preestablished religion drawn out of the past to present us with a *fait accompli*. It would be rather more a matter of finding out what had to be done to master our social circumstances and to locate in the process those transcending images and those adaptive practices which could focus our energies collectively to master our circumstances. This would include readiness to modify and discard old religious models and to create new religious praxis and ideology suitable to our situation, comparable to the Israelite breakthrough into mono-Yahwism on the foundation of old El theology. It would mean being so experimental and radical in our religious formulations that later generations could say of us that we had "founded a new religion."

Yet in one critical and decisive sense we cannot put ourselves in early Israel's position except for analytic and analogical purposes. My characterization above of what it meant "to be religious" in early Israel is necessarily an abstraction from the sum total of early Israelite religious phenomena seen in a certain structural light. I have frankly interpreted Israel's early religion in the only way I can—as a modern observer. We live in a different set of material conditions, differently appropriated by technologies in new social formations. As a result of these changed structural conditions of human life, we experience changed social and intellectual conditions for "being religious." In particular, we live in the aftermath of the Cartesian and Kantian break-ups of the metaphysical and epistemological harmony and unity of perception. We likewise live in the wake of the Hegelian and Marxian departures from ahistoricism and from nonprocessual understandings of the human condition. We are unable to appropriate the powerful religious symbolism out of early Israel in any other way than as moderns for whom radically new techno-economic and social-relational conditions have made us, willingly or not, heirs of the Cartesian-Kantian and Hegelian-Marxian dissolutions of the static, hierarchically layered unity of reality. Our view of religious symbolism is conditioned by a relational and processual understanding of cultural and social evolution. In spite of the sincere intentions of religious conservatives, "believing" and "preserving" scrupulously the biblical formulations simply cannot enable us to think and feel about human community precisely, or even approximately, as ancient Near Eastern and early Israelite peoples thought and felt about it.[641]

The point is that the most ardent attempts to reaffirm the validity of the religious symbolism of early Israel occur within social and intellectual conditions that fundamentally alter the locus and import of the supposed reduplication of those early affirmations. Mono-Yahwistic affirmations that were socially "progressive" in their origins become socially "reactionary" when simplistically reaffirmed today. To purport to believe the same things in different social and intellectual conditions is in fact not to believe the same things at all. Our changed socioeconomic and intellectual-cultural conditions have severed our bondage to the ancient gods, and to Yahweh as well, for Yahweh too fell victim to the process of objectifying and falsifying collective human experience. Yahweh became severed from the experiential base that gave "him" birth and that Yahweh, as a social servomechanism, helped to birth. Yahweh became an idea, even if the highest Idea, and henceforth a problem to the tradition as people struggled to fit the deity back into a suitable social context. It was not perceived that social conditions change and thereby alter the ideas grounded in them. Yahweh had been very much at home in the original social context—an "at homeness" progressively lost as those formative social conditions passed away and new contradictory social conditions arose that step by step turned the socially symbolic deity into a free-floating Idea or Person perceived as "timeless."

56.4 Contribution toward Social Change: The Criterion of Religious Symbols and Organizations

An historical cultural-material and social-evolutionary view of early Israel will free us from trying to duplicate the forms of Israel's life and thought. An historical cultural-material and social-evolutionary view of our own place in human history will enable us more wisely and creatively to meet changed circumstances with the appropriate balance of absorbing and initiating change of our own. If we are to continue to derive symbolic resources from the biblical traditions, our way of relating to early Israel—as to all previous complexes of material conditions, social relations, and religious or philosophical systems—will have to be scientifically informed.[642] A social understanding of early Yahwism might encourage us to see what forms of oppression are inhibiting and frustrating the full development of human life today, what has to be done to change those conditions in specific terms, and what praxis and ideology are needed if we are to develop in the needed direction. If there is something to be retained out of the religious ideology of old Israel, it is certainly not the distorted, alienating line of tradition which absolutizes and falsely projects the traditional religious models into eternal idols and specters of the mind.

With the help of a powerful, evocative religious symbolism, earliest Israel strove for liberated life of a sort realizable under the socioeconomic and intellectual-cultural conditions peculiar to its time and place. Similar struggles in great variety have punctuated the long history that connects us with early Israel. Some of those intervening struggles have been indebted to Israel's symbol system and others have not. We too strive for closer approximations to a fully liberated existence congruent with our circumstances. Our struggles, under the diverse and hybrid intellectual-cultural conditions of modernity, are partially and erratically fueled by the Jewish-Christian symbol system. Rather than naively assuming an overt or necessary connection between these inherited religious symbols and our social aspirations and struggles, it is imperative from moment to moment in the course of conflict that we determine the operational inter-ties between the predominant religions and the current forms of social struggle. In particular, we must assess to what degree and in what respects inherited religion converges on and reinforces social struggle and precisely which social sectors and tendencies religion validates and motivates and which social sectors and tendencies religion invalidates and discourages or obstructs.

It should by now be evident that efforts to draw "religious inspiration" or "biblical values" from the early Israelite heritage will be romantic and utopian unless resolutely correlated to both the ancient and the contemporary cultural-material and social-organizational foundations. The sole God who liberates an egalitarian people was Israel's cipher for the enduring human project: the wisdom and courage to arrange the variable technological options and social relations available to people within determinate ranges, from stage to stage in social evolution, in such a way that the species as a whole can develop its potentialities. The religious symbolism for such a project will have to grow out of an accurate scientific understanding of the actual material conditions we face.

Effective and convincing transcending images will only arise as aspects of the struggle within a specific social sector that is moving to change social relations within the determinate ranges opening up from moment to moment. Whether the transcending images will be compelling or not will depend upon the social setting of the human actors who develop the images and who are confronted by the images. All theologizing will henceforth be a function of social situation, and our judgment about the truth of religious ideology will be a judgment on the promise of particular social tendencies, linked with particular religious symbols, to further the evolution of social relations in a productive way for the maximum number of people. If this seems untenably subjective as a basis for understanding religious truth, the only answer is that at bottom religious truth *always* has been judged by social criteria, either overtly or covertly. What is to be gained by fully accepting this reality is a clearer focus of attention on the appropriate criteria of social advance, which to a historical cultural-material perspective means movement toward subjectively chosen *and* objectively possible social change.

Once we divest ourselves of idealist and supernaturalist notions of independent religious forces abstracted from social relations, the future of religious symbolism remains an open question, as I indicated in Part X in the context of discussing the Marxian expectation that religion will one day die out. In substance my judgment was that we have no certain way of knowing if a religious dimension of social life will survive the discard of religion as a mystifying accompaniment of class rule. Only as we make the necessary surgical removal of socially obstructive religious praxis and ideology will we know what sorts of transcending images and celebrations will develop in future stages of social evolution.[643]

Tentatively I conclude that religion broadly follows changes in social relations which set limits, ranges, or parameters for religious developments. Yet, within the existing limits or parameters of social change, particular symbolic concretions of what is possible and desirable can make decisive differences in the efforts people make to realize changes of one sort or another. Social energies are marshalled or dissipated, social goals are projected or discarded, individual commitments are made or withheld according to proximate symbolic models of what we should be trying realistically to attain. When those models are submerged in archaic networks of tradition, uninformed by scientific analysis and contemporary experience, they are volatile, unpredictable, and next to useless, lacking precisely the calculus of social forces and possibilities which is necessary to participate meaningfully in the social process. Whether Marx was right about the very root of religion consisting of mystification, there is no doubt that the great majority of what passes for religious praxis and ideology serves to mystify and pacify consciousness, lulling it into a far-too-docile compliance with social irrationalities and with the supposed eternal validity of this or that social system. If the social project of humankind depends ultimately upon a greatly awakened and informed populace, only symbolic models that are consciously and intelligibly related to immediate human needs in calculable means-ends relations will be trustworthy and valid.

It is perhaps of some value to our scientific understanding of how religiosocial symbolism functions to recognize that the distinctive monotheistic offshoot from the individuated high gods in the ancient Near East occurred as the ideological correlate of an early experiment in egalitarian retribalization. Exactly how valuable this understanding may prove to be in the sum of our social analytic depends, I think, partly on the results of comparable detailed analyses of the social bases of later Israelite religion and of other religious traditions that have been widely influential in human affairs. The Israelite experiment in egalitarian retribalization was on too limited a scale to succeed, surrounded as it was by elitist societies and penetrated from within by elitist tendencies that overwhelmed it. What we are after today is certainly not any sort of comparable pre-industrial retribalization, which could be no more than a romantic primitivizing form of idealism at best. We are looking for egalitarian social forms that take full account of our advanced and advancing material conditions, social forms in which the cul-de-sac of the nation-state constellation of class divisions with their rampant repression of human life in the service of racism, provincialism, and war will be overcome.

If the replication of Israelite retribalization cannot possibly bring about appropriate egalitarian social forms for our age, it is far more patent that reaffirmations of the Yahwistic ideology of that ancient social system, or of its transformations into Christian or Jewish theology, cannot do so either. Nothing can take the place of analysis and praxis and ideology suitable to our own situation. The analyses, praxes, and ideologies of the past are all instructive, but they are not blueprints or lodestones. The Marxian historical cultural-material approach is not a blueprint or formula but a method, a testable way of approaching our situation as social beings and systematically trying to understand and change it within the limits that each stage of social evolution will permit.

Early Israelite Yahwism is an intriguing case study in the relation of religion to social change. In the short run, Yahwism seems to have been a socially "progressive" force, serving to reinforce the retribalizing endeavors of lower classes in

Canaan. In the long run, however, as we examine the course of Yahwism through biblical times and on into Judaism and Christianity, it appears to have shifted more and more into a socially "reactionary" force, its progressive impetus draining off into sectarian sub-groups or drifting along in uncritical and poorly articulated moods and tendencies in the main social body, but only now and then, as in the prophetic movement, erupting with sustained critical power.

If my line of reasoning about the relation of biblical theology and biblical sociology is correct, the most important contribution of a sociological analysis of early Israel to contemporary religious thought and practice is to close the door firmly and irrevocably on the idealist and supernaturalist illusions still permeating and bedeviling our religious outlook. Yahweh and "his" people Israel must be demystified, deromanticized, dedogmatized and deidolized. Only as we carry through this sociological demythologization of Yahwistic faith, and of its Jewish and Christian derivatives, will those of us who have been formed and nurtured by those curiously ambiguous Jewish and Christian symbols be able to align heart and head, to combine theory and practice. Cogent symbols of historico-social transcendence for the future must illuminate, amid the supersession of social forms through time, *the critical intersection between lawful social process and human freedom.* It is at that intersection, more or less auspicious from moment to moment, where missed and realized opportunities continually emerge for ever larger numbers of us to struggle toward meeting our genuine human needs and actualizing our repressed human potentialities.

Symbol systems claiming to be based on "biblical faith" will be judged by whether they actually clarify the range and contours of exercisable freedom within the context of the unfolding social process. Symbol systems that blur the intersection of social process and human freedom—by talking fuzzy nonsense, by isolating us in our private souls, by positing "unseen" worlds to compensate for the actual world we fear to see, by conditioning us to compete for many small favors instead of cooperating for a few big gains, by cultivating mood and sentiment in place of vision and passion, by instilling resignation in the name of sweetness and sacrifice, by persuading us to accept the humanly unacceptable and to desist from changing what is manifestly changeable, by confirming our fixations to the past and our venturelessness toward the future, by decrying power while feasting on its benefits—all such symbol systems, however venerable and psychically convenient, are bad dreams to be awakened from, cloying relics to be cast away, cruel fetters to be struck off. They are, in a word, the Canaanite idols that Israel smashed when it smashed the Canaanite kings.

Increasingly we humans are thrown together in a process that both narrows and heightens our freedom. Transformations of our social relations and of our ideas are accelerating in tandem with the quickening pace of techno-environmental and techno-economic transformations. Our "higher" cultural accomplishments, religion among them, are swept along in the transformed and transforming social process. In this rapidly complexifying and maturing sociocultural transitional period, all forms of religious faith and practice that fail to grasp and to act upon their connection with and dependence upon the cultural-material evolution of humankind are doomed to irrationality and irrelevance, whatever diversionary consolation they offer at the moment. Forms of religion capable of grasping and acting on that connection and dependence have something to contribute to the next stages in the long struggle for human liberation; and in commitment to that project, they will have something to learn, or to relearn, from the social religion of liberated Israel.[644]

APPENDICES

Appendix A

NOTES TO PART I

1. R. Schlatter, general editor of *The Princeton Studies: Humanistic Scholarship in America,* in "Foreword," *Religion: A Humanistic Field,* by C. A. Holbrook, 1963, p. vii.

2. H. M. Orlinsky, "Whither Biblical Research?" *JBL* 90 (1971) 1. For initial explorations of the social conditioning of biblical hermeneutics, consult N. K. Gottwald and A. C. Wire, eds., *Reader in Biblical Sociology,* 1976 (expanded re-issue of *Radical Religion,* 2/2–3 [1975]).

3. C. A. Holbrook, *Religion: A Humanistic Field,* 1963, p. 39.

4. C. W. Mills, *The Sociological Imagination,* 1959, and *Power, Politics and People: The Collected Essays of C. Wright Mills,* ed. I. L. Horowitz, 1963. For assessments of Mills' contributions to sociology, see I. L. Horowitz, ed., *The New Sociology: Essays in Social Science and Social Theory in Honor of C. Wright Mills,* 1965, pt. 1.

5. P. L. Berger, *Invitation to Sociology: A Humanistic Perspective,* 1963; *The Sacred Canopy: Elements of a Sociological Theory of Religion,* 1967; P. L. Berger and T. Luckmann, *The Social Construction of Reality: A Treatise in the Sociology of Knowledge,* 1966. For a review and interpretation of the course of Berger's intellectual projects as "a paradigmatic career" for illuminating the development of social theory and sociology of religion over the last two decades, see Gordon Clanton, "Peter L. Berger and the Reconstruction of the Sociology of Religion" (Ph.D. diss., Graduate Theological Union, Berkeley, California, 1973).

6. By way of introduction to sociology: A. Inkeles, *What is Sociology?,* 1964; R. S. Rudner, *Philosophy of Social Science,* 1966; G. Lenski and J. Lenski, *Human Societies: An Introduction to Macrosociology,* 2nd ed., 1974; and T. Caplow, *Sociology,* 2nd ed., 1975. The classic issues in social theory are developed in R. Nisbet, *The Sociological Tradition,* 1966, and, with excerpts from major thinkers, in T. Parsons et al., eds., *Theories of Society,* 2 vols., 1961. The present ferment in the discipline is reflected in A. W. Gouldner, *The Coming Crisis of Western Sociology,* 1970, and *For Sociology: Renewal and Critique in Sociology Today,* 1973, as also in T. B. Bottomore, *Sociology as Social Criticism,* 1975. On anthropological theory: M. Harris, *The Rise of Anthropological Theory: A History of Theories of Culture,* 1968. On political theory: S. S. Wolin, *Politics and Vision: Continuity and Innovation in Western Political Thought,* 1960.

7. A somewhat fuller and more bibliographically detailed account of the history and disciplinary boundaries of "Old Testament sociology" will be found in N. K. Gottwald and F. S. Frick, "The Social World of Ancient Israel," *Society of Biblical Literature 1975 Seminar Papers,* vol. 1, pp. 165–178 (an orientation paper for the SBL consultation on the subject of the paper title). A comparable survey of "New Testament sociology" is J. Z. Smith, "The Social Description of Early Christianity," *Religious Studies Review* 1 (1975) 19–25 (with bibliography). Concerning the pre-Islamic Arab bedouins as analogies to early Israel: W. R. Smith, *Lectures on the Religion of the Semites: The Fundamental Institutions,* 3rd ed., with intro. by S. A. Cook, 1927 (reprint with prolegomenon by J. Muilenburg, 1969), and *Kinship and Marriage in Early Arabia,* 2nd ed., 1903; J. Wellhausen, *Reste arabischen Heidentums,* 2nd ed., 1897.

8. M. Weber, *Ancient Judaism,* 1921 (Eng. trans. 1952), and see Weber's *The Sociology of*

Religion, 1922 (Eng. trans. 1963), for a more systematic treatment of the analytic concepts applied to Israel in the first title.

9. W. Rauschenbusch, *Christianity and the Social Crisis,* 1907, chap. 1; and see the editor's introduction to W. Rauschenbusch, *The Righteousness of the Kingdom* (ed. M. L. Stackhouse), 1968. Also, a social study of biblical religion stimulated by the Social Gospel movement: C. C. McCown, *The Genesis of the Social Gospel: The Meaning of the Ideals of Jesus in the Light of Their Antecedents,* 1929. For discussion of early attempts to develop "biblical sociology" under Social Gospel influences, see C. H. Hopkins, *The Rise of the Social Gospel in American Protestantism, 1865–1915,* 1940. Illustrative of a number of surveys and handbooks written to disseminate the Social Gospel view of the Bible is T. G. Soares, *The Social Institutions and Ideals of the Bible,* 1915.

10. L. Wallis, *A Sociological Study of the Bible,* 1912; *God and the Social Process,* 1935; *The Bible Is Human,* 1952. Wallis, although lacking Weber's vast erudition and methodological reflectiveness, appears in many respects as the unacknowledged, and largely unknown, American counterpart of Weber in his intensive efforts to find the social key to ancient Israel. W. C. Graham, *The Prophets and Israel's Culture,* 1934, and W. C. Graham and H. G. May, *Culture and Conscience: An Archaeological Study of the New Religious Past in Ancient Palestine,* 1936. The somewhat better known New Testament scholars at the University of Chicago who adopted a broadly cultural, but only quasi-sociological, approach were S. Mathews, S. J. Case, and H. R. Willoughby. L. E. Keck, "On the Ethos of Early Christians," *JAAR* 42 (1974) 435–452, comments on the continuing pertinence of the social interpretation of early Christianity by Mathews and Case, suggesting how their rather abstract desiderata might be carried forward in an empirical program.

11. K. Koch, *The Growth of the Biblical Tradition: The Form-Critical Method,* 1964–1967 (Eng. trans. 1969), reveals how minimal has been form criticism's direct consideration of Israelite social history. M. Noth, in *A History of Pentateuchal Traditions,* 1948 (Eng. trans. 1972), by far the most sociologically oriented of all the major form-critical and tradition-historical studies of early Israel, nonetheless concludes his inquiry by confessing that his method is unable to find any clear way to account for the social unity in diversity which characterized earliest Israel.

12. A. Alt's fundamental essays on patriarchal religion, law, the settlement, and the monarchy collected with scores of others in his three-volume *Kleine Schriften* (1953/1959; hereafter *KS*) are available in English translation as *Essays on Old Testament History and Religion,* 1966 (hereafter *EOTHR*).

13. W. F. Albright, *From the Stone Age to Christianity,* 2nd ed., 1957, and *History, Archaeology, and Christian Humanism,* 1964. See also Stanley Hardwick, "Change and Constancy in W. F. Albright's Treatment of Early Old Testament History and Religion, 1918—1958" (Ph.D. diss., New York University, 1965).

14. M. Noth, *Das System der zwölf Stämme Israels,* 1930, and, in brief compass, *The History of Israel,* 2nd ed., 1954 (Eng. trans. 1960), pp. 85–138.

15. G. E. Mendenhall, *Law and Covenant in Israel and the Ancient Near East,* 1955 (reprinted in E. F. Campbell, Jr., and D. N. Freedman, eds., *BAR* 3 [1970], pp. 3–53).

16. G. E. Mendenhall, "The Hebrew Conquest of Palestine," *BA* 25 (1962) 66–87 (reprinted in E. F. Campbell, Jr., and D. N. Freedman, eds., *BAR* 3 [1970] 100–120).

17. For a representative, though far from exhaustive, sample of this voluminous technical literature through 1960, see the topically arranged bibliography in R. de Vaux, *Ancient Israel: Its Life and Institutions,* 1958/1960 (Eng. trans. 1961), pp. 519–552. Further publications, including the most recent titles, will be found in P. Nober, ed., "Elenchus Bibliographicus," published annually since 1920 in the periodical *Biblica,* containing by far the

most thorough index of books and articles in biblical research. Less exhaustive, but with brief descriptions of contents (generally in German), is F. Stier, ed., *Internationale Zeitschriftenschau für Bibelwissenschaft und Grenzgebiete,* published biennially since 1951. Valuable for its summaries and critiques of books published in Old Testament studies is the annual *Book List* of the British Society for Old Testament Study (published since 1946).

18. I mention only a few of the most pertinent unpublished doctoral dissertations in chronological order: Stephen H. Bess, "Systems of Land Tenure in Ancient Israel" (Ph.D. diss., University of Michigan, 1963); Paul A. Riemann, "Desert and Return to Desert in the Pre-Exilic Prophets" (Ph.D. diss., Harvard University, 1963); John T. Luke, "Pastoralism and Politics in the Mari Period: A Re-examination of the Character and Political Significance of the Major West Semitic Tribal Groups in the Middle Euphrates" (Ph.D. diss., University of Michigan, 1965); Siegfried Schwertner, 'Das Verheissene Land': Bedeutung und Verständnis des Landes nach den frühen Zeugnissen des Alten Testament" (inaugural dissertation for the doctorate, University of Heidelberg, 1966); W. Eugene Claburn, "Deuteronomy and Collective Behavior" (Ph.D. diss., Princeton University, 1968); Albert E. Glock, "Warfare in Mari and Early Israel" (Ph.D. diss., University of Michigan, 1968); William J. Dumbrell, "The Midianites and Their Transjordanian Successors: Studies in the History, Social Structure, and Political Influence of Related Transjordanian Groupings" (Th.D. diss., Harvard University, 1970); Frank S. Frick, "The City in the Old Testament" (Ph.D. diss., Princeton University, 1970) = *The City in Ancient Israel* (SBLDS, 36), 1977; Dale A. Patrick, "A Study of the Conceptual Models of the Covenant" (Th.D. diss., Graduate Theological Union, Berkeley, Calif., 1971); Robert R. Wilson, "Genealogy and History in the Old Testament" (Ph.D. diss., Yale University, 1972)= *Genealogy and History in the Biblical World* (Yale Near Eastern Researches, 7) 1977; John M. Halligan, "A Critique of the City in the Yahwist Corpus" (Ph.D. diss., University of Notre Dame, 1975); Marvin L. Chaney, "HDL-II and the 'Song of Deborah': Textual, Philological, and Sociological Studies in Judges 5, with Special Reference to the Verbal Occurrences of HDL in Biblical Hebrew" (Ph.D. diss., Harvard University, 1976). Since Chaney is my colleague in the Graduate Theological Union of Berkeley, California, I have had ample opportunity to discuss with him the methods and results of his study and to read early drafts of portions of the dissertation.

19. The most explicitly sociological of these handbooks is R. de Vaux's work cited in note 17, but its chief merit is to state topics and problems and to marshal data rather than to propose synthetic solutions or models. J. Pedersen's widely hailed *Israel: Its Life and Culture,* 4 vols. in 2 bindings, 1926/1940, exhibits a social perspective on premonarchic Israel almost totally derived from notions of Israelite "primitivism" and "nomadism"; nevertheless, his striving to grasp Israel as a totality was exemplary and many of his observations retain their value. Other handbooks (such as G. E. Wright, *Biblical Archaeology,* 2nd ed., 1962; M. Noth, *The Old Testament World,* 1964 [Eng. trans. 1966]; and B. Reicke and L. Rost, eds., *Biblisch-Historisches Handwörterbuch,* 3 vols., 1962–1966), concentrate on archaeology, history, religion, and general culture with strikingly little attention to economics and social structure. The same is true of the three most widely used histories of Israel: M. Noth, *The History of Israel,* 2nd ed., 1954 (Eng. trans. 1960), J. Bright, *A History of Israel,* 2nd ed., 1972, and S. Herrmann, *A History of Israel in Old Testament Times,* 1973 (Eng. trans. 1975). The fullest sociological treatments of certain biblical phenomena, although random and uncoordinated because of the encyclopedia format, are found in U. M. D. Cassuto, B. Mazar, et al., eds., *'Entsiqlōpedyāh Miqrā'ith* (Biblical Encyclopedia; hereafter *EM*), 1955 (Heb.), and in the 16-volume *Encyclopaedia Judaica,* 1972 (hereafter *EJ*).

20. M. Weber, *Ancient Judaism,* 1921 (Eng. trans. 1952), p. 425.

21. H. H. Gerth and D. Martindale, "Preface," *Ancient Judaism* by M. Weber, 1921 (Eng. trans. 1952), p. ix.

NOTES TO PART II

22. Translations of significant extrabiblical texts, with brief introductions and notes, appear in J. A. Pritchard, ed., *Ancient Near Eastern Texts Relating to the Old Testament*, 3rd ed., 1969 (hereafter *ANET*). An orientation to the extrabiblical texts most germane to pre-monarchic Israel, together with extensive bibliography, is available in A. E. Glock, "Early Israel as the Kingdom of Yahweh: The Influence of Archaeological Evidence on the Reconstruction of Religion in Early Israel," *CTM* 41 (1970) 564–569.

23. Qazardi, chief of *'i-ś-r* (Aser? Asher?) is mentioned in Papyrus Anastasi I from the end of the thirteenth century (translation in *ANET*, p. 477, xxiii.5), W. F. Albright, *JAOS* 74 (1954) 222–232, rejects the equation of *'i-ś-r* with the Israelite Asher, but Y. Aharoni, *The Land of the Bible*, 1962 (Eng. trans. 1967), p. 171, argues for the equation.

24. Cultivation of royal estates in Shunem (eventually a town in Issachar) by corvée laborers is reported in a letter from the king of Megiddo to the pharaoh in the fourteenth century (translation of *EA* 365 in A. F. Rainey, *El Amarna Tablets 359–379*, 1970, pp. 25–27). A. Alt, *KS*, III, 1963 (orig. pub. 1924), 169–174, contended that the corvée in Shunem referred to the origins of Israelite Issachar ("hireling") and he has been widely followed in this claim, e.g., M. Noth, *The History of Israel*, 2nd ed., 1954 (Eng. trans. 1960), pp. 78–79, and Y. Aharoni, *The Land of the Bible*, p. 175.

25. The standard edition of the Amarna corpus of diplomatic letters is J. A. Knudtzon, *Die El-Amarna-Tafeln*, 2 vols., 1907–1915, significantly supplemented by A. F. Rainey, *El Amarna Tablets 359–379*, 1970. S. A. B. Mercer, *The Tell El-Amarna Tablets*, 2 vols., 1939, is a faulty edition. Some of the more important letters for biblical studies are translated in *ANET*, pp. 483–490. Much of the voluminous literature on this correspondence is absorbed with simplistic equation of the *'apiru* of the letters with the biblical Hebrews or with simplistic denial of the equation. A reliable introduction to the letters in their sociopolitical setting is E. A. Campbell, Jr., "The Amarna Letters and the Amarna Period," *BAR* 3 (1970) 54–75 = *BA* 23 (1960) 2–22. See fuller bibliography in notes 309 through 312.

26. The contradictory and confusing uses of the genre labels "saga" and "legend" among German- and English-speaking scholars are greatly clarified by the thorough analysis of J. A. Wilcoxen, "Narrative," in *Old Testament Form Criticism* (ed. J. H. Hayes), 1974, pp. 57–98; see also R. M. Hals, "Legend: A Case Study in OT Form-Critical Study," *CBQ* 34 (1972) 166–176.

27. On oral tradition as "time-binding" and writing as "space-binding" and their occasional propitious conjunction (as in early Greece and in early Israel), see the collected essays of H. A. Innis, *The Bias of Communication*, 1951, pp. 3–141.

28. S. Herrmann, *Israel in Egypt* (SBT, Second Series, 27), 1970 (Eng. trans. 1973), pp. 26–27; E. P. Uphill, " Pithom and Raamses: Their Location and Significance," *JNES* 28 (1969) 15–39.

29. V. Harvey, *The Historian and the Believer*, 1966, pp. 49–64, forcefully argues that religious historians in particular have tended to overlook the variety of historical "fields of argument" and the different types of "warrants" that justify moving from data to conclusions (as presented, for example, by S. Toulmin, *The Uses of Argument*, 1958). Harvey's examples of disregard of the varying textures of historical arguments, their relative

"looseness" or "tightness," are taken from New Testament scholarship, but the relevant transfers to equally insensitive Old Testament historical scholarship are easily made.

30. The way in which an observer trying to reconstruct social structure and the interplay of social forces draws selectively from historical data is illustrated by three anthropological/sociological studies of ancient Greece: L. H. Morgan, *Ancient Society*, 1877, chaps. 8–10; G. Thomson, *Studies in Ancient Greek Society: The Pre-Aegean*, 2nd ed., 1954; and A. W. Gouldner, *Enter Plato: Classical Greece and the Origins of Social Theory*, 1966, Part I (published separately as *The Hellenic World: A Sociological Analysis*, 1969). Naturally, the social researcher is obligated to deal responsibly with the historical data used and to ascertain that historical data omitted do not invalidate the sociological conclusions. The sociologist, in other words, has no exemption from producing warrants for the historical conclusions on which sociological reconstructions are built. These warrants may be established by the sociologist working in the historian's role, or they may be derived from some historian(s) whose authority is accepted. The social historian is a historian attentive to data of a certain type. By the same token, the social analyst or social theorist of an ancient society operates as a social historian insofar as the analytic/theoretical project is prefaced by the assembly and assessment of materials from historical sources.

In Jewish historiography, Jacob Katz has pioneered in the application of historical sociology to modern Jewish history, notably in a study of the Jewish Enlightenment; see especially his essay "The Concept of Social History and Its Possible Use in Jewish Historical Research," *SH* 3 (1955) 292–312, and compare his ideal-typical approach to Hasidism and Haskalah in *Tradition and Crisis: Jewish Society at the End of the Middle Ages*, 1961, with his attempt to employ historical sociology in the more traditionally narrative approach of *Out of the Ghetto: The Social Background of Jewish Emancipation, 1770–1820*, 1973. Katz's historical-sociological methodology is critically evaluated by B. Halpern, "Modern Jews and Their History," *Commentary* 56 (1973) 72–74, and by L. J. Silberstein, "Historical Sociology and Jewish Historiography: A Review Essay," *JAAR* 42 (1974) 692–698. For a similar but more ambitious undertaking by the biblical scholar Y. Kaufmann, who attempted to interpret the entire course of Jewish history from the standpoint of historical sociology, see note 640.

31. M. Noth, *A History of Pentateuchal Traditions*, p. 4. In this instance Noth understood the correct question to be the problematic relationship between the forms of the basic themes and the forms of the individual traditions, whereas previous scholars had focused almost entirely on the forms of the discrete traditions. This transposition of the question of form to a more inclusive dialectical level achieved a methodological breakthrough in tradition history that remains unsurpassed, even though Noth was unable to resolve satisfactorily all the far-ranging questions his method permitted him to address in a fundamentally fresh way.

32. M. Weber, *Ancient Judaism*, p. 425.

33. For methodological discussions of where one should locate the beginning of the history of Israel, consult G. E. Mendenhall, "Biblical History in Transition," *The Bible in the Ancient Near East: Essays in Honor of W. F. Albright* (ed. G. E. Wright), 1961, pp. 32–53, and R. de Vaux, "Method in the Study of Early Hebrew History," *The Bible in Modern Scholarship* (ed. J. P. Hyatt), 1965, pp. 15–43 (with responses by G. E. Mendenhall and M. Greenberg); essays on the patriarchs by J. M. Myers, on Moses and the tribal league by E. F. Campbell, Jr., and on the monarchy by G. E. Mendenhall in *Interpretation* 29 (1975) 121–170. For the most lucid and adequate statement of what is meant by "Israel" as an object of historical study, see M. Noth, *The History of Israel*, pp. 1–7. See also J. H. Hayes and J. M. Miller, eds., *Israelite and Judean History*, 1977.

34. H. H. Rowley, "Recent Discovery and the Patriarchal Age," *The Servant of the Lord and*

other Essays on the Old Testatment, 2nd ed. rev., 1965 (orig. pub. 1949–1950), pp. 281–318; R. de Vaux, "The Hebrew Patriarchs and History," *The Bible and the Ancient Near East,* 1971 (orig. pub. 1962–1963), pp. 111–121; J. M. Myers, "The Way of the Fathers,"*Interpretation* 29 (1975) 121–140; T. L. Thompson, *The Historicity of the Patriarchal Narratives: The Quest for the Historical Abraham* (BZAW, 133), 1974; and J. Van Seters, *Abraham in History and Tradition,* 1975.

35. H. Gressmann, *Mose und seine Zeit,* 1913; M. Noth, *A History of Pentateuchal Traditions,* pp. 156–175; R. Smend, *Das Mosebild von H. Ewald bis M. Noth,* 1959; H. Schmid, *Mose: Überlieferung und Geschichte,* 1968. In commenting on Schmid's work, which traces the discussion over the historicity of Moses in German circles from M. Noth onwards, B. Childs remarks that "the highly tentative and theoretical nature of much of the discussion raises a question whether there is a future for continuing the research along these same lines" (*JBL* 88 [1969] 245). Continuing efforts to anchor Moses in a firm historical setting with extrabiblical aids are illustrated by F. Cornelius, "Moses urkundlich," *ZAW* 78 (1966) 75–78, who claims that a high political officer in Egypt named Moses occurs in the Papyrus Salt 214 from the reign of Pharaoh Merneptah. For a recent review of the historical evidence, see G. Widengren, "What Do We Know about Moses?," *Old Testament Essays in Honour of G. Henton Davies* (ed. J. I. Durham and J. R. Porter), 1970, pp. 21–47. J. Dus has set forth a complex of arresting arguments for denying not only the historicity of Moses as a deliverer from Egypt, or as a lawgiver at Sinai, but also that of any so-called Moses group of Israelites originating in Egypt ("Moses or Joshua? On the Problem of the Founder of the Israelite Religion," *RR* 2/2–3 [1975] 26–41, and cf. "Die Stierbild von Bethel und Dan und das Problem der 'Moseschar,' "*AION* 18/2 [1968] 105–137). Although Dus's treatment is at some points brilliantly illuminative of the traditions, I am not as yet fully persuaded by his case—in part because it depends in some measure on the supposition that the early Israelites were nomads and in part because I am not at all certain that he adequately accounts for the transference of the Israelite deliverance traditions from Canaan to Egypt on what could be called grounds of ecclesiastical politics. At any rate Dus's reconstruction is so far-reaching and complex that it deserves a full and rigorous assessment, which I hope to give it eventually in another context. It should be pointed out, however, that Dus and I are in very considerable agreement in stressing that the early Israelite movement was a combined social and religious revolution with a primarily Canaanite locus. The issue on which we diverge, at least for the present, is that Dus denies that there ever was an Egypt-oriented "feeder" revolt among proto-Israelites, whereas I prefer to keep open the probability that there was just such a "feeder" revolt. For fuller detail on Dus's general revolt model see note 148 below.

36. The separation of the Kadesh traditions from the Sinai traditions, with attendant historical conclusions, was first extensively developed by E. Meyer, *Die Israeliten und ihre Nachbarstämme,* 1906, pp. 3–99; see also M. L. Newman, Jr., *The People of the Covenant: A Study of Israel from Moses to the Monarchy,* 1962, pp. 72–101. M. Noth, *A History of Pentateuchal Traditions,* pp. 164–166, reasons that Kadesh's famous springs, being a generally known phenomenon in the southern wilderness, were only arbitrarily connected with specific Israelite traditions about Moses and the wilderness wandering at a fairly late stage in tradition-historical development.

37. M. Noth, *The History of Israel,* pp. 101–104; H.-J. Kraus, *Worship in Israel: A Cultic History of the Old Testament,* 2nd ed., 1962 (Eng. trans. 1966), pp. 101–113; and J. Muilenburg, "The 'Office' of the Prophet in Ancient Israel," *The Bible in Modern Scholarship* (ed. J. P. Hyatt), 1965, pp. 74–97, who believes that at least one significant strain of prophecy in northern Israel was modelled on the office of Moses as cultic mediator or law proclaimer.

38. T. N. D. Mettinger, *Solomonic State Officials: A Study of the Civil Government Officials of the Israelite Monarchy* (CB, Old Testament Series, 5), 1971, chaps. 3–4, 10.

39. The general cultural, intellectual, and literary "enlightenment" triggered by the united monarchy is brilliantly stated by G. von Rad, *Old Testament Theology*, vol. 1, 1957 (Eng. trans. 1962), pp. 48–56. He has, however, overstated the case by playing down a certain capacity for producing connected cultural and intellectual traditional products in the pre-state period, even though those products were still strongly bound to, or at least dominated or influenced by, the cult.

40. O. Eissfeldt, *The Old Testament: An Introduction*, 3rd ed., 1964 (Eng. trans. 1965), and the same author's *Hexateuch-Synopse*, 1962; G. Fohrer, *Introduction to the Old Testament*, 1965 (Eng. trans. 1968). A programmed introduction for students is R. M. Montgomery, *An Introduction to the Source Analysis of the Pentateuch*, 1972. P. E. Ellis, *The Men and Message of the Old Testament*, 1963, pp. 57–72, provides a color chart of the pentateuchal sources for handy reference. It is regularly observed by students that scholars are not unanimous in their detailed identification of the sources. In fact, the frequent discrepancies in the assignment of sources necessarily impels the student to become familiar with the criteria of source separation so that one can at least evaluate provisionally what is at stake in the opposed judgments made by scholars in their source delineations.

41. An instructive introduction to biblical form criticism, with concentration on the Old Testament, is K. Koch, *The Growth of the Biblical Tradition: The Form-Critical Method*, 2nd ed., 1967 (Eng. trans. 1969). Of inestimable value is J. A. Hayes, ed., *Old Testament Form Criticism*, 1974, a careful survey and critique of previous work on major form-critical types methodically pointing to urgent unfinished tasks; it contains sections on the Study of Forms (M. J. Buss), Narrative (J. A. Wilcoxen), Law (W. M. Clark), Prophecy (W. E. March), Psalms (E. Gerstenberger) and Wisdom (J. L. Crenshaw). Also indicative of the massive rethinking of the discipline among form critics is R. Knierim, "Old Testament Form Criticism Reconsidered," *Interpretation* 27 (1973) 435–468. Of much briefer compass than Koch or Hayes is G. M. Tucker, *Form Criticism of the Old Testament*, 1971. The several poetic and prosaic forms are illustrated and discussed in the Old Testament Introductions of O. Eissfeldt and G. Fohrer cited in the previous note. On particular genres: H. Gunkel, *The Legends of Genesis*, 1901 (Eng. trans. reprinted 1964); H. Gunkel, *The Psalms: A Form-Critical Introduction*, 1930 (Eng. trans. 1971); C. Westermann, *Basic Forms of Prophetic Speech*, 2nd ed., 1964 (Eng. trans. 1967).

42. As for tradition history, or the study of the growth of traditions, there has been great diversity among scholars both as to the *scope* of the inquiry (ranging from oral materials alone to the entire body of traditions, from one or a few stages in tradition development to all stages, and from a study of complete traditional units to isolation of particular motifs, concepts, or themes) and as to the *method* of the inquiry (ranging from concentration on one or another single method—conceived as a supplement to or replacement for other methods—to the incorporation of all methods of examining the text in a comprehensive program). D. A. Knight, *Rediscovering the Traditions of Israel: The Development of the Traditio-Historical Research of the Old Testament, with Special Consideration of Scandinavian Contributions* (SBLDS, 9), rev. ed., 1975, identifies the methods and conclusions of German and Scandinavian tradition historians and lucidly proposes an operational definition of the project of tradition history as the study of the precompositional history of the text (excluding compositional analysis and redaction criticism) and involving the complementary operations of critical analysis and historical synthesis (pp. 21–31). Knight follows W. Richter, *Exegese als Literaturwissenschaft: Entwurf einer alttestamentlicher Literaturtheorie und Methodologie*, 1971, in proposing that Old Testament science employ the term "literature

history" (as in contemporary literary sciences) to designate the study of the entire process of the formation and expressive meaning of the traditions, under which tradition history would find its place along with form criticism, literary criticism, redaction criticism, etc.

It is not my intention in this study to critique the method and terminology of tradition history per se. When I refer to "tradition history" and "tradition-historical" I mainly have in mind the work of Noth and von Rad explicated in Part III. Both scholars have vacillated in some measure in their uses of the term "tradition history," although in their major studies on the early Israelite historical traditions they have tended to mean by tradition history the study of the whole history of the literary traditions, both in their oral and in their written phases. In practice, however, von Rad focused chiefly on the compositional stage, demonstrating the architectonic design of the Yahwist's work, while Noth concentrated on the emergent and agglomerating themes, complexes, and tradition units in the oral stage preceding the Yahwist.

43. There has been much explicit and implicit criticism of the inadequacies of form criticism (as well as of literary criticism) from the side of structural linguistics. Until recently the most systematic challenge has surfaced in New Testament studies, particularly in the work of E. Güttgemanns, *Offene Fragen zur Formgeschichte des Evangeliums,* 2nd ed., 1971, and in the journal *Linguistica Biblica,* 1970—(cf. review articles by W. G. Doty in *JAAR* 40 [1972] 521–527; 41 [1973] 114–121. An excellent introduction to the place of structural method in the overall exegetical task is provided by D. Patte, *What Is Structural Exegesis?,* 1976, with applications to New Testament texts. Earlier applications of structural linguistic models to Old Testament texts by C. Lévi-Strauss and by E. Leach are summarized and critiqued by J. Rogerson, "Structural Anthropology and the Old Testament," *BSOAS* 33 (1970) 490–500. Recently more methodologically rigorous applications of structural linguistics to the Old Testament have appeared with R. Barthes et al., *Structural Analysis and Biblical Exegesis* (PTMS, 3), 1974 (including extensive bibliography); H. White, "French Structuralism and Old Testament Narrative Analysis: Roland Barthes," *Semeia* 3 (1975) 99–127; and R. C. Culley, *Studies in the Structure of Hebrew Narratives,* 1976. At the 1974 annual meeting of the American Academy of Religion and the Society of Biblical Literature I had opportunity to discuss some of the historical and sociological implications of White's paper with the author. There appears to be a measure of conjunction, as yet largely unexplored, between the linguistic context isolated by structuralism and the sociohistorical context, in the sense that each points to a larger structure of regularities that finds expression in particular texts. For the moment, social psychology may be the sphere in which the structural linguistic and the sociological approaches initially intersect.

44. In the compendium of sources for premonarchic Israel, I cite references to secondary literature only occasionally in the annotations. In subsequent chapters, where many of the sources are examined with greater fullness, bibliographical references will be provided. The reader's attention is called to two valuable lists of premonarchic sources accompanied by bibliographical notes on secondary literature: J. Bright, *A History of Israel,* 2nd ed., 1972, pp. 142–144, and A. E. Glock, "Early Israel as the Kingdom of Yahweh," *CTM* 41 (1970) 573–577.

45. Against the contention of V. Fritz, "Die sogenannte Liste der besiegten Könige im Josua 12," *ZDPV* 85 (1969) 136–161.

46. G. E. Mendenhall, "The Census Lists of Numbers 1 and 26," *JBL* 77 (1958) 52–66.

47. A. Malamat, "Cushan Rishathaim and the Decline of the Near East around 1200 B.C.," *JNES* 13 (1954) 231–242, identifies this "judge" as a Semitic usurper who ruled Egypt; but see the objections of R. de Vaux, "The Settlement of the Israelites in Southern

Palestine and the Origins of the Tribe of Judah," in *Translating and Understanding the Old Testament* (ed. H. T. Frank and W. L. Reed), 1970, p. 121.

48. M. Noth, "Das Amt des 'Richters Israels,' "*Festschrift A. Bertholet*, 1950, pp. 404–417.

49. M. Noth, "The Background of Judges 17–18," *Israel's Prophetic Heritage: Essays in Honor of James Muilenburg* (ed. B. Anderson and W. Harrelson), 1962, pp. 68–85.

50. M. Noth, *Das System der zwölf Stämme Israels*, 1930, pp. 100–106, 162–170.

51. Z. Kallai, *The Inheritances of the Tribes of Israel: A Study in the Historical Geography of the Land of Israel*, 1967 (Heb.).

52. O. Eissfeldt, *The Old Testament: An Introduction*, 3rd ed., 1964 (Eng. trans. 1966), pp. 218–219.

53. J.-L. Vesco, "Les lois sociales du Livre de l'Alliance (Ex. XX.22–XXIII.19)," *RT* 68 (1968) 241–264, and see further bibliography in note 81.

NOTES TO PART III

54. See E. Shils, "Ideology: I, The Concept and Function of Ideology," *IESS*, vol. 7, 1968, pp. 66–76, for an elaborate Parsons-type definition of ideology which serves as a useful framework for plotting the scope and focus of other definitions. C. Geertz, "Ideology as a Cultural System," in *Ideology and Discontent* (ed. D. E. Apter, 1964), pp. 49–76, surveys social interest and psycho-social strain theories of ideology and argues that, far from there being an "end of ideology," the symbolic value-ordering and energy-mobilizing functions of ideology are enduring aspects of human societies. In an explicitly Marxist vein, L. Althusser, *For Marx*, 1965 (rev. Eng. trans. 1969), p. 252, defines ideology as "the 'lived' relation between men and their world, or a reflected form of this unconscious relation, for instance a 'philosophy,' etc. It is distinguished from a science not by its falsity, for it can be coherent and logical (for instance, theology), but by the fact that the practico-social predominates in it over the theoretical, over knowledge. Historically, it precedes the science that is produced by making an epistemological break with it, but it survives alongside science as an essential element of every social formation, including a socialist and even a communist society" (in the glossary of key terms formulated by Althusser's translator B. Brewster as corrected and interpolated by the author).

55. A. R. Johnson, *The Cultic Prophet in Ancient Israel*, 2nd ed., 1962, pp. 29–30, note 3.

56. E. Durkheim, *The Elementary Forms of the Religious Life*, 1912 (Eng. trans. 1915), pp. 62–63. The Durkheimian background to the British Old Testament scholar's definition of cult is understandable, given the great influence of Durkheim on British structural-functional anthropology. In citing Durkheimian working definitions for the cult, I do not imply acceptance of either Durkheim's mystifying, philosophically idealist notions of social solidarity or his revulsion against diachronics and evolutionary theory. Cf. M. Harris, *The Rise of Anthropological Theory: A History of Theories of Culture*, 1969, chaps. 18–19.

57. A. R. Radcliffe-Brown, "Religion and Society," in *Structure and Function in Primitive Society*, 1952, pp. 153–177, discusses this issue from a structural-functional point of view, characteristically conceding nothing to a diachronic approach except to allow that the factor of historical development leads to institutional differentiation, with the result that independent religious structures of a church-type or sect-type may arise whose relations to the total social structure are often so indirect as to be difficult to establish. M. Harris, *The Rise of Anthropological Theory*, 1968, chap. 19, exposes the Achilles' heel of the structural-

functional approach, namely, its resistance to studying historic change in social systems, both internally and comparatively, in order to establish the kinds and sequences of change in the interacting variables which compose the system. The result is very "weak" forms of explanation which do not predict or retrodict particular constellations of variables but only note certain aspects of system-maintenance felt to be characteristic of all systems. The difficulty with this, as Harris notes, is that "constants cannot explain variables" (p. 531). In employing a broadly structural-functional model to pull together a synoptic view of the Israelite social system in Part VI, I am sensitive to the relatively low level of explanatory power in the model and will deal with that problem theoretically in Parts X and XI. The attention given throughout the study to the historical perspective on early Israel, including how it may have grown out of the pre-conditions of Amarna Canaan (see Parts VIII and IX), should make it clear that I understand diachronics to be absolutely essential to any adequate model of the early Israelite social system.

58. T. Luckmann, *The Invisible Religion: The Problem of Religion in Modern Society,* 1967, identifies ideal-typical stages of social evolution and analyzes at each stage the congruences and incongruences among the comprehensive world-view, the differentiated sacred cosmos, the specialized official religious model(s), and the range of variation in individual appropriation of these social schemes. He argues that because of the modern dissolution of official religious models, coupled with the growing autonomy of differentiated institutions, we are "reverting" toward a more diffuse sacred cosmos which, on the one hand, is highly privatized and eclectic from person to person and, on the other hand, is structurally determined by the rationalized institutions which posit a socialized world-view with a schizophrenic split between the ineluctable institutions and the realm of private "freedom." The diachronic dimension is taken very seriously, but the question of which variable or variables in a social system are responsible for change is not addressed.

59. M. Noth, *A History of Pentateuchal Traditions,* 1948 (Eng. trans. 1972), p. 196.

60. Ibid., p. 197.

61. Noth's methods and conclusions, and their relation to other modes and projects in biblical research, are usefully summarized and evaluated by B. W. Anderson, "Introduction: Martin Noth's Tradition-Historical Approach in the Context of Twentieth-Century Biblical Research," in his translation of Noth's *A History of Pentateuchal Traditions,* 1948 (Eng. trans. 1972), pp. xiii–xxxii, as also by D. A. Knight, *Rediscovering the Traditions of Israel: The Development of the Traditio-Historical Research of the Old Testament, with Special Consideration of Scandinavian Contributions* (SBLDS, 9), rev. ed., 1975, pp. 143–157. Knight's review relates Noth's views on the pentateuchal traditions to his work on the Deuteronomic and Chronicler's Histories and to his reconstruction of the premonarchic history of Israel. Furthermore, Knight perceptively compares and contrasts the respective stances of Noth and von Rad.

62. Noth, *A History of Pentateuchal Traditions,* p. 259.

63. By Tetrateuch Noth refers to the four books Genesis through Numbers, plus portions of Deuteronomy 31–34. He denies that the Tetrateuchal sources J, E, and P extend into Joshua or Judges, a problem to be assessed later in this study. The grounds for his literary analysis were presented in *Überlieferungsgeschichtliche Studien* I, 2nd ed., 1957. He expresses the same view in *A History of Pentateuchal Traditions,* 1948, p. 6, but in an apparent concession to traditional terminology he refers somewhat confusingly to the "Pentateuch," meaning thereby the Tetrateuch of Genesis through Numbers plus parts of Deuteronomy 31–34.

64. Noth, *A History of Pentateuchal Traditions,* p. 2.

65. J. Piaget, *Structuralism,* 1968 (Eng. trans. 1970), p. 140.

66. Noth, *A History of Pentateuchal Traditions,* p. 43.

67. Ibid.

68. G. von Rad, *Genesis: A Commentary* (OTL, 1956 [Eng. trans. 1961]), pp. 13–42.

69. J. Barr, "The Multiplex Nature of the Old Testament Tradition," *Old and New in Interpretation: A Study of the Two Testaments,* 1966, pp. 15–33, warns against a "salvation history"-dominated view of Israelite traditions which tends toward supernaturalistic positivism; see also J. Barr, *The Bible in the Modern World,* 1973. B. Albrektson, *History and the Gods: An Essay on the Idea of Historical Events as Divine Manifestations in the Ancient Near East and in Israel* (CB, Old Testament Series, 1), 1967, explodes the glib assertions of Israel's unique belief in "revelation in history" that have dominated not only popular literature on the Old Testament but wide sectors of biblical scholarship under the rubric of "biblical theology." He does this by showing that all the components of the "revelation in history" complex, purportedly unique to Israel, are duplicated and sometimes exceeded in Near Eastern religions. Albrektson's detailed demonstrations will be presented in XI.52.3 as well as a critique of his altogether inadequate alternative statement of the distinctiveness of Israelite religion.

70. G. von Rad, "The Form-Critical Problem of the Hexateuch," *The Problem of the Hexateuch and Other Essays,* 1966 (orig. pub. 1938), pp. 1–78.

71. Contrary to Noth's claim for a Tetrateuch, von Rad traced the Pentateuchal sources into Joshua. He thus spoke of a Hexateuch consisting of the six books Genesis through Joshua.

72. The attack on the antiquity of the historical credo has taken the form of demonstrating the predominance of Deuteronomic phraseology and concepts in the oldest exemplars which von Rad adduced. T. C. Vriezen, "The Credo in the Old Testament," *Studies on the Psalms* (DOTWSA, 6th meeting), 1963, pp. 5–17, argues that the confessional form isolated by von Rad as specifically Deuteronomic, was never slavishly followed by later prophets, lacks Deuteronomic forerunners, and is only misleadingly called a "credo." L. Rost, "Das kleine geschichtliche Credo," *Das Kleine Credo und andere Studien zum Alten Testament,* 1965, pp. 11–25, assigns the credos to the age of the framework of Deuteronomy and the biography of Jeremiah, possibly as an expression of the historically rooted reform of Josiah. Rost is followed in this by J. P. Hyatt, "Were There an Ancient Historical Credo in Israel and an Independent Sinai Tradition?", *Translating and Understanding the Old Testament: Essays in Honor of Herbert G. May* (ed. H.T. Frank and W. L. Reed, 1970), pp. 152–170. Another line of attack (see note 73) stresses that the historical summaries von Rad grouped together do not form an independent literary type but are elements in other types.

73. C. H. W. Brekelmans, "Het 'historische Credo' van Israel," *TvT* 3 (1963) 1–11, argues that Deuteronomy 6:20–24 is part of a catechesis or religious instruction, Joshua 24:2b–13 part of a covenant formulary, and Deuteronomy 26:5b–9 part of a prayer at the offering of first fruits. By ignoring the full units, von Rad abstracted the common element of historical summaries from different types and erroneously constructed an independent type which had no formal integrity. Brekelmans is followed by Hyatt (see note 72). Although there is considerable force to the Brekelmans-Hyatt argument that there was no historical Credo type per se, the prominence and endurance of certain associated stock themes in these summaries points back toward what D. J. McCarthy, "What Was Israel's Credo?" *LTQ* 4 (1969) 46–53, calls a "commonplace," using the Renaissance rhetorical term, i.e., a skeletal topical list of stock themes which served as the basis for expansion and elaboration in particular expositions or sermons. It is just such a quasi-canonical clustering of stock themes that Noth has hypothesized as the most plausible way to account for the growth of the early historical traditions. We may further conjecture that the "common-

place" historical summaries crop up in Deuteronomic contexts because D was especially dependent on a tradition of preached materials which drew on the "common-place" of historical themes.

74. A. Weiser, *The Old Testament: Its Formation and Development,* 4th ed., 1957 (Eng. trans. 1961), pp. 81–99. E. W. Nicholson, *Exodus and Sinai in History and Tradition,* 1973, has lucidly and succinctly summed up von Rad's case, as well as Noth's modification of it, and has followed Weiser in accounting for the absence of Sinai themes in the historical procla-mations on the basis of fundamental conceptual differences between Sinai type and exodus-settlement type traditions (see especially pp. 23, 26, 33–35).

75. Two works on Old Testament theophanies are J. Jeremias, *Theophanie: Die Geschichte einer alttestamentlichen Gattung* (WMANT, 10, 1965) and J. K. Kuntz, *The Self-Revelation of God,* 1967. Jeremias gives a form-critical and motif analysis which locates the theophany originally in premonarchic victory hymns. Kuntz sets theophany in the theological context of revelation, stresses that divine words as well as descriptions of God's coming are integral to theophany, and locates the theophany in the religious cult primarily at the Jerusalem temple. A penetrating analysis of the theophanic features in the Sinai traditions, together with pertinent cross-references to other parts of the Old Testament, is presented by W. Beyerlin, *Origins and History of the Oldest Sinaitic Traditions,* 1961 (Eng. trans. 1965), pp. 134–143. Beyerlin's astute grasp of the cultic context of theophany does not entail accept-ing other aspects of his reconstruction, e.g., the assumption that the elements of the Sinai tradition go directly back to the desert period, the assumption that the covenant recounted in Exodus 19–24 and 34 was modelled on a suzerainty-vassal treaty, and the assumption that the origin of theophany lies in a brute history outside of and prior to its cultic formulation.

76. I can only cite a small part of the burgeoning literature on covenant. G. Quell on "Diatheke," *TDNT,* vol. 2, 1935 (Eng. trans. 1966), pp. 106–124, is a good introductory orientation to OT *b⁰rîth* which raises questions about the sociopolitical context of the covenant but predates the lively discussion over the international suzerainty-vassal treaty as a model for the Israelite covenant. Advocating the international treaty model for earliest Israel are G. E. Mendenhall, *Law and Covenant in Israel and the Ancient Near East,* 1955 (reprinted in *BAR* 3 [ed. E. F. Campbell, Jr., and D. N. Freedman], 1970, pp. 3–53) and K. Baltzer, *The Covenant Formulary in Old Testament, Jewish and Early Christian Writings,* 2nd rev. ed., 1964 (Eng. trans. 1971). Rejecting the international treaty model for early Israel (but accepting it for the later D formulation of covenant) is D. J. McCarthy in *Treaty and Covenant: A Study in Form in the Ancient Oriental Documents and in the Old Testament* (AB, 21), 1963, and in *Old Testament Covenant: A Survey of Current Opinions,* 1967 (Eng. trans. 1972), as well as D. A. Patrick, "A Study of the Conceptual Models of the Covenant" (Th.D. diss., Graduate Theological Union, Berkeley, California, 1971.

77. The basic work on Israelite law is A. Alt, "The Origins of Israelite Law," in *EOTHR,* 1966 (orig. pub. 1934), pp. 101–171, where the form-critical distinction between "apodic-tic" and "casuistic" laws is illustrated in detail. M. Noth, "The Laws in the Pentateuch: Their Assumptions and Meaning," in *The Laws in the Pentateuch and Other Studies,* 1966 (orig. pub. 1940), pp. 1–107, relates the early laws to his amphictyonic conception of the premonarchic social system. On the administration of justice: L. Köhler, "Justice in the Gate," in *Hebrew Man,* 1953 (Eng. trans. 1956), pp. 127–150; F. C. Fensham, "The Judges and Ancient Israelite Jurisprudence," (DOTWSA, 2nd meeting), 1959, pp. 15–22; D. A. McKenzie, "Judicial Procedure at the Town Gate," *VT 14* (1964) 100–104; H. J. Boecker, *Redeformen des Rechtsleben in Alten Testament* (WMANT, 14), 2nd ed., 1970.

78. E. W. Nicholson, *Exodus and Sinai in History and Tradition,* 1973, touches on the

vulnerability of von Rad's sharp separation between the Exodus and Sinai traditions when he remarks that "a major weakness in von Rad's theory is the belief that the recitation of the saving history was an end in itself " (p. 25), and he aptly cites Weiser's contention that the Sinai event is distinctively and disjunctively both present and absent in various segments of the traditions because "in its setting it represents a particular action in the course of the festival" (A. Weiser, *Introduction to the Old Testament*, p. 86; quoted by Nicholson, p. 34). Nicholson himself goes on to argue that Exodus 19 and 24 were forged out of units originally expressing only a theophany theme, the covenant terminology having been inserted secondarily. He further finds that Exodus 19 is firmly anchored to the exodus theme, whereas Exodus 24:9–11 knows nothing of the exodus tradition and is probably a pre-exodus tradition (chap. 3). In principle, my view of the linkage of theophany-covenant-law in the centralized cult milieu has no difficulty allowing that the formation of the Sinai tradition in Exodus 19—24 was complex and uneven, and even that a "theophany" stage in the formation may have preceded a "covenant" stage. I am, however, unpersuaded by Nicholson that the covenant terminology in Exodus 19—24, 32—34 is the exclusive work of a Deuteronomic editor. Nor do I think that he has shown Exodus 24:9–11 to be a pre-exodus tradition, even on his own argument; at most, his analysis lends credence to the hypothesis that Exodus 24:9–11 was independent of and relatively older than Exodus 19. But what has he shown of the actual dates of origin of the traditions and of their relation to events reported? As with many writers on the Sinai theme, Nicholson tends to translate deliberately reasoned judgments about the affinities, disjunctions, and temporal priorities in tradition units and tradition streams into less securely founded conclusions about the historical events or the loci underlying the traditions.

79. Concerning the developing forms of apodictic instruction lying behind the existing forms of the so-called Decalogues, see J. J. Stamm and M. E. Andrew, *The Ten Commandments in Recent Research* (SBT, 2nd series, 2), 1967, and E. Nielsen, *The Ten Commandments in Perspective* (SBT, 2nd series, 7), 1968.

80. G. Fohrer, *Introduction to the Old Testament*, 1965 (Eng. trans. 1968), p. 130.

81. O. Eissfeldt, *The Old Testament: An Introduction*, 3rd ed., 1964 (Eng. trans. 1965), pp. 212–219. For the sociological setting and implications of the Covenant Code, see A. Menes, *Die vorexilischen Gesetze Israels im Zusammenhang seiner kulturgeschichtlichen Entwicklung* (BZAW, 50), 1928, esp. pp. 20–45; W. Caspari, "Heimat und soziale Wirkung des alt. Bundesbuches," *ZDMG* 83 (1929) 97–120; L. Rost, "Das Bundesbuch," *ZAW* 77 (1965) 255–259; and H. E. von Waldow, "Social Responsibility and Social Structure in Early Israel," *CBQ* 32 (1970) 183–203.

82. On the general phenomenon of the blessing, see J. Pedersen, *Israel: Its Life and Culture*, I–II, 1926, pp. 182–212. On the tribal blessings, see H.-J. Kittel, *Die Stammessprüche Israels: Genesis 49 und Deuteronomium 33 traditionsgeschichtlich untersucht*, 1959, and H.-J. Zobel, *Stammesspruch und Geschichte: Die Angaben der Stammessprüche von Gen 49, Dtn 33 und Jdc 5 über die politischen und kultischen Zustände im damaligen "Israel"* (BZAW, 95, 1965).

83. This view of the life setting of the tribal blessing is influenced by the thesis of A. H. J. Gunneweg, "Über den Sitz im Leben der sog. Stammessprüche," *ZAW* 76 (1964) 244–255, namely, that the word plays and animal comparisons of the blessings are tribal self-descriptions corresponding to the cultic self-predications of Yahweh in the theophany festival to which the blessings are likewise to be assigned. Even if the divine self-predication in the cult has influenced the self-predications of the tribes (and this helps to explain why the blessings were eventually drawn into the central cult), I am not convinced that the covenant of Yahweh with Israel *as a totality* would have encouraged the formulation of *individual* tribal self-predications within the covenant festival proper.

84. The song of triumph in Exodus 15 is situated in the narrative at the crossing of the Sea of Reeds, where it appears twice: in full form attributed to Moses (vss. 1–18), and in abbreviated form attributed to Miriam (vss. 20–21, citing only the opening couplet, probably intended as an *incipit* to indicate that the full song is presupposed). As the story reads, the final editor doubtless meant to say that Miriam took up and repeated the song which Moses and the people first sang. Tradition-historically, however, this double attribution strongly suggests that the song was claimed by one tradition stream for Moses and by another tradition stream for Miriam. On the principle that the actions of traditionally *less* significant figures tend to be transferred and credited to traditionally *more* significant figures in the course of time, coupled with evidence in early Israelite traditions that women were role-typed singers of such songs, it is highly likely that the earliest attribution of the song was to Miriam—a claim so firmly lodged in tradition that it was retained even after the song was credited to Moses. There remains a noticeable contrast between the pale generality of the attribution of the song to Moses and the vivid details of the attribution to Miriam as she takes timbrel in hand among the dancing women.

85. G. von Rad, *Der heilige Krieg im alten Israel,* 3rd ed., 1958; N. K. Gottwald, " 'Holy War' in Deuteronomy: Analysis and Critique," *RE* 61 (1964) 296–310; M. Weippert, " 'Heiliger Krieg' in Israel und Assyrien: Kritische Anmerkungen zu Gerhard von Rads Konzept des 'Heiligen Krieges im Alten Israel,' " *ZAW* 84 (1972) 460–493; N. K. Gottwald, entry on "War, Holy," IDBSV, 1976.

86. S. Mowinckel, *The Psalms in Israel's Worship,* 1962, vol. 1, pp. 78–79; vol. 2, pp. 221–222 (note v).

87. In addition to studies on the cult already referred to in the notes above: G. B. Gray, *Sacrifice in the Old Testament,* 1925; H.-J. Kraus, *Worship in Israel,* 2nd ed., 1962 (Eng. trans. 1966); R. de Vaux, *Studies in Old Testament Sacrifice,* 1964 (Eng. trans. 1964); R. E. Clements, *God and Temple,* 1965. For further titles, see bibliographies in R. de Vaux, *Ancient Israel: Its Life and Institutions,* 1961, pp. 537–552; R. Abba, IDB, vol. 3, 1962, p. 889 (on "Priests and Levites"); and A. Cody, *A History of Old Testament Priesthood,* 1969, xvi–xxvii.

NOTES TO PART IV

88. The tribal allotment traditions are set forth within a series of larger or smaller inclusive editorial frames. I have tried to show these relationships of superordination and subordination by varying degrees of typographical indentation in the summaries of the frames and allotment units. I have also indicated the different modes of characterization: by territories, by boundaries, or by cities. Further, while most of the allotment traditions are lists, some are cast as narratives, including the editorial frames. The allotment lists are noted by *L,* the allotment narratives by *N,* and one composite unit by *LN.* Closely or exactly parallel traditions elsewhere in the Bible are cited by book, chapter, and verse preceded by //, which means "parallels" or "corresponds to."

89. In the allotment lists of Ephraim (Josh. 16:1–3) and in the allotment narrative of Manasseh (Josh. 17:14–18), the phrase "sons of Joseph" or "Josephites" refers in my view to the original unity from which Ephraim and Manasseh subdivided. The actual description of 16:1–3 is clearly that of an Ephraimite boundary, and thus "sons of Joseph" is here used as a deliberate archaism. The narrative of 17:14–18 is assigned by an editor to the Manassite

allotments because it recounts the expansion of Joseph into the regions where Manasseh took form as an offshoot of Joseph, and thus I take "sons of Joseph" to be an accurately placed historical designation in this unit.

90. Judges 2:11—3:6 clearly outlines the interpretive scheme of the editorial framework in which the stories of the major judges are presented. The elements of this scheme are here given the successive sigla F 1–5 (F signifying "frame"): F1=apostasy; F2=oppression; F3=repentance and appeal to Yahweh; F4=deliverance from oppression; F5=rest for the land. The sigla will be used throughout the summaries as shorthand designations for these major themes.

91. N. H. Snaith, "Introduction," *The First and Second Books of Kings* (IB, 1954), vol. 3, pp. 10–12; J. Gray, *I and II Kings* (OTL), 1963, pp. 11–15, 38, 683–686, 705.

92. N. K. Gottwald, "The Book of Deuteronomy," in *IOCB,* 1971, pp. 103–104.

93. M. Noth, *Überlieferungsgeschichtliche Studien I,* 2nd ed., 1957, and briefly noted in his *A History of Pentateuchal Traditions,* 1948 (Eng. trans. 1972), p. 2.

94. G. von Rad, *Studies in Deuteronomy* (SBT, First Series, 9), rev. ed., 1948 (Eng. trans. 1953), pp. 70–73. It has long been suspected that a socioeconomic and political struggle precipitated the Deuteronomic reform. One or another of the following occupational or class groupings have been proposed as the locus of the reform and as the bearers of the Deuteronomic traditions: Levites or priests, prophets, court scribes or officials, army levies, peasants, landed gentry, etc. None of these proposals has been entirely convincing, in part because of uncertainties about the literary history of the book and in part because of considerable gaps in our historical knowledge of the period of the reform. Recently, W. E. Claburn, "The Fiscal Basis of Josiah's Reform," *JBL* 92 (1973) 11–22, has argued that the Deuteronomic reform was principally a reorganization of state finances with the aim of funneling peasant taxes directly to the Jerusalem court for defense expenditures, thereby drastically reducing the share of tax proceeds customarily pocketed by the traditional rural leadership. On this basis, Claburn attempts to show how various constituencies were attracted to the reorganization plan, or "bought off" when necessary, as Josiah balanced contending social groups in an effort to give a modicum of rewards or inducements—if very unequally—to all sectors of the populace. To evaluate Claburn's hypothesis in detail it would be necessary to examine his study on the radical "national liberation" rhetoric and themes of Deuteronomy: "Deuteronomy and Collective Behavior" (Ph.D. diss., Princeton University, 1968). Pending further inquiry, the actual social struggle base of the intense rhetorical and ideological upthrust of Deuteronomy hangs in disputed semi-obscurity.

95. G. E. Wright, "Introduction," *The Book of Deuteronomy* (IB, 1953), vol. 2, pp. 319–320, 323–326; G. von Rad, *Studies in Deuteronomy,* chap. 1. This is not to say that D merely extracted materials from the J/E historical traditions in the way, for instance, that the Chronicler extracted materials from Samuel-Kings. D has his own style, dependent on hortatory cultic forms of expression, and he, or the tradition he draws on, displays considerable freedom toward the historical traditions of Israel, both in detail and in emphasis. For example, W. A. Sumner, "Israel's Encounters with Edom, Moab, Ammon, Sihon and Og according to the Deuteronomist," *VT* 18 (1968) 211–228, is of the view that the historical traditions in Numbers (J/E) and in Deuteronomy on the same topics are in fact dependent on a common ancient body of traditions which they have variously extracted, arranged, and phrased. Even if this should be the case, D would most certainly have known of the existence of J and E (or of redacted J/E), and there is no indication that he intended his much less fully developed account to replace J/E.

96. Wright, *The Book of Deuteronomy,* pp. 326–329.

97. O. Eissfeldt, *The Old Testament: An Introduction,* 3rd ed., 1964 (Eng. trans. 1965), pp. 261–265.

98. I agree with A. Jenks, "The Elohist and North Israelite Traditions" (Ph.D. diss., Harvard University, 1965), pp. 186–194, that strictly on grounds of vocabulary and style it is impossible to identify the continuation of E into Joshua. On tradition-historical and general historical grounds, however, the probability is high that E is present in Joshua. Cf. now A.W. Jenks, *The Elohist and North Israelite Traditions,* 1977.

99. J. A. Soggin, *Joshua: A Commentary* (OTL), 1970 (Eng. trans. 1972), pp. 43–76; see also R. de Vaux, *Histoire ancienne d'Israël: Des Origines à l'Installation en Canaan,* 1971, pp. 556–559, who restricts the role of the Gilgal cult in forming the traditions of conquest.

100. A. Alt, "Josua," *KS,* I, 1953 (orig. pub. 1936), pp. 187–189.

101. O. Eissfeldt, *The Old Testament: An Introduction,* pp. 264–265, attempting to account for the relation between Joshua 11 and Judges 4—5 by means of a triple-source hypothesis, assigns Joshua 11 to J/E, Judges 4 to J, and Judges 5 to L (for "Lay" Source, roughly comparable to J^1 of some other scholars), but he can only give a weak explanation for two Jabins and he concedes that L found the Song of Deborah "already available in written form."

102. Y. Yadin, "Hazor," in *Archaeology and Old Testament Study* (ed. D. Winton Thomas), 1967, pp. 254, 258–259; F. Maass, "Hazor und das Problem der Landnahme," *Von Ugarit nach Qumran* (BZAW, 77), 1958, pp. 105–117.

103. For cartographic representations of these tribal land grants, see A. Aharoni and M. Avi-Yonah, *The Macmillan Bible Atlas,* 1968, Maps 71–73, p. 130.

104. A. Alt argued that all the boundary lists are premonarchic and that the city lists are from the reign of Josiah (c. 620 B.C.), although perhaps based on an earlier monarchic document: "Das System der Stammesgrenzen im Buche Josua," *KS,* I, 1953 (orig. pub. 1927), pp. 193–202, and "Judas Gaue unter Josia," *KS,* II, 1959 (orig. pub. 1925), pp. 276–288. F. M. Cross and G. E. Wright placed the city lists in the time of Jehoshaphat: "The Boundary and Province Lists of the Kingdom of Judah," *JBL* 75 (1956) 202–226.

105. M. Noth, "Studien zu den historisch-geographischen Dokumenten des Josuabuches," *ZDPV* 58 (1935) 185–255, the results of which were incorporated in his commentary *Das Buch Josua* (HAT), 2nd ed., 1953, pp. 73–123.

106. The proper temporal horizon for the southern city lists has been vigorously pursued by several Israeli scholars, within the basic framework of the Alt-Noth-Cross-Wright historico-territorial methodology: Z. Kallai-Kleinmann, "The Town Lists of Judah, Simeon, Benjamin and Dan," *VT* 8 (1958) 134–160, and "Note on the Town Lists of Judah, Simeon, Benjamin and Dan," *VT* 11 (1961) 223–227; Y. Aharoni, "The Province-List of Judah," *VT* 9 (1959) 225–246; B. Mazar, "The Cities of the Territory of Dan," *IEJ* 10 (1960) 65–77; S. Talmon, "The Town Lists of Simeon," *IEJ* 15 (1965) 235–241.

107. Z. Kallai, *The Inheritances of the Tribes of Israel: A Study in the Historical Geography of the Bible,* 1967 (Heb.). His main methods and conclusions are briefly summarized in "The Town Lists of Judah, Simeon, Benjamin and Dan," *VT* 8 (1958), 134–137, and by B. Oded in *Immanuel* 1 (1972), 19–20.

108. On the improbability of an intertribal league drawing up such a document of tribal boundaries, I think S. Mowinckel was right (*Zur Frage nach dokumentarischen Quellen in Josua 13–19* [ANVAOT, 1], 1946, pp. 64–65; see also remarks of H. E. von Waldow, *CBQ* 32 [1970] 190–195). Y. Aharoni, *The Land of the Bible: A Historical Geography,* 1962 (Eng. trans. 1967), pp. 233–234, hypothesizes that the boundary list belongs to the old intertribal alliance of Ephraim, Manasseh, Benjamin, Zebulun, Asher, and Naphtali (for the other tribes he thinks there are no boundaries strictly speaking or they are supplied from David's

time). Aharoni presumably understands these boundaries as having established the claims of the alliance to be "the heir of Canaan." It is not clear, however, why boundaries *internal* to the tribal alliance were necessary to establish such a claim (in contrast to a description of the *outer bounds* of the tribes taken as a whole). I see no evidence of premonarchic Israel making such a comprehensive land claim as opposed to securing and holding actual zones of occupation for cultivation and pasturage. G. Schmitt, *Du sollst keinen Frieden schliessen mit den Bewohnern des Landes: Die Weisungen gegen die Kanaanäer in Israels Geschichte and Geschichtsschreibung* (BWANT, 91), 1970 pp. 83–84, is not persuasive in claiming that only by such a boundary document could the associated tribes have asserted their rights to land while avoiding fatal internecine strife. The arbitration treaties among the Greeks cited by Alt as analogies to the Israelite boundary lists (*KS*, I, 1953, p. 201, note 2) and the arbitration treaties from Ugarit and Hattusas cited by Schmitt (p. 86, note 7) are all instances of determinations reached by central authorities or by bodies designated by central authorities and thus fall short of the mark as analogies to the Israelite situation. I can see no evidence in early Israel for the arbitration of land disputes on the basis of fixed boundaries.

109. The identification of learned priestly collectors as the tradition bearers for the allotment materials partially explains why S. Mowinckel, *Zur Frage nach dokumentarischen Quellen in Josua 13–19*, pp. 25–26, could insist on placing the allotment accounts in the post-exilic P source. There is merit to the suggestion of Cross and Wright (*JBL* 75 [1956] 202) that the so-called Priestly style, both in P and in the allotment traditions, is actually "the official style of the Jerusalem archives" independently excerpted. It is not, however, a sufficient explanation, since many of the distinctive priestly stylistic elements in Joshua 13—19 occur in editorial frames which were probably not contained in the Jerusalem archival version. Apparently, archival and editorial synthesizing styles are alike at work in the shaping of Joshua 13—19. Criteria for determining which biblical traditions stem from priestly circles and which stem from scribal court circles needs more thorough research, cf. T. N. D. Mettinger, *Solomonic State Officials: A Study of the Civil Government Officials of the Israelite Monarchy* (CB, Old Testament Series, 5), 1971, chaps. 4 and 10.

110. S. Talmon, "Judges Chapter 1," in *Studies in the Book of Judges*, 1966, pp. 14–29 (Heb.), analyzes the chapter within its larger Joshua-Judges setting as an instance of the habit of biblical historiography to concentrate supplementary collections of materials at nodular turning points in the narration, of which Judges 17—21, II Samuel 21—24, Jeremiah 52, and Ezra 1 are further instances. These supplementary collections may contain either alternate versions of matters treated in the larger narrative sequences or entirely new materials, or both, and they may be more or less reliable historically. Talmon concludes that Judges 1 contains the more original version of events that are elaborated chiefly in Joshua 10—11, where the conquests in the north and south are represented as a single coordinated process under the command of one man. In fact, the entire sequence Joshua 1 through Judges 12 should be viewed as dealing with the settlement process, many of the materials being duplicate accounts of the same events. He associates Joshua 17:14–18 with Judges 1:22–29 and reconstructs an initial Israelite penetration only into the area around Bethel. Because of land shortage, weaker tribal elements had to cross over the Jordan in an easterly migration in order to find living space, and many intertribal frictions occurred. It was under such pressures that the tribe of Dan split up, part of Benjamin moved to Jabesh-gilead, and the Ephraimite and Manassite colonizations took place in Transjordan. This critical land deficit situation was relieved only when Deborah and Barak provided an opening to the north for settlement as far as the Valley of Esdraelon, a breakthrough which Joshua 11 insists on crediting to Joshua.

In my judgment, however, the presence of Hazor in Joshua 11 distinguishes that battle from the one reported in Judges 4—5. The battle of Merom-Hazor in Joshua 11 (c. 1200?) opened up living space for Israelite or proto-Israelite tribes in upper Galilee, while the battle at Tabor-Kishon in Judges 4—5 (c. 1100 B.C.?) enabled the tribes in upper Galilee and in Samaria to link up. Nevertheless, I agree with Talmon in dissociating Joshua altogether from the battle of Merom-Hazor and would accept his literary analysis to the extent that the account in Joshua 11, building on an older "annalistic" core belonging to the same stock as Judges 1, was "skewed" or "contaminated" by the already existing accounts of the battle of Tabor-Kishon—an event of significance, after all, to many more tribes than was the battle of Merom-Hazor, which may have involved only Naphtali and perhaps also Zebulun and Issachar. At any rate, Talmon's insistence that *conquest and settlement on the land are not two separate processes, but one single process viewed from two angles,* is of great methodological importance, especially considering the manner in which that unity has been obscured by the tradition's passion for attributing the conquest and the programmatic assignment of land to the Ephraimite Joshua (see especially Talmon's remarks on the schematic fictitious two-stage conquest-settlement concepts of the final form of Joshua, pp. 21–22).

111. S. B. Gurewicz, "The Bearing of Judges 1—2:5 on the Authorship of the Book of Judges," *ABR* 7 (1959) 37–40; Talmon, "Judges Chapter 1," p. 19.

112. G. E. Wright. "The Literary and Historical Problems of Joshua 10 and Judges 1," *JNES* 5 (1946) 105–114.

113. In spite of the efforts devoted to the historical clarification of Adonibezek of Bezek by H. W. Hertzberg, "Adonibezek," *JPOS* 6 (1926) 213–221; P. Welten, "Bezeq," *ZDPV* 81 (1965) 138–165; and K.-D. Schunk, "Juda und Jerusalem in vor- und frühisraelitischen Zeit," *Schalom: Studien zu Glaube und Geschichte Israels, A. Jepsen* (AVTR, 51), 1971, pp. 50–57, no coherent solution has yet emerged for a cluster of thorny interrelated problems: a northern or southern location for Bezek; the possible existence of a deity named Bezek; the possible confusion, in one direction or the other, between Adonibezek of Judges 1 and Adonizedek of Joshua 10; the validity of the association of Adonibezek with Jerusalem; the ground for the claim that Jerusalem was captured before David's time; and the Judean or Simeonite locus of the Adonibezek tradition.

114. For a comprehensive review of the data on corvée labor in Canaan and Israel, see A. F. Rainey, "Compulsory Labour Gangs in Ancient Israel," *IEJ* 20 (1970) 191–202.

115. As is frequently the case with archaeological data, the results of recent excavations at Dan (cf. A. Biran, "Tell Dan," *BA* 37 [1974] 26–51) do not correlate in an unambiguous way with the literary records about the seizure of that city by the Danites. There is evidence of minor destruction about 1200 B.C. and a more massive destruction by conflagration about 1050 B.C. If the massive destruction is associated with the Danite attack (cf. Josh. 19:47; Judg. 18:27), a mid-eleventh century date is rather late in the premonarchy to accord with most reconstructions of the period of the Danite migration, leaving either no pre-Philistine period, or a very brief one, to accommodate the phase of Ephraimite counter-pressure on the Amorites in the original homeland of Dan (cf. Judg. 1:35). Furthermore, in spite of Biran's remarks to the contrary, a date of 1050 for the Danite move to the north would allow no measurable lapse of time between the Danite migration and the destruction of Shiloh, which occurred at approximately the same time (Judg. 18:31 presupposes a considerable time span between the founding of the sanctuary at Laish-Dan and the destruction of the sanctuary at Shiloh). Biran also notes that if abundance of collared-rim jars is an Israelite material cultural trait (suggested by R. Amiran, cf. note 127), then Dan was an Israelite city from 1200 to 1050. If so, this would require us to posit that the Danites attacked and expelled fellow-Israelites from Laish-Dan (a point not made by Biran). For

related ambiguities and objective difficulties in assessing archaeological data in relation to biblical data on the Israelite conquest, see the discussion in V.20.

116. G. Schmitt, *Du sollst keinen Frieden schliessen mit den Bewohnern des Landes: Die Weisungen gegen die Kanaanäer in Israels Geschichte und Geschictsschreibung* (BWANT, 91), 1970, obeserving the sobriety and thoroughness of the "negative occupation" accounts in Judges 1:27–36, shrewdly remarks: "It would be best to call the text a statement of accounts (*Rechenschaftsbericht*), if only it were clearer to whom the account was rendered" (p. 79), to which he gives the tentative answer that it may have been an appendix to the boundary document of Joshua 13—19 which was written and deposited in the sanctuary (p. 86). It is my view that the several tribal land acquisitions now reflected confusedly and even fragmentarily in Judges 1 and here and there in Numbers and Joshua were drawn from a once fuller "statement of accounts" to the central government of David compiled in order to limit the regime's exercise of power over the tribes.

117. G. F. Moore, *A Critical and Exegetical Commentary on Judges* (ICC), 1895, pp. 54–56.

118. H. H. Rowley, "Early Levite History and the Question of the Exodus," *JNES* 3 (1944) 73–78, whose views are expanded and put in relation to other theories on the tribal composition of the Exodus Israelites in his *From Joseph to Joshua*, 1950. The insuperable obstacles to conceiving the tribes in Canaan as simply continuous with the group(s) that left Egypt leads J. Bright to say: ". . .it is profitless to ask which of the twelve tribes were in Egypt and participated in the exodus. Although not all of later Israel was there, we shall never find out which elements were by eliminating this or that tribe and settling on the others. We should, indeed, not speak of tribes in Egypt, for there was no tribal system there—only a conglomeration of slaves of various tribal backgrounds" (*A History of Israel*, 2nd ed., 1972, p. 136). M. Noth, *The History of Israel*, 2nd ed., 1954 (Eng. trans. 1960), pp. 117–119, makes similar observations.

119. R. Smend, *Yahweh War and Tribal Confederation: Reflections upon Israel's Earliest History*, 1963 (Eng. trans. 1970), chap. 5.

120. On a pre-D collection of stories of the judges: G. Fohrer, *Introduction to the Old Testament*, 1965 (Eng. trans. 1968), pp. 211–212; W. Beyerlin, "Gattung und Herkunft des Rahmens im Richterbuch," *Weiser Festschrift*, 1963, pp. 1–29. W. Richter, *Traditionsgeschichtliche Untersuchungen zum Richterbuch* (BBB, 18), 2nd ed., 1966, posits the formation in the last half of the ninth century of "a book of deliverers" (*Retterbuch*) in Judges 3—9 composed in large measure of pre-existent traditions, some of them already in the form of sub-collections. This pre-Deuteronomic "book of deliverers," antimonarchic in tone and thrust, aimed to extol the old institutions of Israel eclipsed by the state. Those who trace J/E or like sources, extending from the Pentateuch and Joshua into Judges, naturally assume that there were pre-D versions of some or all of the stories; cf. O. Eissfeldt, *The Old Testament: An Introduction*, pp. 266–267.

NOTES TO PART V

121. Consult J. Bright, *A History of Israel*, 2nd ed., 1972, pp. 121–122, and N. K. Gottwald, *A Light to the Nations: An Introduction to the Old Testament*, 1959, pp. 115–119, for brief reviews of the evidence. H. H. Rowley, *From Joseph to Joshua: Biblical Traditions in the Light of Archaeology*, 1950 (see index under "Chronology"), lays out the complex skein of biblical and extrabiblical data for the chronology of the exodus and the conquest. Although the biblical chronology seems strictly to require a conquest in the period 1450–1400 B.C.,

virtually all historians of the Bible recognize that this traditional chronology is highly schematic, and there is general concurrence that the temporal horizon of the events described in the Book of Joshua (irrespective of the historical veracity of the traditions) is to be located two hundred years later, i.e., c. 1250–1200 B.C.

122. An orientation to types of remains, methods in excavation, and the dating of evidence will be found in G. W. Van Beck, "Archaeology," IDB vol. 1, 1962, pp. 195–207, with important updating by W. G. Dever, "Archaeology," IDBSV, 1976, pp. 44–52. The contributions of archaeology to interpreting the literature of the Old Testament and to reconstructing the history and religion of Israel are conveniently set forth in historical order in G. E. Wright, *Biblical Archaeology,* rev. ed., 1962, although this valuable handbook is by now, unfortunately, seriously dated. Wright has introduced significant tempering judgments into a too facile historical use of archaeology in his essay "What Archaeology Can and Cannot Do," *BA* 34 (1971) 70–76. The extent to which archaeology throws light on the historical origins of a people, either to corroborate or to call into question epics and legends, is a matter of dispute among students of many cultures and nations. R. de Vaux, "On Right and Wrong Uses of Archaeology," in *Near Eastern Archaeology in the Twentieth Century: Essays in Honor of Nelson Glueck* (ed. J. A. Sanders), 1970, pp. 64–80, reviews the divergent opinions and attitudes of scholars on what archaeology tells us of the Trojan War and the Phoenician colonization of the Mediterranean—opinions and attitudes which formally parallel the spectrum of judgments concerning archaeological evidence for the origins of Israel; cf. also M. I. Finley, "Archaeology and History," *Daedalus* (1971) 168–186. I am informed by Lars Heide, a Danish student at Hebrew University in Jerusalem, that a very similar range of discordant opinion exists concerning the relevance of archaeology for Viking prehistory. Heide has recently communicated to me the following titles for treatment of the issue: L. Weibull, *Kritiska undersökningar i Nordens historia omkring år 1000* (Critical Investigations into the History of Scandinavia around 1000 A.D.), 1911; and, in English, J. Brøndsted, *The Vikings,* 1960; P. Sawyer, *The Age of the Vikings,* 1962; and H. Arbman, *The Vikings,* 1966. Heide points out that Sawyer's skepticism about the value of archaeology in illuminating events in Viking prehistory is roughly equivalent to Noth's skepticism concerning the pertinence of archaeological data for reconstructing early Israelite developments.

123. P. W. Lapp, "The Conquest of Palestine in the Light of Archaeology," *CTM* 38 (1967) 283–300; further remarks in *Biblical Archaeology and History,* 1969, pp. 107–111.

124. Bibliographies on the excavations at the sites named in the following paragraphs appear in P. W. Lapp, *CTM* 38 (1967) 283–300; in G. E. Wright, "The Archaeology of Palestine," *The Bible and the Ancient Near East: Essays in Honor of W. F. Albright,* 1961, pp. 73–112; and in A. E. Glock, "Early Israel as the Kingdom of Yahweh: The Influence of Archaeological Evidence on the Reconstruction of Religion in Early Israel," *CTM* 41 (1970) 572–573. The fullest bibliography, arranged in the alphabetical order of the sites, is E. K. Vogel, "Bibliography of Holy Land Sites," *HUCA* 42 (1971) 1–96. P. W. Lapp, "Palestine: Known but Mostly Unknown," *BA* 26 (1963) 121–134, points out that only about one site in two hundred has been the scene of major archaeological work in Palestine and that choice of sites to be excavated occurs largely without any coordinated strategy among the excavators. Very illuminating for the historical uses of archaeology is Lapp's discussion of problems in interpreting and reporting the data which the excavator faces. Y. Aharoni, *The Land of the Bible: A Historical Geography,* 1962 (Eng. trans. 1967), pp. 371–385, provides a list of Palestinian site identifications (excavated and unexcavated) catalogued by ancient name, modern Arabic name, modern Hebrew name, and by location on the Palestine-Syria grid of coordinates used on official maps of the region. Naturally his identification of sites is not

followed in all particulars by other archaeologists and historians. M. Noth, *Das Buch Josua* (HAT), 2nd ed., 1953, pp. 142–151, gives a table of identifications for place names mentioned in the Book of Joshua. Maps of excavated sites in the Canaanite Bronze Age and in the Israelite Iron Age appear in Y. Aharoni and M. Avi-Yonah, *The Macmillan Bible Atlas*, 1968, Maps 17–18. Summaries of the findings at many of the major sites are conveniently published with bibliographies in D. Winton Thomas, ed., *Archaeology and Old Testament Study*, 1967. Useful for its handy summaries of some of the most important work in biblical archaeology in the period 1958–1973, although by no means complete in its coverage, is E. M. Yamauchi, "A Decade and a Half of Archaeology in Israel and Jordan," *JAAR* 42 (1974) 710–726. See also B. Mazar et al., eds., *Encyclopaedia of Archaeological Excavations in the Holy Land*, 2 vols., 1970 (Heb.).

125. Recently the longstanding identification of Debir with Tell Beit Mirsim, first proposed by W. F. Albright, has been sharply challenged. On the basis of soundings at an alternative site, during which water sources were found nearby congruent with the account in Joshua 15:19 and Judges 1:15, supplemented by a reexamination of territorial-historical considerations, M. Kochavi has proposed that ancient Debir was located at Khirbet Rabud, some eight miles SSW of Hebron ("Khirbet Rabud—Ancient Debir," in *Excavations and Studies: Essays in Honour of Prof. Shemuel Yeivin* [Publications of the Institute of Archaeology, Tel Aviv University, 1; ed. Y. Aharoni], 1973, pp. 49–75 [Heb.] = "Khirbet Rabud = Debir," *Tel Aviv* 1 [1974] 2–33).

126. P. W. Lapp, "The Conquest of Palestine in the Light of Archaeology," *CTM* 38 (1967) 287, 290, 292–295, 297–298; *Biblical Archaeology and History*, 1969, pp. 109–110.

127. Lapp, *CTM* 38 (1967) 295–296. R. Amiran, *Ancient Pottery of the Holy Land*, 1963 (Eng. trans. 1969), pp. 191–293, confirms some of Lapp's observations on distinctive features of Israelite pottery. Since, however, historical and sociological interests are secondary in her study, it is difficult to get a conclusive picture of which traits she regards as most typically Israelite. Amiran does comment on an Israelite "predilection for angular pottery shapes" (p. 192), and also notes the probable Israelite origin of "collared-rim" *pithoi*, i.e., large storage jars (pp. 232–233), as well as the association of Phoenician-North Israelite cultural autonomy with bichrome ware (pp. 270–271).

128. K. Kenyon, *Digging up Jericho: The Results of the Jericho Excavation*, 1957, pp. 259–263; *Archaeology in the Holy Land*, 1960, pp. 209–212; G. E. Wright, *Biblical Archaeology*, rev. ed., 1962, pp. 78–80.

129. J. A. Callaway, "New Evidence on the Conquest of 'Ai," *JBL* 87 (1968) 312–320; G. E. Wright, *Biblical Archaeology*, pp. 80–81.

130. J. B. Pritchard, *The Bronze Age Cemetery at Gibeon*, 1963, p. 72; *Gibeon, Where the Sun Stood Still*, 1962, pp. 157–158. Elsewhere the excavator remarks soberly: "The apparent anomalies found in the archaeological results from three sites which figure prominently in the narratives of the first part of Joshua (Jericho, Ai, Gibeon) suggest that we have reached an impasse on the question of supporting the traditional view of the conquest with archaeological undergirding" (J. B. Pritchard, "Culture and History," in *The Bible and Modern Scholarship* [ed. J. P. Hyatt], 1965, p. 319).

131. William G. Dever, one of the new generation of "full-time" Palestinian archaeologists, recent Director of the William Foxwell Albright Institute of Archaeological Research in Jerusalem (1971–1975), was an important informant and stimulant while I was writing the first draft of this chapter in 1968–1969. At the time I was Post-doctoral Research Fellow and Dever was the Archaeological Director at Hebrew Union College Biblical and Archaeological School in Jerusalem, which included the directorship of the excavations at Gezer. As a resource for the resident Fellows, Dever arranged a series of

informal probing conversations with practicing archaeologists, among them Yohanan Aharoni, Ruth Amiran, Joseph Callaway, Moshe and Trude Dothan, Roland de Vaux, and Kathleen Kenyon, in which the discussion centered on the relation between archaeology and historical method in biblical studies. Over the years I have also discussed the same issue repeatedly with Anson F. Rainey of Tel Aviv University. Subsequently, while lecturing in the Overseas Students Program of the Hebrew University in Jerusalem in 1973–1974, I was able to continue my conversations with Dever and Rainey and to consult at length with other field archaeologists on the historical, cultural, and sociological implications of recent finds and methods. My indebtedness to particular archaeologists on specific points is credited at appropriate spots throughout this volume, especially in the notes to Part X. Of course neither Dever nor Rainey, nor the guest archaeologists at HUCBAS in 1968–1969, nor other archaeologists with whom I have talked in 1973–1974, are to be held responsible either for the substance or the detail of my summations of their unpublished views or for my applications of what they conveyed to me.

132. On the chronology of the Philistine entrance into Canaan, cf. G. E. Wright, "Fresh Evidence for the Philistine Story," *BA* 29 (1966) 70–86; W. F. Albright, "The Sea Peoples in Palestine," *CAH*, 1966 (fascicle 51); T. Dothan, *The Philistines and Their Material Culture,* 1967 (Heb. with Eng. summary). For a fuller bibliography on the Philistines, see notes 328–332, 334.

133. On Nephtoah, see Y. Aharoni, *The Land of the Bible,* pp. 172–173. On the Palestinian campaigns of the nineteenth-dynasty pharaohs, see Maps 41–46 in Y. Aharoni and M. Avi-Yonah, *The Macmillan Bible Atlas,* 1968. The Egyptian derivation of biblical Nephtoah is now denied by some Egyptologists, cf. S. Ahituv in *IEJ* 23 (1973) 59–60.

134. The so-called "Israel stele" of Merneptah is translated and annotated in *ANET*, pp. 376–378; see also comments of Y. Aharoni, *The Land of the Bible,* p. 172, and of R. de Vaux, *Histoire ancienne d'Israël: Des Origines à l'Installation en Canaan,* 1971, pp. 366–367, 456–458.

135. G. E. Wright, briefly in *Biblical Archaeology,* pp. 77–78, and, more fully, in *Shechem: The Biography of a Biblical City,* 1965, pp. 123–128.

136. P. W. Lapp, "The Conquest of Palestine in the Light of Archaeology," *CTM* 38 (1967) 298–299. Lapp repeats this claim in a more diffuse form in *Biblical Archaeology and History,* 1969, p. 110: "Inter-city struggles would scarcely have produced a new culture, and a popular revolution would hardly have led to major destructions of large towns." Needless to say, there are numerous unexamined and undemonstrated assumptions and lines of reasoning in Lapp's cover terms, "scarcely" and "hardly." Similarly, E. F. Campbell, Jr., "Moses and the Foundations of Israel," *Interpretation* 29 (1975) 152, asks rhetorically: "Why completely destroy towns which had been liberated from a city-state ruling establishment—especially if many of those who once lived in that town were now among the victors and might very well want to return to their homes?" Campbell, who tends to look favorably on Mendenhall's revolt model, assumes that only archaeological evidence for a "peaceful transition" (such as at Shechem and Debir-Khirbet Rabud) supports the revolt model. That being his premise, he finds no more than fifty percent support for the revolt model from recent archaeological discoveries. As with Lapp, the assumptions and links in the argument are very imprecisely drawn and scarcely argued with reference to the dynamics and urban environmental effects of actual sociopolitical revolutions.

137. G. R. H. Wright, "Tell el-Yehŭdīyah and the Glacis," *ZDPV* 84 (1968) 1–17; P.J. Parr, "The Origin of the Rampart Fortifications of Middle Bronze Age Palestine and Syria," *ZDPV* 84 (1968) 18–45.

138. The general character and coverage of archaeological surveys in Palestine are discussed by Y. Aharoni, *The Land of the Bible,* pp. 91–93.

139. N. Glueck in a series of articles in *Bulletin of the American Schools of Oriental Research:
BASOR* 131 (1953) 6–15; 137 (1955) 10–22; 138 (1955) 7–29; 142 (1956) 17–35; 145 (1957)
11–25; 149 (1958) 8–16; 155 (1959) 2–13. Glueck applied the results historically in "The
Age of Abraham in the Negeb," *BA* 18 (1955) 2–9, and in *Rivers in the Desert: A History of the
Negeb,* 1959. Glueck's surveys are set in the context of continuing archaeological work in the
Negeb by Y. Aharoni, "The Negeb," in *Archaeology and Old Testament Study* (ed. D. Winton
Thomas), 1967, pp. 385–403.

140. N. Glueck, *Explorations in Eastern Palestine I–IV,* issued in *AASOR* 14 (1934); 15
(1935); 18–19 (1939); 25–28 (1951); *The Other Side of Jordan,* 1940; "Transjordan," in
Archaeology and Old Testament Study (ed. D. Winton Thomas), 1967, pp. 429–453, and for
Gilead, see S. Mittmann, *Beiträge zur Siedlungs -und Territorialgeschicte des nördlichen Ostjordanlandes,* 1966.

141. For lower Galilee: A. Saarisalo, *JPOS* 9 (1929) 27–40; 10 (1930) 5–10. For upper
Galilee: Y. Aharoni, *Settlement of the Israelite Tribes in Upper Galilee,* 1959 (Heb.), and
"Problems of the Israelite Conquest in the Light of Archaeological Discoveries," *AS* 2
(1957) 131–150.

142. J. A. Callaway and M. B. Nichol, *BASOR* 183 (1966) 12–19; J. A. Callaway, *JBL* 87
(1968) 315.

143. M. Noth, "Grundsätzliches zur geschichtlichen Deutung archäologischer Befunde
auf dem Boden Palästinas," *PJ* 34 (1938) 7–22; "Hat die Bibel doch recht?" *Festschrift für G.
Dehn,* 1957, pp. 7–22; "Der Beitrag der Archäologie zur Geschichte Israels," *SVT* 7 (1960)
262–282; *The History of Israel,* 2nd ed., 1954 (Eng. trans. 1960), pp. 46–48; *The Old Testament
World,* 4th ed., 1964 (Eng. trans. 1966), pp. 139–144. A lucid methodological discussion on
archaeology and historical method, building on Noth's basic principles, is presented by M.
Weippert, *The Settlement of the Israelite Tribes in Palestine* (SBT, 2nd series, 21), 1967 (Eng.
trans. 1971),pp. 128–136.

144. A. Alt, "The Settlement of the Israelites in Palestine," *EOTHR,* 1966 (orig. pub.
1925), pp. 175–221; "Erwägungen über die Landnahme der Israeliten in Palästina." *KS,* I,
1953 (orig. pub. 1939), pp. 126–175.

145. One of the contributions of G. E. Mendenhall, "The Hebrew Conquest of Palestine," *BAR* 3 (1970) 100–120 = *BA* 25 (1962) 66–87, was his insistence that semi-nomads
and 'apiru must be separated on sociological grounds. Unfortunately, because of the brevity
of the argument, many of the links in his operations and many of the data (especially on
semi-nomads) were not reported by him along with his conclusions. This omission has
proved to be a major factor in the summary dismissal of Mendenhall's proposals about the
"conquest." And on the particular point of semi-nomadism, his more recent *The Tenth
Generation: The Origins of the Biblical Traditions,* 1973, adds no greater clarity and only a little
more detail. It is necessary to draw on the extensive studies of Near Eastern pastoral
nomadism, ancient and modern, in order to further validate, clarify, and nuance
Mendenhall's adumbrations. Precisely that project will be undertaken in VIII.39 of this
study.

146. M. Noth, *The History of Israel,* pp. 68–84, weaves together the diverse data on the
several waves of occupation into a concise synthesis. Fuller treatments of these diverse
"waves" appear in H. H. Rowley, *From Joseph to Joshua,* 1948, and in Y. Aharoni, *The Land of
the Bible,* pp. 174–227.

147. In addition to Noth's full-bodied presentation of the amphictyonic hypothesis in
Das System der zwölf Stämme Israels, 1930, he summed up the main outlines of his theory in
The History of Israel, pp. 85–97. I shall undertake a detailed critique of the amphictyonic
comparative model in VII.31 and 33.

148. The original statement of the revolt model is by G. E. Mendenhall, "The Hebrew Conquest of Palestine," *BA* 25 (1962) 66–87 = *BAR* 3 (1970), pp. 100–120, and is developed somewhat further in his *The Tenth Generation: The Origins of the Biblical Tradition*, 1973 which focuses more on the social system following the revolt than on the revolt proper or on the social conditions which fed into it. Even so, since it is to a large extent only through the consequent system that we can reconstruct the revolt, Mendenhall's recent study furthers the understanding of the formation of Israel in significant ways.

J. L. McKenzie, *The World of the Judges*, 1966, largely accepts Mendenhall's model, adds a few additional instances of its explanatory possibilities, and gives most of his attention to relating the revolt model to Noth's amphictyony, a point which Mendenhall only briefly touched on.

J. Bright, *A History of Israel*, 2nd ed., 1972, shifts from advocacy of a modified conquest model in the first edition to acceptance of the revolt model with minor demurrers. He relies wholly on Mendenhall's presentation, supplying no fresh support, and avoids exploring the sociological implications of the model of the conquest as "an inside job."

M.C. Astour, "The Amarna Age Forerunners of Biblical Anti-Royalism," in *For Max Weinreich on His Seventieth Birthday: Studies in Jewish Languages, Literature, and Society*, 1964, pp. 6–17, seems not to have been familiar with Mendenhall's pioneering article on the revolt model. In stressing sociopolitical and ideological continuity between anti-royalist movements in Amarna Canaan and in early Israel, Astour's analysis coincides partially with Mendenhall's. However, since Astour views both the Amarna 'apiru and the early Israelites as sections of a great West Semitic pastoral nomadic wave of immigration into Canaan, he is decisively prevented from formulating a thesis resembling Mendenhall's view that Israel itself represented an indigenous Canaanite uprising against the city-states.

A. E. Glock, "Early Israel as the Kingdom of Yahweh: The Influence of Archaeological Evidence on the Reconstruction of Religion in Early Israel," *CTM* 41 (1970) 558–605, develops a model of early Israel as a fiercely antiroyalist "counter-culture" (see p. 601, note 264) in which institutions of law and warfare were articulated. Glock's chief interest is in exploring the nonprofessional Israelite form of warfare and the socioeconomic peculiarities of Israelite law. Strangely, although Glock was Mendenhall's student and cites from his mentor's works extensively, there is only one brief reference to Mendenhall's revolt model (p. 599, note 243). In any event, Glock has clearly laid aside the confusions of the pastoral nomadic view of early Israel, and his remarks about the composition of Israel, e.g., "a dissenting and disinherited community of *ḥopshi* (emancipated slaves) and *ḥabirū* (social outcasts)" (p. 577), and "an amalgam of Palestinian peasants" (p. 587), strongly imply that he presupposes the revolt model. Essentially, however, Glock is describing the ideal-typical premonarchic Israelite social order. His views about how that order came into being are only lightly touched upon, and it is uncertain to what degree Mendenhall's conception of the "conquest" has influenced Glock's formulations.

So far as I have been able to determine from the published literature, J. Dus, "Moses or Joshua? On the Problem of the Founder of the Israelite Religion," *RR* 2. 2/3 (1975) 26–41 (orig. pub. in German in *ArO* 39 [1971] 16–45) is the only scholar who has come to the same approximate conclusion as Mendenhall by means of his own independent research, mainly by an analysis of the traditions' testimony to the work of a combined sociopolitical liberator and religious founder at the beginnings of Israelite history. Dus departs from Mendenhall, however, in seeing this liberator-founder as Joshua in Canaan rather than Moses in Egypt. Later, under the influence of the "Mosaic" Danite priesthood, the liberation-founding of Israel was retrojected into Egypt and Moses was invested with the role of liberator-founder (cf. J. Dus. "Die Stierbilder von Bethel und Dan and das Problem der 'Moseschar,' "*AION* 18 [1968] 105–137). The modes and implications of the freeing and unification of the Israelite tribes by means of a great religio-social uprising of Canaanite corvée laborers are worked through far more systematically and relentlessly by Dus than by Mendenhall, e.g., "There lies before us in Exodus 1—24 the report of the first actual ideologically founded sociopolitical revolution in world history" (p. 19).

By and large, however, studies of the Israelite conquest of Canaan since 1962 have either ignored Mendenhall's hypothesis altogether or dismissed it with little more than mockery and caricature. The most extended critique of Mendenhall's position by M. Weippert, *The Settlement of the Israelite Tribes in Palestine* (SBT, Second Series, 21), 1967 (Eng. trans. 1971), 55–126, partially misconstrues Mendenhall's argument about the *'apiru* forerunners of Israel (perhaps pardonably in the light of Mendenhall's terseness), but, more seriously, labors strenuously to buttress a pastoral nomadic model for early Israel with most unconvincing results (cf. review of Weippert's book by Mendenhall in *Biblica* 50 [1969] 432–436). In a review of *The Tenth Generation*, J. A. Sasson (*JBL* 93 [1974] 294–296) notes that Mendenhall elaborates the revolt model set forth earlier in *BA* 25 (1962). Sasson faults Mendenhall for not expressly replying to the "very judicious critique" of his approach by M. Weippert, ignoring the fact that Mendenhall directly and explicitly replied to Weippert in the earlier *Biblica* review. Otherwise, Sasson offers no assessment of the central model, although he comments in some detail, positively and negatively, concerning particular linguistic, exegetical, and historical arguments of Mendenhall. R. de Vaux's compendious *Histoire ancienne d'Israël: Des Origines à l'Installation en Canaan,* 1971, pp. 452–453, manages to summarize and purportedly dismiss Mendenhall's revolt model in less than two pages, while oddly allowing in an aside that certain northern tribes of Israel, mixed with Canaanites, may have served Canaanite princes against whom they revolted when the Joshua group arrived in Canaan. And this is not to mention the steady stream of books on Israelite origins which simply proceed as though a revolt model of the Israelite formation had never been proposed.

In short, if Mendenhall's defense and elaboration of the revolt model has been less than systematic and thorough and if those impressed by its possibilities have been slack in trying their own hand at developing it, the response of the model's critics has been appallingly superficial—as though the revolt model were so manifestly absurd that one need not bother to demonstrate its errors in detail. To date, the revolt model is a suggestive, partially developed explanatory theory about Israelite origins; but not only has that partially developed theory not been rebutted, it has not yet received a rigorous point by point critique. A.J. Hauser, "Israel's Conquest of Palestine: A Peasants' Rebellion?" in *Journal for the Study of the Old Testament* 7 (May 1978) 2–19 is, in my judgment, entirely beside the point in his rejection of the substance (in contrast to some details and forms of argument) in Mendenhall's view. In the same issue is a response to Hauser by Thomas L. Thompson (pp. 20–27) and a rebuttal of Hauser and Thompson by Norman K. Gottwald (pp. 37–52).

149. Mendenhall's sketch of Palestinian politics and society in the Late Bronze Age is very condensed in the initial essay, and only slightly fuller in scattered passages in the recent book, but he bases his description on well-known and secure textual sources. Fuller accounts of the quasi-feudal order established in northern Mesopotamia and in Syria-Palestine, beginning apparently in the north under the Hurrians and extending southward under those who became the Hyksos rulers of Egypt, are available in R. T. O'Callaghan, *Aram Naharaim: A Contribution to the History of Upper Mesopotamia in the Second Millennium B.C.*

(AO, 26), 1948, pp. 51–74, and in W. Helck, *Die Beziehungen Ägyptens zu Vorderasien im 3. und 2. Jahrtausend v. Chr.* (AAb, 5), 1962, pp. 515–535. I shall examine this Canaanite social order in greater detail in Part VIII.

150. I list here only a minimum of sources on the *'apiru,* pending a fuller presentation in Part VIII: E. F. Campbell, Jr., "The Amarna Letters and the Amarna Period," *BAR* 3 (1970) 54–75 = *BA* 23 (1960) 2–22; M. Greenberg, *The Hab/piru (AOS,* 39), 1955, pp. 32–50 for transliterations and translations of the Canaanite texts on the *'apiru,* and pp. 70–76, 85–96 for interpretation and conclusions; M. P. Gray, "The Ḫâbirū-Hebrew Problem," *HUCA* 28 (1958) 135–202.

151. This sociopolitical interpretation of *'apiru* is clearly and concisely stated by E. F. Campbell, Jr., "The Amarna Letters," but his formulation should be recognized as an elaboration of an interpretive tradition, shifting from an ethnic to a sociopolitical understanding, which goes back to B. Landsberger, "Ḫabiru und Lulaḫḫu," *KF* 1 (1930) 321–334.

152. This was a point argued with considerable documentation by A. Alt, "The Settlement of the Israelites in Palestine," *EOTHR,* 1966 (orig. pub. 1925), pp. 175–204. Of course Alt thought that his observation about attenuated city-state control in the highlands buttressed the immigration model of the settlement, but the revolt theorists employ his analysis to support a different reading of Israel's formation in the land.

153. The ultimate Amorite source of Numbers 21:27–30 was claimed by B. Maisler (Mazar), *Untersuchungen zur alten Geschichte und Ethnographie Syriens und Palästinas,* I, 1920, p. 41, but it has been most fully argued by M. Diman (Haran), "An Archaic Remnant in Prophetic Literature," *Yedioth* = *BJPES* 13 (1949) 7–15 (Heb.), who finds that prophetic oracles against Moab in Isaiah 15–16 and Jeremiah 48 derive from a preconquest Amorite elegy and triumphal song dealing with Sihon's defeat of Moab, of which Numbers 21:27–30 is an old exemplar. Recently Haran stated to me in conversation that, were he to re-do the argument, he would probably temper and refine it, but that he sees no reason to alter his original judgment. Mendenhall does not document his identical claim (*BAR* 3 [1970] 114), so it is unclear whether he depended on Mazar and/or on Diman-Haran or reached the conclusion independently. M. Ottosson, *Gilead: Tradition and History* (CB, Old Testament Series, 3), 1969, pp. 62–63, uses tortuous reasoning to deny that the song was Amorite because it does not occur to him that some of the Amorites in Sihon's kingdom could have become Israelites. J. R. Bartlett, "The Historical Reference of Numbers 21:27–30," *PEQ* 101 (1969) 94–100, usefully summarizes and critiques *some* of the prevailing historical reconstructions of the events behind the poem (in particular with reference to precisely when Moab extended its control north of the Arnon River to the vicinity of Heshbon), but curiously he omits reference to the Mazar-Haran hypothesis that the taunt song against Moab is an Amorite composition. He merely rebuts the view that the song was a satire directed against the Amorites. Certainly the Mazar-Haran proposal fits well with Bartlett's contention that the song most probably refers to a single campaign of destruction, and possibly that hypothesis also accords with Bartlett's observation that at least by the time of Eglon, Moab had extended its control well to the north of the Arnon. Bartlett correctly emphasizes that the greatest obstacle to reaching consensus on the historical situation referred to in the song is the problematic text of vs. 30. Likewise, M. Noth, *Numbers* (OTL), 1966 (Eng. trans. 1968), pp. 161–165, discusses the taunt song without attention to the hypothesis that it is an Amorite composition taken over by Israel.

154. Y. Aharoni, *The Land of the Bible,* pp. 191–192, initially directed my attention to the potential significance for the settlement of the Ammonite possession of Og's bedstead and

the possible Aramean origin of Jair, but he interprets both phenomena in terms of an immigration model, i.e., the Ammonites shared a common, anciently rooted tradition with Israelites, and an Aramean group joined the already existing Israelite tribe of Manasseh "in the course of time." J. R. Bartlett, "Sihon and Og," *VT* 20 (1970) 257–277, attempts a tradition history of the Sihon and Og traditions from their emergence among local Transjordanian Israelite groups until, communicated through Gilgal, they passed on into E and D, and, moreover, as a result of the Davidic kingdom's contact with Ammon and Gilead, an alternate form of the Og tradition developed that associated him with the Rephaim and with Rabbath-Ammon. By contrast, the earlier Og tradition had connected him with Amorites at Ashtaroth in Bashan. Here Bartlett misses the significance of Og's iron bedstead, which he construes with many interpreters as a basalt sarcophagus, thereby assuming that the tradition viewed Og as having lived in and having reigned over Rabbath-Ammon. I prefer to construe it as a piece of furniture seized as a war trophy during an Ammonite campaign against Og of Bashan which was put on display in the Ammonite capital. Og is said to be "of the remnant of the Rephaim" (Deut. 3:11), and the Ammonites are said to have destroyed Rephaim=Zamzummim when they settled along the upper reaches of the Jabbok (Deut. 2:20–21). These conquered peoples are reported to have been uncommonly tall (Deut. 2:21), a point underlined by the excessive size of Og's bed (approximately 14' by 6'; Deut. 3:11). This feature of the tradition, when taken too literally, has helped to turn scholars toward the view that it was a sarcophagus (whereas in fact the dimensions are outlandish even for a sarcophagus). Bartlett is probably correct in following the view of F. Schwally and J. Gray that Rephaim, meaning "shades of the dead," was used by the Israelites for "people who were dead and gone, and of whom they knew little" (J. Gray in *Dictionary of the Bible*, 2nd ed., revised by F. Grant and H. Rowley, 1963, p. 842; cited by Bartlett, p. 269, note 2). Of course a methodological distinction must be maintained between the historical grounds of the bedstead tradition and the circumstances of its transmission to Israel, not to mention the embellishment of the motif of "gigantism." Also of apparent relevance to a sociohistorical understanding of the Og tradition is I. Ben-Shem, *The Conquest of Transjordan: A Biblical Study*, 1972 (Heb. with Eng. synopsis), to date available to me only through a short review by T. E. Shea *(CBQ* 36 [1974] 249). Ben-Shem analyzes the Israelite success in overcoming the formidable Og and Sihon by a strategy of isolating them from their vassals before engaging them in battle. Shea makes the terse observation that, contrary to the author's expressed view, Ben-Shem's reconstruction enhances the likelihood "that the relatively small band of Israelite invaders from the south would have been continually augmenting their host with sympathetic vassal states." Unaccountably, however, Shea associates this latter view with Alt and Noth rather than with Mendenhall.

155. Y. Yadin, "And Dan, Why Did He Remain in Ships?" *AJBA* 1 (1968) 9–23 = *Western Galilee and the Coast of Galilee,* 1965, pp. 42–55 (Heb.).

156. M. Weber, *Ancient Judaism,* 1921 (Eng. trans. 1952), p. 75.

157. Ibid.

158. Ibid., p. 79.

159. On Weber's contributions to an understanding of ancient Israel: H.-J. Kraus, *Geschichte der historisch-kritischen Erforschung des Alten Testaments von der Reformation bis zur Gegenwart,* 1956, pp. 294–295; H. H. Hahn, *The Old Testament and Modern Research,* expanded edition, 1966, pp. 159–166; J. Guttmann, "Max Webers Soziologie des Antiken Judentums," *MGWJ* 69 (1925) 195–223. W. Caspari, *Die Gottesgemeinde vom Sinai und das nachmalige Volk Israel: Auseinandersetzungen mit Max Weber,* 1922, took Weber's thesis that

Yahwism developed out of a military confederacy in Canaan seriously enough to make it the foil for stating his defense of the more traditional view that the covenant idea originated in a religious league antedating the settlement.

160. G. E. Mendenhall, *BAR* 3 (1970), pp. 106–107.

161. Mendenhall, *The Tenth Generation*, p. 195.

162. W. R. Goldschmidt, *Comparative Functionalism: An Essay in Anthropological Theory*, 1966, treats the "Malinowskian dilemma." How can one say, as Malinowski does, that every cultural institution must be examined in its whole cultural setting and at the same time justify a cross-cultural comparison of institutions? Goldschmidt concludes that the elements that are comparable are not the institutions but the social functions that can address social problems. It is the problems and the functions that can properly be compared from culture to culture. In my view there is no real solution to the "Malinowskian dilemma" apart from a cultural-material evolutionary perspective on societies, cf. my discussion in X. 49–50.

163. Mendenhall, *The Tenth Generation*, chap. 6.

164. Mendenhall, *BAR* 3 (1970), p. 107.

165. Mendenhall, *The Tenth Generation*, p. 21.

NOTES TO PART VI

166. I. J. Gelb, "Approaches to the Study of Ancient Society," *JAOS* 87 (1967) 4.

167. G. W. Anderson, "Israel: Amphictyony: ʿAM; ḲĀHĀL; ʿEDĀH," in *Translating and Understanding the Old Testament: Essays in Honor of H. G. May* (ed. H. T. Frank and W. L. Reed), 1970, p. 142.

168. A. Malamat, "Tribal Societies: Biblical Genealogies and African Lineage Systems," *AES* 14 (1973) 126–136, in an exploratory application of anthropological data on kinship systems to biblical genealogies, has perceptively pointed out some of the decisive tensions between genealogies that reflect empirical kin connections and pseudo-genealogies that ascribe kinship metaphorically to sociopolitically related groups, which he characterizes as "large-scale projections of real family relationships" (p. 132). It would perhaps be a safer starting point simply to say that pseudo-genealogies are large-scale extensions of kinship tracking schemes used in small-scale social units, i.e., leaving open the question of whether any particular pseudo-genealogy is based on actual small-scale kin relations or is a fabrication without an empirical small-scale foundation. Malamat did not pursue his study into an investigation of how kinship and pseudo-kinship were related in the total Israelite social system vis-à-vis other societies, but his observations are at least amenable to a theoretical understanding of "descent as political ideology" as articulated by M. Sahlins, *Tribesmen*, 1968 (quoted in text, p. 334; cf. note 237 below). See also note 241 below.

169. On the other hand, some interpreters view Jeshurun as originally a reference to deity, eg., "El is upright or trustworthy" (cf. L. Wächter, "Israel und Jeschurun," *Schalom: Studien zu Glaube und Geschichte Israels. A. Jepsen* (AVTR, 51), 1971, pp. 58–64. As a poetic term for Israel, it is sometimes construed as a formation on analogy with Zebulun, while others treat it as a hypocorism, that is, with diminutive ending expressing affection or endearment.

170. A. Besters, " 'Israël' et 'Fils d' Israël' dans les livres historiques (Genèse—II Rois)," *RB* 74 (1967) 5–23.

171. J. Liver, " *ʿĒdāh*," *EM*, vol. 6, 1971, cols. 83–89 (Heb.), and A. Hurwitz, "Linguistic Observations on the Priestly Term *ʿĒdāh* and the Language of P," *Tarbiz* 40 (1971) 261–267

(Heb.; an Eng. summary of the argument appears in *Immanuel* 1 [1972] 21–23). These scholars argue that, since *'ēdāh* is seldom used in later biblical and Talmudic sources, its frequent use in P is surely no bar to its being accepted as an accurate recollection of premonarchic Israelite "assembly." Since, however, there are few references to *'ēdāh* as a popular assembly anywhere outside of P, it seems to me that the argument only shows that *'ēdāh* may have been a premonarchic term, not that it conclusively *was*. Somewhat more cogent evidence is Hurwitz's citation of *'dt 'ilm* ("council of the gods") at Ugarit and the probably parallel ' *ᵃdath-'ēl* ("council of El") in Psalm 82:1. In any event, my point is not to establish the age of the term *'edah* as applied to the popular assembly, but to indicate what evidence exists for such an assembly in premonarchic times by whatever name. Liver's and Hurwitz's studies at least support the likelihood that there was such an institution before the monarchy.

172. Anderson, "Israel: Amphictyony: 'AM; KĀHĀL; 'ĒDÂH," in *Translating and Understanding the Old Testament,* p. 142, note 26, reports that in the after-discussion of his paper at a meeting of the British Society for Old Testament Study, "the suggestion was made ... that the Hebrew equivalent of 'amphictyony' is *šibṭê Yiśrāēl,* i.e., 'the tribes of Israel.' " Anderson finds it no adequate equivalent, but he does not consider how adequately the term might serve for the confederated tribes apart from confirmation or disconfirmation of a specifically amphictyonic league structure.

173. G. Mendenhall, *The Tenth Generation,* 1973, pp. 184–185, after pointing out the root meaning of *shēveṭ,* remarks: "The Hebrew tribe is then, by extension, in a familiar pattern, that over which the staff of office rules. It is an administrative unit within the federation, though it is most probable that such units correspond to already existing social groups which entered the federation as corporate bodies." The organizational implication of *shēveṭ* as "staff " is well put, except for the misleading use of "administrative unit," which implies the very political centralization in Israel which Mendenhall is at pains to deny. Also, the assumption that the tribes entering the federation of Israel were pre-existent corporate units must be cautiously entertained. Allowance must be made for the possibility that such pre-existing units altered their composition or form upon joining Israel, or subsequently, as well as for the possibility that some of the tribes may have been new formations lacking continuity with any single dominant pre-existing social group but rather were composed of several pre-existing groups, plus an indeterminate number of persons cut adrift from membership in any corporate body, all of whom merged into a novel formation. The relative cohesiveness and endurance of the various Israelite tribes would then be in considerable measure a function of the degree of social homogeneity in the groups at the time they became "Israelite."

174. The textual evidence on which the following delimitation of Gilead is based is fully discussed in M. Ottosson, *Gilead: Tradition and History* (CB, Old Testament Series, 3), 1969, especially pp. 15–29, 136–143, 242–253. Ottosson in turn builds critically on previous research into the Gilead problem, especially the work of M. Noth, "Beiträge zur Geschichte des Ostjordanlandes: 1. Das Land Gilead als Siedlungsgebiet israelitischer Sippen," *PJ* 37 (1941) 50–101, and "Gilead und Gad," *ZDPV* 75 (1959) 14–73.

175. C. Hauret, "Aux origines du sacerdoce Danite à-propos de Jud. 18: 30–31," in *Mélanges bibliques rédigés en l'honneur de André Robert,* 1957, pp. 105–113.

176. M. Noth, *The History of Israel,* 2nd ed., 1954 (Eng. trans. 1960), pp. 61–62; and, in greater detail, M. Ottosson, *Gilead,* pp. 138–140.

177. Apparently first proposed by C. Steuernagel, *Die Einwanderung der israelitischen Stämme in Kanaan,* 1901, pp. 15–18, and supported by M. Noth, *The History of Israel,* pp. 63–64.

178. K. Elliger, "Gad," IDB, vol. 2, 1962, p. 333.

179. Y. Aharoni, *The Land of the Bible: A Historical Geography*, 1962 (Eng. trans. 1967), pp. 184–200, 211–245.

180. Valuable in this regard is the proposal of D. Baly, "The Wheat and the Barley, the Oil and the Wine," in *Geographical Companion to the Bible*, 1963, pp. 60–77, that the named tribes of Israel correspond in large measure to "natural regions" (the French *pays*), each having "its own modification of the general bread-wine-oil pattern" of agricultural production, with the result that "each tribe absorbed territory to the limit of that type of agriculture to which it had become accustomed" (p. 75). This factor of regional variation in economic production, correlated to topography, roughly sketched by Baly, has received almost no attention by biblical scholars. Obviously the factors of tribal demographics and of social organization also have to be included as additional correlates to the factor of regional variation in economic production. See X.51 on "A Program of Historical Cultural-Material Research into Early Israel."

181. J. Morgenstern, "Beena Marriage (Matriarchate) in Ancient Israel," *ZAW*, N.F. 6 (1929) 91–110; 8 (1931) 46–58, reviews the linquistic evidence, largely dependent on Arabic cognates, and argues that behind the later understanding of the patrilineal *mishpāḥāh*, from a root meaning "to pour out semen," there lay an older understanding of the root, applied to "concubine" or "beena wife" (perhaps "one into whom semen is poured"?; cf. Heb. *shiphḥāh* for "maid" or "maidservant"). Thus, in Morgenstern's view, *mishpāḥāh* was once a social unit shaped by matrilineal organization. Such a reconstruction rests far more weight on philology than it will bear. Even if *shiphḥāh* and *mishpāḥāh* are from the same root, there is no way of establishing social organizational conclusions without a much better grasp of the history of the development of Northwest Semitic languages than we now have. Even if we go so far as to imagine the development Morgenstern describes as having actually occurred, the old matrilineal rootage of the term may very well have been at a stage of Northwest Semitic linguistic development centuries prior to Israel's emergence, and thus may tell us nothing at all about the *mishpāḥāh* as a social entity in ancient Israel. This general judgment on the philological evidence was confirmed recently in conversation with an authority in Northwest Semitic languages, Jonas Greenfield of the Hebrew University in Jerusalem.

182. W. R. Smith, *Kinship and Marriage in Early Arabia*, 2nd ed., 1903, pp. 41–47. *BDB* may have drawn on the Arabic cognate in translating *ḥayyāh* as "community . . . (i.e., a group of allied families" [p. 312]).

183. A. R. Johnson, "The Primary Meaning of the Root *Gā'al*," *SVT* 1 (1953) 67–77; W. Falk, "Endogamy in Israel," *Tarbiz* 32 (1962) 30–31 (Heb.), comments on *g^e'ullāh* in biblical Israel, making use also of later Jewish and Talmudic sources, with respect to permitted and forbidden marriages, and notes especially the use of the root *qrb* ("to be close") to express eligibility for marriage and the use of the root *rḥq* ("to be far") to express ineligibility for marriage.

184. On Naomi's property, see H. H. Rowley, "The Marriage of Ruth," in *The Servant of the Lord and Other Essays on the Old Testament*, 2nd rev. ed., 1965 (orig. pub. 1947), pp. 180, 183–187 and the bibliography cited there.

185. G. Mendenhall, "The Census Lists of Numbers 1 and 26," *JBL* 77 (1968) 52–66; and cf. C. Schedl, "Biblische Zahlen unglaubwerdig?," *TPQ* 107 (1959) 58–62. For another way of reducing the numbers drastically, consult M. Barnouin, "Tableaux numériques du Livre des Nombres," *RB* 76 (1969) 351–364.

186. Population figures for Amarna Canaan, premonarchic Israel, and even for monarchic Israel, are crude estimates based on sparse data and using virtually none of the

techniques and controls of modern demographic studies, so that the question of the population of ancient Palestine cries out for fresh examination by the collaboration of experts in demographics, climatology, and other relevant disciplines. For a fuller discussion of the problem and bibliography, cf. X.51.4 and note 581.

187. H.-J. Kraus, *Worship in Israel,* 2nd ed., 1962 (Eng. trans. 1966), pp. 76–78.

188. For archaeological data on Israelite houses, see K. Beebe, "Ancient Palestinian Dwellings," *BA* 31 (1968) 35–58 (note comments on "sociological conditions," pp. 56–57), and Y. Shiloh, "The Four-Room House: Its Situation and Function in the Israelite City," *IEJ* 20 (1970) 180–190. See also T. L. McClellan, "Social Organization and Patterns in the Material Culture of Tell Beit Mirsim" (Paper presented to the Social World of Ancient Israel Group at the annual meeting of AAR-SBL, San Francisco, December 30, 1977).

189. M. Fried, *The Evolution of Political Society,* 1967, p. 154, remarks: "If I had to select one word in the vocabulary of anthropology as the single most egregious case of meaninglessness, I would have to pass over 'tribe' in favor of 'race.' I am sure, however, that 'tribe' figures prominently on the list of putative technical terms ranked in order of degree of ambiguity." The current anthropological attempt to give empirical and theoretical specificity to "tribe" is well reported in J. Helm, ed., *Essays on the Problem of Tribe* (Proceedings of the 1967 Annual Spring Meeting of the American Ethnological Society), 1968.

190. R. Walz, "Zum Problem der Domestikation der altweltlichen Cameliden," *ZDMG* 101 (1951) 29–51; W. Dostal, "The Evolution of Bedouin Life," in *L'Antica Società Beduina* (SS, 2), 1959, pp. 11–34 (with excellent bibliography).

191. J. T. Luke, *Pastoralism and Politics in the Mari Period: A Re-examination of the Major West Semitic Tribal Groups in the Middle Euphrates* (Ann Arbor: University Microfilms), 1965. This is the thesis of one of Mendenhall's students on which the latter draws heavily for his understanding of pastoral nomadism in the biblical world. Luke's study remains almost totally unknown to the wider working community of biblical scholars, e.g., M. Weippert (*The Settlement of the Israelite Tribes in Palestine,* SBT, Second Series, 21, 1967 [Eng. trans. 1971], p. 111, note 37) and W. G. Dever ("The Peoples of Palestine in the Middle Bronze I Period," *HTR* 64 [1971] 217, note 45) pointedly note that they have been unable to consult the work of Luke.

192. F. S. Frick, "The Rechabites Reconsidered," *JBL* 90 (1971) 279–287.

193. M. Sahlins, *Tribesmen* (Foundations in Modern Anthropology Series), 1968, p. 14.

194. On the tribe in pre-Roman and Roman antiquity, see W. Kubitschek, "Tribus," *PWRE,* vol. 6A, 2, 1937, cols. 2492–2518. On the Roman *tribus* as the source of the social organizational term "tribe" employed in anthropology and in biblical studies, cf. M. Fried, *The Evolution of Political Society,* pp. 160–161, and G. Mendenhall, *The Tenth Generation,* pp. 184–187.

195. G. E. Dole, "Tribe as the Autonomous Unit," in *Essays on the Problem of Tribe* (ed. J. Helm), 1968, pp. 83–100, suggests that tribe be understood as "a sociocultural autonomous unit." The term should be used, in her view, for social groups that are culture-bearing wholes. Their approximate boundaries can be determined in any given case by noting the politically autonomous social group, i.e., the extent of the group that has the right and power of self-rule, which shows up especially in the system of jural norms that control and integrate the behavior of its members. In treating tribes, Dole argues that we need descriptions of "degrees of tribalism" and not elaborate definitions which will always fail in one way or another to be true to some tribes. She represents the degrees of tribalism by position on a scale expressing both organizational complexity and extent of autonomy (p. 95):

I. Tribe (autonomous groups of people organized primarily by kinship terms)
  A. Egalitarian
    1. Informal unsegmented (unstable band or horde)
    2. Formal unsegmented (stable group without lineal kin division)
    3. Simple segmented (group with lineal kin division)
  B. Ranked
    1. Stratified segmented (aggregate of related kin groups under control of
      a paramount leader; chiefdom)

II. Nation (autonomous group with a centralized government, organized primarily on the
    basis of non-kin relationships)
  A. Simple (a nation comprising a single centralized government): State
  B. Complex (a nation comprising more than one previously autonomous state): Empire

Dole does not include "confederacy" in her scale of degrees of tribalism because a confederacy is not an autonomous unit, but rather "a loose association of political units at any level of complexity that cede their autonomy either temporarily or partially" (p. 95).

196. M. Fried, *The Evolution of Political Society,* p. 164.

197. E. R. Service, *Primitive Social Organization: An Evolutionary Perspective,* 1962, chaps. 3–4; M. Sahlins, "Segmentary Lineage: An Organization of Predatory Expansion," *AA* 63 (1961) 322–345. M. Fried, *The Evolution of Political Society,* pp. 164–167, is not as convinced as Service and Sahlins of an evolutionary typological difference between band and tribe: "It seems possible, e.g., to place both on the same temporal level and level of complexity, with the band representing the semipermanent membership group sharing a common camp, and the tribe constituting the shifting grouping of camps (i.e., bands) that comprises an area of relative peace and that would include demonstrably high frequency of intermarriage" (p. 165). In so arguing, however, Fried scarcely does justice to the cross-cutting associations which distinguish the tribe from the band by greater organizational complexity and cohesion.

198. M. Sahlins, *Tribesmen,* 1968.

199. L. H. Morgan, *Systems of Consanguinity and Affinity in the Human Family* (Smithsonian Institution Contributions to Knowledge, 17), 1871; *Ancient Society,* 1877 (see introduction and annotations by E. B. Leacock in Meridian Books reprint, 1963). For an evaluation of Morgan's accomplishments in the study of kinship, see F. Eggan, "Lewis H. Morgan on Kinship Perspective," in *Essays in the Science of Culture in Honor of L. A. White* (ed. G. E. Dole and R. L. Carneiro), 1960, pp. 179–201.

200. E. B. Leacock, "Introduction" to L. H. Morgan, *Ancient Society* (Meridian Books reprint), 1963, II, pp. viii–xi. The state of modern anthropological field research and theorizing about matrilineality is fully reported in D. M. Schneider and K. Gough, eds., *Matrilineal Kinship,* 1961.

201. W. R. Smith, *Kinship and Marriage in Early Arabia,* 2nd ed., 1903. D. R. Mace, *Hebrew Marriage: A Sociological Study,* 1953, pp. 35–43, sets forth Smith's views in the context of general anthropological theory of the time, and much of the remainder of Mace's book is given to a critique of Smith's conclusions in the light of more recent anthropological studies.

202. K. Elliger, "Das Gesetz Leviticus 18," *ZAW* 67 (1955) 1–25; J. R. Porter, *The Extended Family in the Old Testament* (Occasional Papers in Social and Economic Administration, 6), 1967.

203. R. Fox, *Kinship and Marriage: An Anthropological Perspective,* 1967, pp. 54–55.

204. R. de Vaux, *Ancient Israel: Its Life and Institutions,* 1958/1960 (Eng. trans. 1961), pp. 28–29; W. R. Smith, *Kinship and Marriage in Early Arabia,* pp. 93–98.

205. J. Van Seters, "Jacob's Marriages and Ancient Near Eastern Customs: A Re-examination," *HTR* 62 (1969) 377–395.

206. W. Plautz, "Zur Frage des Mutterrechts im Alten Testaments," *ZAW* 74 (1962) 9–30, finds that the traces of matriarchal society in early Israel are no indication that its social system was matriarchal or that it had been matriarchal in the period prior to its sedentarization in Canaan. Such traces are at most fragmentary survivals from the second or third millennia B.C. and as such occur elsewhere throughout the general Semitic culture, which had long been pervasively patriarchal.

207. M. Noth, "Das Amt des 'Richters Israels,' " *Festschrift für Alfred Bertholet zum 80 Geburtstag,* 1950, pp. 412–413.

208. J. Renger, "*mārat ilim:* Exogamie bei den semitischen Nomaden des 2. Jahrtausends," *AFO* 14 (1973) 103–107.

209. Ibid., 106–107.

210. Ibid., 106.

211. E. B. Tylor, "On a Method of Investigating the Development of Institutions; Applied to Laws of Marriage and Descent," *JRAI* 18 (1889) 267.

212. R. Fox, *Kinship and Marriage: An Anthropological Perspective,* 1967, pp. 175–176, 220.

213. A. de Pury, "Genèse XXXIV et l'histoire," *RB* 71 (1969) 5–49, provides a painstaking literary and historical analysis of Genesis 34. He concurs with S. Lehming, "Zur Überlieferungsgeschichte von Gen. 34," *ZAW* 70 (1958) 228–250, that there are two traditions (already combined in the oral stage) which do not correspond to the usual literary critical sources: (1) a Shechem version in which Dinah is raped by Shechem and the affront is avenged by "the sons of Jacob"; (2) a Hamor version in which Hamor negotiates with "the sons of Jacob" for a connubium with the intent of swindling the Israelites out of their goods—a scheme aborted when, with poetic justice, the near victims take preemptive action and "swindle the swindlers." Moreover, de Pury agrees with Lehming that Simeon and Levi were secondarily inserted in Genesis 34 in order to supply a narrative rationale for the condemnation of those two tribes in the elusive poetry of Genesis 49:5–7. However, on sociological grounds, de Pury strongly contests Lehming's linkage of the tradition with the Israelite amphictyony. He asserts rather that the "sons of Jacob" were a semi-nomadic clan—on the sole grounds that they are pictured as highly mobile—and goes on to suggest that like Issachar and Machir, this group (originally "sons of Israel," later "sons of Jacob") belonged to the general '*apiru* pattern of accommodation with the city-state of Shechem. De Pury takes for granted that '*apiru* were semi-nomads, without demonstration. The difference he sees is that while Issachar and Machir accepted subordinate service under Shechem, "the sons of Israel"="sons of Jacob" refused an inferior status in treaty. The various parts of de Pury's reconstruction must be treated separately. The semi-nomadic component of his interpretation is without foundation. It is highly plausible that Issachar, and less certainly Machir, was subject to Canaanite city-state rule in its beginnings, but that Shechem was the city-state one or both served is undemonstrated. De Pury and Lehming have convincingly excised Simeon and Levi from the original traditions of Genesis 34; if their case is as strong as I believe it to be, they have effectively disposed of the alleged secular tribe of Levi. Instead, Genesis 34 stands out as a composite of reports about two or more contacts and efforts at inter-communalism between Shechem and proto-Israelites. Probably de Pury is right in suggesting that the attachment of the tradition to Jacob came at the genealogical stage of the written tradition, although his case for the origin of the name Israel among this particular proto-Israelite group at Shechem is less clearly established. For

another view of Genesis 34, see J. Pitt-Rivers, *The Fate of Shechem or the Politics of Sex: Essays in the Anthropology of the Mediterranean,* 1977, 126–171.

214. D. Jacobson, *The Social Background of the Old Testament,* 1942, p. 63.

215. E. L. Schusky, *Manual for Kinship Analysis* (Studies in Anthropological Method), 1964, pp. 44–46.

216. Ibid., p. 21.

217. I. C. Brown, *Understanding Other Cultures,* 1963, p. 46.

218. L. H. Morgan, *Ancient Society,* pp. 377–382.

219. Ibid., p. 381.

220. Ibid.

221. C. D. Forde, *Habitat, Economy and Society: A Geographical Introduction to Ethnology,* 5th ed., 1963, pp. 285–307.

222. H. H. Rowley, "Early Levite History and the Question of the Exodus," *JNES* 3 (1944) 73–78: R. Abba, "Priests and Levites," IDB, vol. 3, 1962, pp. 876–889; E. Nielsen, "The Levites in Ancient Israel," *ASTI* 3 (1964) 16–27; A. H. J. Gunneweg, *Leviten und Priester* (FRLANT, 89), 1965; A. Cody, *A History of the Old Testament Priesthood* (AB, 35), 1969; B. A. Levine, "Priests," IDBSV, 1976, pp. 687–690.

223. Or possibly the Rechabites were chariot drivers under the monarchy, cf. F. S. Frick, "The Rechabites Reconsidered," *JBL* 90 (1971) 282–283, see especially footnotes 16–19.

224. M. Sahlins, *Tribesmen,* pp. 20–23.

225. For a review of biblical data and scholarly opinion on Israelite elders, see J. L. McKenzie, "The Elders in the Old Testament," *Biblica* 40 (1959) 522–540. J. Dus, "Die 'Ältesten Israels,' " *CV* 3 (1960) 232–242, and "Die 'Sufeten' Israels," *ArO* 31 (1963) 444–469, outlines the organs of amphictyonic Israel as follows: there were six elders per tribe, constituting seventy-two in all (cf. Num. 11:25–26), who sent representatives to a "college" or "senate" composed of twelve tribal heads, and it was this body that chose the judge, an office conceived by Dus to have been analogous to the Carthaginian *suffete* as ruler or magistrate. Thus, Israel had a republican constitution and was already a state before the monarchy. Dus pieces together his hypothesis with ingenuity, but it depends excessively on asserting a symmetrical model whose supporting evidence is necessarily culled from widely scattered texts. Nor has Dus sufficiently analyzed the alleged grounds for viewing early Israel as an amphictyony and as a state form of political organization. Nevertheless Dus must be highly credited with the intent to apply a comprehensive comparative methodology to the problem. Much can be learned, even from the overabstraction and oversystematizing to which he is prone.

226. M. Sahlins, *Tribesmen,* pp. 86–95; M. Fried, *The Evolution of Political Society,* 1967, pp. 114–118, 182–184; P. Farb, *Man's Rise to Civilization as Shown by the Indians of North America,* 1968, pp. 134–136, 151–152.

227. M. Fried, *The Evolution of Political Society,* p. 170.

228. Ibid., p. 173.

229. E. Service, *Primitive Social Organization,* pp. 113–115.

230. G. Mendenhall, *The Tenth Generation,* 1973, p. 10.

231. Ibid., p. 12, and also note 52 referring to T. B. L. Webster, *From Mycenae to Homer,* 1958, p. 136.

232. Mendenhall, *The Tenth Generation,* p. 14.

233. M. Sahlins, *Tribesmen,* pp. 67–68.

234. In the introductory remarks to this study of Israelite jurisprudence, L. Köhler, "Justice in the Gates," in *Hebrew Man,* 1953 (Eng. trans. 1956), p. 128, perceptively remarks that ". . . the community of life of Palestine depended upon the separate natural divisions

of the country. Each one lived on its own resources and lived to itself. It shaped its own life according to the special needs and laws of its position. The achievement of unity in spite of this depended on the fact that in the individual districts the same conditions and activities led to the same patterns, rather than that there was a unified will of a political kind which worked upon them." When this is viewed not merely in terms of natural conditions, as Köhler seems primarily to have intended it, but also in terms of social conditions and forces, it serves as a useful formulation of the way that regularities in early Israelite social development can be analytically differentiated according to complementary "bottom-up" and "top-down" genetic dynamics.

235. P. A. Munch, "Verwandtschaft und Lokalität in der Gruppendildung der altis-raelitischen Hebräer," *KZSS* 12 (1960) 438–457, accepts the pastoral nomadic origins of Israel and pictures the transition from "kinship" to "locality" as the basis for social organization. In spite of this faulty starting point, Munch exposes aspects of Israelite social organization that accord well with a model of the indigenous Canaanite origins of Israel. He observes, for example, that "the Israelite 'tribes' . . . distinguish themselves from the blood-formations of the bedouins in one essential point, namely, that they are not actual but only supposed kinship groups, and thus they constitute no formations of such groups but rather are *territorial units*" (p. 443). After noting that the tribal names are for the most part names of regions, he continues: "But these tribal spheres are not firmly circumscribed geographical concepts, but rather spheres of power, which fluctuate as the tribes themselves fluctuate" (p.444).

236. Y. Aharoni, *The Land of the Bible,* pp. 184–200, 211–245.

237. M. Sahlins, *Tribesmen,* p. 55.

238. A. Malamat, "Tribal Societies: Biblical Genealogies and African Lineage Systems," *AES* 14 (1973) 126–136; see also note 168 above.

239. Ibid., p. 127.

240. Ibid., p. 129, table 2.

241. The most extensive recent inquiry into the biblical genealogies, M. D. Johnson, *The Purpose of the Biblical Genealogies with Special Reference to the Setting of the Genealogies of Jesus* (SNTSMS, 8), 1969, is disappointing, not because its major focus is on New Testament genealogies, but because the author gives no systematic analysis of the problem of the social organizational levels to which biblical genealogies apply and he brings no social scientific tools to his aid. Still, it contains a useful compendium of basic biblical texts and scholarly views on the genealogies (pp. 3–76) and sums up the Old Testament section with a rough typology of the purposes for which the genealogies were prepared (pp. 77–82). R. R. Wilson, "The Old Testament Genealogies in Recent Research," *JBL* 94 (1975) 169–189, after briefly noting Johnson's too cursory study, singles out Malamat for his service in introducing a systematic method, using internal and external evidence, to the comparative study of biblical and ancient Near Eastern genealogies. Wilson advances the discussion by calling into question the speculativeness of Malamat's reconstruction of "a stereotypical ten-generation depth or a standard four-part structure" (p. 188). Rather than to posit an underlying archetypal genealogical form, he emphasizes the variations in form and function in extant genealogical schemes and observes that "genealogies functioning politically may be different from genealogies functioning in other spheres [e.g., in domestic or religious spheres]. It would be a mistake to ask which of the conflicting genealogies is historically accurate. All of them are accurate when their differing functions are taken into consideration" (p. 182). Citing anthropological studies of genealogies voluminously, Wilson makes a valid point about form-function variability, but speaks rather too carelessly in stating that, depending on function, all genealogies are "historically accurate." He might

better speak of all genealogies as "intelligible" or "plausible" in terms of their functions, since he seems clearly to recognize a difference between "literal" genealogies that closely follow observed kin descent and "metaphorical" genealogies (what I call pseudo-genealogies) that symbolize the relationships of larger groups by eponymous personifications. Wilson's article draws on his "Genealogy and History in the Old Testament" (Ph.D. diss., Yale University, 1972), now published in revised form as *Genealogy and History in the Biblical World* (Yale Near Eastern Researches, 7), 1977.

NOTES TO PART VII

242. M. Noth, *Das System der zwölf Stämme Israels*, 1930 (reprinted 1966).

243. Noth, *Das System*, pp. 122–170; *A History of Pentateuchal Traditions*, 1948 (Eng. trans. 1972); *The History of Israel*, pp. 110–138; "Das Amt des 'Richters Israels,'" *Festschrift für A. Bertholet*, 1950, pp. 404–417. A summary of the relation between the amphictyony and the formation of traditions as viewed by Noth is found in E. W. Nicholson, *Exodus and Sinai in History and Tradition*, 1973, pp. 15–20. See also W. Beyerlin, *Origins and History of the Oldest Sinaitic Traditions*, 1961 (Eng. trans. 1965), pp. 27–35, 112–126, 151–160; J. Dus, "Die altisraelitische amphiktyonische Poesie," *ZAW* 75 (1963) 45–54; J. L. McKenzie, *The World of the Judges*, 1967, chap. 6; M. Newman, *The People of the Covenant: A Study of Israel from Moses to the Monarchy*, 1962.

244. Noth, *Das System der zwölf Stämme Israels*, pp. 3–28; S. Mowinckel, " 'Rahelstämme' und 'Leastämme,' " *Von Ugarit nach Qumran* (BZAW, 77), 1958, 136–150; J. Liver, "The Israelite Tribes," in *WHJP* (ed. B. Mazar), First Series, vol. 3, 1971, pp. 183–211. A survey of some of the leading hypotheses about the identity of the tribes holding membership in the amphictyony appears in A. D. H. Mayes, *Israel in the Period of the Judges* (SBT, Second Series, 29), 1974, pp. 16–34. H. Weippert, "Das geographische System der Stämme Israels," *VT* 23 (1973) 76–89, examines both the positions and sequences of the tribes in lists that do not conform to the main types identified by Noth (i.e., the genealogical system and the system in the Book of Numbers); she tries to account for the departures from "the normal lists" by relating them to three stages of Israel's development: (1) the foundation of the northern tribes; (2) the later insertion of the Transjordan tribes; (3) the still later insertion of Judah and Simeon. Prior to Noth's pace-setting amphictyonic theory, several still useful studies of the tribal lists were published: B. Luther, "Die israelitischen Stämme," *ZAW* 21 (1901) 1–76: G. B. Gray, "The Lists of the Twelve Tribes," *Ex* 5 (1902) 225–240; F. Bönhoff, "Die zwölf Stämme und ihre Bedeutung für die älteste Geschichte des Volkes Israel," *STKM* 9 (1911) 653–663.

245. Noth, *Das System*, pp. 75–80; *The History of Israel*, pp. 88–89.

246. Noth, *Das System*, pp. 107–108; *The History of Israel*, pp. 181–182; cf. also M. Noth, "Die Ansiedlung des Stammes Juda auf dem Boden Palästinas," *PJ* 30 (1934) 31–47.

247. H. Ewald, *Geschichte des Volkes Israel*, I, 3rd ed., 1864, pp. 519–530; H. Gunkel, *Genesis*, 3rd ed., 1910, p. 332; A. Alt, "The God of the Fathers," *EOTHR*, 1966 (orig. pub. 1929), pp. 68–69, 73–75.

248. Noth, *Das System*, pp. 162–170.

249. A. Besters, "Le sanctuaire dans Jud. 19–21," *ETL* 41 (1965) 20–41, finds that the primary elements in these chapters substantiate an amphictyony but not a central sanctuary, whereas the secondary elements endeavor to supply the amphictyony with a central

sanctuary with confusing and contradictory results. J. Dus, "Bethel und Mispa in Jdc. 19—21 und Jdc. 10—12," *OA* 3 (1964) 227–243, contends that Bethel was original to the story in Judges 20—21, while Mizpah was added by means of expansions supplied from its proper appearance in Judges 10—12. S. Talmon, "Judges Chapter 1," in *Studies in the Book of Judges,* 1966, pp. 17–18, 27 (Heb.), and "There Was No *melek* in Israel in Those Days," in *Proceedings of the Fifth World Congress of Jewish Studies,* 1969, p. 40 (Heb.), argues that much shorter accounts of the Danite migration (presently Judges 18) and of the war against Benjamin (presently Judges 19—21) once appeared after Judges 1:34 and Judges 2:1a respectively. Following Talmon's perceptive clues, it may be suggested that an original annalistic core, omitting Micah and the Levite, is visible in Judges 18:1b–2a, 7–12, 27b–29, and that Judges 20:18,31,35a,36 may be bits of an annal, now nearly totally overlaid, which once told of skirmishes between Benjamin and its immediate Israelite neighbors. Noting that Bethel=Bochim ("weeping") is associated with public lament over a national catastrophe both in Judges 2:4–5 and in Judges 20:26; 21:2 and that the only named tribes in Judges 19—21 besides Benjamin are Ephraim and Judah, Talmon proposes that beneath the vastly inflated account may have been the story of fighting between Benjamin and its contiguous Israelite tribal neighbors over scarce land. This suggests a way to get a little closer to the original events which have been so bizarrely elaborated in Judges 19—21, although I do not see any evidence that disputed land claims were the source of the intertribal friction. The rape-murder of the concubine as the actual cause of the conflict is suspicious because of its schematic similarity to the story of the alleged sexual abuse of overnight visitors in Sodom as reported in Genesis 19 (D. S. Bailey, *Homosexuality and the Western Christian Tradition,* 1955, has sharply challenged the traditional homosexual interpretation of the incident). However, Judges 20:31 may contain the clue to the historical situation, for we read there of Benjaminites who periodically attacked fellow-Israelites on the highways in the vicinity of Gibeah and Bethel. The thirty men mentioned as killed in one such attack represent a remarkably modest figure in the midst of the tens and hundreds of thousands of combatants of which the story regularly speaks. Perhaps it was brigandage and murder committed by some Benjaminites, which the tribal elders were unable to stop, that precipitated reprisals and armed clashes between Benjamin and its neighbors Ephraim and Judah. The kernel of the idea that all Israel joined in a war of extermination against Benjamin may have lain in the eventual summoning of the intertribal leadership in order to reach amicable settlement of the affair before it enlarged into extended internecine war. We must envision raids and skirmishes rather than full war, the overall numbers in Judges 19—21 being no more believable than those recounted in the clashes between Gileadites and Ephraimites in Judges 12:1–6. In any case, it is evident that Noth's attempt to retain the twelve-tribe frame of Judges 19—21 as a premonarchic datum is totally shattered by a close scrutiny of the narrative.

250. E. H. Grady, *Epigraphic Sources of the Delphic Amphictyony,* 1931.

251. For available information on the deputies of the Delphic amphictyonic council, see ibid., chaps. 2–3.

252. Noth, *Das System,* pp. 97–104; *The History of Israel,* pp. 98–99.

253. E. A. Speiser, "Background and Function of the Biblical *Nāsī*'," *CBQ* 25 (1963) 111–117, feels that the injunction in Exodus 22:28(27) against cursing a *nāsī*' may mean that the term "was applied also to the head of a combination or confederation of a number of tribes," probably elected by the assembly, whereas Noth reads the same verse as reference to tribal deputies to the amphictyonic council who were given sacral protection.

254. Noth, "Das Amt des 'Richters Israels,' "*Festschrift für A. Bertholet,* 1950, 404–417; *The*

History of Israel, pp. 101–104. Subsequent study of the office of "minor judge" has called into question virtually every one of Noth's conclusions, except for a recognition that the list partially preserved in Judges 10:1–5; 12:7–15 is an independent annalistic literary type distinguishable from the stories of the "major judges." Consequently, a scholarly consensus on the sociopolitical structural position of these leaders seems farther from attainment than ever. Some analysts have stood by Noth's sharp restriction of the office to a legal post, whether in the proclamation of the divine law or in the administration of justice, or in both, so that a clear demarcation between the juridical minor judges and the military major judges is maintained (D. A. McKenzie, "The Judge of Israel," *VT* 17 [1967] 118–121, building on the linguistic study of O. Grether, "Die Bezeichnung 'Richter' für die charismatischen Helden der vorstaatlichen Zeit," *ZAW* 57 [1939] 110–121). More influential are studies based on South Arabian, Ugaritic, and Phoenician-Punic materials enlarging the scope of the *shōphēt*'s activity to "exercising authority, ruling," which might include military and juridical functions by turn. Such a conclusion tends toward the view that major and minor judges were variously filling one office, the differences being partly a matter of which function of the one office is exhibited in any one account and partly a matter of the literary type containing the information, i.e., whether popular narrative or annalistic summation (J. Dus, "Die 'Sufeten Israels' " *ArO* 31 [1963] 444–469; K.-D. Schunck, "Die Richter Israels und ihr Amt," *SVT* 15 [1966] 252–262; A. Malamat, *WHJP,* First Series, vol. 3, 1971, pp. 129–134; A. J. Hauser, "The 'Minor Judges': A re-evaluation," JBL 94 [1975] 190–200). What appeared at first to have been one of the most unshakable of Noth's claims, namely, that the minor judges occupied office in unbroken succession, is now widely questioned if not openly rejected (W. Richter, "Zu den 'Richtern Israels,' " *ZAW* 77 [1965] 40–72; R. de Vaux, *Histoire ancienne d'Israël: La Période des Juges,* 1973, pp. 74, 86).

255. The closest analogy to the minor judge as law proclaimer turns out to be, in Noth's view (cf. *The History of Israel,* p. 103, note 1), not any personnel in the Greek sacral leagues, but rather the Icelandic "law speaker" noted by A. Klostermann, *Der Pentateuch,* 1907, pp. 348–350, 419–423, with respect to Samuel, and by A. Alt, "The Origins of Israelite Law," *EOTHR,* 1966 (orig. pub. 1934), pp.131–132, with respect to the minor judges.

256. Grady, *Epigraphic Sources of the Delphic Amphictyony,* p. 39.

257. Noth, *Das System,* pp. 42–45, 159. W. J. Horwitz, "Were There Twelve Horite Tribes?," *CBQ* 35 (1973) 69–71, beginning with the assumption that there may have been two six-tribe Horite amphictyonies analogous to Noth's hypothesis of two six-tribe ancient Israelite leagues, reconstructs the members of the two Horite leagues as follows: (1) Lotan, Shobal, Zibeon, Anah, Ezer, Dishan; and (2) Anah, Dishon, Hemdan, Eshban, Ithran, Cheran. This exceedingly speculative reconstruction of data in Genesis 36:20–30 depends on omitting Hori as the encompassing eponymn for both leagues, entirely ignoring twelve names included in the genealogy, isolating the second six-tribe roster on the basis of a digression beginning at vs. 24b, and assuming Anah to have belonged simultaneously to two leagues, as Noth assumed in the case of Judah.

258. For details of Augustus's reorganization of amphictyonies, cf. F. Cauer, "Amphiktyonia," *PWRE,* vol. 1, 1894, col. 1932; E. A. Freeman, *History of Federal Government in Greece and Italy,* 2nd ed., 1893, pp. 105–108; J. A. O. Larsen, *Representative Government in Greek and Roman History,* 1955, p. 110–111; O.-W. von Vacano, *The Etruscans in the Ancient World,* 1960, p. 39.

259. V. Ehrenberg, *The Greek State,* 1960, p. 109.

260. An assessment of the social entities in the Keturah and Ishmaelite rosters, based on Arabian and Assyrian sources, suggests that they may be a conglomerate of tribes, cities or settlements, classes or professions, and kingdoms; cf. F. V. Winnett, "The Arabian

Genealogies in the Book of Genesis," *Translating and Understanding the Old Testament* (ed. H. Frank and W. Reed), 1970, pp. 188–196. Winnett dates the lists to the sixth century B.C.

261. M. Noth, *Das System,* pp. 85–86.

262. H. Ewald, *Geschichte des Volkes Israel,* I, 3rd ed., 1864, p. 531, cited by Noth, *Das System,* p. 86.

263. E. Szanto, "Die griechischen Phylen," in *Ausgewählte Abhandlungen von Emil Szanto* (SAWW, 144/5), ed. H. Swoboda, 1906, pp. 254–256, cited by Noth, *Das System,* p. 86.

264. H. Bürgel, *Die pyläisch-delphische Amphiktyonie,* 1877, p. 53, cited by Noth, *Das System,* p. 86.

265. Advocates of an Israelite amphictyony who have cited W. W. Hallo, "A Sumerian Amphictyony," *JCS* 14 (1960) 88–114, as support have been more bewitched by the title of Hallo's article than attentive to the actual findings of his painstaking study of texts from the Ur III Empire (c. 2000 B.C.) that describe the receipt and disbursement of supplies probably destined for the national shrines at Nippur. Hallo sums up his results as follows: "In any one year, the cities of the *bala* [a turn of office in periodic responsibility for delivering the supplies] were theoretically twelve, corresponding to the twelve months, though from year to year a different group might assume the monthly duties, and in a different order. A single *bala* could, however, be divided among two or more cities, if they were small or poor, and, on the other hand, a large and prosperous city might have two or more *bala*-months in a single year" (pp. 93, 96). When, however, Hallo goes on to say that, "with appropriate modifications" (unexplained), this is the same arrangement as in the Mediterranean amphictyonies such as that at Delphi, he cites F. Cauer, *PWRE,* vol. 1, 1894, cols. 1904–1935, a source utterly devoid of mention of a rota system as the possible basis of the size of membership in a Greek amphictyony. Hallo persuasively argues that, at least for a period in the Ur III Empire, the major shrines at Nippur were supported by various cities who delivered supplies on a calendric basis. He does *not,* however, demonstrate that the cities so named ever formed a membership of a fixed number, and certainly not twelve, in a religious league responsible for the upkeep of the shrines through a central council. In fact he shows that at least twenty-five different cities are mentioned in the texts as having had *bala* duties at one time or another (p. 92). Furthermore, although Hallo notes that the *bala* organization was a statist rather than an intertribal scheme, he does not emphasize that it was an organization imposed by Ur imperial policy and thus, if we are to draw analogies from the Greek amphictyonies, they should come from the later stages of the Delphic and Delian amphictyonies when political considerations overrode the older cultic arrangements. All in all, Hallo's claim that "the cities of the *bala* were theoretically twelve" has no foundation in the texts, for such a generalization goes far beyond the empirical situation he describes, i.e., that within a circle of at least twenty-five cities, assignments of supplies for the national shrines at Nippur were made in varying patterns from year to year, so that the shrines were adequately provisioned during all twelve months of the year. In my view that does not an amphictyony make.

266. Grady, *Epigraphic Sources of the Delphic Amphictyony,* chap. 3.

267. J. E. Cirlot, *A Dictionary of Symbols,* 1962, pp. 334–335; cf. remarks and bibliographical references in R. de Vaux, "La thèse de l' 'amphictyonie israélite,' " *HTR* 64 (1971) 422–423, notes 25–26.

268. B. D. Rahtjen, "Philistine and Hebrew Amphictyonies," *JNES* 24 (1965) 100–104.

269. M. Noth, *A History of Pentateuchal Traditions,* 1948, p. 100; cf. also H. Gunkel, *Genesis,* 4th ed., 1917, pp. 329–336, 382–383 and G. von Rad, *Genesis: A Commentary* (OTL), 1956 (Eng. trans. 1961), pp. 287–292, 334–337.

270. Commentators do not deal adequately with the contextual consonance or disso-

nance of the twelve pillars in Exodus 24:4. Noth, however, remarks: "Then the 'blood of the covenant' is sprinkled on the people, not on the twelve representative pillars, which no longer have a part to play" (*Exodus: A Commentary* [OTL], 1959 [Eng. trans. 1962], p. 198).

271. W. Fuss, "II Samuel 24," *ZAW* 74 (1962) 145–164; P. W. Skehan, "Joab's Census: How Far North? (II Sam. 24:6)," *CBQ* 31 (1969) 42–49; on the connection between census and plague, see E. A. Speiser, "Census and Ritual Expiation in Mari and Israel," *BASOR* 149 (1958) 17–25.

272. E. L. Curtis, *The Book of Chronicles* (ICC), 1910, pp. 289–292; W. A. L. Elmslie, *The Book of Chronicles* (CnB), 1916, pp. 153–156; W. Rudolph, *Chronikbücher* (HZAT), 1955, pp. 179–183.

273. Y. Yadin, *The Art of Warfare in Biblical Lands in the Light of Archaeology,* vol. 2, 1963, pp. 275–284.

274. E. L. Curtis, *Chronicles,* pp. 291–292; W. A. L. Elmslie, *Chronicles,* p. 155.

275. I agree with O. Eissfeldt, "Ein gescheiterter Versuch der Wiedervereinigung Israels (2 Sam. 2:12—3:1)," *KS,* III, 1966 (orig. pub. 1951), pp. 132–146, and with Y. Sukenik (Yadin), "Let the Young Men, I Pray Thee, Arise and Play Before Us," *JPOS* 21 (1948) 110–116, in asserting that the passage describes a representative battle of handpicked combatants which was "staged" to decide whether Ishbaal or David would rule over united Israel. From this conclusion, however, they leap too glibly to a harmonization of the twelve combatants with the assumed ancient structural twelvefoldness of the Israelite confederacy.

276. G. E. Wright, "The Provinces of Solomon (I Kings 4:7–19)," *EI* 8 (1967) 58*–68*, convincingly criticizes and supersedes the earlier standard works on Solomon's administrative districts by A. Alt, "Israels Gaue unter Salomo," *KS,* II, 1953 (orig. pub. 1913), pp. 76–89, and by W. F. Albright, "The Administrative Districts of Israel and Judah," *JPOS* 5 (1925) 17–54. T. N. D. Mettinger, *Solomonic State Officials* (CB, Old Testament Series, 5), 1971, pp. 112–121, steers a middle course between Alt's view that Solomon's reorganization adhered conservatively to the old tribal lines and Wright's view of "a radical shift . . . to administrative entities of approximately equal economic capacity" (p. 59). Mettinger plays down the economic factors in reorganization, mistakenly I think, but properly emphasizes political factors such as Solomon's vital interests in breaking up the powerful Joseph tribes.

277. For the argument that Israelite law was not "state law," see M. Noth, "The Laws in the Pentateuch: Their Assumptions and Meaning," *The Laws in the Pentateuch and Other Essays,* 1949 (Eng. trans. 1966), especially pp. 12–20.

278. A. Cody, *A History of Old Testament Priesthood* (AB, 35), 1969, pp. 87–107.

279. W. F. Albright, "The Judicial Reform of Jehoshaphat," *Alexander Marx Jubilee Volume,* 1950, pp. 61–82; W. Rudolph, *Chronikbücher* (HZAT), 1955, pp. 256–258. G. C. Macholz, "Zur Geschicte der Justizorganisation in Juda," *ZAW* 84 (1972) 314–340, concludes that Jehoshaphat's judicial reforms brought about a unitary, carefully interlocking "state" system of justice (II Chron. 19:5–10), possibly with an Egyptian model, on which the Deuteronomists based a further reform that tried to exclude the influence of the king.

280. A. Cody, *A History of Old Testament Priesthood,* p.111.

281. Topographical references and names of tribes speak for the northern provenance of Psalm 68, apparently originally as a cultic piece from the sanctuary on Mt. Tabor, which was given a Jerusalemite reworking; cf. S. Mowinckel, *Der achtundsechzigste Psalm,* 1953, and H.-J. Kraus, *Worship in Ancient Israel,* 2nd. ed., 1962 (Eng. trans. 1966), pp. 166–169.

282. R. Smend, *Yahweh War and Tribal Confederation,* 1963 (Eng. trans. 1970), especially pp. 13–25, who posits an early Israelite "amphictyonic will" expressed in sporadic intertri-

bal military actions that only found embodiment institutionally in the amphictyony proper toward the end of the period of the judges. In some respects similar to Smend's episodic "amphictyonic will" is T. Ishida, "The Leaders of the Tribal Leagues 'Israel' in the Premonarchic Period," *RB* 80 (1973) 514–530, who observes that "the name 'Israel' in the premonarchic time . . . simultaneously indicated the whole as well as a part of the tribal community" (p. 530). Instead of reading "lesser" Israel as a *pars pro toto* usage (i.e., the social whole being seen to inhere in the momentarily operative part), Ishida argues rather that a series of local and ephemeral tribal confederacies, each called "Israel," arose simultaneously or in succession. In so conceptualizing the matter, he does not account for the enduring identity in continuity implied by the single name Israel, nor does he explain how the unlinked "lesser Israels" stood in relation to the one "larger Israel." In fact, it is not clear whether Ishida is articulating the group consciousness and linguistic practice of the Israelites at the time of the judges or whether he is explicating later editorial manipulations in the tradition process, or some combination of those foci. Thus, while there are several cogent points in his treatment, such as the suggestion that "to judge Israel" meant "to muster or to organize Israel for war," Ishida's notion of multiple discrete confederate Israels is not so much a sociopolitical hypothesis as it is a roundabout way of starkly posing the problem of the diffuseness of Israelite organizational cohesion and identity.

283. A. D. H. Mayes, *Israel in the Period of the Judges* (SBT, Second Series, 29), 1974, pp. 84–109.

284. F. Cauer, "Amphiktyonia," *PWRE*, vol. 1, 1894, cols. 1932–1935, surveyed a host of hypotheses about the origin of the Pylaean phase of the Pylaean-Delphic amphictyony, including the view that the organization was the original matrix of Hellenic consciousness, but found them all untenable conjectures for want of reliable information about that early period of Greek history. If fuller historical information is now available, it appears that no one in classical studies has yet applied it to the problem of the origins of the oldest amphictyonies. V. Ehrenberg, *The Greek State*, 1960, in the context of noting economic factors in the formation of amphictyonies (e.g., the prominence of maritime states in the Poseidon-worshipping amphictyonies of Onchestus, Calauria, and Cape Mycale, probably as a means of checking piracy), observes that "we can hardly understand the Amphictyony of Pylae, except by assuming that it was also concerned with the freedom of the pass, which, for political as well as economic reasons, might affect its members" (p. 110). R. G. Boling's hypothesis that the seventh-sixth century B.C. form of the Thessalian League is an apt analogy for early Israelite socioreligious organization is inadequately argued (in *Judges. Introduction, Translation, and Commentary* [The Anchor Bible], 1975, pp. 20–23). The senses in which the Thessalian League was "predecessor" and "nucleus" of the Pylaean-Delphic amphictyony are by no means characteristic of the relation between Israel as a sociopolitical formation and Israel as a religious association. Thessaly was in fact a quasi-feudal territorial state which subjugated, taxed, and conscripted the older populace and which from about 600 B.C. intruded into the already existing amphictyonies of Anthela/Pylae and Delphi in regions of Locris and Phocis situated well beyond the boundaries of Thessaly. Furthermore, the Thessalians linked the two sanctuaries and their festivals to Demeter and Apollo into a single amphictyonic organization and arranged to control the majority of votes on the amphictyonic council through manipulation of their vassals and allies. Boling fails to offer a history of the social, political, military, and religious forms of the Israelite "amphictyony" in order to validate an Israelite analogy to the Thessalian domination of the Pylaean-Delphic amphictyony based on feudal and imperial hegemonies. If anything, the clear distinction between the older Thessalian military-political organization and the subsequent Thessalian

intrusion into the amphictyonic structures appears to be more congruent with R. Smend's view that in Israel the military organization and the amphictyonic organization developed along entirely separate lines that conjoined only at a relatively late premonarchic date. Even at that, the feudal and imperial elements in Thessaly's career find no counterparts in Smend's reconstruction of early Israel. Boling, however, seems to think of the Thessalian sociopolitical and religious-amphictyonic developments as relatively homogeneous and thus a rebuttal of Smend's hypothesis (cf. *Judges*, p. 21, note 29). Methodologically, the one merit in Boling's proposal is that at last a biblical scholar has widened the comparative Greek data to include political-military as well as religious associations. Unfortunately, his attempted analogy between the Thessalian League and the Israelite "amphictyony" is unsustained either in micro- or macrosociological terms. For details of the Thessalian League, see M. Cary, *CAH*, vol. 3, reprinted with corrections, 1929, pp. 598–606, and more fully, J. A. O. Larsen, *Greek Federal States: Their Institutions and History*, 1968, pp. 12–26.

285. J. A. O. Larsen, *Representative Government in Greek and Roman History*, 1955, chap. 2; *Greek Federal States*, 1968, part I, chap. 1.

286. Noth's comprehensive cross-cultural vision and methodological clarity account for the extraordinary tenacity of his amphictyony theory. By comparison, his critics have tended to look parochial and methodologically feeble. Even though they have convincingly rebutted, or at least thrown grave doubt on, Noth's reasoning at point after point, they have failed to propose a comprehensive alternative model of early Israelite society and in fact have shown little interest in societal models, either structural-functional or comparative. This situation is well illustrated by the widely cited anti-amphictyony studies of H. Orlinsky, "The Tribal System of Israel and Related Groups in the Period of the Judges," *OA* 1 (1962) 11–20 =*Studies and Essays in Honor of A. Neuman*, 1962, pp. 375–387, and of G. Fohrer, "Altes Testament—'Amphiktyonie' und 'Bund'?," *TLZ* 91 (1966), cols. 801–816, 893–904. Among the many critics of the amphictyonic scheme, it seems to me that only R. Smend, "Zur Frage der altisraelitischen Amphiktyonie," *EvT* 31 (1971) 623–630, has shown suffi-cient sensitivity to the necessity of formulating an alternative all-Israelite socioreligious design if the amphictyonic model is rejected as improbable. Because he cannot think of an explanatory alternative (except to show holy war and amphictyony as two separately developing institutions, the former older than the latter, which only merged shortly before the rise of the monarchy, cf. *Yahweh War and Tribal Confederation*, 1963 [Eng. trans. 1970]), Smend still adheres cautiously to the amphictyonic model, remarking: "[the thesis of an old Israelite amphictyony] furnishes the most important historical contribution toward an answer to the question of why precisely this Israel was the people of Yahweh, and that in itself is no inconsequential fact" (p. 630). See also the brief update of the discussion in M. C. Astour, "Amphictyony," IDBSV, 1976, pp. 23–25.

287. Indicative of the value of macrosociological control on cross-cultural analysis is the brief but highly penetrating treatment of Greece and Israel as "two seed-bed societies" by T. Parsons, *Societies: Evolutionary and Comparative Perspectives*, 1966, pp. 95–109. Although lacking the literary and historical tools of Noth or of a classical scholar, Parsons skillfully subjects the results of biblical and classical scholarship in broad outline to structural-functional and diachronic-developmental analyses that permit the identification of cross-cultural similarity and differentiation without getting locked into simple either/or choices on single cultural items of the sort that have bedeviled the debate in biblical scholarship over the presence or absence of an Israelite "amphictyony."

NOTES TO PART VIII

288. J. A. Knudtzon, *Die El-Amarna-Tafeln* (with commentary by O. Weber and glossary by E. Ebeling), 2 vols., 1907/1915 (reprinted 1964); A. F. Rainey, *El Amarna Tablets* 359–379, 1970; 2nd ed. rev., 1978.

289. C. F. A. Schaeffer, *Le Palais Royal d'Ugarit*, 5 vols., 1955–1965; A. F. Rainey, "The Social Stratification of Ugarit" (Ph.D. thesis, Brandeis University, 1962); A. F. Rainey, "Family Relationships in Ugarit," *Or* 34 (1965) 10–22, J. Gray, "Feudalism in Ugarit and Early Israel," *ZAW* 64 (1952) 49–55; C. C. Libolt, "The *mudû sarris/sarrati* Texts from Ugarit: An Aspect of Social Structure and Social Process in Ancient Agrarian Society" (Paper presented to the Social World of Ancient Israel Group at the annual meeting of AAR-SBL, San Francisco, December 30, 1977).

290. D. J. Wiseman, *The Alalakh Tablets* (Occasional Publications of the British Institute of Archaeology at Ankara, 2), 1953, and additional texts in *JCS* 8 (1954) 1–30; 12 (1958) 124–129; 13 (1959) 19–33, 50–62. Also, notes on the last two sets of texts by A. Goetze, *JCS* 13 (1959) 34–38, 63–64.

291. *ANET*, 18–22; Y. Aharoni, *The Land of the Bible: A Historical Geography*, 1962 (Eng. trans. 1967), pp. 130–131.

292. *ANET*, 328–329; Aharoni, *The Land of the Bible*, pp. 131–134.

293. J. Prawar and S. N. Eisenstadt, "Feudalism," *IESS*, vol. 3, 1969, pp. 393–403; see also essays on feudalism in ancient Mesopotamia by B. C. Brundage and in ancient Egypt by W. F. Edgerton in *Feudalism in History* (ed. R. Coulborn), 1956, pp. 93–132. See qualifications and reservations on the use of a "feudal" analysis for Canaan in note 299 below.

294. G. R. H. Wright, "Tell el-Yēhudīyah and the Glacis," *ZDPV* 84 (1968) 1–17; P. J. Parr, "The Origin of the Rampart Fortifications of Middle Bronze Age Palestine and Syria," *ZDPV* 84 (1968) 18–45.

295. On the conciliar principle of political organization in the ancient Near East, rather misleadingly dubbed "primitive democracy," see, with respect to Syria-Palestine: J. A. Wilson, "The Assembly of a Phoenician City," *JNES* 4 (1945) 245; H. Reviv, "On Urban Representative Institutions and Self-Government in Syria-Palestine in the Second Half of the Second Millennium B.C.," *JESHO* 12 (1969) 283–297, and with respect to Mesopotamia: T. Jacobsen, "Primitive Democracy in Ancient Mesopotamia," *JNES* 2 (1943) 159–172, and "Early Political Development in Mesopotamia," *ZA* 18 (1957) 91–140; G. Evans, "Ancient Mesopotamian Assemblies," *JAOS* 78 (1958) 1–11; A. L. Oppenheim, "A New Look at the Structure of Mesopotamian Society," *JESHO* 19 (1967) 1–16. I. M. Diakonoff in *Ancient Mesopotamia: Socio-Economic History*, 1969 (article orig. pub. 1957), pp. 182–185, 187–188, 191–193, 200–202, has wisely cautioned in the case of the Mesopotamian Council of Elders and Assembly of Citizens (also the City Ward Assembly) that these institutions should not be simplistically read as broadly democratic, either in their social composition or in the class interests they advocated. Diakonoff claims that the council was the aristocratic organ of an oligarchic ruling class that more or less moderated royal leadership. The councils grew weaker over time, by the reign of Hammurabi serving merely as organs of local administration. On the other hand, the assembly of citizens represented a wider body of freemen sometimes employed by the king as leverage against the more aristocratic interests of the council of elders, who tended to threaten royal dominance of the state. The council in turn struggled to control the popular assembly for its own interests. The kings were able to consolidate their power by using the assemblies against the councils, but, once they were entrenched, kings delivered few benefits to the full body of free citizens, preferring rather

to draw closer once again to the aristocratic elements with whom they worked out mutually supportive alliances. The kings neutralized conciliar oligarchic political power while assuring the basic socioeconomic gains of the upper class under a state-centered mercantile policy, and at the same time they encouraged limited assembly-based "democratic" political power that signally failed to secure socioeconomic protection for weaker and poorer sectors of the free citizenry whose interests were repeatedly sacrificed to mercantile and big land-owning interests. In short," . . . the establishment of the new power [centralized monarchic rule] proved in fact to be beneficial to only quite a small part of the commoners—to those who got promoted in the army or the administration, or to those who were connected with trade, . . . " (pp. 192–193). Accordingly, judgments about the survival of forms of self-government in Palestine during the Amarna period must be based on a diachronic and dialectical social-structural analysis of Syro-Palestine before these nonroyal political organs can be seen as major limitations on monarchic or oligarchic rule, in the rather too facile manner, for example, of H. Reviv in *JESHO* 12 (1969) 283–297.

296. W. F. Albright, "Mitannian Maryannu, 'Chariot Warrior,' and the Canaanite and Egyptian Equivalents," *AFO* 6 (1930/31) 217–221; R. T. O'Callaghan, *Aram Naharaim: A Contribution to the History of Upper Mesopotamia in the Second Millennium B.C.*, 1948, pp. 64–68; W. Helck, *Der Einfluss der Militärführer in der 18. ägyptischen Dynastie* (Untersuchungen zur Geschichte und Altertumskunde Ägyptens, 14), 1939; and *Die Beziehungen Ägyptens zu Vorderasien im 3. und 2. Jahrtausend v. Chr.* (AAb, 5), 1962, pp. 515–526. H. Reviv, "Some Comments on the Maryannu," *IEJ* 22 (1972) 218–228, traces an increasing disintegration of the cohesiveness of the old *maryannu* military aristocracy during the period 1500–1200 B.C. Dynasts, fearful of a concentration of power in the hands of a military caste, began to appoint *maryannu* aristocrats to civilian posts and to draw lower-class elements into the charioteer ranks, a move that tended to sever military performance from the independent wealth formerly necessary to provide and maintain military equipment. M. Heltzer, "Problems of the Social History of Syria in the Late Bronze Age," *La Siria nel Tardo Bronzo* (ed. M. Liverani), 1969, p. 42, adamantly rejects the prevailing view that the *maryannu* were "a privileged aristocratic class of the population in the states of Syria, Palestine and Mitanni in the Late Bronze Age." He insists that in Ugarit *maryannu* owed service duties to the king like all the other royal servants, lived on royal land on conditional holding, and received all their arms and equipment from royal stores. Since Heltzer concedes that royal institutions were probably more highly centralized in Ugarit than elsewhere in Syria, it is not clear how far he would generalize his results about the *maryannu* beyond Ugarit. He rests the problem with the judgment that "a complete reexamination of the *maryannu*-question is urgent" (p. 45).

297. W. Helck, *Die Beziehungen Ägyptens zu Vorderasien*, 1962, pp. 92–108; P. Labib, *Die Herrschaft der Hyksos in Ägypten und ihr Sturz*, 1936; R. Engberg, *The Hyksos Reconsidered*, 1939; J. Van Seters, *The Hyksos: A New Investigation*, 1966; D. B. Redford, "The Hyksos Invasion in History and Tradition," *Or* 39 (1970) 1–51.

298. For a lucid account of Syria-Palestine as a cultural link in the ancient Near East, early sea trade in the region, and the role of chariotry in the age of international relations, see W. S. Smith, *Interconnections in the Ancient Near East: A Study of the Relations Between the Arts of Egypt, the Aegean, and Western Asia,* 1965, pp. 3–37.

299. A vigorous debate among Soviet Assyriologists as to whether the ancient Near East was a feudal society or a slave society has been largely resolved in favor of the latter since the work of V.V. Struve in 1933 (printed in abridged form in I. M. Diakonoff, ed., *Ancient Mesopotamia: Socio-Economic History,* 1969, pp. 17–70). Diakonoff correctly points out, however, that much of the disagreement over "ancient oriental feudalism" has to do with different criteria of feudalism, whether "referring to a socio-economic structure based on

the exploitation of peasants personally dependent on their lord but owning the means of production" or to "a state with a hierarchic structure" *(Ancient Mesopotamia,* p. 202, note 17). If the looser political sense of feudalism is invoked (analogous to S. N. Eisenstadt's "centralized bureaucratic empire"; cf. *The Political Systems of Empires,* 1963 [reprint with new preface 1969]), there can be little doubt that Syro-Palestine was "feudal" in the Amarna Age. If the more technical socioeconomic sense of feudalism is employed, however, the crucial socioeconomic data are much sketchier than we should like, leading to rather different conceptions, for example, of the status of Canaanite peasants, whether as medieval European-type "serfs" or as Roman-like "coloni" (cf. discussion in text under VIII.41.3 and notes 405 through 408). It may be that a more appropriate model than feudalism for understanding pre-Israelite Canaanite society is Marx's analytic concept of "the Asiatic mode of production" as refined and nuanced by recent ethnological and early historical data (see, e.g., E. Mandel, "The Asiatic Mode of Production and the Historical Pre-Conditions for the Rise of Capital," in *The Formation of the Economic Thought of Karl Marx,* 1971, pp. 116–139). I have made some very provisional suggestions as to how this model might apply to ancient Canaan in "Early Israel and 'the Asiatic Mode of Production' in Canaan," *Society of Biblical Literature Seminar Papers,* 1976, pp. 145–154, but my probes of the concept's applicability to Canaan are not yet sufficiently developed or tested to justify complete discard of the admittedly nebulous notion of Canaanite "feudalism."

300. N. K. Gottwald, *All the Kingdoms of the Earth: Israelite Prophecy and International Relations in the Ancient Near East,* 1964, pp. 12–18; G. Steindorff and K. C. Seele, *When Egypt Ruled the East,* 2nd ed., 1956, especially chaps. 3 and 10.

301. M. B. Rowton, "The Topological Factor in the *Ḫapiru* Problem," *Studies in Honor of Benno Landsberger* (Assyriological Studies of the Oriental Institute of the University of Chicago, 16), 1965, pp. 375–387.

302. The above typology of Egyptian imperial and Canaanite feudal sociopolitical symbiosis is particularly indebted to M. A. K. Mohammad, "The Administration of Syro-Palestine during the New Kingdom," *Annales du Service des Antiquités de l'Égypte* [Cairo] 56 (1959) 105–137, and to W. Helck, *Die Beziehungen Ägyptens zu Vorderasien,* 1962, pp. 256–257, 515–535. D. Lorton, *The Juridical Terminology of International Relations in Egyptian Texts through Dynasty XVIII,* 1975, isolates technical juridical terminology from Amarna letters and royal inscriptions of the New Kingdom in order to illuminate the Egyptian view of international law. A pertinent comparative analytic study is S. N. Eisenstadt, *The Political Systems of Empires,* 1963 (reprint with new preface 1969), who reports and synthesizes the results of an ambitious team research project in which pre-modern centralized bureaucratic empires were studied in an effort to identify their basic characteristics as a system type and the social conditions conducive to their development, continuity, and decline. Eisenstadt includes the ancient Egyptian empire in his inventory of empires for which he collects data, the others being: Incas; Aztecs; Hellenistic, Roman, and Byzantine Empires; Persia; China and India: Abbasside, Fatimite, and Ottoman Empires; and European absolutist states. The volume is awash with bibliography and brimming with highly compact codified information to support structural and developmental propositions about bureaucratic empires. Eisenstadt's study is of little use for direct historical study of a particular empire, but of great analytic value in proposing the fundamental socioeconomic, political, and ideological conjunctions that tend to occur in such empires. As such, Eisenstadt's work is suggestive of heuristic perspectives and research strategies appropriate to discerning the bureaucratic imperial system of ancient Egyptian dominion over Canaan.

303. M. W. Several, "Reconsidering the Egyptian Empire in Palestine during the Amarna Period," *PEQ* 104 (1972) 123–133, contends that the Amarna letters do not

document Egyptian imperial decline but rather point up certain abiding imperial problems: inter-city conflict; 'apiru disturbances; disruptions of trade and communication; disregard of imperial orders; bureaucratic incompetence and corruption. Precisely these same problems had existed earlier and continued thereafter. The fuller Amarna references to disruption of trade result from better organization and regularization of trade to replace previous dependence on raids for booty. The Amarna letters give an unrepresentative picture of disorder since normal conditions are less fully reported. As a whole, there is a stable and secure Amarna political environment and a rich material culture, divide-and-conquer tactics work well, Egyptian rule possesses a high degree of legitimacy (its orders were generally followed), envoys are able to deliver diplomatic letters, vassal duties are usually carried out, there is a strong expectation that Egypt will comply with requests for help, and there are fewer destructions of cities in this period than before or after (he does not adequately document this claim). Marvin Chaney points out that the conditions of declining Egyptian rule in Canaan about 1100 B.C. are treated by H. Goedicke, *The Report of Wenamun,* 1975.

Several allows, however, that while the *content* of the Amarna letters does not demonstrate a declining Egyptian empire, the greater *infrequency* of letters from Palestinian vassals (compared with Syrian vassals) in the latter part of the Amarna age may attest Egyptian imperial decline.

At times Several seems to argue toward opposite conclusions from the same data (did trade decline or not?), and he fails adequately to evaluate the total impact over time of the accumulating problems that he treats separately. Nevertheless, I found his approach of value since it challenges accepted conclusions and demands re-evaluation of the evidence. The cautious case I make for a progressive structural weakening of imperialism and feudalism in Canaan is not undermined by Several's overstated broadside, since it is precisely the sort of caveats he tends to exaggerate that I have tried to take into account in describing a very long trajectory of decline over at least two centuries.

304. G. E. Mendenhall, "The Message of Abdi-Ashirta to the Warriors," *JNES* 6 (1947) 123–124. The references to the El Amarna letters hereafter (e.g., EA 74) follow the numbering system of Knudtzon and Rainey in their authoritative editions listed in note 288.

305. I do not share the assurance of P. Artzi, " 'Vox Populi' in the el-Amarna Tablets," *RAAO* 58 (1964) 159–166, that Abdi-Ashirta's speech is straight-out evidence for a full-bodied anti-feudal movement; cf. also M. Liverani, "Implicazioni sociali nella politica di Abdi-Ashirta di Amurru," *RSO* 40 (1965) 367–377.

306. There are considerable variations in the way scholars transliterate the names of the Amarna rulers. I have chosen to follow the transliterations of M. Greenberg, while noting here some of the more common variants: *Abdi-Ashirta* = Abdu-Ashirta = 'Abdu-Ashirta; *ÈR-Ḫeba* = Abdi-Heba = Abdi-Hepa = 'Abdu-Ḫeba = 'Abdu-Ḫepa; *Labaya* = Lab'aya = Lab'ayu; *Rib-addi* = Rib-adda; *Tagi* = Tagu.

307. *ANET,* 529.

308. W. Helck, *Die Beziehungen Ägyptens zu Vorderasien,* pp. 519–520.

309. E. A. Campbell, Jr., "The Amarna Letters and the Amarna Period," *BAR* 3 (1970) 68 = *BA* 23 (1960) 16; H. Klengel, "Aziru von Amurru und seine Rolle in der Geshichte der Amarnazeit," *MIO* 19 (1964) 65–75.

310. See the review and summary of evidence for the linguistic equation *'apiru* = Hebrew(s) in M. Weippert, *The Settlement of the Israelite Tribes* (SBT, Second Series, 21), 1967 (Eng. trans. 1971), pp. 74–82.

311. Cf. the assembled texts on the *'apiru* in translation in J. Bottéro, *Le problème des*

Ḥabiru a la 4e Recontre Assyriologique Internationale (Cahiers de la Société Asiatique, 12), 1954, and in M. Greenberg, *The Ḥab/piru* (AOS, 39), 1955. For summaries and interpretation of the data, see T. J. Meek, *Hebrew Origins*, rev. ed., 1950, pp. 18–48, and M. P. Gray, "The Hâbirū-Hebrew Problem," *HUCA* 29 (1958) 135–202, and for more up-to-date reflections, R. de Vaux, "Le problème des Ḥapiru après quinze années," *JNES* 27 (1968) 221–228, and *Histoire ancienne d'Israël: Des Origines à l'Installation en Canaan*, 1971, pp. 106–112, 202–208. De Vaux's personal conclusion that *'apiru* was, after all, an ethnic designation is scarcely any longer tenable.

312. Possibly a more accurate way of making this point is to say that fundamental economic tendencies in the ancient Near East toward the pauperization of many social sectors led to the peculiar sociopolitical status of *'apiru* as one among several responses to pauperization, including the more vulnerable fates of debt servitude and slavery. N. B. Jankowska, "Extended Family Commune and Civil Self-Government in Arrapḫa in the Fifteenth-Fourteenth Centuries B.C.," *Ancient Mesopotamia* (ed. I. M. Diakonoff), 1969 (Eng. summary of papers orig. pub. 1957–1960), pp. 235–252, links the rise of the *'apiru* as a supplementary labor force at Nuzi to the decline of the economic function of the extended family in the face of the upsurge of specialized production (e.g., fruits and vegetables in agriculture and handicrafts for trade). She concludes " . . . while the 'in-kind' economy predominated, the process of separation of individual households from the family commune was invariably accompanied by growth of credit-and-loan relations. . . . a characteristic feature attesting to an irrevocable disintegration of the earlier ownership conditions: the creditor's rights were recognized by the state as prevailing over the claims of heirs by kin. . . . All known archives in the Near East of the second millennium B.C. provide information on economical shifts of status in the population and on redistribution of ownership rights to real estate, particularly on the loss of property by a high percentage of community members; in our opinion it was this process that gave rise to the multi-tribal crowd of outlaw wanderers from the settled regions . . . [*'apiru*] . . . who got hired as soldiers, were employed by the large estates, got settled on state land, or simply lived by robbery" (pp. 248, 251). Jankowska's account of the *'apiru* at Nuzi should be read in the context of the wide-ranging reconstruction of socioeconomic history in Mesopotamia by V. V. Struve, "The Problem of the Genesis, Development and Disintegration of the Slave Societies in the Ancient Orient," *Ancient Mesopotamia* (ed. I. M. Diakonoff), 1969 (abridgment of article orig. pub. 1933), pp. 17–70, and I. M. Diakonoff, "The Rise of the Despotic State in Ancient Mesopotamia," ibid., 1969 (orig. pub. 1957), pp. 173–203. The above-translated anthology of work by Soviet Assyriologists deliberately omitted any of their contributions to the socioeconomic history of Syria and Palestine; some of the latter is available, however, in *World History* (Academy of Science of the USSR), vol. 1, 1955 (Russ. orig. with subsequent German trans.). Also of interest is the work of the East German scholar B. Brentjes, "Zur socialen Funktion der Kultur im alten Orient unter Berücksichtigung der Lehre W. I. Lenins über die 'Zwei Kulturen,' " *WZMLU* 20 (1971) 29–59.

313. D. J. Wiseman, *The Alalakh Tablets*, 1953, pp. 12, 71–72.

314. *ANET*, 247; Helck, *Die Beziehungen Ägyptens zu Vorderasien*, pp. 528–533.

315. It is now virtually universally agreed that the Sumerian ideogram SA.GAZ (or GAZ) is coextensive and interchangeable with the Akkadian *'apiru*. M. Greenberg, *The Ḥab/piru*, 1955, pp. 88–90, suggests that SA.GAZ was a "pseudo-ideogram" for Akkadian *ṣāggāšu*, influenced by the connotations of West Semitic *šgš*, with the meaning of "disturber" or "one who is restive."

316. EA 87:20–24, as translated by M. Greenberg, *Ḥab/piru*, p. 37.

317. EA 197:2–5, 7–12, 26–34, as translated by M. Greenberg, *Hab/piru*, pp. 43–44.

318. AT = Alalakh Tablet, with numbers supplied according to the enumeration in the official publication of D. J. Wiseman, *The Alalakh Tablets*, 1953, pp. 11–12, 71–72, 79.

319. EA 286:18–20, as translated by Greenberg, *Hab/piru*, p. 47.

320. EA 271:13–21, as translated by Greenberg, *Hab/piru*, p. 46

321. EA 288:43–44, as translated by Greenberg, *Hab/piru*, p. 48.

322. EA 287:29–31, as translated by Greenberg, *Hab/piru*, p. 48.

323. EA 289:5–8, as translated by Greenberg, *Hab/piru*, p. 48.

324. Greenberg, *Hab/piru*, p. 48.

325. *ANET*, 255; W. F. Albright, "The Smaller Beth-shan Stele of Sethos I (1309–1290 B.C.)," *BASOR* 125 (1952) 24–32, and Y. Aharoni, *The Land of the Bible: A Historical Geography*, 1962 (Eng. trans. 1967), pp. 168–169.

326. G. E. Mendenhall, "The Hebrew Conquest of Palestine," *BAR* 3 (1970) 105–107 = *BA* 25 (1962) 71–73, and *The Tenth Generation: The Origins of the Biblical Tradition*, 1973, chap. 5. Mendenhall's sketchy characterization of "withdrawal" from Canaanite society needs to be filled out more discriminatingly by data and categories of the sort initially explored by M. B. Rowton in his analysis of ancient Near Eastern "dimorphic society," under the title of "The Physical Environment and the Problem of the Nomads," *La civilisation de Mari* (ed. J. R. Kupper), 1967, pp. 110–121.

327. E. Hobsbawm, *Bandits*, 1969, first pointed out to me by Marvin L. Chaney.

328. W. F. Albright, "Syria, the Philistines and Phoenicia," *CAH*, rev. ed., 1966, fascicle 51; A. Alt, "Ägyptische Tempel in Palästina und die Landnahme der Philister," *KS*, I, 1953 (orig. pub. 1944), pp. 216–230; J. Bérard, "Philistins et Prehellenes," *RA* 37 (1951) 129–142; G. Bonfante, "Who Were the Philistines?" *AJA* 50 (1946) 251–262; T. Dothan, "Archaeological Reflections on the Philistine Problem," *AS* 2 (1957) 151–164; T. Dothan, *The Philistines and Their Material Culture*, 1967 (Heb. with Eng. summary); R. Hestrin, *The Philistines and Other Sea Peoples* (Israel Museum exhibition catalogue, Heb.-Eng.), 1970; B. Mazar, "The Philistines and the Rise of Israel and Tyre," *Proceedings of the Israel Academy of Sciences* I.7 (1964), pp. 1–15; B. Mazar, "The Philistines and Their Wars with Israel," *WHJP*, 1st series, vol. 3, 1971, pp. 164–179; J. B. Pritchard, "New Evidence on the Role of the Sea Peoples," *The Role of the Phoenicians in the Interaction of Mediterranean Civilizations* (ed. W. A. Ward), 1968, pp. 99–112; G. A. Wainwright, "Caphtor-Cappadocia," *VT* 6 (1956) 199–210; G. A. Wainwright, "Some Early Philistine History," *VT* 9 (1959) 73–84; F. Willesen, "The Philistine Corps of the Scimitar from Gath," *JSS* 3 (1958) 327–335; G. E. Wright, "Philistine Coffins and Mercenaries," *BA* 22 (1959) 53–66; G. E. Wright, " Fresh Evidence for the Philistine Story," *BA* 29 (1966) 70–86.

329. A. Alt, "Ägyptische Tempel in Palästina und die Landnahme der Philister," *KS*, I, 1953 (orig. pub. 1944), p. 228.

330. There is now a strong inclination to locate Ekron at Khirbet el-Muqanna'. A surface survey of potsherds at the site favors the identification, but no excavation has been undertaken, cf. J. Naveh, "Khirbet el-Muqanna'—Ekron," *IEJ* 8 (1958) 87–100, 165–170. For Gath, a succession of sites has been proposed: Tell Sheikh el-'Areini, Tell en-Nejileh, Tell el-Ḥesi, and Tell es-Ṣafi. Occupational and pottery evidence from excavations at the first three sites militates against the identification of Gath with any of them, and the last-named site has yet to be excavated. It is also possible that some of the biblical references to Gath are to another city altogether, as has been argued by B. Mazar, "Gath and Gittaim," *IEJ* 4 (1954) 227–235, but rebutted by H. Kassis (see note 332).

331. On the derivation of *seren/sārān* (?) from Greek *tyrannos,* a Lydian, Phrygian, or Etruscan loan word, cf. H. E. Kassis, *JBL* 84 (1965) 264, nt. 36, and F. Bork, *AFO* 13 (1940)

338; see also entry on *tyrannos* in H. G. Liddell and R. Scott, *A Greek-English Lexicon*, rev. ed., 1940, p. 1836. For the evidence that Philistines and Etruscans were closely related culturally, cf. H. Hencken, *Tarquinia, Villanovans and Early Etruscans,* 1968, p. 146.

332. H. E. Kassis, "Gath and the Structure of the 'Philistine' Society," *JBL* 84 (1965) 259–271.

333. Ibid., p. 268, note 53.

334. For summations on Philistine arms and military organization, cf. Y. Margowsky, "War and Warfare," *EJ*, vol. 16, 1971, col. 271, and Y. Yadin, *The Art of Warfare in Biblical Lands,* vol. 2, 1963, pp. 248–253, 336–345, 354–355; see also titles listed in note 328.

335. The sources I have consulted are not entirely consistent as to the reasons for the technical difficulties in working iron. They cite a number of factors: high or constantly maintained temperature for melting or smelting (the two processes require very different temperatures), adequate draft by bellows, proper amount of carbon to combine with the iron, flux to facilitate smelting, heavy tools to separate out slag from the mass of iron, correct reheating and quenching of the iron in order to harden it, etc. T. T. Read, "Metallurgical Fallacies in Archaeological Literature," *AJA* 38 (1934) 382–389, gives the clearest description for novices, summarizing as follows: ". . . the production of iron from its ores is easy and must have been accomplished very early, but the production of iron of *usable quality* from ores is quite difficult and was not accomplished until long after the art of producing copper and copper alloys was well developed . . . The history of iron is the story of the continuous endeavor of metallurgists to attain a practical mastery over the carbon content of the iron, without knowing that it contained any carbon, or what the effects of carbon are. This concise attempt to explain them is somewhat confusing, because of the simultaneous effect of carbon content, produced by heating, and of hardening, produced by heating and chilling. It is easy to imagine how difficult it must have been to learn how to do it through experiment without understanding the factors in the process, . . . " (p. 387). R. J. Forbes sums up the peculiar challenge of iron-working by stressing the necessity for a happy conjunction of complex technical processes: "The Iron Age is a new metallurgical stage, a technical world of its own. In the Copper Age the stress lies on the *composition* of alloy (or impurities in the metal) but in the Iron Age the properties of the iron are much less determined by its carbon content or accidental or natural impurities, but far more by its *handling*, by the temperature at which it has been heated, by the way and speed of quenching, the time and temperature of tempering or annealing. It is the true age of the smith!" (*Studies in Ancient Technology*, vol. 8, 1964, p. 136; also by Forbes: *Studies in Ancient Technology*, vol. 9, 1964, pp. 175–276; "The Coming of Iron," *Ex Oriente Lux* 9 [1944] 6–14; and *Metallurgy in Antiquity: A Notebook for Archaeologists and Technologists,* 1950. The latter work is reviewed, with enriching bibliographical references and observations, by R. North, "Metallurgy in the Ancient Near East," *Or* 24 [1953] 78–88.) Other works of merit: O. Johannsen, *Geschichte des Eisens*, 3rd ed., 1953; H. Maryon, "Metal Working in the Ancient World," *AJA* 53 (1949) 93–125 (mainly on metal bowls); M. Narkiss, *Metal Crafts in Ancient Palestine,* 1937, pp. 113–125; A. W. Persson, *Eisen und Eisenarbeitung in ältester Zeit,* 1933; T. A. Rickard, "The Primitive Smelting of Iron," *AJA* 43 (1939) 85–101; U. S. Würzburger, "Metals and Mining: Iron," *EJ,* vol. 11, 1971, cols. 1432–1433.

336. Y. Margowsky, "War and Warfare," *EJ,* vol. 16, 1971, cols. 268–269; Y. Yadin, "Chariotry," *EM,* vol. 5, 1968, cols. 462–472 (Heb.); Y. Yadin, "Warfare in the Second Millennium B.C.E.," *WHJP,* 1st series, vol. 2, 1970, pp. 127–159. On the composite bow in particular: W. F. Albright and G. E. Mendenhall, "The Creation of the Composite Bow in Canaanite Mythology," *JNES* 1 (1942) 227–229; Y. Yadin (Sukenik), "The Composite Bow of the Canaanite Goddess Anath," *BASOR* 107 (1947) 11–15.

337. M. B. Rowton, *Studies in Honor of B. Landsberger,* 1965, p. 382.

338. B. Mazar in *WHJP,* 1st series, vol. 3, 1971, pp. 174–175.

339. The excavators of Gibeah (Tell el-Fûl) in 1922–23 and 1933 (W. F. Albright, *AASOR* 4 [1924] 1–160; *BASOR* 52 [1933] 6–12) and in 1964 (P. W. Lapp, *BA* 28 [1965] 2–10) believed that Saul himself built the fortified structure. However, A. Alt, *PJ* 30 (1934) 8–9; *KS*, II, p. 31; III, p. 259, B. Mazar, *EM*, vol. 2, 1954, cols. 412–416 (Heb.), and L.A. Sinclair, *BA* 27 (1964) 52–64, were of the opinion that the Philistines first fortified the site and that Saul made re-use of their fort after driving out the Philistines. The direct archaeological evidence is inconclusive in settling this difference of historical judgment.

340. J. Bright, *A History of Israel,* 2nd ed., 1972, p. 180; W. F. Albright, "Syria, the Philistines and Phoenicia," *CAH,* rev. ed., 1966, p. 32, remarks: "The conquest of Israel by the Philistines about the middle of the 11th century was perhaps dictated mainly by the increasing need of protection for caravans from the desert." In this connection, the close temporal association of the Philistine and Ammonite attacks on Israel (emphasized by M. Noth, *The History of Israel,* pp. 164–178), may well indicate that Philistia and Ammon had converging trading interests, if not an actual alliance, which prompted them to go to war against Israel and perhaps even to collaborate strategically and tactically.

341. A. Alt, "The Formation of the Israelite State," *EOTHR,* 1966 (orig. pub. 1930), p. 235.

342. On Shamgar ben Anath as a non-Semitic name, with varying views as to whether he was an Israelite and concerning his historical locus, see: W. F. Albright, "A Revision of Early Hebrew Chronology," *JPOS* 1 (1921) 55–62; E. Danelius, "Shamgar Ben 'Anath," *JNES* 22 (1963) 191–193; F. C. Fensham, "Shamgar ben 'Anath," *JNES* 20 (1961) 197–198; B. Mazar (Maisler), "Shamgar ben 'Anath," *PEQ* (1934) 192–194; M. Noth, *Die israelitischen Personennamen,* 1928, pp. 122–123; A. van Selms, "Judge Shamgar," *VT* 14 (1964) 294–309.

343. H. W. Hertzberg, *I and II Samuel* (OTL), 2nd rev. ed., 1960 (Eng. trans. 1964), p. 101; see also comments of S. R. Driver, *Notes on the Hebrew Text of the Books of Samuel,* 1890, pp. 75–76.

344. RSV and NEB so translate I Samuel 13:7.

345. Hertzberg, *I and II Samuel,* p. 101.

346. J. P. Overholzer, "The *'ibrîm* in I Samuel," *Studies in the Book of Samuel* (DOTWSA, 3rd meeting), 1960, p. 54.

347. H. P. Smith, *A Critical and Exegetical Commentary on the Books of Samuel* (ICC), 1899, pp. 91–92.

348. Cf. the summary and bibliography on archaeological work in Transjordan by N. Glueck, "Transjordan," *Archaeology and Old Testament Study* (ed. D. Winton Thomas), 1967, pp. 429–453.

349. On Transjordan as a whole: J. A. Thompson, "The Economic Significance of Transjordan in Old Testament Times," *ABR* 6 (1958) 143–168.

On the Ammonites: W. F. Albright, "Some Notes on Ammonite History," *Miscellanea Biblica B. Ubach,* 1954, pp. 131–136; E. F. Campbell, Jr., and G. E. Wright, "Tribal League Shrines in Amman and Shechem," *BA* 32 (1969) 104–116; F. M. Cross, "Epigraphic Notes on the Amman Citadel Inscription," *BASOR* 193 (1969) 13–19; G. Garbini, "Ammonite Inscriptions," *JSS* 19 (1974) 159–168; S. H. Horn, "The Amman Citadel Inscription," *BASOR* 193 (1969) 2–13; S. H. Horn, "Ammon; Ammonites," IDBSV, 1976, p. 20; G. M. Landes, *A History of the Ammonites* (Ph.D. diss., Johns Hopkins University, 1956); G. M. Landes, "The Material Civilization of the Ammonites," *BA* 24 (1961) 66–86; G. M. Landes, "Ammon," IDB, vol. 1, 1962, pp. 108–114; B. Oded, "Ammon," *EM,* vol. 6, 1970, cols.

266–271 (Heb.); B. Oded, "Ammon, Ammonites," *EJ*, vol. 2, 1971, cols. 853–855; H. O. Thompson, "The Biblical Ammonites," *AJBA* 2 (1973) 31–38; H. O. Thompson and F. Zayadine, "The Works of Amminadab," *BA* 37 (1974) 2–19.

On the Moabites: W. F. Albright, "The Oracles of Balaam," *JBL* 63 (1944) 227–230; A. Alt, "Emiter und Moabiter," *KS*, I, 1953 (orig. pub. 1940), pp. 203–215; J. R. Bartlett, "The Moabites and the Edomites," in *Peoples of Old Testatment Times* (ed. D. J. Wiseman), 1973, pp. 229–258; E. D. Grohman, "Moab," IDB vol. 3, 1962, pp. 409–419; J. Liver, "Moab," *EM*, vol. 4, 1962, cols. 707–723 (Heb.); B. Oded, "Moab," *EJ*, vol. 12, 1971, cols, 190–194; W. L. Reed, "The Archaeological History of Elealeh in Moab," *Studies on the Ancient Palestinian World* (ed. J. Wevers and D. Redford), 1972, pp. 18–28; A. H. Van Zyl, *The Moabites* (Pretoria Oriental Series, 3), 1960.

On the Edomites: I. Avishur, "Edom," *EJ*, vol. 6, 1971, cols. 369–372; J. R. Bartlett (see title above under Moabites); J. R. Bartlett, "The Rise and Fall of the Kingdom of Edom," *PEQ* 104 (1972) 26–37; C.-M. Bennett, "An Archaeological Survey of Biblical Edom," *Perspective* 12 (1971) 35–44; C.-M. Bennett, "Edom," IDBSV, 1976, pp. 251–252; F. Buhl, *Geschichte der Edomiter*, 1893; S. Cohen, "Edom," IDB, vol. 2, 1962, pp. 24–26; N. Glueck, "The Civilization of the Edomites," BA 10 (1974) 77–84 = *Bar* 2 (1964) 51–58; N. Glueck, "Edom," EM, vol. 1, 1955, cols. 91–98 (Heb).

350. A. Alt, "The Settlement of the Israelites in Palestine," *EOTHR*, 1966 (orig. pub. 1925), pp. 205–206.

351. A. Alt, "The Formation of the Israelite State in Palestine," *EOTHR*, 1966 (orig. pub. 1930), pp. 259–261.

352. Ibid., pp. 261–263.

353. Ibid., p. 262; on the Edomite king lists, see also J. R. Barlett, "The Edomite King-List of Genesis 36:31–39 and I Chron. 1:43–50," *JTS* 16 (1965) 301–314; J. R. Bartlett, "The Rise and Fall of the Kingdom of Edom," *PEQ* 104 (1972) 26–27; and G. Buccellati, *Cities and Nations of Ancient Syria: An Essay on Political Institutions with Special Reference to the Israelite Kingdoms* (SS, 26), 1967, pp. 125–127.

354. G. E. Mendenhall, *BAR* 3 (1970) 114–115 = *BA* 25 (1962) 81–83.

355. O. Eissfeldt, "Protektorat der Midianiter über ihre Nachbarn im letzten Viertel des 2. Jahrtausends v. Chr.," *JBL* 87 (1968) 383–393; W. F. Albright, "Midianite Donkey Caravans," in *Translating and Understanding the Old Testament* (ed. H. Frank and W. Reed), 1970, pp. 197–205; W. J. Dumbrell, "The Midianites and Their Transjordanian Successors: Studies in the History, Social Structure and Political Influence of Related Transjordanian Groupings" (Th. D. diss., Harvard University, 1970), cf. *VT* 25 (1975) 323–337.

356. G. E. Mendenhall, *The Tenth Generation*, 1973, chap. 6.

357. E. F. Campbell, Jr., and G. E. Wright, "Tribal League Shrines in Amman and Shechem," *BA* 32 (1969) 104–116. Two large cultic structures, rather similar in design, one in northern Israel and one among the Ammonites, are claimed to have been amphictyonic centers for intertribal worship, but it seems to me that the authors' conclusions follow largely from the dubious assumptions of Noth's amphictyonic model (cf. my critique in Part VII). The shrines may or may not have been centers of worship for intertribal associations. Admittedly, the apparent similarity of the structures is a datum calling for further investigation, but a strictly amphictyonic, or even an intertribal, explanation is by no means the only possible one. This is also the view of G. R. H. Wright, "Shechem and League Shrines," *VT* 21 (1971) 572–603, who, in a thorough review of the archaeological evidence on Canaanite-Israelite temples, concludes that neither the free-standing stone pillar nor the courtyard arrangement distinguishes these temples as "amphictyonic."

358. G. E. Mendenhall, *BAR* 3 (1970) 101–105 = *BA* 25 (1962) 67–71, and *The Tenth Generation*, 1973, esp. chaps. 1, 5, and 7.

359. J. T. Luke, *Pastoralism and Politics in the Mari Period: A Re-Examination of the Character and Political Significance of the Major West Semitic Tribal Groups in the Middle Euphrates* (Ann Arbor: University Microfilms), 1965; see also J. T. Luke, "Observations on ARMT XIII 39," *JCS* 24 (1971) 20–23.

360. L. Krader, "Ecology of Central Asian Pastoralism," *SJA* 11 (1955) 301–326.

361. L. Krader, "Pastoralism," *IESS*, vol. 11, 1968, p. 458.

362. E. E. Bacon, "Types of Nomadism in Central and Southwest Asia," *SJA* 10 (1954) 44–68; J. I. Clarke, "Studies of Semi-Nomadism in North Africa,"*EG* 35 (1959) 95–108; see also the interesting attempt to draw together the evidence on pastoral nomadism in these regions and to propose a more refined classificatory typology by D. L. Johnson, *The Nature of Nomadism*, 1969.

363. H. Charles, *Tribus moutonnières du Moyen-Euphrate* (Documents d'Etudes Orientales de L'Institut Français de Damas, 8), 1939.

364. F. S. Frick, "The Rechabites Reconsidered,"*JBL* 90 (1971) 279–287; on the social location of metallurgists, see R. J. Forbes, "The Evolution of the Smith, His Social and Sacred Status," *Studies in Ancient Technology*, vol. 8, 1964, pp. 52–102.

365. A. Haldar, *Who Were the Amorites?* (MANE, 1), 1971, pp. 51–52.

366. A regrettable example of the almost complete neglect of an adequate historical and cultural framework for viewing ancient Near Eastern pastoral nomadism in relation to biblical Israel is M. S. Seale, *The Desert Bible: Nomadic Tribal Culture and Old Testament Interpretation*, 1974. After a cursory and superficial methodological overview, which merely assumes what it purports to demonstrate, Seale treats atomistically a series of biblical texts from the perspective of pre-Islamic Arab texts. As for Seale's competence in rendering and interpreting the Arab texts, I am unable to pass judgment. As for interpretive insight, the book can be read with profit, for many of the exegetical and cultural observations are acute and at times persuasive, but not for the reason Seale thinks, namely, that premonarchic Israel was pastoral nomadic like the pre-Islamic Arabs. In my judgment, the great majority of his "parallels" are in no way premised intrinsically or exclusively on pastoral nomadism, but are indicative of a broad tribal organizational pattern common to early Israel and to some of the pre-Islamic Arabs, and to many sedentary tribes as well. Mention should also be made of J. Van Seters, *Abraham in History and Tradition*, 1975, pp. 13–38. After initially offering some sound and promising observations on nomadism, including a clarification of the distinction between population migration and socioeconomic nomadism, the author unaccountably fails to apply them with consistency in his subsequent analysis of the historical groups in the ancient Near East. More satisfactory is the approach of H. N. Schneidau in *Sacred Discontent: The Bible and Western Tradition*, 1977, pp. 104–172: "The Hebrews against the High Cultures: Pastoral Motifs." Although he vacillates in his definition of nomadism, Schneidau recognizes that the social facts about village agriculture and pastoralism have been greatly transformed into literary motifs and religious types about the true Israelite as "wanderer" and "shepherd."

367. R. J. Braidwood, *Prehistoric Men*, 7th ed., 1967, pp. 81–153; on the physical conditions disposing the neolithic revolution to occur where it did in the ancient Near East, see K. W. Butzer, *CAH*, vol. 1, pt. 1, 1970, pp. 35–62.

368. J. T. Luke, *Pastoralism and Politics in the Mari Period*, pp. 23–24, referring to the studies of Braidwood and Howe in Iraqi Kurdistan (see note 369).

369. C. A. Reed in *Prehistoric Investigations in Iraqi Kurdistan* (Studies in Ancient Oriental Civilization, 31; ed. R. J. Braidwood and B. Howe), 1960, pp. 129–138; see also comments

of editors on "The General Problem," pp. 1–8. On the other hand, J. Mellaart, *CAH*, vol. 1, pt. 1, 1970, pp. 248–254, claims that domestication of animals, beginning with sheep by 9000 B.C., preceded domestication of plants by perhaps two millennia, but he views the domestication of animals as already occurring in settled communities and does not propose a stage of pastoral nomadism prior to the agricultural village. Some of the discrepancy in judgment among prehistorians on this point seems to hinge on differences of opinion over criteria for determining whether animal remains are those of wild or domesticated specimens. L. Braidwood and R. Braidwood, "Current Thoughts on the Beginnings of Food-Production in Southwestern Asia," *MUSJ* 45 (1969) 145–155, observe that it is no longer possible to make a sharp distinction between a food-collecting period and the beginning of domestication and cultivation in prehistoric Palestine, for there is evidence of complete domestication of food plants at points all over the ancient Near East by plus or minus 7000 B.C. The writers view domestication of animals as a part of the same general horizon as the domestication of plants. R. Braidwood, "The Early Village in Southwestern Asia," *JNES* 32 (1973) 34–39, synthesizes the most recent evidence into a fascinating cross-section of early village life throughout the prehistoric Near East.

370. S. Moscati, *The Semites in Ancient History: An Inquiry into the Settlement of the Bedouin and Their Political Establishment,* 1959, p. 29.

371. J. T. Luke, *Pastoralism and Politics in the Mari Period,* p. 24.

372. A. Haldar, *Who Were the Amorites?,* 1971.

373. L. Krader, "Pastoralism," *IESS,* vol. 11, 1968, p. 457.

374. C. D. Forde, *Habitat, Economy and Society: A Geographical Introduction to Ethnology,* 5th ed., 1963, p. 396.

375. Ibid., pp. 287–307.

376. G. Sjoberg, *The Preindustrial City: Past and Present,* 1960, esp. chaps. 2, 5, and 7–8.

377. M. B. Rowton, *Studies in Honor of B. Landsberger,* 1965, pp. 375–387.

378. The Mari Yaminites are so interpreted by J. T. Luke, *Pastoralism and Politics in the Mari Period,* pp. 84–85, 272.

379. D. H. K. Amiran and Y. Ben-Arieh, "Sedentarization of Bedouin in Israel," *IEJ* 13 (1963) 163.

380. F. S. Bodenheimer, "Fauna," IDB, vol. 2, 1962, p. 249; F. S. Bodenheimer, *Animal Life in Palestine,* 1935, p. 118; E. Bilik, "Cattle," *EM,* vol. 2, 1954, cols. 312–316 (Heb.); J. Feliks, "Cattle," *EJ,* vol. 5, 1971, cols. 256–257.

381. Y. Aharoni, *The Land of the Bible,* pp. 178–184.

382. J. L. Mihelic, "Manna," IDB, vol. 3, 1962, p. 260; see also S. E. Loewenstamm, "*Mān,*" *EM,* vol. 5, 1968, cols. 7–10 (Heb.).

383. R. Giveon, *Les bédouins Shosou des documents égyptiens* (DMOA, 18), 1971.

384. Papyrus Anastasi VI; *ANET,* p. 259 (Shosu translated "Bedouin").

385. Giveon, *Les bédouins Shosou,* pp. 240–241.

386. Ibid., pp. 255–257.

387. M. D. Sahlins, *Tribesmen,* 1968, pp. 28–47.

388. Papyrus Anastasi I, xix–xx, xxiii; *ANET,* p. 477 (Shosu translated "Bedouin").

389. Giveon, *Les bédouins Shosou,* pp. 261–264.

390. See note 388 and Amarna letter 318.12 in J. A. Knudtzon, *Die El-Amarna-Tafeln,* 1915, vol. 1, pp. 924–925.

391. *ANET,* p. 247 (Shosu transliterated as "Shasu").

392. Giveon, *Les bédouins Shosou,* pp. 267–271.

393. S. Schwertner, "Das 'Verheissene Land': Bedeutung und Verständnis des Landes nach den frühen Zeugnissen des Alten Testament" (doctoral diss. Heidelberg, 1966)

includes to my knowledge the most thorough and disciplined attempt to date to examine the evidence for pastoral nomadism in the patriarchal, exodus, and settlement traditions. Schwertner's work is well informed by current ethnological studies on nomadism (cf., e.g., "Exkurs: Die Entstehung des Nomadentums," pp. 58–62), including the important distinction between "transmigration" and "transhumance." Schwertner concludes that:(1) there was transmigration and transhumance in the patriarchal groups, although he grants that some or all of the transhumant groups may have been former settled peoples driven into pastoral nomadism, and he is further compelled to regard a number of references to patriarchal land cultivation (such as I have noted in the text above) as later textual intrusions;(2) there was only transmigration and no transhumance in the exodus group, which was an eclectic formation of peoples with a complicated prehistory of underclass incorporation into Egyptian society, and with evidences of many socioeconomic ingredient elements, among which pastoral nomadism is *not* represented;(3) the settlement traditions tell both of transhumant groups (mainly Leah tribes) and of settled agricultural groups (mainly Rachel tribes). It seems to me that Schwertner somewhat overstates the extent of pastoral nomadism in the patriarchal and settlement traditions, since he sometimes aligns biblical texts with transhumance which I read as testimony to transmigration alone. Nonetheless, we agree on many points. In particular, we share the view that the intertribal league of Israel was an eclectic formation of many types of socioeconomic producers. Incidentally, Schwertner refers only once to Mendenhall's revolt model, briefly summarizing it without evaluation and without making any further use of it (p. 132, note 98). The major question with which this incisive analysis leaves me is simply this: What was the objective basis (both in motivation and in socioeconomic conditions) for such diverse socioeconomic groups to cooperate in a single comprehensive socioreligious formation? Unquestionably, Schwertner's thesis deserves publication. I am indebted to the author and to his mentor, Prof. Rolf Rendtorff of the University of Heidelberg, for their initiative in sending me a copy of the dissertation, which would otherwise have escaped my attention, especially since the title unfortunately fails to communicate the significant sociological interest and method that permeate the work.

394. M. Weber, *Ancient Judaism*, 1921 (Eng. trans. 1952), pp. 14–15, 19–21, 56–57, 69–70, argues unpersuasively that in Israelite cities from the beginning there was a military patriciate which lorded it over the rural plebeians, for the evidence he cites is consistently drawn from monarchic times. On the other hand, Weber's argument is not consistently maintained, for elsewhere he notes that the urban military patricians of the coast and plains were the enemies of Israel's peasants and herdsmen (*Ancient Judaism*, p. 54, quoted by Frank S. Frick, "The City in the Old Testament," Ph.D. diss., Princeton University, 1970, p. 222). Cf. S. A. Baron, *The Jewish Community*, 1942, vol. 3, pp. 8–9, who criticizes Weber's thesis of an oligarchy of big landowners in early Israel on the grounds of general Palestinian conditions, but Baron himself misses the revolutionary clash between the Israelite tribal system and the Canaanite city-state system.

395. H. Charles, *Tribus moutonnières du Moyen-Euphrate*, 1939, p. 149, quoted by J. T. Luke in *Pastoralism and Politics in the Mari Period*, p. 29 (translation mine).

396. M. B. Rowton, "The Physical Environment and the Problem of the Nomads," *La Civilization de Mari* (ed. J.-R. Kupper), 1967, p. 116.

397. Rowton has begun to rectify his initially somewhat stereotyped outlook on nomadism by a projected ten-part analysis of pastoral nomadism in the ancient Near East, of which two parts have so far appeared (see my comments in X.51.2 and citations in note 575).

398. J. T. Luke, *Pastoralism and Politics in the Mari Period,* p. 37; M. Liverani, "Memorandum on the Approach to Historiographic Texts," *Or* 42 (1973) 178–194, points out the contrast between city and village as a major set of polar categories in ancient Near Eastern historical texts (see especially pp. 190–191).

399. G. Sjoberg, *The Preindustrial City: Past and Present,* 1960, p. 110.

400. M. D. Sahlins, *Tribesmen,* 1968, pp. 39–40.

401. M. H. Fried, *The Evolution of Political Society: An Essay in Political Anthropology,* 1967, pp. 170–174.

402. W. Helck, "Die Bedrohung Palästinas durch einwandernde Gruppen am Ende der 18. und am Anfang der 19. Dynastie," *VT* 18 (1968) 472–480.

403. Ibid., p. 476.

404. *ANET,* p. 247; and cf. translation and comments by W. Helck, *Die Beziehungen Ägyptens zu Vorderasien im 3. und 2. Jahrtausend v. Chr.,* 1962, p. 528.

405. D. J. Wiseman, *The Alalakh Tablets,* p. 10; I. Mendelsohn, *BASOR* 139 (1955) 10; and see the extensive discussion in M. Dietrich and O. Loretz, "Die soziale Struktur von Alalaḫ und Ugarit (II): Die sozialen Gruppen ḫupše-namê, ḫaniaḫḫe-ekû, eḫele-sūzubu und marjanne nach Texten aus Alalaḫ IV," *WO* 5 (1969) 57–93.

406. W. F. Albright, "Canaanite ḫapši and Hebrew ḥofši," *JPOS* 6 (1926) 107, and "New Canaanite Historical and Mythological Data," *BASOR* 63 (1936) 29.

407. I. Mendelsohn, "The Canaanite Term for 'Free Proletarian,'" *BASOR* 83 (1941) 36–39, and "New Light on the Ḫupšu," *BASOR* 139 (1955) 9–11. On the Roman *colonus* or "tied tenant farmer," see A. H. M. Jones, "The Roman Colonate," *Studies in Ancient Society* (ed. M. Finley), 1974, pp. 288–303. To imply that the model alternatives for understanding the Canaanite *ḫupshu* are solely "serf" or "tied tenant farmer" is of course grossly simplistic. Not only does it ignore the different forms and ranks of serfs and *coloni* at various times and places, but it overlooks additional forms of "dependent or involuntary labor," such as debt-bondsman, helot, and client, as discussed in the sophisticated analysis and interpretation of socioeconomic structure in the Roman Empire by M. I. Finley, *The Ancient Economy,* 1973 (see index under "tenant farmers"). Finley also cautions that the legal status of debt serfdom and tenant farmer in the Roman Empire was more confused and blurred than we, who look at the data through European feudal eyes, tend to recognize.

408. N. P. Lemche, "The 'Hebrew Slave': Comments on the Slave Law of Ex. 21:2–11," *VT* (1975) 140–142, 144, appropriating studies by M. Heltzer and H. Klengel, contends that *ḫupshu* were a group in collective clientage to private persons or kings (generally the latter, called *bnš mlk,* "royal men," along with many other occupational groupings who owed *pilku,* "service duties," to the king), and who served a mainly military function (though some were engaged in crafts or professions). In his view this disallows that the *ḫupshu* were free proletarian peasants (contra Knudtzon and Mendelsohn). M. Heltzer, who has written on the subject almost entirely in Russian, speaks but briefly to the point in his one article available to me, "Problems of the Social History of Syria in the Late Bronze Age," *La Siria nel Tardo Bronzo* (ed. M. Liverani), 1969, pp. 34–35: ". . .the texts of Ugarit tell us about some military service-men of some lower category, *ḫupšu,* but we know very little about them from the sources. However, the data from Alalakh and Byblos tell us more and we can better define their role as royal military men of a lower category. . . .so we must refuse of [sic] the explanation of that term as a 'free proletarian'." Nor have I had access to H. Klengel, *Geschichte Syriens im 2. Jahrtausend,* Teil I, 1965; II, 1969; III, 1970 (in his abbreviated "Probleme einer politischen Geschichte des spätbronzezeitlichen Syrien," *La Siria nel Tardo Bronzo* [ed. M. Liverani], 1969, pp. 15–30, Klengel does not treat the *ḫupshu*

problem). From what I can make of the remarks of Lemche and Heltzer, it appears that their main stress is on denying that the ḫupshu were free proletarians rather than on denying that they were peasants. They were bound to do royal service and were entrusted with plots and provisions by the crown (although Heltzer denies that European-type feudalism held sway in Syria, p. 39). It is less clear that they are denying that ḫupshu worked the land, although this might be taken as the implication of some of their comments about "royal men" doing military or other service. But since the texts seem only to speak of a periodic impressment or call-up to military duty, I see no basis for excluding that between battles the ḫupshu worked their holdings. In the Alalakh Tablets, the ḫupshu are by far the largest enumerated element in the populace, so that if they were not agriculturalists it is by no means clear who did the cultivation of the land. Evidently, the references to the ḫupshu require a complete restudy with a view to more closely determining their identity. To this point, however, I see no compelling reason to modify the hitherto prevailing view that, whatever their degree of personal freedom, the *hupshu* were peasants. It should be noted that the two essays mentioned above by Klengel and Heltzer on the political and social history of Late Bronze Syria provide commendably full and well-annotated bibliographies up to 1969.

409. Commentators on the biblical *hopshī* have noticed that in most of its occurrences it indicates deliverance from a former status of slavery, cf. R. de Vaux, *Ancient Israel*, 1961, p. 88; S. Loewenstamm, "Ḥopshī," *EM*, vol. 3, 1958, cols. 256–257 (Heb.); S. Loewenstamm, "Notes on the Alalakh Tablets," *IEJ* 6 (1956) 217–225; E. A. Speiser, in a review of Wiseman's edition of the Alalakh Tablets, in *JAOS* 74 (1954) esp. pp. 20–21. A. E. Glock, "Early Israel as the Kingdom of Yahweh," *CTM* 41 (1970) 577, describes early Israel "as a dissenting and disinherited community of *hopshi* (emancipated slaves) and *habirū* (social outcasts)." [These two transliterations with a single diacritical mark are as in Glock.] Possibly the strong connotation of emancipation in Hebrew *hopshī*, which is not so markedly present in ḫupshu, derives from the early Israelite success in shattering the Canaanite latifundia system and in freeing ḫupshu, who became members of autonomous extended families in the new Israelite tribal system.

410. E. Marmorstein, "The Origin of Agricultural Feudalism in the Holy Land," *PEQ* 85 (1953) 111–117, describes the *métayage* system in which land is cultivated for a proprietor by an agricultural worker who receives a share of the produce and is extremely vulnerable to debt enslavement and expulsion from the land. This is a useful account of the dynamics of the *métayage* system; it errs historically, however, in viewing the conquest of the land as the imposition of a new Israelite landowning class on indigenous serfs who had formerly served Canaanite masters. Like Weber before him, Marmorstein failed to observe the distinction between premonarchic and monarchic texts. In this respect, E. Neufeld, "The Emergence of a Royal-Urban Society in Ancient Israel," *HUCA* 31 (1960) 31–53, is a far more sociohistorically perceptive account than Marmorstein's. Neufeld focuses on debtor and creditor, town-country enmity, unemployment, and poverty and corruption as evidences of the evolution of striking economic differences stimulated by royal-urban sociopolitical organization.

411. A. F. Rainey, *El Amarna Tablets 359–379*, 1970, pp. 25–27. In my interpretation of the text and its application to Israelite history, I follow A. Alt, "Neues über Palästina aus dem Archiv Amenophis' IV," *KS*, III, 1953 (orig. pub. 1924), pp. 169–174; see also M. Noth, *The History of Israel*, 2nd ed., 1954 (Eng. trans. 1960), pp. 78–79, 81.

NOTES TO PART IX

412. In transcending the *'apiru* status as a social totality, Israel appears nonetheless to have retained a place for thĕ *'apiru* status in at least one of its many forms. N. P. Lemche, "The 'Hebrew Slave': Comments on the Slave Law of Ex. 21:2–11," *VT* 25 (1975) 129–144, building on the views of A. Alt and J. Lewy, has convincingly argued that *'ivrī* in the "slave" law of Exodus 21:2–11 refers to a form of individual service under contract to a master which is formally analogous to the service contracts of *'apiru* at Nuzi in fifteenth- and fourteenth-century Mesopotamia. Whereas the *'apiru* contract at Nuzi was unlimited, except as the *'apiru* found a substitute or was able to pay off the remaining service, the *'ivrī*-contract in Israel was for a stated period of six years. Since *'ivrī* is an appellative for "a person who sells himself as a slave for debt" (p. 138), Lemche concludes that "the thought that the Hebrew [=*'ivrī*] of Ex. 21:2 was necessarily an Israelite must be ruled out, but this does not exclude the possibility that he might have been" (p. 144). Lemche's argument that the *hopshī* (= Akkadian *hupshu*) status to which the *'ivrī* is released after six years is that of a somewhat less onerous form of clientage, rather than to full freedom is a much more disputable contention (pp. 138–142, 144).

413. *ANET,* p. 255; cf. Y. Aharoni, *The Land of the Bible,* 1962 (Eng. trans. 1967), pp. 168–169; W. F. Albright, "The Smaller Beth-shan Stele of Sethos I (1309–1290 B.C.)," *BASOR* 125 (1952) 24–32.

414. J..Dus, "Das Sesshaftswerden der nachmaligen Israeliten im Land Kanaan," *CV* 6 (1963) 263–275.

415. R. H. Smith, "Abram and Melchizedek (Gen. 14:18–20)," *ZAW* 77 (1965) 129–153. Smith's rendering is closely related to W. F. Albright's interpretation in *BASOR* 163 (1961) 52: "Melchizedek, his [Abraham's] allied king." Subsequently, on the basis of a proposal by M. Haran, Albright offered the translation: "Melchizedek, king <of Jerusalem, the king> who was <his> [Abraham's] ally" (*Yahweh and the Gods of Canaan,* 1968, p. 231; the words enclosed by < > are restorations of terms Albright believes were lost from the text by simple haplographies). Incidentally, Albright's ingenious thesis that the *'apiru*-Hebrews were "donkey caravaneers" (ibid., pp. 56–79) seems to me unsubstantiated for three reasons:(1) he did not advance a single text which unambiguously identifies *'apiru* as caravaneers;(2) a caravaneer status for *'apiru* does not adequately explain their militarization to the extent that they were armed auxiliaries in Amarna Canaan; and (3) even if the still contested meaning of "dusty-(footed)" for *'apiru* is accepted, it does not follow that caravaneering would be the only occupation meriting that description. It seems to me that, at most, Albright may possibly have identified another occupational function for some *'apiru*-Hebrews, but hardly for a majority, much less for all. Albright's endeavor is astutely motivated, however, by the perception that "the semi-nomadic hypothesis was correct in some ways, but it failed to solve the problem of how the Patriarchs made their living and what their mode of life was" (ibid., p. 57).

416. R. Clements, *Abraham and David: Genesis 15 and Its Meaning for Israelite Tradition* (SBT, 2nd series, 5), 1967, especially chap. 5.

417. W. F. Albright, "The Names 'Israel' and 'Judah,' " *JBL* 46 (1927) 151–185; W. Caspari, "Die sprächliche und religionsgeschichtliche Bedeutung des Namens Israel," *ZS* 3 (1924) 194–211; R. Coote, "The Meaning of the Name Israel," *HTR* 65 (1972) 137–142; G. A. Danell, *Studies in the Name of Israel in the Old Testament,* 1946; R. Marcus, "The Hebrew Sibilant ŚIN and the Name of YIŚRA'EL," *JBL* 60 (1941) 141–150; M. Noth, *Die israelitische*

Personennamen, 1928, pp. 207–210; E. Sachsse, *Die Bedeutung des Namens Israel,* I, 1910; II, 1922.

418. A contrary view is advanced by A. Lemaire, "Asriel, šr'l, Israël et l'origine de la confédération israélite," *VT* 23 (1973) 239–243, who argues on linguistic grounds that *Asriel,* a clan in Manasseh near Tappuah on the border with Ephraim (*šr'l* in Samarian Ostraca), and *Israel* are two forms of the same name, the initial "demi-consonants" being prosthetic and interchangeable. Lemaire further hypothesizes that the clan gave its name to the confederate entity of greater Israel, in analogy with the canton Schwys that contributed its name to the Swiss confederation and with the small region of Gaul called Franc that gave its name to the nation of France. In spite of the suggestiveness of his observations, several problems are untreated in Lemaire's brief study: (1) Why does MT use two different forms of the name for the clan and for the confederacy? Was this an attempt to hide the derivation of the confederate name from a clan name, and if so, why? Or was it simply a later standardization device to avoid confusing clan and confederacy?; (2) Why was the name for the confederacy drawn from a clan rather than from a tribe? Does this suggest that the first confederating entities were clans rather than tribes?; (3) Why should a clan lacking a major cult center or any known leader of stature have given its name to the confederacy? Lemaire tries to make good this deficiency by suggesting that Shiloh, several miles to the southeast, may have been in the territory of Asriel, but the evidence he offers is weak.

419. M. Noth, *Das System der zwölf Stämme Israels,* 1930, pp. 75–80.

420. "El, the God of Israel," Gen. 33:20. After the proper name Yahweh became the primary designation for deity in Israel, "Yahweh" replaced "El" in the formulary "Yahweh/El, the God of Israel" (e.g., Ex. 5:1; 32:27; Josh. 8:30; 9:18–19; 24:1,23; Judg. 5:3,5). The independent form "the God of Israel" (e.g., Ex. 24:10; Num. 16:9; Josh. 22:16) indicates that the appositional phrase could qualify more than one name for deity (as borne out by Gen. 33:20), and it is likely that Exodus 24:10 points to the older and fuller form "El, the God of Israel." (Cf. B. W. Anderson, "God, Names of," IDB, vol. 2, 1962, p. 413, and M. D. Cassuto, " *'Ēl'elōhē yisrā'ēl,*" *EM,* vol. 1, 1955, cols. 284–285 [Heb.]). I find the view that El Elohe Israel means "El, god of (the patriarch) Israel," which in turn is equivalent to "El, god of your father" (Gen. 46:3), to be highly dubious, since the transfer of the proper name Israel to the patriarch Jacob gives every evidence of being a late secondary phenomenon (contra F. Cross, *Canaanite Myth and Hebrew Epic,* 1973, p. 46, note 13).

421. J. Bright, *A History of Israel,* 2nd ed., 1972, p. 132; E. Nielsen, *Shechem: A Traditio-Historical Investigation,* 1955, pp. 282–283; S. Lehming, "Zur Überlieferungsgeschichte von Gen. 34," *ZAW* 70 (1958) 228–250; A. de Pury, "Genèse XXXIV et l'histoire," *RB* 71 (1969) 5–49. For further exploration of the complex historical and social horizons of Genesis 34, see the discussions in VI.30.3 and VII.32.3 and, in particular, note 213.

422. *ANET,* 376–378; J. Bright, *A History of Israel,* 2nd ed., 1972, pp. 112–113.

423. B. Maisler (Mazar), "Canaan and the Canaanites," *BASOR* 102 (1946) 7–12; A. van Selms, "The Canaanites in the Book of Genesis," *OTS* 12 (1958) 182–213; I. J. Gelb, "The Early History of the West Semitic Peoples," *JCS* 15 (1961) 27–47; J. C. Gibson, "Observations on Some Important Ethnic Terms in the Pentateuch," *JNES* 20 (1961) 217–228.

424. B. Maisler (Mazar), *BASOR* 102 (1946) 7–8; P. Artzi, "Canaan, Canaanite," *EM,* vol. 4, 1962, cols. 196–202 (Heb.); J. Liver, "Canaan in the Bible," *EM,* vol. 4, 1962, cols. 202–204 (Heb.); B. Oded, "Canaan, Land of," *EJ,* vol. 5, 1971, cols. 98–101; R. de Vaux, "Le pays de Canaan," *JAOS* 88 (1968) 23–30.

425. Following E. A. Speiser, "Ethnic Movements in the Near East in the Second Millen-

nium B.C.,"*AASOR* 13 (1933) 26–31; "Hivite," IDB, vol. 2, 1962, p. 615, and "Horite," IDB, vol. 2, 1962, p. 645; "*Ḥorî, Ḥōrîm,*" *EM*, vol. 3, 1958, cols. 57–61 (Heb.). See also S. E. Loewenstamm, "*Ḥivvî,*" *EM*, vol. 3, 1958, cols. 45–47 (Heb.); R. de Vaux, "Les Hurrites de l'histoire et les Horites de la Bible," *RB* 74 (1967) 481–503; and J. Simons, *The Geographical and Topographical Texts of the Old Testament,* 1959, pp. 42–44.

426. N. K. Gottwald, "Amorites," *EJ*, vol. 2, 1971, cols. 877–878; see also Y. Aharoni, *The Land of the Bible,* pp. 59–60, 137, 158–159, 187, who rejects the suggestion of B. Mazar (in "Land of Israel," *EM*, vol. 1, 1955, cols. 694–695 [Heb.]) that the Amorite kingdom of Sihon was colonized by people from Amurru in league with Hittites after the Battle of Kadesh and prefers instead to explain the application of the name "Amorite" to the Transjordanian kingdoms along the line of a progressively southward-shifting geographical restriction of the term Amurru as follows: in Akkadian times for Syria-Palestine as a whole; in the Hyksos era for southern Palestine-Syria; in the Amarna Age for the small kingdom of Amurru in Lebanon; in biblical usage for residents of the mountains and interior regions, virtually coextensive with Canaan.

427. First proposed by B. Maisler (Mazar), "Beth-She 'arim, Gaba, and Harosheth of the Peoples," *HUCA* 24 (1952/53) 81–84, and in *EM*, vol. 3, 1958, cols. 309–310 (Heb.). This view is accepted by Y. Aharoni, *The Land of the Bible,* pp. 201, 203, contra W. F. Albright, "Some Additional Notes on the Song of Deborah," *JPOS* 2 (1922) 284–285.

428. D. Winton Thomas, *SVT* 4 (1958) 8–16; *CBQ* 24 (1962) 154; P. Calderone, *CBQ* 23 (1961) 451–460. My interpretation of Judges 5 is greatly indebted to M. L. Chaney's full-orbed exegetical, historical, and sociological analysis and reconstruction, starting from the philological data, as presented in his unpublished paper "ḤDL-II in I Sam. 2:5; Judg. 5:7; and Deut. 15:11," delivered at the Annual Meeting of the AAR-SBL in Washington, D.C., on October 24, 1974. I have also had the opportunity of reading early drafts of parts of Chaney's Ph.D. dissertation, which treats the same data more exhaustively and with full notes: "ḤDL-II and the 'Song of Deborah': Textual, Philological, and Sociological Studies in Judges 5, with Special Reference to the Verbal Occurrences of ḤDL in Biblical Hebrew" (Ph.D. diss., Harvard University, 1976).

429. W. F. Albright, *BASOR* 163 (1961) 40–43; W. Helck, *Die Beziehungen Ägyptens zu Vorderasien im 3. und 2. Jahrtausend v. Chr.,* 1962, pp. 461–465; A. L. Oppenheim, *Ancient Mesopotamia: Portrait of a Dead Civilization,* 1964, pp. 64, 93, 118–120.

430. F. M. Cross and D. N. Freedman, "The Song of Miriam," *JNES* 14 (1955) 237–250.

431. Ibid., p. 239.

432. E. A. Speiser, " 'People' and 'Nation' of Israel," *JBL* 79 (1960) 157–163; see also L. Rost, "Die Bezeichnungen für Land und Volk im Alten Testament," *Festschrift Otto Procksch,* 1934, pp. 125–148.

433. Speiser, " 'People' and 'Nation,' " p. 158.

434. F. Brown, S. R. Driver, and C. A. Briggs, *A Hebrew and English Lexicon of the Old Testament,* 1906, p. 766 (entries 2 c. and d.).

435. A. Alt, "Meros," *KS,* I, 1953 (orig. pub. 1941), p. 196.

436. E. Täubler, *Biblische Studien: Die Epoche der Richter,* 1958, p. 196.

437. F. M. Cross and D. N. Freedman, "The Song of Miriam," *JNES* 14 (1955) 248–249.

438. Ibid., p. 249. A further instance of *yōshēv* as "ruler(s)" is pointed out by W. G. E. Watson, "David Ousts the City Ruler of Jebus," *VT* 20 (1970) 501–502, who recognizes that *hayᵉvusî yōshēv hāʾārets* in II Samuel 5:6 does not mean "the Jebusites, the inhabitants of the land" (as misconstrued by I Chronicles 11:4–5), but "the Jebusite ruler of the city" (*ʾerets* employed sociopolitically for "city" or "city-state"; cf. p. 502, notes 2 and 3). This rendering

smooths out the grammar and syntax, fits intelligibly within the narrative context, and further explains the awkward repetitive appositions of the Chronicler who did not perceive that *yōshēv* in this context meant "ruler."

439. N. K. Gottwald, *All the Kingdoms of the Earth: Israelite Prophecy and International Relations in the Ancient Near East,* 1964, pp. 214–215.

440. On the architecture of Samaria: G. A. Reisner, C. S. Fisher, and D. G. Lyon, *Harvard Excavations at Samaria,* 1924; J. W. Crowfoot, K. M. Kenyon, and E. L. Sukenik, *The Buildings at Samaria,* 1942. On the decorations and small objects from Samaria displaying the court opulence: J. W. and G. M. Crowfoot, *Early Ivories from Samaria,* 1938; J. W. and G. M. Crowfoot and K. M. Kenyon, *The Objects from Samaria,* 1957. See also R. W. Hamilton, "Architecture," IDB, vol. 1, 1962, p. 213.

441. N. K. Gottwald, *All the Kingdoms of the Earth,* pp. 164–169.

442. Ibid., pp. 165–166.

443. W. Eichrodt, *Ezekiel* (OTL), 1965/1966 (Eng. trans. 1970), pp. 142–143.

444. Ibid., p. 135.

445. J. M. P. Smith, *A Critical and Exegetical Commentary on the Books of Micah, Zephaniah and Nahum* (ICC), 1911, p. 132.

446. M. Noth, *Das Buch Josua* (HAT), 2nd ed., 1953, pp. 53–55; J. Liver, "The Literary History of Josh. 9," *JSS* 8 (1963) 227–243; A. I. Arana, "El pacto con los gabaonitos (Jos. 9) como narración etiológica," *EB* 30 (1971) 161–175; J. Blenkinsopp, *Gibeon and Israel* (Society for Old Testament Study Monograph Series, 2), 1972. Blenkinsopp gives a judicious review of the main problems inherent in the Gibeon traditions and the major proposals for their solution, together with some fresh observations of his own and a copious bibliography. His comments on the formal similarities between the Shechemite-Israelite treaty (Genesis 34) and the Gibeonite-Israelite treaty (Joshua 9) are of particular interest, although not entirely persuasive, e.g., the claim that in Genesis 34 Shechem is the superior treaty partner whereas in Joshua 9 Israel is the superior treaty partner (pp. 37–40).

447. P. J. Kearney, "The Role of the Gibeonites in Deuteronomic History," *CBQ* 35 (1973) 1–19, may be correct, at least in part, in identifying Deuteronomy 29 as an artful play on the covenant with the Gibeonites posited as an "original sin" that threatened to be repeated by later Israel (as, for example, by Hezekiah with respect to the embassy from Merodach-baladan in II Kings 20:12–19). Notwithstanding a number of perceptive textual observations, Kearney is entirely too abrupt in assigning many features of the account in Joshua 9—the deception theme among them—to later stages, or to the final stage, in the tradition formation (pp. 3–6).

448. M. Noth, *Das Buch Josua,* p. 56.

449. J. Blenkinsopp, *Gibeon and Israel,* pp. 32–33.

450. A. Alt, "Meros," *KS,* I, 1953 (orig. pub. 1941), 274–277.

451. G. F. Moore adjudged this portion of the Hebrew text of Judges 18:7 to be "unintelligible" and "incurably corrupt" and remarked that "the RV translation. . .cannot be extorted from the Hebrew text with a rack, and is nonsense when done" (*A Critical and Exegetical Commentary on the Book of Judges* [ICC], 1895, pp. 390–392), whereas R. G. Boling avers that "although the versions later had difficulties with it [the disputed Hebrew text], emendations are unnecessary" (*Judges: Introduction, Translation, and Commentary* [The Anchor Bible], 1975, pp. 260, 263).

452. In connection with Exodus 23:20–33, a passage closely related stylistically and conceptually should be noted in Exodus 34:11–16. F. Langlamet, "Israël et 'l'habitant du pays': Vocabulaire et formules d'Ex. 34:11–16," *RB* 76 (1969) 338–341, singles out *yōshēv*

hā'ārets in 34:12,15 for special comment. Not recognizing, however, the meaning of "lords/rulers" in the collective *yōshēv*, he sees the prohibition against treaties with Canaanites as a rejection of close relations with settled peoples arising from Israel's presumed semi-nomadic bias.

453. J. T. Willis, "The Song of Hannah and Psalm 113," *CBQ* 35 (1973) 139–154, argues forcefully on grounds of Gattung, poetic style, language and thought that both compositions are premonarchic. Observing that the references in I Samuel 2:10 to "king" and "anointed" round out the song of Hannah with "ring" construction (note repetition of the phrase "to lift up the horn"="to exalt the power," vss. 1b, 10b), he concludes that the song must come from a pro-monarchic circle that had in mind "a local 'king' of an Israelite city-state or tribe" (such as Abimelech?, pp. 148–149). This interpretation of the song is difficult to reconcile with its otherwise strongly egalitarian tone (note the plural reference to those placed by Yahweh in the "seat of honor," vs. 8). In fact, Willis does not try to reconcile the clash in sociopolitical ideologies between vs. 10b and the rest of the poem. Nevertheless, this study forcefully reopens the question of whether the original composition ended with vs. 10a or had some form of the present vs. 10b with "ring" composition harking back to vs. 1b. W. F. Albright, *Yahweh and the Gods of Canaan,* 1968, p. 18, has proposed that *malkō,* "his king" of vs. 10, should be vocalized *molkō,* "his [Yahweh's] kingdom," but, as Willis points out, such a reading jars with the parallel "his anointed."

454. See discussion of *hādal* in text above under "Judges 5: Song of Deborah" and refer to note 428.

455. N. K. Gottwald, *Studies in the Book of Lamentations* (SBT, First Series, 14), rev. ed., 1962, pp. 52–62. For the roots of the literary motif of tragic reversal in the funeral song genre, a motif which expands to include any reversal of fortune among the living—for good or for ill—see H. Jahnow, *Das hebräische Leichenlied im Rahmen der Völkerdichtung* (BZAW, 36), 1923, especially chaps. 2 and 3, and consult index under "Einst und Jetzt."

456. On the Winton Thomas-Calderone-Chaney proposal concerning *hādēllū,* see note 428.

457. C. Rabin, "Judges 5:2 and the 'Ideology' of Deborah's War," *JJS* 6 (1955) 129–130, rightly emphasizes that "volunteer" does not do justice to the intertribal obligation to provide troops for mutual defense. "To answer the call with alacrity" includes both the social-structural obligation of the levy and the fact that, unlike an army drafted by a state power, the success of the levy depends on the willing and speedy compliance of the several tribes when summoned. Rabin follows F. Schwally, *Semitische Kriegsaltertümer I: Der heilige Krieg im alten Israel,* 1901, p. 47, in believing that the *nādīv* was originally "the man obliged to fight in war."

458. J. Gray, *Joshua, Judges and Ruth* (CnBN), 1967, p. 276. Whether the *nazir,* "consecrated, dedicated, or separated person," was a formally distinct office in ancient Israel is a vexed question. The Nazirite is connected with warfare in the cases of Samson, Samuel, and Saul. Apparently the commissioning as Nazirite was by a vow uttered either by the parent or by the initiate himself. Long hair and abstention from strong drink were badges of the Nazirite status. Numbers 6 codifies a Nazirite role which says nothing of warfare and seems to have allowed for a short-term "consecration." There is some doubt that we can properly speak of an order of Nazirites in the premonarchic period. The Nazirite may rather have been a category of especially dedicated warriors, but there is no evidence that they fought together, lived together, or were under collective discipline. Possibly any strongly motivated warrior could declare himself a Nazirite for a stated period. In very ancient poetry, Joseph is said to be *nezīr 'ehāv,* "separated from his brothers" or

"consecrated by his brothers" (Gen. 49:26; Deut. 33:16). In these ancient poetic contexts Joseph's "consecration" is marked both by agricultural bounty and by military prowess. That the Joseph tribes as totalities are called "Nazirites" suggests a metaphorical usage of the term but whether a specific class of warriors consigned by vows were recognized as Nazirites in the premonarchic period depends in large measure on how one reads the Samson birth story. Z. Weisman, "The Biblical Nazirite, Its Types and Roots," *Tarbiz* 36 (1967) 207–220 (Heb.), distinguishes between permanent and temporary Nazirites and argues that the earliest temporary type of Nazirite is attested chiefly in the case of Absalom (II Sam. 14:25–26; 15:8). Weisman finds the origin of the Nazirite phenomenon in magic conceptions associated with fear of death in childbirth.

459. G. B. Gray, *A Critical and Exegetical Commentary on the Book of Numbers* (ICC), 1903, p. 288. In 1960 at Jerash in Jordan, I overheard a crew of Arab workmen vociferously singing as they carried earth from a Roman building under excavation to a nearby dump pile. A solo voice alternated with unison responses, and it was obvious that the song functioned to coordinate, motivate, and hasten the work on a very hot summer day. Not knowing Arabic, I was unable to determine the text of the song or to ascertain whether it was a traditional song or one improvised for the occasion. Thus, I am unable to say if the song I heard bore a topical relationship to the work in progress, as is the case with the Song of the Well in Numbers 21:18.

460. Y. Yadin, *The Art of Warfare in Biblical Lands*, 1963, vol. 1, p. 5; vol. 2, pp. 287, 297 (see subject index of plates under "Cavalry").

461. N. K. Gottwald, *All the Kingdoms of the Earth*, p. 254.

462. H.-J. Zobel, *Stammesspruch und Geschichte: Die Angaben der Stammessprüche von Gen 49, Dtn 33, und Jdc 5 über die politischen und kultischen Zustände im damaligen "Israel"* (BZAW, 95), 1965, pp. 98–99; for cattle-raiding among settled peoples, cf. I Chronicles 7:21.

463. R. Smend, *Yahweh War and Tribal Confederation: Reflections upon Israel's Earliest History*, 1963 (Eng. trans. 1970), pp. 98–104.

464. J. Wellhausen, *Prolegomena to the History of Ancient Israel*, 1883 (Eng. trans. 1885), p. 323.

465. H. Gunkel, *Genesis*, 4th ed., 1917, pp. 485–486, followed by R. Smend, *Yahweh War and Tribal Confederation*, p. 104.

466. See note 411 above.

467. W. Krebs, " '. . .sie haben Stiere gelähmt,' (Gen. 49:6)," *ZAW* 78 (1966) 359–361, locates the precise terms, both in Greek and in Arabic, for the practice of hocking the tendons of large animals such as elephants and camels. He notes that in Arabia camels were sometimes interred with the honored dead and apparently the corpses were hocked to keep them from "running away." Later these occasional interments became regular offerings. Krebs makes no attempt to apply these burial or offering practices of hocking animals directly to Geneis 49:6, noting only that in the Old Testament the intent was to deny chariot horses to the enemy, further pointing out that the event implied in Genesis 49:6 is not referred to at all in Genesis 34.

468. N. K. Gottwald, " 'Holy War' in Deuteronomy: Analysis and Critique," *RE* 61 (1964) 296–310; concerning the vow before battle, see F.-M. Abel, "L'anathème de Jéricho et la maison de Rahab," *RB* 57 (1950) 323–324.

469. Gottwald, " 'Holy War' in Deuteronomy," p. 300.

470. *ANET,* 320–321; for historical interpretation, see J. Liver, "The Wars of Mesha, King of Moab," *PEQ* 99 (1967) 14–31.

471. W. Robertson Smith, *Lectures on the Religion of the Semites* (intro. and notes by S. A. Cook), 3rd ed., 1927, p. 641 and cross references (note supplied by S. A. Cook); F.

Schwally, *Semitische Kriegsaltertümer I*, 1901, pp. 29–44 (notes); F.-M. Abel, *RB* 57 (1950) 321–330.

472. Most recently F. Stolz, *Jahwes und Israels Kriege* (ATANT, 60), 1972, pp. 172–187, has summed up Israelite military practices and roles in their hypothetical "nomadic" and "sedentary" cultural phases. The thinness of the data and the arbitrariness of the criteria for distinguishing nomadic and sedentary military methods are embarrassingly evident.

473. *Shorter Encyclopedia of Islam*, 1961, p. 89; *The Encyclopedia of Islam: New Edition*, 1965, vol. 2, pp. 538–539.

474. M. Montgomery Watt, *Islam and the Integration of Society*, 1961, pp. 61–63, 65–67.

475. W. Robertson Smith, *Lectures on the Religion of the Semites*, 3rd ed., 1977, p. 641 (note supplied by S. A. Cook); cf. the reference to a "survival" of *nacī'a* (sacrifice of a choice animal or human captive after battle) cited by C. M. Doughty, *Travels in Arabia Deserta*, 1888, vol. 1, p. 452. At one point, Smith extended the concept of *ḥērem* to include execution of criminals in a sacrificial form (pp. 370–371, note 4).

476. A. Malamat, "The Ban in Mari and in the Bible," *Biblical Essays* (DOTWSA, 9th meeting), 1966, pp. 40–49.

477. Ibid., p. 47.

478. J.-R. Kupper, *Les nomades en Mésopotamie au temps des rois de Mari*, 1957.

479. See notes 359 and 372 and the discussion in VIII.39.2.

480. See notes 367 through 369 and the discussion in VIII.39.2.

481. ARM I 6:18–19, as translated by Malamat, "The Ban in Mari," p. 43 (ARM + numbers indicates the volume, text, and lines in the official publication of the Mari texts: A. Parrot and G. Dossin, eds., *Archives royales de Mari*, 1940–).

482. ARM V 72:11–13, 20–22, as translated by Malamat, "The Ban in Mari," pp. 43–44.

483. M. Weippert, " 'Heiliger Krieg' in Israel und Assyrien: Kritische Anmerkungen zu Gerhard von Rads Konzept des 'Heiligen Krieges im alten Israel,' " *ZAW* 84 (1972) 460–493, shows in detail—by examining Mari, Hittite, and neo-Assyrian statist texts—that all of the characteristics of so-called Yahweh war can likewise be exhibited for "Asshur war" or "Ishtar war" or "Ninurta war."

484. For a discussion of the place of iron in the early Israelite material, cultural, and socioeconomic horizon, see X.51.5–6.

485. W. F. Albright, "A Catalogue of Early Hebrew Lyric Poems (Psalm LXVIII)," *HUCA* 23 (1950/51), part I, 1–39; S. Iwry, "Notes on Psalm 68," *JBL* 71 (1952) 161–165; S. Mowinckel, *Der achtundsechzigste Psalm*, 1953.

486. A. Weiser, *The Psalms* (OTL), 5th rev. ed., 1959 (Eng. trans. 1962), p. 486.

487. M. Buttenwieser, *The Psalms*, 1938, pp. 34–47; H.-J. Kraus, *Psalmen*, 3rd ed., 1966, vol. 1, p. 473.

488. M. Noth, *Das Buch Josua*, 2nd ed., 1953, pp. 60–67; J. Gray, *Joshua, Judges and Ruth*, 1967, pp. 104–107.

489. J. A. Soggin, *Joshua* (OTL), 1970 (Eng. trans. 1972), p. 38.

490. D. J. Wiseman, "Rahab of Jericho," *TB* 14 (1964) 8–11, regards Rahab as a "bar-maid" or "innkeeper" at the city gates who was in semi-official relationship to the court, advising the king of recent arrivals in the city. Not having access to this article, I have derived its argument from K. M. Campbell, "Rahab's Covenant: A Short Note on Josh. 2:9–21," *VT* 22 (1972) 243–244. Accepting Wiseman's interpretation of Rahab's social role, Campbell stresses the political nature of Rahab's act in shifting her allegiance from the king of Jericho to Israel.

491. G. Sjoberg, *The Preindustrial City: Past and Present*, 1960, pp. 133–137. I am indebted to Marvin Chaney, who in lectures at the Graduate Theological Union of Berkeley,

California, and in private conversation, first called my attention to the implications of Sjoberg's analysis of occupational outcasts for an understanding of the Rahab story.

492. Ibid., pp. 135–136.

493. H. Windisch, "Zur Rahabgeschichte," *ZAW* 37 (1917–1918) 188–198, cites two instances from classical antiquity of harlots who were publicly honored for their part in delivering a city to an enemy or in rescuing it from an enemy: in one case, the Romans took the city of Capua in the Second Punic War with the help of a local harlot, Cluvia Faucula; and in the other case, the city of Abydos in the Hellespont expelled an occupying garrison with the aid of a resident harlot. From the source extracts quoted by Windisch, socio-economic factors or motives in the incidents are not discernible.

494. I. J. Gelb, "Hittites," IDB, vol. 2, 1962, p. 613.

495. G. E. Mendenhall, *The Tenth Generation,* 1973, chap. 6.

496. R. de Vaux, "The Settlement of the Israelites in Southern Palestine and the Origins of the Tribe of Judah," *Translating and Understanding the Old Testament* (ed. H. T. Frank and W. L. Reed), 1970, pp. 108–134, in a masterful survey of premonarchic Judah, offers data most obviously congruent with the view that Judah was an indigenous formation from the local populace, in the first instance in the mountains from Bethlehem to Hebron and later extending westward to incorporate peoples in the foothills, and taking its very name from the region itself. De Vaux, however, still under the spell of the notion that Israel had to come *from* somewhere, uses hints that a portion of later Judah immigrated from the south into the vicinity of Arad to hypothesize an initial penetration of peoples from that direction, which became the nucleus for Judah, later enlarged by the inclusion of local Canaanites. But why must the nuclear element in an Israelite tribe always have to be conceived as immigrating? Why should it not be allowed that the nuclear element may have been indigenous and that immigrating elements (and not necessarily from the steppe but also from regions within Canaan proper) were secondary and supplemental? That scholars have not felt free to entertain this latter possibility shows how powerfully the conquest and immigration models have dominated the discussion of Israelite origins, to the extent of determining what questions can be asked and the range of answers that can be entertained.

497. H. Schmidt, "Die Herrschaft Abimelechs," *Judaica* 26 (1970) 1–11.

498. G. E. Wright, *Shechem: The Biography of a Biblical City,* 1965, pp. 80–102; J. Gray, *Joshua, Judges and Ruth,* pp. 317–318.

499. M. Noth, *Das System der zwölf Stämme Israels,* 1930, pp. 65–75, 133–140; M. Noth, *Das Buch Josua* (HAT), 2nd ed., 1953, pp. 135–140; J. A. Soggin, *Joshua* (OTL), 1970 (Eng. trans. 1972), pp. 220–244 (see bibliography cited on pp. 222–223). While recognizing that a religious and sociopolitical confederacy is attested in the text, I of course dissociate myself from the strict amphictyonic interpretation of Joshua 24 advanced by Noth and followed also by Soggin (see my critique of the amphictyonic model for early Israel in Part VII).

500. A distinction between *'allōn* ("oak") and *'ēlāh* ("terebinth") seems firmly attested in Isaiah 6:13 and Hosea 4:13. However, owing to the similarity of sound and of consonantal spelling between *'allōn* and another term generally construed as "terebinth" (*'ēlōn*), it is doubtful how accurately the Massoretic tradition has preserved the original terms in a number of biblical passages. Furthermore, it is to be suspected that many biblical writers used the arboreal names imprecisely, if not interchangeably, and perhaps at times they simply meant "a big tree," without exact knowledge of the species in question. In my view, the variant terms in the Shechem sacred-tree traditions do not provide either corroboration or invalidation of the various cultic reconstructions that have been proposed. Accordingly, I translate all terms by the general expression "sacred tree," indicating in each instance the exact Hebrew word according to MT. On the difficulties of the "oak"/

"terebinth" nomenclature, see M. Zohary, "Flora," IDB, vol. 2, p. 294; J. Trever, "Oak," IDB, vol. 3. p. 575;"Terebinth," IDB, vol. 4, p. 574, and note in particular the remarks of W. F. Albright, *Yahweh and the Gods of Canaan*, 1968, pp. 165–166.

501. There is by now a considerable literature on the subject of the "buried" gods and valuables marked by spirited dispute over the context and meaning of the ritual action: B. Nielsen, "The Burial of the Foreign Gods," *ST* 8 (1954/1955) 103–122 (a black magic ritual of interment of guardian figurines); F. O. Garcia-Treto, "Bethel: The History and Tradition of an Israelite Sanctuary" (Ph.D. diss., Princeton University, 1967); A. de Pury, *Promesse divine et légende cultuelle dans le cycle de Jacob: Une étude à-propos de Genèse 28* (Études Bibliques), 1973 (personal effects deposited as a preparation rite on entering a holy place for worship); O. Keel, "Das Vergraben der 'Fremden Götter,' " *VT* 23 (1973) 305–336 (preparatory rite in holy war to activate the "terror of God" against the enemy). Keel seems justified in stressing that the cultic act is not really a "burial," but rather a "hiding away" or "laying aside" of religious figurines and other valuables. He is also astute in critiquing the pertinence of the various classes of archaeological objects that have been proposed as analogies to the Israelite concealing of god images and costly objects. Nevertheless, there remains an unexplained hiatus between Keel's *formal* account of a rite for removing damaged, outmoded, or rejected sacral objects from use by hiding them in holy ground, on the one hand, and his *contextual* account of how that practice presumably functioned in Israelite holy war, on the other hand.

502. L. Toombs and G. E. Wright, "The Fourth Campaign at Balâṭah (Shechem): The Biblical Traditions of Shechem's Sacred Area," *BASOR* 169 (1963) 27–32, advance the hypothesis that the Israelite holy place with its sacred tree, originally located outside the city (the situation in Jacob's time), was brought within the expanded wall and incorporated in the fortress-temple complex (the situation in the days of Joshua and Abimelech). Although meticulously argued, I think their claim is mistaken. The hypothesis ignores the fact that the Israelite "oak of the soothsayers" is seen by Abimelech to lie outside the walls of the city, and it does not satisfactorily explain how a temple of Baal could be accepted by the Israelites as the site of Joshua's assembly.

W. F. Albright, building on the linguistic study of S. Iwry, subsequently printed in *Textus* 5 (1966) 34–43, has proposed that Judges 9:6 be understood to mean: "By the terebinth (oak) whose location was still shown in Shechem," and that Joshua 24:26 be translated : "In the very place where the terebinth had stood in the sanctuary at Shechem" (cited by Toombs and Wright, ibid., pp. 28–29, note 32). Albright achieves the same basic result as Toombs and Wright in seeing a single holy place and tree at Shechem, but he argues that the tree standing in Jacob's time was no longer standing in the lifetimes of Joshua and Abimelech. This ingenious suggestion strains the linguistic evidence, but it is chiefly objectionable because it flies in the face of the same wider contextual evidence about the existence of two differently located trees as does the Toombs-Wright argument.

B. Mazar, "The 'Place of Shechem'—a Precinct Sacred to the Israelites," *'Erets Shōmrōn*, 1973, pp. 1–7 (Heb.), offers a reading of the Israelite cultic history of Shechem congenial to my own conclusions. He is persuasive in arguing that the Israelite holy place lay at the foot of Mt. Ebal to the north or northwest of Shechem. If so, the holy place was located at least several hundred feet beyond the farthest point reached by the expanded walls of the city.

503. On the source separation in Joshua 24 and the assembly at Shechem: E. Sellin, "Seit welcher Zeit verehrten die nordisraelitischen Stämme Jahwe?," *Oriental Studies for P. Haupt*, 1926, pp. 121–134; M. Noth, *Das Buch Josua* (HAT), 2nd ed., 1953, pp. 15–16, 135–140; J. L'Hour, "L'alliance de Sichem," *RB* 69 (1962) 5–36, 161–184, 350–368; G. Schmitt, *Der Landtag von Sichem* (AZT, First Series, 15), 1964.

504. Y. Aharoni, *The Settlement of the Israelite Tribes in Upper Galilee,* 1957 (Heb.). The results of this survey and the historical implications are discussed by Aharoni in "Problems of the Israelite Conquest in the Light of Archaeological Discovery," *AS* 2 (1957) 131–150. More recently Aharoni has offered a reconstruction of the Israelite occupation from the Plain of Esdraelon northward that shifts the events underlying the Song of Deborah and the conquest of Canaanite cities in the plain to as early at the late thirteenth or early twelfth centuries ("New Aspects of the Israelite Occupation in the North," in *Near Eastern Archaeology in the Twentieth Century: Essays in Honor of Nelson Glueck* [ed. J. A. Sanders], 1970, pp. 254–265).

505. On the premonarchic Jerusalemite traditions: B. Mazar, "Das vordavidische Jerusalem," *JPOS* 10 (1930) 181–191; B. Mazar, "Jerusalem," *EM,* vol. 3, 1958, cols. 793–797 (Heb.); M. Noth, "Jerusalem in the Israelite Tradition," *The Laws of the Pentateuch and Other Essays,* 1966 (orig. pub. 1950), pp. 132–144; K.-D. Schunck, "Juda und Jerusalem in vor- und frühisraelitischen Zeit," *Schalom: Studien zu Glaube und Geschichte Israels, A. Jepsen* (AVTR, 51), 1971, pp. 50–57; S. Talmon, "The Biblical Concept of Jerusalem," *JES* 8 (1971) 300–316. See also titles on Adonibezek and Bezek in note 113 of the present work.

506. M. Noth, "Die fünf Könige in der Höhle von Makkeda," *PJ* 33 (1937) 22–36.

507. There is no certain, or even probable, identification of the site of Meroz. Among the chief proposals have been locations near Hazor in Galilee, near Dothan in Samaria, and on one of the western summits of Mt. Gilboa. Alt (see note 450) did not suggest a particular identification, but simply emphasized that Meroz must have been situated in Manasseh not far removed from the battlefield in the Valley of Esdraelon. M. Chaney, "ḤDL-II and the 'Song of Deborah': Textual, Philological, and Sociological Studies in Judges 5, with Special Reference to the Verbal Occurrences of ḤDL in Biblical Hebrew" (Ph.D. diss., Harvard University, 1976), pp. 97, 100, 212–217, noting the impasse in previous attempts to locate a place called Meroz, has offered a solution which sees *mūzār,* "estranged one," as the original term in Judges 5:23 and taken to refer collectively to the Israelites of Reuben, Gilead, Dan, and Asher, who declined to do battle with the Canaanites (Judg. 15b–17) in contrast to Jael, the Kenite woman, who killed Sisera (Judg. 24–27). An initial reading of Chaney's ingenious proposal convinces me that it must be taken seriously as a genuinely new possibility, which will require evaluation on many levels. Since Chaney reached this conclusion too late in the writing of his dissertation for me to have had opportunity to evaluate fully the complex chain of evidence he employs, I have decided to retain the customary understanding of Meroz as a place name. I remain entirely open, however, to the possibility that Meroz may evaporate altogether as a place name—and thus as an instance of a Canaanite city of grouping in alliance with Israel—while still recognizing that such a politico-military category of Canaanite cities and other social formations did exist.

508. Y. Aharoni, *The Land of the Bible,* p. 241.

509. H. J. Franken, "The Excavations at Deir 'Allā in Jordan," *VT* 10 (1960) 386–393; "The Excavations at Deir 'Allā in Jordan, Second Season," *VT* 11 (1961) 361–372; "The Excavations at Deir 'Allā in Jordan, Third Season," *VT* 12 (1962) 378–382; "Excavations at Deir 'Allā, Season 1964," *VT* 14 (1964) 417–422; *Excavations at Tell Deir 'Allā,* 1968.

510. H. J. Franken, *VT* 10 (1960) 389; *VT* 11 (1961) 371–372; *VT* 14 (1964) 422; *Excavations at Tell Deir 'Allā,* 1968, pp. 4–7.

511. W. F. Albright, "Jethro, Hobab and Reuel in Early Hebrew Tradition," *CBQ* 25 (1963) 7–9; F. C. Fensham, "Did a Treaty Between the Israelites and Kenites Exist?" *BASOR* 175 (1964) 51–54; A. Cody, "Exodus 18:12: Jethro Accepts a Covenant with the Israelites," *Biblica* 49 (1968) 153–166.

512. For advocacy of the Kenite origin of Yahwism, see H. H. Rowley, *From Joseph to*

Joshua, 1950, pp. 149–161, and for rebuttal of the Kenite hypothesis, see C. H. W. Brekelmans, *OTS* 10 (1954) 215–224. See also comments and bibliography in M. Weippert, *The
Settlement of the Israelite Tribes in Palestine* (SBT, Second Series, 21), 1967 (Eng. trans. 1971),
pp. 105–106, note 14.

513. H. Reviv, "Urban Institutions, Personages and Problems of Terminology in Biblical
Presentations of Non-Israelite Cities," *EI* 10 (1971) 258–263 (Heb.), is of methodological
importance in that it approaches biblical technical terms for non-Israelite political offices as
the inexact choices of scribes or redactors addressing Israelite readers who had no proper
framework for understanding how Canaanite urban government operated. Reviv understands *'am hā'ārets* and *bā'ē sha'ar hā'îr* to mean "elders" at Hebron (Gen. 23:7,10,12–13), *nᵉsi'
ha'arets* to mean "nonmonarchic city ruler" at Shechem (Gen. 34:2), *bᵉ'ālîm* to mean
"assembly of citizens" and "elders" at Shechem (Judg. 9:2–3, 6–7, 18,20,23–26), and *sārîm* to
mean "high officials" at Succoth and Penuel (Judg. 8:6,14). The temporal horizons of the
redactions and of the actual Canaanite urban sociopolitical forms presupposed are matters
of so much dispute that Reviv's work is more significant for its effort to bring a consistent
methodology to passages that have been treated atomistically than it is definitive in its
specific conclusions.

514. The still indispensable classic on the Iroquois by the pioneer American anthropologist is L. H. Morgan, *League of the Iroquois,* 1851 (reprinted with intro. by W. N.
Fenton, 1962); see also C. Resek, *Lewis Henry Morgan: American Scholar,* 1960. In the last
century Morgan's work has been deepened, extended, supplemented, and often corrected.
Of pertinence for understanding the structure and history of the league are the following
titles (in chronological order): J. Douglas, "Consolidation of the Iroquois Confederacy,"
JAGS 29 (1897) 41–54; D. C. Scott, "Traditional History of the Confederacy of the Six
Nations," *RSCPT,* 3rd series, 5 (1912), Section II, 195–246; A. C. Parker, "Constitution of
the Five Nations, or the Iroquois Book of the Great Law," *NYSMB* 186 (1916) 1–155
(reprinted in *Parker on the Iroquois,* ed. W. N. Fenton, 1968); J. N. Hewitt, "A Constitutional
League of Peace in the Stone Age of America: The League of the Iroquois and Its
Constitution," *ARSI,* 1918, 527–545; G. S. Snyderman, *Behind the Tree of Peace: A Sociological Analysis of Iroquois Warfare,* 1948; T. R. Henry, *Wilderness Messiah: The Story of Hiawatha
and the Iroquois,* 1955; A. F. C. Wallace, "The Iroquois: A Brief Outline of Their History,"
PH 23 (1956) 15–28; E. Tooker, ed., *Iroquois Culture, History and Prehistory* (proceedings of
the 1965 Conference on Iroquois Research), 1967. On archaeology of the Iroquois, see
note 579 below.

515. O. Eissfeldt, "Protektorat der Midianiter über ihre Nachbarn im letzten Viertel des
2. Jahrtausends v. Chr.," *JBL* 87 (1967) 383–393, proposed that the Midianite nomads, in
the process of shifting from ass to camel nomadism, exercised just such a hegemony or
protectorate over Moab, Edom, and part of Sinai during the period when Israel was taking
root in Canaan. W. J. Dumbrell, "The Midianites and Their Transjordanian Successors:
Studies in the History, Social Structure and Political Influence of Related Transjordanian
Groupings" (Th.D. diss., Harvard University, 1970), posits Midian as a broad-ranging
league, in a manner similar to Eissfeldt, and traces the subsequent league groupings that
emerged one after the other in the same region under the names Ishmaelites, Kedarites,
and Nabateans.

516. *pᵉrāzōn* (Judg. 5:7) and *pirzōnō* (Judg. 5:11) have been customarily translated as a
collective noun meaning "rural populace" or "peasantry," from the root *prz* with a well-
recognized meaning in biblical Hebrew of "open, unwalled" (cf. esp. I Sam. 6:18 where
kōpher hap-pᵉrāzî, "unwalled village," is paired with *'ir mivtsār,* "fortified city"). Many exegetes, on the other hand, have thought that peasants do not fit the military context of the

poem, and some have regarded the reference to *tsidqōth pirzōnō beyisrā'ēl,* "the saving deeds of his peasantry in Israel," as contradictory to the preceding *tsidqōth Yahweh.* Accordingly, in recent years there has been a trend to construe *perāzōn* either as a collective noun for "warriors" for which *perez* in Hab. 3:14 is thought to lend support (cf. W. F. Albright, *Yahweh and the Gods of Canaan,* 1968, p. 43, note 101; P. C. Craigie, *VT* 22 [1972] 350; G. R. Driver, *ALUOS* 4 [1962/63]; M. S. Seale, *JBL* 81 [1962] 343–345), or as an abstract noun for "championship/leadership," its subject being either Israel alone in vss. 7 and 11 or Israel in vs. 7 and Yahweh in vs. 11 (cf. C. Rabin, *JJS* 6 [1955] 127–128; W. Richter, *Traditionsgeschichtliche Untersuchungen zum Richterbuch* [BBB, 18], 1963, p. 95; A. Weiser, *ZAW* 7 [1959] 77). In my judgment the abstract noun "championship/leadership" is syntactically awkward and conceptually dubious in this early poem, while "warriors" is a questionable translation philologically, which leaves "peasantry" as the preferable reading.

517. M. Weber, *The Sociology of Religion,* 4th ed., 1956, chap. 6–7.

518. E. Wolf, *Peasant Wars of the Twentieth Century,* 1966. In private discussions and in class lectures at the Graduate Theological Union, Berkeley, California, Marvin Chaney has applied Wolf's criteria for successful peasant revolutions to the early Israelite peasantry as attested in Joshua, Judges, and other premonarchic sources.

NOTES TO PART X

519. J. Bright, *A History of Israel,* 2nd ed., 1972, pp. 130–139.

520. Ibid., p. 140.

521. *ANET,* 369–371; J. A. Wilson, *The Burden of Egypt,* 1951, pp. 221–228; D. Baly, "The Geography of Monotheism," in *Translating and Understanding the Old Testament* (ed. H. T. Frank and W. L. Reed), 1970, pp. 259–263; on the economic and political factors in Atonism, see H. Kees, *Das Priestertum im ägyptischen Staat,* 1953, pp. 79–88.

522. On the reforms of Urukagina of Lagash: C. J. Gadd, *CAH,* vol. 1/pt. 2, 1971, pp. 139–142, with bibliography cited. The beneficiaries of Urukagina's reforms have been much disputed. V.V. Struve in *Ancient Mesopotamia: Socio-Economic History* (ed. I. M. Diakonoff), 1969 (orig. pub. 1933), pp. 36–40, argued that the new king in Lagash championed a broad democratic base of armed "rank-and-file freemen" (small landholders and lower-rank priests) against the ruling class of big landholders and chief priests, whereas I. M. Diakonoff, *Ancient Mesopotamia,* 1969 (orig. pub. 1957), pp. 189–190, countered with the claim that Urukagina's reform measures were more apparent than substantive, since they were launched primarily to benefit the wealthy citizens and priests while offering no more than symbolic gestures of improved conditions to the lower strata of "freemen." Both scholars concurred that slaves fell outside the scope of the reforms. Struve claimed that in fact slavery was greatly extended in order to reach productivity levels necessary to improve the economic lot of the freemen without cost to the upper classes. Both scholars also agreed that the reforms were incomplete and short-lived, either because Urukagina failed to abolish or limit interest on loans (Struve), or because he never intended to do more than benefit the upper socioeconomic strata (Diakonoff).

523. F. R. Kraus, *Ein Edikt des Königs Ammi-Ṣaduqa von Babylon,* 1958; J. Lewy, "The Biblical Institution of *Derôr* in the Light of Akkadian Documents," *EI* 5 (1958) 21–31; J. Bottéro, "Désordre économique et annulation des dettes en Mésopotamie à l'époque paléo-Babylonienne," *JESHO* 4 (1961) 113–164.

524. See my discussion in X.51 on "A Program of Historical Cultural-Material Research into Early Israel."

525. Cf. e.g., the observations of D. Diringer, *The Alphabet: A Key to the History of Mankind,* 3rd ed., 1968: "The prototype alphabet, which we have referred to as 'Proto-Semitic,' probably originated in the second quarter of the second millennium B.C., i.e., in the Hyksos period now commonly dated 1730–1580 B.C. The political situation in the Near East at that period favored the creation of a 'revolutionary' writing, a script which we can perhaps term 'democratic' (or rather, a 'people's script'), as against the 'theocratic' script of Egypt, Mesopotamia, or China. As with other significant innovations—such as the adoption of the 'Roman' type of writing in England and Germany, the adoption of the decimal system in weights and measures, spelling reform, reform of the monetary system, and so on—alphabetic writing, to begin with, was strongly opposed by the conservative, politically stabilized states and theocratically governed societies. It took centuries till the alphabet established itself, and then only in newly founded states; it doubtless took very many centuries to establish itself in the old states. The nationality of the inventors of the Proto-Semitic alphabet is unknown" (p. 162). While much uncertainty surrounds the origin of the alphabetic script, it is striking that one of the earliest—if not the earliest—of the proto-alphabetic scripts was written by Semitic workers in Egyptian copper mines on the Sinai Peninsula at Serabit el-Khadem, at some time between 1800 and 1500 B.C. We may not know the "nationality" of the inventors, but this Sinaitic setting gives us an important clue to the *socioeconomic status* of some of the earliest experimenters with the alphabetic script. S. Yeivin states: "It should be stressed that it [the alphabetic script] was apparently invented and certainly at first employed by the lower strata of society for their personal everyday use, while the upper classes and learned scribes continued to avail themselves of the 'cultured' systems of Mesopotamian cuneiform, or . . . Egyptian hieroglyphics" (*WHJP*, 1st series, vol. 2, 1970, p. 31; see also S. Yeivin, *RSO* 38 [1963] 284–285, for the rather poorly substantiated suggestion that the invention, or at least the development and spread, of the Proto-Sinaitic alphabet was connected with the biblical patriarchal families). A. R. Millard, "The Practice of Writing in Ancient Israel," *BA* 35 (1972) 98–111, shows that "writing was theoretically within the competence of any ancient Israelite, not the prerogative of an elite professional class alone, and . . . that it was, in fact, quite widely practiced" (p. 111). For fuller details on the invention and spread of the alphabet, see F. M. Cross, "The Origin and Early Evolution of the Alphabet," *EI* 8 (1967) 8*–24*, and P. K. McCarter, "The Early Diffusion of the Alphabet," *BA* 37 (1974) 54–68.

526. G. E. Mendenhall, "The Hebrew Conquest of Palestine," *BAR* 3 (1970) 100–120 = *BA* 25 (1962) 66–87; *The Tenth Generation: The Origins of the Biblical Tradition,* 1973.

527. Mendenhall, *The Tenth Generation,* chap. 3.

528. G. Fohrer, "Zur Einwirkung der gesellschaftlichen Struktur Israels auf seine Religion," *Near Eastern Studies in Honor of W. F. Albright* (ed. H. Goedicke), 1971, pp. 169–185.

529. Ibid., p. 173.

530. Ibid., p. 176.

531. Ibid., pp. 183–184.

532. A lucid critical discrimination of the several meanings of "function" in social-scientific usage will be found in E. Nagel, *The Structure of Science,* 1961, pp. 520–535; a more detailed and fully illustrated analysis and critique of French and British structural functionalism appears in M. Harris, *The Rise of Anthropological Theory: A History of Theories of Culture,* 1968, chaps. 18–19.

533. Nagel emphasizes that functional models need to be more precise about the nature of the system and the state of the system under consideration and more sensitive to the fact that some social items may be both functional and dysfunctional at the same time: " . . . it is

hardly possible to overestimate the importance for the social sciences of recognizing that the imputation of a teleological function to a given variable must always be *relative* to some particular state in some particular system and that, although a given form of social behavior may be functional for certain social attributes, it may also be dysfunctional for many others" (*The Structure of Science,* 1961, p. 532).

534. T. C. Vriezen, *An Outline of Old Testament Theology,* 2nd ed., 1954 (Eng. trans. 1958), pp. 23–25; *The Religion of Ancient Israel,* 1963 (Eng. trans. 1967), pp. 82–83.

535. Reference should also be made to the work of the biblical scholar Antonin Causse, who was influenced in large measure by Durkheim's view of religion as an expression of social solidarity, as well as by L. Lévy-Bruhl's notion of human prelogical mentality that only slowly gave way in historic times to a logical mentality (in Causse's view this occurred in Israel with the Deuteronomist). Causse's debt to Durkheim and Lévy-Bruhl is traced, in a somewhat repetitious and imprecise manner, by S.T. Kimbrough, Jr., "A Non-Weberian Sociological Approach to Israelite Religion," *JNES* 31 (1972) 195–202, and, more fully, in "Une conception sociologique de la religion d'Israël," *RHPR* 49 (1969) 313–330. As to the merit of Causse's work, notably his *Du groupe ethnique à la communauté religieuse,* 1937, it must be said that his efforts at reconstructing the functional fit between early Israelite society and religion were seriously marred by a simplistic identification of early Israel as a homogeneous ethnic community of nomads. Social conflict and disintegration, reflected in religious polemics, were precipitated by the breakup of the old ethnic and occupational homogeneity under the impact of Israelite fusion with Canaanites and socioeconomic diversification into agriculture, crafts, and trade. Peasant conservatism retained elements of the old nomadic outlook on life. Causse's reconstruction was also vitiated by an exaggerated conception of transition from an early collectivism to an individualism emergent in later prophets. By dealing with historical development in the society-religion nexus, however, Causse moved into areas where Durkheim's method was only of limited pertinence. Incidentally, Causse is frequently cited as though his study demonstrated the pastoral nomadic origins of Israel; in truth, Causse merely assumed pastoral nomadic origins as the presupposed base for elaborating his model of the interplay between Israelite society and religion along a time line that moved from unity to diversity and from consensus to confusion and conflict.

536. For a full statement of the evidence on the Hebrew language as a dialect of Canaanite, see Z. S. Harris, *The Development of the Canaanite Dialects,* 1939. By means of isoglosses, Harris studied the structure of Canaanite, including Ugaritic and Hebrew.

537. Durkheim's fundamental work of sociology of religion is *The Elementary Forms of the Religious Life,* 1912 (Eng. trans. 1915), but that work alone may be misleading apart from fuller understanding of his concepts of "social facts" in *The Rules of Sociological Method,* 1895 (Eng. trans. 1938) and of "social solidarity" in its differentiated forms of "mechanical solidarity" and "organic solidarity" in *Division of Labor in Society,* 1893 (Eng. trans. 1933), and in *Suicide,* 1897 (Eng. trans. 1951). I. M. Zeitlin, *Ideology and the Development of Sociological Theory,* 1968, chap. 15, perceptively discusses the interconnections of Durkheim's concepts throughout the course of his intellectual development. Steven Lukes, *Émile Durkheim, His Life and Work: A Historical and Critical Study,* 1973, pp. 237–244, 450–484, situates Durkheim's sociology of religion in biographical and historical context. The impact of Durkheim, and of his pupil Mauss, on structural-functional anthropological theory, particularly in the case of Lévi-Strauss, is discussed by M. Harris, *The Rise of Anthropological Theory,* pp. 464–493. R. N. Bellah, "Durkheim and History," *ASR* 24 (1959) 447–461 (reprinted in R. A. Nisbet, ed., *Emile Durkheim,* 1965, pp. 153–176), argues for a closer

rapprochement between sociology and history in the work of Durkheim than is usually conceded.

538. Durkheim, *The Elementary Forms of the Religious Life,* p. 419.

539. Ibid., p. 8.

540. G. E. Swanson, *The Birth of the Gods: The Origin of Primitive Beliefs,* 1960.

541. Ibid., pp. 18–21.

542. Ibid., p. 63.

543. The method, contents, aims, strengths, and weaknesses of Murdock's Human Relations Area Files (from 1937 to 1949 known as the Cross-Cultural Survey), and including his World Ethnographic Sample and Ethnographic Atlas, are succinctly discussed by M. Harris, *The Rise of Anthropological Theory,* pp. 612–618.

544. J. Freund, *The Sociology of Max Weber,* 1966 (Eng. trans. 1968), relates Weber's sociology of religion to his other special sociologies of economics, politics, law, art, and technique within the framework of his general sociological method.

545. M. Weber, *Ancient Judaism,* 1921 (Eng. trans. 1952).

546. H. H. Gerth and C. W. Mills, eds., *From Max Weber: Essays in Sociology,* 1958; M. Weber, *The Sociology of Religion,* 1922 (Eng. trans. 1963).

547. Weber's most systematic discussion of the social bearers of different kinds of religion is in *The Sociology of Religion,* chaps. 6–8.

548. K. Marx and F. Engels, *The German Ideology* (ed. C. J. Arthur), 1970, p. 42. The original was written in 1845–46 but not published until 1947 in part and 1965 in whole. Arthur's edition is an abridgement and slight revision of the 1965 complete English translation.

549. Ibid., pp. 46–47.

550. Ibid., p. 47.

551. Ibid., pp. 47–48.

552. In their analyses of actual sociohistorical situations Marx and Engels dealt in a more sophisticated and nuanced manner with the complicated skein of interrelated phenomena than could be guessed from mere reference to their summary theoretical statements or from the mechanistic applications of their theory by so-called vulgar Marxists. Especially revealing in this regard is the letter of Engels to Joseph Bloch in 1890 (C. H. Selsam and H. Martel, eds., *Reader in Marxist Philosophy,* 1963, pp. 204–206; cited and commented on by M. Harris, *The Rise of Anthropological Theory,* 1968, pp. 244–245). The French Marxist Louis Althusser, "Contradiction and Overdetermination," *For Marx,* 1965 (essay orig. pub. 1962; Eng. trans. 1969), pp. 89–128, argues that the contradictions at any given moment in a society are open to the impact of structures ranging all the way from the economic base to the ideological superstructure. These influences may pull in opposite directions, thereby impeding the contradiction from surfacing in full force ("historical inhibition"); or they may move toward a conjunction, reinforcing one another, thereby releasing the fullest expression of the contradiction ("revolutionary rupture"). That Marx saw all social factors as internally connected relations within an organic totality—thereby adamantly refusing to isolate factors into unilinear causes, effects, and conditions, but focusing instead on particular social relations as most influential for certain functions, contexts, and developments—is cogently argued by B. Ollman, *Alienation: Marx's Concept of Man in Capitalist Society,* 1971, especially pp. 12–42. Ollman claims that " . . . 'cause' and 'determine' [in Marx] are generally used to point to the effect produced by any entity in changing one or more of the relations that make up other entities. But as each one develops with the direct and indirect aid of everything else, operating on various levels, to single out any aspect as the determin-

ing one can only be a way of emphasizing a particular link in the problem under consideration. Marx is saying that for this factor, in this context, *this* is the influence most worth
noting, the relation which will most aid our comprehension of the relevant characteristics"
(pp. 17–18).

553. There are now two collections in English translation: R. Niebuhr, ed., *Marx and
Engels on Religion,* 1964, and S. K. Padover, trans. and ed., *Karl Marx on Religion,* 1974,
which has fuller materials from Marx, including the important article "On the Jewish
Question" and many private letters. The editors, although making an effort to be fair and
objective in their introductory essays, turn increasingly to a polemical style of deprecation
or rebuttal of the materials they are editing. The volume of secondary literature on the
subject of Marxism and religion seems to have been greater from Christian sources than
from Communist or Marxist sources. Moreover, the greater part of this literature is
superficial, much of it arguing *ad hominem*; cf. titles and annotations under "Marxism and
Religion" in J. Lachs, *Marxist Philosophy: A Bibliographical Guide,* 1967. Bibliography since
1967 can be located in issues of the monthly *AIMS Newsletter* (American Institute of Marxist
Studies). J. Kadenbach, *Das Religionsverständnis von Karl Marx,* 1970, in spite of its liabilities
as a published dissertation (e.g., a certain disjointedness, pedantry, and weakness in
exposition), is rich in bibliography and serves both to lay out the range of Marx's views on
religion and to point up major interconnections with other aspects of his thought within an
overarching philosophic method.

554. Developments in the "new archaeology" are helpfully summed up and case studies
cited by M. Harris, *The Rise of Anthropological Theory,* pp. 675–687. L. R. Binford has been
one of the American pioneers in placing archaeology in a wider social-scientific context. In
his 1962 article on "Archaeology as Anthropology," now reprinted in a collection of his
articles (*An Archaeological Perspective,* 1972), Binford stated programmatically: "Until the
tremendous quantities of data which the archaeologist controls are used in the solution of
problems dealing with cultural evolution and systemic change, we are not only failing to
contribute to the furtherance of the aims of anthropology but retarding the accomplishment of these aims . . . Archaeologists should be among the best qualified to study and
directly test hypotheses concerning the process of evolutionary change, particularly processes of change that are relatively slow, or hypotheses that postulate temporal-processual
priorities as regards total cultural systems. The lack of theoretical concern and rather naive
attempts at explanation which archaeologists currently advance must be modified" (p.31).

555. The limits and possibilities of reconstructing prehistoric religious attitudes, belief,
and practices from material remains are discussed by G. Clark, *Archaeology and Society:
Reconstructing the Prehistoric Past,* 3rd ed., 1957, pp. 232–235, and by G. R. Levy, *Religious
Concepts of the Stone Age and Their Influence upon European Thought,* 1948 (reprinted 1963
with intro. by H. Frankfort), pp. 3–164.

556. N. P. Jacobson, "Marxism and Religious Naturalism," *JR* 29 (1949) 95–113, is a
carefully reasoned and analytically incisive argument advancing the view that the creative
process of labor in which man has developed his history within determinate limits is viewed
by Marx as the source of all human value and, as such, Marx's view is congruent with forms
of religious naturalism that similarly understand the process by which man emerges as an
increasingly value-discriminating but thoroughly this-worldly being. Particularly interesting is his claim that Marx had a clear concept of "transcendence" in the sense that, while
man can move within a range of freedom at any given point in the unfolding human
cultural drama, he is unable to control the overall process which will inevitably confront
him with constantly emerging novelties. Somewhat similar to Jacobson's analysis in its
philosophical range, although more informed by ethical considerations and by the con-

temporary upsurge of Latin American liberation theology, is the brace of articles by G. Pixley, "Justice and Class Struggle: A Challenge for Process Theology," *Process Studies* 4 (1974) 159–175, and by C. Williamson, "Whitehead as Counter-Revolutionary? Toward a Christian-Marxist Dialogue," *Process Studies* 4 (1974) 176–186. From a broadly Marxist philosophical perspective, E. Bloch, *Atheism in Christianity: The Religion of the Exodus and the Kingdom,* 1973, contends that within Jewish-Christian eschatological beliefs and practices there persistently emerges an incisive and potentially effective quality of hope and social commitment and that this orientation toward the future, at once both utopian and capable of practical expression, is detachable from the mistaken idea of the existence of deity.

557. Harris, *The Rise of Anthropological Theory,* especially chaps. 1, 8, and 22.

558. The terms "emic" and "etic" in ethnological theory were coined by the linguist Kenneth Pike on analogy with phon*emic* and phon*etic.* *"Emics"* refers to cultural explanations that draw their criteria from the consciousness of the people in the culture being explained, so that emic statements can be verified or falsified according to their correspondence to or deviation from the understanding of the cultural actors. *"Etics"* refers to cultural explanations whose criteria derive from a body of theory and method shared in a community of scientific observers. These cultural explanations constitute "a corpus of predictions about the behavior of classes of people." Etic statements cannot be verified or falsified by what cultural actors think is true, but only by their predictive success or failure. "Emics" systematically excludes "etics," but "etics" makes room for "emics" insofar as what cultural actors think about their action is part of the data to be accounted for in developing a corpus of predictions about lawful social behavior. See the discussion in Harris, *Anthropological Theory,* chap. 20, and especially the definitions of emics and etics on pp. 571, 575.

559. Harris, *Anthropological Theory,* p. 4. Harris elucidates this Marxian cultural-material strategy at a later point as follows: "What is vital to a science of culture is that an attempt be made to relate such apparently inscrutable phenomena [irrational 'noneconomic' behavior of the sort that Malinowski was fond of pointing out] to the basic techno-economic arrangements by which the total sociocultural system interacts with its natural and cultural habitat. Historical materialism as proposed by Marx did not consist of attempts to explain particular sociocultural systems by reference to individual economic motivations. Nothing could be more contrary to Marx's position. He rather sought to explain the peculiar conditioned forms of a group's collective and individual economic behavior in terms of an adaptive evolutionary sequence. In a modern anthropological formulation, it is the techno-environmental and techno-economic conditions in which the human population finds itself which demand priority of analysis because there exists overwhelming evidence that these are the parts of the total sociocultural system which in the long run and in most cases swing social structure and ideology into functional conformity" (pp. 565–566).

560. By way of illustrating some of the accomplishments of cultural-material research, Harris sums up his own work on cultural-material factors in the differentiated developments of slavery in the United States and in Brazil (*Anthropological Theory,* pp. 242–243), as well as the work of Leslie White, Julian Steward, and Gordon Childe toward a wider cultural-material theory of social evolution, particularly with reference to K. Wittfogel's hydraulic or irrigation hypothesis about human culture (ibid., chaps. 22–23).

561. The fundamental unity of slow cumulative change and rapid cataclysmic change throughout the historico-social process is cogently argued and illustrated by W. F. Wertheim, *Evolution and Revolution: The Rising Waves of Emancipation,* 1974. Wertheim finds an accelerating trend toward emancipation from the forces of nature and from inter-human domination and exploitation over the long course of human history. The movement is

dialectical or pulsating in an unbroken fabric of evolution (slow change), revolution (rapid change), and counter-revolution (temporarily retarded or reversed change). Wertheim further attempts to formulate intellectual and practical criteria for differentiating revolutions and counter-revolutions (both of which fundamentally effect social change), and both from revolts, rebellions, riots, and coups d'état (which do not effect social change).

562. R. McC. Adams, *The Evolution of Urban Society: Early Mesopotamia and Prehispanic Mexico,* 1966, pp. 174–175.

563. G. E. Swanson, *The Birth of the Gods: The Origin of Primitive Beliefs,* 1960, pp. 177–178.

564. Marx and Engels, *The German Ideology,* pp. 46–47; cf. the contrast between emic and etic statements of cultural explanation discussed in note 558. It will be seen that Marx and Engels were strongly opting for an etic cultural explanation as against an emic cultural "nonexplanation" or "pseudo-explanation."

565. On zones of social organization: J. Steward, *Theory of Culture Change,* 1955; M. Sahlins, "Segmentary Lineage: An Organization of Predatory Expansion," *AA* 63 (1961) 322–345; E. Service, *Primitive Social Organization,* 2nd. ed., 1971; M. Fried, *The Evolution of Political Society,* 1967; M. Sahlins, *Tribesmen,* 1968; E. Terray, "Historical Materialism and Segmentary Lineage-based Societies," *Marxism and "Primitive" Societies,* 1969 (Eng. trans. 1972), pp. 95–186.

566. C. Meillassoux, *Anthropologie économique des Gouro de Côte d'Ivoire,* 1964; E. Terray, *Marxism and "Primitive" Societies,* 1969 (Eng. trans. 1972).

567. A. Alt, "The God of the Fathers," in *Essays on Old Testament History and Religion,* 1966 (orig. pub. 1929), pp. 3–100; O. Eissfeldt, "Jahwe Zebaoth," *KS,* III, 1966 (orig. pub. 1950), pp. 103–123; O. Eissfeldt, "El and Yahweh," *JSS* 1 (1956) 25–37; F. M. Cross, "Yahweh and the God of the Patriarchs," *HTR* 55 (1962) 225–259; M. Haran, "The Religion of the Patriarchs: An Attempt at a Synthesis," *ASTI* 4 (1965) 30–55; W. F. Albright, *Yahweh and the Gods of Canaan: A Historical Analysis of Two Contrasting Faiths,* 1968, chaps. 3–4; F. M. Cross, *Canaanite Myth and Hebrew Epic: Essays in the History of the Religion of Israel,* 1973, chaps. 1–3.

568. The linguistic and religio-historical work of F. M. Cross in *Canaanite Myth and Hebrew Epic,* 1973, offers a promising framework and some material results for a further socioreligious inquiry, although his own sociological correlations are disappointingly thin and imprecise.

569. Feedback devices in technology are governors or servomechanisms (e.g., float valves, safety valves, thermostats, etc.) which regulate a machine or process in such manner that a controlled variable (e.g., level, speed, pressure, temperature) is maintained at constant value, or within a desired range of values, by means of a command variable (i.e., a control setting of the feedback regulator). The command is carried out automatically, in spite of external disturbances, by a closed-loop information and response system wherein the feedback device "reads" the state of the controlled variable and adjusts it before that state varies far from the desired constant value or range of values. Norbert Wiener, *The Human Uses of Human Beings: Cybernetics and Society,* 2nd ed., 1954, p. 33, described feedback simply as "the property of being able to adjust future conduct by past performance." Following Wiener's lead, the concept has been applied widely in biology, psychology, economics, and sociology. For example, family counseling techniques developed at the Human Relations Institute in Palo Alto, California, have been formulated according to the analogies of negative feedback in a closed-loop system (good human communication) and of positive feedback in an open-loop system, the so-called vicious circle (bad human communication), cf. P. Watzlewick, ed., *Pragmatics of Human Communication,* 1964.

570. Given the careless polemical use of "reduction" and "reductionist" as "boo-words," it is important to relate reduction in sociological theories of religion to reduction as a fundamental operation in all scientific theory, along the line of H.H. Penner and E.A. Yonan, "Is a Science of Religion Possible?," *JR* 52 (1972) 107–133; "Reduction is defined as the explanation of one theory by some other theory (118). . . . A study of reduction indicates very clearly that what is being reduced is a theory, not a phenomenon or a property (119). . . . The sole purpose of reduction is to offer adequate theoretical explanations and to provide for the continued progress of scientific knowledge (131). . . . Why do scholars of religion remain shy of definitions and theories? It is due to the fact that the 'something' which must be understood cannot in principle be given a definition or theory. Without the construction of theories in which the problems of 'definition,' 'reduction,' and 'explanation' are resolved, this predicament will continue to persist and paralyze all methodological attempts to move beyond existing perspectives that see religion only in terms of the sacred (132). . . . We wish to point out, however, that our argument checks the Fabian tactic of winning a methodological battle by avoiding it (133)." In place of the obscure, methodologically meaningless "definitions" of religion such as "ultimate concern" or "the numinous," Penner and Yonan single out two definitions which they believe satisfy the rules of good definitions (which means propositions that can be tested for verification or falsification): (1) F. Ferré's definition of religion as "one's way of valuing most intensively and comprehensively" and (2) M. Spiro's definition of religion as "a cultural system consisting of culturally patterned interaction with culturally postulated super-human beings" (129). The Penner-Yonan critique of Dilthey's *Verstehen* as a "method" underlying much study in history and phenomenology of religion may be understood as their rejection of an emic approach to explaining cultural phenomena in favor of an etic approach (see notes 558 and 564 above).

571. There exist several valuable compendia of data for making a start on a material-cultural and economic inventory of ancient Canaan/Israel. On archaeological data, see A.G. Barrois, *Manuel d'archéologie biblique*, 2 vols., 1939/1953, a work obviously in need of updating in the light of further archaeological excavations. Daily work, particularly in agriculture and the crafts, is treated in G. Dalman, *Arbeit und Sitte in Palästina,* 7 vols., 1928–1942, although without sufficient discrimination between ancient and modern times. L. Turkowski, "Peasant Agriculture in the Judean Hills," *PEQ* 101 (1969) 21–33, 101–112, reports with astonishing detail on crops, tools, and work processes observed during 1943–1947 primarily in the vicinity of Bethlehem, but with some attention to more northerly and southerly hill regions. To a limited degree, Turkowski comments on changes in agriculture from past to present, but his judgments as to when particular crops, tools, or work processes were introduced into Palestine are random and largely undocumented. With respect to what the author saw with his own eyes and had explained to him by informants, this study is a model of keen observation and thorough reporting.

572. The sorts of correlations that need to be researched between material and socio-religious culture are well illustrated in one circumscribed sphere by E. Neufeld, "Hygiene Conditions in Ancient Israel (Iron Age)," *BA* 34 (1971) 42–66. To be sure, there has been no lack of speculation about hygienic explanations of Israelite dietary and ritual purity laws, but rarely has hygiene been systematically examined as a facet of the actual material-cultural conditions in their total pertinent range, as Neufeld here undertakes in an initial exploratory manner. Although this version of his study is condensed and limited, Neufeld's method is exemplary.

573. A. Alt's essays and articles have been in large part collected in *Kleine Schriften zur*

Geschichte des Volkes Israel, vols. 1–2, 1953; vol. 3, 1959 (abbreviated in notes as *KS*). Several of the most influential of these contributions have been translated as *Essays in Old Testament History and Religion,* 1966 (abbreviated in notes as *EOTHR*). For the origins of Israel, Alt's historico-territorial method is set forth with particular methodological clarity in "The Settlement of the Israelites in Palestine," *EOTHR,* 1966 (orig. pub. 1925), pp. 175–221. Many of Alt's methods and conclusions are well integrated into M. Noth, *The History of Israel,* 2nd ed., 1954 (Eng. trans. 1960), and S. Herrmann, *A History of Israel in Old Testament Times,* 1973 (Eng. trans. 1975).

574. M. B. Rowton, "The Topological Factor in the Ḥapiru Problem," *Studies in Honor of Benno Landsberger* (Assyriological Studies of the Oriental Institute of the University of Chicago, 16), 1965, pp. 375–387.

575. The first two articles in the series on nomadism announced by Rowton are: "Autonomy and Nomadism in Western Asia," *Or* 42 (1973) 247–258, and "Urban Autonomy in a Nomadic Environment," *JNES* 32 (1973) 201–215. The significance of Rowton's undertaking is that, while explicitly acknowledging that he is not a specialist on pastoral nomadism, he recognizes the critical need for specialists in the ancient Near East to avail themselves of what is known about the relevant phenomena from the social sciences and to pose questions and issues which specialists in the pertinent fields can treat in a dialogical relationship with other specialists. From this methodological and programmatic point of view, I regard Rowton's "nomadic project" as exemplary and in a sense parallel to what I am undertaking with reference to the sociology of the religion of early Israel.

576. M. B. Rowton employs "topology" in the following sense: "Topology, viewed here as a subdivision of ecology, denotes the relation between the physical environment and history in all its aspects, that is, not only the economic factor but also the events of history, the military factor, and the social factor" (*Studies in Honor of B. Landsberger,* 1965, p. 375). See also L. Marfoe, "The Emergence of National States in Southern Syria: Aspects of the Political and Ecological Relationships among Highland and Steppe Societies" (Paper presented to the Social World of Ancient Israel Group at the annual meeting of AAR-SBL, San Francisco, December 29, 1977). That geography as a discipline is broadening its outlook and refining its methods in material-cultural and sociological directions will be evident from R. J. Chorley and P. Hagget, *Models in Geography,* 1967, and J. E. Spencer and W. L. Thomas, *Cultural Geography,* 1969. Thus far most biblical geography has been historically oriented, with one valuable "aside" into geology by D. Baly, *The Geography of the Bible,* 1957; rev. ed., 1974. Y. Ben-Arieh, "A Geographical Approach to Historical Geography," *SGI* 7 (1970) 64–95 (Heb.), shows that so-called historical geography of the Bible or of ancient Israel has always been far more "historical" than "geographical," consistently avoiding coming to terms with a systematic initial understanding of the geographical component or base in historical studies. Some of the various ways of analyzing and studying the geographical component in history are indicated by Ben-Arieh.

577. E. Terray, *Marxism in "Primitive" Societies,* 1969 (Eng. trans. 1972), pp. 95–107.

578. Particularly pertinent to a more holistic cultural-material approach to biblical archaeology is the work of A. E. Glock, director of the Concordia-ASOR Excavations at Tell Ta'annak (Jordan). At a seminar of resident fellows at the Albright Institute of Archaeological Research in Jerusalem on May 3, 1974, Glock presented a paper on "Archaeological Systematics" in which he proposed an ethnographic model for Palestinian archaeology. The model views archaeological remains as the deposits of a regional system consisting of paleo-environment, material culture forms in a site, and reconstruction of societal dynamics. The model mandates careful procedures in research design for determining the

site to excavate, researching and reporting the culture, and interpreting the results of excavation and analysis. Glock informs me that this paper is under revision and enlargement and will eventually be published. In the meantime he is preparing an analysis of the pottery from Taanach on the basis of a far more refined and objective method than heretofore employed. The report will be published under the title "Homo Faber: The Pot and the Potter at Taanach," to appear in three parts (I. Fabric Analysis; II. Form Analysis; III. Surface Finish) in *Bulletin of the American Schools of Archaeological Research*. See also A. E. Glock, "Biblical Archaeology—an Emerging Discipline?" in *The Archaeology of Jordan and Other Studies* (ed. L. T. Geraty), 1977.

579. To give only one example in an area with which I have some familiarity, see A. McPherron, "On the Sociology of Ceramics: Pottery Style Clustering, Marital Residence and Cultural Adaptions of an Algonkian-Iroquoian Border," *Iroquois Culture, History and Prehistory* (Proceedings of the 1965 Conference on Iroquois Research, ed. E. Tooker), pp. 101–107. For the significant way in which archaeology has been able to test and to correct both tradition and speculation about Iroquois "prehistory," see W. A. Ritchie, *The Archaeology of New York State*, rev. ed., 1969, and for similar accomplishments with respect to southwest Amer-Indian culture, see J. C. McGregor, *Southwestern Archaeology*, 2nd ed., 1965. In a study of new ways of analyzing and typing Palestinian pottery, based on his excavations at Tell Deir 'Alla (biblical Succoth?), H. J. Franken, "Analysis of Methods of Potmaking in Archaeology," *HTR* 64 (1971) 227–255, has begun to raise questions about the sociological and anthropological applications of more sophisticated pottery analysis: "The combination of analysis of material, method, and tradition reveals the problems these ancient potters faced and how they were solved. This describes the circumstances under which they worked and what was expected from them. In turn we learn something about the community which used the pottery. . . . This [the assignment of the technical analysis to mineralogical and other specialists] should free the archaeologist to do more anthropological study from this raw material—pottery. Mankind is after all the only legitimate reason for digging up the earth" (pp. 254–255). See also note 578 on A. E. Glock's forthcoming report on pottery from Taanach.

580. D. L. Clarke, *Analytical Archaeology*, 1968, comes out strongly for greater conceptual clarity in archaeological synthesis and central theory: "The contemporary study of sociocultural systems has emphasized that the analysis of ancient or modern human units and their products cannot be satisfactorily accomplished in terms of information from single network aspects of these complex systems. The social, psychological, linguistic, religious, economic and material attributes of hominid communities cannot be realistically studied if isolated from the integral context of the sociocultural and environmental system precipitating them in that particular mutually adjusted configuration. It may not be possible for the archaeologist to specify the exact values of these former factors but his analyses must at least take into account their interdependence. . . . Analytical archaeology is therefore primarily a syntactical approach to synthesis and central theory [the largely tacit procedures common to archaeology everywhere], a changing corpus of conceptual frameworks which emphasize that no archaeological study can be better than the ideological assumptions which underlie the development of its arguments" (xiv–xv). See also F. Hole and R. F. Heizer, *An Introduction to Prehistoric Archaeology*, 2nd ed., 1969, especially pt. 5 ("Reconstructing Cultural Subsystems") and pt. 6 ("Theories and Methods of Archaeological Interpretation"); see also the titles referred to in note 554 above.

581. On population figures for biblical Israel, see W. F. Albright, "The Administrative Divisions of Israel and Judah," *JPOS* 5 (1925) 20–25; W. F. Albright, *The Biblical Period*, 2nd

ed., 1955, pp. 59–60, note 75; M. Lurje, *Studien zur Geschichte der wirtschaftlichen und sozialen Verhältnisse im israelitisch-jüdischen Reiche*, 1927, pp. 35–41; A. Lucas, "The Number of Israelites at the Exodus," *PEQ* (1944) 164–168; S. A. Baron, *A Social and Religious History of the Jews*, 2nd ed., 1952, vol. 1, pp. 64, 320–321, note 2; S. A. Baron, "Population," *EJ*, vol. 13, cols. 866–870; and summaries of the state of the discussion among biblical scholars in R. de Vaux, *Ancient Israel*, 1961, pp. 65–67, and in M. Avi-Yonah, " *'Ōklōsyāh* (Population)," *EM*, vol. 1, 1955, cols. 139–146 (Heb.). I was not fully aware of how methodologically impoverished is this inner-biblical discussion on the population of ancient Palestine until a paper on the subject was presented to a seminar on "Problems in the Sociology of the Religion of Ancient Israel" offered in the Graduate Theological Union, Berkeley, California, in 1971–72 in collaboration with my colleague Marvin Chaney. The paper by Dan Dana, a seminary student who had majored in demography in college, introduced the seminar to a methodology for estimating population totals and population density which appears to have been entirely unknown to the biblical scholars who have written on the subject. Using the Köppen system for estimating population climatologically, the student concluded that the population of Palestine (including the plains and hills of West Jordan) at the time of the emergence of Israel was, very generously estimated, not more than 300,000, and probably much smaller (perhaps by one-third). I am unable to make an independent evaluation of the student's conclusions, which he admitted were extremely gross calculations, given the lack of certain critical information. I was at any rate led to suspect that the existing scholarly estimates of the population of ancient Palestine may be on the high side, and became convinced that only as people trained in demographic methods turn their attention to the problem can we hope to make any scientific advance in this vital element for a techno-economic and techno-environmental understanding of early Israel. J. L. Angel, "Ecology and Population in the Eastern Mediterranean," *World Archaeology* 4 (1972) 88–105, uses limited osteological data to study mortality and fertility rates in the region. On the relation of climatology to demographics, see W. von Köppen, *Grundrisse der Klimakunde*, 2nd rev. ed., 1931; R. Geiger and W. von Köppen, eds., *Handbuch der Klimatologie in fünf Bänden*, 1930–1934; C. W. Thornthwaite, "An Approach towards a Rational Classification of Climate," *GR* 38 (1948) 55–94; J. J. Hidore, *A Geography of the Atmosphere*, 1968, chap. 5. Work on the rainfall and climate of Palestine is discussed by N. Rosenau and U. Mané in D. H. K. Amiran et al., eds., *Atlas of Israel*, 2nd (Eng.) ed., 1970, sections IV/2 and 3. Maps that show the climatic regions of Palestine according to the systems of Köppen and Thornthwaite appear in IV/3. For reviews of the field of demography with bibliography, see P. M. Hauser and O. D. Duncan, eds., *The Study of Population: an Inventory and Appraisal*, 1964, and D. Kirk et al., "Population," *IESS*, vol. 12, 1968, pp. 342–388. For discussion of the methods and applications of demography, see D. H. Wrong, *Population and Society*, 3rd ed., 1967, and J. I. Clarke, *Population Geography*, 2nd ed., 1972.

582. See, e.g., Y. Aharoni, "The Settlement of Canaan," *WHJP*, 1st series, vol. 3, 1971, pp. 97–98.

583. While the water tunnel systems in or adjacent to ancient Palestinian cities have been studied fairly intensively, less attention has been given to cisterns, pools, and other water system elements, especially in rural areas, and their relation to problems of hydrology, intensity of land use, and population density and distribution have been almost totally neglected. For elementary remarks on pools and cisterns in ancient Canaan and Israel, see: A.-G. Barrois, *Manuel d'archéologie biblique*, vol. 1, 1939, pp. 239–243; D. R. Hillers, "Cistern," *EJ*, vol. 5, 1971, cols. 578–579; M. Avi-Yonah, "*Bor* (cistern)," *EM*, vol. 2, 1954, cols. 45–47 (Heb.); R. W. Hamilton, "Water Works," *IDB*, vol. 4, 1962, pp. 813–814. Since increasingly numerous examples of lime-plastered waterproof cisterns are being found

from the Late Bronze Age (c. 1500–1200 b.c.) and even from the Middle Bronze Age (c. 2000–1500 b.c.), many field archaeologists are becoming skeptical of the innovative pertinence of this technological advance to the Israelite settlement.

584. On the origins, spread, and distribution of iron in the ancient Near East and Palestine, see: S. Abramsky, "Metals: Iron," *EM*, vol. 5, 1968, cols. 657–661 (Heb.); H. C. Richardson, "Iron, Prehistoric and Ancient," *AJA* 38 (1934) 555–583; G. E. Wright, "Iron: The Date of Its Introduction into Common Use in Palestine," *AJA* 43 (1939) 458–463; J. C. Waldbaum, "The Use of Iron in the Eastern Mediterranean 1200–900 b.c." (Ph.D diss., Harvard University, 1968). For other titles in the voluminous literature on iron in antiquity, particularly concerning the exacting complex of techniques involved in ironworking, see note 335.

585. Two unwalled early Israelite villages excavated in recent years, Khirbet Radanna in Benjamin (on the edge of Ramallah) and Tell Masos in southern Judah (near Beersheba), have helped to fill the gap in our knowledge of what must have been the most common form of Israelite settlement in premonarchic times. So far Khirbet Radanna has been more fully reported, with evidence of very intensive agricultural activity. Cf. J. A. Callaway and R. E. Cooley, "Salvage Excavation at Radanna, in Bireh," *BASOR* 201 (1971) 1–19; F. M. Cross, Jr., and D. N. Freedman, "An Inscribed Jar Handle from Radanna," *BASOR* 201 (1971) 19–22; Y. Aharoni, "Khirbet Radanna and Its Inscription," *IEJ* 21 (1971) 130–135; Y. Aharoni, A. Kempinski, and V. Fritz, "Notes and News: Tel Masos (Khirbet el-Meshâsh)," *IEJ* 22 (1972) 243; *Tell Aviv* 1 (1974) 64–74; 2 (1975).

586. Finding the actual reports on iron objects in the archaeological literature on ancient Israel in the premonarchic period to be strangely meager and imprecise, I began to discuss this problem with field archaeologists, among them Ruth Amiran, William C. Dever, Albert E. Glock, and Yigal Shiloh. Without wishing to hold any of these archaeologists responsible for my interpretations of their remarks, from these discussions I have nevertheless formulated the above possible explanations for the sparseness of archaeological evidence on iron in premonarchic Israel. All of these practicing archaeologists were agreed that iron finds have been inadequately attended to, analyzed, and reported in the past, and that in the future metallurgical specialists will need to be more closely involved in archaeological work. I should add that Beno Rothenberg's metallurgical inquires in the Timna area have been focused almost entirely on copper rather than on iron (B. Rothenberg, *Timna: Valley of the Biblical Copper Mines*, 1972).

587. A. Reifenberg, *The Struggle Between the Desert and the Sown: Rise and Fall of Agriculture in the Levant*, 1955, pp. 35–41, 44–45, 85, 87, 92, 98, in itself a valuable preliminary manual on the history of agriculture in the region, discusses terracing as a measure to combat erosion and to retain rainfall, notes cursorily the distribution of some of the most visible terrace ruins, and records that there is literary evidence on terracing, e.g., detailed instructions on their form and method of construction in the Mishnah (first centuries of the Christian era). E. Orni and E. Efrat, *Geography of Israel*, 3rd rev. ed., 1971, pp. 55, 57, 439–440, and Y. Karmon, *Israel: A Regional Geography*, 1971, p. 98, point out that terracing in this region has always been greatly facilitated by the natural stair-step rock formations of large parts of the hill country. They also indicate how terraces are constructed in modern land-reclamation projects in Israel. B. Golomb and Y. Kedar, "Ancient Agriculture in the Galilee Mountains," *IEJ* 21 (1971) 136–140, briefly describe terracing in relation to other agricultural installations and methods such as strip lynchets, enclosures, and dams. They note that "the system of terraces in Galilee is . . . generally inferior to other types of cultivation and to the kind of terracing found in the Judean Hills" (p. 138). Their explanation that "the inhabitants were small tenant farmers, who lacked the resources for the

construction of elaborate terrace work," does not distinguish which historical period is under discussion, nor does it explain the difference in systems between Galilee and Judah, since presumably Judean cultivators were also small tenant farmers. Their other explanation, namely, geologically unfavorable tilted blocks in Galilee, appears more satisfactory. See also, J. E. Spencer and G. A. Hale, "The Origin, Nature, and Distribution of Agricultural Terracing," *Pacific Viewpoint* 2 (1961) 1–40.

588. Z. Ron, "Agricultural Terraces in the Judean Mountains," *IEJ* 16 (1966) 33–49, 111–122, surveyed only those parts of the Judean hills held by Israel prior to 1967, where he found 56.4 percent of the area covered by agricultural terraces. While not dealing extensively with the history of the observed terracing, Ron did note that at least some of the construction, especially that associated with springs and irrigation structures, can be dated to at least the first century A.D. and perhaps earlier.

589. L. E. Stager has made a study of ancient irrigation agriculture in the Buqei'ah Valley northwest of the Dead Sea. The prospectus of Stager's project was published in *ASOR Newsletter,* No. 2, Sept. 1972, and a short communication of findings appeared in *Archaeology* 27 (1974) 58. The full account appears in L. E. Stager, "Ancient Agriculture in the Judean Desert: A Case Study of the Buqei'ah Valley" (Ph.D. diss., Harvard University, 1975). See also L. E. Stager, "Agriculture," IDBSV, 176, 11–13.

590. C. H. J. de Geus, "The Importance of Archaeological Research into the Palestinian Agricultural Terraces, with an Excursus on the Hebrew Word *gbī**," *PEQ* 107 (1975) 65–74.

591. Ibid., 69.

592. De Geus's optimism about the prospect for dating these ancient terrace and irrigation systems, especially the former, is not shared by most of the archaeologists with whom I have discussed the matter. They emphasize the virtual impossibility of dating ruins, such as rock terraces, that do not normally contain datable objects in sealed loci. They grant that more satisfactory dating is likely where there are single periods of occupation followed by long desertion, as was apparently the case in the Buqei'ah Valley project of L. E. Stager (see note 589). Yet all seemed to agree that progress in unravelling the history of terracing in the land is a desideratum. Since until recently terracing has been treated for the most part in a casual, hit-or-miss manner in Palestinian archaeology, it may be that a systematic approach to the subject will yield substantial results, even if the difficulty of dating particular concentrations of terraces should remain in large measure insurmountable. De Geus refers to an attempt to date terrace walls in Greece by means of sherds found between the stones (J. Bradford, "Ancient Field Systems on Mount Hymettos, Near Athens," *The Antiquaries Journal* 36 [1956] 172–180) and admits that such dating is always provisional, giving no more than a *terminus ad quem*. This leads him to stress a beginning point with irrigation systems that include terrace walls and that are sometimes more satisfactorily datable by means of later structures that cut into the water works.

593. De Geus, "Palestinian Agricultural Terraces," p. 70. Where data on water supply are reasonably complete, it is possible to bring somewhat greater refinement into population calculations. J. Wilkinson, "Ancient Jerusalem: Its Water Supply and Population," *PEQ* 106 (1974) 33–51, posits a population ceiling of 2,500 for Jebusite-Davidic Jerusalem based on the output of the Gihon spring and assuming a modest daily water consumption of twenty liters per head. Holding the consumption figure constant, Wilkinson calculates population ceilings for subsequent periods of Jerusalem's history through Roman times correlated to the progressively improved water supply. For example, he finds that the introduction of the receiving pool Birket el Ḥamra, probably by Solomon, doubled the population ceiling to 5,000, and that the development of the Etam water system in the later

monarchy, which brought water to Jerusalem from the highlands south of Bethlehem, more than doubled the population ceiling to 10,633. Wilkinson also proposes population densities based on the sizes of built-up areas from period to period as determined by archaeological investigations. He admits a number of imponderables, such as the difficulty of determining the amount of water available from cisterns, but the method is clearly formulated and subject to further refinement or correction.

594. De Geus, "Palestinian Agricultural Terraces," p. 70.

595. Methods for collecting and analyzing the seeds and pollen at an excavated site, long employed in prehistoric archaeology, are just beginning to be introduced systematically into Palestinian archaeology of the historical period. Botanists are being included on excavation staffs, and the so-called flotation technique for isolating vegetable matter from soil has been used recently in excavations at Tell Ta'annak and at Tell el-Ḥesi (according to oral reports from A. E. Glock and F. S. Frick); cf. G. W. Dimbleby, "Pollen Analysis." in *The Scientist and Archaeology* (ed. E. Pyddoke), 1963, pp. 56–79, and N. Liphschitz and Y. Waisel, "Dendroarchaeological Investigations in Israel," *IEJ* 23 (1973) 30–36.

596. D. Baly, "The Geography of Monotheism" in *Translating and Understanding the Old Testament* (ed. H. T. Frank and W. L. Reed), 1970, pp. 254–256, effectively rebuts the theory of the desert origins of monotheism; however, after some thrusts in the direction of a cultural-material hypothesis to explain monotheism, and in spite of many interesting observations, Baly is unable in the last resort to formulate a hypothesis or to propose a research strategy toward "the Sociology of Monotheism."

NOTES TO PART XI

597. See the literature cited in R. C. Dentan, *Preface to Old Testament Theology,* 2nd ed., 1963, and in G. Hasel, *Old Testament Theology: Basic Issues in the Current Debate,* 2nd ed., 1975. See also X. Léon-Dufour, ed., *Dictionary of Biblical Theology,* 1962; 2nd ed., 1970 (Eng. trans. 1973), for convenient topical summaries.

598. Among the titles expressing criticism of biblical theology: F. Hesse, "Die Erforschung der Geschichte als theologische Aufgabe," *KD* 4 (1958) 1–19; F. Hesse, "Kerygma oder geschichtliche Wirklichkeit?," *ZThK* 57 (1960) 17–26; J. Barr, *The Semantics of Biblical Language,* 1961; K. Stendahl, "Biblical Theology, Contemporary," IDB, vol. 1, 1962, pp. 418–432; G. Ebeling, "The Meaning of 'Biblical Theology,' " in *Word and Faith,* 1963 (orig. pub. 1955), pp. 79–97; J. Barr, *Old and New in Interpretation,* 1966; N. Gottwald, "W. Eichrodt, Theology of the Old Testament," in *Contemporary Old Testament Theologians* (ed. R. B. Laurin), 1970, pp. 23–62; H.-J. Kraus, *Die Biblische Theologie: Ihre Geschichte und Problematik,* 1970; B. S. Childs, *Biblical Theology in Crisis,* 1970; G. Hasel, *Old Testament Theology: Basic Issues in the Current Debate,* 2nd ed., 1975; J. Barr, "Biblical Theology," IDBSV, 1976, pp. 104–111; D. A. Knight, ed., *Tradition and Theology in the Old Testament,* 1977 (see especially essays by O. H. Steck, P. R. Ackroyd, and H. Gese). For the most part these are not wholesale indictments of the biblical theology movement; they rather single out aspects, tendencies and particular formulations of biblical theology for sharp criticism. My own essay on W. Eichrodt's *Theology of the Old Testament* expressed a nascent sociological critique which at the time was only in embryonic form. Thus, a good deal of the force of the criticism is spent in an inner-disciplinary debate instead of throwing out a direct challenge to the movement's methodological bankruptcy. For example, Hasel's way of dealing with

biblical theology's "crisis of identity" is fairly representative in that he makes brave attempts to reconcile opposed extremes by striking an imprecise average or marking a hypothetical median point between them. Even Childs, who issues an especially devastating frontal attack on biblical theology, ends up to the reader's astonishment by proposing "a new biblical theology" which compounds the methodological pitfalls he has skilfully exposed in "the old biblical theology." The net effect of all this stormy jousting is to show that biblical theology has been unable to answer the questions it set for itself, and, moreover, to expose the entirely logical consequence that the movement's methodological and analytical feebleness does not allow it even to articulate clearly its own failures. Because biblical theology characteristically jumbles together poorly defined issues and mixes up methods for treating those issues with little self-awareness, the questions at issue and the answers offered are often so unclear that sound methodological procedures of verification or falsification cannot be applied.

599. B. Childs, *Biblical Theology in Crisis,* pp. 17–31. The effects of the biblical theology movement on the American church scene were felt in new journals such as *Theology Today* (1944–) and *Interpretation* (1947–) as also in major new educational curricula such as the Christian Faith and Life Curriculum of the Presbyterian Church U.S.A.

600. It seems to me that, in spite of all the will-o'-the-wisps they pursue in trying to relate faith and history and to interconnect Old and New Testaments, W. Eichrodt (*Theology of the Old Testament,* vol. 1, 6th ed., 1959 [Eng. trans. 1967]; vol. 2, 5th ed., 1964 [Eng. trans. 1967]), and G. von Rad (*Old Testament Theology,* vol. 1, 2nd ed., 1957 [Eng. trans. 1961]; vol. 2, 1960 [Eng. trans. 1965]), to give the two outstanding examples, have brilliantly set forth two plausible ways of organizing the multiplex phenomena of Israelite religion. Each offers a significant "map" for plotting these phenomena, Eichrodt in the form of a single architectonic, ideal-typical "cross-section" and von Rad in the form of a number of idea-complexes rooted in separate literary traditions which, in his view, cannot be integrated into a single thought system. Thus, I would stand by most of the positive things I had to say about Eichrodt's undertaking in my essay referred to in note 598. In the end, however, both Eichrodt and von Rad fail disastrously at "theology" because they offer disembodied idea structures unintegrated to the cultural-material and historico-social reality of ancient Israel by means of a clear methodological correlation. We are not shown by them how the structure of Israel's religious ideas was grounded in and correlated to Israel's social system as that system evolved in its techno-economic and techno-environmental setting, i.e., how these religious ideas or testimonies were the ideas and testimonies of actual living, socially evolving beings. Only such a systematic evolutionary correlation will bring that explanatory elucidation to the biblical thought structure(s) which a "the*ology*," a scientific study of the divine manifestation in history, intends to give.

601. M. Smith, "The Common Theology of the Ancient Near East," *JBL* 71 (1952) 135–147. Recently Smith has supplemented his earlier discussion with specific attention to the distinctive elements in early Israel (" On the Differences between the Culture of Israel and the Major Cultures of the Ancient Near East," *JANES* 5 [1973] 389–395). By a "hypothetic-deductive" method he suggests how certain dominant features of Hebrew literature and culture may be seen to follow from the peculiar historical and geographical conditions of early Israel—conditions and developments markedly unlike those of Mesopotamia and Egypt but in many ways similar to the conditions and developments in Phoenicia, Syria, and Greece. Smith steers away from crude determinism and advances tentative hypotheses for further checking. He confesses, however, that for certain features of the religion he has no explanations, such as the jealousy of deity, the hostility toward

images, and the peculiar development of prophecy. It is precisely such phenomena that are illuminated by a social-revolutionary reconstruction of Israelite origins, as I have sought to show and will pointedly formulate in the remainder of this final section of my study.

602. Smith, "Common Theology," p. 137.

603. Ibid., 146.

604. Ibid.

605. Ibid.

606. These highly patternistic views of myth, ritual, and motif diffusion are summarized and related to other similar approaches to the Old Testament by H. H. Hahn, *The Old Testament in Modern Research,* expanded ed., 1966, pp. 78–96. I do not wish to lump together carelessly all such religio-historical studies as valueless pursuits of "parallelomania." H. Gunkel in *Shöpfung und Chaos in Urzeit,* 1895, and H. Gressmann in *Der Messias,* 1929, significantly enlarged scholarly awareness of the antiquity of mythic ideas operative in Israel's environment long before the exile; their historical argumentation was more discriminating than the secondary and popularized uses often made of their conclusions. Moreover, when one compares the trilogy of volumes edited by S. H. Hooke: *Myth and Ritual,* 1933; *The Labyrinth,* 1935; and *Myth, Ritual, and Kingship,* 1958, there is a noticeable moderation of the claims for myth and ritual patternism in the last title of the series (cf. esp. Hooke's essay on "Myth and Ritual: Past and Present," pp. 1–21).

607. B. Albrektson, *History and the Gods: An Essay on the Idea of Historical Events as Divine Manifestations in the Ancient Near East and in Israel* (CB, Old Testament Series, 1), 1967.

608. Ibid., p. 34.

609. Ibid., p. 51.

610. Ibid., p. 67.

611. Ibid., p. 95.

612. Ibid., p. 113.

613. Ibid., pp. 115–116; see also E. Hammershaimb, "History and Cult in the Old Testament," *Near Eastern Studies in Honor of W. F. Albright* (ed. H. Goedicke), 1971, pp. 269–282.

614. Albrektson, *History and the Gods,* p. 118.

615. Ibid., p. 119.

616. Ibid., p. 122.

617. See in particular the lengthy analysis of "The Types of Authority and Imperative Co-ordination" by M. Weber in *The Theory of Social and Economic Organization,* n.d. (Eng. trans. 1947), pp. 324–423, and also pt. 4 of the Introduction by T. Parsons on "The Institutionalization of Authority."

618. M. Fried, *The Evolution of Political Society: An Essay in Political Anthropology,* 1967.

619. I call attention to a certain independently reached formal-structural conjunction between my typology of mono-Yahwism and the monotheistic typologies of A. Bausani, "Can Monotheism Be Taught? (Further Considerations on the Typology of Monotheism)," *Numen* 10 [1963] 167–170, although there is a difference of focus in that Bausani's attention is given to a distinction between primary monotheism (Hebraism and Islam) and secondary monotheism (Christianity and Bahaism).

620. T. Vriezen, *An Outline of Old Testament Theology,* 2nd ed., 1954 (Eng. trans. 1958), pp. 23–25; and refer to my trait typology of mono-Yahwism in the functional model of early Israelite religion proposed in X. 49. 2–3.

621. B. Albrektson, *History and the Gods,* p. 96.

622. F. M. Cross, *Canaanite Myth and Hebrew Epic,* 1973, especially pp. 65–71, which

represents significant refinement and expansion of W. F. Albright's views about the meaning of the name Yahweh, minus Albright's rather grandiose and unpersuasive philosophical interpretations of Mosaic "monotheism."

623. Ibid., pp. 52–60.

624. C. F. Graesser, "Standing Stones in Ancient Palestine," *BA* 35 (1972) 34–64, proposes a comprehensive typology of functions for the numerous plain, unfigured, uninscribed standing stones found in Palestinian excavations. He distinguishes stones marking a legal relationship, stones memorializing the dead, stones commemorating an event and honoring the participants, and stones marking the cultic immanence of the deity. Graesser discusses the difficulties involved in assigning functions, derived from biblical texts and analogously from inscribed steles elsewhere in the Near East, to specific stones variously positioned in relation to nearby structures and variously aligned with other stones.

625. M. B. Rowton, "The Topological Factor in the *Ḥapiru* Problem," *Studies in Honor of B. Landsberger,* 1965, pp. 376, 382, briefly mentions the sociopolitical and military significance of the cliffs and gorges of the Syro-Palestinian highlands, and Marvin Chaney has stressed the pertinence of this point for understanding the frequent metaphor in early Israel of the deity as "rock" or "crag."

626. J. Ouellette, "Le deuxième commandement et le rôle de l'image dans la symbolique religieuse de l'Ancien Testament," *RB* 74 (1967) 504–516.

627. E. E. Urbach, "The Laws of Idolatry in the Light of Historical and Archaeological Facts in the Third Century B.C.E.," *EI* 5 (1958) 189–205 (Heb.), 94*–95* (Eng. summary).

628. As set forth by J. E. Bruns (*God as Woman, Woman as God,* 1973, pp. 35–36), L. M. Russell (*Human Liberation in a Feminist Perspective—a Theology,* 1974, pp. 98–99), and A. M. Bennett (in *Women in a Strange Land,* ed. C. B. Fischer et al., 1974, pp. 113–115), the essential historical case for Elohim as "a plural of bisexuality," is composed of two parts: (1) that *ᵉlohim,* as a plural in general Canaanite and Hebrew usage for pagan gods, referred both to gods and goddesses; and (2) that in Genesis 1:26–27 a parallel is asserted between the bisexuality of deity and the bisexuality of human beings ("Elohim said, 'Let us make persons/human beings in Elohim's own image'. . . male and female Elohim created them"). The first point can be granted. The second point, as a logical exegetical exercise, has as much plausibility as other attempts to "explain" the divine likeness in humans. I am open to exploring it.

The real objections to believing that the writer of Genesis 1 has such a bisexual view of deity in mind lie in the full array of the language employed and in the social context of the writer. As to language, in Genesis 1:26–27 masculine pronouns and masculine verb forms are used throughout for Elohim and for the persons/human beings as a generic totality. If we assume that the writer was pressing against the limits of language and saw no way to thoroughly demasculinize the pronoun and verb usages, even though he/she wished to do so, the difficulty still remains that, as far as we can judge, the socioreligious context of Genesis 1 was in the exilic and postexilic priestly tradition. According to numerous passages in Genesis through Numbers, this priestly tradition gave massive priority to males—as much as, and probably even more than, any other strain of Israelite tradition.

In order to demonstrate that the intent of the writer in Genesis 1 was to demasculinize the conception of God and to assert the equality of men and women in actual socioreligious practice, this inconsistency must be faced and resolved. The only resolution I can presently conceive would be to argue as follows: 1. The author of Genesis 1 was a priestly maverick who tried to persuade fellow religionists of his viewpoint, but did not succeed. Alternatively, the maverick may be regarded as a woman—which, given the social conditions, would only have diminished the likelihood of her interpretation being heard. The failure of the demasculinizing project is concluded from the continuing masculine-centeredness of the priesthood and laity. 2. When the account of creation in Genesis 1 was accepted into priestly tradition, its original demasculinizing project was ignored or obscured. It might even be claimed that masculine pronouns and verb forms avoided in the original text were restored by the priestly editors. If we modify the above hypothesis to assert that the maverick was an earlier figure, outside the priestly tradition, whose work was drawn into priestly circles, we still face the problem of the social context to which the demasculinizing thrust should be assigned. I see no firm basis for assuming the above explanations as more than a faint possibility.

I wish, however, to be understood as arguing only the historical social context and intent of Genesis 1. On the other side, I support fully and unequivocally the right of contemporary women and men to demasculinize biblical lauguage about God for liturgical and theological purposes. In doing so, I think we have to recognize that biblical writers did not share our perspective on feminism and that, even if there were a few mavericks on the subject in ancient Israel, they did not make any measurable dent on a masculine society. The whole point is that social struggle and praxis set the context for religious ideas. We should not be in the least surprised that, lacking the sociohistorical possibilities for a vigorous feminist movement in ancient Israel, there was a similar lack in Israel's thought about God. Where women are not strongly represented in social praxis, there is not going to be any appreciable feminine component in religious thought and praxis, except as a survival from some earlier stage of socioreligious praxis or as a limited compensatory "sop" for women.

Instead of straining after possible "feminine" elements in the overwhelmingly masculine deity of Israel, women and men who care about the future of feminism in our religious communities should be examining the techno-environmental and sociopolitical conditions of ancient Israel to see what parameters actually existed for a feminist movement and to assess the extent to which Israelite women benefited or lost from the transition between elitist hierarchical Canaan and a generally much more egalitarian intertribal Israel. A careful calculus of these gains and losses will ultimately be of far more significance to the contemporary religious feminist movement than attempts to make ancient Israelite religion look more feminist than it actually was. I personally estimate that Israelite women gained much from their break with Canaanite society, but I do not for a moment think that they achieved—or could have achieved under ancient technological and social conditions—what women today are capable of achieving. I would not like to see contemporary religious feminists, and I include myself among them, led into the trap of pinning many hopes on dubious arguments about an ancient Israelite feminism which to this point is more a chimera than a demonstrated reality. For feminists who wish to keep in continuity with their religious heritage, I believe it is sufficient to assert that contemporary feminism in church and synagogue is a logical and necessary extension of the social egalitarian principle of early Israel, which itself did not exhibit any appreciable independent feminist consciousness or praxis.

629. For an introduction to current rethinking of the gender of the biblical deity and of the role of women in Israelite society, see P. Trible, "Depatriarchalizing in Biblical Interpretation," *JAAR* 41 (1973) 30–48; P. Bird, "Images of Women in the Old Testament," *Religion and Sexism* (ed. R. R. Ruether), 1974, pp. 41–88; and P. Hanson, "Masculine Metaphors for God and Sex-Discrimination in the Old Testament," *The Ecumenical Review* 27 (1975) 316–324.

630. M. Weber, *Ancient Judaism*, 1922 (Eng. trans. 1952), pp. 213–218, 297–335, and *The Sociology of Religion*, 1922 (Eng. trans. 1963), pp. 109–115, 138–150, wherein Weber

discusses theodicy in relation to *ressentiment* and salvation hopes among disprivileged classes.

631. H. E. von Waldow, "Social Responsibility and Social Structure in Early Israel," *CBQ* 32 (1970) 182–203, argues for economic equality as the foundation of premonarchic Israel, based on periodic redistribution of land to families within a system of "clan" ownership of land. At that time only a small minority of vulnerable widows, orphans, and resident aliens had to be specifically covered by protective legislation, since everyone else was given clan protection. During the kingdom, however, the clan ownership of land was so undermined by a commercial economy that priestly legislation arose in a reformist attempt to ameliorate the worst abuses of a basically stratified economy. While there are many debatable points in von Waldow's analysis, including the form and range of land redistribution in early days—not to mention the familiar erroneous derivation of the original economic egalitarianism from pastoral nomadism—its value lies in the way it organically connects the development of legislation to the developing social order, all the while perceiving that the theological basis of this legislation is the fact that Yahweh's liberation of Israel from Egypt was a coded symbol for an egalitarian social order: "The liberation from Egypt constitutes Israel's characteristic peculiarity; her attitude toward the destitute is the way to maintain it" (p.202).

632. A. R. Johnson, *The Cultic Prophet in Ancient Israel,* 2nd ed., 1962; and cf. the contrasting views of P. L. Berger, "Charisma and Religious Innovation: The Social Location of Israelite Prophecy," *ASR* 28 (1963) 940–950, and J. G. Williams, "The Social Location of Israelite Prophecy," *JAAR* 37 (1969) 153–165. See also Henri Mottu, "Ideology and Truth in OT Prophecy: A Case Study: Hannaniah against Jeremiah," *RR* 2. 2/3 (1975) 58–67; R. R. Wilson, "Prophecy and Society in Ancient Israel: The Present State of the Inquiry" *SBL Seminar Papers,* 1977, pp. 341–358, provides helpful history of research and formulates methodological problems and areas for future research.

633. A. Cody, *A History of Old Testament Priesthood* (AB, 35), 1969, pp. 1–61; for additional bibliography, see note 222.

634. N. K. Gottwald, *All the Kingdoms of the Earth: Israelite Prophecy and International Relations in the Ancient Near East,* 1964, pp. 16–17; W. F. Edgerton, "The Government and the Governed in the Egyptian Empire," *JNES* 6 (1947) 152–160; cf. also Genesis 47:22 and commentary thereon by J. Skinner, *A Critical and Exegetical Commentary on Genesis* (ICC), 2nd ed., 1930, pp. 500–502, and by J. Vergote, *Joseph en Egypte: Genèse chap. 37–50 à la lumière des études égyptologiques récentes* (OBL, 3), 1959, pp. 190–192.

635. Throughout this study, "equality" and "egalitarianism" do *not* refer to equal biological inheritance or to philosophical theories of the equal value of all persons or to legally established rights of citizenship, but rather to a social-organizational arrangement lacking ranking and stratification. Social stratification means differences in rights of access to the basic resources. M. Fried, *The Evolution of Political Society,* 1967, makes this understanding of egalitarian social structure clear: "Stratification . . . is a system by which the adult members of a society enjoy differential rights of access to basic resources. These resources are the physical things needed to sustain life, either directly (air, water, and food) or indirectly (things that cannot themselves be consumed but are required to obtain other things that are). Outstanding examples of the latter are land, raw materials for tools, water for irrigation, and materials to build a shelter" (p. 52). Citing ethnological evidence from simple societies concerning the socially defined appropriation of these basic resources, Fried identifies a type of social organization which dependably lacks restrictions on equal access to the basic resources, and is therefore "egalitarian" rather than "stratified": "The

evidence for significantly undifferentiated communal access to resources and the relatively permissive attitude toward 'trespass' in simple societies is abundant" (p. 61).

636. M. Buber, *Kingship of God,* 3rd. ed., 1956 (Eng. trans. 1967), p. 97.

637. J. Dus, "Moses or Joshua? (On the Problem of the Founder of Israelite Religion)," *RR* 2. 2/3 (1975) 26–41, originally published in German in *ArO* 39 (1971) 16–45, establishes with admirable clarity that the narratives of Exodus have as their referent the entire Israelite praxis of liberation in Canaan. Dus's further contention that there never was a Moses-led exodus and wilderness wandering—and that Joshua was the religio-social founder of Israel—is more debatable, particularly since Dus is still arguing Israelite origins on a pastoral nomadic model, but his contentions deserve very serious consideration. To my knowledge, no one has yet offered a detailed response or critique of Dus's closely reasoned arguments (cf. notes 35 and 148 for further reference to this important article).

638. For an initial sketch of the socioeconomic history of ancient Israel, together with a basic bibliography, see N. K. Gottwald, "Israel, Social and Economic Development of," in IDBSV, 1976, pp. 465–468.

639. I cite here the interesting study of D. C. Pellett, "Election or Selection? The Historical Basis for the Doctrine of the Election of Israel," *Encounter* 26 (1965) 155–169, which leads off promisingly with the assertion that "It is too naive to be content with the simple assertion that God chose a particular people, for what we really mean is that he chose a particular people as they developed through specific geographical, historical, and sociological factors" (155). Unfortunately, although he touches on many of these "specific factors," and skirts others, Pellett gives no satisfactory cohesive hypothesis about the sociohistorical ground of Israel's "electedness." Following J. Wach's specification of Israel as a "founded" religious group, rather than as a "natural" religious group, Pellett is unable to proceed into the socioeconomic details of Israel's form of "foundedness." At one point he cites Mendenhall's view that invading Israelites were "greatly swelled by additions from the local peasantry" (160). Apparently not fully understanding Mendenhall's point, Pellett construes this to mean that the incoming pastoral nomadic Israelites "assimilated" the local peasants by "the imposition of a national sentiment on an alien people" (quoting from T. H. Robinson, *A History of Israel,* 1932, 1, p. 47). In the end, therefore, Pellett cannot say much more than that "Israel successfully resisted being assimilated because she was able to maintain and strengthen her identity as a particular people, based, not on a geographical area or on purity of race, but on her destiny as the people of Yahweh . . . "(163). It seems to me that in company with the vast majority of such treatments of Israel's "specialness," Pellett has not shown the historical basis of Israel's view of election; he has rather asserted Israel's view of election as the ground of its historical identity and continuity. The question of the roots of the election doctrine is left ultimately untouched except by further referrals to covenant theology and to pastoral nomadic group consciousness.

640. In some respects my view of the religion of ancient Israel as a progressively mystifying surrogate for a lost socioeconomic and cultural unity is convergent with the perspective of Y. Kaufmann in his major early work, *Exile and Alienation: An Historical-Sociological Study of the Jewish Nation from Ancient Times to the Present,* 2 vols., 1928 / 1932 (Heb.). This comprehensive study, together with several periodical articles that foreshadow it, remains largely unknown in contrast to Kaufmann's more technical biblical works. The affinities with my conception of Israel's religion as a dynamic quasi-independent cultural force, increasingly divorced from its generative social roots, will be apparent in the following quotations, which include a bold formulation of the intellectual and cultural plight of the nonreligious Jew: "Religion absorbed all of the Hebrew national

foundations. Because of its powerful influence in the life of the nation, it served to strengthen the national foundations even in exile. Religion gave the nation a mysterious national life in place of the actual national life that it had lost. It gave it a sacred land, a sacred state, and a sacred language in place of the secular land, state, and language that it had lost" ("Democratic Nationalism," *HaShiloah* [July-August 1914] 294 [Heb.]). "The power of religion, whose value for its adherents is absolute, and whose commandments are regarded as absolute obligations, did not cease with the removal of the natural conditions of national existence out of which it had arisen. Because the national factors, which would normally disappear with the abrogation of national reality, were bound up with religious sanctity, they too survived" ("The National Will to Survive," *Miklat* 4 [June-August 1920] 192 [Heb.]). "Our situation is truly tragic: the situation of those who, having lost their religious faith without hope of recovering it, still cling to that entire national universe which depended upon that faith for its life" (ibid., 194; the above three quotations as translated by L. Silberstein, "Religion, Ethnicity and Jewish History: The Contribution of Yehezkel Kaufmann," *JAAR* 42 [1974] 521–523). Kaufmann's work is prodigious in its time scale and audacious in its theorizing; it can scarcely be properly evaluated without a much closer reading than I have so far been able to give it. One thing is clear: the customary unfamiliarity of Christian biblical scholars with Jewish socioreligious theorists will have to be rectified if a sociology of Israel's religion is to be realized in all its potentialities.

641. The modern condition of our being unable to believe in deities and religious constructs with the same degree of "realism" that ancients experienced is brought out by S. Mathews, *The Atonement and the Social Process,* 1930, pp. 30–31, in a distinction between analogies and concepts in terms of the notion of pattern: " . . . a pattern is a social institution or practice used to give content and intelligibility to otherwise unrationalized beliefs [e.g., when practices and roles of an imperial court were used to speak of the relation of God and men]. What the axiom is to mathematics, a pattern is in thought. Later criticism may discover the analogical character of the pattern, but as long as it brings intellectual security and allays intellectual obscurity a pattern is regarded as a fact rather than as a metaphor. . . . The pattern becomes basic to an interpretation, and this interpretation is subject to extensive development. Thus the conception of sovereignty carries within itself such corollaries as the absolute power of the monarch, decrees, law and its violations, trials, sentences, pardon, reward and punishment. . . . That which gives value to the pattern is the fact that men do not regard it as analogical. When its analogical quality is discovered its integrating power disappears. Most religious doubts arise when a pattern is seen to be a metaphor" (quoted by L. E. Keck, "On the Ethos of Early Christians," *JAAR* 42 [1974] 438–439, note 19). Our modern situation can thus be characterized as follows: like all human beings throughout history we require meaning-giving structures of praxis and theory; the scientific revolution, however, has assured that such structures must henceforth be perceived as social and religious metaphors or analogies, rather than as absolutely transparent reflections or copies of objective reality. This, of course, is not to deny that metaphor and analogy operated in ancient thought, nor is it to assert that a metaphorical or analogical perception of socioreligious constructs is any less "serious" or less "important" than a more literal perception.

642. F. Buri, "The Reorientation of Theology in the Light of the Challenge of Sociology," *JAAR* 40 (1972) 304–315, attempts a number of formulations of the "truth" relationship between sociology as science and dogmatics as systematic reflection on the nonobjectifiable self in its conditioned responsibility within a community of other selves. Without entire consistency, Buri seems to be groping toward a conjunction between sociology and theology at the points of social philosophy and philosophical theology:

"Scientific statements within social philosophy and within dogmatics as philosophical theology no longer stand against each other as scientific statements against scientific statements but as faith against faith or as one faith discovering itself in the symbols of another. In understanding the dynamics of differing symbols, one can see different, or perhaps finally common, self-understandings (308). . . . For all that they may avail themselves of a scientific methodology, dogmatics as philosophical theology and sociology as social philosophy have to do with just this non-objectifiable self. And once again, this self never occurs outside of community with other selves (309). . . . In this way, a sociologist may come to see that the personal character of his own being is an unconditional enactment of a self-understanding with an essentially social character which stands in the same transcendent relation which the Christian expresses through his use of the word 'God.' This is possible because faith is nothing else than an expression for the unconditional character of personal responsibility in community. It is even more possible for a philosopher of society to have such a faith than it is for one who adheres to a superstitious church dogmatics (310)." Buri's social existentialism allows him to establish significant ties between sociology and theology, but his existentialist epistemology is such that "faith" remains rather sharply set apart from either context or content.

643. The issue of the future of Christian faith in a classless society is pointedly addressed by H. Morrison, "Theoretical Questions of Marxist-Christian Unity," *RR* 2, no. 4 (1976) 32–36, and by D. Turner, "Marxism and Christian Praxis," *RR* 2, no. 4 (1976) 38–44. Both Morrison and Turner maintain pronounced "high" views of the integrity and validity of Christian truth, but simultaneously they stress that in its views of history and Incarnation, Christianity is radically materialist and therefore congruent, but not identical or simply interchangeable, with Marxism (Turner, for example, says: "If not all Christians are Marxists, certainly their own God is," p. 41). Morrison, stressing the principled atheism of Marxism, asserts that Christians can appropriately be socialists and communists but not Marxists on philosophical grounds. Turner, arguing that Marxist atheism is no intrinsic part of Marxism and that Marxist materialism is firmly set against crude materialism, contends that there is no real philosophical engagement or clash between Christian materialist theism and Marxist materialist atheism because the Marxist rejection of deity lies strictly outside the province of Marxist method and theory and is thus a kind of non sequitur to the body of Marxist truth. Both authors affirm that the precondition of the realization of Christian truth in the world is precisely socialist revolution inasmuch as it is only through socialist revolution that the radical material and egalitarian person-fulfilling promise of Christian faith can move toward fuller actualization (again Turner: "For my part, to retain my orthodoxy as a Christian, to remain in revolutionary continuity with the Church of Christ, I must now be a Marxist," p. 43). They likewise concur that a socialist—or even a fully communist—society is not identical with or exhaustive of the Kingdom of God in Christian terms. Turner adds the provocative observation that Christianity and Marxism each declare that they will be self-abolished when their mission has been completed in the fully redeemed or humanized society toward which they strive.

644. J. P. Miranda, *Marx and the Bible: A Critique of the Philosophy of Oppression,* 1971 (Eng. trans. 1974), is one recent attempt to recover the social referent of biblical religion from within a fully admitted contemporary struggle context. Starting off from the divided mind of papal instructions about whether private or communal property is the biblical-Christian norm, Miranda covers vast tracts of OT and NT, staking out the general claim that the basic biblical norm of property-holding was communal. Granted that the undertaking is on so large a scale that a complete analysis in all details has eluded the author, his method—to start out from the present social struggle in society and church—is the correct method,

while at the same time adhering to sociohistorical-critical criteria in order fully to respect the social and religious phenomena peculiar to each sector of past historical experience. Those who criticize Miranda's "partisanship" or "lack of objectivity" overlook the sly unadmitted and unexamined social presuppositions of many writers on this subject. The issue is not Miranda's "partisanship" but solely whether he has done justice to the biblical data on property-holding. From the side of theology, Dorothee Sölle, *Political Theology*, 1971 (Eng. trans. 1974), emphasizes the collaborative projects of sociologically informed historical criticism and sociopolitical theology: "According to its own projected goals, the historical criticism of the Bible is aimed at emancipation, which follows from the assumption still preserved in the first phase of the Enlightenment that reason and revelation intend the same thing, even if they represent two different approaches. . . . The historical-critical method is not threatened from without by an alleged 'new wave' of scientific and historical hostility, but only by its own characteristic inconsistency, specifically in a three-fold manner: first, because it limits itself and does not include present-day ecclesiastical and social structures and their ideological superstructures; second, because it overlooks the historical mediation of the contents of Christianity; and finally, because it exempts apparently invariable and always valid structures of faith and their appropriation. As long as historical criticism remains true to the Enlightenment spirit in which it is grounded, which means asking critically about historical mediations and conditions, and as long as it preserves the essential features of any historical method (which according to Troeltsch are criticism, analogy, and correlation) then not only does it have nothing to fear from a sociopolitical theology that is consciously committed to the same methodological principles, but on the contrary political theology carries on in the best tradition of liberal theology and preserves precisely the methodological achievements of criticism, analogy, and correlation, while enriching them with refinements from sociology and sociology of knowledge" (pp. 12, 17–18).

Appendix B

1. INDEX OF AUTHORS

2. INDEX OF BIBLICAL REFERENCES

Note: 1. The order of the biblical books in this index arbitrarily conforms to the order found in English translations in the Christian tradition. This order is purely a matter of convenience, since it is assumed that a majority of readers will use English versions employing this sequence. In some respects, the rather different Jewish ordering of the books is historically more accurate, but no existing traditional arrangement of the books corresponds invariably with the chronological order in which the books were written or with the historical periods treated or inferred in the books. In one way or another, every traditional arrangement of the biblical books is an artificial construction. 2. Only English chapter and verse numbers are cited in the index. For treatment of variations in the Hebrew chapter and verse divisions in the body of the book, see the footnote on p. 47.

GENESIS

1	796–97 n.628	24:29	308–10
1:26–27	796 n.628	24:35	452
4:14–22	578	24:53	314
10:8–9	439–40	24:60	279–81
11:27	314	25:1–4	353–54
11:27–30	308–10	25:13–16	353–54
11:29	314	25:20	308–10
12—50	32, 451–53	25:27–28	439–40
12:6	564	25:29–34	452
12:16	452	26	55–56, 493–94
13:5	452	26:12–14	452
14	55–56, 493–94	26:14	452
14:3	219	26:34	560
14:13	219, 494	27:1–4	439–40
14:16	510	27:3	542
14:17	569	27:25–29	452
14:18–20	568–69, 769 n.415	28	777 n.501
15	769 n.416	28:9	304
15:9	452	29:1–30	305
17:20	353–54	29:10	˙308–10
18:1–8	452	29:12	304, 308–10
18:14	697	29:29	304
19	54, 749 n.249	29:31—30:24	240, 359
20:12	314	30:14	452
20:14	452	30:25—31:50	305
21:12	542	32:5	452
21:20–21	439–40	32:7	452
21:27	452	32:15	452
22:20–24	353–54	32:28	108, 495
22:23	308–10	32:30	575
23	55–56, 452, 560	33:15	510
23:7	510, 779 n.513	33:17	575
23:10	779 n.513	33:18—35:8	55–56
23:12–13	779 n.513	33:18b–20	564–65
24:15	304, 314	33:19	520
24:28–29	314	33:20	495, 565, 770 n.420

LEVITICUS

NUMBERS

JOSHUA

JUDGES

II SAMUEL

3. INDEX OF FOREIGN TERMS

Note: 1. For the transliteration of Hebrew terms, the author has chosen a system that stresses approximate accuracy in pronunciation for the benefit of readers who do not know the language. Some features normally represented in transliteration are therefore undistinguished, e.g., the difference between the consonants sāmek and sīn, and the distinction between changeable and unchangeable long vowels.

2. The alphabetical organization of the Index according to the English order of the alphabet is similarly constructed for the aid of non-Hebraists. Abundant cross-references refer to the clustering of words and phrases under their appropriate covering Hebrew verb or noun, e.g., bēth-'āv, see bayith.

3. The various systems of transliteration for Semitic words used in the sources cited are retained unaltered in the text and in the Index.

4. The Index is in three parts: Hebrew, Akkadian, and Other Languages (including Arabic, Egyptian, Greek, Latin, Ugaritic, etc.).

HEBREW

'abbīr, 683
'abbirim, 503
'ad. 505
'ādām, 530
ᵃdath bᵉnē Israel, see 'ēdāh
ᵃdath-'ēl, 741 n.171
'ādōn, 683
'aḥīm, 529
'ālaph, 277
   ᵃlāphīm, 257, 259, 261, 271–78, 280–81,
      284–85, 289, 358–59, 367
   'alphē Israel, 279–80, 289
   'alphē Judah, 269, 267
   'alphē Manasseh, 279–81
   'alphē rᵉvāvāh, 279, 281
   'alphē shā'ōn, 280
   'alphē shin'ān, 280
   'allūph, 272, 277–78, 511
   'allūph nᵉ'ūrīm, 278
   'allūphē Edom, 277, 508, 511–12
   'allūphē Hori, 277, 521
   'allūphē Judah, 277
   'allūphīm, 277–78, 511, 521
   'eleph, 257, 259, 261, 269–78, 281–82, 301,
      305, 307, 315, 319, 330–31, 340, 364,
      511, 654
'allōn, 776 n.500; see also 'ēlōn
'allūph, see 'ālaph
'allūphē, see 'ālaph
'allūphīm, see 'ālaph
'almānōth, 550
'alphē, see 'ālaph
'am, 241, 246–47, 509–10, 740 n.167; 741 n.172

'am bᵉrīth, 239
'ammē bᵉrīth, 239
'am hā 'ārets, 779 n.513
'ammīm, 284, 508–12, 515, 534
'am rav, 420
'am Yahweh, 242
hā 'ām, 242, 510
hā 'ammīm, 515
'ānī, 550
'anshē bᵉrīth, 239
'anshē bēthō, 278
'anshē Israel, 242
ᵃrām, 530
ᵃsaphsuph, 456
 'ᵃsher 'im, 291
'ashpōth, 538
'āsīnū 'immᵉkā ḥesed, 559
ᵃsīrim, 550
'āv, 683; see also bēth-'āv under bayith
'avᵉdēkem, 522
ᵃvīr, 683
'ayil, 511
   'ēlē mō'āv (Moab), 508, 511–12
   'ēlīm, 511

ba'al, 683
   baᵃlē bᵉrīth 'avrām, 239
   baᵃlē ḥitstsīm, 540–41
   baᵃlē Shechem, 564
   baᵃlē yᵉrīḥō, 534
   bᵉ'ālīm, 534, 779 n.513
bā'ē sha'ar hā'īr, 779 n.513
bānīm, see bēn

ḥayyāh, 260–61, 453, 742 n.182
hay-yōshēv, see yāshav
ḥayyīm, 260
ḥbr, 239
   ḥāvēr, 239
   ḥᵃvērim, 239
   hever, 239
   hevrāh, 239
ḥēlō, 508
ḥērem, 507, 543–50, 775 n.475
ḥever, see ḥbr
ḥevrāh, see ḥbr
hithnaddēv, see nādav
ḥivvī, 771 n.425
ḥofši, 767 n.406; see also ḥopshī
ḥopshī, 481, 736 n.148; 768 n.409; 769 n.412;
   see also ḥofši
ḥōri (ḥōrim), 771 n.425

'ibrim, 421, 762 n.346; see also 'ivri
'ivri ('ivrim), 419–22, 494, 562, 769 n.412; see
   also 'ibrim
'īr, 530
   'īr mivtsār, 779 n.516
   'īr nokrī(yyāh), 568
   kᵉ'ahath 'ārē ham-mamlākāh, 523
'īsh milḥāmāh, 683

kᵉ'ahath 'ārē ham-mamlākāh, see 'īr
KAHAL, see qāhāl
kōpher hap-pᵉrāzī, see pᵉrāzōn

lāsheveth, see yāshav
lō' tēshēv, see yāshav

māgēn, 507
maḥsōr kol, 530
mālak, 526, 528, 531
   malk, 697
   malkē 'erets, 513
   malkē kᵉna'an, 503
   malkē tsᵉvā'ōth, 550
   malkō, 773 n.453
   mamlākāh, 241, 510; see also 'īr
   mamlākōth, 510
   mᵉlākīm, 503, 534, 550
   melek, 511, 514, 683, 749 n.249
   mᵉlūkāh, see yōshēv 'al kissē' ham-mᵉlūkāh
   molkō, 773 n.453
mamlākāh, see mālak
mamlākōth, see mālak
mamzēr, 514
mān, 765 n.382
markāvōth, see rākav

markᵉvōth par'ōh, see rākav
mas, 483
   mas 'ōvēd, 483
matstsēvāh, 565, 684
maṭṭeh, 162, 245–46, 258–59, 266–68, 272,
   288–90, 303, 330–31, 399
   maṭṭōth, 245, 250, 266, 285, 289–90
   maṭṭōth 'ᵃvōthām, 289
mᵉhatsᵉtsīm, 507
mᵉhōqᵉqīm, 507
mᵉlākīm, see mālak
melek, see mālak
mᵉrīvāv, 537
mᵉvassᵉrōth, 550
mᵉyuddā', 278
miqdāsh, 565
miqneh, 453
mishpāḥāh, 249–51, 254, 257–71, 274–76, 278,
   281–84, 286–87, 289–90, 292, 301, 303–7,
   315–19, 322, 329–33, 340, 345, 364, 510,
   559–60, 742 n.181
   mishpaḥath 'āvī, 260–61
   mishpaḥath Bichri, 269
   mishpaḥath Elimelech, 269
   mishpaḥath Ephrati, 269, 275
   mishpaḥath Judah, 249
   mishpaḥath Matri, 269
   mishpaḥath maṭṭēh 'āvihā, 266
   mishpaḥath maṭṭēh 'ᵃvihem/'ᵃvihen, 266
   mishpaḥath Punite, 228
   mishpaḥath Tolaite, 288
   mishpaḥath Zeri (Zarhi), 259, 287
   mishpaḥath Zuphi, 283
   mishpāḥōth, 247, 249–50, 257–60, 266–75,
   277, 280–85, 288–90, 292, 301, 319,
   322, 329, 338–40, 367, 549, 558, 561,
   567, 583
      mishpāḥōth Judah, 277
mish-sheveth, see yāshav
mivhar shālishāv, 508
mōdā', 262
molkō, see mālak
mōshᵉkīm bᵉshēveṭ sōphēr, 507
mōshēl, 526
mutstsāv, 565
mūzār, 778 n.507

nādīv, 538–39
   hithnaddēv, 539
   nadīv, 539, 773 n.457
   nᵉdīvē 'ammīm, 510
   nᵉdīvē hā'ām, 539
   nᵉdīvīm, 538–40
nāgīd, 365
nāmōgū, 521

AKKADIAN

OTHER LANGUAGES

4. INDEX OF GEOGRAPHICAL TERMS AND PERSONAL NAMES

Note: 1. Entries in this index are normally defined only when confusion might otherwise arise, as, for example, when two or more persons and/or places bear identical names, e.g., "Jonathan (grandson of Moses)"; "Jonathan (son of Saul)," or "Elon (the Hittite)"; "Elon (a 'minor' judge)"; "Elon (in Zebulun)." Clarifying definitions are also given where the same name is applied to smaller and larger geographical entities, e.g., "Samaria (city)"; "Samaria (region)," and where a personal name functions as a tribal eponym, e.g., "Benjamin (eponymous tribal ancestor)"; "Benjamin (tribal region)." In a few instances very similarly spelled names, easily confused, are also characterized, e.g., "Amman (capital of modern Jordan)"; "Ammon (in ancient Transjordan)."

2. Many of the geographical terms and personal names in this index are also used to designate peoples under various guises as familial, ethnic, cultural, and sociopolitical groupings. All these so-called "gentilic" meanings are entered in the Index of Subjects. They normally appear there either with the same form of the name, e.g., as "Benjamin (tribal region)" in this index and as "Benjamin, tribe of" in the Index of Subjects, or they occur in a gentilic form, e.g., as "Ammon (in ancient Transjordan)" in this index and as "Ammonites" in the Index of Subjects. Sometimes the group meaning of a geographical or personal name is not one cited in biblical or other ancient sources, but is rather a hypothetical construct, e.g., "Abraham" as a personal name in this index and "Abraham group" and "Abraham lineage" in the Index of Subjects, or "Shechem (eponymous ancestor)" as a personal name and "Shechem (city)" as a geographical term in this index and "Shechem, protective association of" and "Shechemite group" in the Index of Subjects.

In addition to the usual cross-references within this index, abundant cross-references to the Index of Subjects have been included. Likewise, it will be noted that the Index of Subjects is itself widely cross-referenced to this Index of Geographical Terms and Personal Names. The result is that by starting from either index it is easy to trace analytically the family relations among these often complex clusters of personal, geographical, and group names.

Since this study is particularly interested in cross-societal comparisons between Israel and other sociohistoric groups, entries in this index are also cross-referenced to analytic regional arrangements of these cross-societal analogies which appear in the Index of Subjects under the entries "Africa, analogies"; "American Indians, analogies"; "Ancient Near East, analogies";"Asia, analogies"; "Europe, analogies."

All cross-references to the Index of Subjects are marked by an asterisk and are always given following all internal cross references, without regard to alphabetization. Thus, under the entry for the city "Jebus" below, "See also Jerusalem; Salem; *Jebusites" indicates that within this index there are additional entries for the same city under "Jerusalem" and "Salem," and it also means that in the Index of Subjects there is an entry for the inhabitants of Jebus who are known as "Jebusites."

Aaron, 288–90

Abdi-Ashirta, 399–400, 402, 409, 482, 758 nn.304–306

Abdi-Heba. *See* ÈR-Heba

Abdon, 53, 138, 306

Abel-Keramim, 137

Abi. *See* Ube

Abimelech (of Gerar), 55

Abimelech (of Manasseh), 53, 137, 200, 258, 298, 306–307, 322 348, 529, 531, 551–52,
563, 565–67, 581, 773 n.453; 776 n.497; 777 n.502

Abner, 365

Abraham, 55, 75–76, 80, 107–109, 120–21, 177, 308–309, 314, 451–52, 493–94, 510, 562, 564, 568–69, 718 n.34; 735 n.139; 769 nn.415–16. *See also* *Abraham group; *Abraham lineage

Absalom, 286, 369, 446, 774 n.458

Abydos (in the .Hellespont), 776 n.493

5. INDEX OF SUBJECTS

Note 1. *The entries in this index are largely of two sorts: (a) historical and literary subjects concerning early Israel and its social and natural environment; (b) social scientific subjects representing the methods and theories used in this study of Israel as a social reality. The index is internally cross-referenced in order to facilitate identification of relationships both within and between these two types of subjects.*

2. *Since many interlocking themes and analytic models are employed in the study, the index supplies summary and analytic entries that group subjects thematically. For example, the social-theoretical dimensions of the study can be seen synoptically by examining the subentries under "Ideal types," while the range and instances of sociohistorical comparisons with Israel can be seen in the list of cross-references under "Analogies, sociopolitical." Anthropological features are highlighted by "Kinship system" and by "Social organization, zones of." Aspects of socioeconomic life in the ancient Near East and Israel are catalogued under headings such as "Foods and crops," "Labor/laborers," "Leaders," and "Technology." The particulars of Israel's social structure can be traced through "Social structure, of premonarchic Israel," and the various stances of Israel and surrounding peoples toward one another can be grasped through entries on "Allies," "Converts," "Enemies," and "Neutrals." Because of their prominence among Israel's neighbors, "Canaanites" and "Egyptians" are developed analytically. Finally, various theological treatments are grouped under "Theology," and the perspectives of sociology of religion appear under "Religion, in human societies" and "Sociology of religion."*

3. *The index is also cross-referenced to the Index of Geographical Terms and Personal Names by means of citations marked with an asterisk. Thus, under the entry "Abraham lineage," the cross-references "See also Lineage; *Abraham" refer respectively to the entry "Lineage" in this Index of Subjects and to "Abraham" in the Index of Geographical Terms and Personal Names. The external cross-references are always given following all internal cross-references, without regard to alphabetization.*

4. *The major languages that are represented by citation of words in this study are noted in this index by the cross-reference "See also Index of Foreign Terms."*

5. *It is recommended that users of this index also read the introductory note to the Index of Geographical Terms and Personal Names.*

Horite tribes, 353, 750 n.257
Ishmaelite tribes, 353–54, 750–51 n.260
Israelite tribes. *See* Amphictyonic model;
    Twelve-tribe system
Mesopotamian city-states at Nippur, 355,
    751 n.265
Philistine city-states, 356, 751 n.268
classical (Graeco-Italian) forms of, 22, 207,
    239, 244, 345, 347–57, 376–86, 750
    n.258; 753–54 n.284
  at Anthela, 348, 350, 753 n.284
  at Calauria, 353, 378–79, 753 n.284
  Delian league, 384–85, 751, n.265
  at Delphi, 348, 350–51, 353, 355, 378–79
    382–83, 749 nn.250–51; 751 nn.
    264–66; 753 n.284
  Etruscan leagues, 345, 347, 353, 385, 750
    n.258
  governing council of, 350–53, 355, 376,
    378–79, 749 n.250; 753 n.284
  Latin leagues, 345, 347, 353, 385
  officers of (amphictyons/president), 350–52,
    376, 749 n.251
  at Onchestus, 753 n.284
  Panionion, 384–85, 753 n.284
  at Pylae, 350–51, 353, 376, 383–84, 751
    n.264; 753 n.284
  Thessalian league, 351, 753–54 n.284
  at Veslinii, 353
  See also Confederacies and leagues; Rota sys-
    tem
Amurru, kingdom of, 399–400, 500–501, 758
    nn.308–309; 771 n.426
Anachronisms. *See* Periodization; Temporal
    distance and refraction
Anah (Horite tribe), 750 n.257. *See also* Horite
    tribes, alleged amphictyony of
Anakim, 132
Analogies for deity:
  epithets and symbols used as,
    bull, 670, 677, 683. *See also* Golden calf
    father-mother, 496, 670, 677, 682-83. *See
      also* Sexuality, of the deity
    heavenly bodies, 518, 670, 677, 682
    judge, 101, 615, 677, 683
    king-sovereign, 57, 90–91, 93–95, 101,
      104–105, 118, 226, 241, 513, 538,
      614–15, 626, 670, 677, 682–83, 697,
      699, 800 n.641
    master/owner/husband, 677, 683. *See also*
      Baal
    mountain, 677, 683..*See also* El Shaddai
    rock/crag, 684, 796 nn.624–25 *See also* Stand-
      ing stones
    sea, 509, 677. *See also* Rahab, sea as primor-
      dial chaos; Yamm
    shepherd, 683
    sir/honored one, 683
    storm phenomena, 677, 682–83
    tree, 511, 677, 683

warrior, 118, 279–82, 615, 677, 682–83. *See
    also* Hosts, armed
  philosophical and theological significance of,
    700–709, 800 n.641
  preferred in the ancient Near East, 670, 677
  preferred in Israel, 670, 677, 682–85
  sociohistorical base of, 611–21, 642–49,
    688–709
  See also High-god pattern; Symbolism, of the
    Yahwistic traditions; Symbolism, reli-
    gious, theories of; Theology
Analogies, sociopolitical, between Israel and
    other societies and states, 22, 608, 659. *See
    also* Africa, analogies; American Indians,
    analogies; Amphictyonic model; Ancient
    Near East, analogies; Asia, analogies;
    Confederacies and leagues; Europe,
    analogies; Greece, ancient, analogies;
    Primitives; Rome, ancient analogies; Un-
    ited States, analogies
Anath, 761 n.336
Ancestor worship. *See* Death, Israelite attitude
    toward
Ancient Near East, analogies to sociopolitical
    forms in Israel. *See* Alalakh; Amalekites;
    Ammonites; Amorites; *'Apiru*; Canaan-
    ites; Edomites; Egyptians; Mari; Midian-
    ites; Philistines; Shosu; Sumeria; Ugarit.
    See also Amphictyonic model; Analogies,
    sociopolitical
Animal husbandry, 39, 206, 292, 294, 297–98,
    389, 416, 437–51, 462, 471, 475–77,
    542–43, 545, 547–49, 614, 765 n.380. *See
    also* Asses; Camels; Cattle, bovine; Domes-
    tication, of animals; Horses; Oxen; Sheep
    and goats
Annals:
  of minor judges, 53, 137–38, 148, 185–86, 750
    n.254
  of tribal battles and occupations (conquest
    annals), 49–50, 134–35, 148–49, 154,
    163–75, 526–28, 543, 563, 568
  life-setting of, 50, 171–75
  tradition history of, 148–49, 173–74, 176,
    179–82, 184–86
  See also Conquest narratives; Judges; Nega-
    tive occupation annals
Anthela, amphictyony of, 348, 350, 753 n.284.
    See also Amphictyony, classical forms of
Anthropological theory, 13, 22, 228, 237–38,
    253, 257, 293–99, 310–313, 317–18,
    323–25, 327–28, 335, 337, 436, 441, 465,
    476, 595, 600, 624, 652, 658, 663, 713 n.6;
    721–22 nn.56–57; 740 nn.162, 168;
    743–44 nn.195–201; 745 n.213; 765–66
    n.393; 782 n.537; 784 n.554; 785
    nn.557–60; 786 nn.565–66; 787 n.570;
    788 n.577; 798 n.635
  See also Social scientific methods, in biblical
    studies; Social theory

Sutu, 478

Swiss Federal Union, 22, 770 n.418. *See also* Confederacies and leagues; Europe, analogies

Sword, 136, 415, 419, 518, 541, 552–53, 655. *See also* Weaponry

Symbiosis, Egyptian-Canaanite. *See* Canaanites, symbiosis of, with Egyptians

Symbolism, of the Yahwistic traditions, 16, 21, 70, 77–78, 83–87, 92–93, 97, 121–24, 155, 214–15, 326, 363, 372–75, 417, 490, 496, 614–15, 618, 627, 646–48, 662, 668, 676–700, 798 n.631; 799 n.637. *See also* Analogies for deity; Biblical theology; Historical consciousness; Historiography, popular/symbolic; Ideology; Salvation paradigms; Symbolism, religious, theory of; Supernatural explanations; Theology

Symbolism, religious, theory of, 624–27, 636–37, 668, 701–703, 800–801 nn.641–42. *See also* Ideology; Religion, in human societies; Sociology of religion; Symbolism, of the Yahwistic traditions

Symmachies, military leagues in Greece. *See* Confederacies and leagues

Sympolities, confederations in Greece. *See* Confederacies and leagues

Synchronics, societal, 31, 100, 228, 230, 288, 290, 332, 335–36, 390, 399, 489, 591, 610, 622–24. *See also* Diachronics, societal

Synthetic social system, early Israel as a, 19, 21, 121–24, 226–33, 325–34, 390, 455–56, 464–65, 489–97, 502, 555–56, 599, 690, 766 n.393. *See also* Egalitarianism, socioeconomic; Retribalization process; Social structure, of premonarchic Israel

Syrians, 232, 415, 459, 462, 478, 499–501, 660, 756 nn.295–96, 298; 757 n.302; 759 n.312; 760 n.328; 763 n.353; 794 n.601. *See also* *Syria

Tabernacle. *See* Tent of meeting. *See also* Temple, at Jerusalem

Tabernacles, festival of. *See* Festivals

Tallensi, 312. *See also* Africa, analogies; Primitives

Talmud, 741 n.171; 742 n.183; 791 n.587. *See also* Jews/Judaism

Taunt Song against Heshbon, 48, 215, 217, 556, 738 n.153

Taxation, 158, 212–14, 363, 365–66, 368–69, 371–72, 407, 430, 444, 449–50, 460, 464, 466, 468–69, 475, 545, 547, 662, 727 n.94; 753 n.284. *See also* Corvée; Draft, military; Surplus labor products

Technology:
  agricultural/pastoral (tools/water systems/ terraces), 297, 419, 445–46, 465–66, 548–49, 650–51, 653, 655–63, *See also*

Agriculture

craft (ceramics/metallurgy), 196, 201, 217, 292, 465–66, 548–50, 613, 650–51, 653, 657–58, 661, 761 n.335. *See also* Iron; Pottery

military (weaponry), 212, 319, 392–93, 414–15, 417–18, 542–43, 547–50, 65ᵉ, 697. *See also* Weaponry

in models of social and religious change, 299, 334, 465, 598, 631–36, 638–39, 641–63, 697, 785 n.559. *See also* Social change; Social evolution

See also Cultural-material inventory; Economic organization; Labor/laborers; Surplus labor products

Temple

in Ammon, 763 n.357

at Gaza, 138

at Jerusalem, 140, 143, 243, 279–80, 371–73, 508, 522, 548, 551, 575; 724 n.75; 726 n.87; 752 n.281

at Shechem, 137, 564–66, 763 n.357; 777 n.502

at Shiloh, 283, 730 n.115

See also Holy places

Temporal distance/refraction, of traditions, 20, 27–30, 32–38, 41–42, 47, 63, 76, 84, 87, 93, 120–21, 125, 154–55, 162–63, 187, 208, 217, 308–310, 333–34, 365–66, 370, 375, 451–54, 493, 498–99, 731–32 n.121; 736 n.148. *See also* Canonical traditions; Geographical schematization; Pan-Israelite framework

Tenant farmers, 481–82, 542, 558, 722 n.63; 723 n.71; 757 n.299; 767 n.407; 791–92 n.587. *See also* Colonate; Feudalism; Peasants; Serfs

Tent, as indicator of pastoral nomadism, 136, 195, 440–41. *See also* Living quarters

Tent of meeting, 161, 370, 603. *See also* Ark; Temple, at Jerusalem

Terah lineage, 309. *See also* Lineage; *Terah

Teraphim, 138, 291

Terebinth. *See* Trees, sacred

Terraces, agricultural, 297, 598, 658–61, 791–92 nn.587–92. *See also* Agriculture; Cultural-material inventory; Technology, agricultural; Water systems

Territorial lists, 56, 132–33, 155–63, 182–84, 274–75. *See also* Allotment traditions; Boundary inventories; City lists

Territorial states, in Syro-Palestine, 426–34. *See also* National states; State; Territoriality

Territoriality, concept of, 56, 157–59, 162, 173–75, 179–83, 247, 253–56, 368–69, 427, 471, 528, 747 n.235. *See also* Territorial states

Tetrateuch, 722 n.63; 723 n.71. *See also* Hexateuch; Pentateuch

Textiles, 454, 499, 506, 543, 558, 561, 563. *See also* Labor/laborers, types of: dye workers/traders; linen workers

Themes, of the early Israelite traditions. *See* Basic themes

Theodicy, in Weber, 628, 687, 797–98 n.630

Theology. *See* Analogies for deity; Biblical theology; Common theology, of the ancient Near East; Existentialist theology; High-god pattern; Individuated high gods; Liberation theology; Monotheism; Mono-Yahwism; Moral-theological interpretations of history;Naturalism, religious; Neo-Orthodox theology; Political theology; Process theology; Sociology of religion; Supernatural explanations; Symbolism, of the Yahwistic traditions; Transcendence

Theophany, 57–58, 89–105, 109–115, 118–19, 131, 144, 185, 280–82, 550, 683, 724 n.75; 725 nn.78, 83. *See also* Covenant; Law; Sinai theme

Thessalian league, 351, 753–54 n.284. *See also* Amphictyony, classical forms of; Confederacies and leagues

Timber, 212, 396, 515. *See also* Commerce

Tinkers. *See* Labor/laborers, types of

Tirzah, protective association of, 268. *See also* *Tirzah

Tolaites, protective association of, 288. *See also* *Tola

Tonga, 324–25. *See also* Africa, analogies

"Top-down" model, of Israel's social system, 327–34, 747 n.234. *See also* "Bottom-up" model; Social structure, of premonarchic Israel

Topological method, of Rowton, 652–53, 757 n.301; 788 n.576; 796 n.625. *See also* Geography; Historico-territorial method

Town/village, in the ancient Near East/Canaan and Israel

　archaeology of, 656–57, 791 n.585

　beginnings of, 441–42, 765 n.369

　as focus of the tribal countryside, 159, 231, 406, 408, 435, 438, 451, 461–62, 470–73, 491, 528, 568–70, 764 n.366; 767 n.398; 779 n.516

　as locus of Israelite protective association of families, 257, 269–70, 316, 561, 613, 656

　as lowest level of state administration, 408, 412, 466–73, 527–28

　as a residency arrangement, 291, 466–73, 528, 766 n.396

　See also Canaanites, village tribalism among; Countryside; State; Tribe

Trade. *See* Barter; Commerce. *See also* Labor/laborers, types of: merchants

Tradition formation, in premonarchic Israel

　centralization and harmonization in, 63, 69–71, 81–92, 105–110, 141–42, 145–75 *passim*, 176–87, 197–98, 207–209

　centralized traditions, 70–71, 81–82, 145–75 *passim*, 176–86

　localized traditions, 70–71, 81–82, 145–75 *passim*, 176–79

　See also Cult, relation between centralized and local forms of

　cultic-ideological foundations of, 4–5, 27–30, 47, 58, 63–125, 129, 141–42, 146–48, 152, 154–55, 179–81, 191, 202, 204, 207–208, 221–23, 229, 320, 451, 584, 687, 691, 748 n.243

　lay traditions, 69–71, 78–79, 109–110, 122–24

　priestly traditions, 69–71, 78–79, 109–110

　periodization and schematization in. *See* Geographical schematization; Periodization; Temporal distance/refraction

　See also Canonical traditions; Historiography, documentary; Historiography, popular/symbolic; Pentateuch

Tradition history, 29, 45–47, 64, 72–79, 82, 101, 140, 146, 149, 151–52, 162, 183, 187, 204, 221–24, 247–48, 360, 605, 717 n.31; 718 n. 36; 719–20 n.42; 726 n.84. *See also* Form criticism; Literary criticism

Trajectory, social and historical. *See* Diachronics, societal

Transcendence

　as a contemporary theological category, 703, 800–802 nn.642–44

　as a symbolic function of sociohistorical experience, 601, 637, 640, 645, 648, 688–709, 784–85 n.556; 801–802 nn.643–44

　as a theological category in the ancient Near East, 599–601, 670–78

　as a theological category in Israel, 599–602, 645, 669–91, 697–98

　See also High-god pattern; Objectification; Projection; Reduction; Symbolism, religious, theory of; Theology

Transhumant pastoralism, 231, 294, 437, 444–48, 451–53, 455–57, 459–64, 466–67, 471, 474, 476–78, 480, 483–85, 491, 493, 497, 555, 584–85, 643, 661, 765 nn.373–74; 766 n.393. *See also* Nomadism, pastoral; Semi-nomadism

Transport, 414, 440–441, 444, 505–507. *See also* Commerce; Labor/laborers, types of: caravaneers

Treaties, 14, 49, 55, 131, 134–35, 164, 191, 193–94, 198, 200, 204–205, 216, 226, 304, 311–12, 321, 400, 418, 493, 520, 522–25, 529–30, 533–34, 568–74, 571–74, 576–83, 596, 745 n.213; 769 n.415; 772 nn.446–47, 452; 775 n.490; 778 n.511.*See also* Covenant

508, 512, 515–18, 521–22, 527–29,
532–40, 548, 550, 554, 561, 564–67,
572–73, 580, 585, 595–96, 600, 603–604,
614–16, 619, 627, 630, 644–45, 671, 674,
679–94, 696–97, 700, 702, 704–706, 708,
770 n.420; 780 n.516; 786 n.567; 795
n.622. *See also* Analogies for deity; Cult;
El; El Elohe Israel; El Shaddai; High-god
pattern; Mono-Yahwism; Symbolism, of
the Yahwistic traditions

Yahwism. *See* Mono-Yahwism

Yahwist. *See* J

Yahwistic Israel, successor to Elohistic Israel
and continuities with Elohistic Israel, 21, 33,
43–44, 107, 333, 494–97, 555, 564–67,
584, 644–45, 662
demarcated from Canaanite society, 21, 32,
43–44, 202–203, 489–92, 556, 644
demarcated from Exodus proto-Israelites,
38–40, 42–44
distinctive new features of, 33–34, 489–92,
496–97
See also Elohistic Israel; Mono-Yahwism;
Yahweh

Yaminites, of Mari, 546, 765 n.378. *See also*
Mari

Yamm, 509. *See also* Rahab, the sea as primordial chaos

Yauri, 215. *See also* Jair, group or protective
association of

Zamzummim, 739 n.154. *See also* Ammonites;
Rephaim

Zarhi. *See* Zerah

Zebulun, tribe of, 50, 53, 133–36, 138, 156, 163,
169–70, 246, 268, 276, 307, 346, 366–67,
507, 527–28, 542, 728 n.108; 730 n.110;
740 n. 169. *See also* *Zebulun (eponymous
tribal ancestor); *Zebulun (tribal region)

Zerah, protective association of, 259, 275, 287,
561. *See also* *Zerah

Zibeon (Horite tribe), 750 n.257. *See also* Horite
tribes, alleged amphictyony of

Ziphites, protective association of, 277

Zodiac, 355, 751 nn.264, 267. *See also* Twelve,
the number

Zuphites, protective association of, 283

Epilogue

Since completion of the body of this work, recent publications by others and further thoughts of my own have prompted some concluding observations in conversation with current lines of inquiry that relate to my overall socioreligious model for early Israel. Here and there I extend my purview to include previously overlooked older studies. I shall organize these remarks according to the sequence of topics treated in the foregoing text.

Part III. The Cultic-Ideological Framework of the Sources.

My adoption of the general pentateuchal model of Noth presupposes that the centralized growth of the early traditions in Genesis through Numbers (and probably also underlying Joshua 1—12 and Judges 1) is in itself compelling and thus requires no support whatsoever from Noth's unconvincing model of the amphictyony. This means that while I deny a central cult in the sense of a single sanctuary functioning like a Mediterranean amphictyonic center, I do posit a central cult in the sense that a body of Yahwistic beliefs and practices developed under the aegis of the Levites in such fashion that a schema of the traditions was shaped and given general acknowledgement within the Israelite confederacy prior to the monarchy.

Criticisms of the literary side of Noth's reconstruction of early Israel, as pointedly voiced for example by Thomas L. Thompson,[1] focus on the arbitrariness of Noth's identification of nuclear themes, doubts about the germinative creativity of these themes in the whole fund of traditions, the predominance of a narrow form critical/historico-territorial orientation over an allegedly more appropriate literary critical/sociological orientation in evaluating the traditions, and even the unlikelihood of the centralization and standardization of traditions in the absence of specifically amphictyonic institutions. The reservations that I share on some of these points are, I believe, expressed in my elastic manner of adopting Noth's version of the cultic-ideological framework for the early traditions. I do not, however, find the sum of these objections—and particularly the last named—decisive against the clear advantages of Noth's literary strategy. I take seriously that in committing themselves to the religion of Yahweh, the Israelite tribes consented to a centralized tradition-building tendency and process which they were able to contribute to by the inclusion of localized materials but which bore the crucial imprint of the Levites as cultic and intellectual leaders of the confederacy.

That I do not follow Noth's literary schema slavishly should be evident from my preference for the view that portions of the J/E sources have survived in Joshua and Judges. I follow the broad outlines of Noth's schema because I find it more convincing and adequate to account for the agglomeration of the early traditions than any other I am aware of. I am prepared to entertain other ways of conceptualizing the growth of the early traditions, as, for example, in Claus Westermann's fascinating endeavor to locate the mixed family/clan, tribal, and state horizons of the patriarchal stories,[2] whose method incidentally is not unlike the way I approach the patriarchal accounts (cf. e.g., pp. 308–313). The base line for such literary/sociological analyses is that—whatever their forms—they must explain how a decentralized social movement developed a complex and extensively integrated body of traditions prior to the introduction of central government, scribal schools, and state-sponsored religion.

Part V.   Models of the Israelite Settlement in Canaan.

Advocacy of the three major models (conquest, immigration, and revolt) seems to have reached an impasse which the flood of archaeological, literary, and historical studies has not succeeded in breaking through. Confidence in the older models of the conquest and immigration continues to erode, while the more recent revolt model has yet to be set on a broad enough base to be convincing to most scholars. One detects also aversion and impatience toward the harsh polemical garb in which the models have frequently been dressed, resulting in more heat than light on the subject.

It has of course been my intention in this volume to present a version of the revolt model that simultaneously attends to all classes of relevant evidence (and as much of the content of each class as I can muster) while remaining open to correction and revision. Here I wish only to single out one recent corroborative contribution on the subject of the revolt model and to reply to some recently published objections to the model. It should by now be clear that while one may speak of "the Mendenhall-Gottwald model" in a very broad generic sense, the fact is that Mendenhall and I, proceeding from the same evidence, have agreed only partially on methods and have produced versions of the revolt model that are different in significant respects.

Marvin L. Chaney reviews the data for and against the major settlement models and emerges with a succinct, closely argued, and temperate defense of an amended revolt model.[3] He persuasively answers the chief objections leveled against the most widely published form of the model and shows that they largely disappear when Mendenhall's argumentation is amended so as to give nuanced emphasis to the conjunction of interacting geographical, technological, sociological, political, and ideological factors operative in early Israel.

In his fundamental conception of social revolutionary early Israel, Chaney is much closer to the theoretical design and method advanced in this work than he is to the direction in which Mendenhall has pushed the model in his recent work.[4]

Chaney contends, as do I, that the revolt model explains little when Yahwistic ideology is isolated and hypostatized. In any event, it is of great utility for a proper focusing of the discussion that we now have in brief compass a pointed, lucid, and systematic presentation of a refined version of the revolt model which clears away foolish misconceptions and promotes a honing of the kinds of arguments and the classes of evidence that will improve the chances for verification or for falsification of the hypothesis. I find it particularly significant that Chaney sets high standards for a dialogue among those who espouse the revolt model with the promise that the hypothesis can be refined and self-corrected.

Valuable also in Chaney's discussion is his application to the Amarna/early Israelite data of four heuristic categories from sociology. Three of these categories are referred to in the text and Notes to this work on the basis of my contacts with Chaney in conversations and lectures (see citations below). It is fitting that Chaney has now put the outlines of his proposals into print as a prod to further research. Briefly, the categories are as follows: (1) Gerhard Lenski's concept of the opportunity for and incentive to innovation in *frontier areas* is used to illuminate the burst of Israelite economy and culture in the central highlands in Iron I; (2) Eric Wolf's schemata of the conditions conducive to *peasant revolt* are shown to be almost, if not entirely, satisfied by what we know of early Israel (cf. above pp. 585–586, 780 n.518; (3) Gideon Sjoberg's specification of the socially subversive role of *occupational outcasts* in preindustrial cities becomes a way of clarifying Rahab's role in Joshua 2 (cf. above, pp. 557, 775–776 n.491); (4) Eric Hobsbawm's typology of *social banditry* is applied to the Amarna *'apiru* so as to open up a determinate range of socioeconomic and political options for understanding their possible role(s) and function(s), in a manner somewhat analogous to, but more precise than, M. B. Rowton's work on "the parasocial element" in dimorphic society[5] (cf. above pp. 408–409, 760 n.327).

Two of the most frequent objections to the revolt model are, firstly, that it has no foundation in the texts and, secondly, that it is the imposition of a modern notion on an ancient situation totally foreign to conceptions of social revolution. Precisely such rebuttals appear, for example, in two of the most recent assessments of the revolt model. J. Maxwell Miller objects that

> The "peasants' revolt" model seems to be a modern construct superimposed upon the biblical traditions. . . .The theory that Israel emerged from a Palestinian peasants' revolt finds no basis in the biblical materials, whether one considers the oldest discernible strata of the conquest tradition or the final canonical account. . . .There is not the slightest hint in the biblical traditions regarding the revolution which supposedly brought Israel into existence.[6]

Similarly, Alan J. Hauser protests that

> The uniqueness he describes [for ancient Israel], however, derives from the modern views of religion and revolution which Mendenhall has uncritically transplanted into

the context of ancient society. . . . If it is the case that most of later Israel derived from
the indigenous population of Canaan, who joined with the small exodus-Sinai group
and rebelled against their overlords, it is a curious anomaly that there is no trace in
the biblical traditions of a massive conversion and uprising such as Mendenhall
proposes. Even granting Mendenhall's claim [about the monarchic filtering out of
the reality of Israel's revolutionary origins], one would still expect that there would be
tacit, covert, and inadvertent hints as to the real nature of the conquest that could be
uncovered by careful analysis of the traditions.[7]

As noted in my published response to Hauser, I believe that there is now a
sufficient corpus of carefully reasoned literature, singling out specific early Israelite texts and elucidating them by means of specific sociological concepts, to
provide far more evidence for a revolt model than the minimal "hints" Miller and
Hauser seek. Chaney's analysis of the literary/sociological strata in Joshua 2 is a
fine case in point, standing in persuasive continuity with many of the texts given
sociological illumination in the published work of Mendenhall and in Part IX
especially of this volume. Hopefully it will not be long before Chaney's superb
philological, historical, and sociological dissertation on Judges 5 will be in print (cf.
pp. 504, 771 n.428). I would also add the probing textual insights in the articles of
Jan Dus, although these often lack the necessary depth of treatment to give full
support to his perceptive conceptual apparatus (cf. above pp. 718 n.35; 736
n.148; 769 n.414; 779 n.637).

Only as more and more texts are elucidated by a combination of traditional
critical and sociologically critical methods is it likely that the bugaboo of "imported
alien concepts" will be laid to rest. As I have argued in my criticism of some typical
misstatements of the society-religion nexus in ancient Israel—as exhibited in the
work of John Bright and Georg Fohrer, and even in the work of Mendenhall
himself when he wanders from sociological premises—there is no more inherent
reason for sociological methods and theories to be "superimpositions" on ancient
society than for historico-critical methods to be "superimpositions" on ancient
texts (cf. above pp. 592–607). Any given historico-critical approach to a text may
be a failure, and so may any particular sociological approach to early Israelite
society by way of texts or archaeological data. In neither case is it the method per se
that is at fault. In most instances it is either a bad execution of method, or an
attempt to do something with the method that cannot be done, or a failure to
recognize the limits of the data. We face a valid problematic: What are appropriate
sociological methods and constructs for analyzing biblical texts and archaeological
remains in order to uncover early Israelite social realia and processes? Aspects of
this problematic are further discussed in my recent reply to the critical assessments of the revolt model by Alan J. Hauser and Thomas L. Thompson,[8] and in a
forthcoming essay on general methodological considerations in social scientific
study of ancient Israel.[9]

Part VII.   Models of the Social Structure (II): All Israel, Amphictyony or Confederacy?

In my efforts to undertake a fresh examination of the Mediterranean amphictyonies, I deplored the apparent paucity of work on Greek amphictyonies in the last several decades. In reading the stimulating work of C. H. J. de Geus (discussed below under Part IX), my attention was drawn to a previously unnoted study by Fritz R. Wüst published in 1954/55.[10]

Wüst evaluates the two Greek traditions that explained the meaning of "amphictyony" and the origins of the institution in quite different ways: (1) that its proper form was *amphiktiones*, referring to "inhabitants of surrounding districts" who joined in a cultic union at Delphi; and (2) that its proper form was *amphiktuones*, referring to its founder Amphiktyon, who established a cultic union at Anthela/Pylae. As I noted earlier (pp. 348, 350–351), Anthela/Pylae and Delphi were successive locations of the Pylaean-Delphic amphictyony, and for a time served as simultaneous centers of the cultic formation. Wüst believes, on linguistic and historical grounds, that the proper name of Amphiktyon from Pylae was the actual origin of the term and that Delphic devotees later altered the spelling of the proper name so as to form the appellative, "dwellers around" or "neighboring associates," with the deliberate intent of obscuring the older specifically Pylaean origins of the amphictyony.

This Pylaean-Delphic amphictyony went through three phases of development: 1. It was at first the tribe of Amphiktyon, named for its eponymous founder, which established a sanctuary at Pylae in pre-Dorian (Ionian?) times, probably toward the end of the sixteenth century B.C., 2. The venerable old sanctuary became the center for a cultic league of Dorian tribes devoted to Demeter at Pylae and eventually also to Apollo at Delphi. 3. In historical times, the members of this Dorian amphictyony ceased to be tribes and came to be city-states as centralized political institutions spread throughout Greece. The Delphic cult site eventually totally displaced the Pylaean cult site within the amphictyony.

Wüst observes the distribution of the use of the term amphictyony and finds that it is never employed without qualification for any cultic association other than Pylae-Delphi. Strabo referred to the sacral leagues at Onchestus and Calauria as "a kind of amphictyony" or as "amphictyonic," i.e., bearing some resemblances to *the* amphictyony at Delphi-Pylae. For all the other sacral leagues, only the term "amphictyons" is occasionally used, in which case it always refers to the cultic officials and never to the association itself or to its member states. Moreover, the member states are never specified by number or by name.

With the above evidence in mind, Wüst denies flatly that the institutional category of "amphictyony" was ever recognized by the Greeks, there having been only *one* amphictyony and *many* sacral leagues that on certain points only could be described with amphictyonic terminology, but even then only rather sparsely. If Wüst is correct about his linguistic data, he has shown that even within the Greek world the sacral unions did not present a sufficient similarity to have acquired a single covering technical term. This suggests, if I read him rightly, that one might have just as much trouble showing that any other Greek sacral league was typologically analogous to *the* sole amphictyony of Pylae-Delphi as Noth had in demonstrating that the Israelite confederacy was like *the* sole Greek amphictyony. This I take to be the thrust of de Geus's less than lucid conclusions on the import of Wüst's research (cf. pp. 193–195 of the work discussed under Part IX below).

A further pertinent aspect of Wüst's study is his careful examination of the function of the number *twelve* in the amphictyony and the other sacral leagues. It is his contention that twelve did indeed have a decisive constitutional and operational function in the Pylaean-Delphic union. He believes that the indispensability of twelve arose because of the historical fact that the original cult of the tribe of Amphiktyon had exactly twelve cultic officials and this number remained prescriptive throughout the later tribal and statist phases of the amphictyony. Strictly speaking, this does not mean that there were twelve and only twelve tribes or states that participated in the union, as demonstrated by the various ways in which many more than twelve city-states could in fact participate in electing the twenty-four *hieromnemones* (12 x 2). What it does mean is that the founding number of twelve retained a cultic sanctity and had to be reflected in structural features of the amphictyony, fictitiously if necessary, however many actual political units took part in its life at any one moment.

Interestingly, Wüst also observes that the Panionion in Asia Minor was, according to Herodotus, composed of precisely twelve parts or divisions which could not possibly be enlarged, even as a practical measure to incorporate additional mixed elements in the populace. Herodotus explains that before the members of the Panionion colonized Asia Minor they had already constituted twelve parts or sections in Achaia. Wüst underlines the connection between the cultic necessity for twelve both among the putative Ionian tribalists of Amphiktyon and the Ionian precursors of the Panionion when they still lived in mainland Greece. In an aside he further notes that the political subdivisions of ancient Athens included four *phylen* ("tribes"), each broken down into three *trittyn* (lit. "thirds"; "phratries"?), i.e., 4 x 3 = 12.

As for an explanation of this presumed Ionian political/cultic predilection for twelve, Wüst finds no hypothesis among the Greek observers of the phenomenon and he offers none himself. He leaves the matter at the level of "historical accident" in the sense that both *the* amphictyony and the Panionion in their earliest phases showed a stipulated division into twelve officials and parts respectively and that this remained a division to which they scrupulously adhered. Striking is the fact that Wüst finds no data and makes no speculative claims for the notion that twelve was normative in order to fill a twelve-month rota system for supporting the central sanctuary. Thus the fullest discussion I have found of the prescriptive function of twelve in the Greek cult fails to corroborate Noth's view of an obligatory rota system and also discovers the number twelve to have been normative only in two of the Greek sacral leagues, with an aside that the twelve-member Etruscan league may have been influenced by the Panionion.

Finally, Wüst proposes that rather than being of wide influence on other sacral leagues, the sole amphictyony of ancient Greece was rather more influential in passing on aspects of its structure to the fifth century political/military formations of the oath-bound confederation of Greeks against Persia and of the Athenian sea league, and also in the same century to a new form of the *symmachy* (military alliance or league) among Greek city-states involving three or more parties. Whether this line of structural continuity extended on from the amphictyony through the oath-bound confederation, the Athenian sea league, and the multi-party military alliance to find eventual expression in the *koine eirene* (common peace) of the fourth century in Greece, Wüst declines to make judgment without further study.

At the close of Part VII, I urged further inquiry into the Mediterranean amphictyonies and allowed that Noth's case might conceivably be strengthened by a re-examination of the evidence. It is evident, however, in the light of the painstaking scrutiny of the subject by Wüst, that the aptness of Noth's analogy diminishes still further, indeed almost to the vanishing point.

Part VIII. Comparative Social Systems and Economic Modes: The Sociohistoric Matrices of Liberated Israel.

Of the several topics treated in this part of my study, I want to comment generally on pastoral nomadism and specifically on M. B. Rowton's continuing project on dimorphic social structure and enclosed nomadism.

An exceedingly heartening development, which can only bring greater clarity into our search for the social origins of Israel, is the present far-reaching re-examination of the previous enormous, uncritical claims for pastoral nomadism as a factor in ancient Near Eastern culture and history—and especially as a cover explanation for all manner of phenomena in early Israel, including many of its most distinctive features. When I published my 1974 essay disclaiming that the first Israelites were pastoral nomads in any quantitatively or qualitatively significant sense I was somewhat of a lone voice among biblical scholars. Apart from a few critics who had challenged the long-regnant "nomadic ideal" as a norm in Israelite religion, only Mendenhall—who first alerted me to the issue—had made measurable attempts to challenge the still prevalent view that the Israelites had "obviously" been pastoral nomads since they exhibited tribal traits. On this point

Mendenhall was drawing heavily on the unpublished study of Mari pastoralism by his student John Tracey Luke. A study by Frank S. Frick in 1971, which showed that the supposedly intractably nomadic Rechabites were more probably traveling smiths, went largely unnoticed (cf. above p. 743 n.192).

In the last few years, however, a virtual polar shift in attitudes toward the pan-nomadic hypothesis has occurred among American scholars working on Israelite origins. There is much less evidence that "the news" about nomadism has significantly affected the European scene, where biblical scholars are generally out of touch with the social sciences (but cf. two important exceptions commented on below). Virtually all American historians of early Israel seem to have been impressed by the belated "discovery" of the overwhelming arguments against pan-nomadism that have been the common knowledge of prehistorians and ethnologists for decades. It was merely the strategic good fortune of a few of us biblical scholars to have paid attention to those developments in the study of nomadism and to have applied them to the ancient Near East and to early Israel. At a minimum it is now customary to throw down a warning flag whenever nomadic categories are invoked to explain any aspect of ancient Israel and to require fresh validation of all such claims. In the first flush of the new awareness there are even those who appear to deny that pastoral nomadism existed in ancient Israel, a view which has sometimes been attributed to me, although I do not see how it is possible to draw that conclusion from what I have written.

Typical of the total reassessment and drastic reduction of nomadism as a major creative factor in early Israel are the views of William G. Dever and W. Malcolm Clark on the patriarchal traditions and of J. Maxwell Miller on the occupation of Canaan as expressed in the recent compendious survey of Israelite and Judean history published in the Westminster Old Testament Library.[11] It is also striking that the Dutch scholar de Geus, having familiarized himself with the scientific literature on nomadism, takes as a leitmotif of his study on Israelite origins that pastoral nomadism simply cannot begin to account for the major outlines of early biblical history or for the structural peculiarities of Israelite life and thought. It is in large measure due to his consistent adherence to that methodological principle that de Geus is able to strike out on new paths in the exploration of Israelite beginnings. Earlier I mentioned the apparently isolated European instance of the German scholar Siegfried Schwertner, who in 1966 scrutinized the early traditions of Israel only to find a minimal nomadic content (cf. above pp. 765–766 n.393).

Yet precisely at this juncture, as a hitherto neglected truth about early Israel comes to sudden acceptance—even to "popularity"!—it is necessary to sound a few cautions. One must not, for example, overstate either the extent of our knowledge of ancient Near Eastern nomadism nor the precision of our conceptual apparatus for understanding nomadism in its total range and endless permutations. A close reading of the literature by prehistorians and ethnologists discloses that they are far from having reached an altogether satisfactory and agreed upon nomenclature for characterizing different forms of nomadism. While there is general consensus on specifying camel nomadism as "full nomadism," the terms "semi-nomadism" and "transhumant pastoralism" are used with variable meanings, and most would recognize that sheep and goat nomadism may be "full-time" without being "fully developed" nomadism. The disagreements over terms and concepts that I describe among biblical scholars (cf. above pp. 445–446) sometimes seem duplicated or echoed among specialists on nomadism. The all-important difference is that the specialists for the most part define or characterize as carefully as they can what it is that they are labeling by one term or another, whereas biblical scholars have seldom shown scrupulosity in clarifying the cluster of traits they were choosing to label as one form or another of nomadism. It is one of the merits of M. B. Rowton's series on enclosed nomadism in the ancient Near East that he strives toward clarity and consistency in nomenclature, even when it may be doubted that the great time ranges he covers and the sources he must rely upon lend themselves to the precision he seeks.[12]

Even more unsettling are the problems in making analogies between presently observed nomads and nomads in ancient times. One authority cautions that domestication of animals, marginality of exploited lands and resources, migrations over long distances with seasonal changes, and forms of tribal structure (all of which are often extrapolated from modern nomads to prehistoric nomads), may not have taken the same forms or have carried the same structural weight then as they have in modern pastoral nomadic settings.[13] Of course for analogies to the historical ancient Near East, within which Israel falls, we do have written records, but it does not take much effort in reading Allan Gilbert's provocative essay to realize how superficially we often make assumptions about the less well known nomadism of the ancient Near East by extrapolation from the better known nomadism of the present. As carefully, for example, as Rowton has done his historical and ecological study of pastoral nomadism in the Near East over millennia of time, other arguable choices from the broad range of possible adaptations on each of the subtopics noted by Gilbert could easily have skewed Rowton's interpretations in markedly different directions. Moreover, if it is true that all modern nomads are descendants of groups that have either lived through a phase of full nomadism or have been heavily influenced by full nomadism, that recognition alone must give us pause as we approach ancient forms of nomadism that knew nothing whatever of the much fuller exploitation of pastoral nomadism, which was to become possible with the domesticated camel after a satisfactory form of saddle was invented in the first Christian centuries.

These cautions are not at all intended to discourage further study of ancient Near Eastern pastoral nomadism but only to warn us against assuming that it is a subject easily mastered and disposed of. I continue to believe that pastoral nomadism had a relatively small role to play in the total Israelite social structure on all levels, but it did have a role (especially on the eastern and southern frontier regions), and it can be understood properly only if the gaps and indeterminations in our knowledge—not simply about specifically Israelite data but about the ancient nomadic forms themselves—are securely held in mind at the same time we work systematically to reduce them.

In the meantime, Rowton's ambitious project on social dimorphism and enclosed nomadism is nearing completion, available now in thirteen out of sixteen planned installments. Regrettably these studies are scattered through several periodicals and Rowton's listing of them according to topical coherence does not correspond to the chronological order of their appearance.[14] It is obviously a project that mushroomed in the course of its execution, with the result that the later articles are conceptually clearer and better related to one another than the earlier articles. In spite of helpful summaries and cross-references, an overview of the Rowton articles available to me does not make for ready understanding of how Rowton intends the plethora of materials on dimorphic societies to be integrated theoretically. Hopefully the last three installments of the series will provide greater help in this respect.

There is no question in my mind that, following Owen Lattimore's distinction between "open" and "closed" nomadism in China, Rowton has established his basic thesis: Near Eastern nomadism in its many forms, ancient and modern, evinces the persistent characteristic of being economically and sociopolitically integrated into sedentary society. This follows from the topological reality that the pastoral nomadic ecologies in the Near East are distributed in checkered and erratic patterns both along the fringes of, and in bulges and enclaves within, the regions of rainfall and irrigation agriculture.

The great immediate value of Rowton's series is that he has gathered empirical evidence and presented it in vivid topological form that encourages us to visualize the interplay of pastoral and agricultural pursuits throughout the Mesopotamian valley over centuries of time. Syro-Palestine is much less fully treated, and mainly in terms of the 'apiru, apparently in large part due to a division of labor, since Rowton cites the work of M. Liverani on a dimorphic analysis of Syro-Palestinian society as complementing his own Mesopotamian analysis.[15] A compact summary of the major results of Rowton's project, drawn up at a later point than my own summary in the body of this book (cf. above pp. 466–473), is offered by W. G. Dever from the point of view of an archaeologist.[16]

The problems I continue to have with Rowton's conceptual model are much the same as those I expressed when I had seen only the first few installments. His conceptual model manages to grasp only part of the issues that arise if his basic thesis of dimorphism is correct, as I believe it to be. For example, although Rowton convincingly validates that the morphemes of sedentary agriculture and nomadic pastoralism intermix extensively in the Near East, he does not provide an adequate basis for understanding their unity as a functional whole. The unity projected on the level of topology and ecology is only thinly extended into the sociopolitical realm. Even though one can read virtually everything descriptive in the articles as contradictory or neutral toward the old nomadic infiltration model, Rowton unaccountably retains the covert notion that nomadism comes from out of the desert to impinge on the settled areas. This impingement is more sophisticated and generally less traumatic than formerly imagined. The effect, however, is that pastoral nomads stand apart from the settled lands. To the degree that they are in the settled lands they are out of their usual place, at least sociopolitically. This unexamined assumption particularly affects the way Rowton looks at the sociopolitical totality of which settled and nomadic peoples form functional segments. He has yet to deal adequately with the reality that pastoral nomadism developed out of the settled community as a branch of its socioeconomic life.

In Rowton's conception of the dimorphic society the emphasis falls one-sidedly on the pastoral nomadic component. We learn of the embarrassment and difficulty the nomads create for settled authorities. Much less is said about the problem that the state represents for nomads and farmers alike. We hear much about how nomads and settled folk live side by side and about how one and the same group is often divided into nomadic and settled sections, i.e., "integrated tribes." We hear almost nothing about how the village/countryside environment forms the ground of mediation for settled and nomadic peoples and what face the rural hinterland as a whole presents to the state. We are made aware that the state, for example at Mari, takes steps to control nomads by appointing officials to deal with them and by influencing the internal choice of tribal heads, and we are also informed of many instances in which nomadic peoples lay hold of the government itself in order to form a "dimorphic state" (as I have treated the Midianites, cf. above pp. 431–433, 462–463, 779 n.515). In short, what is largely unexplored by Rowton is how the existence of the state affected the basic producers of the hinterland in whatever forms they lived and worked, whether as farmers, pastoralists, artisans, etc., and particularly what were the intended and unintended consequences of state policy in shaping nomadism quantitatively and qualitatively as part of the village-based hinterland.

At one level we can simply be appreciative of the rich documentation for the basic thesis and not expect Rowton to cover everything. On the other hand, to the degree that he wishes to deal with social groups such as the 'apiru—and even the biblical Israelites, as announced for the sixteenth and final article of the series (as also briefly in the twelfth and thirteenth articles)—it is needful that Rowton have as adequate a sociopolitical conceptual grid as he has a topological and economic grid. His illuminative probes into the phenomena of "tribal seepage," "tribal disintegration," "retribalization," and "social ethnonyms" (terms that oscillate between gentilic and social meanings) explicitly intend to throw light on the spheres of social organization and political structure. Consequently it is not enough for him to treat "tribal society" (largely equated with nomadism) so fully, while giving only a bare description of "urban society" as "nontribal society." I believe that on all the above topical points Rowton could give us a much more satisfying account were he to deal with the persistence of basically tribal institutions in the non-nomadic countryside ruled over by the state. In sum, the sophistication of the nomadic analysis in Rowton is not matched by a requisite sophistication (including attention to theory and content) in his characterization of urbanism = state = nontribal society.

Part IX.   A New Egalitarian Canaanite Society: Liberated Israel vis-à-vis Indigenous Peoples.

C. H. J. de Geus, whose study of early Israelite agricultural terraces I used with profit in Part X, has now published a revised and expanded version of his doctoral dissertation.[17] In the strictest sense it is a critical rebuttal of the presuppositions and conclusions of Noth's model of the amphictyony. Yet de Geus has actually produced a work much broader in scope and much more constructive than a mere refutation of Noth's model. De Geus's volume could appropriately be treated in connection with most of the parts of my study but I choose to place it here because it is his articulation of Israel vis-à-vis Canaan that seems to me the crucial dimension of his work.

The reasons for the methodological and substantive trenchancy of de Geus's presentation are in my opinion three-fold:

1. De Geus rightly perceives that Noth's model is an exceedingly comprehensive version of early Israelite socioreligious structure, especially as it has been elaborated by others over nearly forty years. Accordingly, it cannot be set aside without a fresh and thorough examination of all the data concerning earliest Israel. To reject Noth's construct of early Israel is therefore necessarily to turn oneself in another direction paradigmatically and to be prepared to struggle with what can be authentically said about the early Israelite totality and not merely to fixate on what Noth incorrectly concluded.

2. In seeking to lay the foundations of a more adequate paradigm for the emergent structure of early Israel, and operating all the while from a basis of wide familiarity with anthropological literature, de Geus firmly argues that the hypothesis of the pastoral nomadic origins of Israel is altogether bankrupt, unsupported as it is both by the content of the biblical materials and by cultural anthropology. This not only means that de Geus rejects the nomadic model for early Israel, but that he is impelled to make sense of the tribal data about Israel as a people who had

been much longer in the land than supposed and whose peculiar subcultural identity was achieved while they were a part of the general culture and society of ancient Canaan. Thus, while de Geus's study is not a large work, he does feel obliged to assess and to make at least preliminary judgments on most of the aspects of early Israel that must be addressed if a comprehensive model of Israel is to replace the discredited amphictyonic, conquest, and pastoral nomadic models.

3. De Geus further emphasizes that the amphictyonic model is through and through a religious model, culminating a long practice of conceptualizing the origin and distinctiveness of early Israel as primarily or exclusively religious. One of the most fascinating aspects of his study is the careful preliminary situating of Noth's amphictyonic theory in a history of interpretation going back as far as Eduard Meyer (in his methodological essay of 1881). Over the decades the debate about the character of early Israel has revolved around two poles: those who see Israel as distinctively shaped *by religion alone* and those who see Israel as distinctively shaped *by "national," or broadly sociocultural experience,* of which religion was but one aspect. The "religion alone" tendency may be said to have triumphed in Noth's encompassing and greatly refined version of a theory that had been foreshadowed and even rudimentarily advanced by others before him. In reaching this conclusion, de Geus points out that Noth himself did not attribute any significant sociopolitical functions to the amphictyony, but that the subsequent secondary extensions of the amphictyony as an institution into society and politics have been the work of followers who wanted to give still wider explanatory meanings to the hypothesis, including the notion that the amphictyony represented the middle evolutionary term between tribe and state.

With respect to this "religion alone" program, de Geus insists that history knows no instances of religion by itself creating an entire people, although religion may very well be a prominent factor among others in popular/national origins and it may become important and pivotal as a political force under particular circumstances. As for the secondary extensions of the amphictyony into social and political structure, de Geus follows the line of anthropological theory that regards the tribe as an evolutionary cul-de-sac, since nearly always the state arises not as an extension of the tribe but as a negation and transcending of the tribe.

In sum, de Geus's desiderata for a new model of early Israel, following the above principled criteria, are that it must be *comprehensive,* taking into account the whole range of data Noth struggled with and also the data he overlooked. A new model must also be *indigenous* (or *inner-Canaanite*) in the sense that it must explain the emergence of Israel as a long-time factor in Canaan. Finally, it must be *ethnic* (I prefer *subcultural*) in that it must spell out the total basis and range of the consciousness of Israel's unity in all aspects of its life and not in religion abstracted from the social totality. The upshot in de Geus's presentation is a kind of prolegomenon to—and initial sketch of—an *indigenous ethnic model* of early Israel, although he does not propose a name for the view he espouses. His study stops short of proposing an actual program for clarifying and giving content to a new model.

In this explication of de Geus's requirements for a model of early Israel it can be seen that they are close to my own, although rather differently phrased and nuanced. In the light of the great extent of agreement we share on the design of early Israel, it is surprising to me that at the point where de Geus approaches the revolt model he summarily rejects it and veers away in an "ethnic" direction as though that were an obvious counterposition to social revolution. Why is this so? In no more than one paragraph, de Geus gives three reasons for his denial that early Israel was a social revolutionary phenomenon: (1) Mendenhall's hypothesis "simplifies the various problems," for which he gives the sole example of a too-easy equation of 'apiru = Hebrew = Israelite; (2) Mendenhall's view does not allow for the roots of Israel to stretch back into an ethnic demarcation between Israelites and Canaanites; (3) Mendenhall's conception of "a nation and a state being formed as a result of social revolt, class war and a movement of mass conversion, seems altogether too idealistic and romantic!", which conception he sees as merely another twist to the unacceptable "primacy of religion" as an explanation for the rallying together of this revolutionary people. It is manifest that de Geus knows only of the revolt model as advanced by Mendenhall.[18]

It is my contention that de Geus far too readily surrenders the sociopolitical inquiry into the matrix of early Israel once he meets objectionable features in Mendenhall's way of viewing matters. A kind of unspoken taboo about social revolutionary categories seems to block his way quite as emphatically as the fixed idea of pastoral nomadism blocked so many inquirers over past decades. In answer to his tersely stated objections, it may be pointedly remarked: 1. A simplistic or blanket equation of 'apiru = Hebrew = Israelite is not necessary to the revolt model (cf. Chaney's treatment of 'apiru in terms of social banditry as noted under Part V of the Epilogue, and see my text above, pp. 401–409, 419–425, 476–485, and especially, 489–497). 2. A revolt model has no need to deny that the great majority of the ingredient peoples of Israel had been long in the land and that they had achieved identity as a recognized sector or segment of the populace. 3. Once it is concurred that religion working independently doest not create peoples, it can nonetheless be shown that peoples have repeatedly emerged as potent factors in history as the result of a cohesive mix of socioeconomics, politics, and religion. Often the identity of a people has been rooted in its polarization against a dominant society that despises and oppresses it and against which it struggles with the outcome that its consciousness of self is fortified in the struggle. It simply is not consistent with the carefulness of de Geus's work that he should dismiss this matter in one sentence by using the bald labels "social revolt," "class war," and "mass conversion," instead of unpacking them contextually by means of a comparative historical analysis.

In my view there is a significant point of contact, and a possible bridge, between de Geus's ethnic understanding of early Israel and the social revolutionary understanding of early Israel that I have advanced in this study. De Geus uses the term "ethnic" with some reluctance, for in his attempt at a precise characterization of what it means in the case of Israel he displays sensitivity to its astonishing ambiguity when left unqualified. He seems at least implicitly aware that a careless monolithic and univocal perception of "ethnic" (both biologically and culturally) has been a gravely damaging part of the negative legacy of the pastoral nomadic hypothesis. De Geus wants to avoid this kind of bloc-ethnicity concept, which does more to abort inquiry than to stimulate it.

Rightly unhappy with Herodotus's definition of a people by criteria of blood, language, and religion, de Geus argues that peoplehood is shaped in a particular culture and a particular social organization,[19] a point regrettably obscured by the overstating of the role of religion in early Israel. Using the Latin conceptual terms, *connubium* and *forum*, de Geus suggests that an endogamous population focused in an ethico-juridical and aesthetic-cultural community became the distinctive people Israel. He here finds affinity with the typology of tribalism espoused by Gertrude Dole whose work I too drew upon (cf. above pp. 743–744 n. 195). For de Geus religion did not create this Israelite peoplehood, but it did give expression and reinforcement to what Israelites already cherished and incorporated in their collective life.

> One might say, then, that a people is determined by the limits within which something is accepted, appreciated, admired or disapproved. In this context Von Grunebaum speaks of an admiring, disapproving or censuring "ever present public."[20]

It is expressly at this juncture that questions arise about the basis for the differentiation of such an ethnos or subculture in ancient Canaan. There would appear to be nothing "idealistic" or "romantic" about proposing social conflict as one influential factor in precipitating this subculture, especially if other bodies of evidence lead in that direction. Given his finely textured sense of "ethnic," for de Geus to say that Israel had been in Canaan for a long time and had developed ethnic differentiation from other peoples in Canaan does not in any principled way preclude that the differentiation may have emerged as a function of conflict over sociopolitical organization. Especially so when we consider that what is "accepted, appreciated, admired" prominently in early Israel is free agriculture among roughly equal extended families banded together in self-defense, and that what is "disapproved" is state-imposed taxes, corvée, and military draft in order to promote a wealthy elite.

In my judgment it would be advisable for de Geus to look at evidence for peoples/tribes who have had major sociopolitical conflict components in their origins and/or histories, such as the Kurds of Iraq and Turkey, the Ibos of Nigeria, and the Iroquois of New York State. My guess is that, given sufficient refinement for the specific cases, precisely the abruptly rejected categories of "social revolt," "civil war," and "mass conversion" will be found to have analytical value not to be improved upon by softer or fuzzier terms. In this respect, Rowton's case for "social ethnonyms" that waver between denotations of a particular group and of a social function or stance, may in fact point toward situations in the ancient Near East in which a people may be simultaneously viewed (1) from the point of view of their demarcation from others as a recognized population group, and (2) from the point of view of their demarcation from others typologically in terms of their socioeconomic and political function or style, e.g. merchants, brigands, mercenaries, revolutionaries, etc. Obviously the functional meaning of the term may become severed from the specific group reference and the memory of the sociopolitical matrix of the group may be obscured or lost, and vice versa.

Ethnicity has for too long been allowed a loose and slippery function as an explanatory category that, airily suspended above or beyond sociopolitical history, explains precious little until it is more exactly characterized from case to case.[21] The publication of de Geus's work gives us grounds to re-examine the whole conception of early Israel as an ethnic group. It is my contention that in doing so the social revolutionary and religious revolutionary dimensions of early Israel will not appear so arbitrary and imposed as de Geus and many others imply after little more than a cursory glance at the evidence.

Finally, on a number of points developed in Parts VI–VIII in my work, de Geus's treatment provides confirmation and supplementation. Especially striking is our independently reached conclusion that the twelve-tribe system containing Joseph/Levi is *more recent* than the twelve-tribe system containing Manasseh/Ephraim,[22] except that I date the Joseph/Levi version shortly after Solomon's administrative reorganization of his kingdom, and de Geus dates it after the downfall of the northern kingdom. Incidentally, de Geus presents a vigorously argued case for Joseph as a late monarchic tribal name, whereas I have preferred to see it as an archaic term conveniently revived for a symbolic/ideological version of the twelve tribes once the practical political foundations of the earlier system were undermined by Solomon. My case for the antiquity of Joseph, resting in large measure on Joshua 17:14–18, will certainly have to be reassessed in the light of de Geus's sharp critique.

Likewise, de Geus's analysis of family, clan, and tribe corresponds in several particulars to my own but also exhibits differences that should serve further inquiry.[23] He finds the typical extended family size to have been much smaller than I posit. In this de Geus works mainly from archaeological evidence, whereas I proceed from a population estimate based on the conjectured number of generations living in a household and an average number of children per marriage.

Closer study should be able to narrow this difference in estimates. He also grants only the sixty some clans given in the census lists of Numbers for the whole of Israel, whereas I regard the *mishpāḥāh* names in those lists as fragmentary and further propose, following Mendenhall's method of treating the lists, that approximately forty clans per tribe was customary.

Furthermore, while describing the *mishpāḥôth* correctly as "voluntarily endogamic," de Geus does not show awareness of the frequency of appearance of *exogamous clans* among tribes the world over, and thus he does not consider what may have been the contributing causes and resulting functions in the peculiarly Israelite *endogamous "clan"* = my "protective association of extended families." De Geus admirably perceives that the tribal organization of early Israel entirely suits a rainfall agricultural society, and he offers a useful comparison with south Arabian tribes in pre/Christian times. It would be possible to mention many additional issues on which de Geus adds valuable details, but I shall refer for the moment only to his citation of I Samuel 9:12 as evidence of the religious function of the *mishpāḥāh*, a text I did not consider in my own analysis of that topic (cf. above pp. 282–284).

Part X. The Religion of the New Egalitarian Society: Idealist, Structural-Functional, and Historical Cultural-Material Models.

In my study the case for the relevance of historical cultural-material macrosociological theory is mediated extensively through the work of neo-evolutionists such as the anthropologist Marvin Harris and the sociologist Gerhard Lenski. I wish to add to this mediation an incisive article by Lenski which is cast in the frame of a critical rebuttal of the arguments of Robert Nisbet that neo-evolutionary theory in the social sciences rests upon a muddled unscientific metaphor of organic growth.[24] When proper place is made for the distinction between general and specific evolution, and when prediction is cast in probabilistic rather than mechanical deterministic form, all of the leading premises of neo-evolutionism that Nisbet believes to have been demolished are in fact fully alive because, as Lenski demonstrates, those premises alone do justice to the materials of archaeology, history, and sociology. These neo-evolutionist premises are that change is natural, directional, immanent, continuous and cumulative, necessary, and proceeds from uniform causes. Those who find it difficult to see that a cultural-material approach to an historical entity like ancient Israel is apposite will do well to read Lenski's compact and principled defense of neo-evolutionist method and theory, which is not of course a blanket defense of every application and result—as though neo-evolutionism yields mathematical or mechanical formulas that operate automatically.

The use of macrosociological theory in early Israelite studies remains minimal.

H. J. Kraus has published a survey of socioreligious research in Old Testament studies that is fairly exemplary of the interests and biases of most biblical scholars.[25] Surprisingly, Kraus recognizes only one correct practitioner of the method of socioreligious research into early Israel, and that is Max Weber. Weber is favored because, unlike Auguste Comte who was positivist and Karl Marx who was determinist, he allowed that society and religion were interdependent and not mere functions one of the other. Durkheim is no alternative for Kraus because he really never broke free of positivism, and the same is true of Antonin Causse, who used Durkheim's method in his social study of Israel. Kraus expressly objects concerning Causse that "here the development of the religion of Israel and of the Old Testament belief in God turns into a function of social development."[26]

Exactly what is wrong with treating religion as a function of society is never made explicit by Kraus, since his strategy in refuting Causse and confirming Weber is to focus on the historical and religious weaknesses in the content of Causse's reconstruction and to single out the productive insights of Weber's detailed reconstruction, which were carried on in the work of Alt and Noth on the Israelite covenant league. Now there is no doubt in my mind that Weber did give us a richer and over-all more accurate account of early Israel than did Causse, but that certainly cannot be attributed to the simplistic formulations of social and religious functions that Kraus identifies in the work of the two scholars. To be convincing Kraus would have to show us that there is an intrinsic connection between their respective views of the relation between social and religious functions and the accuracy of their sociohistorical reconstructions. Another way to put this is to say that I do not agree, as Kraus implies, that Weber takes the religion of Israel any more seriously or autonomously than does Causse. Causse is less adequate not because of his general theory of social and religious functions but because he pinned his whole conceptualization on the weak foundation of the pastoral nomadic hypothesis, whereas Weber employed a many-stringed conceptual instrument developed through broad and detailed studies of many societies.

Kraus displays, I regret to say, a persisting failure of the humanist scholar—as well as the theologian—to see that any study cast in the form of socioreligious research and theory will inevitably treat religion as a function of society. If it does not, socioreligious inquiry fails to deliver results that are any other than conclusions imported from other disciplines. Such conclusions and the procedures yielding them would be merely redundant. Kraus does not address in the slightest the weak unclarified connection that Weber leaves between religion as the function of society and society as the function of religion. In a formal sense I have granted Weber's point in my discussion, but have further stressed that we do not possess a true scientific explanatory theory if we cannot say more about the mediations between the two types of functions and specifically about how they mix and interact and how one or the other has priority in particular streams of socioreligious development (cf. above pp. 627–631, 634–635, 645–646).

To be sure, Kraus has limited himself to the epoch of social scientific study of ancient Israel that closed with Weber. This limitation seems to be much more, however, than a chronological convenience. Kraus speaks of no further worthy work in this field since Weber, other than allusion to J. Wach, who has little to say on ancient Israel, and one is left wondering how someone today might "resume the life work of Max Weber" in order "to achieve that objectivity and flexibility of research and conceptualization which is appropriate to the ambivalent phenomena of a religious sociology."[27]

How the concerns of Weber might be taken up and extended is at least suggested in an article by Kazuhiko Sumiya in which he picks up neglected aspects of Weber's interest in modern-day socialism as a potential form of "emissary prophecy."[28] Sumiya makes specific application of Weberian categories to the thought and practice of Mao Tse-tung in leading the Chinese revolution. In conclusion, Sumiya offers provocative parallels between the Long March in the Chinese revolution and the Exodus and Wandering in the early Israelite revolution.

In what could have been a rather vague juxtaposition of superficial similarities, the author is at pains to pinpoint his comparisons with as much exactitude as possible. He begins with a model of how Mao led a revolution based on a very careful analysis of all the elements of the old order and what it would take to replace them in a new order, and especially what appeals and strategies were appropriate to the various sectors of peasants who stood to profit from change. Mao then sought to insure that the elements of the coming order were worked into the actual practice of peasants and soldiers as they struggled against the old order. Sumiya sees this thoroughgoing reshaping of a traditional society in all its dimensions as the sort of universal ascetic rationalization process that Weber identified in Western history and that he saw lacking in China, although he studied with fascination the glimmerings of such a process in the T'ai P'ing Rebellion (the Great Peaceful Heavenly Kingdom) of 1850–64.

Mao analyzed that what bound people to the old order was a system of four authorities: (1) *political authority* and its embodiment in the landlord system; (2) *clan authority* in all its ancestral ties reaching into the household; (3) *religious authority* unfolding in a hierarchy of gods and their manifestations in sociopolitical authority figures; (4) *authority of the husband*, which added yet another form of domination of women over and above the three previous authorities. Mao concluded that the political authority system must be broken by force, but that the other authority systems could only be dissolved in the course of new social relations. Paradoxically, however, to acquire and execute the necessary force

against the political authorities, it was necessary that people already be loosened in
status from the other, more sociocultural authorities.

> . . . his [Mao's] ideological position—destroying the privileged *status* of the landlord
> class, eradicating the inferiority complex that resulted from the pariah-like status of
> the peasant class, and thus stimulating their political consciousness—was directed
> toward utilizing the peculiar dynamics of what Weber called a "status situation."[29]

Mao's approach to the inseparable connection of the status problem with political
revolution was expressed by his "The Four Firsts":

> When treating the relationship between weapons and men, the human factor is to be
> given first priority; when dealing with political maneuvers in relation to other types
> of stratagems, the political are placed first; within a political maneuver, when dealing
> with the relationship between bureaucratic and ideological matters, the ideological
> comes first; and in ideological matters, when relating living thought and thought
> from written sources, the living thought is primary.[30]

On the basis of this analysis of obstacles, goals, and methods, Mao was able to
address and to overcome what had been intractable features resisting large-scale
change in China: contending *local loyalties* and feelings of unbridgeable *ethnic
differences* between long-time inhabitants of regions and later settlers. The key role
of the Long March was that it brought the ascetic discipline of military life into
fruitful interaction with masses of peasantry as large communities of people
travelled and fought their way over thousands of miles in a great strategic retreat.
The universal ascetic rationalization process of the Chinese revolution released
the Chinese people from the oriental "garden of magic" in terms of criteria that
correspond closely to Weber's understanding of "emissary prophecy."

Sumiya's own comments on the parallel with Israel are brief and not notably
informed by the historical and literary actualities in the reports of the Exodus.
Given the problematic historicity of the Exodus—and our lack of much information about it even as a sociopolitical process—I think we make better use of
Sumiya's insights if we try to see which, if any, of the obstacles, goals, and methods
of the Chinese peasant revolution show up in Israelite origins insofar as Israel
grew out of a peasant revolution in a traditional society wherein socioeconomic,
political, cultural, and religious/ideological dimensions all played a part.

It has long been noted that localism plagued the confederate experience of
early Israel, constantly weighing against the tendencies toward unification. It is
also to be assumed that among the lower-class sectors of Canaan who came to form
Israel there were groups with various ethnic identities (using ethnic in the
sociocultural manner of de Geus) who were only able to feel at home with one
another as some transcending status situation became a real option for them. To
these factors we may add the prominence of religious ideology for the emergent
people of Israel.

Is it possible that the analogy of the Chinese revolution, mediated through the rationalization and status categories of Weber, can suggest one way to envision the relation of society and religion in early Israel? The analogy would propose as an initial hypothesis that Israel began to concretize as a wide movement of dis-privileged peoples, largely peasant, who were seeking political change, i.e., the overthrow of a concretely oppressive system that intruded destructively into their lives. Religion was the form that their ideology took as they struggled to achieve a self-validating status sense different from their inferior status in Canaanite ideol-ogy. Yahwism reversed former sociopolitical values and validated a broad com-munity of persons of different regions, techno-economic modes, and cultural traits by casting their community both on the level of autonomous socioeconomic and political action and on the level of ultimate values and goals expressed ethically and religiously. In some sense, then, early Israel's social revolution, like the Chinese, may be conceived as achieving its success by simultaneously attacking and replacing clan and religious authorities as well as political authorities. This analogy would also compel us to ask anew whether early Israel also opposed "authority of the husband," or at least qualified or redirected that authority.

These two levels of attack and displacement (the socioeconomic/political *and* the familial/cultural/religious) intersected and reinforced one another in early Israel-ite experience. The religion focused expressly on legitimating institutions for the regularization and perpetuation of free agricultural production among equals. Just as Mao's ideological warfare cannot be separated from the whole sociopoliti-cal revolution he led, so the religious ideology of early Israel stemmed from the total revolutionary unrest and at the same time fueled that unrest and gave it a persisting confidence in a new status for the formerly disprivileged. A dialectical analysis of the revolutionary process thus suggests ways of mediating and nuanc-ing the unadorned disjunctive statements of Weber that sometimes religion is the function of society and sometimes society is the function of religion. They are functions of one another always, and in very complex ways that differ from social moment to social moment, but never are they interconnected in such a fashion that ideologies and religions stand apart from and prior to socially bonded and conflicting persons.

Part XI. Biblical Theology or Biblical Sociology?

I want finally to comment on two articles that treat aspects of the religion of early Israel along lines developed in the closing section of this volume. Both studies take as a point of departure the kind of "faith against culture" motif associated with G. E. Wright's profile of ancient Israel that had formative impact on the biblical theology movement, expecially in its American expressions.

Lynn Clapham[31] and Walter Brueggemann[32] both take note of major ways in which Wright's sharp counterposing of "historical" Israelite Yahwism over against "naturalistic" Canaanite baalism has proven to be indefensible in the light of subsequent research and reflection. Each of them explores a different facet of the inadequate paradigm of "faith against culture/history against nature," delineating variously how the biblical world view integrates the supposedly irreconcilable polarities which Clapham calls "historical" and "mythopoeic" thought and which Brueggemann characterizes as "salvation" and "blessing" paradigms. Clapham turns his attention to the quest for those forward thrusts in ancient Near Eastern religious thought that likely provided the conditions for the special Israelite religious mutation. Brueggemann focuses instead on inner-Israelite theological developments and tackles the thorny conjunction between Israelite religious novelty and the problem of the sexuality/asexuality of the deity.

Taking his clues from the important research on early Israelite religious motifs and imagery executed by Frank Moore Cross and his students Patrick D. Miller, Jr., and Paul D. Hanson, Clapham notes that the most distinctive "historical" conceptualization of Yahweh, namely as Divine Warrior and King, is from earliest times deeply entangled with mythopoeic representations. Likewise, ancient Near Eastern religious thought was much more directly concerned with political historical affairs than the biblical theology movement recognized. On this point, Clapham resonates approvingly with the work of Bertil Albrektson cited in my treatment of the subject (cf. above pp. 671–677, 679–680, 682, 685–686).

This religion-historical realization leads Clapham to focus on the sector of ancient Near Eastern religious thought closest to the point of departure for ancient Israelite religion, namely, among those gods most often pictured as warriors and executors of the divine assembly who are notably involved with politics and warfare. Making use of the theogonic schemes in the Babylonian *Enuma Elish*, the *Praeparatio evangelica* of Eusebius, and the *Theogony* of Hesiod, he posits that the warrior god-type is typical of a "younger" generation of deities ("political gods") who in the second millennium B.C. increasingly pushed the "older" generation of deities ("theogonic gods") into the background both in cult and in symbolism.

In this connection Clapham draws upon T. Jacobsen's observations[33] that already in Sumerian religion in the third millennium B.C. we can trace a tendency in representations of the gods to move from an initial nature-oriented "intransitive" stage to a human-oriented "transitive" stage, a movement in which the divine shifts from being a mere numinous manifestation restricted to discrete phenomena to being a power operative through a range of phenomena with willful ends in mind that have profound effects in history as in nature. Clapham points out that among the young political gods, some of them such as Enki, Kothar, Zeus, and El are far removed from their antecedents in nature.

The specific vehicle by which the transcending warrior god-type was transmitted to Israel Clapham believes to have been the "special 'clan-deity' or 'God of the Fathers' relationship between the patriarchs and Yahweh." [34] This connection provided the extra burst of transcendence or "transitivity" for lifting Israelite religion farther beyond mythopoeic thought than any other cult in the ancient Near East. He follows Cross, as do I, in suggesting that Yahweh, arising as an epithet for El, became a separate deity who eventually ousted El as head of the divine assembly. I would stress, however, that Yahweh did not simply "oust" El but, in a more complicated maneuver, also "absorbed" or "preempted" El attributes and functions in a new constellation of traits and spheres of interest and even retained the generic name El (ohim).

Clapham's delineation of the theological precursors of Israelite Yahwism is promising but necessarily more schematic than is desirable. In the ancient Near East, particular gods are not always easily assignable as "older" or "younger." The "transitive/intransitive" stages are evidently not merely chronologically successive or irreversible in direction of development. His remarks about El in relation to Baal and Yahweh hint at the possibility that a deity first appearing as a "younger" god may have lapsed into "old age" in the face of new challengers, and that this aging process may have happened again and again. It may even be that the same deity "aged" and "rejuvenated" more than once in its lifetime. It is likely that the systematic theogonic blueprints used by Clapham have schematized and compressed developments that were much more diffuse and cyclical or undulatory in reality. Rather than to prejudge chronology by referring to "older" and "younger" gods, we perhaps ought to speak of "descendent/recessive" gods and "ascendent/dominant" gods. Nonetheless, having granted cautions and qualifications, the kind of tendency Clapham identifies does seem present in ancient Near Eastern religion, especially when one takes into account the richly elaborated description of that process in Sumerian religion. In principle it should be possible to do for other ancient Near Eastern religions what Jacobsen did for Sumerian religion, with the proviso of course that gaps in our information about some of these cults and gods—regrettably so in southern Canaan—may make the task very difficult of execution. At any rate we are able to see that Yahweh is a plausible further development of trends already at work in ancient Near Eastern religion and thus neither an import from outside the region or a mere construct of a narrow group of intellectuals.

I find Clapham's hypothesis about the patriarchal deity as the bridging mechanism between other "transitive" gods and Yahweh to be problematic for all the reasons I have cited as impediments to gaining any clear historical or social locus for the patriarchal figures. That Yahweh split off from El in one of the communities dimly articulated in the patriarchal traditions is difficult to substantiate. To my mind the differentiation and elevation of Yahweh entailed enormous communal energies and struggles that imply a much larger social organization than is reflected in the patriarchal traditions. So it seems to me far in excess of the evidence for Clapham to speak of "Israel's founding clan." There is a clue, I believe, in the apparent fact that the first groupings of people who chose the name Israel were not yet worshipers of Yahweh but rather still worshipers of El. Probability tips in my view toward the likelihood that a confederation of El-worshiping Israelites first conceived Yahweh as a divine being independent of and superior to El and entirely capable of taking over El's functions and name.

It seems to me more promising to focus on the kind of sociopolitical milieu that might have precipitated the hyper-development of a "younger" transcendent warrior god in Israelite Canaan. T. Jacobsen offers some crucial considerations about the shift from "intransitive" to "transitive" deities which Clapham does not take into account in his article. Commenting on the specific coloration of divine powers as they grew more anthropomorphic and "transitive," Jacobsen asserts:

> The tendency for the human response [to the numinous powers] to take color as negative or positive from the values inherent in the situation in which the numinous power was encountered could not but act to single out for special attention certain situations and certain powers which were recognized as good and approachable. . . To some such process of natural selection we may ascribe *the marked uniformity* with which the major deities of the older Mesopotamian pantheon prove, on closer inspection, to be *powers or activities of primary economic importance to their worshipers*. . . That the major deities of the Sumerian pantheon are powers in phenomena and activities of primary economic importance also means, of course, that they differ in character from region to region, as natural conditions give prominence now to one, now to another type of economy (italics mine).[35]

Jacobsen then goes on to detail the gods and their economic spheres according to the several regions of ancient Sumeria: the hunting and fishing marshlands, the bovine-herding country along the Euphrates, the sheep-herding grassy steppe in the center of southern Babylonia, and the cereal-growing zones farthest north. Lastly, he introduces the factor of new centralizing sociopolitical patterns that prompted a more integrated patterning of the divine world:

> . . . it is a temptation to remodel the image of the numinous ever closer to the heart's desire, to see it more and more under human forms, to soften estrangement in its stark otherness by seeing it under *familiar images taken from human society and human interrelations,* so as to broaden the basis for community and contact. In ancient Mesopotamia this tendency early led to the development of a finely spun, closely interwoven, and complete pattern. This guided the human response to the numinous into *channels parallel to those developed for relations of dependence in human society.* Thus, in a progressively more differentiated, stratified and complex society, the image of the numinous powers, individually and as a functioning group, was subtly molded into *the likeness of an earthly landed aristocracy.* In blunt fact *the gods came to be part of society, the ruling caste exercising all basic economic and political functions of the country* (italics mine).[36]

I believe it can be reasonably hypothesized that the periodic appearance of "younger" gods corresponded in large measure to new techno-economic and sociopolitical developments that disrupted old orders and shifted power to different segments of the populace. These "ascendent/dominant" gods show a relative disengagement from particular aspects of nature in parallel with the mounting cultural control that the human community was gaining over nature. In particular, "political" gods were increasingly prominent because the shifts in social organization and political control were more frequent and fateful than the modifications in the "ground bass" of nature. Guy Swanson's hypothesis about monotheistic high gods tending to appear in societies with three or more sovereign groups is relevant at this point (cf. above pp. 625–627, 639–641).

Accordingly, whether Yahweh emerged in one of the patriarchal communities or among a confedrate group of Israelites, we should probably look for the precipitating mechanism in a techno-economic and sociopolitical context. In my view this context is well supplied by a restive peasant movement that was retribalizing in the face of city-state opposition and that was struggling to develop free rainfall agriculture, with modest irrigation possibilities, under precarious conditions in the hill country of Canaan (cf. above Part X, chap. 51, esp. pp. 660–663). The mythopoeic/culture-affirming/blessing elements *endure* in Yahwism because the peasant movement depended in the long run on a successful agricultural conquest of nature. The historical/transcendent/salvation elements *predominate* in Yahwism because the peasant movement arose in intense sociopolitical conflict and depended in the short run on a successful military defense against the old elites. Thus resulted the peculiar hybrid of Israelite continuity and discontinuity with Canaanite culture and religion. Immediate short-run needs led to a maximization of Yahweh's political-military competence, but the long-run needs for conquest of nature guaranteed a simultaneous expression of Yahweh's affirmation of agriculture, population increase, social prosperity, and an indigenous people's culture. Yahweh was the especially potent and eruptive "younger" (indeed, "upstart"!) god that "he" was because Israel was an especially determined and eruptive "younger/upstart" movement in great need of ideological legitimation, morale-building, and culture-affirmation for its daring undertaking.

Brueggemann elaborates in two directions on the discussions in biblical theology about Israel's religious uniqueness: (1) the social vision and social criticism implicit in Israel's view of God, and (2) the purport of the asexuality/sexuality of Yahweh both for Israel itself and for biblical theologians. While maintaining the basic aim of G. E. Wright to formulate adequately the distinctiveness of Israelite opposition to culture religion, Brueggemann astutely widens and nuances the project.

Employing Mendenhall and Gottwald he argues that the early covenantal faith of Israel entailed egalitarian social organization so foundationally that what Israel opposed in Canaan was not merely a form of nature religion but a hierarchic social structure. Moreover, he faults the simplism and distortion resulting from asserting the asexuality of Yahweh as the symbolic protection of Yahweh's transcendence over culture while at the same time naively using masculine imagery for Yahweh ("how exceedingly difficult it is to prevent *asexuality* from in fact being the imagery of *masculinity*").[37] Brueggemann deals frontally with the problem I formulate and emphasize by putting all masculine pronouns for Yahweh in quotation marks (as explained above, pp. 684–685, and practiced from that point on to the end of the book).

Brueggemann is particularly effective in exposing the sly assumptions of many biblical theologians that masculinity = virility = historical action = covenant faith = "good," while femininity = weakness = cultural passivity = natural evolutionism = "bad." He shows the dubiousness of this set of polar equations and values by noting that Yahweh's masculinity often affirms continuity and culture, e.g., Yahweh as "father" is both a sociopolitical and a natural/familial metaphor, applicable to divine control over history and nature. Moreover, Yahweh's overlooked femininity is fully located within a covenantal context and stresses aspects of the blessing/"fecundity" paradigm that Claus Westermann has emphasized as the persisting companion theme to the salvation/"virility" paradigm.

Brueggemann sums up the present state of thinking on these inner-Israelite theological tensions vis-à-vis Canaan by articulating a paradigm with two parallel terms that lead to differing theological perspectives, sexual metaphors, and forms of social organization:

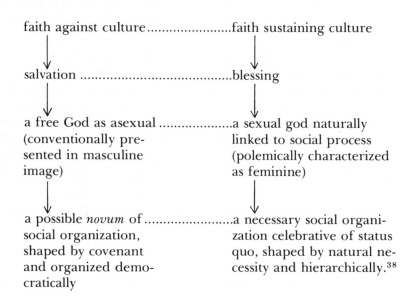

faith against culture......................faith sustaining culture

salvation ....blessing

a free God as asexual ....a sexual god naturally
(conventionally pre-   linked to social process
sented in masculine   (polemically characterized
image)   as feminine)

a possible *novum* of........................a necessary social organi-
social organization,   zation celebrative of status
shaped by covenant   quo, shaped by natural ne-
and organized demo-   cessity and hierarchically.[38]
cratically

The major problem that Brueggemann sees in this paradigm (signalled by his terms "conventionally" and "polemically") is its stereotypical use of masculinity/ femininity to assert the promissory and conserving aspects of deity respectively. The real issue in his view is not the sexuality of deity after all but the relationship in which Yahweh stands to human culture. In the wake of the sociohistorical work of Mendenhall and Gottwald, Brueggemann claims that

> . . . it is no longer a question of mythological against historical religion but a question of hierarchical, oppressive social reality and the possibility of covenant. . . .the issues of distinctiveness and againstness in the future will increasingly be expressed and understood in terms of sociological issues. That is, what Israel has to say about God will be more intentionally presented in terms of competing social visions. Wright had not been unaware of these matters, but the stress of his work is upon mytho-religious rather than sociopolitical questions. What is at issue, then, is not the sexuality of God but the way in which *different gods* are understood to sanction *different social visions.*[39]

Further summing up what is actually at stake in the discussion, Brueggemann asserts:

> . . . the program of againstness is not really interested in the issue of sexuality or asexuality of God as such. Rather, the interest is the contrast between a *covenantal* view of reality and a *noncovenantal* or *anticovenantal* view of reality, each of which depends upon a *notion of God* and each of which contains a *derivative social vision.*[40]

The argument is many-stranded and finely nuanced in its studied effort to show that the already complicated set of Israelite theological interests has gotten incredibly tangled up with the differing agendas of modern interpreters concerning religion, culture, and sexuality. Brueggemann is effective in purging the Israelite imagery surrounding sexuality/asexuality of some of these entanglements so that it can be looked at more objectively and imaginatively. Brueggemann also properly introduces the dimension of social organization and social vision, without which no discussion of these issues has sufficient anchorage.

My own assessment is that Brueggemann has been less successful in his clarification of the relevance of social organization for Israel's theology than in his clarification of the relevance of sexuality. This is partly due to his decision to focus primarily on the sexuality/asexuality issue. However, where he does comment on the implications of social organization for theology, Brueggemann has not been able to disengage Israelite social organization sufficiently from a heavily theologized notion of covenant. In this respect he follows the lead of the "religion alone" theorists over the decades (as traced and elucidated by de Geus; cf. the discussion under Part IX of the Epilogue), a perspective retained not only by Wright but also by most of his critics and also by Mendenhall in his formulations of the religion-society nexus in early Israel. This orientation has apparently led Brueggemann in summarizing an earlier published version of sections of Part XI of this work to conclude that I give the same prominence and accent to Israel's early covenantal religion as does Mendenhall. Brueggemann has correctly grasped my point about Israel's guarded attitude toward sexuality as a locus for religious symbolization when he says

> Gottwald . . . asserts that the notion of gods/goddesses having sexuality makes the natural processes the source of life and vitality. And since those natural processes are controlled by the priestly-royal establishment, the power of life is monopolized precisely by the forces of affluence and order which inevitably will be oppressive.[41]

However, he then goes on to inferences and implications which are not those that I would care to make:

> The issue [for Gottwald] is rather whether this God works in *sexual* ways so that God is continuous with the normal social and natural processes, or whether this God works in *covenantal* ways and is discontinuous both from natural processes and the social apparatus. . . . Gottwald argues that the sexuality of God (masculine or feminine) finally leads to social conservatism and legitimization of hierarchy and its implicit oppression. The asexuality of Yahweh means that social cohesion happens not naturally but only by intentional, historical covenanting.[42]

While I applaud Brueggemann's intention and direction of movement, it is *not* my view that in early Israel God was thought of as discontinuous with natural processes and the social apparatus as such. In fact, Yahweh was correspondent to and continuous with the natural processes on which the Israelite peasants depended, and "he" was correspondent to and continuous with the social apparatus of retribalization. The political hierarchy/oppression complex that Israel opposed was not exhaustive of nor simply identical with natural processes and/or with social processes. Israel made the claim in its own retribalizing social activity that nature and history were both malleable and good: they belonged to Yahweh and to the people of Yahweh. Sexuality, as an aspect of the natural and social whole, was likewise good.

Consequently, I believe that we must say that "covenantal" thinking in early Israel was not faith against culture but, more accurately, *faith sustaining Israelite retribalizing culture against Canaanite hierarchic culture*. In other words, in terms of Brueggemann's paradigm, I would move the sociocultural component up the scale to the very first level in that the religion of Yahweh was intrinsically sociocultural from its inception. There simply never was a moment in Israelite Yahwism when its theological assertions were only or primarily *against* culture, whether the Canaanite culture or culture in general. From the start Israelite Yahwism *affirmed and sustained an alternative way of appropriating natural and social goods through an alternative culture*. The requisite reverse side of this project of affirmation and sustenance was the deliberate invalidation of the dominant culture with its ingrained misappropriations of natural and social goods in a hierarchic state order.

The combative stance of Yahweh is the combative stance of the defender and champion of one cultural order against another cultural order that directly threatened the emergence and viability of "his" people as an intertribal egalitarian sovereign community.

Within the framework of two contending forms of social organization, sexuality as a religious dimension of life was an explosive many-sided issue. Sexuality was both fundamental to Israelite retribalization and simultaneously the human mode that the dominant culture exploited in religion and in society. Thus, I agree with Brueggemann that sexuality/asexuality in the deity is a secondary question that follows from the faith/culture dynamics generated by the socioeconomic and political conflict. For this perspective to have its full effect, however, it is absolutely essential to grasp the faith/culture dynamics not as an abstract division between faith and culture but as the sharp juxtaposition of one faith/culture nexus against another faith/culture nexus in a contest over the appropriation of the same natural and social goods. In this way the correctness of Brueggemann's claim is vindicated and sharpened: Israel's "distinctiveness/againstness" syndrome can only be unravelled intelligibly by explicating the forms of social organization through which Israel came into existence. Thus, as I argued in Part XI, the valid intention of biblical theology can only be fulfilled by "biblical sociology."

In this connection a word about "covenant" is in order. In my work above I do give prominence to the covenant, for example, as one mode in the early cultic program of Israel (Part III) and as an element in the complex of Israel's theological thought (Part XI), as well as in its role as a sociopolitical linking device for the confederating tribal peoples of Israel (Parts VII, IX). Nevertheless, I believe it to be a grave methodological error to elevate "covenant" to the level of an all-controlling theological category for understanding early Israel, an error quite as obstructive in its consequences as adopting "amphictyony" as the all-controlling institutional category in early Israel.

The danger is that the covenantal category can too easily carry the implication that the suzerain-vassal treaty model was operative for premonarchic Israel. That assumption simply cannot be taken as proved. I continue to believe with Dennis McCarthy, among others, that the treaty model was not operative in Israel before the time of Deuteronomy and that the sociopolitical analogue for the early Israelite covenant theology was the confederating linkage among tribal peoples. In other words, neither the sociopolitical covenant nor its religious conceptualization was drawn from the world of international politics but rather from the direct experience of confederating people in the process of their retribalization over against the power centers of the ancient Near East. The Israelite covenant was therefore a revolutionary concept forged in the immediate experience of the lower classes and not a direct borrowing from the concepts of international treaty-making. The Israelite covenant was garbed in international treaty dress only after Israel itself became a monarchy and entered into the conventions and formalities of international relations as a direct participant.

This understanding carries the weighty inference that *"covenant" as an historical and theological category does not oppose or transcend culture and nature*. Covenant is of course "intentional" and "historical," but that does not make it "unnatural" or "anticultural" (or even "noncultural"). Israel's covenant was simply another way of organizing society for the appropriation of nature and the generation of a more satisfying social life. Covenant action in the retribalizing project was "abnormal" with respect to the flow of hierarchic social processes in Canaan, but its aim was to seize natural and social processes for what it conceived to be far more human benefits than the Canaanite religiopolitical order permitted. In short, the critique of "faith against culture" that Clapham and Brueggemann have both undertaken needs to be carried through more rigorously and consistently until the entire biblical theological abstract superstructure is overturned and the religion of early Israel is seen as an intelligible social product, its distinctiveness significantly correlated point by point with the intentionality and instrumentalization of its social program.

I realize that what I am calling for is an enormous methodological shift for biblical scholars. It is not easy to shift from thinking of cultural and social realities deriving from beliefs about God to thinking of cultural and social realities as the matrices for spawning correlative beliefs about God. When Brueggemann, for example, says, "the interest is the contrast between a covenantal view of reality and a noncovenantal or anticovenantal view of reality, each of which *depends* upon a notion of God and each of which contains a *derivative* social vision" (my italics and omitting Brueggemann's italics),[43] his articulation of the proposition by the key terms "depends" and "derivative" is certainly defensible in the humanistic framework that stresses philosophical or religious ideas as the fundamental constituents and determinants for cultural and social life. That, however, is but one approach and not the broadest and most important one. What the social scientific approach contributes is the recognition that all ideas, even the highest and most encompassing, have social matrices and are triggered and shaped in the dynamics of cultural and social development. That being my approach, I would find it more appropriate to restate Brueggemann's formulation as follows: for early Israel the interest is the contrast between an egalitarian view of reality and an hierarchic view of reality, each of which *comes to expression and is indirectly reinforced* in a notion of God and each of which is *embodied and directly enforced* in a form of sociopolitical organization.

Brueggemann closes his provocative study with cautions directed to two types of biblical scholarship:

> Thus scholarship concerned with radical social criticism informed by covenant (Mendenhall, Gottwald) needs to be more attentive to the freedom of images and the

awareness that the various images, in their great variety, do indeed turn the central paradigm in various directions. Conversely, scholarship concerned with the meaning of language and metaphor (Wilder, TeSelle) needs to be more attentive to the faith which transforms every metaphor and every language in the service of the central paradigm.[44]

If the firm core of Israel's "covenantal" faith is in fact an *egalitarian paradigm,* it is precisely one of my aims to acknowledge the rich mutiplicity of religious imagery generated by an astonishing range of cultural and sociopolitical experiences entailed in the upthrust of this egalitarian people into ancient Near Eastern history.

In this vein, it is clear that literary tools of various sorts will greatly enrich our perception of the remarkable expressiveness of Israel's central egalitarian paradigm. Employing rhetorical criticism and metaphor (with its two levels of "vehicle" and "tenor"), Phyllis Trible has recently argued that Israel's "God male and female" sums up and gives impetus to many surprising expressions of feminine as well as of masculine freedom and initiative which simplistic "faith against culture" and "patriarchal hierarchic" models have entirely missed or deliberately suppressed.[45] I consider her study one way of carrying out a strategy of feminism (meaning for her not "a narrow focus upon women, but rather a critique of culture in light of misogyny)[46] in biblical studies which I both invite and urge (cf. above pp. 684–685, 796–797 n.628). By her rhetorical method, Trible conjures a biblical literary world congruent with a central egalitarian paradigm, so that the body of her work provokes urgent social situational questions: What forms of egalitarian social organization, in what times and spaces, in ancient Israel were the matrices of these expressions of feminine creativity? And what forms of hierarchic social organization in biblical times and later were responsible for subordinating and obscuring these expressions of feminine creativity?

Notes to the Epilogue

1. Thomas L. Thompson, "The Joseph and Moses Narratives," *Israelite and Judaean History* (ed. J. H. Hayes and J. Maxwell Miller), 1977, pp. 174–180, who draws on the criticisms of Noth by H. Schmidt, G. Fohrer, V. Fritz, H. Cazelles, R. De Vaux, W. Beyerlin, and R. Smend, Jr. Cf. also R. Polzin, "Martin Noth's *A History of Pentateuchal Traditions,*" *BASOR* 121 (1976), 113–120, which presents an appreciative and judicious evaluation from the perspective of structuralism.

2. Claus Westermann, "Arten der Erzählung in der Genesis," *Forschung am Alten Testament: Gesammelte Studien* (Theologische Bücherei, 24) 1964, pp. 9–91; idem *Genesis 12–50* (Erträge der Forschung 48) 1975, and see the cautious approval of this method as a movement "beyond Gunkel and Noth" by W. Malcolm Clark, "The Patriarchal Traditions," *Israelite and Judaean History* (ed. J. H. Hayes and J. Maxwell Miller), 1977, pp. 140–142.

3. Marvin L. Chaney, "Ancient Palestinian Peasant Movements and the Formation of Premonarchic Israel," *BA*, projected for publication in two installments in forthcoming issues.

4. I refer particularly to G. E. Mendenhall, "The Conflict between Value Systems and Social Control," *Unity and Diversity: Essays in the History, Literature, and Religion of the Ancient Near East* (ed. H. Goedicke and J. J. M. Roberts), 1975, pp. 169–180; idem, "Social Organization in Early Israel," *Magnalia Dei, The Mighty Acts of God: Essays on the Bible and Archaeology in Memory of G. Ernest Wright* (ed. F. M. Cross, W. E. Lemke, and P. D. Miller), 1976, pp. 132–151; idem, "'Change and Decay in All Around I See': Conquest, Covenant, and *The Tenth Generation*," *BA* 39 (1976) 152–157. As socioreligious theorist, Mendenhall's over-isolation and hypostatization of the ideological factors in early Israel prompt him, for example, in "'Change and Decay. . .'" to reduce drastically the military-political component in the Israelite social revolution almost to the vanishing point and to picture the Israelites as stepping relatively unhindered into a vacuum resulting from the self-destructive collapse of the Canaanite sociopolitical order. Particularly in "The Conflict between Value Systems and Social Control," Mendenhall appears to be explicit about operating with an unresolved mixture of the Lutheran concept of the two kingdoms and a form of unclarified anarchism which, in my view, clouds his conceptual and theoretical grasp of the Israelite social revolution which, ironically, he himself has done so much historically to uncover and elucidate in many particulars (cf. above pp. 220–233, 599–602). By contrast, as social historian, Mendenhall continues in the above articles to introduce valuable insights and to display a much more astute and balanced understanding of the social locus of ideology in "Migration Theories vs. Culture Change as an Explanation for Early Israel," *Society of Biblical Literature Seminar Papers* (1976), pp. 135–143.

5. See below under Note 14, item xiii.

6. J. Maxwell Miller, "The Israelite Occupation of Canaan," *Israelite and Judaean History*, 1977, p. 279. The quoted remarks have as their context Miller's survey and evaluation of "possible approaches to historical reconstruction," pp. 262–277.

7. Alan J. Hauser, "Israel's Conquest of Palestine: A Peasants' Rebellion?" *Journal for the Study of the Old Testament* 7 (May 1978) 7, 10.

8. N. K. Gottwald, "The Hypothesis of the Revolutionary Origins of Ancient Israel: A Response to Hauser and Thompson," *Journal for the Study of the Old Testament* 7 (May 1978), 39–52.

9. N. K. Gottwald, "Sociological Method in the Study of Ancient Israel," *Encounter with the Text: Issues in Hermeneutics with Special Reference to Genesis 25–35* (ed. M. J. Buss; prepared by a task group on Method and its History under the aegis of the SBL Form Criticism seminar), *Semeia Supplements*, forthcoming.

10. Fritz R. Wüst, "Amphiktyonie, Eidgenossenschaft, Symmachie," *Historia* 3 (1954/55) 129–153.

11. W. G. Dever and W. M. Clark, "The Patriarchal Traditions," *Israelite and Judaean History*, pp. 104–120, 141–142, and J. Maxwell Miller, "The Israelite Occupation of Canaan," *Israelite and Judaean History*, pp. 267–270, 277–279.

12. See especially the terminological discussions in the articles cited in Note 14, items i-iii, vi.

13. Allan S. Gilbert, "Modern Nomads and Prehistoric Pastoralists: The Limits of Analogy," *JANES* 7 (1975) 53–71.

14. The first twelve installments by M. B. Rowton dealing with "the role of dimorphic structure and topology in the history of Western Asia" are listed by the author in "logical sequence" in *Oriens Antiquus* 15 (1976) 17–18, note 4, to which a thirteenth part may now be added. I have marked with an asterisk those installments to which I have had access in

preparing the above evaluation. (i) *"Autonomy and Nomadism in Western Asia," *Or* 42 (1973) 247–258; (ii) *"Urban Autonomy in a Nomadic Environment," *JNES* 32 (1973) 201–215; (iii) *"Enclosed Nomadism," *JESHO* 17 (1974), 1–30; (iv) "Dimorphic Structure and the Tribal Elite," *Studia Instituti Anthropos* 30 (1976), no pagination; (v) *"The Abu Amurrim," *Iraq* 31 (1969) 68–73; (vi) *"Dimorphic Structure and Topology," *OA* 15 (1976) 17–31; (vii) *"The Physical Environment and the Problem of the Nomads," *La Civilisation de Mari* (ed. J.-R. Kupper), 1967, pp. 109–121; (viii) *"The Woodlands of Ancient Western Asia," *JNES* 26 (1967) 261–277; (ix) "The Role of the Watercourses in the Growth of Mesopotamian Civilization," *Alter Orient und Altes Testament* 1 (1969) 307–316; (x) *"Watercourses and Water Rights in the Official Correspondence from Larsa and Isin," *JCS* 21 (1967) 267–274; (xi) *"The Topological Factor in the *Hapiru* Problem," *Studies in Honor of Benno Landsberger* (Assyriological Studies of the Oriental Institute of the University of Chicago, 16), 1965, pp. 375–387; (xii) *"Dimorphic Structure and the Problem of the 'apiru-'ibrim," *JNES* 35 (1976) 13–20; (xiii) *"Dimorphic Structure and the Parasocial Element," *JNES* 36 (1977) 181–198.

15. M. B. Rowton, *OA* 15 (1976) 30, referring in particular to M. Liverani, "Per una considerazione storica del problema amorreo," *OA* 9 (1970) 5–27; idem, "The Amorites," *Peoples of Old Testament Times* (ed. D. J. Wiseman), 1973, pp. 100–133.

16. W. G. Dever, "The Patriarchal Traditions," *Israelite and Judaean History*, pp. 105–108, 113–114, 116–17.

17. C. H. J. de Geus, *The Tribes of Israel: An Investigation into Some of the Presuppositions of Martin Noth's Amphictyony Hypothesis* (Studia Semitica Neerlandica, 18), 1976.

18. Ibid., pp. 184, 187.

19. Ibid., pp. 156–164.

20. Ibid., p. 164.

21. "The term *ethnic* has its derivation from the Greek *ethnos* meaning a tribe or race, but *ethnic group* has come to be more closely associated with *ethos* or *custom* as the latter is now analyzed and understood in terms of social learning and social inheritance, as against former conceptions of biological and genetic determination of culture patterns" (M. M. Tumin in *A Dictionary of the Social Sciences*, [ed. J. Gould and W. L. Kolb], 1964, p. 244). C. F. Ware, "Ethnic Communities," *Encyclopaedia of the Social Sciences*, vol. 5, 1931, pp. 607–613, discusses several ways in which ethnic communities are known to have originated, as well as factors working for their cohesive perpetuation. H. S. Morris, "Ethnic Groups," *IESS*, vol. 5, 1968, pp. 167–172 recounts a brief history of the study of ethnic groups and analyzes ethnic groups in stratified (in relation to castes and classes) and nonstratified societies. Comments Morris: "The sections of an ethnically and culturally divided population may, according to circumstances, be institutionalized groups related to one another in a system of stratification, or they may be groups living side by side and related in other ways. Ethnic divisions may simply be categories of the population. . .who are beginning to lose [or to gain?—N.K.G.] a sense of ethnic separateness. It is, therefore, always important to be sure what is the exact sociological status of an ethnic or cultural division. Clarity in analysis depends upon it," *IESS*, vol 5, p. 168.

22. C. H. J. de Geus, *The Tribes of Israel*, pp. 69–119.

23. Ibid., pp. 133–150.

24. Gerhard Lenski, "History and Social Change," *American Journal of Sociology* 82 (1976) 548–564, being a critical review and point-by-point rejoinder to Robert A. Nisbet, *Social Change and History: Aspects of the Western Theory of Development*, 1969.

25. Hans-Joachim Kraus, "Die Anfänge der religionssoziologischen Forschungen in der alttestamentlichen Wissenschaft," *Biblisch-theologische Aufsätze*, 1972, pp. 296–310 (unfortunately, the third through the fifth pages of this essay are mispaginated and disordered

and therefore the whole must be read in the following order: pp. 296–297, 300, 299, 298, 301–310).

26. Ibid., p. 303. With reference to Causse, S. T. Kimbrough, Jr., whose articles on Causse I refer to on p. 782 n.535, advises me that his book *Old Testament Religion in Sociological Perspective* is being published in English in 1978 in the series "Studies in Oriental Religions" by Harrassowitz Verlag in Wiesbaden, Germany and that it "attempts a careful analysis in particular of the work of Antonin Causse."

27. H.-J. Kraus, "Die Anfänge der religionssoziologischen Forshungen," p. 310.

28. Kazuhiko Sumiya, "The Long March and the Exodus: 'The Thought of Mao Tse-tung' and the Contemporary Significance of 'Emissary Prophecy,'" *China and Ourselves* (ed. B. Douglas and R. Terrill), 1970, pp. 189–223.

29. Ibid., p. 200. On the importance for early Israel of ideology to address its "status situation," see my remarks in "Early Israel and the Canaanite Socioeconomic System," *BA*, forthcoming issue, which is a revision of "Early Israel and 'the Asiatic Mode of Production' in Canaan," *Society of Biblical Literature Seminar Papers* (1976), pp. 145–154.

30. Sumiya, pp. 200–201.

31. Lynn Clapham, "Mythopoeic Antecedents of the Biblical World-View and Their Transformation in Early Israelite Thought," *Magnalia Dei; The Mighty Acts of God: Essays on the Bible and Archaeology in Memory of G. Ernest Wright* (ed. F. M. Cross, W. E. Lemke, and P. D. Miller), 1976, pp. 108–119.

32. Walter Brueggemann, "Israel's Social Criticism and Yahweh's Sexuality," *JAAR Supplement* 45/3 (Sept. 1977) B: 739–772.

33. Thorkild Jacobsen, "Formative Tendencies in Sumerian Religion," *The Bible and the Ancient Near East: Essays in Honor of William Foxwell Albright* (ed. G. E. Wright), 1961, pp. 267–278.

34. L. Clapham, "Mythopoeic Antecedents," pp. 117–118.

35. T. Jacobsen, "Formative Tendencies," p. 271.

36. Ibid., p. 274.

37. W. Brueggemann, "Israel's Social Criticism," p. 746.

38. Ibid., p. 751.

39. Ibid., pp. 751, 753.

40. Ibid., pp. 758–759.

41. Ibid., pp. 749–750.

42. Ibid., p. 750.

43. Ibid., pp. 758–759.

44. Ibid., p. 765.

45. Phyllis Trible, *God and the Rhetoric of Sexuality,* 1978.

46. Ibid., p. 7.